THE THERMODYNAMICS PROBLEM SOLVER®

REGISTERED TRADEMARK

Staff of Research and Education Association,
Dr. M. Fogiel, Director

REA
Research and Education Association
505 Eighth Avenue
New York, N. Y. 10018

THE THERMODYNAMICS PROBLEM SOLVER®

Printed in the United States of America

Library of Congress Catalog Card Number 84-61810

International Standard Book Number 0-87891-555-9

WHAT THIS BOOK IS FOR

Students have generally found thermodynamics a difficult subject to understand and learn. Despite the publication of hundreds of textbooks in this field, each one intended to provide an improvement over previous textbooks, students continue to remain perplexed as a result of the numerous conditions that must often be remembered and correlated in solving a problem. Various possible interpretations of terms used in thermodynamics have also contributed to much of the difficulties experienced by students.

In a study of the problem, REA found the following basic reasons underlying students' difficulties with thermodynamics taught in schools:

(a) No systematic rules of analysis have been developed which students may follow in a step-by-step manner to solve the usual problems encountered. This results from the fact that the numerous different conditions and principles which may be involved in a problem, lead to many possible different methods of solution. To prescribe a set of rules to be followed for each of the possible variations, would involve an enormous number of rules and steps to be searched through by students, and this task would perhaps be more burdensome than solving the problem directly with some accompanying trial and error to find the correct solution route.

(b) Textbooks currently available will usually explain a given principle in a few pages written by a professional who has an insight in the subject matter that is not shared by students. The explanations are often written in an abstract manner which leaves the students confused as to the application of the principle. The explanations given are not sufficiently detailed and extensive to make the student aware of the wide range of applications and different aspects of the principle being studied. The numerous possible variations of principles and their applications are usually not discussed, and it is left for the students to discover these for themselves while doing exercises. Accordingly, the average student is expected to rediscover that which has been long known and practiced, but not published or explained extensively.

(c) The examples usually following the explanation of a topic are too few in number and too simple to enable the student to obtain a thorough grasp of the principles involved. The explanations do not provide sufficient basis to enable a student to solve problems that may be subsequently assigned for homework or given on examinations.

The examples are presented in abbreviated form which leaves out much material between steps, and requires that students derive the omitted material themselves. As a result, students find the examples difficult to understand--contrary to the purpose of the examples.

Examples are, furthermore, often worded in a confusing manner. They do not state the problem and then present the solution. Instead, they pass through a general discussion, never revealing what is to be solved for.

Examples, also, do not always include diagrams/graphs, wherever appropriate, and students do not obtain the training to draw diagrams or graphs to simplify and organize their thinking.

(d) Students can learn the subject only by doing the exercises themselves and reviewing them in class, to obtain experience in applying the principles with their different ramifications.

In doing the exercises by themselves, students find that they are required to devote considerably more time to thermodynamics than to other subjects of comparable credits, because they are uncertain with regard to the selection and application of the theorems and principles involved. It is also often necessary for students to discover those "tricks" not revealed in their texts (or review books), that make it possible to solve problems easily. Students must usually resort to methods of trial-and-error to discover these "tricks", and as a result they find that they may sometimes spend several hours to solve a single problem.

(e) When reviewing the exercises in classrooms, instructors usually request students to take turns in writing solutions on the boards and explaining them to the class. Students often find it difficult to explain in a manner that holds the interest of the class, and enables the remaining students to follow the material written on the boards. The remaining students seated in the class are, furthermore, too occupied with copying the material from the boards, to listen to the oral explanations and concentrate on the methods of solution.

This book is intended to aid students in thermodynamics to overcome the difficulties described, by supplying detailed illustrations of the solution methods which are usually not apparent to students. The solution methods are illustrated by problems selected from those that are most often assigned for class work and given on examinations. The problems are arranged in order of complexity to enable students to learn and understand a particular topic by reviewing the problems in sequence. The problems are illustrated with detailed step-by-step explanations, to save the students the large amount of time that is often needed to fill in the gaps that are usually found between steps of illustrations in textbooks or review/outline books.

The staff of REA considers thermodynamics a subject that is best learned by allowing students to view the methods of analysis and solution techniques themselves. This approach to learning the subject matter is similar to that practiced in various scientific laboratories, particularly in the medical fields.

In using this book, students may review and study the illustrated problems at their own pace; they are not limited to the time allowed for explaining problems on the board in class.

When students want to look up a particular type of problem and solution, they can readily locate it in the book by referring to the index which has been extensively prepared. It is also possible to locate a particular type of problem by glancing at just the material within the boxed portions. To facilitate rapid scanning of the problems, each problem has a heavy border around it. Furthermore, each problem is identified with a number immediately above the problem at the right-hand margin.

To obtain maximum benefit from the book, students should familiarize themselves with the section, "How To Use This Book," located in the front pages.

To meet the objectives of this book, staff members of REA have selected problems usually encountered in assignments and examinations, and have solved each problem meticulously to illustrate the steps which are difficult for students to comprehend. Special gratitude is expressed to them for their efforts in this area, as well as to the numerous contributors who devoted brief periods of time to this work.

Gratitude is also expressed to the many persons involved in the difficult task of typing the manuscript with its endless changes, and to the REA art staff who prepared the numerous detailed illustrations together with the layout and physical features of the book.

The difficult task of coordinating the efforts of all persons was carried out by Carl Fuchs. His conscientious work deserves much appreciation. He also trained and supervised art and production personnel in the preparation of the book for printing.

Finally, special thanks are due to Helen Kaufmann for her unique talents to render those difficult border-line decisions and constructive suggestions related to the design and organization of the book.

Max Fogiel, Ph.D.
Program Director

HOW TO USE THIS BOOK

This book can be an invaluable aid to students in thermodynamics as a supplement to their textbooks. The book is subdivided into 14 chapters, each dealing with a separate topic. The subject matter is developed beginning with work and heat, ideal gas processes, entropy and second law, irreversibility and availability, equations of state and extends through vapor power and refrigeration cycles, mixtures and solutions, chemical reactions and equilibrium. Also included are problems in flow through nozzles and blade passages, heat transfer and statistical thermodynamics. An extensive number of applications have been included, since these appear to be more troublesome to students.

TO LEARN AND UNDERSTAND A TOPIC THOROUGHLY

1. Refer to your class text and read the section pertaining to the topic. You should become acquainted with the principles discussed there. These principles, however, may not be clear to you at that time.

2. Then locate the topic you are looking for by referring to the "Table of Contents" in front of this book, "The Thermodynamics Problem Solver."

3. Turn to the page where the topic begins and review the problems under each topic, in the order given. For each topic, the problems are arranged in order of complexity, from the simplest to the more difficult. Some problems may appear similar to others, but each problem has been selected to illustrate a different point or solution method.

To learn and understand a topic thoroughly and retain its contents, it will be generally necessary for students to review the problems several times. Repeated review is essential in order to gain experience in recognizing the principles that should be applied, and in selecting the best solution technique.

TO FIND A PARTICULAR PROBLEM

To locate one or more problems related to a particular subject matter, refer to the index. In using the index, be certain to note that the numbers given there refer to problem numbers, not page numbers. This arrangement of the index is intended to facilitate finding a problem more rapidily, since two or more problems may appear on a page.

If a particular type of problem cannot be found readily, it is recommended that the student refer to the "Table of Contents" in the front pages, and then turn to the chapter which is applicable to the problem being sought. By scanning or glancing at the material that is boxed, it will generally be possible to find problems related to the one being sought, without consuming considerable time. After the problems have been located, the solutions can be reviewed and studied in detail. For this purpose of locating problems rapidly, students should acquaint themselves with the organization of the book as found in the "Table of Contents".

In preparing for an exam, it is useful to find the topics to be covered in the exam from the "Table of Contents," and then review the problems under those topics several times. This should equip the student with what might be needed for the exam.

CONTENTS

Chapter No. **Page No.**

4 ENTROPY AND THE SECOND LAW OF THERMODYNAMICS 151

5 IRREVERSIBILITY AND AVAILABILITY 222

6 THERMODYNAMIC RELATIONS 264

7 IDEAL AND REAL GAS PROCESSES AND RELATIONS 328

8 VAPOR POWER AND REFRIGERATION CYCLES 397

CHAPTER 1

THERMODYNAMIC PROPERTIES AND STATE OF PURE SUBSTANCES

PRESSURE AND TEMPERATURE

• PROBLEM 1-1

Calculate the absolute pressure for a system, given a gauge pressure of 1.5 MPa and a barometric pressure (atmospheric pressure) of 104 kPa.

Solution: The thermodynamic pressure P is defined as the total normal force per unit area exerted by the system on its boundary. It is also called the absolute pressure. The pressure of a system is usually measured with a gauge by using the atmospheric pressure as the reference point. The absolute pressure is related to the gauge pressure in the following manner:

absolute pressure = atmospheric pressure + gauge pressure

$$P_{abs} = P_{atm} + P_{gauge}$$

Given:

$$P_{atm} = 104 \text{ kPa} \text{ \{where kPa = kilo Pascal\}}$$

and

$$P_{gauge} = 1.5 \text{ MPa} \text{ \{where MPa = mega Pascal\}}$$
$$= 1.5 \times 1000 \text{ kPa}$$
$$= 1500 \text{ kPa}$$

$$P_{abs} = 1500 + 104$$
$$= 1604 \text{ kPa}$$

$$= \frac{1604}{1000} \text{ MPa}$$

$$P_{abs} = 1.604 \text{ MPa}$$

• PROBLEM 1-2

An open end mercurial manometer shown below in the figure is connected to a gas tank. The mercury meniscus in the left leg of the manometer is opposite 33.8 cm on the meter stick; in the right leg it is opposite 16.2 cm. Atmospheric pressure is 747 mm Hg. Find the pressure of the gas.

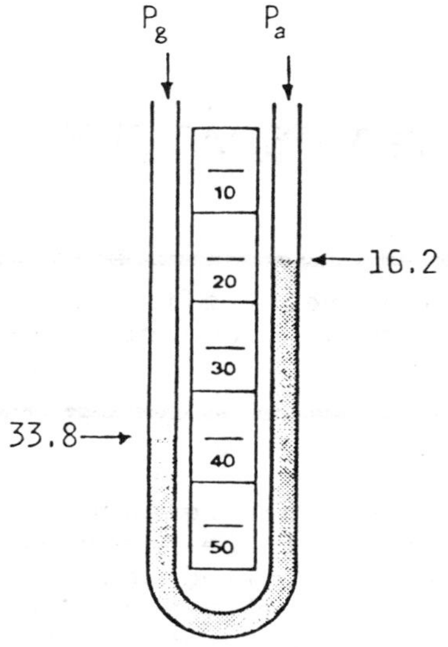

Solution: Always equate pressures at the lower liquid surface, that is, $P_g = P_a + P_{Hg}$. The gas pressure is greater than atmospheric pressure as shown in the figure. The figure shows the gas supporting both the mercury and the atmosphere.

The difference between atmospheric and gas pressures is always equal to the difference in levels of the mercury in the two legs of the manometer. This difference is 33.8 - 16.2 = 17.6, or 176 mm. Since the gas pressure is greater than atmospheric pressure,

$$P_g - P_a = 176 \text{ mm Hg}$$

$$P_a = 747 \text{ mm Hg}$$

$$P_g = 747 + 176.0$$

$$= 923 \text{ mm Hg.}$$

• PROBLEM 1-3

The density of liquid gallium is 6.09 g/cm^3 at 35°C. If this element is employed in a barometer instead of mercury, what is the height of a column of gallium sustained in the barometer at 1 atm. pressure?

Solution: The gallium column can be computed by the use of the relation:

$$(h_{Ga})(d_{Ga}) = (h_{Hg})(d_{Hg})$$

where

h = height of a column,
d = density,

therefore

$$h_{Ga} = \frac{(h_{Hg})(d_{Hg})}{(d_{Ga})}$$

1 atm pressure = h_{Hg} = 760 mm Hg = 76.0 cm Hg. The density of mercury = d_{Hg} = 13.6 gm/cm^3. Therefore,

$$h_{Ga} = \frac{(76.0 \text{ cm Hg})(13.6 \text{ gm/cm}^3)}{(6.09 \text{ gm/cm}^3)}$$

$$= 169.7 \text{ cm Ga} = 1697 \text{ mm Ga}$$

• PROBLEM 1-4

A piston weighs 4.3 kgs and has a cross sectional area of 450 mm^2. Determine the pressure that is exerted by this piston on the gas in the chamber, as shown in the figure. Assume gravitational acceleration 'g' to be 9.81 m/sec^2.

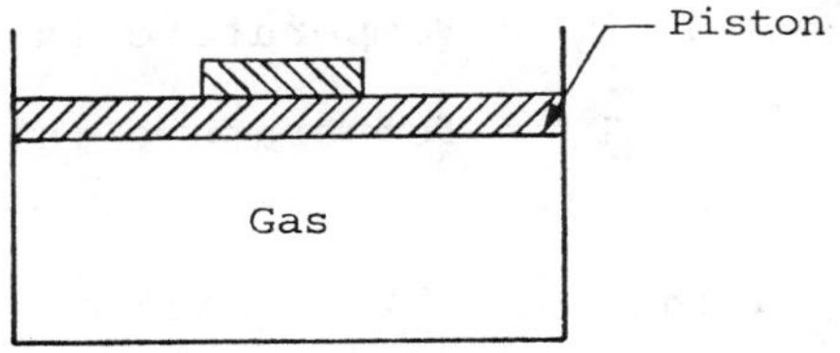

Solution: From Newton's Law

$$F = mg$$

where

F = Force in Newtons (N)

m = Mass in kilograms (kg)

g = acceleration in m/sec^2

therefore

$$F = 4.3 \times 9.81$$
$$= 42.18 \text{ N}$$

then

$$P = \frac{\text{Force}}{\text{Area}}$$

$$= \frac{42.18}{4.5 \times 10^{-4}} \frac{N}{m^2}$$

$$= 9.37 \times 10^4 \text{ N/m}^2 = 9.37 \times 10^4 \text{Pa}$$

or

$$P = 9.37 \times 10^4 \text{Pa} \times \frac{1\text{kPa}}{1000\text{Pa}} = 93.7 \text{ kPa}$$

• PROBLEM 1-5

The temperature of a given gas is -10°C. What are the equivalent Fahrenheit and absolute Kelvin scale readings?

Solution: (a) The Fahrenheit and Celsius scales are related by the following equation:

$$T_F = 32 + \frac{9}{5} T_c \qquad (1)$$

where

T_F = Temperature in degrees Fahrenheit

T_c = Temperature in degrees Celsius

Therefore, using Eq. (1) we can convert -10°C to °F.

$$T_F = 32 + \frac{9}{5}(-10)$$

$$= 32 + (-18)$$

$$= 14°F$$

(b) 0°C is equivalent to 273°K, where

K = absolute Kelvin scale

To convert from °C to °K, the relationship

$$T_K = 273 + T_c$$

is used. The problem above indicates that $T_c = -10°$.

Therefore

$$T_K = 273 + (-10)$$

$$= 273-10 = 263°$$

• PROBLEM 1-6

If the temperature of the air in a chemistry laboratory is ambient (77°F), what is the equivalent scale in Kelvin?

Solution: The Kelvin and Fahrenheit scales are related by the following equation:

$$T_K = 273 + T_C \quad (1)$$

Convert 77° Fahrenheit (°F) to Celsius (°C). Then convert Celsius (°C) to the absolute temperature scale, Kelvin (°K).

$$\frac{T_F - 32}{9} = \frac{T_C}{5}$$

$$\frac{77 - 32}{9} = \frac{T_C}{5}$$

or

$$5(77 - 32) = 9T_C$$

$$5\,(45) = 9T_C$$

$$T_C = 25°$$

From eq. 1

$$T_K = 273 + T_C$$

$$T_K = 273 + 25$$

$$T_K = 298° \ .$$

• PROBLEM 1-7

> Calculate the temperature of a fluid when both a Fahrenheit and a Celsius thermometer are immersed in it, under the following conditions: a) the numerical reading is identical in both thermometers and b) the Fahrenheit reading is numerically twice that of the Celsius reading. Express the values in °R and °K.

Solution: The Fahrenheit scale is related to the Celsius scale by the equation

$$T_C = \left(\frac{T_F - 32}{1.8}\right) \qquad (1)$$

where

T_C = temperature in the Celsius scale

T_F = temperature in the Farenheit scale

a)

$$T_C = T_F = T$$

Using Eq. (1)

$$T = \left(\frac{T - 32}{1.8}\right)$$

Solving for T

$$1.8\,T - T = -32$$

$$\therefore\ T = \frac{-32}{0.8} = -40$$

Therefore,

$$T = -40°C \text{ or } T = -40°F$$

The relations between the absolute temperature scales and the conventional scales are given by

$$T_{F_{abs}} = T_F + 460 \qquad (2)$$

The Fahrenheit absolute scale $T_{F_{abs}}$ is also called the Rankine scale (symbol R) and the Centigrade absolute scale is called the Kelvin scale (symbol K), and

$$T_R = 1.8\ T_K \qquad (3)$$

Using Eq. (2)

$$T_R = T_F + 460$$

$$= -40 + 460$$

$$T_R = 420$$

From Eq. (3),
$$T_K = \frac{T_R}{1.8}$$

$$T_K = \frac{420}{1.8}$$

$$= 233.33$$

b) Using Eq. (1)

$$T_C = \frac{(2T_C - 32)}{1.8}$$

Solving for T_C

$$1.8T_C - 2T_C = -32$$

$$\therefore\ T_C = \frac{-32}{-0.2}$$

$$= 160$$

Given $T_F = 2T_C$

$$\therefore\ T_F = 2 \times 160$$

$$T_F = 320$$

Using Eqs. (2) and (3)

$$T_R = T_F + 460$$

$$= 320 + 460$$

$$T_R = 780$$

and $$T_K = \frac{T_R}{1.8}$$

$$= \frac{780}{1.8}$$

$$T_K = 433.33$$

IDEAL GAS BEHAVIOR

• PROBLEM 1-8

The following substances are described by the given states.

a) Carbon Monoxide at 45°C, 4MPa
b) Carbon Dioxide at 15°C, 7MPa
c) Water at 40°C, 5kPa.

Can ideal gas behavior be assumed at the given states? Indicate the reasons for your answer.

Solution: a) Carbon Monoxide:

$$T \text{ given} = 45°C$$

$$= 273.15 + 45 = 318.15°K.$$

The critical temperature T_{CR} for CO, (from tables) is

$$T_{CR} = 133K$$

Since T given $\geq 2T_{CR}$ $(318.15 \geq 2 \times 133)$ and the pressure is less than 10 MPa, it is reasonable to assume ideal gas behavior.

b) Carbon Dioxide:

$$T \text{ given} = 15°C$$

$$= 273.15 + 15°$$

$$= 288.15°K$$

The critical temperature from tables for CO_2 is

$$T_{CR} = 304.2°K$$

In this case, T given $\leq 2T_{CR}$.

Therefore, it is unreasonable to assume ideal gas behavior in this case.

c) Water:

The saturation pressure P_{sat} from the steam tables at the given temperature is 7.384 kPa.

$$P_{sat} = 7.384 \text{ kPa}$$

$$P_{given} = 5.0 \text{ kPa}$$

Since the given pressure is lower than the pressure of the saturated vapor, it is reasonable to assume ideal gas behavior. In this case water lies in the superheated region.

• PROBLEM 1-9

The following substances are described by the given state:

a) Oxygen at 30°C and 1.0 MPa
b) Nitrogen at -100°C and 10 MPa
c) Water at 40°C and 10 kPa.

Determine whether it is reasonable to assume that the given substance behaves as an ideal gas at the specified state.

Solution: A gas will behave ideally if its compressibility factor Z is equal to or very close to unity:

a) Oxygen: From the tables of critical constants, the critical temperature for oxygen is

$$T_{CR} = 154.8°K$$

and the critical pressure

$$P_{CR} = 5.08 \text{ MPa}.$$

The reduced temperature $T_r = \frac{T}{T_{CR}}$ and

the reduced pressure $P_r = \frac{P}{P_{CR}}$ (1)

From the given state, T = 273.15 + 30

$$= 303.15°K$$

From Eq. (1), $$T_r = \frac{303.15}{154.8}$$

$$= 1.96$$

and

$$P_r = \frac{1.0}{5.08}$$

$$= 0.197$$

Using the compressibility factor chart, the compressibility factor Z = 0.989 for oxygen.

For an ideal gas, the compressibility factor Z is obviously unity under all conditions, whereas for a real gas, the value of Z may be less or more than unity.

Since $Z = 0.989 \cong 1$ for oxygen, ideal gas assumption is reasonable.

b) Nitrogen: Proceeding as in case a)

$$P_r = \frac{P}{P_{CR}}$$

$$= \frac{10.0}{3.39}$$

$$= 2.95$$

$$T_r = \frac{T}{T_{CR}}$$

$$= \frac{173.15}{126.2}$$

$$= 1.372$$

From the compressibility factor chart, using the above T_r and P_r for nitrogen,

$$Z = 0.72 << 1$$

Since $Z << 1$ it is not reasonable to assume ideal gas behavior.

c) Water: Water behaves as an ideal gas only when it is in the superheated region.

From steam tables, for T = 40°C

$$P_{sat} = 7.384 \text{ kPa}$$

(compressed liquid region).

Since $P_{given} > P_{sat}$, (10 kPa > 7.384 kPa)

it is not reasonable to assume ideal gas behavior.

IDEAL GAS EQUATION OF STATE

• PROBLEM 1-10

Assuming steam to be an ideal gas, obtain its specific volume and density at a pressure of 90 lb/in^2 and a temperature of 650°F.

Table

Gas	Chemical symbol	Molecular weight	Gas constant ft-lb/lb_mR	Specific heat B/lb		Specific heat ratio
		M	R	C_V	C_P	k
Air		28.95	53.35	0.172	0.240	1.40
Carbon dioxide	CO_2	44.00	35.13	0.160	0.205	1.28
Hydrogen	H_2	2.016	766.80	2.44	3.42	1.40
Nitrogen	N_2	28.02	55.16	0.176	0.247	1.40
Oxygen	O_2	32.0	48.31	0.155	0.217	1.40
Steam	H_2O	18.016	85.81	0.36	0.46	1.28

Solution:

$$\text{Given } P = 90 \text{ lb/in}^2$$

$$= 90 \frac{\text{lb}}{\text{in}^2} \times 12^2 \frac{\text{in}^2}{\text{ft}^2}$$

$$= 12960 \text{ lb/ft}$$

$$T_R = T_F + 460$$

$$= 650 + 460$$

$$T_R = 1110°R$$

The specific gas constant R is related to the universal gas constant $\overline{R}$ through its molecular weight M in the following manner.

$$R = \frac{\bar{R}}{M} \qquad (1)$$

From the table, M for steam = 18.016

$$R = \frac{1545.3}{18.016} \; \frac{\text{ft-lb/lbm.mole °R}}{\text{lbm/lbm.mole}}$$

$$= 85.77 \text{ ft-lb/lbm °R}$$

$$v = \frac{RT}{P} \qquad (2)$$

$$\rho = \frac{1}{V} \qquad (3)$$

where v = specific volume of steam

ρ = density of steam

From Eq. (2)

$$v = \frac{85.77 \text{ ft-lb/lbm-°R} \times 1110\text{°R}}{12960 \text{ lb/ft}^2}$$

$$= 7.34 \; \frac{\text{ft}^3}{\text{lbm}}$$

From Eq (3)

$$\rho = \frac{1}{7.34 \text{ ft}^3\text{/lbm}}$$

$$= 0.136 \; \frac{\text{lbm}}{\text{ft}^3}$$

By interpolation from the steam tables, the values of v and ρ are 7.26 $\frac{\text{ft}^3}{\text{lbm}}$ and 0.1355 $\frac{\text{lbm}}{\text{ft}^3}$ respectively.

• PROBLEM 1-11

Find the mass of air in a closed chamber measuring 35 ft × 20 ft χ 10 ft, when the pressure is 17 lb/in^2 and the temperature is 75°F. Assume air to be an ideal gas.

Solution: The pressure $P = 17 \frac{\text{lb}}{\text{in}^2} \times 12^2 \frac{\text{in}^2}{\text{ft}^2}$

$$= 2448 \; \frac{\text{lb}}{\text{ft}^2}$$

The volume V of the room $= 35 \times 20 \times 10$

$$= 7000 \text{ ft}^3.$$

$$T_R = T_F + 460$$

$$= 75 + 460$$

$$T_R = 535°$$

$$R = \frac{\overline{R}}{M}$$

where $\overline{R}$ = universal gas constant

R = specific gas constant

M = molecular weight

$$\overline{R} = 1545.3 \frac{\text{ft-lb}}{\text{lbm.mol-°R}}$$

$$M \text{ for air} = 28.97 \text{ lbm/lbm.mol}$$

$$R = \frac{1545.3 \text{ ft-lb/lbm.mol-°R}}{28.97 \text{ lbm/lbm.mol}}$$

An ideal gas is a simple compressible substance and is defined as one whose thermal equation of state is given by

$$PV = mRT$$

where P = pressure

V = volume

m = mass

R = specific gas constant

T = temperature

$$m = \frac{PV}{RT}$$

$$= \frac{2448 \text{ lb/ft}^2 \times 7000 \text{ ft}^3}{53.27 \text{ ft-lb/lbm-°R} \times 535°\text{R}}$$

$$= 601 \text{ lbm.}$$

• PROBLEM 1-12

A 0.2 m^3 container holds oxygen at 70°C and 25 bars. Calculate the amount of oxygen in the container if the atmospheric pressure is 1 bar.

Solution: For an ideal gas, the thermal equation of state is given by

$$PV = mRT$$

where

$$P = \text{Pressure} = 25+1 = 26 \text{ bars}$$

$$V = \text{Volume} = 0.2 \text{ m}^3.$$

$$R = \frac{\bar{R}}{M}$$

$$= \frac{8314.3 \text{ J/kg.mol-°K}}{32 \text{ kg/kg.mol}}$$

$$= 259.8 \text{ J/kg-°K}$$

$$= 259.8 \text{ N-m/kg-°K}$$

$$T = 273 + 70 = 343°\text{K}$$

$$m = \frac{PV}{RT}$$

$$= \frac{26 \text{ bars} \times 10^5 \dfrac{\text{N/m}^2}{\text{bar}} \times 0.2 \text{ m}^3}{259.8 \text{ N-m/kg-°K} \times 343°\text{K}}$$

$$= 5.8354 \text{ kg}$$

• PROBLEM 1-13

Calculate the volume of a cylinder which contains 60 lbm of carbon dioxide at 230°F and 23 psig pressure. Assume atmospheric pressure to be 14.7 psia.

Solution: The ideal gas equation for m pounds of gas occupying a total volume V is

$$PV = mRT \tag{1}$$

where P is the absolute pressure, and is the sum of the atmospheric pressure and gauge pressure.

$$\therefore P = 14.7 + 23$$

$$= 37.7 \text{ psia}$$

$$= 37.7 \frac{lb}{in^2} \times 144 \frac{in^2}{ft^2}$$

$$= 5429 \frac{lb}{ft^2}$$

$$T = 230 + 460$$

$$= 690°R$$

Using Eq. (1)

$$V = \frac{mRT}{P}$$

$$= \frac{60 \text{ lbm} \times 35.1 \text{ ft-lb/lbm-°R} \times 690°R}{5429 \text{ lb/ft}^2}$$

$$= 268 \text{ ft}^3.$$

• PROBLEM 1-14

Determine the mass and specific volume of argon gas in a vessel at 150 kPa and 20°C. The vessel is spherical and has a radius of 5m.

Solution: For an ideal gas, the equation of state is given by PV = mRT

$$\therefore m = \frac{PV}{RT} \qquad (1)$$

The specific gas constant for argon is

$$R = \frac{\overline{R}}{M}$$

where

$$\overline{R} = 8.3143 \text{ kJ/kg.mol-°K}$$

$$M = 39.95 \text{ kg/kg.mole (for argon)}$$

$$\therefore R = \frac{8.3143 \text{ kJ/kg.mol-°K}}{39.95 \text{ kg/kg.mol}}$$

$$= 0.20813 \text{ kJ/kg -°K}$$

$$= 0.20813 \text{ kN-m/kg-°K}$$

$$T = 20 + 273$$

$$= 293°K$$

The volume V of the spherical vessel is

$$V = \frac{4}{3}\pi r^3$$

$$= \frac{4}{3}\pi(5)^3$$

$$= 523.6 \text{ m}^3$$

$$P = 150 \text{ kPa}$$

$$= 150 \text{ kN/m}^2$$

Using these values in Eq. (1)

$$m = \frac{150 \text{ kN/m}^2 \times 523.6 \text{ m}^3}{0.20813 \text{ kN-m/kg-°K} \times 293°K}$$

$$= 1288 \text{ kg.}$$

The specific volume is given by $v = \frac{V}{m}$

$$v = \frac{523.6 \text{ m}^3}{1288 \text{ kg}}$$

$$= 0.4065 \text{ m}^3/\text{kg.}$$

• PROBLEM 1-15

The gauge pressure in an automobile tire when measured during winter at 32°F was 30 pounds per square inch (psi). The same tire was used during the summer, and its temperature rose to 122°F. If we assume that the volume of the tire did not change, and no air leaked out between winter and summer, what is the new pressure as measured on the gauge?

Solution: From one season to another, the only properties of the gas that will change are pressure and temperature. The mass (hence the number of moles) and the volume will remain the same. If it is assumed that this gas is ideal, then

$$PV = n\bar{R}T \qquad (1)$$

where

P = Pressure of the gas
V = Volume of the gas
n = number of moles

$\bar{R}$ = gas constant
T = Temperature of the gas.

Rearranging equation (1) to solve for P gives,

$$P = (n/V)\bar{R}T. \tag{2}$$

Since n and V are constant, equation (2) shows that pressure is directly proportional to temperature. That is, $P/T = n\bar{R}/V$ = constant. Therefore,

$$\frac{P_1}{T_1} = \frac{P_2}{T_2} = \frac{n_1\bar{R}}{V_1} = \frac{n_2\bar{R}}{V_2} \tag{3}$$

where

P_1 = initial pressure
T_1 = initial temperature
P_2 = final pressure
T_2 = final temperature

n_1 and n_2 are initial and final moles respectively. V_1 and V_2 are initial and final volume respectively.

The moles and volume are not changing; therefore, $n_1 = n_2$ and $V_1 = V_2$. Consequently, equation (3) can be written as

$$\frac{P_1}{T_1} = \frac{P_2}{T_2}. \tag{4}$$

Before equation (4) can be used, the pressure and temperature must be in absolute scales.

$$\frac{T_C}{5} = \frac{T_F - 32}{9} \tag{5}$$

and

$$P = 14.7 \text{ psia} + \text{psig} \tag{6}$$

where T_C = temperature in degrees centigrade
T_F = temperature in degrees fahrenheit
Psia = absolute psi
Psig = gauge psi

Using equations (5) and (6),

$$122°F = 50°C = (50 + 273)°K = 323°K$$

and

$$P = 14.7 + 30 = 44.7 \text{ psia} .$$

These can now be inserted into equation (4) to give,

$$\frac{44.7}{273} = \frac{P_2}{323} .$$

Therefore,

$$P_2 = \left[\frac{(44.7)(323)}{273}\right] \text{psia}$$

$$= 52.9 \text{ psia}$$

or from equation (6),

$$52.9 \text{ psia} = 14.7 \text{ psia} + x \text{ psig}$$

$$P_2 = (52.9 - 14.7)\text{psig}$$

$$= 38.2 \text{ psig}$$

• PROBLEM 1-16

> A pioneer aeronaut is planning the design of a hot-air balloon. What volume of air at 100°C should be used if the balloon is to have a gross lifting power of 200 kg (defined as the mass of displaced air minus the mass of hot air)? The ambient temperature and pressure are 25°C and 1 atm, and the average molecular weight of air is 29 g/mole, whereas that of the hot air is 32 g/mol (due to the presence of some CO_2).

Solution: Since $n = \frac{\text{weight or mass}}{\text{molecular weight}} = m/M$ = number of moles, the ideal gas equation can be written as

$$PV = \frac{m}{M}\bar{R}T \qquad (1)$$

where
P = pressure
V = volume
$\bar{R}$ = gas constant
T = temperature in °K

The problem states that $m_{air} - m_{hot\ air} = 200$ kg or 2×10^5 gm.

From equation (1)

$$m_{air} = \frac{VPM_{air}}{\bar{R}T_{air}}$$

$$m_{hot\ air} = \frac{VPM_{hot\ air}}{\bar{R}T_{hot\ air}}$$

$$m_{air} - m_{hot\ air} = \frac{VP}{\bar{R}}\left(\frac{M_{air}}{T_{air}} - \frac{M_{hot\ air}}{T_{hot\ air}}\right) = 2 \times 10^5 \text{ gm}$$

$$2 \times 10^5 \text{ gm} = \frac{VP}{\bar{R}}\left(\frac{M_{air}}{T_{air}} - \frac{M_{hot\ air}}{T_{hot\ air}}\right)$$

and

$$V = \frac{2 \times 10^5 \text{ gm} \times \bar{R}}{P\left(\frac{M_{air}}{T_{air}} - \frac{M_{hot\ air}}{T_{hot\ air}}\right)}$$

$$= \frac{(2 \times 10^5 \text{ gm})(0.082 \text{ liters atm } {}^\circ K^{-1} \text{ mole}^{-1})}{1 \text{ atm}\left(\frac{29 \text{ g mole}^{-1}}{298^\circ K} - \frac{32 \text{ g mole}^{-1}}{373^\circ K}\right)}$$

$$= \frac{(2 \times 10^5 \text{ gm})(0.082 \text{ liters atm } {}^\circ K^{-1} \text{ mole}^{-1})}{1 \text{ atm}(0.0115) \text{ g mole}^{-1}/{}^\circ K}$$

$$V = 1.42 \times 10^6 \text{ liters.}$$

• PROBLEM 1-17

A container having a volume of 2.5 ft^3 initially contains oxygen gas at a pressure of 125 psia and a temperature of 75°F. Oxygen then leaks from the container until the pressure drops to 100 psia, while the temperature remains the same. Assuming ideal gas behavior, determine how many pounds of oxygen leaked out of the container.

Solution: For an ideal gas

$$m_1 = \frac{P_1V_1}{RT_1}$$

$$m_2 = \frac{P_2V_2}{RT_2}$$

For oxygen $R = \frac{1545.3 \text{ ft-lb/lbm.mol-}^\circ R}{32 \text{ lbm/lbm.mol}}$

a) $P_1 = 125$ psia

$T_1 = 75 + 460$

$= 535°R$

$V_1 = 2.5 \text{ ft}^3$

$$m_1 = \frac{125 \text{ lb/in}^2 \times 12^2 \text{ in}^2/\text{ft}^2 \times 2.5 \text{ ft}^3}{48.3 \text{ ft-lb/lbm-°R} \times 535°\text{R}}$$

$= 1.74 \text{ lbm}$

b) $P_2 = 100 \text{ psia}$

$T_2 = T_1 = 535°R$

$V_2 = V_1 = 2.5 \text{ ft}^3$

$$m_2 = \frac{100 \text{ lb/in}^2 \times 12^2 \text{ in}^2/\text{ft}^2 \times 2.5 \text{ ft}^3}{48.3 \text{ ft-lb/lbm-°R} \times 535°\text{R}}$$

$= 1.393 \text{ lbm}$

Therefore $m_2 - m_1 = 1.393 - 1.74$

$= -0.347 \text{ lbm}$

The negative sign in the answer simply means that the final amount of oxygen in the cylinder is less than the initial amount in the cylinder.

TABLES OF THERMODYNAMIC PROPERTIES

• PROBLEM 1-18

Given the following states of water:

(a) At 10 MPa and an entropy of 3.3 kJ/kg-°K

(b) At 320°C and 5.6 MPa

(c) With a specific volume of 0.10 m^3/kg at 1.0 MPa

Determine whether water is a compressed liquid, superheated vapor, saturated liquid, saturated vapor, or a mixture of saturated liquid and vapor, in each case. If the state is determined to be a mixture, determine the quality. If it is not a mixture, determine an additional property at that state.

P(MPa)	T(°C)	v(m^3/kg)	u(kJ/kg)	h(kJ/kg)
10	300	0.0013972	1328.4	1342.3
10	305.21	0.001423	1358.8	1373.1
10	311.06	0.0014524	1393.0	1407.6

Table 1.

P(MPa)	T(°C)
5	263.99
5.6	270.98
6	275.64

Table 2.

Solution: a) For the given pressure, the entropy of the saturated liquid (s_f) and vapor (s_g) can be obtained from steam tables.

$$s_f = 3.3596 \text{ kJ/kg-°K}$$

$$s_g = 5.6141 \text{ kJ/kg-°K}$$

Since the given value for the entropy is less than that for the saturated liquid

$$3.3 < 3.3596,$$

the state of the substance is compressed liquid. The additional properties obtained by interpolation are shown in Table 1.

b) First the value of the saturation temperature at the given pressure is obtained from the steam tables by interpolation, as shown in table 2.

Comparing the given temperature with the saturation temperature,

$$T_{given} > T_{sat} \qquad (320 > 270.98)$$

The substance lies in the superheated region. The other properties can then be evaluated using the steam tables. Since the steam tables do not give values for the properties at 5.6 MPa, 320°C, interpolation is done as follows:

First the values for a pressure of 5.0 MPa, 320°C are calculated from the steam tables. These values are summarised in Table 3.

P(MPa)	T(°C)	v(m^3/kg)	u(kJ/kg)	h(kJ/kg)	s(kJ/kg-°K)
5.0	300	0.04532	2698.0	2924.5	6.2084
5.0	320	0.04797	2742.28	2982.1	6.3048
5.0	350	0.05194	2808.7	3068.4	6.4493

Table 3.

P(MPa)	T(°C)	v(m^3/kg)	u(kJ/kg)	h(kJ/kg)	s(kJ/kg-°K)
6.0	300	0.03616	2667.2	2884.2	6.0674
6.0	320	0.03859	2716.16	2947.7	6.1738
6.0	350	0.04223	2789.6	3043.0	6.3335

Table 4.

T(°C)	P(MPa)	v(m^3/kg)	u(kJ/kg)	h(kJ/kg)	s(kJ/kg-°K)
320	5.0	0.04797	2742.28	2982.1	6.3048
320	5.6	0.04234	2726.6	2961.46	6.2262
320	6.0	0.03859	2716.16	2947.7	6.1738

Table 5.

The properties at 6.0 MPa, 320°C are then evaluated in the same manner, as shown in Table 4.

Now from values in Table 3 and 4, Table 5 is formed by interpolation.

The values enclosed within boxes in Table 5 are the desired properties.

c) Using the steam tables and proceeding in the same manner as in parts (a) and (b), at P = 1.0 MPa

$$v_f = 0.001127 \text{ m}^3/\text{kg}$$

$$v_g = 0.19444 \ m^3/kg.$$

Comparing the value given for the specific volume with those for the saturated liquid and vapor it is evident that

$$v_f < v_{given} < v_g$$

$$(0.001127 < 0.1 < 0.19444)$$

and thus the substance is a mixture of saturated liquid and vapor. The quality can now be calculated using the equation

$$v = v_f + x(v_g - v_f) \qquad (1)$$

The quality x is then given by

$$x = \frac{v - v_f}{v_g - v_f}$$

$$= \frac{0.1 - 0.001127}{0.19444 - 0.001127}$$

$$= 0.5115$$

• PROBLEM 1-19

a) Calculate the specific volume of water at 1.0 MPa with an internal energy of 3200 kJ/kg.

b) Determine the enthalpy of freon-12 at 1.0843 MPa and 30°C.

c) Determine the specific volume of freon-12 at 1.0 MPa with an entropy of 0.91 kJ/kg-°K.

In addition, show for each case whether it is a liquid, vapor, or a mixture. Is it reasonable to assume ideal gas behavior in each case?

Solution: a) Using the given values, the internal energy u_g for a saturated vapor can be obtained from the steam tables.

$$u_g = 2{,}583 \ kJ/kg.$$

Since the given value of the internal energy is greater than the one obtained from the table

$$u_{given} = 3200 \ kJ/kg > u_g = 2583.6 \ kJ/kg,$$

the state is superheated vapor.

From the superheated steam tables, the specific volume is

$$v = 0.2921 \ m^3/kg \text{ (by interpolation)}$$

To check for ideal gas behavior the temperature must be known, and is obtained from the steam tables to be

$$T = 369.9°C = 643.1°K$$

If $T_{given} \geq 2T_{cr}$ then ideal gas assumption is reasonable at relatively low pressures ($P \leq 10$ MPa). From the table of the critical constants, for water

$$T_{cr} = 647.3°K$$

Thus

$$T_{given} \leq 2T_{cr} \quad (643.1 << 1,294.6).$$

Therefore it is not reasonable to assume ideal gas behavior.

b) From the freon-12 tables at 30°C, the saturation pressure is given as

$$P_{sat} = 0.7449 \text{ MPa}.$$

Since the given value for the pressure is greater than the saturation pressure at the given temperature ,

$$P_{given} = 1.0843 \text{ MPa} < P_{sat} = 0.7449 \text{ MPa},$$

the state is compressed liquid.

From the same freon-12 table, the enthalpy for the liquid phase is

$$h = h_f = 64.539 \text{ kJ/kg}.$$

This value is obtained by using the temperature and not the pressure, since the enthalpy is a function of the temperature. In this case the substance does not lie in the superheated region so ideal gas approximations are not reasonable.

c) From the saturated freon-12 tables at the given pressure, the entropies for the liquid and vapor states are given as

$$S_f = 0.2767 \text{ kJ/kg-K}; \ S_g = 0.6816 \text{ kJ/kg-°K}$$

(by interpolation)

Since the given value for the entropy is greater than the entropy for the saturated vapor state:

$$S_{given} = 0.91 \text{ kJ/kg-°K} > S_g = 0.6816 \text{ kJ/kg-°K},$$

the vapor is superheated.

From the superheated freon-12 tables, the specific volume is

$$v = 0.027667 \text{ m}^3/\text{kg} \qquad \text{(by interpolation)}$$

To check for ideal gas behavior the temperature is required. This is obtained from the freon-12 tables.

$$T = 154.9°C = 428°K$$

If $T_{given} \geq 2T_{cr}$ then ideal gas approximations are reasonable at relatively low pressures. From the table of critical constants, for freon-12

$$T_{cr} = 384.7°K$$

Since

$$T_{given} \leq 2T_{cr} \quad (428 < 769.4),$$

it is not reasonable to assume ideal gas behavior.

• PROBLEM 1-20

Given:

a) Water at 200°C and 10 MPa,

b) Water at 200°C and 1.0 MPa,

c) Ammonia at 30°C and a specific volume of 0.10 m^3/kg.

Determine for each case whether the substance is a compressed liquid, superheated vapor, saturated liquid, saturated vapor, or a mixture of saturated liquid and saturated vapor, by using the steam tables. Determine the quality if the state is a mixture and determine an additional independent property if the state is superheated.

Solution: a) Since both the temperature and pressure are given, either one of the following conditions will have to be satisfied. If $P_{given} > P_{saturated}$ at T_{given}, then the substance is located in the compressed liquid region, or if $P_{given} < P_{saturated}$ at T_{given}, then the given substance is in the superheated region.

From the steam tables, at T = 200°C

$$P_{sat} = 1.5538 \text{ MPa}$$

and

$$P_{given} > P_{sat} \quad (10 \text{ MPa} > 1.5538 \text{ MPa})$$

Thus the substance is in the compressed region.

An additional independent property is v.

From steam tables, at T = 200°C and P = 10 MPa,

$$v = 0.001148 \text{ m}^3/\text{kg}$$

b) As in (a), from the steam tables, at T = 200°C

$$P_{sat} = 1.5538 \text{ MPa}$$

and

$$P_{given} < P_{sat} \quad (1.0 \text{ MPa} < 1.5539 \text{ MPa})$$

Thus the substance is in the superheated region.

An additional independent property is v.

From the superheated steam tables, at T = 200°C and P = 1.0 MPa

$$v = 0.2060 \text{ m}^3/\text{kg}.$$

c) From the ammonia tables, at T = 30°C

$$v_f = 0.001680 \text{ m}^3/\text{kg}$$

$$v_g = 0.1106 \text{ m}^3/\text{kg}$$

The specific volume given in the problem lies between the two values obtained from the tables:

$$v_f < v_{given} < v_g$$

making the substance a mixture of saturated liquid and vapor.

The quality is calculated using the equation

$$v = v_f + x(v_g - v_f) \tag{1}$$

solving for x,

$$x = \frac{v - v_f}{v_g - v_f} = \frac{0.10 - 0.001680}{0.1106 - 0.001680} = 0.9027$$

$$x = 0.9027 \times 100 = 90.27\%$$

• **PROBLEM 1-21**

A cylinder contains 3 kg of water and water vapor mixture in equilibrium at a pressure of 500 kN/m^2. The volume of the cylinder is 1 m^3.

Calculate:

(a) the temperature of the mixture,

(b) the volume and mass of water and

(c) the volume and mass of vapor.

Solution: The mixture is saturated because the water and water vapor exist in equilibrium. The saturation temperature

$$T_{sat} \text{ at } P = 500 \text{ kN/m}^2 \text{ is } 424.95°K$$

(or 151.8°C).

b) The specific volume of the mixture $= \frac{V}{m} = v$

$$v = \frac{1}{3} = 0.3333 \text{ m}^3/\text{kg}$$

$$v = v_f + xv_{fg}$$

where v_g = specific volume of the saturated vapor

v_f = specific volume of the saturated liquid,

$v_{fg} = v_g - v_f$ and

x = quality of the mixture

$$\therefore\ 0.3333 = 0.0011 + 0.3737x$$

$$x = \frac{0.3322}{0.3737}$$

$$= 0.889.$$

The mass of liquid $= 3(1-x)$

$= 0.333$ kg.

The volume of liquid $= m_f v_f$

$= 0.333 \times 0.0011$

$= 0.000366 \text{ m}^3$

$= 0.366$ liter

c) The mass of vapor = mx = 0.889 × 3

$$= 2.667 \text{ kg}$$

The volume of vapor = $m_g v_g$

$$= 2.667\ (0.3737 + 0.0011)$$

$$= 2.667 \times 0.3748$$

$$\simeq 0.9995 \text{ m}^3$$

• PROBLEM 1-22

A cylinder contains 30 lbm of liquid water and water vapor mixture in equilibrium at a pressure of 100 lbf/in^2. If the volume of the cylinder is 10 ft^3 calculate

(a) the volume and mass of liquid

(b) the volume and mass of vapor

Solution: The specific volume is calculated first using the formula

$$v = \frac{V}{m}$$

$$= \frac{10.0}{3.0} = 3.333 \text{ ft}^3/\text{lbm}$$

The quality can now be calculated, using the following equation:

$$v = v_g - (1-x)v_{fg}$$

where

v_g = specific volume of saturated vapor

v_f = specific volume of saturated liquid

$$v_{fg} = v_g - v_f$$

Thus, from steam tables,

$$3.333 = 4.432 - (1-x)4.414$$

$$(1-x) = \frac{1.099}{4.414} = 0.249$$

solving for x gives

$$x = 0.751$$

(a) The mass of liquid is given by the formula

$$m_l = m_T(1-x)$$

where

m_l = mass of liquid

m_T = total mass

substituting the numerical values

$$m_l = 3 \text{ lbm}(0.249) = 0.747 \text{ lbm}.$$

The volume of liquid is

$$V_{liq} = m_l v_f$$

The value of v_f is obtained from the steam tables at the given state, as

$$v_f = 0.01774 \text{ ft}^3/\text{lbm}$$

Therefore

$$V_{liq} = 0.747(0.01774) = 0.0133 \text{ ft}^3.$$

(b) The mass of the vapor is

$$m_v = m_T x$$

where m_v = mass of vapor

m_T = total mass of water

x = quality

substituting the numerical values

$$m_v = 3 \text{ lbm}(0.751) = 2.253 \text{ lbm}.$$

The volume of the vapor is

$$V_{vap} = m_{vap} v_g$$

where v_g is obtained from the steam tables at the given state as

$$v_g = 4.432 \text{ ft}^3/\text{lbm}$$

Therefore

$$V_{vap} = 2.253(4.432) = 9.99 \text{ ft}^3$$

• PROBLEM 1-23

A cylinder which has a volume of 0.4 m^3 holds 2.0 kg of a mixture of liquid water and water vapor. The mixture is in equilibrium at a pressure of 6 bar (0.6 MPa).

Calculate:

1) The volume and mass of liquid

2) The volume and mass of vapor

Solution: First calculate the specific volume

$$v = \frac{0.4}{2.0}$$

$$= 0.20 \text{ m}^3/\text{kg}$$

From the steam tables

$$v_{fg} = 0.3157 - 0.001101$$

$$= 0.3146$$

The quality can be calculated using the equations

$$v = v_g - (1-x)v_{fg}$$

$$0.20 = 0.3157 - (1-x)0.3146$$

$$1-x = \frac{0.1157}{0.3146}$$

$$= 0.3678$$

$$x = 0.6322$$

The mass of the liquid is given by

$$m_{liq} = m(1-x)$$

$$= 2.0(0.3678)$$

$$= 0.7356 \text{ kg}$$

The mass of vapor is given by

$$m_{vap} = mx$$

$$= 2.0\ (0.6322)$$

$$= 1.2644\ \text{kg}$$

The volume of liquid is

$$V_{liq} = m_{liq}\ v_f$$

$$= 0.7356\ (0.001101)$$

$$= 0.0008\ \text{m}^3$$

The volume of the vapor is

$$V_{vap} = m_{vap}\ v_g$$

$$= 1.2644\ (0.3157)$$

$$= 0.3992\ \text{m}^3.$$

• PROBLEM 1-24

A cylinder which contains 3 pounds of saturated liquid water at a constant pressure of 30 psia is heated until the quality of the mixture is 70 per cent.

Calculate:

a) the initial temperature,

b) the final pressure and temperature, and

c) the volume change of the mixture.

Solution: a) In a saturation state there is only one saturation temperature for a given pressure. From the saturation pressure table (steam tables) for water, the saturation temperature corresponding to 30 psia is 250.34°F.

b) Since the fluid is not completely vaporized, the pressure and temperature remain equal to the initial values of 30 psia and 250.34°F.

c) The volume and enthalpy changes are computed from the basic relations $\Delta V = m(v_2 - v_1)$ and $\Delta H = m(h_2 - h_1)$, where 1 and 2 represent the initial and final states. The initial specific volume and specific enthalpy are read directly from the steam tables in terms of v_f and h_f. These values are

$$v_1 = v_f = 0.017 \text{ ft}^3/\text{lb} \quad \text{and} \quad h_1 = h_f = 218.93 \text{ Btu/lb}$$

The values of v_2 and h_2 must be calculated on a basis of a liquid-vapor mixture of 70 percent quality. Hence

$$v_2 = v_f + xv_{fg} = 0.017 + 0.70(13.75 - 0.017) = 9.63 \text{ ft}^3/\text{lb}$$

$$h_2 = h_f + xh_{fg} = 218.9 + 0.70(945.4) = 880.7 \text{ Btu/lb}$$

Consequently,

$$\Delta V = 3 \text{ lb} \times (9.63 - 0.02) \text{ ft}^3/\text{lb} = 28.8 \text{ ft}^3$$

$$\Delta H = 3 \text{ lb} \times (880.7 - 218.9) \text{ Btu/lb} = 1985 \text{ Btu}$$

CHAPTER 2

WORK AND HEAT

WORK INTERACTIONS

• PROBLEM 2-1

A ball falling in a vacuum requires 1 second to reach the ground. Can adiabatic work interaction be considered during the first 0.5 sec of the fall when the ball is chosen as the system?

Solution: Since the weight is falling in a vacuum, it does not affect its surroundings in any way. There is no external effect, and so the interaction is not adiabatic work.

• PROBLEM 2-2

A falling weight is used to operate a generator as shown in the figure. The power generated is converted to heat by a resistor. Can this be considered an adiabatic work interaction? Neglect all losses in the process.

Solution: The process can be divided into two systems as shown in the figure. The external effect to system A is system B, where the weight falls and operates a generator. Let system A be inversed by replacing it with a motor having a weight attached to its shaft. Then system B can be made to undergo the same process where its external effect will be an equivalent rise in the level of the weight. Since the inverse is possible, this example is an adiabatic work interaction.

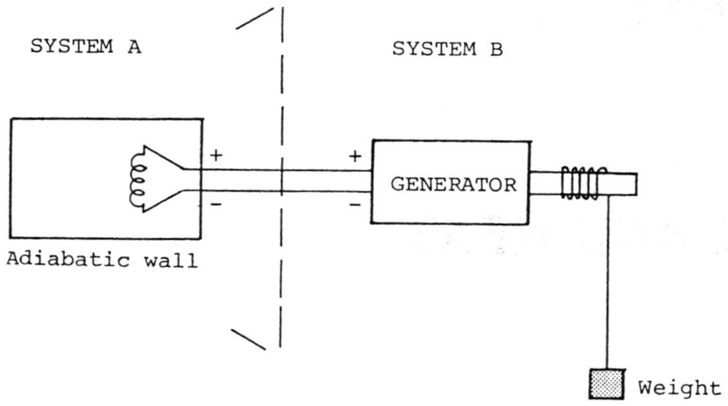

WORK DONE ON THE MOVING BOUNDARIES OF A SYSTEM

• PROBLEM 2-3

The figure shows a chamber containing 0.04 m^3 of a gas. The initial pressure which is supplied by weights on the piston is 200 kPa. Keeping this pressure constant the chamber is heated until the volume of the gas is 0.1 m^3. Considering the gas in the chamber as a system, a) calculate the work done by the system.

While heating is going on, weights are removed from the piston in such a way that the relation between pressure and volume is given by the expression

b) $PV = \text{constant} = P_1V_1 = P_2V_2$

c) $PV^{1.3} = \text{constant}.$

Calculate the work done in both cases if the initial conditions are the same and the final volume is 0.1 m^3.

d) Let the piston be fixed so that the volume remains constant. For the same initial conditions calculate the work done if heat is removed from the system and the pressure drops to 100 kPa.

Solution: a) Since the pressure is constant ,

$$ {}_1W_2 = \int_1^2 \delta W = \int_1^2 PdV $$

$$ = P(V_2 - V_1) $$

$$_1W_2 = 200 \text{ kPa} \times (0.1 - 0.04)\text{m}^3$$

$$= 12.0 \text{ kJ}$$

The work done by the system = 12.0 kJ

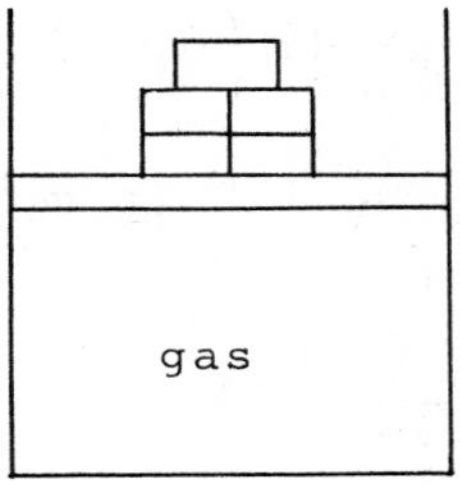

b) Determine the final pressure first.

$$P_2 = \frac{P_1V_1}{V_2}$$

$$= 200 \times \frac{0.04}{0.10}$$

$$= 80 \text{ kPa}$$

$$_1W_2 = \int_1^2 PdV$$

Substitute $P = \text{constant}/V = \dfrac{P_1V_1}{V}$ into this equation,

$$_1W_2 = P_1V_1 \int_1^2 \frac{dV}{V} = P_1V_1 \ln \frac{V_2}{V_1}$$

$$= 200 \text{ kPa} \times 0.04 \text{ m}^3 \times \ln \frac{0.10}{0.04}$$

$$= 7.33 \text{ kJ}$$

The work done in this case = 7.33 kJ.

c) First solve for the general case of PV^n = constant

$$PV^n = \text{constant} = P_1V_1{}^n = P_2V_2{}^n$$

$$P = \frac{\text{constant}}{V^n} = \frac{P_1V_1{}^n}{V^n}$$

$$= \frac{P_2V_2{}^n}{V^n}$$

$$
{}_1W_2 = \int_1^2 PdV = \text{constant} \int_1^2 \frac{dv}{V^n}
$$

$$
= \text{constant} \left[\frac{V^{-n+1}}{-n+1} \right]_1^2
$$

$$
= \frac{\text{constant}}{1-n} \left(V_2{}^{1-n} - V_1{}^{1-n} \right)
$$

$$
= \frac{(P_2V_2{}^nV_2{}^{1-n}) - (P_1V_1{}^nV_1{}^{1-n})}{1-n}
$$

$$
= \frac{P_2V_2 - P_1V_1}{1-n}
$$

In this case

$$
P_2 = 200 \left(\frac{0.04}{0.10} \right)^{1.3}
$$

$$
= 60.77 \text{ kPa}
$$

$$
{}_1W_2 = \frac{P_2V_2 - P_1V_1}{1 - 1.3}
$$

$$
= \frac{60.77 \times 0.1 - 200 \times 0.04}{1 - 1.3}
$$

$$
= 6.41 \text{ kJ}
$$

The work done for this case = 6.41 kJ.

d) Since $\delta W = PdV$

for a quasiequilibrium process, the work is zero, because in this case there is no change in volume.

• PROBLEM 2-4

Air inside a chamber is heated from an initial volume and pressure of 1.0 ft^3 and 1500 psia respectively to a final volume of 8.0 ft^3. Calculate the total work done by the gas if the expansion process is quasi-static and given by the relation $PV^{1.4}$ = constant.

Solution: Since the process is quasi static the work done by the gas is

$$W_{12} = \int_1^2 p\,dV . \qquad (1)$$

Since $pV^{1.4}$ = constant,

$$p = \frac{\text{constant}}{V^{1.4}}$$

$$= \frac{p_1 V_1^{1.4}}{V^{1.4}}$$

$$= \frac{p_2 V_2^{1.4}}{V^{1.4}}$$

Substituting into Eq.(1), gives

$$W_{12} = \text{constant} \int_1^2 \frac{dV}{V^{1.4}}$$

$$= \frac{\text{constant}}{1 - 1.4} (V_2^{1-1.4} - V_1^{1-1.4})$$

$$= \frac{p_1 V_1^{1.4}}{1 - 1.4} (V_2^{1-1.4} - V_1^{1-1.4})$$

$$= \frac{(1500 \times 144)(1.0)^{1.4}}{1 - 1.4} (8^{1-1.4} - 1.0^{1-1.4})$$

$$= 305{,}000 \text{ ft-lbf.}$$

The total amount of work done by the gas is 305,000 ft-lbf.

• PROBLEM 2-5

A liquid is compressed isothermally inside a chamber. Obtain an expression for the total amount of work required if the compression process is quasistatic and is given by the equation

$$\ln \frac{V}{V_0} = -A(p - p_0)$$

where A, V_0 and p_0 are constants.

Solution: Since the process is quasi-static, the work done is

$$W = \int_1^2 p\,dV$$

Since $\ln(V/V_0) = -A(p - p_0)$,

$$dV = -AV\,dp.$$

Therefore,

$$W = -A\int_1^2 Vp\,dp.$$

To perform the integration, the expression for V has to be a function of p.

In general, the volume of a liquid is not sensitive to a change in pressure. Hence, assuming constant V in the integration,

$$W = -AV\int_1^2 p\,dp$$

$$= -\frac{AV}{2}(p_2^2 - p_1^2).$$

Since A and V are positive quantities, W will be negative if p_2 is greater than p_1. This is consistent with the convention that work is done to a system in a compression process. The values for A and V will be different for different substances.

• PROBLEM 2-6

A container with a plunger compresses one lb-mol of an ideal gas from 1 atmosphere pressure to 10 atmospheres. Calculate the amount of work done if the process is considered to be polytropic. Assume the temperature to be 273°K and k for the process to be 1.4. All losses are neglected.

Solution: Determine the initial volume of the gas, from the ideal gas equation of state.

$$V = \frac{nRT}{P} \qquad (1)$$

Convert all units to lb-mol, lb_f, ft, and °R. In these units:

$n = 1$ lb-mol

$R = 1545$ ft-lb_f/lb-mol°R

$T = 273°K = 492°R$

$P = 1$ atm $= 2.12 \times 10^3$ lb_f/ft^2.

Therefore

$$V = \frac{1 \times 1545 \times 492}{2.12 \times 10^3} \quad \frac{(\text{lb-mol})[\text{ft-lb}_f/(\text{lb-mol}°\text{R})](°\text{R})}{(\text{lb}_f/\text{ft}^2)}$$

or

$$V = 359 \text{ ft}^3$$

The constant K for the polytropic process can be calculated from the initial conditions

$$K = P_1 V_1^{\,k}$$

$$= (2.12 \times 10^3)(359)^{1.4}$$

$$= 7.85 \times 10^6$$

Assuming that the compression occurs without acceleration of the piston, the following equation can be used to calculate the work of compression

$$W = \int_{V_1}^{V_2} P_{sys} \, dV_{sys} \qquad (2)$$

The pressure of the system and the volume are related by the polytropic conditions.

$$P_{sys} = \frac{K}{V_{sys}^k}$$

Therefore

$$W = \int_{V_1}^{V_2} \frac{K}{V_{sys}^k} \, dV_{sys} = K \int_{V_1}^{V_2} \frac{dV_{sys}}{V_{sys}^k}$$

for $k \neq 1.0$ the integral becomes:

$$W = \frac{K}{1 - k}\left(\frac{1}{V^{1-k}}\right)\Bigg]_{V_1}^{V_2} = \frac{K}{1 - k}[V_2^{k-1} - V_1^{k-1}]$$

This expression may be simplified as follows:

$$W = \frac{1}{1 - k}[KV_2^{k-1} - KV_1^{k-1}] = \frac{1}{1 - k}[P_2 V_2^k V_2^{k-1} - P_1 V_1^k V_1^{k-1}]$$

or

$$W = \left[\frac{P_2 V_2 - P_1 V_1}{1 - k}\right]$$

All that is needed to allow evaluation of W are the final conditions. The final pressure is specified to be 10 atm or 2.12×10^4 lb_f/ft^2. The final volume is obtained from the polytropic relation:

$$V_2 = \left(\frac{K}{P_2}\right)^{1/k} = \left(\frac{7.85 \times 10^6}{2.12 \times 10^4}\right)^{1/1.4} ft^3 = 68.5 \ ft^3$$

Thus:

$$W = \left[\frac{(2.12 \times 10^4)(68.5) - (2.12 \times 10^3)(359)}{(1 - 1.4)}\right] \frac{lb_f}{ft^2} \ ft^3$$

or

$$W = -1.73 \times 10^6 \ ft\text{-}lb_f$$

where the negative sign indicates that work is required to perform the compression.

• PROBLEM 2-7

A vessel with a piston contains one pound mole of an ideal gas. The gas is expanded at a constant temperature of 100°F from 20 atm pressure to 5 atm. Assuming losses to be negligible, calculate the work done for the following cases:

a) The expansion rate is large against a pressure of 1 atm.

b) The expansion rate is negligible.

c) The expansion rate is so large that it approaches infinity.

Solution: a) The resisting pressure is 1 atm.

$$W = \int_{V_1}^{V_2} P_r dV$$

$$= P_r (V_2 - V_1)$$

$$= P_r RT\left(\frac{1}{P_2} - \frac{1}{P_1}\right)$$

$$= [(14.7)(144)](0.73)(460 + 100) \left[\frac{1}{5} - \frac{1}{20}\right] \frac{1}{778}$$

$$= 166.7 \ Btu/lb \ mole$$

b) Since there is hardly any rate of expansion, i.e. the resisting pressure is equal to that of the system, therefore

$$W = \int_{V_1}^{V_2} \frac{RT}{V}\, dV$$

$$= RT \ln \frac{V_2}{V_1}$$

$$= -RT \ln \frac{P_2}{P_1}$$

$$= -(1.987)(460 + 100) \ln \frac{5}{20}$$

$$= 1546 \text{ Btu/lb mole.}$$

c) Since the resisting pressure is equal to zero

$$W = 0.$$

• PROBLEM 2-8

A vessel with a frictionless piston contains 1 ft^3 of a gas at 200 psia. The piston is held in position by applying an external force. Calculate the amount of work done if:

a) This external force is released gradually until the volume is doubled in such a way that PV is always a constant.

b) If the external force is released suddenly to half its initial value.

Solution: a) The process carried out is a reversible one, and

$$W = \int_{V_1}^{V_2} P\, dV$$

Since

$$PV = k(\text{const}) \qquad P = \frac{k}{V}$$

and

$$W = k \int_{V_1}^{V_2} \frac{dV}{V} = k \ln \frac{V_2}{V_1}$$

But

$$k = PV = P_1V_1 = (200)(144)(1) = 28{,}800 \ (\text{ft-lb}_f)$$

$$V_1 = 1(\text{ft})^3 \qquad \text{and} \qquad V_2 = 2(\text{ft})^3$$

Therefore

$$W = 28{,}800 \ln 2 = 19{,}930(\text{ft-lb}_f)$$

The final pressure will be

$$P_2 = \frac{k}{V_2} = \frac{28,800}{2} = 14,400(lb_f)/(ft)^2 \text{ or } 100(psia)$$

b) The force exerted is constant and is equal to a pressure of 100 (psia). After half the initial force has been removed, the gas will undergo a sudden expansion. Eventually the system will return to an equilibrium condition identical with the final state attained in the reversible process. Thus ΔV will be the same as before, and the net work accomplished will equal the equivalent external pressure times the volume change, or

$$W = (100)(144)(2 - 1) = 14,400(ft\text{-}lb_f)$$

This process is clearly irreversible, and compared with the reversible process is said to have an efficiency of

$$\frac{14,400}{19,930} = 0.723 \text{ or } 72.3 \text{ percent}$$

• PROBLEM 2-9

A cylinder with a frictionless piston contains 0.05 m^3 of gas at 60 kPa. The spring holding the piston is now in tension. The cylinder is heated until the volume rises to 0.2 m^3 and pressure rises to 180 kPa. Assuming no losses in the system, and the force on the spring to vary linearly with length, compute a) the amount of work done by the gas. b) the amount of work done if the system consists of the gas, the piston and the spring. Assume P_{atm} = 100kPa.

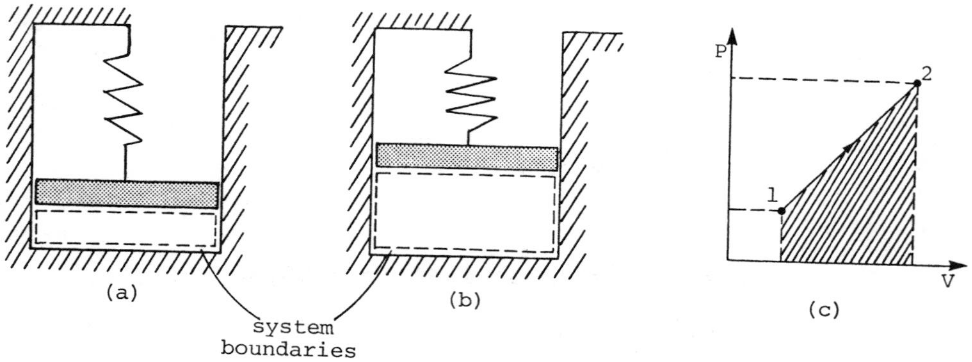

Figure 1. (a) Initially; (b) After heat has been applied; (c) P-V diagram

Solution: a) The spring is in tension in this case because the weight of the piston acts downward when the atmospheric pressure is greater than the internal pressure. It is given that

$$F_{spring} = kx \quad \text{(linear variation)}$$

Also

$$P = \frac{F}{A} = \frac{kx}{A} \tag{1}$$

From Eq. (1) it is obvious that the pressure also varies linearly with displacement.

Hence in the evaluation of the work done by the system, the pressure can be taken as the average of the initial and final pressures.

The work done is

$$W_{12} = \int_1^2 PdV$$

$$= \frac{(P_2 + P_1)}{2}\left[V_2 - V_1\right]$$

$$= \frac{(180 + 60)}{2}\left[0.2 - 0.05\right]$$

$$= 18 \text{ kJ}$$

b)

$$W_{12} = \int_{V_1}^{V_2} PdV$$

$$= P(V_2 - V_1)$$

$$= 100(0.2 - 0.05) = 15 \text{ kJ}$$

• PROBLEM 2-10

A container having an area of 1 ft^2 and a volume of 5 ft^3 holds 2 ft^3 of an ideal gas at a pressure of 10 atm. An external force is applied to keep the 1440 lb piston in position in the container, which is open to the atmosphere of 1 atm, pressure. When the external force is released the piston rises frictionlessly up the container. The gas in the container is always kept at the same temperature.
a) What will be the velocity of the piston as it moves.
b) What is the total vertical displacement of the piston.

Solution: The effective pressure of the surroundings is

$$P_{surr} = P_{atm} + \frac{\text{weight of piston}}{\text{area of piston}}$$

$$= 14.7 \text{ psia} + \frac{1440 \text{ lb}_f}{144 \text{ in}^2}$$

$$= 24.7 \text{ psia.}$$

To obtain the total work done by the gas on the piston and atmosphere, use the equation for the work done during an isothermal expansion,

$$W = nRT \ln \frac{V_2}{V_1}$$

But

$$nRT = P_1V_1$$

$$\therefore W = (10 \text{ atm} \times 2 \text{ ft}^3) \ln \left(\frac{5.0}{2.0}\right)$$

$$= 18.4 \text{ atm ft}^3$$

$$= 3.88 \times 10^4 \text{ ft-lb}_f$$

From this, a certain amount must be used to move the effective surrounding pressure.

$$W_s = \int P_s \, dV_{sys}$$

$$= 24.7 \frac{\text{lb}_f}{\text{in}^2} \times 3 \text{ ft}^3$$

$$= 1.07 \times 10^4 \text{ ft-lb}_f$$

$$\therefore (3.88 \times 10^4 - 1.07 \times 10^4) = 2.81 \times 10^4 \text{ ft-lb}_f$$

of energy is used to accelerate the piston.

The change in kinetic energy of the piston is 2.81×10^4 ft-lb_f which means that

$$\left(\frac{1}{2}\right) \frac{MV^2}{g_c} = 2.81 \times 10^4 \text{ ft-lb}_f$$

$$\text{or} \quad \left(\frac{1}{2}\right) \frac{1440 \text{ lbm sec}^2}{32.2 \text{ ft}} V^2 = 2.81 \times 10^4 \text{ ft-lb}_f$$

$$V^2 = 1255 \text{ ft}^2/\text{sec}^2$$

$V = 35.4$ ft/sec at the container exit.

b) At the highest point or maximum rise of the piston, potential energy = kinetic energy imparted to it. ∴ At the maximum height

$$PE = \frac{MgZ}{g_c} = WZ$$

$$= 2.81 \times 10^4 \text{ ft} - lb_f$$

$$\text{weight} = 1440 \; lb_f$$

$$Z_{max} = \frac{2.81 \times 10^4}{1440}$$

$= 19.5$ ft above the top of the container.

• PROBLEM 2-11

An elastic balloon filled with Hydrogen gas has a diameter of 0.3m and an internal pressure of 150 kPa. The gas is then heated as shown in the figure to a diameter of 0.4m and a pressure of 200 kPa. During the process, the pressure is proportional to the balloon's diameter. Calculate (a) the work done by the gas during the process, (b) the work done by the balloon on the atmoshere. Assume atmospheric pressure to be 100 kPa.

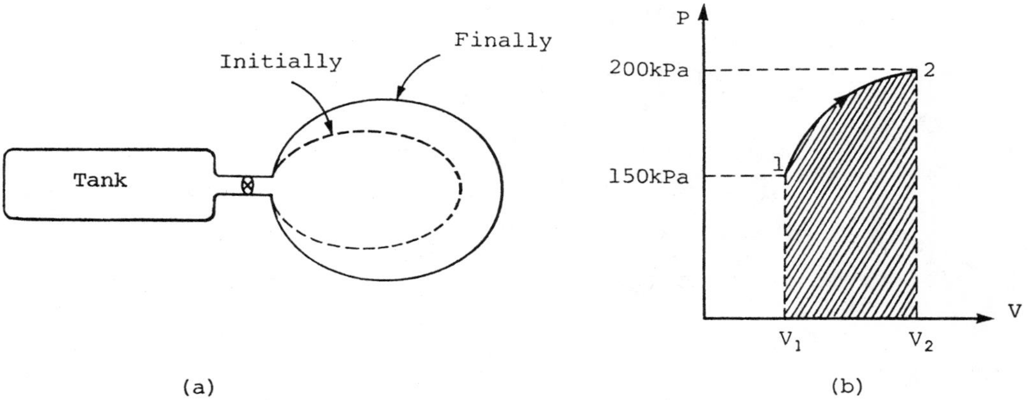

Figure. Inflation of an elastic balloon: (a) schematic, (b) P-V diagram

Solution: (a) First the initial and final volumes of the balloon must be calculated, using the equation

$$V = \frac{4}{3}\pi r^3 = \frac{1}{6}\pi d^3 \qquad (1)$$

Hence

$$V_1 = \frac{1}{6} \times 3.1416 \times (0.3)^3 = 0.0141 \text{ m}^3$$

$$V_2 = \frac{1}{6} \times 3.1416 \times (0.4)^3 = 0.0335 \text{ m}^3$$

The work done by the gas is represented by the area under the curve in Fig. 1(b).

$$W_{12} = \int_1^2 PdV \qquad (2)$$

And

$$P = \text{Const} \times d = \text{const} \times \left[\frac{6V}{\pi}\right]^{1/3}$$

where d is the diameter obtained from Eq. (1)

but $\frac{6}{\pi}$ is also a constant and

$$P = C \times (V)^{1/3}$$

where C is a general constant for the equation.

Solving for C obtain

$$C = \frac{P_1}{(V_1)^{1/3}} = \frac{P_2}{(V_2)^{1/3}}$$

substituting into (2)

$$W = C\int_{V_1}^{V_2} V^{1/3}\, dV$$

$$= \frac{3}{4} C\left[(V_2)^{4/3} - (V_1)^{4/3}\right]$$

$$= \frac{3}{4}\left[P_2V_2 - P_1V_1\right]$$

$$= 3.438 \text{ kJ}$$

(b) The pressure this time is constant, having the value $P_{atm} = 100$ kPa

From part(a)

$$V_1 = 0.0141\text{m}^3, \quad V_2 = 0.0335\text{m}^3$$

and

$$W_{12} = \int_1^2 PdV = P\int_1^2 dV$$

$$= P(V_2 - V_1)$$

$$= 100 \times (0.0335 - 0.0141) = 1.94 \text{ kJ}$$

• PROBLEM 2-12

The figure shows a container having 4kgs of saturated water at 35°C. It also has a frictionless piston with a cross sectional area of 0.06 m^2 initially resting on the stops enclosing a volume of 0.03 m^3. To raise this piston against atmospheric pressure, a pressure of 300 kPa has to be applied. On moving the piston upwards, it will encounter a linear spring when the contained volume is 0.075 m^3. To deflect this spring 1 m, the force required is 360 kN. If the final pressure is 7 MPa, determine

a) the final state of water, and

b) the work done during the process.

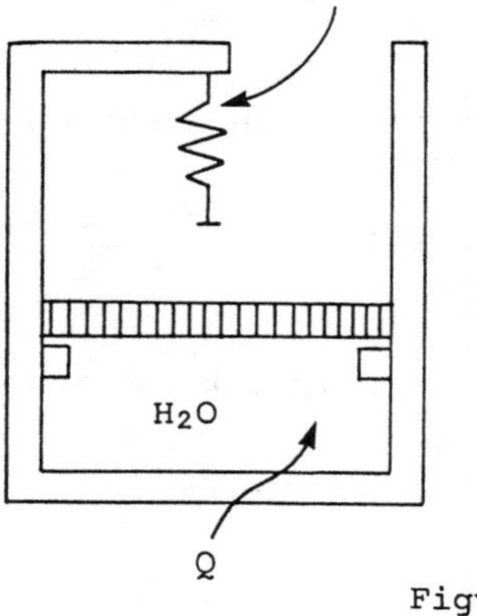

Figure 1

Solution: a) In this problem, the final mass inside the container will be the same as the initial mass since no additional mass is added or extracted from the system. However as a result of the heat transfer, the volume changes, and hence the specific volume also changes and will be different at the final state from that at the initial state. In order to calculate the final specific volume, the final volume of the container must be found first.

The final volume is (3 denotes the final state)

$$V_3 = V_2 + A\Delta h \tag{1}$$

where Δh is the height the piston moves after it touches the spring.

Then from the following equations

$$F = A\Delta P$$

and

$$F = k\Delta h \quad \text{where } k = \text{spring constant}$$

a relation for Δh can be obtained in terms of the pressure (P) and area (A) as

$$\Delta h = \frac{A\Delta P}{k} \tag{2}$$

since the spring is linear, the force will be linear which in turn implies that the pressure in going from state 2 (just before it touches the spring) to the final state 3, will change linearly. Thus,

$$\Delta P = P_3 - P_2,$$

and Eq. (2) will become

$$\Delta h = \frac{A^2(P_3 - P_2)}{k}$$

Substituting the above relation into Eq. (1) and solving, one gets

$$V_3 = V_2 + A^2\left(\frac{P_3 - P_2}{k}\right)$$

$$= 0.075 + (0.06)^2\left(\frac{7{,}000-300}{360}\right)$$

$$= 0.142 \text{ m}^3.$$

Solving for the specific volume at the final state

$$v_3 = \frac{V_3}{m} = \frac{0.142}{4} = 0.0355 \text{ m}^3/\text{kg}.$$

From the steam tables at P = 7 MPa,

$$v_g = 0.02737 \text{ m}^3/\text{kg}.$$

Since

$$v_3 = 0.0355 \text{ m}^3/\text{kg} > v_g = 0.02737 \text{ m}^3/\text{kg}$$

the final state lies in the superheated region. The process can then be plotted on a pressure-volume diagram as illustrated in Figure 2.

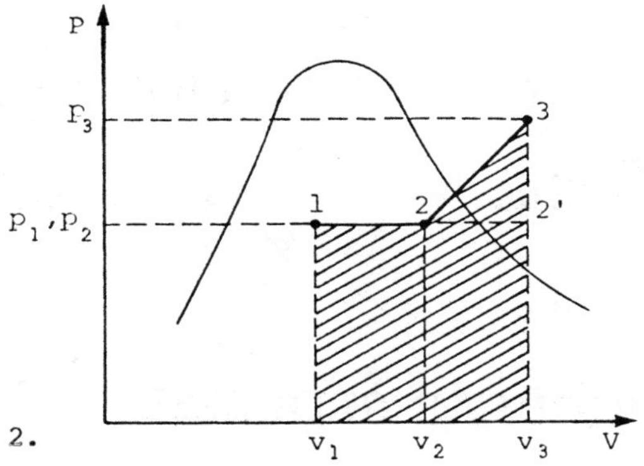

Figure 2.

b) The work done in going from state 1 to state 3 is

$$W_{1-3} = W_{12} + W_{23} \tag{3}$$

where

$$W_{12} = \int_1^2 PdV = P\int_{V_1}^{V_2} dV \tag{4}$$

because the pressure is constant from state 1 to state 2 as shown in Fig. 2.

However, in going from state 2 to state 3 the pressure varies. Since this change is linear the pressure can be assumed to be the average of the pressures at state 2 and state 3. The work done is

$$W_{12} = \int_2^3 PdV = \frac{P_3 - P_2}{2}\int_{V_2}^{V_3} dV \tag{5}$$

substituting (4) and (5) in Eq. (3),

$$W_{1-3} = P\int_{V_1}^{V_2} dV + \frac{P_3 - P_2}{2}\int_{V_2}^{V_3} dV$$

$$= P(V_2 - V_1) + \frac{P_3 - P_2}{2}(V_3 - V_2)$$

$$= 300\ (0.075-0.03) + \frac{7000-300}{2}\ (0.1420-0.075)$$

$$= 237.95 \text{ kJ}$$

Note that the work could have also been calculated graphically from Figure 2, by calculating the shaded area under the curve. The procedure would be.

(1) Calculate the area of the rectangle $12V_1V_2$.

(2) Calculate the area of the rectangle $22'V_2V_3$.

(3) Calculate the area of the triangle 232'.

(4) The total work is the sum of the above three areas.

This value will be identical with the one obtained earlier.

WORK FOR PARTICULAR PROCESSES

• PROBLEM 2-13

How many joules are equivalent to one lit-atm of work?

Solution: For 76.00-cm column of mercury (density = 13.596 gm/cm^3) supported by the atmosphere,

$$M/A = (76\ \text{cm})(13.6\ \text{gm/cm}^3) = 1033\ \text{gm/cm}^2 = 1.033\ \text{kgm/cm}^2.$$

Hence

$$P_x = Mg/A = (1.033\ \text{kgm/cm}^2)(9.81\ \text{meter/sec}^2)$$

$$= 10.13\ \text{kgm-meter/sec}^2\text{-cm}^2 = 10.13\ \text{newton/cm}^2;$$

and one lit-atm will represent

$$P_x\Delta V = (10.13\ \text{newton/cm}^2)(1000\ \text{cm}^3) = 10130\ \text{newton-cm}$$

$$= 101.3\ \text{newton-meter} = 101.3\ \text{joule}.$$

• PROBLEM 2-14

Calculate the work done by a perfect gas during an adiabatic frictionless process when its temperature changes from 200°F to 300°F. The molecular weight of the gas is 34.0 and the specific heat at constant pressure is given by the expression Cp = 0.212 + 0.000059T.

Solution: $$T_{Rankine} = T_{Farenheit} + 460$$

$$\therefore\ T_1 = 460 + 200° = 660°R$$

$$T_2 = 460 + 300° = 760°R$$

Since the process is frictionless, heat loss = 0.

Gas constant R = 1.985 Btu/lb mole°R

Molecular weight = 34.0

$$\frac{R}{W} = \frac{1.985}{34.0} = 0.058$$

∴ Work done

$$W = \int_{T_1}^{T_2} (0.058 - Cp)dT$$

$$= \int_{660}^{760} (\frac{1.985}{34.0} - 0.212 - 0.000059T)dT$$

$$= \int_{660}^{760} (-0.1536 - 0.000059T)dT$$

$$= (-0.1536)(760-660) - (\frac{0.000059}{2})(760^2-660^2)$$

$$= -15.36 - 4.19$$

$$= -19.55 \text{ Btu/lb.}$$

• PROBLEM 2-15

During a process the volume of a unit weight system changes from 5 cu. ft to 3 cu. ft.(a) Calculate the work done for this process if $P = \frac{500}{V} + 0.060\ V^3$, where P is the pressure and v is the specific volume. (b) Also calculate the work done for the process if frictional losses are neglected.

Solution: (a) When losses are taken into account the work done for a process which involves a unit weight system is

$$W + J = \int PdV$$

$$= \int_{V_A=5}^{V_B=5} (\frac{500}{V} + 0.060\ V^3)dV$$

$$= \left[500(\ln 3 - \ln 5) + \frac{0.060}{4}(3^4-5^4)\right] \times (0.1850)$$

$$= -48.8 \text{ Btu/lb}$$

$$\therefore W = (-48.8 - J) \text{ Btu/lb.}$$

(b) If frictional losses are neglected, J = 0

$$W = \int PdV = -48.8 \text{ Btu/lb.}$$

• PROBLEM 2-16

An air compressor compresses air from 15 psia to 75 psia according to the relation $PV^{1.3}$ = constant along the path of compression.

a) Calculate the work done during the compression process if the entrance and exit velocities are assumed to be the same.

b) Also calculate the shaft work of the compressor. Take specific volume of air to be 13.1 cu ft/lb.

Solution: a) The work done $w = \int_{V_1}^{V_2} pdv.$

Given $$pv^{1.3} = C = p_1v_1 = p_2v_2 \qquad (1)$$

$$\therefore p = \frac{C}{v^{1.3}} = Cv^{-1.3} \qquad (2)$$

But $$p_1v_1^{1.3} = p_2v_2^{1.3}$$

$$\therefore v_2^{1.3} = \left(\frac{p_1}{p_2}\right) v_1^{1.3}$$

$$v_2 = \left(\frac{p_1}{p_2}\right)^{\frac{1}{1.3}} v_1 \qquad (3)$$

$$= \left(\frac{15}{75}\right)^{\frac{1}{1.3}} \times 13.1 \text{ cu. ft}$$

$$= 3.8 \text{ cu. ft.}$$

From Eq. (2)

$${}_1W_2 = \int_{V_1}^{V_2} Cv^{-1.3} \, dv$$

$$= \left[\frac{C_{v_2}^{-0.3}}{-0.3}\right]_{V_1}^{V_2} \qquad (4)$$

From Eq. (1) and (4)

$$W = \frac{p_2 v_2^{1.3} \times v_2^{-0.3} - p_1 v_1^{1.3} \times v_1^{-0.3}}{-0.3}$$

$$= \frac{p_2 v_2 - p_1 v_1}{-0.3}$$

$$= \frac{12^2}{0.3} (15 \times 13.1 - 75 \times 3.8)$$

$$= \frac{-144 \times 88.5}{0.3}$$

$$= -42,480 \text{ ft lb per lb.}$$

b) In this case the work done by the shaft (Ws), i.e. the power required to drive the shaft is to be determined.

$$W_s = -\int_{P_1}^{P_2} v\,dp + \frac{V_1^2 - \cancel{V_2^2}}{2\beta} \!\!\!\nearrow^O + \frac{g}{\beta}(Z_1 - \cancel{Z_2}) \!\!\!\nearrow^O$$

$$= -\int_{P_1}^{P_2} v\,dp$$

$$p^{\frac{1}{1.3}} v = C^{\frac{1}{1.3}}$$

$$v = (C)^{\frac{1}{1.3}} (p)^{-\frac{1}{1.3}}$$

$$\therefore W_s = -C^{\frac{1}{1.3}} \int_{P_1}^{P_2} p^{-\frac{1}{1.3}}\,dp$$

$$= -C^{\frac{1}{1.3}} \left(\frac{p_2^{-\frac{1}{1.3}+1} - p_1^{-\frac{1}{1.3}+1}}{-\frac{1}{1.3} + 1} \right)$$

$$= \frac{-p_2 v_2 - p_1 v_1}{-\frac{1}{1.3} + 1}$$

$$= -1.3 \left(\frac{p_2 v_2 - p_1 v_1}{1.3 - 1} \right)$$

$$= -4.34 \,(p_2 v_2 - p_1 v_1)$$

$$= 12^2 \times (-4.34)(75 \times 3.8 - 15 \times 13.1)$$

$$= 55224 \text{ ft lb per lb.}$$

Due to losses, the work done in each case is not the same.

• PROBLEM 2-17

> $0.1 m^3$ of a ferromagnetic substance is kept at a constant temperature of 4°K while the magnetic field is increased from 0 to $\frac{4\pi}{10}$ weber/m^2. Obtain an expression for the work required if the substance follows the Curie equation of state. Assume $C = 4\pi \times 10^9$ weber - °K/amp-m.

Solution: A Curie substance is any simple magnetic substance obeying the equation of state MT = CH (1)

where M = mass

T = temperature

H = strength of the applied magnetic field

C = Curie constant

Unit work dW = VHdM (2)

Combining (1) and (2)

$$dW = \frac{VT}{C} MdM$$

$$\therefore W = \int_{M_1}^{M_2} \frac{VT}{C} MdM$$

$$= \frac{VT}{2C}(M_2^2 - M_1^2)$$

$$= \frac{(0.1)(4)(4\pi)^2(10^{-2})}{(2)(4\pi)(10^{-9})} \left[\frac{(m^3)(°K)(webers/m^2)^2}{(webers\text{-}°K/amp\text{-}m)}\right]$$

$$= (8 \times 10^6)\pi \text{ webers-amp}$$

$$= (8 \times 10^6)\pi \text{ N-m.}$$

Prove that the work required to stretch a wire of length ℓ within the elastic region is given by the equation $W = -0.5AE\ell(\varepsilon)^2$.

A is the cross sectional area of the wire,
E is the Young's Modulus, and ε the unit strain.

Solution: From Hooke's law

$$\text{stress } \sigma = \frac{T}{A}$$

$$= E\varepsilon \qquad (1)$$

where T = tension in the wire

From the definition of strain

$$d\varepsilon = \frac{\delta}{\ell}$$

where δ = deformation of wire due to the tension

$$\delta = dL$$

or $$d\varepsilon = \frac{dL}{\ell} \qquad (2)$$

$$dL = \ell d\varepsilon \qquad (3)$$

Solving in Eq. (1) for the tension T gives

$$T = AE\varepsilon \qquad (4)$$

Hence when the length of the wire changes by an amount dL, the work done by the system is

$$\delta W = -TdL$$

Substituting Eqs. (3) and (4) into the above equation

$$\delta W = -AE\varepsilon\ell d\varepsilon$$

For finite changes

$$W_{12} = \int_1^2 - AE\varepsilon\ell d\varepsilon$$

$$= - AE\ell \int_0^{\varepsilon} \varepsilon d\varepsilon$$

$$= \frac{-AE\ell(\varepsilon)^2}{2}$$

$$= -0.5\ AE\ell(\varepsilon)^2$$

• PROBLEM 2-19

An 18 inch electrical conductor carries a current of 20 amps. A constant force moves this conductor with a velocity of 20 ft/sec orthogonally across a magnetic field. Find this force and the rate of work done if the flux density is 2 $Webers/m^2$.

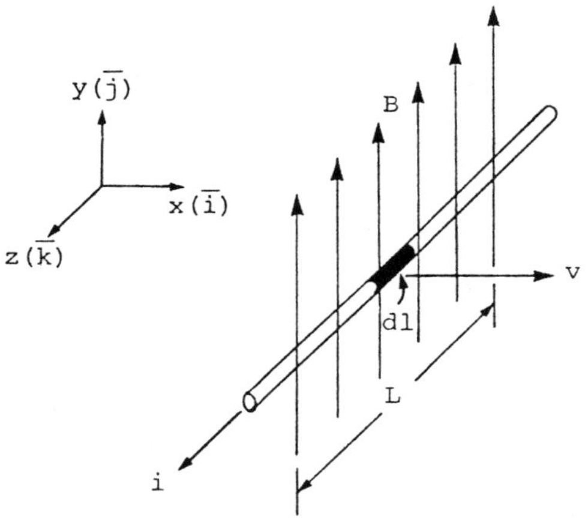

Figure. A conductor moving in a magnetic field

Solution: Amperes law relates a force to a movement of charge. If a charge q moves with a known velocity v and experiences a force in the absence of an electrostatic field, the force is then due to a magnetic field B and is related by the vector equation

$$F = qv \times B \tag{1}$$

However, this force tends to create a current flow (i) in the direction shown in the figure, because the force has the tendancy to try and displace the charges which are in the conductor. Considering a small element of length dl on the conductor, the following can be written.

$$dqv = idt \frac{dl}{dt} = idl,$$

or for finite changes

$$qv = \int idl \tag{2}$$

Substituting Eq. (2) into Eq. (1) gives for the force

$$F = \int_0^L idl \times B = -iBL\hat{i} \tag{3}$$

The rate of work then can be obtained, using the equation

$$W = F \cdot V$$

or since the expression for the force is known (Eq. 3) it can be substituted into the relation for work. Taking the dot product,

$$W = -(iBL\hat{i}) \cdot v\hat{i} = -iBLv \ . \qquad (4)$$

In order to substitute the values in the equations and to obtain a meaningful answer the units have to be consistent. Therefore, convert all the units into one system. (The S I system is used here.)

Hence

$$L = 18 \text{ in} \times 2.540 \frac{\text{cm}}{\text{in}} \times \frac{1\text{m}}{100\text{cm}} = 0.4572 \text{ m}$$

$$v = 25 \frac{\text{ft}}{\text{sec}} \times 30.48 \frac{\text{cm}}{\text{ft}} \times \frac{1\text{m}}{100\text{cm}} = 7.62 \text{ m/sec.}$$

Substituting L into Eq. (3), the force is

$$F = iBL\hat{i}$$

$$= (20 \text{ amp})(2 \text{ Weber/m}^2)(0.4572\text{m})$$

$$= 18.288 \text{ Newtons} \quad (\text{in x-direction})$$

In this problem the thermodynamic system under consideration is the conductor and the work is done on the conductor by the magnetic field. Thus the work done <u>on</u> the conductor by the force exerted externally on it is then given by Eq. (4) but with a positive sign.

Hence

$$W = +iBLv$$

$$= (20 \text{ amp})(2 \text{ Weber/m}^2)(0.4572\text{m})(7.62 \text{ m/sec})$$

$$= 139.35 \text{ Watts.}$$

• PROBLEM 2-20

A wire frame equipped with a slide wire S shown in the figure, is dipped into a vessel containing soap solution. A soap film is then formed by moving the slide wire S away from leg b. Let F be the constant force applied to move the slide wire, and σ be the surface tension of the soap film.

a) Prove that the work done to overcome the resisting surface tension is given by the equation $W = \sigma \ell b$.

b) Calculate the work done when b = 10 cm, ℓ = 6 cm, and σ = 25 dynes/cm.

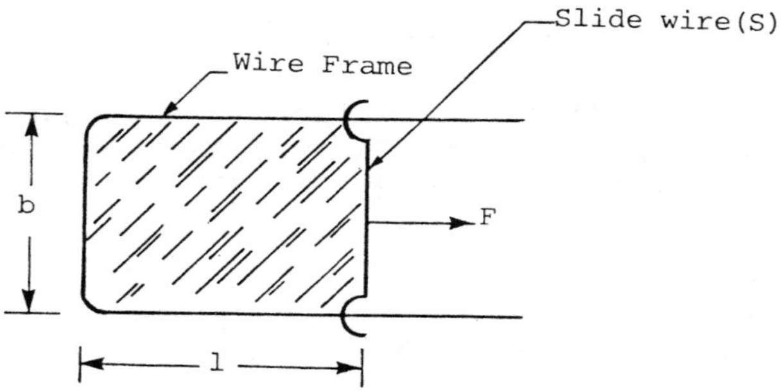

Solution: When the wire S moves along the frame the area of the film is changed and work is done on or by the film. The work is done as a result of the pressure that is being applied because of the force F, and the change in area. Thus when the area changes by an amount dA, the work done on the system is

$$\delta W = PdA \qquad (1)$$

However

$$P = \frac{F}{A}$$

where P = pressure, F = force, and A = area

and Eq. (1) becomes

$$\delta W = \frac{F}{A}dA \qquad (2)$$

Also using T = F, where T = tension, the equation for surface tension σ is

$$\sigma = \frac{T}{A} \rightarrow T = \sigma A$$

Eq. (2) becomes

$$\delta W = \sigma dA.$$

Since the force applied is constant, the surface tension is also constant. Thus for finite changes

$$W_{12} = \int_1^2 \sigma dA = \sigma(A_2 - A_1) \qquad (3)$$

where $A_1 = 0$ (wire is initially closed $\ell = 0$)

and $A_2 = \ell \cdot b$

Hence Eq. (3) becomes

$$W_{12} = \sigma \cdot \ell \cdot b = \sigma A \quad (4)$$

b) For the given values of b, ℓ, and σ when substituted in (4), the work is

$$W = \sigma \cdot \ell \cdot b = (25)(6)(10) = 1,500 \text{ dyne-cm.}$$

HEAT

• PROBLEM 2-21

A refrigerator is a common device used in every home. Examine the following systems regarding the direction of heat transfer.

(a) The refrigerator alone

(b) The room the refrigerator is located in.

Solution: (a) In order to keep the products stored inside the refrigerator at a lower temperature, heat must be absorbed from the products stored (through the evaporator) and rejected to the atmosphere. In fact this is the principle for a refrigeration cycle. Therefore, as far as heat transfer is concerned, heat is transferred from the refrigerator (the system) and thus Q = -Q.

(b) From the statement made in part(a), heat is rejected from the refrigerator to the room. The heat transfer is done through the condenser which is so arranged that the air in the room flows past the condenser by natural convection. As a result of that, heat is added to the room and the heat transfer is positive (Q = +Q) for the system under consideration. This explains why the room where the refrigerator is usually located, is always warmer than the other rooms.

• PROBLEM 2-22

Calculate the heat transferred when 100J of work is done on a system consisting of 1 mole of an ideal gas. At constant temperature, $\Delta E = 0$ for the expansion of an ideal gas.

Solution: A statement of the first law of thermodynamics is expressed as

$$\Delta E = q - w$$

where ΔE = change in internal energy of the system

q = quantity of heat

w = work done

In this problem, work is done on the system and so w is negative. (Note that we are adopting the convention that work done on the system is negative.) Since $\Delta E = 0$ for an isothermal expansion of an ideal gas,

$$\Delta E = 0 = q - w$$

$$\therefore\ q = w$$

or

$$q = -100J$$

As a result, 100J of heat must be transferred from the system to maintain isothermal conditions.

• PROBLEM 2-23

What can you say about the following statements if one has an adiabatic process in which there is no heat transfer between the system and the surroundings, either because the system is well insulated or because the process occurs very rapidly?

1. $q = +w$
2. $q = 0$
3. $\Delta E = q$
4. $\Delta E = w$
5. $P\Delta V = 0$

Solution: In an adiabatic system there is no heat flow into or out of the system, thus $q = 0$

1. This statement gives q to be +w but this can only happen when $\Delta E = 0$ since for instance $\Delta E = q - w$ for isothermal expansion of an ideal gas.
2. Statement (2) is correct since $q = 0$ for the process.
3. This statement indicates $\Delta E = q$, but this can only happen,

as in the case when one expands a gas into a vacuum, when $w = 0$.

4. Since $\Delta E = q - w$, ΔE will be equal to w only when $q = 2w$ so that

$$\Delta E = 2w - w = w$$

5. $\Delta E = q - w$

$$= q - P\Delta V$$

Thus for $P\Delta V$ to be zero, ΔE must be equal to q such that

$$\Delta E = \Delta E - P\Delta V$$

$$\therefore P\Delta V = 0$$

CHAPTER 3

ENERGY AND THE FIRST LAW OF THERMODYNAMICS

THE FIRST LAW FOR CONSTANT MASS SYSTEMS

• PROBLEM 3-1

When 100 kJ of work is done on a closed system during a process, the total energy of the system increases by 55.0 kJ. Calculate how much heat is either added or removed from the system?

Solution: In accordance with the principle of energy conservation, a net energy transfer to a system results in an equal increase of internal energy stored in the system. This may be written as

$$Q = \Delta E + W \tag{1}$$

where Q is the heat transferred to the system during the process.

W is the work transferred from the system during the process.

ΔE is the change in the internal energy of the system during the process, and all these terms are expressed in the same units.

Eq. (1) is the usual statement of the First Law. It says that in any change of state the heat supplied to a system is equal to the increase of internal energy in the system plus the work done by the system.

Considering work done on a system as positive, from Eq. (1)

$$Q + (+100.0) = +55.0$$

$$Q = +55.0 - 100.0$$

$$= -45.0 \text{ kJ}$$

From the result, due to the negative sign, 45.0 kJ of energy in the form of heat is removed from the system during the process.

• PROBLEM 3-2

A group of twenty executives attend a board meeting in a room which measures 20 ft by 20 ft and has a 10 ft ceiling. Assume that each person occupies 2.5 ft^3 and gives out about 375 Btu of heat per hour. Calculate the air temperature rise occurring within 15 min of the start of the conference if the room is completely sealed and insulated. Take c_v for air as 0.1715 Btu/lbm°F.

Solution: Take the air in the room as a thermodynamic system and assume that the people are adding heat to the air in a constant-volume process. The room volume is

$$V_{room} = 20 \times 20 \times 10 = 4000 \text{ ft}^3$$

The volume of air is obtained by subtracting the volume occupied by the people:

$$V_{air} = 4000 - (20)(2.5) = 3950 \text{ ft}^3$$

Assuming that the constant-volume heat-addition process starts at standard atmospheric conditions of 14.7 psia and 70°F, the mass of air is

$$m = \frac{pV}{RT} = \frac{(14.7)(144)(3950)}{(53.35)(530)} = 295 \text{ lbm}$$

For the constant-volume process,

$$c_v \approx \left(\frac{\Delta u}{\Delta T}\right)_v$$

and

$$\Delta U_v = mc_v \Delta T_v \qquad (1)$$

The change in internal energy of the air is equal to the heat added by the people, since

$$Q + W = \Delta U \qquad (2)$$

and there is presumably no work done on the air. Thus

$$\Delta U = (20)(375) = 7500 \text{ Btu/hr}$$

or, for a 15-min period,

$$\Delta U = \frac{15}{60} (7500) = 1875 \text{ Btu}$$

The temperature increase is now calculated from Eq. (1) as

$$\Delta T = \frac{\Delta U}{mc_v} = \frac{1875}{(295)(0.1715)} = 37°F$$

• PROBLEM 3-3

A container which has a volume of 0.1 m^3 is fitted with a plunger enclosing 0.5 kg of steam at 0.4 MPa. Calculate the amount of heat transferred and the work done when the steam is heated to 300°C at constant pressure.

Solution: For this system changes in kinetic and potential energy are not significant. Therefore

$$Q = m(u_2 - u_1) + W$$

$$W = \int_1^2 P\, dV = P \int_1^2 dV = P(V_2 - V_1) = m(P_2 v_2 - P_1 v_1)$$

Therefore

$$Q = m(u_2 - u_1) + m(P_2 v_2 - P_1 v_1) = m(h_2 - h_1)$$

$$v_1 = \frac{V_1}{m} = \frac{0.1}{0.5} = 0.2 = 0.001084 + x_1(0.4614)$$

$$x_1 = \frac{0.1989}{0.4614} = 0.4311$$

Then

$$h_1 = h_f + x_1 h_{fg}$$

$$= 604.74 + 0.4311 \times 2133.8 = 1524.6$$

$$h_2 = 3066.8$$

$$Q = 0.5\ (3066.8 - 1524.6) = 771.1 \text{ kJ}$$

$$W = mP\ (v_2 - v_1) = 0.5 \times 400\ (0.6548 - 0.2)$$

$$= 91.0 \text{ kJ}$$

Therefore

$$U_2 - U_1 = Q - W = 771.1 - 91.0 = 680.1 \text{ kJ}$$

The heat transfer can be calculated from u_1 and u_2 by using

$$Q = m(u_2 - u_1) + W$$

$$u_1 = u_f + x_1 u_{fg}$$

$$= 604.31 + 0.4311 \times 1949.3 = 1444.6$$

$$u_2 = 2804.8$$

and

$$Q = 0.5\ (2804.8 - 1444.6) + 91.0 = 771.1 \text{ kJ}$$

• PROBLEM 3-4

A medical ampule containing dextrose (liquid water) at 1000 psia, 100°F and having a volume of 0.3 in^3 is placed in a cylinder having a volume of 1 ft^3. A vacuum is created in the cylinder and the capsule is broken. Dextrose now evaporates and fills the cylinder. Calculate the final quality of the water-vapor mixture in the cylinder if it reaches a final equilibrium temperature of 100°F. b) Also calculate the heat transfer with the surroundings.

Solution: The inside surface of the cylinder is chosen as the boundary of the system. This surface is stationary and so W = O. From the first law,

$$Q + W = \Delta U \qquad (1)$$

$$Q = \Delta U = m(u_2 - u_1) \qquad (2)$$

$$V_1 = 0.3 \text{ in.}^3 = 1.735 \times 10^{-4} \text{ ft}^3.$$

Using the compressed-liquid tables for water

$$v_1 = 0.016132 - 5.2 \times 10^{-5} = 0.016080 \text{ ft}^3/\text{lb}_m$$

$$h_1 = 67.97 + 2.64 = 70.61 \text{ Btu/lb}_m$$

Furthermore,

$$u_1 = h_1 - p_1 v_1 = 70.61 - \frac{(1000)(144)(0.01608)}{778}$$

$$= 67.64 \text{ Btu/lb}_m$$

The mass of water is

$$m = \frac{V_1}{v_1} = \frac{1.735 \times 10^{-4}}{1.608 \times 10^{-2}} = 0.0108 \text{ lb}_m$$

The final specific volume is, thus,

$$v_2 = \frac{V_2}{m} = \frac{1}{0.0108} = 92.5 \text{ ft}^3/\text{lb}_m$$

The final state is determined by entering the steam tables with the known values of T_2(100°F) and v_2. At 100°F, $v_g = 350.4 \text{ ft}^3/\text{lb}_m$, so that a mixture of vapor and liquid is obtained since $v_2 < v_g$. Thus,

$$v_2 = v_{f_2} + x_2 v_{fg_2}$$

Using the properties from the saturation-temperature table

$$92.5 = 0.01613 + x_2(350.3)$$

and

$$x_2 = 0.264$$

The final internal energy is now obtained from this same table. Since internal energy is not tabulated directly, use the relation

$$u_2 = h_2 - p_2 v_2 \qquad (3)$$

The final enthalpy is

$$h_2 = h_{f_2} + x_2 h_{fg_2}$$

$$= 67.97 + (0.264)(1037.2)$$

$$= 342 \text{ Btu/lb}_m$$

Then, from Eq. (3), since the saturation pressure is 0.9492 psia at 100°F,

$$u_2 = 342 - \frac{(0.9492)(144)(92.5)}{778}$$

$$u_2 = 326 \text{ Btu/lb}_m$$

The heat transfer is now calculated using Eq. (2)

$$Q = (0.0108)(326 - 67.6)$$

$$= 2.79 \text{ Btu}$$

The positive sign on the heat transfer indicates that 2.79 Btu of heat must be supplied to the large container to maintain the vapor at 100°F during the expansion-evaporation process.

• PROBLEM 3-5

5 lbm of water at 200°F and 2 psia pressure is heated to a temperature of 1200°F. Calculate the amount of heat transferred at constant volume by

a) using the steam tables.

b) using the perfect gas approximation.

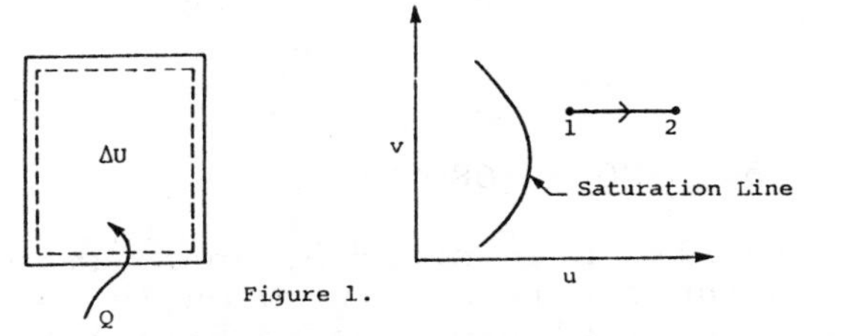

Figure 1.

(a) The control mass (b) The process representation

Solution: Define a control mass consisting of the 5 lbm of water. As in fig. 1a, energy inflow as heat will be considered positive, and there is also no work involved. The only energy possessed by the system is its internal energy U, so the energy balance, made over the time for the state change to take place, is

Q	=	ΔU
energy input		increase in energy storage

Here

$$\Delta U = m(u_2 - u_1)$$

where u_1 and u_2 represent the internal energy in the initial and final states.

Idealise that the substance is in a state of thermodynamic equilibrium at the start of the process and in another such state at the end of the process. The equation of state for water, treated as a simple compressible substance can then be employed. For the initial state, from the steam tables

$$P_1 = 2 \text{ psia} \qquad u_1 = 1080 \text{ Btu/lbm}$$

$$T_1 = 200°F \qquad v_1 = 198 \text{ ft}^3/\text{lbm}$$

Fig. 1b gives the process representation which helps in fixing the final state of the process. From the steam tables the final state is

$$v_2 = 198 \text{ ft}^3/\text{lbm} \quad P_2 = 5 \text{ psia}$$

$$T_2 = 1200°F \qquad u_2 = 1440 \text{ Btu/lbm}$$

Substituting into the energy balance

$$Q = 5 \text{ lbm} \times (1440 - 1080) \text{ Btu/lbm} = 1800 \text{ Btu}$$

b) The energy balance is the same (Fig. 1), i.e.

$$Q = m(u_2 - u_1)$$

H_2O vapor can be taken as a perfect gas, with $c_v = 0.336$ Btu/ lbm-°R, then

$$u_2 - u_1 = c_v(T_2 - T_1) = 0.336 \times (1660 - 660) = 336 \text{ Btu/lbm}$$

and

$$Q = 5 \times 336 = 1680 \text{ Btu}$$

Note that this result is in error by approximately 7 percent in comparison to the exact value previously determined as 1800 Btu. Now, the final pressure is calculated from the equation

$$Pv = RT \tag{1}$$

which gives

$$\frac{P_2}{P_1} = \frac{T_2}{T_1}$$

Hence,

$$P_2 = \frac{1660}{660} \times 2 = 5.03 \text{ psia}$$

If access to the exact property tabulations for water vapor was not given the specific volume could be estimated using equation (1). For water R = 85.58 ft-lbf/lbm-°R. Then at state 1

$$v_1 = \frac{RT_1}{P_1} = 85.58 \times \frac{(200 + 460)}{2 \times 144} = 196 \text{ ft}^3\text{/lbm}$$

which is within about 1 percent of the tabulated value.

The applicability of the perfect gas approximation can be checked by computing the value of $Z \equiv \frac{PV}{RT}$ at states 1 and 2. Using the state data obtained in part (a)

$$Z_1 = \frac{P_1 v_1}{RT_1} = \frac{2 \times 144 \times 198}{85.58 \times (200 + 460)} = 1.01$$

$$Z_2 = \frac{P_2 v_2}{RT_2} = \frac{5 \times 144 \times 198}{85.58 \times (1200 + 460)} = 1.003$$

Note that both values are very close to unity. Since both states have the same density, the state of higher temperature

(2) should more closely resemble the perfect gas, and this is indeed the case. The main error in the simplified analysis is not the assumption that Pv = RT, but the idealization that c_v is constant over the wide range of temperatures involved.

• PROBLEM 3-6

Refrigerant 12 (Freon 12) at 20 psia and 30°F is compressed to 140 psia and 150°F during a compression stroke. For a pound of this refrigerant (a) calculate the work done during compression, (b) the heat removed during compression.

Solution: (a) From the table of thermodynamic properties for refrigerant 12, the original and final specific volumes are, 2.0884 and 0.33350 cu ft/lb respectively. For the process

$$\frac{140}{20} = \left(\frac{2.0884}{0.33350}\right)^n$$

or

$$7 = 6.262^n \quad \text{and} \quad n = 1.0607$$

The work of compression equals

$$W = \frac{P_2v_2 - P_1v_1}{1-n} = \frac{144}{1-1.067}(140 \times 0.3335 - 20 \times 2.0884)$$

or

$$W = -11{,}670 \text{ ft-lb}$$

(b)

$$u_2 - u_1 = \left(h_2 - \frac{P_2v_2}{J}\right) - \left(h_1 - \frac{P_1v_1}{J}\right)$$

$$= \left(95.709 - \frac{144 \times 140 \times 0.33350}{778}\right) - \left(81.842 - \frac{144 \times 20 \times 2.0884}{778}\right)$$

$$= 12.941 \text{ Btu}$$

Then

$$Q = u_2 - u_1 + \frac{W}{J} = 12.941 - \frac{11{,}670}{778} = -2.059 \text{ Btu/lb}$$

The above values of heat and work are approximate, but they are the nearest values obtainable without a knowledge of the actual compression process.

• PROBLEM 3-7

Heat is transferred to steam at 50 lbf in a cylinder having a volume of 2 ft³. The temperature of steam rises from 300°F to 500°F while the pressure remains constant. Calculate (a) the heat transfer, (b) the work done, and (c) the change in internal energy for the above process. Assume the system to be a closed one.

Solution: Since the system is a closed one, the changes in kinetic and potential energy can be neglected.

$$Q = m(u_2 - u_1) + W$$

$$W = \int_1^2 P\,dV = P\int_1^2 dV = P(V_2 - V_1) = m(P_2v_2 - P_1v_1)$$

Therefore

$$Q = m(u_2 - u_1) + m(P_2v_2 - P_1v_1) = m(h_2 - h_1)$$

$$m = \frac{V_1}{v_1} = \frac{2}{8.773} = 0.228 \text{ lbm}$$

$$h_1 = 1184.3 \qquad h_2 = 1283.9,$$

(a) $$Q = 0.228(1283.9 - 1184.3) = 22.7 \text{ Btu}$$

(b) $$W = mP(v_2 - v_1) = \frac{0.228 \times 50 \times 144}{778}(11.309 - 8.773)$$

$$= 5.34 \text{ Btu}$$

(c) $$U_2 - U_1 = {}_1Q_2 - {}_1W_2 = 22.7 - 5.3 = 17.4 \text{ Btu}$$

This can be checked by finding u_1 and u_2

$$u_1 = h_1 - P_1v_1 = 1184.3 - \frac{50 \times 144 \times 8.773}{778}$$

$$= 1103.0 \text{ Btu/lbm}$$

$$u_2 = h_2 - P_2v_2 = 1283.9 - \frac{50 \times 144 \times 11.309}{778}$$

$$= 1179.1 \text{ Btu/lbm}$$

$$U_2 - U_1 = m(u_2 - u_1) = 0.228(1179.2 - 1103.0) = 17.4 \text{ Btu}$$

• PROBLEM 3-8

Heat is transferred to a cylinder having a volume of $5m^3$ containing 0.05 m^3 of saturated liquid water and 4.95 m^3 of saturated water vapor at 0.1 MPa, until the cylinder is filled with saturated vapor. Calculate the amount of heat transferred for the process.

Solution: The total mass within the vessel is taken as the system. From the first law

$$Q = U_2 - U_1 + m\frac{(V_2^2 - V_1^2)}{2} + mg(Z_2 - Z_1) + {}_1W_2$$

Since changes in kinetic and potential energy are not involved, this reduces to

$${}_1Q_2 = U_2 - U_1 + {}_1W_2$$

The work for this process is zero; therefore

$${}_1Q_2 = U_2 - U_1$$

The thermodynamic properties can be found from the steam tables. The initial internal energy U_1 is the sum of the initial internal energy of the liquid and the vapor

$$U_1 = m_{1liq}u_{1liq} + m_{1vap}u_{1vap}$$

$$m_{1liq} = \frac{V_{liq}}{v_f} = \frac{0.05}{0.001043} = 47.94 \text{ kg}$$

$$m_{1vap} = \frac{V_{vap}}{v_g} = \frac{4.95}{1.6940} = 2.92 \text{ kg}$$

$$U_1 = 47.94\ (417.36) + 2.92\ (2506.1) = 27326 \text{ kJ}$$

To determine u_2 we need to know two thermodynamic properties, since this determines the final state. The properties we know are the quality, x = 100%, and v_2, the final specific volume, which can readily be determined.

$$m = m_{1liq} + m_{1vap} = 47.94 + 2.92 = 50.86 \text{ kg}$$

$$v_2 = \frac{V}{m} = \frac{5.0}{50.86} = 0.09831 \text{ m}^3/\text{kg}$$

From the steam tables it is found, by interpolation, that at a pressure of 2.03 MPa, $v_g = 0.09831 \text{ m}^3/\text{kg}$. The final pressure of the steam is 2.03 MPa. Then,

$$u_2 = 2600.5 \text{ kJ/kg}$$

$$U_2 = mu_2 = 50.86\ (2600.5) = 132261 \text{ kJ}$$

$$_1Q_2 = U_2 - U_1 = 132261 - 27326 = 104935 \text{ kJ}$$

• PROBLEM 3-9

> A rigid vessel which has a volume of $0.5 m^3$ is filled with Freon-12 at 0.5 MPa, 50°C. It is then heated until the Freon-12 is fully saturated vapor. Calculate the heat transfer for this process.

Solution: It is known from the statement of the problem that the state of the substance at the end of the process (state 2) is saturated vapor, and from the Freon-12 tables it can be obtained that the state at the beginning of the process (state 1) is superheated vapor.

The First Law for this system is

$$_1Q_2 = U_2 - U_1 + {}_1W_2 \quad \text{where } {}_1W_2 = 0 \tag{1}$$

Values for the internal energy are needed to compute the heat transfer. However the Freon-12 tables do not give values for the internal energy, and thus the relation

$$u = h - Pv \tag{2}$$

can be used to obtain values of the internal energy, using the enthalpy, the specific volume, and the pressure.

From the Freon-12 tables,

State 1:

$$v_1 = 0.040911 \text{ m}^3/\text{kg}; \; h_1 = 217.484 \text{ kJ/kg}$$

From Eq. (2)

$$u_1 = 217.484 - (500)(0.040911) = 197.028 \text{ kJ/kg}$$

State 2: At this state, the only information available is the state of the substance. However this is a rigid container meaning that the volume as well as the mass of the Freon-12 will remain constant, throughout the process, which implies that the specific volume of Freon-12 will be the same at both states, because

$$v = \frac{V}{m} ; \tag{3}$$

and so

$$v_2 = v_1 = v_g = 0.040911$$

Now that enough information is available the other necessary values can be obtained directly from the Freon-12 tables. These values are

$$h_2 = h_g = 191.602 \text{ kJ/kg; } P = 0.4233 \text{ MPa}$$

Then using Eq. (2)

$$u_2 = 191.602 - (423.3)(0.040911) = 174.284 \text{ kJ/kg}$$

The mass of the Freon-12 is then given from (3) as

$$m = \frac{V}{v} = \frac{0.5}{0.040911} = 12.22 \text{ kg}$$

Eq. (1) then, written on a mass basis gives

$$_1Q_2 = m(u_2 - u_1)$$

$$= 12.22\ (174.284 - 197.028)$$

$$= -277.93 \text{ kJ}$$

The minus sign indicates that heat is extracted from the system.

• PROBLEM 3-10

A piston-cylinder system contains three lbm of water in the saturated-liquid state at 100 psia. Heat is added to the water in such a way that pressure always remains a constant during the process. Calculate (a) the work done by the water and (b) the energy required to bring the water to the saturated vapor state.

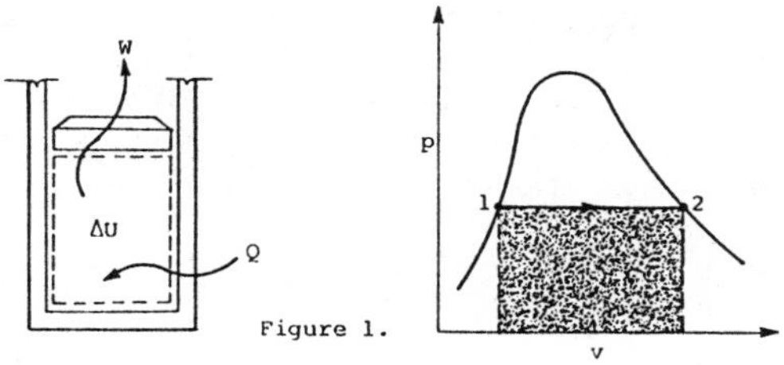

Figure 1.

(a) The control mass (b) The process representation

Solution: The water or the water plus the piston can be selected as the control mass. Since the energy transfer to the water is the only thing that is of concern, and the piston is merely a means for maintaining the constant pressure, only the water is taken as the control mass. The change of state is depicted by the process representation, which is shown on a P-v plane in the figure.

In order to solve the problem idealize that the changes in the gravitational potential energy of the water are negligible in comparison with the changes in the internal energy. Idealize further that the presence of the gravitational field does not significantly alter the behavior of the water molecules, so that the relationships between the thermodynamic properties are the same as if the water were truly a simple compressible substance. In short, idealize that the water behaves like a simple compressible substance and is in equilibrium states at the start and end of the process.

Employing these idealizations, the energy balance, made over the period for the process to occur, is

Q	=	W	+	ΔU
energy input		energy output		increase in energy storage

where

$$\Delta U = m(u_2 - u_1)$$

Fixing the initial and final states from the steam tables, at the initial state (saturated liquid at 100 psia)

$P_1 = 100$ psia $\qquad T_1 = 327.81°F$

$u_1 = 298.08$ Btu/lbm $\qquad v_1 = 0.01774\ ft^3/lbm$

and at the final state (saturated vapor at 100 psia)

$P_2 = 100$ psia $\qquad T_2 = 327.81°F$

$u_2 = 1105.2$ Btu/lbm $\qquad v_2 = 4.432\ ft^3/lbm$

Note that the volume occupied by the water increases tremendously.

Now the net energy added to the water could be computed but as yet is not possible to tell how much is added as heat and how much is taken away as work. The fact that the pressure remains constant during the process allows to compute the work very simply. The work done by the water is

$$W = \int_1^2 dW = \int_1^2 P\ dV = M \int_1^2 P\ dv$$

Since the pressure is constant,

$$W = mP(v_2 - v_1)$$

The work done is therefore

$$W = 3\ lbm \times 100\ lbf/in^2 \times 144\ in^2/ft^2 \times (4.432 - 0.017)\ ft^3/lbm$$

$$= 191{,}000 \text{ ft-lbf} \times \frac{1 \text{ Btu}}{778 \text{ ft-lbf}} = 245 \text{ Btu}$$

Finally the energy added as heat can be calculated:

$$Q = 245 \text{ Btu} + 3 \text{ lbm} \times (1105.2 - 298.08) \text{ Btu/lbm} = 2665 \text{ Btu}$$

The energy transfer as heat could have been calculated directly if it was noticed that it is expressible as

$$Q = m[P(v_2 - v_1) + (u_2 - u_1)] = m(h_2 - h_1)$$

Note that the energy transfer as heat (per unit of mass) to a simple compressible substance during a constant pressure process is equal to the increase in its enthalpy.

Values for h_1 and h_2 could have been obtained from the steam tables.

The energy transfer as heat required to evaporate a unit of mass of a simple compressible substance at constant pressure is therefore simply $h_g - h_f = h_{fg}$ and is sometimes called the enthalpy of evaporation of that substance. Note that it depends on pressure and vanishes at the critical point.

• PROBLEM 3-11

A piston-cylinder system is used to compress 2 lbm of a gas from 14 ft^3 to a volume of 9 ft^3 at a constant pressure of 2000 lbf/ft^2. It is found that the internal energy decreases by 6000 ft-lbf during the process. Calculate the amount of heat transferred to or from the gas during the compression.

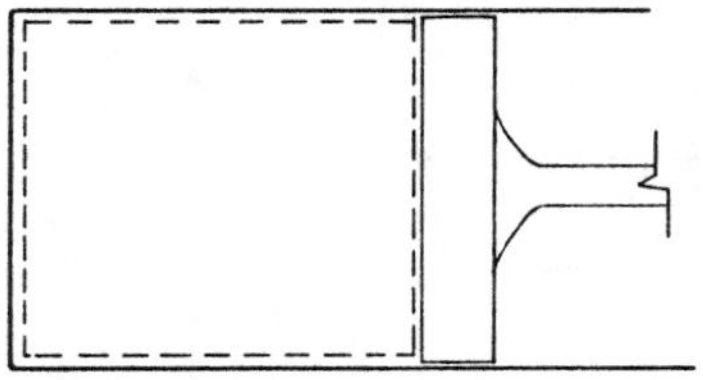

Fig. 1. The control mass

Solution: For the system, the gas alone is considered as the control mass. It is clear from the problem statement that energy will be put into the system as work, and so choose the sign of positive work as indicated in the figure. It may not be immediately clear which way the energy transfer as heat takes place; define Q to be positive as an energy input, and indicate this on the figure. Also assume that the only system energy is its internal energy U. In terms of the system and symbols of Figure 1, the energy balance is then

$$\underset{\text{energy input}}{W + Q} = \underset{\text{increase in energy storage}}{\Delta U}$$

where $\Delta U = U_2 - U_1$ and the subscripts 1 and 2 denote the initial and final states. The internal energy change is known and Q can be computed from the energy balance if W can be evaluated. The work done on a gas during compression is

$$W = -\int_1^2 P\,dV$$

Since the pressure P is constant, integrate and obtain

$$W = P(V_1 - V_2) = 2000\ \text{lbf/ft}^2 \times (14-9)\ \text{ft}^3 = 10{,}000\ \text{ft-lbf}$$

Solving Eq. (1) for Q,

$$Q = \Delta U - W = -6000 - 10{,}000 = -16{,}000\ \text{ft-lbf}$$

The minus number means that the actual direction of energy transfer as heat was incorrect. The answer is that 16,000 ft-lbf of energy was transferred as heat from the gas.

• PROBLEM 3-12

Determine the final equilibrium state when 2 lbm of saturated liquid mercury at 1 psia is mixed with 4 lbm of mercury vapor at 1 psia and 1400°F. During the process the pressure in the cylinder is kept constant and no energy is lost between the cylinder and mercury.

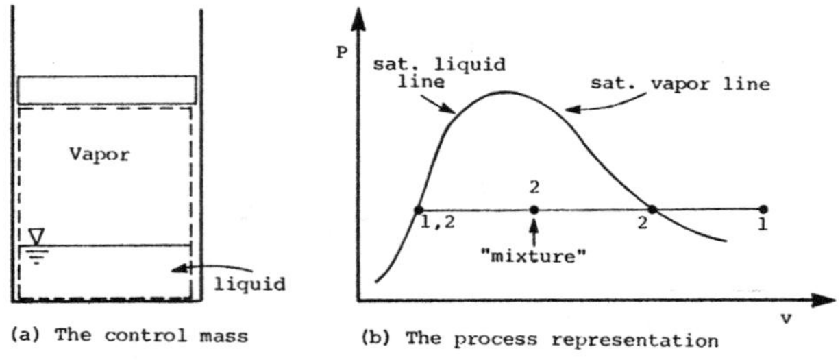

Fig. 1.

Solution: Since the amount of liquid might change during the process, the liquid or only the vapor cannot be taken as the control mass. Instead take the entire 6 lbm of mercury. By assumption, no energy transfer as heat occurs, but the volume is expected to change, resulting in an energy transfer as work. The only energy stored within the control mass is the internal energy of the mercury; the energy balance, made over the time for the process to take place, is therefore (Fig. 1)

W	=	ΔU
energy input		increase in energy storage

where

$$\Delta U = U_2 - U_1$$

The work calculation is made easy by the fact that the pressure is constant. When the piston moves an amount dx, the energy transfer as work from the environment to the control mass is

$$dW = PAdx = -P\ dV$$

Integrating,

$$W = \int_1^2 -P\ dV = P(V_1 - V_2)$$

Combining with the energy balance, obtain

$$U_2 + PV_2 = U_1 + PV_1 \tag{1}$$

Table 1. Properties of Saturated Mercury

		Enthalpy, Btu/lbm		
P, psia	*T, °F*	*Sat. liq.*	*Evap.*	*Sat. vap.*
0.010	233.57	6.668	127.732	134.400
0.020	259.88	7.532	127.614	135.146
0.030	276.22	8.068	127.540	135.608
0.050	297.97	8.778	127.442	136.220
0.100	329.73	9.814	127.300	137.114
0.200	364.25	10.936	127.144	138.080
0.300	385.92	11.639	127.047	138.686
0.400	401.98	12.159	126.975	139.134
0.500	415.00	12.568	126.916	139.484
0.600	425.82	12.929	126.868	139.797
0.800	443.50	13.500	126.788	140.288
1.00	457.72	13.959	126.724	140.683
2.00	504.93	15.476	126.512	141.988
3.00	535.25	16.439	126.377	142.816
5.00	575.7	17.741	126.193	143.934

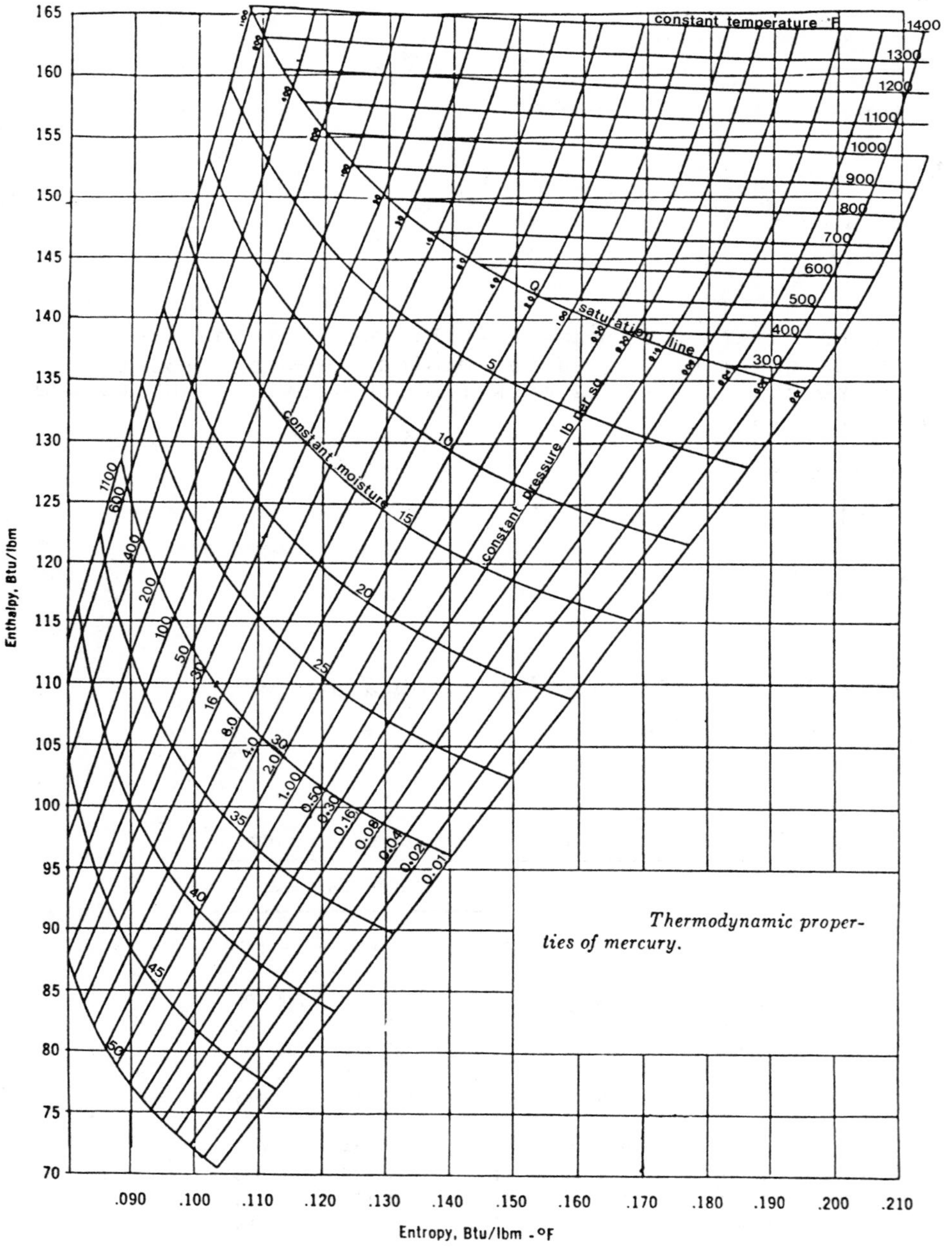

Thermodynamic properties of mercury.

Fig. 2

To evaluate the initial terms assume that the liquid is in an equilibrium state and the vapor is in an equilibrium state, even though they are not in equilibrium with one another. The graphical and tabular equations of state, Fig. 2 and the Table for the thermodynamic properties of saturated mercury, may then be employed for each phase. Since the available equation-of-state information is in terms of the enthalpy property, express the right-hand side of Eq. (1) as

$$U_1 + PV_1 = M_{l_1}u_{l_1} + M_{v_1}u_{v_1} + P(M_{l_1}v_{l_1} + M_{v_1}v_{v_1})$$

$$= M_{l_1}h_{l_1} + M_{v_1}h_{v_1}$$

Now, from the tables, the initial liquid enthalpy is (saturated liquid at 1 psia, Table 1)

$$h_{l_1} = 13.96 \text{ Btu/lbm}$$

$$T_1 = 457.7°F$$

The initial vapor enthalpy is found from Fig. 2 as

$$h_{v_1} = 164 \text{ Btu/lbm}$$

Substituting the numbers,

$$U_1 + PV_1 = 2 \times 13.96 + 4 \times 164 = 684 \text{ Btu}$$

The final state is a state of equilibrium, for which

$$U_2 + PV_2 = M(u + Pv)_2 = Mh_2$$

The enthalpy in the final state is therefore

$$h_2 = \frac{684 \text{ Btu}}{6 \text{ lbm}} = 114 \text{ Btu/lbm}$$

The final pressure and enthalpy may be used to fix the final state. Upon inspection of Fig. 2 the final state is a mixture of saturated liquid and vapor at 1 psia and the "moisture" $(1 - x)$ is about 21 percent (0.79 quality). Alternatively, the information in Table 1, could have been used.

$$114 = (1 - x_2) \times 13.96 + x_2 \times 140.7$$

$$x_2 = 0.79$$

• **PROBLEM 3-13**

A partition separates the two compartments of an insulated vessel as shown in the figure. Compartment A contains 2 kg of water at 200°C, 5 MPa and compartment B contains 0.983 kg of water at 200°C, 0.1 MPa. The partition is removed and the water in both the compartments fill up the entire vessel. Determine the final pressure, and the heat transfer involved in the mixing process, if the final temperature is 200°C.

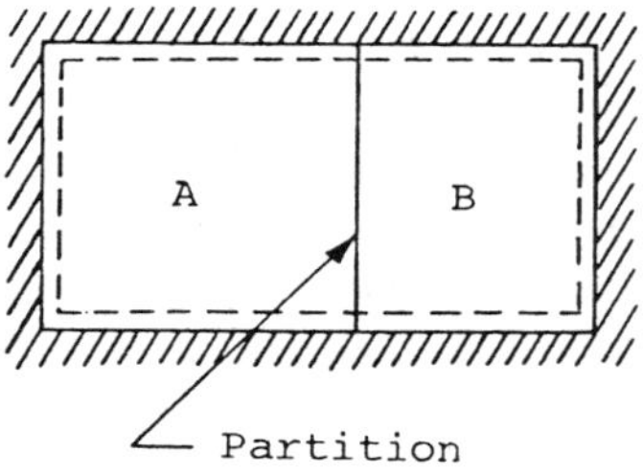

Solution: (a) If there was another independent property known for the final state, then the pressure could have been obtained from the steam tables since one property (temperature) is already known. Furthermore looking at the given information, one can see that another independent property can be calculated at the final state. That property is the specific volume. Let subscripts A, B, and F denote the states in chambers A and B, and the final state respectively.

First the state of the water must be found in the two chambers

Chamber A: compressed liquid ($P_{given} > P_{sat.}$)

$$v_A = 0.001153 \text{ m}^3/\text{kg}; \quad u_A = 848.1 \text{ kJ/kg}$$

Chamber B: superheated vapor ($P_{given} < P_{sat.}$)

$$v_B = 2.172 \text{ m}^3/\text{kg}; \quad u_B = 2658.1 \text{ kJ/kg}.$$

The volume of the container is

$$V = V_A + V_B$$

where

$$V = mv \tag{1}$$

Thus

$$V_F = m_A v_A + m_B v_B = (2)(0.001153)+(0.983)(2.172)$$

$$= 2.1374 \text{ m}^3$$

The total mass is

$$m_F = m_A + m_B = 2 + 0.983 = 2.983 \text{ kg}$$

Hence from Eq. (1)

$$v_F = \frac{V_F}{m} = \frac{2.1374}{2.983} = 0.7165$$

The temperature and specific volume are now known for the final state. With these values and the steam tables the final state lies in the superheated region. Therefore

$$P_F = 0.3 \text{ MPa}$$

$$u_F = 2650.7 \text{ kJ/kg.}$$

(b) Now consider the inside surface of the whole container as a system. The first law is then,

$$Q_{12} = U_2 - U_1 + \cancel{W}^{=0}$$

or on a per mass basis

$$Q_{12} = m_F u_F - (m_A u_A + m_B u_B)$$

$$= (2.983)(2650.7)-[(2)(848.1)+(0.983)(2658.1)]$$

$$= 3597.9 \text{ kJ}$$

• PROBLEM 3-14

A piston cylinder arrangement having an enclosed volume of 0.1 m^3 holds Freon-12 at 500 kPa and 70°C. The piston is held in position by a pin while the pressure is raised to 600 kPa. Keeping this pressure constant, the pin is released and additional heat is transferred until the temperature reaches 80°C. Calculate the total heat transferred during the process to the system.

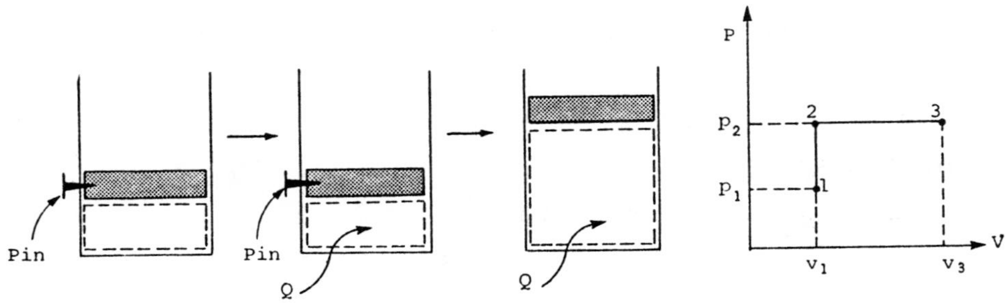

(a) (b)

Figure 1. (a) Schematic representation. (b) P-V diagram (superheated region)

Solution: Referring to Figure 1(b), and using the Freon-12 tables for the given data, we have,

State 1: $T = 70°C$ and $P = 500$ kPa

$v_1 = 0.044184\ m^3/kg$, $h_1 = 231.161$ kJ/kg

State 2: $P = 600$ kPa (constant volume process, $v_2 = v_1$)

From the saturated Freon-12 tables,

$v_g = 0.0293\ m^3/kg$,

so the substance lies in the superheated region ($v_2 > v_g$). Also

$T_{sat} = 130°C$, and obtain

$h_2 = 272.231$ kJ/kg

State 3: $T = 80°C$ and $P = 600$ kPa

$v_3 = 0.037653\ m^3/kg$, $h_3 = 237.027$ kJ/kg

From Fig. 1 it is evident that this is a constant mass process and one that can be separated into two different processes; a constant volume process (state 1 to 2), and a constant pressure process (state 2 to 3).

The mass is first obtained, using

$$m = \frac{V}{v} = \frac{0.10}{0.044184} = 2.2633 \text{ kg}$$

from the First Law of Thermodynamics,

$$Q_{12} = U_2 - U_1 + (K.E.) + (P.E.) + W_{12} \qquad (1)$$

Neglecting potential and kinetic energy and writing on a mass basis, becomes

$$Q_{12} = m(u_2 - u_1) + W_{12} \qquad (2)$$

Divide the entire process into two different processes.
State 1 to 2: This is a constant volume process, and so

$$W_{12} = 0$$

Noting that there are no values for u in the tables the equation

$$u = h - Pv \tag{3}$$

is substituted into Equation (2) giving

$$Q_{12} = m[(h_2-h_1) - v_1(P_2-P_1)] + W_{12} \tag{4}$$

Substituting the obtained values in Eq. (4)

$$Q_{12} = 2.2633[(272.231-231.161) - 0.044184(600-500)]$$

$$= +82.9536 \text{ kJ}$$

State 2 to 3: This is a constant pressure process and the work done is given by

$$W_{23} = \int_2^3 PdV = P(V_3 - V_2) = mP(v_3 - v_2)$$

$$= 2.2633(600)(0.037653 - 0.044184)$$

$$= -8.8690 \text{ kJ}$$

The minus sign indicates that work was done on the system.

Combine Equations (3) and (2) to obtain

$$Q_{12} = m[(h_3 - h_2)-P(v_3- v_2)] + W_{12}$$

$$= 2.2633[(237.027-272.231)-600(0.037653-0.044184)]+(-8.8690)$$

$$= -79.6772 \text{ kJ}$$

The total heat transfer

$$Q_{TOT} = Q_{12} + Q_{23}$$

$$= (+82.9536 \text{ kJ})+(-79.6772 \text{ kJ})$$

$$= +3.2764 \text{ kJ}$$

The plus sign indicates that heat was transferred to the system.

• PROBLEM 3-15

Two identical, well insulated piston cylinder devices of 100 cm^2 area are placed as shown in the figure. Both have metallic pistons and connecting rods. The first cylinder contains gaseous helium at 2 atm and the second contains gaseous helium at 1 atm. The temperature in both cylinders is 0°C. When the stopper is removed the pressures will become identical and all oscillations will cease.

(a) Calculate the final temperatures after the oscillations cease, if the gas is assumed to be ideal with a constant C_v. Also neglect the masses of cylinders and pistons.

(b) Calculate the final temperatures for the same situation, but with well insulated pistons and connecting rods of low thermal conductivity.

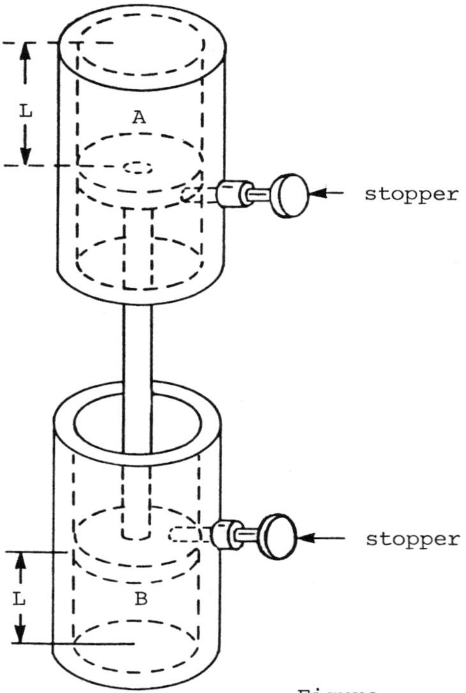

Figure

Solution: (a) Choose the gases in compartments A and B as systems A and B, respectively. Since these are simple systems, denote the energies by $\underline{U}$ instead of $\underline{E}$. Since the mass and initial temperature are known for the gas in each compartment, the final temperature can be calculated for each compartment, if the final energy - or energy change - of each compartment is first determined. Thus, from the equations

$$\underline{PV} = NRT \tag{1}$$

$$\underline{U} = N \int C_v dT + NU_o \tag{2}$$

as applied for each system, give

$$N_A = \frac{P_{Ai}\underline{V}_{Ai}}{RT_{Ai}} \tag{3}$$

$$N_B = \frac{P_{Bi}\underline{V}_{Bi}}{RT_{Bi}} \tag{4}$$

$$T_{Af} = T_{Ai} + \frac{\underline{U}_{Af} - \underline{U}_{Ai}}{N_A C_v} \tag{5}$$

and

$$T_{Bf} = T_{Bi} + \frac{\underline{U}_{Bf} - \underline{U}_{Bi}}{N_B C_v} \tag{6}$$

where $\underline{U}_{Af}$ and $\underline{U}_{Bf}$ are the only unknowns ($\underline{U}_{Ai}$ and $\underline{U}_{Bi}$ can be chosen at will because $\underline{U}_0$ in Eq. (2) is an arbitrary constant).

Since the pistons and shaft have been assumed to be good conductors of heat, the final temperatures of compartments A and B will be equal:

$$T_{Af} = T_{Bf}$$

To determine the energy change, apply the First Law, to system A:

$$\underline{U}_{Af} - \underline{U}_{Ai} = Q_A - W_A \tag{7}$$

The work done by this system is equal to the work done on the gas in B and the frictional work done on the walls of A and B, or

$$W_A = -W_B - W_{WA} - W_{WB} \tag{8}$$

where W_B is the work done by the gas in B and W_{WA} is the work done by the wall of A, etc. Now consider the wall of A as the system and apply the First Law to this system:

$$\Delta\underline{U}_{WA} = Q_{WA} - W_{WA} \tag{9}$$

If we neglect the change in energy of the wall, the frictional work done by the gas on the wall will be transmitted back to the gas in the form of a heat interaction; that is

$$Q_{WA} = W_{WA} \tag{10}$$

and furthermore,

$$Q_{A} = -Q_{WA} - Q_{AB} \tag{11}$$

where Q_{AB} is the heat conducted from A to B through the pistons. Substituting Equations (8), (10), and (11) into Equation (7)

$$\Delta \underline{U}_{A} = W_{B} + W_{WB} - Q_{AB} \tag{12}$$

By analogy to Eqs. (10) and (11) as applied to the walls of B,

$$W_{WB} = Q_{WB} = - Q_{B} + Q_{AB} \tag{13}$$

and by analogy to Eq. (9),

$$W_{B} - Q_{B} = - \Delta \underline{U}_{B} \tag{14}$$

Eq. (12) becomes

$$\Delta \underline{U}_{A} = - \Delta \underline{U}_{B} \tag{15}$$

Equation (15) could have been stated at the outset because the composite system A + B is equivalent to an isolated system; this result, however, may not have been immediately obvious. Combining Eq. (15) with Eqs. (5) and (6), and making use of the fact that $T_{Af} = T_{Bf}$; obtain

$$T_{f} = \frac{N_{A}T_{Ai} + N_{B}T_{Bi}}{N_{A} + N_{B}} \tag{16}$$

or, for this special case wherein $T_{Ai} = T_{Bi} = T_{i}$,

$$T_{f} = T_{i} = 0°C$$

Now use hindsight to reevaluate the problem. A qualitative feeling for the path in that the frictional work was involved, but the path could not be described quantitatively because the coefficient of friction of either piston-cylinder was not known. Nevertheless, the final conditions were determined and, therefore, it was possible to describe the path to find the solution. Such a situation would be expected if the end state was independent of the path. This is obviously the case in the present example: Since the composite system A + B is an isolated simple system, there is only one state to which it can go, and that is the one for which $\underline{U} = \underline{U}_{Ai} + \underline{U}_{Bi}$ and

$T = T_{Af} = T_{Bf}$. For an ideal gas, $\underline{U}$ is a unique function of T and N and, thus, the final temperature can be determined.

(b) The composite system of A + B is no longer a simple system because it contains an internal adiabatic wall. Therefore, the final composite cannot be described by a single equilibrium state; instead, the final conditions will depend on the path of the process.

Eqs. (5) through (15) are still valid. Combining Eqs. (5) and (6) with Eq. (15) results in

$$N_A C_v (T_{Af} - T_{Ai}) + N_B C_v (T_{Bf} - T_{Bi}) = 0 \tag{17}$$

which now gives one equation in two unknowns, T_{Af} and T_{Bf}. One can try to juggle the other equations to find another relationship between T_{Af} and T_{Bf}, but until some assumptions are made regarding the path, all efforts will be in vain.

If no information on the coefficient of friction is known the engineering judgment to simplify the situation while obtaining a close approximation to the actual conditions will have to be used.

Assume that there is friction only in compartment B. This will give a lower bound for T_{Af} and an upper bound for T_{Bf}. The case of friction only in compartment A can then be treated, which will give an upper bound for T_{Af}.

If there is no friction in compartment A and if the assumption that the process is quasi-static (i.e., no pressure gradients within the compartment can be made for) the simple system of the gas in A

$$d\underline{U}_A = -dW_A = -P_A d\underline{V}_A \tag{18}$$

Since

$$dW_{WA} = dQ_A = dQ_{AB} = 0$$

$$N_A C_v dT_A = -N_A R\left(dT_A - \frac{T_A}{P_A} dP_A\right) \tag{19}$$

or

$$\left(\frac{C_v + R}{R}\right)\frac{dT_A}{T_A} = \frac{dP_A}{P_A} \tag{20}$$

Integrating between initial and final conditions,

$$\frac{T_{Af}}{T_{Ai}} = \left(\frac{P_{Af}}{P_{Ai}}\right)^{R/(C_v+R)} \tag{21}$$

Eqs. (21) and (17) give two equations in three unknowns,

T_{Af}, T_{Bf}, and $P_{Af} = P_f$. The final pressure can be eliminated in the following manner.

Since

$$\underline{V}_{Af} + \underline{V}_{Bf} = \underline{V}_{Ai} + \underline{V}_{Bi} = \underline{V}_T \tag{22}$$

and $\underline{V}_T$ is known, substitution of Eq. (1) into Eq. (22) gives

$$\underline{V}_T = (N_A T_{Af} + N_B T_{Bf})\frac{R}{P_f} \tag{23}$$

Eq. (2) along with Eqs. (21) and (17) give us three equations in these unknowns.

$$P_f = \frac{P_{Ai}\underline{V}_{Ai} + P_{Bi}V_{Bi}}{\underline{V}_{Ai} + \underline{V}_{Bi}} = 1.5 \text{ atm}$$

From Eq. (21), with $C_v = 3$ cal/g-mol °K

$$T_{Af} = \left(\frac{1.5}{2}\right)^{0.4} T_{Ai} = 243°K$$

From Eq. (17)

$$T_{Bf} = 334°K$$

If it is assumed that there is friction only in compartment A, then one can find that $T_{Bf} = 318°K$. Since in the actual case the friction is distributed between A and B, a better approximation might be $T_{Bf} = (318 + 334)/2 = 326°K$ and $T_{Af} = 246°K$.

The fact that the adiabatic wall prevents a direct solution to the problem in the absence of a complete description of the path is sometimes referred to as the "adiabatic dilemma". In fact, it is no dilemma at all, but results from the difference between heat and work interactions.

INTERNAL ENERGY, ENTHALPY, AND SPECIFIC HEAT OF IDEAL GASES

• PROBLEM 3-16

A container holds 5 lbm of water as shown in the figure. (a) Calculate the change in specific and total internal energy if the total work input is 3890 ft-lbf. Assume the system is adiabatic. (b) If 0.1 Btu/lbm of heat is lost, then what is the change in the internal energy?

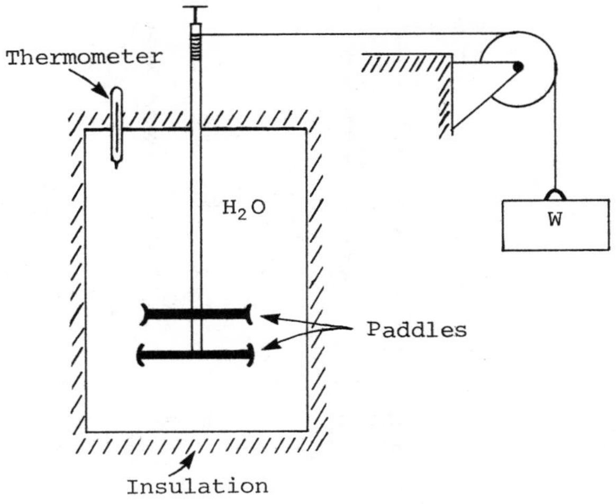

Solution: Assume heat flow in to be positive and work in as negative. Since ΔK.E. and ΔP.E. are zero for both cases, the energy balance for the system is

First law: $Q = \Delta U + W$

(a) Adiabatic: $Q = 0$

$\Delta U = W = 3890 \text{ ft-lbf} = 5 \text{ Btu}$

$\Delta u = 1 \text{ Btu/lbm}$

(b) $Q = -0.5 \text{ Btu}$

$-0.5 = \Delta U - 5$

$\Delta U = 4.5 \text{ Btu}$

$\Delta u = 0.9 \text{ Btu/lbm}$

• PROBLEM 3-17

The figure shows a system having a paddle wheel which does work. The system is adiabatic and at constant pressure. It contains 0.3 lbm of air at 20 psia, and after it receives 14,004 ft-lbf of work the temperature rises from 500°R to 750°R. Calculate a) the total work, b) the mechanical work, c) the changes in internal energy and d) the enthalpy change for the system.

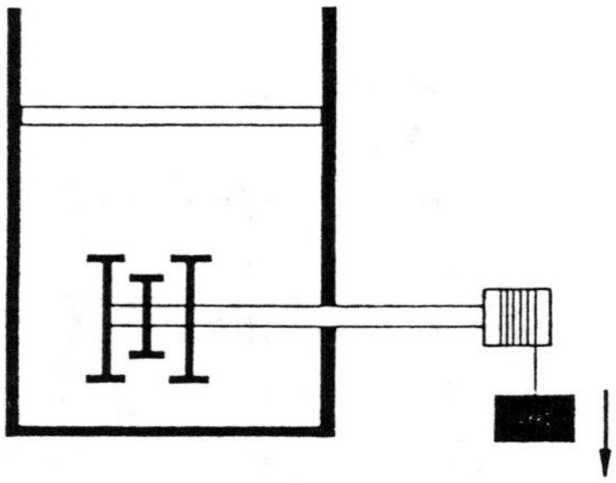

<u>Solution</u>: a) The work done $W = \int_1^2 mpdv = mp(v_2 - v_1)$

From the ideal gas equation $v_1 = \frac{RT_1}{P_1}$

$$= \frac{(53.34)(500)}{(20)(144)}$$

$$= 9.253 \text{ ft}^3/\text{lbm}$$

and

$$V_2 = \frac{RT_2}{P_2} = \frac{(53.34)(750)}{(20)\ (144)}$$

$$= 13.88 \text{ ft}^3/\text{lbm}$$

$$W = \frac{(0.3)(20)(144)(13.88 - 9.253)}{778}$$

$$= 5.13 \text{ Btu}$$

(c) The change in internal energy $\Delta u = mc_v(T_2 - T_1)$

$$= (0.3)(0.1714)(250) = 12.87 \text{ Btu}$$

(d) The change in enthalpy $H = mc_p(T - T)$

$$= (0.3)(0.24)(250)$$

$$= 18.0 \text{ Btu}$$

(b) From the above values, the mechanical work can be calculated.

Given W = 14004 ft-lbf

= 18 Btu

$\therefore\ \Sigma W = 5.13 - 18$

$= -12.87$ Btu

• PROBLEM 3-18

To vaporise 1 mole of water at 1 atm pressure and 100°C, 9.71 kcal of heat is required. a) Calculate the change in enthalpy and total energy for this vaporisation process. b) If one mole of steam condenses at 100°C and 1 atm pressure then what is the change in enthalpy and total energy for the process?

Solution: a) Given that the pressure is maintained at 1 atm.

$$\therefore \Delta H = 9.71 \text{ kcal/mole}$$

The volume of the liquid vaporized, $V_l \cong 18$ ml.

The volume of 1 mole of the gas produced, $V_g \cong 25{,}000$ ml.

Since V_g is much larger than V_l,

$$P\Delta V = P(V_g - V_l) \cong PV_g = RT$$

$$= (2)(373)$$

$$= 746 \text{ cal/mole}$$

$$\cong 0.75 \text{ kcal/mole}$$

$$\Delta H = \Delta E + P\Delta V$$

The change in total energy $= \Delta H - P\Delta V$

$$= 9.71 - 0.75$$

$$= 8.96 \text{ kcal/mole.}$$

b) When we consider condensation there will be an output of heat, $\therefore \Delta H = -9.71$ kcal/mole. Condensation will have a decrease in volume, so that

$$P\Delta V \cong P(-V_G) = -RT = -0.75 \text{ kcal/mole}$$

Then

$$\Delta E = \Delta H - P\Delta V$$

$$= -9.71 - (-0.75)$$

$$= -8.96 \text{ kcal/mole.}$$

Water is continuously spilling over a water tank at a height of 100 m from ground level.

a) Calculate the potential energy of the water at the top of the tank with respect to its base.

b) Calculate the kinetic energy of the water just before it strikes the floor.

c) After the water enters the flow below, what change has occurred to its state?

Calculate for 1 kg of water in all three cases, assuming that there is no energy exchange with the surroundings.

Solution: Since there is no energy exchange Q and W = 0

$$\Delta U + \Delta E_K + \Delta E_P = 0 \qquad (1)$$

E_K = kinetic energy

E_P = potential energy

U = internal energy.

Equation (1) can be applied to any point of the fall.

$$E_P = \frac{mzg}{g_c} = \frac{1(kg) \times 100(m) \times 9.8066(m)/(s)^2}{1(kg)(m)/(N)(s)^2}$$

where g has been taken as the standard value. This gives

$$E_P = 980.66(N \cdot m) \qquad \text{or} \qquad 980.66(J)$$

b) During the free fall of the water no mechanism exists for conversion of potential or kinetic energy into internal energy. Thus ΔU must be zero, and

$$\Delta E_K + \Delta E_P = E_{K_2} - E_{K_1} + E_{P_2} - E_{P_1} = 0$$

For practical purposes take $E_{K_1} = 0$ and $E_{P_2} = 0$. Then

$$E_{K_2} = E_{P_1} = 980.66(J)$$

c) As the 1(kg) of water strikes the bottom and joins with other masses of water to form a flow, there is much turbulence, which has the effect of converting kinetic energy into internal energy. During this process ΔE_P is essentially zero. Therefore

$$\Delta U + \Delta E_K = 0 \qquad \text{or} \qquad \Delta U = E_{K_2} - E_{K_3}$$

However, the velocity is assumed to be small, and therefore E_{K_3} is negligible. Thus

$$\Delta U = E_{K_2} = 980.66(J)$$

• PROBLEM 3-20

Calculate the change of enthalpy as 1 lbm of oxygen is heated from 500 R to 2000 R. Also calculate the average specific heat for the process.

Solution: Using the specific-heat equation and integrating the equation $dH = MC_{po}dt$, we obtain

$$\bar{h}_2 - \bar{h}_1 = \int_{T_1}^{T_2} \bar{C}_{po} dT = \int_{T_1}^{T_2} 11.515\ dT - \frac{172 dT}{T^{\frac{1}{2}}} + 1530 \frac{dT}{T}$$

$$\bar{h}_2 - \bar{h}_1 = 11.515(T_2 - T_1) - 172 \times 2(T_2^{\frac{1}{2}} - T_1^{\frac{1}{2}}) + 1530 \ln \frac{T_2}{T_1}$$

$$\bar{h}_{2000} - \bar{h}_{500} = 17,280 - 7690 + 2120 = 11,710 \text{ Btu/lb-mole}$$

$$h_{2000} - h_{500} = \frac{\bar{h}_{2000} - \bar{h}_{500}}{M} = \frac{11,710}{32} = 366 \text{ Btu/lbm}$$

The average specific heat for any process is defined by the relation

$$C_{p(av)} = \frac{\int_{T_1}^{T_2} C_p dT}{T_2 - T_1}$$

Therefore the average specific heat is

$$C_{p(av)} = \frac{366 \text{ Btu/lbm}}{(2000 - 500)\ {}^\circ R} = 0.244 \text{ Btu/lbm}\ {}^\circ R$$

• PROBLEM 3-21

Calculate the heat added when one mole of carbon dioxide is heated at constant volume from 540 to 3540 F.

Solution: Since the temperature is much higher than the critical temperature, the compressibility factor can be taken as 1. The specific heat can be calculated from the relationship

$$C_v = C_p - \frac{R_o}{J} \text{ Btu/lb/°F}$$

and $$d'Q = NC_v dT$$

Then

$$d'Q = N(C_p - 1.985)\ dT$$

$$d'Q = 1\left(16.2 - \frac{6.53 \times 10^3}{T} + \frac{1.41 \times 10^6}{T^2} - 1.985\right) dT$$

Hence,

$$Q = 14.215(4000-1000) - 6.53\times10^3 \ln\left(\frac{4000}{1000}\right) - 1.41\times10^6\left(\frac{1}{4000} - \frac{1}{1000}\right)$$

$$= 42{,}645 - 9053 + 1058 = 34{,}650 \text{ Btu}$$

Alternate Solution: At the mean temperature of 2500 R,

$$C_v = (16.2 - 1.985) - \frac{6.53 \times 10^3}{2500} + \frac{1.41 \times 10^6}{2500^2}$$

$$= 14.215 - 2.612 + 0.226 = 11.829 \text{ Btu/lbm-°F}$$

Then

$$Q = NC_v(T_2 - T_1) = 1 \times 11.829 \times 3000 = 35{,}487 \text{ Btu}$$

• PROBLEM 3-22

A pressure vessel contains an inert gas at a temperature of 140°F and a pressure of 10 atm. The vessel is then heated until the pressure becomes 20 atm. For one pound mole of the inert gas, calculate a) q, the heat transfer per unit mass. b) ΔE, the change in total energy, c) ΔH, the change in internal energy.

Solution: The specific heat of the gas at constant volume, C_V, is given approximately as

$$C_V = 1.09 + 3.72 \times 10^{-3} T \text{ Btu/(lb mole)(°R)}$$

where T is in degrees Rankine. The equation of state for the gas over the range under consideration may be expressed by

$$PV = (1 - 0.01\ P)RT$$

Also

$$\left(\frac{\partial E}{\partial T}\right)_V = C_V$$

$$\Delta E = \int_{T_1}^{T_2} C_V dT = 1.09\ \Delta T + (1.86 \times 10^{-3})(T_2^2 - T_1^2)$$

since

$$PV = (1 - 0.01P)RT$$

then

$$\frac{V_1}{R} = \frac{(1 - 0.01P_1)T_1}{P_1} = \frac{V_2}{R} = \frac{(1 - 0.01P_2)T_2}{P_2}$$

$$T_2 = \frac{1 - (0.01)(10)(600)(20)}{(10)1 - (0.01)(20)} = 1350°R$$

Therefore

$$\Delta E = 3540 \text{ Btu}$$

$$w_V = 0$$

$$q = \Delta E = 3540 \text{ Btu}$$

$$\Delta H_V = \Delta E + \Delta(PV) = \Delta E + (P_2V_2 - P_1V_1)$$

$$\Delta H_V = \Delta E - (1 - 0.01P_2)RT_2 - (1 - 0.01P_1)RT_1$$

$$\Delta H_V = 4610 \text{ Btu}$$

• PROBLEM 3-23

A container with an air tight piston is at a pressure of 100 psia and a temperature of 70°F. The piston moves up when 100 Btu of heat is transferred and the volume changes from 0.5 ft^3 to 2.0 ft^3.

Assuming perfect gas behavior, calculate a) the change in internal energy, b) the final temperature and c) the heat capacity of the process.

Solution: For a simple system

$$\Delta U = Q - W$$

Assuming the system behaves ideally:

$$\Delta U = Q - p\int_{V_1}^{V_2} dV$$

where p is a constant. Then

$$\Delta U = 100 - \frac{100 \times 144}{778}\int_{0.5}^{2.0} dV$$

1 BTU ≅ 778 ft lbf, and so

$$\Delta U = 100 - 18.5(2.0 - 0.5) = 72.2 \text{ Btu}$$

From the perfect gas laws:

$$\frac{p_1 V_1}{T_1} = \frac{p_2 V_2}{T_2}$$

Hence

$$T_2 = \frac{T_1 V_2}{V_1} = \frac{(70 + 460)(2.0)}{0.5} = 2120°R$$

$$t_2 = \underline{1660°F}$$

Since the process is at constant pressure then $\overline{C}_p$ is the heat capacity desired.

$$\overline{C}_p = \frac{\Delta Q}{\Delta T} = \frac{100}{2120 - 530} = 0.0629 \text{ Btu/°R}$$

c) $$dQ = C_p dt = dh$$

$$_1Q_2 = h_2 - h_1 = 66 \text{ Btu per lbm.}$$

To produce an increase of enthalpy either heat or work should be done.

Since heat transferred = 66 Btu/lbm, the value of work is also equal to 66 Btu.

• PROBLEM 3-24

A gas at 100°F has a specific heat at constant pressure of 0.28 Btu/lbm-°F. Independent of pressure, for every degree rise in temperature the c_p increases by 0.0005 Btu.

Assuming one pound of the gas a) Calculate the change of enthalpy if the temperature rises by 200°F. b) Calculate Δpv in Btu/lbm if C_v is less by 0.08 Btu/lbm-°F.

c) How much heat is to be added and how much work is to be performed to produce the same enthalpy change?

Solution: $dh = C_p dt$

where C_p = specific heat at constant pressure

h = specific enthalpy

$$C_p = 0.28 + 0.0005\,(t - 100)$$

$$h_2 - h_1 = \int_{t_1}^{t_2} C_p dt$$

$$= \int_{t_1}^{t_2} (0.23 + 0.0005t)\, dt$$

$$= \int_{t_1}^{t_2} 0.23\, dt + \int_{t_1}^{t_2} 0.0005t\, dt$$

$$= 0.23(t_2 - t_1) + 0.00025(t_2^2 - t_1^2)$$

$$= 0.23(300-100) + 0.00025(90{,}000-10{,}000)$$

$$= 46 + 20$$

$$= 66 \text{ Btu/lbm},$$

b) $$h = u + pv$$

$$h_2 - h_1 = (u_2 + p_2v_2) - (u_1 + p_1v_1)$$

$$= (u_2 - u_1) + (p_2v_2 - p_1v_1)$$

$$\int_{t_1}^{t_2} c_p dt = \int_{t_1}^{t_2} c_v dt + \Delta pv$$

$$\Delta pv = \int_{t_1}^{t_2} c_p dt - \int_{t_1}^{t_2} c_v dt$$

$$= \int_{t_1}^{t_2} (0.23+0.0005t)dt - \int_{t_1}^{t_2} (0.15+0.0005t)dt$$

$$= \int_{t_1}^{t_2} 0.08\, dt$$

$$= 0.08(t_2 - t_1)$$

$$= 0.08(300 - 100)$$

$$= 16 \text{ Btu/lbm}$$

Ten cubic feet of air are cooled at a constant pressure of 80 psia. The initial temperature was 180°F and the final temperature after cooling is 100°F. Calculate

a) the external work done in foot pounds,

b) the change of internal energy,

c) the heat abstracted, and

d) the change in enthalpy.

Solution: From the ideal gas equation

$$P_1V_1 = mRT_1$$

$$80 \times 144 \times 10 = M \times 53.35\ (180 + 459.7)$$

$$\therefore M = 3.38 \text{ lb of air}$$

a) Work $\quad {}_1W_2 = P(V_2 - V_1)$

and for a constant pressure process,

$$PV_1 = mRT_1 \text{ and } PV_2 = mRT_2$$

$$ {}_1W_2 = mR(T_2 - T_1)$$

$$= 3.38 \times 53.35\ (559.7 - 639.7)$$

$$= -14425.8 \text{ ft-lb}$$

The negative sign indicates that there was compression, i.e. work was done on the gas.

b) $\Delta U = U_2 - U_1 = mc_v\ (T_2 - T_1)$

$$U_2 - U_1 = 3.38 \times 0.171\ (559.7 - 639.7)$$

$$= -46.3 \text{ Btu}$$

which means that there is a decrease in internal energy.

c) $\quad {}_1Q_2 = mc_p\ (T_2 - T_1)$

$$= 3.38 \times 0.240\ (559.7 - 639.7)$$

$$= -64.9 \text{ Btu}$$

which means that heat has been removed.

d) $\quad H_2 - H_1 = {}_1Q_2 = -64.9$ Btu. i.e., there is a decrease in enthalpy.

• PROBLEM 3-26

> One pound of a gas in a piston cylinder arrangement undergoes compression from 500 psia to 50 psia. The initial volume of the gas is 3 cu. ft per lb. The variation of p and v is such that $pv^{1.4}$ is a constant. Calculate the change in internal energy if the work performed is equal to the amount of heat transferred to the surroundings.

Solution: The work done can be obtained from the equation

$$W = \int_{v_1}^{v_2} p\,dv \tag{1}$$

Given

$$pv^{1.4} = \text{constant};\ p = Cv^{-n} = Cv^{-1.4}$$

$$pv^n = c = p_1 v_1^n = p_2 v_2^n \tag{2}$$

From (1)

$$W = \int_{v_1}^{v_2} Cv^{-n}\,dv.$$

$$= \left.\frac{cv^{-n+1}}{-n+1}\right|_{v_1}^{v_2}$$

$$= \frac{Cv_2^{1-n} - Cv_1^{1-n}}{1-n}$$

From (2)

$$W = \frac{p_2 v_2^n v_2^{1-n} - p_1 v_1^n v_1^{1-n}}{1-n}$$

$$= \frac{p_2 v_2 - p_1 v_1}{1-n}$$

$$= \frac{p_1 v_1 - p_2 v_2}{n-1} \tag{3}$$

To calculate the value of v_2

$$p_1 v_1^n = p_2 v_2^n$$

$$\therefore\ v_2 = \left(\frac{p_1}{p_2}\right)^{1/n} v_1$$

$$= \left(\frac{500}{50}\right)^{\frac{1}{1.4}} \times 3$$

$$= 15.54 \text{ ft}^3/\text{lbm}$$

From (3)

$$W = \frac{(144 \times 500 \times 3) - (144 \times 50 \times 15.54)}{1.4 - 1}$$

$$= 260280 \text{ ft lbf/lbm}$$

$$= \frac{260280}{777.9} \text{ Btu/lbm}$$

$$= \underline{335 \text{ Btu/lbm}}$$

Given that Q, the total heat transferred, is equal to the work done,

i.e. $Q = -W$

$$Q - \int_{v_1}^{v_2} pdv = u_2 - u_1$$

$$-W - \int_{v_1}^{v_2} pdv = u_2 - u_1$$

$$-2 \int_{v_1}^{v_2} pdv = u_2 - u_1$$

where u is the internal energy. ∴ the change in internal energy.

$$\therefore u_2 - u_1 = -2 \times 380 = -760 \text{ Btu/lbm}$$

• PROBLEM 3-27

1 gm-mole of carbon dioxide is heated from 500°C to 1000°C at a) constant volume, and b) constant pressure. Assuming ideal gas behavior calculate the heat transferred, the work done, the change in energy, and the change in enthalpy for the two processes.

Solution: a) When heating is done at constant volume, the work done will be zero and there will only be a change in internal energy.

$$Q = \Delta E = \int C_v dT$$

The heat capacity data for CO_2 is given in terms of C_p. It becomes easier to evaluate ΔH first.

According to Eq. (1)

$$\Delta H = \int C_v dT + \int R dT = \int (C_v + R) dT = \int C_p dT \qquad (1)$$

for a constant-volume process in an ideal gas system. The change in enthalpy may be evaluated either from the empirical constants given in the table for Molal heat capacities of gases, or from the mean heat capacity data between 298°K (25°C) and temperature T°K.

A mean heat capacity between 500°C and 1000°C may be evaluated by substituting the empirical constants for carbon dioxide into the equation

$$C_{pm} = a + \frac{b}{2}(T_2 - T_1) + \frac{c}{3}(T_2^2 + T_2 T_1 + T_1)^2$$

$$C_{pm} = 6.214 + (10.396 \times 10^{-3})(1237 + 573)/2$$
$$- (3.545 \times 10^{-6})[(1237)^2 + (1237)(573) + (573)^2]/3$$

$$= 6.214 + 9.60 - 3.18 = 12.64 \text{ cal/(gram mole) (°K)}$$

$$\Delta H = (12.64)(1000 - 500) = 6320 \text{ cal/gram mole}$$

Using the mean heat capacities between 25°C and temperature t,

	cal/gram mole
ΔH between 25°C and 1000°C = (11.92)(1000-25) =	11,620
ΔH between 25°C and 500°C = (10.77)(500-25) =	5,110
ΔH between 1000°C and 500°C =	6,510

Using the latter value for ΔH,

$$Q = \Delta E = \Delta H - v\Delta p = \Delta H - R\Delta T$$

$$= 6510 - (1.987)(1000 - 500) = 5516 \text{ cal/gram mole}$$

b) Constant Pressure: At constant pressure,

$$w = p\Delta v = R\Delta T = (1.987)(1000 - 500) = 994 \text{ cal/gram mole}$$

$$Q = \Delta E + p\Delta v = \Delta H = 6510 \text{ cal/gram mole}$$

$$\Delta E = \Delta H - p\Delta v = \Delta H - R\Delta T$$

$$= 6510 - 994 = 5516 \text{ cal/gram mole.}$$

• **PROBLEM 3-28**

A cylinder piston arrangement compresses air at 70°F and 14.7 psia to 294 psia. The compression follows a reversible process defined by the relation $PV^{1.3} = C$. (a) Calculate the work performed and the heat transferred in this case. (b) Also calculate the specific heat. In this case the specific heat is considered to be a constant. $Q - W = \Delta E = \Delta U$

Solution: (a) The differential change of state for a stationary closed system in general is given by,

$$dQ - dW = dU$$

$$dQ = dU + dW \tag{1}$$

dQ for a stationary closed system undergoing a change of state quasi-statically is given by

$$dQ = dU + pdv$$

$$\therefore\ dW = pdv \tag{2}$$

$$dQ = c_v dT + pdv \tag{3}$$

$$dW = pdv \qquad pv^n = C = p_1 v_1^n = p_2 v_2^n$$

$$= Cv^{-n}\,dv \qquad \therefore\ p = Cv^{-n}$$

$$_1W_2 = \int_{v_1}^{v_2} Cv^{-n}\,dv$$

$$= C\left.\frac{v^{-n+1}}{-n+1}\right|_{v_1}^{v_2}$$

$$= \frac{Cv_2^{1-n} - Cv_1^{1-n}}{1-n}$$

$$= \frac{p_2 v_2^n v_2^{1-n} - p_1 v_1^n v_1^{1-n}}{1-n}$$

$$= \frac{p_2 v_2 - p_1 v_1}{1-n}$$

$$= \frac{p_1 v_1}{1-n}\left(\frac{p_2 v_2}{p_1 v_1} - 1\right)$$

$$= \frac{RT_1}{1-n}\left[\left(\frac{p_2}{p_1}\right)^{\frac{n-1}{n}} - 1\right]$$

$$ {}_1W_2 = \frac{53.34 \times 530}{-.3}\left[\left(\frac{294}{14.7}\right)^{.3/1.3} - 1\right] $$

$$ = -\frac{53.34 \times 530 \times 0.998}{0.3} $$

$$ = -93{,}800 \text{ ft-lbm} $$

$$ \therefore \; {}_1W_2 = -120.4 \text{ Btu.} $$

Now

$$ dQ = c_v \, dT + pdv $$

$$ \therefore \; {}_1Q_2 = c_v(T_2 - T_1) + \int_{v_1}^{v_2} pdv \qquad\qquad T_2 = T_1\left(\frac{p_2}{p_1}\right)^{\frac{n-1}{n}} $$

$$ = .173(1057 - 530) - 120.4 \qquad\qquad \therefore \; T_2 = 530 \times 20^{0.231} $$

$$ = 91.3 - 120.4 \qquad\qquad = 530 \times 1.998 $$

$$ {}_1Q_2 = -29.1 \text{ Btu.} \qquad\qquad = 1057°R $$

(b)

$$ dQ = c_n dT $$

$$ {}_1Q_2 = c_n(T_2 - T_1) $$

and

$$ c_n = \frac{Q}{T_2 - T_1} $$

$$ = \frac{-29.1}{527} $$

$$ = -0.0552 \text{ Btu/lb degree.} $$

CONSERVATION OF MASS

• PROBLEM 3-29

Calculate the mass rate of flow of air through a pipeline with an inside diameter of 3.5 in. if the average velocity of air at 80°F and 20 psia is 110 ft/min.

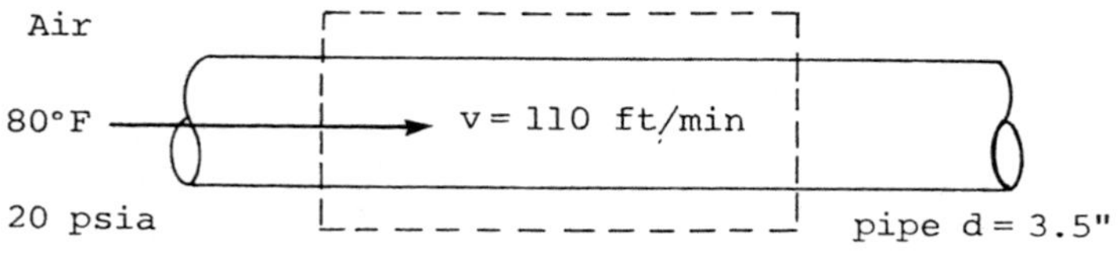

Solution: Using the ideal gas equation

$$Pv = RT \quad (1)$$

And from the conservation of mass

$$\dot{m} = \rho AV \quad (2)$$

where V = velocity of air = 110 ft/min

A = area of cross section of the pipe

ρ = density of air

From (2)

$$\dot{m} = \frac{1}{v} AV \quad (3)$$

where v = specific volume of air

From (3) $v = \frac{AV}{\dot{m}}$

Combining Eq. (3) and (1), gives

$$\frac{PAV}{\dot{m}} = RT$$

$$\dot{m} = \frac{P}{RT} \cdot AV$$

$$\dot{m} = \frac{20 \times 144}{\left(\frac{1545}{29}\right)(80+460)} \cdot \frac{\pi\left(\frac{3.5}{12}\right)^2}{4} \times 110$$

$$= \frac{20 \times 144 \times \pi}{(53.41)(540)} \times \frac{0.085}{4} \times 110$$

$$\dot{m} = \underline{0.733} \text{ lbm/min.}$$

• PROBLEM 3-30

Steam enters a heat exchanger at 1.4 MPa and 300°C, where it condenses on the outside of some tubes. The condensed steam leaves the heat exchanger as liquid at 1.4 MPa and 150°C with a flow rate of 5,000 kg/hr. The steam is condensed by water passing through the tubes. The water enters the heat exchanger at 20°C and experiences a temperature rise of 20°C before leaving. Assuming the heat exchanger to be adiabatic, determine the flow rate of water required.

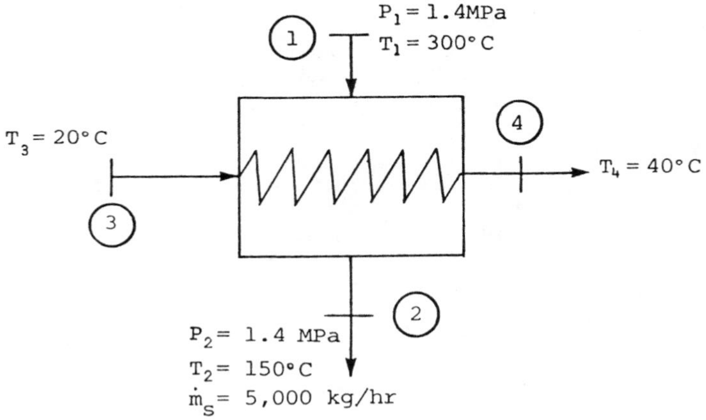

Solution: This is a steady-state-steady-flow process. The First Law written for the control volume, is

$$\dot{Q}_{c.v.} + \Sigma\dot{m}_i h_i = \Sigma\dot{m}_e h_e + \dot{W}_{c.v.} \qquad (1)$$

Since the heat exchanger is assumed to be adiabatic, $\dot{Q}_{c.v.} = 0$, and also because there is no work done on or by the system $\dot{W}_{c.v.} = 0$. Eq. (1) reduces to,

$$\Sigma\dot{m}_i h_i = \Sigma\dot{m}_e h_e$$

Referring to the accompanying figure for the different states, and denoting $\dot{m}_s$ as the mass flow rate of steam and $\dot{m}_w$ as the mass flow rate of the cooling water obtain

$$m_1 h_1 + m_3 h_3 = m_2 h_2 + m_4 h_4$$

But

$$m_s = m_1 = m_2$$

and

$$m_w = m_3 = m_4$$

Hence

$$m_s(h_1 - h_2) = m_w(h_4 - h_3)$$

$$m_w = \left[\frac{(h_1 - h_2)}{(h_4 - h_3)}\right] m_s \qquad (2)$$

Using the steam tables:

State 1: The gas at state 1 is in the superheated region.

$$h_1 = 3{,}040.4 \text{ kJ/kg}$$

State 2: $h_2 = h_f = 632.20$ kJ/kg (liquid at T = 150°C)

State 3: $h_3 = h_f = 83.96$ kJ/kg (liquid at T = 20°C)

State 4: $h_4 = h_f = 167.57$ kJ/kg (liquid at T = 40°C)

substituting into Equation (2), gives

$$m_w = \left[\frac{(3{,}040.4 - 632.20)}{(167.57 - 83.96)}\right] 5{,}000$$

$$= 144{,}013.8 \text{ kg/hr.}$$

$$= 2{,}400.2 \text{ kg/min.}$$

$$= 40.0 \text{ kg/sec.}$$

THE FIRST LAW FOR OPEN STEADY - STATE, STEADY - FLOW SYSTEMS

• PROBLEM 3-31

A fluid having a flow rate of 5 lbm/sec passes through a pipe where heat is transferred at the rate of 50 Btu/sec. How much work can be done by this system if the velocity, enthalpy and height at the entrance are 100 ft/sec, 1000 Btu/lbm, and 100 ft respectively. At the exit the values of these quantities are 50 ft/sec, 1020 Btu/lbm, and 0 ft. What is the area of the inlet of the pipe if the specific volume of the fluid is 15 ft^3/lbm.

Solution: The equation to be used to calculate the above is

$$\Delta q - \Delta W = (h_2 - h_1) + \frac{V_2^2 - V_1^2}{2Jg_c} + \frac{g}{g_c}\frac{Z_2 - Z_1}{J}$$

where

q = heat transfer per unit mass

w = work transfer per unit mass

h = specific enthalpy

g = acceleration due to gravity

g_c = constant that relates force, mass, length and time in Newton's second law of motion

J = Joules equivalent.

Hence

$$\frac{50}{5} - \Delta w = (1{,}020 - 1{,}000) + \frac{50^2 - 100^2}{2(32.2)(778)} + \frac{32.2}{32.2}\left(\frac{0 - 100}{778}\right)$$

$$10 - \Delta w = 20 - 0.15 - 0.13$$

$$\Delta w = -9.7 \text{ Btu/lbm}$$

This answer, when multiplied by the mass-flow rate (pounds mass per second), has the dimension of power.

$$\text{Power} = -48.5 \text{ Btu/sec}$$

Note that work (or power) must be supplied to the system, a condition indicated by the negative sign of ΔW.

From the equation below

$$\text{The area } A = \frac{\dot{m}_f v}{V} = \frac{5(15)}{100} = 0.75 \text{ ft}^2$$

• PROBLEM 3-32

> An air compressor takes in 2 ft^3/lb of air at 15 psia and compresses it to a pressure of 110 psia. The specific volume at discharge is 0.5 ft^3/lb. Calculate the amount of heat transferred if the increase in internal energy is 40 Btu/lb and the work done is 70 Btu/lb.

Solution: The different forms of energy to be considered in this case are the flow energy, internal energy, work and heat. For unit mass (1 lb) of a substance.

$$W_1 = \frac{p_1 v_1}{J}$$

$$= \frac{15 \times 12^2 \times 2}{778}$$

$$= 5.55 \text{ Btu/lb.}$$

$$W_2 = \frac{p_2 v_2}{J}$$

$$= \frac{(110) \times 12^2 \times 0.5}{778}$$

$$= 10.18 \text{ Btu/lb.}$$

$$\therefore \ \Delta W_f = W_2 - W_1 = 10.18 - 5.55 = 4.63 \text{ Btu/lb.}$$

In any case of compression, work must be done on the air to compress it and work therefore is negative in this case.

$$W = -70 \text{ Btu/lb.}$$

The change in internal energy is

$$\Delta u = u_2 - u_1 = 40 \text{ Btu/lb}$$

The total heat transfer Q can be given by

$$Q = \Delta u + \Delta W_f + W$$

$$= 40 + 4.63 + (-70)$$

$$= -25.37 \text{ Btu/lb.}$$

The negative sign shows that heat is given out during the process, and air compressors usually have water jackets for the purpose of cooling the air during compression.

• PROBLEM 3-33

A pump has a 2 in. diameter outlet pipe which is 5 ft above the inlet pipe. Brine at 15°F and 14 psia enters the pump through the 3 in inlet pipe and leaves at 45 psia. Assuming no losses calculate the power required to maintain a flow rate of 200 gallons per minute. The specific gravity of brine is 1.20 lb/ft³.

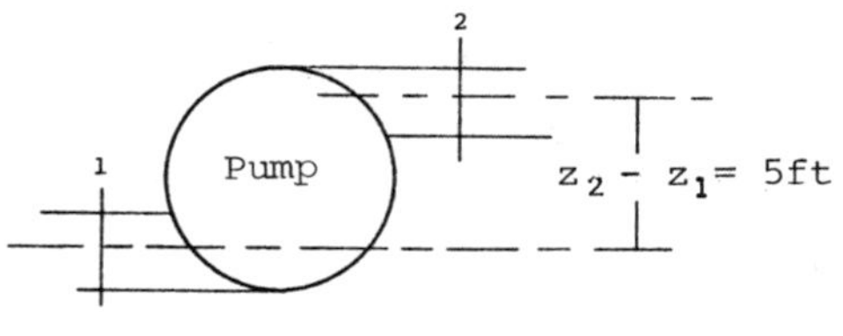

Solution: This is an example of an extension of the first law to open systems across the boundary of which there will be mass flow in addition to the possibility of heat and work transfer. Assume steady-flow conditions.

The work input

$$W_{in} = \int_1^2 vdp + \frac{V_2^2 - V_1^2}{2g_c} + \frac{g}{g_c}(Z_2 - Z_1) \qquad (1)$$

Since brine is incompressible, i.e. v = const. and using the continuity equation to obtain the velocities, the work input can be easily calculated using equation (1).

The mass rate of flow

$$M = \frac{200}{60} \times \frac{231}{1728} \times 62.4 \times 1.20 \quad \left[\frac{gal}{sec}\right] \left[\frac{in^3}{gal}\right] \left[\frac{ft^3}{in^3}\right] \left[\frac{lb}{ft^3}\right]$$

$$= 33.4 \text{ lb/sec.}$$

$$V_1 = \frac{M}{\rho A_1}$$

$$= \frac{33.4 \times 4 \times 12^2}{1.20 \times (62.4) \times \pi \times 3^2}$$

$$= 9.1 \text{ fps}$$

$$V_2 = \frac{M}{\rho A_2} = \frac{\rho A_1 V_1}{\rho A_2} = \left(\frac{D_1}{D_2}\right)^2 V_1$$

$$= \left(\frac{3}{2}\right)^2 \times 9.1$$

$$= 20.5 \text{ ft/sec.}$$

$$\therefore W_{in} = v(p_2 - p_1) + \frac{(V_2 - V_1)(V_2 + V_1)}{2g_c} + \frac{g}{g_c}(Z_2 - Z_1)$$

$$= \frac{1}{1.2 \times 62.4}(45-14)144 + \frac{11.4(29.6)}{2 \times 32.2} + \frac{32.2}{32.2} \times 5$$

$$= 59.7 + 5.2 + 5 = 69.9 \text{ ft-lbf/lbm}$$

The power required to do this quantity of work is

$$P = M W_{in}$$

$$= \frac{33.4 \times 69.9}{550}$$

$$= 4.245 \text{ hp.}$$

• PROBLEM 3-34

Oil having a density of 50 lbm/ft³ is pumped through a pipeline 9000 ft. long. Calculate the work needed for this purpose if losses are 3 ft-lbf/lbm per 100 ft. (Refer to the figure.)

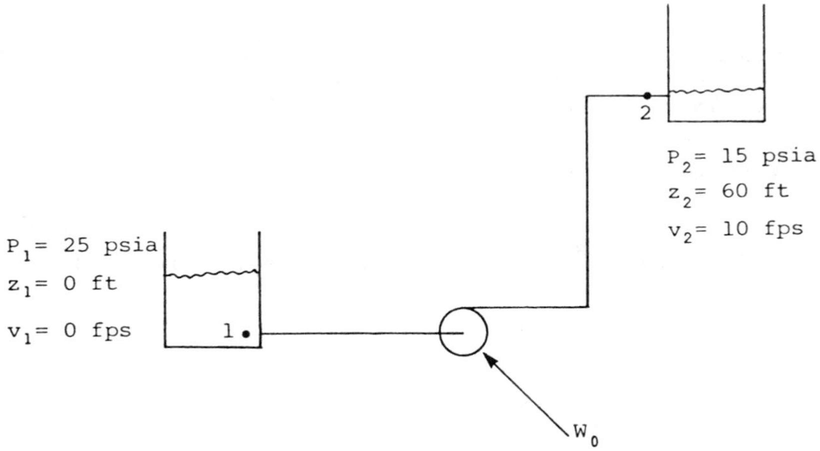

Solution: Taking into consideration the different forms of energy and losses,

$$\frac{\Delta p}{\rho} + \Delta KE + \Delta PE + W + \text{losses} = 0$$

$$\frac{P_2 - P_1}{\rho} + \frac{V_2{}^2 - V_1{}^2}{2\ g_c} + \frac{(Z_2 - Z_1)}{g_c}\ g + W + \text{losses} = 0 \qquad (1)$$

Substituting the values,

$$\frac{(15-25)\ \frac{\text{lbf}}{\text{in}^2} \times 144\ \frac{\text{in}^2}{\text{ft}^2}}{50\ \frac{\text{lbm}}{\text{ft}^3}} + \frac{(10^2 - 0^2)\ \frac{\text{ft}^2}{\text{sec}^2}}{2 \times 32.2\ \frac{\text{ft lbm}}{\text{sec}^2 \text{lbf}}}$$

$$+ \frac{(60-0)\ \text{ft}\ \frac{32.2\ \text{ft}}{\text{sec}^2}}{32.2\ \frac{\text{ft lbm}}{\text{sec}^2\ \text{lbf}}} + W + 9000\ \text{ft} \times \frac{3\ \text{ft-lbf}}{100\ \text{ft}}$$

or

$$-\ 28.8 + 1.55 + 60 + W + 270 = 0$$

$$\therefore\ W = -302.75\ \text{ft-lbf/lbm}$$

The negative sign shows that the work done is transferred to the system.

• PROBLEM 3-35

Calculate the total work transfer that takes place for a process as shown in the figure.

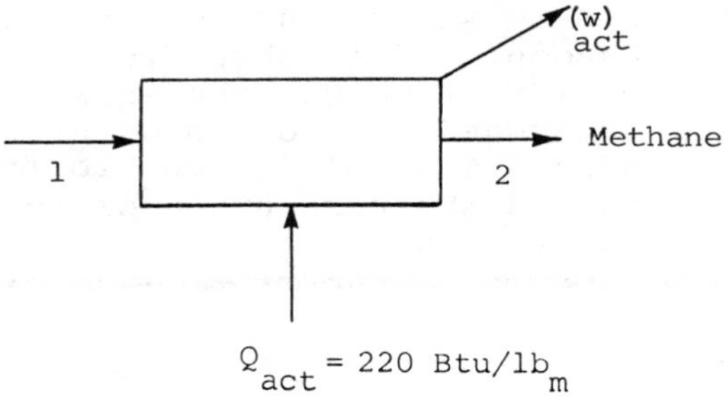

$T_1 = -50°F$	$T_2 = +70°F$
$P_1 = 650$ psia	$P_2 = 25$ psia
$H_1 = 300$ Btu/lb_m	$H_2 = 410$ Btu/lb_m
$S_1 = 1.0$ Btu/lb_m°R	$S_2 = 1.65$ Btu/lb_m°R
$Z_1 = 100$ ft	$Z_2 = 100$ ft
$V_1 = 450$ ft/sec	$V_2 = 150$ ft/sec

Solution: Taking into consideration the different forms of energy

$$Q_{act} - (W)_{act} = \Delta H + \Delta KE + \Delta PE$$

$$= H_2 - H_1 + \frac{V_2^2 - V_1^2}{2\, g_c} + (Z_2 - Z_1)\frac{g}{g_c}$$

$$220\,\frac{\text{Btu}}{\text{lb}_m} - (W)_{act} = (410-300)\,\frac{\text{Btu}}{\text{lb}_m} + \frac{(150^2-450^2)\,\frac{\text{ft}^2}{\text{sec}^2}}{2 \times \frac{32.2\ \text{ft lb}_m}{\text{sec}^2\ \text{lb}_f}}$$

$$\times \frac{1\ \text{Btu}}{778\ \text{ft-lbf}} + \frac{(100-100)\,\frac{32.2\ \text{ft}}{\text{sec}^2}}{\frac{32.2\ \text{ft-lb}_m}{\text{sec}^2\ \text{lb}_f}}$$

$$220 - W_{act} = 110 + (-3.6) + 0$$

$$\therefore\ -W_{act} = -113.6\ \text{Btu/lb}_m$$

$$W_{act} = 113.6 \text{ Btu/lb}_m$$

• PROBLEM 3-36

Snow from a pavement is scooped up to a height of 10 ft by an endless bucket-scoop, and is then dropped into a container. At the highest point, the snow moves at 3 ft/sec. A total of 33 HP is needed to scoop snow at the rate of 100 lb/sec. Assuming a loss of 10% due to friction, calculate the total work done and the percentage of total work needed to melt and break up the snow.

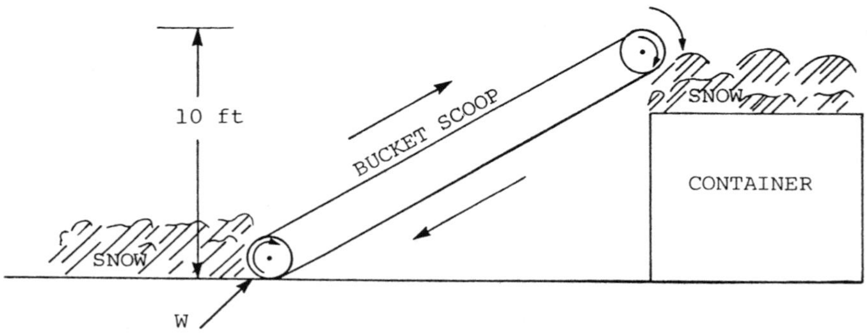

DIAGRAM OF A BUCKET-SCOOP SYSTEM.

Solution: This system involves changes in potential, and kinetic energy plus an enthalpy change of the "flowing" material.

The total work,

$$W = \left[\frac{g}{g_c}(Z_1 - Z_2) + \frac{1}{2g_c}(V_1^2 - V_2^2) + (h_1 - h_2)\right]\dot{m}$$

V_1 is obviously zero since the snow is at rest until picked up, h_2 is greater than h_1 since frictional energy goes into the snow to melt it. Then (if the energy needed to melt a pound of snow is 144 Btu)

$$W = -\left(10 \text{ ft-lbf/lbm} + \frac{3^2}{64.4} + 0.1 \times 144 \times 778\right) 100 \text{ lbm/sec}$$

$$= -(10 + 0.14 + 11{,}200)100 \text{ ft-lbf/sec} \times \frac{1}{550} \text{ HP-sec/ft-lbf}$$

$$= 20.4 \text{ HP}$$

The input to the scoops is 33 HP so that the 12.6 HP not

included goes into breaking the snow out of its banks, or 12.6/33 = 39.3% of the total work input.

• PROBLEM 3-37

For the data given in the figure, calculate the change in energy, Δe for 1 kg of steam.

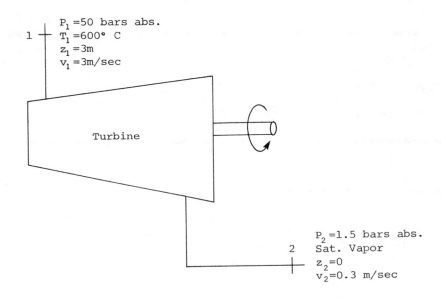

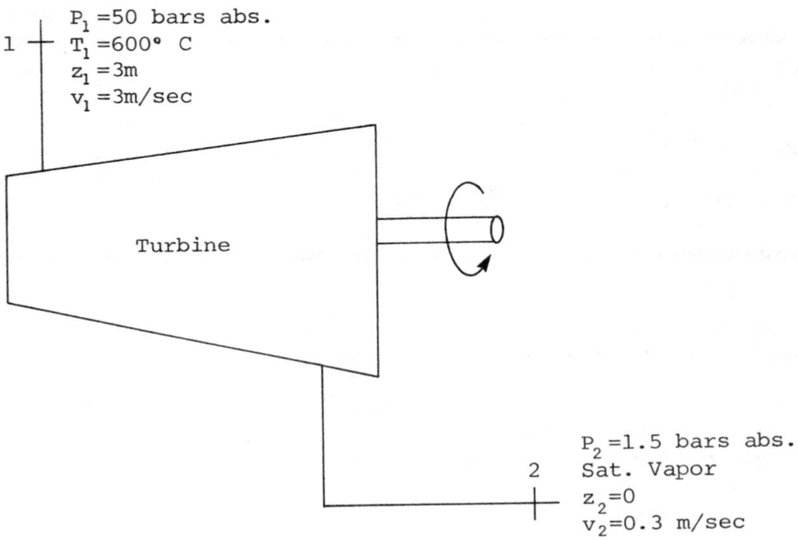

Solution:

From the steam tables

$$u_1 = 3273.0 \text{ j/gm}$$

$$v_1 = 78.69 \text{ cm}^3\text{/gm}$$

$$u_2 = 2519.7 \text{ j/gm}$$

$$v_2 = 1159.3 \text{ j/gm}$$

$$\Delta e = \Delta(u + \tfrac{1}{2}V^2 + gz) = \Delta u + \Delta\tfrac{1}{2}V^2 + \Delta gz \qquad (1)$$

$$\Delta u = u_2 - u_1 = 2519.7 - 3273.0 = -753.3 \text{ j/gm}$$

$$= -753{,}300 \text{ j/kg}$$

$$\Delta\tfrac{1}{2}V^2 = \tfrac{1}{2}(V_2^2 - V_1^2) = -\tfrac{1}{2}(9 - 0.09)1 = -4.455 \text{ j/kg}$$

Units:

$$m^2/sec^2 \times 1(N\text{-}sec^2/kg\text{-}m) \rightarrow N\text{-}m/kg \rightarrow j/kg$$

$$\Delta gz = g(z_2 - z_1) = -9.8(3 - 0)1 = -29.4 \text{ j/kg}$$

Then Eq. (1) gives

$$\Delta e = -753{,}300 - 4.455 - 29.4$$

$$= -753{,}333.85 \text{ J/kg}$$

$$= -753.34 \text{ kJ/kg.}$$

• PROBLEM 3-38

Steam enters an adiabatic turbine in a boiler at a pressure of 1000 psia and 1000 F, and leaves at 3 psia. The turbine inlet is higher than the exit by 10 ft. Calculate (a) the turbine work/unit mass of steam and (b) the effect in percentage, each term has on the turbine work, if the inlet steam velocity is 50 ft/sec and the exit velocity is 1000 ft/sec.

Solution: (a) The turbine work under reversible adiabatic conditions is given by the equation,

$$w_1 = (h_2 - h_3)_s + (K.E._2 - K.E._3) + (P.E._2 - P.E._3)$$

$$h_2 = 1505.9 \text{ Btu/lbm} \qquad s_2 = 1.6530 \text{ Btu/lbm-R}$$

$$s_3 = s_2 = s_g - (1 - x)s_{fg}$$

$$1.6530 = 1.8861 - (1 - x)1.6852; \qquad (1 - x) = 0.1383$$

$$h_3 = h_g - (1 - x)h_{fg} = 1122.5 - (0.1383)(1013.1)$$

$$h_3 = 982.36 \text{ Btu/lbm}$$

$$w_t = (1505.9 - 982.36) + \frac{50^2 - 1000^2}{2g_c J} + \frac{10}{778}\left(\frac{32.17}{32.17}\right)$$

$$w_t = 523.54 - 19.95 + 0.0128 = 503.6 \text{ Btu/lbm}$$

total energy available for work = 543.5 Btu/lbm

(b)

$$(\Delta h) = \left(\frac{523.54}{543.5}\right)(100) = 96.3 \text{ percent}$$

$$(\Delta K.E.) = \left(\frac{19.95}{543.5}\right)(100) = 3.6 \text{ percent}$$

$$(\Delta P.E.) = \left(\frac{0.0128}{543.5}\right)(100) = 0.1 \text{ percent}$$

• PROBLEM 3-39

As indicated in the figure, steam enters a steam turbine at 400 psia and 700 F and at a rate of 440,000 lb/hr; and 255,000 lb of steam per hr are extracted at 35 psia and 290 F. (These conditions can be measured because the steam is superheated.) The remainder of the steam passes through the turbine and exhausts at 1 in. Hg abs with a velocity of 500 ft/sec. (Although the exhaust pressure can be measured, it is difficult to measure the moisture content of steam at very low pressure. The exit velocity can be approximated by a knowledge of the flow area, the mass rate of flow, and the approximate specific volume.) The horsepower delivered by the turbine is 44,000 hp. Determine the specific enthalpy of the exhaust steam.
(Take $g = 32.174 \frac{m}{lb^2}$, $J = 778.16 \frac{ft.lb}{Btu}$)

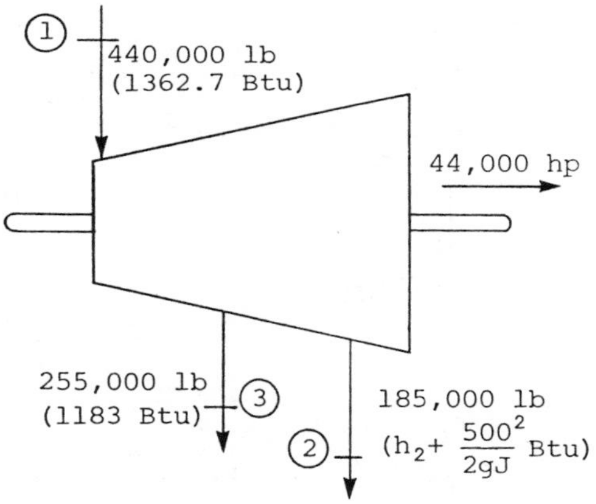

Solution: The specific enthalpy for each state is shown in parenthesis in the figure. There will be a small amount of heat lost from the turbine, generally less than 1 Btu/lb. This heat loss is neglected in the energy balance. The energy entering the system

$$m_1 h_1 = 440{,}000 \times 1362.7 = 599{,}600{,}000 \text{ Btu/hr}$$

The energy leaving the system is

$$W_{turb} + m_3 h_3 + (m_1 - m_3)\left[h_2 - \frac{V_2^2}{2gJ}\right]$$

$$= 44{,}000 \times 2544 + 255{,}000 \times 1183 + (440{,}000 - 255{,}000)\left(h_2 + \frac{500^2}{2gJ}\right)$$

$$= 111{,}900{,}000 + 301{,}700{,}000 + 185{,}000\ h_2 + 925{,}000$$

$$= 414{,}500{,}000 + 185{,}000\ h_2$$

When the energy entering the system is equated to the energy leaving, the result is

$$599{,}600{,}000 = 414{,}500{,}000 + 185{,}000\ h_2$$

Hence,

$$h_2 = 1000 \text{ Btu/lb}$$

• PROBLEM 3-40

10,000 lbm/min of air expands polytropically from 60 psia and 2000 F to 15 psia in a turbine. Calculate the work and heat in S.I. units if the value of the exponent n is taken as 1.75.

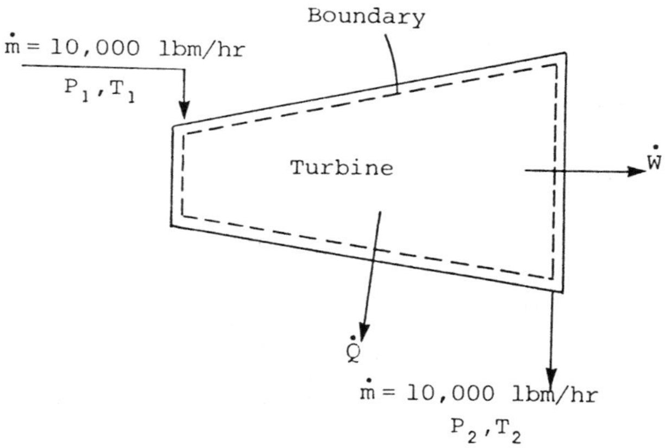

Solution: From the first law energy in will be equal to energy out.

$$\dot{m}h_1 = \dot{m}h_2 + \dot{W} + \dot{Q}$$

$$h_1 - h_2 = c_p(T_1 - T_2)$$

$$\dot{Q} = \dot{m}c_n(T_2 - T_1)$$

The outlet temperature and the specific heat must be

calculated before the problem can be solved.

$$T_2 = T_1\left(\frac{p_2}{p_1}\right)^{(n-1)/n} = 2460\left(\frac{15}{60}\right)^{0.75/1.75} = 1360 \text{ R}$$

$$c_n = \frac{0.24 - (1.75)(0.1714)}{-0.75} = +\ 0.080 \text{ Btu/lbm-R}$$

$$\dot{Q} = \dot{m}c_n(T_2 - T_1) = (10{,}000)(0.08)(1360 - 2460)$$

$$\dot{Q} = -8.8 \times 10^5 \text{ Btu/min} \quad \text{or heat loss}$$

$$(h_1 - h_2) = c_p(T_1 - T_2) = (0.24)(2460-1360) = 264 \text{ Btu/lbm}$$

$$\dot{W} = \dot{m}(h_1 - h_2) - \dot{Q} = (10{,}000)(264) - 8.8 \times 10^5$$

$$\dot{W} = 1.76 \times 10^6 \text{ Btu/min} = 4.15 \times 10^4 \text{ hp}$$

There are 1.055 kJ/Btu and also 0.746 kW/hp.

$$\dot{Q} = (8.8\times10^5) \text{ Btu/min} \times 1.055 \text{ kJ/Btu} \times \frac{1}{60} \text{ min/sec} = 1.547 \times 10^4 \text{kW}$$

$$\dot{W} = (4.15 \times 10^4) \text{ hp} \times 0.746 \text{ kW/hp} = 3.096 \times 10^4 \text{ kW}$$

There is only one set of units for power, and the energy form must be reduced to its final form.

• PROBLEM 3-41

The given data is for a steam power plant as shown in the figure.

Location	Pressure	Temperature or Quality
Boiler exit	400 lbf/in^2	600F
At turbine entry	380 lbf/in^2	560F
At turbine exit, condenser entry	2 lbf/in^2	93%
Leaving condenser, entering pump	1.9 lbf/in^2	115F

If the pump work is 3 Btu/lbm, calculate the following per pound mass.

(a) Heat transfer between boiler and turbine

(b) Turbine work

(c) Heat transfer in condenser

(d) Heat transfer in boiler.

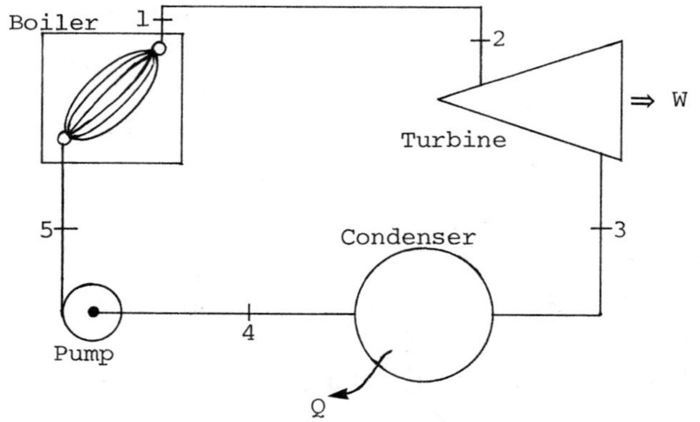

A simple steam power plant

Solution: For the turbine

$$q_{turb} + h_2 + \frac{\overline{V}_2^2}{2g_c} + \frac{g}{g_c} Z_2 = w_{turb} + h_3 + \frac{\overline{V}_3^2}{2g_c} + \frac{g}{g_c} Z_3$$

For the boiler (no work is involved)

$$q_{boiler} + h_5 + \frac{\overline{V}_5^2}{2g_c} + \frac{g}{g_c} Z_5 = h_1 + \frac{\overline{V}_1^2}{2g_c} + \frac{g}{g_c} Z_1$$

We might also use the alternate but equally acceptable notation

$$q_{turb} = {}_2q_3 \qquad q_{boiler} = {}_5q_1$$

Assume that changes in kinetic and potential energy are negligible.

The following property values are obtained from the steam tables, where the subscripts refer to the figure.

$h_1 = 1306.9$ Btu/lbm

$h_2 = 1285.2$ Btu/lbm

$h_3 = 1116.2 - 0.07(1022.2) = 1044.7$ Btu/lbm

$h_4 = 82.9$ Btu/lbm

(a) For the pipe line between boiler and turbine,

$${}_1q_2 + h_1 = h_2$$

$${}_1q_2 = h_2 - h_1 = 1285.2 - 1306.9 = 21.7 \text{ Btu/lbm}$$

(b) A turbine is essentially an adiabatic machine, and therefore

$$h_2 = h_3 + {}_2w_3$$

$${}_2w_3 = 1285.3 - 1044.7 = 240.6 \text{ Btu/lbm}$$

(c) For the condenser the work is zero.

$${}_3q_4 + h_3 = h_4$$

$${}_3q_4 = 82.9 - 1044.7 = -961.8 \text{ Btu/lbm}$$

(d) The enthalpy at point 5 may be found by considering the steady-flow energy equation across the pump

$${}_4w_5 + h_4 = h_5$$

$$h_5 = 3.0 + 82.9 = 85.9 \text{ Btu/lbm}$$

(e) For the boiler

$${}_5q_1 + h_5 = h_1$$

$${}_5q_1 = 1306.9 - 85.9 = 1221.0 \text{ Btu/lbm}$$

• PROBLEM 3-42

A water cooled compressor has Freon-12 entering as saturated vapor at -30°C. The refrigerant leaves the compressor at 800 kPa. The refrigerant flow rate is 0.9 kg/min and the cooling water results in a heat transfer rate of 140 kJ/min from the refrigerant. The power input tc the compressor is 3kW. Determine the exit temperature of Freon-12.

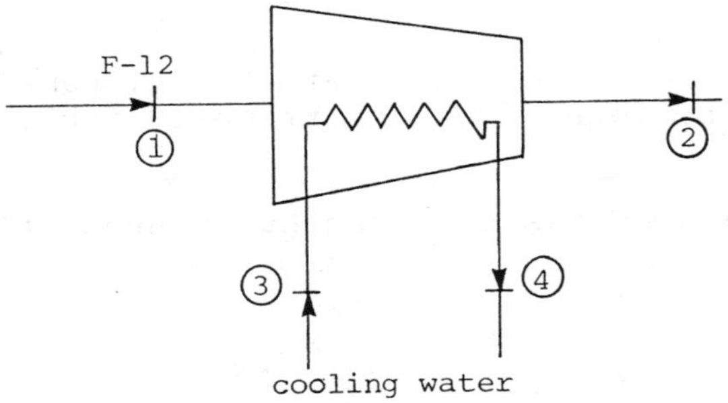

Solution: Referring to the figure for the states, the following are obtained.

State 1: saturated liquid, T = -30°C

$$h_1 = 174.076 \text{ kJ/kg}$$

The First Law written for Freon-12 is

$$Q + \dot{m}_1 h_1 = \dot{m}_2 h_2 + \dot{W}_{cv}$$

Solving for h_2,

$$h_2 = \frac{Q_{cv.} + \dot{m}_1 h_1 + W_{cv.}}{\dot{m}_2}$$

substituting the given and calculated data,

$$h_2 = \frac{-140 + \left(\frac{0.9 \text{ kg/min}}{60 \text{ min/sec}}\right)(174.076) + 3}{\left(\frac{0.9 \text{ kg/min}}{60 \text{ min/sec}}\right)}$$

$$= 218.74 \text{ kJ/kg}$$

h (kJ/kg)	T°C
213.290	50.0
218.740	57.49
220.558	60.0

Since two independent properties are known, namely P and h, a third (T) can be found from the Freon-12 tables.

The value T = 57.49°C was obtained by interpolation.

• PROBLEM 3-43

Steam enters the nozzle of a steam turbine with a velocity of 10 ft/sec at a pressure of 500 psia and a temperature of 1000°F. At the nozzle discharge the pressure and temperature are 300°F and 1 atm. Calculate the discharge velocity. Refer to the Figure.

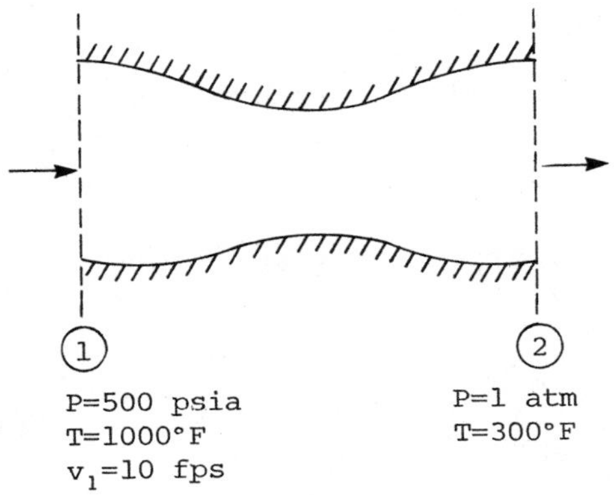

(a) The control volume

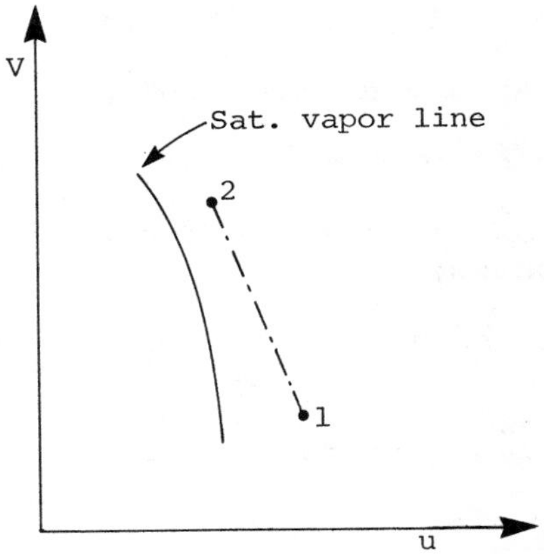

(b) The process representation

Solution: In nozzles, the frictional effects between the fluid and the walls have to be taken into consideration. By choosing the boundary of the control volume as shown in Figure (a), this effect becomes internal. In this case if the flow is steady, the frictional effect can be neglected, i.e. it is not necessary to take into account what is going on within the control volume. Also assume that the control volume is adiabatic, so that no energy transfer as heat takes place across the control-volume boundaries. This does not mean that no energy transfer as heat takes place within the control volume, but any such transfer would not be involved in a steady-flow steady-state analysis.

The conservation-of-mass principle implies that the flow rate is the same at sections 1 and 2. In applying this principle assume that the flow is one dimensional at 1 and 2, which means that the properties are uniform across the sections. The energy per unit of mass is taken as

$$e = u + \frac{V^2}{2g_c}$$

In evaluating u as a function of the temperature and pressure assume that the motion in no way alters the thermodynamic equations of state. In microscopic terms, even though the fluid is accelerating, the molecules behave locally as if there were no bulk motion. Also neglect any differences in the potential energy of position of the entering and emergent flows.

The internal process is quite complicated. However, only the states of the fluid at 1 and 2 need to be known.

Several important simplifying idealizations have been made, and they are

a) Steady flow steady state

b) Adiabatic control volume

c) One-dimensional flow at 1 and 2

d) Equation of state the same as for a simple compressible substance

e) Changes in the potential energy of position negligible

With these idealizations, application of the conservation-of-energy principle to the control volume gives, on a rate basis,

$$\dot{M}\left(u + Pv + \frac{V^2}{2g_c}\right)_1 - \dot{M}\left(u + Pv + \frac{V^2}{2g_c}\right)_2 = 0$$

energy-inflow rate   energy-outflow rate   energy-storage rate

Solving for the discharge kinetic energy per unit of mass,

$$\frac{V_2{}^2}{2g_c} = \frac{V_1{}^2}{2g_c} + [(u + Pv)_1 - (u + Pv)_2]$$

The intensive thermodynamic states are fixed by the temperature and pressure measurements (steam tables)

$T_1 = 1000°F$	$T_2 = 300°F$
$P_1 = 500$ psia	$P_2 = 14.7$ psia
$u_1 = 1360$ Btu/lbm	$u_2 = 1110$ Btu/lbm
$v_1 = 1.7$ ft^3/lbm	$v_2 = 31$ ft^3/lbm

Hence

$$h_1 = (u_1 + P_1v_1) = 1520 \text{ Btu/lbm}$$

$$h_2 = (u_2 + P_2v_2) = 1193 \text{ Btu/lbm}$$

Then

$$\frac{V_1{}^2}{2g_c} = \frac{10^2}{2 \times 32.2} \text{ (ft}^2\text{/sec}^2\text{)/(ft-lbm/lbf-sec}^2\text{)}$$

$$= 1.55 \text{ ft-lbf/lbm} = 2 \times 10^{-3} \text{ Btu/lbm}$$

$$\frac{V_2{}^2}{2g_c} = 2 \times 10^{-3} + 1520 - 1193 = 327 \text{ Btu/lbm} = 254{,}000 \text{ ft-lbf/lbm}$$

$$V_2 = \sqrt{2 \times 32.2 \text{ ft-lbm/lbf-sec}^2 \times 254{,}000 \text{ ft-lbf/lbm}} = 4100 \text{ ft/sec}$$

• **PROBLEM 3-44**

Air at 100°F and 100 atm is passed into a storage tank from a large high pressure vessel, at the rate of 0.05 moles/min, in order to increase the flow of water from the tank. The tank contains 50 ft^3 of air at 1 atm and 50°F and 50 ft^3 of liquid. When the pressure in the tank becomes 5 atm, the liquid is released at the rate of 5 ft^3/min.

Calculate the air temperature when the pressure reaches 5 atm and when the liquid has been drained completely.

Neglect all losses and assume air to be an ideal gas with C_v = 5 Btu/lb-mol°F.

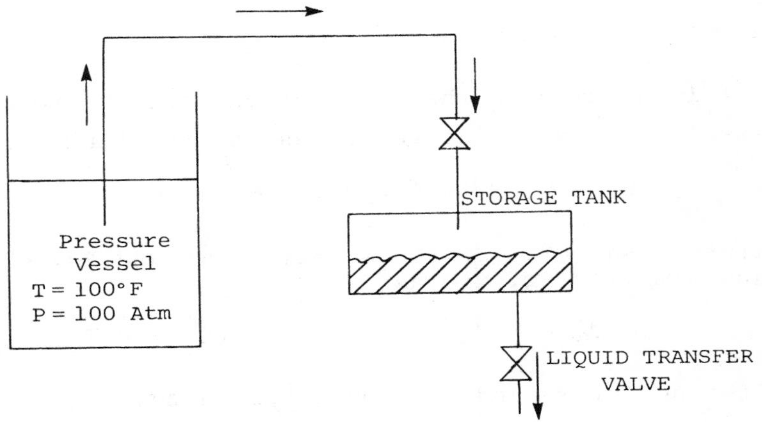

Solution: The process can be divided into two periods. (1) The period during which the pressure rises from 1 to 5 atm and the volume of the gas in the tank is constant, and (2) the period during which liquid is drained.

(1) The most convenient system is the gas in the tank at any time, which is an open simple system with constant volume. The temperature of this system is related to the energy and moles by the equation,

$$\underline{U} = N\int C_v dt + NU_0 \tag{1}$$

and to the pressure, volume, and moles by the equation

$$PV = NRT. \tag{2}$$

The energy may be related to the moles by using the First Law for an open system. These three relationships can be solved simultaneously for the temperature as a function of pressure.

Using the integrated form of the equation,

$$dU = dQ_\sigma - dW_\sigma + \sum_e h_e dm_e - \sum_i h_i dm_i \quad (3)$$

the First Law for an open system in the absence of body force fields, becomes

$$\Delta \underline{U} = Q_\sigma - W_\sigma + \int h_e dn_e \quad (4)$$

where

$$Q_\sigma = 0$$

$$W_\sigma = 0$$

$$h_e = u + P_e v = \text{constant}$$

and

$$\int dn_e = N_2 - N_1$$

where it is assumed in the h_e relation that the volume of the vessel is large relative to that of the tank. Thus

$$\underline{U}_2 - \underline{U}_1 = (u + P_e v)(N_2 - N_1) \quad (5)$$

Substituting Eq. (1) for the energy terms and Eq. (2) for $P_e v$, and simplifying, yields

$$N_2 C_v T_2 - N_1 C_v T_1 = (N_2 - N_1)(C_v + R)T_e \quad (6)$$

Substituting for N_2 and N_1, and rearranging,

$$T_2 = \frac{\kappa T_e}{1 + \dfrac{P_1}{P_2}\left[\kappa\left(\dfrac{T_e}{T_1}\right) - 1\right]} \quad (7)$$

where

$$\kappa = \frac{C_v + R}{C_v}$$

Thus,

$$T_2 = \frac{(1.4)(560)}{1 + (\frac{1}{5})[1.4(\frac{560}{510}) - 1]} = 709°R \text{ or } 249°F$$

Also

$$N_2 = \frac{P_2 \underline{V}_2}{RT_2} = \frac{(5)(50)}{(0.730)(709)} = 0.48$$

The final temperature of the gas is higher than that of either the initial temperature or the temperature of the incoming gas. In the limit where $P_2 \gg P_1$, the temperature approaches κT_e, independent of the initial conditions in the tank.

Step (2): If the system is again chosen as all of the gas in the tank at any time, the analysis is similar to that of Step (1) except that the volume of this system is changing continuously. As a result of this complication, $W_\sigma = \int P\,d\underline{V}$ cannot be evaluated until the pressure-volume history is determined. In this case, the differential form of the First Law for an open system, Eq. (3), is more convenient.

Thus,

$$d\underline{U} = dQ_\sigma - dW_\sigma + h_e dn_e \tag{8}$$

where

$$d\underline{U} = N\,dU + U\,dN$$

$$dQ_\sigma = 0$$

$$dW_\sigma = p\,d\underline{V}$$

$$dn_e = dN$$

$$h_e = u + P_e v = u + RT_e$$

so that

$$N\,dU + (U - u - RT_e)dN + P\,d\underline{V} = 0 \tag{9}$$

and

$$\frac{dT}{T} + \left(1 - \frac{\kappa T_e}{T}\right)\frac{dN}{N} + \frac{R}{C_v}\frac{d\underline{V}}{\underline{V}} = 0 \tag{10}$$

Since

$$dN = 0.05\ dt; \qquad N = 0.48 + 0.05\ t$$

and

$$d\underline{V} = 5\ dt; \qquad \underline{V} = 50 + 5\ t$$

Eq. (10) becomes

$$\frac{dT}{T} + \left(1 - \frac{\kappa T_e}{T.}\right)\frac{dt}{9.6 + t} + \left(\frac{R}{C_v}\right)\left(\frac{dt}{10 + t}\right) = 0$$

Integration of this equation from t = 0 to 10 min yields the final temperature; T = 544°R or 84°F.

THE FIRST LAW FOR CLOSED UNIFORM - STATE, UNIFORM - FLOW SYSTEMS

• PROBLEM 3-45

A steam pipe containing saturated steam at 100 psia is connected to an empty cylinder. What will be the final state of the steam if the cylinder is filled with steam at the same pressure as the pipe?

Solution: Since the cylinder is empty at time zero, $m_1 = 0$ and $u_1 = 0$, while $e_f = h$, the enthalpy of the fluid in the reservoir. Then the equation

$$Q_{cv} + \Sigma m_i h_i = \Sigma m_e h_e + (m_2 u_2 - m_1 u_1) + W_{12}$$

reduces to

$$m_2 u_2 = m_2 e_f$$

From the steam tables for 100 psia saturated steam,

$$h = 1187.2 \text{ Btu/lb}_m \qquad T = 328°F$$

The final conditions in the tank are

$$P_2 = 100 \text{ psia} \qquad u_2 = e_f = 1187.2 \text{ Btu/lb}_m$$

Interpolating in the steam tables for these values,

$$T_2 \approx 540°F \qquad (P_2 = 100 \text{ psia})$$

The temperature rise from compression of the steam in the container is

$$540° - 328° = 212°F$$

Thus, the steam in the container is highly superheated although the steam in the reservoir is not.

• PROBLEM 3-46

A well insulated cylinder of volume V contains gas initially at a temperature T_o and pressure p_o. External gas at a temperature T_1 is passed into the cylinder. This flow rate decreases exponentially with time according to $\dot{m} = m_o e^{-at}$. Neglecting kinetic energy of the gas and assuming ideal gas behavior, calculate the temperature and pressure of the gas in the cylinder as a function of time. Assume the gases have constant specific heats.

Solution: Since the cylinder is well insulated, Q = 0; there is also no external shaft work, i.e. W = 0; hence the equation

$$\frac{dE}{dt} = \sum_i h_i^o \frac{dm_i}{dt} + \frac{\delta Q}{dt} - \frac{\delta W}{dt} \qquad (1)$$

becomes

$$\frac{dE}{dt} = h^o \frac{dm}{dt} = h^o \dot{m}_o e^{-at}$$

On integrating and using the condition $E = E_o$ at $t = 0$

$$E = E_o + \frac{h^o \dot{m}_o}{a} (1 - e^{-at})$$

where E_o is the initial energy of the cylinder at the beginning of the charging process.

As both the kinetic and potential energies are negligible,

$$Mu = M_o u_o + \frac{\dot{m}_o}{a} (1 - e^{-at}) (u_1 + p_1 v_1)$$

Further, from conservation of mass obtained by integrating the mass flow rate equation

$$M = M_o + \frac{\dot{m}_o(1 - e^{-at})}{a}$$

Eliminating M between these two expressions yields

$$\{M_o + \frac{\dot{m}_o}{a} (1 - e^{-at})\}u - M_o u_o = \frac{\dot{m}_o}{a} (1 - e^{-at})(u_1 + RT_1)$$

hence

$$M_o c_v(T - T_o) = \frac{\dot{m}_o}{a} (1 - e^{-at})\{c_v(T_1 - T) + RT_1\}$$

i.e.

$$T = \frac{M_o c_v T_o + \frac{\dot{m}_o}{a} (1 - e^{-at}) c_p T_1}{\{M_o + \frac{\dot{m}_o}{a} (1 - e^{-at})\}c_v}$$

whence

$$p = \frac{MRT}{V} = \frac{R}{Vc_v} \{M_o c_v T_o + \frac{\dot{m}_o}{a} (1 - e^{-at}) c_p T_1\}$$

$$= p_o + \frac{\dot{m}_o R}{aV} (1 - e^{-at}) \gamma T_1$$

Notice that if the mass inflow is large compared to the initial mass in the cylinder the temperature inside the cylinder tends to γT_1 on fully charged, i.e. as t tends to infinity. If the tank is evacuated initially, the temperature inside the cylinder becomes independent of time and is equal to γT_1 throughout the entire charging process.

For the case where the charging is effected by a high pressure main, the charging process will stop when the pressure inside the cylinder reaches that of the main. The charging time can be found by setting $p = p_1$ in the pressure relation; hence the final temperature can be obtained.

• PROBLEM 3-47

A 1 ft^3 cylinder containing an ideal gas at a pressure of 10 atm is kept in a larger tank at a pressure of 1 atm and 535°R. Calculate the work done, heat transferred and the change in internal energy if

(a) the gas starts leaking slowly such that the cylinder and gas still remains at a constant temperature.

(b) If the cylinder is insulated and the process is adiabatic.

(c) If the valve is suddenly opened and the tank pressure above a hypothetical piston falls to atmospheric pressure. The cylinder is insulated and the process is adiabatic.

(d) If the process is polytropic with n=1.3.

Solution: a) The process describes the system as that quantity of gas remaining in the cylinder at the final pressure and temperature. During the process this quantity of gas may be considered as separated from the remaining cylinder contents by a free-floating piston. In this case, the pressure decreases very slowly so that the process can be considered as an isothermal reversible expansion of an ideal gas.

From the ideal gas law, the quantity of gas remaining in the cylinder at the final temperature and pressure is

$$m = p_2 v_2 / RT_2 = (1)(1)/(0.73)(535) \text{ lb moles}$$

According to Eq. (1),

$$w = RT\int_{v_1}^{v_2} \frac{dv}{v} = RT\ln\left(\frac{v_2}{v_1}\right) = RT\ln\left(\frac{p_1}{p_2}\right) \qquad (1)$$

the work performed is

$$w = mRT\ln(p_1/p_2) = \frac{(1.987)(535)}{(0.73)(535)}\ \ln(10) = 6.30 \text{ Btu}$$

Since the process is isothermal,

$$\Delta E = 0$$

for any ideal gas; then the heat transferred is equal to the work done.

$$Q = w = 6.30 \text{ Btu}$$

b) If the leak is sufficiently slow that the process can be considered reversible, the final temperature may be determined from Eq. (2)

$$\frac{T_2}{T_1} = \left(\frac{P_2}{P_1}\right)^{\frac{R}{Cp}} \qquad (2)$$

For a monatomic, ideal gas with a temperature independent C_v of 3 Btu/(lb mole)(°R) and a C_p of 5 Btu/(lb mole)(°R),

$$T_2/T_1 = (1/10)^{2/5} = 0.398$$

where an approximate value of 2 Btu/(lb mole)(°R) has been used for the gas constant R. Therefore

$$T_2 = (0.398)(535) = 213°R \text{ or } -247°F$$

The quantity of gas remaining in the cylinder at the end of the process is

$$m = (1)(1)/(0.73)(213) \text{ lb moles}$$

According to Eq. (3) the work is

$$w = c_v T_1 \left[1 - \left(\frac{P_2}{P_1}\right)^{R/Cp}\right] \qquad (3)$$

$$= \frac{(3)(535)}{(0.73)(213)}\ (1 - 0.398) = 6.21 \text{ Btu}$$

In this case, Q is zero and

$$\Delta E = -w$$

or

$$\Delta E = \frac{(3)(213 - 535)}{(0.73)(213)} = -6.21 \text{ Btu}$$

If the fluid were an ideal gas with a temperature

independent C_v of 5 Btu/(lb mole)(°R) and a C_p of 7 Btu/(lb mole)(°R), the final temperature and the energy changes would have different numerical values. In this case, the final temperature would be

$$T_2 = (535)/(10)^{2/7} = 535/1.93 = 277°R \text{ or } -183°F$$

The quantity of gas remaining in the cylinder at the end of the process would be

$$m = (1)(1)/(0.73)(277) \text{ lb moles}$$

and the work done would be

$$w = \frac{(5)(535)}{(0.73)(277)}(1 - 1/1.93) = 6.38 \text{ Btu}$$

(c) In this case the process is irreversible, and the final temperature is determined by Eq. (4).

$$\frac{T_2}{T_1} = \frac{C_v/R + Pa/P_1}{C_v/R + Pa/P_2} \tag{4}$$

For an ideal gas with a temperature independent C_v of 3 Btu/(lb mole)(°R) and a C_p of 5 Btu/(lb mole)(°R),

$$\frac{T_2}{T_1} = \frac{(3/2) + (1/10)}{(3/2) + 1/1} = \frac{1.60}{2.50} = 0.640$$

$$T_2 = (535)(0.640) = 342°R \text{ or } -118°F$$

The quantity of gas remaining in the cylinder is

$$m = (1)(1)/(0.73)(342) \text{ lb moles}$$

In this case, w and $-\Delta E$ are given by Eq. (5).

$$w = P_a\left[\frac{RT_2}{P_2} - \frac{RT_1}{P_1}\right] = -\Delta E = C_v T\left[1 - \frac{T_2}{T_1}\right] \tag{5}$$

$$= \frac{(3)(535)}{(0.73)(342)}(1 - 0.640) = 2.31 \text{ Btu}$$

For an ideal gas with a temperature independent C_v of 5 Btu/(lb mole)(°R) and a C_p of 7 Btu/(lb mole)(°R), the final temperature would be

$$\frac{T_2}{T_1} = \frac{(5/2) + (1/10)}{(5/2) + 1/1} = \frac{2.6}{3.5} = 0.743$$

$$T_2 = (535)(0.743) = 397°R \text{ or } -63°F$$

The work done would be

$$w = -\Delta E = \frac{(5)(535)(1 - 0.743)}{(0.73)(397)} = 2.37 \text{ Btu}$$

(d) In this case the final temperature is given by Eq. (6).

$$\frac{T_2}{T_1} = \left(\frac{P_2}{P_1}\right)^{(n-1)/n} \tag{6}$$

$$= (1/10)^{0.3/1.3} = 0.587$$

$$T_2 = (535)(0.587) = 314°R \text{ or } -146°F$$

The number of moles remaining in the cylinder is

$$m = (1)(1)/(0.73)(314) \text{ lb moles}$$

The work is given by Eq. (7).

$$w = \frac{p_1 v_1}{n-1}\left[1 - \frac{P_2}{P_1}^{(n-1)/n}\right] \tag{7}$$

$$= \frac{(1.987)(535)}{(0.73)(314)(1.3 - 1)}(1 - 0.587) = 6.42 \text{ Btu}$$

For an ideal gas with a temperature independent C_v of 3 Btu/(lb mole)(°R), the change in internal energy is

$$\Delta E = \frac{(3)(314 - 535)}{(0.73)(314)} = -2.89 \text{ Btu}$$

From the general energy balance

$$Q = \Delta E + w$$

$$Q = -2.89 + 6.42 = 3.53 \text{ Btu}$$

For an ideal gas with a temperature independent C_v of 5 Btu/(lb mole)(°R),

$$\Delta E = \frac{(5)(314 - 535)}{(9.73)(314)} = -4.81 \text{ Btu}$$

and

$$Q = -4.81 + 6.42 = 1.61 \text{ Btu}$$

• **PROBLEM 3-48**

A well insulated cylinder having a volume of 20 ft^3 contains 3.0 lb of air at 40 psia. Due to a leak some of the air escapes. Determine the amount of air left if the pressure inside the tank is 20 psia when the leak is fixed. Assume specific enthalpy h = 1.4 u = 0.24 T = 0.0045 pv, where u and h are in Btu/lbm, T is in °R, p in psfa and v in ft^3/lb.

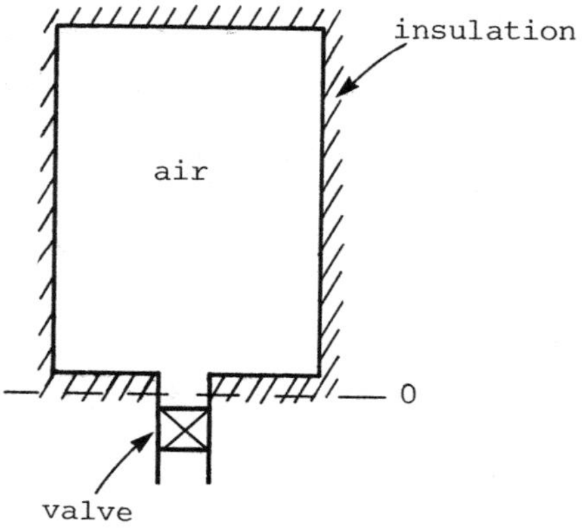

Solution: Define the open system as being the region within the cylinder. The mass of air remaining in the cylinder at 20 psia will depend on the temperature, and the temperature will be influenced by the energy removed from the system by means of the outflowing air; the first step is to set up an energy balance for the system. Since the properties of the air crossing the system boundary vary, the differential form of the energy balance must be used. As an infinitesimal mass of air, δm_0, flows out of the system, the mass of the air within the system m changes by an amount dm. Since mass δm_0 leaves the system, $\delta m_0 = -dm$. Since Q = 0 and W = 0,

$$\begin{bmatrix}\text{Decrease in stored}\\ \text{energy of air in}\\ \text{cylinder}\end{bmatrix} = \begin{bmatrix}\text{stored energy of}\\ \delta m_0 \text{ leaving}\\ \text{cylinder}\end{bmatrix} + \begin{bmatrix}\text{flow work of}\\ \delta m_0 \text{ leaving}\\ \text{cylinder}\end{bmatrix}$$

$$-dU = e_0\delta m_0 + p_0v_0\delta m_0 = (e_0 + p_0v_0)\delta m_0$$

where a property without a subscript is a property of the air in the cylinder. Potential energy changes can be neglected. Section 0 is located just upstream of the small valve opening so that KE_0 is negligibly small, $e_0 = u_0$ and the last equation becomes

$$-dU = (u_0 + p_0v_0)\delta m_0$$

Since the properties of the air leaving are the same as those of the air in the tank, $u_0 = u$, $p_0 = p$, and $v_0 = v$. Recalling also that $\delta m_0 = -dm$,

$$-dU = -(u + pv)dm$$

$$d(mu) = (u + pv)dm$$

$$m\,du + u\,dm = (u + pv)dm$$

$$m\,du = pv\,dm$$

Specific internal energy can be expressed in terms of pv as

$$u = \frac{0.0045}{1.4}pv\left[\frac{\text{Btu}}{\text{lb}_m}\right] = \frac{778(0.0045)}{1.4}pv\left[\frac{\text{ft-lb}_f}{\text{lb}_m}\right] = 2.5pv\left[\frac{\text{ft-lb}_f}{\text{lb}_m}\right]$$

so that $du = 2.5\,d(pv)$, and the energy balance becomes

$$2.5m\,d(pv) = pv\,dm$$

$$\frac{dm}{m} = 2.5\frac{d(pv)}{pv}$$

$$\ln\frac{m_f}{m_i} = 2.5\ln\left(\frac{p_f v_f}{p_i v_i}\right)$$

$$\frac{m_f}{m_i} = \left(\frac{p_f v_f}{p_i v_i}\right)^{2.5} = \left(\frac{p_f V_f m_i}{m_f p_i V_i}\right)^{2.5}$$

But the tank volume is constant, $V_f = V_i$, so

$$\frac{m_f}{m_i} = \left(\frac{p_f}{p_i}\right)^{2.5}\left(\frac{m_i}{m_f}\right)^{2.5}$$

$$\frac{m_f}{m_i} = \left(\frac{p_f}{p_i}\right)^{2.5/3.5} = \left(\frac{20}{40}\right)^{0.714} = 0.609$$

$$m_f = 0.609m_i = 0.609(3) = 1.83\ \text{lb}_m$$

• PROBLEM 3-49

A cylinder having a volume of 1 ft^3 contains air at 1 atm and 70°F. A compressor evacuates the cylinder at one atm and operates isothermally at 70°F. Calculate the total work done by the compressor which is assumed to operate reversibly. Also assume ideal gas behavior.

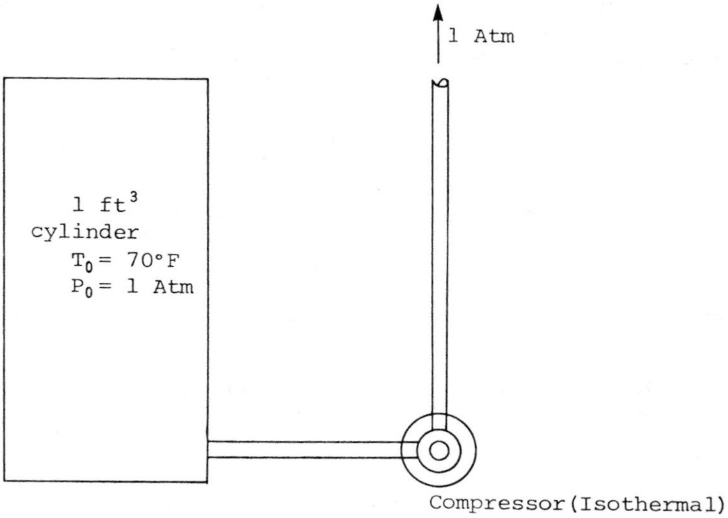

Solution: If it is assumed that the amount of air processed during one cycle of the compressor is small in relation to the total quantity of air expelled, then the work of any one cycle can be treated as a differential and the properties within the tank can be assumed to vary smoothly with the amount of air expelled. Thus, for a differential amount processed, the work done by the gas on the compressor is given by the equation

$$\frac{\delta w}{\delta n} = -\int_B^c V\,dP = -\int_{P_1}^{P_2} V\,dP \tag{1}$$

or

$$dW = -dn \int_{P_t}^{P_a} V\,dP \tag{2}$$

where P_a is the discharge pressure (1 atm) and P_t is the compressor pressure during the cycle under consideration.

Introducing the ideal gas law and integrating,

$$dW = RT \ln\left(\frac{P_t}{P_a}\right) dn \tag{3}$$

Since the amount of gas processed, dn, is equal to the decrease in gas in the tank, -dN, and since

$$dN = \frac{V_t}{RT}\,dP_t \tag{4}$$

Eq. (3) becomes

$$dW = -\underline{V}_t \ln\left(\frac{P_t}{P_a}\right) dP_t \tag{5}$$

Integrating between $P_t = 1$ atm and $P_t = 0$,

$$W = -\underline{V}_t [P_t \ln P_t - P_t]_1^0 = -\underline{V}_t \cdot (1 \text{ atm}) \tag{6}$$

Substituting the values, the work done by the compressor is 2117 ft-lb.

• PROBLEM 3-50

A cylinder piston arrangement as shown in the figure is made of a non heat conducting material. The cylinder has a volume of 3 ft^3 and is connected to a steam source at 100 psia and 500°F. The piston is held in position by air at 20 psia and a cooling coil is placed in the cylinder to maintain a constant air temperature of 100°F. Determine the final temperature of the steam if the valve is opened until the pressure in the cylinder falls to 100 psia.

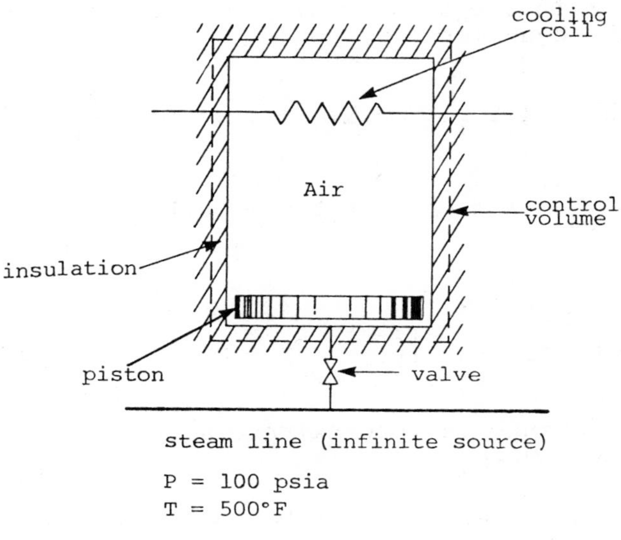

Solution: The thermodynamic system is chosen as the air, steam, and piston inside the cylinder. Even though the cylinder is insulated, heat is being removed by the action of the cooling coil. The amount of heat removed is calculated by determining the heat transfer when the given quantity of air is compressed isothermally from 20 psia to 100 psia. The mass of air is

$$m_a = \frac{pV}{RT} = \frac{(20)(144)(3)}{(53.35)(560)} = 0.289\ lb_m$$

The work done on the gas is

$$W_a = \int -p\,dV = -\int_{V_1}^{V_2} mRT\frac{dV}{V} = -\ mRT\ \ln\frac{V_2}{V_1}$$

Since the temperature remains constant, $V_2/V_1 = p_1/p_2$, so that the work is

$$W_a = mRT\ \ln\frac{p_1}{p_2}$$

$$= -(0.289)(53.35)(560)\ \ln\frac{20}{100}$$

$$= 13{,}850\ ft\text{-}lb_f = 17.8\ Btu$$

For the air

$$Q_a + W_a = \Delta U_a$$

But since T_a = const., $\Delta U_a = 0$ and

$$Q_a = -W_a = -17.8\ Btu$$

This heat transfer is the total heat loss from the control volume. Write the equation

$$m_i(h_i + K.E._i + P.E._i + \ldots) + \frac{d'Q}{d\tau} + \frac{dWext}{d\tau}$$

$$= \left(\frac{dE}{d\tau}\right)_\sigma + \dot{m}_e(h_e + K.E._e + P.E._e + \ldots)$$

in integral form as

$$\int \dot{m}_i h_i d\tau + Q = \int\left(\frac{dE}{d\tau}\right)_\sigma d\tau = m_{2_s}u_{2_s} - m_{1_s}u_{1_s} \quad (1)$$

since there is no change in internal energy of the air in the control volume. Here,

$$\int \dot{m}_i d\tau = m_{2_s}$$

so that, finally, since $m_{1_s} = 0$,

$$m_{2_s}(h_i - u_{2_s}) = -Q \quad (2)$$

The final volume of the steam is

$$V_{2_s} = 3 - V_{a_2} = 3.0 - \frac{3}{5} = 2.4\ ft^3$$

and the mass of steam is

$$m_{2_s} = \frac{V_{2_s}}{v_{2_s}}$$

Equation (2) thus becomes, with h_i = 1279.1 Btu/lb_m and Q = -17.8 Btu,

$$\frac{2.4}{v_{2_s}}(1279.1 - u_{2_s}) = 17.8 \qquad (3)$$

Equation (3) must be solved by trial and error with the use of the superheat steam tables. The result is

$$T_{2_s} = 536°F$$

which is the final temperature of the steam.

• PROBLEM 3-51

In a pneumatic lift air is initially contained in a 10 ft^3 steel tank at 80°F and 100 psia. Lifting occurs when a valve allows this air into a cylinder which initially contains air at 1 atm, 60°F. The cylinder has an initial volume of 0.5 ft^3, a cross sectional area of 1 ft^2 and a lifting height of 3 ft. A cylinder pressure of 50 psia is maintained while the load is lifted up 3 ft. Air continues to flow into the cylinder after the load has reached the maximum lifting height and finally the pressure in the tank and cylinder will be equal and the air will attain a uniform temperature of 60°F.

(a) Calculate the final air temperature.

(b) Calculate the amount of energy transferred as heat from the tank walls to the air.

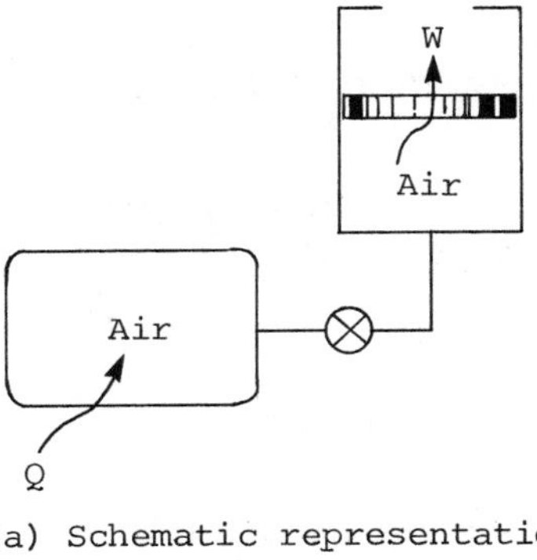

(a) Schematic representation

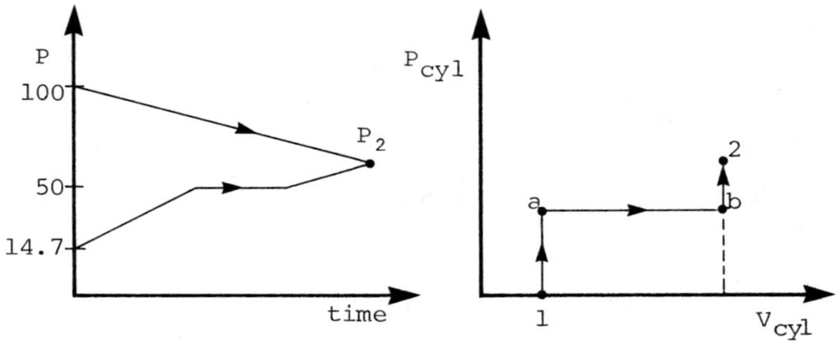

(b) The process representation

Solution: (a) In making the energy balance consider the time period from the start to the end, where the air is in equilibrium throughout the system, and the load is at its highest point. Take the air as the control mass, and consider the energy flows indicated in the figure. The energy balance is

Q	=	W	+	ΔU
energy input		energy output		increase in energy storage

In order to calculate Q first evaluate ΔU and W. The work computation is facilitated by consideration of the process representation. Work will be done by the control mass on the piston only when the piston is moving, and during this period the cylinder pressure is assumed to remain at 50 psia. During this period the force exerted by the gas on the piston is 144 × 50 = 7200 lbf, and the piston moves a distance of 3 ft. Hence

$$W = 7200 \times 3 = 21{,}600 \text{ ft-lbf}/(778 \text{ ft-lbf/Btu})$$

$$= 27.8 \text{ Btu}$$

Idealizing that the air behaves as a perfect gas, enough information to establish the initial and final air states completely is available. For air:

$$c_v = 0.171 \text{ Btu/lbm-°R} \qquad R = 53.3 \text{ ft-lbf/lbm-°R}$$

Initial state:

Tank air 80°F(=540°R), 100 psia

$$p = \frac{1}{v} = \frac{P}{RT} = \frac{100 \times 144}{53.3 \times 540} = 0.498 \text{ lbm/ft}^3$$

Hence

$$M_t = 10 \times 0.498 = 4.98 \text{ lbm}$$

Using the equation, $u_1 - u_0 = c_v(T_1 - T_0)$ (1)

with $T_0 = 0°F = 460°R$,

$$u_t = 0.171 \times (540 - 460) = 13.7 \text{ Btu/lbm}$$

Hence

$$U_t = Mu = 4.98 \times 13.7 = 68.1 \text{ Btu}$$

Cylinder air 60°F (= 520°R), 14.7 psia

$$\rho = \frac{P}{RT} = \frac{14.7 \times 144}{53.3 \times 520} = 0.0764 \text{ lbm/ft}^3$$

$$M_c = 0.5 \times 0.0764 = 0.038 \text{ lbm}$$

$$u_c = 0.171 \times (520 - 460) = 10.3 \text{ Btu/lbm}$$

$$U_c = 0.038 \times 10.3 = 0.39 \text{ Btu}$$

So, the total mass and energy in the initial configuration are

$$M = 4.98 + 0.038 = 5.02 \text{ lbm}$$

$$U_1 = 68.1 + 0.39 = 68.5 \text{ Btu}$$

Final state: All air at 60°F (520°R)

The total final volume is

$$V = 10.00 + 0.5 + 3.0 = 13.5 \text{ ft}^3$$

Hence the final density is

$$\rho_2 = \frac{M}{V} = \frac{5.02}{13.5} = 0.372 \text{ lbm/ft}^3$$

The final pressure is,

$$P_2 = \rho_2 RT_2 = 0.372 \times 53.3 \times 520 = 10,400 \text{ lbf/ft}^3$$

$$= 71.7 \text{ psia}$$

(b) The final specific internal energy is [Eq. (1)]

$$u_2 = 0.171 \times (520 - 460) = 10.3 \text{ Btu/lbm}$$

So

$$U_2 = Mu_2 = 5.02 \times 10.3 = 52.0 \text{ Btu}$$

Now calculate the internal energy increase as

$$\Delta U = U_2 - U_1 = 52.0 - 68.5 = -16.5 \text{ Btu}$$

(The minus sign indicates that the internal energy actually

decreases.) Substituting for W and ΔU in the energy balance,

$$Q = 27.8 + (-16.5) = 11.3 \text{ Btu}$$

• PROBLEM 3-52

An insulated tank with a volume of $0.5 m^3$ contains air at 100 kPa and 25°C. The tank is connected through a valve to a large compressed air line. The air in the line is maintained at 700 kPa and 120°C. The valve is then opened and air is allowed to flow into the tank until the tank pressure becomes 500 kPa. At that point the valve is closed. Determine the mass of air that enters, and the final temperature of the air in the tank.

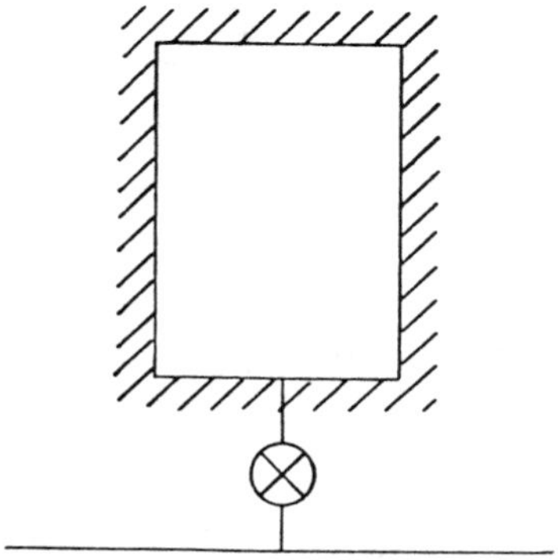

$P_L = 700$ kPa

$T_L = 120°C = 393.15$ K

Solution: This is a uniform-state, uniform-flow problem with mass entering the system. In order to calculate this mass, first calculate the mass that was originally in the system (before the valve was opened). Assuming air to behave ideally in the equation of state.

$$m = \frac{PV}{RT} \quad \text{and } R = 0.287 \text{ kJ/kg-°K}$$

for the mass of air get

(The subscript: i stands for "in", F stands for "Final", I stands for "Initial", and L stands for "Line".

$$m_I = \frac{P_I V_I}{R\ T_I} = \frac{100 \times 0.5}{0.287 \times 298.15} = 0.5843 \text{ kg} \qquad (1)$$

The mass that enters the system is given by the equation

$$m_i = m_F - m_I \tag{2}$$

But

$$m_F = \frac{P_F V_F}{RT_F} \tag{3}$$

which has two unknowns (m_F, T_F).

The First Law is then written for the system, (a closed one in this case), on a mass basis as:

$$Q_{c.v.} + \Sigma m_i h_i = \Sigma m_e h_e + m_F u_F - m_I u_I + W_{c.v.} \tag{4}$$

Now, the following conditions hold.

(i) There is no work done on or by the system

$$W_{12} = 0$$

(ii) Since the tank is insulated

$$Q_{12} = 0$$

(iii) No mass leaves the system

$$m_e = 0$$

(iv) The ideal gas equations

$$du = c_{v_0}\, dT \text{ and } dh = c_{p_0}\, dT$$

will be used with

$$c_{v_0} = 0.7165 \text{ and } c_{p_0} = 1.0035 \text{ kJ/kg-°K}$$

(v) The volume is constant throughout the process. With the above conditions in mind, Equation (4) takes the following form

$$m_i c_{p_0} T_L = m_F c_{v_0} T_F - m_I c_{v_0} T_I, \tag{5}$$

which upon substitution of Equations (1), (2), and (3) and rearranging,

$$o = \left[\left(\frac{P_F V}{RT_F}\right) C_{v_0} T_F - \left(\frac{P_I V}{RT_I}\right) c_{v_0} T_I\right]$$

$$- \left[\frac{P_F V}{RT_F} - \frac{P_I V}{RT_I}\right] C_{p_0} T_L$$

multiply both sides by $\frac{R}{C_{v_0} V}$, and substitute the given and calculated values to get

$$o = (P_F - P_I) - \left[\frac{P_F}{T_F} - \frac{P_I}{T_I}\right]\left(\frac{C_{p_0}}{C_{v_0}}\right)T_L$$

$$= (500-100) - \left[\frac{500}{T_F} - \frac{100}{298.15}\right]\left(\frac{1.0035}{0.7165}\right) \times 393.15$$

$$= 584.682 - \frac{275,314.7418}{T_F}$$

solving for T_F, obtain

$$T_F = \frac{275,314.7418}{584.682} = 470.88\text{K} = 197.73°\text{C}$$

Now that the final temperature is obtained; from Equation (3), the final mass is

$$m_F = \frac{P_F V}{RT_F} = \frac{500 \times 0.5}{0.287 \times 470.88} = 1.8499 \text{ kg}$$

By Eq. (2)

$$m_i = m_F - m_I$$

$$= 1.8499 - 0.5843$$

$$= 1.2656 \text{ kg}$$

• PROBLEM 3-53

A piston cylinder arrangement is connected with a line to a large tank containing air at 20°C, 300 kPa - as shown in the figure. Initially the cylinder contains 0.1m³ of air at 40°C, and the mass of the piston is such that a pressure of 200 kPa is required to raise it. The valve is then opened and air is allowed to flow into the cylinder until its volume doubles, at which time the valve closes. Assuming air to be an ideal gas, and no heat transfer occurring during the process, calculate the final temperature of the air in the cylinder.

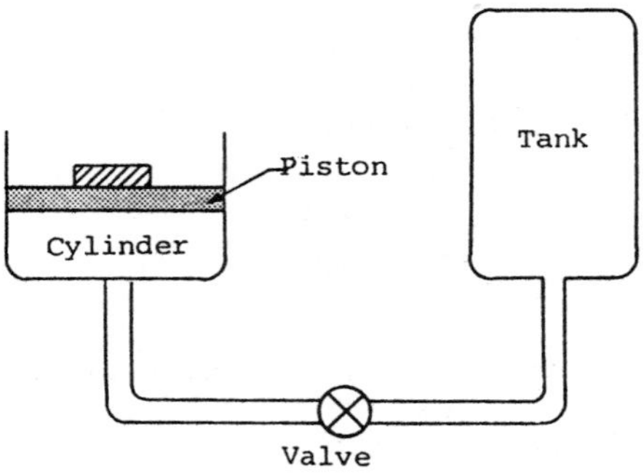

Solution: The mass inside the cylinder initially is obtained by use of the ideal gas equation of state,

$$m_1 = \frac{P_1V_1}{RT_1} \qquad (R_{air} = 0.287 \text{ kJ/kgK})$$

$$= \frac{200 \times 0.1}{0.297 \times 313.15} = 0.2225 \text{ kg}$$

when the valve opens the volume doubles and becomes

$$V_2 = 2V_1 = 2 \times 0.1 = 0.2 \text{ m}^3$$

and

$$m_2 = \frac{P_2V_2}{RT_2}$$

The first law for this case on a per mass basis is

$$Q_{c.v.} + m_ih_i = m_eh_e + m_2u_2 - m_1u_1 + W_{c.v.} \qquad (1)$$

where $\quad Q_{c.v.} = 0$ (given)

and $\quad m_eh_e = 0$ (no mass is leaving from the cylinder)

Furthermore the work for this process is the work done in moving the piston from state 1 to state 2

$$W_{c.v.} = \int_1^2 PdV = P(V_2-V_1) = 200(0.2-0.1) = 20 \text{ kJ}$$

Assuming constant specific heats,

$$du = c_{v_0}dT \quad \text{and} \quad dh = c_{p_0}dT$$

where for air $c_{v_0} = 0.7165$ kJ/kgK and

$$c_{p_0} = 1.0035 \text{ kJ/kgK}$$

Hence Eq. (1) takes the form

$$m_ic_{p_0}T_L = m_2c_{v_0}T_2 - m_1c_{v_0}T_1 + W_{12}$$

where the subscript L refers to the air in the line.

Solving for T_2 in the above equation one gets

$$T_2 = \frac{m_ic_{p_0}T_L + m_1c_{v_0}T_1 - W_{12}}{m_2c_{v_0}} \qquad (2)$$

where $m_i = m_2 - m_1$ (mass entering the cylinder)

This equation cannot be solved because it has two unknowns.

But from the ideal gas equation of state

$$T = \frac{P_2V_2}{m_2R} \tag{3}$$

Equations (2) and (3) involve the same two unknowns. M_2 and T_2 (since $P_2 = P_1$) and thus can be solved simultaneously, for the two unknowns.

Substituting Eq. (3) into Eq. (2),

$$\frac{P_2V_2}{M_2R} = \frac{(m_2-m_1)c_{p_0}T_L + m_1c_{v_0}T_1 - W_{12}}{m_2c_{v_0}}$$

Solving for m

$$m_2 = \frac{P_2V_2c_{v_0} + R[m_1(c_{p_0}T_L - c_{v_0}T_1) + W_{12}]}{Rc_{p_0}T_L}$$

$$= \frac{(200)(0.2)(0.7165)}{(0.287)(1.0035)(293.15)}$$

$$+ \frac{0.287[0.2225(1.0035 \times 293.15 - 0.7165 \times 313.15) + 20]}{(0.287)(1.0035)(293.15)}$$

$$= 0.4602 \text{ kg}$$

Substituting this value into Eq. (3), the final temperature in the cylinder is obtained.

$$T_2 = \frac{P_2V_2}{m_2R} = \frac{(200)(0.2)}{(0.4602)(0.287)}$$

$$= 302.85 \text{ K}$$

or $$T_2 = 302.85 - 273.15 = 29.7°C$$

• PROBLEM 3-54

SCUBA tanks normally have a volume of 1 ft^3 and contain air at 50 psia and 75°F after it is used. Assume that they are recharged by connecting them to a pipeline at 100 psia and 120°F. Air is passed into each tank until the pressure in it is 1000 psia. Calculate the amount of air added and the total amount of air in the tank at the end of filling if

(a) the tank is filled slowly and the final temperature of air in the tank is the same as the room temperature (75°F).

(b) If the tanks are filled rapidly, so that the process is adiabatic.
Assume air obeys the ideal gas equation of state and
$C_v = 4.4 + 1.5 \times 10^{-3}T$ cal/g-mol°K.

Solution: (a) Determine the mass of air remaining in the SCUBA (Self Contained Underwater Breathing Apparatus) tank at the beginning of the filling:

$$M = \frac{V}{v}$$

where v is obtained from the ideal-gas equation of state and the known initial pressure and temperature:

$$v = \frac{RT}{P}$$

where $R = 1545$ ft-lb_f/lb-mol°R

$P = 50$ psia $= 7.20 \times 10^3$ lb_f/ft^2

$T = 75°F = 535°R$

Therefore,

$$v = \frac{(1545)(535)(\text{ft-lb}_f)°R/(\text{lb-mol}°R)}{7.20 \times 10^3 \qquad (\text{lb}_f/\text{ft}^2)}$$

$$= 115 \text{ ft}^3/\text{lb-mol}$$

$$= 3.96 \text{ ft}^3/\text{lb}_m$$

Thus the amount of air left in each tank is:

$$M = \frac{1 \text{ ft}^3}{3.96 \text{ ft}^3/\text{lb}_m} = 0.254 \text{ lb}_m$$

At the end of the filling operation

$$P_{end} = 1000 \text{ psia} = 1.44 \times 10^5 \text{lb}_f/\text{ft}^2$$

$$T_{end} = 75°F = 535°R$$

Therefore

$$v_{end} = \frac{RT_{end}}{P_{end}} = \frac{(1545)(535)}{1.44 \times 10^5} \text{ ft}^3/\text{lb-mol}$$

$$= 5.72 \text{ ft}^3/\text{lb-mol} = 0.197 \text{ ft}^3/\text{lb}_m$$

and

$$M_{end} = \frac{1\ ft^3}{0.197\ ft^3/lb_m} = 5.07\ lb_m$$

The amount of air needed to fill each cylinder is then the difference between M_{end} and $M_{initial}$:

$$\Delta M = 5.07\ lb_m - 0.25\ lb_m = 4.82\ lb_m$$

(b) For the adiabatic filling the final temperature is unknown. Thus determine T_{end}. Since P_{end} is still 1000 psia, determination of any other end property will give the desired temperature. The additional property to be determined is the internal energy (or, equivalently, the enthalpy). Begin by picking a system for analysis and applying the energy equation to the system and process (as shown in the figure).

Several choices of systems are available for this problem. Choice of the tank, the valve, and their contents as the system will lead to the most direct solution of the problem. Now assume that potential and kinetic energy changes are negligible during the filling process. In addition, no mass leaves the system during the filling operation, so that the energy equation around the system can be written as:

$$(h\delta M)_{in} + \delta Q - \delta W = d(Mu)_{sys}$$

The filling operation is adiabatic, so that $\delta Q = 0$. In addition, since no shaft passes through the system boundaries, and the system boundaries are rigid and immobile, $\delta W = 0$ and the energy equation reduced to:

$$h\delta M_{in} = d(Mu)_{sys}$$

Now this result must be integrated over the entire filling operation:

$$\int h\delta M_{in} = \int d(Mu)_{sys}$$

h_{in} is the enthalpy of the air entering the system, in this case, the enthalpy of the air in the supply pipeline. Since the supply pipeline conditions do not change during the filling operation, h_{in} is constant and may be removed from under the integral of the left-hand side. The integral of δM_{in} is the total amount of mass which enters the tank. The integral of the right-hand side is the total change in (Mu_{sys}) during the process.

$$h_{in}(M_{in}) = [(Mu)_{end} - (Mu)_{begin}]_{sys}$$

or

$$h_{in}M_{in} = [M_{end}u_{end} - M_{begin}u_{begin}]_{sys}$$

M_{in} may be eliminated by means of the mass balance:

$$M_{in} = M_{end} - M_{begin}$$

Substitution into the energy balance then gives:

$$h_{in}[M_{end} - M_{begin}]_{sys} = [M_{end}u_{end} - M_{begin}u_{begin}]_{sys}$$

or

$$M_{end}[h_{in} - u_{end}] = M_{begin}[h_{in} - u_{begin}] \qquad (1)$$

Equation (1) contains five distinct variables: M_{end}, M_{begin}, h_{in}, u_{begin}, and u_{end}. M_{begin} is already known. h_{in} and u_{in} can be evaluated from the known pressure and temperature of these materials. Thus equation (1) contains two unknowns, and more equations will have to be developed before determining the missing unknowns. Relate the final mass of air in the cylinder to the cylinder volume by means of the final specific volume:

$$M_{end} = \frac{v_{tank}}{v_{end}} \qquad (2)$$

Equation (2) however adds another variable u_{end} to the system of equations and there is still one more unknown than the number of equations. The final specific volume, in turn, may be related to the final temperature and (known) pressure by means of the ideal-gas equation of state:

$$v_{end} = \frac{RT_{end}}{P_{end}(\text{mol wt})} \qquad (3)$$

Although equation (3) adds a fourth unknown, T_{end}, to our system of equations, the closing equation is now obtained by using the law which states that the specific internal energy of a gas which obeys the ideal-gas equation of state is a function only of the gas's temperature:

$$u_{end} = f(T_{end}) \qquad (4)$$

Since equation (4) adds no new unknowns, our system of equations is now complete. There are four equations with four unknowns. However, before solving these equations, develop the functional form indicated in equation (4):

The constant-volume heat capacity C_v is defined by:

$$C_v = \left(\frac{\partial u}{\partial T}\right)_v$$

As indicated, however, the constant-volume restriction is unnecessary for a gas which obeys the ideal-gas equation of state. Thus for this problem:

$$\frac{du}{dT} = C_v$$

or

$$du = C_v dT \qquad (5)$$

Now arbitrarily assign a reference state internal energy: u = 0 at T = 75°F. The internal energy at any other temperature is then obtained from the integral of equation (5)

$$u(T) = \int_{T=75°F}^{T} C_v dT$$

Substituting the expression for C_v,

$$C_v = [4.4 + 8.35 \times 10^{-4} T(°R)^{-1}] \frac{Btu}{lb_m °R}$$

then gives

$$u(T) = \int_{535}^{T} [4.4 + 8.35 \times 10^{-4} T(°R)^{-1}] dT \frac{Btu}{lb_m °R}$$

$$= \{4.4[T - 535°R] + 4.18 \times 10^{-4}[T^2 - (535°R)^2]°R^{-1}\} \frac{Btu}{lb_m °R}$$

or

$$u(T) = [4.4T(°R)^{-1} + 4.18 \times 10^{-4} T^2 (°R)^{-2} - 2470] \frac{Btu}{lb_m} \qquad (6)$$

The enthalpy is obtained from:

$$h(T) = u(T) + Pv$$

$$= u(T) + RT$$

or

$$h(T) = [6.4T(°R)^{-1} + 4.18 \times 10^{-4} T^2 (°R)^{-2} - 2470] \frac{Btu}{lb_m} \qquad (7)$$

Therefore:

$$u_{begin} = 0 \text{ Btu/lb}_m$$

$$h_{in} = h(585°R) = 1213\ Btu/lb_m$$

and

$$M_{begin} = 0.254\ lb_m$$

Thus the system of equations to be solved can now be expressed as:

$$M_{end}\left[1213\ \frac{Btu}{lb_m} - u_{end}\right] = 0.254\ lb_m[1213 - 0]\ \frac{Btu}{lb_m}$$

or

$$M_{end}\left[1213\ \frac{Btu}{lb_m} - u_{end}\right] = 296\ Btu \qquad (8)$$

$$M_{end} = \frac{1\ ft^3}{v_{end}} \qquad (9)$$

$$v_{end} = \frac{1545}{29} \times \frac{T}{1.44 \times 10^5}\ \frac{ft\text{-}lb_f}{lb_m(lb_f/ft^2)}$$

or

$$v_{end} = 3.70 \times 10^{-4} T\left(\frac{ft^3}{lb_m °R}\right) \qquad (10)$$

and

$$u_{end} = [4.4\ T_{end}(°R)^{-1} + 4.18 \times 10^{-4} T_{end}^2(°R)^{-2} - 2470]\frac{Btu}{lb_m} \qquad (11)$$

Equation (11) is non-linear in temperature. A simple direct solution of equations (8) through (11) cannot be used. Therefore reduce the system of equations to a single non-linear equation in T_{end} and this equation can be solved by appropriate means.

Eliminate M_{end} between equations (8) and (9)

$$\frac{(1213\ Btu/lb_m - u_{end})ft^3}{v_{end}} = 296\ Btu \qquad (12)$$

v_{end} is now eliminated between (12) and (10)

$$\frac{(1213\ Btu/lb_m - u_{end})\ ft^3}{3.70 \times 10^{-4}\ T_{end} ft^3/(lb_m °R)} = 296\ Btu$$

or

$$(1213 \text{ Btu/lb}_m - u_{end}) = 1.09 \times 10^{-1} T_{end} \frac{\text{Btu}}{\text{lb}_m {}^\circ\text{R}} \tag{13}$$

u_{end} is then eliminated between (13) and (11) to give a single equation in T_{end}:

$$[3684 - 4.4T_{end}({}^\circ\text{R})^{-1} - 4.18 \times 10^{-4} T_{end}^2({}^\circ\text{R}^{-2})]\frac{\text{Btu}}{\text{lb}_m} \tag{14}$$

$$= 1.09 \times 10^{-1} T_{end} \frac{\text{Btu}}{\text{lb}_m {}^\circ\text{R}}$$

Although this equation is nonlinear in T_{end}, it is only quadratic, and thus the use of the quadratic formula appears the most direct means of solution. Equation (14) may be rearranged to:

$$4.18 \times 10^{-4} T_{end}^2({}^\circ\text{R}^{-2}) + 4.5\ T_{end}({}^\circ\text{R})^{-1} - 3684 = 0$$

Application of the quadratic formula yields:

$$T_{end} = \frac{-4.5 + \sqrt{(4.5)^2 + (4)(3684)(4.18 \times 10^{-4})}}{2 \times 4.18 \times 10^{-4}} {}^\circ\text{R}$$

or

$$T_{end} = 765{}^\circ\text{R}$$

Thus: $$v_{end} = 0.283 \text{ ft}^3/\text{lb}_m$$

and

$$M_{end} = 3.53 \text{ lb}_m$$

The mass added during filling is

$$M_{end} - M_{begin} = (3.53 - 0.254) \text{ lb}_m = 3.28 \text{ lb}_m$$

CHAPTER 4

ENTROPY AND THE SECOND LAW OF THERMODYNAMICS

REVERSIBLE PROCESSES AND CYCLES

• **PROBLEM 4-1**

A Carnot engine operates between the temperatures 1000°F and 50°F, producing 120 Btu of work. Calculate the heat input to the engine.

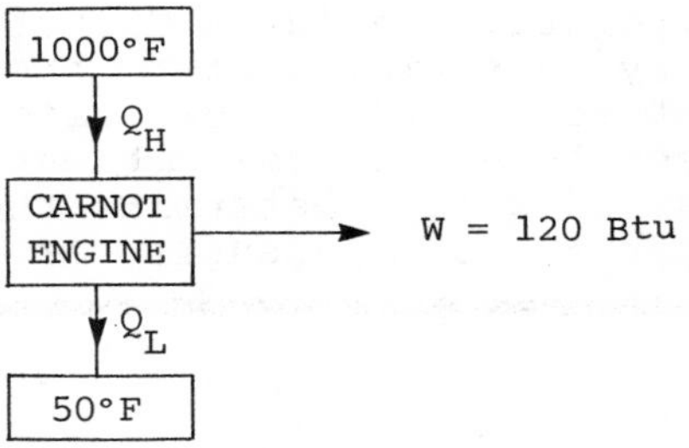

Solution: The first law of thermodynamics yields

$$Q_H - Q_L = W \quad (1)$$

where

Q_H = Heat input

Q_L = Heat output

W = Work done = 120 Btu

From the definition of absolute thermodynamic temperature scale,

$$\frac{Q_H}{Q_L} = \frac{T_H}{T_L} \qquad (2)$$

Solving equations (1) and (2) for Q_H,

$$Q_H - Q_H \frac{T_L}{T_H} = W$$

or

$$Q_H = \frac{W}{1-T_L/T_H} \qquad (3)$$

$T_H = 1000 + 460 = 1460°R$

$T_L = 50 + 460 = 510°R$

Substituting these values in equation (3),

$$Q_H = \frac{120}{1-(510/1460)} = 184.4 \text{ Btu}$$

• PROBLEM 4-2

The temperature inside a Carnot refrigerator is maintained at 5°C by rejecting heat to the surroundings at an ambient temperature of 27°C. The inside temperature is now decreased to -13°C, the ambient temperature remaining constant at 27°C. Determine the percent increase in work input for the same quantity of heat Q_L removed.

Solution: Using the first law of thermodynamics and the definition of the absolute thermodynamic scale of temperature,

$$Q_H - Q_L = W \qquad (1)$$

and

$$\frac{Q_H}{Q_L} = \frac{T_H}{T_L} \qquad (2)$$

Solving for Q in equation (2) and substituting in equation (1),

$$W = Q_L \left(\frac{T_H}{T_L} - 1\right) \qquad (3)$$

When the refrigerator operates between 5°C and 27°C,

$$T_H = 273 + 27 = 300°K$$

$$T_L = 273 + 5 = 278°K$$

$$W_1 = Q_L \left(\frac{300}{278} - 1\right) = 0.0791\ Q_L$$

When the refrigerator works between -13°C and 27°C,

$$T_H = 273 + 27 = 300°K$$

$$T_L = 273 - 13 = 260°K$$

$$W_2 = Q_L \left(\frac{300}{260} - 1\right) = 0.1538\ Q_L$$

The percent increase in work input is then given by

$$\frac{W_2 - W_1}{W_1} \times 100 = \left(\frac{0.1538\ Q_L - 0.0791\ Q_L}{0.0791\ Q_L}\right) \times 100$$

$$= 94.5\%$$

• PROBLEM 4-3

A reversible cyclic device does work, while exchanging heat with three constant temperature reservoirs as illustrated in the figure. The three reservoirs 1, 2, and 3 are at temperatures of 1000°K, 300°K, and 500°K respectively. It is known that 400 kJ of heat are transferred from reservoir 1 to the device, and the total work done by the cyclic device is 100 kJ. Determine both the magnitude and direction of the heat transfer with the other two reservoirs.

Solution: Applying the first law of thermodynamics to this system

$$Q_{TOT} = W_{TOT}$$

or

$$Q_1 + Q_2 + Q_3 = W_{Device}$$

Substituting the known values

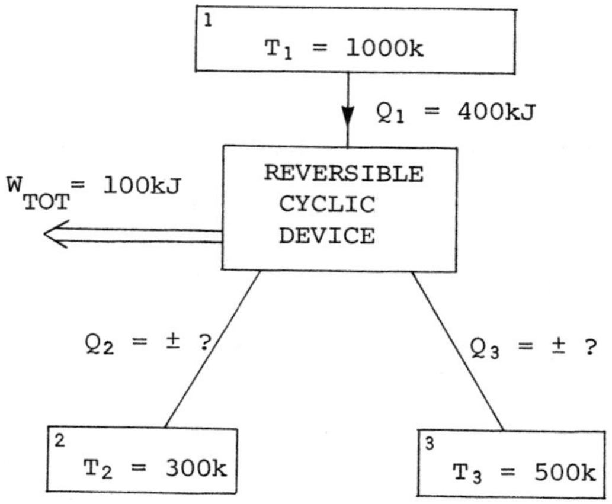

$$400 + Q_2 + Q_3 = 100 \qquad (1)$$

Since Eq. (1) is an equation with two unknowns, a second equation must be obtained. From the second law of thermodynamics

$$\int \frac{dQ}{T}\bigg|_{rev} = 0$$

or

$$\frac{Q_1}{T_1} + \frac{Q_2}{T_2} + \frac{Q_3}{T_3} = 0$$

Substituting the known values

$$\frac{400}{1000} + \frac{Q_2}{300} + \frac{Q_3}{500} = 0$$

or

$$0.4 + \frac{Q_2}{300} + \frac{Q_3}{500} = 0 \qquad (2)$$

Eqs. (1) and (2) have the same two unknowns, and can therefore be solved simultaneously. Solving for Q_2 in Eq. (1) and substituting into Eq. (2) gives:

$$0.4 + \left(\frac{-300-Q_3}{300}\right) + \frac{Q_3}{500} = 0$$

or

$$0.4 - 1 - \frac{2Q_3}{1500} = 0$$

Solving for Q_3,

$$Q_3 = -450 \text{ kJ}$$

From Eq. (1) then

$$Q_2 = -300 - Q_3$$
$$= -300 - (-450)$$
$$= +150 \text{ kJ}$$

Therefore 150 kJ of heat is transferred from reservoir 2 to the device, and 450 kJ of heat are rejected from the device to reservoir 3. As a check Q_{TOT} must equal W_{TOT},

$$400 + 150 - 450 = 100$$

which is a true statement.

• PROBLEM 4-4

> One kg of water is initially located 100m above a very large lake. The water, the lake, and the air are at a uniform temperature of 20°C. Then the one kg of water falls into the lake, mixing and coming to equilibrium with it. Determine the entropy change associated with this process.

Solution: For a combined system of the water, the lake, and the air

$$U_F - U_I = (P.E.)_I - (P.E.)_F$$

However at the final state (at equilibrium) the potential energy (P.E.) is zero. Thus

$$U_F - U_I = (P.E.)_I = mgh$$

where

$$m = 1 \text{ kg}$$
$$g = 9.81 \text{ m/sec}^2$$
$$h = 100 \text{ m}$$

Also for the change in entropy

$$ds = \frac{1}{T}(du + Pdv) \cong \frac{1}{T}\,du \tag{1}$$

Integrating Eq. (1),

$$\int ds = \Delta s = \frac{1}{T}\int du$$

$$= \frac{1}{T}(U_F - U_I)$$

$$= \frac{1}{T}(mgh)$$

Substituting the known values

$$\Delta s = \frac{1}{293}(1.0 \times 9.81 \times 100)$$

$$= 3.346 \text{ J/°K}$$

ENTROPY CHANGE IN REVERSIBLE AND IRREVERSIBLE PROCESSES

• PROBLEM 4-5

An adiabatic system, open to the atmosphere which has a pressure of 14.7 psia, consists of 1.0 lbm of ice at 32°F and 6 lbm of liquid water at 80°F. Assuming a constant specific heat C_p = 1.0 Btu/lbm-°F for water, and the latent heat of fusion for ice to be 144 Btu/lbm, determine the final temperature of the system and the change in entropy for the spontaneous adiabatic process.

Solution: Since the process is adiabatic, the change in enthalpy is zero, thus,

$$\Delta H\Big|_{P = \text{const.}} = 0$$

or

$$(m\Delta h)_{ice} + (m\Delta h)_{water} = 0 \qquad (1)$$

Let the final temperature be T. Then equation (1) can be written as

$$144 \text{ Btu/lbm} \times 1 \text{ lbm} + (T°F - 32°F) \times 1.0 \text{ Btu/lbm-°F} \times 1.0 \text{ lbm}$$
$$+ (T°F - 80°F) \times 1.0 \text{ Btu/lbm-°F} \times 6 \text{ lbm} = 0$$

or

$$7T - 368 = 0$$

$$T = 52.6°F$$

The change in entropy is given by

$$\Delta S_{system} = \Delta S_{ice} + \Delta S_{water}$$

where

ΔS_{ice} = ΔS due to melting ice at constant temperature

+ ΔS due to heating melted ice from 32°F to 52.6°F

$$= \frac{144 \times 1.0}{32 + 460} + 1.0 \ln\left(\frac{52.6 + 460}{32 + 460}\right) \times 1.0$$

$$= 0.292 + 0.041$$

$$= +0.333 \text{ Btu/°R}$$

ΔS_{water} = ΔS due to cooling from 80°F to 52.6°F

$$= 1.0 \ln\left(\frac{52.6 + 460}{80 + 460}\right) \times 6.0$$

$$= -0.312 \text{ Btu/°R}$$

Thus,

$$\Delta S_{system} = +0.333 - 0.312 = +0.021 \text{ Btu/°R.}$$

The positive sign indicates that the entropy of the system has increased due to the irreversible process.

• PROBLEM 4-6

One lbm of saturated water is initially at 100°F. It then undergoes an isothermal process until the final pressure of the water is 3000 psia. Calculate the entropy change for the water by (a) using data from the steam tables and (b) using the experimental expansion coefficient $\beta = 205 \times 10^{-6} \, °R^{-1}$, assumed constant for the given change in pressure.

Solution: (a) Since all the calculations will be made on the basis of large increments, they will be approximate. Therefore assume the liquid to be incompressible, with the isothermal bulk modulus given by

$$\kappa_T = -v\left(\frac{\partial v}{\partial P}\right)_T = 0 \qquad (1)$$

and the change in entropy given by

T °F	v_f ft³/lbm	Δv_f ft³/lbm	$\Delta v/\Delta T$ ft³/lbm-°R
120	0.01620	0.0012	3×10^{-6}
80	0.01608		

$$ds = C_p \frac{dT}{T} - \left(\frac{\partial v}{\partial T}\right) dP \qquad (2)$$

Next approximate the value of $\left(\frac{\partial v}{\partial T}\right)_P$ using the steam tables as follows:

For this range of temperatures, the saturation pressure changes very little and therefore the value obtained is virtually at constant pressure. Neglecting the initial pressure (P_1 = 0.95 psia) because it is small compared to the final pressure, and integrating Eq. (2),

$$\int ds = \Delta s = -\int \left(\frac{\partial v}{\partial T}\right)_P dP$$

$$= -\left(\frac{\Delta v}{\Delta T}\right)_P \Delta P$$

substituting the numerical values, and converting to the proper units

$$\Delta s = -(3 \times 10^{-6})\left(\frac{3000 \times 144}{778}\right)$$

$$= -1.665 \times 10^{-3} \text{ Btu/lbm-°R}$$

In the steam tables, for compressed water, a more accurate value of -1.79×10^{-3} Btu/lbm-°R is obtained. The calculated value is therefore only an approximation, and a correction method has to be applied for a more accurate value.

(b) Since T = constant, Eq. (2) and the relation

$$\left(\frac{\partial v}{\partial T}\right)_P = v\beta$$

combined, give

$$ds = -v\beta dP$$

or

$$\Delta s = -v\beta\Delta P$$

$$= -\frac{(0.01613)(205 \times 10^{-6})(3000-0.95)(144)}{778}$$

$$= -1.77 \times 10^{-3} \text{ Btu/lbm-°R.}$$

• PROBLEM 4-7

A reversible cyclic heat engine is used to cool an aluminum block having a mass of 5 kg, from 40°C to 20°C by reversibly transferring heat from it as shown in the figure. The room air, which is at 20°C serves as a constant temperature sink for the engine. What is the change in entropy for the block and for the room air? Also calculate the work done by the engine. Assume for aluminum C_p = 400 J/kg-°K.

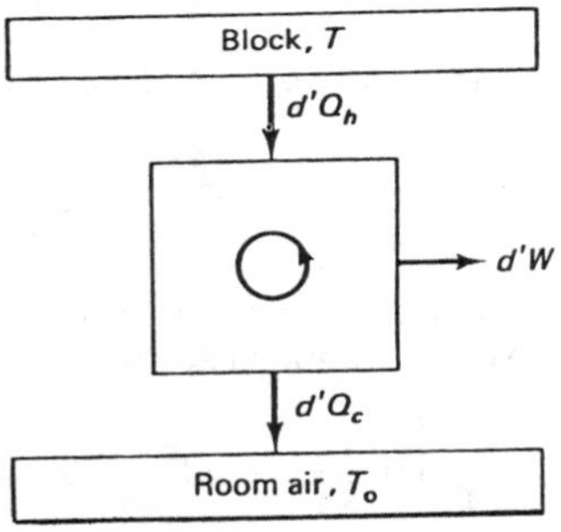

Solution: The block is cooled reversibly, therefore

$$ds = \left(\frac{dQ}{T}\right)_{revers.} \tag{1}$$

where dQ is the heat transferred to the block. However we can also write

$$dQ = mC_p dT \tag{2}$$

Combining Eqs. (1) and (2),

$$ds = mC_p \frac{dT}{T}$$

Integrating

$$(s_2 - s_1)_{block} = mC_p \ln\left(\frac{T_2}{T_1}\right)$$

$$= 5(400)\ \ln\left(\frac{293}{313}\right)$$

$$= -134\ J/°K.$$

The process is reversible, and if the system is taken to be the block, the engine, and the room air then this system is adiabatic and $dQ = 0$. In turn for an adiabatic system in a reversible process, the change in entropy is zero. Therefore for the room air

$$(s_2 - s_1)_{air} = -(s_2 - s_1)_{block} = +134\ J/°K$$

To calculate the work, consider the efficiency of a completely reversible engine.

$$\eta_{rev} = 1 - \frac{T_0}{T} \tag{3}$$

and

$$\eta_{rev} = \frac{dW}{dQ_h} = \frac{-dW}{mC_p dT} \tag{4}$$

Equating (3) and (4) and solving for dW obtain

$$dW = mC_p T_0 \frac{dT}{T} - mC_p dT \tag{5}$$

Integrating Eq. (5) as the temperature changes from $T_1 = 313°K$ to $T_2 = 293°K$, the total work is obtained

$$W = mC_p \ln \frac{T_2}{T_1} - mC_p\ (T_2 - T_1)$$

$$= 5(400)\ \ln\left(\frac{293}{313}\right) - 5(400)(293-313)$$

$$= -39{,}260 + 40{,}000$$

$$= 740\ J.$$

• PROBLEM 4-8

A 34 kg steel casting at a temperature of 427°C is quenched in 136 kg of oil initially at 21°C. Assuming no heat losses and the steel casting and oil to have constant specific heats of 0.5024 and 2.5121 kJ/kg-°K respectively, determine the change in entropy for a system consisting of the oil and casting.

Solution: In this process, since there are no heat losses, whatever heat is rejected from the hotter medium is going to be added to the colder medium making the total energy of the oil and steel, zero. Therefore

$$Q_{cast} = Q_{oil}$$

or

$$m_c C_p (T_1 - T_F) = m_0 C_p (T_F - T_1) \quad (1)$$

Substituting the numerical values into Eq. (1)

$$34(0.5024)(427 - T_F) = 136(2.5121)(T_F - 21)$$

or

$$7,293.84 - 17.08T_F = 341.65T_F - 7,174.56$$

Solving for T_F

$$T_F = \frac{14,468.40}{358.73}$$

$$= 40.3°C.$$

The change in entropy for the system is

$$(\Delta S)_{syst.} = (\Delta S)_{oil} + (\Delta S)_{cast.} \quad (2)$$

where for the oil

$$(\Delta S)_{oil} = \int \frac{mdQ}{T} = m\,C_p \int \frac{dT}{T}$$

$$= m\,C_p \ln \frac{T_2}{T_1}$$

or

$$(\Delta S)_{oil} = (136)(2.5121) \ln \left(\frac{313.3}{294}\right)$$

$$= 21.72 \text{ kJ/°K}$$

For the steel casting, following the same procedure

$$(\Delta S)_{cast.} = m_c C_p \ln \left(\frac{T_2}{T_1}\right)$$

$$= 34(0.5024) \ln \left(\frac{313.3}{700}\right)$$

$$= -13.73 \text{ kJ/°K}.$$

Then from Eq. (2)

$$(\Delta S)_{syst.} = 21.72 - 13.73 = 7.99 \text{ kJ/°K}.$$

• **PROBLEM 4-9**

Derive an equation for the entropy change of an ideal gas undergoing any reversible or irreversible process, by using the definition for the change in entropy

$$ds = \frac{\delta q}{T}$$

along any reversible path connecting the same end states. Assume constant specific heats.

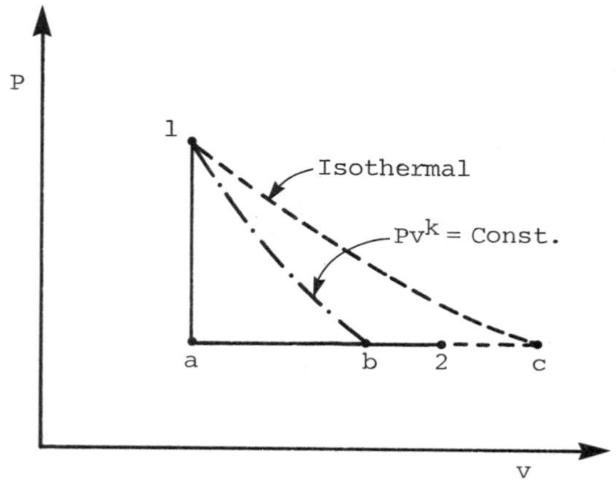

Solution: Entropy is a property, and for a pure substance is determined by any two independent properties, regardless of the motion or position of the system. Therefore it does not matter whether the substance is in a closed system, or is flowing into, out of, or through an open system. Also the change in entropy depends only on the end states and not on the path connecting them.

The figure depicts three of the possible reversible paths between the two states (1 and 2). The derivation will therefore be made for these three reversible paths.

Path 1→a→2:

$$ds = \left(\frac{\delta q}{T}\right)_{1\to a} + \left(\frac{\delta q}{T}\right)_{a\to 2} \tag{1}$$

Path 1→a represents a constant volume process. Hence for an ideal gas

$$\delta q_{1\to a} = du_{1\to a} = C_v dT\Big|_{1\to a} \tag{2}$$

Path a→2 is a constant pressure process. Hence for an ideal gas

$$\delta q_{a\to 2} = dh_{a\to 2} = C_p dT\Big|_{a\to 2} \tag{3}$$

Substituting Eqs. (2) and (3) into Eq. (1),

$$ds = \left(C_v \frac{dT}{T}\right)_{1\to a} + \left(C_p \frac{dT}{T}\right)_{a\to 2} \tag{4}$$

Integrating

$$\Delta S = C_v \ln \frac{T_a}{T_1} + C_p \ln \frac{T_2}{T_a} \tag{5}$$

From the ideal gas equation

$$Pv = RT \tag{6}$$

at states 1, a, and 2 obtain

$$\frac{T_a}{T_1} = \frac{P_a}{P_1} = \frac{P_2}{P_1} \tag{7}$$

and

$$\frac{T_2}{T_a} = \frac{v_2}{v_a} = \frac{v_2}{v_1} \tag{8}$$

Substituting these relations into Eq. (5) gives

$$\Delta S_{1\to 2} = C_v \ln \frac{P_2}{P_1} + C_p \ln \frac{v_2}{v_1} \tag{9}$$

Path 1→b→2:

$$ds = \left(\frac{\delta q}{T}\right)_{1\to b} + \left(\frac{\delta q}{T}\right)_{b\to 2} \tag{10}$$

Path 1→b represents an adiabatic process. Hence

$$\delta q_{1\to b} = 0 \tag{11}$$

Path b→2 represents a constant pressure process. Thus

$$\delta q_{1\to b} = dh_{1\to b} = C_p\, dT\Big|_{1\to b} \tag{12}$$

Substituting (11) and (12) into (10)

$$ds = 0 + \left(C_p \frac{dT}{T}\right)_{1\to b} \tag{13}$$

Integrating

$$\Delta S = C_p \ln \frac{T_2}{T_b} \tag{14}$$

From Eq. (6)

$$\frac{T_2}{T_b} = \frac{v_2}{v_b} \tag{15}$$

Substituting (15) into (14)

$$\Delta S = C_p \ln \frac{v_2}{v_b} = C_p \ln \frac{v_2/v_1}{v_b/v_1} \tag{16}$$

Path 1→c→2

$$ds = \left(\frac{\delta q}{T}\right)_{1\to c} + \left(\frac{\delta q}{T}\right)_{c\to 2} \tag{17}$$

Path 1→c represents an isothermal process. Hence

$$\delta q_{1\to c} = \delta w_{1\to c} = PdV \tag{18}$$

Path c→2 represents a constant pressure process. Hence

$$d\delta_{c\to 2} = dh_{c\to 2} = C_p \, dT\Big|_{c\to 2} \tag{19}$$

Substituting Eqs. (18) and (19) into Eq. (17)

$$ds = \left(\frac{PdV}{T}\right)_{1\to c} + \left(C_p \frac{dT}{T}\right)_{c\to 2} \tag{20}$$

For an ideal gas however, from Eq. (6)

$$P = \frac{RT}{v} \tag{21}$$

Substituting Eq. (21) into Eq. (20) and integrating

$$\Delta S = \frac{RT_1}{T_1}\int_1^c \frac{dV}{v} + C_p\int_c^2 \frac{dT}{T}$$

$$= R \ln \frac{v_c}{v_1} + C_p \ln \frac{T_c}{T_1} \tag{22}$$

From Eq. (6)

$$\frac{v_c}{v_1} = \frac{P_1}{P_c} = \frac{P_1}{P_2}$$

and

$$\frac{T_c}{T_1} = \frac{T_2}{T_1}$$

Substituting these relations into Eq. (22),

$$\Delta S = R \ln \frac{P_1}{P_2} + C_p \ln \frac{T_2}{T_1} \tag{23}$$

The three equations (Eqs. (9), (16), (23)) will give the same result for the change in entropy between the two end states for any reversible or irreversible process.

ENTROPY CHANGE OF IDEAL GASES

• PROBLEM 4-10

Three kilograms of air are at an initial state of 100 kPa, 300°K. The air is then compressed polytropically with n = 2.56, to a final pressure of 500 kPa. Assuming constant specific heats, calculate the change in entropy using the three ideal gas equations.

Solution: The three different equation which give the change in entropy for an ideal gas are

$$\Delta S = mC_v \ln\left(\frac{T_2}{T_1}\right) + mR \ln\left(\frac{V_2}{V_1}\right) \tag{1}$$

$$\Delta S = mC_p \ln\left(\frac{T_2}{T_1}\right) - mR \ln\left(\frac{P_2}{P_1}\right) \tag{2}$$

and

$$\Delta S = m\,C_n \ln\left(\frac{T_2}{T_1}\right) \tag{3}$$

where C_n is the polytropic specific heat defined as

$$C_n = \frac{C_p - nC_v}{1-n} \tag{4}$$

In all three equations the temperatures at both states is involved. To find the temperature at state 2 the following expression is used.

$$T_2 = T_1 \left(\frac{P_2}{P_1}\right)^{\frac{n-1}{n}}$$

Substituting the numerical values

$$T_2 = 300\left(\frac{500}{100}\right)^{(2.56-1)/2.56}$$

$$= 300\,(5)^{0.6094}$$

$$= 800°K.$$

Using the ideal gas equation of state

$$PV = mRT$$

the volumes at the two states are then calculated as

$$V_1 = \frac{mRT_1}{P_1}$$

$$= \frac{3(0.287)(300)}{100}$$

$$= 2.583 \text{ m}^3$$

and

$$V_2 = \frac{mRT_2}{P_2}$$

$$= \frac{3(0.287)(800)}{500}$$

$$= 1.378 \text{ m}^3.$$

Also from Eq. (4)

$$C_n = \frac{1.0035-2.56(0.717)}{1-2.56}$$

$$= 0.534 \text{ kJ/kg-°K}.$$

Eq. (1) gives

$$\Delta S = 3(0.717) \ln \left(\frac{800}{300}\right) + 3(0.287) \ln \left(\frac{1.378}{2.583}\right)$$

$$= 1.57 \text{ kJ/°K}.$$

Eq. (2) gives

$$\Delta S = 3(1.0035) \ln \left(\frac{800}{300}\right) - 3(0.287) \ln \left(\frac{500}{100}\right)$$

$$= 1.57 \text{ kJ/°K}.$$

Eq. (3) gives

$$\Delta S = 3(0.534) \ln \left(\frac{800}{300}\right)$$

$$= 1.57 \text{ kJ/°K}$$

All three equations give the same result, as should be expected.

• PROBLEM 4-11

Calculate the change in specific entropy of 1 lbm of air when it is compressed from 14 psia, 60°F to 84 psia and 460°F.

Solution: Assume a reversible process between the two state points. Thus

$$\frac{T_2}{T_1} = \left(\frac{P_2}{P_1}\right)^{\frac{(n-1)}{n}}$$

$$\frac{920}{520} = \left(\frac{84}{14}\right)^{\frac{(n-1)}{n}}$$

$$1.769 = (6)^{\frac{(n-1)}{n}}$$

Hence

$$\frac{n-1}{n} = 0.3185$$

$$n = 1.467$$

For a polytropic process

$$C_n = C_v + \frac{R}{J(1-n)}$$

$$= 0.1715 + \frac{53.35}{(1-1.467)778}$$

$$= 0.1715 - 0.1467$$

$$= 0.0248 \text{ Btu/lbm-°R}$$

Then $S_2 - S_1 = mC_n \ln \frac{T_2}{T_1}$

$$= 1 \times 0.0248 \ln \left(\frac{920}{520}\right)$$

$$= 0.01416 \text{ Btu/°R}$$

The change in entropy is

$$\Delta S = 0.01416 \text{ Btu/°R}$$

• PROBLEM 4-12

Helium is heated reversibly at constant pressure from 18 psia, 80F to 200 F in a steady flow system. Calculate the change in entropy per pound of helium for this process.

Solution: The first law for a steady flow system in differential form is

$$\delta q = dh + dKE + dPE + \delta w \tag{1}$$

For a reversible steady-flow process

$$\delta w = -vdp - dKE - dPE \tag{2}$$

From (1) and (2)

$$\delta q = dh + dKE + dPE - vdp - dKE - dPE$$

For a constant pressure process $dp = 0$

$$\therefore \ \delta q = dh$$

For a steady flow system $dS = 0$ and $\delta m_1 = \delta m_2$

The expression for dS of an open system is

$$dS = \left(\frac{\delta Q}{T}\right)_{rev} + S_1\delta m_1 - S_2\delta m_2$$

$$dS = 0 = \left(\frac{\delta Q}{T}\right)_{rev} + (S_1 - S_2)\delta m$$

$$S_2 - S_1 = \int_1^2 \frac{\delta q}{T} = \int_1^2 \frac{dh}{T} = \int_1^2 \frac{C_p\,dT}{T}$$

for helium, $C_p = 1.25$ Btu/lb°F

$= 1.25$ Btu/lb°R

$$\Delta S = C_p \ln \frac{T_2}{T_1}$$

$$= 1.25 \ln\left(\frac{660}{540}\right)$$

$= 0.251$ Btu/lb-°R.

• PROBLEM 4-13

A gas having a constant volume specific heat equal to (4.52 + 0.00737T)Btu/lbm-°F is initially at 175°F. Heat is then added to the gas in a constant volume process until its temperature rises to 200° F. Calculate the change in entropy associated with this process.

Solution: In this case, C_v, for the gas is in the form

$$C_v = a + bT$$

where

$$a = 4.52$$

and

$$b = 0.00737$$

The entropy change per unit mass is given as

$$\Delta S = \int_a^b C_p \frac{dT}{T} = \int_a^b \left(\frac{a+bT}{T}\right) dT$$

$$= \int_a^b a \frac{dT}{T} + \int_a^b \frac{bT}{T}\, dT$$

Integration yields

$$\Delta S = a \ln\left(\frac{T_b}{T_a}\right) + b(T_b - T_a)$$

$$= 4.52 \ln\left(\frac{660}{635}\right) + 0.00737(200-175)$$

$$= 0.1745 + 0.1843$$

$$= 0.3588 \text{ Btu/lbm.}$$

• PROBLEM 4-14

An ideal gas at an initial state of 4.1 atm, 38°C is expanded irreversibly to a final state of 2 atm, 4.4°C. Assuming the specific heats of the gas to be C_p = 0.5150 and C_v = 0.3098 kJ/kg-°K calculate the change in entropy.

Solution: The change in entropy for a reversible or irreversible process is given by the relation

$$ds = \frac{1}{T}\,du + \frac{P}{T}\,dv \tag{1}$$

However for an ideal gas

$$du = C_v\,dT \tag{2}$$

and

$$\frac{P}{T} = \frac{R}{v} = \frac{C_p - C_v}{v} \tag{3}$$

Substituting Eqs. (2) and (3) into Eq. (1),

$$\int_1^2 ds = C_v\int_1^2 \frac{dT}{T} + (C_p - C_v)\int_1^2 \frac{dv}{v}$$

Integrating gives

$$\Delta s_{1\to 2} = C_v \ln\left(\frac{T_2}{T_1}\right) + (C_p - C_v)\ln\left(\frac{v_2}{v_1}\right) \tag{4}$$

The specific volumes at the initial and final states are then calculated as follows. From Eq. (3)

$$v = \frac{(C_p - C_v)T}{P}$$

or

$$v_1 = \frac{(0.5150-0.3098)\times 311}{4.1\times 101}$$

$$= 0.1541\ m^3/kg$$

and

$$v_2 = \frac{(0.5150-0.3098)\times 277.4}{2\times 101}$$

$$= 0.2818\ m^3/kg$$

Substituting all the numerical values into Eq. (4),

$$\Delta s_{1\to 2} = 0.3098\ \ln\left(\frac{277.4}{311}\right) + (0.5150-0.3098)\ln\left(\frac{0.2818}{0.1541}\right)$$

$$= -0.0354 + 0.1239$$

$$= 0.0885\ kJ/kg\text{-}^\circ K$$

• PROBLEM 4-15

> Ten grams of argon gas at an initial pressure and temperature of 608 kPa, 300°K respectively undergo a change of state at constant internal energy until the final volume is three times the initial occupied volume. Assuming ideal gas behavior determine the final state (pressure and temperature), and the entropy change of the gas due to the change of state.

Solution: For a perfect gas, the internal energy is a function of the temperature only.

$$u = f(T)$$

Assuming constant internal energy, follows that the temperature must also be a constant. Therefore for a change of state at constant internal energy.

$$T_2 = T_1 = 300°K.$$

Since we have assumed ideal gas behavior

$$P_1V_1 = mRT_1 \quad (1)$$

$$P_2V_2 = mRT_2 \quad (2)$$

However $T_2 = T_1$, $V_2 = 3V_1$, and m = constant. Combining Eqs. (2) and (1) and solving for P_2,

$$P_2 = \frac{P_1}{3} = \frac{608}{3} = 202.7\text{kPa}$$

The change in entropy is given by the equation

$$s_2 - s_1 = C_p \ln\frac{T_2}{T_1} - R\ln\frac{P_2}{P_1} \quad (3)$$

Since $T_2 = T_1$, Eq. (3) reduces to

$$s_2 - s_1 = -R\ln\frac{P_2}{P_1} \quad (4)$$

where for argon gas R = 0.20813 kJ/kg-°K.

Substituting the numerical values into Eq. (4)

$$s_2 - s_1 = -(0.20813)\ln\left(\frac{202.7}{608}\right)$$

$$= +0.2286 \text{ kJ/kg-°K}$$

$$= +228.6 \text{ J/kg-°K}$$

For 10 g of argon gas

$$\Delta S = S_2 - S_1 = m(s_2 - s_1)$$

$$= \frac{10(228.6)}{1000}$$

$$= +2.286 \text{ J/°K}$$

• PROBLEM 4-16

Air at 70°F and 90 psia is enclosed inside an insulated cylinder, as shown in the figure, by a piston having a cross sectional area of 25 in². Initially the piston is held stationary by a stop and has a weight of 125 lbf on it. The piston is then released and moves upwards. Calculate the change of entropy produced by the process resulting from the piston release.

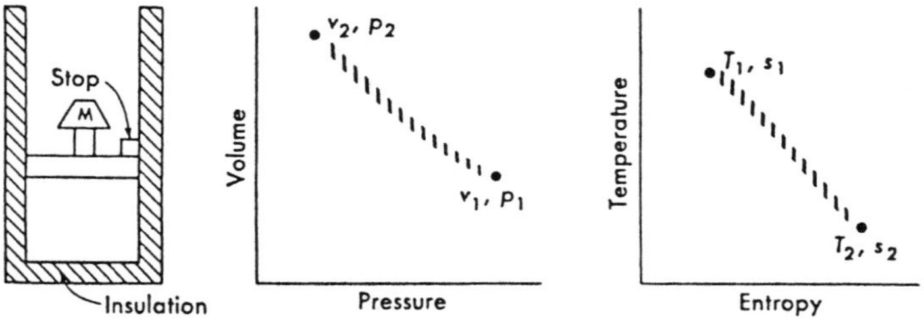

An Irreversible Adiabatic Process.

Solution: The piston would be raised as a result of the expanding gas due to the difference in pressure on the two sides of the piston. The piston would stop rising when the forces on the two sides of the piston have equalized. The weight of the piston creates a pressure on the enclosed gas.

This pressure is

$$P = \frac{M}{A} = \frac{125}{25} = 5 \text{ lbf/in}^2$$

This pressure along with atmospheric pressure gives a value for the pressure at the end of the process

$$P_2 = P + P_{atm}$$

$$P_2 = 5 + 15 = 20 \text{ lbf/in}^2 = 2880 \text{ lbf/ft}^2$$

The change in entropy for an ideal gas is given by the equation

$$\Delta s_{1\to 2} = C_p \ln \frac{v_2}{v_1} + C_v \ln \frac{P_2}{P_1} \qquad (1)$$

From the table of the critical constants, for air

$$C_p = 0.240 \text{ Btu/lbm-°R}$$

$$C_v = 0.171 \text{ Btu/lbm-°R}$$

$$R = 53.34 \text{ ft-lbf/lbm-°R}$$

However, the specific volumes must be calculated first before we can solve for $\Delta s_{1\to2}$. At state 1,

$$v_1 = \frac{RT_1}{P_1}$$

where

$$T_1 = 70 + 460 = 530°R$$

$$P_1 = 90 \text{ lbf/in}^2 \times 144 \frac{\text{in}^2}{\text{ft}^2} = 12{,}960 \text{ lbf/ft}^2$$

Then

$$v_1 = \frac{53.34(530)}{12{,}960} = 2.2 \text{ ft}^3\text{/lbm}$$

Since the cylinder is insulated $Q_{1\to2} = 0$ and the first law gives

$$-W_{1\to2} = \Delta u = \frac{P_2v_2 - P_1v_1}{k-1} \qquad (2)$$

where

$$k = 1.4 \quad \text{(for air)}$$

Substituting the numerical values, Eq. (2) becomes

$$-W_{1\to2} = \frac{1}{0.4}\left[2880v_2 - (12{,}960)(2.2)\right]$$

or

$$W_{1\to2} = 7200v_2 - 71{,}280 \qquad (3)$$

However the work can also be evaluated by using the formula

$$W_{1\to2} = F \times h \qquad (4)$$

where

$$F = M = 125 \text{ lbf}$$

and

$$h = \text{height} = \frac{v_2}{A} - \frac{v_1}{A} = \frac{v_2 - v_1}{A}$$

$$A = 25 \text{ in}^2 \times \frac{1 \text{ ft}^2}{144 \text{ in}^2} = 0.1736 \text{ ft}^2$$

From Eq. (4) then

$$W_{1\to2} = 125 \left[\frac{v_2 - v_1}{0.1736}\right]$$

or

$$W_{1\to2} = 720 \; v_2 - 720(2.2)$$

$$W_{1\to2} = 720 \; v_2 - 1584 \qquad (5)$$

Equating the two values of $W_{1\to2}$ in (5) and (3) and solving for v_2 gives,

$$720 \; v_2 - 1584 = - 7200 \; v_2 + 71280$$

$$7920 \; v_2 = 72864$$

$$\therefore \; v_2 = 9.2 \text{ ft}^3/\text{lbm}$$

From Eq. (1) then

$$\Delta s_{1\to2} = 0.240 \ln \left(\frac{9.2}{2.2}\right) + 0.171 \ln \left(\frac{20}{90}\right)$$

$$= 0.0862 \text{ Btu/lbm-°R}$$

• PROBLEM 4-17

An ideal gas undergoes an isothermal expansion in which its volume doubles. For one mole of this gas calculate the change in entropy for the surroundings if the process is assumed to be reversible.

Solution: For any reversible isothermal process, the surrounding temperature and the system temperature must be the same

$$\therefore \; (\Delta S)_{surr} = \frac{(q_{rev})_{surr}}{T}$$

The surroundings absorb the heat that is given up by the system

$$\therefore (\Delta S)_{surr} = - \frac{(q_{rev})_{sys}}{T}$$

$$(q_{rev})_{sys} = T(\Delta S)_{sys}$$

$$\therefore \ (\Delta S)_{surr} = -T \frac{(\Delta S)_{sys}}{T}$$

$$= -\ (\Delta S)_{sys}$$

$$(S_2 - S_1)_{sys} = C_{v_0} \ln\left(\frac{T_2}{T_1}\right) + \bar{R} \ln\left(\frac{V_2}{V_1}\right)$$

$$= \bar{R} \ln(2)$$

$$(\Delta S)_{surr} = -1.38 \text{ cal/mole-°K}$$

• PROBLEM 4-18

A high temperature reservoir at 538°C is brought into thermal communication with a lower temperature reservoir at 260°C, and as a result 1055 kJ of heat are transferred from the high to the low temperature reservoir. Determine the change in entropy of the universe, resulting from the heat-exchange process between the two reservoirs.

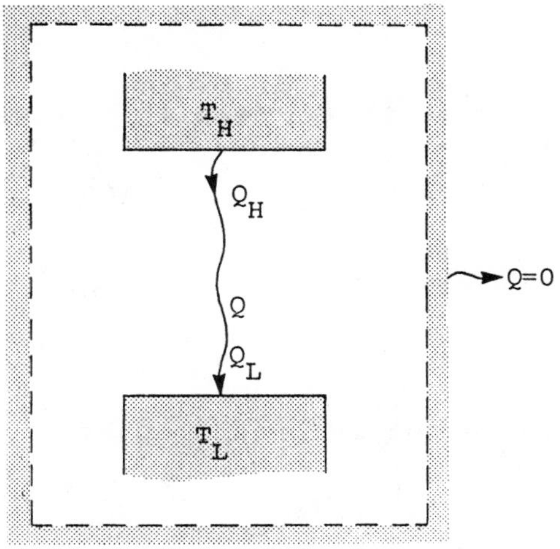

Figure 1. Heat transfer across finite temperature difference is irreversible and produces increase in entropy.

Solution: The change in entropy of the universe is the algebraic sum of the change in entropy of the high and low temperature reservoirs, considered separately. Therefore

$$(\Delta S)_{univ.} = (\Delta S)_{high} + (\Delta S)_{low} \tag{1}$$

Assuming an isothermal process for both bodies

$$\Delta S = \frac{Q}{T}$$

where Q, for the high temperature reservoir is -1,055 kJ (since heat is rejected from it), and for the low temperature reservoir Q = +1,055 kJ (since heat is added to it).

Therefore

$$(\Delta S)_{high} = \frac{Q_H}{T_H}$$

$$= \frac{-1055}{811}$$

$$= -1.30 \text{ kJ/°K}$$

and

$$(\Delta S)_{low} = \frac{Q_L}{T_L}$$

$$= \frac{1055}{533}$$

$$= 1.98 \text{ kJ/°K}$$

From Eq. (1), the change in entropy for the universe is

$$(\Delta S)_{univ.} = -1.30 + 1.98$$

$$= 0.68 \text{ kJ/°K}$$

The heat transfer in this case is irreversible, since it involves heat transfer across a finite temperature difference. All real processes are irreversible, and because of the inability to eliminate all dissipative effects there will be an increase in entropy of the universe whenever an irreversible process occurs.

PRINCIPLE OF THE INCREASE OF ENTROPY

• PROBLEM 4-19

A device compresses isothermally 1 lb mole/hr of ideal gas at 1000°R and releases 3000 Btu of heat which is transferred to another 1 lb mole/hr of ideal gas which expands isothermally from 2.72 atm to 1 atm. Is it possible to have such a device? Assume the process to be reversible.

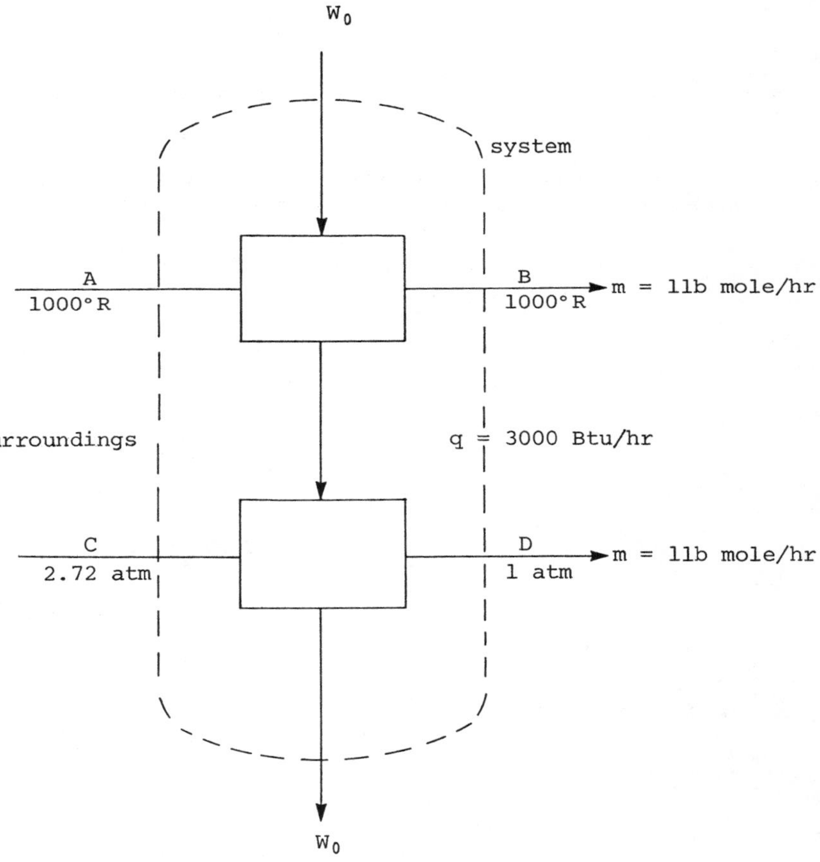

Solution: For the process A-B

$$Q = \frac{-q}{m}$$

$$= \frac{-3000}{1}$$

$$= -3000 \text{ Btu/lb mole}$$

$$\Delta S = \int \frac{dQ}{T}$$

$$= \frac{-3000}{1000}$$

$$= -3 \text{ Btu/lb mole-°R}$$

For the process C-D

$$Q = +\frac{q}{\dot{m}}$$

$$= \frac{3000}{1}$$

$$= +3000 \text{ Btu/lb mole}$$

Here the value of T is not known. The ΔS equation for an isothermal expansion process will be used, to obtain T

$$\Delta S = \int \frac{dQ}{T}$$

$$= \int \frac{dWo}{T}$$

$$= -R \ln \frac{P_2}{P_1}$$

$$= -2 \ln \frac{1}{2.72}$$

$$= 2 \text{ Btu/lb mole-°R}$$

For the surroundings

$$\Delta S = \int \frac{dQ}{T}$$

$$= 0$$

When the universe is considered

$$(\dot{m}\Delta S)_{univ.} = (\dot{m}\Delta S)_{sys.} + (\dot{m}\Delta S)_{surr.}$$

$$= (1)(-3) + (1)(2) + 0$$

$$= -1 \text{ Btu/hr-°R}$$

This process violates the second law because ΔS for the universe is negative, which means that the process cannot take place and such a device is not possible.

● **PROBLEM 4-20**

Is it theoretically possible to devise a steady-flow compressor which requires no shaft-power input if the following conditions are known? Two lbm/sec of CO_2 at 200 psia, 120°F are compressed to 300 psia, and emerge at 20°F, simply by transferring heat at the rate of 60 Btu/sec from the device to a cold reservoir maintained at -140°F. Potential and kinetic energies are not significant.

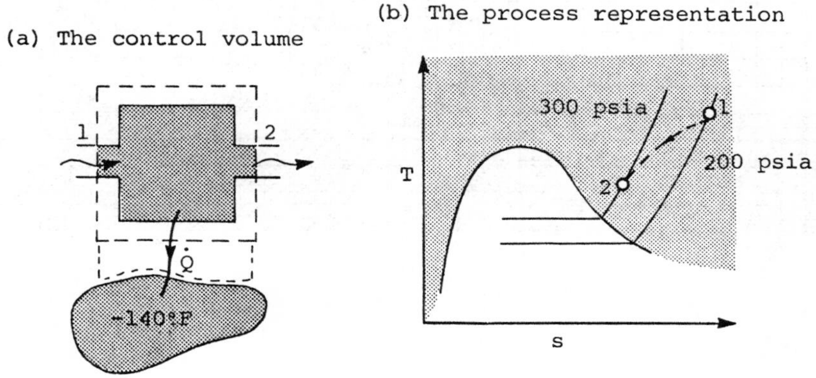

Figure 1. Analysis of inventor's claim

Solution: This compressor is theoretically possible only if it does not violate either the first or second laws of thermodynamics. Assuming that the flows are one-dimensional at the inlet and exit, and also that the CO_2 is in equilibrium states at these points from figure 2 obtain,

at $T_1 = 120°F$, $P_1 = 200$ lbf/in^2

$$h_1 = 318 \text{ Btu/lbm}$$

$$s_1 = 1.315 \text{ Btu/lbm-°R}$$

at $T_2 = 20°F$, $P_2 = 300$ lbf/in^2

$$h_2 = 288 \text{ Btu/lbm}$$

$$s_2 = 1.240 \text{ Btu/lbm-°R}$$

From the first law of thermodynamics, on a rate basis

$$\dot{m}(h_2 - h_1) + \dot{Q} = 0$$

or substituting the numerical values

$$2(288-318) + 60 = 0 \text{ Btu/sec}$$

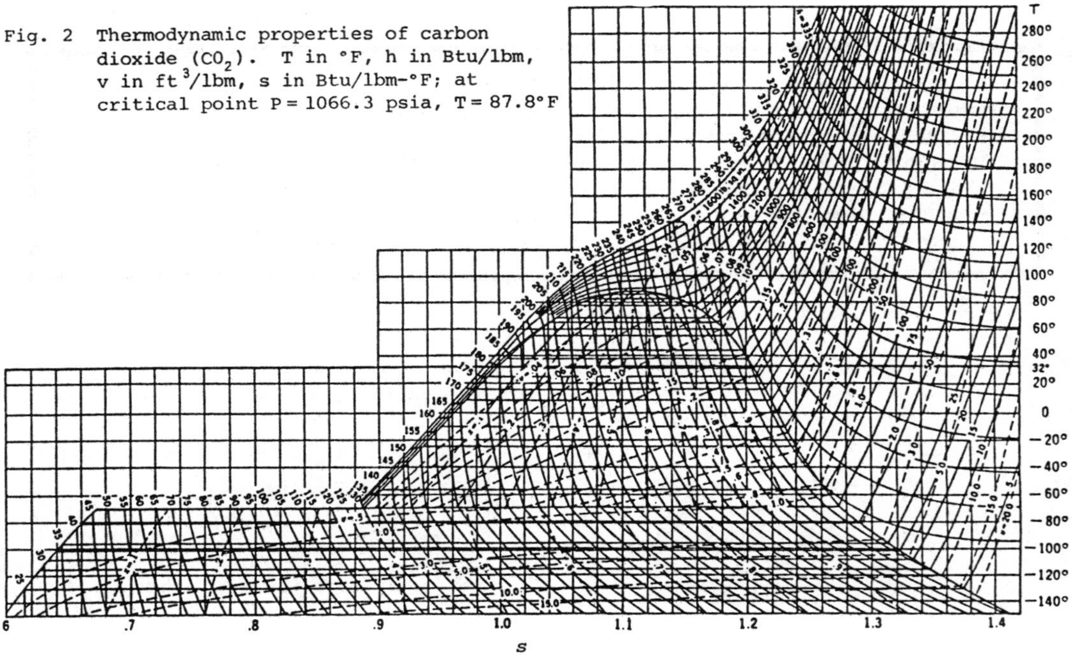

Fig. 2 Thermodynamic properties of carbon dioxide (CO_2). T in °F, h in Btu/lbm, v in ft^3/lbm, s in Btu/lbm-°F; at critical point P = 1066.3 psia, T = 87.8°F

which is true. Therefore the compressor is not an energy producing device, and so it does not violate the first law.

For the control volume, the entropy production rate is given as

$$\dot{P}_s = \dot{m}(s_2 - s_1) + \frac{\dot{Q}}{T_{res.}}$$

where $T_{res.} = -140°F = 320°R$. Thus

$$\dot{P}_s = 2(1.240-1.315) + \frac{60}{320}$$

$$= -0.150 + 0.188$$

$$= +0.038 \text{ Btu/°R-sec}$$

The rate of entropy production is indeed positive. Therefore it can be concluded that since the device does not violate neither the first nor the second law of thermodynamics, it is theoretically possible to build such a compressor.

One lbm/min of steam initially at 14.7 psia, 284.5°F is compressed in a water cooled compressor to a final state of 150 psia, 1200°F. The cooling water enters at 284.5°F and a mass flowrate of 0.465 lbm/min, and leaves at 500°F. For a combined system of the steam and the cooling water, calculate the change in entropy of the universe for the process.

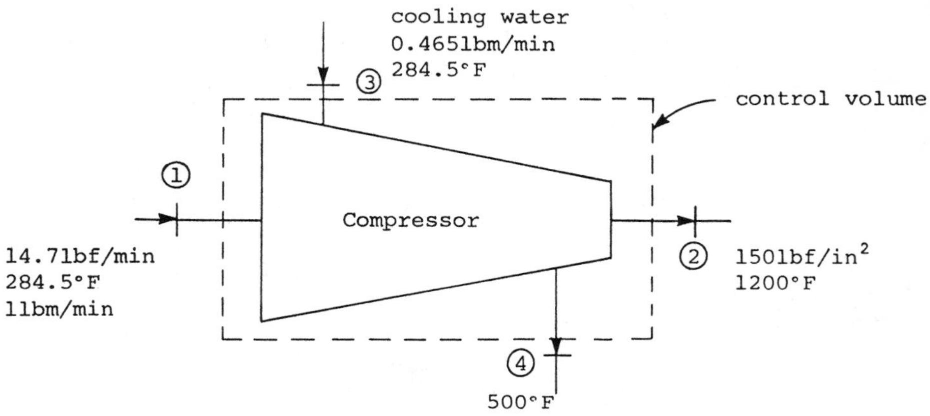

Fig. 1

Solution: For a control volume consisting of the steam and the cooling water as shown in Fig. 1, there is no energy entering or leaving the control volume. Therefore for this process

$$(m\Delta s)_u = (m\Delta s)_w + (m\Delta s)_{st} \tag{1}$$

For the water (C_p = 1 Btu/lbm-°R)

$$(\Delta s)_w = \int \frac{dQ}{T} = C_p \ln \frac{T_4}{T_3}$$

$$= 1 \ln \left(\frac{960}{744.5}\right)$$

$$= +0.254 \text{ Btu/lbm-°R}$$

or

$$(m\Delta s)_w = (0.465)(0.254) = 0.1181 \text{ Btu/min-°R} \tag{2}$$

For the steam, using the superheated steam tables obtain

$$s_1 = 1.8052 \text{ Btu/lbm-°R}$$

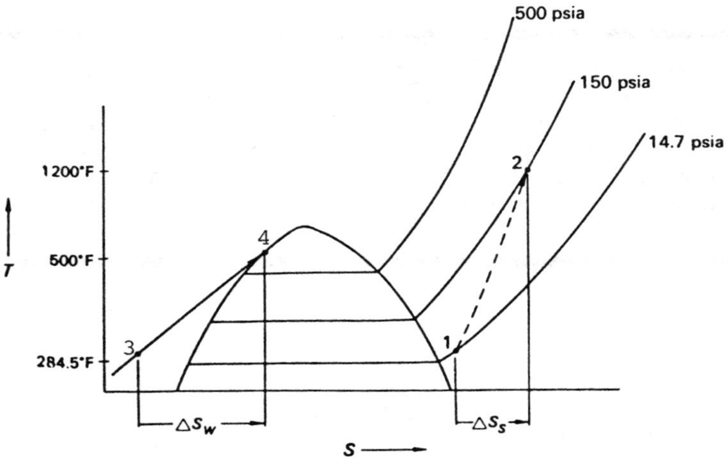

Fig. 2

$$s_2 = 1.9397 \text{ Btu/lbm-°R}$$

Then

$$(\Delta s)_{st} = s_2 - s_1$$
$$= 1.9397 - 1.8052$$
$$= +0.1345 \text{ Btu/lbm-°R}$$

or

$$(m\Delta s)_{st} = (1)(0.1345) = +0.1345 \text{ Btu/min-°R} \qquad (3)$$

Substituting (2) and (3) into Eq. (1)

$$(m\Delta s)_u = 0.1181 + 0.1345$$
$$= +0.2526 \text{ Btu/min-°R}$$

The process is shown on a T-s diagram.

• PROBLEM 4-22

An insulated chamber containing oxygen, is divided equally into two by a partition, as shown in Fig. 1. Part A of the chamber contains 1 lb-mole at 1 atm, 984°R while part B contains 1 lb-mole at 1 atm, 492°R. The partition is then removed allowing the oxygen in A and B to mix and attain the same temperature. Draw the T-S diagram for this process, and calculate the change in entropy of the universe.

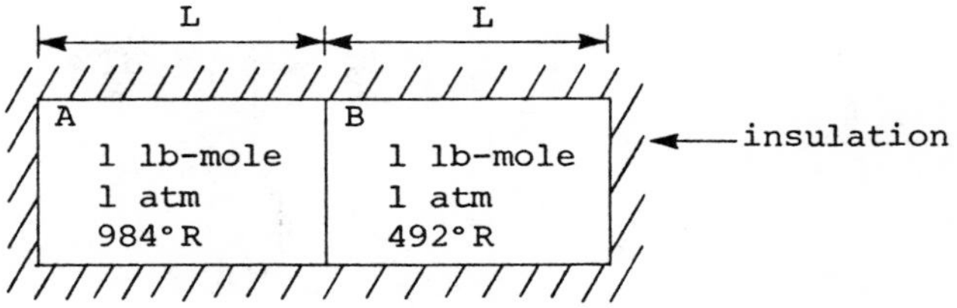

Fig. 1

Solution: This system is a closed system and involves unbalanced temperature forces. When the partition is removed the oxygen in A will cool to a final temperature T_2 and heat the oxygen in B to T_2. For this process $W_{1\to 2} = 0$ and since the chamber is insulated $Q_{1\to 2} = 0$. From the first law then

$$(\Delta u)_{syst} = 0$$

or

$$(m\Delta u)_{syst.} = m_A \Delta u_{A\to 2} + m_B \Delta u_{B\to 2} \qquad (1)$$

Assuming ideal gas behavior with constant specific heats, and using the relation

$$\Delta u = C_v \Delta T$$

Eq. (1) becomes

$$m_A C_v \Delta T_{A\to 2} + m_B C_v \Delta T_{B\to 2} = 0 \qquad (2)$$

However because both gases are O_2

$$(\Delta S)_{mix} = 0$$

Also since points A, B, and 2 all lie on the same isobar, an isobaric reversible path can be used to evaluate $(m\Delta S)_A$ and $(m\Delta S)_B$.

Therefore

$$\Delta S_A = \int \frac{dQ}{T} = \int C_p \frac{dT}{T}$$

$$= C_p \ln \frac{T_2}{T_A}$$

$$= 7 \ln \left(\frac{738}{984}\right)$$

$$= -2.01 \text{ Btu/lb-mole-°R}$$

and

$$\Delta S_B = \int \frac{dQ}{T} = \int C_p \frac{dT}{T}$$

$$= C_p \ln \frac{T_2}{T_B}$$

$$= 7 \ln \left(\frac{738}{492}\right)$$

$$= +2.84 \text{ Btu/lb mole-°R}$$

or since $m_A = m_B$ and the C_v is the same since there is only oxygen involved, Eq. (2) becomes

$$\Delta T_{A\to 2} + \Delta T_{B\to 2} = 0$$

or

$$(T_2 - T_A) + (T_2 - T_B) = 0$$

Solving for T_2

$$T_2 = \frac{T_A + T_B}{2}$$

$$= \frac{984 + 492}{2}$$

$$= 738°R$$

The T-S diagram can then be sketched as shown in Fig. 2.

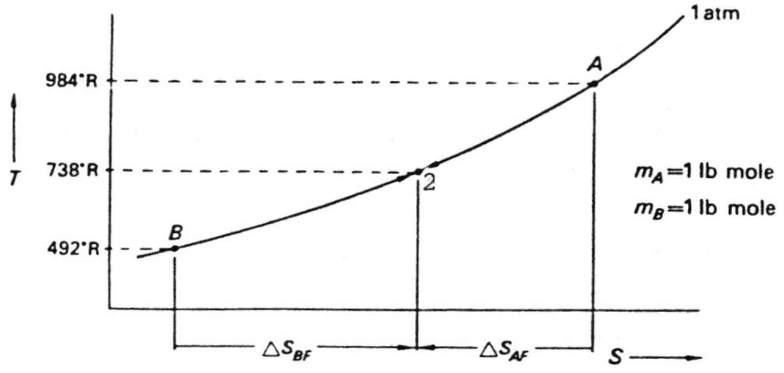

Fig. 2

The change in entropy of the universe for this process is

$$(m\Delta S)_u = (m\Delta S)_A + (m\Delta S)_B + (m\Delta S)_{mix} \quad (3)$$

Substituting into Eq. (3)

$$(m\Delta S)_u = (1)(-2.01) + (1)(2.84) + 0$$

$$= +0.83 \text{ Btu/°R}$$

The entropy increase of the universe shows that as a result of the unbalanced temperature forces the system lost the ability to do work.

EFFICIENCY

• PROBLEM 4-23

A cylinder contains 1500 lbm of air initially at 15 psia, 500°R. Energy is then added to the air and as a result the temperature increases to 540°R. Calculate the entropy creation in the universe, (a) if the energy supplied to the air is from a heat reservoir at 300°F alone, and (b) if the energy supplied to the air is from a work reservoir alone. Assume air to behave as an ideal gas with $C_v = 0.171$ Btu/lbm-°R.

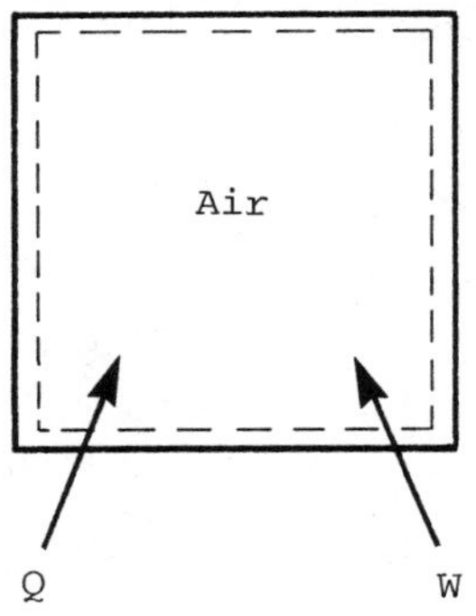

Solution: This is a constant mass constant volume process, and therefore $v_2 = v_1$. From the first law of thermodynamics, the net energy input ($E_{1\to2}$) is

$$E\Big|_{in} = Q_{12} - W_{12} = U_2 - U_1 = m(u_2 - u_1) \tag{1}$$

For an ideal gas with constant specific heats,

$$u_2 - u_1 = C_v(T_2 - T_1) \tag{2}$$

Substituting Eq. (2) into Eq. (1), obtain

$$E\Big|_{in} = mC_v(T_2 - T_1)$$

$$= 1500(0.171)(540-500)$$

$$= 10,260 \text{ Btu}$$

(a) If heat is the only source of energy ($W_{1\to 2} = 0$), then

$$E\Big|_{in} = Q_{1\to 2} = 10,260 \text{ Btu}$$

Therefore,

$$Q_H = -10,260 \text{ Btu}$$

From the second law of thermodynamics

$$\Delta S_u = \Delta S_{air} + \Delta S_H \qquad (3)$$

For an ideal gas

$$s_2 - s_1 = C_v \ln \frac{T_2}{T_1} + R \ln \frac{v_2}{v_1}$$

But $v_2 = v_1$, and so

$$s_2 - s_1 = C_v \ln \frac{T_2}{T_1}$$

Therefore, for air

$$\Delta S_{air} = mC_v \ln \frac{T_2}{T_1}$$

$$= 1500(0.171) \ln \left(\frac{540}{500}\right)$$

$$= 19.74 \text{ Btu/°R}$$

For a heat reservoir, the change in entropy is given by

$$\Delta S_H = \frac{Q_H}{T_H}$$

$$= \frac{-10,260}{760}$$

$$= -13.5 \text{ Btu/°R}$$

From Eq. (3) then

$$\Delta S_u = 19.74 - 13.5$$

$$= 6.24 \text{ Btu/°R}$$

(b) If the energy supplied is from a work reservoir alone ($Q_{1\to2} = 0$), then from the second law of thermodynamics

$$\Delta S_u = \Delta S_{air} + \Delta S_w \tag{4}$$

But $\Delta S_w = 0$ and thus

$$\Delta S_u = \Delta S_{air}$$

$$= 19.74 \text{ Btu/°R}$$

• PROBLEM 4-24

> The heat engine of a thermal power station can be approximated by a Carnot cycle operating between 650°F and 150°F. If the maximum rise in the cooling water is restricted to 50°F, and the power output is 1×10^6kW, at what rate must the cooling water be supplied?

Solution: The net power produced by the station is

$$\dot{W}_{net} = 1 \times 10^6 \text{kW}$$

$$= 1 \times 10^9 \text{W}$$

$$= 5.69 \times 10^7 \text{ Btu/min}$$

For this cycle, the thermal efficiency is given as

$$\eta = \frac{T_H - T_L}{T_H}$$

$$= \frac{1110-610}{1110} = 0.45$$

Also

$$\eta = \frac{\dot{W}_{net}}{\dot{Q}_H} \tag{1}$$

Since $\dot{W}_{net}$ and η are both known

$$\dot{Q}_H = \frac{\dot{W}_{net}}{\eta}$$

$$= \frac{5.69 \times 10^7}{0.45}$$

$$= 1.26 \times 10^8 \text{ Btu/min}$$

From the overall energy balance

$$\dot{W}_{net} = \dot{Q}_H + \dot{Q}_L$$

or

$$\dot{Q}_L = -(\dot{Q}_H - \dot{W}_{net})$$

$$= -(1.26 \times 10^8 - 5.69 \times 10^7)$$

$$= -6.9 \times 10^7 \text{ Btu/min}$$

Considering only the cooling water and doing an energy balance gives

$$\dot{Q}_w = -\dot{Q}_L = \dot{m}_w(C_p \Delta T)_w \qquad (2)$$

since all $\dot{Q}_L$ must be transferred to the cooling water. For water C_p = 1 Btu/lbm and ΔT = 50°F. Therefore, solving for $\dot{m}_w$ in Eq (2) gives

$$\dot{m}_w = \frac{6.9 \times 10^7}{50}$$

$$= 1.38 \times 10^6 \text{ lbm/min}$$

or

$$\dot{m}_w = 1.66 \times 10^5 \text{ gal/min}$$

• PROBLEM 4-25

The heat engine shown in the figure is supplied with 10,000 Btu/hr of heat from a high temperature reservoir at 3,000°R while the working fluid is at 1000°F. The engine rejects 8,000 Btu/hr of heat to a lower temperature reservoir at 500°R and the working fluid is at 140°F. Calculate the actual efficiency of the engine. What fraction is this (a) of the internally reversible efficiency and (b) of the external reversible efficiency?

Solution: The actual cycle efficiency is given by

$$\eta_{act.} = \frac{W_{out}}{Q_{in}} = \frac{Q_{in} - Q_{out}}{Q_{in}}$$

or

$$\eta_{act.} = \frac{10{,}000 - 8000}{10{,}000} = 0.20$$

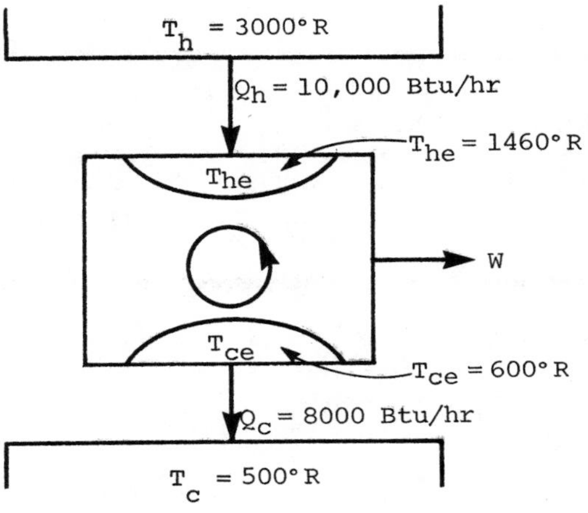

(a) The internal reversible efficiency is

$$\eta_{\substack{int.\\rev}} = 1 - \frac{T_{ce}}{T_{he}}$$

$$= 1 - \frac{600}{1460}$$

$$= 0.59$$

Therefore the fraction of internally reversible efficiency is

$$\frac{\eta_{act}}{\eta_{\substack{int.\\rev}}} = \frac{0.20}{0.59} = 0.34$$

(b) The external reversible efficiency is

$$\eta_{\substack{ext.\\rev.}} = \frac{T_h - T_c}{T_h}$$

$$= 1 - \frac{500}{3000}$$

$$= 0.83$$

Hence the fraction of external reversible efficiency is

$$\frac{\eta_{act}}{\eta_{\substack{ext.\\rev.}}} = \frac{0.20}{0.83} = 0.24$$

Freon-12 is compressed in an adiabatic steady-state, steady-flow process from an initial state of 0.30 MPa, 0°C to a final pressure of 1.40 MPa. If 7.2 kJ/sec is the work required for this compression process, determine the efficiency of the compressor assuming a mass flow rate of 0.2 kg/s.

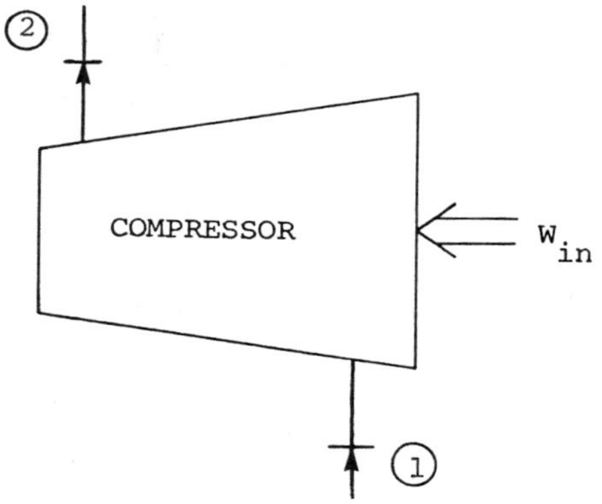

Solution: From the continuity equation,

$$\dot{m}_1 = \dot{m}_2 = \dot{m} \tag{1}$$

From the first law written for this system

$$w_s = h_1 - h_{2s} \tag{2}$$

where the subscript 2s denotes the isentropic process

From the second law

$$s_{2s} = s_1 \tag{3}$$

Furthermore the efficiency for a compressor is given by the equation

$$\eta_{comp.} = \frac{W_s}{W_a} = \frac{h_1 - h_{2s}}{W_a} \tag{4}$$

The only unknowns in Eq. (4) are the enthalpies at states 1 and 2, since the actual work input to the compressor (W_a) is given.

Hence the state of the substance must be determined both at the entrance and exit, and then the values for the enthalpies can be obtained from the Freon-12 tables. So proceed as follows.

State 1: $P_{sat} = 0.3086 > P_{given} = 0.3$ thus the state is superheated vapor and

$$h_1 = 187.583 \text{ kJ/kg}; \; s_1 = 0.6984 \text{ kJ/kg-K}$$

State 2: $s_{2s} = 0.6984$ kJ/kg-K $> s_g = 0.6773$ kJ/kg-K (P=1.4MPa) the state is superheated vapor and

$$h_{2s} = 215.11 \text{ kJ/kg} \quad \text{(by interpolation)}$$

substituting all the above values into Eq. (4) and noting that

$$W_a = (W_{comp})/\dot{m} = \frac{-7.2}{0.2} = -36 \text{ kJ/kg}$$

the efficiency is found to be

$$\eta = \frac{187.583-215.11}{-36} = 0.7646$$

or

$$\eta = 0.7646 \times 100 = 76.46\%$$

THE SECOND LAW FOR OPEN STEADY - STATE, STEADY - FLOW SYSTEMS

• PROBLEM 4-27

Air at 30°C, 200 kPa enters a nozzle in steady flow. The nozzle discharges into a space which is at a pressure of 100 kPa. Determine (a) the maximum velocity at the nozzle exit, and (b) the exit velocity if the nozzle has an efficiency of 95%.

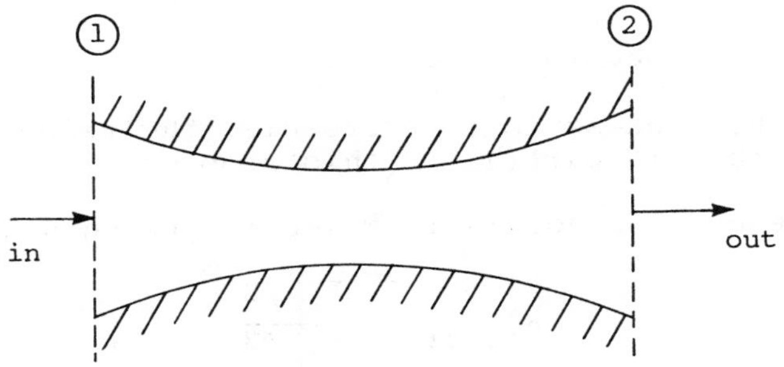

Solution: (a) The maximum velocity can be reached, when the process in the nozzle is both reversible and adiabatic, because then there is neither heat transfer nor friction to slow the air down.

Assuming air to behave as an ideal gas, from the isentropic relations for ideal gases.

$$\frac{P_1}{P_2} = \left(\frac{P_{r_1}}{P_{r_2}}\right)_{s=\text{const.}} \quad (1)$$

From the air tables, at the entrance plane

$$P_{r_1} = 1.4366$$

Solving for P_{r_2} from Eq. (1)

$$P_{r_2} = \frac{P_2}{P_1} \times P_{r_1} = \frac{100}{200} \times 1.4366$$

$$= 0.7183$$

Then with P_{r_2} known, the temperature at the exit plane is (from the air tables)

$$T_2 = 248.5°K = -24.6°C$$

Assuming the velocity of the air to be negligible at the entrance, and writing the first law for the control volume one gets

$$h_1 + \frac{V_1^2}{2}{}^{\cong 0} = h_2 + \frac{V_2^2}{2}$$

or

$$V_2 = \sqrt{2(h_1 - h_2)} \quad (2)$$

Since enough information is known or has been calculated, from air tables the enthalpies at both states can be obtained as

$$h_1 = 303.2 \text{ kJ/kg}; \; h_2 = 248.55 \text{ kJ/kg}$$

Then from (2)

$$V_2 = \sqrt{2(303.2 - 248.5) \times \frac{1{,}000 \text{ kgm}^2/\text{s}^2}{1 \text{ kJ}}}$$

$$= 330.76 \text{ m/sec}$$

(b) Since the process is irreversible, the velocity is going to be less than in part(a) of this problem.

The efficiency of a nozzle is given by the equation

$$\eta_{\text{nozzle}} = \frac{(V_a)^2/2}{(V_s)^2/2}$$

where the subscripts a and s stand for the actual and isentropic processes respectively.

Solving for V_a in the above equation

$$V_a = \sqrt{2(\eta \times \frac{V_s^2}{2})} = \sqrt{2(0.95 \times \frac{(330.76)^2}{2})}$$

$$= 322.38 \text{ m/sec.}$$

• PROBLEM 4-28

Water at 15 kPa, 40°C enters a pump and leaves after the pressure has been raised to 5 MPa. Assuming the process to be reversible and adiabatic determine the temperature of the water at the exit of the pump.

Solution: Consider as the system, the pump with a steady flow in and out. From the first law

$$q + h_i + \frac{V_i^2}{2} + gZ_i = h_e + \frac{V_e^2}{2} + gZ_e + w$$

Neglecting potential and kinetic energies

$$q + h_i = h_e + w \tag{1}$$

The process is reversible and adiabatic, hence

$$q = 0$$

and

$$s_e = s_i$$

Eq. (1) then becomes

$$h_e - h_i = -w \tag{2}$$

Using the relation

$$Tds = dh - vdP$$

Eq. (2) becomes

$$h_e - h_i = -\int vdP \tag{3}$$

Assuming constant specific volume and substituting Eq. (3) into Eq. (2) and integrating

$$w_p = -v_1(P_2 - P_1) \qquad (4)$$

where the subscripts 1 and 2, stand for the inlet and exit states. From the steam tables, at $T_1 = 40°C$

$$v_1 = 0.001008 \text{ m}^3/\text{kg}$$

Substituting into Eq. (4)

$$w_p = -0.001008(5000 - 15)$$

$$= -5.02 \text{ kJ/kg}$$

Also from the steam tables at T = 40°C

$$h_1 = h_f = 167.57 \text{ kJ/kg}$$

From Eq. (2)

$$h_2 = h_1 - w_p$$

$$= 167.57 + 5.02$$

$$= 172.59 \text{ kJ/kg.}$$

From the compressed liquid table at P_2 = 5MPa and h_2, by interpolation

$$T_2 = 40.15°C$$

Note that the temperature does not change very much, and in many cases constant temperature is assumed.

• PROBLEM 4-29

Steam at 500°F and 100 lbf/in² enters a steam turbine with a velocity of 200 ft/sec. The outlet steam has a velocity of 600 ft/sec and a pressure of 20 lbf/in². If the process is reversible and adiabatic, calculate the work per pound of steam.

Solution: The steady flow energy equation for this process can be written as

$$h_i + \frac{V_i^2}{2g_c} = h_e + \frac{V_e^2}{2g_c} + w$$

The example is one of steady-flow, reversible, adiabatic

process, $s_e = s_i$ and entropy and pressure for the final state are known.

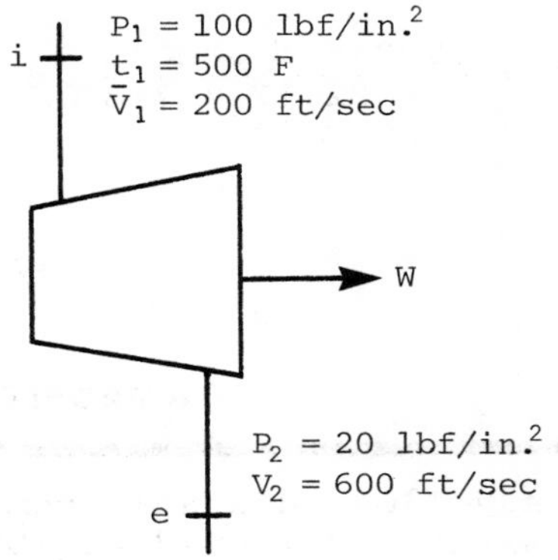

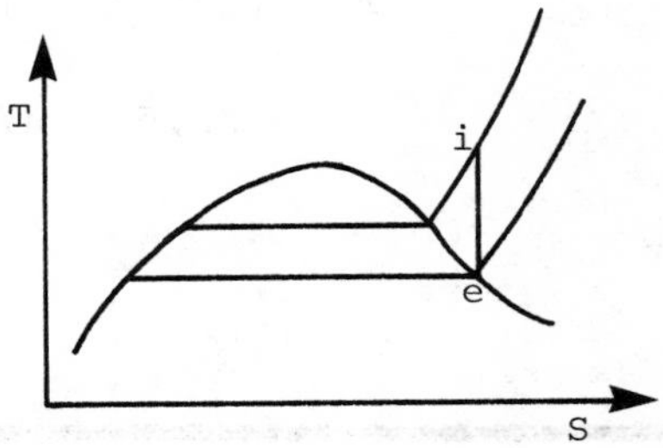

From the steam tables

$$h_i = 1279.1 \text{ Btu/lbm}$$

$$s_i = 1.7085 \text{ Btu/lbm R}$$

For the final state

$$P_e = 20 \text{ lbf/in}^2$$

$$s_e = s_i = 1.7085 \text{ Btu/lbm R.}$$

From these values the quality and enthalpy leaving the turbine can be determined, as follows:

$$s_e = 1.7085$$

$$= s_g - (1-x)_e s_{fg}$$

$$= 1.7319-(1-x)_e \, 1.3962$$

or

$$(1-x)_e = \frac{0.0234}{1.3962}$$

$$= 0.01676$$

Then

$$h_e = h_g - (1-x)_e h_{fg}$$

$$= 1156.3 - 0.01676\ (960.1)$$

$$= 1140.2 \text{ Btu/lbm}$$

Using the steady flow energy equation, the work per pound of steam for this process can be calculated, as

$$w = 1279.1 - 1140.2 + \frac{(200)^2 - (600)^2}{2 \times 32.17 \times 778}$$

$$= 132.5 \text{ Btu/lbm.}$$

• PROBLEM 4-30

> Water enters a steady state steady flow adiabatic pump having an efficiency of 70% as saturated liquid at 100°F, and leaves the pump at 3000 psia. Assuming the process to be adiabatic, calculate the actual pump work.

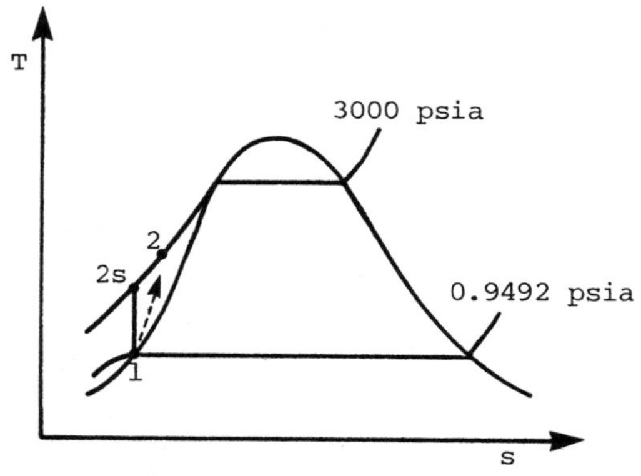

Solution: Assume water to be incompressible

Let η_p = adiabatic pump efficiency.

Then

$$w_{act} = \frac{w_{rev}}{\eta_p}$$

Where w = work transfer/unit mass

$$w_{rev} = -\int_1^2 vdP$$

$$\cong -v(P_2 - P_1)$$

From the steam tables,

P_1 = saturation pressure at 100°F = 0.9492 psia

$v = v_f$ at 100°F = 0.01613 ft^3/lbm

Substituting in Eq. (1)

$$w_{rev} = \frac{0.01613 \times (3000-0.9492) \times 144}{778} \text{ Btu/lbm}$$

$$= -8.95 \text{ Btu/lbm}$$

Therefore

$$w_{act} = -\frac{8.95}{0.7}$$

$$= -12.8 \text{ Btu/lbm}$$

The actual pump work = -12.8 Btu/lbm.

• PROBLEM 4-31

At the inlet of a turbine, nitrogen enters at 3000 psia and 540°R. Assuming the turbine to have an adiabatic efficiency of 80% calculate the actual work required for the turbine.

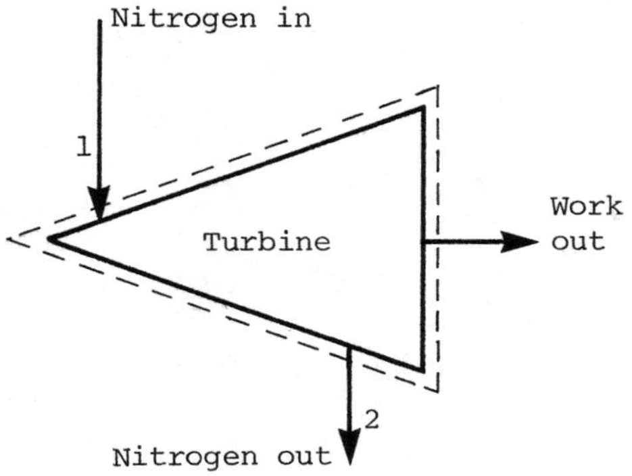

Fig. 1

Solution: From the definition of the turbine efficiency

$$w_{act} = \eta w_{rev} \tag{1}$$

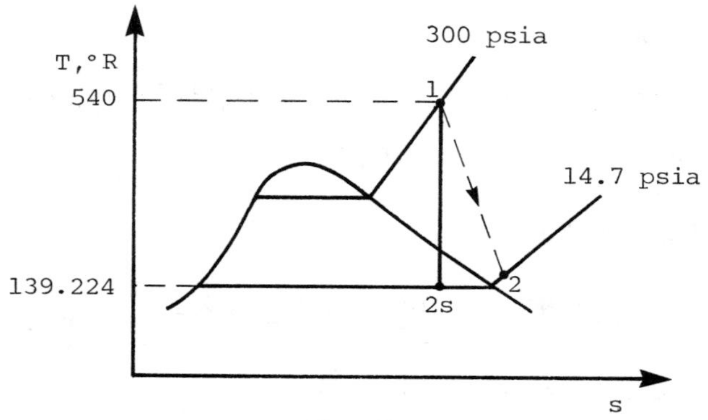

Fig. 2

From the first law, for a reversible process, neglecting kinetic and potential energies and referring to Fig. 2

$$w_{rev} = h_1 - h_{2s} \tag{2}$$

From the nitrogen tables at state 1

$$h_1 = 119.735 \text{ Btu/lbm}$$

$$s_1 = 1.23089 \text{ Btu/lbm-°R}$$

Since this is a reversible process

$$s_2 = s_1 = 1.23089 \text{ Btu/lbm-°R}$$

and state 2s is found to be a mixture of liquid and vapor. Therefore at state 2

$$s_{2s} = s_f + X_{2s}\, s_{fg} \tag{3}$$

From the nitrogen tables at 14.7 psia

$$s_f = 0.67850 \text{ Btu/lbm-°R}$$

$$s_g = 1.29290 \text{ Btu/lbm-°R}$$

$$h_f = -52.243 \text{ Btu/lbm}$$

$$h_g = 33.218 \text{ Btu/lbm}$$

From Eq. (3) solving for X_{2s}, obtain

$$X_{2s} = \frac{s_{2s} - s_f}{s_{fg}}$$

$$= \frac{1.23089 - 0.67850}{1.29290 - 0.67850}$$

$$= 0.8991$$

Then at state 2

$$h_{2s} = h_f + X_{2s} h_{fg}$$

$$= -52.243 + 0.8991(33.218 + 52.243)$$

$$= 24.595 \text{ Btu/lbm}$$

Substituting into Eq. (2), obtain

$$w_{rev} = 119.735 - 24.595$$

$$= 95.140 \text{ Btu/lbm}$$

Then from Eq. (1), the actual work is

$$w_{act} = 0.8(95.140) = 76.112 \text{ Btu/lbm}$$

• PROBLEM 4-32

Calculate the quality and work for a steady flow and nonflow process, when three pounds per second of steam expand isentropically from 300 lbf/in², 700°F to a final temperature of 200°F.

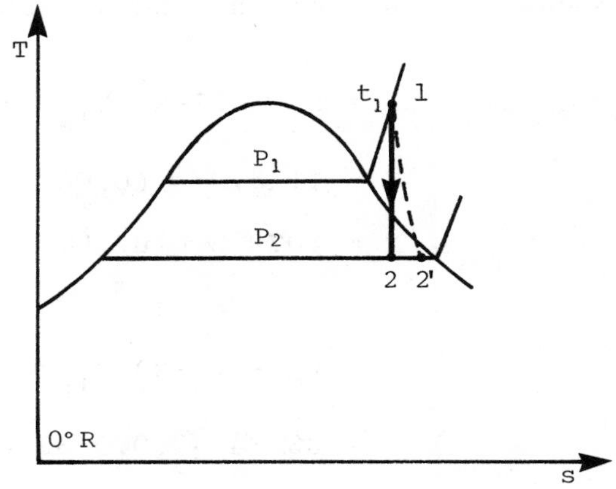

Solution: The process is depicted on a T-s diagram as shown in the figure. From the superheated steam tables obtain

$$s_1 = 1.6751 \text{ Btu/lbm-°R}, \quad h_1 = 1368.3 \text{ Btu/lbm}$$

$$v_1 = 2.227 \text{ ft}^3/\text{lbm}$$

Since this is an isentropic process

$$s_2 = s_1 = 1.6751 \text{ Btu/lbm-°R}$$

and state 2 is in the mixture region. From the steam tables then (at T_2)

$$s_f = 0.2938 \text{ Btu/lbm-°R}$$

$$s_{fg} = 1.4824 \quad ''$$

$$s_g = 1.7762 \quad ''$$

$$h_f = 167.99 \text{ Btu/lbm}; \; v_f = 0.01663 \text{ ft}^3/\text{lbm}$$

$$h_{fg} = 977.9 \quad '' \; ; \quad v_{fg} = 33.62 \quad ''$$

$$h_g = 1145.9 \quad '' \; ; \quad v_g = 33.64 \quad ''$$

The quality can then be calculated using the equation

$$s_2 = [s_g - (1-x)s_{fg}]_2$$

or

$$1.6751 = 1.7762 - (1-x)(1.4824)$$

solving for x

$$x = 0.9318 = 93.18\%$$

Now that the quality is known h_2 and v_2 can be obtained as follows

$$h_2 = h_g - (1-x)\, h_{fg}$$

$$= 1145.9 - (0.0682)(977.9)$$

$$= 1079.2 \text{ Btu/lbm}$$

and

$$v_2 = v_g - (1-x)\, v_{fg}$$

$$= 33.64 - (0.0682)(33.62)$$

$$= 31.35 \text{ ft}^3/\text{lbm}$$

For the steady flow isentropic process, the work is

$$w = h_1 - h_2 \qquad (1)$$

$$=- 1368.3 - 1079.2 = 289.1 \text{ Btu/lbm}$$

or

$$W = \dot{m}w = (3)(289.1) = 867.3 \text{ Btu/sec}$$

For the nonflow isentropic process, the work is

$$w = u_1 - u_2 \qquad (2)$$

The internal energies as states 1 and 2 are then evaluated by using the relation

$$u = h - Pv$$

At state 1

$$u_1 = h_1 - P_1v_1$$

$$= 1368.3 - \frac{300(144)(2.227)}{778}$$

$$= 1244.6 \text{ Btu/lbm}$$

At state 2, $P_2 = 11.526 \text{ lbf/in}^2$,

$$u_2 = h_2 - P_2v_2$$

$$= 1079.2 - \frac{(11.526)(144)(31.35)}{778}$$

$$= 1012.3 \text{ Btu/lbm}$$

Substituting into Eq. (2)

$$w = 1244.6 - 1012.3 = 232.3 \text{ Btu/lbm}$$

or

$$W = 3(232.3) = 696.9 \text{ Btu/sec.}$$

• PROBLEM 4-33

The adiabatic compression efficiency of an air compressor operating under steady state, steady flow conditions is known to be 70%. Assuming air to behave ideally determine the temperature of the air leaving the compressor and the compression work requirements in kJ/kg, if the conditions at the entrance are 101kPa and 300K, and the pressure of the stream leaving is 505 kPa.

Solution: Since this problem involves an irreversible process, from the given data it is obvious that the problem cannot be solved by just applying the first law. Thus another method will have to be employed.

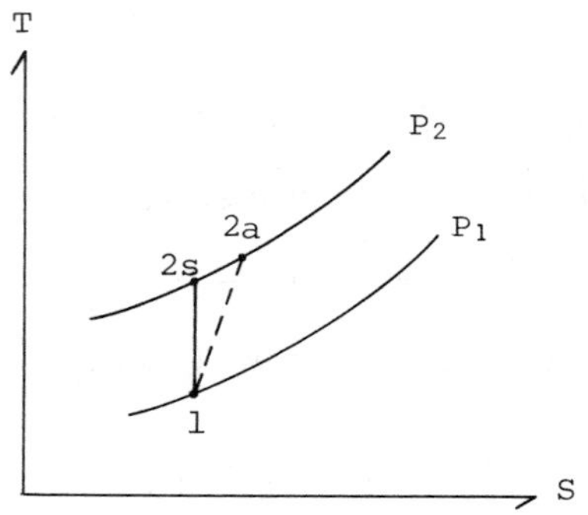

T-S diagram for the process.

Let the subscripts "s" and "a" represent the isentropic and actual process respectively, and refer to the figure for the states. Since this is a steady state-steady flow process, with one stream entering and one leaving, from continuity

$$m_1 = m_2$$

Also since the process is adiabatic, there is no heat transfer and thus

$$Q = 0$$

With the above statements in mind write the first law for the system as

$$w = (h_1 - h_2)$$

But for an ideal gas

$$dh = C_{p0} dT$$

and Equation (1) takes the form

$$w = C_{p0}(T_1 - T_2) \tag{1}$$

From the equation

$$Pv^k = P_1 v_1^{\ k} = P_2 v_2^{\ k} = \text{constant}$$

and the ideal gas equation of state, the following equation is obtained for an isentropic process.

$$\frac{T_{2s}}{T_1} = \left(\frac{P_{2s}}{P_1}\right)^{(k-1)/k} \tag{2}$$

Solving for T_{2s} obtain

$$T_{2s} = T_1 \left(\frac{P_{2s}}{P_1}\right)^{(k-1)/k}$$

$$= 300 \left(\frac{505}{101}\right)^{(1.4-1)/1.4}$$

$$= 475.15K$$

Having the temperature for the isentropic process, the work of isentropic compression can be evaluated, but the work for the irreversible process cannot be evaluated because the actual temperature at state 2 is not known.

Since the efficiency is given, the relation

$$\eta = \frac{w_s}{w_a} = \frac{C_{p_0}(T_1 - T_{2s})}{C_{p_0}(T_1 - T_{2a})} \tag{3}$$

is obtained.

Simplifying Equation (3) obtain

$$0.70 = \frac{T_1 - T_{2s}}{T_1 - T_{2a}}$$

Solving for T_{2a} get

$$T_{2a} = T_1 - \left(\frac{T_1 - T_{2s}}{0.70}\right)$$

$$= 300 - \left(\frac{300-475.15}{0.70}\right)$$

$$= 550.21 \text{ K.}$$

Equation (1) then gives, for the actual process,

$$w_a = C_{p_0}(T_1 - T_{2a})$$

$$= 1.0035(300-550.21)$$

$$= -2.51.08 \text{ kJ/kg.}$$

The minus sign indicates that work is done on the compressor, as expected.

• PROBLEM 4-34

The unit shown in Fig. 1 is used to produce drinking water from sea water by a vapor-compression desalination process. Seawater (3.5% salt) enters the unit and is preheated by countercurrent contact with the drinking water and the waste brine. The preheated seawater then enters the evaporator at 1 atm, where a portion is boiled off by condensing steam. The condensing steam leaves the evaporator at 105°C and is compressed adiabatically to 1.5 bar, and is then cooled to produce the drinking water. If the compressor has an efficiency of 60%, calculate the temperature at the outlet of the compressor and the work of compression per kilogram of drinking water formed.

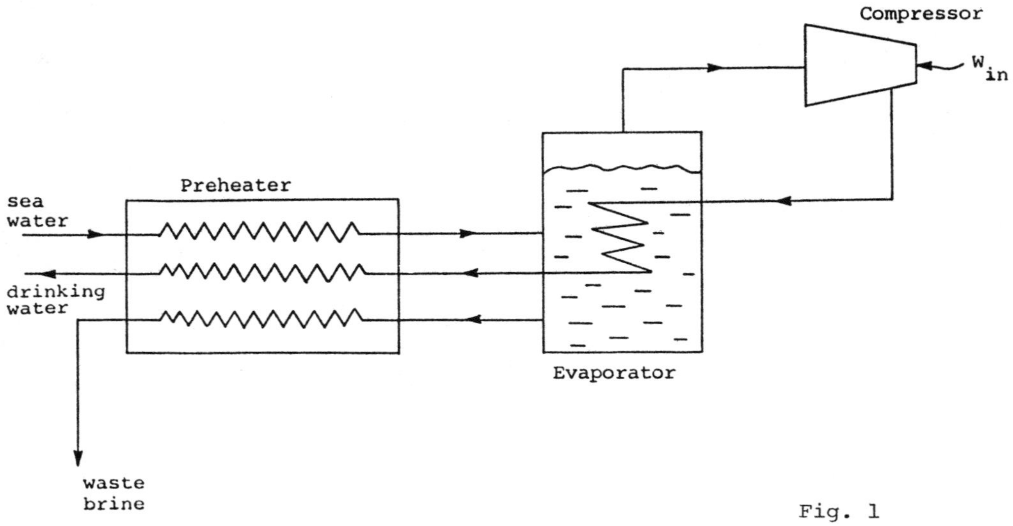

Fig. 1

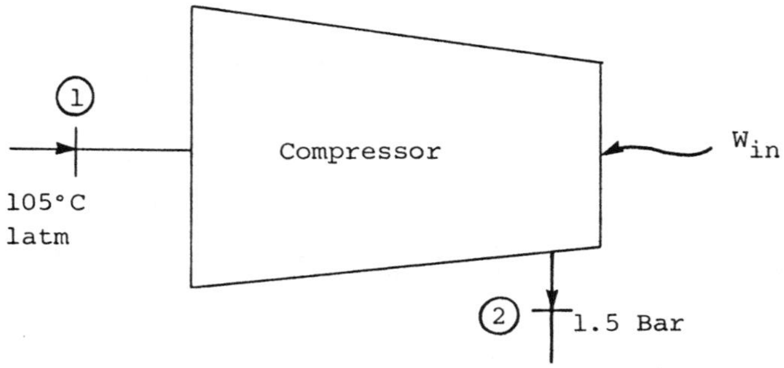

Fig. 2

Solution: Consider the compressor as a separate unit receiving steam at 105°C, 1 atm and discharging it at 1.5 Bar, as shown in Fig. 2.

Then consider as the system, the compressor and its contents. Neglecting potential and kinetic energies the energy balance for this system is

$$q - w = \Delta h = h_e - h_i \tag{1}$$

where the subscripts e and i stand for the exit and inlet states respectively.

However the process is adiabatic (q = 0) and so Eq. (1) reduces to

$$-w = \Delta h \tag{2}$$

The pressure at the exit (P_2 = 1.5 Bar) is known. Therefore determination of any other system property at the exit will fix the state, and so the temperature of the outlet steam can be obtained.

Since the compressor efficiency is known to be 60%, the ratio of the actual work of compression to that needed if the compression were reversible is

$$\frac{w_{rev}}{w_{act}} = 0.60$$

or

$$w_{act} = \frac{w_{rev}}{0.60} \tag{3}$$

For the reversible process, the entropy balance can be written as

$$(s_i - s_e)\delta m + \int_A \frac{\delta q}{T}\, dA = 0$$

For the reversible process $\delta q = 0$, and the entropy balance can be reduced to

$$s_i = s_e$$

From the steam tables at state 1

$$s_1 = s_2 = 7.2844 \text{ kJ/kg-°K}$$

$$h_1 = 2685 \text{ kJ/kg}$$

At state 2, using the outlet pressure and entropy, from the steam tables

$$(h_2)_{rev} = 2760 \text{ kJ/kg}$$

From Eq. (2), for the reversible process

$$(\Delta h)_{rev} = (h_2)_{rev} - h_1$$

$$= 2760-2685$$

$$= 75 \text{ kJ/kg}$$

or

$$w_{rev} = -75 \text{ kJ/kg}$$

From Eq. (3)

$$w_{act} = \frac{-75}{0.60} = -125 \text{ kJ/kg}$$

Since the energy balance is independent of any irreversibility involved in the process

$$(\Delta h)_{act} = -w_{act} = 125 \text{ kJ/kg}$$

From Eq. (1)

$$(h_2)_{act} = \Delta h + h_1$$

$$= 125 + 2685$$

$$= 2810 \text{ kJ/kg}$$

Now that the exit enthalpy and pressure are known they fix the exit state. Therefore from the steam tables

$$T_2 = 168°C$$

which is the temperature leaving the compressor.

• **PROBLEM 4-35**

Air at 14.7 psia, 540°R is cooled to a lower temperature, by exchanging heat with nitrogen at 15 psia, 300°R, in a steady-state steady-flow heat exchanger as shown in the figure. Assuming air and nitrogen to behave ideally with constant specific heats of C_p = 0.240 Btu/lbm-°R and C_p = 0.284 Btu/lbm-°R respectively, calculate the mass flow rate of the nitrogen, and the temperature of the air at the exit.

Solution: Neglecting kinetic and potential energies, pressure drops, and heat transfer between the heat exchanger and surroundings, from the first law

$$\dot{m}_{air}(h_1 - h_2) = \dot{m}_N(h_4 - h_3) \qquad (1)$$

From the property relation for an ideal gas with constant specific heats

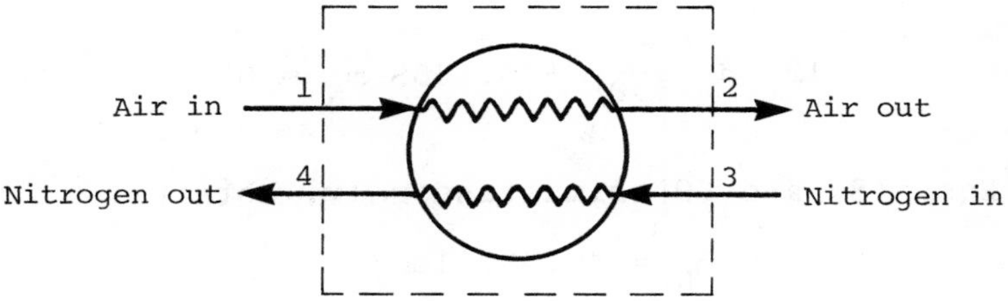

$$\Delta h = C_p \Delta T \tag{2}$$

Substituting Eq. (2) into Eq. (1), gives

$$\dot{m}_{air} C_{pa}(T_1 - T_2) = \dot{m}_N C_{pN}(T_4 - T_3) \tag{3}$$

From the second law of thermodynamics

$$\Delta\dot{S} = \dot{m}_{air}(s_2 - s_1) + \dot{m}_N(s_4 - s_3) \tag{4}$$

For a reversible process $\Delta\dot{S} = 0$ and so

$$\dot{m}_{air}(s_2 - s_1) + \dot{m}_N(s_4 - s_3) = 0 \tag{5}$$

For an ideal gas

$$s_2 - s_1 = C_{pa} \ln \frac{T_2}{T_1}$$

and (6)

$$s_4 - s_3 = C_{pN} \ln \frac{T_4}{T_3}$$

Substituting (6) into (5) obtain

$$\dot{m}_{air} C_{pa} \ln \frac{T_2}{T_1} + \dot{m}_N C_{pN} \ln \frac{T_4}{T_3} = 0 \tag{7}$$

Eqs. (3) and (7) are two equations with three unknowns, namely $\dot{m}_N$, T_2, and T_4. However, in order to get the lowest temperature of T_2, we should get the highest temperature for T_4 which can be only 540°R (the temperature of the entering air). Then substituting all the known numerical values into Eqs. (4) and (7) obtain

$$50(0.24)(540 - T_2) = \dot{m}_N(0.248)(540-300)$$

or

$$6480-12T_2 = 59.52\,\dot{m}_N \tag{8}$$

Also

$$50(0.24)\ln\left(\frac{T_2}{540}\right) + \dot{m}_N(0.248)\ln\left(\frac{540}{300}\right) = 0$$

or

$$12 \ln\left(\frac{T_2}{540}\right) + 0.1458\, \dot{m}_N = 0 \qquad (9)$$

Solving Eqs. (8) and (9) simultaneously, obtain

$$\dot{m}_N = 48.387 \text{ lbm/s}$$

and

$$T_2 = 300°R$$

• PROBLEM 4-36

An adiabatic turbine operates with a throttle governor as shown in the figure. Steam approaches the throttle governor with a mass flow rate of 2.0 kg/sec at a pressure of 10 MPa and a temperature of 500°C. The steam leaves the turbine with a pressure of 1.0 MPa. If the isentropic turbine efficiency is 80% and the power output is 700 kW, what is the pressure leaving the throttle governor?

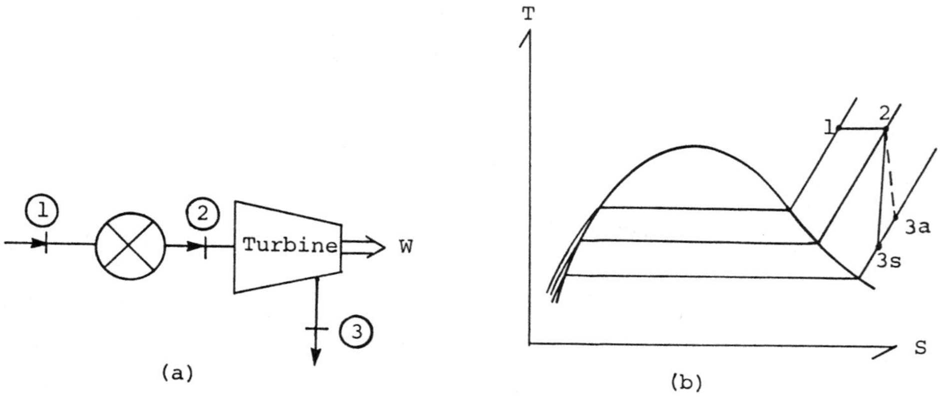

(a) Schematic diagram; (b) T-S diagram (not drawn to scale)

Solution: Let the subscripts "s" and "a" represent the isentropic (reversible process), and the actual (irreversible process) respectively and refer to the figure for the different states. The process from state 1 to state 2 is a throttling process. Therefore from the superheated steam tables

$$h_2 = h_1 = 3{,}373.7 \text{ kJ/kg}$$

From the continuity equation

$$\dot{m}_1 = \dot{m}_2 = \dot{m}_3 = \dot{m} \tag{1}$$

since there is only one flow entering and leaving the system. From the definition of the turbine efficiency

$$\eta \equiv \frac{w_a}{w_s}$$

we can solve for the isentropic work, since the actual work output is known. Hence

$$w_s = \frac{w_a}{\eta} \tag{2}$$

where

$$w_a = (\text{Power}) \div (\text{mass flow-rate})$$

$$= \frac{700}{2} = 350 \text{ kJ/kg}$$

Then from Eq. (2)

$$w_s = \frac{350}{0.8} = 437.5 \text{ kJ/kg}$$

From the first law of thermodynamics, for a reversible process

$$Q + \dot{m}_2 h_2 = \dot{m}_3 h_3 + \dot{W}_s \tag{3}$$

Since the process is adiabatic Q = 0, and because of Eq. (1), Eq. (3) becomes

$$\frac{\dot{W}_s}{\dot{m}} = h_{3s} - h_2$$

or

$$h_{3s} = h_2 - w_s$$

$$= 3373.7 - 437.5$$

$$= 2936.2 \text{ kJ/kg}$$

From the steam tables at $P_3 = 1.0$ MPa and h_{3s}, we find that the steam is superheated. From the superheated steam tables then, obtain

$$T_{3s} = 247.21°\text{C}$$

$$s_{3s} = 6.9118 \text{ kJ/kg-°K}$$

From the second law, however

$$s_2 = s_{3S} = 6.9118 \text{ kJ/kg-°K}$$

Now two properties are known at state 2; the enthalpy and the entropy. Therefore a third, pressure in this case, can be directly obtained from the steam tables at the known values of the two properties. The procedure, however, is going to be a trial and error one because of the structure of the steam tables, and goes as follows.

1. Assume a pressure less than the pressure before the throttle governor.
2. Using the value of the entropy at state 2 (s_2) and the superheated steam tables obtain the temperature at state 2 (T_2)
3. Using the value of the enthalpy at state 2 (h_2) and the superheated steam tables obtain the temperature at state 2 (T_2)
4. Compare the temperatures obtained in steps 2. and 3. If they are the same, or very close to each other, then the pressure assumed is the final pressure. If not, repeat the whole procedure, until the temperatures based on the enthalpy and entropy agree.

The trials are as follows.

First trial: Assume $P_2 = 4.5$ MPa

$T_2 = 461.96°C$ (based on s_2)

$T_2 = 471.67°C$ (based on h_2)

Second trial: Assume $P_2 = 5$ MPa

$T_2 = 479.6°C$ (based on s_2)

$T_2 = 474.4°C$ (based on h_2)

Third trial: Assume $P_2 = 4.8$ MPa

$T_2 = 472.61°C$ (based on s_2)

$T_2 = 473.34°C$ (based on h_2)

Therefore, from these trials it can be concluded that

$$P_2 \cong 4.8 \text{ MPa}$$

• PROBLEM 4-37

A piston cylinder arrangement contains saturated Freon-12 at -10°C. The vapor is then compressed to a final pressure of 1.6 MPa. If the process is assumed to be reversible and adiabatic calculate the work per kilogram of Freon-12 for this process.

Solution: From the first law of thermodynamics,

$$q_{1\to2} = u_2 - u_1 + w_{1\to2} = 0$$

However, this process is adiabatic ($q_{1\to2} = 0$) and so

$$w_{1\to2} = u_1 - u_2 \qquad (1)$$

Since this is a reversible and adiabatic process,

$$s_1 = s_2.$$

From the Freon-12 tables at state 1

$$s_1 = s_2 = 0.7014 \text{ kJ/kg-°K}$$

Since the tables do not give values for the specific internal energy, using the relationship

$$u_1 = h_1 - P_1 v_1$$

with

$$h_1 = 183.058 \text{ kJ/kg}$$

$$P_1 = 219.1 \text{ kPa}$$

and

$$v_1 = 0.076646 \text{ m}^3\text{/kg}$$

obtain

$$u_1 = 183.058 - (219.1)(0.076646)$$

$$= 166.265 \text{ kJ/kg}$$

At state 2, from the superheat tables for Freon-12

$$T_2 = 72.2°C; \; h_2 = 218.564 \text{ kJ/kg}$$

$$v_2 = 0.011382 \text{ m}^3\text{/kg}$$

Then

$$u_2 = 218.564 - (1600)(0.011382)$$

$$= 200.352 \text{ kJ/kg}$$

From Eq. (1)

$$w_{1\to2} = u_1 - u_2$$

$$= 166.265 - 200.352$$

$$= -34.087 \text{ kJ/kg}$$

The minus sign indicates that work was done on the system.

• PROBLEM 4-38

The tank shown in the figure is insulated and has a volume of $0.5m^3$. Initially the valve is closed and the tank contains air at 900kPa, 20°C. The valve is then opened allowing some of the air to escape until the pressure inside the tank drops to 150kPa. Assuming the air remaining inside the tank to have undergone a reversible adiabatic expansion, determine the final temperature inside the tank, and the amount of air withdrawn.

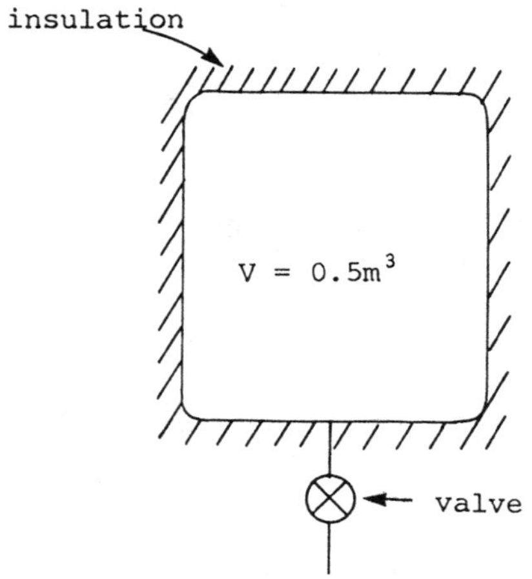

Solution: Assume that air behaves according to the ideal gas equation of state

$$PV = mRT \tag{1}$$

where for air R = 0.287 kJ/kg-°K.

Since the air remaining inside has undergone a reversible

adiabatic process, then

$$s_2 = s_1$$

From the isentropic relation, for an ideal gas

$$\frac{T_2}{T_1} = \left(\frac{P_2}{P_1}\right)^{(k-1)/k}$$

where k = 1.4, solving for T_2

$$T_2 = T_1\left(\frac{P_2}{P_1}\right)^{(k-1)/k}$$

$$= 293\left(\frac{150}{900}\right)^{(1.4-1)/1.4}$$

$$= 175.61°K$$

The amount of air withdrawn is

$$m_e = m_1 - m_2 \qquad (2)$$

From Eq. (1), at state 1

$$m_1 = \frac{P_1 V}{RT_1}$$

$$= \frac{900(0.5)}{0.287(293)}$$

$$= 5.35 \text{ kg}$$

At state 2

$$m_2 = \frac{P_2 V}{RT_2}$$

$$= \frac{150(0.5)}{0.287(175.61)}$$

$$= 1.49 \text{ kg}$$

From Eq. (2), then

$$m_e = 5.35 - 1.49 = 3.86 \text{ kg}$$

Therefore 3.86 kg of air were withdrawn from the tank.

Tank A has a volume of 0.2 m^3 and contains air initially at 2.0 MPa, 400K. Cylinder B has a volume of 0.1 m^3 and contains air initially at 0.15 MPa, 300K. The pressure of 0.15 MPa is required to balance the weight of the piston and atmospheric pressure on B. The connecting valve is then opened and air is allowed to flow from A to B, until the pressure in A falls to 0.15 MPa. Assuming air to behave as an ideal gas, and the air remaining in A to have gone through a reversible adiabatic expansion, compute (a) the mass of air finally in A and B, and (b) the final temperature of the air in B. Refer to the figure for the schematic representation.

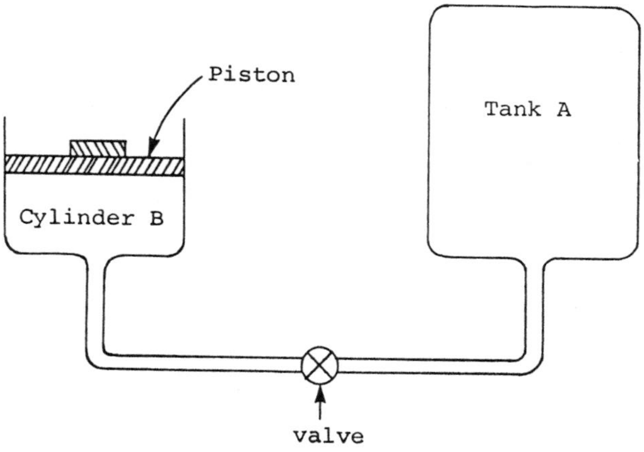

Solution: (a) In order to calculate the final mass in either the container or the cylinder, the initial mass has to be known.

From the ideal gas equation of state

$$m = \frac{PV}{RT} \quad \text{where } R_{air} = 0.287 \text{ kJ/kg-K} \tag{1}$$

Before the valve opens (state 1):

Tank A:

$$m_{A1} = \frac{P_1V_1}{RT_1} = \frac{(2000)(0.2)}{(0.287)(400)} = 3.4843 \text{ kg}$$

Cylinder B:

$$m_{B1} = \frac{P_1V_1}{RT_1} = \frac{(150)(0.1)}{(0.287)(300)} = 0.1742 \text{ kg.}$$

After the valve opens (state 2):

Tank A:

In order to calculate the mass in tank A at the final state (state 2), the temperature inside tank A must be calculated, so that Eq. (1) can be used. Since it has been assumed that the air remaining in tank A has gone through a reversible adiabatic process

$$s_2 = s_1.$$

From the isentropic relation

$$\frac{T_2}{T_1} = \left(\frac{P_2}{P_1}\right)^{(k-1)/k} \qquad k = 1.4 \text{ (air)} \qquad (2)$$

solving for $T_2\big|_A$ in Eq. (2) yields

$$T_2\Big|_A = T_1 \left(\frac{P_2}{P_1}\right)^{(k-1)/k}$$

$$= 400 \left(\frac{150}{2000}\right)^{(1.4-1)/1.4}$$

$$= 190.83 \text{ K.}$$

From Eq. (1)

$$m_{A_2} = \frac{P_2V_2}{RT_2} = \frac{(150)(0.2)}{(0.287)(190.83)} = 0.5478 \text{ kg.}$$

Cylinder B

The final mass in cylinder B will be the mass that was originally there before the valve was opened plus the mass that was allowed to escape from tank A when the valve opened. Thus

$$m_{B_2} = m_{B_1} + m_{Ae} \qquad (3)$$

where

$$m_{Ae} = m_{A_1} - m_{A_2}$$

$$= 3.4843 - 0.5478$$

$$= 2.9365 \text{ kg}$$

From Eq. (3)

$$m_{B_2} = m_{B_1} + m_{Ae} = 0.1742 + 2.9365 = 3.1107 \text{ kg}$$

(b) The first law written for this system (tank A and cylinder B) is

$$Q_{12} = U_2 - U_1 + W_{12} \qquad (4)$$

where $Q_{12} = 0$ (adiabatic process). Also the work done, in moving the piston in cylinder B from the initial to the final volume, is

$$W_{12} = \int_1^2 PdV = P(V_{B_2} - V_{B_1})$$

substituting the above expression for work and expressing on a per mass basis, Eq. (4) takes the form

$$0 = (m_{A_2}u_{A_2} + m_{B_2}u_{B_2}) - (m_{A_1}u_{A_1} + m_{B_1}u_{B_1}) + mP(v_2 - v_1)$$

or

$$m_{A_2}u_{A_2} - m_{A_1}u_{A_1} + m_{B_2}u_{B_2} - m_{B_1}u_{B_1} + mP(v_{B_2} - v_{B_1}) = 0$$

Using the relation

$$u = h - Pv$$

the above equation becomes

$$m_{A_2}u_{A_2} - m_{A_1}u_{A_1} + m_{B_2}h_{B_2} - m_{B_1}h_{B_1} = 0 \qquad (5)$$

Since air was assumed to behave ideally, the relations (assuming constant specific heats)

$$dh = C_{po}dT \quad \text{and} \quad du = C_{vo}dT$$

can be substituted into Eq. (5) to give

$$m_{A_2}C_{vo}T_{A_2} - m_{A_1}C_{vo}T_{A_1} + m_{B_2}C_{po}T_{B_2} - m_{B_1}C_{po}T_{B_1} = 0$$

The only unknown in the above equation is the temperature in cylinder B, after the valve was closed. Thus, using the values for the different masses as was obtained in part (a) of this problem, and taking the specific heats as

$$C_{vo} = 0.7165 \text{ kJ/kg-K}, \; C_{po} = 1.0035 \text{ kJ/kg-K}$$

solving for T_{B_2} gives

$$T_{B_2} = \frac{m_{A_1}C_{vo}T_{A_1} - m_{A_2}C_{vo}T_{A_2} + m_{B_1}C_{po}T_{B_1}}{m_{B_2}C_{po}}$$

$$= \frac{(3.4843)(0.7165)(400)-(0.5478)(0.7165)(190.83)}{(3.1107)(1.0035)}$$

$$+ \frac{(0.1742)(1.0035)(300)}{(3.1107)(1.0035)}$$

$$= 312.71 \text{ K}$$

Thus there was a temperature rise of approximately twelve degrees.

Note that the answer could have been obtained using Eq. (5), with values for the enthalpies and internal energies obtained from the air tables. The procedure would be to solve for the unknown enthalpy, and then go back to the air tables to find the corresponding temperature at the calculated enthalpy. This procedure however would involve more numerical calculations, even though it would give a more accurate value.

THE SECOND LAW FOR CLOSED UNIFORM - STATE, UNIFORM - FLOW SYSTEMS

• PROBLEM 4-40

Two rigid and perfectly insulated tanks, are connected by a small pipe and valve. Tank A has a volume of 0.5 m^3 and initially contains water at 1.0MPa, 400°C. Tank B has a volume of 0.6 m^3 and initially contains water at 0.1MPa, 250°C. The valve is then opened and water flows from tank A to tank B until the pressure inside tank A is 0.6 MPa, and then the valve is closed. What is the final pressure in tank B?

Solution: First determine the state of the substance in both tanks, before the valve is opened. Let this be state 1.

From the steam tables for each tank:

State 1

Tank A: Initial state is superheated vapor

$$T_{sat.} = 179.91°C < T_{given} = 400°C$$

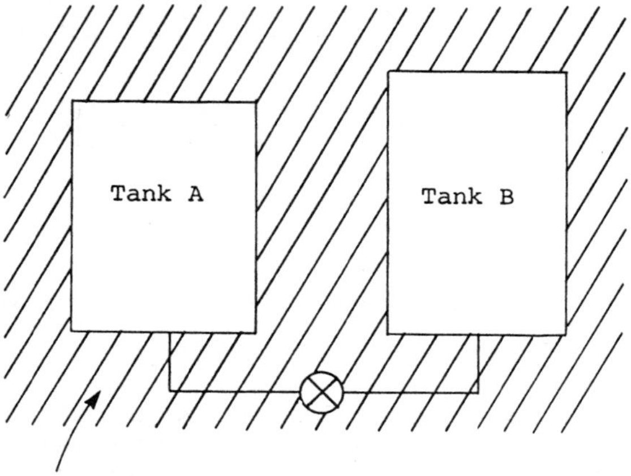

Therefore, from the superheated steam tables

$$v_{A_1} = 0.3066 \text{ m}^3/\text{kg}$$

$$h_{A_1} = 3263.9 \text{ kJ/kg}$$

$$u_{A_1} = 2957.3 \text{ kJ/kg}$$

$$s_{A_1} = 7.4651 \text{ kJ/kg-°K}$$

Tank B: Initial state is superheated vapor

$$T_{sat} = 99.63°C < T_{given} = 250°C$$

Therefore,

$$v_{B_1} = 2.406 \text{ m}^3/\text{kg}$$

$$h_{B_1} = 2,974.3 \text{ kJ/kg}$$

$$u_{B_1} = 2,733.7 \text{ kJ/kg}$$

$$s_{B_1} = 8.0333 \text{ kJ/kg-°K}$$

Because the containers are insulated

$$Q = 0$$

Furthermore assume that everything remaining in tank A goes through a reversible adiabatic process.

Hence

$$s_{A_2} = s_{A_1} = 7.4651 \text{ kJ/kg-°K}$$

After the valve has been opened and closed again (when the pressure in tank A reaches 0.6 MPa), the two tanks have reached a new state.

State 2

Tank A: Two independent properties are known at this state, and so the state of the substance can be determined as follows:

Using the steam tables at P = 0.6 MPa

$$(s_f)_{A_2} = 1.9312 \text{ kJ/kg-°K}$$

$$(s_g)_{A_2} = 6.76 \text{ kJ/kg-°K}$$

Since $s_{A_2} > (s_g)_{A_2}$ the substance is superheated.

From the superheated steam tables then

$$T_{A_2} = 326.64°C$$

$$v_{A_2} = 0.4556 \text{ m}^3/\text{kg}$$

$$u_{A_2} = 2843.72 \text{ kJ/kg}$$

$$h_{A_2} = 3117.06 \text{ kJ/kg}$$

Tank B: Since not enough information is available, state 2 cannot be determined for the substance inside tank B.

However the mass in both tanks can be calculated at both states as follows.

$$m_{A_1} = \frac{V_A}{v_{A_1}} = \frac{0.5}{0.3066} = 1.6308 \text{ kg}$$

$$m_{A_2} = \frac{V_A}{v_{A_2}} = \frac{0.5}{0.4556} = 1.0975 \text{ kg}$$

$$m_{B_1} = \frac{V_B}{v_{B_1}} = \frac{0.6}{2.406} = 0.2494 \text{ kg}$$

At state 2 the mass of water in tank B equals the initial mass in the tank plus the mass of water entered while the valve was kept open. Therefore

$$m_{B_2} = m_{B_1} + m_{Ae}$$

$$= m_{B_1} + (m_{A_1} - m_{A_2})$$

$$= 0.2494 + (1.6308 - 1.0975)$$

$$= 0.7827 \text{ kg}$$

From the first law

$$Q_{1\to2} = U_2 - U_1 + W_{1\to2} \qquad (1)$$

For this process, however, $Q_{1\to2} = 0$ and $W_{1\to2} = 0$. Therefore

$$U_2 - U_1 = 0$$

or on a per mass basis

$$(m_A u_A + m_B u_B)_2 - (m_A u_A + m_B u_B)_1 = 0 \qquad (2)$$

The only unknown in Eq. (2) is the specific internal energy of the water inside tank B at state 2.

Solving for u_{B_2} obtain

$$u_{B_2} = \frac{m_{A_1}u_{A_1} + m_{B_1}u_{B_1} - m_{A_2}u_{A_2}}{m_{B_2}}$$

$$= \frac{(1.6308)(2957.3) + (0.2494)(2733.7)}{0.7827}$$

$$- \frac{(1.0975)(2843.72)}{0.7827}$$

$$= 3{,}045.31 \text{ kJ/kg}$$

At state 2, inside tank B, the specific volume can be calculated as follows:

$$v_{B_2} = \frac{V_B}{m_{B_2}} = \frac{0.6}{0.7827} = 0.7666 \text{ m}^3/\text{kg}$$

Now two independant properties, namely the specific internal energy and specific internal volume are known. Therefore a third property can be obtained for the substance at that state, using the property relation

$$u = h - Pv \qquad (2)$$

and the steam tables. The solution is a trial and error one, and goes as follows:

First trial: Assume $P = 0.4MPa$

From the superheated steam tables

$$h = 3262.8 \text{ kJ/kg}$$

From Eq. (2)

$$u = 2956.16 \text{ kJ/kg}$$

$$u_{B_2} = 3045.31 > u = 2956.16$$

Second trial: Assume $P = 0.5MPa$

From the superheated steam tables

$$h = 3614.1 \text{ kJ/kg}$$

From Eq. (2)

$$u = 3230.80 \text{ kJ/kg}$$

$$u_{B_2} = 3045.31 < u = 3230.80$$

From these trials it is clear that the final pressure must lie between the two assumed values. The reason is that one of the trials gives a value lower than the actual value for the specific internal energy, and the other gives a higher value.

Therefore it can be concluded that

$$0.4MPa < P_{B_2} < 0.5MPa$$

Or by interpolation

$$P \cong 0.43 \text{ MPa}$$

CHAPTER 5

IRREVERSIBILITY AND AVAILABILITY

REVERSIBLE WORK

• PROBLEM 5-1

Air at 150 lbf/in^2, 150°F and a velocity of 300 ft/sec is expanded in a gas turbine and leaves at 50 lbf/in^2, 40°F and 200 ft/sec. Assuming no heat losses and air to be an ideal gas with constant specific heats, calculate the reversible work per pound of air done, and the actual work done by the turbine.

Solution: A typical turbine consists of (1) a nozzle which accelerates the air flow converting internal energy and flow work to kinetic energy, and (2) a rotor which slows down the fluid, extracting energy from the air as work.

The reversible work done for a steady state process can be calculated from the equation

$$W_{rev} = (h_i - h_e) - T_o(S_i - S_e) + \frac{V_1{}^2 - V_e{}^2}{2g_c} + (Z_1 - Z_e)\frac{g}{g_c}$$

$$= (h_i - h_e) - T_o(S_i - s_e) + \frac{V_i{}^2 - V_e{}^2}{2g_c}$$

$$= C_{po}(T_i - T_e) - T_o\left(C_{po}\ln\frac{T_i}{T_e} - R\ln\frac{P_i}{P_e}\right) + \frac{V_1{}^2 - V_e{}^2}{2g_c}$$

$$= 0.240(610 - 500) - 537(0.240 \ln\frac{610}{500} -$$

$$\left.\frac{53.3}{778}\ \ln \frac{150}{50}\right) + \frac{(300)^2 - (200)^2}{64.34 \times 778}$$

$$= 26.4 + 14.8 + 1.0$$

$$= 42.2 \text{ Btu/lbm}$$

The actual work of the turbine is obtained from the steady-flow energy equation

$$W = (h_i - h_e) + \frac{V_1^2 - V_2^2}{2g_c}$$

$$= 0.240(610 - 500) + \frac{(300)^2 - (200)^2}{64.34 \times 778}$$

$$= 26.4 + 1$$

$$= 27.4 \text{ Btu/lbm}$$

• PROBLEM 5-2

Calculate the minimum power required to cool 100 lb moles/min of air from 550°R to 500°R when the surrounding temperature is 550°R.

Solution: Apply the equation

$$W = T_o \Delta S - \Delta H \qquad (1)$$

to 1 pound mole of air. Assume the heat capacity as 7 Btu/(lb mole)(°R)

$$\therefore\ \Delta S = -7 \ln (550/500)$$

$$= -\ 0.666 \text{ Btu/(lb mole)(°R)}$$

$$\Delta H = 7(500 - 550) = -350 \text{ Btu/(lb mole)}$$

The minimum work required is

$$W_{min} = (550)(-0.666) + 350$$

$$= -16 \text{ Btu/(lb mole)}.$$

For 100 lb moles of air per minute

$$W_{min} = (-16)(100) = -1600 \text{ Btu/min}.$$

$$= -37.7 \text{ hp}.$$

• PROBLEM 5-3

Air at an initial state of 100 psia and 800°R is expanded in a cylinder to a final pressure of 10 psia, along a polytropic path with n = 1.3. Assuming the process to be adiabatic, and air to behave as an ideal gas, calculate the friction of the process per lbm of air.

Solution: The friction of the process is the difference between the actual work done during the process and maximum possible work or the reversible work. Therefore

$$F = w_{rev} - w_{act} \tag{1}$$

Noting that Q = 0, the actual or irreversible work equals

$$w_{act} = u_1 - u_2 = c_v(T_2 - T_1) \tag{2}$$

The temperature T_2 at the end of the expansion is found using the relation

$$T_2 = T_1\left(\frac{P_2}{P_1}\right)^{\frac{n-1}{n}}$$

$$= 800\left(\frac{1}{10}\right)^{0.230}$$

$$= 470°R$$

Then by Eq. (2), with c_v = 0.172 Btu/lbm-°R

$$w_{act} = 0.172(800-470)$$

$$= 56.6 \text{ Btu/lbm}$$

The reversible work for this system is given as

$$w_{rev} = \frac{P_2v_2 - P_1v_1}{1-n} = \frac{R(T_2 - T_1)}{1-n}$$

$$= \frac{1.986(800-470)}{29(0.3)}$$

$$= 75.4 \text{ Btu/lbm.}$$

Then from Eq. (1)

$$F = 75.4 - 56.6 = 18.8 \text{ Btu/lbm}$$

which is the frictional force

• **PROBLEM 5-4**

An air compressor is used to compress air from atmospheric conditions (14 psia, 60°F) to 70 psia, 120°F in a steady-state, steady-flow process. Calculate the minimum work required per pound of air to drive the compressor.

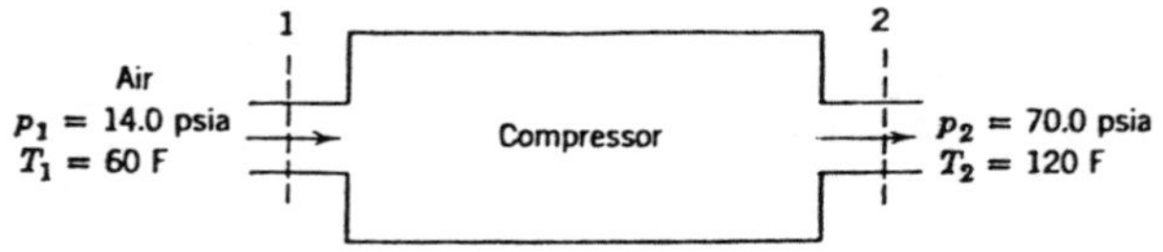

Solution: For a compression process, $W_{max} < 0$ because work must be supplied to the system. Therefore

$$-w_{max} = \text{minimum } w_{in}$$

Neglecting kinetic and potential energies, it can be written for the reversible work (w_{max})

$$w_{max} = (h_1 - T_0S_1) - (h_2 - T_0S_2)$$

$$= (h_1 - h_2)\ T_0(S_1 - S_2) \quad (1)$$

where

$$T_0 = 60 + 460 = 520°R$$

Assuming constant specific heats, and treating air as an ideal gas Eq. (1) takes the form

$$w_{max} = C_p(T_2 - T_1) - T_0\int_2^1 ds \quad (2)$$

However, from the relation

$$Tds = dh - vdP$$

Eq. (2) can be written as,

$$w_{max} = C_p(T_2 - T_1) - T_0\left[\int_2^1 \frac{dh}{T} - \int_2^1 \frac{vdP}{T}\right]$$

or after integration, and the fact that

$$v = \frac{RT}{P}$$

$$w_{max} = C_p(T_2 - T_1) - T_0\left[C_p \ln\left(\frac{T_1}{T_2}\right) - R\ln\left(\frac{P_1}{P_2}\right)\right] \quad (3)$$

for air

$$C_p = 0.24 \text{ Btu/lbm-°R}$$

$$R = 0.0686 \text{ Btu/lbm-°R}$$

Substituting the numerical values into Eq. (3), obtain

$$w_{max} = 0.24(60-120)-520\left[0.24 \ln\left(\frac{520}{580}\right) - 0.0686 \ln\left(\frac{14}{70}\right)\right]$$

$$= -14.4 - 520 [-0.0262 + 0.1104]$$

$$= -58.2 \text{ Btu/lbm}$$

Since $w_{max} = -58.2$ Btu/lbm or $w_{in} \geq 58.2$ Btu/lbm, it follows that the minimum work input is 58.2 Btu/lbm.

• PROBLEM 5-5

Steam initially at 500°F, 100 psia enters a steady-state, steady-flow system with negligible velocity. It leaves the system with a velocity of 500 ft/sec, at a mass flow rate of 8000 lbm/hr. If the conditions at the exit are 15 psia, 240°F and heat is exchanged only with the surroundings at 60°F, calculate the maximum power output.

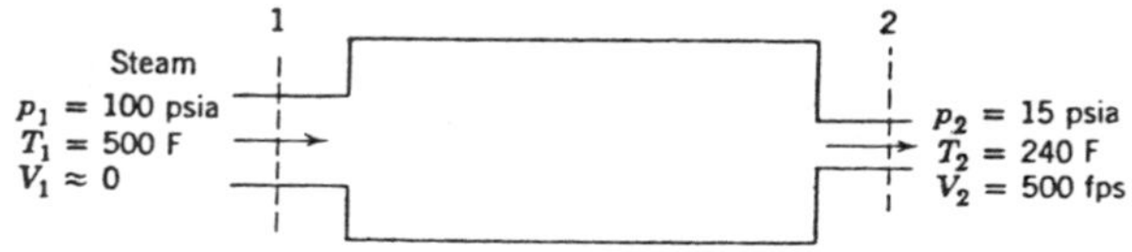

Solution: The maximum power output that the system is able to perform is

$$P_{max} = \dot{m}w_{max} = \dot{m}w_{rev} \qquad (1)$$

For a steady-state, steady-flow system exchanging heat only with the atmosphere, the reversible work is

$$w_{rev} = (h_1 - T_0 s_1 + \frac{V_1^2}{2g} + gZ_1) - (h_2 - T_0 s_2 + \frac{V_2^2}{2} + gZ_2) \qquad (2)$$

In this case, changes in potential energy can be neglected as well as the initial kinetic energy (since $V_1 \cong 0$). Then Eq. (2) becomes

$$w_{rev} = (h_1 - T_0 s_1) - (h_2 + \frac{V_2^2}{2g} - T_0 s_2)$$

or

$$w_{rev} = (h_1 - h_2) - T_0(s_1 - s_2) - \frac{V_2^2}{2g} \qquad (3)$$

From the steam tables then at states 1 and 2

$$h_1 = 1279.1 \text{ Btu/lbm}$$

$$h_2 = 1164.1 \text{ Btu/lbm}$$

$$s_1 = 1.7085 \text{ Btu/lbm-°R}$$

$$s_2 = 1.7742 \text{ Btu/lbm-°R}$$

Substituting these values into Eq. (3),

$$w_{rev} = (1279.1 - 1164.1) - 520(1.7085 - 1.7742) - \frac{(500)^2}{50000}$$

$$= 144.2 \text{ Btu/lbm}$$

Then from Eq. (1)

$$P_{max} = \frac{8000(144.2)}{2545} = 453 \text{ hP}$$

It should be noted that an actual machine operating at these specified end conditions will produce less power on account of irreversibilities. Also it does not make any difference what kind of mechanism is used for producing this much power, because this power output cannot be exceeded.

IRREVERSIBILITY

• PROBLEM 5-6

Determine the irreversibility per kg of Freon-12 flow, associated with an expansion valve (see figure). Freon-12 enters at 1.2 MPa, 30°C and is expanded to 100 kPa.

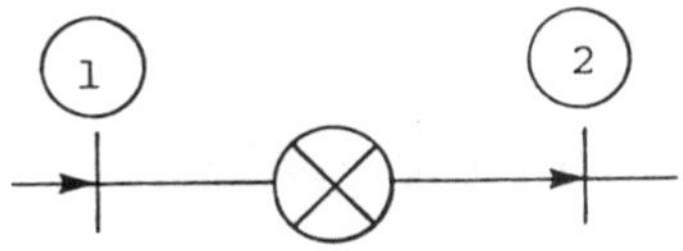

Solution: Consider a control volume around the expansion valve. This is a throttling process, and for such a process both the work and heat transfer are zero. The irreversibility for such a process (steady-state-steady-flow) can be found using the equation

$$I = m_2 T_0 s_2 - m_1 T_0 s_1 \;, \quad T_0 = 298.15K$$

or

$$\frac{I}{m_1} = T_0(s_2 - s_1) \tag{1}$$

The only unknown in the above equation is the entropy at the two states, and can be obtained using the given information along with the Freon-12 tables.

State 1: From the tables it is easily seen that this state lies in the compressed region ($P_{sat} < P_{given}$) and thus

$$s_1 = s_f = 0.2397 \text{ kJ/kg K}$$

State 2: The given information is insufficient to obtain the value for the entropy from the tables. However, for a throttling process the enthalpy at the the entrance and exit will be the same. Using this, the state at 2 can be obtained. From the Freon-12 tables

$$h_2 = h_1 = h_f = 64.539 \text{ kJ/kg.}$$

By inspection one gets that state two lies in the mixture region, and so the quality must be calculated, using the equation

$$x = \frac{h_4 - h_f}{h_{fg}}$$

where

$$h_f = 8.854 \text{ kJ/kg}$$

$$h_{fg} = 165.222 \text{ kJ/kg}$$

Hence

$$x = \frac{64.539-8.854}{165.222} = 0.3370$$

Then the entropy can be obtained from

$$s_2 = s_f + xs_{fg}$$

where

$$s_f = 0.0371 \text{ kJ/kg K}$$

$$s_{fg} = 0.6795 \text{ kJ/kg K}$$

Hence $\quad s_2 = 0.0371 + (0.3370)(0.6795)$

$$= 0.2661 \text{ kJ/kgK}$$

Substituting the value for entropy into Eq. (1), gives the irreversibility per kg of Freon-12

$$\frac{I}{m} = T_0(s_2 - s_1) = 298.15(0.2661 - 0.2397)$$

$$= 7.8712 \text{ kJ/kg}$$

• **PROBLEM 5-7**

Air at 14 psia and 80°F is allowed into a compressor having an efficiency of 70 per cent and a pressure ratio of 3. Calculate the irreversibility per pound of air.

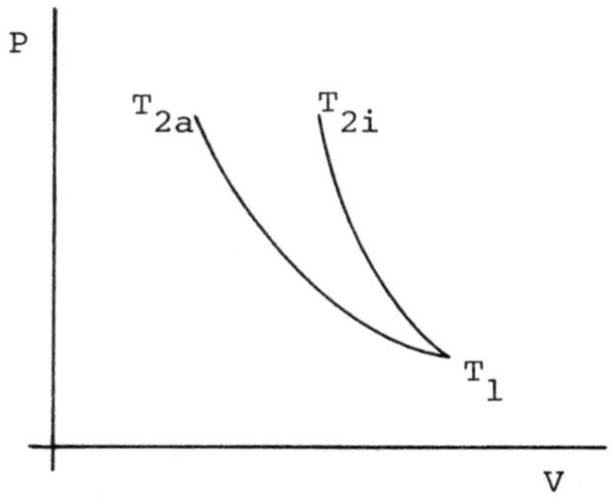

Solution: The irreversibility for the process is

$$i = T_0 \Delta s \Big)_{syst.}$$

Since the inlet temperature of air is not given, assume the inlet air temperature to equal the temperature of the surrounding atmosphere. To calculate Δs, the end states of the process have to be determined. Since the process is adiabatic, the final state can be calculated from the initial state and the work done. The work done can be obtained from the compressor efficiency and the isentropic (ideal) work. The ideal work can be obtained by using the first law. The change in temperature here is very small, hence the following values can be used.

$$C_p = 0.24 \text{ Btu/lb-f and } k = 1.4$$

The temperature at stage 2 is then

$$T_{2i} = T_1\left(\frac{P_2}{P_1}\right)^{\left(\frac{k-1}{k}\right)}$$

$$= (460 + 80)(3)^{\frac{1.4-1}{1.4}}$$

$$= (540)(3)^{0.286}$$

$$= 739 \text{ R}$$

$$\text{Input work})_i = h_2 - h_1$$

$$= C_p(T_2 - T_1)$$

$$= 0.24(739-540)$$

$$= 47.76 \text{ Btu/lbm}$$

$$\text{Input work})_a = \frac{\text{input work})_i}{\eta}$$

where η = efficiency

$$= \frac{47.76}{0.7}$$

$$= 68.2 \text{ Btu/lbm}$$

$$T_{2a} - T_1 = \frac{h_{2a} - h_i}{C_p} = \frac{\text{input work}_a}{C_p}$$

$$= \frac{68.2}{0.24}$$

$$= 284 \text{ R}$$

$$T_{2a} = T_1 + 284$$

$$= 540 + 284$$

$$= 824 \text{ R}$$

$$\Delta s = s_{2a} - s_1 = \int_1^{2a} ds = \int_1^{2a} \frac{dh}{h} - \int_1^{2a} \frac{vdp}{T}$$

$$= C_p \ln \frac{T_{2a}}{T_1} - R \ln \frac{P_2}{P_1}$$

$$= 0.24 \ln \frac{824}{540} - \frac{53.3}{778} \ln 3$$

$$= 0.0262 \text{ Btu/lbm-°R}$$

$$\therefore\ i = T_0 \Delta s$$

$$= 540 \times (0.0262)$$

$$= 14.15 \text{ Btu/lbm}$$

This shows that when 68.2 B/lb of energy is added to the air as work, 14.15 B/lb is wasted or cannot be reconverted to work. For the reversible process 47.76 B/lb of work is required and the entire amount can be reconverted into work by reversing the process.

• PROBLEM 5-8

A 0.1 m diameter, 0.1 m high solid copper cylinder is initially at 180°C. It is then placed in a room and is allowed to cool to a final temperature of 30°C. Assuming copper to have a density of 8954 kJ/kg-°K, calculate the heat transfer and the irreversibility of the process if the temperature of the surroundings (T_0) is 25°C.

Solution: Consider as the system, the copper cylinder alone. After a period of time the cylinder will cool, as a result of heat transfer from the cylinder to the surroundings. From the first law of thermodynamics it can be written

$$Q = \Delta U - W .$$

Noting that there is no work involved in this process, the first law reduces to

$$Q = \Delta U \tag{1}$$

Assuming constant specific heats, and noting that the internal energy is not a function of volume, we can write

$$du = C_v dT$$

and for a specified mass m

$$dU = mC_v dT \tag{2}$$

Integrating between states 1 and 2

$$\Delta U = U_2 - U_1 = mC_v(T_2 - T_1) \tag{3}$$

where

$$c_v = 0.4 \text{ kJ/kg-°K}$$

$$T_2 = 30 + 273 = 303°K$$

$$T_1 = 180 + 273 = 453°K$$

and

$$m = \rho V$$

For a cylinder

$$V = \frac{\pi d^2 h}{4}$$

$$= \frac{\pi(0.1)^2(0.1)}{4}$$

$$= 7.85 \times 10^{-4} m^3$$

Then

$$m = 8954\ (7.85 \times 10^{-4}) = 7.029 \text{ kg}$$

substituting the numerical values into Eq. (3), obtain

$$\Delta U = 7.029 \times 0.4\ (303 - 453)$$

$$= -421.74 \text{ kJ}$$

and from Eq. (1)

$$Q = \Delta U = -421.74 \text{ kJ}$$

The minus sign indicates that heat was lost by the cylinder as expected.

The irreversibility for any process is given as

$$I = \Sigma m_e T_0 s_e - \Sigma m_i T_0 s_i + m_2 T_0 s_2 - m_1 T_0 s_1 - Q_{c.v.} \quad (4)$$

However for this system

$$m_e T_0 s_e = 0 \ ; \quad m_i T_0 s_i = 0$$

since neither mass leaves nor enters the system.

Therefore Eq. (4) reduces to

$$I = mT_0(s_2 - s_1) - Q_{c.v.}$$

or

$$I = mT_0 \Delta S)_{syst.} - Q_{c.v.} \quad (4a)$$

The specific enthalpies however, s_2 and s_1, cannot be calculated directly or obtained from any table. We can however write

$$\Delta S = m\left[C_v \ln\left(\frac{T_2}{T_1}\right) + R \ln\left(\frac{v_2}{v_1}\right)\right] \tag{5}$$

But $v_2 = v_1$ and Eq. (5) becomes

$$\Delta S = mC_v \ln\left(\frac{T_2}{T_1}\right)$$

$$= 7.029 \times 0.4 \ln\left(\frac{303}{453}\right)$$

$$= -1.1307 \text{ kJ/°K}$$

From Eq. (4a)

$$I = 298(-1.1307) - (-421.74)$$

$$= 84.79 \text{ kJ}$$

• PROBLEM 5-9

Consider a turbine in a large power plant. Steam enters at a pressure of 5 MPa and a temperature of 500°C. Some of the steam is extracted from the turbine at 1 MPa and 300°C and rejected into a high pressure heater. At another stage of the turbine some more steam at 100 kPa and 99.63°C is extracted and rejected into a low pressure heater. The remaining steam leaves the turbine at 5kPa with an enthalpy of 2200 kJ/kg. Assuming $m_2/m_1 = 0.13$ and $m_3/m_1 = 0.1$ compute the irreversibility of the turbine.

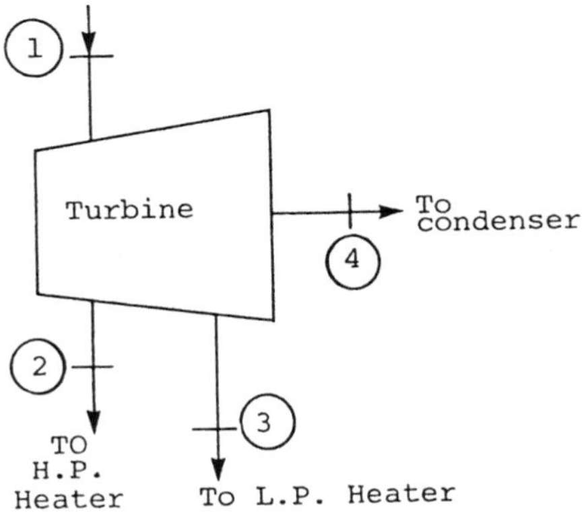

Solution: The irreversibility in this case is given by the equation

$$I = \Sigma m_e T_0 s_e - \Sigma m_i T_0 s_i - Q_{c.v.}$$

where $T_0 = 298.15°K$

$Q_{c.v.} = 0$ (Assume an adiabatic turbine)

or $I = m_4 T_0 s_4 + m_3 T_0 s_3 + m_2 T_0 s_2 - m_1 T_0 s_1$

Dividing by the mass (m_1) entering the turbine, the above equation takes the following form

$$\frac{I}{m_1} = T_0\left(\frac{m_4}{m_1}s_4 + \frac{m_2}{m_1}s_3 + \frac{m_2}{m_1}s_2 - s_1\right) \quad (1)$$

From continuity

$$m_4 = m_1 - m_2 - m_3.$$

Dividing by m_1 and substituting the given information

$$\frac{m_4}{m_1} = 1 - \frac{m_2}{m_1} - \frac{m_3}{m_1}$$

$$= 1-0.13-0.10$$

$$= 0.77$$

The specific entropies at the different states must next be calculated.

State 1: $s_1 = 6.9759$ kJ/kg K (superheated vapor)

State 2: $s_2 = 7.1229$ kJ/kg K (superheated vapor)

State 3: $s_3 = s_g = 7.3594$ kJ/kg K (saturated vapor)

State 4: The enthalpy given for this pressure (5 kpa) lies in the mixture region, and so the entropy must lie in that region as well. The information given for this state is insufficient to obtain the value for the entropy at this state. But the quality x can be calculated using the enthalpy and the steam tables.

$$x = \frac{h-h_f}{h_{fg}}$$

where

$$h_f = 137.82 \text{ kJ/kg}$$

$$h_{fg} = 2,423.7 \text{ kJ/kg.}$$

Thus

$$x = \frac{2200 - 137.82}{2423.7}$$

$$= 0.8508$$

Knowing the quality, the entropy can be calculated.

$$s_4 = s_f + xs_{fg}$$

where $s_f = 0.4764$ kJ/kg K

$$S_{fg} = 7.9187 \text{ kJ/kg K}$$

Thus

$$s_4 = 0.4764 + (0.8508)(7.9187)$$

$$= 7.2136 \text{ kJ/kg K}$$

Substituting the above values in Eq. (1), the irreversibility per kg of steam entering the turbine is

$$\frac{I}{m_1} = 298.15\Big[(0.77)(7.2136) + (0.10)(7.3595) + (0.13)(7.1229) - 6.9759\Big]$$

$$= 298.15\ (0.2405)$$

$$= 71.70 \text{ kJ/kg}$$

• PROBLEM 5-10

Heat from the surroundings which remain at a fixed temperature of 1200°R, is added to 0.03 lbm of helium initially at 550°R, 10 atm., at constant pressure. The helium then expands reversibly and adiabatically to a final pressure of 1 atm and a temperature of 550°R. Assuming constant specific heats and the helium to behave as an ideal gas, calculate the irreversibility for the process.

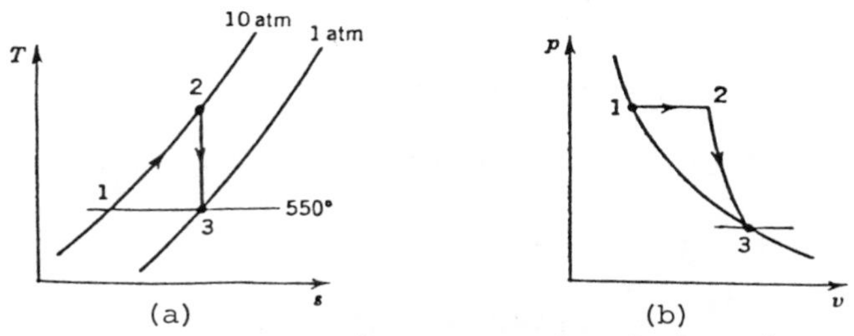

Complex process (perfect gas).

Solution: The figure suggests that the process can be broken into two steps. Process 1-2 is a constant pressure process, and process 2-3 is a constant entropy process. Therefore for the irreversibility of the overall process

$$I_{1\to 3} = I_{1\to 2} + I_{2\to 3} \tag{1}$$

for process $1\to 2$

$$I_{1\to 2} = T_0 \Delta S_{1\to 2} - Q_{1\to 2} \tag{2}$$

and for process $2\to 3$, which is a reversible process as stated by the problem

$$I_{2\to 3} = 0 \tag{3}$$

substituting Eqs.(2) and (3) into (1)

$$I_{1\to 3} = \Delta S_{1\to 2} - \left(\frac{Q}{T_0}\right)_{1\to 2} \tag{4}$$

The change in entropy for process $1\to 2$ is

$$\Delta S_{1\to 2} = mC_p \ln\left(\frac{T_2}{T_1}\right) - mR \ln\left(\frac{P_2}{P_1}\right)$$

But $P_2 = P_1$ and thus

$$\Delta S_{1\to 2} = mC_p \ln\left(\frac{T_2}{T_1}\right) \tag{5}$$

Since constant heat capacities have been assumed the relation

$$\frac{T_2}{T_3} = \left(\frac{P_2}{P_3}\right)^{\frac{\gamma-1}{\gamma}}$$

where for helium

$$\gamma = 1.667$$

is used to find the temperature at state 2.

$$T_2 = 550 \left(\frac{10}{1}\right)^{\frac{1.667-1}{1.667}}$$

$$= 1382°R$$

From the table of critical constants, for helium

$$C_p = 1.240 \text{ Btu/lbm-°R}$$

$$C_v = 0.7442 \text{ Btu/lbm-°R}$$

Then from Eq. (5)

$$\Delta S_{1\to 2} = 0.03 \times 1.240 \ln \left(\frac{1382}{550}\right)$$

$$= 0.03428 \text{ Btu/°R}$$

The only unknown in Eq. (4) is the heat transfer $Q_{1\to 2}$.

From the first law of thermodynamics

$$Q_{1\to 2} = \Delta U_{1\to 2} + W_{1\to 2}$$

$$= mC_v(T_2 - T_1) + P(V_2 - V_1) \quad (6)$$

for the initial volume

$$V_1 = \frac{mRT_1}{P_1}$$

$$= \frac{0.03(386)(550)}{10(14.7)(144)}$$

$$= 0.3010 \text{ ft}^3$$

For V_2

$$V_2 = V_1\left(\frac{T_2}{T_1}\right)$$

$$= 0.3010 \left(\frac{1382}{550}\right)$$

$$= 0.7564 \text{ ft}^3$$

Substituting the numerical values into Eq. (6)

$$Q_{1\to 2} = 0.03 \times 0.7442(1382-550)$$

$$+ \frac{10(14.7)(144)(0.7564-0.3010)}{778.2}$$

$$= 18.38 + 12.38$$

$$= 30.96 \text{ Btu}$$

Eq. (2) then gives

$$I_{1\to 3} = 1200(0.03428) - 30.96$$

$$= 10.176 \text{ Btu}$$

Two identical blocks of aluminum are initially at 1300°K and 400°K respectively. The two blocks are then brought into thermal communication and they attain the same temperature. Assuming that the specific heat of aluminum is 0.9 kJ/kg-°K, calculate the irreversibility of the process if the mass of each of the blocks is 5 kgs.

Solution: Let A represent the 1300°K block, and B the 400°K block. For the two blocks to attain the same final temperature, when the two blocks are brought into thermal communication heat is going to be rejected from the hotter to the colder block. Furthermore since there is no work involved in the process, the heat rejected by the higher temperature block is going to be received by the lower temperature block. Hence

$$Q_H = Q_L \tag{1}$$

Note that in reality some of the heat is going to be lost to the environment, but for our purposes it is assumed to be negligible compared to that between the two blocks.

The irreversibility for such a process is equal to the product of the net entropy change of the process and the temperature of the surroundings. Therefore it is directly related to the second law of thermodynamics and we can write

$$I = T_0 \Delta S)_{net} \tag{2}$$

where

$$\Delta S)_{net} = \Delta S_A + \Delta S_B$$

From the second law of thermodynamics, for the entropy change of a substance, following the ideal gas equation of state, is

$$\Delta S = m\left[C_p \ln\left(\frac{T_2}{T_1}\right) - R \ln\left(\frac{P_2}{P_1}\right)\right] \tag{3}$$

However

$$P_2 = P_1$$

and so Eq. (2) reduces to

$$\Delta S = mC_p \ln\left(\frac{T_2}{T_1}\right) \tag{4}$$

For each of the two blocks

$$\Delta S_A = mC_p \ln\left(\frac{T_2}{T_{A_1}}\right)$$

and

$$\Delta S_B = mC_p \ln\left(\frac{T_2}{T_{B_1}}\right)$$

Substituting into Eq. (2)

$$I = mC_p\ T_0 \left[\ln\left(\frac{T_2}{T_{A_1}}\right) + \ln\left(\frac{T_2}{T_{B_1}}\right)\right] \qquad (5)$$

where T_0 is the temperature of the environment, assumed to be 298°K.

The equilibrium temperature must then be evaluated

$$(T_{B_2} = T_{A_2} = T_2)$$

Since we have assumed constant specific heats it can be written for this process

$$Q = mC_p\ (T_2 - T_1) \qquad (6)$$

Substituting Eq. (6) into Eq. (1) yields

$$mC_p(T_{A_1} - T_2) = mC_p(T_2 - T_{B_1})$$

or solving for T_2

$$T_2 = \frac{T_{A_1} + T_{B_1}}{2}$$

$$= \frac{1300 + 400}{2}$$

$$= 850°K$$

Finally substituting all the numerical values into Eq. (5), obtain

$$I = 5 \times 0.9 \times 298\left[\ln\left(\frac{850}{1300}\right) + \ln\left(\frac{850}{400}\right)\right]$$

$$= 1341(0.3289)$$

$$= 441.1 \text{ kJ}$$

Saturated vapor steam at 100 kPa is mixed with a stream of water at 15°C, in a steady-flow mixing process. The result is a hot water supply of 3.5 kg/sec at 90°C. Assuming the process to be adiabatic calculate the irreversibility rate of the mixing process.

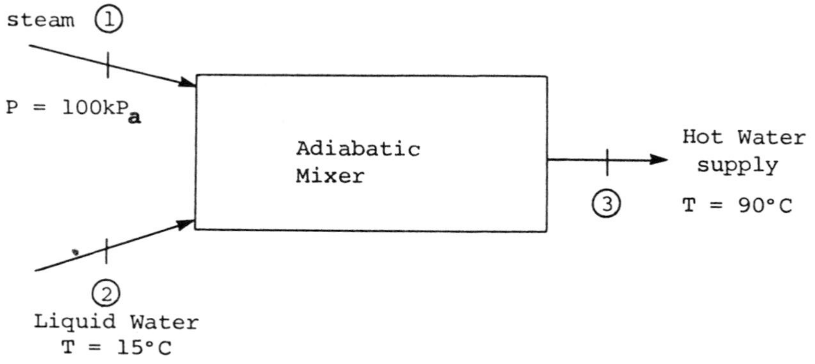

Solution: Let the subscripts e, i, and o stand for the exit, inlet, and surrounding states, respectively. For the steady-state, steady-flow process the irreversibility is given as

$$\dot{I} = T_0\left[\Sigma \dot{m}_e s_e - \Sigma \dot{m}_i s_i\right] - \dot{Q}_{c.v.} \quad (1)$$

However this process is adiabatic and therefore

$$\dot{Q}_{c.v.} = 0$$

Then Eq. (1) reduces to

$$\dot{I} = T_0\left[\Sigma \dot{m}_e s_e - \Sigma \dot{m}_i s_i\right] \quad (2)$$

Referring to the figure

$$\dot{I} = T_0(\dot{m}_3 s_3 - \dot{m}_1 s_1 - \dot{m}_2 s_2) \quad (3)$$

To solve Eq. (3) the mass flow rates must first be obtained. Noting that there is no work done on or by the system, from the first law

$$\dot{m}_3 h_3 = \dot{m}_1 h_1 + \dot{m}_2 h_2 \quad (4)$$

From the conservation of mass equation

$$\dot{m}_3 = \dot{m}_1 + \dot{m}_2 \quad (5)$$

From the steam tables, the enthalpies at the three stages are found to be

$$h_1 = h_g = 2675.5 \text{ kJ/kg} \qquad (\text{at } P = 100 \text{ kPa})$$

$$h_2 = h_f = 62.99 \text{ kJ/kg} \qquad (\text{at } T = 15°C)$$

$$h_3 = h_f = 376.92 \text{ kJ/kg} \qquad (\text{at } T = 90°C)$$

Substituting these values into Eq. (4), obtain

$$(376.92)\dot{m}_3 = (2675.5)\dot{m}_1 + (62.99)\dot{m}_2 \tag{6}$$

From Eq. (5), noting that $\dot{m}_3 = 3.5$ kg/sec

$$\dot{m}_2 = 3.5 - \dot{m}_1 \tag{7}$$

Substituting this expression into Eq. (6),

$$(376.92)(3.5) = (2675.5)\dot{m}_1 + (62.99)(3.5 - \dot{m}_1)$$

solving for $\dot{m}_1$, yields

$$(2612.51)\dot{m}_1 = 1098.76$$

or

$$\dot{m}_1 = 0.421 \text{ kg/sec}$$

From Eq. (7), then

$$\dot{m}_2 = 3.079 \text{ kg/sec}$$

From the steam tables, at the different stages

$$s_1 = s_g = 7.3594 \text{ kJ/kg-°K} \qquad (\text{at } P = 100\text{kPa})$$

$$s_2 = s_f = 0.2245 \text{ kJ/kg-°K} \qquad (\text{at } T = 15°C)$$

$$s_3 = s_f = 1.1925 \text{ kJ/kg-°K} \qquad (\text{at } T = 90°C)$$

Assuming the surroundings to be at 25°C or

$$T_0 = 25°C = 298°K$$

from Eq. (3)

$$\dot{I} = 298\left[(3.5)(1.1925) - (0.421)(7.3594) - (3.079)(0.2245)\right]$$

$$= 298(0.384)$$

$$= 114.5 \text{ kW}$$

• **PROBLEM 5-13**

An evacuated and insulated container with a volume of $0.5m^3$ is attached through a valve to a line carrying steam at 1.2 MPa, 350°C. The valve is then opened in order to fill the container with steam, and when the pressure inside the container reaches 1.2 MPa the valve closes. Calculate the mass entering the container and the irreversibility associated with this process.

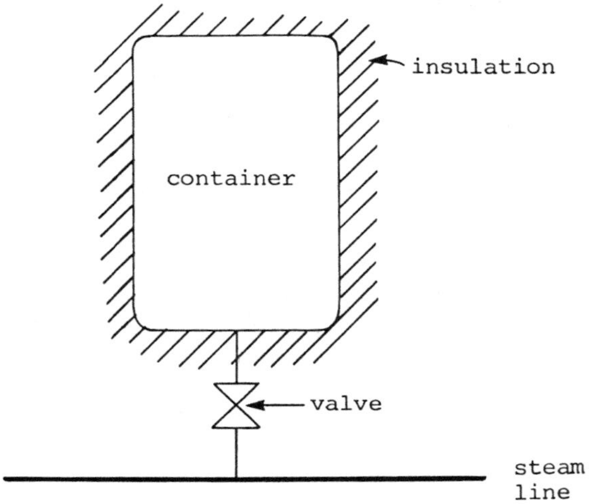

Solution: Irreversibility is called the difference between the reversible work W_{rev}, and that done by the control volume, or actual work associated with irreversible processes. Hence

$$I = W_{rev} - W_{c.v.}$$

For the process involved, however, there is no work done on or by the control volume; hence

$$I = W_{rev} \tag{1}$$

Noting that the cylinder is insulated $Q = 0$ and neglecting potential and kinetic energies, we can write for W_{rev}

$$W_{rev} = \Sigma m_i \left[h_i - T_0 s_i\right] - \Sigma m_e \left[h_e - T_0 s_e\right] - \left[m_2(u_2 - T_0 s_2) - m_1(u_1 - T_0 s_1)\right] \tag{2}$$

However the following conditions hold. Initially the container is evacuated and so

$$m_1 = 0$$

Also no mass is leaving the container, and thus

$$m_e = 0$$

Then it follows that the mass finally inside the container must be equal to that entering. Hence

$$m_i = m_2 = m$$

Therefore Eq. (1) reduces to

$$W_{rev} = m\left[(h_i - u_2) - T_0(s_i - s_2)\right] \quad (3)$$

From the first law, written for this process

$$m_i h_i - m_e h_e = m_2 u_2 - m_1 u_1$$

or because of the previous conditions

$$h_i = u_2$$

substituting for u_2 into Eq. (3), obtain

$$W_{rev} = mT_0(s_2 - s_i)$$

Then from Eq. (1)

$$I = mT_0(s_2 - s_i) \quad (4)$$

From the steam tables for the steam in the line at P = 1.2MPa, T = 350°C

$$u_2 = h_i = 3153.6 \text{ kJ/kg}$$

$$s_i = 7.2121 \text{ kJ/kg-°K}$$

At state 2 we know

$$P = 1.2\text{MPa}, \; u_2 = 3153.6 \text{ kJ/kg}$$

From the steam tables then (by interpolation)

$$v_2 = 0.3016 \text{ m}^3\text{/kg}$$

$$s_2 = 7.7236 \text{ kJ/kg-°K}$$

Then for the mass finally inside the container

$$m_2 = m = \frac{V}{v_2} = \frac{0.5}{0.3016} = 1.658 \text{ kg}$$

For the irreversibility, from Eq. (4)

$$I = 1.658 \times 298(7.7236-7.2121)$$

$$= 258.72 \text{ kJ}$$

AVAILABILITY

• PROBLEM 5-14

A container contains compressed air at 620 kPa, 27°C. If atmospheric conditions are 103 kPa and 27°C calculate the work potential per kg of air.

Solution: The availability for a system neglecting kinetic and potential energies is

$$A.E. = (W_{rev})_{max} - W_{surr.}$$

$$= (U_1 + P_0V_1 - T_0S_1) - (U_\infty + P_0V_\infty - T_0S_\infty)$$

$$= (U_1 - U_\infty) + P_0(V_1 - V_\infty) - T_0(S_1 - S_\infty)$$

However $U_1 = U_\infty$ and hence

$$A.E. = P_0(V_1 - V_\infty) - T_0(S_1 - S_\infty) \tag{1}$$

Assuming air to behave ideally

$$V = \frac{RT}{P}$$

and

$$\Delta S = R \ln \frac{P_1}{P_0} \quad \text{(for this case)}$$

Substituting into Eq. (1) and rearranging

$$A.E. = P_0RT_0\left(\frac{1}{P_1} - \frac{1}{P_0}\right) + T_0R \ln\left(\frac{P_1}{P_0}\right)$$

$$= RT_0\left(\frac{P_0}{P_1} - 1\right) + RT_0 \ln\left(\frac{P_1}{P_0}\right) \tag{2}$$

for air

$$R = 0.287 \text{ kJ/kg-°K}$$

Therefore from Eq. (2)

$$A.E. = 0.287(300)\left(\frac{103}{620} - 1\right)$$

$$+ 0.287(300) \ln\left(\frac{620}{103}\right)$$

$$= 82.75 \text{ kJ/kg}$$

• PROBLEM 5-15

Determine the available energy that can be associated with a 10 m^3 perfect vacuum and its surroundings at a pressure of 0.100 MPa and at a temperature of 300K.

Solution: The Equation of availability for any system is given as

$$\phi = (u + P_0 v - T_0 s) - (u_0 + P_0 v_0 - T_0 s_0) \qquad (1)$$

$$= (u-u_0) + P_0(v-v_0) - T_0(s-s_0)$$

For a perfect vacuum

$$m = 0,\ (u-u_0) = 0,\ (s-s_0) = 0,\ v_0 = 0$$

so the only terms left for the computation of the available energy are the initial pressure (or pressure of the surroundings), and the volume that this vacuum takes in space.

With these in mind get

$$\phi = P_0 v$$

$$= (0.10) \times (10) \times 10^6 \text{ N-m}$$

$$= 1,000 \text{ kJ}$$

• PROBLEM 5-16

In a particular flow system 1 lbm of saturated water at 400°F is heated at constant pressure until it is saturated vapor. If the reservoir temperature is 40°F, calculate the availability of the heat transferred to the water. Assume the process to be reversible and the heat of vaporisation at 400°F to be 826.0 Btu/lbm.

Solution: In a constant pressure process, the work is zero, and the reversible heat

$$Q_{rev} = h_{fg} = \text{the heat of vaporisation.}$$

This process is reversible, and so

$$Q_{rev} = \int_1^2 Tds$$

The entropy change is

$$\Delta S = \frac{Q_{rev}}{T_A} = \frac{h_{fg}}{T_A}$$

The availability of heat is obtained by

$$A.E. = \int_{S_1}^{S_2} Tds - T_0 \Delta s$$

or

$$A.E. = h_{fg} - \frac{T_0}{T_A} h_{fg}$$

$$= (1 - \frac{T_0}{T_A}) h_{fg}$$

Using the given values of T_A, T_0, and h_{fg}, [Note: 40F = 500R],

$$A.E. = (1 - \frac{500}{960})826$$

$$= 396 \text{ Btu}$$

The amount of heat now available for conversion to work in reference to the reservoir at 40°F is 396 Btu.

• **PROBLEM 5-17**

An automobile battery is able to deliver 5.2 MJ of electrical energy to start a car. Suppose compressed air at 7MPa, 25°C were to be used for doing the same work. What will be the volume of the tank required in order for the compressed air to have an availability of 5.2 MJ?

Solution: The availability of air at 7 MPa, 25°C is given by

$$\phi = (u-u_0) - T_0(s-s_0) + P_0(v-v_0)$$

where

$$v = \frac{RT}{P}$$

$$= \frac{0.287 \times 298.15}{7000}$$

$$= 0.01222 \text{ m}^3/\text{kg}$$

$$v_0 = \frac{RT_0}{P_0}$$

$$= \frac{0.287 \times 298.15}{100}$$

$$= 0.8557 \text{ m}^3/\text{kg}.$$

$$\therefore \ \phi = 0 - 298.15\left(0 - 0.287 \ln \frac{7000}{100}\right)$$

$$+ 100\ (0.01222 - 0.8557)$$

$$= 279.2 \text{ kJ/kg}$$

For an availability of 5.2 MJ, the mass of air required is

$$m = \frac{5.2\text{MJ}}{\phi} = \frac{5200\text{kJ}}{279.2\text{kJ/kg}}$$

$$= 18.625 \text{ kg}$$

The volume of the tank then is,

$$V = mv$$

$$= 18.625\ (0.01222)$$

$$= 0.2276 \text{ m}^3.$$

• PROBLEM 5-18

Calculate the specific availability function ϕ for steam at a pressure of 100 lb/in^2 and a temperature of 1000°F in an environment of pressure 14.7 lb/in^2 and a temperature of 60°F. Also calculate the specific availability of steam in a process having the same initial state as given above and whose final state is at a pressure of 40 lb/in^2 and a temperature of 500°F.

Solution: For $P = 100\ lb/in^2$ and

$T = 1000°F$,

from the steam tables;

$v = 8.656\ ft^3/lbm$

$h = 1530.8\ Btu/lbm$

$s = 1.9193\ Btu/lbm\text{-}°R$

Using the equation:

$$u = h - Pv$$

obtain

$$u = 1530.8\ \frac{Btu}{lbm} - 100 \times 144\ \frac{lb}{ft^2} \times 8.656\ \frac{ft^3}{lbm} \times \frac{1}{778}(ft\ lb/Btu)^{-1}$$

$$= 1370.6\ \frac{Btu}{lbm}$$

and $\phi = u + P_0 v - T_0 s$

$$\phi = 1370.6\ \frac{Btu}{lbm} + 14.7 \times 144\ \frac{lb}{ft^2} \times 8.656\ \frac{ft^3}{lbm} \times \frac{1}{778\ ft\ lb/Btu}$$

$$- 520°R \times 1.9193\ \frac{Btu}{lbm°R}$$

$$= 396.2\ \frac{Btu}{lbm}$$

∴ The specific availability function $\phi = 396.2\ \frac{Btu}{lbm}$.

For the final state; i.e. at $P = 40\ lb/in^2$

$T = 500°F$,

from the steam tables,

$$u_2 = 14.168\ \frac{ft^3}{lbm}$$

$$h_2 = 1284.8\ \frac{Btu}{lbm}$$

$$s_2 = 1.8140\ \frac{Btu}{lbm°R}$$

from which $u_2 = 1179.9$ Btu/lbm.

Using the same procedure

$$\phi_2 = 275.2\ \frac{Btu}{lbm}$$

The specific availability of any process is

$$\Delta\phi = \phi_1 - \phi_2$$

$$= (396.2 - 275.2)\ \frac{\text{Btu}}{\text{lbm}}$$

$$= 121.0\ \frac{\text{Btu}}{\text{lbm}}$$

which means that for one pound mass of steam the maximum useful work for any process between these end states is 121.0 Btu.

• PROBLEM 5-19

A turbine takes in air at 825K, 690 kPa and expands it to 138 kPa and 585K. Assuming air to be an ideal gas, calculate

a) the available energy of the air taken in ,

b) the loss of available energy in the turbine,and

c) T_0, the isentropic exit temperature, or, the lowest available temperature.

Solution: a) The available energy of the air taken in can be obtained from the equation

$$(\text{A.E.})_{1-0} = h_1 - h_0$$

$$h_1 - h_0 = c_p(T_1 - T_0)$$

but

$$\frac{T_0}{T_1} = \left(\frac{P_0}{P_1}\right)^{\frac{(k-1)}{k}} \qquad (1)$$

$$T_0 = 825\left(\frac{138}{690}\right)^{\frac{0.4}{1.4}}$$

$$= 520.9\ \text{K}$$

Therefore

$$(\text{A.E.})_{1-0} = 1.0046(825 - 520.9)$$

$$= 305.5\ \text{kJ/kg}$$

b) The loss of available energy in the turbine can be obtained from the equation

$$(A.E.)_{loss} = T_0(s_0 - s_2)$$

$$= -T_0(s_2 - s_0)$$

and

$$(s_2 - s_0) = c_p \ln\left(\frac{T_2}{T_0}\right)$$

$$= 1.0046 \ln\left(\frac{585}{520.9}\right)$$

$$s_2 - s_0 = 0.1160 \text{ kJ/kg-K}$$

$$\therefore (A.E.)_{loss} = -(520.9)(0.1160)$$

$$= -60.4 \text{ kJ/kg}$$

c) From equation (1) the lowest available temperature is 520.9K.

• PROBLEM 5-20

A chamber is divided into two equal compartments each holding 100 lbm of water at a pressure of 25 psia, and at temperatures of 140°F and 240°F respectively. Heat is then transferred between the two compartments until their temperature equalizes. If the lowest available sink temperature (refrigerator) is 40°F, and water is assumed to have a constant specific heat of 1.0 Btu/lb-°F, calculate the decrease in available energy associated with the process.

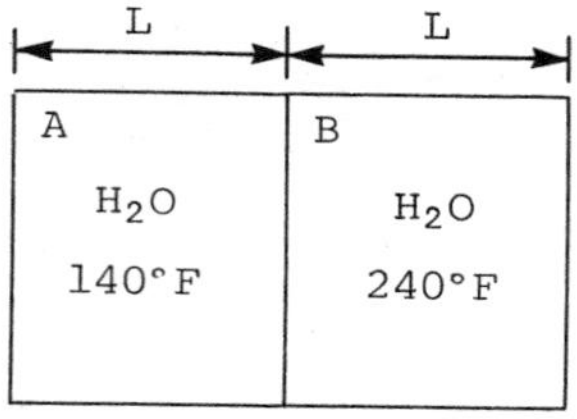

Solution: When heat transfer is involved between two systems, when a temperature equalization process occurs, the heat rejected by the hot reservoir is equal to the heat received by the cold reservoir.

Therefore

$$mc_p \Delta T_{high} = mc_p \Delta T_{low}$$

However the masses are equal, and since water is present in both compartments, the specific heats are the same and so

$$T_B - T_2 = T_2 - T_A$$

where T_2 is the equalization temperature, and is the same for compartments A and B.

The change in unavailable energy for the high temperature medium (compartment B) is,

$$U.E.\Big|_B = T_L \Delta S_B$$

$$= mc_p T_L \int_{T_1}^{T_2} \frac{dT}{T} \qquad (2)$$

or

$$U.E.\Big|_B = mc_p T_L \ln \frac{T_2}{T_B}$$

$$= 100(1)(500) \ln \left(\frac{650}{700}\right)$$

$$= -3705 \text{ Btu}$$

The change in unavailable energy for the low temperature medium (compartment A) is,

$$U.E.\Big|_A = mc_p T_L \ln \left(\frac{T_2}{T_A}\right)$$

$$= 100(1)(500) \ln \left(\frac{650}{600}\right)$$

$$= 4000 \text{ Btu.}$$

solving for T_2,

$$T_2 = \frac{T_B + T_A}{2}$$

$$= \frac{240 + 140}{2}$$

$$= 190°F = 650°R$$

The available energy is defined as

$$A.E. = Q - U.E. \quad (1)$$

where

Q = heat transfer for the system

$U.E.$ = unavailable energy

The heat transferred is

$$Q_{in} = Q_{out} = mc_p(T_B - T_2)$$

$$= (100)(1)(700 - 650)$$

$$= 5000 \text{ Btu}$$

From Eq. (1) for compartment A

$$A.E.\Big|_A = 5000 - 4000 = +1000 \text{ Btu}$$

and for compartment B

$$A.E.\Big|_B = -5000 - (-3705) = -1295 \text{ Btu}$$

The energy and entropy values are summarized in the following table.

Medium	Q	U.E	A.E	ΔS
Hot	−5000	−3705	−1295	−7.41
Cold	+5000	+4000	+1000	+8.00
Mixture	0	+295	−295	+0.59

No heat is added or rejected from the mixture as a whole, but the heat transfer between the two compartments increased the unavailable energy of the mixture at the expense of the available energy oı the constituents.

In a Babcock and Wilcox boiler, water evaporates at a constant temperature of 400°F. Hot gases from a fire having a specific heat of 0.24 Btu/lbm°F and a temperature of 2000°F transfer heat to the boiler. The final temperature of the gases is 1000°F. On the basis of a pound of water evaporated, calculate the increase in entropy of the combined system. Take the latent heat of water to be 826.0 Btu/lbm.

b) If the temperature of the surroundings is 80°F calculate the increase in unavailable energy due to this irreversible heat transfer.

Solution: a) The entropy change of the combined system of gas and water, is the entropy change of the parts of the system which can be found by assuming in each case a reversible process between the actual end states of the individual systems.

Since the temperature of water is constant, the entropy change is

$$\Delta s = \frac{Q}{T} = \frac{826}{860} = 0.965 \text{ Btu/°R}$$

For the gas, per pound of water evaporated Q = -826 Btu.

$$\therefore \ \Delta s_g = \int_{rev} \frac{dQ}{T} = mc_p \int \frac{dT}{T}$$

$$= mc_p(\ln T_2 - \ln T_1)$$

$$= \frac{Q}{\Delta T_g} (\ln T_2 - \ln T_1)$$

$$= 0.826 (\ln 1460 - \ln 1260)$$

$$= -0.431 \text{ Btu/R}$$

The total change is $\Delta s = \Delta s_w + \Delta s_g$

$$= 0.965 - 0.431$$

$$= 0.534 \text{ Btu/R.}$$

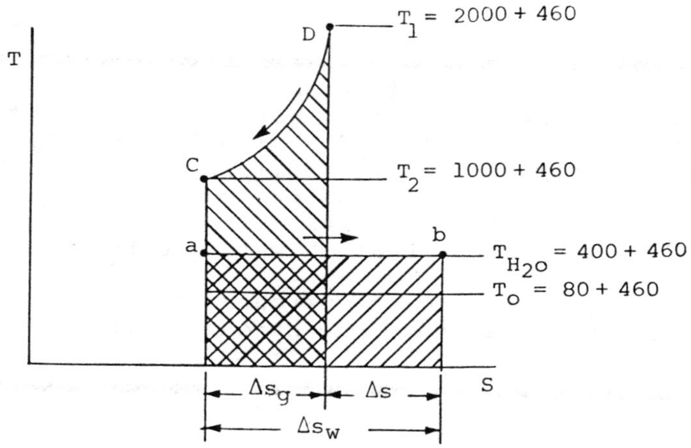

b)

The two assumed reversible processes are shown in the T-S diagram. In this figure the gas is cooled from D to C by transferring heat to the evaporating water, which changes from a to b. Next consider the heat from the gas to be transferred reversibly to a reversible heat engine. The heat engine will receive the heat along the path C-D. This is because the reversible heat transfer requires zero temperature difference as each increment of heat is transferred. In the figure, the heat engine will reject at T_0 a heat quantity $T_0\Delta s_{CD}$ or $-T\Delta s_g$. The increase in unavailable energy due to this transfer of heat from gas to water is

$$T_0\Delta s_w - (-T_0\Delta s_g) = T_0\Delta s$$

where Δs is for the combined system as shown in part a).

$$T_0\Delta s = 540\ (0.534)$$

$$= 289 \text{ Btu}$$

$$Q - T_0\Delta s_g = 826 - 540\ (0.431) = 594 \text{ Btu}$$

Therefore due to the irreversible transfer of heat there is a loss of

$$\frac{289}{594} \times 100$$

= 49% of the available energy.

• PROBLEM 5-22

Superheated steam enters an adiabatic turbine at 400 lbf/in^2, 600°F and leaves at a pressure of 50 lbf/in^2 and a quality of 99.5%. If the temperature of the surroundings (T_0) is 60°F, calculate the turbine efficiency, effectiveness, and loss of available energy.

Solution: The efficiency of the turbine is defined as

$$\eta = \frac{w_{act}}{w_{ideal}} \tag{1}$$

where

$$w_{act} = w_{12a}$$

$$w_{ideal} = w_{12i}$$

From the steam tables, at the entrance of the turbine

$P_1 = 400\ lbf/in^2$ $\quad T_1 = 600°F$

$h_1 = 1306.9\ Btu/lbm$ $\quad s_1 = 1.5894\ Btu/lbm\text{-}°R$

At the exit, from the Mollier chart

$P_2 = 50\ lbf/in^2$ $\quad x = 0.995$

$h_2 = 1169.5\ Btu/lbm$ $\quad s_2 = 1.6522\ Btu/lbm\text{-}°R$

For the isentropic expansion (ideal case) from the Mollier diagram

$P_{2i} = 50\ lbf/in^2$ $\quad x = 0.995$

$h_{2i} = 1122\ Btu/lbm$ $\quad s_{2i} = s_1 = 1.5894\ Btu/lbm\text{-}°R$

With these values and Q = 0

$$w_{12a} = h_1 - h_2$$

$$= 1306.9 - 1169.5 = 137.4\ Btu/lbm$$

and

$$w_{12} = h_1 - h_{2i}$$

$$= 1306.9 - 1122$$

$$= 184.9\ Btu/lbm.$$

Then from Eq. (1)

$$\eta = \frac{137.4}{184.9} = 0.745 = 74.5\%$$

The effectiveness of a turbine is defined as the ratio of the actual work over the specific availability function

$$\varepsilon = \left| \frac{w_{12a}}{\phi} \right| \tag{2}$$

The availability function is

$$\phi = g_{2a} - g_1 \tag{3}$$

where

$$g \equiv h - T_0 s = \text{Gibbs function}$$

Then

$$g_1 = h_1 - T_0 s_1$$

$$= 1306.9 - (520)(1.5894)$$

$$= 480.4 \text{ Btu/lbm}$$

$$g_{2a} = h_{2a} - T_0 s_{2a}$$

$$= 1169.5 - (520)(1.6522)$$

$$= 310.4 \text{ Btu/lbm}$$

From Eq. (3)

$$\phi = 310.4 - 480.4 = -170 \text{ Btu/lbm}$$

From Eq. (2)

$$\varepsilon = \left|\frac{137.4}{-170}\right| = 0.81 = 81\%$$

The loss of available energy is defined as

$$\Delta(\text{A.E.}) = w_{12a} + \phi$$

$$= 137.4 - 170$$

$$= -32.6 \text{ Btu/lbm.}$$

A piston-cylinder device has an initial contained volume of 0.1 ft^3 and contains steam at an initial state of 160 psia, 500°F. The steam is then expanded to 20 psia, and as a result of this process 0.50 Btu of heat is transferred to the system. Assuming atmospheric conditions to be 14.7 psia, 80°F calculate

(a) the actual useful work done by the system, and

(b) the change in availability during the process.

Solution: (a) Actual useful work is called the difference between the total work that the system is capable of doing and the work done in moving the piston against the atmosphere or the PdV work. Hence

$$W_{use} = W_{tot} - W_{atm} \tag{1}$$

From the conservation of energy equation

$$W_{tot} = m(u_2 - u_1) - Q \tag{2}$$

and for the boundary work

$$W_{atm} = -P_0(V_2 - V_1) \tag{3}$$

where

$$P_0 = 14.7 \text{ psia}$$

Substituting Eq. (2) and (3) into Eq. (1), obtain

$$W_{use} = m(u_2 - u_1) - Q + P_0(V_2 - V_1) \tag{4}$$

From the steam tables at 500°F and 160 psia

$$u_1 = 1171.2 \text{ Btu/lbm}$$

$$v_1 = 3.44 \text{ ft}^3\text{/lbm}$$

$$s_1 = 1.6518 \text{ Btu/lbm-°R}$$

The mass of the system is then

$$m = \frac{V_1}{v_1} = \frac{0.1}{3.44} = 0.0291 \text{ lbm}$$

The final state can then be determined in the following matter

$$v_2 = v_1\left(\frac{V_2}{V_1}\right)$$

$$= 0.0291\left(\frac{0.65}{0.1}\right)$$

$$= 22.36\ ft^3/lbm$$

Then from the superheated steam tables at 20 psia and a specific volume of 22.36 ft^3/lbm

$$T_2 = 300°F$$

$$u_2 = 1108.7\ Btu/lbm$$

$$s_2 = 1.7805\ Btu/lbm\text{-}°R$$

Substituting the numerical values into Eq. (4)

$$W_{use} = 0.0291(1108.7 - 1171.2) - (-0.5) + \frac{14.7(0.65-0.1)(144)}{778}$$

$$= -1.82 + 0.50 + 1.50 = -0.82\ Btu$$

(b) The change in availability, associated with this process, is found using the equation

$$\phi = (U_2 - U_1) + P_0(V_2 - V_1) - T_0(S_2 - S_1)$$

or on a per mass basis

$$\phi = m(u_2 - u_1) + P_0(V_2 - V_1) - mT_0(s_2 - s_1)$$

$$= -1.82 + 1.50 - 0.0291(540)(1.7805 - 1.6518)$$

$$= -2.34\ Btu.$$

The availability is also known as the maximum useful work. For this process the actual useful work is approximately 35% of the maximum useful work.

• PROBLEM 5-24

A cylinder contains 10 lbm of water at 240°F. Ten more lbm of water at 140°F are mixed with the previous ten inside the cylinder at a constant pressure of 30 lbf/in^2. Assuming a reference temperature of 40°F and a constant pressure specific heat of 1.0 Btu/lbm-°F, determine the change in available and unavailable energies when the temperatures are equalized.

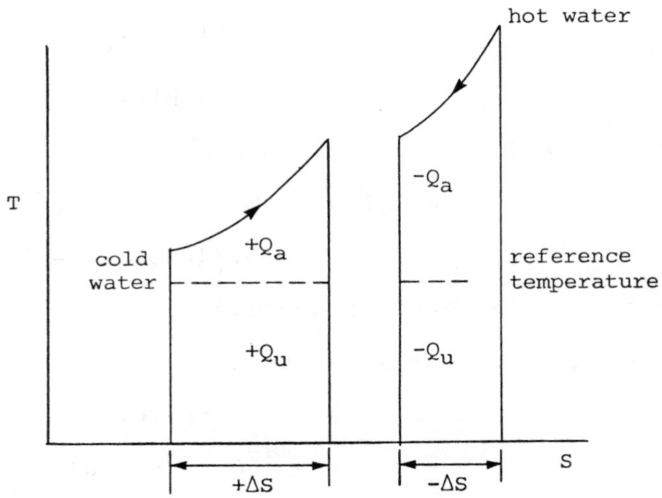

FIG. Change in entropy when hot water is mixed with cold water.

Solution: The final temperature T_F must be determined first. Noting that whatever heat was lost by the higher temperature water, was added to the lower temperature water

$$Q_{in} = Q_{out}$$

or since both masses are the same

$$T_A - T_F = T_F - T_B$$

or solving for T_F

$$T_F = \frac{T_A + T_B}{2}$$

$$= \frac{240 + 140}{2}$$

$$= 190°F = 650°R$$

For the hot water

$$Q = mc_p(T_2 - T_1)$$

$$= 10(1)(650 - 700)$$

$$= -500 \text{ Btu}$$

$$\Delta S = mc_p \ln\left(\frac{T_2}{T_A}\right)$$

$$= 10(1)\ln\left(\frac{650}{700}\right)$$

$$= -0.74 \text{ Btu/°R}$$

For the change in unavailable energy

$$\Delta(\text{U.E.}) = \Delta S T_0$$

$$= -0.74(500) = -370 \text{ Btu}$$

The minus sign indicates a decrease.

For the change in available energy

$$\Delta(\text{A.E.}) = Q - \Delta(\text{U.E.})$$

$$= -500 - (-370)$$

$$= -130 \text{ Btu}$$

Next consider the cold water

$$Q = mc_p(T_2 - T_B)$$

$$= 10(1)(650 - 600)$$

$$= +500 \text{ Btu}$$

$$\Delta S = mc_p \ln\left(\frac{T_2}{T_A}\right)$$

$$= 10(1)\ln\left(\frac{650}{600}\right)$$

$$= 0.795 \text{ Btu/°R}$$

For the unavailable energy

$$\Delta(\text{U.E.}) = \Delta S T_0$$

$$= 0.795(500)$$

$$= 398 \text{ Btu}$$

For the available energy

$$\Delta(\text{A.E.}) = Q - \Delta(\text{U.E.})$$

$$= 500 - 398$$

$$= +102 \text{ Btu}$$

The total change in the available energy is

$$\Delta(\text{A.E.})_{\text{Tot}} = \Delta(\text{A.E.})_{\text{cold}} + \Delta(\text{A.E.})_{\text{hot}}$$

$$= 102 - 130$$

$$= -28 \text{ Btu} \quad \text{(decrease)}$$

The total change in the unavailable energy is

$$\Delta(\text{U.E.})_{\text{Tot}} = \Delta(\text{U.E.})_{\text{cold}} + \Delta(\text{U.E.})_{\text{hot}}$$

$$= 398 - 370$$

$$= 28 \text{ Btu} \quad \text{(increase)}$$

The change in entropy of the two quantities is shown in the figure, and the net change in entropy is found to be 0.055 Btu/°R.

• PROBLEM 5-25

Hot gases with a mean specific heat of 0.26 Btu/lbm-°F leave a gas turbine at 1200°F and are used to heat water in a constant pressure heater. Water enters the heater at 200°F and its temperature rises as a result of heat transfer with the gases. At the exit of the heater the temperature and mass flowrate of the gases are measured to be 300°F and 200,000 lbm/hr respectively, and the mass flowrate of water is measured to be 250,000 lbm/hr. Assuming the lowest available sink temperature to be 100°F and water to have a mean specific heat of 1.02 Btu/lbm-°F determine the available and unavailable energies for the process.

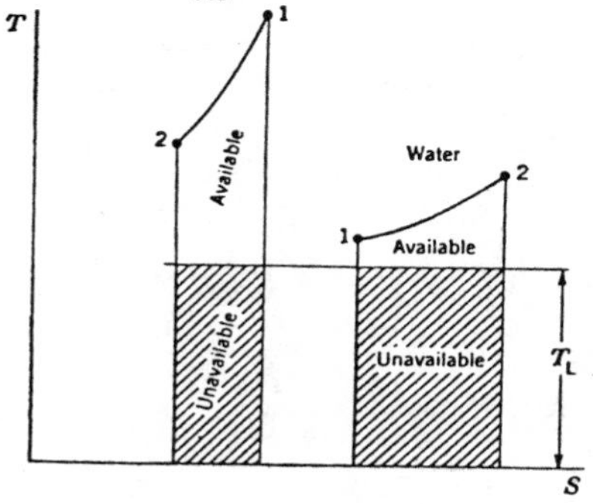

Figure 1. Irreresible Heat Transfer

Solution: In this process, the heat lost by the hot gases which serve as the heat reservoir, are added to the water which is the system. Therefore

$$Q_{gas} = Q_{water}$$

or

$$m_g c_p (T_1 - T_2)_{gas} = m_w c_p (T_2 - T_1)_w \qquad (1)$$

Since the temperature at the exit of heater is not known (for water), solving for $T_2)_w$ gives

$$T_2\Big)_w = \frac{\dot{m}_g c_p (T_1 - T_2)_g}{\dot{m}_w c_p} + T_1\Big)_w$$

$$= \frac{200{,}000(0.26)(1200-300)}{250{,}000(1.02)} + 200$$

$$= 183.6 + 200$$

$$= 383.6°F = 843.6°R$$

Fig. 1 shows the available and unavailable energies associated with the process. For the gas the unavailable energy is

$$\phi_u = Q_u = T_L m c_x \ln\left(\frac{T_1}{T_2}\right)$$

$$= (560)(200{,}000)(0.26) \ln\left(\frac{1660}{760}\right)$$

$$= 22{,}850{,}000 \text{ Btu/hr}$$

The available energy is defined as the difference between the heat transferred to the system and the unavailable energy

$$\phi_a = Q_a = Q - \phi_u \qquad (2)$$

Where

$$Q = m_g c_x (T_1 - T_2)_g$$

$$= 200{,}000 \times 0.26(1200 - 300)$$

$$= 46{,}800{,}000 \text{ Btu/hr}$$

Then from Eq. (2), for the gas

$$\phi_a = 46{,}800{,}000 - 22{,}850{,}000$$

$$= 23{,}950{,}000 \text{ Btu/hr}$$

For the water (system)

$$\phi_u = T_L m_w c_x \ln\left(\frac{T_2}{T_1}\right)$$

$$= 560(250{,}000)(1.02) \ln \left(\frac{843.6}{660}\right)$$

$$= 34{,}700{,}000 \text{ Btu/hr.}$$

From Eq. (2), for the water

$$\phi_a = 46{,}800{,}000 - 34{,}700{,}000$$

$$= 12{,}100{,}000 \text{ Btu/hr}$$

For this process

$$\Delta\phi_a = \phi_g - \phi_w$$

$$= 23{,}950{,}000 - 12{,}100{,}000$$

$$= 11{,}850{,}000 \text{ Btu/hr}$$

Therefore in the heat transfer-process, the available energy decreased by the amount $\Delta\phi_a$ and the unavailable energy increased by the same amount. Hence the loss of available energy is 11,850,000 Btu/hr.

CHAPTER 6

THERMODYNAMIC RELATIONS

MAXWELL RELATIONS, GIBS AND HELMHOLTZ FUNCTIONS

• PROBLEM 6-1

Using the Maxwell equation

$$\left(\frac{\partial T}{\partial v}\right)_s = -\left(\frac{\partial p}{\partial s}\right)_v \quad (1)$$

and the mathematical relation

$$\left(\frac{\partial x}{\partial y}\right)_z \left(\frac{\partial y}{\partial z}\right)_x \left(\frac{\partial z}{\partial x}\right)_y = -1 \quad (2)$$

derive the remaining Maxwell relations.

Solution: In principle, functional relations or equations of state exist between any two properties and any other property of a substance. The exact forms of only a few of these are known. So general thermodynamic relations, between partial derivatives of properties are used very extensively. There are four Maxwell equations altogether. One of them is given in the problem, and the rest that will have to be derived are

a) $$\left(\frac{\partial s}{\partial v}\right)_T = \left(\frac{\partial p}{\partial T}\right)_v$$

b) $$\left(\frac{\partial v}{\partial T}\right)_p = -\left(\frac{\partial s}{\partial p}\right)_T$$

and

c) $$\left(\frac{\partial T}{\partial p}\right)_s = \left(\frac{\partial v}{\partial s}\right)_p$$

Each of these four equations express a different relation between p, v, T, and s.

Dividing Eq. (2) by any of the partial derivatives, say $\left(\frac{\partial z}{\partial x}\right)_y$ one obtains

$$\left(\frac{\partial x}{\partial y}\right)_z \left(\frac{\partial y}{\partial z}\right)_x = -\left(\frac{\partial x}{\partial z}\right)_y$$

or $$\left(\frac{\partial x}{\partial z}\right)_y = -\left(\frac{\partial x}{\partial y}\right)_z \left(\frac{\partial y}{\partial z}\right)_x \tag{3}$$

In Eq. (3) x, y, and z are three variables, where one is always dependent on the other two. Thus there are only two independent variables.

a) Let

$$x = s,\ y = T,\ \text{and } z = v$$

Then Eq. (3) takes the form

$$\left(\frac{\partial s}{\partial v}\right)_T = -\left(\frac{\partial s}{\partial T}\right)_v \left(\frac{\partial T}{\partial v}\right)_s$$

From the given Maxwell relation however

$$\left(\frac{\partial T}{\partial v}\right)_s = -\left(\frac{\partial P}{\partial s}\right)_v$$

and so

$$\left(\frac{\partial s}{\partial v}\right)_T = \left(\frac{\partial s}{\partial T}\right)_v \left(\frac{\partial P}{\partial s}\right)_v = \left(\frac{\partial P}{\partial v}\right)_v$$

or

$$\left(\frac{\partial s}{\partial v}\right)_T = \left(\frac{\partial P}{\partial v}\right)_v$$

which is the second Maxwell relation.

b) Letting x = v, y = p, and z = T, Eq. (3) is written as

$$\left(\frac{\partial v}{\partial T}\right)_P = -\left(\frac{\partial v}{\partial P}\right)_T \left(\frac{\partial P}{\partial T}\right)_v$$

From the second Maxwell relation, which was derived

$$\left(\frac{\partial P}{\partial T}\right)_v = \left(\frac{\partial s}{\partial v}\right)_T$$

and thus

$$\left(\frac{\partial v}{\partial T}\right)_p = -\left(\frac{\partial v}{\partial P}\right)_T\left(\frac{\partial s}{\partial v}\right)_T = -\left(\frac{\partial s}{\partial P}\right)_T$$

or

$$\left(\frac{\partial v}{\partial T}\right)_P = -\left(\frac{\partial s}{\partial p}\right)_T$$

This is the third Maxwell relation.

c) Letting x = T, y = s, and Z = p, Eq. (3) takes the form

$$\left(\frac{\partial T}{\partial p}\right)_s = -\left(\frac{\partial T}{\partial s}\right)_p\left(\frac{\partial s}{\partial P}\right)_T$$

From the third Maxwell relation, derived in (b)

$$\left(\frac{\partial s}{\partial p}\right)_T = \left(\frac{\partial v}{\partial T}\right)_p$$

and thus

$$\left(\frac{\partial T}{\partial p}\right)_s = \left(\frac{\partial T}{\partial s}\right)_p\left(\frac{\partial v}{\partial T}\right)_p = \left(\frac{\partial v}{\partial s}\right)_p$$

or

$$\left(\frac{\partial T}{\partial p}\right)_s = \left(\frac{\partial v}{\partial s}\right)_p$$

which is the fourth Maxwell relation.

In all four Maxwell relations it is seen that for the three properties that are involved, one is always dependent on the other two.

• PROBLEM 6-2

Show that more than one function can be transformed to the Gibbs function. The Gibbs function is given as

$$L\begin{bmatrix} & U & \\ S, & & V\end{bmatrix} = G(T, -p, N_i)$$

Solution: The Gibbs function allows to determine the equilibrium composition of any reactive mixture of known pressure and temperature, regardless of whether or not these were kept constant during all of the reaction. Since the electrochemical potential relates the change in the Gibbs function of a mixture, considered as nonreacting, to changes in the amounts of its constituents, it too is very important in chemical thermodynamics.

Since we are looking for one or more functions we can write

$$\psi = \psi(T,-p,N_i)$$

Now $$F = F(T,V,N_i)$$

We need only replace V by -p. This is possible since p is conjugate to V. Then

$$L\begin{bmatrix}F\\V\end{bmatrix} = \left(1 - V\frac{\partial}{\partial V}\right)F$$

$$= U - TS - V\frac{\partial F}{\partial V}$$

$$= U - TS + pV$$

$$= H - TS$$

$$L\begin{bmatrix}F\\V\end{bmatrix} = G(T,-p,N_i)$$

In the same manner, it can be shown, since $H = H(S, -p, N_i)$, that

$$L\begin{bmatrix}H\\S\end{bmatrix} = G(T,-p,N_i)$$

Consequently

$$L\begin{bmatrix}F\\V\end{bmatrix} = L\begin{bmatrix}H\\S\end{bmatrix} = L\begin{bmatrix}U\\S,V\end{bmatrix} = G(T,-p,N_i)$$

• PROBLEM 6-3

Given the following data for diamond and graphite at 25°C and 1 atm

	Diamond	Graphite	Units
$\bar{g}$	1.233	0	Btu/lb mol-°R
v	0.00456	0.00712	ft^3/lbm
β_T	0.16×10^{-6}	3.0×10^{-6}	atm^{-1}

determine the pressure that is needed to make diamonds from graphite at 25°C.

Solution: Graphite and diamond can exist in equilibrium at a particular pressure when both have the same value of the Gibbs function. At 1 atm. pressure the Gibbs function of the diamond is greater than that of Graphite but the rate of increase in the Gibbs function with respect to pressure is greater for the graphite than the diamond. Therefore at some pressure, the two will exist in equilibrium.

Consider the relation

$$dg = v\,dP - s\,dT$$

Since it is a process that takes place at constant temperature this reduces to

$$dg_T = v\,dP_T \qquad (1)$$

Now at any pressure P and the given temperature the specific volume can be found from the following relation, which utilizes the isothermal compressibility factor.

$$v = v^o + \int_{P=1}^{P} \left(\frac{\partial v}{\partial P}\right)_T dP = v^o + \int_{P=1}^{P} \frac{v}{v}\left(\frac{\partial v}{\partial P}\right)_T dP = v^o - \int_{P=1}^{P} v\beta_T\,dP$$

(2)

The superscript ^{o} will be used in this example to indicate the properties at a pressure of 1 atm and a temperature of 25 C.

The specific volume changes only slightly with pressure, so that $v \approx v^o$. Also, assume that β_T is constant and that we are considering a pressure of many atmospheres. With these assumptions this equation can be integrated to give

$$v = v^o - v^o\beta_T P = v^o(1 - \beta_T P) \qquad (3)$$

Substitute this into Eq. (1)

$$dg_T = [v^o(1 - \beta_T P)]dP_T \qquad (4)$$

$$g - g^o = v^o(P - P^o) - v^o\beta_T \frac{(P^2 - P^{o2})}{2}$$

Assume that $P^o << P$ this reduces to

$$g - g^o = v^o\left[P - \frac{\beta_T P^2}{2}\right] \qquad (5)$$

For the graphite, $g^o = 0$ and

$$g_G = v_G^{\,o}\left[P - (\beta_T)_G \frac{P^2}{2}\right]$$

For the diamond, g^o has a definite value and we have

$$g_D = g_D^o + v_D^o\left[P - (\beta_T)_D \frac{P^2}{2}\right]$$

But, at equilibrium the Gibbs function of the graphite and diamond are equal.

$$g_G = g_D$$

Therefore,

$$v_G^o\left[P - (\beta_T)_G \frac{P^2}{2}\right] = g_D^o + v_D^o\left[P - (\beta_T)_D \frac{P^2}{2}\right]$$

$$(v_G^o - v_D^o)P - [v_G^o(\beta_T)_G - v_D^o(\beta_T)_D] \frac{P^2}{2} = g_D^o$$

$$(0.00712 - 0.00456)P$$
$$- (0.00712 \times 3.0 \times 10^{-6} - 0.00456 \times 0.16 \times 10^{-6}) \frac{P^2}{2}$$
$$= \frac{1233}{12} \times \frac{778}{14.7 \times 144}$$

Solving this for P

$$P = 15{,}500 \text{ atm}$$

That is, at 15,500 atm, 25 C, graphite and diamond can exist in equilibrium, and the possibility exists for conversion from graphite to diamonds.

THE CLAUSIUS - CLAPEYRON EQUATION

• PROBLEM 6-4

Derive the Clausius-Clapeyron equation by using the Maxwell relations. Consider the change of state from saturated liquid to saturated vapor of a pure substance.

Solution: The Clausius-Clapeyron equation is a very important relation which involves the saturation pressure and temperature, the specific volumes, and the change of enthalpy associated with a change of phase. With the use of the Clausius-Clapeyron equation a change in a property which cannot be measured directly can be determined if the other properties are known. The derivation of this equation is as follows.

Consider the Maxwell relation

$$\left(\frac{\partial P}{\partial T}\right)_v = \left(\frac{\partial s}{\partial v}\right)_T \quad (1)$$

As the substance changes from saturated-liquid to saturated-vapor it undergoes an isothermal process. Also in the saturation region the pressure and temperature are independent of the volume. Therefore the left hand side of Eq. (1) can be written as

$$\left(\frac{\partial P}{\partial T}\right)_v = \left(\frac{dP}{dT}\right)_{sat}$$

and the right hand side of Eq. (1) can be written as

$$\left(\frac{\partial s}{\partial v}\right)_T = \frac{\Delta s}{\Delta v} = \frac{s_g - s_f}{v_g - v_f} = \frac{s_{fg}}{v_{fg}}$$

Eq. (1) then becomes

$$\left(\frac{dP}{dT}\right)_{sat} = \frac{s_{fg}}{v_{fg}} \quad (2)$$

For the heat added in a constant-pressure vaporization process, the first law gives

$$Q = \Delta u - w$$

$$= u_g - u_f + P(v_g - v_f) \quad (3)$$

From the relation

$$h = u + Pv$$

Eq. (3) takes the form

$$Q = h_g - h_f = h_{fg} \quad (4)$$

However for the isothermal process

$$Q = T(s_g - s_f) = Ts_{fg} \quad (5)$$

From Eqs. (4) and (5)

$$s_{fg} = \frac{h_{fg}}{T} \quad (6)$$

Substituting Eq. (6) into (2) gives

$$\left(\frac{dP}{dT}\right)_{sat} = \frac{h_{fg}}{Tv_{fg}}$$

or

$$\left(\frac{dP}{dT}\right)_{sat} = \frac{s_g - s_f}{v_g - v_f} = \frac{h_g - h_f}{T(v_g - v_f)}$$

which is the standard form of the Clausius-Clapeyron equation. In general, for any change of state the Clausius-Clapeyron equation can be written as

$$\left(\frac{dP}{dT}\right)_{sat} = \frac{s_b - s_a}{v_g - v_a} = \frac{h_b - h_a}{T(v_b - v_a)}$$

where the subscripts a and b designate any two phases.

• PROBLEM 6-5

Determine the melting point increase of ice, due to an increase of pressure of 1 atm. Assume that at 0°C the specific volumes of water and ice are 0.001000 and 0.001091 m^3/kg respectively and the latent heat of fusion is 334 kJ/kg.

Solution: The Clausius-Clapeyron equation is written as

$$dT = \frac{T_{sat} V_{sf} dP}{h_{sf}} \qquad (1)$$

where

$$T_{sat} = 0°C + 273.15 = 273.15°K$$

$$V_{sf} = 0.001000 - 0.001091 = -0.000091 \text{ m}^3/\text{kg}$$

$$h_{sf} = 334 \text{ kJ/kg}$$

and

$$dP = 1 \text{ atm} = 101.325 \text{ kN/m}^2$$

Therefore

$$dT = \frac{273.15(-0.000091)(101.325)}{334}$$

$$= -0.00753°K$$

• PROBLEM 6-6

Calculate Δh_{vap} of liquid oxygen if it boils at 90.15°K and has a vapor pressure of 2.5 atm at 100°K.

Solution: When the temperature is more than 50°C below the critical temperature, the specific volume of the liquid is negligible when compared with the volume of the vapor with which it is in equilibrium. Therefore assume that the specific volume of liquid oxygen is negligible and the vapor to behave as an ideal gas.

The Clausius-Clapeyron equation then becomes

$$\frac{dP}{dT} = \frac{\Delta h_{vap}}{Tv_{vap}} = \frac{\Delta h_v}{TRT/P} = \frac{\Delta h_v P}{RT^2}$$

$$\frac{dP}{P} = \frac{\Delta h_v}{R} \cdot \frac{dT}{T^2} \qquad (1)$$

Assume Δh_v to be a constant. Integrate equation (1)

$$\ln\left(\frac{P_2}{P_1}\right) = \frac{\Delta h_v}{R}\left(\frac{1}{T_1} - \frac{1}{T_2}\right) \qquad (2)$$

$$\ln\left(\frac{2.50}{1.00}\right) = \frac{\Delta h_v}{1.98\ \text{cal/mol°K}}\left(\frac{1}{90.15\text{°K}} - \frac{1}{100\text{°K}}\right)$$

$$\Delta h_v = 1658\ \frac{\text{cal}}{\text{g-mol}}$$

• PROBLEM 6-7

> On a very cold day in Alaska the temperature is measured to be -60°C. Assuming atmospheric pressure to be 100 kPa, calculate the value of the saturation pressure of the water vapor in the air.

Solution: This problem could easily be done by using the steam tables for the compressed liquid. However, the values in the table do not go below -40° C. The differences in enthalpy between the solid and gas states are relatively constant in this range. Therefore the Clausius-Clapeyron equation can be used with limits at -40° C and -60° C.

Hence

$$\int_1^2 \frac{dP}{P} = \int_1^2 \frac{h_{ig}\, dT}{RT^2} \qquad (1)$$

or

$$\ln\left(\frac{P_2}{P_1}\right) = \frac{h_{ig}}{R}\left[\frac{T_2 - T_1}{T_1 T_2}\right] \qquad (2)$$

For water vapor

$$R = 0.46152 \text{ kJ/kg-°K}$$

From the steam tables at T = -40°C

$$h_{ig} = 2838.9 \text{ kJ/kg}; \; P_2 = 0.0129 \text{ kPa}$$

For the consistency of units

$$T_2 = -40 + 273.2 = 233.2°\text{K}$$

$$T_1 = -60 + 273.2 = 213.2°\text{K}$$

Eq. (2) then gives

$$\ln\left(\frac{P_2}{P_1}\right) = \frac{2838.9}{0.46152}\left[\frac{233.2 - 213.2}{233.2 \times 213.2}\right]$$

$$= 2.4744$$

or

$$\frac{P_2}{P_1} = 11.87$$

Then

$$\frac{0.0129}{P_1} = 11.87$$

or

$$P_1 = 0.00109 \text{ kPa}$$

• **PROBLEM 6-8**

What is the pressure inside a boiler which contains liquid water and steam at a temperature of 225°F. Assume that the enthalpy of vaporization of water at 212°F, 1 atm is 970.3 Btu/lbm and the specific volume of the vapor and liquid phases are 26.80 and 0.01672 ft^3/lbm respectively.

Solution: An equation that relates the slope of the saturation pressure-temperature line with the latent heat and the change in volume during a phase transformation is the Clausius-Clapeyron equation. This relation is useful for checking the consistency of measurements or for calculating one of these properties given data on the other two.

The Clausius-Clapeyron equation can be written in the form

$$dP = \frac{\Delta h_v}{\Delta v} \cdot \frac{dT}{T} \tag{1}$$

where the values of Δh_v and Δv are assumed to be constant over small temperature differences. Therefore Eq. (1) can be integrated to yield

$$P_2 - P_1 = \frac{\Delta h_v}{\Delta v} \ln\left(\frac{T_2}{T_1}\right) \tag{2}$$

From the statement of the problem

$$\Delta h_v = 970.3 \frac{Btu}{lbm} \times 778 \frac{ft\text{-}lbf}{Btu} = 754{,}893.4 \text{ ft-lbf/lbm}$$

$$\Delta v = v_g - v_l$$

$$= 26.80 - 0.01672$$

$$= 26.78328 \cong 26.78 \text{ ft}^3/\text{lbm}$$

$$T_1 = 212 + 460 = 672°R$$

$$T_2 = 225 + 460 = 685°R$$

For the consistency of units

$$P_1 = 1 \text{ atm} \times \frac{14.7 \text{ lbf/in}^2}{1 \text{ atm}} \times \frac{144 \text{ in}^2}{\text{ft}^2} = 2116 \text{ lbf/ft}^2$$

From Eq. (1) then

$$P_2 - 2116 = \frac{754{,}893.4}{26.78} \times \ln\left(\frac{685}{672}\right)$$

$$= 540.11$$

or

$$P_2 = 540.11 + 2116 = 2656.11 \text{ lbf/ft}^2$$

or

$$P_2 = 18.45 \text{ lbf/in}^2$$

• PROBLEM 6-9

An ice skating rink contains ice at -10°C. Calculate the pressure that an ice skate blade must exert to allow smooth ice skating at this temperature. Assume that Δh_{fusion} = 1440 cal/g-mol.

$$\rho_{liq} = 1.0\ g/_{cm^3}\ ,\ \rho_{ice} = 0.917\ gm/_{cm^3}$$

Solution: When pressure is exerted by the skate blade on the ice, a thin layer of ice melts and the skate blade glides over this thin lubricating layer.

The Clausius-Clapeyron equation will be used to solve this problem.

$$\left(\frac{dP}{dT}\right)_{eq} = \frac{\Delta h}{\Delta v T}$$

Multiply by dT and integrate:

$$\int_{P_1}^{P_2} dP = \int_{T_1}^{T_2} \frac{\Delta h}{\Delta v}\frac{dT}{T}$$

or

$$P_2 - P_1 = \frac{\Delta h}{\Delta v} \ln\left(\frac{T_2}{T_1}\right) \qquad \text{(a)}$$

But at P = 1 atm, T_1 = 0°C. Since P_2 is desired at which T_2 = -10°C, use equation (a) directly: For the consistency of units

$$P_1 = 1 \text{ atm} = 1.013 \times 10^5 \text{ N/m}^2$$

$$T_1 = 0°C = 273°K$$

$$T_2 = -10°C = 263°K$$

$$\Delta h = 1440 \text{ cal/g-mol} = 3.34 \times 10^5 \text{ J/kg} = 3.34 \times 10^5 \text{ Nm/kg}$$

$$v^{liq} = \frac{1}{\rho_L} = 1 \text{ cm}^3/\text{gm} = 1.000 \times 10^{-3} \text{ m}^3/\text{kg}$$

$$v^{sol} = \frac{1}{\rho_S} = 1.091 \text{ cm}^3/\text{gm} = 1.091 \times 10^{-3} \text{ m}^3/\text{kg}$$

Therefore

$$P_2 - 1.013 \times 10^5 (\text{N/m}^2) = \frac{3.34 \times 10^5 \text{ Nm/kg}}{(1.000 - 1.091) \times 10^{-3} \text{ m}^3/\text{kg}} \ln\left(\frac{263}{273}\right)$$

$$= \left[-\frac{3.34 \times 10^5}{9.1 \times 10^{-5}} \ln (0.963)\right] \text{N/m}^2$$

$$P_2 - 1.01 \times 10^5 \text{ N/m}^2 = 1.38 \times 10^8 \text{ N/m}^2$$

or

$$P_2 = 1.38 \times 10^8 \text{ N/m}^2 = 1.36 \times 10^3 \text{ atm} = 20.0 \times 10^3 \text{psi}$$

This pressure is clearly quite high and is achieved with the ice skate blade by having only a small portion of the blade surface contact the ice at any given time.

• PROBLEM 6-10

Show that the vaporization line and sublimation line for water do not have the same slopes at the triple point.

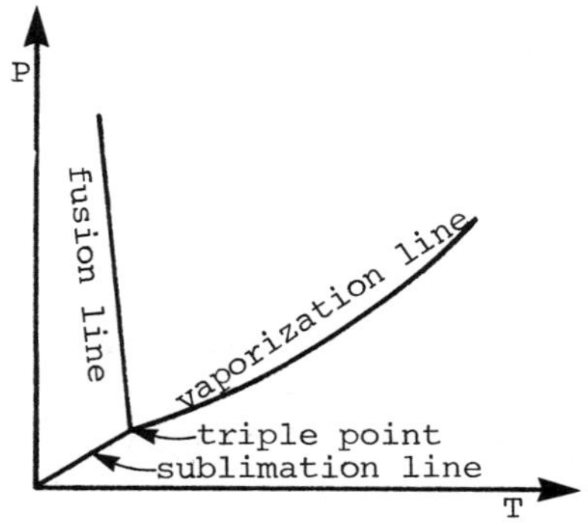

Solution: Let the slopes be $\frac{dp}{dT}$ for the sublimation and vaporization lines. If the slopes are not the same then

$$\left(\frac{dp}{dT}\right)_{sub} - \left(\frac{dp}{dT}\right)_{vap} \neq 0.$$

At the triple point

$$\frac{h_{fg}}{T_C} = s_{fg}$$

and

$$\frac{h_{ig}}{T_c} = s_{ig}$$

where the subscripts, i, f, and g denote the solid, liquid, and vapor states respectively.

Using the Clausius-Clapeyron equation

$$\left(\frac{dp}{dT}\right)_{sub} - \left(\frac{dp}{dT}\right)_{vap} = \frac{s_{ig}}{v_{fg}} - \frac{s_{fg}}{v_{fg}}$$

At the triple point, $s_{ig} = s_{if} + s_{fg}$ and

$$V_{ig} = V_{if} + V_{fg}$$

$$\left(\frac{dp}{dT}\right)_{sub_{T.P.}} - \left(\frac{dp}{dT}\right)_{vap_{T.P.}}$$

$$= \frac{(s_{if} + s_{fg})V_{fg} - s_{fg}(V_{if} + V_{fg})}{V_{fg}(V_{if} + V_{fg})}$$

$$= \frac{s_{if} V_{fg} - s_{fg} V_{if}}{V_{fg}(V_{if} + V_{fg})}$$

Noting that s_{if} is smaller than s_{fg}, and V_{if} is much smaller than V_{fg}, the above expression can be approximated as

$$\left(\frac{dP}{dT}\right)_{sub_{T.P.}} - \left(\frac{dP}{dT}\right)_{vap_{T.P.}} \cong \frac{s_{if}}{V_{fg}}$$

Since both s_{if} and V_{fg} are positive, the slope of the sublimation line is greater than that of the vaporization line at the triple point.

ENTHALPY, ENTROPY, AND INTERNAL ENERGY

• PROBLEM 6-11

Express $(\partial h/\partial P)_g$ in terms of P, v, T, C_p, C_v, and absolute entropy, s.

Solution: Begin by substituting the dh property relation for the dh term in the numerator:

$$\left(\frac{\partial h}{\partial P}\right)_g = T\left(\frac{\partial s}{\partial P}\right)_g + v\left(\frac{\partial P}{\partial P}\right)_g = T\left(\frac{\partial s}{\partial P}\right)_g + v$$

Now bring g into the derivatives by application of the triple-product expansion.

$$\left(\frac{\partial h}{\partial P}\right)_g = -T\frac{\left(\frac{\partial g}{\partial P}\right)_s}{\left(\frac{\partial g}{\partial s}\right)_P} + v$$

Now eliminate g with the dg property relation:

$$\left(\frac{\partial h}{\partial P}\right)_g = -T\left[\frac{-s\left(\frac{\partial T}{\partial P}\right)_s + v}{\left(-s\frac{\partial T}{\partial s}\right)_P + v\left(\frac{\partial P}{\partial s}\right)_P}\right] + v$$

But $(\partial P/\partial s)_P = 0$, thus

$$\left(\frac{\partial h}{\partial P}\right)_g = -T\left[\frac{-s\left(\frac{\partial T}{\partial P}\right)_s + v}{-s\left(\frac{\partial T}{\partial s}\right)_P}\right] + v$$

$$= -T\left[\left(\frac{\partial T}{\partial P}\right)_s\left(\frac{\partial s}{\partial T}\right)_P - \frac{v}{s}\left(\frac{\partial s}{\partial T}\right)_P\right] + v$$

Now use the triple product on the first term in parentheses:

$$= T\left[\left(\frac{\partial s}{\partial P}\right)_T + \frac{v}{s}\left(\frac{\partial s}{\partial T}\right)_P\right] + v$$

But $(\partial s/\partial P)_T = -(\partial v/\partial T)_P$ from the Maxwell equations, and

$$\left(\frac{\partial s}{\partial T}\right)_P = \frac{C_P}{T}$$

Thus the derivative is finally expressed as

$$\left(\frac{\partial h}{\partial P}\right)_g = -T\left(\frac{\partial v}{\partial T}\right)_P + v\left(\frac{C_P}{s} + 1\right)$$

The absolute entropy cannot be reduced, so this is the simplest form possible.

• PROBLEM 6-12

Obtain an expression for the entropy change as a function of pressure and temperature

Solution: Writing the first law in differential form for a reversible nonflow process with 1 pound of ideal gas as the system, gives:

$$Tds = du + p\,\frac{dv}{J} \tag{1}$$

Differentiating the enthalpy equation $h = u + \frac{pv}{J}$ gives:

$$dh = du + \frac{pdv}{J} + \frac{vdp}{J} \tag{2}$$

or

$$du + \frac{pdv}{J} = dh - \frac{vdp}{J} \qquad (3)$$

Substituting the value of du + pdv/J of equation (3) into equation (1) gives:

$$Tds = dh - v\,\frac{dp}{J} \qquad (4)$$

But $dh = c_p dT$, and $v = RT/p$.

Thus

$$Tds = C_p dT - \frac{RT}{J}\frac{dp}{p} \qquad (5)$$

Dividing by T gives the required expression:

$$ds = c_p\,\frac{dT}{T} - \frac{R}{J}\frac{dp}{p}$$

• PROBLEM 6-13

a) Express dh as a function of C_p, C_v, P, v, and T, and

b) Express ds in terms of dT and dP.

Solution: a) dh can be expressed in terms of dT and dP or dv, or dv and dP, but dT and dP will yield the simplest expression. The property relation for dh is

$$dh = T\,ds + v\,dP$$

Assume that

$$h = h(T,P)$$

The total differential for enthalpy may be expressed as

$$dh = \left(\frac{\partial h}{\partial T}\right)_P dT + \left(\frac{\partial h}{\partial P}\right)_T dP$$

But

$$\left(\frac{\partial h}{\partial T}\right)_P = C_P$$

Therefore

$$dh = C_P dT + \left(\frac{\partial h}{\partial P}\right)_T dP$$

$(\partial h/\partial P)_T$ can be determined from division of the dh property relation by dP at constant T to yield

$$\left(\frac{\partial h}{\partial P}\right)_T = \left(\frac{\partial s}{\partial P}\right)_T + v$$

From the Maxwell relations

$$\left(\frac{\partial s}{\partial P}\right)_T = -\left(\frac{\partial v}{\partial T}\right)_P$$

which is substituted into the last equation to yield

$$\left(\frac{\partial h}{\partial P}\right)_T = -T\left(\frac{\partial v}{\partial T}\right)_P + v$$

The desired expression for dH then becomes

$$dh = C_P dT + \left[v - T\left(\frac{\partial v}{\partial T}\right)_P\right] dP$$

b) Let s = s(T,P). Therefore,

$$ds = \left(\frac{\partial s}{\partial T}\right)_P dT + \left(\frac{\partial s}{\partial P}\right)_T dP$$

but from the Maxwell relation,

$$\left(\frac{\partial s}{\partial P}\right)_T = -\left(\frac{\partial v}{\partial T}\right)_P$$

so

$$ds = \left(\frac{\partial s}{\partial T}\right)_P dT - \left(\frac{\partial v}{\partial T}\right)_P dP$$

$(\partial s/\partial T)_P$ is evaluated from the enthalpy property relation:

$$dh = T\,ds + v\,dP$$

by dividing by dT at constant P. That is,

$$\left(\frac{\partial h}{\partial T}\right)_P = T\left(\frac{\partial s}{\partial T}\right)_P$$

But

$$\left(\frac{\partial h}{\partial T}\right)_P = C_P$$

Therefore,

$$\left(\frac{\partial s}{\partial T}\right)_P = \frac{1}{T} C_P$$

so

$$ds = \frac{C_P}{T} dT - \left(\frac{\partial v}{\partial T}\right)_P dP$$

which is the desired relation for ds in terms of dP and dT.

• PROBLEM 6-14

Derive a general expression for the change of enthalpy, internal energy, and entropy of a substance following the equation of state

$$\left(\frac{\partial v}{\partial T}\right)_P = \frac{R}{P} - \frac{C}{T^4}$$

This substance has a constant pressure specific heat along isobar P_x (shown in the figure) given by the relation

$$C_p = A + BT$$

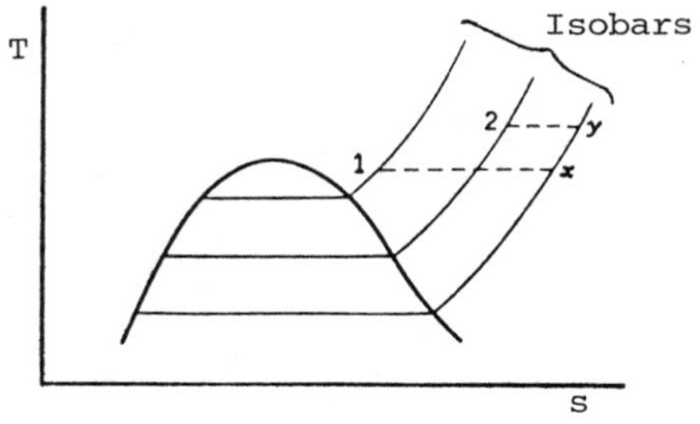

T-s diagram

Solution: The change in enthalpy between 1 and 2 is equal to the change in enthalpy along path 1-x-y-2. (Refer to the figure)

$$h_2 - h_1 = (h_2 - h_y) + (h_y - h_x) + (h_x - h_1) \quad (1)$$

$$h_2 - h_1 = \int_{P_y=P_x}^{P_2} \left[v - T\left(\frac{\partial v}{\partial T}\right)_P\right] dP_T + \int_{T_x=T_1}^{T_y=T_2} C_p dT_p$$

$$+ \int_{P_1}^{P_x=P_y} \left[v - T\left(\frac{\partial v}{\partial T}\right)_P\right] dP_T \quad (2)$$

Since the equation of state is explicit in v, then

$$(h_2 - h_y)_T = \int_y^2 \left[v - T\left(\frac{\partial v}{\partial T}\right)_P \right] dP_T \qquad (3)$$

From the equation of state

$$\left(\frac{\partial v}{\partial T}\right)_P = \frac{R}{P} + \frac{3C}{T^4} \qquad (4)$$

Therefore Eq. (3) becomes

$$(h_2 - h_y)_T = \int_y^2 \left[v - T_2\left(\frac{R}{P} + \frac{3C}{T^4}\right) \right] dP$$

$$= \int_y^2 - \frac{4C}{T_2^3}\, dP$$

$$= - \frac{4C}{T_2^3}(P_2 - P_y) \qquad (5)$$

In a similar fashion

$$h_x - h_1 = - \frac{4C}{T_1^3}(P_x - P_1) \qquad (6)$$

Then for $h_y - h_x$ we have

$$h_y - h_x = \int_{T_x=T_1}^{T_y=T_2} C_P\, dT = \int_{T_x=T_1}^{T_y=T_2} (A + BT)\, dT$$

$$= A(T_2 - T_1) + \frac{B}{2}(T_2^2 - T_1^2)$$

Therefore, substituting into Eq. (1)

$$h_2 - h_1 = -\frac{4C}{T_2^3}(P_2 - P_x) + A(T_2 - T_1) + \frac{B}{2}(T_2^2 - T_1^2) - \frac{4C}{T_1^3}(P_x - P_1)$$

$$= A(T_2 - T_1) + \frac{B}{2}(T_2^2 - T_1^2) - 4C\left[\frac{(P_2 - P_x)}{T_2^3} - \frac{(P_1 - P_x)}{T_1^3}\right]$$

For the internal energy

$$u_2 - u_1 = h_2 - h_1 - (P_2v_2 - P_1v_1)$$

$$= (A - R)(T_2 - T_1) + \frac{B}{2}(T_2^2 - T_1^2)$$

$$- 3C\left(\frac{P_2}{T_2^3} - \frac{P_1}{T_1^3}\right) + 4CP_x\left(\frac{1}{T_2^3} - \frac{1}{T_1^3}\right)$$

The change in entropy between 1 and 2 is equal to the change in entropy along the path 1-x-y-2.

$$s_2 - s_1 = (s_2 - s_y) + (s_y - s_x) + (s_x - s_1) \qquad (7)$$

Therefore

$$s_2 - s_1 = -\int_{P_y=P_x}^{P_2} \left(\frac{\partial v}{\partial T}\right)_P dP_T + \int_{T_x=T_1}^{T_y=T_2} C_p \frac{dT_P}{T} - \int_{P_1}^{P_x} \left(\frac{\partial v}{\partial T}\right)_P dP_T \qquad (8)$$

where

$$s_2 - s_y = -\int_y^2 \left(\frac{\partial v}{\partial T}\right)_P dP$$

$$= -\int_y^2 \left(\frac{R}{P} + \frac{3C}{T^4}\right) dP$$

$$= -R \ln \frac{P_2}{P_y} - \frac{3C}{T_2{}^4}(P_2 - P_y)$$

But $P_y = P_x$ and so

$$s_2 - s_y = -R \ln \frac{P_2}{P_x} - \frac{3C}{T_2{}^4}(P_2 - P_x)$$

In a similar fashion

$$s_x - s_1 = -R \ln \frac{P_x}{P_1} - \frac{3C}{T_1{}^4}(P_x - P_1)$$

Then for $s_y - s_x$

$$s_y - s_x = \int_{T_x=T_1}^{T_y=T_2} C_p \frac{dT}{T} = \int_{T_x=T_1}^{T_y=T_2} (A + BT)\frac{dT}{T} = A \ln \frac{T_2}{T_1} + B(T_2 - T_1)$$

Therefore, substituting into Eq. (7)

$$s_2 - s_1 = -R \ln \frac{P_2}{P_x} - \frac{3C}{T_2{}^4}(P_2 - P_x) + A \ln \frac{T_2}{T_1} + B(T_2 - T_1) - R \ln \frac{P_x}{P_1} - \frac{3C}{T_1{}^4}(P_x - P_1)$$

$$s_2 - s_1 = -R \ln \frac{P_2}{P_1} - 3C\left[\frac{(P_2 - P_x)}{T_2{}^4} - \frac{(P_1 - P_x)}{T_1{}^4}\right] + A \ln \frac{T_2}{T_1} + B(T_2 - T_1)$$

a) Start with the entropy function s = f(T,v) and derive the general expression for the entropy change

$$ds = c_v \frac{dT}{T} + \left(\frac{\partial P}{\partial T}\right)_v dv$$

b) Use the function s = f(T,P) and obtain the general expression

$$ds = C_p \frac{dT}{T} - \left(\frac{\partial v}{\partial T}\right)_P dP$$

Solution: a) Since s = f(T,v) it follows from mathematical relations that

$$ds = \left(\frac{\partial s}{\partial T}\right)_v dT + \left(\frac{\partial s}{\partial v}\right)_T dv \quad (1)$$

solving for ds in the property relation

$$du = Tds - Pdv$$

one gets

$$ds = \frac{1}{T}(du + pdv) \quad (2)$$

since u = f(T,v), then

$$du = \left(\frac{\partial u}{\partial T}\right)_v dT + \left(\frac{\partial u}{\partial v}\right)_T dv$$

substitute this relation into Eq. (2) and write

$$ds = \frac{1}{T}\left[\left(\frac{\partial u}{\partial T}\right)_v dT + \left(\frac{\partial u}{\partial v}\right)_T dv + Pdv\right]$$

or rearranging

$$ds = \frac{1}{T}\left(\frac{\partial u}{\partial T}\right)_v dT + \frac{1}{T}\left[\left(\frac{\partial u}{\partial v}\right)_T + P\right] dv \quad (3)$$

Equating coefficients with (1) we obtain

$$\left(\frac{\partial s}{\partial T}\right)_v = \frac{1}{T}\left(\frac{\partial u}{\partial T}\right)_v = \frac{1}{T} c_v$$

and

$$\left(\frac{\partial s}{\partial v}\right)_T = \frac{1}{T}\left[\left(\frac{\partial u}{\partial v}\right)_T + P\right] dv$$

Because of the above, the relation for ds can be written as

$$ds = \frac{1}{T} c_v dT + \left(\frac{\partial s}{\partial v}\right)_T dv \qquad (4)$$

Finally using the Maxwell relation

$$\left(\frac{\partial s}{\partial v}\right)_T = \left(\frac{\partial P}{\partial T}\right)_v$$

Eq. (4) can be written as

$$ds = \frac{c_v}{T} dT + \left(\frac{\partial P}{\partial T}\right)_v dv$$

b) The approach is quite similar to that used in developing the relation of part a). However, this time the entropy is given as $s = f(T,P)$. Then

$$ds = \left(\frac{\partial s}{\partial T}\right)_P dT + \left(\frac{\partial s}{\partial P}\right)_T dP \qquad (5)$$

The property relation

$$dh = Tds + vdP$$

will be used. Solving for ds in this relation we obtain

$$ds = \frac{1}{T}\left[dh - vdP\right] \qquad (6)$$

since $h = f(T,P)$, then

$$dh = \left(\frac{\partial h}{\partial T}\right)_P dT + \left(\frac{\partial h}{\partial P}\right)_T dP$$

substituting this relation into (6) one gets

$$ds = \frac{1}{T}\left[\left(\frac{\partial h}{\partial T}\right)_P dT + \left(\frac{\partial h}{\partial P}\right)_T dP - vdP\right]$$

Rearrangement of this equation gives

$$ds = \frac{1}{T}\left(\frac{\partial h}{\partial T}\right)_P dt + \frac{1}{T}\left[\left(\frac{\partial h}{\partial P}\right)_T - \upsilon\ dp\right]$$

Equating coefficients with (5) gives

$$\left(\frac{\partial s}{\partial T}\right)_P = \frac{1}{T}\left(\frac{\partial h}{\partial T}\right)_P = \frac{1}{T}\,Cp$$

and

$$\left(\frac{\partial s}{\partial T}\right)_T = \left[\frac{1}{T}\left(\frac{\partial h}{\partial P}\right)_T - \upsilon\right]$$

Because of the above two equations, the relation for $s = f(P,T)$ can be written as

$$ds = \frac{1}{T}\,CpdT + \left(\frac{\partial s}{\partial P}\right)_T dP \tag{7}$$

Finally, using the Maxwell relation

$$\left(\frac{\partial s}{\partial P}\right)_T = -\left(\frac{\partial \upsilon}{\partial T}\right)_P$$

Eq. (7) can be written in the following form.

$$ds = \frac{Cp}{T}\,dT - \left(\frac{\partial \upsilon}{\partial T}\right)_P dP\ ,$$

which is the desired expression.

• PROBLEM 6-16

The P,v,T relation of a real gas is represented with reasonable accuracy by the relation

$$v = \frac{RT}{P} + b - \frac{a}{RT}$$

where a and b are constants. For this gas find the change in enthalpy and entropy along an isothermal path between pressures P_1 and P_2.

Solution: The change in enthalpy is given by the second term of Eq. (1)

$$(h_2 - h_1)_T = \int_1^2 \left[v - T\left(\frac{\partial v}{\partial T}\right)_P\right] dP \tag{1}$$

The equation of state is explicit in v. Hence $(\partial v/\partial T)_P = R/P + a/RT^2$, and

$$v - T\left(\frac{\partial v}{\partial T}\right)_P = \frac{RT}{P} + b - \frac{a}{RT} - T\left(\frac{R}{P} + \frac{a}{RT^2}\right) = b - \frac{2a}{RT}$$

Therefore,

$$(h_2 - h_1)_T = \left(b - \frac{2a}{RT}\right)(P_2 - P_1)$$

To evaluate the entropy change choose the equation

$$ds = \frac{CpdT}{T} - \left(\frac{\partial r}{\partial T}\right)_P dp$$

because it requires an equation of state explicit in v. Hence

$$(s_2 - s_1)_T = -\int_1^2 \left(\frac{\partial v}{\partial T}\right)_P dP = -\int_1^2 \left(\frac{R}{P} + \frac{a}{RT^2}\right) dP$$

$$= -R \ln \frac{P_2}{P_1} - \frac{a(P_2 - P_1)}{RT^2}$$

• PROBLEM 6-17

Derive a relation for the change of internal energy of a pure substance as a function of the temperature and specific volume.

Solution: Note that

$$u = u(T,P)$$

Therefore

$$du = \left(\frac{\partial u}{\partial T}\right)_v dT + \left(\frac{\partial u}{\partial v}\right)_T dv \qquad (1)$$

For a pure substance

$$Tds = du + Pdv \qquad (2)$$

dividing by T Eq. (2) becomes

$$ds = \frac{du}{T} + \frac{P}{T} dv \qquad (3)$$

Also

$$\left(\frac{\partial u}{\partial T}\right)_v = c_v$$

and Eq. (1) becomes

$$du = c_v \, dT + \left(\frac{\partial u}{\partial v}\right)_T dv \tag{4}$$

substituting Eq. (4) into Eq. (3) and rearranging, gives

$$ds = c_v \frac{dT}{T} + \left[\frac{1}{T}\left(\frac{\partial u}{\partial v}\right)_T + \frac{P}{T}\right] dv \tag{5}$$

However the entropy may be written as a function of the independent variables T and v

$$s = s(T,v)$$

and

$$ds = \left(\frac{\partial s}{\partial T}\right)_v dT + \left(\frac{\partial s}{\partial v}\right)_T dv \tag{6}$$

Eqs. (5) and (6) are the same equation. Therefore equating coefficients gives

$$\left(\frac{\partial s}{\partial T}\right)_v = \frac{C_V}{T} \tag{7}$$

and

$$\left(\frac{\partial s}{\partial v}\right)_T = \frac{1}{T}\left[\left(\frac{\partial u}{\partial v}\right)_T + P\right] \tag{8}$$

Using the Maxwell relation

$$\left(\frac{\partial P}{\partial T}\right)_v = \left(\frac{\partial s}{\partial v}\right)_T$$

and substituting into Eq. (8) gives

$$\left(\frac{\partial P}{\partial T}\right)_v = \frac{1}{T}\left[\left(\frac{\partial u}{\partial v}\right)_T + P\right]$$

or after rearrangement

$$\left(\frac{\partial u}{\partial v}\right)_T = T\left(\frac{\partial P}{\partial T}\right)_v - P \tag{9}$$

substituting Eq. (9) into Eq. (4) yields

$$du = c_v dT + \left[T\left(\frac{\partial P}{\partial T}\right)_v - P\right] dv$$

• PROBLEM 6-18

Show that for any gas which obeys the Van der Waals equation of state

$$\left[P + \frac{a}{v^2}\right](v - b) = RT \qquad (1)$$

the relation

$$\left(\frac{\partial u}{\partial v}\right)_T = \frac{a}{v^2}$$

is true.

<u>Solution</u>: From the first law of thermodynamics

$$du = dq - dw$$

But

$$dw = Pdv \quad \text{and} \quad ds = \frac{dq}{T}$$

$$\therefore \; du = Tds - Pdv \qquad (2)$$

Differentiating Eq. (2) partially with respect to v, and keeping T constant, it becomes

$$\left(\frac{\partial u}{\partial v}\right)_T = T\left(\frac{\partial s}{\partial v}\right)_T - P \qquad (3)$$

Using the Maxwell relation,

$$\left(\frac{\partial s}{\partial v}\right)_T = \left(\frac{\partial P}{\partial T}\right)_v$$

Eq. (3) becomes

$$\left(\frac{\partial u}{\partial v}\right)_T = T\left(\frac{\partial P}{\partial T}\right)_v - P \qquad (4)$$

From the Van der Waals equation of state (Eq. (1))

$$\left(\frac{\partial P}{\partial T}\right)_v = \frac{R}{v-b}$$

Rearranging Eq. (1)

$$\frac{R}{v-b} = \left[P + \frac{a}{v^2}\right]\frac{1}{T} \qquad (5)$$

Therefore

$$\left(\frac{\partial u}{\partial v}\right)_T = T\left(P + \frac{a}{v^2}\right)\frac{1}{T} - P$$

$$= P + \frac{a}{v^2} - P$$

or

$$\left(\frac{\partial u}{\partial v}\right)_T = \frac{a}{v^2}$$

• PROBLEM 6-19

a) Derive the expression $\left(\frac{\partial E}{\partial T}\right)_P = C_P - P\left(\frac{\partial V}{\partial T}\right)_P$

b) Calculate $(C_P - C_V)$ for Al at 25°C.

Density of Al = 2.702×10^3 kg m^{-3}

Mass of Al = 26.98×10^{-3} kg mol^{-1}

$\alpha = 69 \times 10^{-6}\ K^{-1}$

$\beta = 1.34 \times 10^{-6}\ atm^{-1}$

Solution: a) The internal energy, E, is a function of temperature and volume. That is

$$E = f(T,V)$$

$$dE = \left(\frac{\partial E}{\partial T}\right)_V dT + \left(\frac{\partial E}{\partial V}\right)_T dV$$

Divide by dT to obtain,

$$\left(\frac{\partial E}{\partial T}\right)_P = \left(\frac{\partial E}{\partial T}\right)_V + \left(\frac{\partial E}{\partial V}\right)_T \left(\frac{\partial V}{\partial T}\right)_P \qquad (1)$$

By definition, the heat capacity at constant pressure, $C_P = \left(\frac{\partial H}{\partial T}\right)_P$ and the heat capacity at constant volume,

$$C_V = \left(\frac{\partial E}{\partial T}\right)_V$$

∴ Equation (1) becomes

$$\left(\frac{\partial E}{\partial T}\right)_P = C_V + \left(\frac{\partial E}{\partial V}\right)_T \left(\frac{\partial V}{\partial T}\right)_P \tag{2}$$

Now,

$$C_P - C_V = \left(\frac{\partial H}{\partial T}\right)_P - \left(\frac{\partial E}{\partial T}\right)_V \tag{3}$$

But, $H = E + PV$

Therefore,

$$\left(\frac{\partial H}{\partial T}\right)_P = \left(\frac{\partial E}{\partial T}\right)_P + P\left(\frac{\partial V}{\partial T}\right)_P$$

Substituting this into equation (3) changes it to

$$C_P - C_V = \left(\frac{\partial E}{\partial T}\right)_P + P\left(\frac{\partial V}{\partial T}\right)_P - \left(\frac{\partial E}{\partial T}\right)_V \tag{4}$$

$$C_P - C_V = \left(\frac{\partial E}{\partial T}\right)_V + \left(\frac{\partial E}{\partial V}\right)_T \left(\frac{\partial V}{\partial T}\right)_P + P\left(\frac{\partial V}{\partial T}\right)_P - \left(\frac{\partial V}{\partial T}\right)_V$$

$$= \left(\frac{\partial V}{\partial T}\right)_P \left[\left(\frac{\partial E}{\partial V}\right)_T + P\right]$$

Solving for C_V gives

$$C_V = C_P - \left[P + \left(\frac{\partial E}{\partial V}\right)_T\right]\left(\frac{\partial V}{\partial T}\right)_P \tag{5}$$

Using equation (5), equation (2) can be written as

$$\left(\frac{\partial E}{\partial T}\right)_P = C_P - \left[P + \left(\frac{\partial E}{\partial V}\right)_T\right]\left(\frac{\partial V}{\partial T}\right)_P + \left(\frac{\partial E}{\partial V}\right)_T \left(\frac{\partial V}{\partial T}\right)_P$$

$$= C_P - P\left(\frac{\partial V}{\partial T}\right)_P - \left(\frac{\partial E}{\partial V}\right)_T \left(\frac{\partial V}{\partial T}\right)_P + \left(\frac{\partial E}{\partial V}\right)_T \left(\frac{\partial V}{\partial T}\right)_P$$

Hence,

$$\left(\frac{\partial E}{\partial T}\right)_P = C_P - P\left(\frac{\partial V}{\partial T}\right)_P$$

b) Since

$$E = f(V,T)$$

$$dE = \left(\frac{\partial E}{\partial T}\right)_V dT + \left(\frac{\partial E}{\partial V}\right)_T dV$$

where E = internal energy

V = volume

and T = temperature

f means "a function of".

But dq = dE + PdV

where q = heat and P = pressure

$$\therefore \; dq = \left(\frac{\partial E}{\partial T}\right)_V dT + \left[P + \left(\frac{\partial E}{\partial V}\right)_T\right] dV \qquad (6)$$

By definition,

$$C_V = \left(\frac{\partial E}{\partial T}\right)_V \quad \text{and} \quad C_P = \left(\frac{\partial q}{\partial T}\right)_P$$

Divide equation (6) through by dT,

$$\left(\frac{dq}{dT}\right)_P = \left(\frac{\partial E}{\partial T}\right)_V + \left[P + \left(\frac{\partial E}{\partial V}\right)_T\right] \left(\frac{\partial V}{\partial T}\right)_P$$

$$C_P = C_V + \left[P + \left(\frac{\partial E}{\partial V}\right)_T\right] \left(\frac{\partial V}{\partial T}\right)_P$$

or

$$C_P - C_V = \left[P + \left(\frac{\partial E}{\partial V}\right)_T\right] \left(\frac{\partial V}{\partial T}\right)_P \qquad (7)$$

For an ideal gas,

$$\left(\frac{\partial E}{\partial V}\right)_T = 0 \text{ and } \left(\frac{\partial V}{\partial T}\right)_P = \frac{R}{P}$$

$$C_P - C_V = [P + 0]\,\frac{R}{P} = \frac{PR}{P} \text{ or } C_P - C_V = R$$

One unit of R = liter atm K^{-1} mol^{-1}

$$\text{liter} = \text{volume} = \frac{\text{mass}}{\text{density}} = \frac{m}{\rho}$$

K is given by α and atm is given by β

$$\therefore \; C_P - C_V = R = \frac{\alpha^2 VT}{\beta} \qquad (8)$$

Substituting the respective values into equation (8) gives

$$\text{Volume} = \frac{26.98 \times 10^{-3} \ \frac{\text{kg}}{\text{mole}}}{2.702 \times 10^{3} \ \frac{\text{kg}}{\text{m}^3}}$$

$$C_P - C_V = \frac{(69 \times 10^{-6} \ K^{-1})^2}{(1.34 \times 10^{-6} \text{atm}^{-1})} \ \frac{26.98 \times 10^{-3} \ \frac{\text{kg}}{\text{mole}} \ (298°K)}{2.702 \times 10^{-3} \ \frac{\text{kg}}{\text{m}^3}}$$

$$= 10.57 \times 10^{-6} \ \frac{\text{m}^3 \ \text{atm}}{\text{mole K}}$$

$$= 10.57 \times 10^{-6} \ \text{m}^3 \ \text{atm mol}^{-1} \ K^{-1}$$

To convert the answer from m^3 atm to Joules use the ratio of the different values for the gas constant R.

SPECIFIC HEAT RELATIONS

• PROBLEM 6-20

Using the first law of thermodynamics obtain an expression for the heat capacity C at constant volume in the form

$$C_V = - \left(\frac{\partial E}{\partial V}\right)_T \left(\frac{\partial V}{\partial T}\right)_E$$

Solution: The heat capacity C is defined as the temperature rise dT by 1 degree when a small amount of heat dq is added to the system.

i.e.

$$C = {}^{dq}/dt$$

But

$$dq = dE + pdV$$

where dE = small change in Internal Energy

P = Pressure

dV = small change in volume

$$\therefore \quad C = \frac{dE + pdV}{dT} \tag{1}$$

The heat capacity C at constant volume is obtained from equation (1) when dV = 0

$$\therefore \quad C_V = \left(\frac{\partial E}{\partial T}\right)_V$$

Thus, the internal energy, E is a function of both the volume and the temperature. This dependence can be written as

$$E = f(V,T)$$

where V = volume and T = Temperature.

Differentiating yields

$$dE = \left(\frac{\partial E}{\partial T}\right)_V dT + \left(\frac{\partial E}{\partial V}\right)_T dV$$

Divide throughout by dT keeping E constant

$$0 = \left(\frac{\partial E}{\partial T}\right)_V + \left(\frac{\partial E}{\partial V}\right)_T \left(\frac{\partial V}{\partial T}\right)_E$$

$$\left(\frac{\partial E}{\partial T}\right)_V = -\left(\frac{\partial E}{\partial V}\right)_T \left(\frac{\partial V}{\partial T}\right)_E$$

$$C_V = -\left(\frac{\partial E}{\partial V}\right)_T \left(\frac{\partial V}{\partial T}\right)_E$$

• **PROBLEM 6-21**

The specific heat for a certain substance in the temperature range 40 to 1800°F, and at low pressure is given by the following equation.

$$C_p = 0.1 + \frac{100}{T} + \frac{T}{10,000}$$

where C_p is in B/lb-F and T in °R. Calculate a) The mean specific heat C_p between 40 and 1040 F. b) $\bar{C}_p$ between 40 and 540 F. c) $\bar{C}_p$ at 40,540 and 1040 F, and d) h at 14.5 psia, 740 F, if h = 28.0 B/lb at 14.5 psia.

Solution: The mean specific heat

$$\bar{C}_p = \frac{\int_1^2 C_p \, dT}{T_2 - T_1}$$

The mean specific heat $\bar{C}_p$ for the temperature range of 40F (500R) to 1040F (1500R), is

$$\bar{C}_p = \int_1^2 \frac{\left(0.1 + \frac{100}{T} + \frac{T}{10,000}\right) dT}{T_2 - T_1}$$

$$= \frac{0.1(T_2 - T_1) + 100 \ln (T_2/T_1) + (T_2^2 - T_1^2)/20,000}{T_2 - T_1}$$

$$= 0.1 + \frac{100}{T_2 - T_1} \ln \frac{T_2}{T_1} + \frac{T_2 + T_1}{20,000} \qquad (1)$$

$$= 0.1 + \frac{100}{1500 - 500} \ln \frac{1500}{500} + \frac{1500 + 500}{20,000} = 0.1 + 0.1098 + 0.1$$

$$= 0.310 \text{ B/lb-F}$$

b) Substituting in equation (1) the values of $T_1 = 500$ R and $T_2 = 1000$ R,

$$\bar{C}_p = 0.1 + \frac{100}{1000 - 500} \ln \frac{1000}{500} + \frac{1000 + 500}{20,000}$$

$$= 0.1 + 0.1386 + 0.075 = 0.314 \text{ B/lb-F}$$

c) Substituting the proper temperatures into the given expression for C_p,

$$C_{p,40F} = 0.1 + \frac{100}{500} + \frac{500}{10,000} = 0.35 \text{ B/lb-F}$$

$$C_{p,540F} = 0.1 + \frac{100}{1000} + \frac{1000}{10,000} = 0.30 \text{ B/lb-F}$$

$$C_{p,1040F} = 0.1 + \frac{100}{1500} + \frac{1500}{10,000} = 0.317 \text{ B/lb-F}$$

d) Considering h as a function of p and T,

$$dh = \left(\frac{\partial h}{\partial T}\right)_p dT + \left(\frac{\partial h}{\partial p}\right)_T dp = C_p dT + \left(\frac{\partial h}{\partial p}\right)_T dp$$

Letting subscripts 1 and 2 denote the conditions at 14.5 psia, 40 F, and at 14.5 psia, 740 F, respectively,

$$h_2 = h_1 + \int_1^2 dh = h_1 + \int_1^2 \left[c_p dT + \left(\frac{\partial h}{\partial p}\right)_T\right] dp$$

Since the pressure is the same at states 1 and 2, the second term in the integrand is zero, so that

$$h_2 = h_1 + \int_1^2 C_p dT = h_1 + \int_1^2 \left[0.1 + \frac{100}{T} + \frac{T}{10,000}\right] dT$$

$$= h_1 + 0.1(T_2 - T_1) + 100 \ln \frac{T_2}{T_1} + \frac{T_2^2 - T_1^2}{20,000}$$

$$= 28.0 + 0.1(1200 - 500) + 100 \ln \frac{1200}{500} + \frac{(1200)^2 - (500)^2}{20,000}$$

$$= 28.0 + 70 + 87.5 + 59.5 = 245 \text{ B/lb}$$

Note that the definition of specific heat involves a temperature difference or differential and the units can be interchangeably B/lb-F or B/lb-R. $T_R = T_F + 460$. Therefore $dT_R = dT_F$. The size of a degree is the same on the Rankine and Fahrenheit scale hence a change in temperature has the same value on both scales.

JOULE - THOMSON COEFFICIENT

• PROBLEM 6-22

a) Develop an expression for the Joule-Thomson coefficient in terms of the properties of a substance.

b) Derive a relation for the Joule-Thomson coefficient for a gas, obeying the equation of state

$$Pv = ZRT$$

Solution: a) The Joule-Thomson coefficient is by definition

$$\mu_J = \left(\frac{\partial T}{\partial P}\right)_h \quad (1)$$

Because $s = f(P,T)$ it follows that

$$ds = \left(\frac{\partial s}{\partial P}\right)_T dP + \left(\frac{\partial s}{\partial T}\right)_P dT \quad (2)$$

Substituting the above relation into the property relation

$$dh = Tds + vdP$$

obtain

$$dh = T\left[\left(\frac{\partial s}{\partial P}\right)_T dP + \left(\frac{\partial s}{\partial T}\right)_P dT\right] + vdP$$

or rearranging

$$dh = T\left(\frac{\partial s}{\partial T}\right)_P dT + \left[T\left(\frac{\partial s}{\partial P}\right)_T + v\right] dP \qquad (3)$$

Using the Maxwell relation

$$\left(\frac{\partial s}{\partial P}\right)_T = -\left(\frac{\partial v}{\partial T}\right)_P$$

Eq. (3) becomes

$$dh = T\left(\frac{\partial s}{\partial T}\right)_P dT + \left[v - T\left(\frac{\partial v}{\partial T}\right)_T\right] dP \qquad (4)$$

And

$$C_p \equiv \left(\frac{\partial s}{\partial T}\right)_P$$

Solving for dT gives

$$dT = \frac{1}{C_p} dh + \frac{1}{C_p}\left[T\left(\frac{\partial v}{\partial T}\right)_P - v\right] dP \qquad (5)$$

Since $T = f(h,P)$ it follows that

$$dT = \left(\frac{\partial T}{\partial h}\right)_P dh + \left(\frac{\partial T}{\partial P}\right)_h dP \qquad (6)$$

Equating coefficients in (5) and (6) gives

$$\frac{1}{C_p} = \left(\frac{\partial T}{\partial h}\right)_P$$

and

$$\left(\frac{\partial T}{\partial P}\right)_h = \frac{1}{C_p}\left[T\left(\frac{\partial v}{\partial T}\right)_P - v\right] \qquad (7)$$

From equation (1) and (7)

$$\mu_J = \frac{1}{C_p}\left[T\left(\frac{\partial v}{\partial T}\right)_P - v\right] \qquad (8)$$

Noting that

$$\alpha = \frac{1}{v}\left(\frac{\partial v}{\partial T}\right)_P$$

Eq. (8) can be written as

$$\mu_J = \frac{v}{C_p} \left[T\alpha - 1 \right]$$

b) Solving for the specific volume in the equation

$$Pv = ZRT$$

one gets

$$v = \frac{ZRT}{P} \tag{9}$$

Differentiating this relation with respect to temperature at constant pressure gives

$$\left(\frac{\partial v}{\partial T}\right)_P = \frac{ZR}{P} + \frac{RT}{P} \left(\frac{\partial Z}{\partial T}\right)_P$$

Substituting into Eq. (8) we obtain

$$\mu_J = \frac{1}{C_p} \left[\frac{ZRT}{P} + \frac{RT^2}{P} \left(\frac{\partial Z}{\partial T}\right)_P - v \right]$$

and using (9), the above relation reduces to

$$\mu_J = \frac{1}{C_p} \left[\frac{RT^2}{P} \left(\frac{\partial Z}{\partial T}\right)_P \right]$$

or

$$\mu_J = \frac{RT^2}{C_p P} \left(\frac{\partial Z}{\partial T}\right)_P$$

• PROBLEM 6-23

Steam at 1000 kPa, 350°C, is throttled slowly to 300 kPa. Neglecting potential and kinetic energies calculate the average Joule Thomson coefficient for this process.

Solution: The Joule-Thomson coefficient is given by

$$\mu_J = \left(\frac{\partial T}{\partial P}\right)_h$$

However, the average Joule-Thomson coefficient is required and the above relation can be written as

$$\mu_J \cong \left(\frac{\Delta T}{\Delta P}\right)_h$$

Since this is a throttling process the first law of thermodynamics gives

$$h_{exit} = h_{in}$$

From the superheated steam tables at

$$P = 1000 \text{ kPa}, \quad T = 350°C$$

the enthalpy is given as

$$h = 3,157.7 \text{ kJ/kg}$$

Again from the superheated steam tables at $P_2 = 300$ kPa and h = 3,157.7 kJ/kg the temperature of steam is obtained to be

$$T_2 \cong 338.7°C$$

Then

$$\Delta T = T_2 - T_1$$

$$= 611.85 - 623.15$$

$$= -11.3°K$$

and

$$\Delta P = P_2 - P_1$$

$$= 300 - 1000$$

$$= -700 \text{ kPa.}$$

Thus

$$\mu_J = \frac{-11.3}{-700} = 0.0161 \text{ °K/kPa}$$

VOLUME EXPANSIVITY AND ISOTHERMAL AND ADIABATIC COMPRESSIBILITY

• PROBLEM 6-24

Using the relation

$$\left(\frac{\partial C_p}{\partial p}\right)_T = -T\left(\frac{\partial^2 v}{\partial T^2}\right)_P \qquad (1)$$

and the definition for the volume expansivity α, derive a relation between the constant specific heat and the volume expansivity, a) assuming variable α, and b) constant α.

Solution: The volume expansivity α is by definition

$$\alpha \equiv \frac{1}{V}\left(\frac{\partial V}{\partial T}\right)_P = \frac{1}{v}\left(\frac{\partial v}{\partial T}\right)_P \qquad (2)$$

a) Eq. (1) can be written as

$$\left(\frac{\partial C_p}{\partial p}\right)_T = -T\left[\frac{\partial}{\partial T}\left(\frac{\partial v}{\partial T}\right)_p\right]_p$$

However $\left(\frac{\partial v}{\partial T}\right)_p$ can be written as $v\alpha$ and so the wanted relation is

$$\left(\frac{\partial C_p}{\partial p}\right)_T = -T\left[\frac{\partial(v\alpha)}{\partial T}\right]_p \qquad (3)$$

b) Assuming α = constant (3) can be written as

$$\left(\frac{\partial C_p}{\partial p}\right)_T = -T\alpha\left(\frac{\partial v}{\partial T}\right)_p$$

but

$$\left(\frac{\partial v}{\partial T}\right)_p = v\alpha \qquad \text{and so}$$

$$\left(\frac{\partial C_p}{\partial p}\right)_T = -Tv\alpha^2$$

• PROBLEM 6-25

a) Using the first law of thermodynamics, along with the continuity equation, show that for an isentropic process the velocity of sound in a fluid is given by the relation

$$c^2 = \left(\frac{\partial P}{\partial \rho}\right)_s$$

b) Using the result obtained in part (a) derive a relation for the speed of sound in a fluid, undergoing an isentropic process, in terms of its density and adiabatic compressibility β_s

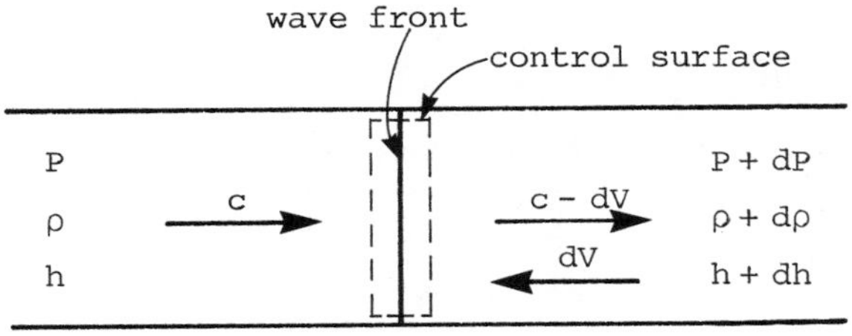

Solution: a) Using the first law of thermodynamics for the control surface shown in the figure

$$h + \frac{c^2}{2} = (h + dh) + \frac{(c - dv)^2}{2}$$

assuming an adiabatic and isentropic process.

Expanding this equation,

$$h + \frac{c^2}{2} = h + dh + \frac{c^2}{2} - \frac{cdv}{2} + \frac{dV^2}{2}$$

cancelling like terms and noting that dv^2 is small compared to dv, the above equation reduces to

$$dh - cdv = 0 \tag{1}$$

The continuity equation for this control volume is

$$\rho cA = (\rho + d\rho)(c - dV)A \ .$$

Expanding this equation and cancelling like terms, it reduces to

$$cd\rho - \rho dv = 0 \tag{2}$$

Since this is an isentropic process the property relation between the enthalpy and entropy will be useful

$$Tds = dh - vdP$$

Since,

$$v = \frac{1}{\rho}$$

$$Tds = dh - \frac{dP}{\rho}$$

For ds = 0

$$dh - \frac{dP}{\rho} = 0 \tag{3}$$

Combining (1) and (3) gives the relation

$$\frac{dP}{\rho} - cdV = 0 \tag{4}$$

solving for dV in both (2) and (4) one has

$$dv = \frac{cd\rho}{\rho}$$

and

$$dv = \frac{dP}{\rho c}$$

Combining these two equations the following relation is obtained

$$\frac{cd\rho}{\rho} = \frac{dP}{\rho c}$$

Therefore

$$c^2 = \frac{dP}{d\rho} \tag{5}$$

But since the process is isentropic the above relation is better written in the form of a partial derivative

$$c^2 = \left(\frac{\partial P}{\partial \rho}\right)_s$$

b) Consider Equation (5) in part (a). From elementary calculus and the fact that

$$\rho = \frac{1}{v}$$

it follows that

$$d\rho = -\frac{1}{v^2}\, dv$$

Substituting this relation into (5) for $d\rho$,

$$c^2 = -v^2 \frac{dP}{dv},$$

or in partial differential form

$$c^2 = -v^2 \left(\frac{\partial P}{\partial v}\right)_s \tag{6}$$

The definition of the adiabatic compressibility is

$$\beta_s \equiv -\frac{1}{v}\left(\frac{\partial v}{\partial P}\right)_s$$

But the reciprocal of β_s (the adiabatic bulk modulus B_s) is given as

$$B_s = -v \left(\frac{\partial P}{\partial v}\right)_s \tag{7}$$

Substituting (7) into (6) one obtains

$$c^2 = B_s v = B_s \frac{1}{\rho}$$

But

$$B_s = \frac{1}{\beta_s}$$

and thus

$$c^2 = \frac{1}{\beta_s \rho}$$

or

$$c = \sqrt{1/\beta_s \rho}$$

EQUATIONS OF STATE

• PROBLEM 6-26

A certain substance obeys the van der Waals equation, and its constants a and b are known. Name six types of properties or coefficients that may be calculated for this substance, using the above information.

Solution: If van der Waals forces are included the equation

used is

$$\left(P + \frac{n^2a}{V^2}\right)(V-nb) = nRT$$

where P = pressure

n = moles

V = volume

a and b = constants

R = gas constant

T = temperature.

Looking at the above equation it is possible to compute (a), P, V, or T if the other two are known. (b) Its critical point. At the critical point the P, T and V in the equation are replaced by P_c, T_c and V_c, respectively. P_c is the critical pressure, V_c, the critical volume, and T_c, the critical temperature. Since the van der Waals constants, a and b are known it is possible to express the critical pressure, temperature and volume in terms of these constants. Thus

$$V_c = 3b; \; P_c = \frac{a}{27b^2}; \; T_c = \frac{8a}{27bR}$$

c) The vapor pressure of the liquid; d) Compressibility factor, Z.

Z is written as $\frac{P_cV_c}{RT_c}$; e) The heat of vaporization;

f) Coefficient of thermal expansion.

• PROBLEM 6-27

Determine the numerical values of $(\partial V/\partial T)_P$ at 140°F and a specific volume of 2.100 cu ft per lb for (a) a perfect gas with a molecular weight of 70.9, and (b) a van der Waals gas of the same molecular weight for which $\alpha = 4.88$ (psi) $(ft^3/lb)^2$ and $\beta = 0.0127$ ft^3/lb.

Solution: a) For a perfect gas, $(\partial V/\partial T)_P = b/P = bV/bT = V/T$

$$(\partial V/\partial T)_P = 2.100/(460 + 140) = 0.00350 \text{ (cu ft per lb)/°R}$$

b) For the van der Waals gas,

$$b = \frac{10.73}{70.9} = 0.1514 \text{ (psi)(cu ft per lb)/°R}$$

Therefore

$$(\partial V/\partial T)_P = \frac{bV^3(V - \beta)}{bTV^3 - 2\alpha(V - \beta)^2}$$

$$= \frac{(0.1514)\ (2.100)^3\ (2.100 - 0.0127)}{(0.1514)\ (600)\ (2.100)^3 - 2(4.88)\ (2.100 - 0.0127)^2}$$

$$= \frac{2.925}{841.0 - 42.5} = 0.00366 \text{ (cu ft per lb)/°R.}$$

• PROBLEM 6-28

A gas obeys the van der Waals equation, with P_c = 30 atm and T_c = 200°C. The compressibility factor PV/RT will be more than one (at P = 50 atm, T = 250°C; at P = 1 atm, T = 100°C; P = 500 atm, T = 500°C; none of these). Calculate the van der Waals constant b for this gas.

Solution: For a compressibility factor greater than unity, P = 500 atm and T = 500°C (that is the highest P and T) are chosen. The constant b = $V_c/3$. It is known that

$$\frac{P_c V_c}{RT_c} = \frac{\left(\frac{a}{27b^2}\right)\left(3b\right)}{R\left(\frac{8a}{27Rb}\right)} = \frac{3}{8}$$

for a van der Waals gas. Therefore,

$$V_c = \frac{3RT_c}{8P_c} = \frac{(3)(.082)(473°K)}{(8)(30 \text{ atm})}$$

$$V_c = 0.4848 \text{ and } b = \frac{0.4848}{3} = 0.162 \text{ liter/mole.}$$

The van der Waals constants for gases A,B, and C are:

Gas	a, liters^2-atm/mole	b, liters/mole
A	4.0	0.027
B	12.0	0.030
C	6.0	0.032

Which gas has (a) the highest critical temperature, (b) the largest molecular volume, and (c) most ideal general behavior around STP?

Solution: The van der Waals equation is

$$\left(P + \frac{n^2a}{V^2}\right)\left(V - nb\right) = nRT$$

where
P = pressure
T = temperature
V = volume
n = number of moles.

a and b are van der Waals constants.

(a) It is known that T_c, the critical temperature is proportional to the ratio a/b . Computing the a/b ratios for the three gases yields:

for gas A $\frac{4.0}{0.027} = 148.15$

for gas B $\frac{12.0}{0.030} = 400$

for gas C $\frac{6.0}{0.032} = 187.5$

Since the ratio for gas B is the largest, gas B has the largest T_c. This question could have been answered by mere inspection. It can be seen that the constant b has almost the same value for the three gases. So, the larger a value means greater intermolecular forces. A larger T_c would be needed to overcome them. Since gas B has the largest a value, its T_c will be the largest.

(b) The constant b is proportional to V_c . Therefore gas C has the largest V_c.

(c) The b values are almost the same. Therefore ideality will be determined by the a values. Looking at the original equation, it can be seen that it is near ideality for values of the constants close to zero. Since gas A has the smallest a value, it should be the most ideal in behavior. Remember that for ideality, the expression is PV = nRT.

• PROBLEM 6-30

Some P-V plots are shown below for a gas that obeys the van der Waals equation. Calculate the constants a and b for this gas. Since your calculation is necessarily approximate, it is necessary to show very clearly just how you have obtained numbers from the graph below and how you have used them. Give the units of a and b also. (HINT: The 300°C isotherm is closest to critical point.)

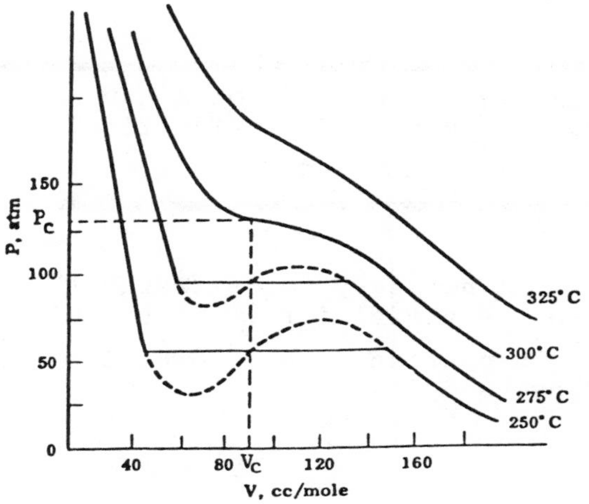

Solution: Since this problem requires approximate values, it is not necessary to interpolate or extrapolate. For the purposes of the problem, the 300°C isotherm (which is the closest to the critical point) is good enough.

Isotherm means, for any pressure and volume on that line, the temperature remains the same (300°C in this case). The terms P_c and V_c can be estimated from the point of inflection. Therefore $P_c \cong 130$ atm, $V_c \cong 90$ cm^3/mole and $T_c = 300°C = 573°K$.

For a van der Waals gas, $V_c = 3b$ and $P_c = \frac{a}{27b^2}$.

A system of two equations and two unknowns can now be

presented. Thus,

$$90 = 3b \tag{1}$$

and

$$130 = \frac{a}{27b^2} \tag{2}$$

From (1) $b = 90/3 = 30\ cm^3/mole$. Substituting this value into (2),

$$130 = \frac{a}{27\times 30^2}\ .$$

$$a = (130 \times 27 \times 30^2)cc^2\ atm/mole^2$$

$$= 3159000\ cc^2\ atm/moles^2$$

$$= 3.16 \times 10^6\ cc^2\ atm/moles^2.$$

• PROBLEM 6-31

Express the Boyle temperature of a van der Waals gas in terms of the constants a,b, and R. The final expression for T_B must contain only a,b, and R.

Solution: It is not easy to rearrange the van der Waals equation into the virial form, which would allow T_B to be evaluated by inspection. Therefore, the van der Waals equation to be used is

$$P = \frac{nRT}{V-nb} - \frac{n^2a}{V^2} \tag{1}$$

where P = pressure, V = volume, n = number of moles, T = temperature and R = gas constant. Multiplying both sides of equation (1) by V gives

$$PV = nRT\left(\frac{V}{V-nb}\right) - \frac{n^2a}{V} \tag{2}$$

Differentiating equation (2) partially with respect to P, keeping T constant, gives

$$\left(\frac{\partial(PV)}{\partial P}\right)_T = \left[\frac{nRT}{V-nb} - \frac{nRTV}{(V-nb)^2} + \frac{n^2a}{V^2}\right]\left(\frac{\partial V}{\partial P}\right)_T \tag{3}$$

At $P = 0$, $\left[\frac{\partial(PV)}{\partial P}\right]_T = 0$. Therefore,

$$\left[\frac{nRT}{V-nb} - \frac{nRTV}{(V-nb)^2} + \frac{n^2a}{V^2}\right]\left(\frac{\partial V}{\partial P}\right)_T = 0 \qquad (4)$$

Under all conditions $(\partial V/\partial P)_T < 0$; therefore, the expression in square brackets in equation (4) must equal to zero. That is

$$\frac{nRT}{V-nb} - \frac{nRTV}{(V-nb)^2} + \frac{n^2a}{V^2} = 0 \qquad (5)$$

Multiplying equation (5) through by $V^2(V-nb)^2$ gives

$$nRTV^2(V - nb) - nRTV^3 + n^2a(V - nb)^2 = 0$$

or

$$nRTV^2(V-nb) - nRTV^3 = -n^2a(V-nb)^2.$$

Therefore,

$$RT = \frac{a}{b}\left[\frac{V-nb}{V}\right]^2 = \frac{a}{b}\left[\frac{V}{V} - \frac{nb}{V}\right]^2$$

$$= \frac{a}{b}\left[1 - \frac{nb}{V}\right]^2 \qquad (6)$$

At the Boyle point $T = T_B$, $P = 0$ and $V = \infty$, so $RT_B = a/b$

or

$$T_B = \frac{a}{Rb} .$$

Another method of doing this is to set $n/V = c$. So, the van der Waals equation of state becomes

$$P = \frac{cRT}{1-bc} - ac^2 \qquad (7)$$

From equation (7),

$$PV = n\left[\frac{RT}{1-bc} - ac\right] \qquad (8)$$

Using the chain rule to differentiate equation (8) partially with respect to P gives

$$\left(\frac{\partial(PV)}{\partial P}\right)_T = \left(\frac{\partial(PV)}{\partial c}\right)_T \left(\frac{\partial c}{\partial P}\right)_T = n\left[\frac{bRT}{(1-bc)^2} - a\right]\left(\frac{\partial c}{\partial P}\right)_T . \qquad (9)$$

Observe that $\left(\frac{\partial c}{\partial P}\right)_T = \frac{1}{(\partial P/\partial c)_T} = \left(\frac{\partial P}{\partial c}\right)_T^{-1}$. From equation (7),

$$\left(\frac{\partial P}{\partial c}\right)_T = \left[\frac{bcRT}{(1-bc)^2} + \frac{RT}{1-bc} - 2ac\right]^{-1} \qquad (10)$$

Observe that equation (10) reduces to

$$RT \quad \text{as} \quad P \to 0 \quad \text{and} \quad c \to 0 \quad \text{or} \quad \left(\frac{\partial c}{\partial P}\right)_T = 1/RT\ .$$

Since $1/RT \neq 0$ and $n \neq 0$, the term in the square brackets in equation (9) must vanish at $c = 0$ and $T = T_B$. That is,

$$bRT_B - a = 0 \qquad (11)$$

Solving for T_B changes equation (11) to

$$T_B = \frac{a}{bR}\ .$$

• PROBLEM 6-32

What is the work needed to compress methane in a compressor from an initial pressure of 1 atm to a final pressure of 100 atm, at a constant temperature of 25°C. Use the van der Waals equation of state.

Solution: From the van der Waals equation of state

$$P = \frac{RT}{V-b} - \frac{a}{V^2} \qquad (1)$$

Differentiating Eq. (1) gives

$$dP = \left[-\frac{RT}{(V-b)^2} + \frac{2a}{V^3}\right] dV \qquad (2)$$

For the shaft work, w_s

$$-w_s = \int_{P_1}^{P_2} vdP$$

$$= \int_{V_1}^{V_2} V\left[-\frac{RT}{(V-b)^2} + \frac{2a}{V^3}\right] dV \qquad (3)$$

Integrating Eq. (3), obtain

$$-w_s = RT\ln\frac{V_2-b}{V_1-b} - RT\left(\frac{b}{V_2-b} - \frac{b}{V_1-b}\right) + 2a\left(\frac{1}{V_2} - \frac{1}{V_1}\right) \qquad (4)$$

The van der Waals constants expressed in terms of atm, ft^3, lb-mol, and °K are given as

$$a = 581.2$$

$$b = 0.6855$$

The gas constant R is (in the same units as above)

$$R = 1.3145$$

The solution is a trial-and-error one. After solving in Eq. (1), the values of V_1 and V_2 are found to be

$$V_1 = 391 \text{ ft}^3$$

$$V_2 = 3.16 \text{ ft}^3$$

Substituting these values into Eq. (4) gives

$$w_s = -1731 \text{ atm-ft}^3/\text{lb-mol}$$

$$= -4720 \text{ Btu/lb mol}$$

The negative sign indicates that work must be put into the compressor.

• PROBLEM 6-33

Estimate the pressure which would be exerted by 8.2 lb of CO in a 1-ft^3 container at -78°F, employing (a) the ideal-gas equation, (b) the van der Waals equation of state, and (c) the Redlich-Kwong equation.

Solution: The temperature of -78°F is equal to 382°R. The specific volume of the gas is 1/8.2 = 0.122 ft^3/lb.

a) The pressure is computed directly from the ideal-gas equation as

$$P = \frac{RT}{v} = \frac{1545(382)}{28(0.122)(144)} = 1200 \text{ psia} = 81.7 \text{ atm}$$

b) The constants for the van der Waals equation are found from tables. For CO we find that a = 372 atm-ft^6/(lb-mol)^2 and b = 0.63 ft^3/lb-mol. In this system of units the value of R_u will be 0.730 atm-ft^3/(lb-mol)(°R). In addition, the specific volume to be used is 0.122(28) = 3.42 ft^3/lb-mol. Substitution of these values in the proper equation leads to

$$\left(P + \frac{a}{v^2}\right)(v - b) = RT$$

$$\left[P + \frac{372}{(3.42)^2}\right](3.42 - 0.63) = 0.73(382)$$

The solution of this equation gives the pressure to be 68.2 atm.

c) The specific volume is 3.42 ft^3 /lb-mol and the temperature is 382°R. The constants a and b are found from a constant conversion chart to be 5870 atm $(ft^6)(R)^{1/2}/(lb\text{-}mol)^2$ and 0.4395 ft^3/lb-mol, respectively.

Making the proper substitutions,

$$P = \frac{RT}{v - b} - \frac{a}{T^{1/2}v(v + b)}$$

$$= \frac{0.73(382)}{3.42 - 0.440} - \frac{5870}{(382)^{1/2}(3.42)(3.42 + 0.440)}$$

$$= 70.8 \text{ atm}$$

• PROBLEM 6-34

a) Estimate the Boyle temperature for a certain non-ideal gas whose equation of state is

$$P\overline{V} = RT + APT - BP,$$

where $\overline{V}$ is the molar volume and A and B are constants.

b) Determine whether this gas has a critical point.

Solution: Rearranging the equation $P\overline{V} = RT + APT - BP$ gives

$$P\overline{V} - APT + BP = RT$$

or

$$P(\overline{V} - AT + B) = RT .$$

Solving for P yields

$$P = \frac{RT}{\overline{V}-AT+B} \tag{1}$$

$$= \frac{RT}{\overline{V}(1-(AT/\overline{V})+(B/\overline{V}))}$$

$$P = \frac{RT}{\overline{V}(1+(B-AT)/\overline{V})}$$

$$P\overline{V} = \frac{RT}{[1 + (B-AT)/\overline{V}]} \tag{2}$$

Consider the term $|(B-AT)/\overline{V}|$ to be very much less than 1, then equation (2) can be rewritten as,

$$P\overline{V} = RT[1 - (B-AT)/\overline{V}] \tag{3}$$

The Boyle temperature of a gas according to one definition is the temperature, T_B, at which

$$\lim_{\overline{V}\to\infty} \left[\frac{\partial(P\overline{V})}{\partial(1/\overline{V})}\right]_T = 0$$

at which point $P = 0$ and $T = T_B$. Thus, from equation (3),

$$B - AT_B = 0$$

or

$$T_B = B/A.$$

b) To be able to ascertain whether a gas has a critical point, the first and second derivative of the equation of state for such a gas with respect to V at constant T must vanish. Therefore from (1)

$$\left(\frac{\partial P}{\partial \overline{V}}\right)_T = \frac{-RT}{(\overline{V}-AT+B)^2} \tag{4}$$

$$\left(\frac{\partial^2 P}{\partial \overline{V}^2}\right)_T = \frac{2RT}{(\overline{V}-AT+B)^3} \tag{5}$$

At the critical point $(\partial P/\partial \overline{V})_T = 0$ and $(\partial^2 P/\partial \overline{V}^2)_T = 0$. The right hand sides of (4) and (5) can only be 0 if $T = 0$ or $\overline{V} - AT + B$ is infinite. Therefore this gas does not have a true critical point.

• PROBLEM 6-35

> At high pressures and temperatures a quite good equation of state is $P(V - nb) = nRT$, where b is a constant. Find $(\partial V/\partial T)_P$ and $(\partial V/\partial P)_T$ from this equation and hence dV in terms of P, T, V-nb, dT and dP.

Solution: Expanding the given equation of state, $P(V - nb) = nRT$, gives $PV - Pnb = nRT$ and rearranging to solve for V gives

$$V = \frac{nRT}{P} + nb \qquad (1)$$

where V = volume, n = number of moles, P = pressure, R = gas constant and T = temperature. Differentiating equation (1) with respect to T and keeping P constant yields

$$\left(\frac{\partial V}{\partial T}\right)_P = \frac{nR}{P} \qquad (2)$$

But $P = \frac{nRT}{V-nb}$. Therefore, $\left(\frac{\partial V}{\partial T}\right)_P = \frac{nR}{\left[\frac{nRT}{V-nb}\right]} = \frac{nR}{nRT} \times \left(V - nb\right)$

$$= \frac{V-nb}{T} \qquad (2a)$$

Note that the subscript P signifies that the pressure is being held constant while equation (1) is being differentiated. Now, differentiating with respect to P and holding T constant gives

$$\left(\frac{\partial V}{\partial P}\right)_T = - \frac{nRT}{P^2} = - \left(\frac{nRT}{P}\right) \frac{1}{P} \qquad (3)$$

Observe that equation (1) can be rearranged to give $V-nb = \frac{nRT}{P}$.

Therefore,

$$\left(\frac{\partial V}{\partial P}\right)_T = - \left(\frac{nRT}{P}\right) \frac{1}{P} = -(V - nb) \frac{1}{P} \qquad (3a)$$

Volume as a function of pressure and temperature can be represented as

$$V = f(P,T) . \qquad (4)$$

If the volume is a property of the system for which $P(V - nb) = nRT$, then it has an exact differential,

$$dV = \left(\frac{\partial V}{\partial P}\right)_T dP + \left(\frac{\partial V}{\partial T}\right)_P dT \qquad (5)$$

using equations (2a) and (3a), equation (5) becomes

$$dV = - \left(\frac{V-nb}{P}\right) dP + \left(\frac{V-nb}{T}\right) dT$$

$$= (V-nb)\left[- \frac{dP}{P} + \frac{dT}{T}\right].$$

• **PROBLEM 6-36**

Determine the equation of state for a certain hypothetical gas whose thermal coefficient of expansion is

$$\alpha = \frac{1}{V}\left(\frac{\partial V}{\partial T}\right)_P = k_1\left(\frac{C_P}{C_V}\right)T^{(C_P/C_V)-1}$$

and the coefficient of isothermal compressibility is

$$\beta = -\frac{1}{V}\left(\frac{\partial V}{\partial P}\right)_T = \frac{k_2}{P}.$$

In this problem, assume that C_P, C_V, k_1 and k_2 are constants.

Solution: If temperature, T and pressure, P are chosen to be independent variables, then, volume, V is some function of T and P. Thus,

$$V = f(T,P).$$

Writing the change in volume in differential form gives

$$dV = \left(\frac{\partial V}{\partial T}\right)_P dT + \left(\frac{\partial V}{\partial P}\right)_T dP \tag{1}$$

The quantities $\left(\frac{\partial V}{\partial T}\right)_P$ and $\left(\frac{\partial V}{\partial P}\right)_T$ can be determined using α and β

$$\alpha = \frac{1}{V}\left(\frac{\partial V}{\partial T}\right)_P = k_1\left(\frac{C_P}{C_V}\right)T^{(C_P/C_V)-1}$$

or

$$\left(\frac{\partial V}{\partial T}\right)_P = \frac{k_1 C_P T^{(C_P/C_V)-1}\,V}{C_V} \tag{2}$$

$$\beta = -\frac{1}{V}\left(\frac{\partial V}{\partial P}\right)_T = \frac{k_2}{P}$$

or

$$\left(\frac{\partial V}{\partial P}\right)_T = \frac{-k_2 V}{P} \tag{3}$$

Substituting equations (2) and (3) into equation (1) yields

$$dV = \frac{k_1 C_P T^{(C_P/C_V)-1} V}{C_V} dT - \frac{k_2 V}{P} dP$$

or

$$\frac{dV}{V} = k_1 \frac{C_P}{C_V} T^{(C_P/C_V)-1} dT - k_2 \frac{dP}{P} \qquad (4)$$

Integrating equation (4) gives

$$\ln V = k_1 \frac{C_P}{C_V} \cdot \frac{C_V}{C_P} T^{C_P/C_V} - k_2 \ln P + \text{constant}$$

$$\ln V = k_1 T^{C_P/C_V} - K_2 \ln P + \text{constant}$$

or

$$P^{k_2} V = k \exp\left(k_1 T^{(C_P/C_V)}\right)$$

Hence the desired equation of state is

$$P^{k_2} V = k \exp\left(k_1 T^{C_P/C_V}\right).$$

• PROBLEM 6-37

An equation of state due to Dieterici is

$$P(V - nb')\exp \frac{na'}{RTV} = nRT \qquad (1)$$

Evaluate the constants a' and b' in terms of the critical constants P_c, V_c, and T_c of a gas.

Solution: Rearranging equation (1) to solve for P gives

$$P = \frac{nRT}{V - nb'} e^{na'/RTV}$$

For 1 mole,

$$P = \frac{RT}{V - b'} e^{a'/RTV} \qquad (2)$$

where P = pressure, R = gas constant, V = volume and T = temperature. Differentiating equation (2) with respect to V gives

$$\frac{dP}{dV} = -\frac{P}{V - b'} + \frac{a'P}{RTV^2} \tag{3}$$

and

$$\frac{d^2P}{dV^2} = \frac{a'^2P}{(RTV^2)^2} - \frac{2a'P}{RTV^3} \tag{4}$$

At some point on a P-V diagram, the curve is horizontal and this part can be mathematically expressed as $dP/dV = 0$. Also, the highest temperature (maximum) at which such a horizontal line can still exist is called the critical temperature and at this point

$$\frac{d^2P}{dV^2} = 0 .$$

So, using these two conditions for equations (3) and (4), they can be rewritten as

$$0 = -\frac{P}{V - b'} + \frac{a'P}{RTV^2} \tag{3a}$$

$$0 = \frac{a'^2P}{(RTV^2)^2} - \frac{2a'P}{RTV^3} \tag{4a}$$

Since there are two equations and two unknowns, the equations can be solved simultaneously. Simplifying equation (4a), it becomes

$$a'\left(\frac{a'P}{R^2T^2V^4} - \frac{2P}{RTV^3}\right) = 0$$

From this, observe that there are two possible values for a'. That is, $a' = 0$ and $a' = 2RT_cV_c$. The trivial solution is discarded, so that $a' = 2RT_cV_c$. Putting this into equation (3a) gives

$$0 = -\frac{P}{V_c - b'} + \frac{2RT_cV_cP}{RT_cV^2_c}$$

or

$$0 = -\frac{P}{V_c - b'} + \frac{2P}{V_c} = P\left(-\frac{1}{V_c-b'} + \frac{2}{V_c}\right)$$

From this,

$$-\frac{1}{V_c-b'} + \frac{2}{V_c} = 0 \quad \text{or}$$

$$\frac{1}{V_c-b'} = \frac{2}{V_c} \tag{5}$$

The reciprocal of equation (5) is

$$V_c - b' = \frac{V_c}{2} ,$$

or

$$-b' = \frac{V_c}{2} - V_c = -\frac{V_c}{2} .$$

$$b' = \frac{V_c}{2} .$$

• PROBLEM 6-38

Consider an equation of state in the form

$$P = \frac{RT}{V - b} \cdot e^{-A/RT^{3/2}\overline{V}}$$

for an arbitrary gas. Show that the critical constants are given by

$$T_c = \left(\frac{A}{4bR}\right)^{2/3} ,$$

$$\overline{V}_c = 2b \quad \text{and} \quad P_c = \frac{R}{b}\left(\frac{A}{4bR}\right)^{2/3} e^{-2}$$

Solution:

$$P = \frac{RT}{(\overline{V} - b)} \cdot e^{-A/RT^{3/2}\,\overline{V}} \tag{1}$$

Differentiate equation (1) twice with respect to $\overline{V}$ at constant temperature, T to generate two new equations. That is,

$$\left(\frac{\partial P}{\partial \overline{V}}\right)_T = \frac{RT}{(\overline{V} - b)} e^{-A/RT^{3/2}\,\overline{V}}\left(\frac{A}{RT^{3/2}\,\overline{V}^2} - \frac{1}{(\overline{V} - b)}\right) \tag{2}$$

and

$$\left(\frac{\partial^2 P}{\partial \overline{V}^2}\right)_T = \left\{\left[\frac{A}{RT^{3/2}\,\overline{V}^2} - \frac{1}{(\overline{V} - b)}\right]\left[\frac{-1}{(\overline{V} - b)^2} + \frac{A}{RT^{3/2}\,\overline{V}^2}\right] + \left(\frac{1}{(\overline{V} - b)}\right)\left[\frac{-2A}{RT^{3/2}\,\overline{V}^3} + \frac{1}{(\overline{V} - b)^2}\right]\right\} RTe^{-A/RT^{3/2}\,\overline{V}} \tag{3}$$

The first and second derivatives disappear at the critical point, therefore

$$\left(\frac{\partial P}{\partial \overline{V}}\right)_T = 0 \quad \text{and} \quad \left(\frac{\partial^2 P}{\partial \overline{V}^2}\right)_T = 0$$

From equation (2), since $\frac{RT}{(\overline{V} - b)} e^{-A/RT^{3/2}\,\overline{V}}$ can not be zero, then

$$\frac{A}{RT_c^{3/2}\,\overline{V}_c^2} - \frac{1}{\overline{V}_c - b} = 0 \;. \tag{4}$$

In equation (3), the first term is also zero; consequently, the second term will disappear only when

$$\frac{-2A}{RT_c^{3/2}\,V_b^3} + \frac{1}{(\overline{V}_c - b)^2} = 0 \tag{5}$$

Dividing equation (4) by equation (5) yields

$$\frac{2}{V_c} = \frac{1}{(\overline{V}_c - b)}$$

$$2(\overline{V}_c - b) = V_c$$

$$2\overline{V}_c - 2b = V_c$$

and

$$\overline{V}_c = 2b \tag{6}$$

Substituting equation (6) into equation (4) gives

$$\frac{A}{RT_c^{3/2}(2b)^2} - \frac{1}{2b - b} = 0$$

$$\frac{A}{RT_c^{3/2}\,4b^2} - \frac{1}{b} = 0$$

$$RT_c^{3/2}\,4b^2 - Ab = 0$$

$$RT_c^{3/2}\,4b - A = 0$$

$$T_c^{3/2} = \frac{A}{4bR}$$

or

$$T_c = \left(\frac{A}{4bR}\right)^{2/3}$$

Combining equations (6), (7), and (1) gives

$$P_c = \frac{R\left(\frac{A}{4bR}\right)^{2/3}}{(2b - b)} e^{-A/R(A/4BR)2b}$$

or

$$P_c = \frac{R}{b}\left(\frac{A}{4bR}\right)^{2/3} e^{-2} .$$

• PROBLEM 6-39

Derive the relations between the constants a, b, and R of the Berthelot equation,

$$P = \frac{RT}{(\overline{V} - b)} - \frac{a}{T\overline{V}^2} ,$$

and the critical parameters. Express the equation of state in terms of reduced variables.

Solution:

$$P = \frac{RT}{(\overline{V} - b)} - \frac{a}{T\overline{V}^2} \tag{1}$$

Taking the first derivative with respect to V at constant temperature gives

$$\left(\frac{\partial P}{\partial \overline{V}}\right)_T = \frac{-RT}{(\overline{V} - b)^2} + \frac{2a}{T\overline{V}^3} \tag{2}$$

The second derivative is

$$\left(\frac{\partial^2 P}{\partial \overline{V}^2}\right)_T = \frac{2RT}{(\overline{V} - b)^3} - \frac{6a}{T\overline{V}^4} \tag{3}$$

Applying the critical isotherm conditions, that the partial derivatives with respect to volume at constant temperature is zero, equations (2) and (3) become

$$\left(\frac{\partial P}{\partial \overline{V}}\right)_T = \frac{-RT}{(\overline{V} - b)^2} + \frac{2a}{T\overline{V}^3} = 0 \tag{4}$$

and

$$\left(\frac{\partial^2 P}{\partial \overline{V}^2}\right)_T = \frac{2RT}{(\overline{V} - b)^3} - \frac{6a}{T\overline{V}^4} = 0 . \tag{5}$$

Solving equations (4) and (5) simultaneously yields

$$\frac{2}{\overline{V}_c - b} = \frac{3}{\overline{V}_c}$$

$$3(\overline{V}_c - b) = 2\overline{V}_c$$

$$3\overline{V}_c - 3b = 2\overline{V}_c$$

$$3b = \overline{V}_c$$

$$b = \overline{V}_c/3 \ .$$

Substitute $b = \overline{V}_c/3$ into equation (4) and solve for a. That is,

$$\frac{-RT_c}{\left(\overline{V}_c - \overline{V}_c/3\right)^2} + \frac{2a}{T_c\overline{V}_c^3} = 0$$

or

$$2a\overline{V}_c^2(1 - \tfrac{1}{3})^2 - RT_c^2\ \overline{V}_c^3 = 0$$

$$2a = \frac{RT_c^2\ \overline{V}_c^3}{\frac{4}{9}\ \overline{V}_c^2}$$

$$2a = \frac{9RT_c^2\ \overline{V}_c}{4}$$

$$a = \frac{9RT_c^2\ \overline{V}_c}{8} \qquad (5)$$

Substituting $a = 9RT_c^2\ \overline{V}_c/8$ and $b = \overline{V}_c/3$ into equation (1) gives

$$P_c = \frac{RT_c}{\left(\overline{V}_c - \overline{V}_c/3\right)} - \frac{\frac{9RT_c^2\overline{V}_c}{8}}{(T_c)(\overline{V}_c^2)}$$

$$= \frac{RT_c}{\overline{V}_c(1 - \frac{1}{3})} - \frac{9RT_c^2\ \overline{V}_c}{8T_c\ \overline{V}_c^2}$$

$$= \frac{RT_c}{\frac{2}{3}\ \overline{V}_c} - \frac{9RT_c}{8\overline{V}_c}$$

$$P_c = \frac{3RT_c}{2\overline{V}_c} - \frac{9RT_c}{8\overline{V}_c}$$

$$= \frac{12RT_c - 9RT_c}{8\overline{V}_c}$$

$$P_c = \frac{3RT_c}{8\overline{V}_c}$$

and

$$R = \frac{8P_c\overline{V}_c}{3T_c}$$

Substituting $R = 8P_c\overline{V}_c/3T_c$ into (5) gives

$$a = \frac{9(8P_cV_c)T_c^2\ \overline{V}_c}{24T_c}$$

or

$$a = 3P_c\overline{V}_c^2T_c$$

Now, define the reduced variables as π, ϕ and θ , corresponding to reduced pressure, volume and temperature respectively.

$$\pi = \frac{P}{P_c} \qquad (6)$$

$$\phi = \frac{\overline{V}}{\overline{V}_c} \qquad (7)$$

and

$$\theta = \frac{T}{T_c} \qquad (8)$$

From equation (6) $P = \pi P_c$ and from equations (7) and (8)

$\overline{V} = \phi\overline{V}_c$ and $T = \theta T_c$ respectively.

Substituting $P = \pi P_c$, $\overline{V} = \phi\overline{V}_c$, $T = \theta T_c$, R, b and a into equation (1) gives

$$\pi P_c = \frac{\frac{8\ P_c\overline{V}_c}{3T_c}(\theta T_c)}{\phi\overline{V}_c - \overline{V}_c/3} - \frac{3P_c\overline{V}_c^2\ T_c}{\theta T_c\ \phi^2\ \overline{V}^2}$$

$$= \frac{8P_c\overline{V}_c\theta T_c}{3T_c\overline{V}_c(\phi-\frac{1}{3})} - \frac{3P_c}{\theta\phi^2}$$

$$\pi P_c = \frac{8P_c\theta}{3(\phi-\frac{1}{3})} - \frac{3P_c}{\theta\phi^2}$$

or

$$\pi = \frac{8\theta}{3\phi - 1} - \frac{3}{\theta\phi^2} \tag{9}$$

Equation (9) is the equation of state in terms of reduced variables.

• PROBLEM 6-40

Carbon dioxide is assumed to follow the equation of state

$$\left(P + \frac{n}{V^2 T^{\frac{1}{2}}}\right)(v-m) = RT$$

where n and m are constants for any gas. Given that the critical pressure and temperature of carbon dioxide are 72.9 atm and 304.2°K respectively, determine the compressibility factor of the gas at 100°C and at a volume of 6.948 cubic decimeters per kilogram.

Solution:

$$\left(P + \frac{n}{V^2 T^{\frac{1}{2}}}\right)(V-m) = RT$$

solving for P gives

$$P = \frac{RT}{V-m} - \frac{n}{V^2 T^{\frac{1}{2}}} \tag{2}$$

Differentiate equation (2) twice with respect to V at constant T and set them equal to zero because at the critical point

$$\left(\frac{\partial P}{\partial V}\right)_T = \left(\frac{\partial^2 P}{\partial V^2}\right)_T = 0$$

Therefore at the critical point

$$\left(\frac{\partial P}{\partial V}\right)_T = -\frac{RT_c}{(V_c - m)^2} + 2\frac{n}{V_c^3 T_c^{\frac{1}{2}}} = 0 \tag{3}$$

$$\left(\frac{\partial^2 P}{\partial V^2}\right)_T = \frac{2RT_c}{(V_c - m)^3} - 6\frac{n}{V_c^4 T_c^{\frac{1}{2}}} = 0 \tag{4}$$

Equation (3) can also be written as

$$\frac{RT_c}{(V_c - m)^2} = \frac{n}{T_c^{\frac{1}{2}}} \frac{2}{V_c^3} \tag{5}$$

and equation (4) as

$$\frac{RT_c}{(V_c - m)^3} = \frac{n}{T_c^{\frac{1}{2}}} \frac{3}{V_c^{\;4}} \qquad (6)$$

Divide equation (5) by equation (6) to get

$$V_c - m = \tfrac{2}{3} V_c$$

from which

$$m = \tfrac{1}{3} V_c$$

where V_c is the critical volume. Substitute the value of m into equation (5) and solve for n

$$\frac{RT_c}{\left(V_c^2 - 2mV_c + m^2\right)} = \frac{n}{T_c^{\frac{1}{2}}} \frac{2}{V_c^3}$$

or

$$n = \frac{RT_c^{3/2} V_c^3}{2V_c^2 - \frac{4}{3} V^2 + \frac{2}{9} V^2}$$

$$= \frac{RT_c^{3/2} V_c^3}{V_c^2(2 - \frac{4}{3} + \frac{2}{9})}$$

$$= \frac{RT_c^{3/2} V_c^3}{V_c^2(\frac{8}{9})}$$

$$= \frac{9RT_c^{3/2} V_c}{8} \qquad (7)$$

Equation (2) becomes at the critical point

$$P_c = \frac{RT_c}{V_c - m} - \frac{n}{V_c^2 T_c^{\frac{1}{2}}}$$

where P_c is the critical pressure

$$P_c = \frac{RT_c}{V_c - m} - \frac{9/8\ RT^{3/2} V_c}{V_c^2 T_c^{\frac{1}{2}}}$$

$$= \frac{3}{2} \frac{RT_c}{V_c} - \frac{9}{8} \frac{RT_c}{V_c}$$

$$= \frac{3}{8} \frac{RT_c}{V_c}$$

or

$$\frac{P_c V_c}{RT_c} = \frac{3}{8} \tag{8}$$

CO_2 has a molecular weight of 44 g mol^{-1}

$$V = 6.948\left(\frac{(dm)^3}{kg}\right)\left(\frac{10^3 cm^3}{(dm)^3}\right)\left(\frac{0.044\ kg}{mol}\right)$$

$$= 3.057 \times 10^2\ cm^3/mol.$$

From equation (8)

$$V_c = \frac{3}{8}\ \frac{RT_c}{P_c}$$

$$= \frac{3}{8} \times \frac{(82.05\ cm^3 atm/°K^{-1}\ mol^{-1})(304.2°K)}{72.9\ atm}$$

$$= 128.3\ cm^3\ mol^{-1}$$

Remember that $m = V_c/3$

$$= \frac{128.3\ cm^3\ mol^{-1}}{3}$$

$$= 42.79\ cm^3\ mol^{-1}$$

From equation (7)

$$n = \frac{(9)(82.05\ cm^3 atm\ °K^{-1} mol^{-1})(304.2°K)^{3/2}\ (128.3\ cm^3 mol^{-1})}{8}$$

$$= 6.28 \times 10^7\ \frac{cm^6\ atm\ K^{\frac{1}{2}}}{mol^2}$$

Solving for P using equation (2) gives

$$P = \left[\frac{(82.05\ cm^3 atm\ K^{-1} mol^{-1})(373°K)}{(3.057 \times 10^2 cm^3/mol)-(42.79\ cm^3/mol)}\right]$$

$$-\left[\frac{6.28 \times 10^7 cm^6\, atm\ K^{\frac{1}{2}}/mol^2}{(3.057 \times 10^2 cm^3/mol)^2 (373°K)^{\frac{1}{2}}}\right]$$

$$= 81.57\ atm.$$

By definition the compressibility factor Z is given as

$$Z = \frac{PV}{RT}$$

$$= \frac{(81.57\ \text{atm})(3.057 \times 10^2\ \text{cm}^3/\text{mol})}{(82.05\ \text{cm}^3\ \text{atm}°\text{K}^{-1}\text{mol}^{-1})(373°\text{K})}$$

$$= 0.815.$$

• PROBLEM 6-41

A magnesium alloy, at 600°F is stretched isentropically by 1.0×10^{-2} in./in. What is the stress that results, and how does it differ from the stress produced by an isothermal stress of the same amount . Assume the alloy to follow the Hooke equation of state with the following constants.

$$Y_t = 6.5 \times 10^6\ \text{lbf/in}^2$$

$$\alpha = 16 \times 10^{-6}\ (1/°\text{F})$$

$$C_\sigma = 0.242\ \text{Btu/lbm-°F}$$

$$\rho = 109\ \text{lbm/ft}^3$$

Solution: The change in temperature with such a strain is given by the equation

$$C_\sigma \ln\left(\frac{T_2}{T_1}\right) = \beta(e_2 - e_1) \qquad (1)$$

where

$$e_2 = \text{final stretch} = 1.0 \times 10^{-2}\ \text{in/in}$$

$$e_1 = \text{initial stretch} = 0\ \text{in/in}$$

and

$$\beta = -Y_t\ \alpha$$

For the consistency of units

$$C_\sigma = 0.242\ \frac{\text{Btu}}{\text{lbm-°F}} \times 778\ \frac{\text{ft-lbf}}{\text{Btu}} \times \frac{12\ \text{in}}{\text{ft}} \times 109\ \frac{\text{lbm}}{\text{ft}^3} \times \frac{1\ \text{ft}^3}{1728\ \text{in}^3}$$

$$= 142.51\ \text{ft-lbf/in}^2\text{-lbm-°F}.$$

Substitution of the numerical values into Eq. (1), yields

$$142.5 \ln\left(\frac{T_2}{T_1}\right) = -6.5 \times 10^6\ (16 \times 10^{-6})(1 \times 10^{-2})$$

or

$$\ln\left(\frac{T_2}{T_1}\right) = -0.0073$$

For such a small number

$$\ln\left(\frac{T_2}{T_1}\right) \cong \left(\frac{T_2}{T_1}\right) - 1$$

so that

$$\frac{T_2}{T_1} = -0.0073 + 1 = 0.9927$$

solving for T_2,

$$T_2 = 600(0.9927) = 595.62°F$$

To compute the stress, the thermoelastic equation of state

$$\sigma = Y_t[e - \alpha(T - T_0)] \qquad (2)$$

will be used with T_0 arbitrarily set at 600°F.

Then

$$\sigma = 6.5 \times 10^6 \left[0.01 - (16 \times 10^{-6})(595.62\text{-}600)\right]$$

$$= 654{,}455.52 \text{ lbf/in}^2.$$

In the case of an isothermal stretch

$$T = T_0$$

and the stress, from Eq. (2), is calculated to be

$$\sigma = (6.5 \times 10^6)(0.01) = 65000 \text{ lbf/in}^2$$

The difference of 460 psi out of 60,000 is probably below the level of measurement of most testing machines, so that the method of stretch is not important for this type of material. Actually, this is generally true of metals, while, with rubbers and synthetics, disregarding the way in which a tensile test is run may produce a serious error in prediction of stress and strain characteristics. Such elastomers are, however, usually governed by equations more complex than the Hooke form.

CHAPTER 7

IDEAL AND REAL GAS PROCESSES AND RELATIONS

IDEAL GAS PROCESSES INVOLVING THE FIRST AND SECOND LAWS OF THERMODYNAMICS

• PROBLEM 7-1

Two pounds of oxygen undergo a polytropic process in which they are compressed from an initial state of 14 psia and 70°F, to a final pressure of 98 psia along a path for which $PV^{1.3} = C$. Using the polytropic equation calculate, (a) the heat transferred, and (b) the change of entropy for this process. Assume that for oxygen

$$R = 0.062 \text{ Btu/lbm-°R}$$

$$c_p = 0.217 \text{ Btu/lbm-°R}$$

Solution: (a) The heat transfer for the process can be found in two ways. Either by using the first law

$$Q_{1\to2} = \Delta U_{1\to2} - W_{1\to2} \tag{1}$$

or by using the polytropic equation

$$Q_{1\to2} = mc_n(T_2 - T_1) \tag{2}$$

where

$$c_n = c_v\left(\frac{k-n}{1-n}\right) \tag{3}$$

However by definition

$$c_v = c_p - R = 0.217 - 0.062 = 0.1550 \text{ Btu/lbm-°R}$$

and

$$k = \frac{c_p}{c_v} = \frac{0.2170}{0.1550} = 1.4$$

Then from Eq. (3)

$$c_n = 0.1550\left(\frac{1.4 - 1.3}{1 - 1.3}\right)$$

$$= -0.052 \text{ Btu/lbm-°R}$$

The temperature at state 1 expressed in °R is

$$T_1 = 70 + 460 = 530°R$$

At state two

$$T_2 = T_1\left(\frac{P_2}{P_1}\right)^{(n-1)/n}$$

$$= 530\left(\frac{98}{14}\right)^{(1.3-1)/1.3}$$

$$= 830°R$$

Therefore from Eq. (2)

$$Q_{1\to 2} = 2(-0.052)(830 - 530)$$

$$= -31.2 \text{ Btu}$$

(b) For the change in entropy the polytropic equation can be written as

$$\Delta S = s_2 - s_1 = mc_n \ln \frac{T_2}{T_1}$$

$$= 2(-0.052) \ln \left(\frac{830}{530}\right)$$

$$= -0.0466 \text{ Btu/°R}$$

• PROBLEM 7-2

Air at an initial pressure and temperature of 1 bar and 17°C respectively is contained inside a cylinder. The air is then compressed polytropically, along a path for which n = 1.30, until the final pressure inside the cylinder is 5 bars. What is the heat transferred per kg of air for this process?

Solution: This problem involves a closed system. Therefore the first law written for this process is

$$q_{1\to2} + w_{1\to2} = \Delta u \tag{1}$$

In Eq. (1) both $q_{1\to2}$ and $w_{1\to2}$ are unknown. Since $q_{1\to2}$ cannot be calculated independently, $w_{1\to2}$ must be evaluated using the relation which applies in this case,

$$dw_{1\to2} = -P\ dv \tag{2}$$

For this process

$$Pv^n = c$$

Therefore

$$w_{1\to2} = -\int P\ dv = -\int cv^{-n}\ dv$$

$$= \frac{c(v_2)^{1-n} - c(v_1)^{1-n}}{n-1}$$

$$= \frac{P_2v_2 - P_1v_1}{n-1} = \frac{R(T_2 - T_1)}{n-1} \tag{3}$$

For air

$$R = 0.287\ \text{kJ/kg-°K}$$

Also because air is essentially an ideal gas in the range of pressures and temperatures involved, the ideal gas equation for a polytropic process

$$\frac{T_2}{T_1} = \frac{P_2}{P_1}^{(n-1)/n} \tag{3}$$

can be used to find the temperature at state 2.

Therefore, solving for T_2 in Eq. (3) gives,

$$T_2 = T_1\left(\frac{P_2}{P_1}\right)^{(n-1)/n}$$

$$= 290\left(\frac{5}{1}\right)^{(1.3-1)/1.3}$$

$$= 420.43°\text{K}$$

From Eq. (3) then

$$w_{1\to 2} = \frac{0.287(420.43-290)}{1.3-1}$$

$$= 124.78 \text{ kJ/kg.}$$

The specific internal energy change for an ideal gas is

$$\Delta u = c_v \Delta T$$

or

$$u_2 - u_1 = c_v(T_2 - T_1)$$

where $c_v = 0.7165$ kJ/kg-°K (for air)

Substituting the numerical values

$$\Delta u = u_2 - u_1 = 0.7165(420.43 - 290)$$

$$= 93.45 \text{ kJ/kg}$$

Then solving for $q_{1\to 2}$ in Eq. (1) gives

$$q_{1\to 2} = \Delta u - w_{1\to 2}$$

$$= 93.45 - 124.78$$

$$= -31.33 \text{ kJ/kg}$$

The negative sign indicates that heat was removed from the gas during the compression process.

• PROBLEM 7-3

An ideal gas is enclosed inside a chamber with a volume of 0.1 ft^3 at 115°C, 690kPa. It then expands isentropically to a final pressure of 138kPa. Calculate the work done during the process, assuming that for this gas

$$c_v = 0.7201 \text{ kJ/kg-°K}$$

$$c_p = 1.0048 \text{ kJ/kg-°K}$$

Solution: Since the process is isentropic

$$s_2 = s_1$$

The process is adiabatic, and thus

$$Q_{1\to2} = 0$$

The first law applied to this system is

$$Q_{1\to2} = m(u_2 - u_1) + w_{1\to2} = 0 \tag{1}$$

or

$$w_{1\to2} = -m(u_2 - u_1) \tag{2}$$

Since the specific heats, for this process, are constant

$$du = c_v dT$$

or

$$u_2 - u_1 = c_v(T_2 - T_1)$$

Then Eq. (2) becomes

$$w_{1\to2} = -mc_v(T_2 - T_1) \tag{3}$$

For this process

$$P_1V_1^{\gamma} = P_2V_2^{\gamma} \tag{4}$$

where

$$\gamma = \frac{c_p}{c_v} = \frac{1.0048}{0.7201} = 1.3954$$

Solving for V_2 in Eq. (4) gives,

$$V_2 = V_1\left(\frac{P_1}{P_2}\right)^{1/\gamma}$$

$$= 0.1 \left(\frac{690}{138}\right)^{1/1.3954}$$

$$= 0.317\,^3\text{ft}$$

or

$$v_2 = 0.317\text{ ft}^3 \times 0.028317 \frac{\text{m}^3}{\text{ft}^3} = 8.98 \times 10^{-3}\text{ m}^3$$

For an isentropic process

$$T_1V_1^{\gamma-1} = T_2V_2^{\gamma-1}$$

or

$$T_2 = T_1\left(\frac{V_1}{V_2}\right)^{\gamma-1}$$

where

$$T_1 = 115 + 273.15 = 388.15°K$$

Therefore

$$T_2 = 388.15\left(\frac{0.1}{0.317}\right)^{1.3954-1}$$

$$= 245.97°K$$

or $$T_2 = -27.18°C$$

The mass of the system can be obtained by using the ideal gas equation of state. Therefore

$$m = \frac{P_2 V_2}{RT_2} \qquad (5)$$

where

$$R = c_p - c_v = 1.0048-0.7201$$

$$= 0.2847 \text{ kJ/kg-°K}$$

From Eq. (5), then

$$m = \frac{138(8.98 \times 10^{-3})}{0.2847(245.97)}$$

$$= 0.0177 \text{ kg}$$

Then from Eq. (3)

$$W_{1\to 2} = -0.0177(0.7201)(245.97-388.15)$$

$$= 1.8122 \text{ kJ}$$

• PROBLEM 7-4

A chamber contains 5 lbm of an ideal gas, initially at a temperature of 100°F. The gas then undergoes a reversible isobaric process during which 500 Btu are added to the gas as heat. Determine the final temperature of the gas, assuming that the following properties of the gas are known.

$R = 0.0641$ Btu/lbm-°R [0.2684 kJ/kg-°K]

$k = 1.147$

Solution: Since the gas is not stated the specific heats are found from the equations

$$c_v = \frac{R}{k-1} \qquad (1)$$

and

$$c_p = R + c_v \qquad (2)$$

Also $T_1 = 100°F + 460 = 560°R \quad [311.11°K]$

Substituting the numerical values into Eq. (1), gives

$$c_v = \frac{0.0641}{(1.147-1)}$$

$$= 0.4361 \text{ Btu/lbm-°R} \quad [1.8257 \text{ kJ/kg-°K}]$$

From Eq. (2), then

$$c_p = 0.0641 + 0.4361$$

$$= 0.5 \text{ Btu/lbm-°R} \quad [2.0942 \text{ kJ/kg-°K}]$$

Then, write the first law for an ideal gas for this case. Therefore

$$Q = mc_p dT = mc_p(T_2 - T_1)$$

or solving for T_2, gives

$$T_2 = \frac{Q}{mc_p} + T_1$$

$$= \frac{500}{(5)(0.5)} + 560 = 760°R \quad (422.2°K]$$

This temperature expressed in °F is

$$T_2 = 300°F \quad [149.1°C]$$

• PROBLEM 7-5

A piston and cylinder arrangement has an initial volume of 1.5 ft^3 and contains air at 400 psia. The air is then expanded reversibly at a constant temperature of 85°F. What is the work and heat transferred of the process if the final volume of the air inside the cylinder is 4 ft^3. Assume the temperature of the surroundings to be 85°F.

Solution: The mass of the system is constant throughout the process, and can be determined using the ideal gas equation of state

$$m = \frac{PV}{RT} \qquad (1)$$

Direct substitution of the numerical values into Eq. (1) will give the amount of air present in the process. However, in substituting the numbers care must be taken so that the units are consistent. Hence

$$P_1 = 400 \frac{\text{lbf}}{\text{in}^2} \times \frac{144 \text{ in}^2}{1 \text{ ft}^2} = 57,600 \text{ lbf/ft}^2$$

$$T_1 = 85°\text{F} + 460 = 545°\text{R}$$

$$R = 53.34 \frac{\text{ft-lbf}}{\text{lbm°R}} \text{ (from table of contents)}$$

Substituting into Eq. (1)

$$m = \frac{57,600 \times 1.5}{53.34 \times 545} = 2.972 \text{ lbm}$$

Since this is an isothermal process, the pressure at state 2 can be determined by applying Eq. (1) at states 1 and 2 (after solving for T).

Therefore,

$$T = \frac{P_1V_1}{mR} = \frac{P_2V_2}{mR} = \text{constant}$$

Solving for P_2

$$P_2 = P_1\left(\frac{V_1}{V_2}\right) = 400 \left(\frac{1.5}{4}\right) = 150 \text{ lbf/in}^2$$

Since this is a reversible isothermal process, the work can be calculated using

$$W_{1\to2} = \int_1^2 PdV \qquad (2)$$

where the path 1→2 for this process is given by

$$PV = mRT$$

Substituting into Eq. (2)

$$W_{1\to2} = \int_1^2 \frac{mRT}{V} dV = mRT \int_{V_1}^{V_2} \frac{dV}{V}$$

$$= mRT \ln \frac{V_2}{V_1}$$

$$= (2.972 \times 53.34 \times 545) \ln \frac{4}{1.5}$$

$$= 84,740.64 \text{ ft-lbf} \times \frac{1 \text{ Btu}}{778 \text{ ft-lbf}}$$

$$= 108.92 \text{ Btu}$$

The heat transferred to or from the system can be found by using the energy equation,

$$Q = -\Delta U + W$$

However for the ideal gas undergoing an isothermal process the change in internal energy is

$$\Delta U = 0$$

and so

$$Q = W = 108.92 \text{ Btu}$$

• PROBLEM 7-6

A block of copper is at an initial pressure and temperature of 1 atm and 520°R respectively. The pressure is then increased to 1000 atm in a reversible isothermal process. Find (a) the change in internal energy, (b) the change in entropy, (c) the heat absorbed, and (d) the work done, all per unit mass.

Solution: (a) Since the temperature is constant

$$(u_2 - u_1)_T = -\beta \nu_o T(P_2 - P_1) + \frac{\kappa \nu_o}{2}(P_2^2 - P_1^2) \qquad (1)$$

where

$$\beta = 2.8 \times 10^{-5}/°R$$

$$\kappa = 5.9 \times 10^{-8} \text{ in}^2/\text{lbm} = 4.1 \times 10^{-10} \text{ ft}^2/\text{lbm}$$

$$\nu_o = \frac{1}{\rho} = \frac{1}{550} = 1.82 \times 10^{-3} \text{ ft}^3/\text{lbm}$$

For the consistency of units,

$$P_1 = 1 \text{ atm} = 14.7 \text{ lbf/in}^2 = 2116.8 \text{ lbf/ft}^2$$

$$P_2 = 1000 \text{ atm} = 2{,}116{,}800 \text{ lbf/ft}^2$$

Substituting the numerical values into Eq. (1)

$$(u_2 - u_1)_T = -(2.8 \times 10^{-5})(1.82 \times 10^{-3})(530)(2{,}116{,}800 - 2116.8)$$

$$+ \frac{(4.1 \times 10^{-10})(1.82 \times 10^{-3})}{2}\left[(2116800)^2 - (2116.8)^2\right]$$

$$= -56.016 + 1.6649$$

$$= -54.35 \text{ ft-lbf/lbm}$$

$$= -69.86 \times 10^{-3} \text{ Btu/lbm}$$

(b) The change in entropy can be found using the equation

$$(s_2 - s_1)_T = -\beta\nu_o(P_2 - P_1)$$

$$= -(2.8 \times 10^{-5})(1.82 \times 10^{-3})(2116800 - 2116.8)$$

$$= 0.1078 \text{ ft-lbf/lbm-°R}$$

$$= 1.39 \times 10^{-4} \text{ Btu/lbm-°R}$$

(c) Since the process is reversible, the heat absorbed is

$$q = T(s_2 - s_1) = -\beta\nu_o T(P_2 - P_1)$$

$$= -(2.8 \times 10^{-5})(1.82 \times 10^{-3})(530)(2,116,800-2,116.8)$$

$$= -56.016 \text{ ft-lbf/lbm}$$

$$= -72 \times 10^{-3} \text{ Btu/lbm}$$

(d) From the first law of thermodynamics

$$w = q - \Delta u$$

$$= -72 \times 10^{-3} - (-69.86 \times 10^{-3})$$

$$= -2.14 \times 10^{-3} \text{ Btu/lbm}$$

Eq. (1) is a statement of the combined first and second laws, the first term on the right being equal to $T(s_2 - s_1)$, and the second term being equal to w.

• PROBLEM 7-7

1. An ideal gas initially at 70°C and 1 bar undergoes the following reversible processes, completing a cycle.

(a) The gas is compressed adiabatically to 150°C (1→2)

(b) It is then cooled at constant pressure from 150°C to 70°C (2→3)

(c) Finally the gas is expanded at constant temperature to a final pressure of 1 bar (3→1)

Assuming that for the gas $c_v = \frac{3}{2}\bar{R}$, calculate Δh, Δu, w, and q for the entire cycle on a per gm-mole basis.

2. Repeat the calculations assuming an efficiency of 80% for each cycle.

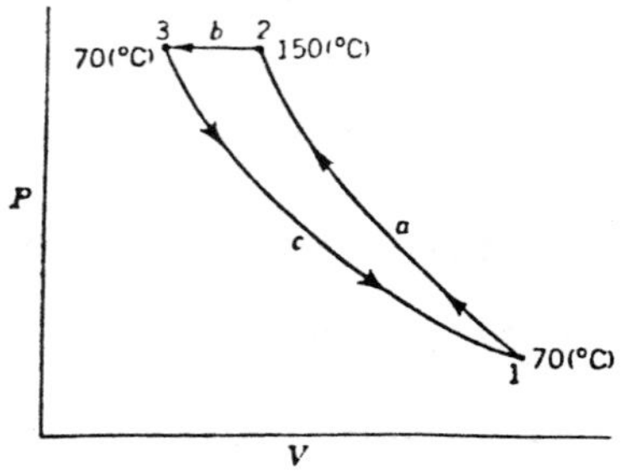

Solution: 1. The cycle is represented on a P-V diagram as shown in the figure. To calculate q, w, Δu, and Δh for the entire cycle, first calculate these quantities for each of the processes and then use the following equations.

$$q\Big|_{cycle} = q_{1\to2} + q_{2\to3} + q_{3\to1} \tag{1}$$

$$w\Big|_{cycle} = w_{1\to2} + w_{2\to3} + w_{3\to1} \tag{2}$$

$$\Delta u\Big|_{cycle} = \Delta u_{1\to2} + \Delta u_{2\to3} + \Delta u_{3\to1} \tag{3}$$

$$\Delta h\Big|_{cycle} = \Delta h_{1\to2} + \Delta h_{2\to3} + \Delta h_{3\to1}$$

For an ideal gas

$$\overline{R} = c_p - c_v$$

or

$$c_p = c_v + \overline{R}$$

For the cycle, using Eqs. (1), (2), (3), and (4)

$$q = 0 - 1663 + 1495 = -168 \text{ J/g mol}$$

$$w = -998 - 665 + 1495 = -168 \text{ J/g mol}$$

$$\Delta u = 998 - 998 + 0 = 0$$

$$\Delta h = 1663 - 1663 + 0 = 0$$

It is very important that Δu and Δh are both zero for the entire cycle, since the initial and final states are identical. Also the fact that q and w are equal proves the first law applied to the cycle, since Δu = 0.

2. If the same changes in state are carried out by irreversible processes, the property changes for the steps will be identical with those already calculated. However the values of q and w will be different.

Then for this gas

$$c_p = \frac{3}{2}\bar{R} + \bar{R} = \frac{5}{2}\bar{R}$$

where $\bar{R} = 8.314$ J/g mol-°K

Therefore

$$c_v = \frac{3}{2}(8.314) = 12.471 \text{ J/g-mol-°K}$$

$$c_p = \frac{5}{2}(8.314) = 20.785 \text{ J/g mol-°K}$$

(a) For an ideal gas undergoing adiabatic compression

$$Q = 0$$

From the first law

$$\Delta u = -w = c_v \Delta T = 12.471(150\text{-}70) = 998 \text{ J/g mol}$$

$$\Delta h = c_p \Delta T = 20.785(150\text{-}70) = 1{,}663 \text{ J/g mol.}$$

(b) For a constant pressure process

$$\Delta h = Q = \int c_p dT$$

or

$$\Delta h = c_p \Delta T = 20.785(70\text{-}150) = -1663 \text{ J/g mol}$$

Also

$$\Delta u = c_v \Delta T = 12.471(70\text{-}150) = -998 \text{ J/g mol}$$

From the first law

$$w = q - \Delta u = -1663 - (-998) = -665 \text{ J/g mol}$$

(c) For an isothermal process Δu and Δh are zero for ideal gases. Then for such a process

$$q = w = \bar{R}T \ln \frac{P_3}{P_1} \qquad (4)$$

However $P_3 = P_2$ and

$$P_2 = P_1\left(\frac{T_2}{T_1}\right)^{\gamma/(\gamma-1)}$$

where $\gamma = \frac{c_p}{c_v} = \frac{20.785}{12.471} = 1.67$

Therefore

$$P_2 = 1\left(\frac{273 + 150}{273 + 70}\right)^{2.5}$$

$$= 1.689 \text{ bars}$$

From Eq. (4), then

$$q = 8.314(343) \ln \left(\frac{1.689}{1}\right)$$

$$= 1,495 \text{ J/g mol.}$$

(a) For an 80% efficient process

$$w = \frac{w_{rev}}{\eta} = \frac{-998}{0.80} = -1248 \text{ J/g mol}$$

Since Δu is still the same, from the first law, and since the process can no longer be adiabatic,

$$q = \Delta u + w = 998 - 1248 = -250 \text{ J/g mol}$$

(b)

$$w = \frac{w_{rev}}{\eta} = \frac{-665}{0.80} = -831 \text{ J/g mol}$$

and

$$q = \Delta u + w = -998-831 = -1829 \text{ J/g mol}$$

(c) In this process work is done by the system, and so the irreversible work must be less than the reversible work. Hence

$$w = (w_{rev})\eta = 1495(0.80) = 1196 \text{ J/g mol}$$

and

$$q = \Delta u + w = 0 + 1196 = 1196 \text{ J/g mol}$$

For the entire cycle $\Delta u = \Delta h = 0$, but

$$q = -250 - 1829 + 1196 = -883 \text{ J/g mol}$$

$$w = -1248 - 831 + 1196 = -883 \text{ J/g mol}$$

	Reversible				Irreversible			
	Δu	Δh	q	w	Δu	Δh	q	w
process a....	998	1,663	0	−998	998	1,663	−250	−1,248
process b....	−998	−1,663	−1,663	−665	−998	−1,663	−1,829	−831
process c....	0	0	1,495	1,495	0	0	1,196	1,196
cycle........	0	0	−168	−168	0	0	−883	−883

These results are shown in the accompanying table for comparing the reversible and irreversible processes. All values are in J/g mol of gas.

• PROBLEM 7-8

A reversible and isothermal compressor is used to continuously compress helium initially at 540°R and 12 atm, to a final pressure of 180 atm. Calculate the work per mole of helium needed to operate the compressor, and the quantity of heat to be removed from the compressor if helium is assumed to behave (a) as an ideal gas, or (b) according to the equation of state

$$Pv = RT - \frac{a}{T}P + bP$$

where

$$a = 11.13 \text{ °R-ft}^3\text{/lb-mol}$$

$$b = 0.2445 \text{ ft}^3\text{/lb-mol}$$

$$R = 1.987 \text{ Btu/lb-mol-°R}$$

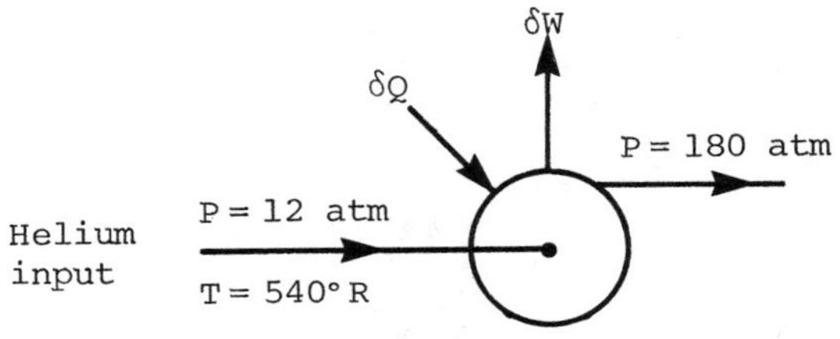

Fig. 1

Solution: In solving this problem, consider a control volume around the compressor, as shown in Fig. 1. Then write the energy and entropy balances around the compressor. Energy balance:

$$\left(h + \frac{V^2}{2g_c} + \frac{gZ}{g_c}\right)\delta m_{in} - \left(h + \frac{V^2}{2g_c} + \frac{gZ}{g_c}\right)\delta m_{out}$$

$$+ \delta Q - \delta W = d(me)_{syst.}$$

Entropy balance:

$$(s\delta m)_{in} - (s\delta m)_{out} + \frac{\delta Q + \delta LW}{T_{syst.}} = d(ms)_{syst.}$$

Since the compressor operates under steady-state conditions, the following can be assumed.

1. $d(me)_{syst.} = d(ms)_{syst.} = 0$

2. $\delta m_{in} = \delta m_{out}$

Since the compressor operates reversibly

$$\delta LW = 0$$

Neglecting potential and kinetic energies, the energy and entropy equations reduce to

$$\text{Energy:} \quad \Delta h = q - w \tag{1}$$

$$\text{Entropy:} \quad \Delta s = \frac{q}{T_{syst}} \tag{2}$$

However, $T_{syst.} = 540°R$

From Eq. (2), solving for q

$$q = T_{syst}(\Delta s) = 540(\Delta s) \tag{3}$$

To find the values of q and w, first calculate Δs for the process and use Eq. (3) to determine q. Then obtain Δh and use Eq. (1) to solve for w. To make the solution clearer sketch the compression process on a P-T diagram, as follows.

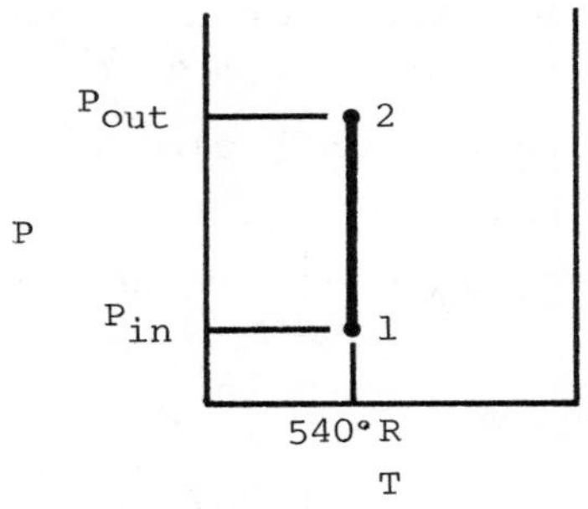

Fig. 2

From the P-T diagram it is evident that there is no change in temperature. Therefore a simple one step integration from P_{in} to P_{out} at constant temperature (T = 540°R) is sufficient to calculate Δh and Δs. Furthermore

$$(\Delta h_{1\to 2})_T = \int_{P_1}^{P_2} \left[v - T\left(\frac{\partial v}{\partial T}\right)_P \right] dP \qquad (4)$$

and

$$(\Delta s_{1\to 2})_T = -\int_{P_1}^{P_2} \left(\frac{\partial v}{\partial T}\right)_P dP \qquad (5)$$

which are the governing equations for evaluating Δh and Δs for this process, using the different equations of state that apply to the process.

(a) Ideal gas behavior

$$Pv = RT$$

and

$$\left(\frac{\partial v}{\partial T}\right)_P = \frac{R}{P} = \frac{v}{T} \qquad (6)$$

Hence

$$T\left(\frac{\partial v}{\partial T}\right)_P = v \qquad (7)$$

Substituting Eq. (7) into Eq. (4), yields

$$(\Delta h_{1\to 2})_T = \int_{P_1}^{P_2} \left[T\left(\frac{\partial v}{\partial T}\right)_P - T\left(\frac{\partial v}{\partial T}\right)_P \right] dP$$

$$= \int 0 \; dP$$

$$= 0$$

That is, the change in enthalpy for an isothermal compression of an ideal gas is zero.

Substituting Eq. (6) into Eq. (5), yields,

$$(\Delta s_{1\to 2})_T = -\int_{P_1}^{P_2} \frac{R}{P}\, dP$$

$$= -R \ln \frac{P_2}{P_1}$$

$$= -1.987 \ln \left(\frac{180}{12}\right)$$

$$= -5.36 \text{ Btu/lb mol-°R}$$

Using Eq. (3),

$$q = 540(-5.36)$$

$$= -2{,}900 \text{ Btu/lb mol}$$

From Eq. (1) then

$$q - w = 0$$

or

$$q = w = -2{,}900 \text{ Btu/lb mol}$$

(b) Real gas behavior

$$Pv = RT + \left[-\frac{a}{T} + b\right] P$$

or

$$v = \frac{RT}{P} + \left(b - \frac{a}{T}\right) \qquad (8)$$

Then

$$\left(\frac{\partial v}{\partial T}\right)_P = \frac{R}{P} + \frac{a}{T^2} \qquad (9)$$

Substituting Eqs. (8) and (9) into Eq. (4) gives

$$(\Delta h_{1\to 2})_T = \int_{P_1}^{P_2} \left(b - \frac{2a}{T}\right) dP$$

$$= \left(b - \frac{2a}{T}\right)(P_2 - P_1)$$

$$= \left(0.2445 - \frac{2 \times 11.13}{540}\right)\left(180-12\right)$$

$$= (0.2032)(180-12)$$

$$= 34.1 \text{ ft}^3 \text{ atm/lb mol}$$

or

$$\left(\Delta h_{1\to 2}\right)_T = \frac{34.1 \text{ ft}^3\text{atm}}{\text{lb mol}} \times \frac{14.7 \text{ psi}}{\text{atm}} \times \frac{144 \text{ in}^2}{\text{ft}^2} \times \frac{\text{Btu}}{778 \text{ lbf-ft}}$$

$$= 93.5 \text{ Btu/lb mol.}$$

Substituting Eq. (9) into Eq. (5) yields

$$\left(\Delta s_{1\to 2}\right)_T = -\int_{P_1}^{P_2} \left(\frac{R}{P} + \frac{a}{T^2}\right) dP$$

$$= R \ln \frac{P_2}{P_1} - \frac{a}{T^2} P_2 - P_1)$$

$$= 1.987 \ln \left(\frac{180}{12}\right) - \frac{11.13}{(540)^2}(180-12)$$

$$= -5.36 - \frac{11.13}{(540)^2}(180-12)\left[\frac{(144)(14.7)}{778}\right]$$

$$= -5.36 - 0.0175$$

$$= -5.38 \text{ Btu/lb mol-°R}$$

Substitute this value into Eq. (3) to obtain

$$q = 540(-5.38)$$

$$= -2{,}910 \text{ Btu/lb mol.}$$

With this value for q and the value obtained for Δh from Eq. (1) get

$$\Delta h = q - w$$

or

$$w = q - \Delta h$$

$$= -2910-93$$

$$= -3003 \text{ Btu/lb mol}$$

• PROBLEM 7-9

Helium initially at 300°K and 12.2 Bar, enters an adiabatic and reversible compressor and is continuously compressed to a pressure of 182.4 Bar. Determine the outlet temperature of the gas, and calculate the amount of work per mole of helium that must be supplied to the compressor, in order to maintain an outlet pressure of 182.4 Bar if (a) helium behaves as an ideal gas, and (b) according to the equation of state

$$Pv = RT + \left(b - \frac{a}{T}\right)P$$

where

$$a = 0.385 \text{ m}^3 \text{ °K/kg mol}$$

$$b = 0.0153 \text{ m}^3 \text{ /kg mol}$$

Assume constant specific heats.

Solution: Consider the control volume to be the compressor and its contents. Then write the energy and entropy balances around the compressor.

Energy:

$$\left(h + \frac{V^2}{2g_c} + \frac{gZ}{g_c}\right)_{in} \delta m_{in} - \left(h + \frac{V^2}{2g_c} + \frac{gZ}{g_c}\right)_{out} \delta m_{out}$$

$$+ \delta Q - \delta W = d(me)_{sys.}$$

However since the compressor operates at steady-state, $d(me)_{sys} = d(ms)_{sys} = \delta m_{in} - \delta m_{out} = 0$. Also because this is an adiabatic compressor $\delta q = \delta lw = 0$. Assuming potential and kinetic energy changes in the compressor to be negligible, the energy equation reduces to

$$\Delta h_{1-2} = -w \qquad (1)$$

For the Entropy balance

$$(s\delta m)_{in} - (s\delta m)_{out} + \int_{area} \frac{\delta q dA}{T} + \int_{volume} \frac{\delta lw dV}{T} = d(Ms)_{syst}$$

However with the assumptions made previously the entropy equation reduces to

$$\Delta s_{1\to 2} = 0 \qquad (2)$$

Eq. (2) implies that the entropy of the material leaving the compressor is equal to the entropy of the material entering the compressor. This condition can be used to calculate the temperature of the material leaving the compressor. Then by knowing the temperature at the exit, $\Delta h_{1\to 2}$ can be calculated, which in turn, gives the work that must be supplied.

(a) The ideal gas equation of state is

$$Pv = RT$$

The final T and P of an ideal gas (with constant c_p) undergoing an isentropic process are related according to the expression

$$c_p \ln \frac{T_2}{T_1} = R \ln \frac{P_2}{P_1}$$

or

$$\frac{T_2}{T_1} = \left(\frac{P_2}{P_1}\right)^{R/c_p}$$

Solving for T_2

$$T_2 = T_1\left(\frac{P_2}{P_1}\right)^{R/c_p}$$

$$= 300 \left(\frac{182.4}{12.2}\right)^{(8.31/20.9)}$$

$$= 886°K.$$

The total change in enthalpy can be calculated using the formula

$$\Delta h_{1-2} = \int_{T_1}^{T_2} c_p dT$$

$$= c_p(T_2 - T_1)$$

$$= 2.09(886-300) \times 10^4$$

$$= 1.22 \times 10^7 \text{ J/kg-mol.}$$

(b) Using the real gas equation of state

$$Pv = RT + \left[(b - a/T)\right] P$$

complicates the problem. Now a value of T_2 must be found such that the change of entropy from the initial to the final state is zero. This, however, can be done only by a trial-and-error solution, as follows:

1. An initial value for T_2 is guessed, usually close to the value obtained by the ideal gas equation.

2. Knowing P_1, T_1, P_2, and T_2 the value of Δs_{1-2} can be calculated.

3. The last guess of T_2 is then corrected.

4. Steps 2 and 3 are repeated until a value of T_2 has been found that makes Δs_{1-2} equal to zero.

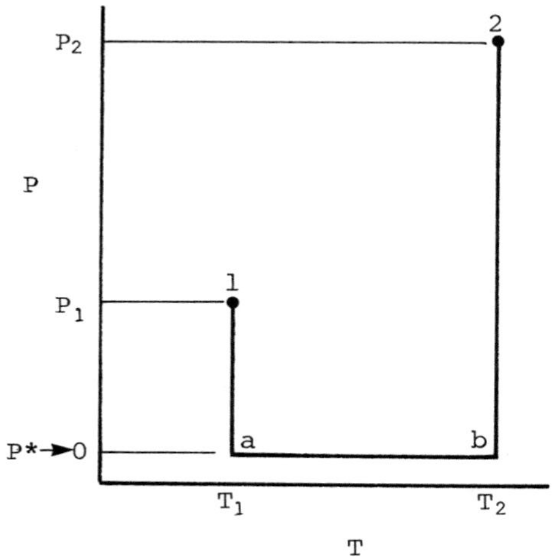

Fig. 1

To make the solution clearer a three-step path is sketched as shown in Fig. 1 for the evaluation of Δs. This is a P-T diagram.

The total change in entropy is

$$\Delta s_{1-2} = \Delta s_{1-a} + \Delta s_{a-b} + \Delta s_{b-2}$$

where

$$\Delta s_{1-2} = \int_{P_1}^{P^*} -\left(\frac{\partial v}{\partial T}\right)_P dP \qquad (3)$$

$$\Delta s_{a-b} = \int_{T_1}^{T_2} \frac{c_p^*}{T} dT \qquad (4)$$

$$\Delta s_{b-2} = \int_{P^*}^{P_2} -\left(\frac{\partial v}{\partial T}\right)_P dP \qquad (5)$$

where P* is a very low pressure approaching zero.

The quantity $\frac{\partial v}{\partial T}$ is

$$\frac{\partial v}{\partial T} = \frac{R}{P} + \frac{a}{T^2} \tag{6}$$

Substituting (6) into (3) gives

$$\Delta s_{1-2} = \int_{P_1}^{P*} - \left(\frac{R}{P} + \frac{a}{T^2}\right) dP = -R \ln \frac{P*}{P_1} - \underbrace{\frac{a}{T_1{}^2}(P* - P_2)}_{\cong 0} \tag{7}$$

$$\Delta s_{a\to b} = c_p* \ln \frac{T_2}{T_1} \tag{8}$$

Substitution of Eq. (6) into (5) gives

$$\Delta s_{b\to a} = \int_{P*}^{P_1} - \left(\frac{R}{P} + \frac{a}{T^2}\right) dP$$

$$= -R \ln \frac{P_2}{P*} - \frac{a}{T_2{}^2}(P_2 - P*) \tag{9}$$

Combining Eqs. (7), (8), and (9) gives

$$\Delta s_{1\to 2} = -R \ln \frac{P_2}{P_1} + c_p* \ln \frac{T_2}{T_1} + \frac{aP_1}{T_1{}^2} - \frac{aP_2}{T_2{}^2}$$

which upon substitution of the numerical values results in

$$\Delta s_{1\to 2} = -8310 \ln \frac{182.4}{12.2} + 2.09 \times 10^4 \ln \frac{T_2}{300} + \frac{(0.385)(1.22 \times 10^6)}{(300)^2}$$

$$- (0.385)(1.82 \times 10^7) \frac{1}{T_2{}^2}$$

or

$$\Delta s_{1\to 2} = -22{,}500 \frac{J}{\text{kg-mol}^\circ\text{K}} + 2.09 \times 10^4 \ln \frac{T_2}{300} - \frac{7.0 \times 10^6}{T_2{}^2} \ {}^\circ\text{K/kg-mol} \tag{10}$$

In Eq. (10) $\Delta s_{1\to 2}$ is a function of the temperature T_2. To solve this equation the following table is set up, where values of T_2 are assumed and values for $\Delta s_{1\to 2}$ are calculated.

Table 1

assumed T_2	$\frac{T_2}{300}$	$C_p^* \ln \frac{T_2}{300}, \frac{J}{\text{kg-mol}^\circ\text{K}}$	$\frac{7.0 \times 10^6}{T_2}, \frac{J}{\text{kg-mol}^\circ\text{K}}$	$\Delta S_{1-2}, \frac{J}{\text{kg-mol}^\circ\text{K}}$
860	2.87	2.195×10^4	9.5	−540
883	2.94	22500	9.4	~0

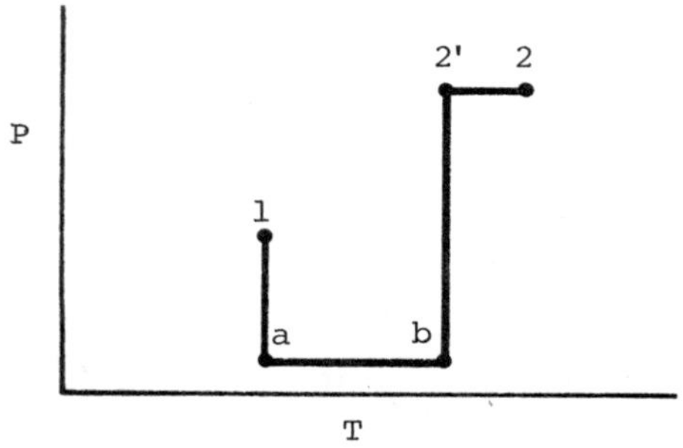

Fig. 2

The value T_2 = 860°K is that obtained for the ideal gas approximation. However this value substituted into Eq. (10) does not give a value of zero for the change in entropy (as shown in the table). Therefore another value, greater or lower, must be guessed for the temperature in order to give $\Delta s_{1\to 2} = 0$. However, the guessing of different numbers can result in lengthy and unnecessary calculations. Hence, a more systematic reasoning can be used to find a second guess for T_2. To do that, first draw a step path similar to Fig. 1 using as the final temperature, the temperature we are searching for. This will result in Fig. 2 where T_2' is the temperature T_2' = 860°K. In Fig. 2, point 2 is the point where $\Delta s_{1\to 2} = 0$. Until the point 2'

$$\Delta s_{1\to 2'} = -540 \text{ J/kg-mol°K (from the table).}$$

This implies that for $\Delta s_{1\to 2}$ to equal to zero, $\Delta s_{2'\to 2}$ must equal +540 J/kg-mol°K since

$$\Delta s_{1\to 2} = \Delta s_{1\to 2'} + \Delta s_{2'\to 2}$$

or

$$0 = -540 + \Delta s_{2'\to 2}$$

and

$$\Delta s_{2'\to 2} = +540 \text{ J/kg-mol°K}$$

However $\Delta s\big)_P$ is given by

$$\Delta s\big)_P = \int_{T_2'}^{T_2} \frac{c_p}{T}\, dT$$

since the process 2→2' is a constant pressure process. Thus

$$\Delta s_{2'\to 2} = c_p \ln \frac{T_2}{T_2'}$$

or

$$540 = 2.09 \times 10^4 \left[\ln \left(\frac{T_2}{860} \right) \right]$$

and

$$\ln \left(\frac{T_2}{860} \right) = 0.0258$$

Taking the antilogarithm gives

$$\frac{T_2}{860} = 1.0262$$

or

$$T_2 = 882.51 \cong 883°K$$

Now using this value for T_2, and substituting it into Eq. (10) results in the second value of the Table, which is

$$\Delta s \cong 0 \; .$$

Now that the temperature at state 2 is known, the change of enthalpy for the gas can be calculated as

$$\Delta h_{1\to 2} = \Delta h_{1\to a} + \Delta h_{a\to b} + \Delta h_{b\to 2} \tag{11}$$

where

$$\begin{aligned} \Delta h_{1\to a} &= \int_{P_1}^{P*} \left[v - T \left(\frac{\partial v}{\partial T} \right)_P \right] dP \\ &= \left(b - \frac{2a}{T_1} \right) (P* - P_1) \\ &= \left[0.0153 - \frac{2(0.385)}{300} \right] (0-12.2) \\ &= -0.1553 \text{ J/kg-mol} \end{aligned}$$

$$\begin{aligned} \Delta h_{a\to b} &= \int_{T_1}^{T_2} c_p^* \, dT = c_p^* \, (T_2 - T_1) \\ &= 2.09 \times 10^4 \, (883-300) \\ &= 1.22 \times 10^7 \text{ J/kg-mol} \end{aligned}$$

and

$$\begin{aligned} \Delta h_{b\to 2} &= \int_{P*}^{P_2} \left[v - T \left(\frac{\partial v}{\partial T} \right)_P \right] dP \\ &= \left[b - \frac{2a}{T_2} \right] (P_2 - P*) \\ &= \left[0.0153 - \frac{2(0.385)}{883} \right] (182.4 - 0) \\ &= 2.6317 \text{ J/kg-mol.} \end{aligned}$$

Substituting these values into Eq. (11), yields

$$\Delta h_{1\to 2} = -0.1553 + 1.22 \times 10^7 + 2.6317$$

$$= 1.22 \times 10^7 \text{ J/kg-mol}$$

From Eq. (1) then, the work is found to be

$$w = -1.22 \times 10^7 \text{ J/kg-mol}$$

THE AIR TABLES

• PROBLEM 7-10

One pound mass of dry air expands reversibly and adiabatically from an initial state of 900°R, 100 psia to a final pressure of 10 psia. Calculate the final temperature of the air, and show that the ratio of the two relative volumes is equal to the isentropic volume ratio.

Solution: (a) This problem can be solved by either assuming ideal gas behavior and constant specific heats or using the air tables. However since the latter gives more accurate results since it also takes into account the changes in the specific heats we choose to use the air tables. Then from the tables, at state 1

$$T_1 = 900°R \quad [500°K] \quad P_{r_1} = 8.411$$

Since this is a reversible and adiabatic process

$$\frac{P_{r_2}}{P_{r_1}} = \frac{P_2}{P_1} \tag{1}$$

or

$$P_{r_2} = P_{r_1}\left(\frac{P_2}{P_1}\right)$$

Substituting the numerical values, gives

$$P_{r_2} = 8.411\left(\frac{10}{100}\right) = 0.8411$$

For this value for the reduced pressure at state 2, the air tables give a temperature

$$T_2 \cong 468°R \quad [260°K]$$

which is the desired temperature

(b) Eq. (1) can be converted into a volume ratio by substituting the relation

$$P = \frac{RT}{v}$$

which gives

$$\left.\frac{T_2/v_2}{T_1/v_1}\right]_{s=\text{const.}} = \frac{P_{r_2}}{P_{r_1}}$$

or

$$\left.\frac{v_1}{v_2}\right]_{s=\text{const.}} = \frac{P_{r_1}/T_2}{P_{r_2}/T_1} \qquad (2)$$

The form of Eq. (2) suggests a definition for the relative volume v_r as

$$v_r = \frac{PT}{P_r} \qquad (3)$$

Substituting Eq. (3) into Eq. (2), obtain

$$\left.\frac{v_1}{v_2}\right]_{s=\text{const.}} = \frac{v_{r_1}}{v_{r_2}}$$

• PROBLEM 7-11

One pound of dry air initially at 14.7 psia and 60.3F is compressed in a reversible adiabatic nonflow process through a volume ratio (compression ratio) of 6. Determine the final state of the air and calculate the work required for the process.

Solution: From the tables of air at low pressure, at T = 520°R at the initial state (State 1)

$$v_{r_1} = 158.58 \quad u_1 = 88.62 \text{ Btu/lbm} \quad P_{r_1} = 1.2147$$

Since the volume ratio $\frac{v_1}{v_2}$ is known the following equation can be written

$$\frac{v_{r_2}}{v_{r_1}} = \frac{v_2}{v_1}$$

or

$$v_{r_2} = \frac{v_{r_1}}{v_1/v_2}$$

$$= \frac{158.58}{6} = 26.43$$

For this value of v_{r_2}, the air tables give

$$T_2 = 1050°R$$

$$u_2 = 181.47 \text{ Btu/lbm}$$

$$P_{r_2} = 14.686$$

The pressure ratio at states 1 and 2 is

$$\frac{P_{r_2}}{P_{r_1}} = \frac{P_2}{P_1}$$

Solving for the pressure at state 2 gives

$$P_2 = P_1\left(\frac{P_{r_2}}{P_{r_1}}\right)$$

$$= 14.7\left(\frac{14.686}{1.2147}\right)$$

$$= 178 \text{ psia}$$

Since two independent properties have been found the final state is considered completely defined. However as a check, using the relation

$$h = u + Pv$$

the value for h must be the same as the one given in the air tables. Therefore

$$h_2 = u_2 + Pv_2$$

$$= u_2 + \frac{RT_2}{MW}$$

$$= 181.47 + \frac{1.986 \times 1050}{29}$$

$$= 253.4 \text{ Btu/lbm}$$

which checks the value given in the air tables. This is an adiabatic process, hence

$$Q_{1\to 2} = 0$$

From the first law

$$w_{1\to 2} = u_1 - u_2$$

$$= 88.62 - 181.47$$

$$= -92.85 \text{ Btu/lbm}$$

• PROBLEM 7-12

Air is expanded reversibly and adiabatically from an initial state of 150 lbf/in^2, 2100°F to a final pressure of 17 lbf/in^2. Calculate the changes in enthalpy and specific volume of the air by using

(a) The perfect gas laws with constant specific heats.

(b) The air tables.

Solution: (a) The change in the specific volume is given as

$$\Delta v = v_2 - v_1 \qquad (1)$$

At state 1, using the ideal gas equation of state, obtain

$$P_1 v_1 = RT_1$$

or

$$v_1 = \frac{RT_1}{P_1}$$

where

$$R = 53.34 \text{ ft-lbf/lbm-°R}$$

$$P_1 = 150 \frac{\text{lbf}}{\text{in}^2} \times \frac{144 \text{ in}^2}{\text{ft}^2} = 21{,}600 \text{ lbf/ft}^2$$

$$T_1 = 2100°\text{F} + 460 = 2560°\text{R}$$

Therefore

$$v_1 = \frac{(53.34)(2560)}{(21{,}600)} = 6.3218 \text{ ft}^3/\text{lbm}$$

At state 2 the temperature is unknown. However solving for v_2 in the relation

$$p_1 v_1^k = P_2 v_2^k$$

gives

$$v_2 = v_1 \left(\frac{P_1}{P_2}\right)^{1/k}$$

where

$$k = 1.4 \quad \text{(for air)}$$

Then

$$v_2 = 6.3218 \left(\frac{21{,}600}{(17)(144)}\right)^{1/1.4} = 29.9433 \text{ ft}^3/\text{lbm}$$

Then by Eq. (1)

$$\Delta v = 29.9433 - 6.3218 = 23.6215 \text{ ft}^3/\text{lbm}$$

The change in enthalpy is given as

$$\Delta h = c_p \Delta T = c_p(T_2 - T_1) \tag{2}$$

At state 2 the temperature is unknown. However in the relation

$$\frac{p_1 v_1}{T_1} = \frac{P_2 v_2}{T_2}$$

solving for T_2 gives

$$T_2 = T_1\left(\frac{P_2 v_2}{P_1 v_1}\right)$$

$$= 2560 \left(\frac{2448 \times 29.9433}{21600 \times 6.3218}\right)$$

$$= 1374.2°R = 914.2°F$$

For a constant specific heat $c_p = 0.240$ Btu/lbm-°R Eq. (2) gives

$$\Delta h = 0.240\ (1,374.2 - 2,560) = -284.59 \text{ Btu/lbm}$$

(b) Using the air tables is more accurate because it takes into account the changes in the specific heats. Then from the air tables at $T_1 = 2560°R$

$$h_1 = 663.0 \text{ Btu/lbm} \qquad P_{r_1} = 481$$

For a reversible adiabatic process

$$\frac{P_{r2}}{P_{r_1}} = \frac{P_2}{P_1}$$

or

$$P_{r_2} = P_{r_1}\left(\frac{P_2}{P_1}\right)$$

$$= 481 \left(\frac{17}{150}\right)$$

$$= 54.51$$

Then from the air tables at $P_{r_2} = 54.51$

$$T_2 = 1490.4°R \qquad h_2 = 366.65 \text{ Btu/lbm}$$

Therefore

$$\Delta h_{1\to 2} = h_2 - h_1$$

$$= 366.65 - 663.0$$

$$= -296.35 \text{ Btu/lbm}$$

From part (a) the specific volume at state 1 is $v_1 = 6.3218 \text{ ft}^3/\text{lbm}$

At state 2 using the ideal gas equation of state

$$v_2 = \frac{RT_2}{P_2}$$

$$= \frac{(53.34)(1490.4)}{2448}$$

$$= 32.4746 \text{ ft}^3/\text{lbm}$$

Then by Eq. (1)

$$\Delta v = 32.4746 - 6.3218 = 26.1528 \text{ ft}^3/\text{lbm}$$

THE GENERALIZED COMPRESSIBILITY FACTOR CHART

• PROBLEM 7-13

What is the pressure of carbon dioxide (CO_2) at 200°F and a specific volume of 0.20 ft³/lbm?

Solution: From the table of the critical constants, for CO_2,

$$T_{cr} = 547.6°R$$

$$V_{cr} = 1.53 \text{ ft}^3/\text{lbm-mole} = 0.0348 \text{ ft}^3/\text{lbm}$$

$$Z_{cr} = 0.279$$

Converting to reduced temperature and volume obtain,

$$T_r = \frac{T}{T_{cr}} = \frac{660}{547.6} = 1.203$$

$$v_r = \frac{v}{v_{cr}} = \frac{0.20}{0.0348} = 5.747$$

Then

$$v_r' = v_r Z_{cr} = 5.747(0.279) = 1.63$$

From the generalized compressibility factor's chart at T_r and v_r', obtain

$$Z = 0.87$$

Hence

$$P = \frac{ZRT}{v}$$

$$= \frac{0.87(35.12)(660)}{0.20 \times 144}$$

$$= 700 \text{ psia.}$$

• PROBLEM 7-14

What is the volume of a container required, to store 1500 lbm of ethane (C_2H_6) at 160°F and a pressure of 1100 psig (gage pressure)?

Solution: To compute the required volume, the equation of state for real gases

$$Pv = ZRT \quad (1)$$

has to be used. A value of Z is found from the compressibility factors chart at the reduced pressure and temperature. Then all the values are substituted into Eq. (1) and the equation is solved for v. Since the pressure is given in gage reading, we have to convert to absolute pressure. Thus

$$P_{abs} = P_{atm} + P_{gage}$$

or

$$P_{abs} = 14.7 + 1100 = 1114 \text{ psi}$$

From the table of critical constants, for ethane

$$T_{cr} = 550°R$$

$$P_{cr} = 48.2 \text{ atm} \times \frac{14.7 \text{ lbf/in}^2}{1 \text{ atm}} = 708.54 \text{ lbf/in}^2$$

$$R = 1542.6 \text{ ft-lbf/lb mole-°R}$$

and

$$MW = 30.07 \text{ lbm/lb mole}$$

Therefore,

$$T_r = \frac{T}{T_{cr}} = \frac{620}{550} = 1.127$$

and

$$P_r = \frac{P_{abs}}{P_{cr}} = \frac{1114}{708.54} = 1.572$$

Then from the compressibility factors chart

$$Z = 0.49$$

Substituting into Eq. (1) and solving for v gives

$$v = \frac{ZRT}{P}$$

$$= \frac{(0.49)(1542.6)(620)}{1114}$$

$$= 420.68 \frac{\text{ft-in}^2}{\text{lb mole}} \times \frac{1 \text{ ft}^2}{144 \text{ in}^2} = 2.9214 \text{ ft}^3/\text{lb-mole}$$

Solving for the volume

$$V = v \times \frac{m}{MW}$$

$$= 2.9214 \frac{\text{ft}^3}{\text{lb-mole}} \times \frac{1500 \text{ lbm}}{30.07 \text{ lbm/lb mole}}$$

$$= 145.73 \text{ ft}^3$$

• PROBLEM 7-15

A chamber contains 3 lb of nitrogen at 5,000 psia and 392°F. Using the figure below, determine the final pressure of the nitrogen inside the chamber if the temperature is lowered to 32°F. Assume R to be constant.

Solution: Since the chamber is closed (nothing enters or leaves the system), the mass of nitrogen is constant. Therefore the equation of state can be written for states 1 and 2 as,

$$m = \frac{P_1 V_1}{Z_1 R T_1} \qquad (1)$$

and

$$m = \frac{P_2 V_2}{Z_2 R T_2} \qquad (2)$$

Combining Eqs. (1) and (2), yields

$$mR = \frac{P_1V_1}{Z_1T_1} = \frac{P_2V_2}{Z_2T_2}$$

or solving for P_2,

$$P_2 = \frac{P_1Z_2T_2}{Z_1T_1} \qquad (3)$$

Where

$$T_1 = 392°F + 460 = 852°R$$

and

$$T_2 = 32°F + 460 = 492°R$$

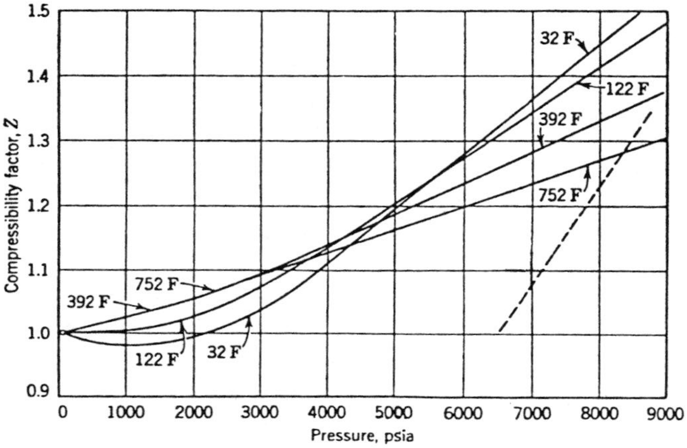

Eq. (3) has two unknowns, and will have to be solved by using a trial-and-error solution along with the compressibility factor chart. From the figure, the value of Z_1 (at 5000 psia, 392°F) is approximately 1.19. Since the final pressure is unknown, assume that it is P_2 = 3000 psia, for which Z_2 = 1.04. Then from Eq. (3)

$$P_2 = \frac{5000(1.04)(492)}{(1.19)(852)} = 2{,}523.4 \text{ psia}$$

For this pressure, however, the compressibility factor as found from the figure is Z_2 = 1.02. Hence the assumed pressure is too high.

Next assume P_2 = 2400 psia. From the figure $Z_2 \cong 1.01$, and by Eq. (3)

$$P_2 = \frac{5000(1.01)(492)}{(1.19)(852)} = 2{,}450.6 \text{ psia}$$

which is close to the assumed pressure. Thus this is the approximate final pressure. If greater accuracy is needed, more trials and a more precise compressibility chart will have to be used.

Pure methane initially at 3000 psi, 65°F enters a pipeline of 12-in inside diameter, at a rate of 70 lbm/sec. Using the generalized compressibility factor chart, calculate the inlet density and initial velocity of methane.

Solution: The direct solution is based on the real gas equation of state

$$Pv = ZRT \qquad (1)$$

since

$$\rho = \frac{1}{v}$$

the equation of state becomes

$$\rho = \frac{P}{ZRT} \qquad (2)$$

where

ρ = density

Z = compressibility factor

$\bar{R}$ = 1545 ft-lbf/lb-mol-°R

Express

$$P = 3000 \text{ lbf/in}^2 = 4.32 \times 10^5 \text{ lbf/ft}^2$$

$$T = 65 + 460 = 525°R$$

From the table of critical constants for methane

MW = 16 lbm/lb-mol

T_c = 343.9°R

$P_c = 9.70 \times 10^4$ lbf/ft^2

Then the ideal gas constant (in mass units) is expressed as

$$R = \bar{R}/(MW) = 1545/(16) = 96.7 \text{ ft-lbf/lbm-°R}$$

To use the generalized charts, the reduced temperature and pressure of the incoming methane must first be evaluated.

$$T_r = \frac{T}{T_c} = \frac{525}{343.9} = 1.53$$

$$P_r = \frac{P}{P_c} = \frac{4.32 \times 10^5}{9.70 \times 10^4} = 4.46$$

Then according to the compressibility factor chart for these conditions

$$Z = 0.82$$

From Eq. (2) then

$$\rho = \frac{4.32 \times 10^5}{(0.82)(96.7)(525)} = 10.37 \text{ lbm/ft}^3$$

The velocity then can be found using the formula

$$\dot{m} = \rho VA$$

Solving for V gives

$$V = \frac{\dot{m}}{\rho A}$$

where

$$A = \frac{\pi d^2}{4} = \frac{\pi(1)^2}{4} = 0.785 \text{ ft}^2$$

The velocity is then

$$V = \frac{70}{(10.3)(0.785)} = 8.6575 \text{ ft/sec}$$

• PROBLEM 7-17

A cylinder having a volume of 10 ft^3, has a safe working pressure of 500 psig (gage pressure). What is the maximum operating temperature for the cylinder if it contains 1 lb-mole of propane?

Solution: Since the temperature is not given, a trial-and-error solution is required to find the temperature T that will satisfy both the compressibility factor chart and the equation of state

$$Z = \frac{PV}{RT} \quad (1)$$

where

$$P = P_{gage} + P_{atm} = 500 + 14.7 = 514.7 \text{ psi} \cong 515 \text{ psi}$$

$$R = 1543.15 \text{ ft-lbf/lb mole-°R} \times \frac{1 \text{ ft}^2}{144 \text{ in}^2}$$

$$= 10.73 \text{ ft}^3\text{.lbf/lb mole-°R in}^2$$

From the table of critical constants for C_3H_8

$$T_{cr} = 370°K = 666°R$$

$$P_{cr} = 42.1 \text{ atm} = 619 \text{ lbf/in}^2$$

Then

$$P_r = \frac{P}{P_{cr}} = \frac{515}{619} = 0.833$$

and

$$T_r = \frac{T}{T_{cr}}$$

or

$$T = T_r \times T_{cr} = 666°R \times T_r \quad (2)$$

Then Eq. (1) becomes

$$Z = \frac{515 \times 10}{10.73\ T} = \frac{479}{T} \quad (3)$$

Now the trial-and-error solution can be started as follows:
First trial: Guess $T_r = 1.2$. Then from the compressibility factor chart at $P_r = 0.833$ get

$$Z = 0.83 .$$

From (2)

$$T = 666 \times 1.2 = 799°R$$

Substitute this value of T into Eq. (3), and obtain

$$Z = \frac{479}{799} = 0.6$$

Since this value of Z(=0.6) and that obtained from the compressibility factor chart (0.83) are not the same,

another value for T_r will have to be guessed, and the same procedure be followed:

Second trial: Use the last value of Z to choose an improved value of T_r at $P_r = 0.833$. Let $T_r = 1.00$. Then

$$Z = 0.6 \quad \text{(From chart)}$$

$$T = 666°R$$

$$Z = 0.72 \quad \text{(From Eq. (3))}$$

Third trial: Let $T_r = 1.06$. Then

$$Z = 0.72 \text{ (From chart)}$$

$$T = 706°R$$

$$Z = 0.68 \text{ (From Eq. (3))}$$

Fourth trial: Let $T_r = 1.04$. Then

$$Z = 0.68 \text{ (From chart)}$$

$$T = 692°R$$

$$Z = 0.693 \text{ (From Eq. (3))}$$

Fifth trial: Let $T_r = 1.042$. Then

$$Z = 0.693 \text{ (From chart)}$$

$$T = 694°R$$

$$Z = 0.692 \text{ (From Eq. (3))}$$

Since both values of Z are the same, it can be concluded that this is the final temperature required. Hence

$$T_{max} = 694°R = 234°F$$

THE GENERALIZED ENTHALPY DEVIATION CHART

• PROBLEM 7-18

A closed system contains pure ammonia (NH_3) at an initial pressure and temperature of 1640 psia and 1460°R respectively. The ammonia then undergoes an isothermal expansion to a final pressure of 820 psia. Using the generalized enthalpy correction chart calculate the change in specific enthalpy.

Solution: The first step in solving this problem is to convert to reduced pressures and temperatures, since we are going to use the enthalpy correction charts. For ammonia

$$P_{cr} = 1640 \text{ psia}$$

$$T_{cr} = 730°R$$

$$MW = 17.02$$

Therefore

$$P_{r_1} = \frac{P_1}{P_{cr}} = \frac{1640}{1640} = 1.0$$

$$P_{r_2} = \frac{P_2}{P_{cr}} = \frac{820}{1640} = 0.5$$

$$T_{r_1} = \frac{T_1}{T_{cr}} = \frac{1460}{730} = 2.0$$

$$T_{r_2} = T_{r_1} = 2.0$$

The enthalpy values given in the generalized enthalpy correction chart are the differences between the properties of a gas assumed to be ideal and its actual properties. For the ideal gas state the properties are denoted by an asterisk. To use the chart, the change in specific enthalpy is expected to be

$$h_2 - h_1 = -(h^* - h)_2 + (h_2^* - h_1^*) + (h^* - h)_1 \qquad (1)$$

Assuming constant specific heats and introducing molar quantities for the corrections, Eq. (1) becomes

$$h_2 - h_1 = -\left(\frac{\bar{h}^* - \bar{h}}{T_c}\right)_2 \frac{T_c}{MW} + c_p\Delta T + \left(\frac{\bar{h}^* - \bar{h}}{T_c}\right)_1 \frac{T_c}{MW} \qquad (2)$$

However since this is an isothermal process, $\Delta T = 0$, and hence

$$h_2^* - h_1^* = c_p\Delta T = 0$$

Eq. (2) then becomes

$$h_2 - h_1 = -\left(\frac{\bar{h}^* - \bar{h}}{T_c}\right)_2 \frac{T_c}{MW} + \left(\frac{\bar{h}^* - \bar{h}}{T_c}\right)_1 \frac{T_c}{MW} \qquad (3)$$

From the enthalpy correction chart

$$\left(\frac{\bar{h}^* - \bar{h}}{T_c}\right)_1 = 0.65$$

$$\left(\frac{\bar{h}^* - \bar{h}}{T_c}\right)_2 = 0.33$$

Substituting into Eq. (3)

$$h_2 - h_1 = -(0.33)\left(\frac{730}{17.02}\right) + 0 + (0.65)\left(\frac{730}{17.02}\right)$$

$$= -14.15 + 27.88$$

$$= 13.73 \text{ Btu/lbm.}$$

• PROBLEM 7-19

Ethylene gas at an initial state of 22.8 MPa, 338.4°K undergoes a reversible and isobaric process in which it is cooled to 169.2°K. Using the generalized correction chart calculate the change in enthalpy for the process. Assume that at this pressure

$$c_p = 1.4329 \text{ kJ/kg-°K}$$

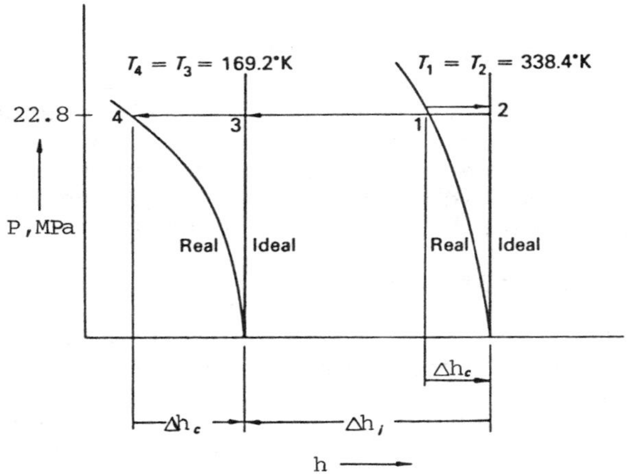

Solution: To facilitate the solution, first draw the calculation path on a P-h diagram as shown in the figure. From this diagram, for the real process, the change in enthalpy can be calculated as

$$(\Delta\bar{h})_{1\to4} = \left[(\Delta\bar{h}_c)_{1\to2} + (\Delta\bar{h}_i)_{2\to3}\right] - (\Delta\bar{h}_c)_{3\to4} \quad (1)$$

where

$(\Delta\bar{h}_c)_{1\to2}$, $(\Delta\bar{h}_c)_{3\to4}$ are obtained from the enthalpy correction chart and $(\bar{h}_i)_{2\to3}$ is calculated using the relation

$$(\Delta h_i)_{2\to3} = c_p\Delta T = c_p(T_3 - T_2) \quad (2)$$

assuming constant specific heats.

From the table of critical constants for ethylene

$$T_c = 282°K$$

$$P_c = 5.12 \text{ MPa}$$

$$MW = 28.05 \text{ kg/kg mole}$$

To use the generalized charts the reduced temperatures and pressures of ethylene must first be evaluated. At the initial state

$$P_{r1} = \frac{P_1}{P_c} = \frac{22.8}{5.12} = 4.5$$

$$T_{r1} = \frac{T_1}{T_c} = \frac{338.4}{282} = 1.2$$

From the enthalpy correction chart

$$\frac{\bar{h}_2 - \bar{h}_1}{T_c} = 27.2 \text{ kJ/kg mol-°K}$$

or

$$(\Delta\bar{h}_c)_{1\to2} = 27.2(282) = 7{,}670.4 \text{ kJ/kg mol.}$$

At the final state

$$P_{r3} = P_{r1} = 4.5 \text{ (isobaric process)}$$

$$T_{r3} = \frac{T_3}{T_c} = \frac{169.2}{282} = 0.6$$

From the enthalpy correction chart

$$\frac{\bar{h}_3 - \bar{h}_4}{T_c} = 56.5 \text{ kJ/kg mol-°K}$$

Then

$$(\Delta\bar{h}_c)_{3\to4} = \left(\frac{\bar{h}_3 - \bar{h}_4}{T_c}\right) T_c$$

$$= 56.5(282) = 15{,}933 \quad \text{kJ/kg mole}$$

From Eq. (2)

$$(\Delta h_i)_{2\to3} = 1.4329(169.2 - 338.4)$$

$$= -242.45 \text{ kJ/kg}$$

or

$$(\Delta\bar{h}_i)_{2\to3} = (\Delta h_i)_{2\to3} \times MW$$

$$= (-242.45)(28.05) = -6800.7 \text{ kg/kg mol}$$

Finally, substituting the numerical values into Eq. (1)

$$(\Delta\bar{h})_{1\to4} = \left[7{,}670.4 + (-6800.7)\right] - 15933$$

$$= -15063.3 \text{ kJ/kg mol}$$

or on a per mass basis

$$(\Delta h)_{1\to 4} = (\Delta \bar{h})_{1\to 4} \times \frac{1}{MW}$$

$$= (-15{,}063.3)\left(\frac{1}{28.05}\right)$$

$$= -537 \text{ kJ/kg.}$$

• PROBLEM 7-20

Carbon dioxide enters a heater at 995 lbf/in^2, 80°F and is heated until its temperature at the exit is 900°F. Assuming the carbon dioxide to have undergone a constant pressure, steady-flow process calculate the heating required per pound of CO_2.

Solution: Neglecting kinetic and potential energies, the heat transfer for this process (from the first law) is

$$Q = h_2 - h_1 \tag{1}$$

and hence the problem reduces to one of determining the change in enthalpy by using the generalized enthalpy charts. First from the table of critical constants for CO_2

$$P_c = 72.9 \text{ atm} = 1070 \text{ lbf/in}^2$$

$$T_c = 548°R$$

Because the tables use reduced pressure and temperatures, and also absolute Rankine temperatures, the following conversions must be performed

$$T_1 = 80°F + 460 = 540°R$$

$$T_2 = 900°F + 460 = 1360°R$$

$$P_{r_1} = P_{r_2} = \frac{P}{P_c} = \frac{995}{1070} = 0.93$$

$$T_{r_1} = \frac{T_1}{T_c} = \frac{540}{548} = 0.98$$

$$T_{r_2} = \frac{T_2}{T_c} = \frac{1360}{548} = 2.48$$

Then at state 1, from the generalized enthalpy chart

$$\frac{\bar{h}_1^* - \bar{h}_1}{T_c} = 3.80 \text{ Btu/lb mole-°R}$$

or

$$\bar{h}_1^* - \bar{h}_1 = 3.80\ T_c = 3.80(548) = 2082.4 \text{ Btu/lb mole}$$

At state 2

$$\frac{\bar{h}_2^* - \bar{h}_2}{T_c} = 0.32 \text{ Btu/lb mole-°R}$$

or

$$\bar{h}_2^* - \bar{h}_2 = 0.32(T_c) = 0.32(548) = 175.36 \text{ Btu/lbmole-°R}$$

Assuming constant specific heats, $\bar{c}_p = 8.91$ Btu/lb mole-°R, the value of $\bar{h}_2^* - \bar{h}_1^*$ can be evaluated using

$$\bar{h}_2^* - \bar{h}_1^* = \bar{c}_p(T_2^* - T_1^*) \qquad (2)$$

(The variation in $\bar{c}_p$ with temperature can be taken into account when necessary). From (2)

$$\bar{h}_2^* - \bar{h}_1^* = 8.91(1360 - 540) = 7{,}306.2 \text{ Btu/lb mole.}$$

Then from Eq. (1)

$$Q = h_2 - h_1 = -(\bar{h}_2^* - \bar{h}_2) + (\bar{h}_1^* - \bar{h}_1) + (\bar{h}_2^* - \bar{h}_1^*)$$

$$= -175.36 + 2082.4 + 7{,}306.2$$

$$= 9{,}213.24 \text{ Btu/lb mole}$$

If the value of the heat transferred is required on a per mass basis, then

$$Q = 9{,}213.24 \frac{\text{Btu}}{\text{lb mole}} \times \frac{1 \text{ lb mole}}{44.01 \text{ lbm}} = 209.34 \text{ Btu/lbm}$$

• PROBLEM 7-21

Oxygen initially at 13.8 MPa, 15.5°C is throttled in a steady-flow process to a final pressure of 1.38 MPa. Assuming the process to be adiabatic, determine the final temperature of oxygen.

Solution: Since the process is adiabatic

$$Q_{1\to 2} = 0$$

For a throttling process, $h_1 = h_2$. To account for real gas behavior

$$h_1^* - (h^* - h)_1 = h_2^* - (h^* - h)_2$$

or

$$h_2 - h_1 = -(h^* - h)_2 + (h_2^* - h_1^*) + (h^* - h)_1 = 0 \quad (1)$$

Since the temperature change is moderate, $(h_2^* - h_1^*)$ can be evaluated using the relationship

$$dh^* = c_p dT$$

or

$$h_2^* - h_1^* = c_p(T_2 - T_1) \quad (2)$$

with $c_p = 0.9216$ kJ/kg-°K

For oxygen

$$T_c = 154.8°K$$

$$P_c = 5.08 \text{ MPa}$$

$$R = 0.25983 \text{ kJ/kg-°K}$$

$$MW = 32$$

Converting to reduced pressure and temperature

$$P_{r_1} = \frac{P_1}{P_c} = \frac{13.8}{5.08} = 2.72$$

$$T_{r_1} = \frac{T_1}{T_c} = \frac{288.65}{154.8} = 1.87$$

$$P_{r_2} = \frac{P_2}{P_c} = \frac{1.38}{5.08} = 0.274$$

From the generalized enthalpy deviation chart

$$\frac{(\bar{h}^* - \bar{h})_1}{T_c} = 7.12 \text{ kJ/kg mol-°K}$$

and

$$(h^* - h)_1 = \frac{(\bar{h}^* - \bar{h})_1}{T_c} \times \frac{T_c}{MW}$$

$$= 7.12 \left(\frac{154.8}{32}\right)$$

$$= 34.44 \text{ kJ/kg}$$

Eq. (1) can also be written as

$$h_2^* - h_1^* = (h_2^* - h_2) - (h_1^* - h_1) \qquad (3)$$

This relation however, has more than one unknown and hence a trial-and-error solution must be used since there are no other equations applicable to the process. The procedure goes as follows

(a) Assume a temperature for state 2 and convert to reduced temperature.

(b) Calculate $(h_2^* - h_1^*)$ using Eq. (2), and using the generalized enthalpy correction chart determine $(h_2^* - h_2)$.

(c) Substitute the values obtained in (b) and the value of $(h_1^* - h_1)$ into Eq. (3)

(d) If the right hand side (RHS) equals the left hand side (LHS), the assumed temperature is the correct final temperature. If not, then repeat the procedure until a satisfactory value for T_2 has been found. Therefore, assume $T_2 = 244.4°K$

$$T_{r_2} = \frac{244.4}{154.8} = 1.58$$

$$(h_2^* - h_1^*) = 0.9216(244.4 - 288.65)$$

$$= -40.78 \text{ kJ/kg}$$

$$\left(\frac{\overline{h}^* - \overline{h}}{T_c}\right)_2 = 1.15 \text{ kJ/kg mol-°K}$$

$$(h^* - h)_2 = 1.15\left(\frac{154.8}{32}\right)$$

$$= 5.56 \text{ kJ/kg}$$

Substituting into (3)

$$-40.75 \stackrel{?}{=} 5.56 - 34.44$$

$$-40.75 \neq 28.88$$

This indicates that the assumed value of T_2 was too low. After more trials the final temperature is found to be

$$T_2 = 259.4°K = -13.71°C$$

• PROBLEM 7-22

A container having a volume of 0.3 m^3 contains nitrogen gas initially at 10 MPa, 200 K. Heat is then transferred to the nitrogen until its temperature becomes 350 K. Using the generalized charts determine the final pressure and heat transfer for the nitrogen.

Solution: Since no mass enters or leaves the system the mass can be calculated using the equation of state for real gases.

$$m = \frac{PV}{ZRT} \tag{1}$$

Let the subscripts 1 and 2 represent the states before and after the heat transfer has occurred. To obtain a value for Z at state 1 the generalized compressibility factor chart will be used. To use the chart, however, the reduced pressure and temperature will have to be known at that state.

Therefore

$$P_{r_1} = \frac{P_1}{P_{critical}}$$

and

$$T_{r_1} = \frac{T_1}{T_{critical}}$$

From the table of critical constants

$$P_{critical} = 3.39 \text{ MPa}; \; T_{critical} = 126.2°K$$

Hence

$$P_{r_1} = \frac{10}{3.39} = 2.94$$

$$T_{r_1} = \frac{200}{126.2} = 1.58$$

Then from the generalized compressibility factor chart

$$Z_1 \cong 0.85$$

From Eq. (1) then

$$m = \frac{P_1V_1}{Z_1RT_1} = \frac{(10,000)(0.3)}{(0.85)(0.2968)(200)} = 59.46 \text{ kg}$$

Since it is more efficient to work with moles instead of mass, we can express m in numbers of moles (n)

$$n = \frac{\text{mass}}{\text{Molecular Weight}} = \frac{59.46}{28.013} = 2.12 \text{ moles}$$

Eq. (1) then becomes

$$n = \frac{PV}{Z\bar{R}T} \tag{2}$$

where

$$\bar{R} = 8.31434 \text{ kNm/kmol-°K}$$

At state 2 Eq. (2) is

$$n_2 = \frac{P_2V_2}{Z_2\bar{R}T_2} \tag{3}$$

In this equation, however, there are two unknowns, the pressure and the coefficient Z_2. Therefore the equation will have to be solved by trial and error, using the generalized compressibility factor chart. However because the chart uses reduced pressure and temperature, express Eq. (3) in terms of P_r, as follows.

$$n_2Z_2\bar{R}T_2 = P_2V_2$$

or

$$2.12 \times Z_2 \times 8.31434 \times 350 = P_2 \times 0.3$$

$$6169.24\ Z_2 = 0.3P_2$$

Divide both sides by $P_{critical}$ and obtain

$$1.8198\ Z_2 = 0.3\ P_{r_2}$$

or

$$P_{r_2} = 6.0661\ Z_2 \tag{4}$$

Also the reduced temperature at 2 is

$$T_{r_2} = \frac{350}{126.2} = 2.77$$

Now that all the necessary information has been obtained, we can proceed with the trial and error solution, as follows.

First trial: Assume $P_{r_2} = 6.3$. From the generalized compressibility factor chart at T_{r_2}, obtain

$$Z_2 = 1.07$$

Substitute this value into Eq. (4) and obtain

$$P_{r_2} = 6.0661\ (1.07) = 6.4907 > 6.3$$

Thus the assumed and calculated values for P_{r_2} are not the same.

Second trial: Assume $P_{r_2} = 6.5$. From the generalized chart at T_{r_2} obtain $Z_2 = 1.08$

Substitute into Eq. (4) and obtain

$$P_{r_2} = 6.0661(1.08) = 6.5514 \cong 6.5.$$

This time the assumed and calculated values for P_{r_2} are very close. Therefore a fair approximation is $P_{r_2} = 6.53$.

From

$$P_{r_2} = \frac{P_2}{P_{critical}}$$

solving for P_2

$$P_2 = P_{r_2} \times P_{critical} = 6.53 \times 3.39 = 22.14 \text{ MPa}$$

• PROBLEM 7-23

Methane is stored at low temperature inside a tank having a volume of 1.5 m^3. Initially the tank is at a pressure of 8 atm and contains 30% liquid and 70% vapor on a volume basis. How much heat must be transferred to the tank from the surroundings, so that the pressure inside the tank rises to 100 atm?

Solution: The first law written for this process gives

$$Q_{1\to2} = m(u_2 - u_1) + \overset{\cong 0}{\cancel{W_{1\to2}}} \qquad (1)$$

From the relation

$$u = h - Pv$$

Eq. (1) becomes

$$Q_{1\to2} = m\left[(h_2 - P_2v_2) - (h_1 - P_1v_1)\right]$$

or

$$Q_{1\to2} = m(h_2 - h_1) - V(P_2 - P_1) \qquad (2)$$

Then convert the pressures to the same units that the temperature is. Thus

$$P_1 = 8 \text{ atm} \times 101.325 \frac{\text{kPa}}{\text{atm}} = 810.6 \text{ kPa}$$

$$P_2 = 100 \text{ atm} \times 101.325 \frac{\text{kPa}}{\text{atm}} \times \frac{1 \text{ MPa}}{1000 \text{ kPa}} = 10.13 \text{ MPa}$$

In Eq. (2)

$$V(P_2 - P_1) = 1.5(10,132.5 - 810.6) = 13,982.85 \text{ kJ} \quad (2a)$$

and

$$h_2 - h_1 = -(h_2{}^* - h_2) + (h_2{}^* - h_1{}^*) + (h_1{}^* - h_1) \quad (3)$$

where $(h_2{}^* - h_2)$, $(h_1{}^* - h_1)$ are found using the enthalpy deviation chart, and $(h_2{}^* - h_1{}^*)$ is obtained using the relation (assuming constant specific heats)

$$dh^* = c_p dT$$

or

$$h_2{}^* - h_1{}^* = c_p(T_2 - T_1) \quad (4)$$

However, in order to calculate these quantities, the temperatures at states 1 and 2 must be found first.

Since the percentage of the volumes are given it can be written

$$V_1)_{liq} = 0.3V = 0.3(1.5) = 0.45 \text{ m}^3$$

and

$$V_1)_{vap} = 0.7V = 0.7(1.5) = 1.05 \text{ m}^3$$

From the table of the critical constants, for methane

$$P_c = 45.8 \text{ atm} \qquad T_c = 191.1°K$$

$$R = 0.51835 \text{ kJ/kg-°K} \qquad c_p = 2.2537 \text{ kJ/kg-°K}$$

$$MW = 16.04 \text{ kg/kg-mole}$$

Since methane is saturated, from the compressibility factor chart at

$$P_{r_1} = \frac{P_1}{P_c} = \frac{8}{45.8} = 0.1747$$

and on the saturated gas line, obtain

$$T_{r_1})_{sat} = 0.8$$

Then using the formula

$$T_{r_1} = \frac{T_1}{T_c}$$

gives

$$T_1 = T_r)_{sat} \times T_c = 0.8 \times 191.1 = 152.8°K$$

The compressibility factor chart then gives two values for Z; one for the liquid state and one for the vapor state.

Therefore

$$Z_1)_{liq} = 0.025, \; Z_1)_{vap} = 0.84$$

The specific volume can be computed now at state one, as

$$v_1 = \frac{V}{m} \tag{5}$$

The only unknown in Eq. (5) is the mass of methane. However,

$$m_1 = m_1)_{liq} + m_1)_{vap} \tag{6}$$

where

$$m_1)_{liq} = \frac{V_{liq}}{v_{liq}}$$

and (7)

$$m_1)_{vap} = \frac{V_{vap}}{v_{vap}}$$

From the equation of state

$$Pv = ZRT$$

solving for v at state 1 gives

$$v_1)_{liq} = \frac{Z_1)_{liq}RT_1}{P_1} = \frac{0.025(0.51835)(152.8)}{810.6} = 0.0024 \text{ m}^3/\text{kg}$$

and

$$v_1)_{vap} = \frac{Z_1)_{vap}RT_1}{P_1} = \frac{0.84(0.51835)(152.8)}{810.6} = 0.0821 \text{ m}^3/\text{kg}$$

Then from Eq. (7)

$$m_1)_{liq} = \frac{V_1)_{liq}}{v_1)_{liq}} = \frac{0.45}{0.0024} = 187.5 \text{ kg}$$

and

$$m_1)_{vap} = \frac{V_1)_{vap}}{v_1)_{vap}} = \frac{1.05}{0.0821} = 12.79 \text{ kg}$$

Substituting into Eq. (6), gives

$$m_1 = 187.5 + 12.79 = 200.29 \text{ kg}$$

Since no mass enters or leaves the system, the mass at state 2 is the same as that at state 1.

Then

$$m_2 = m_1 = m = 200.29 \text{ kg}$$

Also

$$v_2 = v_1 = v = \frac{V}{m} = \frac{1.5}{200.29} = 0.007489 \text{ m}^3/\text{kg}$$

The equation of state applied at state 2 is

$$P_2 v_2 = Z_2 R T_2$$

Substituting the numerical values gives

$$10132.5 \times 0.007489 = Z_2(0.51835)T_2$$

or

$$Z_2 T_2 = 146.392$$

Divide by T_c to obtain

$$Z_2 T_{r_2} = 0.7660 \qquad (8)$$

Eq. (8) has two unknowns, and will have to be solved by trial-and-error, using the compressibility factor chart, along with the information known for state 2.

At state 2

$$P_{r_2} = \frac{P_2}{P_c} = \frac{100}{45.8} = 2.1834$$

<u>First trial</u>: Assume T_2 = 200K

Then

$$T_{r_2} = \frac{200}{191.1} = 1.0466$$

From the compressibility factor chart at P_{r_2}, T_{r_2}

$$Z_2 = 0.34$$

From Eq. (8)

$$Z_2 = 0.7319$$

<u>Second trial</u>: Assume T_2 = 250°K

Then

$$T_{r_2} = \frac{250}{191.1} = 1.3082$$

From the compressibility factor chart at P_{r_2}, T_{r_2}

$$Z_2 = 0.69$$

From Eq. (8)

$$Z_2 = 0.5855$$

Third trial: Assume $T_2 = 240°K$

Then

$$T_{r_2} = \frac{240}{191.1} = 1.2559$$

From the compressibility factor chart at P_{r_2}, T_{r_2}

$$Z_2 = 0.62$$

From Eq. (8)

$$Z_2 = 0.6099$$

Fourth trial: Assume $T_2 = 235°K$

Then

$$T_{r_2} = \frac{235}{191.1} = 1.2297$$

From the compressibility factor chart at P_{r_2}, T_{r_2}

$$Z_2 = 0.60$$

From Eq. (8)

$$Z_2 = 0.6229$$

From the above trials it is clear that the temperature lies between 235°K and 240°K. Then

$$T_2 \cong 238°K$$

or

$$T_{r_2} = \frac{238}{191.1} = 1.2454$$

Now that the temperatures are known at both states the enthalpies can be calculated, by using the enthalpy correction chart. Therefore

$$h_a^* - h_b = \left[\left(\frac{\bar{h}_a^* - \bar{h}_b}{T_c}\right) T_c\right] \frac{1}{MW} \tag{9}$$

From the chart

$$\left(\frac{\bar{h}_2^* - \bar{h}_2}{T_c}\right) T_c = 17.5 \text{ kJ/kmol-°K}$$

From Eq. (9)

$$h_2^* - h_2 = 17.5 \left(\frac{191.1}{16.04}\right) = 208.5 \text{ kJ/kg} \tag{9a}$$

At state 1 methane is saturated liquid and vapor, thus

$$(h_1^* - h_1) = (h_1^* - h_{l_1}) - x_1(h_{v_1} - h_{l_1}) \tag{10}$$

where

$$x_1 = \frac{m_{vap}}{m} = \frac{12.79}{200.20} = 0.0639 \tag{10a}$$

From the enthalpy deviation chart at the saturated liquid line and T_{r_1}

$$\frac{\bar{h}_1^* - \bar{h}_{l_1}}{T_c} = 47.5 \text{ kJ/kmol-°K}$$

and from Eq. (9)

$$h_1^* - h_{l_1} = 47.5\left(\frac{191.1}{16.04}\right) = 565.91 \text{ kJ/kg} \tag{11}$$

From the chart again, at the saturated gas line and T_{r_1}

$$\frac{\bar{h}^*{}_1 - \bar{h}_{v_1}}{T_c} = 3.5 \text{ kJ/kmol-°K}$$

and from Eq. (9)

$$h_1^* - h_{l_1} = 3.5\left(\frac{191.1}{16.04}\right) = 41.69 \text{ kJ/kg} \tag{12}$$

Substituting (10a), (11), and (12) into (10), obtain

$$\begin{aligned} h_1^* - h_1 &= 565.91 - 0.0639(565.91 - 41.69) \qquad (13) \\ &= 532.41 \text{ kJ/kg} \end{aligned}$$

Also from Eq. (4)

$$h_2^* - h_1^* = 2.2537(238-152.8) = 192.1 \text{ kJ/kg} \tag{14}$$

Then substitute (9a), (13), and (14) into (3), to obtain

$$\begin{aligned} h_2 - h_1 &= -(208.5) + 192.1 + 532.41 \\ &= 516.01 \text{ kJ/kg} \end{aligned}$$

Substituting the numerical value of the above expression, and of expression (2a) into (2), obtain

$$\begin{aligned} Q_{1\to 2} &= 200.29(516.01) - 13,982.85 \\ &= 89,368.79 \text{ kJ} \end{aligned}$$

THE GENERALIZED ENTROPY DEVIATION CHART

• PROBLEM 7-24

A gas initially at 700 psia, 540°R runs through a heat exchanger and heat is added to the gas until it leaves the heat exchanger at 650 psia and 1000°R. Using the generalized enthalpy and entropy charts calculate the heat transfer to the gas and the change in entropy of the system. Assume the gas to have the following properties

$$\bar{M} = 31 \text{ lbm/lbmole} \qquad P_c = 900 \text{ psia} \qquad T_c = 540°R$$

$$c_p = 0.50 \text{ Btu/lbm-°R (at low pressure)}$$

Solution: First check the inlet state 1 to see if the perfect-gas model is appropriate.

$$P_{r_1} = \frac{P}{P_c} = \frac{700}{900} = 0.779$$

$$T_{r_1} = \frac{T}{T_c} = \frac{540}{540} = 1.000$$

Checking on the generalized compressibility chart, Z = 0.6 so that the conditions are not those of the perfect gas (Z = 1.0), and we must use the generalized enthalpy chart to calculate the enthalpy change. For the exit state 2 we have

$$P_{r_2} = \frac{P}{P_c} = \frac{650}{900} = 0.723$$

$$T_{r_2} = \frac{T}{T_c} = \frac{1000}{540} = 1.85$$

An energy balance gives the heat input per unit mass as

$$Q = h_2 - h_1$$

From the generalized enthalpy chart,

$$\frac{\hat{h}_{pg} - \hat{h}_1}{T_c} = 2.7 \text{ cal/gmole°K} = 2.7 \text{ Btu/lbmole-°R}$$

Then,

$$h_1 = \frac{\hat{h}_{pg} - 2.7T_c}{\hat{M}} = h_{pg_1} - \frac{2.7 \times 540}{31} = (h_{pg_1} - 47) \text{ Btu/lbm}$$

Similarly,

$$h_2 = h_{pg_2} - \frac{0.55 \times 540}{31} = (h_{pg_2} - 10) \text{ Btu/lbm}$$

So,

$$Q = h_2 - h_1 = (h_{pg2} - h_{pg1}) - 10 + 47$$

$$Q = c_p(T_2 - T_1) + 37 = 0.5 \times (1000 - 540) + 33 = 267 \text{ Btu/lbm}$$

Note that h_{pg} is evaluated using the low-pressure (ideal gas) value for c_p. If the perfect-gas approximation had been used, the error would have been about 15 percent. The entropy change can be calculated in a similar manner from the generalized entropy chart.

$$s_2 - s_1 = (s_2 - s_1)_{pg} + \frac{1.9 - 0.27}{31}$$

$$= 0.36 \text{ Btu/lbm-°R.}$$

• PROBLEM 7-25

Methane (CH_4) undergoes a steady-flow isobaric process and as a result its temperature changes from 688°R to 516°R. If the pressure is 1346 psia, determine the change in specific entropy by using the generalized entropy deviation chart.

Table 1: Empirical Equations for Specific Heat Capacities of the Ideal Gas State°

$$c_p = A + BT + CT^2 + D/(T)^{1/2}, \text{ Btu/lb}_m\text{°F}$$

$$c_v = c_p - R/J, \text{ Btu/lb}_m\text{°F}$$

Gas	Temperature range (°R)	A	$B \times 10^{-5}$	$C \times 10^{-9}$	D	For T = 70°F c_p	c_v	γ	R/J
air	400 to 1200	0.2405	−1.186	20.1	0	0.240	0.171	1.40	0.0685
	1200 to 4000	0.2459	3.22	−3.74	−0.833				
CO	400 to 1200	0.2534	−2.35	26.88	0	0.249	0.178	1.40	0.0709
	1200 to 4000	0.2763	3.04	−3.89	−1.5				
CO_2	400 to 4000	0.328	3.2	−4.4	−3.33	0.199	0.154	1.29	0.0451
H_2	400 to 1000	2.853	145	−883	0	0.341	2.43	1.41	0.9850
	1000 to 2500	3.447	−4.7	70.3	0				
	2500 to 4000	2.841	45	−31.2	0				
H_2O	400 to 1800	0.4267	2.425	23.85	0	0.446	0.331	1.37	0.1102
	1800 to 4000	0.3275	14.67	−13.59	0				
N_2	400 to 1200	0.2510	−1.63	20.4	0	0.248	0.177	1.40	0.0709
	1200 to 4000	0.2192	4.38	−5.14	−0.124				
O_2	400 to 1200	0.213	0.188	20.3	0	0.220	0.158	1.39	0.0621
	1200 to 4000	0.340	−0.36	0.616	−3.19				
CH_4	400 to 1000	0.453	0.62	268.8	0	0.532	0.408	1.30	0.1238
	1000 to 4000	1.152	32.58	−41.29	− 22.42				
C_8H_{18}	400 to 1200	0.0693	52.6	0	0	0.348	0.331	1.05	0.0174
$C_{12}H_{26}$	400 to 1200	0.0510	52.2	0	0	0.328	0.316	1.04	0.0117

Solution: From the table of critical constants, for methane

$$P_c = 673 \text{ psia}$$

$$T_c = 343.9°R$$

$$MW = 16.03$$

Convert to reduced pressures and temperatures

$$P_{r_1} = \frac{P_1}{P_c} = \frac{1346}{673} = 2.0$$

$$P_{r_2} = P_{r_1} = 2.0$$

$$T_{r_1} = \frac{T_1}{T_c} = \frac{688}{343.9} = 2.0$$

$$T_{r_2} = \frac{T_2}{T_c} = \frac{516}{343.9} = 1.5$$

The change in specific enthalpy is expected as

$$s_2 - s_1 = \left[s_2* - (s* - s)_2\right] - \left[s_1* - (s* - s)_1\right]$$

$$= -(s* - s)_2 + (s_2* - s_1*) + (s* - s)_1 \qquad (1)$$

Assuming variable specific heats

$$s_2* - s_1* = \int_{T_1}^{T_2} \frac{c_p}{T}\, dT - \frac{R}{J} \ln \frac{P_2}{P_1} \qquad (2)$$

But $P_2 = P_1$, hence

$$s_2* - s_1* = \int_{T_1}^{T_2} \frac{c_p}{T}\, dT \qquad (3)$$

From the accompanying table

$$c_p = 0.453 + 0.62 \times 10^{-5}T + 268.8 \times 10^{-9}T^2 \text{ Btu/lbm-°F}$$

Substituting into Eq. (3) and integrating

$$s_2* - s_1* = 0.453 \ln \frac{516}{688} + 0.62 \times 10^{-5}(516-688)$$

$$+ \frac{268.8 \times 10^{-9}}{2}\left[(516)^2 - (688)^2\right]$$

$$= -0.1322 \text{ Btu/lbm-°R}$$

From the generalized entropy chart

$$(s^* - s)_2 = \left(\frac{\bar{s}^* - \bar{s}^*}{MW}\right)$$

$$= \frac{1.14}{16.03}$$

$$= 0.0711 \text{ Btu/lbm-°R}$$

$$(s^* - s)_1 = \left(\frac{\bar{s}^* - \bar{s}}{MW}\right)_1$$

$$= \frac{0.55}{16.03}$$

$$= 0.0343 \text{ Btu/lbm-°R}$$

Substituting the numerical values into Eq. (1), obtain

$$s_2 - s_1 = -(0.0711) + (-0.1322) + (0.0343)$$

$$= -0.169 \text{ Btu/lbm-°R}$$

• PROBLEM 7-26

Ethylene gas initially at 338.4°K, 1 atm is compressed reversibly and isothermally to a final pressure of 225 atm. Calculate the change in entropy for the real-gas compression process, by first drawing the calculation path for the process on a P-S diagram.

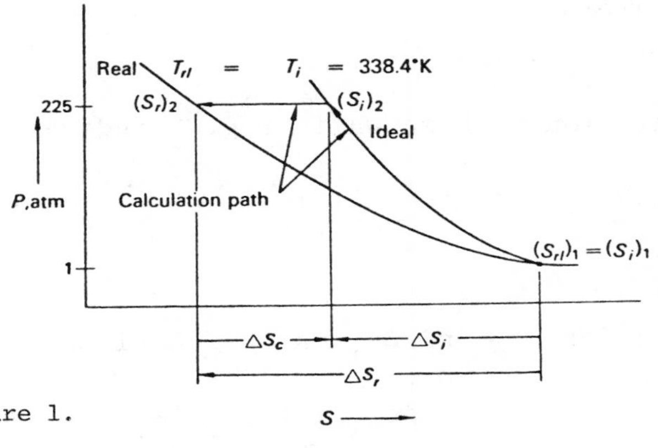

Figure 1.

Solution: First check states 1 and 2 to see if the perfect gas model is appropriate. From the table of critical constants, for ethylene

$$P_{cr} = 50 \text{ atm} \qquad T_{cr} = 282°K$$

$$R = 1.9854 \text{ Btu/lb mole-°R} \qquad [8.3144 \text{ kJ/kg°K}]$$

Then

$$P_{r_1} = \frac{P_1}{P_{cr}} = \frac{1}{50} = 0.02$$

$$T_{r_1} = \frac{T_1}{T_{cr}} = \frac{338.4}{282} = 1.2$$

checking on the generalized compressibility chart

$$Z \cong 1$$

so that at state 1 the conditions are those for the perfect gas. For the exit state

$$P_{r_2} = \frac{P_2}{P_{cr}} = \frac{225}{50} = 4.5$$

$$T_{r_2} = T_{r_1} = 1.2$$

Checking on the generalized compressibility chart

$$Z = 0.65$$

so that at state 2 the conditions are not those for the perfect gas ($Z = 1$). Now the calculation path can be drawn as shown in Fig. 1. To calculate Δs for the real gas compression process, $(\Delta s_{rl})_{1\to 2}$, first calculate $(\Delta s_i)_{1\to 2}$ for the compression of an ideal gas from 1 to 225 atm and subtract Δs_c (obtained from the entropy correction chart) from the result.

The calculation path shown in Fig. 1 indicates that

$$(s_{rl})_1 = (s_i)_1 \to (s_i)_2 \to (s_{rl})_2$$

The arrows for Δs_c and Δs_i on the abscissa indicate that

$$\Delta s_{rl} = \Delta s_i - \Delta s_c$$

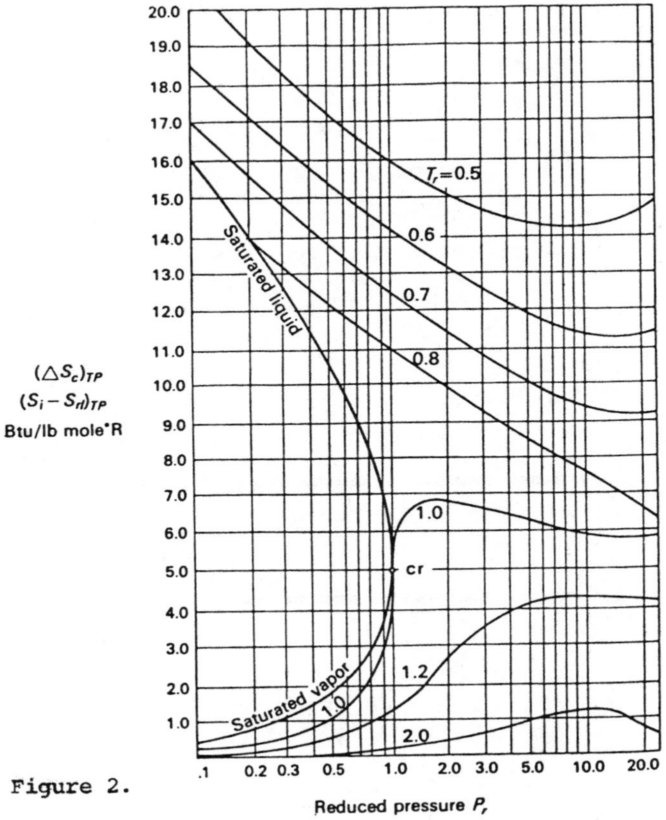

Figure 2.

Since all the needed information is known the solution of the problem proceeds as follows

Ideal gas path:

$$\Delta s_i = \int \frac{dQ}{T} = \int \frac{dW_0}{T} = -\int \frac{VdP}{T}$$

$$= -R\int \frac{dP}{P} + -R \ln \frac{P_2}{P_1}$$

Substituting the numerical values

$$\Delta s_i = -1.9854 \ln \left(\frac{225}{.1}\right) = -10.75 \text{ Btu/lb mole°R}$$

or

$$(s_i)_2 - (s_i)_1 = -10.75 \text{ Btu/lb mole-°R } [-45.03 \text{ kJ/kg-mole°K}]$$

From the Δs correction chart at P_{r2}, T_{r2} obtain

$$\Delta S_c = (s_i - s_{rl})_2 = +4.0 \text{ Btu/lb-mole°R } [+16.75 \text{ kJ/kg-mole-°K}]$$

For the real-gas compression process,

$$(\Delta s_{rl})_{1\to 2} = \Delta s_i - \Delta s_c$$

$$= (s_i)_2 - (s_i)_1 - [(s_i)_2 - (s_{rl})_2]$$

$$= (s_{rl})_2 - (s_i)_1$$

$$= -10.75 - (+4.0)$$

$$= -14.75 \text{ Btu/lb-mole°R} \quad [-61.78 \text{ kJ/kg-mole-°K}]$$

• PROBLEM 7-27

Ethylene gas enters a turbine at 225 atm, 338.4°K and expands reversibly and adiabatically to a final pressure of 100 atm. What is the temperature of the gas at the exit of the turbine?

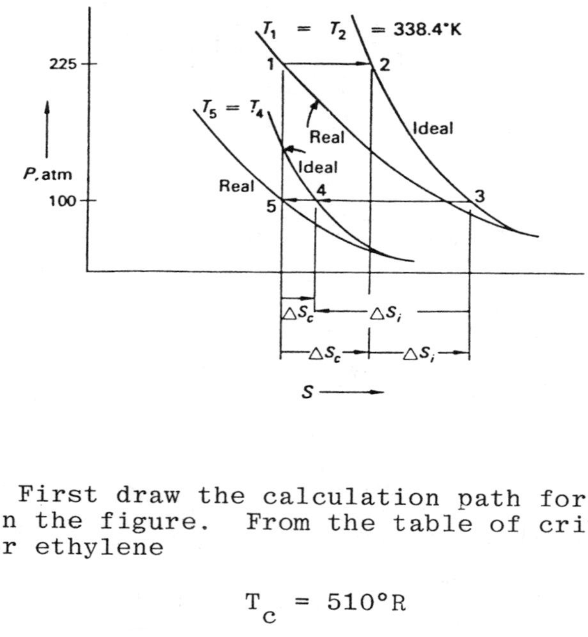

Solution: First draw the calculation path for the process as shown in the figure. From the table of critical constants obtain, for ethylene

$$T_c = 510°R$$

$$P_c = 50.5 \text{ atm}$$

$$\overline{c}_p = 8.53 \text{ Btu/lb mole-°R}$$

Converting to absolute Rankine scale

$$T_1 = \frac{9}{5}(338.4) = 609.12°R$$

Also

$$T_{r1} = \frac{T_1}{T_c} = \frac{609.12}{510} = 1.2$$

$$T_{r1} = \frac{P_1}{P_c} = \frac{225}{50.5} = 4.5$$

At state 2

$$P_{r2} = \frac{P_2}{P_c} = \frac{100}{50.5} = 2$$

$$T_{r4} = \frac{T_4}{T_c} = \frac{T_4}{282}$$

Now using Fig. 1, the following equations can be written for Δs. (Let the subscript i stand for the ideal gas, and rl for the real gas.)

Path 1-2: From the entropy deviation chart

$$\Delta s_c = 4.0 \text{ Btu/lbmole-°R}$$

Path 2-3:

$$\Delta s_i = -R \ln \frac{P_3}{P_2} = -2 \ln \frac{100}{225} = +1.62 \text{ Btu/lbmole°R}$$

Path 3-4:

$$\Delta s_i = \bar{c}_p \ln \frac{T_4}{T_3} = 8.53 \ln \frac{T_4}{609.12}$$

Path 4-5: The value of Δs_c must be obtained. The change in entropy for the real gas is

$$(\Delta s_{rl})_{1\to5} = (\Delta s_c)_{1\to2} + (\Delta s_i)_{2\to3} + (\Delta s_i)_{3\to4} - (\Delta s_c)_{4\to5} = 0$$

Substituting the numerical values gives

$$4 + 1.62 + 8.53 \ln \frac{T_4}{609.12} - (\Delta s_c)_{4\to5} = 0$$

Rearranging, gives

$$8.53 \ln \frac{T_4}{609.12} - (\Delta s_c)_{4\to5} + 5.62 = 0$$

or

$$(\Delta s_c)_{4\to5} = 5.62 + 8.53 \ln \frac{T_4}{609.12} \qquad (1)$$

The above equation has two unknowns and therefore must be solved by employing a trial-and-error solution, along with the use of the entropy deviation chart. The procedure is as follows.

1. Assume a temperature T_4, and convert it to a reduced temperature.

2. Using T_{r_4} and P_{r_4} obtain a value for $(\Delta s_c)_{4\to 5}$ from the entropy deviation chart.

3. Using the assumed temperature T_4 (in °R) calculate $(\Delta s)_{4\to 5}$ using Eq. (1).

4. Compare the values obtained in 3 and 4. If they are equal, this is the final temperature. If they are not, assume another temperature and follow the same procedure until a satisfactory temperature has been found that gives a value of $(\Delta s_c)_{4\to 5} = 0$ in both 3 and 4.

Following this path we have

First trial: Assume $T_4 = 550°R$

$$T_{r_4} = \frac{550}{510} = 1.08$$

From the entropy deviation chart

$$(\Delta s)_{4\to 5} = 4.8 \text{ Btu/lbmol-°R}$$

From Eq. (1)

$$(\Delta s)_{4\to 5} = 4.75 \text{ Btu/lbmol-°R}$$

<u>Second trial</u>: Assume $T_4 = 530°R$

$$T_{r_4} = \frac{530}{510} = 1.04$$

From the entropy deviation chart

$$(\Delta s)_{4\to 5} = 5.2 \text{ Btu/lbmol-°R}$$

From Eq. (1)

$$(\Delta s)_{4\to 5} = 4.44 \text{ Btu/lbmol-°R}$$

<u>Third trial</u>: Assume $T_4 = 560°R$

$$T_{r_4} = \frac{560}{510} = 1.09$$

From the entropy deviation chart

$$(\Delta s_c)_{4\to 5} = 4.5 \text{ Btu/lbmol-°R}$$

From Eq. (1)

$$(\Delta s_c)_{4\to5} = 4.9 \text{ Btu/lbmol-°R}$$

From the above trials the following table can be formed.

T °R	$(\Delta s_c)_{4\to s}$ from entropy deviation chart	$(\Delta s_c)_{4\to s}$ from Eg. (1)
530	5.2 Btu/lbmole-°R	4.44 Btu/lbmole-°R
550	4.8 Btu/lbmole-°R	4.75 Btu/lbmole-°R
560	4.5 Btu/lbmole-°R	4.90 Btu/lbmole-°R

From this table it can be seen that the temperature which would give $(\Delta s)_{4\to5}$ the same value for both the entropy deviation chart and Eq. (1), lies between 530°R and 550°R, closest to 550°R.

FUGACITY AND THE GENERALIZED FUGACITY CHART

• PROBLEM 7-28

What is the fugacity of water at a temperature of 298°K and a pressure of $10^7 N/m^2$? Assume that the following properties are known, for water at 298°K.

$$\rho = 997 \text{ kg/m}^3$$

$$MW = 18.02 \text{ kg/kg mol}$$

$$P_c = \text{vapor pressure} = 3{,}160 \text{ N/m}^2$$

Solution: Since the vapor pressure at 298°K is low we may assume that

$$f = P = 3160 \text{ N/m}^2$$

However, to obtain the fugacity at 298°K and 10^7N/m^2 the equation

$$\left(\frac{\partial \ln f}{\partial P}\right)_T = \frac{v}{RT}$$

will be used.

Integrating, yields

$$RT \ln \frac{f_2}{f_1} = v(P_2 - P_1)$$

or

$$\ln \frac{f_2}{f_1} = \frac{v}{RT}(P_2 - P_1)$$

Substituting the numerical values

$$\ln \frac{f_2}{f_1} = \frac{18.02}{8.3143(298)(997)(1000)}(10^7 - 3160)$$

$$= 0.073$$

Then

$$f_2 = 1.076 \times 3160 = 3400 \text{ N/m}^2$$

• PROBLEM 7-29

Carbon dioxide obeys the reduced Berthelot equation reasonably well

$$z = \frac{PV}{RT} = 1 + \frac{9}{128}\frac{PT_c}{P_cT}\left[1 - 6\frac{T_c^2}{T^2}\right]$$

Given: $T_c = 304.3$ K and $P_c = 73.0$ atm, calculate the fugacity of carbon dioxide at a temperature of 150°C and pressure of 50 atm.

Solution: By definition, $d\,\ell n\, f = d\,\ell n\, P + \frac{1}{RT}\left(V - V_{id}\right) dP$. On substituting the solution for V from the given equation and using the relation $V_{id} = \frac{RT}{P}$ yields

$$d\ \ell n\ f = d\ \ell n\ P + \frac{9T_c}{128\ P_c T}\left(1 - 6\ \frac{T_c^2}{T^2}\right) dP \qquad (1)$$

where f = fugacity
P = pressure
T_c = critical temperature or temperature at the critical point
T = 150 C or 423 K

Note that at a pressure approaching zero, the fugacity can be equated to the pressure, P.

Therefore, the integration of equation (1) gives

$$\ell n\ f = \ell n\ P + \frac{9\ T_c}{128\ P_c T}\left(1 - 6\ \frac{T_c^2}{T^2}\right) P$$

Substituting the numerical values

$$\ell n\ f = \ell n\ 50 + \frac{(9)(304.3)}{(128)(73.0)(423)}\left(1\ \ \frac{6(304.3)^2}{(423)^2}\right) 50$$

$$= 3.91 + (0.0006929)(-2.105)50$$

and $f = 46.4$ atm.

• PROBLEM 7-30

Use two simplified forms of the van der Waals equation of state, one is with $b = 0$ and the other with $a = 0$, to find an explicit expression for the fugacity of ammonia in each case when the pressure is 10 atm. The van der Waals constants for NH_3 are a/dm^6 atm $mol^{-2} = 4.170$ and $100b/dm^3\ mol^{-1} = 3.707$. Use these values to assess the contributions to the fugacity of the two aspects of non-ideality.

Solution: The van der Waals equation of state is given by

$$\left(P = \frac{n^2 a}{V^2}\right)(V - nb) = nRT \qquad (1)$$

where P = Pressure of the gas
n = Number of moles
V = Volume of the gas
T = Temperature of the gas
R = Gas constant
a and b = constants.

When a = 0, equation (1) becomes

$$P(V - nb) = nRT$$

$$\therefore P = \frac{nRT}{V-nb}$$

For one mole, $P = \dfrac{RT}{V-b}$ (2)

When b = 0, the equation becomes

$$\left(P + \frac{n^2a}{V^2}\right)V = nRT$$

$$\therefore P = \frac{nRT}{V} - \frac{n^2a}{V^2}$$

For one mole, $P = \dfrac{RT}{V} - \dfrac{a}{V^2}$ (3)

or $$V^2 - \frac{VRT}{P} + \frac{a}{P} = 0 \quad (4)$$

Solve for V in equation (4) (using the quadratic formula).

That is $V = \dfrac{-b \pm\sqrt{b^2 - 4ac}}{2a}$. Note that the a and b in the quadratic formula are just the coefficients of V^2 and V respectively.

Therefore, $$V = \frac{\dfrac{RT}{P} \pm\sqrt{\dfrac{R^2T^2}{P^2} - \dfrac{4a}{P}}}{2} \quad (5)$$

Discarding the negative solution, equation (5) becomes

$$V = \frac{\left[\dfrac{RT}{P} + \dfrac{R^2T^2}{P^2} - \dfrac{4a}{P}\right]^{1/2}}{2}$$

Upon rearranging,

$$V = \frac{RT}{2P}\left[1 + \left(1 - \frac{4aP}{R^2T^2}\right)^{1/2}\right] \quad (6)$$

If deviation from ideality is small, the term $\dfrac{4aP}{R^2T^2}$ in equation (6) is small. Therefore, $\left(1 - \frac{4a}{R^2T^2}\right)^{1/2}$ can be

approximated by $1 - \frac{2aP}{R^2T^2}$. (7)

Now, fugacity $f = P \exp \int_0^P [(Z - 1)/P]dP$ (8)

where Z = compression factor. Because of the small deviation from ideality, this can be approximated by

$1 - \frac{aP}{R^2T^2}$.

Therefore equation (8) becomes $P \exp\left(\frac{-aP}{R^2T^2}\right)$. (9)

Remember that this is for the condition, b = 0.

Recall that when $a = 0,\ P = \frac{RT}{V - b}$

$$\therefore\ PV - Pb = RT$$

$$\text{and } PV = RT + Pb$$

$$\therefore\ V = \frac{RT}{P} + b$$

So, Z can be approximated by $1 + \frac{Pb}{RT}$. Therefore,

$$f = P \exp \int_0^P (b/RT)dP = P \exp(Pb/RT) \qquad (10)$$

Using the data given, equation (9) becomes

$$f = (10\text{ atm})\exp\left[\frac{-(4.17\text{ dm}^6\text{ atm mol}^{-2})(10\text{ atm})}{(0.082\text{ dm}^3\text{ atm K}^{-1}\text{ mol}^{-1})^2(298°\text{K})^2}\right]$$

$$\therefore\ f = (10\text{ atm})\exp(-0.0698) = 10\left(e^{-0.0698}\right)$$

$$f = (10)(0.93) = 9.3\text{ atm}$$

Also equation (10) becomes

$$f = (10\text{ atm})\exp\left[\frac{(0.037)(10)}{(0.082)(298)}\right]$$

$$\therefore\ f = (10)\exp(0.0151) = 10\left(e^{0.0151}\right)$$

$\therefore$ f = (10)(1.02) = 10.2 atm.

The results show that the effect of the constant a is to reduce the fugacity and that of constant b is to increase it. This agrees with the relation of these parameters to the attractive and repulsive interactions respectively.

• PROBLEM 7-31

Ethane initially at 1 atm, 317°K undergoes a reversible, isothermal steady-flow process until the pressure rises to 68 atm. Using the generalized fugacity chart calculate the work and heat interactions for 1 kg of ethane.

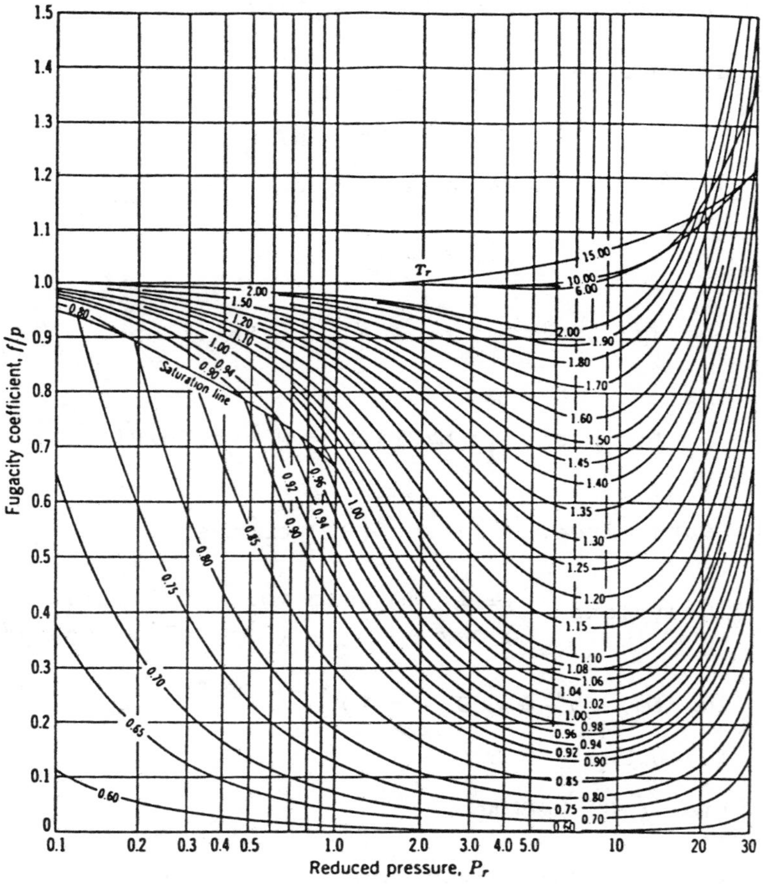

Fig. 1 Generalized fugacity coefficient chart.

Solution: For ethane, using the table of critical constants,

$$T_c = 305.48°K$$

$$P_c = 48.20 \text{ atm.}$$

$$Z_c = 0.285$$

$$MW = 30 \text{ kg/kgmol}$$

Converting to reduced pressure and temperature yields

$$T_{r_1} = T_{r_2} = \frac{T}{T_c} = \frac{317}{305.48} = 1.037$$

$$P_{r_1} = \frac{P_1}{P_c} = \frac{1}{48.2} = 0.0208$$

$$P_{r_2} = \frac{P_2}{P_c} = \frac{68}{48.2} = 1.412$$

From the generalized enthalpy chart

$$\left(\frac{\bar{h}^* - \bar{h}}{T_c}\right)_1 < 0.01 \cong 0 \qquad (1)$$

and

$$\left(\frac{\bar{h}^* - \bar{h}}{T_c}\right)_2 = 31.4 \qquad (2)$$

where $\bar{h}^*$ denotes the enthalpy as the pressure approaches zero. For this problem $\bar{h}_1^* = \bar{h}_2^*$ since as the pressure approaches zero (p-0), the enthalpy is only a function of temperature. Also from (1)

$$\bar{h}_1 \cong \bar{h}_1^*$$

Therefore

$$\bar{h}_1 - \bar{h}_2 = -(\bar{h}^* - \bar{h})_1 + (\bar{h}_2^* - \bar{h}_1^*) + (\bar{h}^* - \bar{h})_2$$

$$\cong \bar{h}_2^* - \bar{h}_2$$

$$= \left(\frac{\bar{h}^* - \bar{h}}{T_c}\right)_2 T_c \qquad (3)$$

Substituting the numerical values into Eq. (3) gives,

$$\bar{h}_1 - \bar{h}_2 = 31.4\ (305.48)$$

$$= 9{,}060 \text{ kJ/kgmol}$$

or on a per mass basis,

$$h_1 - h_2 = (\overline{h}_1 - \overline{h}_2) \times \frac{1}{MW}$$

$$= \frac{9{,}060}{30}$$

$$= 302 \text{ kJ/kg}$$

For a reversible and isothermal compression, the work interaction is given by the formula

$$w = g_1 - g_2 = \frac{\overline{R}T}{MW} \ln \left(\frac{f_1}{f_2}\right) \qquad (4)$$

where

g = Gibbs function

f = fugacity coefficient

From the accompanying figure

$$\frac{f_1}{P_1} = 1.0$$

$$\frac{f_2}{P_2} = 0.58$$

Since $P_1 = 1$ atm it follows that $f_1 = 1$ and since $P_2 = 68$ atm,

$$f_2 = P_2\left(\frac{f_2}{P_2}\right)$$

$$= 68(0.58)$$

$$= 39.44$$

Substituting into Eq. (4)

$$w = \frac{8.3143 \times 305.4}{30} \ln \left(\frac{1}{39.44}\right)$$

$$= -311 \text{ kJ/kg}$$

From the first law, assuming negligible kinetic and potential energies

$$q = (h_2 - h_1) + w$$

$$= -(h_1 - h_2) + w$$

$$= -302 - 311$$

$$= -613 \text{ kJ/kg.}$$

CHAPTER 8

VAPOR POWER AND REFRIGERATION CYCLES

THE RANKINE CYCLE

• **PROBLEM 8-1**

Calculate the heat supplied, the turbine work, and the pump work per kg of steam in a Rankine cycle where steam leaves the boiler at 4 MPa, 400°C, and the condenser operates at a pressure of 10 kPa. Also, compute the cycle efficiency. Assume the processes in the turbine and pump to be reversible and adiabatic.

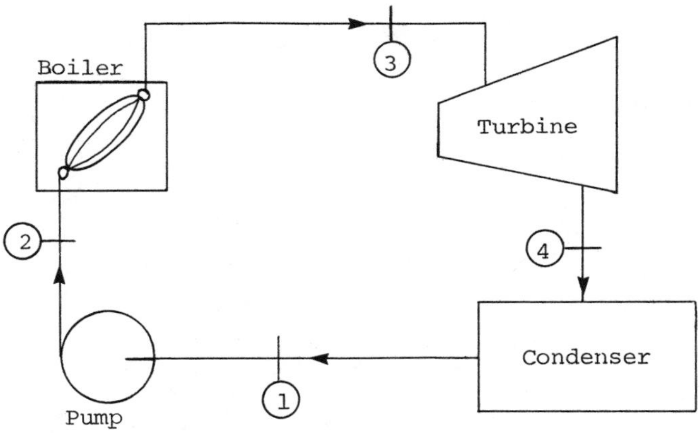

Solution: Assume all the processes to be steady-state, steady-flow and consider a control surface around each of the components under analysis. (Refer to the figure.)

First consider a control surface around the pump. Since the pump is adiabatic, from the first law

$$w_p = h_2 - h_1 \qquad (1)$$

Assuming a reversible pump, from the second law

$$s_2 = s_1$$

To obtain the enthalpy change in a reversible adiabatic process in a liquid, use the general property relation

$$Tds = dh - vdP$$

Since ds = 0

$$\Delta h = v\Delta P$$

or

$$w_p = h_2 - h_1 = v_1(P_2 - P_1)$$

$$= 0.00101(4000-10)$$

$$= 4 \text{ kJ/kg}$$

and

$$h_1 = h_f = 191.8$$

$$h_2 = 191.8 + 4 = 195.8 \text{ kJ/kg}$$

Now consider the boiler. Since no work is done,

$$q_{in} = h_3 - h_2 \qquad (2)$$

From the steam tables

$$h_3 = 3213.6 \text{ kJ/kg}$$

Thus from Eq. (2)

$$q_{in} = 3213.6-195.8$$

$$= 3017.8 \text{ kJ/kg}$$

For the reversible adiabatic process in the turbine

$$w_t = h_3 - h_4 \qquad (3)$$

and

$$s_3 = s_4$$

From the steam tables

$$s_3 = 6.7690 \text{ kJ/kg-}^{o}\text{K}$$

With this value, the state at 4 lies in the mixture region (at the pressure of 10 kPa) and hence the quality must be calculated. Therefore

$$x_4 = \frac{s_4 - s_f}{s_{fg}}$$

$$= \frac{6.7690-0.6493}{7.5009}$$

$$= 0.8159$$

The enthalpy at state 4 is then computed as

$$h_4 = h_f - x_4 h_{fg}$$

$$= 191.83 - (0.8159)(2392.8)$$

$$= 2144.1 \text{ kJ/kg}$$

Substituting the values of h_3 and h_4 into Eq. (3) gives

$$w_t = 3213.6 - 2144.1$$

$$= 1065.5 \text{ kJ/kg}$$

The efficiency of the Rankine cycle is given as

$$\eta_{th} = \frac{w_{net}}{q_{in}} \tag{4}$$

where

$$w_{net} = w_T + w_P$$

$$= 1069.5-4$$

$$= 1065.5 \text{ kJ/kg}$$

Then

$$\eta_{th} = \frac{1065.5}{3017.8} = 0.353$$

or

$$\eta_{th} = 35.3\%$$

• **PROBLEM 8-2**

In a Rankine cycle, steam at 6.89 MPa, 516°C enters the turbine with an initial velocity of 30.48 m/sec and leaves at 20.68 kPa with a velocity of 91.44 m/sec. If the mass flow rate of the steam is 136,078 kg/hr, compute the thermal efficiency of the cycle and the net power produced in horsepower.

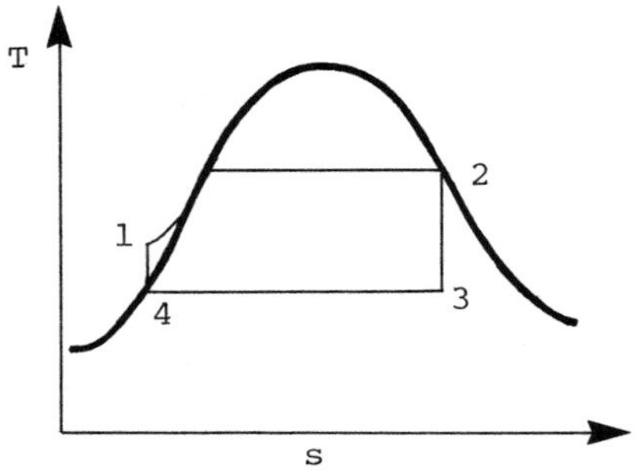

Solution: The figure shows the Rankine cycle on a T-s diagram. The efficiency of the Rankine cycle is given as

$$\eta_{th} = \frac{w_{net}}{q_{in}} \qquad (1)$$

where w_{net} is the sum of the work produced by the turbine and the work used by the pump. Hence

$$w_{net} = \Sigma w = w_t + w_p \qquad (2)$$

q_{in} is the heat added to the system in the boiler, or

$$q_{in} = h_2 - h_1 \qquad (3)$$

First consider the turbine. From the first law of thermodynamics

$$w_t = (h_2 - h_3) + \frac{V_2^2 - V_3^2}{2} \qquad (4)$$

From the steam tables at P_2, obtain

$$h_2 = 3449.3 \text{ kJ/kg}$$

$$s_2 = 6.8538 \text{ kJ/kg-°K}$$

Process 2→3 is isentropic, hence

$$s_3 = s_2$$

Furthermore, the state at 3 is a mixture of vapor and liquid. Thus, the quality at 3 is found as

$$x_3 = \frac{s_3 - s_f}{s_{fg}}$$

$$= \frac{6.8538-0.8403}{7.0578}$$

$$= 0.8522$$

Then

$$h_3 = h_f + x_3 h_{fg}$$

$$= 254.19 + 0.8522(2356.67)$$

$$= 2262.54 \text{ kJ/kg.}$$

From Eq. (4), then

$$w_t = (3449.3-2262.54)$$

$$+ \frac{(30.48)^2-(91.44)^2}{2\times 1000}$$

$$= 1183.0 \text{ kJ/kg}$$

Now consider the pump. The pump work is

$$-w_p = v_1 \Delta P = v_1(P_4 - P_1)$$

$$= 0.001018(6890-20.68)$$

$$= 6.993 \text{ kJ/kg.}$$

From Eq. (2), then

$$\Sigma w = 1183-6.993 = 1176 \text{ kJ/kg}$$

Next consider the boiler. Since no work is done it can be written

$$q_{in} = h_2 - h_1$$

$$= 3449.3-261.44$$

$$= 3187.86 \text{ kJ/kg}$$

Finally, using Eq. (1) obtain

$$\eta_{th} = \frac{1176}{3187.86} = 0.368$$

or

$$\eta_{th} = 36.89\%$$

The net power produced is

$$\dot{W} = \dot{m}w_{net}$$

$$= 136{,}078(1{,}176)$$

$$= 160{,}027{,}728 \text{ W}$$

$$= 59{,}590 \text{ hp}$$

• PROBLEM 8-3

1. Compute (a) the work input to the pump, (b) the heat added in the boiler, (c) the work produced by the turbine, (d) the heat transferred from the condenser, and (e) the thermal efficiency of the open Rankine cycle described in Fig. 1, if the pump and turbine are both adiabatic and their isentropic efficiencies are 60% and 80% respectively. Assume steady-state, steady-flow conditions and negligible kinetic and potential energies.

2. Compare the efficiency of the Rankine cycle with that of a Carnot cycle operating between the same temperature limits.

(a)

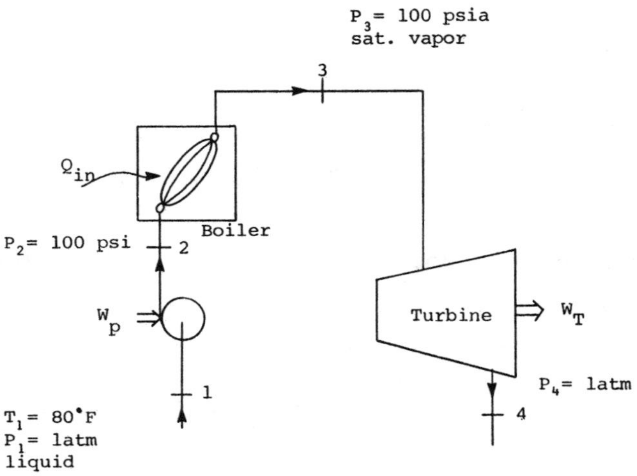

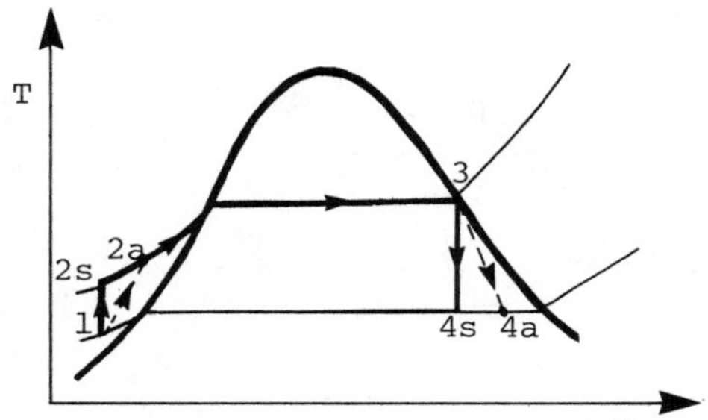

(b)

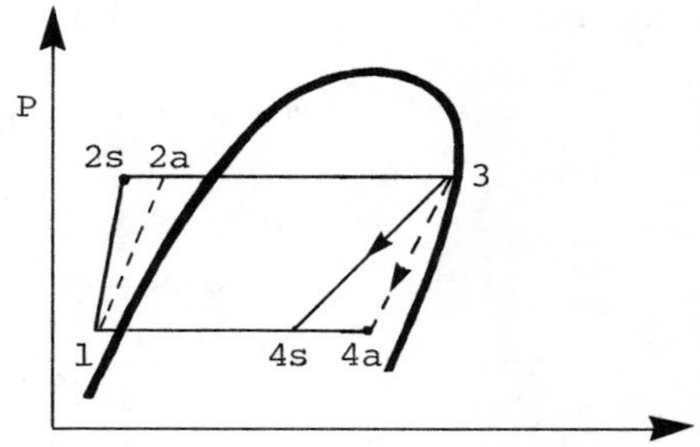

(c)

Fig. 1. A simple open Rankine cycle.

Solution: (a) Using the energy balance for the pump yields

$$w_p = h_2 - h_1$$

where w_p = total shaft-work input for each unit of mass handled by the pump.

Treat water as an incompressible liquid. Using the equation

$$h_2 - h_1 = c(T_2 - T_1) + (P_2 - P_1)v \tag{1}$$

w_p for an ideal adiabatic pump is

$$w_{ps} = v(P_{2s} - P_1) \quad \text{(isentropic process)}$$

From the steam tables $v = 0.0161$ ft^3/lbm.

$$\therefore \; w_{ps} = 0.0161 \times (100 - 14.7) \times \frac{144}{778}$$

$$= 0.253 \text{ Btu/lbm}$$

$\therefore$ The pump requires

$$w_p = \frac{w_{ps}}{\eta_s}$$

$$= \frac{0.253}{0.6}$$

$$= 0.42 \text{ Btu/lbm}$$

h_2 is determined from the equation

$$h_2 = h_1 + w_p$$

$$= 48.06 + 0.42$$

$$= 48.48 \text{ Btu/lbm}$$

T_2 may be found from Eq. (1) as

$$T_2 = T_1 + \frac{(h_2 - h_1) - v(P_2 - P_1)}{c}$$

$$= 80 + \frac{0.42 - 0.25}{1.0}$$

$$= 80.2°F$$

(b) From the steam tables, h_3 = 1187.2 Btu/lbm. Doing an energy balance on the boiler,

$$q_b = h_3 - h_2$$

$$= 1187.2 - 48.48$$

$$= 1138.7 \text{ Btu/lbm}$$

Here q_b is the energy transferred as heat to the boiler per lbm of water.

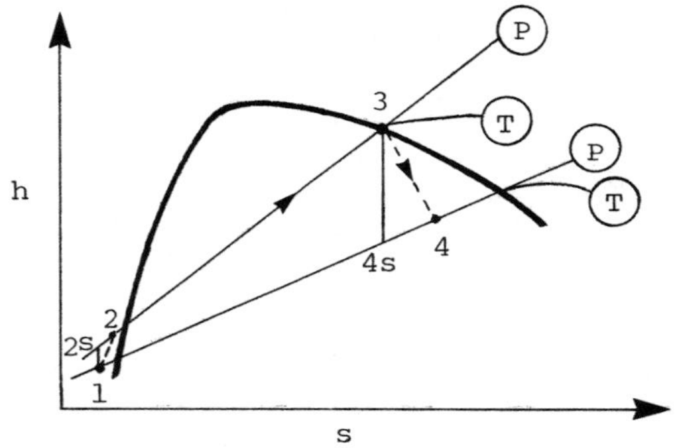

Fig. 2. Process representation on the h-s plane.

(c) Next consider an energy balance on the turbine,

$$w_t = h_3 - h_4$$

To determine state 4, first fix state 4s.

From the steam tables

$$s_3 = 1.6026 \text{ Btu/lbm-°R}$$

$$s_{f_4} = 0.3120 \text{ Btu/lbm-°R}$$

$$s_{g_4} = 1.7566 \text{ Btu/lbm-°R}$$

$$s_{fg_4} = s_{g_4} - s_{f_4}$$

$$= 1.4446 \text{ Btu/lbm-°R}$$

Since $s_{4s} = s_3$

$$s_{4s} = (1 - x_{4s})\, s_{f_4} + x_{4s}\, s_{g_4}$$

$$= s_{f_4} + x_{4s}\, s_{fg_4}$$

$$x_{4s} = \frac{1.6026 - 0.3120}{1.4446}$$

$$= 0.893$$

From the steam tables

$$h_{f_4} = 180.07 \text{ Btu/lbm}$$

$$h_{fg_4} = 970.3 \text{ Btu/lbm}$$

$$\therefore\ h_{s_4} = h_{f_4} + x_4 h_{fg_4}$$

$$= 180 + (0.893 \times 970.3)$$

$$= 1046 \text{ Btu/lbm}$$

$$\therefore\ w_{ts} = h_3 - h_{4s}$$

$$= 1187 - 1046$$

$$= 141 \text{ Btu/lbm}$$

from which

$$w_t = w_{ts}\, \eta_s$$

$$= 141 \times 0.8$$

$$= 112 \text{ Btu/lbm}$$

and

$$h_4 = h_3 - w_t$$

$$= 1187 - 112$$

$$= 1075 \text{ Btu/lbm}$$

The actual discharge quality is

$$x_4 = \frac{h_4 - h_{f_4}}{h_{fg_4}}$$

$$= \frac{1075 - 180}{970}$$

$$= 0.922$$

One attractive feature of a vapor power plant is that the part of the turbine work required to drive the pump is only a very small fraction of the turbine-work output. Here the back-work ratio (bwr) is

$$\text{bwr} = \frac{w_p}{w_t}$$

$$= \frac{0.4}{112}$$

$$\approx 0.004$$

(d) Since $P_1 = P_4$, we can have a closed cycle by adding a condenser. By this, the efficiency of the system will not change if states 1 and 2 are kept fixed. The energy transferred as heat from the condenser is obtained by taking the overall energy balance.

$$q_c = q_b - w_{net}$$

$$= 1139 - 111.6$$

$$= 1027 \text{ Btu/lbm.}$$

The series of processes is shown in Fig. 2. This plot shows the back work ratio as the respective enthalpy changes for the pump and turbine processes.

(e) The energy conversion efficiency of the plant is

$$\eta = \frac{w_{net}}{q_b}$$

$$= \frac{112-0.4}{1139}$$

$$= 0.099$$

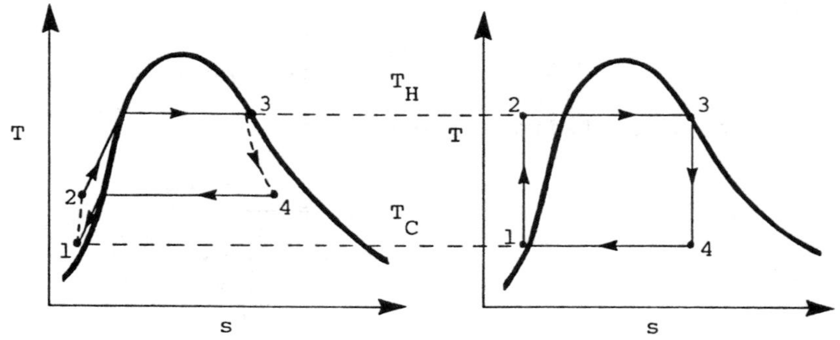

Fig. 3. Comparison with a Carnot cycle.

2. For the Carnot cycle operating between the same temperature limits,

$$\eta = 1 - \frac{540}{788}$$

$$= 0.315$$

The difference in efficiency is due to the fact that the temperatures at which energy is transferred as heat to and from the working fluid are more widelv separated for the Carnot cycle. (Ref. Fig. 3.)

Summarizing the results:

1.

(a) $w_t = 112$ Btu/lbm

(b) $w_p = 0.4$ Btu/lbm

(c) $q_b = 1139$ Btu/lbm

(d) $q_c = 1027$ Btu/lbm

(e) $\eta = 0.099$

2. $\eta = 0.315$

THE REHEAT CYCLE

• PROBLEM 8-4

Steam at 3MPa, 300°C leaves the boiler and enters the high pressure turbine (in a reheat cycle) and is expanded to 300kPa. The steam is then reheated to 300°C and expanded in the second stage turbine to 10kPa. What is the efficiency of the cycle if it is assumed to be internally reversible?

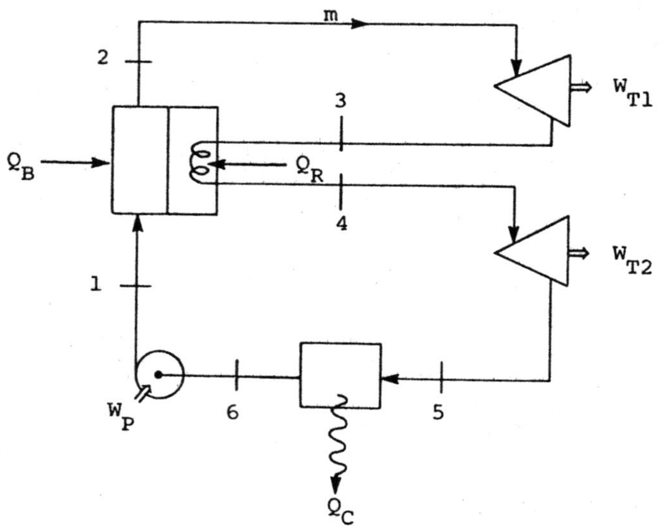

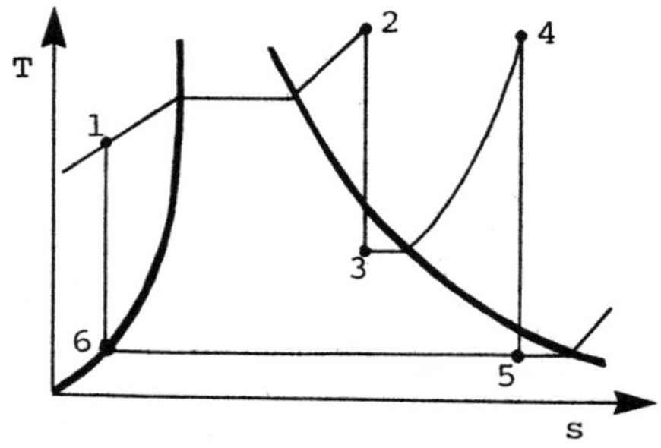

Solution: The efficiency η can be obtained from the following equation;

$$\eta = \frac{\dot{W}_{t_1} + \dot{W}_{t_2} - \dot{W}_p}{\dot{Q}_b + \dot{Q}_r} \tag{1}$$

To calculate $\dot{W}_{t_1}$ assume that the turbine is adiabatic and neglect kinetic and potential energy changes. Applying the first law to the turbine,

$$\dot{W}_{t_1} = \dot{m}(h_2 - h_3)$$

From the steam tables,

$$h_2 = 2993.5 \text{ kJ/kg}$$

$$s_2 = 6.5390 \text{ kJ/kg-}^{\circ}\text{K}$$

To find h_3, for the internally reversible adiabatic process $2 \rightarrow 3$

$$s_2 = s_3 = 6.5390 \text{ kJ/kg-}^{\circ}\text{K}$$

At state 3,

$$s_{f_3} = 1.6718 \text{ kJ/kg-}^{\circ}\text{K} \qquad h_{f_3} = 561.47 \text{ kJ/kg}$$

$$s_{fg_3} = 5.3201 \text{ kJ/kg-}^{\circ}\text{K} \qquad h_{fg_3} = 2163.8 \text{ kJ/kg}$$

$$s_{g_3} = 6.9919 \text{ kJ/kg-}^{\circ}\text{K} \qquad h_{g_3} = 2725.3 \text{ kJ/kg}$$

$$s_2 = s_3 = s_{f_3} + x_3 s_{fg_3}$$

$$6.5390 = 1.6718 + x_3(5.3201)$$

$$x_3 = 0.915$$

$$h_3 = h_{f_3} + x_3 h_{fg_3}$$

$$h_3 = 561.47 + 0.915\ (2163.8)$$

$$h_3 = 2542 \text{ kJ/kg}$$

$$\frac{\dot{W}_{t_1}}{\dot{m}} = h_2 - h_3$$

$$= 2993.5 - 2542$$

$$= 452 \text{ kJ/kg}$$

Similarly, to find $\dot{W}_{t_2}$

$$\dot{W}_{t_2} = \dot{m}(h_4 - h_5)$$

From the steam tables,

$$h_4 = 3069.3 \text{ kJ/kg}$$

$$s_4 = 7.7022 \text{ kJ/kg-}^{\circ}\text{K}$$

To find h_5, note that

$$s_4 = s_5$$

At state 5

$$s_{f_5} = 0.6493 \text{ kJ/kg-}^{\circ}\text{K}$$

$$h_{f_5} = 191.83 \text{ kJ/kg}$$

$$s_{fg_5} = 7.5009 \text{ kJ/kg-}^{\circ}\text{K}$$

$$h_{fg_5} = 2392.8 \text{ kJ/kg}$$

$$s_{g_5} = 8.1502 \text{ kJ/kg-}^{\circ}\text{K}$$

$$h_{g_5} = 2584.7 \text{ kJ/kg}$$

$$s_4 = s_5 = s_{f_5} + x_5 s_{fg_5}$$

$$x_5 = 0.949$$

$$h_5 = h_{f_5} + x_5 h_{fg_5}$$

$$h_5 = 191.83 + 0.949(2392.8)$$

$$h_5 = 2463 \text{ kJ/kg}$$

$$\therefore \quad \frac{\dot{W}_{t2}}{\dot{m}} = h_4 - h_5$$

$$= 3069.3 - 2463$$

$$= 606 \text{ kJ/kg}$$

To obtain $\dot{W}_p$, assume that $\dot{W}_p = \dot{m}v_6(p_1 - p_6)$

From the steam tables, $v_6 = v_{f_6}$

$$= 1.0102 \times 10^{-3} \text{m}^3\text{/kg}.$$

Thus
$$\frac{\dot{W}_p}{\dot{m}} = 1.0102\ (30-0.1)10^5 \times 10^{-6}$$

$$= 3.0 \text{ kJ/kg}$$

To obtain $\dot{Q}_b$, use

$$\dot{Q}_b = \dot{m}(h_2 - h_1)$$

$$h_1 = h_6 + \frac{\dot{W}_p}{\dot{m}}$$

$$= 191.8 + 3.0$$

$$= 194.8 \text{ kJ/kg}$$

$$\frac{\dot{Q}_b}{\dot{m}} = 2993.5 - 194.8$$

$$= 2799 \text{ kJ/kg}$$

To find $\dot{Q}_r$

$$\dot{Q}_r = \dot{m}(h_4 - h_3)$$

$$\frac{\dot{Q}_r}{\dot{m}} = 3069.3 - 2542$$

$$= 527 \text{ kJ/kg}$$

From Eq. (1) then

$$\eta = \frac{452 + 606 - 3}{2799 + 527}$$

$$= 0.317$$

• PROBLEM 8-5

In the reheat cycle shown in Fig. 1, steam is supplied to the high pressure turbine at 1100 lbf/in^2, 740°F and is expanded to 200 lbf/in^2. After the expansion the steam is reheated to 720°F and is then expanded in the low pressure turbine to 1 lbf/in^2. (a) Determine the enthalpy and entropy of the successive states of steam and plot them on an h-s diagram, (b) compute the low and high pressure isentropic turbine work, and (c) calculate the thermal efficiency and the rate of steam of the cycle. Assume the turbines and pump to be adiabatic.

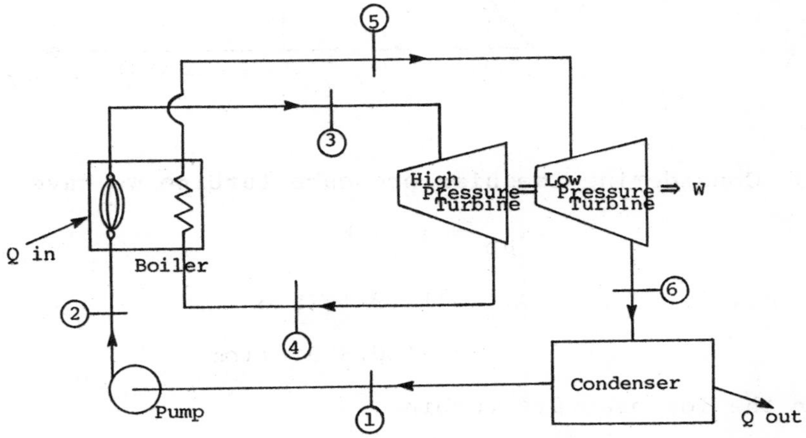

Fig. 1. A simple reheat cycle

Solution: The pump work is

$$w_p \simeq v_1(P_2 - P_1)/J$$

$$= \frac{0.01614 \times 144(1100-1)}{778}$$

$$= 3.29 \text{ Btu/lbm}$$

(a) From the steam tables at 1 psia

$$h_1 = h_f = 69.1 \text{ Btu/lbm}$$

At state 2 then, the enthalpy is

$$h_2 = 69.1 + 3.29 = 72.39 \text{ Btu/lbm}$$

Now, using the value for h_2 and the steam tables (or Mollier chart) the values of the enthalpy and entropy at the successive states of the cycle are obtained and plotted on the h-s diagram, shown in Fig. 2.

Figure 2 h-s diagram

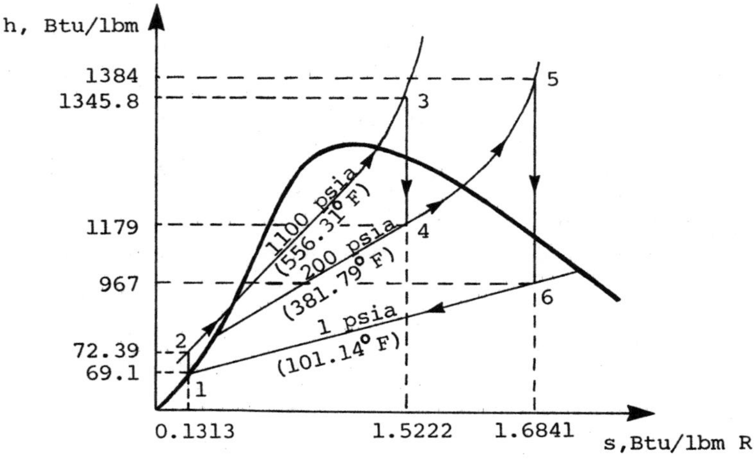

(b) Considering the high pressure turbine we have

$$-w_{hp} = h_4 - h_3$$

$$= 1179-1345.8$$

$$= -166.8 \text{ Btu/lbm}$$

For the low pressure turbine

$$-w_{lp} = h_6 - h_5$$

$$= 967 - 1384$$

$$= -417 \text{ Btu/lbm}$$

(c) The efficiency of the reheat cycle is

$$\eta_{th} = \frac{w_{net}}{(h_3 - h_2) + (h_5 - h_4)}$$

$$= \frac{166.8 + 417 - 3.29}{(1345.8 - 72.39) + (1384 - 1179)}$$

$$= 0.393$$

The rate of steam for 1 hp is

$$1 \text{ hp} = 2545 \text{ Btu/hr}$$

$$sr = \frac{2545}{w_{net}} = \frac{2545}{580.51} = 4.39 \text{ lbm/hp-hr}$$

THE REGENERATIVE CYCLE

• PROBLEM 8-6

Steam at 300 psi abs. and 700°F leaves the boiler and enters the first stage of the turbine, which has an efficiency of 80%. Some of the steam is extracted from the first stage turbine at 30 psi abs. and is rejected into a feedwater heater. The remainder of the steam is expanded to 0.491 psi in the second stage turbine, which has an efficiency of 75%.
(a) Compute the net work and the efficiency of the cycle.
(b) Compare this cycle with one having no heater. Refer to the figure.

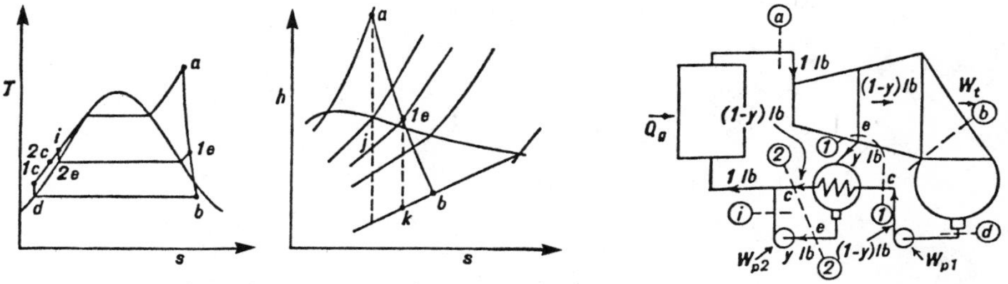

Fig. 1. Analysis of Regenerative Cycle

Solution: (a) Assume that the liquid leaving the coil of the heater and the drip leaving the heater are both at the temperature corresponding to the saturated state at the pressure of the extraction stage. Also assume that compression in the pumps is isentropic and that the turbines are adiabatic.

Using the steam tables, at the different states

Saturation temperature at 30 lb/in.^{2}	250.3 °F
Enthalpy of condensate leaving condenser, h_d	47.05 Btu/lb
Entropy of condensate leaving condenser, s_d	0.0914 Btu/lb °F
Entropy of liquid entering heater, s_{1c}	0.0914 Btu/lb °F
Pressure of liquid entering heater	300lb/in.^{2}
Enthalpy of liquid entering heater, h_{1c}	47.95 Btu/lb
The liquid leaves the heater coils at 300 lb/in.^{2} and 250.3 °F	
Enthalpy of liquid leaving coils, h_{2c}	219.4 Btu/lb
Enthalpy of drip from heater, h_{2c}	218.8 Btu/lb

In figure 1,

$$P_a = 300 \text{ lbf/in.}^2$$

$$T_a = 700\ ^\circ F$$

$$P_j = 30 \text{ lbf/in}^2$$

$$h_a = 1368.3 \text{ Btu/lbm}$$

$$h_j = 1146.9 \text{ Btu/lbm}$$

$$s_a = 1.6751 \text{ Btu/lbm-}^\circ R$$

$$s_j = 1.6751 \text{ Btu/lbm-}^\circ R$$

Therefore, from the definition of the efficiency of the first stage turbine

$$h_{1e} = h_a - 0.80\ (h_a - h_j)$$

$$= 1191.2 \text{ Btu/lbm}$$

Using the equation

$$y = \frac{h_{2c} - h_{1c}}{h_{1e} - h_{2e} + h_{2c} - h_{1c}}$$

$$y = 0.15$$

For the work delivered by the turbine

$$w_t = h_a - h_{1e} + (1-y)\ 0.75\ (h_{1e} - h_k)$$

assuming velocities at a and 1e are negligible.

State k is described by the pressure 0.491 psi, and by the entropy, which is that of state 1e

$$s_k = 1.7361\ \text{Btu/lbm-}^{\circ}\text{R}$$

From the steam tables, obtain

$$h_k = 933.4\ \text{Btu/lbm}$$

By substituting, obtain

$$w_t = 341.3\ \text{Btu/lbm}$$

The negative work of the cycle is

$$w_{p_1} + w_{p_2} = (1-y)(h_{1c} - h_d) + y(h_i - h_{2e})$$

Using the steam tables

$$w_{p_1} + w_{p_2} = 0.9\ \text{Btu/lbm}$$

The net work of the cycle is

$$w_{net} = w_t - (w_{p_1} + w_{p_2}) = 340.4\ \text{Btu/lbm}$$

Let q_g = the heat added to the fluid in the steam generator per pound of steam generated, or

$$q_g = h_a - (1-y)\ h_{2c} - yh_i$$

$$= 1368.3 - 0.85 \times 219.4 - 0.15 \times 219.6$$

$$= 1148.9\ \text{Btu/lbm}$$

For every kilowatt-hour of work delivered, the heat supplied is

$$1148.9 \times \frac{3412.8}{340.4}$$

$$= 11{,}520\ \text{Btu/kw-hr}$$

and the cycle efficiency is

$$\eta = \frac{w_{net}}{q_g}$$

$$= \frac{340.4}{1148.9}$$

$$= 29.6\%$$

(b) If no steam was extracted for feedwater heating then the whole quantity of liquid fed to the steam generator will be in a state corresponding to section 1c. Then the heat added to the fluid per pound of steam generated would be

$$h_a - h_{1c} = 1368.3 - 47.95$$

$$= 1320.3 \text{ Btu/lbm}$$

The work done when each pound of fluid passes through the turbine would be

$$h_a - h_b = h_a - h_{1e} + 0.75\,(h_{1e} - h_k)$$

$$= 177.1 + 193.3$$

$$= 370.4 \text{ Btu/lbm}$$

The total work of the cycle = the work delivered by the turbine - feedpump work

$$w_{net} = 370.4 - (h_{1c} - h_d)$$

$$= 370.4 - 0.9$$

$$= 369.5 \text{ Btu/lbm}$$

The heat supplied per kilowatt hour of work delivered would be

$$1320.3 \times 3412.8/369.5 = 12{,}195 \text{ Btu/kw-hr}$$

When extracted steam was used to heat the feedwater, the heat supplied was 11,520 Btu/kw-hr.

Therefore the saving due to regenerative heating is

$$\frac{12{,}195 - 11{,}520}{12{,}195}$$

$$= 5.5\%$$

• PROBLEM 8-7

A vapor power cycle operates between the upper and lower limits of 3.45 MPa and 14 kPa respectively. Steam at 371°C enters the high pressure turbine and leaves at 690 kPa, at which point some of the steam is extracted and rejected to an open feedwater heater. The remaining steam is expanded in the low pressure turbine to 14 kPa. Assuming the processes in the turbines and pumps to be isentropic, calculate the thermal efficiency of the cycle.

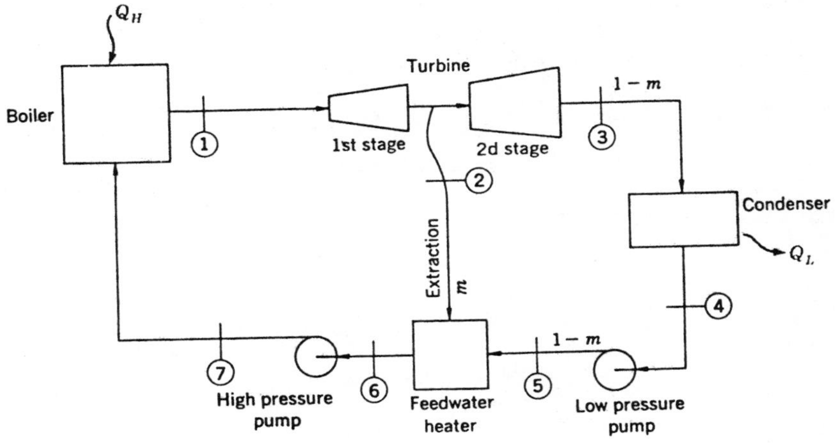

Fig. 1. Regenerative cycle with one open feedwater heater.

Solution: This cycle is shown in the figure. Since at least one open feedwater heater is employed, it is a regenerative steam cycle. The efficiency of the cycle is

$$\eta_{th} = \frac{W_{net}}{Q_H} \quad (1)$$

where

$$W_{net} = W_t + W_p$$

$$Q_H = \text{heat added in the boiler}$$

Assuming the processes in the turbines and pumps to be adiabatic, we can write for the turbines

$$w_t = m_1(h_1-h_2) + m_3(h_2-h_3) \quad (2)$$

and for the pumps

$$-w_p = m_4(h_5-h_4) + m_7(h_7-h_6) \quad (3)$$

In the boiler, since no work is done

$$Q_H = m_1(h_1-h_7) \quad (4)$$

Substituting Eqs. (2), (3), and (4) into (1) yields

$$\eta_{th} = \frac{m_1(h_1-h_2) + m_3(h_2-h_3) - m_4(h_5-h_4) - m_7(h_7-h_6)}{m_1(h_1-h_7)} \quad (5)$$

Therefore, evaluating the different mass flow rates and the enthalpies at the different states and substituting them into Eq. (5) gives the efficiency of the cycle.

For isentropic expansion in the turbine

$$s_1 = s_2 = s_3$$

Using the Mollier diagram, obtain

$$h_1 = 3198.25 \text{ kJ/kg}$$

$$h_2 = 2777.24 \text{ kJ/kg}$$

$$h_3 = 2174.81 \text{ kJ/kg}$$

$$h_4 = 218.62 \text{ kJ/kg}$$

Consider the low-pressure pump, which raises the pressure of the water coming out of the condenser from 14 kPa to 690 kPa. Therefore

$$h_5 - h_4 = v_4(P_5 - P_4)$$

$$= 0.001007(690-14)$$

$$= 0.6807 \text{ kJ/kg}$$

Hence

$$h_5 = 218.62 + 0.6807 = 219.3 \text{ kJ/kg}$$

Assuming the open feedwater heater to be ideal

$$P_2 = P_5 = P_6$$

Also, at point 6 we assume saturated liquid conditions to exist. Then from the steam tables (at 694 kPa)

$$h_6 = 694.1 \text{ kJ/kg}$$

For the high-pressure pump

$$h_7 - h_6 = v_6(P_7 - P_6)$$

$$= 0.001107(3450-690)$$

$$= 3.055 \text{ kJ/kg}$$

Thus

$$h_7 = 694.1 + 3.055 = 697.15 \text{ kJ/kg}$$

Now the mass flow rates must be evaluated. For this consider the open feedwater heater. Let m be the extraction mass. Then let $m_1 = 1$. Hence

$$m_2 = m$$

$$m_3 = m_4 = m_5 = 1-m$$

$$m_6 = m_7 = m_1 = 1$$

The energy balance on the feedwater heater is

$$mh_2 + (1-m)h_5 = 1(h_6)$$

Substituting the numerical values for the enthalpies

$$(2777.24)m + (219.3)(1-m) = 694.1$$

Solving for m gives

$$m = 0.1856 \text{ kg extracted/kg total flow}$$

Then $m_2 = 0.1856$, $m_3 = m_4 = m_5 = 0.8144$

Finally, substituting all the numerical values into Eq. (5) yields

$$\eta_{th} = \frac{1}{3198.25-697.15}\Big[1(3198.25-2777.24) + (0.8144)(2777.25-2174.81)-(0.8144)(219.3-218.62)-(1)(697.15-694.1)\Big]$$

$$= \frac{908.03}{2501.1}$$

$$= 0.3631$$

or

$$\eta_{th} = 36.31\%$$

• PROBLEM 8-8

The regenerative feedwater heating cycle shown in the figure employs one open and one closed heater operating at 10 psia and 50 psia respectively. If steam is supplied at 400 psia, 500°F and leaves the condenser at 2 in. Hg. abs., calculate the thermal efficiency of the ideal cycle, neglecting pump work.

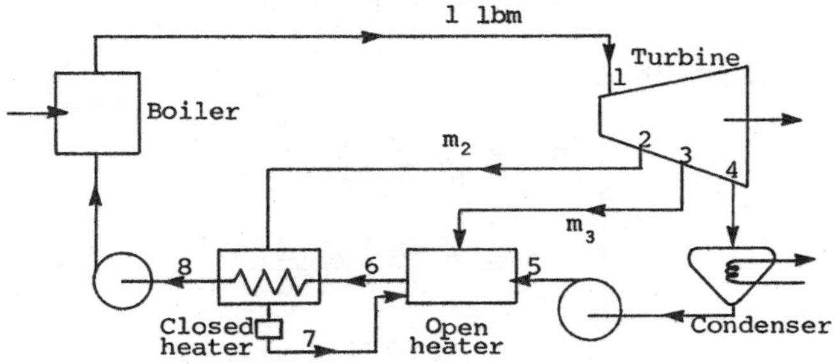

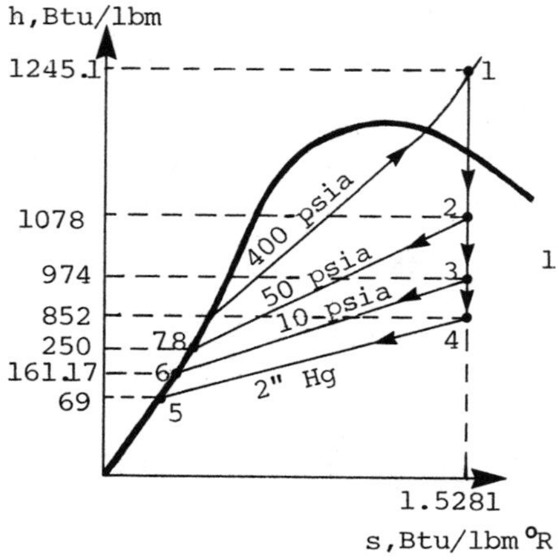

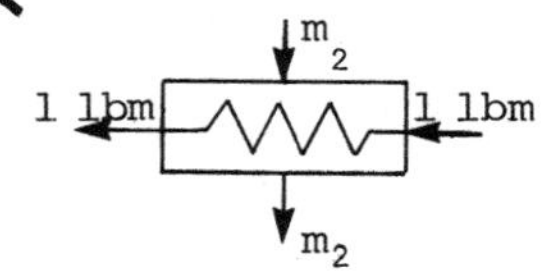

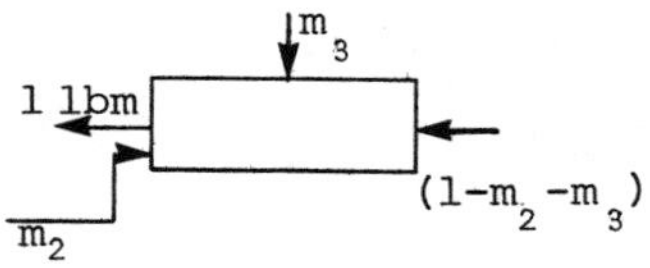

Solution: In solving this problem, first calculate the enthalpies at all the states noting that

$$s_1 = s_2 = s_3 = s_4$$

and using the given information. Note that

$$P_2 = 50 \text{ psia}$$

$$P_3 = 10 \text{ psia}$$

$$P_4 = 2 \text{ in Hg} = 0.9823 \text{ psia}$$

Using the steam tables, all the values are obtained and plotted on the h-s diagram shown in the figure. Next, assume that 1 lbm enters the turbine, and make an energy balance on the closed heater.

$$m_2h_2 + m_6h_6 = m_7h_7 + m_8h_8 \tag{1}$$

However, because the heater is closed

$$m_2 = m_7$$

$$m_6 = m_8 = 1 \text{ lbm}$$

Therefore Eq. (1) becomes

$$m_2h_2 - m_2h_7 = h_8 - h_6$$

Solving for m_2 yields

$$m_2 = \frac{h_8 - h_6}{h_2 - h_7}$$

$$= \frac{250-161.17}{1078-250}$$

$$= 0.1075 \text{ lbm/lbm}$$

Considering the open feedwater heater, write the energy balance as

$$m_2h_7 + (1-m_2-m_3)h_5 + m_3h_3 = m_6h_6$$

or

$$0.1075(250) + (1-0.1075-m_3)(69) + m_2(974) = 1(161.17)$$

Solving for m_3 yields

$$m_3 = 0.0802 \text{ lbm/lbm}$$

The thermal efficiency is

$$\eta_{th} = \frac{w_{net}}{h_1 - h_8} \qquad (2)$$

The work done is

$$-w = m_1(h_2-h_1) + (m_1-m_2)(h_3-h_2) + (m_1-m_2-m_3)(h_4-h_3)$$

$$= 1(1078-1245) + (1-0.1075)(974-1078)$$

$$+ (1-0.1075-0.0802)(852-974)$$

$$= -359 \text{ Btu/lbm}$$

Substituting in Eq. (2) gives

$$\eta_{th} = \frac{359}{1245-250}$$

$$= 0.361$$

$$= 36.1\%$$

• PROBLEM 8-9

The flow diagram for a steam power cycle with two stages of open regenerative feedwater heating is illustrated below. Using the information given, compute the mass flow rates of the extraction steam (at the two extraction points) per unit mass flow through the boiler, i.e., compute (a) m_2/m_1 and (b) m_3/m_1, assuming the isentropic efficiency of all three pumps to be 80%.

$P_1 = P_{10} = 5$ MPa	$P_2 = P_8 = P_9 = 1$ MPa	$P_3 = P_6 = P_7 =$ 100 kPa
$T_1 = 500°C$	$T_2 = 300°C$	$h_3 = 2675.5$ kJ/kg
$h_1 = 3433.6$ kJ/kg	$h_2 = 3051.2$ kJ/kg	

$h_5 = 137.8$ kJ/kg	$T_9 = 179.91°C$ (sat. liq.)	$P_4 = P_5 = 5$ kPa
$T_7 = 99.63°C$ (sat. liq.)		$h_4 = 2200$ kJ/kg.

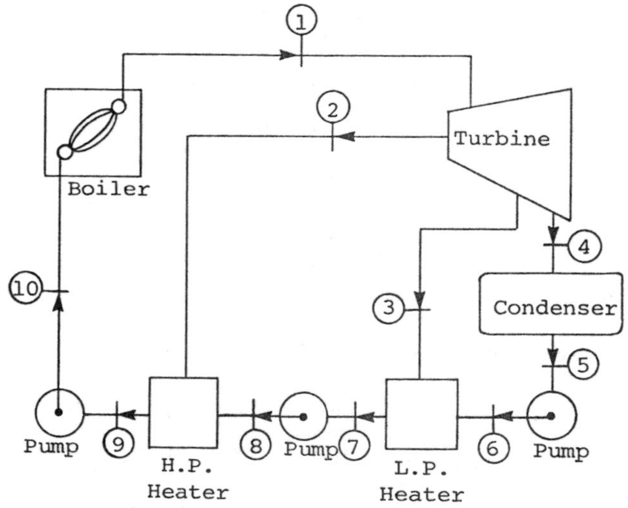

Solution: (a) First consider the high pressure feedwater heater alone, and write the equations that apply to this control volume.

Continuity: $m_8 = m_9 - m_2 \qquad (m_9 = m_1)$ (1)

First law: $m_8 h_8 = m_9 h_9 - m_2 h_2$ (2)

Dividing (1) and (2) by the mass flow at 1 (through the boiler) one gets

$$\frac{m_8}{m_1} = 1 - \frac{m_2}{m_1} \tag{3}$$

and

$$\frac{m_8}{m_1} h_8 = h_9 - \frac{m_2}{m_1} h_2 \tag{4}$$

Substituting Eq. (3) into Eq. (4) obtain

$$\left(1 - \frac{m_2}{m_1}\right) h_8 = h_9 - \frac{m_2}{m_1} h_2$$

or solving for $\frac{m_2}{m_1}$

$$\frac{m_2}{m_1} = \frac{h_8 - h_9}{h_8 - h_2} \tag{5}$$

Now that the mass flow rate has been expressed in terms of the enthalpies, all that is needed to be done is to determine the enthalpies at the different states, using the information given and the steam tables.

State 2: $h_2 = 3051.2$ kJ/kg (given)

State 8: At this state the pressure of the steam is the only known property. But for a pump, the difference in enthalpy between the entering and the leaving stream is almost the same, differing only by the amount of the work done by the pump. Assuming the fluid to be incompressible, it can be written (for an isentropic pump)

$$h_{exit} = h_{in} + \int v dP \tag{6}$$

But this is not an isentropic pump, and irreversibilities are involved, making the work required to drive the pump more than that in the isentropic case. Since the efficiency is known, Eq. (6) can be written as

$$h_8 = h_7 + \frac{v_7(P_8 - P_7)}{\eta_{pump}}$$

At state 7, $h_7 = h_f = 417.48$ kJ/kg and

$$v_7 = v_f = 0.001044 \text{ m}^3/\text{kg}$$

Substituting in the above expression

$$h_8 = 417.48 + \frac{0.001044(1000-100)}{0.8}$$

$$= 418.65 \text{ kJ/kg}$$

State 9: $h_9 = h_f = 762.82$ kJ/kg (saturated liquid)

Substituting into Eq. (5)

$$\frac{m_2}{m_1} = \frac{h_8 - h_9}{h_8 - h_2}$$

$$= \frac{418.65 - 762.82}{418.65 - 3051.2}$$

$$= 0.1307$$

(b) Now the second mass flow rate will be calculated in a similar way. Consider a control volume around the low pressure feedwater heater and write the equations that apply.

Continuity: $m_6 = m_7 - m_3$ (7)

First law: $m_6h_6 = m_7h_7 - m_3h_3$ (8)

From continuity it is known that $m_7 = m_8 = m_1 - m_2$ and $m_6 = m_1 - m_2 - m_3$ (considering a control volume around the turbine, since $m_6 = m_5 = m_4$). Taking the above into consideration, Eq. (8) takes the form

$$(m_1 - m_2 - m_3)h_6 = (m_1 - m_2)h_7 - m_3h_3$$

Dividing by m_1 (mass flow through the boiler) gives

$$(1 - \frac{m_2}{m_1} - \frac{m_3}{m_1})h_6 = (1 - \frac{m_2}{m_1})h_7 - \frac{m_3}{m_1}h_3$$

Solving for $\frac{m_3}{m_1}$

$$\frac{m_3}{m_1} = \frac{(1 - \frac{m_2}{m_1})(h_7 - h_6)}{(h_3 - h_6)} \quad (9)$$

The enthalpies at the different states must then be calculated.

State 3: $h_3 = 2675.5$ kJ/kg (given)

State 6: This is the same process as the one at state 7. Recalling from part (a) and using Eq. (6) one gets

$$h_6 = h_5 + \frac{v_5(P_6 - P_5)}{\eta_{pump}} \quad (10)$$

At state 5, $h_5 = 137.8$ kJ/kg (given)

$$v_5 = v_f = 0.001005$$

Substituting into Eq. (10), obtain for the enthalpy at state 6

$$h_6 = 137.8 + \frac{0.001005(100-5)}{0.8}$$

$$= 137.92 \text{ kJ/kg}$$

State 7: $h_7 = 417.48$ kJ/kg (from part (a))

Substituting into Eq. (9) yields

$$\frac{m_3}{m_1} = \frac{(1-0.1307)(417.48-137.92)}{(2675.5-137.92)}$$

$$= 0.0958$$

Summarizing,

$$\frac{m_2}{m_1} = 0.1307$$

$$\frac{m_3}{m_1} = 0.0958$$

OTHER VAPOR POWER CYCLES

• PROBLEM 8-10

A power cycle using steam as the working fluid involves one stage of reheat and one stage of regeneration as shown in the figure. The efficiencies for the high and low pressure turbines are 87% and 86%, respectively. Neglecting pump work and assuming the steam leaving the condenser and the open feedwater heater to be saturated liquid, determine the cycle efficiency for the following conditions.

$T_1 = T_3 = 400°C$, $P_1 = P_8 = 4.0$ MPa, $P_2 = P_3 = P_6 = P_7 = 0.4$MPa

and $P_4 = P_5 = 10$kPa.

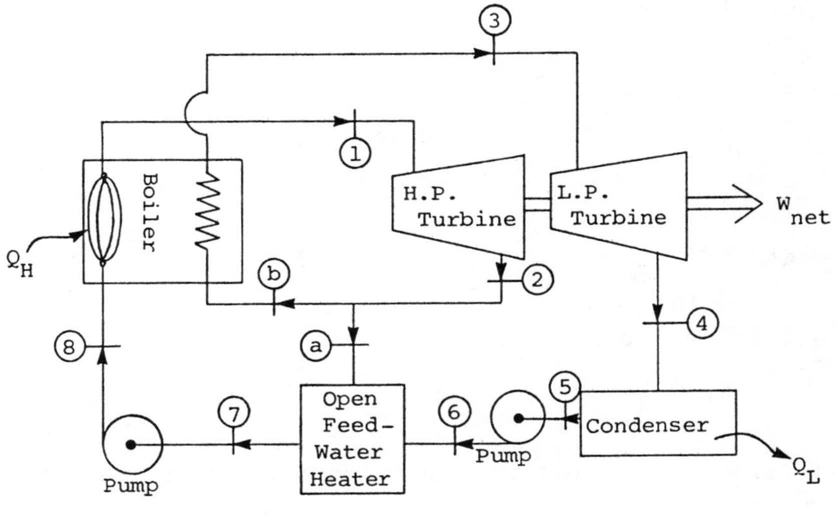

(a)

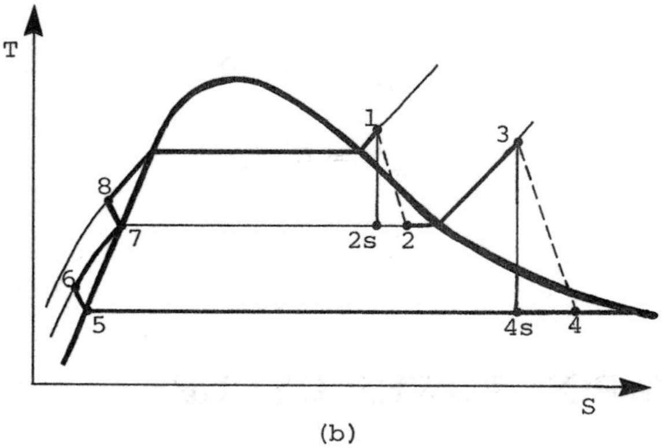

(b)

Solution: The efficiency of the cycle is given by the equation

$$\eta = \frac{w_{net}}{q_H} \tag{1}$$

where

$$w_{net} = w_t \Big|_{H.P.} + w_t \Big|_{L.P.} \tag{2}$$

and q_H is the heat added to the boiler. In order to solve this problem, w_{net} and q_H will have to be evaluated. First, consider the high pressure turbine alone and write the equations that apply.

$$\text{Continuity:} \quad m_i = m_e \qquad (i = \text{in},\ e = \text{exit}) \tag{3}$$

$$\text{1st Law:} \quad \cancel{Q}^{\,0} + m_i h_i = m_e h_e + w \tag{4}$$

$$\text{Second Law:} \quad s_i = s_e \tag{5}$$

The state of the steam has to be found, at the entrance and exit states.

State 1 is in the superheated region, and from the superheated steam tables and given conditions

$$h_1 = 3213.6 \text{ kJ/kg}, \qquad s_1 = 6.7690 \text{ kJ/kg-}^0\text{K}$$

State 2 is in the mixture region, and thus the quality will have to be calculated as

$$x_2 = \frac{s_2 - s_f}{s_g - s_f}$$

with values $s_2 = s_1 = 6.7690$ kJ/kgK, and

$$s_f = 1.7766 \text{ kJ/kg-}^0\text{K}, \quad S_g = 6.8959 \text{ kJ/kg-}^0\text{K}$$

Thus
$$x_2 = \frac{6.7690 - 1.7766}{6.8959 - 1.7766}$$
$$= 0.9752$$

Now that the quality is known, the enthalpy at state 2 can be calculated. From the steam tables, $h_f = 604.74$ kJ/kg and $h_g = 2738.6$ kJ/kg. Thus

$$h_{2s} = h_f + x_2(h_g - h_f) \quad (6)$$
$$= 604.74 + 0.9752(2738.6 - 604.74)$$
$$= 2685.7 \text{ kJ/kg}$$

Note that this is the enthalpy for the reversible process (isentropic) in the turbine. Since this is an irreversible process and since the efficiency is known, the work for this process can be obtained using the equation

$$\eta_t = \frac{W_a}{W_s} = \frac{m_1(h_1 - h_2)}{m_2(h_1 - h_{2s})} \quad (7)$$

From Equation (3) and upon substitution of obtained values, solving for h_2 gives

$$h_2 = h_1 - \eta(h_1 - h_{2s})$$
$$= 3213.6 - 0.87(3213.6 - 2685.7)$$
$$= 2754.3 \text{ kJ/kg}$$

From Eq. (4), solving for the work per unit mass

$$\left.\frac{W_t}{m_1}\right|_{\text{H.P.}} = h_1 - h_2$$
$$= 3213.6 - 2754.3$$
$$= 459.3 \text{ kJ/kg}$$

A similar process is used for the low pressure turbine. The equations that apply here are the same as before, with continuity being the only exception, written as

$$m_3 = m_4$$

where
$$m_3 = m_2 - m_a$$

The first law is written (per kg of steam entering) as

$$\left.\frac{W_t}{m_1}\right|_{L.P.} = \frac{m_3}{m_1}(h_3 - h_4) \tag{8}$$

The mass ratio will have to be calculated as well as the enthalpies, in order to solve for the work of the low pressure turbine.

Noting that there is the feedwater heater where the different mass flow rates meet, take a control volume around it and write the equations that apply.

Continuity: $m_7 = m_a + m_6$ (9)

First Law: $m_7h_7 = m_ah_a + m_6h_6$ (10)

Note that $m_6 = m_3$, $m_7 = m_1$, and $h_a = h_2$. With this in mind, Eq. (9) becomes (solving for $\frac{m_a}{m_7}$)

$$\frac{m_a}{m_7} = \frac{m_a}{m_1} = 1 - \frac{m_3}{m_1}$$

and Eq. (10) becomes (solving for h_7)

$$h_7 = \frac{m_a}{m_1} h_2 + \frac{m_3}{m_1} h_6$$

$$= \left(1 - \frac{m_3}{m_1}\right) h_2 + \frac{m_3}{m_1} h_6 \tag{11}$$

From Eq. (11)

$$\frac{m_3}{m_1} = \frac{(h_7 - h_2)}{(h_6 - h_2)}$$

Substituting into Eq. (8) get

$$\left.\frac{W_t}{m_1}\right|_{L.P.} = \left(\frac{h_7 - h_2}{h_6 - h_2}\right)(h_3 - h_4)$$

Neglecting pump work and using the steam tables, obtain

State 3: $h_3 = 3273.4$ kJ/kg, $s_3 = 7.8985$ kJ/kg-^{0}K

State 6: $h_6 = h_5 = h_f = 191.83$ kJ/kg

State 7: $h_7 = h_f = 604.74$ kJ/kg

State 4: This is in the mixture region, so the quality has to be calculated first with $s_f = 0.6493$ kJ/kg-^{0}K $s_g = 8.1502$ kJ/kg-^{0}K

$$x_4 = \frac{s_4 - s_f}{s_f - s_g}$$

$$= \frac{7.8985 - 0.6493}{8.1502 - 0.6493}$$

$$= 0.9664$$

The enthalpy at state 4 with

$$h_f = 191.83 \text{ kJ/kg}, \; h_g = 2584.7 \text{ kJ/kg}$$

is then

$$h_{4s} = h_f + x_4(h_g - h_f)$$

$$= 191.83 + 0.9664(2584.7-191.83)$$

$$= 2504.3 \text{ kJ/kg},$$

remembering that this is the isentropic enthalpy. For the irreversible process with an efficiency of 86%, for the low pressure turbine

$$h_4 = h_3 - \eta(h_3 - h_{4s})$$

$$= 3273.4-0.86(3273.4-2504.3)$$

$$= 2611.9 \text{ kJ/kg}$$

Hence

$$\left.\frac{W_t}{m_1}\right|_{L.P.} = \left[\frac{604.74 - 2754.3}{191.83 - 2754.3}\right](3273.4 - 2611.9)$$

$$= 554.91 \text{ kJ/kg}$$

From Eq. (1) $\frac{W_{net}}{m_1}$ can be calculated as

$$\frac{W_{net}}{m_1} = 459.34 + 554.91$$

$$= 1014.25 \text{ kJ/kg}.$$

Next, q_H or rather Q_H/m, will have to be evaluated. To do that, consider the boiler alone, and write the equations that apply.

First Law: $Q_H + m_8 h_8 + m_b h_2 = m_3 h_3 + m_1 h_1$ (W=0)

$$\text{or} \quad \left.\frac{Q_H}{m_1}\right|_b = (h_1 - h_8) + \frac{m_3}{m_1}(h_3 - h_2)$$

substituting the calculated values yields

$$\left.\frac{Q_H}{m_1}\right|_b = (3213.6 - 604.74) + 0.8389(3273.4 - 2754.3)$$

$$= 3044.3 \text{ kJ/kg}$$

Now, substitution of all the needed information into Eq. (1) gives

$$\eta_{cycle} = \frac{1014.25}{3044.3}$$

$$= 0.3332$$

or

$$\eta_{cycle} = 33.32\%$$

• PROBLEM 8-11

Consider the combined reheat and regenerative cycle shown in the accompanying figure. Assuming that the processes in the pumps and turbines are reversible and adiabatic, compute the thermal efficiency of the cycle. Assume that the working fluid is steam with the following properties known:

$P_1 = 6.20$ MPa, $P_2 = 2.1$ MPa, $T_6 = T_7 = 65°C$

$T_1 = 460°C$, $P_3 = 620$ kPa,

$P_5 = 207$ kPa,

States 7, 9, 11, 13 are saturated liquid.

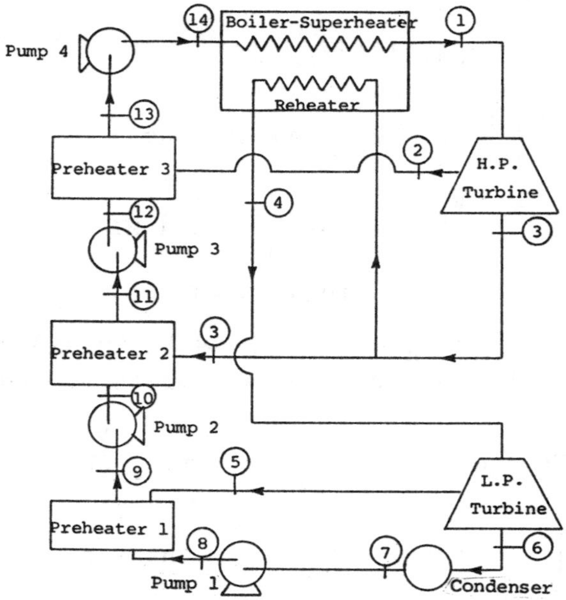

Solution: Because 14 different states occur in this cycle, it is efficient to calculate the enthalpies and entropies at these states before starting the problem.

Using the steam tables along with the given information, the following are obtained.

Table 1

	P (kPa)	T (C)	h (kJ/kg)	s kJ/kg-k)
1	6200	460	3323.05	6.7343
2	2100	299	3014.50	6.7343
3	620	160	2756.31	6.7343
4	2100	443	3356.42	7.8209
5	207	282	3030.78	7.8209
6	25.03	65	2618.75	7.8310
7	25.03	65	272.06	0.8935
8	207			
9	207	121	509.19	1.5414
10	620			
11	620	160	676.05	1.9438
12	2100			
13	2100	214	919.87	2.4698
14	620			

Note that the enthalpy and entropy at states 8, 10, 12, and 14 cannot be calculated directly from the steam tables.

The efficiency of the cycle is given as

$$\eta = \frac{W_{net}}{Q_{in}} \tag{1}$$

where

$$W_{net} = \Sigma W_t + \Sigma W_p \tag{2}$$

$$Q_{in} = Q_b + Q_r \tag{3}$$

However, because of the number of pumps and the number of streams leaving the turbines, W_{net} can be calculated from an overall energy balance around the cycle. Hence

$$W_{net} = Q_b + Q_r + Q_c \tag{4}$$

Because of the number of streams involved, the work and heat will be calculated per 1 kg through the condenser.

First consider an energy balance around the condenser.

$$q_c = h_6 - h_7 \tag{5}$$

$$= 2618.75 - 272.06$$

$$= 2{,}346.69 \text{ kJ/kg}$$

Consider next an energy balance around the boiler

$$Q_b = m_1 h_1 - m_{14} h_{14}$$

or per 1 kg through the condenser

$$Q_b' = \frac{m_1}{m_7} h_1 - \frac{m_{14}}{m_7} h_{14} \qquad (6)$$

Then consider the reheater. An energy balance gives

$$Q_r = m_4 h_4 - m_4 h_3$$

or per 1 kg through the condenser

$$Q_r' = \frac{m_4}{m_7} h_4 - \frac{m_4}{m_7} h_3 \qquad (7)$$

To evaluate Eqs. (6) and (7), the mass flow rates and the unknown enthalpies must first be computed. Let

$$m' = \frac{\text{kg. through part. equipment}}{\text{kg. through condenser}}$$

Consider an energy balance around preheater 1.

$$m_8' h_8 + m_5' h_5 = m_9' h_9 \qquad (8)$$

A mass balance gives

$$m_8' + m_5' = m_9' \qquad (9)$$

Substituting Eq. (9) into into Eq. (8) and solving for m_5' gives

$$m_5' = m_8' \left(\frac{h_9 - h_8}{h_5 - h_9} \right)$$

but $m_8' = 1$, hence

$$m_5' = \frac{h_9 - h_8}{h_5 - h_9} \qquad (10)$$

The enthalpy at 8 (h_8) is obtained from the pump work as

$$-w_p = \Delta h = h_8 - h_7 = \int v dP$$

$$= v_7 (P_8 - P_7)$$

$$= 0.001011(207-25.03)$$

$$= 0.184 \text{ kJ/kg}$$

or $$h_8 = 272.24 \text{ kJ/kg}$$

Substituting into Eq. (10)

$$m'_5 = \frac{509.19-272.24}{3030.78 - 509.19}$$

$$= 0.0940 \text{ kg/kg through cond.}$$

$$m'_9 = 1 + 0.094 = 1.094 \text{ kg/kg through cond.}$$

The enthalpy at 10 (entering preheater 2) is

$$\Delta h = h_{10} - h_9$$

$$= v_9(P_{10} - P_9)$$

$$= 0.001061(620-207)$$

$$= 0.4382$$

or $$h_{10} = 509.63 \text{ kJ/kg}$$

Consider an energy and mass balance around preheater 2.

$$m'_{10}h_{10} + m'_3 h_3 = m'_{11}h_{11}$$

and

$$m'_{10} + m'_3 = m'_{11} \qquad (11)$$

Solving for m'_3 gives

$$m'_3 = m'_{10}\left(\frac{h_{11} - h_{10}}{h_3 - h_{11}}\right)$$

But

$$m'_{10} = m'_9 = 1.094$$

Therefore

$$m'_3 = 1.094\left(\frac{676.05-509.63}{2756.31-676.05}\right)$$

$$= 0.087 \text{ kg/kg through cond.}$$

and from Eq. (11)

$$m'_{11} = 1.094 + 0.087$$

$$= 1.181 \text{ kg/kg through cond.}$$

The same procedure is followed for preheater 3.

$$\Delta h = h_{12} - h_{11}$$

$$= v_{11}(P_{12} - P_{11})$$

$$= 0.001105(2100-620)$$

$$= 1.6354 \text{ kJ/kg}$$

or

$$h_{12} = 677.68 \text{ kJ/kg}$$

Then

$$m'_{12}h_{12} + m'_2h_2 = m'_{13}h_{13} \quad (12)$$

$$m'_{13} = m'_{12} + m'_2 \quad (13)$$

Solving for m'_2 in Eq. (12) gives

$$m'_2 = m'_{12}\left(\frac{h_{13} - h_{12}}{h_2 - h_{13}}\right)$$

but

$$m'_{12} = m'_{11} = 1.181$$

Thus

$$m'_2 = 1.181\left(\frac{919.87-677.68}{3014.5-919.87}\right)$$

$$= 0.136 \text{ kg/kg through cond.}$$

and from Eq. (13)

$$m'_{13} = m'_{14} = 1.181 + 0.136$$

$$= 1.317 \text{ kg/kg through cond.}$$

The enthalpy of the liquid entering the boiler is obtained by considering the work of pump 4.

$$-w_p = h_{14} - h_{13}$$

$$= v_{13}(P_{14} - P_{13})$$

$$= 0.001180(6200-2100)$$

$$= 4.838 \text{ kJ/kg}$$

or $$h_{14} = 924.71 \text{ kJ/kg}$$

The mass flow rate through the reheater is obtained by considering a mass balance around the low pressure turbine.

$$m'_4 = m'_6 + m'_5$$

$$= 1.0 + 0.094$$

$$= 1.094 \text{ kg/kg through cond.}$$

The different mass flow rates are shown in Table 2.

Table 2

State	m' (kg/kg through cond.)	h (kJ/kg)
1	1.317	3,323.05
2	0.136	3,014.50
3	0.087	2,756.31
4	1.094	3,356.42
5	0.094	3,030.78
6	1.000	2,618.75
7	1.000	272.06
8	1.000	272.24
9	1.094	509.19
10	1.094	509.63
11	1.181	676.05
12	1.181	677.68
13	1.317	919.87
14	1.317	924.71

Using Eq. (5) and values from Table 2 obtain

$$Q'_b = 1.317\ [3323.06 - 924.71] \qquad (14)$$

$$= 3158.63 \text{ kJ/kg through cond.}$$

From Eq. (6) and values from Table 2 obtain

$$Q'_r = 1.094\ [3356.42 - 2756.31] \qquad (15)$$

$$= 656.52 \text{ kJ/kg through cond.}$$

Substituting the numerical values of Eqs. (5), (14), and (15) into Eq. (4) gives

$$w'_{net} = 3158.63 + 656.52 - 2346.99$$

$$= 1468.16 \text{ kJ/kg through cond.}$$

From Eq. (3)

$$Q'_{in} = 3158.63 + 656.52$$

$$= 3815.15 \text{ kJ/kg through cond.}$$

Finally, from Eq. (1)

$$\eta = \frac{1468.16}{3815.15}$$

$$= 0.3848$$

$$= 38.48\%$$

• **PROBLEM 8-12**

Steam leaves the boiler in a steam turbine plant at 2 MPa, 300°C and is expanded to 3.5kPa before entering the condenser. Compare the following four cycles:

1. A superheated Rankine cycle.

2. A reheat cycle, with steam reheated to 300°C at the pressure where it becomes saturated vapor.

3. A regenerative cycle, with an open feedwater heater operating at the pressure where steam becomes saturated vapor.

4. A regenerative cycle, with a closed feedwater heater operating at the pressure where steam becomes saturated vapor.

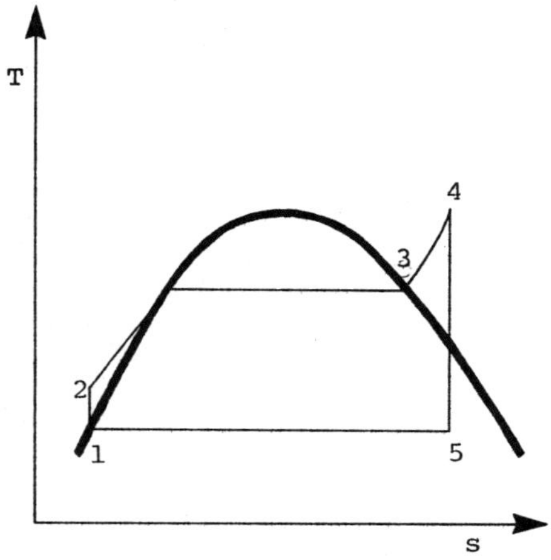

Fig. 1. Rankine Cycle

Solution: 1. Referring to Figure (1), the steam tables show that

$$h_4 = 3025 \text{ kJ/kg}$$

$$s_4 = 6.768 \text{ kJ/kg-}^0\text{K}$$

At P = 3.5 kPa

$$s_g = 8.521 \text{ kJ/kg-}^0\text{K}$$

$$s_f = 0.391 \text{ kJ/kg-}^0\text{K}$$

Since $s_5 = s_4$, steam at 5 is a mixture of liquid and vapor. The quality is found as

$$x_5 = \frac{s_5 - s_f}{s_{fg}}$$

$$= \frac{6.768 - 0.391}{8.130}$$

$$= 0.785$$

Therefore

$$h_5 = h_f + x_5 h_{fg}$$

$$= 112 + 0.785(2438)$$

$$= 2023 \text{ kJ/kg}$$

hence

$$w_{45} = h_4 - h_5$$

$$= 3025 - 2023$$

$$= 1002 \text{ kJ/kg}$$

Now

$$w_{12} = h_1 - h_2$$

$$\cong v_f(p_1 - p_2)$$

$$= 0.0010(0.0035 - 2) \times 10^3 \text{ kJ/kg}$$

$$= -2 \text{ kJ/kg}$$

Therefore the net work output is

$$w = w_{45} + w_{12} = 1000 \text{ kJ/kg}$$

Heat input is

$$q_{42} = h_4 - h_2$$

But

$$h_2 = h_1 - w_{12} = 112 + 2 = 114 \text{ kJ/kg}$$

therefore

$$q_{42} = 3025 - 114 = 2911 \text{ kJ/kg}$$

Thus,

$$\eta = \frac{w}{q_{42}} = \frac{1000}{2911} = 0.344$$

Also

$$\text{Specific Steam Consumption} = \frac{3600}{w} = \frac{3600}{1000} = 3.6 \text{ kg/kW h}$$

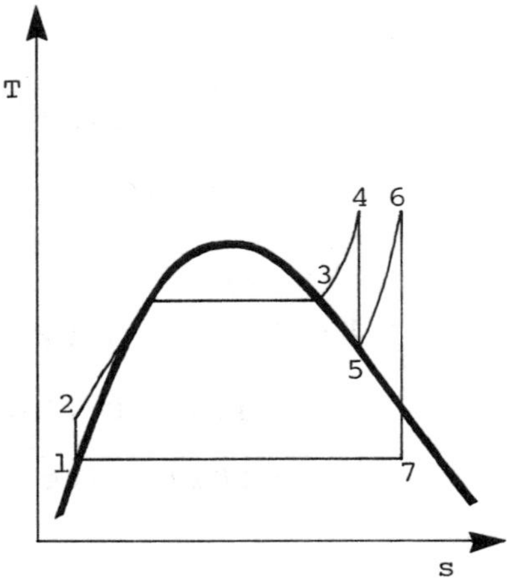

Fig. 2. Reheat Cycle

2. Refer to Fig. 2, and note that since

$$s_5 = s_{sat} = s_4 = 6.768 \text{ kJ/kg-}^0\text{K}$$

the pressure at reheat point 5 can be found using the steam tables. Interpolating between 0.55 MPa and 0.6 MPa gives

$$P_5 = 0.588 \text{ MPa}$$

Then

$$h_5 = 2753 + \frac{0.588 - 0.55}{0.60 - 0.55}(2757 - 2753)$$

$$= 2753 + \frac{0.038}{0.05} \times 4$$

$$= 2756 \text{ kJ/kg}$$

As 6 and 5 are on the same isobar, by interpolation

$$h_6 = 3065 + \frac{0.588 - 0.5}{0.60 - 0.5}(3062 - 3065)$$

$$= 3065 + \frac{0.088}{0.1}(-3)$$

$$= 3062.4 \text{ kJ/kg}$$

$$s_6 = 7.460 + 0.88\,(7.373 - 7.460)$$

$$= 7.460 + 0.88\,(-0.087)$$

$$= 7.384 \text{ kJ/kg-}^0\text{K}$$

At P = 3.5 kPa

$$s_g = 8.521 \text{ kJ/kg-}^0\text{K}$$

$$s_f = 0.391 \text{ kJ/kg-}^0\text{K}$$

Since $s_7 = s_6$, the quality at 7 is found as

$$x_7 = \frac{7.384 - 0.391}{8.130} = 0.86$$

Then

$$h_7 = 112 + 0.86(2438)$$

$$= 112 + 2095 = 2207 \text{ kJ/kg}$$

The net work output is given by

$$w = w_{45} + w_{67} + w_{12}$$

$$= (3025 - 2765) + (3062.4 - 2207) - 2$$

$$= 1122.4$$

The heat input is

$$q = q_{42} + q_{65}$$

$$= 2911 + (h_6 - h_5)$$

$$= 2911 + (3062.4 - 2756)$$

$$= 3217.4$$

Therefore

$$\eta = \frac{1122.4}{3217.4} = 0.349$$

and

$$\text{s.s.c.} = \frac{3600}{w} = \frac{3600}{1122.4} = 3.2 \text{ kg/kW h}$$

(a)

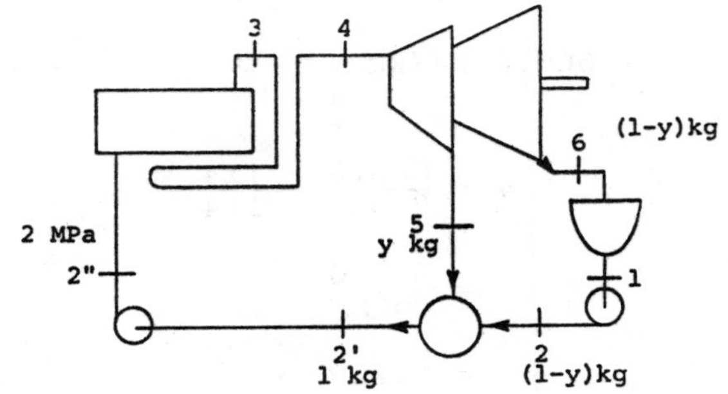

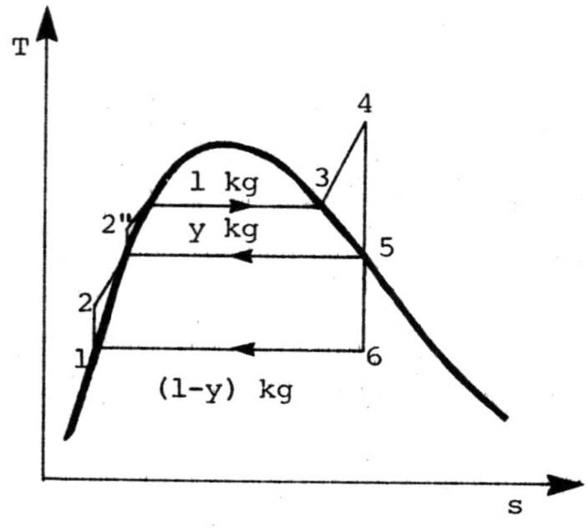

(b)

Fig. 3 Regenerative cycle.

3. Refer to Figures 3(a) and 3(b). The work is as in (b)

$$w_{45} = 269 \text{ kJ/kg}$$

Next determine the amount of steam bled off at 5. Consider an energy balance for the open feedwater heater with

$$h_{2'} = yh_S - (1-y)h_2$$

which gives

$$y = \frac{h_{2'} - h_2}{h_5 - h_2}$$

To find the value for h_2', enter the steam tables. At 5 the pressure is known (P = 0.588 MPa) and the state of the steam is given as saturated vapor. Therefore by interpolating between the values of 0.5 MPa and 0.6 MPa, obtain

$$h_{2'} = 656 + \frac{0.588 - 0.55}{0.60 - 0.55}(670 - 656)$$

$$= 656 + \frac{0.038}{0.05} \times 14$$

$$= 666.6 \text{ kJ/kg}$$

Then

$$y = \frac{666.6 - 114}{2756 - 114}$$

$$= \frac{552.6}{2642}$$

$$= 0.209$$

Hence

$$w_{56} = (1 - y)(h_5 - h_6)$$
$$= 0.791(2756 - 2023)$$
$$= 580 \text{ kJ/kg}$$

also

$$w_{2'2''} = v_f(p_{2'} - p_{2''})$$
$$= 0.0011(0.588 - 2) \times 10^3$$
$$= -1.1 \times 1.412$$
$$= -1.55 \text{ kJ/kg}$$

Therefore

$$w = w_{45} + w_{56} + w_{12} + w_{2'2''}$$
$$= 269 + 580 - 0.791 \times 2 - 1.55$$
$$= 845.87 \text{ kJ/kg}$$

The heat input is

$$q_{42''} = 3025 - (666.6 + 1.55)$$
$$= 2356.8 \text{ kJ/kg}$$

The efficiency of this cycle is

$$\eta = \frac{w}{q_{42''}} = \frac{845.87}{2356.8} = 0.3595$$

and

$$\text{s.s.c.} = \frac{3600}{w} = \frac{3600}{845.9} = 4.25 \text{ kg/kW h}$$

(a)

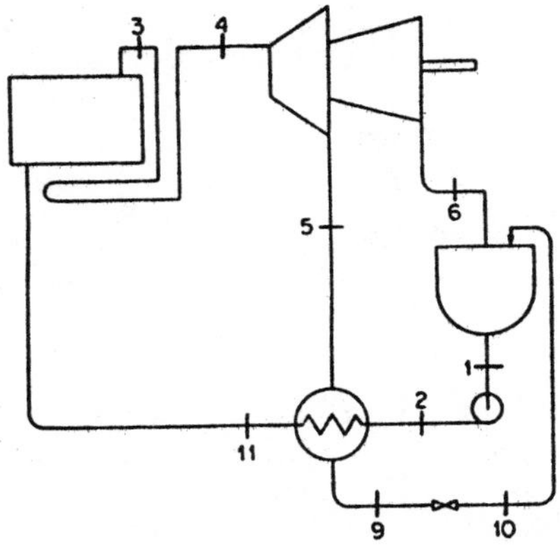

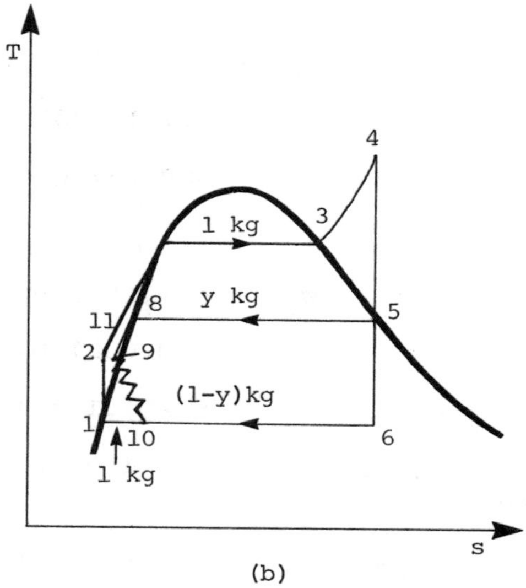

Fig. 4. A Regenerative cycle with closed heater.

4. Refer to Figures 4(a) and 4(b). The work is as in part (b)

$$w_{45} = 269 \text{ kJ/kg}$$

Heat balance for the heater as a closed system gives

$$1.h_{11} + yh_9 = 1.h_2 + yh_5$$

giving

$$y = \frac{h_{11} - h_2}{h_5 - h_9}$$

Now in finding the enthalpies in the feed line, it is usual to make the following assumptions:

i. Neglect the feed pump term.

ii. Assume the enthalpy of the compressed liquid to be the same as that of the saturated liquid at the same temperature.

iii. Assume the states of the condensate extracted from the turbine, before and after throttling, to be the same as that of the saturated liquid at the lower pressure of the throttled liquid.

Using these assumptions

$$h_2 = h_1$$

$$h_{11} = h_8$$

$$h_9 = h_{10} = h_1$$

whence

$$y = \frac{h_8 - h_1}{h_5 - h_1}$$

$$= \frac{666.6 - 112}{2756 - 112} = 0.209 \text{ kJ/kg}$$

Also

$$w_{56} = 580 \text{ kJ/kg}$$

Therefore

$$w = w_{45} + w_{56} + w_{12}$$

$$= 269 + 580 - 2 = 847 \text{ kJ/kg}$$

Heat input $q_{411} = 2358.4$ kJ/kg

Then

$$\eta = \frac{w}{q_{411}} = \frac{847}{2358.4} = 0.360$$

and

$$\text{s.s.c.} = \frac{3600}{w} = \frac{3600}{847} = 4.25 \text{ kg/kW h}$$

• PROBLEM 8-13

In a simple power plant, steam leaves the boiler at 87 psia, 560°F and is expanded adiabatically in the turbine to a final pressure of 15 psia. Determine the ratio of the net work produced to the heat added in the cycle $\left(\frac{W_{net}}{Q_{in}}\right)$ if the cycle is (a) an ideal Rankine cycle, (b) an irreversible Rankine cycle with an increase in entropy of 0.0500 Btu/lbm-°R during the expansion in the turbine, (c) a Carnot cycle operating between the same maximum and minimum temperatures. (d) Compare the cycles in (a) and (b) to the Carnot cycle.

Solution: (a) For the Rankine cycle, the heat added during the process of heating the water in the boiler is

$$q_{in} = h_3 - h_2 \tag{1}$$

where h_3 and h_2 are the enthalpies of the working fluid after and before the boiler respectively. From the steam tables

$$h_3 = 1310.2 \text{ Btu/lbm}$$

$$h_2 = 181.1 \text{ Btu/lbm}$$

Substituting into Eq. (1)

$$q_{in} = 1310.2 - 181.1$$

$$= 1129.1 \text{ Btu/lbm}$$

The net work for the cycle is given as

$$w_{net} = \Sigma w = w_t + w_p \tag{2}$$

Consider the turbine

$$w_t = h_3 - h_4 \tag{3}$$

where h_3 and h_4 are the enthalpies before and after the turbine, respectively. From the steam tables

$$h_4 = h_g = 1150.8 \text{ Btu/lbm} \quad (P = 15 \text{ psia})$$

$$s_4 = s_g = 1.7550 \text{ Btu/lbm-°R}$$

Substituting into Eq. (3)

$$w_t = 1310.2 - 1150.8$$

$$= 159.4 \text{ Btu/lbm}$$

For the pump

$$w_p = v_1(P_2 - P_1)$$

$$= \frac{0.01672(87 - 15) \times 144}{778}$$

$$= 0.22 \text{ Btu/lbm}$$

(Note that $w_p << w_t$, and in many cases w_p is neglected.)

Substituting into Eq. (2)

$$w_{net} = 159.4 - 0.22$$

$$= 159.18 \text{ Btu/lbm}$$

Then

$$\frac{w_{net}}{q_{in}} = \frac{159.18}{1129.1} = 0.141$$

(b) For the cycle with the increase in entropy, the heat added during the cycle is the same as in part (a), since the entropy increase happens during the expansion in the turbine. However, for this cycle

$$s_4' = s_4 + \Delta s$$

$$= 1.7550 + 0.05$$

$$= 1.8050 \text{ Btu/lbm-°R}$$

With this increase in entropy, and P = 15 psia, at the exit of the turbine the steam is slightly superheated. From the superheated steam tables obtain

$$h_4' = 1186.3 \text{ Btu/lbm}$$

and

$$w_t = h_3 - h_4'$$

$$= 1310.2 - 1186.3$$

$$= 123.9 \text{ Btu/lbm}$$

The turbine work is as in part (a). Therefore

$$w_{net} = 123.9 - 0.22 = 123.68 \text{ Btu/lbm}$$

Hence

$$\frac{w_{net}}{q_{in}} = \frac{123.68}{1129.1} = 0.110$$

(c) For the Carnot cycle

$$\frac{w_{net}}{q_{in}} = \frac{T_{max} - T_{min}}{T_{max}}$$

where

T_{max} = temperature after the boiler

$$= 560 + 460 = 1020°R$$

$$T_{min} = \text{temperature in the condenser}$$

$$= 213 + 460 = 673°R$$

Hence

$$\frac{w_{net}}{q_{in}} = \frac{1020 - 673}{1020} = 0.340$$

(d) Comparing as ratios,

$$\frac{\text{Ideal Rankine}}{\text{Carnot}} = \frac{0.141}{0.340} = 0.415$$

$$\frac{\text{Irrev. Rankine}}{\text{Carnot}} = \frac{0.110}{0.340} = 0.324$$

• PROBLEM 8-14

A steam turbo-generator having an efficiency of 98% receives steam at 10.34 MPa, 538°C and expands it to 6.89 kPa with the exhaust steam leaving at a velocity of 122 m/sec. When the mass flow rate is 137,000 kg/hr, 40,000 kW of power are produced and mechanical losses in the turbine total to 447.6 kW. Compute (a) the rate of steam, based on shaft output, (b) the internal engine efficiency, (c) the enthalpy of the exhaust steam, and (d) the amount of excess heat that must be removed in the condenser because of losses in the turbine.

Solution: (a) Since irreversibilities are involved, the shaft output is

$$\text{Shaft output} = \frac{P}{\eta}$$

$$= \frac{40,000}{0.98}$$

$$= 40,816.33 \text{ kW}$$

The steam rate is

$$\text{steam rate} = \frac{\dot{m}}{\text{Shaft output}}$$

$$= \frac{137,000}{40,816.33}$$

$$= 3.36 \text{ kg/shaft kw-hr}$$

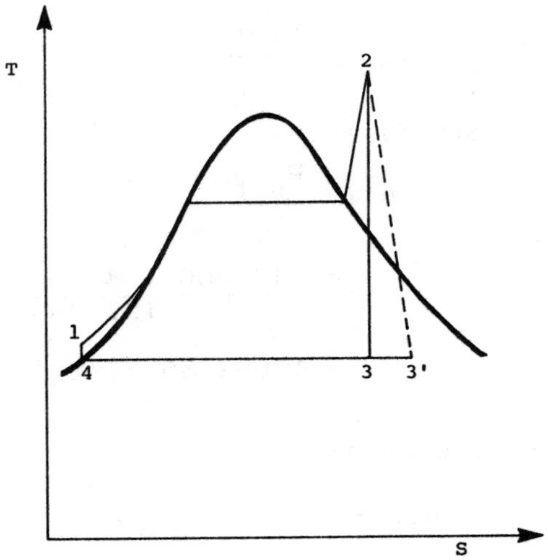

T-S diagram for actual vapor cycle.

(b) Referring to the figure and using the steam tables,

$$h_2 = 4,465.97 \text{ kj/kg}$$

$$s_3 = s_2 = 6.6993 \text{ kJ/kg-}^{\circ}\text{K}$$

State 3 is in the mixture region. Hence

$$s_f = 0.5520 \text{ kJ/kg-}^{\circ}\text{K}$$

$$s_g = 8.2865 \text{ kJ/kg-}^{\circ}\text{K}$$

Therefore, solving for the quality at 3

$$x_3 = \frac{s_3 - s_f}{s_g - s_f}$$

$$= \frac{6.6993 - 0.5520}{8.2865 - 0.5520}$$

$$= 0.7948$$

Hence

$$h_3 = h_f + x_3(h_g - h_f)$$

$$= 161.23 + 0.7948(2571.55 - 161.23)$$

$$= 2,076.95 \text{ kJ/kg}$$

The internal engine efficiency is given as

$$\eta_{int} = \frac{w_{int}}{w_{th}} \qquad (1)$$

The internal work is

$$w_{int} = \frac{P_{net}}{\dot{m}}$$

$$= \frac{(40,000 + 447.6) \times 3,600}{137,000}$$

$$= 1,062.85 \text{ kJ/kg}$$

The theoretical work is

$$w_{th} = h_2 - h_3$$

$$= 3,465.97 - 2,076.95$$

$$= 1389.02 \text{ kJ/kg}$$

Substituting into Eq. (1) yields

$$\eta_{int} = \frac{1062.85}{1389.02} = 0.7652$$

or

$$\eta_{int} = 76.52\%$$

(c) To find the enthalpy at the exhaust of the turbine, write an energy balance for the turbine.

$$h_2 = h_3' + w_{int} + \frac{V^2}{2 \times 1,000}$$

Solving for h_3'

$$h_3' = 3465.97 - 1062.85 - \frac{(122)^2}{2 \times 1000}$$

$$= 2395.68 \text{ kJ/kg}$$

(d) The excess heat to be removed from the condenser is

$$Q_{exc} = \dot{m}(h_3^* - h_3)$$

where h^* = stagnation enthalpy at exit

$$h^* = h_3' + \frac{V^2}{2 \times 1000}$$

$$= 2395.68 + 7.442$$

$$= 2403.12 \text{ kJ/kg}$$

Therefore

$$\dot{Q}_{exc} = 137{,}000\ (2403.12 - 2076.95)$$

$$= 44{,}685{,}564.15 \text{ kJ/hr}$$

$$= 12{,}412.66 \text{ kJ/sec}$$

• PROBLEM 8-15

> Saturated mercury vapor at 538°C flows into the mercury turbine in a mercury steam power plant and leaves it at 316°C. Cooling water for the steam condenser is available at 16°C, and saturated steam at 316°C is supplied to the steam turbine after it has been heated in the mercury condenser, which serves as the steam boiler. Neglecting pump work and assuming the mercury and steam to undergo a Rankine cycle with reversible processes, calculate the thermal efficiency of the combined plant.

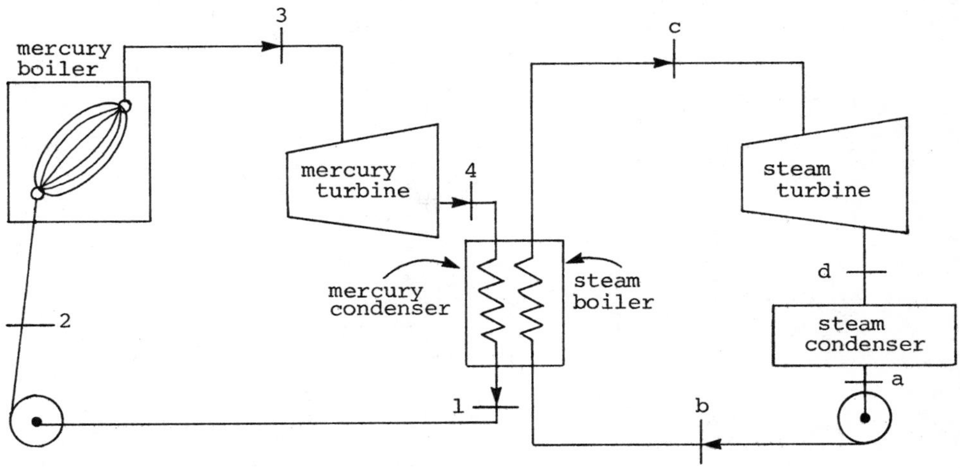

(a)

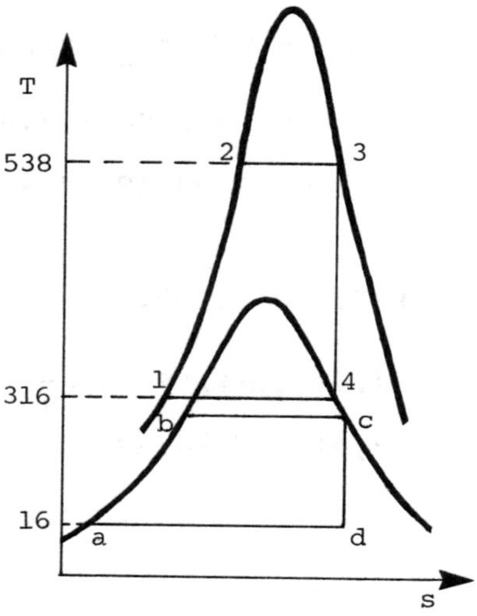

(b)

Solution: To solve this problem, consider the two cycles separately. Refer to the figure and consider the mercury cycle first. Using the mercury tables, the enthalpy of the mercury vapor entering the turbine is

$$h_3 = 361.28 \text{ kJ/kg} \qquad \text{(mercury)}$$

and the entropy is

$$s_3 = 0.5024 \text{ kJ/kg-°K} \quad \text{(mercury)}$$

At the exit of the mercury turbine, the state lies in the mixture region. The quality at that state is

$$x_4 = \frac{s_4 - s_f}{s_g - s_f}$$

$$= \frac{0.5024 - 0.1047}{0.6029 - 0.1047}$$

$$= 0.7983$$

The enthalpy at state 4 is then found to be

$$h_4 = h_f + x_4(h_g - h_f)$$

$$= 43.13 + 0.7983(336.43 - 43.13)$$

$$= 277.27 \text{ kJ/kg} \quad \text{(mercury)}$$

Also from the mercury tables

$$h_1 = h_f = 43.08 \text{ kJ/kg} \quad \text{(mercury)}$$

Next consider the steam cycle. From the steam tables at 316°C

$$h_c = 2711.62 \text{ kJ/kg} \quad \text{(steam)}$$

$$s_c = s_d = 5.5714 \text{ kJ/kg-}^{\circ}\text{K} \quad \text{(steam)}$$

At the exit of the steam turbine, the steam is in the mixture region. Hence

$$x_d = \frac{s_d - s_f}{s_g - s_f}$$

$$= \frac{5.5714 - 0.2324}{8.7705 - 0.2324}$$

$$= 0.6253$$

The enthalpy at the exit of the turbine is then found to be (T = 16°C)

$$h_d = h_f + x_d(h_g - h_f)$$

$$= 67.18 + 0.6253(2530.74 - 67.18)$$

$$= 1607.64 \text{ kJ/kg} \quad \text{(steam)}$$

Also from the steam tables

$$h_a = h_f = 65.27 \text{ kJ/kg}$$

The thermal efficiency for the binary-vapor heat cycle is

$$\eta_{th} = \frac{(h_3 - h_4) + \frac{m_w}{m_m}(h_c - h_d)}{h_3 - h_1} \qquad (1)$$

where $\frac{m_w}{m_m}$ is yet to be determined. Assume a flow of 1 lbm of mercury and write an energy balance for the mercury condenser (or steam boiler).

$$m_m h_4 + m_w h_b = m_m h_1 + m_w h_c$$

Dividing by m_m gives

$$h_4 + \frac{m_w}{m_m} h_b = h_1 + \frac{m_w}{m_m} h_c$$

Solving for $\frac{m_w}{m_m}$ gives

$$\frac{m_w}{m_m} = \frac{h_4 - h_1}{h_c - h_a}$$

$$= \frac{277.27 - 43.08}{2711.62 - 65.27}$$

$$= 0.0885 \text{ kg steam/kg mercury}$$

Substituting into Eq. (1)

$$\eta_{th} = \frac{(361.28 - 277.27) + 0.0885(2711.62 - 1607.64)}{361.28 - 43.08}$$

$$= \frac{181.71}{318.20}$$

$$= 0.5711$$

$$= 57.11\%$$

THE VAPOR CARNOT CYCLE

• PROBLEM 8-16

Assuming that the efficiency of the Carnot cycle is a function of the temperature limits only, derive the expression for the thermal efficiency of this cycle as

$$\eta_{th} = 1 - \frac{T_L}{T_H}$$

Refer to the accompanying figure. Assume ideal gas behavior.

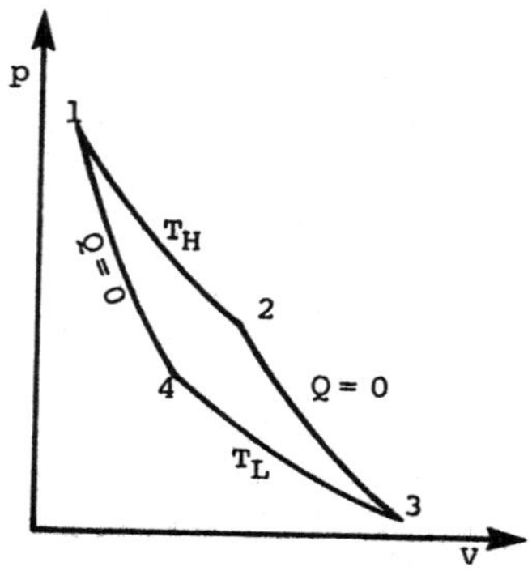

Solution: The thermal efficiency is by definition

$$\eta_{th} = \frac{\int \delta W}{Q_{in}} = \frac{W}{Q_{in}} \qquad (1)$$

From the first law

$$\int \delta W = \int \delta Q = Q_{in} - Q_{out} \qquad (2)$$

Substituting Eq. (2) into Eq. (1) gives

$$\eta_{th} = \frac{Q_{in} - Q_{out}}{Q_{in}}$$

or

$$\eta_{th} = 1 - \frac{Q_L}{Q_H}$$

where Q_{in} or Q_H and Q_{out} or Q_L stand for the total heat transferred from the reservoir at T_H to the engine and from the engine to the reservoir at T_L, respectively. All the heat added to the working fluid during the cycle is added during the isothermal expansion 1-2, during which the temperature of the working fluid is T_H (or lower than this by only an infinitesimal amount). Applying the first law to the system during the reversible isothermal expansion 1-2,

$$Q_H = U_2 - U_1 + W$$

For an ideal gas, internal energy is a function of temperature only; therefore $\Delta U = 0$ for an isothermal process. Also, for a reversible process of a closed system, $W = \int pdV$

$$Q_H = 0 + \int_1^2 p\, dV$$

Substituting for p from the ideal-gas equation of state, and noting that m, R, and T are constant for this process,

$$Q_H = 0 + \int_1^2 \frac{mRT}{V}\, dV = mRT \int_1^2 \frac{dV}{V} = mRT_H \ln \frac{V_2}{V_1}$$

By the same reasoning,

$$Q_L = U_3 - U_4 - W = 0 - \int_3^4 pdV = -mRT_L \ln \frac{V_4}{V_3} = mRT_L \ln \frac{V_3}{V_4}$$

Substituting these values for Q_H and Q_L into the expression obtained above for thermal efficiency,

$$\eta = 1 - \frac{Q_L}{Q_H} = 1 - \frac{mRT_L \ln(V_3/V_4)}{mRT_H \ln(V_2/V_1)} = 1 - \frac{T_L \ln(V_3/V_4)}{T_H \ln(V_2/V_1)}$$

For the reversible adiabatic processes 2-3 and 4-1 of the ideal-gas working substance, at least if the ratio of specific heats is constant,

$$\frac{V_3}{V_2} = \left(\frac{T_2}{T_3}\right)^{1/(k-1)} = \left(\frac{T_H}{T_L}\right)^{1/(k-1)} \qquad \text{and}$$

$$\frac{V_4}{V_1} = \left(\frac{T_1}{T_4}\right)^{1/(k-1)} = \left(\frac{T_H}{T_L}\right)^{1/(k-1)}$$

Therefore

$$\frac{V_3}{V_2} = \frac{V_4}{V_1}$$

and

$$\frac{V_3}{V_4} = \frac{V_2}{V_1}$$

Hence the expression for thermal efficiency reduces to

$$\eta = 1 - \frac{T_L}{T_H}$$

Note that the thermal efficiency of a Carnot cycle using an ideal gas as a working fluid increases as the ratio of T_H to T_L increases. Writing the efficiency expression as

$$\eta = \frac{T_H - T_L}{T_H}$$

shows that, for a given temperature of either reservoir, the efficiency is increased by increasing the temperature difference between the reservoirs.

• PROBLEM 8-17

In a Carnot engine, using 0.05 kg of air as the working fluid, the maximum cycle temperature and pressure are 940°K and 8.4 MPa respectively. What is the maximum cylinder volume if the minimum temperature during the cycle is 300°K and the addition of heat to the air is 4.2 kJ? Assume ideal gas behavior.

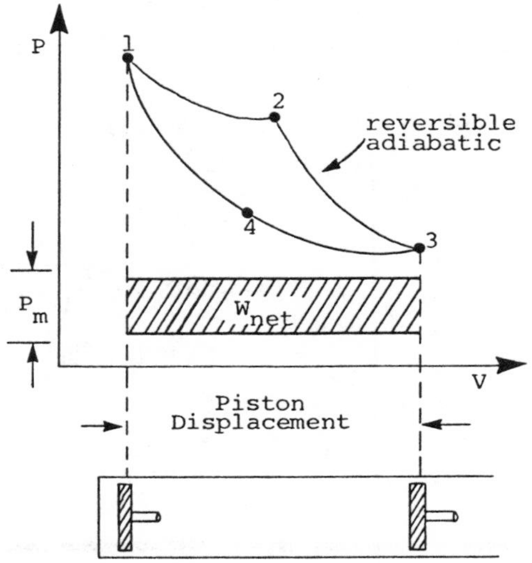

Solution: From the accompanying figure note that the maximum temperature and pressure occur at state 1, and the maximum volume occurs at state 3. Following process 1-2-3, the maximum cylinder volume (V_3) can easily be obtained. First, at state 1

$$V_1 = \frac{mRT_1}{P_1}$$

$$= \frac{0.05(0.287)(940)}{8.4 \times 10^3}$$

$$= 1.606 \times 10^{-3} m^3$$

Since the heat added to the air is known we can write

$$Q_{in} = P_1V_1 \ln \left(\frac{V_2}{V_1}\right)$$

or

$$4.2 = 8{,}400(1.606 \times 10^{-3}) \ln \left(\frac{V_2}{1.606 \times 10^{-3}}\right)$$

Solving for V_2 obtain

$$V_2 = 2.193 \times 10^{-3} m^3$$

Also

$$T_2 = T_{max} = 940°K$$

Since process 2-3 is reversible and adiabatic

$$\frac{V_3}{V_2} = \left(\frac{T_2}{T_3}\right)^{1/(k-1)}$$

or

$$V_3 = V_2\left(\frac{T_2}{T_3}\right)^{1/(k-1)}$$

$$= 2.193 \times 10^{-3}\left(\frac{940}{300}\right)^{1/(1.4-1)}$$

$$= 3.811 \times 10^{-2} m^3$$

• PROBLEM 8-18

The source and sink temperatures of a Carnot steam cycle are 316°C and 16°C respectively. Assuming the internal engine efficiency of the turbine to be 80% and that of the compressor to be 60%, determine the thermal efficiency of the cycle and the ratio of turbine work to compressor work.

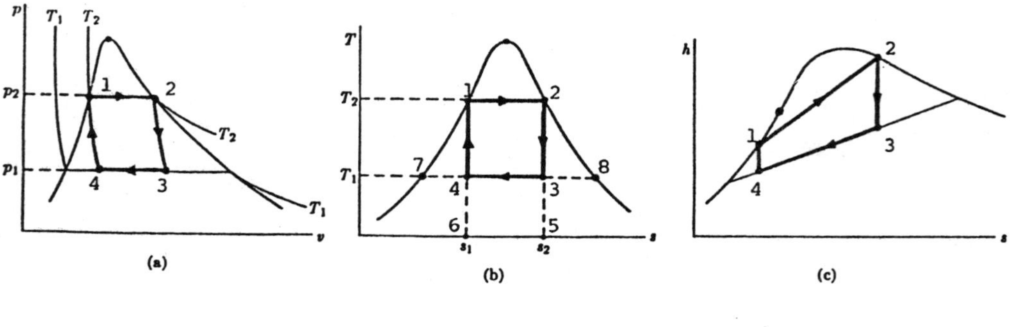

Carnot cycle in (a) a p-v diagram, (b) a T-s diagram, (c) an h-s diagram.

<u>Solution</u>: Referring to the figure, the thermal efficiency of the cycle can be written as

$$\eta_{th} = \frac{(h_2 - h_{1'}) - (h_{3'} - h_4)}{h_2 - h_1'} \quad (1)$$

where $h_{1'}$ and h_3' are the enthalpies for the irreversible processes at states 1 and 3. To obtain these enthalpies, first the enthalpies for the isentropic processes must be evaluated.

For the isentropic turbine, using the steam table obtain

$$h_2 = 2711.2 \text{ kJ/kg}$$

$$s_2 = s_3 = 5.5714 \text{ kJ/kg-°K}$$

At 3, $s_f < s_3 < s_g$. Therefore, the quality at 3 is

$$x_3 = \frac{s_3 - s_f}{s_{fg}}$$

$$= \frac{5.5714 - 0.2324}{8.5381}$$

$$= 0.625$$

Hence

$$h_3 = h_g - (1-x_3)\, h_{fg}$$

$$= 2530.7 - (1-0.625)(2465.3)$$

$$= 1,606.2 \text{ kJ/kg}$$

Since the internal engine efficiency of the turbine is 80%, the actual enthalpy leaving the turbine is

$$h_{3'} = h_2 - \eta_{int}(h_2 - h_3)$$

$$= 2711.2 - 0.8(2711.2 - 1606.2)$$

$$= 1827.2 \text{ kJ/kg}$$

Similarly, for the isentropic compressor, using the steam tables

$$h_1 = 1435.1 \text{ kJ/kg}$$

$$s_1 = s_4 = 3.4043 \text{ kJ/kg-°K}$$

At 4, $s_f < s_4 < s_g$. Therefore, the quality at 4 is

$$x_4 = \frac{s_4 - s_f}{s_{fg}}$$

$$= \frac{3.4043 - 0.2324}{8.5381}$$

$$= 0.372$$

Hence

$$h_4 = h_g - (1-x_4)h_{fg}$$

$$= 2530.7 - (1-0.372)(2465.3)$$

$$= 982.5 \text{ kJ/kg}$$

For the actual enthalpy after compression

$$h_{1'} = h_4 + \frac{1}{\eta_{int}} (h_1 - h_4)$$

$$= 982.5 + \frac{1}{0.6} (1435.1 - 982.5)$$

$$= 1736.8 \text{ kJ/kg}$$

The internal work done by the turbine is

$$w_t = h_2 - h_{3'}$$

$$= 2711.2 - 1827.2$$

$$= 884 \text{ kJ/kg}$$

The internal work done by the compressor is

$$w_c = h_{1'} - h_4$$

$$= 1736.8 - 982.5$$

$$= 754.3 \text{ kJ/kg}$$

The work ratio is

$$\frac{w_t}{w_c} = \frac{884}{754.3} = 1.17$$

From Eq. (1), the thermal efficiency of the cycle is

$$\eta_{th} = \frac{(2711.2 - 1736.8) - (1827.2 - 982.5)}{2711.2 - 1736.8}$$

$$= \frac{129.9}{974.4}$$

$$= 0.13$$

VAPOR REFRIGERATION CYCLES

• PROBLEM 8-19

A refrigeration plant is to operate with an evaporator saturation temperature of 0°F while removing 10,000 Btu/hr from a cold room. The condenser is to be cooled by water so that the saturation temperature can be kept at 76°F. The refrigerant is ammonia.

(a) Assuming the plant works on a cycle like that in the figure, find its coefficient of performance and compare this with the coefficient of performance for a Carnot refrigerating machine to do the same job.

(b) If the volumetric efficiency of the compressor is 70 percent, how much piston displacement per minute will be needed?

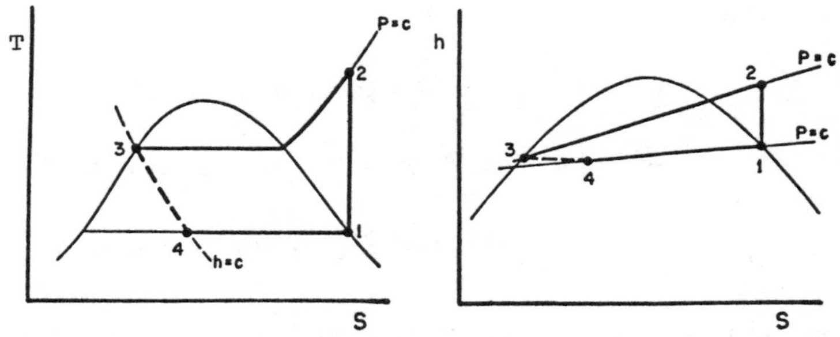

Fig. 1 Vapor-compression refrigerator cycle.

Solution: (a) Referring to the figure, on a basis of one pound of fluid the heat transferred in the evaporator is

$$q_e = h_1 - h_4 \text{ Btu/lb}$$

The net work to the cycle is the compressor work, given by

$$w_c = h_2 - h_1 \text{ Btu/lb}$$

The enthalpy values are obtained from the ammonia tables:

$$h_1 = h_g \text{ at } 0°F = 611.8 \text{ Btu/lb}$$

$$h_2 = h \text{ at } s_1 \text{ and } p_2$$

$$s_1 = s_g \text{ at } 0°F = 1.3352 \text{ Btu/lb°R}$$

$$p_2 = \text{saturation pressure at } 76°F = 143.0 \text{ psia}$$

$$h_2 = 704.4 \text{ Btu/lb}$$

$$h_3 = h_f \text{ at } 76°F = 127.4 \text{ Btu/lb}$$

$$h_4 = h_3 = 127.4 \text{ Btu/lb}$$

$$(CP) = \frac{q_e}{w_c} = \frac{h_1 - h_4}{h_2 - h_1} = \frac{484.4}{92.6} = 5.23$$

For a Carnot refrigerator

$$(CP) = \frac{T_2}{T_1 - T_2} = \frac{460}{76} = 6.05$$

(b) The piston displacement required is given by

$$(PD) = \frac{wv_1}{\eta_v}$$

where w is the refrigerant flow rate, lb/min. The flow rate is found from the time rate of heat flow to the refrigerant, and the value of q_e:

$$w = \frac{10{,}000/60}{484.4} = 0.344 \text{ lb/min}$$

$$v_1 = v_g \text{ at } 0°F = 9.116 \text{ cu ft/lb}$$

$$(PD) = \frac{(0.344)(9.116)}{0.70} = 4.48 \text{ cu ft/min}$$

A refinement sometimes used for refrigeration through a wide range of temperature is a cascade arrangement in which the condenser of one plant is the evaporator of another, so the heat-pumping process takes place in two stages. This is the reverse of the binary vapor power cycle process.

• PROBLEM 8-20

A simple compression refrigeration cycle, as shown in the figure, is operating with Freon-12 as the working fluid under the following given conditions.

$P_1 = P_4 = 100$ kPa $\qquad P_2 = P_3 = 1.20$ MPa

$T_2 = 80°C \qquad T_3 = 30°C$

State 1: saturated vapor.

Determine the coefficient of performance of this refrigerator.

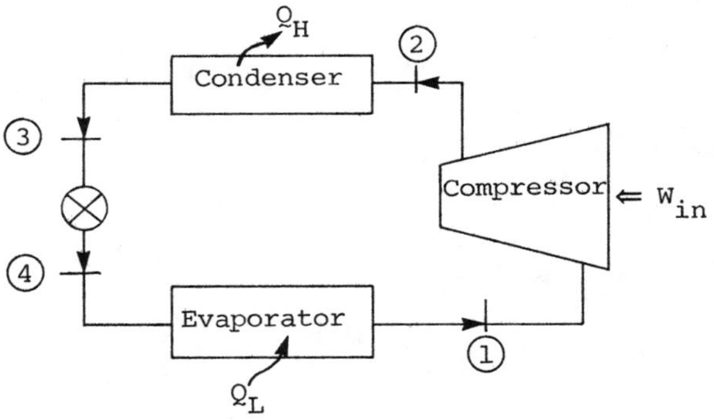

Solution: The coefficient of performance (β) for a refrigeration cycle is given as

$$C.O.P. = \beta = \frac{q_L}{w_{in}} \tag{1}$$

To calculate β, the heat transferred to the evaporator and the work input to the compressor must be calculated. Assuming an adiabatic and reversible compressor, from the first law of thermodynamics

$$\cancel{Q}^{\,0} + m_1 h_1 = m_2 h_2 + w_{in}$$

or on a unit mass basis

$$w_{in} = -w_{c.v.} = h_2 - h_1 \tag{2}$$

From the Freon-12 tables, at state 1 (saturated vapor)

$$h_1 = h_g = 174.076 \text{ kJ/kg}$$

and at state 2 (superheated vapor)

$$h_2 = 230.398 \text{ kJ/kg}$$

Substituting into Eq. (2) obtain

$$w_{in} = 230.398 - 174.076$$

$$= 56.322 \text{ kJ/kg}$$

To find q_L, consider the evaporator and write an energy balance for the control volume.

$$Q_{c.v.} + m_4 h_4 = m_1 h_1 + \cancel{W}^{\,0}_{c.v.}$$

or on a mass basis

$$q_{in} = -q_{c.v.} = h_1 - h_4 \qquad (3)$$

From the Freon-12 tables, at state 4 (saturated liquid)

$$h_4 = h_3 = h_f = 64.539 \text{ kJ/kg}$$

Substituting into Eq. (3) yields

$$q_{in} = 174.076 - 64.539$$

$$= 109.537 \text{ kJ/kg}$$

Substitution in Eq. (1) then gives

$$\beta = \frac{109.537}{56.322} = 1.945$$

• PROBLEM 8-21

The working pressure of the evaporator, in the vapor compression refrigerator shown in the figure, is 16 psia with Freon-12 as the working fluid, leaving the evaporator at -17.78°C and entering the compressor at -12.2°C. The refrigerant leaves the condenser as saturated liquid at 21°C and enters the expansion valve at 20°C. Heat losses from the compressor amount to 1.8 Btu/lbm while the work input to the compressor is 23 Btu/lbm. If 10 tons of refrigeration are produced and 0.5 Btu/lbm of heat are lost in the piping between the compressor and condenser, compute the heat rejected from the condenser per minute.

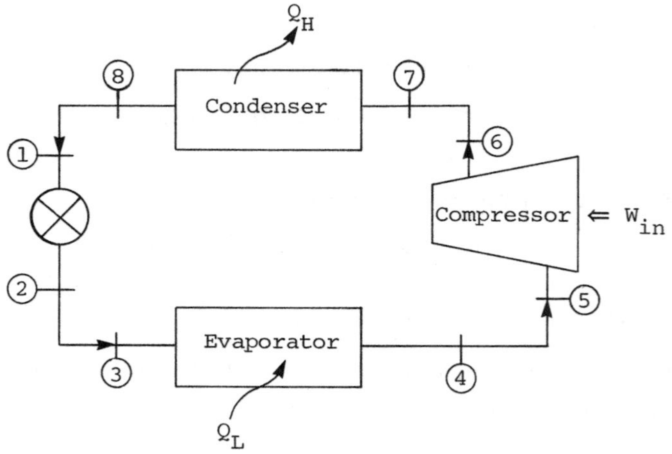

Fig. 1. Schematic representation

Solution: To find the heat rejected from the condenser per minute, first find the heat rejected from the condenser per pound of mass, using

$$q_H = h_7 - h_8 \tag{1}$$

Then find the heat absorbed in the evaporator (the refrigeration) per pound of mass, using

$$q_L = h_4 - h_3 \tag{2}$$

Since we know that 10 tons of refrigeration are produced, we can find the mass flow rate as

$$\dot{m} = \frac{10 \text{ tons} \times 12{,}000 \text{ Btu/hr}}{q_L} \tag{3}$$

After all this information has been obtained we can find the heat rejected from the condenser per minute by using

$$\dot{Q}_H = \dot{m}q_H \tag{4}$$

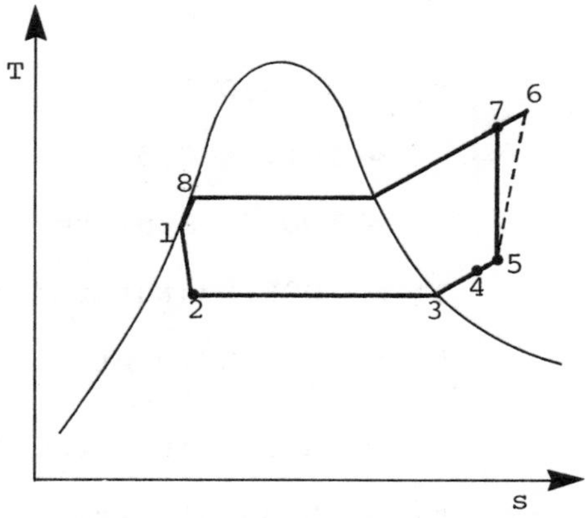

Fig. 2

The numerical solution is as follows. First sketch the cyclic process on a T-s diagram as shown in Figure 2. Then, referring to Figure 2, enter the Freon-12 tables and obtain the various properties at the different states.

State 4: $P_4 = 16 \text{ lbf/in}^2$, $T_4 = 0°F$

State 4 is found to be superheated vapor, hence

$$h_4 = 78.58 \text{ Btu/lbm}$$

State 5: $P_5 = 16 \text{ lbf/in}^2$, $T_5 = 10°F$

State 5 is superheated vapor, hence

$$h_5 = 79.94 \text{ Btu/lbm}$$

State 6: To find the enthalpy at state 6, note that the enthalpy increase due to compression work is

$$\Delta h = h_6 - h_5 = q - w$$

or

$$h_6 - h_5 = -1.8 - (-23)$$

$$= 21.2 \text{ Btu/lbm}$$

Solving for h_6, obtain

$$h_6 = 21.2 + 79.94$$

$$= 101.14 \text{ Btu/lbm}$$

State 7: To find the enthalpy of the fluid entering the condenser, note that 0.5 Btu/lbm of heat are lost in the piping between the compressor and condenser.

Therefore

$$h_7 = h_6 - 0.5$$

$$= 101.14-0.5$$

$$= 100.64 \text{ Btu/lbm}$$

State 8: $T_8 = 70°F$, saturated liquid

$$h_8 = h_f = 23.9 \text{ Btu/lbm}$$

State 1: $T_1 = 68°F$, saturated liquid

$$h_1 = 23.43 \text{ Btu/lbm}$$

State 2, 3: Throttling process

$$h_3 = h_2 = h_1 = 23.43 \text{ Btu/lbm}$$

Now that all the information needed has been obtained, we can solve the numerical part of the problem. Substituting into Eq. (1), obtain

$$q_H = 100.64-23.9$$

$$= 76.74 \text{ Btu/lbm}$$

From Eq. (2)

$$q_L = 78.58 - 23.43$$

$$= 55.2 \text{ Btu/lbm}$$

The mass flowrate of refrigerant is, from Eq. (2),

$$\dot{m} = \frac{10 \times 12000}{55.2}$$

$$= 2{,}173.91 \text{ lbm/hr}$$

$$= 36.3 \text{ lbm/min}$$

Finally, from Eq. (3)

$$\dot{Q}_H = \dot{m} q_H$$

$$= 36.3\ (76.74)$$

$$= 2785.6 \text{ Btu/min}$$

• PROBLEM 8-22

The vapor compression refrigeration system shown in the figure uses Freon-12 as its working fluid. The pressures before and after the compressor are 28 lbf/in^2 and 130 lbf/in^2, respectively. State 3 is saturated liquid and there is 20°F of subcooling before the fluid is throttled. (a) Determine the coefficient of performance of this cycle, (b) determine the coefficient of performance of the cycle without subcooling, and (c) compute the increased refrigerating effect and the increased work of the cycle with subcooling.

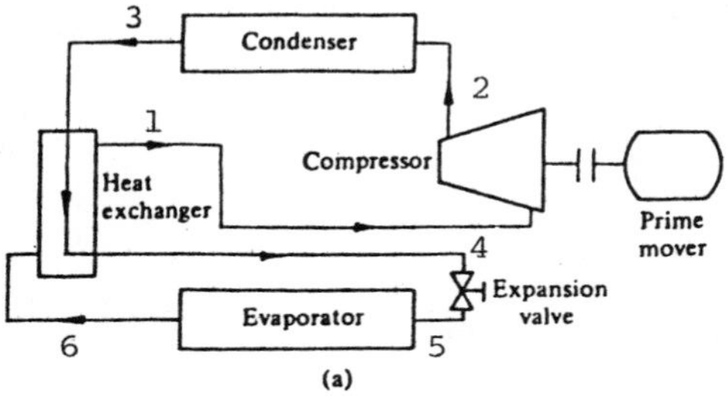

(a)

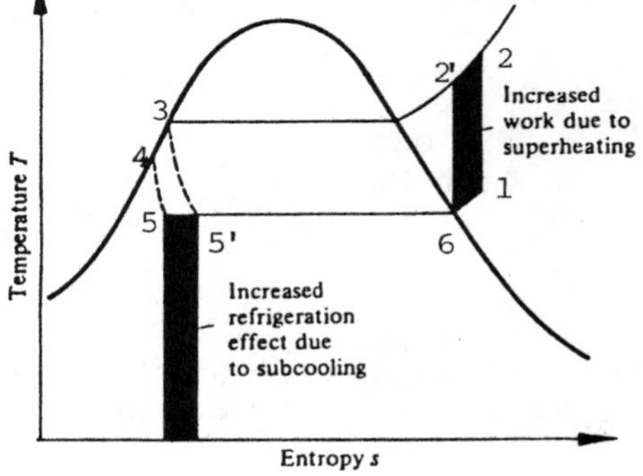

(b)

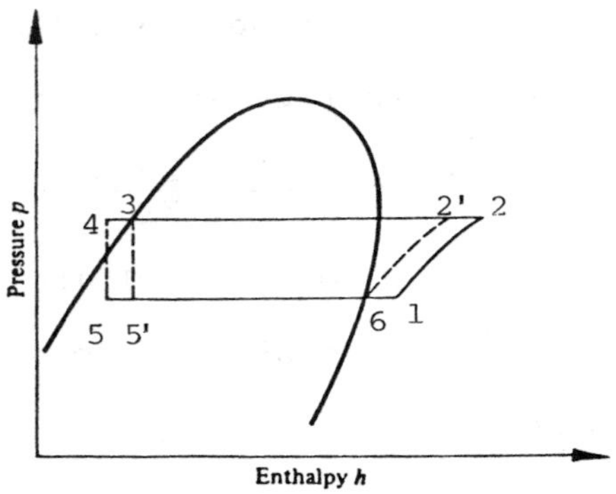

(c)

Solution: The accompanying figure shows the cycle representation on the T-s and P-h diagrams. On these diagrams there are two cycles depicted. Cycle 1-2-3-4-5-6, which involves subcooling, and cycle 1-2'-3-5'-6, which is the cycle without subcooling.

The coefficient of performance is given as

$$\beta = \frac{q_{in}}{w} \quad (1)$$

(a) In order to find the C.O.P. of the refrigeration cycle using subcooling, the enthalpies at all the states must first be calculated. Begin at state 3 since it is known that we have saturated liquid at P = 130 lbf/in^2. Hence

$$h_3 = h_f = 30.859 \text{ Btu/lbm}$$

The saturated temperature of the liquid at state 6 is 99°F, hence the subcooled temperature at state 4 is

$$T_{sub} = T_{sat} - 20°F = 79°F$$

At T_4 = 79°F

$$h_4 = h_f = 26.132 \text{ Btu/lbm}$$

Process 4-5 is a throttling process. Hence

$$h_5 = h_4 = 26.132 \text{ Btu/lbm}$$

At the exit of the evaporator the fluid is saturated vapor. Thus at P_6 = 28 lbf/in^2

$$h_6 = h_g = 78.06 \text{ Btu/lbm}$$

To find the enthalpy at state 1, write an energy balance for the subcooling heat exchanger.

$$m(h_1 - h_6) = m(h_3 - h_4)$$

Solving for h_1 gives

$$h_1 = h_6 + (h_3 - h_4)$$

$$= 78.06 + (30.859 - 26.132)$$

$$= 82.787 \text{ Btu/lbm}$$

State 1 is in the superheated region. From the superheat Freon-12 tables

$$s_1 = 0.17760 \text{ Btu/lbm-°R}$$

Assuming the processes in the compressor to be reversible,

$$s_2 = s_1 = 0.17760 \text{ Btu/lbm-°R}$$

At $P_2 = 130$ lbf/in^2 and s_2, obtain from the Freon-12 tables

$$h_2 = 95.4 \text{ Btu/lbm}$$

Then

$$w_c = h_2 - h_1$$

$$= 95.4 - 82.78$$

$$= 12.62 \text{ Btu/lbm}$$

and

$$q_{in} = h_6 - h_5$$

$$= 78.06 - 26.13$$

$$= 51.93 \text{ Btu/lbm}$$

Substituting into Eq. (1) yields

$$\beta = \frac{51.93}{12.62} = 4.11$$

(b) For the cycle without subcooling

$$h_{5'} = h_3 = 30.859 \text{ Btu/lbm}$$

$$s_{2'} = s_6 = 0.16818 \text{ Btu/lbm-°R}$$

$$h_{2'} = 89.5 \text{ Btu/lbm}$$

Then

$$w_c = h_{2'} - h_6$$

$$= 89.5 - 78.06$$

$$= 11.44 \text{ Btu/lbm}$$

and

$$q_{in} = h_6 - h_5,$$

$$= 78.06 - 30.859$$

$$= 47.20 \text{ Btu/lbm}$$

Substitution into Eq. (1) yields

$$\beta = \frac{47.20}{11.44} = 4.14$$

(c) The increase in refrigeration effect is

$$\text{R.E.} = \frac{q_{sub} - q_{st}}{q_{st}} \times 100$$

$$= \frac{51.93 - 47.2}{47.2} \times 100$$

$$= 10\%$$

The increase in work is

$$\text{I.W.} = \frac{w_{sub} - w_{st}}{w_{st}} \times 100$$

$$= \frac{12.62 - 11.4}{11.4} \times 100$$

$$= 10.87\%$$

• PROBLEM 8-23

A standard vapor compression refrigeration cycle uses Freon-22 as the working fluid to provide 3 tons of cooling capacity. If the condenser operates at 140°F and the evaporator operates at 50°F, compute (a) the mass flow rate of the Freon-22, (b) the horsepower required for the compressor, and (c) the heat transferred in the condenser. Assume the compression process to be reversible and adiabatic.

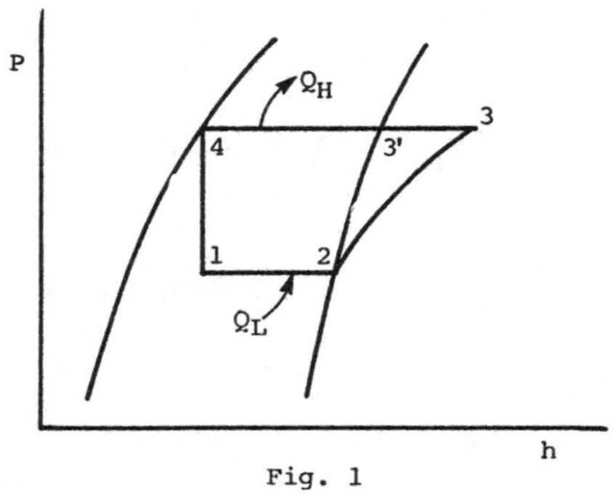

Fig. 1

Solution: Since the process has been assume to be reversible and adiabatic, it will also be isentropic. Assuming the throttling process to be adiabatic, then it is also isenthalpic (constant enthalpy). Furthermore, assume that the condenser and evaporator operate at constant pressure. Then this cycle can be plotted on a P-h diagram as shown in Figure 1.

The values of the various properties at the different states shown in Figure 1 are taken from the P-h diagram for Freon-22, as shown in Figure 2. The procedure is as follows.

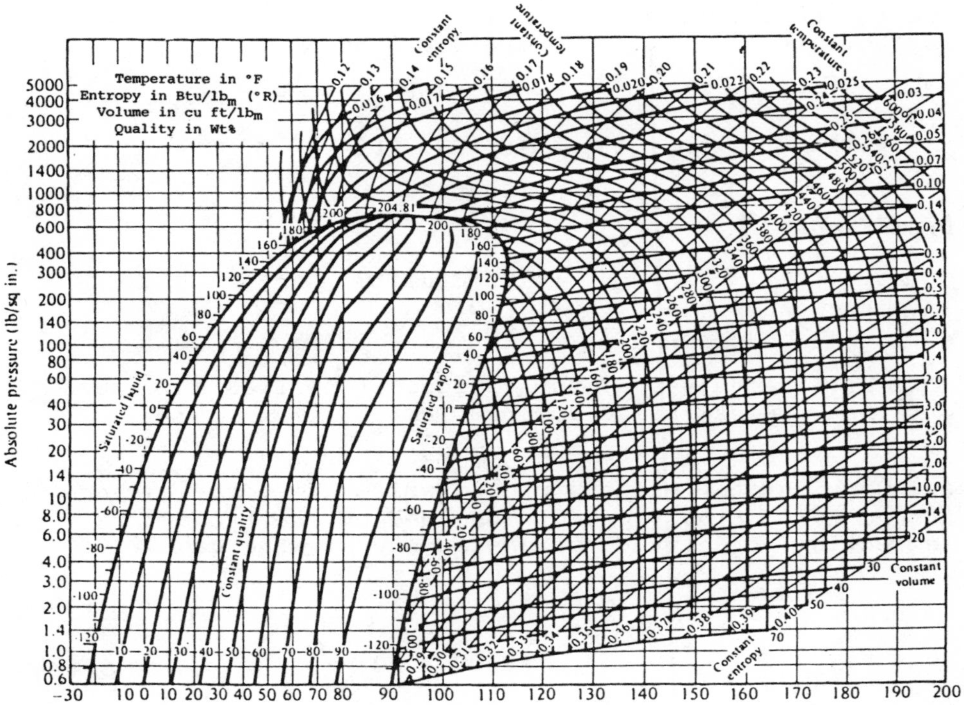

Fig. 2. Pressure-enthalpy diagram for "Freon"-22 refrigerant.

At state 3' the temperature is known to be 140°F, and the state is saturated vapor. Therefore, from Figure 2

$$P_{3'} = P_3 = 350 \text{ psia}$$

At state 4

$$P_4 = P_{3'} = 350 \text{ psia}$$

$$T_4 = T_{3'} = 140°F$$

Hence $$h_4 = 52 \text{ Btu/lbm}$$

At state 1, since process 1-4 is isenthalpic

$$h_1 = h_4 = 52 \text{ Btu/lbm}$$

At state 2 the temperature is known to be 50°C, and the state is saturated vapor. Hence from Figure 2

$$P_2 = 100 \text{ psia}$$

$$h_2 = 109 \text{ Btu/lbm}$$

$$s_2 = 0.218 \text{ Btu/lbm-°R}$$

State 3: Process 2-3 is an isentropic process and state 3, due to the compression, lies in the superheated region. Furthermore, $P_3 = P_{3'} = 350$ psia. Hence

$$s_3 = s_2 = 0.218 \text{ Btu/lbm-°R}$$

$$h_2 = 109 \text{ Btu/lbm}$$

From Figure 2

$$h_2 = 123 \text{ Btu/lbm}$$

$$T_2 = 180°F$$

Now that the values of the various properties have been obtained, we can solve the problem.

(a) Consider the evaporator, and write an energy balance around it to find the heat absorbed by the Freon-22. Neglecting potential and kinetic energies, we can write

$$q_L = h_2 - h_1$$

$$= 109 - 52$$

$$= 57 \text{ Btu/lbm}$$

It is known, however, that the evaporator is to absorb 3 tons or 36,000 Btu/hr. Hence, the required mass flow rate is

$$\dot{m} = \frac{\dot{Q}_L}{q_L}$$

$$= \frac{36,000}{57}$$

$$= 631.58 \text{ lbm/hr}$$

(b) Consider the compressor, and write an energy balance around it, neglecting potential and kinetic energies.

$$-w = h_3 - h_2$$

$$= 123 - 109$$

$$= 14 \text{ Btu/lbm}$$

or

$$w = -14 \text{ Btu/lbm}$$

The total work production is

$$\dot{W} = \dot{m}w$$

$$= 631.58\ (-14)$$

$$= -8842.12 \text{ Btu/hr}$$

However, 1 hp = 2545 Btu/hr, and hence the compressor will need

$$P = \frac{8842.12}{2545} = 3.48 \text{ hp}$$

(c) The heat load of the condenser can be computed in two ways: either by writing an energy balance around it, or by writing the overall energy balance around the refrigerator. Here the second way is used. Hence

$$\dot{W} = \dot{Q}_H + \dot{Q}_L$$

Solving for $\dot{Q}_H$ gives

$$\dot{Q}_H = \dot{W} - \dot{Q}_L$$

$$= -8842.12 - 36,000$$

$$= -44842.12 \text{ Btu/hr}$$

The heat transferred per unit mass is

$$q_H = \frac{\dot{Q}_H}{\dot{m}}$$

$$= \frac{-44842.12}{631.58}$$

$$= 71 \text{ Btu/lbm}$$

The vapor compression refrigeration cycle shown in the figure uses Freon-12 as its working fluid, and operates under the following given conditions.

$$P_1 = P_4 = P_5 = P_6 = 308.6 \text{ kPa}$$

$$P_2 = P_3 = 1.2 \text{ MPa}$$

$$T_3 = 30°C, \text{ state 1 is saturated vapor}$$

Assuming that the adiabatic compressor's efficiency is 80%, determine the compression work required per kJ of refrigeration.

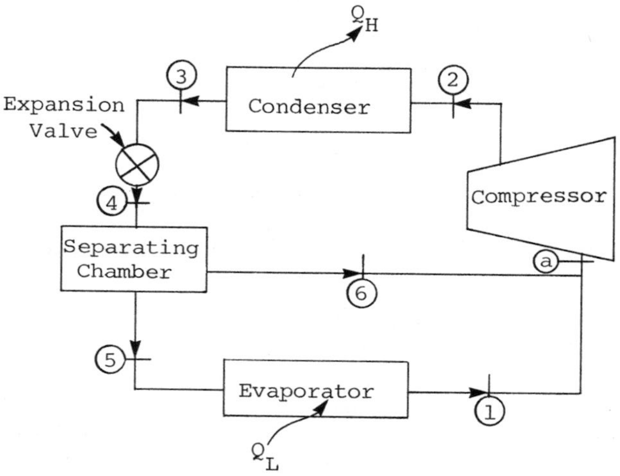

Solution: This problem is solved by computing both the work input to the compressor and the heat added in the evaporator. First consider the compressor and write the first and second laws of thermodynamics for the reversible process.

First law: $$m_a h_a = m_2 h_2 + w_{a-2} \tag{1}$$

Second law: $$s_2 = s_a \tag{2}$$

From the steam tables, obtain the properties at the different states.

State 1: saturated vapor (given), $P_1 = 308.6$ kPa

$$h_a \simeq h_1 = h_g = 187.397 \text{ kJ/kg}$$

$$s_a = s_1 = s_g = 0.6960 \text{ kJ/kg-°K}$$

State 2: superheated vapor ($P_2 = 1.2$ MPa, $s_2 = s_a$)

$$h_2 = 211.52 \text{ kJ/kg}$$

Solving for $\frac{w}{m}$ in Eq. (1), obtain

$$\left.\frac{w}{m}\right|_{comp.} = h_2 - h_a$$

$$= 211.52 - 187.397$$

$$= 24.123 \text{ kJ/kg}$$

However, this is the work that would be needed if the process in the compressor was reversible. Since irreversibilities are involved, the equation involving the adiabatic compressor efficiency can be used.

$$\eta_{comp.} = \frac{w_s}{w_a}$$

Solving for the actual work per unit mass gives

$$\left.\frac{w_a}{m}\right|_{comp} = \frac{w_{s/m}}{\eta} \times \frac{1}{\eta}$$

$$= \frac{24.123}{0.80}$$

$$= 30.154 \text{ kJ/kg}$$

Now consider the evaporator. From the first law, get

$$Q_H + m_5 h_5 = m_1 h_1 \qquad (3)$$

or

$$\frac{Q_H}{m} = h_1 - h_5 \qquad (4)$$

However

$$h_6 \cong h_1 = 187.397 \text{ kJ/kg}$$

$$h_3 = h_4 \cong h_5 = 64.539 \text{ kJ/kg}$$

Substituting into Eq. (4) yields

$$\left.\frac{Q}{m}\right|_{ev} = 187.397 - 64.539$$

$$= 122.858 \text{ kJ/kg}$$

Hence

$$\frac{W/m}{Q/m} = \frac{30.15}{122.858} = 0.2454$$

$\therefore$ W = 0.2454 kJ/kg of refrigeration.

• **PROBLEM 8-25**

Freon-12 enters the compressor of a refrigeration power cycle at a pressure of 261 kPa dry saturated, and leaves at 961 kPa. After leaving the condenser, the fluid is then subcooled to 20°C, and is throttled before entering the evaporator. Sketch the P-h and T-s diagrams for the cycle, and calculate the coefficient of performance of the refrigerator.

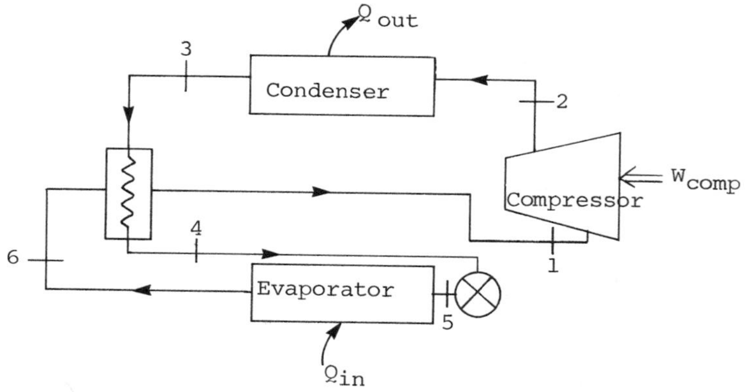

Fig. 1. Schematic Representation.

Solution: The coefficient of performance of a refrigeration power cycle is given as

$$\beta = \text{C.O.P.} = \frac{q_{in}}{w_{in}} \tag{1}$$

where

$$q_{in} = h_1 - h_5 \tag{2}$$

$$w_{in} = h_2 - h_1 \tag{3}$$

First compute the enthalpies at states 1 and 2. From the Freon-12 tables at P = 261 kPa, T_{sat} = 268.15°K,

$$h_1 = h_g = 185.38 \text{ kJ/kg}$$

$$s_1 = s_g = 0.6991 \text{ kJ/kg-}^{\circ}\text{K}$$

At state 2, $P_2 = 961$ kPa and $s_2 = s_1$. Hence the state is superheated. $(s_2 > s_g)$

$$h_2 = 208.51 \text{ kJ/kg}$$

Next find the enthalpy at state 5 as follows.

$$h_5 = h_4$$

since process 4→5 is a throttling process. Then for a subcooled liquid

$$h_{sub} - h_{sat} = v_f(P_{sub} - P_{sat})$$

Hence

$$h_4 - h_3 = v_3(P_4 - P_3) \qquad (4)$$

From the Freon-12 tables at T = 20°C

$$P_3 = P_{sat} = 567.3 \text{ kPa}$$

At $P_4 = 961$ kPa

$$h_3 = h_{sat} = 74.59 \text{ kJ/kg}$$

$$v_3 = v_f = 0.000789 \text{ m}^3\text{/kg}$$

Substituting into Eq. (4) yields

$$h_4 = 74.59 + 0.000789\ (961-567.3)$$

$$= 74.90 \text{ kJ/kg}$$

Thus $\qquad h_5 = h_4 = 74.90$ kJ/kg

Substituting Eqs. (2) and (3) into Eq. (1),

$$\beta = \frac{h_1 - h_5}{h_2 - h_1}$$

$$= \frac{185.38 - 74.90}{208.51 - 185.38}$$

$$= 4.78$$

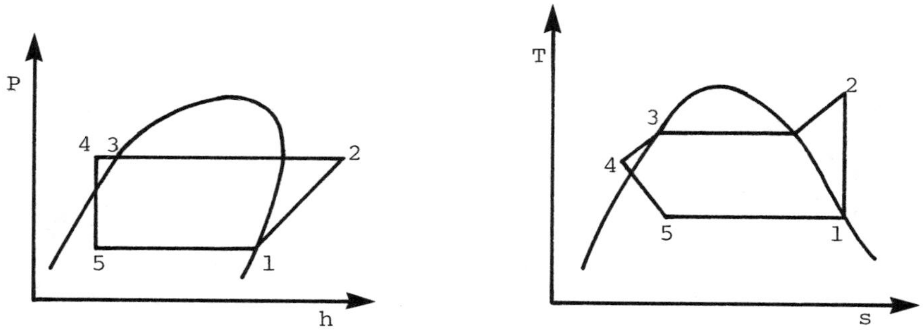

Fig. 2

Now that all the information is known, the P-h and T-s diagrams can be sketched as shown in Figure 2.

• **PROBLEM 8-26**

In the refrigeration cycle shown in Figure 1, Freon-12 is used as the working fluid. The heat exchanger uses the cold vapor leaving the evaporator to cool the liquid entering the expansion valve. The working temperature of the evaporator is -25°C, with Freon-12 leaving the evaporator as saturated vapor at -25°C. The fluid leaves the heat exchanger at 20°C and is compressed in the compressor to 1.2 MPa. Liquid leaves the condenser at 1.2 MPa, 45°C. Calculate (a) the work input to the compressor, (b) the heat transfer in the evaporator, and (c) the coefficient of performance of the cycle. Assume the compression process to be reversible and adiabatic.

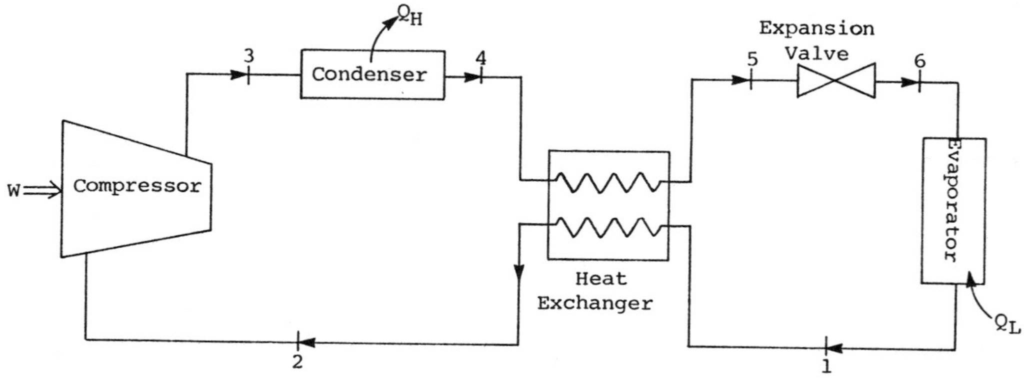

Fig. 1. Schematic representation of the cycle.

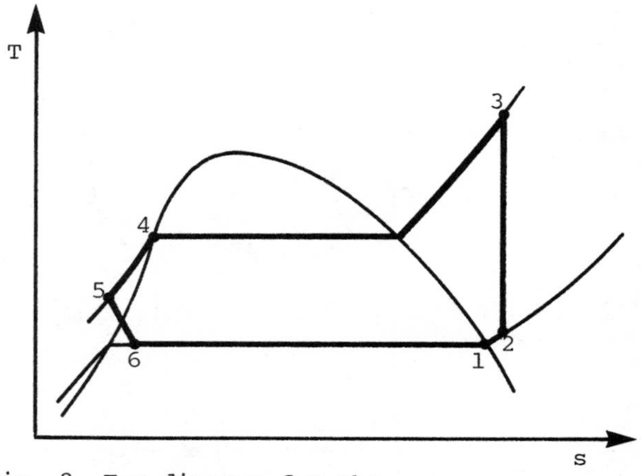

Fig. 2 T-s diagram for the process.

Solution: (a) Assume the condenser, the evaporator, and the heat exchanger to be constant pressure devices. Therefore, referring to Figures 1 and 2,

$$P_1 = P_2 = P_6$$

$$P_3 = P_4 = P_5 = 1.2 \text{ MPa}$$

Consider a control volume around the compressor. From the first law of thermodynamics, we can write on a per mass basis (neglecting potential and kinetic energies)

$$q_{c.v.} + h_2 = h_3 + w_{c.v.}$$

Since the process is adiabatic

$$w_{c.v.} = h_2 - h_3 \qquad (1)$$

Next find the enthalpies at states 2 and 3, as follows. State 1 is saturated vapor, and from the saturated Freon-12 tables at -25°C

$$P_1 = 0.1237 \text{ MPa}$$

$$h_1 = h_g = 176.352 \text{ kJ/kg}$$

However, $P_2 = P_1$ and $T_2 = 20°C$. From the Freon-12 tables we see that state 2 lies in the superheated region. Hence from the superheated Freon-12 tables, by interpolation

$$h_2 = 203.34 \text{ kJ/kg}$$

$$s_2 = 0.8134 \text{ kJ/kg-°K}$$

Since the process has been assumed reversible, $s_3 = s_2$. From the superheated Freon-12 tables at $s_3 = 0.8134$ kJ/kg-°K and $P_3 = 1.2$ MPa,

$$h_3 = 253.19 \text{ kJ/kg}$$

$$T_3 = 110.3°C$$

Substituting into Eq. (1), obtain

$$w_c = 203.34 - 253.19$$

$$= -49.85 \text{ kJ/kg}$$

The negative sign indicates that work was done on the control volume (compressor).

(b) Consider a control volume around the evaporator. Neglecting potential and kinetic energies, and noting that there is no work done on the control volume, write

$$q_L = h_1 - h_6 \qquad (2)$$

The enthalpy at state 1 is known from part (a) to be

$$h_1 = 176.352 \text{ kJ/kg}$$

To find the enthalpy at state 6, proceed as follows. Consider a control volume around the heat exchanger.

$$h_4 - h_5 = h_2 - h_1 \qquad (3)$$

The fluid at state 4 is saturated liquid. From the saturated Freon-12 tables at $T_4 = 45°C$,

$$h_4 = h_f = 79.647 \text{ kJ/kg}$$

Then from Eq. (3), solving for h_5

$$h_5 = h_4 - h_2 + h_1$$

$$= 79.647 - 203.34 + 176.352$$

$$= 52.64 \text{ kJ/kg}$$

Process 5-6 is a throttling process. Hence

$$h_6 = h_5 = 52.64 \text{ kJ/kg}$$

Substituting into Eq. (2), obtain

$$q_L = 176.352 - 52.64$$

$$= 123.71 \text{ kJ/kg}$$

(c) The coefficient of performance of the cycle is defined as

$$\beta = \frac{q_L}{w_c}$$

$$= \frac{123.71}{49.85}$$

$$= 2.48$$

• PROBLEM 8-27

Compute the ratio of mass flow rate through the power loop to that through the refrigeration loop required such that the turbine will produce just enough power to drive the compressor in the ideal dual-loop cycle shown in the figure. Take Freon-12 as the working fluid with the following known conditions.

State 1: T = 110°C, saturated vapor

State 3: T = 50°C, saturated liquid

State 8: T = -15°C, saturated vapor.

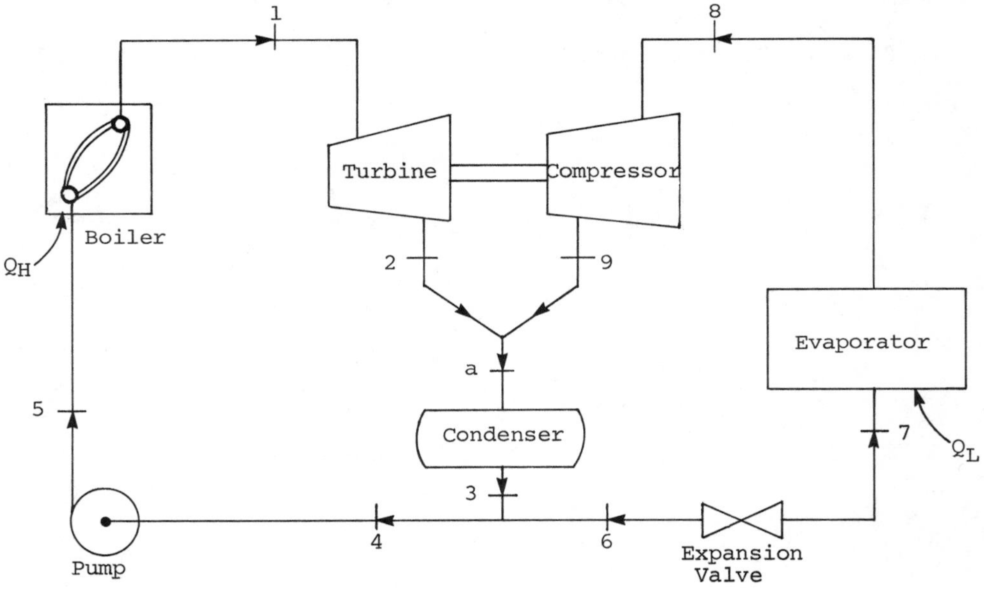

Solution: Consider a control volume consisting of both the compressor and the turbine. Since the turbine must produce just enough power to drive the compressor, we can write

$$W_t = W_c$$

or

$$\dot{m}_1 h_1 - \dot{m}_2 h_2 = \dot{m}_9 h_9 - \dot{m}_8 h_8$$

or

$$\dot{m}_1 h_1 + \dot{m}_8 h_8 = \dot{m}_2 h_2 + \dot{m}_9 h_9 \quad (1)$$

From continuity

$$\dot{m}_1 = \dot{m}_2 = \dot{m}_p$$

and

$$\dot{m}_8 = \dot{m}_9 = \dot{m}_r$$

Eq. (1) then becomes

$$\dot{m}_p h_1 + \dot{m}_r h_8 = \dot{m}_p h_2 + \dot{m}_r h_9$$

Solving for $\dot{m}_p/\dot{m}_r$

$$\frac{\dot{m}_p}{\dot{m}_r} = \frac{h_9 - h_8}{h_1 - h_2} \quad (2)$$

From the Freon-12 tables, obtain the following:

At $T_1 = 110°C$, saturated vapor

$$P_1 = P_5 = 3.9784 \text{ MPa}$$

$$h_1 = h_g = 196.484 \text{ kJ/kg}$$

$$s_1 = s_g = 0.6064 \text{ kJ/kg-°K}$$

At $T_3 = 50°C$, saturated liquid

$$P_3 = P_2 = P_9 = 1.2193 \text{ MPa}$$

$$P_4 = P_6 = P_3 = 1.2193 \text{ MPa}$$

$$h_7 = h_3 = h_f = 84.868 \text{ kJ/kg}$$

At $T_8 = -15°C$, saturated vapor

$$P_8 = P_7 = 0.1826 \text{ MPa}$$

$$h_8 = 180.846 \text{ kJ/kg}$$

$$s_8 = s_g = 0.7046 \text{ kJ/kg-°K}$$

At the exit of the compressor

$$P_9 = 1.2193 \text{ MPa}$$

$$s_9 = s_8 = 0.7046 \text{ kJ/kg-°K}$$

From the superheated Freon-12 tables, by interpolation

$$T_9 = 60.16°C$$

$$h_9 = 214.61 \text{ kJ/kg}$$

At the exit of the turbine

$$P_2 = 1.2193 \text{ MPa}$$

$$s_2 = s_1 = 0.6064 \text{ kJ/kg-°K}$$

The state is in the mixture region. From the saturated Freon-12 tables

$$s_f = 0.3034 \text{ kJ/kg-°K}$$

$$s_{fg} = 0.3758 \text{ kJ/kg-°K}$$

The quality at state 2 is found as

$$x_2 = \frac{s_2 - s_f}{s_{fg}}$$

$$= \frac{0.6064 - 0.3034}{0.3758}$$

$$= 0.8063$$

Then the enthalpy at state 2 can be found as

$$h_2 = h_f + x_2 h_{fg}$$

$$= 84.868 + 0.8063(121.430)$$

$$= 182.78 \text{ kJ/kg.}$$

Substituting the numerical values into Eq. (2), obtain

$$\frac{\dot{m}_p}{\dot{m}_r} = \frac{214.61 - 180.85}{196.48 - 182.78}$$

$$= 2.4642$$

• PROBLEM 8-28

The two-stage cascade refrigeration unit shown in Figure 1 is used to maintain a room at a temperature of -160°F. Freon-503 is used in the low temperature cycle (cycle II) and Freon-22 is used in the high temperature cycle

(cycle I). The working temperatures of the evaporator and condenser are -180°F and 100°F, respectively. The temperature at the entrance of the expansion valve in cycle II is -30°F and the temperature at the exit of the expansion valve in cycle I is -50°F. Assuming the processes in the compressors to be reversible and adiabatic, compute the compressor horsepower for both cycles if the refrigerator absorbs 28,000 Btu/hr from the room.

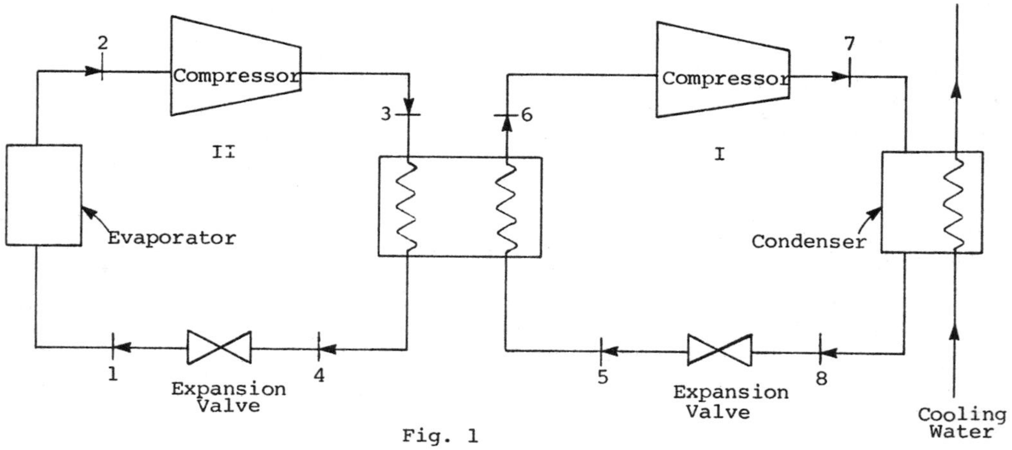

Fig. 1

Solution: First consider the low temperature cycle (cycle II), and plot the cycle on a P-h diagram as shown in Figure 2. Referring to Figure 2, and using Figure 4 obtain

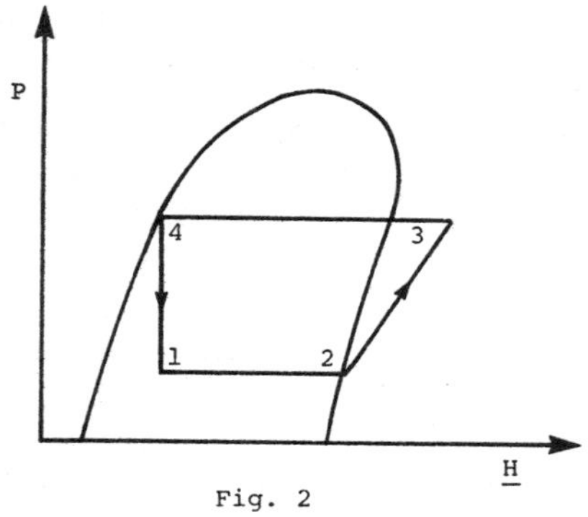

Fig. 2

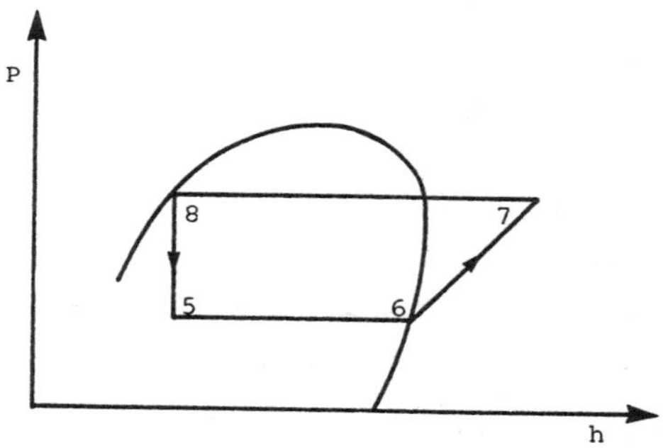

Fig. 3

State 4: $T_4 = -30°F$, saturated liquid

$P_4 = 150$ psia

$h_4 = 3$ Btu/lbm

State 2: $T_2 = -180°F$, saturated vapor

$P_2 = 2.1$ psia

$h_2 = 48$ Btu/lbm

$s_2 = 0.198$ Btu/lbm-°R

State 1: $h_1 = h_4 = 3$ Btu/lbm

State 3: $s_3 = s_2, \quad P_3 = P_4$

$h_3 = 88$ Btu/lbm

$T_3 = 110°F$

The heat absorbed in the evaporator per lbm of refrigerant is

$$q_L = h_2 - h_1$$
$$= 48 - 3$$
$$= 45 \text{ Btu/lbm}$$

Since 28,000 Btu/hr are absorbed from the room, the mass flow rate of refrigerant in cycle II is

$$\dot{m} = \frac{\dot{Q}_L}{q_L}$$
$$= \frac{28,000}{45}$$
$$= 622 \text{ lbm/hr}$$

The work done by the compressor per lbm of refrigerant is

$$-w_c = h_3 - h_2$$
$$= 88-48$$
$$= 40 \text{ Btu/lbm}$$

The total load is

$$-\dot{W}_c = \dot{m}(-w_c)$$
$$= 622(40)$$
$$= 24,880 \text{ Btu/hr}$$

or

$$-\dot{W}_c = \frac{24,880}{2545}$$

$$= 9.8 \text{ hp}$$

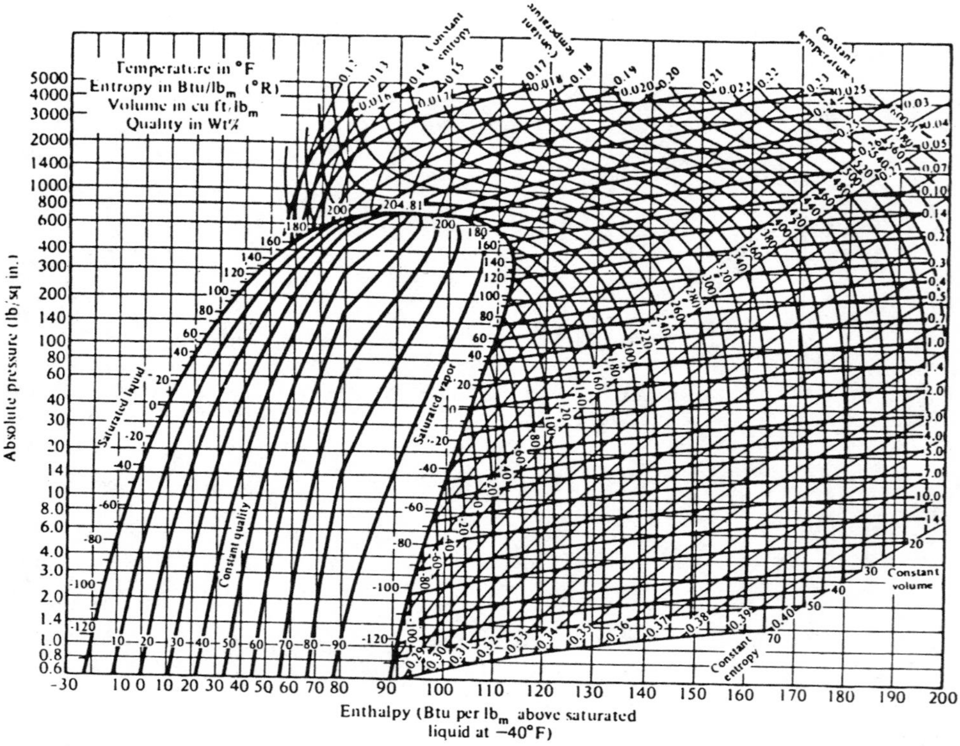

Fig. 4 Pressure-enthalpy diagram for "Freon" refrigerant.

To find the heat rejected in the low-temperature condenser, proceed as follows.

$$-q_H = h_3 - h_4$$

$$= 88-3$$

$$= 85 \text{ Btu/lbm}$$

and

$$-\dot{Q}_H = \dot{m}(-q_H)$$

$$= 622(85)$$

$$= 52,870 \text{ Btu/hr}$$

Now consider the high-temperature cycle (cycle I) using Freon-22. Plotting the P-h diagram as shown in Figure 3 and using Figure 4, obtain

State 8: $T_8 = 100^0F$

$P_8 = 220$ psia

$h_8 = 39$ Btu/lbm

State 6: $T_6 = -50^0F$

$P_6 = 14$ psia

$s_6 = 0.243$ Btu/lbm-^0R

$h_6 = 99$ Btu/lbm

State 5: $T_5 = -150^0F$

$P_5 = 14$ psia

$h_5 = 39$ Btu/lbm

State 7: $P_7 = 220$ psia

$s_7 = s_6 = 0.243$ Btu/lbm-^0R

$h_7 = 133$ Btu/lbm

$T_7 = 200^0F$

In this cycle, however, the total heat absorbed in the high temperature evaporator equals the heat discharged by the low-temperature condenser, which was found to be 52,870 Btu/hr. Therefore, the mass flow rate of refrigerant in the Freon-22 cycle is

$$\dot{m} = \frac{\dot{Q}_L}{q_L}$$

$$= \frac{52,870}{99 - 39}$$

$$= 881 \text{ lbm/hr}$$

The work for the high temperature cycle is

$$-w_c = h_7 - h_6$$

$$= 133-99$$

$$= 34 \text{ Btu/lbm}$$

and

$$-\dot{W}_c = -w_c\dot{m}$$

$$= 34(881)$$

$$= 29{,}954 \text{ Btu/hr}$$

or

$$-\dot{W}_c = \frac{29{,}954}{2545}$$

$$= 11.8 \text{ hp.}$$

The total power needed to drive both compressors in the system is the sum of the works from both cycles, which is 21.6 hp.

CHAPTER 9

AIR STANDARD POWER AND REFRIGERATION CYCLES

AIR - STANDARD CYCLES

• PROBLEM 9-1

A certain air cycle is designed such that air is first heated at a constant volume until its pressure is twice the initial value. The air is then heated at constant pressure until its volume is doubled. The cycle is completed by cooling first at constant volume and then at constant pressure. If, for air, $k = \frac{7}{5}$ (where $k = C_p/C_v$), calculate the thermal efficiency of the cycle.

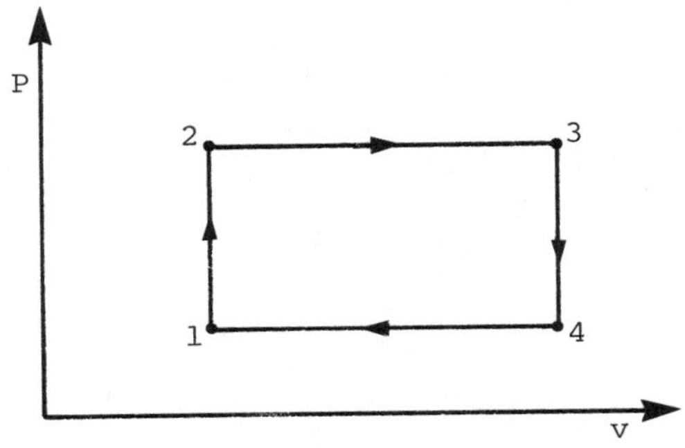

Solution: The cycle is represented on the P-v diagram as shown in the figure.

Process 1-2 is the constant volume heat addition process.
Process 2-3 is the constant pressure heat addition process.
Process 3-4 is the constant volume cooling process and
Process 4-1 is the constant pressure cooling process.

The thermal efficiency of the cycle is

$$\eta_{th} = \frac{Q_s - Q_r}{Q_s} = 1 - \frac{Q_r}{Q_s} \tag{1}$$

where Q_s = heat supplied

Q_r = heat rejected

Q_s and Q_r are

$$Q_s = C_v(T_2 - T_1) + C_p(T_3 - T_2) \tag{2}$$

$$Q_r = C_v(T_3 - T_4) + C_p(T_4 - T_1) \tag{3}$$

where C_v and C_p are specific heats at constant volume and constant pressure, respectively.

Process 1-2 is at constant volume. Hence from the ideal gas relations,

$$\frac{P_1}{T_1} = \frac{P_2}{T_2}$$

or

$$T_2 = T_1\left(\frac{P_2}{P_1}\right)$$

but, given $P_2 = 2P_1$,

therefore,

$$T_2 = 2T_1 \tag{4}$$

Process 2-3 is at constant pressure.

Hence

$$\frac{v_2}{T_2} = \frac{v_3}{T_3}$$

or

$$T_3 = T_2\left(\frac{v_3}{v_2}\right)$$

but, $v_3 = 2v_2$.

Therefore,

$$T_3 = 2T_2$$

$$= 4T_1 \tag{5}$$

Process 4-1 is at constant pressure.

Hence,

$$\frac{v_1}{T_1} = \frac{v_4}{T_4}$$

or

$$T_4 = T_1\left(\frac{v_4}{v_1}\right)$$

but, $\frac{v_4}{v_1} = 2.$

Therefore, $$T_4 = 2T_1 \tag{6}$$

Substituting equations (4), (5) and (6) into equations (2) and (3),

$$Q_s = C_v(2T_1-T_1) + C_p(4T_1-2T_1)$$

$$= C_vT_1 + C_p(2T_1)$$

$$Q_s = T_1(C_v + 2C_p)$$

and

$$Q_r = C_v(4T_1-2T_1) + C_p(2T_1-T_1)$$

$$= T_1(2C_v + C_p)$$

Substituting the values into equation (1),

$$\eta_{th} = 1 - \frac{T_1(C_p + 2C_v)}{T_1(2C_p + C_v)}$$

$$= 1 - \frac{k + 2}{2k+1}$$

Substituting $k = \frac{7}{5}$,

$$\eta_{th} = 1 - \left(\frac{\frac{7}{5} + 2}{2\left(\frac{7}{5}\right) + 1}\right)$$

$$= 1 - \frac{17}{19} = \frac{2}{19}$$

• PROBLEM 9-2

In an air-standard cycle, air at 70°F and 14.7 psia is initially heated at constant volume till the pressure is 30 psia, and then heated at constant pressure till the temperature is 1600°F. The cycle is completed by first expanding isentropically to 14.7 psia and then cooling at constant pressure. Determine the thermal efficiency of the cycle.

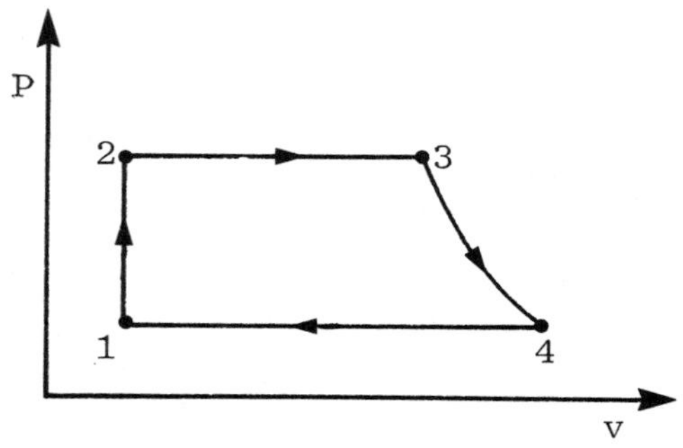

Solution: Referring to the figure, processes 1-2 and 2-3 are heat addition processes, and process 4-1 is the heat rejection process.

Given, state 1:

$$T_1 = 70°F$$

$$= 530°R$$

$$p_1 = 14.7 \text{ psia}$$

Since the process 1-2 is a constant volume process,

$$\frac{p_1}{T_1} = \frac{p_2}{T_2}$$

and hence,

$$T_2 = T_1\left(\frac{p_2}{p_1}\right)$$

$$= 530 \left(\frac{30}{14.7}\right)$$

$$= 1082°R$$

Therefore, state 2:

$$T_2 = 1082°R$$

$$p_2 = 30 \text{ psia}$$

State 3 is given as

$$T_3 = 2060°R$$

$$p_3 = p_2 = 30 \text{ psia}$$

Consider the isentropic expansion process 3-4. The temperature at state 4 is given by

$$T_4 = T_3\left(\frac{p_4}{p_3}\right)^{\frac{k-1}{k}}$$

$$= 2060 \left(\frac{14.7}{30}\right)^{\frac{1.4-1}{1.4}}$$

$$= 1680°R$$

Therefore, state 4:

$$T_4 = 1680°R$$

$$p_4 = 14.7 \text{ psia}$$

The heat added during the cycle is

$$q_A = C_v(T_2-T_1) + C_p(T_3-T_2)$$

$$= 0.171(1082-530) + 0.24(2060-1082)$$

$$= 329 \text{ Btu/lbm}$$

The heat rejected during the cycle is

$$q_R = C_p(T_4-T_1)$$

$$q_R = 0.24(1680-530)$$

$$= 276 \text{ Btu/lbm}$$

The thermal efficiency of the cycle is defined as

$$\eta_{th} = \frac{q_A - q_R}{q_A}$$

$$= 1 - \frac{q_R}{q_A}$$

$$= 1 - \frac{276}{329}$$

$$= 0.16$$

or $\eta_{th} = 16\%$

THE CARNOT CYCLE

• PROBLEM 9-3

Temperature, pressure and volume of air at the end of isentropic compression in an air standard Carnot heat engine cycle are 600°F, 275 psia and 4 ft³, respectively. If the ratio of isothermal expansion $r_e = 3$ and the ratio of isentropic compression $r_K = 6$, calculate

(a) the pressure and temperature at the other states of the Carnot cycle,

(b) the heat supplied and rejected by the cycle,

(c) the efficiency of the cycle, and

(d) the mean effective pressure.

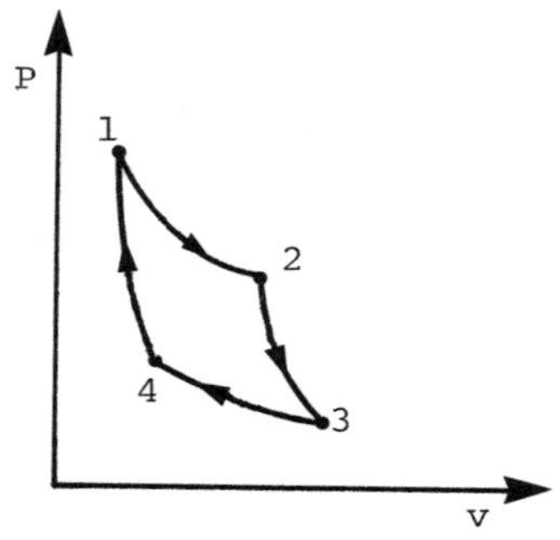

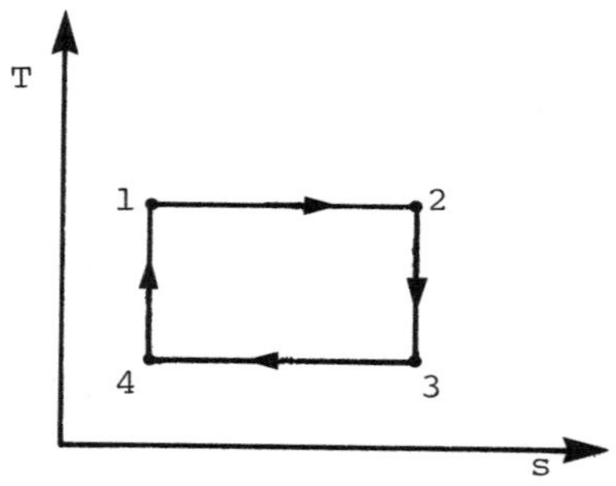

Solution: Consider the figure. The processes 1-2 and 3-4 are isothermal while 2-3 and 4-1 are isentropic processes.

The isothermal expansion ratio is defined as

$$r_e = \frac{V_2}{V_1} = \frac{V_3}{V_4} = 3$$

and the isentropic compression ratio is defined as

$$r_K = \frac{V_3}{V_2} = \frac{V_4}{V_1} = 6$$

Given state 1 is

$$T_1 = 600°F = 1060°R$$

$$P_1 = 275 \text{ psia}$$

$$V_1 = 4 \text{ ft}^3$$

(a) The temperature at state 2 is same as that at state 1, because the process 1-2 is isothermal.

Therefore, $T_2 = T_1 = 600°F$.

For the isothermal process 1-2, the pressure at state 2 is given by

$$P_2 = P_1\left(\frac{V_1}{V_2}\right)$$

$$= 275\left(\frac{1}{3}\right)$$

$$= 91.67 \text{ psia.}$$

For the isentropic process 2-3,

$$P_3 = P_2\left(\frac{V_2}{V_3}\right)^k$$

$$T_3 = T_2\left(\frac{V_2}{V_3}\right)^{k-1}$$

where $k = C_p/C_v$ and

$$k = 1.4 \text{ for air}$$

Substituting the values,

$$P_3 = 91.67\left(\frac{1}{6}\right)^{1.4}$$

$$= 7.46 \text{ psia}$$

$$T_3 = 1060\left(\frac{1}{6}\right)^{0.4}$$

$$= 517.67°R$$

or, $T_3 = 57.7°F$

The temperature at state 4 is same as that at state 3, because the process 3-4 is isothermal.

Therefore, $T_4 = T_3 = 57.7°F$

For the isothermal process 3-4, the pressure at state 4 is given by

$$P_4 = P_3\left(\frac{V_3}{V_4}\right)$$

$$= 7.46 \times 3$$

$$= 22.38 \text{ psia}$$

The calculations can be verified by finding out the temperature and pressure at state 1, by considering the isentropic compression process 4-1 and the previously obtained state 4 properties. The temperature and pressure at state 1 should coincide with the given values.

The four states of the Carnot cycle are:

State	Temperature	Pressure
1	600°F	275 psia
2	600°F	91.67 psia
3	57.7°F	7.46 psia
4	57.7°F	22.38 psia

(b) Heat is supplied to the cycle during process 1-2 and is rejected during process 3-4.

Heat transferred during process 1-2 is given by

$$Q_S = \frac{mRT_1}{J} \ln\left(\frac{V_2}{V_1}\right)$$

$$= \frac{P_1V_1}{J} \ln\left(\frac{V_2}{V_1}\right)$$

Substituting the values,

$$Q_S = \frac{275 \times 144 \times 4}{778} \ln(3)$$

$$= 223.7 \text{ Btu}$$

Heat rejected during process 3-4 is

$$Q_R = \frac{mRT_3}{J} \ln\left(\frac{V_4}{V_3}\right)$$

$$= \frac{P_1V_1T_3}{JT_1} \ln\left(\frac{V_4}{V_3}\right)$$

or

$$Q_R = \frac{275 \times 144 \times 4 \times 517.7}{778 \times 1060} \ln\left(\frac{1}{3}\right)$$

$$= -109.2 \text{ Btu}$$

The negative sign indicates that heat is rejected from the system.

(c) The thermal efficiency of the cycle is given by

$$\eta_{th} = \frac{T_1 - T_4}{T_1}$$

$$= \frac{1060-517.7}{1060} = 51\%$$

(d) The mean effective pressure is given by

$$\text{mep} = \frac{W}{V_3 - V_1}$$

where

$$W = \Sigma Q = 223.7-109.2$$

$$= 114.5 \text{ Btu}$$

$V_3 = 3V_4$ from the expansion and compression ratios

$$= 18 \times V_1$$

$$= 72 \text{ ft}^3$$

Therefore,

$$\text{mep} = \frac{114.5 \times 778}{(72-4)\ 144}$$

$$= 9.1 \text{ psia}$$

• PROBLEM 9-4

A Carnot heat engine cycle using steam as the working fluid operates between the temperatures 560°F and 70°F. All the processes are steady-state steady-flow. The fluid states at the beginning and end of the isothermal heat-addition process are saturated liquid and saturated vapor, respectively. Calculate the thermal efficiency of the cycle and the ratio of turbine work to compressor work.

Solution: Consider the figure. The process a-b is a reversible isothermal heat-addition process. The temperature during this process is 560°F, i.e., 1020°R, and is constant.

The process b-c is the reversible isentropic expansion process. Here the temperature drops from 560°F to 70°F. This process takes place in a turbine to produce work.

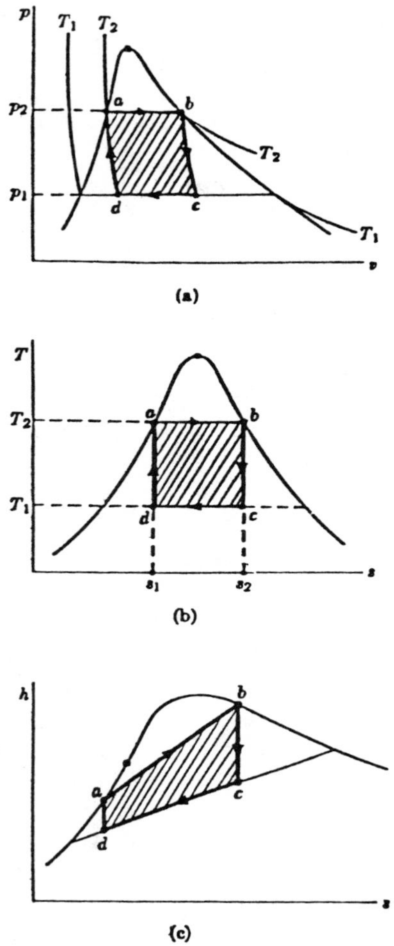
p
T1
T2
p2
p1
a
b
c
d
v
(a)
T
T2
T1
s1
s2
s
(b)
h
s
(c)

Fig.1

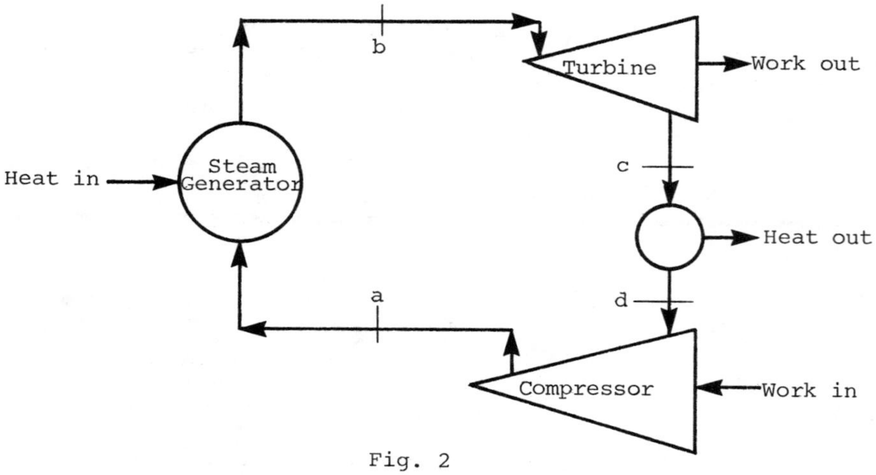
b
Turbine
Work out
c
Heat in
Steam
Generator
Heat out
a
d
Compressor
Work in

Fig. 2

The process c-d is the reversible isothermal process where heat is rejected at a temperature of 70° F (530° R).

The process d-a is the reversible isentropic compression process. This process takes place in a compressor, so work is being done on the working fluid. Here the temperature rises to 560°F.

The thermal efficiency of the Carnot cycle is given by

$$\eta_{th} = \frac{T_1 - T_2}{T_1}$$

where T_1 = isothermal heat-addition-temperature

T_2 = isothermal heat-rejection-temperature

Substituting the values,

$$\eta_{th} = \frac{1020-530}{1020}$$

$$= 0.48$$

i.e., $\eta_{th} = 48\%$

Referring to the figure and from steam tables, the condition of steam at state b is

(enthalpy) h_b = 1187.7 Btu/lbm

(entropy) s_b = 1.3757 Btu/lbm-°R

During the process b-c, the entropy remains constant. Therefore, $s_c = s_b$ = 1.3757 Btu/lbm-°R.

The quality of steam at the state C is given by

$$x_c = \frac{s_c - s_f}{s_{fg}}$$

where s_c = entropy at state C

s_f = saturated liquid entropy at 70°F

s_{fg} = evaporation entropy at 70°F

x_c = quality of steam of state C

Substituting,

$$x_c = \frac{1.3757-0.0745}{1.9900}$$

$$= 0.654$$

Therefore, the enthalpy of steam at state C is

$$h_c = h_f + x_c h_{fg}$$

where h_f = enthalpy of saturated water at 70°F

h_{fg} = enthalpy of evaporation at 70°F

Substituting the values,

$$h_c = 38.052 + 0.654 \times 1054$$
$$= 727.37 \text{ Btu/lbm}$$

The work produced by the turbine is given by $W_{turb} = \left(h_b - h_c\right)$

i.e., $$W_{turb} = 1187.7 - 727.37$$
$$= 460.33 \text{ Btu/lbm}$$

The condition of steam at state a is

$$h_a = 562.4 \text{ Btu/lbm}$$

$$s_a = 0.7625 \text{ Btu/lbm-°R}$$

During the process d-a, the entropy remains constant. Therefore, $s_d = s_a = 0.7625$ Btu/lbm°R.

The quality of steam at state d is given by

$$x_d = \frac{s_d - s_f}{s_{fg}}$$

Substituting the values,

$$x_d = \frac{0.7625 - 0.0745}{1.9900}$$
$$= 0.346$$

Therefore, the enthalpy of steam at state d is

$$h_d = h_f + x_d h_{fg}$$
$$= 38.052 + 0.346 \times 1054$$
$$= 402.74 \text{ Btu/lbm}$$

The work done by the compressor is $(h_a - h_d)$

i.e., $$W_{comp} = h_a - h_d$$

Substituting,

$$w_{comp} = 562.4 - 402.74$$

$$= 159.66 \text{ Btu/lbm.}$$

Therefore, the ratio of turbine work to compressor work is,

$$\frac{w_{turb}}{w_{comp}} = \frac{460.33}{159.66}$$

$$= 2.88$$

• PROBLEM 9-5

A Carnot cycle engine using steam as the working fluid works between the pressures of 962.75 psia and 2.89 psia. The steam consists of saturated vapor at the end of isothermal expansion and saturated liquid at the end of isentropic compression. Determine the thermal efficiency, turbine and pump work, net work, heat rejected and the work ratio for the cycle per lbm of water, assuming (a) all the processes to be reversible, (b) the adiabatic efficiency of the turbine and pump to be 80%. Compare the reversible and irreversible cycles.

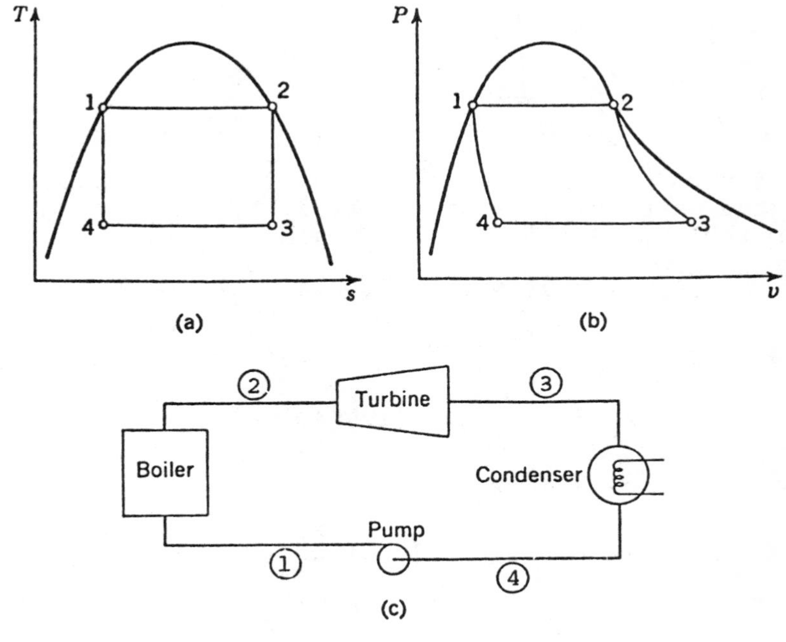

Fig. 1. The vapor Carnot cycle: 1-2, isothermal isobaric heat addition; 2-3, isentropic expansion; 3-4, isothermal heat rejection; 4-1, isentropic compression.

Solution: For a Carnot cycle operating on steam, the pressures are constant during the isothermal processes for the condition given in the problem. The corresponding saturation temperatures are found from steam tables.

$$T_1 = 540°F = 1000°R \text{ (isothermal expansion)}$$

$$T_3 = 140°F = 600°R \text{ (isothermal compression)}$$

(a) Since the temperatures of the two reversible isothermal heat-transfer processes are known, the thermal efficiency of the cycle can be found as

$$\eta_{th} = \frac{T_H - T_L}{T_H}$$

$$= \frac{1000-600}{1000}$$

$$= 0.4$$

$$= 40\%$$

The turbine work can be found as

$$W_{turb.} = W_{2-3} = -(h_3-h_2) \quad (1)$$

and the pump work as

$$W_{pump} = W_{4-1} = -(h_1-h_4) \quad (2)$$

In order to evaluate eqs. (1) and (2), it is necessary to find the enthalpies at states 1, 2, 3, and 4. Using the steam table at T = 540° F, we obtain

$$s_1 = s_4 = s_f = 0.7374 \text{ Btu/lbm-°R}$$

$$h_1 = h_f = 536.6 \text{ Btu/lbm}$$

$$s_2 = s_3 = s_g = 1.3942 \text{ Btu/lbm-°R}$$

$$h_2 = h_g = 1193.2 \text{ Btu/lbm}$$

However, at state 3, T_3 = 140° F and

$$s_f = 0.1984 \text{ Btu/lbm-°R}$$

$$s_g = 1.8895 \text{ Btu/lbm-°R}$$

Because $s_f < s_3 < s_g$, it is necessary to find the quality.

Hence

$$x_3 = \frac{s_3 - s_f}{s_g - s_f}$$

$$= \frac{1.3942-0.1984}{1.8895-0.1984}$$

$$= 0.7072$$

The enthalpy at state 3 can now be found from the expression

$$h_3 = h_f + x_3 h_{fg}$$

with $h_f = 107.89$ Btu/lbm

$$h_{fg} = 1014.1 \text{ Btu/lbm}$$

$$h_3 = 107.89 + 0.7072(1014.1)$$

$$= 825.06 \text{ Btu/lbm}$$

Similarly, at state 4,

$$x_4 = \frac{s_4 - s_f}{s_g - s_f}$$

$$= \frac{0.7374-0.1984}{1.8895-0.1984}$$

$$= 0.3187$$

The enthalpy at 4 is

$$h_4 = h_f + x_4 h_{fg}$$

$$= 107.89 + 0.3187(1014.1)$$

$$= 431.08 \text{ Btu/lbm.}$$

From eq. (1), for the turbine work,

$$W_{turb.} = -(825.06-1193.2) = 368.14 \text{ Btu/lbm}$$

and from eq. (2), for the pump work,

$$W_{pump} = -(536.6-431.08) = -105.52 \text{ Btu/lbm}$$

The net work of the cycle is the algebraic sum of the turbine and pump works. Therefore,

$$\Sigma W = W_{turb.} + W_{pump}$$

$$= 368.14 - 105.52$$

$$= 262.62 \text{ Btu/lbm}$$

Note that the net work of the cycle can also be found using the relation

$$\Sigma W = \eta_{th} (Q_A) \qquad (3)$$

which relates the net work and heat added to the system through the thermal efficiency.

Heat is added to the system during the boiler process and can be found as

$$Q_A = Q_{1\rightarrow 2} = h_2 - h_1 = T_H(s_2 - s_1)$$

or

$$Q_A = 1193.2 - 536.6$$

$$= 656.6 \text{ Btu/lbm}$$

As a check, using eq. (3),

$$\Sigma W = 0.40\ (656.6) = 262.64 \text{ Btu/lbm}$$

The work ratio is defined as the ratio of the net work produced by the system to the total net positive work produced (the turbine work), or

$$R_w = \frac{\Sigma W}{\Sigma W_{turb.}}$$

$$= \frac{262.64}{368.14}$$

$$= 0.7134$$

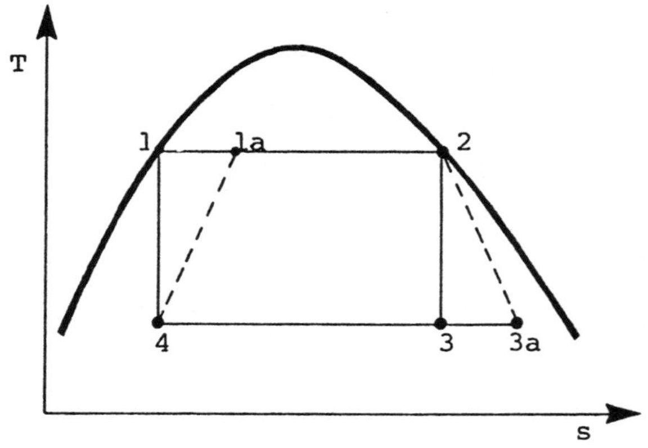

Fig. 2. Basic Carnot cycle with irreversible processes.

(b) Assume that states 1 and 3 are those affected by the irreversibilities, while states 2 and 4 remain the same as in (a).

Fig. 2 shows the process depicted on a temperature entropy diagram. The dotted lines indicate an irreversible process between the equilibrium and states 2 and 3a, and 4 and 1a. The enthalpies at the new states, due to the irreversibilities, can be found from the definition of adiabatic efficiency:

$$\eta_{ad} = \frac{W_a}{W_s} \quad \text{(for a work-producing process)}$$

and

$$\eta_{ad} = \frac{W_s}{W_a} \quad \text{(for a work-absorbing process)}$$

Therefore ,

$$0.80 = \frac{h_2 - h_{3a}}{h_2 - h_3}$$

$$= \frac{1193.2 - h_{3a}}{1193.2 - 825.06}$$

or

$$h_{3a} = 898.69 \text{ Btu/lbm}$$

Then the actual turbine work is

$$W_a\Big|_{turb.} = -(h_{3a} - h_2)$$

$$= -(898.69 - 1193.2)$$

$$= 294.51 \text{ Btu/lbm.}$$

Similarly,

$$0.80 = \frac{h_1 - h_4}{h_{1a} - h_4}$$

$$= \frac{536.6 - 431.08}{h_{1a} - 431.08}$$

or

$$h_{1a} = 562.98$$

Then the actual pump work is

$$W_a\Big|_{pump} = -(h_{1a} - h_4)$$

$$= -(562.98 - 431.08)$$

$$= -131.90 \text{ Btu/lbm}$$

The net work of this cycle is

$$\Sigma W = 294.51 - 131.90$$

$$= 162.61 \text{ Btu/lbm}$$

The work ratio is

$$R_w = \frac{162.61}{294.51} = 0.5521$$

The heat added is

$$Q_A = h_2 - h_{1a}$$

$$= 1193.2 - 562.98$$

$$= 630.22 \text{ Btu/lbm.}$$

Since this is not a reversible cycle, the thermal efficiency of the cycle cannot be found from the temperatures of the cycle alone. However, from eq.(3),

$$\eta_{th} = \frac{\Sigma W}{Q_A}$$

$$= \frac{162.61}{630.22} \times 100$$

$$= 25.80\%$$

	Reversible	Irreversible
η_{th}	40.0%	25.80%
W_{turb}	368.14 Btu/lbm	294.51 Btu/lbm
W_{pump}	-105.52 Btu/lbm	-131.90 Btu/lbm
ΣW	262.64 Btu/lbm	162.61 Btu/lbm
Q_A	656.6 Btu/lbm	630.22 Btu/lbm
R_W	0.7134	0.5521

The two cycles are compared as shown in the table.

• PROBLEM 9-6

An air standard Carnot cycle has a constant highest compression ratio R_c and lower temperature T_1. If the isentropic compression ratio r is variable, determine the required condition for the maximum work in terms of this ratio.

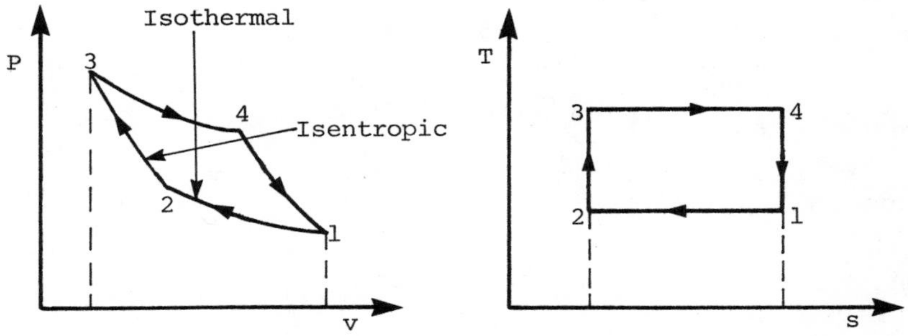

Solution: The total compression ratio of a Carnot cycle is defined as

$$R_c = \frac{v_1}{v_3}$$

and the isentropic compression ratio as

$$r = \frac{v_2}{v_3}$$

Applying the isentropic process law for points 2 and 3,

$$\frac{T_2}{T_3} = \left(\frac{v_3}{v_2}\right)^{k-1} \quad (1)$$

where k = ratio of specific heats of air, $(k = C_p/C_v)$

From isentropic process 4-1,

$$\frac{T_4}{T_1} = \left(\frac{v_1}{v_4}\right)^{k-1} \quad (2)$$

But from isothermal process,

$$T_1 = T_2 \quad \text{and} \quad T_3 = T_4$$

Therefore, from equations (1) and (2),

$$\frac{v_2}{v_3} = \frac{v_1}{v_4}$$

or

$$\frac{v_1}{v_2} = \frac{v_4}{v_3} \tag{3}$$

$$\frac{R_c}{r} = \frac{v_1}{v_3} \times \frac{v_3}{v_2} = \frac{v_1}{v_2} \tag{4}$$

The work done during the cycle is given by

$$W = Q_s - Q_r \tag{5}$$

where W = work done

Q_s = heat supplied

Q_r = heat rejected.

Heat is supplied during the isothermal process 3-4. It is given as

$$Q_s = \frac{P_3 v_3}{J} \ln\left(\frac{v_4}{v_3}\right)$$

$$= \frac{RT_3}{J} \ln\left(\frac{v_4}{v_3}\right)$$

Heat is rejected during the isothermal process 1-2. It is given as

$$Q_r = \frac{P_2 v_2}{J} \ln\left(\frac{v_1}{v_2}\right)$$

$$= \frac{RT_2}{J} \ln\left(\frac{v_1}{v_2}\right)$$

Substituting into equation (5),

$$W = \frac{R}{J}\left[T_3 \ln\left(\frac{v_4}{v_3}\right) - T_2 \ln\left(\frac{v_1}{v_2}\right)\right]$$

Substituting equations (3) and (4),

$$W = \frac{R}{J}\left[T_3 \ln\left(\frac{R_c}{r}\right) - T_2 \ln\left(\frac{R_c}{r}\right)\right]$$

$$= \frac{R}{J} \ln\left(\frac{R_c}{r}\right)\left(T_3 - T_2\right)$$

From equation (1),

$$T_3 = T_2 \left(\frac{v_2}{v_3}\right)^{k-1}$$

$$= T_2 (r)^{k-1}$$

Therefore, $(T_3 - T_2) = T_2(r^{k-1} - 1)$.

But $T_2 = T_1$ from isothermal process 1-2.

Therefore, $(T_3 - T_2) = T_1(r^{k-1} - 1)$

Substituting $(T_3 - T_2) = T_1(r^{k-1} - 1)$ into the simplified form of equation (5),

$$W = \frac{R}{J} \ln\left(\frac{R_c}{r}\right) T_1(r^{k-1} - 1)$$

In this equation, only r is a variable, and all other terms are constants.

Differentiating with respect to r, the condition for maximum work is

$$\frac{dw}{dr} = 0$$

i.e., $$\frac{RT_1}{J}\left[\ln\left(\frac{R_c}{r}\right)(k-1)r^{k-2} + (r^{k-1} - 1)\frac{r}{R_c}\left(\frac{-R_c}{r^2}\right)\right] = 0$$

$$(k-1)\, r^{k-2} \ln\left(\frac{R_c}{r}\right) - r^{k-2} + \frac{1}{r} = 0$$

Multiplying by r,

$$(k-1)\, r^{k-1} \ln\left(\frac{R_c}{r}\right) - r^{k-1} + 1 = 0$$

Dividing by (r^{k-1}),

$$(k-1) \ln\left(\frac{R_c}{r}\right) + \frac{1}{r^{k-1}} - 1 = 0$$

This is the required condition for maximum work for the given conditions (in terms of r).

THE OTTO CYCLE

• PROBLEM 9-7

1. One kilogram of air at 101.35 kPa, 21°C is compressed in an Otto cycle with a compression ratio of 7 to 1. During the combustion process, 953.66 kJ of heat is added to the air. Compute (a) the specific volume, pressure, and temperature at the four points in the cycle, (b) the air standard efficiency, and (c) the mep (mean effective pressure) and hp of the engine, if it uses 1 kg/min of air.

2. Calculate the efficiency for a Carnot cycle operating between the maximum and minimum temperatures of the Otto cycle.

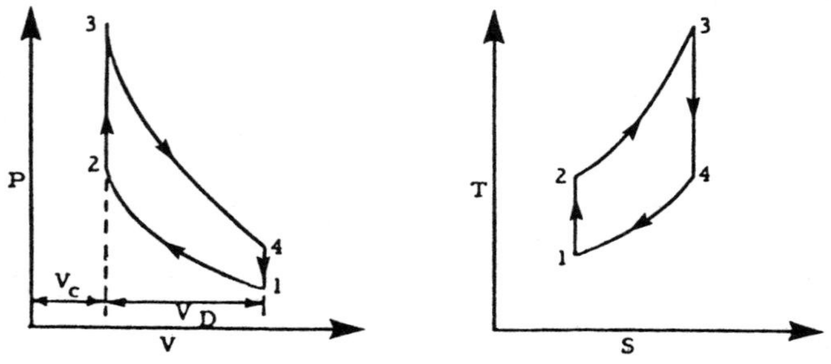

Fig. 1. Otto Cycle.

Solution: 1. At state 1,

$$P_1 = 101.35 \text{ kPa}$$

$$T_1 = 294°K$$

The specific volume, v_1, is determined by using the perfect gas equation of state.

$$v_1 = \frac{RT_1}{P_1}$$

$$= \frac{0.287\ (294)}{101.35}$$

$$= 0.8325 \text{ m}^3/\text{kg}.$$

At 2, the specific volume can be obtained by using the compression ratio.

$$\frac{v_2}{v_1} = \frac{1}{7}$$

or

$$v_2 = \frac{v_1}{7}$$

$$= \frac{0.8325}{7}$$

$$= 0.1189 \text{ m}^3/\text{kg}$$

The pressure (P_2) is obtained from the isentropic relation

$$P_2 = P_1\left(\frac{v_1}{v_2}\right)^k$$

$$= 101.35\left(\frac{0.8325}{0.1189}\right)^{1.4}$$

$$= 1{,}545.6 \text{ kPa}$$

The temperature (T_2) is

$$T_2 = T_1\left(\frac{v_1}{v_2}\right)^{k-1}$$

$$= 294\left(\frac{0.8325}{0.1189}\right)^{1.4-1}$$

$$= 640.4°K$$

At state 3, $v_3 = v_2 = 0.1189 \text{ m}^3/\text{kg}$. The temperature here can be calculated from the quantity of heat supplied since

$$Q_{in} = mc_v(T_3 - T_2)$$

or solving for T_3,

$$T_3 = \frac{Q_{in}}{mc_v} + T_2$$

$$= \frac{953.66}{1(0.7243)} + 640.4$$

$$= 1957.1°K$$

The pressure (P_3) is

$$P_3 = \frac{RT_3}{v_3}$$

$$= \frac{0.287(1957.1)}{0.1189}$$

$$= 4{,}724 \text{ kPa}$$

At 4, $v_4 = v_1 = 0.8325 \text{ m}^3/\text{kg}$,

and the pressure is $P_4 = P_3\left(\frac{v_3}{v_4}\right)^k$

$$= 4724\left(\frac{0.1189}{0.8325}\right)^{1.4}$$

$$= 309.7 \text{ kPa}$$

The temperature T_4 is

$$T_4 = T_3\left(\frac{v_3}{v_4}\right)^{k-1}$$

$$= 1957.1\left(\frac{0.1189}{0.8325}\right)^{1.4-1} = 898.5°K$$

(b) The efficiency of the Otto cycle is defined as

$$\eta = \frac{Q_{in}-Q_{out}}{Q_{in}} \times 100 \qquad (1)$$

where

$$Q_{in} = 953.66 \text{ kJ}$$

and

$$Q_{out} = mc_v(T_4 - T_1)$$

$$= 1(0.7243)(898.5-274)$$

$$= 452.3 \text{ kJ}$$

Therefore,

$$\eta = \frac{953.66-452.3}{953.66} \times 100$$

$$= 53\%$$

(c) The mep is

$$\text{mep} = \frac{W_{net}}{v_1 - v_2}$$

where

$$W_{net} = q_{in} - q_{out}$$

$$= 953.66 - 452.3$$

$$= 501.36 \text{ kJ}$$

Thus

$$\text{mep} = \frac{501.36}{0.8325-0.1189} = 702.6 \text{ kPa}$$

The horsepower is

$$\text{hp} = \dot{m}W_{net} = 501.36 \text{ kW}$$

$$= 5.2 \text{ hp.}$$

2. The maximum and minimum temperatures of the Otto cycle are

$$T_{max} = 1957.1°K$$

$$T_{min} = 294°K$$

The Carnot cycle efficiency is

$$\eta = \frac{T_{max} - T_{min}}{T_{max}} \times 100$$

$$= \frac{1957.1-294}{1957.1} \times 100$$

$$= 85\%$$

which is comparatively higher than the Otto cycle efficiency.

• PROBLEM 9-8

An Otto cycle engine has an initial air pressure and temperature of 14.7 psia and 60°F. 750 Btu of heat is supplied per lbm of air at the end of compression. The compression ratio is 7. Find (a) temperature and pressure at all salient points. (b) the thermal efficiency and the mean effective pressure for the cycle. Assume ideal conditions.

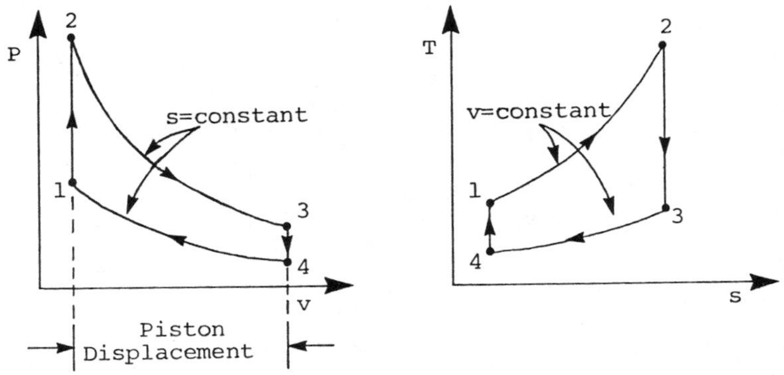

The air-standard Otto cycle.

Solution: Consider a piston-cylinder assembly containing air. The initial state is at the beginning of the isentropic compression. This state is shown in the figure as point 4.

(a) The compression ratio is defined as

$$R_c = \frac{v_3}{v_2} = \frac{v_4}{v_1}$$

where R_c = compression ratio

Therefore, $R_c = 7$

Consider the isentropic compression process 4-1.

$$\frac{T_1}{T_4} = \left(\frac{v_4}{v_1}\right)^{k-1}$$

where k = ratio of specific heats $\left(\frac{C_p}{C_v}\right)$

$$\frac{p_1}{p_4} = \left(\frac{v_4}{v_1}\right)^k$$

Therefore, the temperature at state 1 is

$$T_1 = T_4\left(\frac{v_4}{v_1}\right)^{k-1}$$

Substituting the values,

$$T_4 = (460+60)^\circ R = 520^\circ R$$

$$\left(\frac{v_4}{v_1}\right) = 7$$

$$k = 1.4 \text{ for air}$$

$$T_1 = 520(7)^{1.4-1}$$

$$= 1133^\circ R \ (673^\circ F)$$

Similarly, the pressure at state 1 is

$$P_1 = P_4\left(\frac{v_4}{v_1}\right)^k$$

$$= 14.7\ (7)^{1.4}$$

$$= 224 \text{ psia}$$

Consider the constant volume heat addition process 1-2. Heat supplied during the process 1-2 is given by

$$Q_s = C_v(T_2-T_1)$$

where Q_s = heat supplied

c_v = constant volume specific heat of air (0.171 Btu/lbm°R)

Substituting the values and calculating for T_2,

$$750 = 0.171\ (T_2-1133)$$

or $$T_2 = \frac{750}{0.171} + 1133$$

$$= 5519°R \ (5059°F)$$

The pressure at state 2 is given by

$$\frac{P_2}{T_2} = \frac{P_1}{T_1}$$

for constant volume process 1-2.

Therefore, $$P_2 = \frac{P_1 T_2}{T_1}$$

$$= \frac{224 \times 5519}{1133}$$

i.e., $$P_2 = 1091 \text{ psia}$$

Consider the isentropic expansion process 2-3. The pressure and temperature at state 3 can be found from the isentropic relations.

$$\frac{P_3}{P_2} = \left(\frac{v_2}{v_3}\right)^k$$

$$\frac{T_3}{T_2} = \left(\frac{v_2}{v_3}\right)^{k-1}$$

Therefore,

$$P_3 = P_2 \left(\frac{1}{R_c}\right)^k$$

$$= 1091 \left(\frac{1}{7}\right)^{1.4}$$

$$P_3 = 71.6 \text{ psia}$$

$$T_3 = T_2 \left(\frac{1}{R_c}\right)^{k-1}$$

$$= 5519 \left(\frac{1}{7}\right)^{0.4}$$

$$T_3 = 2534°R \ (2074°F)$$

The calculations can be verified by calculating the pressure and temperature at state 4 from the constant volume heat rejection process (3-4) relations.

Therefore, the pressure and temperature at all the salient points of the Otto cycle are:

STATE	PRESSURE psia	TEMPERATURE °F
1	224	673
2	1091	5059
3	71.6	2074
4	14.7	60

(b) The thermal efficiency of the cycle is given by

$$\eta_{th} = 1 - \frac{T_4}{T_1}$$

$$= 1 - \frac{1}{(R_c)^{k-1}}$$

Substituting the values,

$$\eta_{th} = 1 - \frac{1}{(7)^{1.4-1}}$$

$$= 0.541$$

The mean effective pressure is defined as

$$mep = \frac{\text{Net work done}}{\text{Stroke volume}}$$

$$\text{Net work done} = \eta_{th} \times Q_s$$

$$= 0.541 \times 750$$

$$= 405.75 \text{ Btu}$$

Stroke volume is defined as $v_4 - v_1$.

$$v_4 - v_1 = v_1\left(\frac{v_4}{v_1} - 1\right)$$

$$= v_1(R_c - 1)$$

The volume at state 1 is given from the ideal gas equation.

$$v_1 = \frac{RT_1}{P_1}$$

$$= 53.34 \times \frac{1133}{224 \times 144}$$

$$= 1.87 \text{ ft}^3/\text{lbm}$$

Therefore, stroke volume is $1.87(7-1) = 11.22 \text{ ft}^3/\text{lbm}$.

Substituting into the equation for mep,

$$mep = \frac{405.75 \times 778}{11.22 \times 144}$$

$$= 195.4 \text{ psi}$$

• PROBLEM 9-9

> Air at 14 lbf/in², 540°R is supplied to an open Otto cycle with a compression ratio of 9. The maximum temperature for the cycle is 2500°F. Compute the amount of heat supplied and rejected per lbm of air, the total work done per lbm of air, and the thermal efficiency of the cycle. Use the air tables to solve the problem.

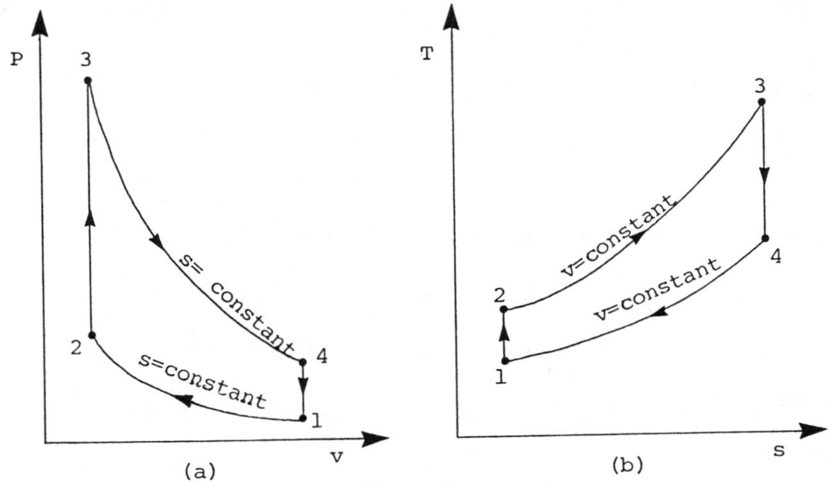

Fig. 1.

Solution: The air tables result in a more accurate answer than the use of the ideal gas equation of state does. This is due to the fact that the air tables take into account the variation of the specific heats due to the difference in temperatures, whereas the ideal gas equation does not.

From the air tables at $T_1 = 540°R$,

$$v_{r1} = 144.32$$

$$u_1 = 92.04 \text{ Btu/lbm}$$

Process 1-2 is an isentropic process. Therefore, from the isentropic relations,

$$v_{r_2} = v_{r_1}\left(\frac{V_2}{V_1}\right)$$

$$= 144.32\left(\frac{1}{9}\right)$$

$$= 16.04$$

From the air tables at $v_{r_2} = 16.04$,

$$T_2 = 1,264.8°R$$

$$u_2 = 221.19 \text{ Btu/lbm}$$

At $T_3 = 2500°F = 2960°R$,

$$v_{r_3} = 1.233$$

$$u_3 = 576.1 \text{ Btu/lbm}$$

Process 3-4 is also an isentropic process. Hence

$$v_{r_4} = v_{r_3}\left(\frac{V_4}{V_3}\right)$$

$$= 1.233\ (9)$$

$$= 11.10$$

Then at $v_{r_4} = 11.10$, the air tables give

$$T_4 = 1443.26°R$$

$$u_4 = 255.32 \text{ Btu/lbm}$$

Heat is supplied during process 2-3 and is rejected during process 1-4. For the heat added,

$$q_{2-3} = u_3 - u_2$$

$$= 576.1 - 221.19$$

$$= 354.91 \text{ Btu/lbm}$$

The heat rejected is

$$-q_{4-1} = u_4 - u_1$$

$$= 255.32 - 92.04$$

$$= 163.28 \text{ Btu/lbm}$$

The net work produced is

$$w_{net} = q_{2-?} + q_{4-1}$$

$$= 354.91 - 163.28$$

$$= 191.63 \text{ Btu/lbm}$$

The efficiency of the cycle is

$$\eta_{th} = \frac{w_{net}}{q_{in}}$$

$$= \frac{191.63}{354.91}$$

$$= 0.54$$

$$= 54\%.$$

• PROBLEM 9-10

> An air standard Otto cycle of 48% thermal efficiency has air at 25°C and 1 bar at the beginning of the isentropic compression. Calculate the temperature and pressure of air at the end of the isentropic compression process.

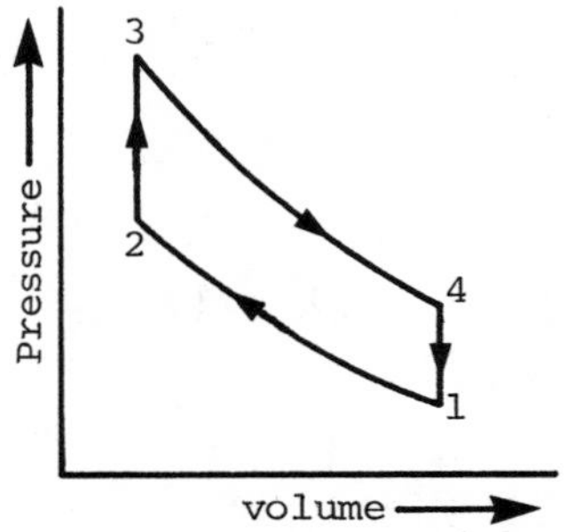

Solution: The figure shows the Otto cycle on a P-v diagram. 1-2 is the isentropic compression process. It is necessary to know the compression ratio $\left(\frac{V_1}{V_2}\right)$ in order to determine the state 2 from the isentropic process relations. The compression ratio can be obtained from the equation of thermal efficiency.

$$\eta_{th} = 1 - \frac{1}{R_c^{\,k-1}}$$

where η_{th} = thermal efficiency

R_c = compression ratio

k = ratio of specific heats (1.4 for air)

Substituting the values and calculating for R_c,

$$0.48 = 1 - \frac{1}{R_c^{0.4}}$$

$$R_c^{-0.4} = 1-0.48$$

$$R_c = 5.13$$

i.e.,

$$\frac{V_1}{V_2} = 5.13$$

For the isentropic process 1-2,

$$\frac{P_2}{P_1} = \left(\frac{V_1}{V_2}\right)^k$$

Therefore,

$$P_2 = P_1 \left(\frac{V_1}{V_2}\right)^k$$

Substituting the values,

$$P_2 = 1(5.13)^{1.4}$$

$$= 9.87 \text{ bars}$$

For the isentropic process 1-2,

$$\frac{T_2}{T_1} = \left(\frac{V_1}{V_2}\right)^{k-1}$$

Therefore,

$$T_2 = T_1 \left(\frac{V_1}{V_2}\right)^{k-1}$$

$$= (25 + 273)(5.13)^{1.4-1}$$

$$T_2 = 573°K = 300°C$$

Therefore, the temperature and pressure at the end of the isentropic compression are 300°C and 9.87 bars, respectively.

• PROBLEM 9-11

An air standard Otto cycle in which the salient points are 1, 2, 3 and 4 has fixed upper and lower limits of absolute temperatures T_3 and T_1, respectively. If maximum work per unit mass of air is to be done, show that

(a) the compression ratio $R_c = \left(\frac{T_3}{T_1}\right)^{\frac{1}{2(k-1)}}$

(b) the intermediate temperature $T_2 = T_4 = \sqrt{T_1 T_3}$

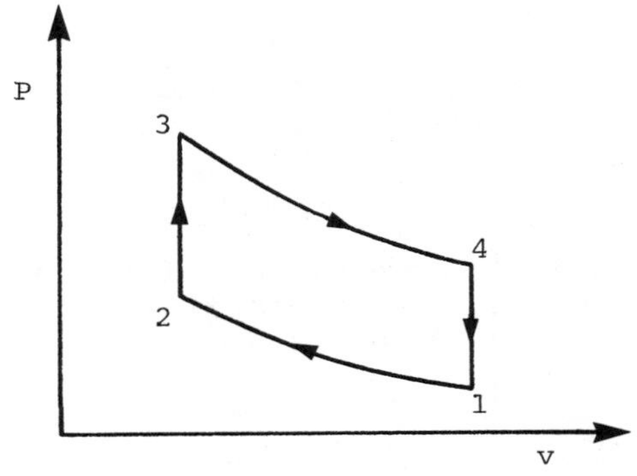

Solution: The net work done during a cycle is given by

$$W_{net} = Q_s - Q_r$$

where W_{net} = net work done

Q_s = heat supplied

Q_r = heat rejected

Heat is added during the constant volume process 2-3.

So, for unit mass of air,

$$Q_s = C_v(T_3 - T_2)$$

where C_v = constant volume specific heat.

Heat is rejected during the constant volume process 4-1, so for unit mass of air,

$$Q_r = C_v(T_4 - T_1)$$

Therefore,

$$W_{net} = C_v(T_3-T_2) - C_v(T_4-T_1)$$

$$= C_v[T_3-T_2-T_4+T_1] \qquad (1)$$

For the isentropic compression process 1-2,

$$\frac{T_2}{T_1} = \left(\frac{v_1}{v_2}\right)^{k-1}$$

where k = ratio of specific heats

Therefore, the temperature at state 2, in terms of T_1 and the compression ratio (R_c), is

$$T_2 = T_1\left(\frac{v_1}{v_2}\right)^{k-1}$$

$$= T_1(R_c)^{k-1} \qquad (2)$$

Similarly, from the consideration of the isentropic expansion process 3-4, the temperature at state 4, in terms of T_3 and compression ratio (R_c), is

$$T_4 = \frac{T_3}{R_c^{k-1}} \qquad (3)$$

Substituting the values of T_2 and T_4 into equation (1),

$$W_{net} = C_v\left[T_3 + T_1 - T_1R_c^{k-1} - \frac{T_3}{R_c^{k-1}}\right]$$

Since T_1 and T_3 are fixed for the given cycle, the net work is a function of R_c only. The net work will be maximum when

$$\frac{d(W_{net})}{dR_c} = 0$$

Hence, taking the derivative of the above expression,

$$\frac{d(W_{net})}{dR_c} = -T_1(k-1)R_c^{k-2} + T_3(k-1)R_c^{-k} = 0$$

Simplifying,

$$T_1R_c^{k-2} = T_3R_c^{-k}$$

i.e., $$R_c^{2k-2} = \frac{T_3}{T_1}$$

$$R_c^{2(k-1)} = \frac{T_3}{T_1}$$

Therefore,

$$R_c = \left(\frac{T_3}{T_1}\right)^{\frac{1}{2(k-1)}}$$

(b) The compression ratio for maximum work output is

$$R_c = \left(\frac{T_3}{T_1}\right)^{\frac{1}{2(k-1)}}$$

Equation (2) states that

$$T_2 = T_1(R_c)^{k-1}$$

Substituting the value of R_c,

$$T_2 = T_1\left[\left(\frac{T_3}{T_1}\right)^{\frac{1}{2(k-1)}}\right]^{k-1}$$

i.e.,

$$T_2 = T_1\left(\frac{T_3}{T_1}\right)^{\frac{1}{2}}$$

$$= \sqrt{T_1 T_3}$$

Similarly, from equation (3),

$$T_4 = \frac{T_3}{R_c^{k-1}} = T_3\ R_c^{-(k-1)}$$

Substituting the value of R_c,

$$T_4 = T_3\left[\left(\frac{T_3}{T_1}\right)^{-(k-1)}\right]^{\frac{1}{2(k-1)}}$$

$$= T_3\left(\frac{T_3}{T_1}\right)^{-\frac{1}{2}}$$

$$= T_3\left(\frac{T_1}{T_3}\right)^{\frac{1}{2}}$$

i.e.,

$$T_4 = \sqrt{T_1 T_3}$$

Therefore, for maximum work output,

$$T_2 = T_4 = \sqrt{T_1 T_3}$$

THE DIESEL CYCLE

• PROBLEM 9-12

Consider an air standard Diesel cycle. At the beginning of compression the temperature is 300°K and the pressure is 101.35 kPa. If the compression ratio is 15 and during the process 1860 kJ/kg of air are added as heat, calculate; (a) the maximum cycle pressure and temperature, (b) the thermal efficiency of the cycle, and (c) the mep.

Solution: Referring to the figure for the states, and using the ideal gas equation of state

$$Pv = RT \tag{1}$$

the specific volume at state d is

$$v_d = \frac{RT_d}{P_d}$$

$$= \frac{0.287(300)}{101.35}$$

$$= 0.8495 \text{ m}^3/\text{kg}$$

Process c→d is an isochoric (constant volume) process. Hence

$$v_c = v_d = 0.8495 \text{ m}^3/\text{kg}$$

The compression ratio is

$$r_v = \frac{v_d}{v_a} = 15$$

or

$$= \frac{v_d}{15}$$

$$= \frac{0.8495}{15}$$

$$= 0.0566 \text{ m}^3/\text{kg}$$

Process d→a is an isentropic process. Therefore,

$$\frac{T_a}{T_d} = \left(\frac{v_d}{v_a}\right)^{k-1}$$

or

$$T_a = 300\left(\frac{0.8495}{0.0566}\right)^{1.4-1}$$

$$= 886.5°\text{K}$$

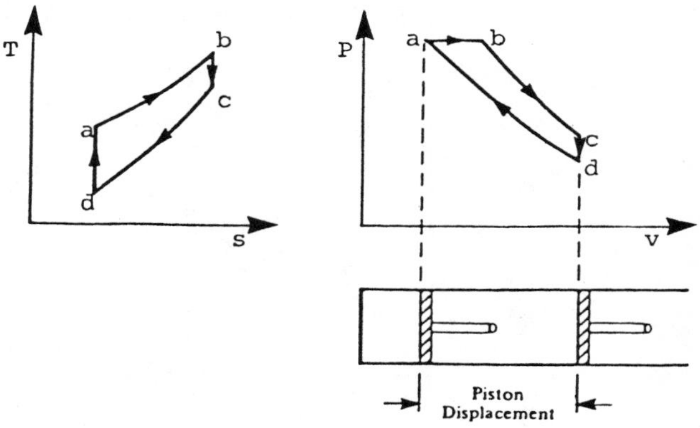

Fig. 1. Diesel Cycle

Also,

$$\frac{P_a}{P_d} = \left(\frac{v_d}{v_a}\right)^k$$

or

$$P_a = 101.35 \left(\frac{0.8495}{0.0566}\right)^{1.4}$$

$$= 4,495 \text{ kPa}$$

$$\therefore \; P_{max} = P_a = 4,495 \text{ kPa}$$

The maximum temperature can be obtained as follows. From the first law, assuming constant specific heats, the heat supplied is

$$Q_{in} = Q_{ab} = C_p \, (T_b - T_a)$$

or

$$T_b = \frac{Q_{ab}}{C_p} + T_a$$

$$= \frac{1860}{1.0035} + 886.5$$

$$= 2,740°K$$

$$\therefore \; T_{max} = T_b = 2,740°K$$

(b) The thermal efficiency of the Diesel cycle is

$$\eta_{th} = 1 - \frac{(T_c - T_d)}{k(T_b - T_a)} \tag{2}$$

T_c can be obtained from the isentropic relation

$$\frac{T_b}{T_c} = \left(\frac{v_c}{v_b}\right)^{k-1} \tag{3}$$

where

$$v_b = \frac{RT_b}{P_b} \qquad \text{from equation (1)}$$

$$= \frac{0.287(2{,}740)}{4{,}495}$$

$$= 0.1749 \text{ m}^3/\text{kg}$$

Substituting into (3),

$$\frac{T_b}{T_c} = \left(\frac{0.8495}{0.1749}\right)^{1.4-1}$$

or

$$\frac{T_b}{T_c} = 1.88$$

Solving for T_c,

$$T_c = \frac{2{,}740}{1.88}$$

$$= 1{,}457.5°\text{K}$$

From Eq. (2), then,

$$\eta_{th} = 1 - \frac{(1{,}457.5-300)}{1.4(2{,}740-886.5)}$$

$$= 1 - \frac{1{,}157.5}{2{,}594.9}$$

$$= 0.554$$

(c) The mean effective pressure (mep) is defined as

$$\text{mep} = \frac{W_{net}}{v_d - v_a} \tag{4}$$

where

$$W_{net} = \eta_{th}\, Q_{in}$$

$$= 0.554\ (1860)$$

$$= 1030.44 \text{ kJ/kg}$$

Substituting into (4),

$$\text{mep} = \frac{1030.44}{(0.8495-0.0566)}$$

$$= 1299.6 \text{ kPa}$$

• PROBLEM 9-13

Determine the work output per kilogram mass of air and the thermal efficiency of an air-standard Diesel cycle with a cutoff ratio (r_c) of 2 and r_v = 15, assuming that the inlet conditions are 101.35 kPa and 21°C.

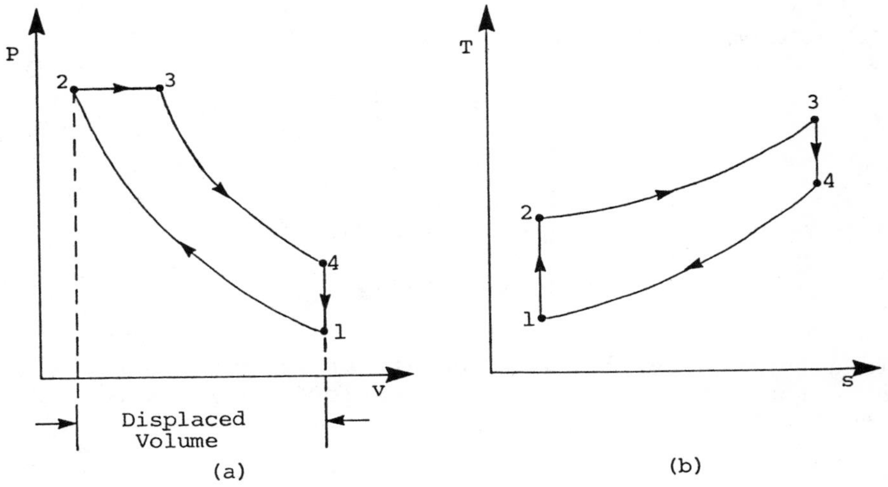

Fig. 1. Cycle diagrams for air-standard diesel cycle. (a) p-V diagram; (b) T-s diagram.

Solution: Referring to the accompanying figure, the condition at state 1 is:

$$T_1 = 21°C = 294°K$$

$$P_1 = 101.35 \text{ kPa.}$$

Process 1-2 is isentropic and hence

$$\frac{T_2}{T_1} = \left(\frac{V_1}{V_2}\right)^{k-1} \qquad (1)$$

But, given that the compression ratio

$$r_v = \frac{v_1}{v_2} = 15$$

thus eq. (1) becomes

$$\frac{T_2}{T_1} = (r_v)^{k-1}$$

or

$$T_2 = 294(15)^{1.4-1} = 868.5°K$$

For the constant-pressure heat-addition process (2-3),

$$\frac{v_3}{v_2} = \frac{T_3}{T_2} \qquad (2)$$

But the cut off ratio r_c is defined as $r_c = \frac{V_3}{V_2}$

Hence from equation (2),

$$r_c = \frac{T_3}{T_2}$$

or

$$T_3 = T_2(r_c)$$

$$= 868.5\ (2.0)$$

$$= 1737°K$$

To determine the temperature at the end of the power stroke, note that process 3-4 is an isentropic process. Hence from the isentropic relation

$$\frac{T_4}{T_3} = \left(\frac{v_3}{v_4}\right)^{k-1}$$

$$T_4 = T_3\left(\frac{v_3}{v_4}\right)^{k-1} \qquad (3)$$

From the figure, $v_1 = v_4$, hence

$$\frac{v_3}{v_4} = \frac{v_3}{v_1} = \frac{v_3/v_2}{v_1/v_2} = \frac{2}{15}$$

Then from eq. (3),

$$T_4 = 1737\left(\frac{2}{15}\right)^{0.4} = 776°K$$

The work output is defined as

$$w = q_H - q_L \qquad (4)$$

where q_H = heat added during the constant pressure process 2-3.

q_L = heat rejected during the constant volume process 4-1.

Assuming specific heats to be constant, eq. (4) can be written as

$$w = c_p(T_3 - T_2) - c_v(T_4 - T_1)$$

$$= 1.0035(1737-868.5) - 0.7165(776-294)$$

$$= 871.54 - 345.35$$

$$= 526.19 \text{ kJ/kg}$$

The thermal efficiency of the cycle is

$$\eta_{th} = \frac{w}{q_H}$$

$$= \frac{526.19}{871.54}$$

$$= 0.6037$$

or

$$\eta_{th} = 60.37\%$$

• PROBLEM 9-14

An air standard ideal Diesel engine (k for air = 1.4) operates with a pressure and temperature at the start of the compression stroke of 14.7 psia and 550°R. If the cut-off ratio and clearance volume are 2.5 and 1.0 ft^3, respectively, calculate

(a) Pressure, temperature and specific volume at the 4 states of the cycle

(b) the clearance

(c) the thermal efficiency

(d) mep for the cycle.

Solution: Referring to the figure, the pressure and temperature at state 1 are given as

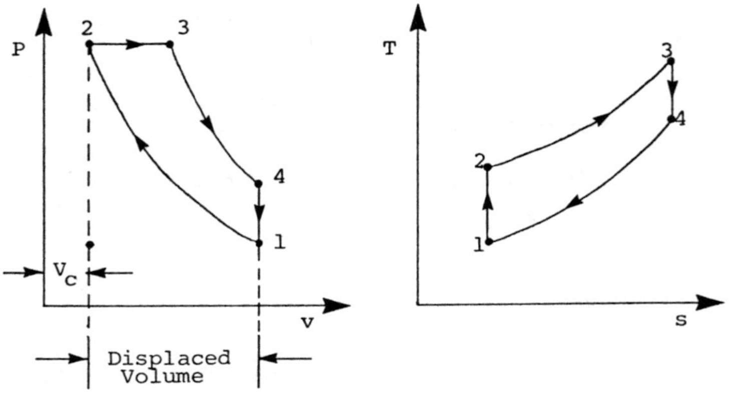

Representation of the Diesel cycle.

$$P_1 = 14.7 \text{ psia}$$

$$T_1 = 550°R$$

Therefore, the specific volume at state 1 can be obtained by using the perfect gas equation of state

$$v_1 = \frac{RT_1}{P_1}$$

Substituting the values,

$$v_1 = \frac{53.35 \times 550}{14.7 \times 144}$$

$$= 13.86 \text{ ft}^3/\text{lbm}$$

At state 2, given $v_2 = 1.0$ ft^3/lbm.

Pressure P_2 can be obtained from the isentropic compression process relation

$$\frac{P_2}{P_1} = \left(\frac{v_1}{v_2}\right)^k$$

Therefore,

$$P_2 = 14.7 \left(\frac{13.86}{1.0}\right)^{1.4}$$

$$= 583 \text{ psia}$$

The temperature T_2 is given by

$$\frac{T_2}{T_1} = \left(\frac{v_1}{v_2}\right)^{k-1}$$

Therefore,

$$T_2 = 550 \left(\frac{13.86}{1}\right)^{0.4}$$

$$= 1574°R$$

At 3, the specific volume is obtained using the cutoff ratio.

$$r_c = \frac{v_3}{v_2} = 2.5$$

or

$$v_3 = 2.5\ v_2$$

$$= 2.5 \times 1.0$$

$$= 2.5\ ft^3/lbm$$

The temperature at state 3 can be obtained from the constant pressure process relation

$$\frac{v_3}{T_3} = \frac{v_2}{T_2}$$

or

$$T_3 = T_2 \frac{v_3}{v_2}$$

$$= 1574 \times 2.5$$

$$= 3935°R$$

Since the process 2-3 is a constant pressure process,

$$P_2 = P_3 = 583 \text{ psia}$$

At state 4, $v_4 = v_1 = 13.86\ ft^3/lbm$.

The temperature T_4 is obtained from the isentropic relation

$$\frac{T_4}{T_3} = \left(\frac{v_3}{v_4}\right)^{k-1}$$

or

$$T_4 = 3935 \left(\frac{2.5}{13.86}\right)^{0.4}$$

$$= 1983°R$$

The pressure P_4 is

$$P_4 = P_3\left(\frac{v_3}{v_4}\right)^{k}$$

$$= 583 \left(\frac{2.5}{13.86}\right)^{1.4}$$

$$= 53 \text{ psia}$$

Therefore, the 4 states are:

STATE	PRESSURE psia	TEMPERATURE °R	SP. VOLUME ft^3/lbm
1	14.7	550	13.86
2	583	1574	1.0
3	583	3935	2.5
4	53	1983	13.86

(b) The clearance is obtained by using the equation

$$v_c = Cv_D$$

where C = clearance

v_C = clearance volume

v_D = piston displacement volume

The piston displacement volume is given by

$$v_D = v_1 - v_2$$

$$= 13.86 - 1$$

$$= 12.86 \text{ ft}^3/\text{lbm}$$

Therefore,

$$C = \frac{v_C}{v_D}$$

$$= \frac{1}{12.86} \quad (\text{since } v_C = v_2)$$

$$= 0.078$$

i.e.,

$$C = 7.8\%$$

(c) The thermal efficiency can be obtained using the heat quantities. Hence

$$\eta_{th} = \frac{q_{in} - q_{out}}{q_{in}} \times 100\%$$

where

$$q_{in} = C_p(T_3 - T_2)$$

$$= 0.24(3935-1574)$$

$$= 566.64 \text{ Btu/lbm}$$

and

$$q_{out} = C_v(T_4 - T_1)$$

$$= 0.173(1983-550)$$

$$= 247.91 \text{ Btu/lbm}$$

Therefore,

$$\eta_{th} = \frac{566.64 - 247.91}{566.64} \times 100\%$$

$$= 56.25\%$$

(d) The mean effective pressure (mep) of the cycle is

$$mep = \frac{w_{net}}{v_1 - v_2}$$

where

$$w_{net} = q_{in} - q_{out}$$

$$= 566.64-247.91$$

$$= 318.73 \text{ Btu/lbm}$$

Therefore,

$$mep = \frac{318.73}{13.86-1} \times 778$$

$$= 19282 \text{ lbf/ft}^2$$

$$= 134 \text{ psi.}$$

• PROBLEM 9-15

An oil engine has six cylinders, each of 4.5 in bore and 5.0 in stroke. They work on a theoretical Diesel cycle. The initial pressure and temperature of the air are 14.7 psia and 75°F. The clearance volume is 10% of the stroke volume. The temperature reached during the combustion is 2700°F. Find the following:

(a) compression ratio

(b) pressure and temperature at the end of compression

(c) the thermal efficiency

(d) the H.P. of engine if the working speed is 2200 rpm.

Use air tables to solve the problem.

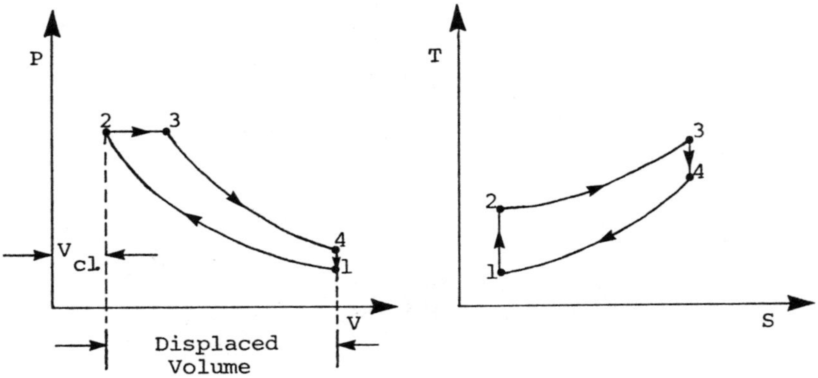

Diesel cycle

Solution: (a) Referring to the P-v diagram, the stroke volume or displaced volume is $(V_1 - V_2)$ and the clearance volume is V_2.

Given $$\frac{V_2}{V_1 - V_2} = 0.1$$

i.e., $$\frac{1}{\left(\frac{V_1}{V_2}\right) - 1} = 0.1$$

But $\frac{V_1}{V_2}$ = compression ratio (r_c).

Thus, $$\frac{1}{r_c - 1} = 0.1$$

or $$r_c - 1 = 10$$

Therefore, $r_c = 11$.

(b) Assuming ideal gas behavior, the specific volume at state 1 is given by

$$v_1 = \frac{RT_1}{P_1}$$

$$= \frac{53.35 \times 535}{14.7 \times 144}$$

$$= 13.48 \text{ ft}^3/\text{lbm}$$

Thus, the specific volume at state 2 is

$$v_2 = \frac{v_1}{r_c}$$

$$= \frac{13.48}{11}$$

$$= 1.225 \text{ ft}^3/\text{lbm}$$

The pressure and temperature at state 2 can be obtained by using air tables as follows.

From the air tables at T = 535°R ,

$$v_{r_1} = 147.89$$

$$P_{r_1} = 1.34$$

$$u_1 = 91.19 \text{ Btu/lbm}$$

Then, from the compression ratio,

$$v_{r_2} = v_{r_1}\left(\frac{v_2}{v_1}\right)$$

$$= \frac{147.89}{11}$$

$$= 13.44$$

Corresponding to this value of v_{r_2}, from the tables,

$$T_2 = 1348°R$$

$$P_{r_2} = 37.19$$

$$h_2 = 329.45 \text{ Btu/lbm}$$

The pressure at state 2 is given by the relation

$$\frac{P_2}{P_1} = \frac{P_{r_2}}{P_{r_1}}$$

Therefore,

$$P_2 = 14.7\left(\frac{37.19}{1.34}\right)$$

$$= 408 \text{ psia}$$

(c) The thermal efficiency of the cycle is given by

$$\eta_{th} = 1 - \frac{q_{out}}{q_{in}}$$

$$= 1 - \frac{u_4 - u_1}{h_3 - h_2}$$

The values of u_1 and h_2 are known from the previous table readings.

The temperature during the combustion reaches 2700°F,

i.e., $$T_3 = (2700 + 460)°R$$
$$= 3160°R$$

Corresponding to this temperature,

$$h_3 = 837.7 \text{ Btu/lbm}$$
$$v_{r_3} = 0.995$$

From the perfect gas law, the specific volume at state 3 is

$$v_3 = \frac{RT_3}{P_3} = \frac{RT_3}{P_2}$$

$$= \frac{53.35 \times 3160}{408 \times 144} = 2.87 \text{ ft}^3/\text{lbm}$$

and $$v_{r_4} = v_{r_3}\left(\frac{v_4}{v_3}\right) = v_{r_3}\left(\frac{v_1}{v_3}\right)$$

$$= 0.995\left(\frac{13.48}{2.87}\right)$$

$$= 4.67.$$

From the air tables at $v_{r_4} = 4.67$,

the corresponding values are

$$T_4 = 1940°R$$

$$u_4 = 355.12 \text{ Btu/lbm}$$

Substituting the values into the equation for thermal efficiency,

$$\eta_{th} = 1 - \left(\frac{355.12 - 91.19}{837.7 - 329.45}\right)$$

$$= 1 - \left(\frac{263.93}{508.25}\right)$$

$$= 0.48$$

i.e., $$\eta_{th} = 48\%$$

(d) The net work output per cycle is given by

$$W = mw$$

where m = total mass of air used per cycle in all six cylinders

w = work output of one cylinder per cycle

w is given by

$$w = q_{in} - q_{out}$$

$$= 508.25 - 263.93$$

$$w = 244.32 \text{ Btu/lbm}$$

m is given by

$$m = 6 \times \frac{V_1}{v_1}$$

where V_1 = total volume of the cylinder

= clearance volume + displacement volume

= 1.1×(displacement volume)

$$= 1.1 \left[\frac{\pi}{4} \times \left(\frac{4.5}{12}\right)^2 \times \frac{5}{12}\right]$$

$$V_1 = 0.05062 \text{ ft}^3$$

Therefore,

$$m = 6 \times \frac{0.05062}{13.48}$$

$$= 0.02253 \text{ lbm/cycle}$$

Therefore,

$$W = 0.02253 \times 244.32$$

$$= 5.506 \text{ Btu/cycle}$$

Therefore the H.P. of the engine is

$$\text{H.P.} = W \times \frac{\text{rpm}}{2}$$

since there is 1 cycle for every 2 revolutions.

$$\text{H.P.} = 5.506 \times \frac{2200}{2} \times \frac{60}{2545}$$

$$= 142.8 \text{ hp}$$

THE DUAL CYCLE

• PROBLEM 9-16

The compression ratio of an air-standard dual cycle is 9. The conditions at the beginning of compression are 14.7 psi, 80°F; and during the process, 450 Btu/lbm of heat are added at constant volume, and 350 Btu/lbm of heat are added at constant pressure. Determine the maximum temperature and pressure, the thermal efficiency and the mep of the cycle.

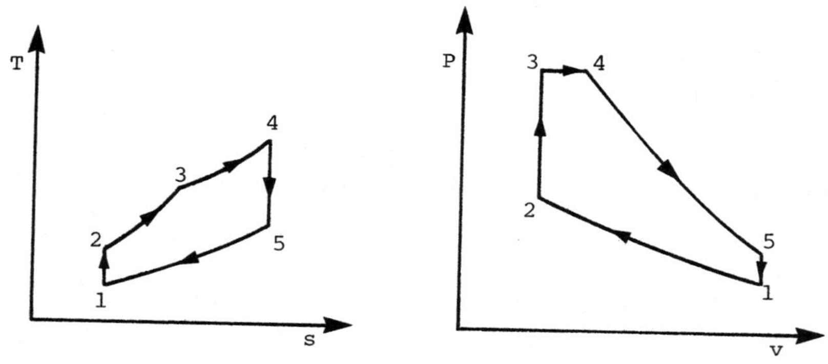

Solution: Referring to the accompanying figure, note that the maximum temperature occurs at point 4 and the maximum pressure occurs at point 3. However since the only state known is state 1, first find the pressure and temperature at state 2.

Process 1-2 is an isentropic process. Hence

$$\frac{P_2}{P_1} = \left(\frac{v_1}{v_2}\right)^k$$

But, the compression ratio is

$$\frac{v_1}{v_2} = r_v = 9$$

Therefore ,

$$P_2 = P_1(r_v)^{1.4}$$

$$= 14.7\ (9)^{1.4}$$

$$= 318.61 \text{ psi}$$

The temperature T_2 is

$$T_2 = T_1(r_v)^{k-1}$$

$$= 540\ (9)^{1.4-1}$$

$$= 1300°R$$

Process 2-3 is a constant-volume process. Therefore, for the constant volume heating process,

$$(q_{in})_V = c_v(T_3-T_2)$$

or

$$T_3 = \frac{q_{in}}{c_v} + T_2$$

$$= \frac{450}{0.1715} + 1300$$

$$= 3924$$

The pressure P_3 is

$$P_3 = P_2\left(\frac{T_3}{T_2}\right)$$

$$= 318.61\ \left(\frac{3924}{1300}\right)$$

$$= 962 \text{ psi}$$

$$\therefore \quad P_{max} = P_3 = P_4 = 962 \text{ psi}$$

To find the temperature at point 4, consider the constant-pressure heating process 3-4 .

$$(q_{in})_P = c_p(T_4-T_3)$$

or

$$T_4 = \frac{q_{in}}{c_p} + T_3$$

$$= \frac{350}{0.24} + 3924$$

$$= 5382°R$$

$$\therefore \quad T_{max} = T_4 = 5382°R$$

The thermal efficiency of the dual cycle is

$$\eta_{th} = \frac{W_{net}}{Q_{in}} = \frac{Q_{in}-Q_{out}}{Q_{in}} \qquad (1)$$

where

$$Q_{in} = 450 + 350 = 800 \text{ Btu (for 1 lbm air)}$$

$$Q_{out} = c_v(T_5 - T_1) \qquad (2)$$

The temperature at 5 is

$$\frac{T_5}{T_4} = \left(\frac{v_4}{v_5}\right)^{k-1}$$

or

$$T_5 = T_4\left(\frac{v_4}{v_5}\right)^{0.4} \qquad (3)$$

Also,

$$\frac{v_4}{v_3} = \frac{T_4}{T_3}$$

$$= \frac{5382}{3924} = 1.372$$

$$\frac{v_5}{v_3} = \frac{v_1}{v_2} = 9$$

Hence

$$\frac{v_4}{v_5} = \frac{v_4/v_3}{v_5/v_3} = \frac{1.372}{9} = 0.1524$$

From eq. (3), then

$$T_5 = 5382(0.1524)^{0.4} = 2536°R$$

Substituting into eq. (2),

$$Q_{out} = (0.1715)(2536-540)$$

$$= 342.3 \text{ Btu}$$

Finally, from eq. (1),

$$\eta_{th} = \frac{800-342.3}{800} = 0.572$$

or

$$\eta_{th} = 57.2\%$$

The mep (mean effective pressure) is defined as

$$mep = \frac{W_{net}}{v_1 - v_2} \qquad (4)$$

with

$$v_1 = \frac{RT_1}{P_1}$$

$$= \frac{53.35(540)}{14.7 \times 144}$$

$$= 13.61 \ ft^3/lbm$$

and

$$v_2 = \frac{v_1}{9}$$

$$= \frac{13.61}{9}$$

$$= 1.51 \ ft^3/lbm$$

From eq. (4),

$$mep = \left(\frac{800-342.3}{13.61-1.51}\right) \times 778$$

$$= 29429 \ lbf/ft^2$$

$$= 204.4 \ psi$$

• PROBLEM 9-17

At the beginning of compression in an air-standard dual cycle, the pressure and temperature of the air are 100 kPa and 27°C. During the isentropic compression process, the volume of the air is reduced from 0.0708 m^3 to 0.0042 m^3, and during the constant pressure process, the temperature of the air is increased from 1149°C to 1593°C. Compute (a) the cutoff and compression ratios, (b) the heat added and rejected, and (c) the thermal efficiency for the cycle, using the air tables.

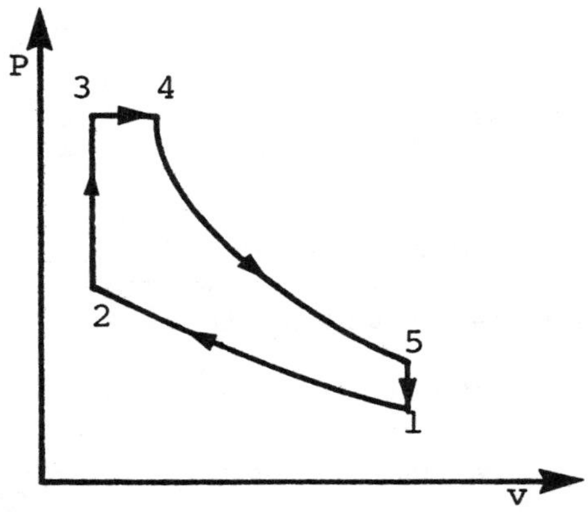

(a)

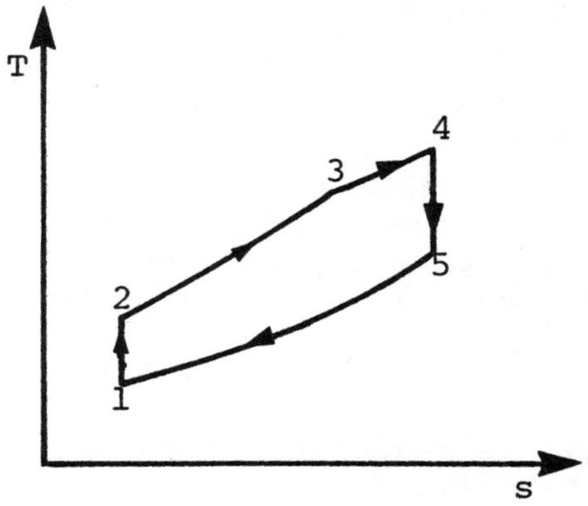

(b)

Solution: (a) The cutoff ratio is, by definition,

$$r_{cut.} = \frac{V_4}{V_3} \quad (1)$$

and the compression ratio is

$$r_v = \frac{V_1}{V_2} \quad (2)$$

Referring to the accompanying figure and using the given data, note that

$$T_3 = 1149°C = 1422°K$$

$$T_4 = 1593°C = 1866°K$$

$$V_3 = 0.0042 \text{ m}^3$$

and

$$P_3 = P_4.$$

Process 3-4 is a constant pressure process and so

$$\frac{V_4}{V_3} = \frac{T_4}{T_3}$$

or

$$V_4 = V_3\left(\frac{T_4}{T_3}\right)$$

$$= 0.0042 \left(\frac{1866}{1422}\right)$$

$$= 0.0055 \text{ m}^3$$

From eq. (1),

$$r_{cut} = \frac{0.0055}{0.0042} = 1.31$$

and from eq. (2),

$$r_v = \frac{0.0708}{0.0042} = 16.86$$

(b) In the cycle, heat is added during processes 2-3 and 3-4, and is rejected during process 5-1 (as shown in the figure). The heat added to the system in the cycle is

$$Q_{in} = m\left[(u_3-u_2) + (h_4-h_3)\right] \quad (3)$$

Heat is rejected during the constant volume process 5-1 and can be found as

$$Q_{out} = m(u_5-u_1) \quad (4)$$

From the given data,

$$T_1 = 27°C = 300°K$$

$$V_1 = 0.0708 \text{ m}^3$$

Using the air tables, the relative volume at 1 is

$$v_{r_1} = 144.32$$

From the relation

$$\frac{v_{r_2}}{v_{r_1}} = \frac{V_2}{V_1}$$

obtain

$$v_{r_2} = v_{r_1}\left(\frac{V_2}{V_1}\right)$$

$$= 144.32\left(\frac{0.0042}{0.0708}\right)$$

$$= 8.56$$

For this value of v_{r_2}, from the air tables,

$$T_2 = 875°K = 605°C$$

$$u_2 = 656.46 \text{ kJ/kg}$$

and from the known values for T_3 and T_4,

$$u_3 = 1133.93 \text{ kJ/kg}$$

$$h_3 = 1542.14 \text{ kJ/kg}$$

$$h_4 = 2085.96 \text{ kJ/kg}$$

The mass of air at the beginning of compression is found by using the ideal gas equation of state.

$$m = \frac{P_1 V_1}{RT_1}$$

$$= \frac{100(0.0708)}{0.287(300)}$$

$$= 0.0822 \text{ kg}$$

Substituting the numerical values into eq. (3),

$$Q_{in} = 0.0822\left[(1133.93-656.46) + (2085.96-1542.14)\right]$$

$$= 0.0822(477.47 + 543.82)$$

$$\therefore \quad Q_{in} = 83.95 \text{ kJ}$$

Next consider the heat rejected by the system during the constant volume process 5-1.

At 4, the relative volume is found from the air tables to be

$$v_{r_4} = 0.812$$

and since $$V_5 = 0.0708\ m^3,$$

$$v_{r_5} = v_{r_4}\left(\frac{V_5}{V_4}\right)$$

$$= 0.812 \left(\frac{0.0708}{0.0055}\right)$$

$$= 10.45.$$

For this relative volume, using the air tables, obtain

$$T_5 = 819°K$$

$$u_5 = 607.87\ kJ/kg$$

$$u_1 = 214.09\ kJ/kg$$

From eq. (4), then

$$Q_{out} = 0.0822\ (607.87-214.09)$$

$$= 32.37\ kJ$$

(c) The thermal efficiency of the cycle is

$$\eta_{th} = \frac{Q_{in}-Q_{out}}{Q_{in}}$$

$$= \frac{83.95-32.37}{83.95}$$

$$= 0.614$$

or

$$\eta_{th} = 61.4\%$$

• PROBLEM 9-18

A dual cycle engine has a temperature and pressure at the beginning of isentropic compression of 180°F and 14.7 psia. The compression ratio is 10 and the maximum pressure is 1030 psia. The total heat supplied per lbm of air is 720 Btu. Determine the following:

(a) pressure and temperature at all the salient points

(b) air standard efficiency.

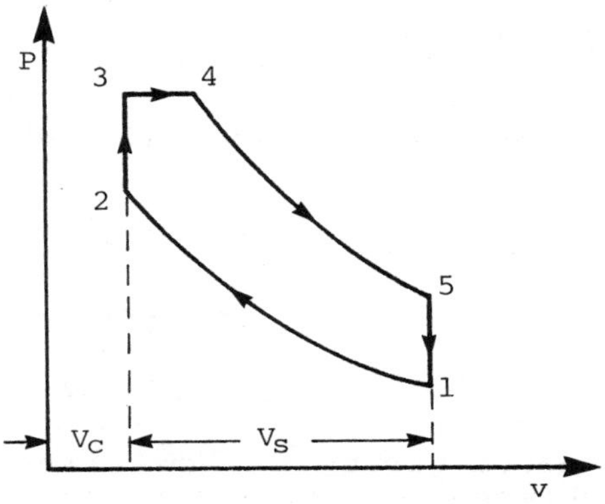

Solution: In a dual cycle, the heat is supplied to the compressed air partly at constant volume and partly at constant pressure.

Given, the pressure and temperature of air at the beginning of isentropic compression,

i.e.,
$$P_1 = 14.7 \text{ psia}$$
$$T_1 = 180°F$$
$$= (180 + 460) = 640°R$$

The pressure and temperature after isentropic compression are

$$P_2 = P_1\left(\frac{V_1}{V_2}\right)^k \quad (k_{air} = 1.4)$$

$$= 14.7\ (10)^{1.4} \quad = 369.25 \text{ psia}$$

$$T_2 = T_1\left(\frac{V_1}{V_2}\right)^{k-1}$$

$$= 640\ (10)^{1.4-1} \quad = 1608°R$$

The pressure after the constant volume heating is the maximum pressure of the cycle.

Therefore, $\quad P_3 = 1030$ psia

Since 2-3 is a constant volume heat addition process, on the basis of the perfect-gas equation,

$$T_3 = T_2 \frac{P_3}{P_2}$$

$$= 1608 \left(\frac{1030}{369.25}\right)$$

$$= 4485°R$$

Assuming constant specific heats, the heat added at constant volume is given by

$$Q_1 = C_v(T_3 - T_2)$$

$$= 0.171(4485-1608)$$

$$= 491.97 \text{ Btu/lbm}$$

Therefore, heat added during constant pressure process is the difference between the total heat supplied and the heat supplied during constant volume heat addition process.

i.e., $\quad Q_2$ (heat added at constant pressure)

$$= 720-491.97$$

$$= 228.03 \text{ Btu/lbm}$$

i.e., $\quad C_p(T_4 - T_3) = 228.03$

Substituting the values of C_p and T_3 and evaluating the value of T_4,

$$0.24\ (T_4 - 4485) = 228.03$$

$$T_4 = \frac{228.03}{0.24} + 4485$$

$$= 5435°R$$

Since 3-4 is a constant pressure heat addition process, the cut-off ratio is given by

$$r_{cut} = \frac{V_4}{V_3} = \frac{T_4}{T_3}$$

$$= \frac{5435}{4485}$$

$$= 1.212$$

Therefore, the expansion ratio

$$R_e = \frac{V_5}{V_4} = \frac{V_5}{V_2} \times \frac{V_3}{V_4}$$

since $V_2 = V_3$

But $\frac{V_5}{V_2} = \frac{V_1}{V_2}$ = compression ratio

Therefore, $R_e = \frac{10}{1.212}$

$$= 8.251$$

Process 4-5 is an isentropic expansion process. Thus, the pressure and temperature at the end of expansion, i.e., P_5 and T_5, are given by the isentropic relationships

$$P_5 = P_4\left(\frac{V_4}{V_5}\right)^k$$

$$= P_4\left(\frac{1}{R_e}\right)^k$$

$$= \frac{1030}{(8.251)^{1.4}}$$

i.e., $P_5 = 53.67$ psia

and $T_5 = T_4\left(\frac{V_4}{V_5}\right)^{k-1}$

$$= T_4\left(\frac{1}{R_e}\right)^{k-1}$$

$$= \frac{5435}{(8.251)^{1.4-1}}$$

i.e., $T_5 = 2337°R$

(b) Heat rejected during constant volume heat rejection process 5-1 is given by (assuming constant specific heats)

$$Q_r = C_v(T_5-T_1)$$

$$= 0.171(2337-640)$$

$$= 290.19 \text{ Btu/lbm}$$

and the heat supplied ,

$$Q_s = 720 \text{ Btu/lbm}$$

Therefore, the thermal efficiency of the cycle is

$$\eta_{th} = \frac{Q_s - Q_r}{Q_s}$$

$$= 1 - \frac{Q_r}{Q_s}$$

$$= 1 - \frac{290.19}{720}$$

$$= 0.5969$$

i.e., $\eta_{th} = 59.69\%$

• PROBLEM 9-19

A dual cycle oil engine has a compression ratio of 10 and an expansion ratio of 5.5. The air pressure and temperature are initially 14.7 psia and 540° R. The heat supplied at constant pressure is twice the heat supplied at constant volume. If the expansion and compression follow the law $PV^{1\,3}$ = constant, compute the following:

(a) Pressure and temperature at all salient points

(b) Mean effective pressure of the cycle

(c) Efficiency of the cycle

(d) H.P. of the engine, if there are 500 cycles/min.

Take the bore of the cylinder to be 10 in and stroke length of the piston to be 16 in.

Solution: Given the pressure and temperature of air at the beginning of isentropic compression process to be

$$P_1 = 14.7 \text{ psia}$$

$$T_1 = 540°R$$

the pressure and temperature after compression are

$$P_2 = P_1\left(\frac{V_1}{V_2}\right)^n \qquad (n = 1.3)$$

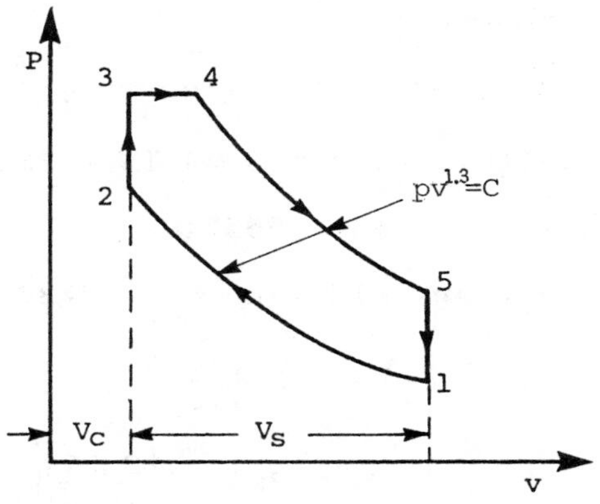

$$= 14.7\ (10)^{1.3}$$

$$P_2 = 293.3 \text{ psia}$$

and $$T_2 = T_1\left(\frac{V_1}{V_2}\right)^{n-1}$$

$$= 540(10)^{1.3-1}$$

$$= 1077°R$$

Given that heat added during constant pressure process is twice that of during constant volume, then, for constant specific heats,

$$C_p(T_4-T_3) = 2C_v(T_3-T_2) \qquad (1)$$

Now consider the constant pressure process 3-4. From ideal gas relations,

$$\frac{T_4}{T_3} = \frac{V_4}{V_3} = \frac{V_4}{V_5} \times \frac{V_5}{V_3}$$

But, since $V_1 = V_5$ and $V_2 = V_3$

and $\frac{V_5}{V_4}$ = expansion ratio = 5.5 ,

$$\frac{T_4}{T_3} = \frac{V_1}{V_2} \times \frac{V_4}{V_5}$$

$$= \frac{10}{5.5}$$

$$= 1.82$$

or $$T_4 = 1.82\ T_3$$

Substituting into equation (1),

$$0.24\,(1.82\,T_2 - T_3) = 2 \times 0.17\,(T_3 - 1077)$$

i.e., $$(0.24)(0.82\,T_3) = 0.34\,T_3 - 366.18$$

or $$T_3 = 2557°R$$

and from the constant volume process 2-3,

$$P_3 = P_2\left(\frac{T_3}{T_2}\right)$$

$$= 293.3\left(\frac{2557}{1077}\right)$$

$$= 696.35 \text{ psia}$$

For the state 4,

$$P_4 = P_3 = 696.35 \text{ psia}$$

and $$T_4 = 1.82\,T_3$$

$$= 1.82\,(2557)$$

$$= 4654°R$$

For the state 5,

$$P_5 = P_4\left(\frac{V_4}{V_5}\right)^n$$

$$= \frac{696.35}{(5.5)^{1.3}}$$

$$= 75.92 \text{ psia}$$

and

$$T_5 = T_4\left(\frac{V_4}{V_5}\right)^{n-1}$$

$$= \frac{4654}{(5.5)^{1.3-1}}$$

$$= 2791°R$$

(b) The mean effective pressure of the cycle is given by

$$\text{mep} = \frac{1}{(R_c - 1)}\left[P_3(\rho - 1) + \frac{P_4\rho - P_5 R_c}{n-1} - \frac{P_2 - P_1 R_c}{n-1}\right]$$

where R_c = compression ratio

ρ = cut-off ratio $\left(\frac{V_4}{V_3}\right)$

Substituting the values,

$$\text{mep} = \left[\frac{1}{(10.1)} \quad 696.35(1.82-1) + \frac{696.35(1.82) - 75.92(10)}{(1.3-1)} - \frac{293.3-14.7(10)}{(1.3-1)}\right]$$

$= 197.47$ psia.

(c) The stroke volume is

$$V_s = \frac{\pi}{4} d^2 \times L$$

$$= \frac{\pi}{4}\left(\frac{10}{12}\right)^2\left(\frac{16}{12}\right)$$

$$= 0.7272 \text{ ft}^3$$

The work done per cycle is

$$W = (\text{mep})(V_s)$$

$$= \frac{197.47 \times 144 \times 0.7272}{778}$$

$$= 26.58 \text{ Btu/cycle}$$

The volume of air at state 1 is given by

$$V_1 = V_s + V_c$$

$$= \left(\frac{R_c}{R_c-1}\right)V_s$$

$$= \frac{10}{9}(0.7272)$$

i.e., $V_1 = 0.808 \text{ ft}^3$

Mass of air per cycle is given by the perfect gas equation,

$$m = \frac{P_1V_1}{RT_1}$$

$$= \frac{14.7 \times 0.808 \times 144}{53.35 \times 540}$$

$$= 0.05937 \text{ lbm/cycle.}$$

The heat supplied per cycle is

$$Q = m\left[C_v(T_3-T_2) + C_p(T_4-T_3)\right]$$

$$= 3\ mC_v(T_3 - T_2) \qquad \text{from eq. (1)}$$

$$= 3 \times 0.05937 \times 0.171\ (2557-1077)$$

$$= 45.08 \text{ Btu/cycle}$$

Therefore, the thermal efficiency of the cycle is

$$\eta_{th} = \frac{26.58}{45.08}$$

$$= 0.5896$$

or

$$\eta_{th} = 58.96\%$$

(d) The work done per minute is

= work done per cycle × number of cycles per minute

$$= 26.58 \times 500$$

$$= 13290 \text{ Btu/min}$$

Therefore, HP of the engine is

$$\frac{13290}{42.42} = 313.3 \text{ HP}$$

THE BRAYTON CYCLE

• PROBLEM 9-20

The adiabatic efficiencies of the compressor and turbine used in an air-standard Brayton cycle are 85% and 90%, respectively. If the cycle operates between 14.7 and 55 psia and if the maximum and minimum temperatures are 1500°F and 80°F, respectively, compute the thermal efficiency of the cycle. Assume constant specific heats.

Solution: Use the accompanying figure to refer to the different states. The thermal efficiency of the cycle is calculated using the formula

$$\eta_{th} = \frac{W_{act}}{Q_H} \qquad (1)$$

where

$$W_{act} = W_{turb.} + W_{comp.} \qquad (2)$$

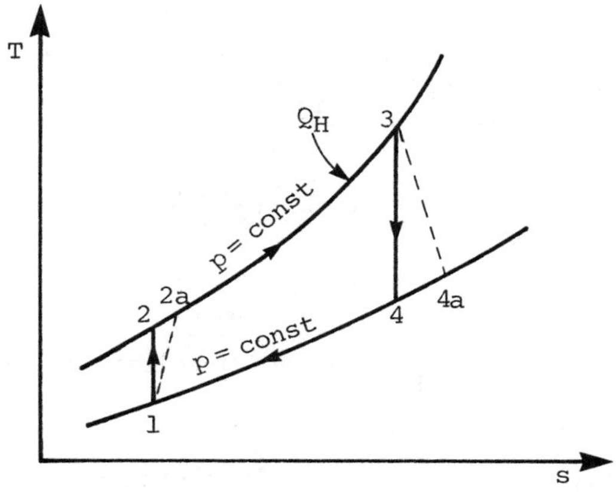

For this problem, the processes in the turbine and compressor are not reversible, and so the work done will be less than the work of the processes were reversible. Using the given efficiencies, it can be written

$$W_{act}\Big|_{turb.} = \eta_{turb.} \times W_{theo.}\Big|_{turb.} \tag{3}$$

and

$$W_{act}\Big|_{comp.} = \frac{W_{theo.}\Big|_{comp.}}{\eta_{comp}} \tag{4}$$

where

$$W_{theo.}\Big|_{turb.} = h_3 - h_4 = c_p(T_3 - T_4) \tag{5}$$

and

$$-W_{theo.}\Big|_{comp.} = h_2 - h_1 = c_p(T_2 - T_1) \tag{6}$$

To find the temperatures at states 2 and 4, use the isentropic relation

$$\frac{T_a}{T_b} = \left(\frac{P_a}{P_b}\right)^{\frac{k-1}{k}}$$

At state 2 ,

$$T_2 = T_1\left(\frac{P_2}{P_1}\right)^{\frac{k-1}{k}}$$

$$= 540\left(\frac{55}{14.7}\right)^{0.286}$$

$$= 787.6°R$$

At state 4,

$$T_4 = T_3\left(\frac{P_4}{P_3}\right)^{\frac{k-1}{k}}$$

$$= 1960 \left(\frac{14.7}{55}\right)^{0.286}$$

$$= 1343.9°R$$

With these values, and c_p = 0.24 Btu/lbm-°R, from eqs. (5) and (6),

$$w_{theo.}\Big|_{turb.} = 0.24(1960-1343.9)$$

$$= 147.9 \text{ Btu/lbm}$$

and

$$-w_{theo.}\Big|_{comp.} = 0.24\ (787.6-540)$$

$$= 59.42 \text{ Btu/lbm}$$

Substituting into eqs. (3) and (4),

$$w_{act}\Big|_{turb.} = 0.90\ (147.9) = 133.1 \text{ Btu/lbm}$$

$$-w_{act}\Big|_{comp.} = \frac{59.42}{0.85} = 69.9 \text{ Btu/lbm}$$

From eq. (2), then

$$w_{act} = 133.1-69.9 = 63.2 \text{ Btu/lbm}$$

The only term unknown in eq. (1) is the heat added to the system during process 2-3 (Q_H). However,

$$q_H = h_3-h_{2a} = c_p(T_3-T_{2a}) \qquad (7)$$

where T_{2a} is the actual temperature at state 2, and can be found using the efficiency of the compressor. Hence

$$\eta_{comp} = \frac{T_2-T_1}{T_{2a}-T_1} = 0.85$$

or

$$T_{2a} = \left(\frac{T_2-T_1}{0.85}\right) + T_1$$

$$= \left(\frac{787.6-540}{0.85}\right) + 540$$

$$= 831.3°R$$

Eq. (7) then gives

$$q_H = 0.24\ (1960-831.3)$$

$$= 270.89$$

Finally, using eq. (1), the efficiency of the cycle is calculated as

$$\eta_{th} = \frac{63.2}{270.89} = 0.233$$

or

$$\eta_{th} = 23.3\%$$

• PROBLEM 9-21

A regenerator of 75 percent effectiveness is used in an air-standard Brayton cycle working between pressures of 15 psia and 75 psia, as shown in Figure 1. Determine the work per pound of air and the efficiency of the cycle if the maximum and minimum temperatures of the cycle are 1700°R and 550°R, respectively.

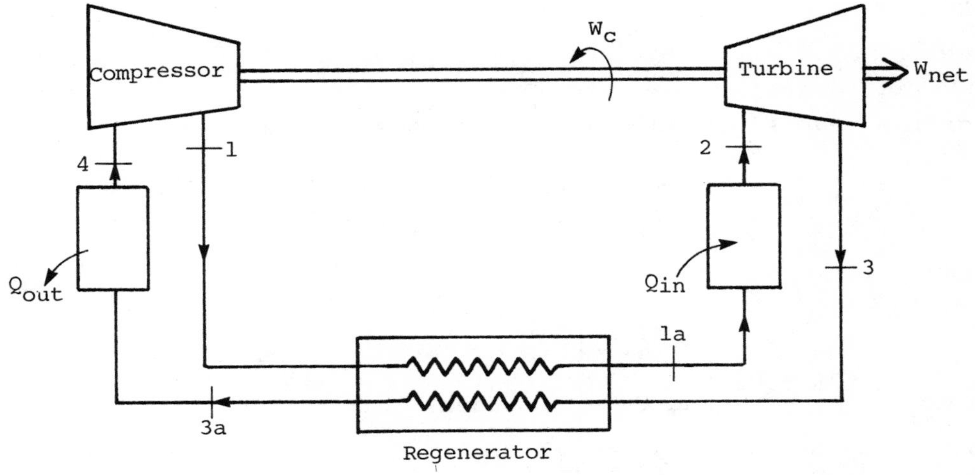

(a)

Solution: By adding a regenerator or heat exchanger to transfer heat from the turbine exhaust gas to the gas leaving

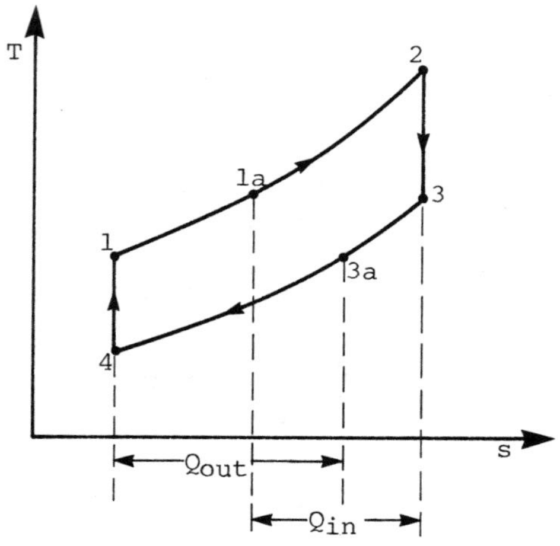

(b)

Fig. 1 Brayton cycle with regenerator.

the compressor, the heat supplied externally is reduced, and therefore the efficiency of the cycle is increased. To solve this problem, first consider the idealized cycle without a regenerator. From Fig. 2, the minimum temperature occurs at 4 and the maximum at 2. Furthermore, the heat added and the heat taken out are

$$Q_{in} = c_p(T_2 - T_1) \tag{1}$$

and

$$Q_{out} = c_p(T_3 - T_4) \tag{2}$$

For the reversible adiabatic processes 4-1 and 2-3,

$$\frac{T_1}{T_4} = \left(\frac{P_1}{P_4}\right)^{(k-1)/k} \tag{3}$$

and

$$\frac{T_2}{T_3} = \left(\frac{P_2}{P_3}\right)^{(k-1)/k} \tag{4}$$

However, $P_1 = P_2$ and $P_3 = P_4$. Then

$$\frac{P_1}{P_4} = \frac{P_2}{P_3} = \frac{75}{15} = 5$$

From eq. (3),

$$T_1 = 550(5)^{(1.4-1)/1.4}$$

$$= 870°R$$

From eq. (4),

$$T_3 = \frac{1700}{(5)^{(1.4-1)/1.4}}$$

$$= 1075°R$$

From eq. (1), with c_p = 0.24 Btu/lbm-°R,

$$Q_{in} = 0.24(1700-870) = 199 \text{ Btu/lbm}$$

and from eq. (2),

$$Q_{out} = 0.24\ (1075-550) = 126 \text{ Btu/lbm}$$

Hence

$$W_{net} = Q_{in}-Q_{out}$$

$$= 199-126$$

$$= 73 \text{ Btu/lbm}$$

When the regenerator is added, the maximum temperature to which the cold gas can be heated is the temperature of the hot gas entering the exchanger. However, this could be achieved only with an infinitely large heat exchanger operating reversibly. In a real case the temperature at 1a cannot reach the temperature at 3. To determine the temperature at 1a, the effectiveness of the regenerator is used. Therefore,

$$e = \frac{T_{1a}-T_1}{T_3-T_1}$$

Since e = 75%, solving for T_{1a} gives

$$T_{1a} = e(T_3-T_1) + T_1$$

$$= 0.75(1075-870) + 870$$

$$= 1024°R$$

To obtain the temperature at 3a, perform an energy balance for the regenerator.

$$c_p(T_{1a}-T_1) = c_p(T_3-T_{3a})$$

or

$$T_{1a}-T_1 = T_3-T_{3a}$$

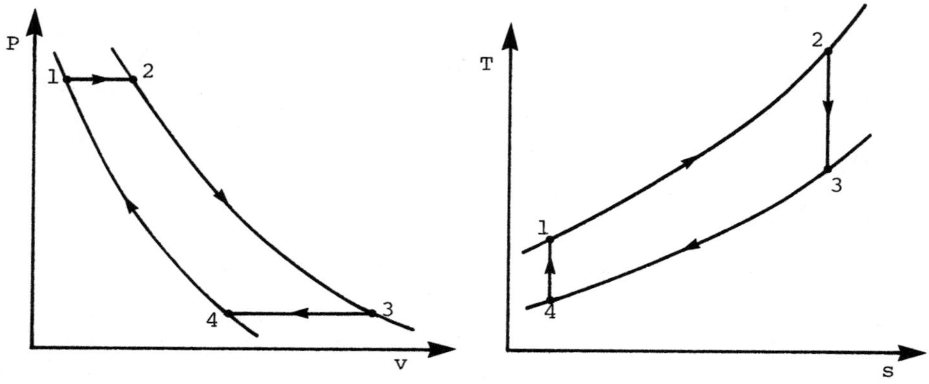

Fig. 2 Brayton cycle without regenerator.

Solving for T_{3a},

$$T_{3a} = -(T_{1a} - T_1) + T_3$$

$$= -(1024-870) + 1075$$

$$= 921°R$$

Then for the actual cycle,

$$Q_{in} = c_p(T_2 - T_{1a})$$

$$= 0.24(1700-1024)$$

$$= 162 \text{ Btu/lbm}$$

and

$$Q_{out} = c_p(T_{3a} - T_4)$$

$$= 0.24(921-550)$$

$$= 89 \text{ Btu/lbm}$$

$$W_{net} = 162-89 = 73 \text{ Btu/lbm.}$$

The efficiency is

$$\eta = \frac{W_{net}}{Q_{in}}$$

$$= \frac{73}{162}$$

$$= 0.45$$

or

$$\eta = 45\%$$

Compare this efficiency with 36.7% for the same cycle without a regenerator.

• PROBLEM 9-22

An internally reversible air-standard Brayton cycle receives air at 27°C and 103 kPa. The upper limits of pressure and temperature of the cycle are 517 kPa and 316°C. Determine the thermal efficiency of the cycle, assuming constant specific heats.

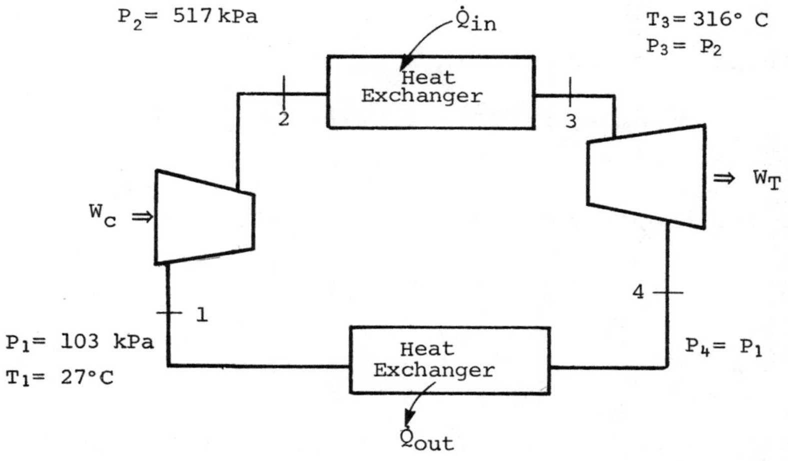

(a)

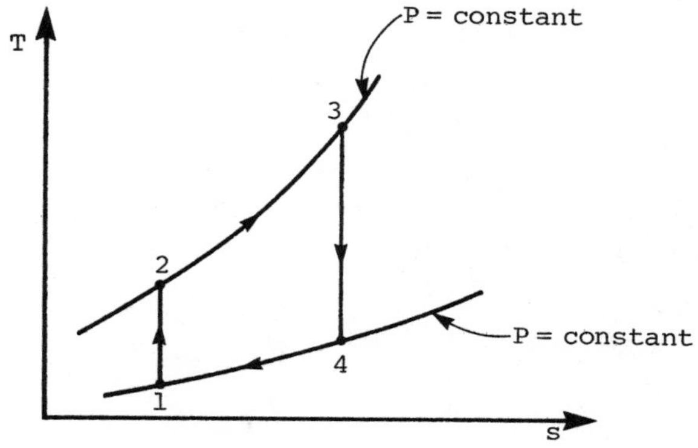

(b)

Representation of the Brayton Cycle.

Solution: The efficiency of the cycle is defined as

$$\eta = \frac{W_{net}}{Q_{added}} \tag{1}$$

where

$$W_{net} = W_t + W_c \tag{2}$$

$$Q_{added} = Q_{in}$$

Therefore, in order to calculate the cycle efficiency, the turbine and compressor work, as well as the heat added to the the air, must be determined. Next, consider the compressor and turbine to be adiabatic, and since it has been assumed that they are internally reversible, the expansion and compression processes are isentropic. For the turbine,

$$W_{turb.} = h_3 - h_4 = c_p(T_3 - T_4) \tag{3}$$

and for the compressor,

$$W_{compr.} = h_1 - h_2 = c_p(T_1 - T_2) \tag{4}$$

Using the isentropic relation

$$\frac{T_a}{T_b} = \left(\frac{p_a}{p_b}\right)^{(\gamma-1)/\gamma}$$

the temperature at the end of compression can be found as

$$T_2 = T_1\left(\frac{P_2}{P_1}\right)^{(\gamma-1)/\gamma}$$

$$= 300 \left(\frac{517}{103}\right)^{(1.4-1)/1.4}$$

$$= 475.67°K$$

and at the end of expansion,

$$T_4 = T_3\left(\frac{P_4}{P_3}\right)^{(\gamma-1)/\gamma}$$

$$= 589 \left(\frac{103}{517}\right)^{(1.4-1)/1.4}$$

$$= 371.47°K$$

From eq. (3), with c_p = 1.0035 kJ/kg,

$$W_{turb.} = 1.0035(589-371.47)$$

$$= 218.3 \text{ kJ/kg}$$

From eq. (4),

$$W_{compr.} = 1.0035(300-475.67)$$

$$= -176.3 \text{ kJ/}^{\circ}\text{K}$$

The heat per kg added to the air is

$$Q_{in} = h_3-h_2 = c_p(T_3-T_2)$$

or

$$Q_{in} = 1.0035\ (589-475.67)$$

$$= 113.73 \text{ kJ/kg}$$

From eq. (2),

$$W_{net} = 218.3 - 176.3 = 42 \text{ kJ/kg}$$

Finally, using eq. (1), the cycle efficiency is found to be

$$\eta = \frac{42}{113.73} = 0.369$$

or

$$\eta = 36.9\%$$

Note that the efficiency of the cycle could have also been found using the formula

$$\eta = 1 - \left(\frac{P_1}{P_2}\right)^{(\gamma-1)/\gamma}$$

$$= 1 - \left(\frac{103}{517}\right)^{(1.4-1)/1.4}$$

$$= 0.369$$

$$= 36.9\%.$$

• PROBLEM 9-23

Air is compressed from 15 psia, 80°F, to 90 psia. Compare the work done and the heat transferred per pound of air according to the following processes:

(a) reversible adiabatic,

(b) reversible isothermal, and

(c) reversible $pv^{1.3}$ = constant.

Solution: From the equation of state for air,

$$P_1V_1 = RT_1$$
$$= (53.34)(540)$$

The index for this reversible adiabatic process is taken as 1.4 (u , k = 1.4 for air).

The work done during the compression process is given by

$$W_k = \frac{k}{k-1} RT \left[\left(\frac{P_2}{P_1}\right)^{\frac{k-1}{k}} - 1 \right]$$

$$= \frac{1.4}{0.4} (53.34)(540) \left[\left(\frac{90}{15}\right)^{\frac{(1.4-1)}{1.4}} - 1 \right]$$

$$= (100813)(1.67-1)$$

$$= 67,545 \text{ ft lb/lb}$$

For a reversible isothermal process, the work done is

$$W_t = RT \ln \frac{P_2}{P_1}$$

$$= (53.34)(540) \ln \frac{90}{15}$$

$$= 51,609 \text{ ft lb/lb}$$

For a reversible $pv^{1.3}$ = constant process, the work is obtained by using n = 1.3.

$$W_n = \frac{1.3}{0.3} (53.34)(540) \left[\left(\frac{90}{15}\right)^{\frac{1.3\ 1}{1.3}} - 1 \right]$$

$$= (124,816)(1.51 - 1)$$

$$= 63{,}656 \text{ ft lb/lb}$$

The heat transfer for an adiabatic process = 0. For the polytropic process, the heat transferred is

$$Q = c_v \left(\frac{k-n}{1-n}\right) \left(T_2 - T_1\right)$$

$$= c_v \left(\frac{k-n}{1-n}\right) T_1 \left(\frac{T_2}{T_1} - 1\right)$$

$$= c_v \left(\frac{k-n}{1-n}\right) T_1 \left[\left(\frac{P_2}{P_1}\right)^{\frac{n-1}{n}} - 1\right]$$

$$= (0.171) \frac{(1.4-1.3)}{(1-1.3)} (540)(1.51 - 1)$$

$$= -16.0 \text{ Btu/lb.}$$

The heat transferred from the air is 16.0 Btu/lb. For an isothermal process with a perfect gas, the heat transfer is equal to the work. In this case, the heat transferred from the air is 51,609 ft lb/lb or 66.3 Btu/lb.

Most tests on reciprocating air compressors with water-cooled cylinders show that it is practical to cool the air during compression to correspond to a polytropic exponent n in the vicinity of 1.3. The usefulness of cooling for a work reduction in the compression process is clearly shown in this example.

• PROBLEM 9-24

A single-stage double-acting air compressor having a clearance of 6.25% and a stroke volume of 0.06 m^3 draws in air at 100 kPa and delivers it at 700 kPa. The compression follows the law $PV^{1.3}$ = constant. If the compressor operates at 400 rpm, calculate the power required and the volume of air delivered per second.

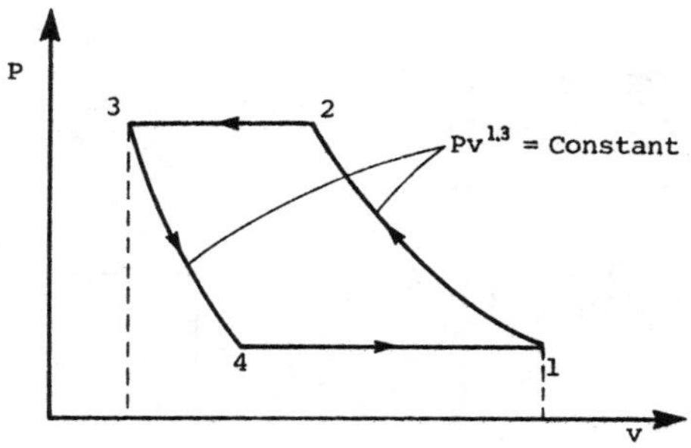

Solution: A double-acting reciprocating air compressor has two delivery strokes per revolution of the crankshaft. Hence there are two cycles (i.e., one occurring on each side of the piston) per revolution of the crankshaft.

Referring to the figure, the work required per cycle is given by

$$W_{cycle} = \frac{n}{(n-1)} P_1(V_1-V_4)\left[\left(\frac{P_2}{P_1}\right)^{\frac{n-1}{n}} -1\right]$$

where n = index of compression

(V_1-V_4) = volume of air taken in

From the figure,

$$V_1 = (V_1-V_3) + V_3$$

where V_1-V_3 = stroke volume

V_3 = clearance volume

$$V_3 = \frac{6.25}{100} \times 0.06$$

$$= 0.00375 \text{ m}^3$$

Hence, $V_1 = 0.06 + 0.00375$

$$= 0.06375 \text{ m}^3.$$

From the isentropic process 3-4,

$$V_4 = V_3\left(\frac{P_3}{P_4}\right)^{\frac{1}{n}}$$

$$= 0.00375 \left(\frac{700}{100}\right)^{\frac{1}{1.3}}$$

$$= 0.01675 \text{ m}^3$$

hence, $V_1-V_4 = 0.06375-0.01675$

$$= 0.047 \text{ m}^3$$

Therefore,

$$W_{cycle} = \frac{1.3}{(1.3-1)}(100)(0.047)\left[\left(\frac{700}{100}\right)^{\frac{1.3-1}{1.3}} -1\right]$$

$$= 11.54 \text{ kNm}$$

The power required to run the compressor at 400 rpm is

$$W = 11.54 \times 2 \times \frac{400}{60}$$

$$= 153.87 \text{ kW}$$

The volume of air delivered per cycle is

$$V_d = V_2 - V_3$$

From the isentropic process relation for the process 1-2,

$$V_2 = V_1 \left(\frac{P_1}{P_2}\right)^{\frac{1}{n}}$$

$$= 0.06375 \left(\frac{100}{700}\right)^{\frac{1}{1.3}}$$

$$= 0.01427 \text{ m}^3$$

Therefore,

$$V_d = 0.01427 - 0.00375$$

$$= 0.01052 \text{ m}^3$$

Therefore, volume of air delivered per second is

$$0.01052 \times 2 \times \frac{400}{60}$$

$$= 0.14 \text{ m}^3/\text{s}$$

• PROBLEM 9-25

An air compressor takes in air at 14.7 psia and 72°F and compresses it isentropically to 55 psia. If the clearance volume is $\frac{1}{16}$th of the stroke volume, determine

(a) the stoke volume in cubic feet per minute to compress 80 ft^3/min of air at inlet conditions,

(b) the volumetric efficiency, and

(c) the power needed to run the compressor.

Assume the expansion process to be isentropic.

Solution: The piston displacement or stroke volume may be

defined as the volume swept out by the piston as it moves from the center of the top to the center of the bottom.

Referring to the figure, the stroke volume is $(V_2 - V_4)$ and the clearance volume is V_4.

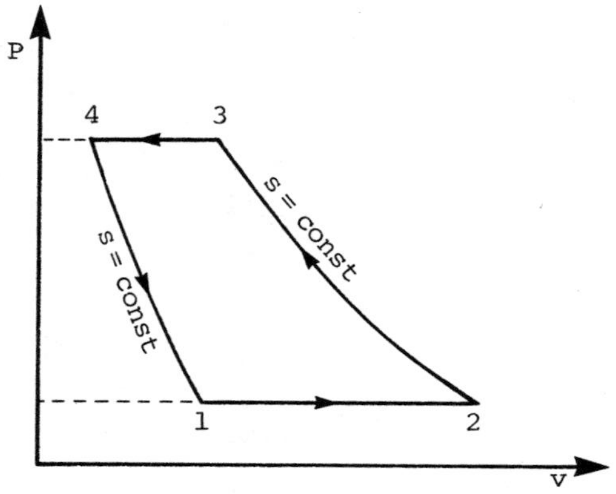

Volume of air drawn into the cylinder per minute is

$$V_2 - V_1 = 80 \text{ ft}^3/\text{min}. \tag{1}$$

Given,

$$V_4 = \frac{1}{16}\left(V_2 - V_4\right)$$

or

$$V_4 = \frac{1}{17} V_2 \tag{2}$$

From the isentropic compression process 2-3,

$$\frac{V_2}{V_3} = \left(\frac{p_3}{p_2}\right)^{\frac{1}{k}}$$

$$= \left(\frac{55}{14.7}\right)^{\frac{1}{1\ 4}}$$

i.e.,

$$\frac{V_2}{V_3} = 2.566 \tag{3}$$

From the isentropic expansion process 4-1,

$$\frac{V_1}{V_4} = \left(\frac{P_4}{P_1}\right)^{\frac{1}{k}}$$

$$= \left(\frac{55}{14.7}\right)^{\frac{1}{1.4}}$$

$$\frac{V_1}{V_4} = 2.566 \qquad (4)$$

Substituting equations (1) and (2) into (4) to calculate V_2,

$$\frac{V_2 - 80}{\left(\frac{1}{17}\right) V_2} = 2.566$$

Simplifying, $V_2 = 94.22 \text{ ft}^3/\text{min}$

From equation (1), $V_1 = 14.22 \text{ ft}^3/\text{min}$

and from equation (2), $V_4 = 5.54 \text{ ft}^3/\text{min}$.

Therefore, the stroke volume $V_2 - V_4 = 94.22 - 5.54$

$= 88.68 \text{ ft}^3/\text{min}$

(b) The volumetric efficiency is given as

$$\eta = \frac{V_2 - V_1}{V_2 - V_4}$$

$$= \frac{94.22 - 14.22}{94.22 - 5.54} \times 100\%$$

$$= 90.2\%$$

(c) The power required is given by

$$W = \frac{k}{k-1} P_2(V_2 - V_1) \left[\left(\frac{P_3}{P_2}\right)^{\frac{k-1}{k}} - 1 \right]$$

$$= \frac{1.4}{(1.4-1)}(14.7 \times 144)(80) \left[\left(\frac{55}{14.7}\right)^{\frac{1.4-1}{1.4}} - 1 \right]$$

i.e., $W = 271398$ ft-lbf/min.

or $W = 8.22$ hp

• PROBLEM 9-26

A reciprocating refrigeration compressor uses Freon-12 as the refrigerant. The gas enters at 20 lbf/in², 60°F and is compressed to 180 lbf/in². The single cylinder compressor has a bore of 2.0 in, a stroke of 2.5 in and a rpm of 1800. Calculate the volumetric efficiency of this compressor if the mass rate of flow of refrigerant is 2.5 lbm/min.

Solution: The volumetric efficiency of a reciprocating compressor may be defined as

$$\eta = \frac{\text{actual mass of gas compressed per cycle}}{\text{mass of gas occupying stroke volume at inlet conditions}}$$

The mass of refrigerant occupying stroke volume at inlet conditions is given by the product of stroke volume and the density of the refrigerant at 20 psia and 60°F.

At 20 psia and 60°F, the refrigerant Freon-12 is in the superheated region.

From the tables, its specific volume $v = 2.234\ ft^3/lbm$

The stroke volume is given by

$$\frac{\pi}{4} d^2 l$$

$$= \frac{\pi}{4}\left(\frac{2}{12}\right)^2\left(\frac{2.5}{12}\right)$$

$$= 4.545 \times 10^{-3}\ ft^3$$

Therefore, the mass of refrigerant occupying stroke volume is

$$\frac{4.545 \times 10^{-3}}{2.234} = 2.03 \times 10^{-3}\ lbm$$

The actual mass of refrigerant compressed per cycle is

$$\frac{2.5}{1800} = 1.389 \times 10^{-3}\ lbm$$

Therefore, the volumetric efficiency is

$$\frac{1.389 \times 10^{-3}}{2.03 \times 10^{-3}} \times 100\%$$

$$= 68.4\%.$$

• PROBLEM 9-27

A 12 × 15 in double acting air compressor draws in air at 14 psia and 90°F (point 1 in figure). It has a clearance of 5%, runs at 150 rpm, and discharges at 50 psia. Compression is taken as polytropic, with n = 1.3.

(a) Calculate an approximate value for the free air from conventional volumetric efficiency.

(b) As air passes through the compressor, calculate the heat transferred,

(c) the change of enthalpy, and

(d) the conventional HP.

(e) Using air tables, calculate the available part of the heat for t_o = 60°F.

Take atmospheric pressure and temperature to be 14.7 psia and 70°F, respectively.

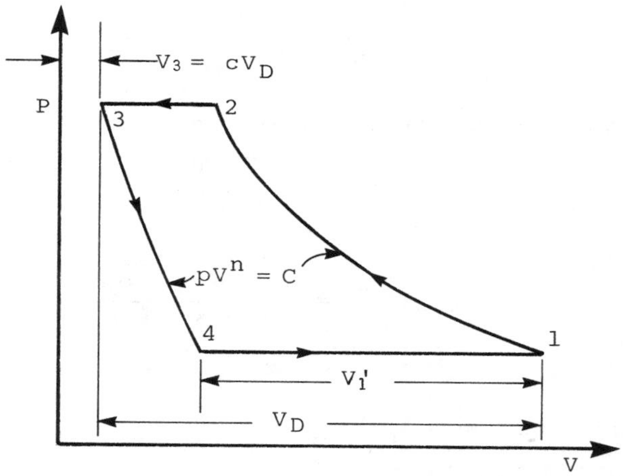

Solution: Since the compressor is double acting,

$$N = 2 \times 150$$
$$= 300$$

The displacement

$$V_D = \frac{\pi D^2}{4} \times L \times N$$
$$= \frac{\pi \times (12)^2 \times 15 \times 300}{4 \times 1728}$$
$$= 294.5 \text{ cfm.}$$

The volumetric efficiency

$$\eta_v = 1 + C - C\left(\frac{P_2}{P_1}\right)^{\frac{1}{n}}$$

$$= 1.05 - 0.05\left(\frac{50}{14}\right)^{\frac{1}{1.3}}$$

$$= 0.9169$$

$$= 91.69\ \%$$

The volume drawn in per minute =

$$V_1{}^1 = \eta_V V_D$$

$$= 0.9169 \times 294.5$$

$$= 270 \text{ cfm}$$

which is measured at 14 psia and 90°F at point 1.

Using subscript o for atmospheric air ,

$$\frac{p_o V_o}{T_o} = \frac{p_1 V_1{}^1}{T_1}$$

The approximate volume of free air is

$$V_o = \frac{p_1 V_1{}^1 T_o}{T_1 p_o}$$

$$= \frac{14 \times 270 \times 530}{550 \times 14.7}$$

$$= 247.8 \text{ cfm}$$

(b) To obtain the heat,

$$T_2 = T_1\left(\frac{P_2}{P_1}\right)^{\frac{(n-1)}{n}}$$

$$= 550\left(\frac{50}{14}\right)^{\frac{(1.3-1)}{1.3}}$$

$$= 738°R$$

$$= 278°F$$

$$m^1 = \frac{p_1 V_1{}^1}{RT_1}$$

$$= \frac{14 \times 144 \times 270}{53.3 \times 550}$$

$$= 18.57 \text{ lb/min}$$

$c_v = 0.1714$ for air

$k = 1.4$

Then

$$c_n = c_v \left(\frac{k-n}{1-n}\right)$$

$$= \frac{0.1714 \times (1.4-1.3)}{1-1.3}$$

$$= -0.0572 \text{ Btu/lb.}$$

$$Q = m'c_n \, \Delta T$$

$$= 18.57 \times (-0.0572) \times (738-550)$$

$$= -199.7 \text{ Btu/min}$$

which means that heat is rejected.

(c) Change of enthalpy for $c_p = 0.24$ is

$$\Delta H = m'c_p \, \Delta T$$

$$= 18.57 \times 0.24 \times (738 \times -550)$$

$$= 837.9 \text{ Btu/min}$$

(d) For work, the equation is

$$W = - \Delta H + Q$$

$$= -837.9-199.7$$

$$= -1037.6 \text{ Btu/min.}$$

Therefore, $$HP = \frac{1037.6}{42.4}$$

$$= 24.5 \text{ hp.} \quad \{\text{since } 42.4 \text{ Btu/hp-min}\}$$

(e) From the air tables, $s_1 = 0.60514$

$s_2 = 0.67599$

∴ change in entropy

$$\Delta s = s_2 - s_1 - \frac{R}{J} \ln \frac{p_2}{p_1}$$

$$= 0.67599 - 0.60514 - 0.0685 \ln \frac{50}{14}$$

or $$\Delta s = -0.01635 \text{ Btu/lb-°R}$$

i.e., there is a decrease in entropy.

Unavailable heat, of the total amount of heat is

$$E_u = m' T_o \Delta\bar{s}$$

$$= -(18.57)(520)(0.01635)$$

$$= -157.88 \text{ Btu/min}$$

$$E_a = -199.7 + 157.88$$

$$= -41.8 \text{ Btu/min}$$

is the available part of the heat.

THE GAS TURBINE CYCLE

• PROBLEM 9-28

A gas turbine cycle with a stage of reheat and regeneration operates under the conditions given below, as illustrated in the figure. The turbine efficiencies are 86%, and the compressor efficiency is 81%. Furthermore, the work output of the high pressure turbine is just enough to drive the compressor. Determine the pressure at which the reheater operates.

$T_1 = T_3 = 1300°K$, $T_6 = 3000°K$, $P_1 = P_7 = P_8 = 450$ kPa,

$P_4 = P_5 = P_6 = 100$ kPa

Solution: In solving this problem, note that the pressure drop in the reheater is very small, and thus neglected in this problem. That means the pressures at states two and three are assumed to be equal, and thus only the pressure at state two will have to be calculated.

First consider the compressor alone. For the reversible (isentropic, subscript s) process it can be written

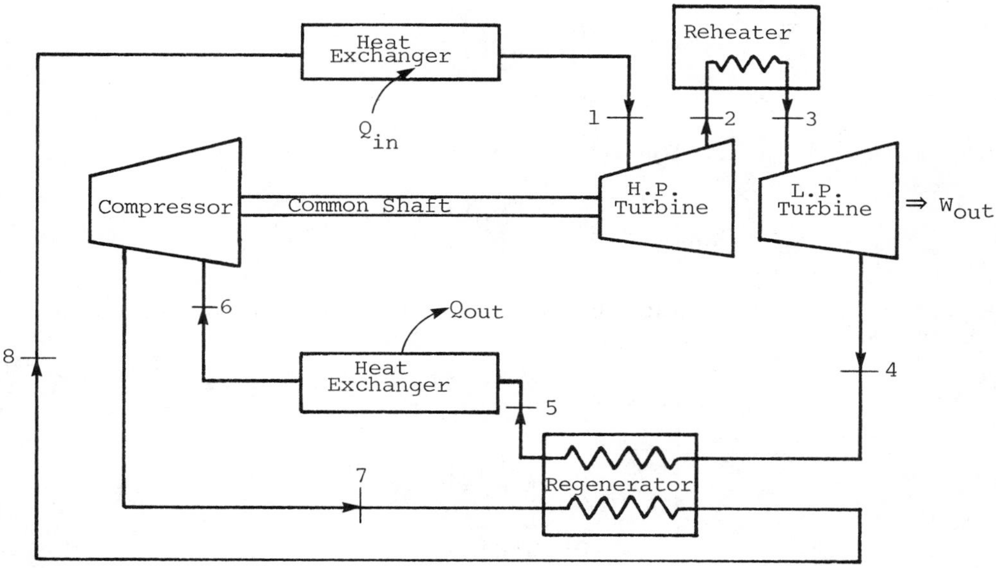

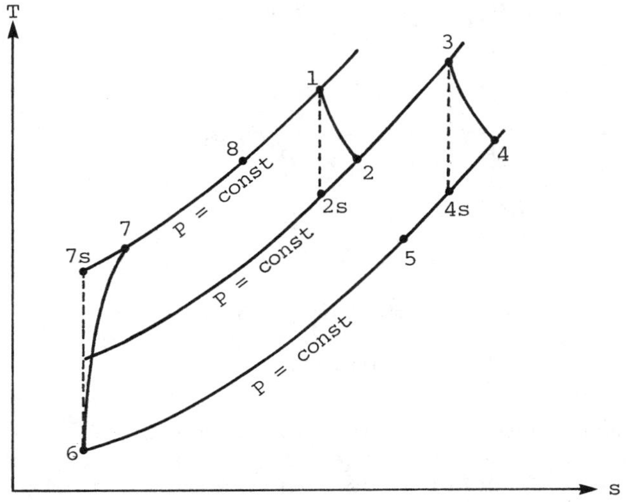

$$\frac{T_{se}}{T_i} = \left(\frac{P_e}{P_i}\right)^{(k-1)/k} \qquad (1)$$

or solving for T_{7s} and substituting the given values,

$$T_{7s} = T_6 \left(\frac{P_7}{P_6}\right)^{(k-1)/k} \qquad \text{(for air } k = 1.4\text{)}$$

$$= 300 \left(\frac{450}{100}\right)^{(1.4-1)/1.4}$$

$$= 461.1^\circ K$$

Then, using the equation of the compressor efficiency,

$$\eta_{comp} = \frac{W_s}{W_a} = \frac{mC_p(T_{7s}-T_6)}{mC_p(T_7 - T_6)}$$

the temperature and thus the work for the actual process can be found as

$$T_7 = T_6 + \left(\frac{T_{7s}-T_6}{\eta}\right)$$

$$= 300 + \left(\frac{461.1-300}{0.81}\right)$$

$$= 498.9^\circ K$$

Since the work output of the high pressure turbine just equals the work input to the compressor, then

$$W_{turb.}\Big|_{H.P.} = W_{comp.}$$

or

$$mC_p(T_1-T_2) = mC_p(T_7-T_6)$$

Solving for T_2, one gets

$$T_2 = T_6-T_7 + T_1$$

$$= 300-498.9 + 1300$$

$$= 1101.1^\circ K$$

Now, if the temperature for the isentropic process can be found at state two, then the use of the isentropic relation given by equation (1) will give the pressure at the entrance of the reheater, since the pressure is the same for both the reversible and irreversible processes.

Considering the high pressure turbine alone, and since the efficiency of the turbine is known and also given by the equation

$$\eta_{turb} = \frac{W_a}{W_s} = \frac{mC_p(T_1-T_2)}{mC_p(T_1-T_{2s})}$$

the temperature for the reversible process at state two is found to be

$$T_{2s} = T_1 + \left(\frac{T_2- T_1}{\eta}\right)$$

$$= 1300 + \left(\frac{1101.1-1300}{0.86} \right)$$

$$= 1068.7° K.$$

Then solving for P_2 in equation (1) gives:

$$P_2 = P_1 \left(\frac{T_{2s}}{T_1} \right)^{k/(k-1)}$$

$$= 450 \left(\frac{1068.7}{1300} \right)^{1.4/(1.4-1)}$$

$$= 226.7 \text{ kPa}.$$

• PROBLEM 9-29

1. In an air standard gas turbine cycle, air at 14.5 psia and 70°F is first compressed to 80 psia in a compressor of 82 percent efficiency. The hot air leaving the combustion chamber at 1250°F is expanded back to 14.5 psia in a turbine of 85 percent efficiency.

Determine (a) compressor and turbine work quantities, and (b) thermal efficiency of the cycle.

2. If a regenerator is inserted into the cycle to heat the air leaving the compressor to 650°F, determine the thermal efficiency of the cycle and the effectiveness of the regenerator.

Solution: Referring to the T-s diagram, points (5) and (6) refer to the second part of the problem where a regenerator is inserted.

Using air tables to solve the problem to get better accuracy,

for the given inlet state 1,

$$T_1 = 70°F = 530°R$$

$$p_1 = 14.5 \text{ psia}$$

from the air tables, corresponding,

$$p_{r_1} = 1.2983$$

$$h_1 = 126.66 \text{ Btu/lbm}$$

The relative pressure at the compressor outlet, that is, at state 2, is given by

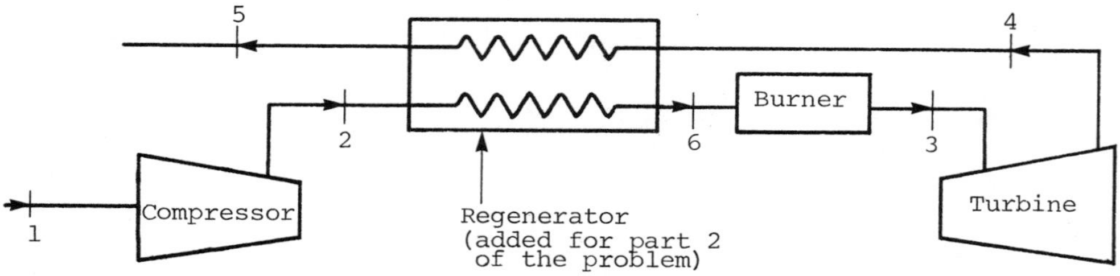

(a)

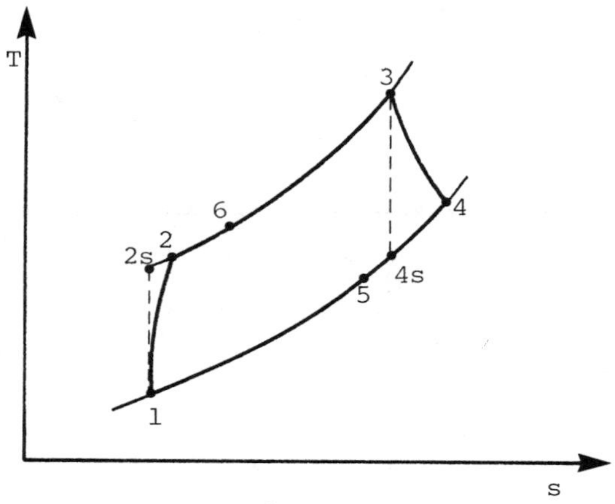

(b)

$$p_{r_2} = p_{r_1}\left(\frac{p_2}{p_1}\right)$$

$$= 1.2983\left(\frac{80}{14.5}\right)$$

$$= 7.163$$

The enthalpy at state 2s corresponding to p_{r_2} can be approximated by interpolation.

$$h_{2s} = 206.57 \text{ Btu/lb}$$

From the definition of the efficiency of the compressor,

$$h_2 = h_1 + \frac{h_{2s}-h_1}{\eta_{comp}}$$

$$= 126.66 + \frac{206.57-126.66}{0.82}$$

$$h_2 = 224.11 \text{ Btu/lbm}$$

Given $T_3 = 1250°F$

$= 1710°R$,

the corresponding values from the air tables are

$$p_{r_3} = 93.156$$

$$h_3 = 425.30$$

Hence

$$p_{r_4} = p_{r_3}\left(\frac{p_4}{p_3}\right)$$

$$= 93.156\left(\frac{14.5}{80}\right)$$

$$p_{r_4} = 16.88$$

Again employing the air tables ,

$$h_{4s} = 263.57 \text{ Btu/lbm}$$

$$T_{4s} = 1090°R$$

From the definition of the efficiency of the turbine,

$$h_4 = h_3 - \eta_{turb}(h_3 - h_{4s})$$

$$= 425.3 - 0.85(425.3 - 263.57)$$

$$= 287.83 \text{ Btu/lbm}$$

Therefore , the compressor work quantity is

$$h_2 - h_1 = 224.11 - 126.66$$

$$= 97.45 \text{ Btu/lbm.}$$

The turbine work quantity is

$$h_3 - h_4 = 425.30 - 287.83$$

$$= 137.47 \text{ Btu/lbm}$$

(b) The thermal efficiency of the cycle is given by

$$\eta_{th} = \frac{(h_3 - h_4) - (h_2 - h_1)}{h_3 - h_2}$$

$$= \frac{(425.30 - 287.83) - (224.11 - 126.66)}{425.30 - 224.11} \times 100\%$$

$$= 19.89\%$$

2. By inserting a regenerator, the net work done by the cycle remains unchanged, whereas the heat input is reduced.

The enthalpy of air at T_6 = 650°F = 1110°R is

$$h_6 = 269 \text{ Btu/lbm}$$

Therefore, the net heat transferred to the system is

$$q = h_3 - h_6$$

$$= 425.3 - 269$$

$$= 156.3 \text{ Btu/lbm}$$

Therefore, thermal efficiency of the regenerative cycle is

$$\eta_{th} = \frac{137.47 - 97.45}{156.3} \times 100\%$$

$$= 25.6\%$$

The effectiveness of the regenerator is given by

$$e = \frac{h_6 - h_2}{h_4 - h_2}$$

$$= \frac{269 - 224.11}{287.83 - 224.11}$$

$$= 0.7044$$

i.e., $e = 70.44$ percent.

• PROBLEM 9-30

An air-standard gas-turbine engine operates on an overall pressure ratio of 4 and between the temperature limits of 70°F and 1600°F. Assuming constant specific heats, evaluate the compressor work, turbine work and thermal efficiency for each of the modifications below. Assume optimum stage pressure ratios, perfect intercooling and perfect reheating.

(a) Ideal cycle.

(b) The efficiencies of compressor and turbine are 0.82 and 0.92, respectively.

(c) To modify (b), a regenerator of effectiveness 0.65 is added.

(d) To modify (c), a two stage compressor with intercooler is inserted.

(e) To modify (c), a two stage turbine with reheater is inserted.

(f) To modify (e), a two stage compressor with inter-cooler is inserted.

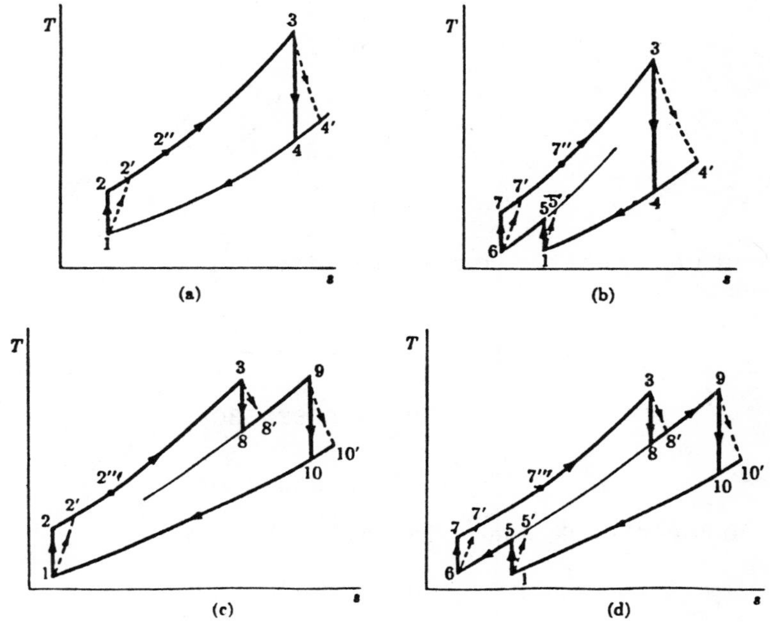

Solution: (a) For the ideal Brayton cycle, the temperature at the inlet to the compressor, i.e., $T_1 = 70°F$

or $$T_1 = (70 + 460) = 530°R$$

The temperature at the compressor outlet, i.e., T_2, can be obtained from the isentropic relation

$$T_2 = T_1 \left(\frac{P_2}{P_1}\right)^{\frac{k-1}{k}}$$

where

$$\frac{P_2}{P_1} = \text{pressure ratio}$$

$$k = \text{ratio of specific heats}$$

Thus,

$$T_2 = 530(4)^{\frac{1.4-1}{1.4}}$$

$$= 788°R$$

The temperature at the inlet to the turbine is

$$T_3 = (1600 + 460)$$

$$= 2060°R$$

The temperature at the turbine outlet, T_4, is given by

$$T_4 = T_3\left(\frac{P_4}{P_3}\right)^{\frac{k-1}{k}}$$

$$= 2060\left(\frac{1}{4}\right)^{\frac{1.4-1}{1.4}}$$

$$T_4 = 1386°R$$

For constant specific heats, the isentropic work done in the compressor is

$$w_c = c_p(T_2 - T_1)$$

$$= 0.24\ (788-530)$$

$$w_c = 61.92\ \text{Btu/lbm}$$

The isentropic work done in the turbine is

$$w_t = c_p(T_3 - T_4)$$

$$= 0.24(2060-1386)$$

$$w_t = 161.76\ \text{Btu/lbm}$$

The heat added during the combustion process is

$$q_A = c_p(T_3 - T_2)$$

$$= 0.24(2060-788)$$

$$= 305.28\ \text{Btu/lbm}$$

Then, the thermal efficiency is given by

$$\eta_{th} = \frac{w_t - w_c}{q_A}$$

$$= \frac{161.76-61.92}{305.28}$$

$$= 0.327$$

i.e., $\eta_{th} = 32.7\%$

(b) Considering the efficiencies of compressor and turbine, the corresponding cycle is 1-2'-3-4'-1, as shown in figure (a).

The temperature at the end of compression is given by

$$T_{2'} = T_1 + \frac{1}{\eta_c}(T_2 - T_1)$$

$$= 530 + \frac{1}{0.82}(788-530)$$

$$T_{2'} = 845°R$$

The temperature at the turbine outlet is given by

$$T_{4'} = T_3 - \eta_t(T_3 - T_4)$$

$$= 2060-0.92(2060-1386)$$

$$T_{4'} = 1440°R$$

Then, the compressor work is

$$w_c = c_p(T_{2'} - T_1)$$

$$= 0.24(845-530)$$

$$w_c = 75.6 \text{ Btu/lbm}$$

The turbine work is

$$w_t = c_p(T_3 - T_{4'})$$

$$= 0.24(2060-1440)$$

$$w_t = 148.8 \text{ Btu/lbm}$$

The heat added during the combustion process 2'-3 is

$$q_A = c_p(T_3 - T_{2'})$$

$$= 0.24(2060-845)$$

$$= 291.6 \text{ Btu/lbm}$$

Then, the thermal efficiency is

$$\eta_{th} = \frac{w_t - w_c}{q_A}$$

$$= \frac{148.8-75.6}{291.6}$$

$$= 0.251$$

i.e., $$\eta_{th} = 25.1\%$$

(c) By adding a regenerator to part (b), the compressor work and turbine work are unaffected. Hence they remain the same as in part (b),

i.e., $$w_c = 75.6 \text{ Btu/lbm}$$

$$w_t = 148.8 \text{ Btu/lbm}$$

The temperature of the air leaving the regenerator and entering the combustor is

$$T_{2''} = T_{2'} + \varepsilon(T_{4'} - T_{2'})$$

$$= 845 + 0.65(1440-845)$$

$$T_{2''} = 1232°R$$

Therefore, the heat added in the combustor is

$$q_A = c_p(T_3 - T_{2''})$$

$$= 0.24(2060-1232)$$

$$= 198.72 \text{ Btu/lbm}$$

The thermal efficiency is

$$\eta_{th} = \frac{w_t - w_c}{q_A}$$

$$= \frac{148.8-75.6}{198.72}$$

$$= 0.368$$

i.e., $$\eta_{th} = 36.8\%$$

(d) Figure (b) represents the cycle with two stage compression, intercooling and regeneration along with the efficiencies of compressors and turbine.

In order to minimize the compressor work, the pressure ratio across each stage must be the same. This requires the pressure ratio across each stage to be the square root of the overall pressure ratio.

Thus $$\frac{p_5}{p_1} = \frac{p_7}{p_6} = \sqrt{4}$$

i.e., $$\frac{p_5}{p_1} = \frac{p_7}{p_6} = 2$$

For the first stage of compression, consider the isentropic process 1-5.

Temperature at state 5 is given by

$$T_5 = T_1\left(\frac{p_5}{p_1}\right)^{\frac{k-1}{k}}$$

$$= 530\ (2)^{\frac{1.4-1}{1.4}}$$

$$= 646°R$$

Then for the actual process 1-5', the temperature at state 5' is given by

$$T_{5'} = T_1 + \frac{1}{\eta_c}(T_5 - T_1)$$

$$= 530 + \frac{1}{0.82}(646-530)$$

$$= 671°R$$

Since the intercooler is ideal, the temperature at the inlet of the second stage of compression is T_6 = 530°R, and from the conditions of optimum pressure ratio, the temperature at state 7',

i.e., $$T_{7'} = T_{5'} = 671°R$$

The temperature of the air leaving the regenerator and entering the combustor is

$$T_{7''} = T_{7'} + \varepsilon(T_{4'} - T_{7'})$$

$$= 671 + 0.65(1440-671)$$

i.e., $$T_{7''} = 1171°R$$

The compressor work is given by

$$w_c = c_p[(T_{5'} - T_1) + (T_{7'} - T_6)]$$

$$= 0.24[(671-530) + (671-530)]$$

$$= 67.68 \text{ Btu/lbm}$$

The turbine work remains unaffected.

$$w_t = 148.8 \text{ Btu/lbm}$$

The heat added during the combustion process 7"-3 is

$$q_A = c_p(T_3 - T_{7''})$$

$$= 0.24(2060-1171)$$

$$= 213.36 \text{ Btu/lbm}$$

The thermal efficiency is

$$\eta_{th} = \frac{w_t - w_c}{q_A}$$

$$= \frac{148.8-67.68}{213.36}$$

$$= 0.38$$

i.e., $\eta_{th} = 38\%$

(e) Figure (c) represents the cycle with two stage expansion, reheating and regeneration along with the efficiencies of the compressor and turbines.

From the consideration of optimum stage pressure ratios,

$$\frac{p_3}{p_8} = \frac{p_9}{p_{10}} = 2$$

For the first stage of expansion, consider the isentropic process 3-8.

Temperature at state 8 is given by

$$T_8 = T_3 \left(\frac{p_8}{p_3}\right)^{\frac{k-1}{k}}$$

$$= 2060 \left(\frac{1}{2}\right)^{\frac{1.4-1}{1.4}}$$

$$= 1690°\text{R}$$

Then for the actual expansion process 3-8', the temperature at state 8' is given by

$$T_{8'} = T_3 - \eta_t(T_3 - T_8)$$

$$= 2060-0.92(2060-1690)$$

$$= 1720°\text{R}$$

Since the reheater is ideal, the temperature at the second state turbine inlet is $T_9 = T_3 = 2060°\text{R}$, and from the conditions of optimum pressure ratio, the temperature at state 10',

i.e., $T_{10'} = T_{8'} = 1720°\text{R}$

The compressor work remains same as in part (b),

i.e., $w_c = 75.6$ Btu/lbm

The turbine work is

$$w_t = 2\ c_p(T_3 - T_{8'})$$

$$= 2 \times 0.24(2060-1720)$$

$$= 163.2 \text{ Btu/lbm}$$

The temperature of air leaving the regenerator is

$$T_{2'''} = T_{2'} + \varepsilon(T_{10'} - T_{2'})$$

$$= 845 + 0.65(1720-845)$$

$$= 1414°R$$

Therefore, the heat added is

$$q_A = c_p\left[(T_3 - T_{2'''}) + (T_9 - T_{8'})\right]$$

$$= 0.24\left[(2060-1414) + (2060-1720)\right]$$

$$= 236.64 \text{ Btu/lbm}$$

Therefore, the thermal efficiency is

$$\eta_{th} = \frac{w_t - w_c}{q_A}$$

$$= \frac{163.2-75.6}{236.64}$$

$$= 0.37$$

i.e., $\eta_{th} = 37\%$

(f) Figure (d) represents the cycle with two stage compression and two stage expansion.

The compressor work is the same as in part (d),

i.e., $w_c = 67.68$ Btu/lbm

The turbine work is the same as in part (e),

i.e., $w_t = 163.2$ Btu/lbm

The temperature of the air leaving the regenerator and entering the combustor is

$$T_{7'''} = T_{7'} + \varepsilon(T_{10'} - T_{7'})$$

$$= 671 + 0.65(1720-671)$$

$$= 1353°R$$

Therefore, heat added is

$$q_A = c_p \left[(T_3 - T_{7'''}) + (T_9 - T_{8'})\right]$$

$$= 0.24 \left[(2060-1353) + (2060-1720)\right]$$

i.e., $$q_A = 251.28 \text{ Btu/lbm}$$

Therefore, the thermal efficiency is

$$\eta_{th} = \frac{w_t - w_c}{q_A}$$

$$= \frac{163.2-67.68}{251.28}$$

$$= 0.38$$

i.e., $$\eta_{th} = 38\%$$

THE JET PROPULSION CYCLE

• PROBLEM 9-31

A turbo-jet unit consists of a single stage compressor, a single stage turbine and a nozzle. The pressure and temperature at the inlet of the compressor are 7 psia and -30°F. The pressure at the outlet of the compressor is 70 psia. The maximum temperature limit for the engine is 1800°F. Assuming an inlet velocity of 275 ft/s and the compression and expansion processes to be isentropic, estimate the thrust for 1 lbm/s of air flow, and the heat input per pound mass of air. Assume constant specific heats.

Solution: Referring to the figure, the compressor inlet conditions, i.e., state 1, are

$$T_1 = -30°F = 430°R$$

$$P_1 = 7 \text{ psia}$$

velocity of air $V_1 = 275$ ft/s

The compressor outlet conditions can be determined from isentropic relationships.

Fig. 1. Gas-turbine cycle for jet propulsion. (a) Schematic, (b) T-s diagram.

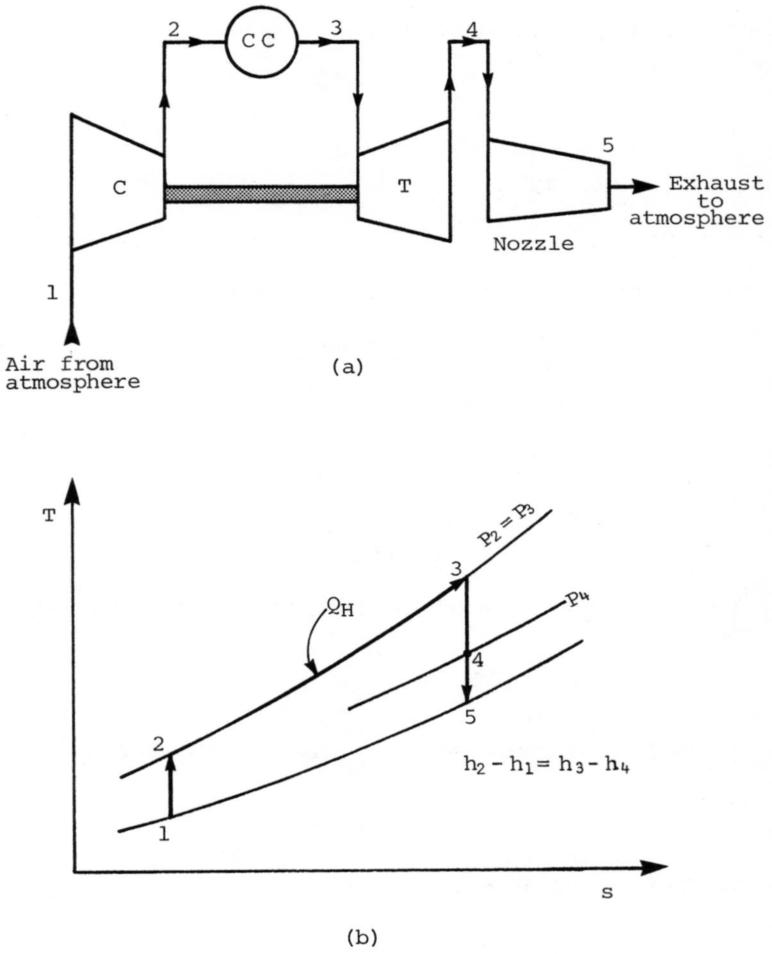

$$T_2 = T_1\left(\frac{p_2}{p_1}\right)^{\frac{k-1}{k}}$$

$$= 430\left(\frac{70}{7}\right)^{\frac{1.4-1}{1.4}}$$

$$= 830°R$$

In a turbo-jet unit, the turbine produces just sufficient power to drive the compressor by partial expansion of the hot compressed air.

Then, since the work of the compressor and that of the turbine are equal,

$$h_2 - h_1 = h_3 - h_4$$

and for constant specific heats,

$$T_2 - T_1 = T_3 - T_4$$

or $T_4 = T_3 + T_1 - T_2$

$= 2260 + 430 - 830$

$T_4 = 1860°R$

For the isentropic turbine-exhaust nozzle process,

$$T_5 = T_3 \left(\frac{p_5}{p_3}\right)^{\frac{k-1}{k}}$$

$$= 2260 \left(\frac{7}{70}\right)^{\frac{1.4-1}{1.4}}$$

$$= 1171°R$$

Applying the conservation of energy principles for the nozzle,

$$h_4 + \frac{V_4^2}{2g} = h_5 + \frac{V_5^2}{2g}$$

V_4 is very small compared to V_5. Hence, neglecting V_4,

$$V_5 = \left[2g(h_4 - h_5)\right]^{\frac{1}{2}}$$

and for constant specific heats

$$V_5 = \left[2gc_p(T_4 - T_5)\right]^{\frac{1}{2}}$$

$$= \left[2(32.2)(0.24)(1860-1171)(778)\right]^{\frac{1}{2}}$$

$$= 2878 \text{ ft/s}$$

The thrust is given by

$$T = F = \frac{\dot{m}}{g}(V_1 - V_5)$$

$$= \frac{(1)(275-2878)}{32.2}$$

$$= -80.84 \text{ lbf}$$

The negative sign shows that the thrust is in the opposite direction of the velocity. Assuming that the turbo-jet unit moves with a velocity equal to the inlet air velocity, the power developed by the thrust force is

$$P = TV_1$$

$$= (80.84)(275)$$

$$= 22231 \text{ ft-lbf/s}$$

i.e.,

$$P = 40.42 \text{ hp}$$

The heat added per pound mass of air is

$$q = h_3 - h_2$$

$$= c_p(T_3 - T_2)$$

$$= 0.24(2260-830)$$

i.e.,

$$q = 343 \text{ Btu/lbm.}$$

• PROBLEM 9-32

A jet-propelled plane is flying with a velocity of 650 ft/s, at an altitude of 17,000 ft ($p = 7.0$ psia, $T = 460°R$). The incoming air has a mass flow rate of 30 lbm/second and is decelerated to a negligible velocity in a diffuser of pressure coefficient 0.9. After raising the pressure of the air by 6 times in a compressor, the air is sent into a combustion chamber where the temperature of the combustion products is 1850°F. After expanding in the turbine, the gases continue to expand in the nozzle to a pressure of 9 psia. The isentropic efficiencies of the compressor, turbine and nozzle are 0.8, 0.84 and 0.9, respectively. If the enthalpy of combustion of the fuel $\Delta h° = -20{,}000$ Btu/lbm, and assuming that the products of combustion have the same properties as air, determine

(a) the power required to drive the compressor,

(b) the fuel-air ratio on a mass basis,

(c) the velocity of gases at the nozzle exit, and

(d) the thrust and thrust power developed by the engine.

Solution: (a) In a jet-propelled plane engine, the power required to drive the compressor is equal to the power developed by the turbine.

Referring to the figure, the incoming air conditions, i.e., at state 1, are

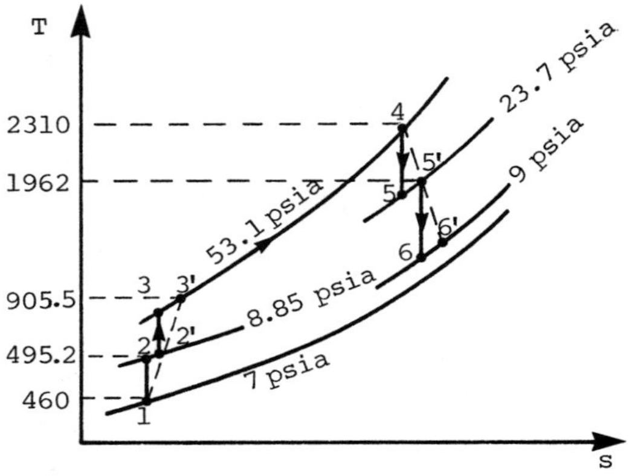

$$T_1 = 460°R$$

$$P_1 = 7.0 \text{ psia}$$

velocity of air $V_1 = 650$ ft/s

From the air tables, corresponding to $T_1 = 460°R$,

$$h_1 = 109.9 \text{ Btu/lbm of air}$$

As the velocity of air is decelerated to a negligible velocity in the diffuser,

$$h_2 = h_{2'} = h_1 + \frac{V_1^{\,2}}{2g}$$

$$= 109.9 + \frac{(650)^2}{2 \times 32.2 \times 778}$$

$$= 118.33 \text{ Btu/lbm of air}$$

Corresponding to this value of enthalpy of air,

$$T_2 = 495.2°R$$

$$P_{r2'} = P_{r2} = 1.0252$$

For isentropic flow in the diffuser,

$$\frac{P_2}{P_1} = \left(\frac{T_2}{T_1}\right)^{\frac{k}{k-1}}$$

or $$P_2 = P_1\left(\frac{T_2}{T_1}\right)^{\frac{k}{k-1}}$$

$$= 7\left(\frac{495.2}{460}\right)^{\frac{1.4}{1.4-1}}$$

$$= 9.06 \text{ psia}$$

From the definition of the pressure coefficient of the diffuser,

$$P_{2'} = P_1 + \eta_d (P_2 - P_1)$$

where

$$\eta_d = \text{pressure coefficient of diffuser}$$

Therefore,

$$P_{2'} = 7 + 0.9(9.06-7)$$

$$= 8.85 \text{ psia}$$

At the end of the isentropic compression process in the compressor, the relative pressure is given by

$$P_{r_3} = \left(\frac{P_3}{P_{2'}}\right) P_{r_{2'}}$$

where $\frac{P_3}{P_{2'}}$ is the pressure ratio of the compressor

Hence $$P_{r_3} = (6)(1.0252)$$

$$= 6.1512$$

Corresponding to this value of relative pressure, the enthalpy is

$$h_3 = 197.76 \text{ Btu/lbm of air}$$

From the definition of isentropic efficiency of the compressor, the enthalpy of air at the end of the compression is

$$h_{3'} = h_{2'} + \frac{h_3 - h_{2'}}{\eta_c}$$

$$= 118.33 + \left(\frac{197.76-118.33}{0.8}\right)$$

$$= 217.62 \text{ Btu/lbm of air}$$

Corresponding to this value of enthalpy, the temperature is

$$T_{3'} = 905.5°R$$

$$P_{3'} = P_3 = 6 \times 8.85$$

$$= 53.1 \text{ psia}$$

The work done on the compressor is given by the change in enthalpy, i.e.,

$$w = h_{3'} - h_{2'}$$

$$= 217.62 - 118.33$$

$$= 99.29 \text{ Btu/lbm of air}$$

The power required to run the compressor is given by

$$\dot{m}_a (h_{3'} - h_{2'})$$

where $\dot{m}_a$ = mass flow rate of air

Hence power required is $\dfrac{30(99.29) \times 3600}{2545}$

$$= 4214 \text{ hp}$$

or the power generated by the turbine is 4214 hp.

(b) Applying the first law of thermodynamics to the combustion process, and neglecting the kinetic energy terms, yields

$$\dot{m}_a (h_{3'} - h^\circ)_a + \dot{m}_f (-\Delta h^\circ)_f = (\dot{m}_a + \dot{m}_f)(h_4 - h^\circ)_p$$

where superscript (^{0}) refers to the standard state at 77°F, and subscripts a, f and P refer to air, fuel and combustion products, respectively. Assuming that the fuel is introduced at 77°F,

the above equation may be written as

$$(h_{3'} - h^\circ)_a + \frac{\dot{m}_f}{\dot{m}_a}(-\Delta h^\circ)_f = \left(1 + \frac{\dot{m}_f}{\dot{m}_a}\right)(h_4 - h^\circ)_p$$

At T_4 = 1850°F = 2310°R, the corresponding values are

h_4 = 591.69 Btu/lbm

P_{r_4} = 313.84

At T = 77°F = 537°R,

h° = 128.1 Btu/lbm

Substituting the values into the above equation and noting that the properties of the products are the same as those of air,

$$(217.62 - 128.1) + \frac{\dot{m}_f}{\dot{m}_a}(20{,}000) = \left(1 + \frac{\dot{m}_f}{\dot{m}_a}\right)(591.69 - 128.1)$$

Solving for $\frac{\dot{m}_f}{\dot{m}_a}$,

$$\frac{\dot{m}_f}{\dot{m}_a} = 0.01915$$

The ratio $$\frac{\dot{m}_a}{\dot{m}_p} = \frac{\dot{m}_a}{\dot{m}_a + \dot{m}_f}$$

$$= \frac{1}{1 + \frac{\dot{m}_f}{\dot{m}_a}}$$

$$= \frac{1}{1+0.01915} = 0.9812$$

(c) The work developed in the turbine, in terms of unit mass of products, is given by the product of work developed per unit mass of air and $\frac{\dot{m}_a}{\dot{m}_p}$

$$= 99.29 \times 0.9812$$

$$= 97.42 \text{ Btu/lbm of products}$$

Therefore, the enthalpy at the exit of the turbine is

$$h_{5'} = h_4 - 97.42$$

$$= 591.69 - 97.42$$

$$= 494.27 \text{ Btu/lbm of products}$$

Temperature and relative pressure corresponding to this enthalpy are

$$T_{5'} = 1962°R$$

$$P_{r_{5'}} = 161.24$$

For the isentropic expansion process ,

$$h_5 = h_4 - \left(\frac{h_4 - h_{5'}}{\eta_t}\right)$$

$$= 591.69 - \left(\frac{97.42}{0.84}\right)$$

$$= 475.71 \text{ Btu/lbm of products}$$

At h_5 = 475.71 Btu/lbm of products, the corresponding relative pressure is P_{r_5} = 140.06 .

At the end of the isentropic expansion process , the pressure is given by

$$P_5 = P_{5'} = P_4\left(\frac{P_{r_5}}{P_{r_4}}\right)$$

$$= 53.1\left(\frac{140.06}{313.84}\right)$$

$$= 23.7 \text{ psia}$$

The relative pressure at the end of the nozzle is

$$P_{r_6} = \left(\frac{P_6}{P_{5'}}\right) P_{r_5'}$$

$$= \frac{9}{23.7}\ (161.24)$$

$$P_{r_6} = 61.23$$

Then the corresponding value of enthalpy,

i.e., the enthalpy of gases at the nozzle exit is, from tables, h_6 = 378.65 Btu/lbm of products.

The velocity at the nozzle exit is given by

$$V_{6'} = \eta_n \sqrt{2g(h_{5'}-h_6)}$$

$$= 0.9\ \sqrt{2 \times 32.2(494.27-378.65)(778)}$$

$$= 2166 \text{ ft/s}$$

(d) Neglecting the difference in pressure forces on the turbo-jet and assuming that the momentum of the fuel at entrance is negligible, the thrust force is given by

$$F = \frac{\dot{m}_a}{g}\left[\left(1 + \frac{\dot{m}_f}{\dot{m}_a}\right) V_{6'} - V_1\right]$$

$$= \frac{30}{32.2}\ \left[(1 + 0.01915)2166-650\right]$$

$$= 1451 \text{ lbf}$$

and the thrust power is

$$P = \frac{FV_1}{550}$$

$$= \frac{1451 \times 650}{550}$$

$$= 1715 \text{ hp}$$

If the plant in this problem had been a turbo-prop engine, the turbine would have had to supply the power required by the propeller as well as the compressor power. The analysis would have been unchanged in other respects, except for adding the propeller thrust at the end.

THE AIR - STANDARD REFRIGERATION CYCLE

• PROBLEM 9-33

An air refrigeration system operating on a Bell-Coleman cycle is required to produce 3 tons of refrigeration with a cooler pressure of 70 psia and a refrigerator pressure of 14.7 psia. The temperature of air leaving the cooler is 70°F and the air leaving the room is 30°F. If the machine runs at 140 working strokes per minute, determine

(a) the horse power required, and

(b) the volumes of compression and expansion cylinders.

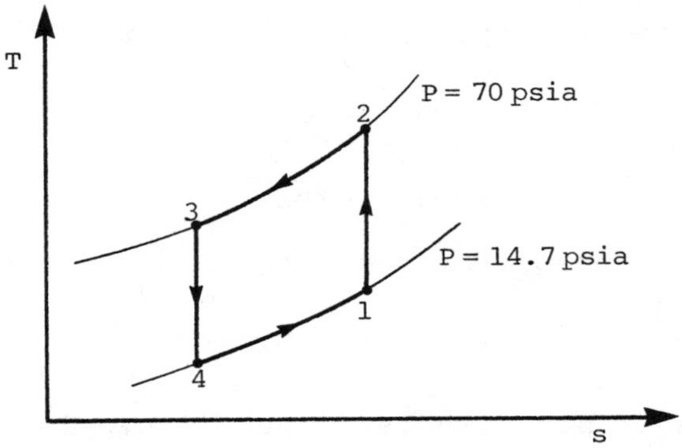

Solution: Given the pressure and temperature of air leaving the cooler as

$$P_3 = 70 \text{ psia}$$

$$T_3 = 70°F = 530°R,$$

for the isentropic expansion process 3-4, the temperature at state 4 is given by the isentropic relation

$$T_4 = T_3\left(\frac{P_4}{P_3}\right)^{\frac{k-1}{k}}$$

$$= 530\left(\frac{14.7}{70}\right)^{\frac{1.4-1}{1.4}}$$

i.e., $T_4 = 339°R$

(a) The coefficient of performance (COP) defined as

$$COP = \frac{Q}{W}$$

where Q = refrigeration effect

W = net work supplied

COP is also given by

$$COP = \frac{T_4}{T_3 - T_4}$$

Therefore , from the two relations,

$$\frac{Q}{W} = \frac{T_4}{T_3 - T_4}$$

or

$$W = Q\,\frac{(T_3 - T_4)}{T_4}$$

Substituting the values, (1 ton = 200 Btu/min)

$$W = 3 \times 200\,\frac{(530-339)}{339} \times 778$$

$$= 263005 \text{ ft-lbf}$$

Therefore, the horsepower required to drive the machine

is $\frac{263005}{33000} = 7.97$ hp

(b) The mass of air circulated per minute is given by the heat equation

$$Q = mc_p(\Delta T)$$

Applying this equation to process 4-1 , where heat is absorbed at the rate of 3 tons , and writing yhe above equation for m,

$$m = \frac{Q}{c_p(T_1 - T_4)}$$

$$= \frac{3 \times 200}{0.24(490-339)}$$

or $$m = 16.56 \text{ lbm/min.}$$

The mass of air per cycle is given by

(mass of air per minute)/(number of working strokes per min)

Therefore, mass of air per cycle is

$$\frac{16.56}{140} = 0.1183 \text{ lbm/cycle.}$$

The volume of the compressor cyclinder is the volume of air at state 1.

It can be obtained from the perfect gas equation,

$$V_1 = \frac{mRT_1}{P_1}$$

$$= \frac{0.1183 \times 53.35 \times 490}{14.7 \times 144}$$

$$V_1 = 1.46 \text{ ft}^3$$

The volume of the expansion cylinder is the volume at state 4.

Since process 4-1 is a constant pressure process, from the ideal gas relations,

$$V_4 = V_1\left(\frac{T_4}{T_1}\right)$$

$$= 1.46 \left(\frac{339}{490}\right)$$

$$V_4 = 1.01 \text{ ft}^3$$

• PROBLEM 9-34

In a refrigeration plant, air is drawn from a room at 70°F and 14.7 psia and compressed to 70 psia in a compressor having an adiabatic efficiency of 0.78. The air is then cooled to 30°F in the cooler before expanding, in a turbine with an efficiency of 0.82, to the room pressure. Using air tables, calculate

(a) the air temperature at the compressor and turbine exits,

(b) the coefficient of performance (COP), and

(c) the power required, if 120 lbm/min of air flows through the refrigerator.

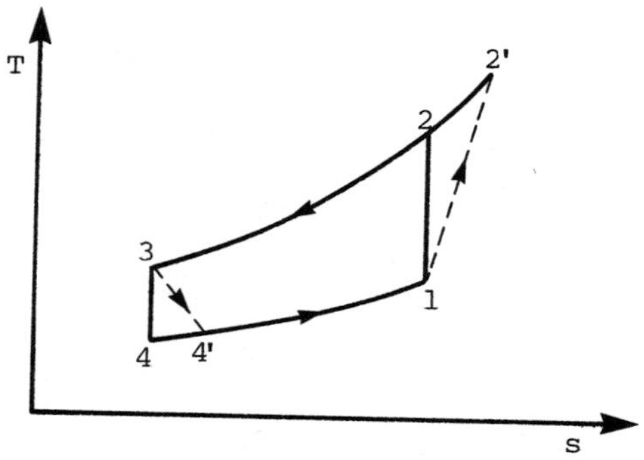

Solution: (a) Given, the pressure and temperature of air at the inlet to the compressor are

$$p_1 = 14.7 \text{ psia}$$

$$T_1 = 70°F = 530°R$$

From the air tables, the relative pressure at state 1 is

$$p_{r_1} = 1.2998$$

Considering the isentropic compression process 1-2, the relative pressure at state 2 is given by the relation

$$p_{r_2} = p_{r_1}\left(\frac{p_2}{p_1}\right)$$

$$= 1.2998 \left(\frac{70}{14.7}\right)$$

$$= 6.1895$$

From the air tables, the corresponding temperature is

$$T_2 = 826°R$$

Taking adiabatic efficiency of the compressor into consideration, the temperature of the air at the end of compression is given by

$$T_{2'} = T_1 + \frac{1}{\eta_c}(T_2 - T_1)$$

$$= 530 + \frac{1}{0.78}(826-530)$$

$$= 910°R$$

Similarly, the temperature of air leaving the turbine can be obtained by considering the expansion process 3-4. Given, the pressure and temperature of air at the turbine inlet are

$$p_3 = 70 \text{ psia}$$

$$T_3 = 30°F = 490°R$$

From the air tables, the relative pressure at state 3 is

$$p_{r_3} = 0.9886$$

Considering the isentropic expansion process 3-4, the relative pressure at state 4 is given by

$$p_{r_4} = p_{r_3}\left(\frac{p_4}{p_3}\right)$$

$$= 0.9886 \left(\frac{14.7}{70}\right)$$

$$= 0.2076$$

The corresponding temperature T_4, from air tables, is

$$T_4 = 313°R$$

Taking the efficiency of the turbine into consideration, the actual temperature of air leaving the turbine is given by

$$T_4 = T_3 - \eta_t (T_3 - T_4)$$

$$= 490-0.82(490-313)$$

$$= 345°R$$

(b) The net work done during the cycle is

(compressor work) - (turbine work)

$$= (h_{2'}-h_1) - (h_3-h_{4'})$$

Since the temperatures at all the four states are known from part (a), the corresponding enthalpies can be obtained from air tables.

Therefore, from air tables,

$$h_1 = 126.7 \text{ Btu/lbm}$$

$$h_{2'} = 218.7 \text{ Btu/lbm}$$

$$h_3 = 117.1 \text{ Btu/lbm}$$

$$h_4 = 82.5 \text{ Btu/lbm}$$

Therefore, net work done during the cycle is

$$w_{net} = (218.7-126.7) - (117.1-82.5)$$

$$= 57.4 \text{ Btu/lbm}$$

The refrigeration effect per cycle is given by

$$q_R = h_1 - h_4,$$

$$= 126.7-82.5$$

$$= 44.2 \text{ Btu/lbm}$$

The coefficient of performance is given by

$$COP = \frac{q_R}{W_{net}}$$

$$= \frac{44.2}{57.4}$$

$$= 0.77$$

(c) The power required is given by

Power = (mass flow rate) × (net work done)

$$= 120 \frac{\text{lbm}}{\text{min}} \times 60 \frac{\text{min}}{\text{hr}} \times 57.4 \frac{\text{Btu}}{\text{lbm}} \times \frac{1}{3413 \frac{\text{Btu}}{\text{kW - hr}}}$$

$$= 121 \text{ kW}.$$

• PROBLEM 9-35

A turbo-propeller aeroplane has an air cycle system which is fed with compressed air. The air is bled off the compressor of the main power unit at 65 psia and 850°R. After cooling, the compressed air reaches the turbine at 60 psia and 550°R. The adiabatic efficiency of the turbine is 70%. The pressure of the air at the turbine exit is 14 psia. If the flow rate to the turbine, under maximum conditions, is 50 lbm/min, calculate

(a) the air temperature at the turbine exit,

(b) power output of the turbine, and

(c) Tons of refrigeration, if the temperature of the air exhausting out of the cabin is 75°F.

Solution: Refer to the figure for a T-s representation of the problem.

Process 1-2' takes place in the main compressor, and air at state given by point 2', i.e., at 65 psia and 850°R, is bled-off for refrigeration.

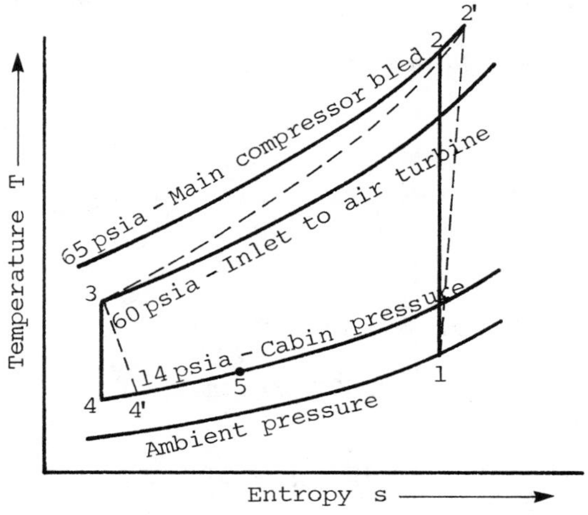

Process 2'-3 takes place in a heat exchanger (cooler), and air at 60 psia (there is a pressure drop of 5 psia in the cooler) and 550°R is available at point 3 for expansion in the turbine.

Process 3-4' is the expansion process in the turbine. The turbine exit pressure p_4 = 14 psia.

Process 4'-5 is indicative of the cabin heat load absorption. The pressure in the cabin is maintained at 14 psia.

(a) The air temperature at the turbine exit is the temperature at point 4', i.e., $T_{4'}$.

Consider the isentropic expansion process 3-4. The temperature at state 4 is given by the relation

$$T_4 = T_3\left(\frac{p_4}{p_3}\right)^{\frac{k-1}{k}}$$

For air, the coefficient of expansion k = 1.4. Therefore,

$$T_4 = 550\left(\frac{14}{60}\right)^{\frac{1.4-1}{1.4}}$$

$$= 363°R$$

Considering the adiabatic efficiency of the turbine, the actual exit temperature $T_{4'}$ is

$$T_{4'} = T_3 - \eta_t(T_3 - T_4)$$

$$= 550 - 0.7(550-363)$$

$$= 419°R$$

(b) The power output of the turbine is given by

$$\text{Power} = mc_p(T_3 - T_{4'})$$

where

$$m = \text{mass flow rate of air}$$

hence

$$\text{Power} = 50 \times 0.24\ (550-419)$$

$$= 1572\ \text{Btu/min}$$

$$= \frac{1572}{42.42} = 37\ \text{hp}$$

(c) Refrigeration produced in the cabin is given by

$$q_R = mc_p(T_5 - T_{4'})$$

$$= 50 \times 0.24\ \left[(75+460) - 419\right]$$

$$= 1392\ \text{Btu/min}$$

$$= \frac{1392}{200} = 6.96\ \text{tons}\ (1\ \text{ton} = 200\ \text{Btu/min.})$$

$$\cong 7\ \text{tons}$$

• PROBLEM 9-36

A jet plane has a simple air cycle air cooling system. The aircraft flies at 620 mph at an altitude of 17,000 ft, where the ambient air pressure and temperature are 9.0 psia and 460°R. The incoming air is decelerated to a negligible velocity in a diffuser of pressure coefficient 0.8. After raising the air pressure by 3 times in a compressor with an adiabatic efficiency of 80%, the air is cooled to 150°F in a heat exchanger. The pressure drop through the heat exchanger is 5 psi. The air is then expanded to 14.7 psia in a turbine having an adiabatic efficiency of 85%. If the cooling load is 1 ton when the cockpit is maintained at 70°F, calculate

(a) the pressure and temperature of air entering and leaving the compressor,

(b) the air flow rate, and

(c) the COP of the cycle.

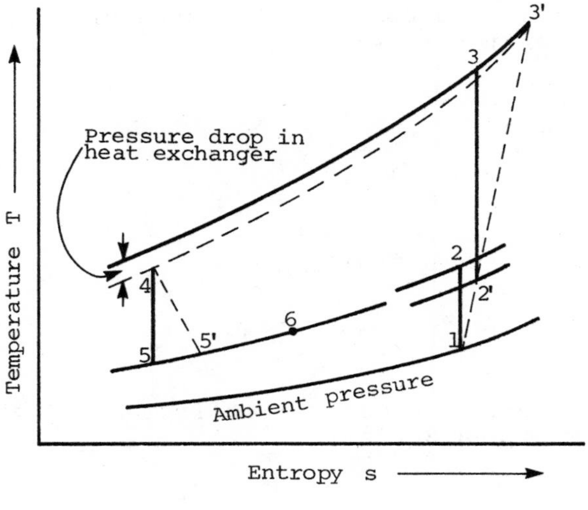

Solution: (a) Referring to the figure, process 1-2' is the ramming process in the diffuser. In the diffuser, the total energy remains unchanged, if the process is assumed to be adiabatic while pressure of the air increases. A perfect ram action would proceed along a path such as 1-2, shown in the figure. But due to irreversibilities, the actual state is indicated by point 2'. which shows increase in entropy and decrease in pressure (relative to point 2).

Kinetic energy of the outside air, relative to aircraft, is expressed as follows:

$$KE = \frac{V^2}{2gJ}$$

$$= \frac{\left(\frac{620 \times 5280}{3600}\right)^2}{2 \times 32.2 \times 778}$$

$$= 16.5 \text{ Btu/lbm}$$

Therefore, from the energy equation,

$$h_2 - h_1 = 16.5 \text{ Btu/lbm}$$

Assuming air to be a perfect gas with constant apecific heats, the temperature at state 2 is given by

$$c_p(T_2 - T_1) = h_2 - h_1$$

$$0.24(T_2 - 460) = 16.5$$

or

$$T_2 = \frac{16.5}{0.24} + 460$$

$$= 529°R$$

For the isentropic process 1-2, the pressure at state 2 is given by the isentropic relation

$$\frac{p_2}{p_1} = \left(\frac{T_2}{T_1}\right)^{\frac{k}{k-1}}$$

Hence,

$$p_2 = 9\left(\frac{529}{460}\right)^{\frac{1.4}{1.4-1}}$$

$$= 14.7 \text{ psia}$$

From the definition of pressure coefficient of the diffuser, the pressure at state 2' is

$$p_{2'} = p_1 + \eta d(p_2 - p_1)$$

$$= 9.0 + 0.8(14.7 - 9.0)$$

$$= 13.6 \text{ psia}$$

Thus, the pressure and temperature of air entering the compressor are 13.6 psia and 529°R. Consider the isentropic compression process 2'-3. The temperature at the end of isentropic compression is given by

$$T_3 = T_{2'}\left(\frac{p_3}{p_{2'}}\right)^{\frac{k-1}{k}}$$

$$= 529(3)^{\frac{1.4-1}{1.4}}$$

$$= 724°R$$

From the definition of adiabatic efficiency of a compressor, the temperature at the end of actual compression is

$$T_{3'} = T_{2'} + \frac{\left(T_3 - T_{2'}\right)}{\eta_c}$$

$$= 529 + \frac{(724-529)}{0.8}$$

$$= 773°R.$$

The pressure of air leaving the compressor is

$$p_3 = 3p_{2'}$$

$$= 3(13.6)$$

$$= 40.8 \text{ psia}$$

(b) There is a pressure drop of 5 psi in the heat exchanger (cooler). Therefore, the pressure available at the entrance to the cooling turbine is

$$p_4 = p_3 - 5$$

$$= 40.8 - 5$$

$$= 35.8 \text{ psia}$$

The temperature of air at entry to turbine is

$$T_4 = 150°F$$

$$= 610°R$$

The exit pressure from the cooling turbine is

$$p_5 = 14.7 \text{ psia}$$

For isentropic expansion through the turbine, the exit temperature is given by the isentropic relation

$$T_5 = T_4 \left(\frac{p_5}{p_4}\right)^{\frac{k-1}{k}}$$

$$= 610 \left(\frac{14.7}{35.8}\right)^{\frac{1.4-1}{1.4}}$$

$$= 473°R$$

From the definition of adiabatic efficiency of a turbine, the temperature at the end of actual expansion is

$$T_{5'} = T_4 - \eta_t (T_4 - T_5)$$

$$= 610 - 0.85(610 - 473)$$

$$= 494$$

The quantity of air supplied per minute for 1 ton of refrigeration load is given by the equation

$$Q = mc_p(T_6 - T_{5'})$$

or

$$m = \frac{Q}{c_p(T_6 - T_{5'})}$$

$$= \frac{1 \times 200}{0.24(530 - 494)} \quad (1 \text{ ton} = 200 \text{ Btu/lbm})$$

$$= 23 \text{ lbm/min}$$

(c) The COP of the plant is given by

$$\text{COP} = \frac{\text{Refrigeration obtained}}{\text{net work done}}$$

$$= \frac{Q}{m\left[c_p(T_{3'}-T_{2'})-c_p(T_4-T_{5'})\right]}$$

$$= \frac{1 \times 200}{23 \times 0.24\left[(773-529)-(640-494)\right]}$$

$$= 0.37$$

CHAPTER 10

MIXTURES AND SOLUTIONS

DEFINITIONS OF IDEAL GAS MIXTURES

• PROBLEM 10-1

A cubic foot of air, which is considered as a mixture of ideal gases, has the following chemical composition at 80°F and 14.7 psia.

Component	N_2	O_2	Argon	CO_2
Mole %	78.02	20.99	0.94	0.05

Calculate (a) partial pressure, partial volume, volume percent and weight per cent of each component gas, and (b) the average molecular weight and density of air.

Solution: A relationship between the component pressure P_i of an ideal-gas mixture and its mole fraction y_i is given by

$$\frac{p_i}{p_t} = y_i$$

or,

$$p_i = p_t y_i$$

where

p_t = total pressure of the mixture

That is, the component pressure of each gas equals the mole fraction times the total pressure.

Substituting values for different components,

$$P(N_2) = (14.7)(0.7802) = 11.469 \text{ psia}$$

$$P(O_2) = (14.7)(0.2099) = 3.086 \text{ psia}$$

$$P(\text{Argon}) = (14.7)(0.0094) = 0.138 \text{ psia}$$

$$P(CO_2) = (14.7)(0.0005) = 0.007 \text{ psia}$$

The partial volume of each gas component equals the mole fraction times the total volume. But the total volume is given as 1 ft^3. Therefore, the partial volume of each component is equal to its mole fraction.

The volume percent of each component gas is equal to its mole percent because each mole of an ideal gas occupies the same volume at the same temperature and pressure. The volume percent can be obtained from

$$\frac{V_i}{V_{mixture}} \times 100\%$$

Weight percent of a component is given by

$$\text{Weight percent of component } i = \frac{(\text{component weight of } i) \times 100\%}{\text{total weight of mixture}}$$

Component weight is the product of the mole fraction and its molecular weight. The total weight of the mixture is the sum of all component weights.

Therefore,

$$\text{Weight percent of component } i = \frac{y_i \times \text{molecular wt. of } i}{\Sigma(y_i \times \text{molecular wt. of } i)} \times 100\%$$

The total weight of the mixture is

$$\Sigma(y_i \times \text{molecular wt. of } i)$$

$$= (0.7802 \times 28) + (0.2099 \times 32) + (0.0094 \times 39.94)$$

$$+ (0.0005 \times 44)$$

$$= 28.96$$

Therefore,

$$\text{weight \% of } N_2 = \frac{(0.7802)(28)}{28.96} \times 100\% = 75.43\%$$

$$\text{weight \% of } O_2 = \frac{(0.2099)(32)}{28.96} \times 100\% = 23.19\%$$

$$\text{weight \% of Argon} = \frac{(0.0094)(39.94)}{28.96} \times 100\% = 1.30\%$$

$$\text{weight \% of } CO_2 = \frac{(0.0005)(44)}{28.96} \times 100\% = 0.08\%$$

(b) The average molecular weight of a gas mixture is the total weight of one mole of the mixture, which is $\Sigma(y_i \times \text{molecular wt. of } i)$

This value has already been calculated as 28.96.

The density of the mixture is given by the ideal gas equation

$$\rho = \frac{P}{RT}(\text{average molecular wt.})$$

$$= \frac{14.7 \times 144 \times 28.96}{1545 \times 540}$$

$$= 0.0735 \text{ lbm/ft}^3$$

• PROBLEM 10-2

Consider a mixture consisting of 25% CO_2, 60% H_2 and 15% O_2 by volume. (a) Calculate the mass fractions and the gas constant R for this mixture. (b) Calculate the density of the mixture and the partial pressures of the constituents if the mixture is at 60 psia and 70°F. (c) Suppose the mixture is placed in a closed tank, and all of the oxygen is absorbed by the tank walls, while the temperature is maintained at 70°F. Calculate the new mass fraction, mole fraction and the new total pressure.

MIXTURE CALCULATION

Component	$\psi_i = x_i$, *lbmole / lbmole mixture*		M_i, *lbm / lbmole*		m_i *lbm / lbmole mixture*	m_i/M *lbm / lbm mixture*
O_2	0.15	×	32.0	=	4.80	0.282
H_2	0.60	×	2.016	=	1.21	0.071
CO_2	0.25	×	44.01	=	11.00	0.647
					M = 17.01 lbm/lbmole	1.000

Solution: A perfect gas mixture will have identical volumes and mole fractions. The mixture calculation is carried out as shown in the following table. The gas constant for this mixture is

$$R = \frac{R_u}{M}$$

$$= \frac{15.45}{17.01}$$

$$= 90.8 \text{ ft-lbf/lbm-°R.}$$

In the table, H_2 has the largest mole fraction but has the least mass fraction.

(b) The density of the mixture is given by the ideal gas relation

$$\rho = \frac{P}{RT}$$

$$= \frac{60 \times 144}{90.9 \times (70 + 460)}$$

$$= 0.180 \text{ lbm/ft}^3.$$

The partial pressures of the constituent gases are given by $P_i = \chi_i P$.

$$P_{O_2} = 0.15 \times 60$$

$$= 9 \text{ psia}$$

$$P_{H_2} = 0.60 \times 60$$

$$= 36 \text{ psia}$$

$$P_{CO_2} = 0.25 \times 60$$

$$= 15 \text{ psia.}$$

(c) The new total pressure $P = P_{H_2} + P_{CO_2}$.

The constituent partial pressures depend only on the number of moles of each one present, the temperature and the volume. Hence the H_2 and CO_2 partial pressures are unchanged. Therefore, the new total pressure is

$$P = 36 + 15$$

$$P = 51 \text{ psia.}$$

To calculate the new mass fractions and mole fractions:

$$\frac{m_{H_2}}{M} = \frac{0.071}{1-0.282}$$

$$= 0.099$$

$$\frac{m_{CO_2}}{M} = \frac{0.647}{1-0.282}$$

$$= 0.901$$

Mole fractions:

$$\chi_{H_2} = \frac{P_{H_2}}{P} = \frac{36}{51}$$

$$= 0.706$$

$$\chi_{CO_2} = \frac{P_{CO_2}}{P}$$

$$= \frac{15}{51}$$

$$= 0.294$$

• PROBLEM 10-3

A mixture of 4 lbm of CO_2 and 3 lbm of N_2 is stored in a tank with a volume of 5 ft^3. The temperature of the mixture is maintained at 80°F. Evaluate (a) the total pressure of the mixture, (b) the mole fraction of both the gases, (c) the molecular weight of the mixture, and (d) the apparent specific gas constant of the mixture.

Solution: (a) By Dalton's law of additive pressures, the total pressure of the mixture is the sum of the partial pressures of constituent gases. From the ideal gas equation of state, the partial pressures of the constituents at the temperature and volume of the mixture are obtained.

$$P = \frac{mR_uT}{VM}$$

$$P(CO_2) = \frac{4 \text{ lbm}}{5 \text{ ft}^3} \times \frac{1545 \text{ ft-lb/lb-mole-°R}}{44 \text{ lb/lb-mole}} \times \frac{540\text{°R}}{144 \text{ in}^2/\text{ft}^2}$$

$$= 105.34 \text{ psia}$$

$$P(N_2) = \frac{3 \text{ lbm}}{5 \text{ ft}^3} \times \frac{1545 \text{ ft-lb/lbm-mole-°R}}{28 \text{ lb/lb-mole}} \times \frac{540\text{°R}}{144 \text{ in}^2/\text{ft}^2}$$

$$= 124.15 \text{ psia.}$$

Therefore, the total pressure of the mixture is

$$P(\text{total}) = P(CO_2) + P(N_2)$$
$$= 105.34 + 124.15$$
$$= 229.49 \text{ psia}$$

(b) Number of moles present in a gas is given by

$$n = \frac{\text{mass of gas}}{\text{molecular weight}}$$

Therefore, number of moles of CO_2 is

$$n(CO_2) = \frac{4 \text{ lbm}}{44 \text{ lb/lb-mole}}$$
$$= 0.0909 \text{ lb-mole}$$

and number of moles of N_2 is

$$n(N_2) = \frac{3 \text{ lbm}}{28 \text{ lb/lb-mole}}$$
$$= 0.1071 \text{ lb-mole}$$

Therefore, number of moles of mixture is

$$n(\text{mixture}) = n(CO_2) + n(N_2)$$
$$= 0.0909 + 0.1071$$
$$= 0.198$$

From the definition of mole fraction,

$$x(CO_2) = \frac{n(CO_2)}{n(\text{mixture})}$$
$$= \frac{0.0909}{0.198}$$
$$= 0.459$$

and $$x(N_2) = \frac{n(N_2)}{n(\text{mixture})}$$
$$= \frac{0.1071}{0.198}$$
$$= 0.541$$

(c) The molecular weight of the mixture is given by the definition of a mole.

$$M = \frac{m}{n}$$

$$M(\text{mixture}) = \frac{4+3}{0.198}$$

$$= 35.35 \text{ lbm/lb-mole}$$

(d) The apparent specific gas constant is given by

$$R = \frac{R_u}{M}$$

Therefore, the specific gas constant of the mixture is

$$R = \frac{1545}{35.35}$$

$$= 43.7 \frac{\text{ft-lb}}{\text{lbm-°R}}$$

• PROBLEM 10-4

A gas mixture at 1 atm and 10°C consists of 75 percent hydrogen and 25 percent nitrogen by volume. The mixture is compressed from an initial volume of 7.07 m^3 to a final volume of 28.32 litres. The final pressure, measured at a temperature of 50°C, is 350 atm. Compare values with those calculated from

(a) an ideal gas mixture

(b) an ideal solution obeying the law of additive pressures, and

(c) an ideal solution obeying the law of additive volumes.

Solution: (a) The number of moles of each gas will remain constant throughout, because an ideal gas mixture behaves as an ideal gas.

$$P_2 = P_1 \frac{V_1 T_2}{V_2 T_1}$$

$$= 1.0 \times \frac{7.07}{0.02832} \times \frac{323}{283}$$

$$= 285 \text{ atm.}$$

(b) Using the law of additive pressures in conjunction with van der Waals equation,

$$p = RT\left(\Sigma \frac{y_i}{v_m - y_i b_i}\right) - \frac{1}{v_m^2} \Sigma a_i y_i^2$$

where

y_i = mole fraction of the component gas

v_m = molar volume of the mixture

a_i and b_i are van der Waals gas constants.

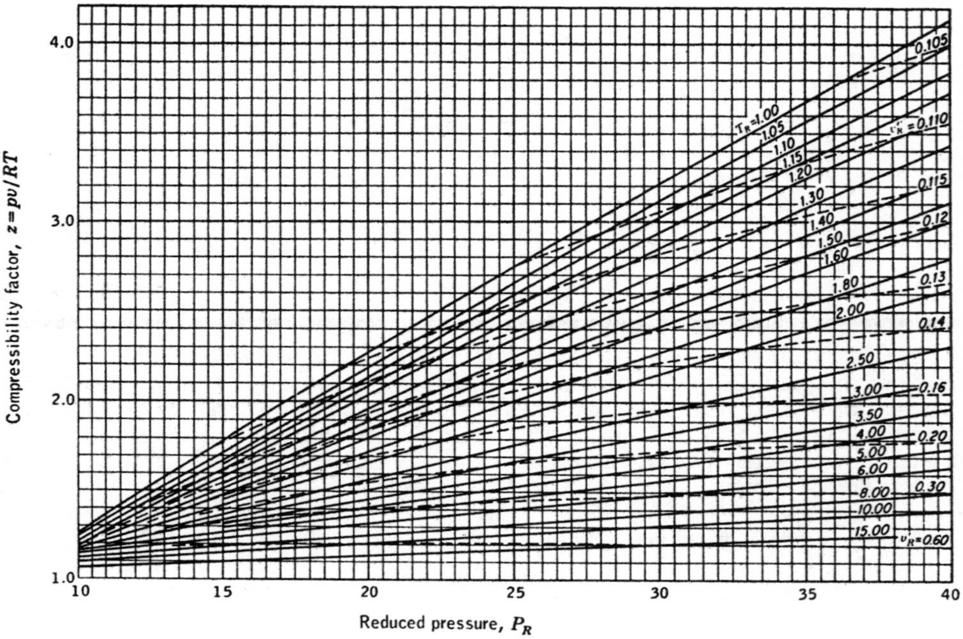

Figure Compressibility chart, high-pressure range.

From the ideal gas equation, the number of moles in the mixture is given by

$$N = \frac{pV}{RT}$$

$$= \frac{1 \times 101.325 \times 7.07}{8.3143 \times 283}$$

$$= 0.304 \text{ kmol.}$$

The molar volume at the end of compression is

$$v_m = \frac{V}{N} = \frac{28.32}{304.0} = 0.0931 \text{ l/mol.}$$

Therefore

$$p = \frac{8.3143}{101.325} \times 323\left(\frac{0.75}{0.0931-0.75 \times 0.0265} + \frac{0.25}{0.0931-0.25 \times 0.0385}\right)$$

$$- \frac{1}{(0.0931)^2}\,(0.244 \times 0.75^2 + 1.347 \times 0.25^2)$$

$$= 325.5 \text{ atm.}$$

(c) Using van der Waals equation,

$$0.75\ v_H + 0.25\ v_N = 0.0931$$

$$v_H = 0.1241 - 0.333\ v_N$$

To solve for v_H, trial values of v_N are taken in the above equation. Then p is calculated for each gas using the van der Waals equation. The trial values are correct when there is equality of the pressures computed for the two gases.

Assuming $v_N = 0.095$ l/mol

$$v_H = 0.0923 \text{ l/mol}$$

the pressures then calculated using van der Waals equation are

$$p_N = 330 \text{ atm}$$

$$p_H = 367 \text{ atm.}$$

From the results, it is clear that p_N has to be increased and p_H has to be reduced (i.e., by decreasing v_N and increasing v_H). Carrying out the procedure, the final values for v_N and v_H are

$$v_N = 0.0881 \text{ l/mol.}$$

$$v_H = 0.0947 \text{ l/mol.}$$

$$p_N = 363 \text{ atm.}$$

$$p_H = 364 \text{ atm}$$

$$P_{average} = \frac{363 + 364}{2} = 363.5 \text{ atm.}$$

(b) Using the generalized Z - chart,

assume p = 350 atm.

Then for hydrogen, the reduced temperature and pressure are

$$T_r = \frac{T}{T_{cr}} = \frac{323}{33.2} = 9.73$$

$$P_r = \frac{P}{P_{cr}} = \frac{350}{12.8} = 27.3$$

Then $$Z_H = 1.30$$

For nitrogen:

$$T_r = \frac{323}{126} = 2.56$$

$$P_r = \frac{350}{33.5} = 10.44$$

for which

$$Z_N = 1.18.$$

$$Z_{mixture} = 0.75 \times 1.30 + 0.25 \times 1.18 = 1.270$$

whence

$$p = \frac{1.27 \times 8.3143 \times 323}{0.0931 \times 101.325}$$

$$= 361 \text{ atm.}$$

The iteration process is to be continued until the assumed and computed pressure values are close enough.

Next try p = 361 atm, and proceed as before.

$$Z_H = 1.31$$

$$Z_N = 1.17$$

$$Z_{mixture} = 0.75 \times 1.31 + 0.25 \times 1.17$$

$$= 1.274$$

$$\therefore \quad p = 361 \times \frac{1.274}{1.27}$$

$$= 362 \text{ atm.}$$

(c) With the generalized Z chart,

$$Z_i = \frac{p_i v_i}{RT}$$

$$v_i = \frac{v_m}{\chi_i}$$

$$Z_i = \frac{p_i v_m}{\chi_i RT}$$

Thus

$$Z_H = \frac{0.0931\ p_H}{0.75 \times 8.3143 \times 323}$$

Simplifying,

$$p_H = 213.5\ Z_H$$

Assume $p_H = 250$ atm

$$T_r = 9.73$$

$$P_r = \frac{250}{12.8}$$

$$= 19.53$$

$$Z_H = 1.21 \quad \text{(from generalized Z-chart)}$$

But Z_H obtained from the assumed value of P_H is

$$= \frac{250}{213.5}$$

$$= 1.17$$

∴ to increase the computed value of Z_H, the assumed P_H is increased.

As the next guess, the value of p_H may be taken from the expression derived above, by substituting the value found from the generalized Z chart in the last trial into this relation.

∴ the value of p_H to be used $= 213.5 \times 1.21$

$= 258$ atm.

Using this value of p_H,

$$p_r = \frac{258}{12.9}$$

$$= 20.0$$

From the generalized Z-chart,

$$Z_H = 1.21$$

$$p_N = 71.1\ Z_N$$

Assuming $P_N = 100$ atm,

$$Z_N = \frac{100}{71.1}$$

$$= 1.406$$

$$T_r = 2.56$$

$$\therefore\ P_r = \frac{100}{33.5} = 2.98$$

$$\therefore\ Z_N = 1.025 \quad \text{from generalized Z chart.}$$

As for the next trial,

$$P_N = 71.1 \times 1.025$$

$$= 72.9 \text{ atm}$$

$$p_r = \frac{72.9}{33.5}$$

$$= 2.175$$

$$\therefore\ Z_N = 0.98$$

For the next trial take

$$p_N = 71.1 \times 0.98$$

$$= 69.6 \text{ atm}$$

$$p_r = \frac{69.6}{33.5}$$

$$= 2.08$$

$$Z_N = 0.98$$

$$\therefore\ p = 258 + 69.6$$

$$= 327.6 \text{ atm.}$$

Comparing all the results, we see that the ideal gas assumption is the most erractic.

• PROBLEM 10-5

Oxygen at 80°F and 60 psia is maintained in a tank with a volume of 20 cu. ft. Under isothermal conditions, nitrogen is introduced into the tank until the total pressure is 100 psia. Calculate the mass and partial volume of each gas.

Solution: From the ideal gas relation, the number of moles of oxygen is given by

$$N_0 = \frac{p_0 V}{RT}$$

$$= \frac{144 \times 60 \times 20}{1545 \times 540}$$

$$= 0.2071 \text{ moles.}$$

One mole of oxygen has a mass of 32 lb. The total mass of oxygen is 0.2071×32

$$= 6.63 \text{ lb.}$$

From Dalton's law of additive pressure, the partial pressure of nitrogen is the difference between the total pressure of the mixture and the partial pressure of oxygen. Therefore, the partial pressure of nitrogen is

$$p = 100-60$$

$$= 40 \text{ psia}$$

The number of moles of nitrogen is given by

$$N_n = \frac{P_n V}{RT}$$

$$= \frac{144 \times 40 \times 20}{1545 \times 540}$$

$$= 0.1381 \text{ moles.}$$

One mole of nitrogen has a mass of 28 lbs. The total mass of nitrogen is 0.138×28

$$= 3.87 \text{ lbs.}$$

(b) The partial volume of oxygen, $V = \frac{N_0 RT}{p_t}$

$$= \frac{0.2071 \times 1545 \times 540}{144 \times 110}$$

$$= 10.91 \text{ cu. ft.}$$

The partial volume of nitrogen is $20-10.91 = 9.09$ cu. ft.

• **PROBLEM 10-6**

> An oxygen cylinder at 35 psia and 80°F contains 0.9 lb of oxygen. If nitrogen is added to the cylinder to increase the cylinder pressure to 45 psia at the same temperature, find the mass of nitrogen added.

Solution: Both gases, i.e. oxygen and nitrogen, occupy the same volume and have the same temperature. Then, from the ideal gas equation,

$$pV = NR_uT$$

or

$$\frac{p}{N} = \frac{R_uT}{V}$$

$$\frac{p_{O_2}}{N_{O_2}} = \frac{R_uT}{V} = \frac{p_{N_2}}{N_{N_2}}$$

Therefore the number of moles of nitrogen is given by

$$N_{N_2} = N_{O_2}\left(\frac{P_{N_2}}{P_{O_2}}\right)$$

The number of oxygen moles is given by

$$N_{O_2} = \frac{m}{M}$$

where m = mass of oxygen

M = molecular weight of oxygen

Therefore,

$$N_{O_2} = \frac{0.9}{32}$$

$$= 0.02813 \text{ lb.mol}$$

The partial pressure of nitrogen is given by

$$P_{N_2} = P_t - P_{O_2}$$

$$= 45-35$$

$$= 10 \text{ psia}$$

Substituting the values into the equation for the number of moles of nitrogen,

$$N_{N_2} = 0.02813\left(\frac{10}{35}\right)$$

$$= 0.00804 \text{ lb-mol}$$

Therefore, the mass of nitrogen added is given by

$$m = NM$$

$$= 0.00804(28)$$

$$= 0.225 \text{ lb.}$$

• PROBLEM 10-7

A mixture of 21% O_2 and 79% N_2 is cooled to 80°K, 0.1 MPa pressure. Determine the composition of the liquid and vapor phases for this condition. Use the Raoult's Rule - Ideal Gas model to solve the problem.

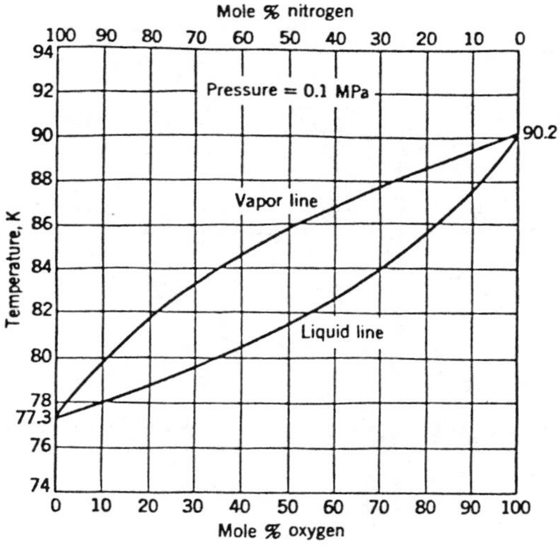

Solution: From the tables,

$$P_{sat_{N_2}} = 0.1370 \text{ MPa}$$

$$P_{sat_{O_2}} = 0.03006 \text{ MPa}$$

Using the following equations, the composition in each phase may be solved for.

$$\left[x_{N_2}\right]\left[P_{sat_{N_2}}\right] = \left[y_{N_2}\right](P)$$

$$\left[x_{O_2}\right]\left[P_{sat_{O_2}}\right] = \left[y_{O_2}\right](P)$$

Therefore, at 80°K, 0.1 MPa pressure,

$$[x_{N_2}](0.137) = [y_{N_2}](0.1)$$

$$[x_{O_2}](0.03006) = [y_{O_2}](0.1)$$

But

$$x_{N_2} + x_{O_2} = 1$$

$$y_{N_2} + y_{O_2} = 1$$

After substitution for y_{N_2} and y_{O_2}, the following equation is obtained :

$$\frac{0.137}{0.1}[x_{N_2}] + \frac{0.03006}{0.1}[x_{O_2}] = 1$$

$$1.37(x_{N_2}) + 0.3006\,(1-x_{N_2}) = 1$$

Solving for x_{N_2},

$$x_{N_2} = \frac{0.6994}{1.069} = 0.65$$

$$y_{N_2} = \frac{x_{N_2} \times 0.137}{0.1} = \frac{0.65 \times 0.137}{0.1} = 0.89$$

PROPERTIES OF IDEAL GAS MIXTURES

• PROBLEM 10-8

A mixture of 4 lbm of CO_2 and 3 lbm of N_2 is stored in a tank with a volume of 5 ft^3. The temperature and total pressure of the mixture are 80°F and 229.5 psia. Evaluate the entropy, internal energy, enthalpy, and the constant pressure and constant volume specific heat capacities.

Solution: In evaluating the entropy, internal enegy and enthalpy a datum-state of zero entropy and zero internal energy at 14.7 psia and 0°F (460°R) is chosen.

i.e., $s_0 = u_0 = 0$ at $T_0 = 460°R$ and $p_0 = 14.7$ psia

The entropy of CO_2 relative to the datum-state is

$$s(CO_2) = \frac{m(CO_2)}{m(\text{mixture})} \left[\int_{T_0}^{T} c_p \frac{dT}{T} - \int_{p_0}^{p} R \frac{dp}{p} \right]$$

$$= \frac{m(CO_2)}{m(\text{mixture})} \left[c_p \ln \frac{T}{T_0} - R \ln \frac{p}{p_0} \right]$$

(The positive sign in front of the first integral is due to an increase in entropy by raising the temperature. The negative sign in front of the second integral is due to a decrease in entropy by raising the pressure.)

The gas constant R for CO_2 is 35.12 $\frac{\text{ft-lbf}}{\text{lbm.°R}}$

and c_p for CO_2 is 0.203 $\frac{\text{Btu}}{\text{lbm.°R}}$

Substituting the values,

$$s(CO_2) = \frac{4}{7} \left[0.203 \ln \left(\frac{540}{460}\right) - \frac{35.12}{778} \ln \left(\frac{229.5}{14.7}\right) \right]$$

$$= -0.0523 \text{ Btu/lbm.°R}$$

Similarly, the entropy of N_2 is

$$s(N_2) = \frac{3}{7} \left[0.248 \ln \left(\frac{540}{460}\right) - \frac{55.12}{778} \ln \left(\frac{229.5}{14.7}\right) \right]$$

$$= -0.0664 \text{ Btu/lbm.°R}$$

Therefore, the entropy of the mixture is

$$s(\text{mixture}) = s(CO_2) + s(N_2)$$

$$= -0.0523 - 0.0664$$

$$= -0.1187 \text{ Btu/lbm.°R}$$

Since the gases are assumed to be ideal gases, the internal energy and enthalpy are functions of temperature only.

The internal energy of CO_2 relative to datum-state is

$$u(CO_2) = \frac{m(CO_2)}{m(\text{mixture})} c_v \int_{T_0}^{T} dT$$

$$= \frac{m(CO_2)}{m(\text{mixture})} c_v (T - T_0)$$

$$= \frac{4}{7} (0.158)(540-460)$$

$$= 7.22 \text{ Btu/lbm}$$

Similarly, the internal energy of N_2 relative to datum-state is

$$u(N_2) = \frac{m(N_2)}{m(\text{mixture})} c_v(T-T_0)$$

$$= \frac{3}{7}(0.177)(540-460)$$

$$= 6.07 \text{ Btu/lbm.}$$

Therefore, the internal energy of the mixture relative to the datum-state is

$$u(\text{mixture}) = u(CO_2) + u(N_2)$$

$$= 7.22 + 6.07$$

$$= 13.29 \text{ Btu/lbm.}$$

The enthalpy of CO_2 relative to the datum state is

$$h(CO_2) = \frac{m(CO_2)}{m(\text{mixture})}\left[c_p \int_{T_0}^{T} dT + RT_0\right]$$

$$= \frac{4}{7}\left[0.203(540-460) + \frac{35.12}{778}(460)\right]$$

$$= 21.15 \text{ Btu/lbm}$$

Similarly, the enthalpy of N_2 is

$$h(N_2) = \frac{3}{7}\left[0.248(540-460) + \frac{55.12}{778}(460)\right]$$

$$= 22.47 \text{ Btu/lbm}$$

Therefore, the enthalpy of the mixture is

$$h(\text{mixture}) = h(CO_2) + h(N_2)$$

$$= 21.15 + 22.47$$

$$= 43.62 \text{ Btu/lbm.}$$

The constant pressure specific heat of the mixture is given by

$$c_p = \frac{(mc_p)_{CO_2} + (mc_p)_{N_2}}{m(\text{mixture})}$$

$$= \frac{4(0.203) + 3(0.248)}{7}$$

$$= 0.222 \text{ Btu/lbm} - {}^0R$$

The constant volume specific heat of the mixture is given by

$$c_v = \frac{(mc_v)_{CO_2} + (mc_v)_{N_2}}{m(\text{mixture})}$$

$$= \frac{4(0.158) + 3(0.177)}{7}$$

$$= 0.166 \text{ Btu/lbm} - {}^0R$$

• PROBLEM 10-9

The exhaust gases from an engine are analyzed and found to have the following composition on a volumetric basis.

CO_2 - - - - - - - 10%

H_2O - - - - - - - 13%

CO - - - - - - - 2%

O_2 - - - - - - - 3%

N_2 - - - - - - - 72%

The gas pressure and temperature are 100 kPa and 300°C respectively. Subsequent to leaving the engine, the gas is cooled. Determine (a) the temperature at which water will start to condense, and (b) the value of the specific heat ratio, k, for this mixture. Assume constant specific heats.

Table 1.

constit-uent	mole fraction $y_i = n_i/n$		Molecular Weight (MW)		Mass kg per K mol of Mixture.
CO_2	0.10	x	44.01	=	4.4010
H_2O	0.13	x	18.015	=	2.3420
CO	0.02	x	28.01	=	0.5602
O_2	0.03	x	31.99	=	0.9597
N_2	0.72	x	28.013	=	+20.1694
					28.4323

Table 2.

Constit-uents	c_{p_0} KJ/kgK	c_{v_0} kJ/kgK	mass fraction m_i/m
CO_2	0.8418	0.6529	0.1548
H_2O	1.8723	1.4108	0.0824
CO	1.0413	0.7445	0.0197
O_2	0.9216	0.6618	0.0338
N_2	1.0416	0.7448	0.7094

Solution: It is very convenient to use Table 1 and Table 2 in solving this problem.

$$(M.W.)_{mixt.} = 28.43 \text{ kg/kmol}$$

(a) From the equation

$$y_i = \frac{p_i}{p_T}$$

the partial pressure can be obtained for the water in the mixture as

$$p_w = y_i \times p_T$$

$$= 0.13 \times 100$$

$$= 13 \text{ kPa}$$

From the steam tables, the dew point temperature (the temperature at which water vapor will start to condense) is found to be

$$T_{D.P.} = 50.71°C$$

The specific heat ratio k for the mixture is given by the equation

$$k = \frac{c_{p_0}}{c_{v_0}} \quad (1)$$

Thus the specific heats at constant pressure and volume will have to be calculated. The specific heat at constant pressure is given as

$$\left(c_{p_0}\right)_{mixt.} = \Sigma \frac{m_i}{m} c_{p_i}$$

$$= (0.1548 \times 0.8418) + (0.0824 \times 1.8723) + (0.0197 \times 1.04143)$$

$$(0.0338 \times 0.9216) + (0.7094 \times 1.0416)$$

$$= 1.0752 \text{ kJ/kg} - {}^0K$$

Then from the equations

$$c_{p_0} - c_{v_0} = R$$

and $$(R)_{mixt.} = \frac{\bar{R}}{(M.W.)_{mixt}} \qquad (\bar{R} = 8.31434 \text{ kJ/kg} - {}^0K)$$

$$= \frac{8.31434}{28.43}$$

$$= 0.2924$$

the value for the specific heat at constant volume is

$$(c_{v_0})_{mixt.} = (c_{p_0})_{mixt.} - (R)_{mixt.}$$

$$= 1.0752-0.2924$$

$$= 0.7828 \text{ kJ/kg} - {}^0\text{K}$$

Substituting into Equation (1),

$$k = \frac{1.0752}{0.7828}$$

$$= 1.3736$$

Note that the specific heat at constant volume could also have been found using the equation

$$(c_{v_0})_{mixt.} = \Sigma \frac{m_i}{m} c_{v_i}$$

which would have given the same result.

• PROBLEM 10-10

An ideal gas mixture consists of 1 mole of oxygen and 2 moles of nitrogen at 90°F and 13.5 psia.

(a) If each constituent gas is assigned a datum-state value of zero entropy at 14.7 psia and 0°F, calculate the entropy of the mixture.

(b) Determine the change in internal energy and entropy if the mixture is cooled to 40°F at constant volume.

Assume that the heat capacities are constant for the temperature range of interest and have the following valves:

$C_{p_{oxygen}} = 7.01$ $\qquad$ $C_{v_{oxygen}} = 5.02$

$C_{p_{nitrogen}} = 6.96$ $\qquad$ $C_{v_{nitrogen}} = 4.97$

Solution: (a) Given the number of moles of oxygen as

$$n_O = 1 \text{ mole}$$

and number of moles of nitrogen as

$$n_N = 2 \text{ moles}$$

Therefore, the mole fractions are

$$x_O = \frac{1}{3}$$

and

$$x_N = \frac{2}{3}$$

The corresponding partial pressures are

$$p_O = x_O P$$

$$= \frac{1}{3}(13.5)$$

$$= 4.5 \text{ psia}$$

and

$$p_N = x_N P$$

$$= \frac{2}{3}(13.5)$$

$$= 9.0 \text{ psia}$$

The entropy of each gas constituent is given by

$$ds_i = C_{p_i} \frac{dT}{T} - R_u \frac{dP_i}{P_i}$$

Therefore, the entropy of oxygen relative to the datum state is

$$s_O = \Delta s_O = C_{p_O} \int_d^a \frac{dT}{T} - R_u \int_d^a \frac{dP}{P}$$

where the limits d and a denote datum and actual states, respectively.

Integrating and substituting the limits,

$$s_O = 7.01 \ln \frac{550}{460} - 1.986 \ln \frac{4.5}{14.7}$$

$$= 3.60 \text{ Btu/lb-mole} - {}^0\text{R}$$

Similarly, the entropy of nitrogen relative to datum state is

$$s_N = \Delta s_N = C_{p_N} \int_d^a \frac{dT}{T} - R_u \int_d^a \frac{dP}{P}$$

$$= 6.96 \ln \frac{550}{460} - 1.986 \ln \frac{9.0}{14.7}$$

$$= 2.22 \text{ Btu/lb-mole} - {}^0\text{R}$$

The entropy of the mixture is given by

$$S = n_O s_O + n_N s_N$$

$$= 1(3.60) + 2(2.22)$$

$$= 8.04 \text{ Btu/°R}$$

(b) The change in internal energy of the mixture is given by

$$\Delta U = (n_O C_{vO} + n_N C_{vN})(T_2 - T_1)$$

where

C_{vO} = constant volume specific heat of oxygen

C_{vN} = constant volume specific heat of nitrogen

Substituting the values,

$$\Delta U = \left[1(5.02) + 2(4.97)\right](40-90)$$

$$= -748 \text{ Btu}$$

The change in entropy of the mixture is given by integrating the equation

$$dS = (n_O C_{vO} + n_N C_{vN}) \frac{dT}{T} + R_u \frac{dv}{v}$$

But since the colling process is taking place at constant volume, $dv = 0$.

Therefore, $$dS = (n_O C_{vO} + n_N C_{vN}) \frac{dT}{T}$$

Integrating and substituting the limits,

$$\Delta S = \left[1(5.02) + 2(4.97)\right] \ln \frac{500}{550}$$

$$= -1.426 \text{ Btu/°R}$$

• PROBLEM 10-11

A mixture of 6 mol of helium and 4 mol of nitrogen is at 170°F and 120 psia. If this mixture is expanded isentropically to 25 psia, find

(a) the final temperature of the mixture, and

(b) the entropy change for each constituent gas.

Assume all gases are ideal.

Solution: The total entropy change of the mixture is given by

$$ds = \left[\chi_{He} \, c_{PHe} + \chi_N \, c_{PN_2} \right] \frac{dT}{T} - R_u \frac{dp}{p}$$

But for an isentropic expansion process, ds = 0.

Therefore,

$$\left[\chi_{He} \, c_{PHe} + \chi_{N_2} \, c_{PN_2} \right] \frac{dT}{T} = R_u \frac{dp}{p}$$

Assuming the heat capacities to be constant in the expansion range and integrating the above equation yields

$$\left[\chi_{He} \, c_{PHe} + \chi_{N_2} \, c_{PN_2} \right] \ln \frac{T_2}{T_1} = R_u \ln \frac{P_2}{P_1}$$

Taking

$$c_{P_{He}} = \frac{5}{2} R_u$$

and

$$c_{P_{N_2}} = \frac{7}{2} R_u ,$$

substituting the values of the known variables into the above equation and evaluating for T_2,

$$\left[0.6 \left(\frac{5}{2} R_u \right) + 0.4 \left(\frac{7}{2} R_u \right) \right] \ln \frac{T_2}{630} = R_u \ln \frac{25}{120}$$

$$2.9 \ln \frac{T_2}{630} = \ln \frac{25}{120}$$

Therefore,

$$T_2 = 366.8°R$$

(b) The specific entropy changes of the individual gases in the mixture are given by

$$\Delta s_i = c_{pi} \ln \left(\frac{T_2}{T_1} \right) - R_u \ln \left(\frac{p_{i_2}}{p_{i_1}} \right)$$

Since the mole fraction of either gas does not change during the process, the ratio of partial pressures in this equation is the same as the ratio of total pressures of the mixture.

$$\text{i.e.,} \quad \frac{p_{i_2}}{p_{i_1}} = \frac{p_2}{p_1}$$

The entropy change of helium is

$$\Delta s_{He} = n_{He} \left[c_{PHe} \ln \frac{T_2}{T_1} - R_u \ln \frac{P_2}{P_1} \right]$$

$$= 6\left[\frac{5}{2}(1.986)\ \ln\frac{366.8}{630} - 1.986\ \ln\frac{25}{120}\right]$$

$$= 2.578\ \text{Btu}/°\text{R}$$

The entropy change of nitrogen is

$$\Delta s_{N_2} = n_{N_2}\left[c_{p_{N_2}}\ \ln\frac{T_2}{T_1} - R_u\ \ln\frac{p_2}{p_1}\right]$$

$$= 4\left[\frac{7}{2}(1.986)\ \ln\frac{366.8}{630} - 1.986\ \ln\frac{25}{120}\right]$$

$$= -2.578\ \text{Btu}/°\text{R}.$$

It is clear that the entropy of N_2 decreases while the entropy of He increases in the isentropic expansion process. The reverse is true for isentropic compression process.

• PROBLEM 10-12

An air-water-vapor mixture at 1 atm and 75°F has a relative humidity of 0.45. For this mixture, calculate the specific humidity, the dew point and the partial pressures.

Solution: The relative humidity ϕ is the ratio of the actual partial pressure of water vapor to the saturation partial pressure of water vapor.

$$\phi = \frac{P_v}{P_g}$$

$$= 0.45$$

From steam tables, at 75°F the pressure of saturated water vapor P_g is 0.430 psia.

$\therefore$ P_v, the actual water partial pressure

$$= \phi \times p_g$$

$$= 0.45 \times 0.430$$

$$= 0.1935\ \text{psia}.$$

The partial pressure of dry air, $P_a = 14.7 - 0.1935$

$$= 14.5065\ \text{psia}$$

Using the equation

$$\gamma = \frac{(R_a T/P_a)}{(R_w T/P_w)}$$

$$= 0.622 \frac{P_w}{P_a}$$

$$= \frac{0.622 \times 0.1935}{14.5065}$$

$$= 8.297 \times 10^{-3} \text{ lbm water/lbm air.}$$

The temperature at which the mixture becomes saturated, or condensation begins, when a mixture of dry air and water vapor is cooled at constant pressure from an unsaturated state, is called the dew point temperature.

From steam tables, the dew point temperature

$$= 52.15^{\circ}\text{F}.$$

• PROBLEM 10-13

A mixture of ideal gases consisting of 0.4 mole fraction of N_2 and 0.6 mole fraction of argon is flowing at a rate of 2500 lbm/hr through a heat exchanger, where its temperature is increased from 80°F to 450°F. Assuming that the heating process takes place at a constant pressure of 14.7 psia, determine the rate of heat addition.

Solution: This is a steady-state, steady-flow process in which there is no work transfer. Neglecting the changes in kinetic energy and potential energy, the first law applied to a steady flow process yields

$$\mathring{Q} = \frac{\mathring{m}(h_2 - h_1)}{M}$$

where

h_2 = enthalpy of the mixture at 450°F

h_1 = enthalpy of the mixture at 80°F

$\mathring{m}$ = mass flow rate of mixture

M = molecular weight of mixture.

For an ideal-gas mixture of fixed proportions and of constant specific heat capacity,

$$\dot{Q} = \frac{\dot{m}}{M} c_p(T_2 - T_1)$$

where

c_p = constant pressure specific heat capacity of the mixture

The molecular weight of the mixture is given by

$$M = \Sigma X_i M_i$$

$$= 0.4(28) + 0.6(39.95)$$

$$= 35.17 \text{ lbm/lbmol.}$$

The constant pressure specific heat capacity of the mixture is given by

$$c_p = \Sigma X_i c_{pi}$$

Taking c_p for N_2 as $\frac{7}{2} R_u$,

and for argon as $\frac{5}{2} R_u$,

$$c_p = 0.4\left(\frac{7}{2} R_u\right) + 0.6\left(\frac{5}{2} R_u\right)$$

$$= 2.9\, R_u$$

$$= 2.9\,(1.986)$$

$$= 5.759 \text{ Btu/lb-mol} - {}^0\text{R}$$

Substituting the values into the equation for the rate of heat addition gives

$$\dot{Q} = \frac{2500(5.759)(450-80)}{35.17}$$

$$= 151466.45 \text{ Btu/hr.}$$

AIR - VAPOR MIXTURES

• PROBLEM 10-14

A rigid insulation tank, consisting of two compartments separated by a wall, has 1 mole of oxygen at 35 psia and 65^0F in one compartment, and 2 moles of nitrogen at 14 psia and 120^0F in the other compartment. If the partition is removed to allow the gases to mix adiabatically, calculate

(a) the equilibrium temperature and pressure of the mixture, and

(b) the change in entropy for each gas and for the mixing process.

Solution: For the low pressures involved, the gases are assumed to behave as ideal gases. Since both the heat transfer and work done are zero, the first law for a closed system dictates that $\Delta U = 0$,

i.e.,
$$n_O c_{vO}(T_f - T_O) + n_N c_{vN}(T_f - T_N) = 0$$

where the subscripts O, N and f denote oxygen, nitrogen and final state, respectively.

Substituting the values,

$$1(5.02)(T_f - 65) + 2(4.97)(T_f - 120) = 0$$

Therefore,
$$T_f = 101.5°F$$

The final pressure is determined from the ideal gas relation $PV = nR_uT$. The total volume is the sum of the volumes of the original compartments, which may also be determined from the same equation.

Hence, volume of the original oxygen compartment is

$$V_O = \frac{n_O R_u T_O}{p_O}$$

$$= \frac{1(1545)(525)}{35(144)}$$

$$= 161 \text{ ft}^3$$

and volume of original nitrogen compartment

$$V_N = \frac{n_N R_u T_N}{p_N}$$

$$= \frac{2(1545)(580)}{14(144)}$$

$$= 889 \text{ ft}^3$$

Therefore, the total volume of the tank is

$$V = V_O + V_N$$

$$= 161 + 889$$

$$= 1050 \text{ ft}^3$$

Then the mixture pressure is

$$p = \frac{nR_O T}{V}$$

$$= \frac{3(1545)(561.5)}{1050(144)}$$

$$= 17.2 \text{ psia}$$

(b) The change in entropy of each constituent gas is found by

$$\Delta s = (\Delta s \text{ from change in temperature})$$

$$+ (\Delta s \text{ from change in volume})$$

i.e., $$\Delta s = c_v \ln \frac{T_2}{T_1} + R_u \ln \frac{v_2}{v_1}$$

Therefore, the change in entropy of oxygen is

$$\Delta S_O = n_O \Delta s_O = 1\left[5.02 \ln \frac{561.5}{525} + 1.986 \ln \frac{1050}{161}\right]$$

$$= 4.06 \text{ Btu/°R}$$

Similarly, for nitrogen,

$$\Delta S_N = n_N \Delta s_N = 2\left[4.97 \ln \frac{561.5}{580} + 1.986 \ln \frac{1050}{889}\right]$$

$$= 0.34 \text{ Btu/°R}$$

The change in entropy for the process is

$$\Delta S = \Delta S_O + \Delta S_N$$

$$= 4.06 + 0.34$$

$$= 4.4 \text{ Btu/°R}.$$

• PROBLEM 10-15

An air-vapor mixture having a volume of 2500 ft^3 is at 75°F and 14.7 psia, and has a relative humidity of 50%. Compute (a) the humidity ratio, (b) the dew-point, (c) the mass of air, and (d) the mass of water vapor.

Solution: (a) The relative humidity is defined as

$$\phi = \frac{p_v}{p_g}$$

where p_v = vapor pressure of the mixture

p_g = saturated vapor pressure

Saturation pressure corresponding to 75°F is

$$p_g = 0.430 \text{ psia}$$

Therefore

$$p_v = \phi p_g$$

$$= 0.5(0.430)$$

$$= 0.215 \text{ psia}$$

The humidity ratio ω is given by

$$\omega = 0.622 \frac{p_v}{p_t - p_v}$$

$$= 0.622 \left(\frac{0.215}{14.7 - 0.215}\right)$$

$$= 0.00923 \text{ lbm water/lbm dry air}$$

(b) The dew-point temperature is the saturation temperature of water corresponding to the vapor pressure p_v (=0.215 psia).

From steam tables,

Dew Point Temperature (DPT) = 55°F

(c) The mass of air is given by the ideal gas equation

$$m_a = \frac{p_a V}{R_a T}$$

where $p_a = p_t - p_v = 14.485$ psia

$V = 2500 \text{ ft}^3$

$R_a = 53.35$ ft.lbf/lbm°R

$T = 75°F = 535°R$

Substituting the values,

$$m_a = \frac{(14.485)(144)(2500)}{(53.35)(535)}$$

$$= 182.7 \text{ lbm}$$

(d) The humidity ratio is defined as

$$\omega = \frac{m_v}{m_a}$$

Therefore, mass of vapor is

$$m_v = (\omega)(m_a)$$

$$= 0.00923\ (182.7)$$

$$= 1.69 \text{ lbm.}$$

• PROBLEM 10-16

A sling-psychrometer reads 85°F DBT and 65°F WBT (DBT = Dry bulb temp., WBT = Wet bulb temp.). Calculate the following:

(a) Specific humidity (b) Relative humidity (c) Dew point temperature.

Assume atmospheric pressure to be 14.7 psia.

Solution: In a sling-psychrometer, an adiabatic saturation process takes place, and the given DBT and WBT correspond to the inlet and outlet temperatures i.e., unsaturated mixture and saturated mixture temperatures, respectively.

(a) The specific humidity of the saturated mixture ω_2 is given by

$$\omega_2 = 0.622 \frac{p_{v_2}}{p_t - p_{v_2}}$$

where p_{v_2} = saturation vapor pressure at the WBT.

p_t = total pressure

From steam tables, the saturation vapor pressure at temperature 65°F is 0.3057 psia.

Hence $$\omega_2 = 0.622 \left(\frac{0.3057}{14.7-0.3057}\right)$$

$$= 0.0132 \text{ lbm water/lbm dry air}$$

The specific humidity of the air is given by

$$\omega_1 = \frac{c_{pa}(T_2-T_1) + \omega_2 h_{fg_2}}{h_{v_1}-h_{f_2}}$$

where c_{pa} = constant pressure specific heat of air

h_{fg_2} = evaporation enthalpy of water at 65°F

h_{v_1} = saturated vapor enthalpy at 85°F

h_{f_2} = saturated water enthalpy at 65°F

From the steam tables,

$$h_{fg_2} = 1056.8 \text{ Btu/lbm}$$

$$h_{f_2} = 33.09 \text{ Btu/lbm}$$

$$h_{v_1} = 1098.6 \text{ Btu/lbm}$$

Substituting into the equation for ω_1,

$$\omega_1 = \frac{0.24(65-85) + 0.0132(1056.8)}{(1098.6-33.09)}$$

$$= 0.00859 \text{ lbm water/lbm dry air}$$

(b) The specific humidity of the unsaturated mixture is also given by

$$\omega_1 = 0.622 \frac{p_{v_1}}{p_t-p_{v_1}}$$

where p_{v_1} = saturation vapor pressure at DBT.

The above equation can be written as

$$p_{v_1} = \frac{p_t(\omega_1)}{0.622 + \omega_1}$$

$$= \frac{(14.7)(0.00859)}{0.622 + 0.00859}$$

$$= 0.2002 \text{ psia}$$

The relative humidity of the unsaturated mixture is given by

$$\phi_1 = \frac{p_{v_1}}{p_{g_1}}$$

where p_{g_1} = saturation pressure at DBT.

From steam tables, p_{g_1} = 0.5964 psia.

Therefore,

$$\phi_1 = \frac{0.2002}{0.5964}$$

$$= 0.3357$$

$$= 33.57\%$$

(c) The dew point temperature corresponds to the saturation temperature of water vapor in the mixture of air and water vapor.

The partial pressure of the vapor is

$$p_{v_1} = 0.2002 \text{ psia}$$

The corresponding saturation temperature gives the dew point temperature (DPT).

From steam tables,

$$DPT = 53.1°F$$

• PROBLEM 10-17

A tank contains saturated air-vapor mixture at 240°F and 55 psia. If the mixture contains 1 lb of dry air, calculate the volume of the tank and the mass of water vapor in the mixture.

Solution: The volume of the tank is the volume occupied by 1 lb of dry air at its partial pressure. From Dalton's law, the partial pressure of air (p_a) is

$$p_a = p_t - p_v$$

where p_t = total pressure

p_v = partial pressure of vapor

But it is given that the mixture is saturated.

Therefore, p_v = saturation vapor pressure at 240°F

= 24.97 psia

Therefore, p_a = 55-24.97

= 30.03 psia.

The volume occupied by 1 lb of air at 30.03 psia is given by the ideal gas equation,

$$V = \frac{m_a R_a T}{M_a p_a}$$

where m_a = mass of air

M_a = molecular wt. of air

R_a = gas constant of air

Substituting,

$$V = \frac{1(1545)(700)}{29(30.03)(144)}$$

$$= 8.62 \text{ ft}^3$$

Therefore, the volume of the tank is 8.62 ft^3.

Also, this is the volume occupied by vapor.

The mass of water vapor is given by

$$m_v = \frac{V}{v_v}$$

where v_v = specific volume of saturated vapor.

From saturation steam tables,

$$v_v = 16.33 \text{ ft}^3\text{/lbm}$$

Therefore, mass of vapor is

$$m_v = \frac{8.62}{16.33}$$

$$= 0.528 \text{ lbm.}$$

• PROBLEM 10-18

A rigid tank contains 1 lbm of air and 0.2 lbm of saturated water vapor at 250°F. Determine the volume of the tank and the total pressure of the air-vapor mixture.

Solution: The volume of the tank is the volume occupied by the 0.2 lbm of saturated water vapor at 250°F. From saturation steam tables, the saturation pressure (p_v) and specific volume of saturated vapor (v_g) at 250°F are

$$p_v = 29.82 \text{ psia}$$

$$v_g = 13.83 \text{ ft}^3/\text{lbm}$$

Therefore, the volume occupied by 0.2 lbm of saturated vapor is V = 0.2(13.83)

$$= 2.766 \text{ ft}^3$$

Therefore, the volume of the tank is $V = 2.766 \text{ ft}^3$.

From Dalton's law of additive pressures, it can be inferred that each gas acts independently of the others present in the mixture.

Then, the total pressure of the mixture is equal to the sum of the pressures exerted by the vapor and air. The volume occupied by air is equal to the tank volume. Then, from the ideal gas equation, the partial pressure of the air is

$$p_a = \frac{m_a R_a T}{V}$$

$$= \frac{1(53.35)(710)}{(2.766)(144)}$$

$$= 95.1 \text{ psia}$$

Therefore, the total pressure of the mixture is

$$p_t = p_v + p_a$$

$$= 29.82 + 95.1$$

$$= 124.92 \text{ psia.}$$

• PROBLEM 10-19

The metal beaker of a dew-point apparatus is gradually cooled from room temperature, 75°F. When the beaker temperature reaches 60°F, the moisture of the room air starts condensing on it. Assuming the room air to be at 14.7 psia, determine (a) the partial pressure of vapor, and (b) the parts by mass of vapor in the room air.

Solution: The temperature at which the moisture in the air starts condensing is the dew-point temperature. Therefore, the dew-point temperature is given as 60°F. The partial pressure of the water vapor in the room air is equal to the saturation pressure corresponding to the dew-point temperature, 60°F.

From saturation steam tables,

$$p_v = 0.2563 \text{ psia}$$

Therefore, the partial pressure of vapor is 0.2563 psia.

(b) Dalton's law of partial pressures states that

$$P = p_a + p_v$$

where P = total pressure (room pressure, 14.7 psia)

p_a = partial pressure of dry air

Therefore, the partial pressure of dry air is

$$p_a = 14.7-0.2563$$

$$= 14.4437 \text{ psia}$$

From the definition of mole fraction,

$$\chi_a = \frac{n_a}{n} = \frac{p_a}{p}$$

and

$$\chi_v = \frac{n_v}{n} = \frac{p_v}{p}$$

From the definition of molecular weight,

$$m = nM$$

Therefore, the parts by mass are

$$\frac{m_a}{m} = \frac{n_a M_a}{nM} = \frac{p_a M_a}{PM}$$

and

$$\frac{m_v}{m} = \frac{n_v M_v}{nM} = \frac{p_v M_v}{PM}$$

Therefore,

$$\frac{m_a}{m_v} = \frac{p_a M_a}{p_v M_v}$$

$$= \frac{(14.4437)(29)}{(0.2563)(18)}$$

$$= 90.8$$

Then,

$$\frac{m_a + m_v}{m_v} = \frac{m_a}{m_v} + 1 = 90.8 + 1$$

$$= 91.8$$

But $$m_a + m_v = m$$

Therefore, the parts by mass of vapor in the room air is

$$\frac{m_v}{m} = \frac{1}{91.8}$$

$$= 0.01089.$$

• PROBLEM 10-20

An air-vapor mixture consisting of 1 lbm of dry air and 0.015 lbm of vapor is at 85°F and 20 psia. Find the partial pressure of water vapor.

Solution: It is unknown whether the mixture is saturated or not. The maximum partial pressure of vapor is the saturation pressure of the vapor corresponding to the mixture temperature.

Therefore, the maximum partial pressure of vapor that could be exerted is (from Steam Tables at 85°F)

$$p_v = 0.5964 \text{ psia}$$

If the water vapor is in the superheated state, then the partial pressure is given by

$$p_v = \chi_v p_t$$

where χ_v = mole-fraction of vapor

p_t = total pressure

The mole-fraction of the vapor is defined as

$$\chi_v = \frac{(m_v/M_v)}{(m_v/M_v) + (m_a/M_a)}$$

where

m = mass

M = molecular weight

Therefore,

$$\chi_v = \frac{(0.015/18)}{(0.015/18) + (1/29)}$$

$$= 0.023596$$

The partial pressure of the vapor is

$$p_v = 0.023596(20)$$

$$= 0.4719 \text{ psia}$$

Since this pressure is less than the saturated pressure, the vapor must be superheated.

Therefore, the partial pressure of the vapor is 0.4719 psia.

• PROBLEM 10-21

A saturated air-water-vapor mixture is at -80°F and 14.7 psia. Determine its humidity ratio.

Solution: Humidity ratio is defined as

$$\omega = 0.622 \frac{p_v}{p_t - p_v}$$

where p_v = partial vapor pressure

But since the mixture is saturated,

$$p_v = \text{saturation vapor pressure}$$

But the saturated steam tables do not give saturation pressures for temperatures less than -40°F. However, it can be noticed that the evaporation enthalpy (h_{fg}) is relatively constant in this range. Taking the evaporation enthalpy (h_{fg}) as constant, the saturation pressure at -80°F (380°R) can be found by integrating the equation

$$\frac{dP}{P} = \frac{(h_g - h_f)}{RT}\left(\frac{dT}{T}\right)$$

between the limits of -80°F and -40°F.

Integrating,

$$\int_1^2 \frac{dP}{P} = \int_1^2 \frac{h_{fg}}{R} \frac{dT}{T^2}$$

$$\ln \frac{P_2}{P_1} = \frac{h_{fg}}{R}\left(\frac{T_2 - T_1}{T_1 T_2}\right)$$

From steam tables,

at $T_2 = -40^0F = 420^0R$

$P_2 = 0.0019$ psia

and $h_{fg} = 1221$ Btu/lbm

Substituting the values into the above equation ,

$$\ln\left(\frac{0.0019}{P_1}\right) = \frac{1221}{(1.986/18.02)}\left[\frac{420-380}{(420)(380)}\right]$$

$$= 2.7766$$

$$\frac{0.0019}{P_1} \Rightarrow e^{2.7766}$$

$$= 16.065$$

Therefore,

$$P_1 = \frac{0.0019}{16.065}$$

$$= 1.18 \times 10^{-4} \text{ psia}$$

P_1 is the saturation vapor pressure,

i.e., $P_1 = P_v$

Substituting the values into the equation for the humidity ratio,

$$\omega = 0.622\ \frac{1.18 \times 10^{-4}}{14.7-1.18 \times 10^{-4}}$$

$$= 4.99 \times 10^{-6} \text{ lbm water/lbm dry air}$$

• PROBLEM 10-22

A certain sample of room air at 14.7 psia has dry-bulb and wet-bulb temperatures of 80^0F and 70^0F, respectively. Calculate (a) vapor pressure, (b) relative humidity, (c) specific humidity, (d) density of dry air, (e) density of the vapor in the mixture, and (f) enthalpy of the mixture/lbm dry air.

Solution: (a) The saturation vapor pressure at the wet-bulb temperature of 70°F can be obtained from steam tables.

From the saturation steam tables,

$$p_{vw} = 0.3632 \text{ psia}$$

The vapor pressure of the room air may be obtained from the equation

$$p_{vd} = p_{vw} - \frac{(p_t - p_{v\omega})(T_d - T_\omega)}{2800 - 1.3\ T_\omega}$$

The subscripts d and w defer to the dry-bulb temperature and wet-bulb temperature conditions.

$$p_v = \text{vapor pressure}$$

$$p_t = \text{total pressure}$$

Substituting the values into the above equation,

$$p_{vd} = 0.3632 - \frac{(14.7 - 0.3632)(80 - 70)}{2800 - 1.3(70)}$$

$$= 0.3103 \text{ psia}$$

(b) For a dry-bulb temperature of 80°F, the saturation vapor pressure in the mixture is obtained from saturation steam tables.

$$p_{gd} = 0.5073 \text{ psia}$$

The relative humidity is defined as

$$\phi = \frac{p_{vd}}{p_{gd}}$$

$$= \frac{0.3103}{0.5073}$$

$$= 0.612$$

(c) Assume the water vapor and air in the mixture to be ideal gases. Then the specific humidity is given by

$$\omega = 0.622 \frac{p_{vd}}{p_t - p_{vd}}$$

$$= 0.622 \times \frac{0.3103}{14.7 - 0.3103}$$

$$= 0.0134 \text{ lbm water/lbm dry air}$$

(d) The density of dry air is given by the ideal gas equation

$$\rho_a = \frac{p_t - p_{vd}}{R_a T_d}$$

$$= \frac{(14.7-0.3103)(144)}{(53.35)(540)}$$

$$= 0.072 \text{ lbm/ft}^3$$

(e) The specific humidity is defined as

$$\omega = \frac{m_v}{m_a}$$

Since both the vapor and dry air occupy the same total volume, the mass ratio can be replaced by the ratio of densities,

i.e.,
$$\omega = \frac{\rho_v}{\rho_a}$$

Therefore, vapor density $\rho_v = \omega\rho_a$

$$= 0.0134(0.072)$$

$$= 0.00096 \text{ lbm/ft}^3$$

(f) The enthalpy of the mixture is the sum of the enthalpies of the dry air and water vapor (Gibbs-Dalton law).

The enthalpy of the mixture per lbm of dry air is given by

$$h = h_a + \omega h_v$$

where h_a = enthalpy of dry air (h_a can be written as $C_{pa}T_d$

where C_{pa} = constant pressure specific heat of air)

and h_v = enthalpy of saturated vapor at 80°F

From saturated steam tables,

$$h_v = 1096.4 \text{ Btu/lbm}$$

Therefore,

$$h = (0.24)(80) + (0.0134)(1096.4)$$

$$= 33.89 \text{ Btu/lbm of dry air}$$

It is important to note the complete arbitrariness of this enthalpy value. The enthalpy of the air was chosen to be zero at 0°F, and the enthalpy of the water vapor, on the basis of the steam tables, is zero as a saturated liquid at 32°F. If differences in enthalpies are to be calculated for engineering purposes, the enthalpy at each state must be based on the same reference values.

An air-vapor mixture consisting of 1 lbm of air and 0.92 lbm of water vapor is isentropically compressed from 45 psia and 240°F to 90 psia. For this process determine (a) the final temperature, and (b) the change in entropy of each constituent.

Solution: The number of air moles present in 1 lbm is given by

$$n_a = \frac{m_a}{M_a}$$

where m_a = mass of air

M_a = molecular weight of air

$$n_a = \frac{1}{29}$$

$$= 0.03448 \text{ lb mole}$$

Similarly, the number of moles of water vapor in 0.92 lbm is

$$n_w = \frac{m_w}{M_w}$$

$$= \frac{0.92}{18}$$

$$= 0.05111 \text{ lb mole}$$

The mole fraction of air χ_a is

$$\chi_a = \frac{n_a}{n_a + n_w}$$

$$= \frac{0.03448}{0.03448 + 0.05111}$$

$$= 0.403$$

and

$$\chi_w = 1 - \chi_a$$

$$= 1 - 0.403$$

$$= 0.597$$

The total entropy change of the mixture is given by

$$ds = (\chi_a c_{pa} + \chi_w c_{pw}) \frac{dT}{T} - R_u \frac{dp}{p}$$

But for isentropic compression process $ds = 0$

Therefore

$$\left(x_a\ c_{Pa} + x_w\ c_{Pw}\right) \frac{dT}{T} = R_u \frac{dP}{P}$$

Assuming the heat capacities to be constant in the compression range, after integration, the above equation is

$$(\chi_a c_{pa} + \chi_w\ c_{pw}) \ln \left(\frac{T_2}{T_1}\right) = R_u \ln \left(\frac{p_2}{p_1}\right)$$

$$\left[0.403\ (7.01) + 0.597\ (7.95)\right] \ln \left(\frac{T_2}{T_1}\right) = 1.986 \ln \left(\frac{90}{45}\right)$$

i.e., $\ln \left(\frac{T_2}{700}\right) = 0.2623 \ln (2)$

or $T_2 = 700(2)^{0.2623}$

$= 840°R\ (380°F)$

(b) The entropy changes of the individual gases in the mixture are given by

$$\Delta s_i = c_{pi} \ln \left(\frac{T_2}{T_1}\right) - R_u \ln \left(\frac{p_{2i}}{p_{1i}}\right)$$

Since the mole fraction of either gas does not change during the process, the ratio of partial pressures in this equation is the same as the ratio of total pressures of the mixture,

i.e., $\frac{p_{2i}}{p_{1i}} = \frac{p_2}{p_1}$

Then the change in specific entropy of air is

$$\Delta s_a = c_{pa} \ln \left(\frac{T_2}{T_1}\right) - R_u \ln \left(\frac{p_2}{p_1}\right)$$

$$= 7.01 \ln \left(\frac{840}{700}\right) - 1.986 \ln \left(\frac{90}{45}\right)$$

$= -0.0985$ Btu/lb mole°R

The total change in entropy of air is

$$\Delta S_a = n_a \Delta s_a$$

$= 0.03448(-0.0985)$

$$= -0.0034 \text{ Btu/°R}$$

Since the overall process is isentropic, the sum of ΔS for air and vapor should be zero. Therefore, the change in entropy of vapor is equal to $-\Delta S_a$

i.e.,
$$\Delta S_w = -\Delta S_a$$
$$= 0.0034 \text{ Btu/°R}$$

The change in specific entropy of vapor is

$$\Delta s_w = \frac{\Delta S_w}{n_w}$$
$$= \frac{0.0034}{0.0511}$$
$$= 0.0665 \text{ Btu/lb-mole-°R}$$

AIR CONDITIONING PROCESSES

• PROBLEM 10-24

An air-vapor mixture, initially at 60°F and 55 percent relative humidity, is heated until its temperature reaches 85°F. Determine

(a) the initial and final specific humidities,

(b) the final relative humidity, and

(c) the amount of heat added per lbm of dry air.

Assume the mixture to be at a pressure of 14.7 psia.

Solution: (a) Heating an air-vapor mixture at constant specific humidity, i.e., without any change in its moisture content, is called a sensible heating process. Therefore, the initial and final specific humidities are equal.

The specific humidity at the initial stage is given by

$$\omega = 0.622 \frac{p_v}{p_t - p_v}$$

where p_v = partial vapor pressure

p_t = total pressure

The partial vapor pressure is given by the definition of relative humidity

$$\phi = \frac{p_v}{p_g}$$

p_g = saturation vapor pressure

Therefore,

$$p_v = p_g(\phi)$$

The value of p_g can be obtained from saturated steam tables.

For T = 60°F, p_g = 0.2563 psia

Substituting,

$$p_v = 0.2563\ (0.55)$$

$$= 0.141 \text{ psia}$$

Substituting the values into the equation for specific humidity,

$$\omega = 0.622\left(\frac{0.141}{14.7-0.141}\right)$$

$$= 0.00602 \text{ lbm vapor/lbm dry air}$$

(b) At the final state, i.e., at T = 85°F, the specific humidity is 0.00602 lbm vapor/lbm dry air,

i.e., $$p_v = 0.141 \text{ psia}$$

The saturation pressure at temperature 85°F is

$$p_g = 0.5964 \text{ psia}$$

Therefore, the relative humidity

$$\phi = \frac{p_v}{p_g}$$

$$= \frac{0.141}{0.5964}$$

$$= 0.2364$$

i.e., $$\phi = 23.64 \text{ percent}$$

(c) The amount of heat added per lbm of dry air is given by

$$Q = H_2 - H_1$$

where H_2 = final state enthalpy

H_1 = initial state enthalpy

Enthalpy of the mixture can be written as

$$H = h_a + \omega h_v$$

$$= c_{pa}T + \omega h_v$$

where c_{pa} = constant pressure specific heat of air

h_v = saturated vapor enthalpy

Therefore, $(H_2-H_1) = c_{pa}(T_2-T_1) + \omega(h_{v2}-h_{v1})$

$$= 0.24(85-60) + 0.00602(1098.6-1087.7)$$

i.e., $Q = 6.1$ Btu/lbm of dry air.

• PROBLEM 10-25

Atmospheric air at 29.92 in Hg pressure and dry bulb and wet bulb temperatures of 60°F and 50°F, respectively, is heated in a heating coil to 80°F. Determine the wet bulb temperature, relative humidity and specific humidity of the air leaving the heating coil. Also calculate the sensible heat added per lbm of dry air. Solve the problem with the help of the psychrometric chart.

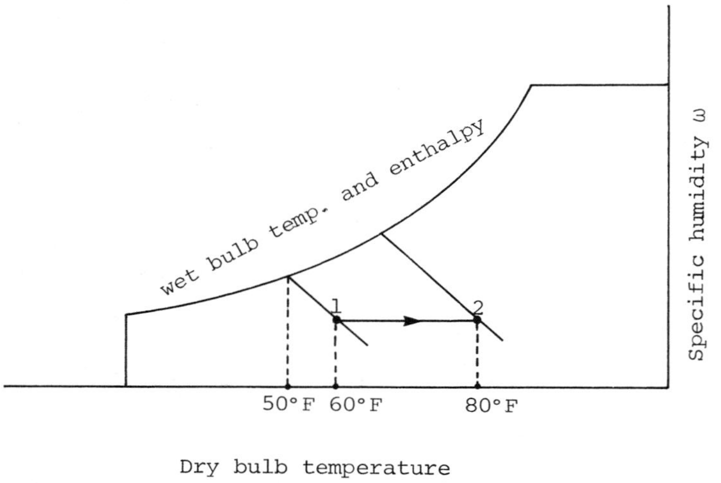

Solution: Referring to the figure. the dry bulb temperature

(60^0F) and wet bulb temperature (50^0F) lines intersect at point 1, which locates the condition of the entering air. Draw a horizontal line from point 1 to cut the 80^0F dry bulb temperature line at point 2. The sensible heating process is indicated by the line 1-2. The condition at which air comes out of the heating coil is represented by point 2.

Reading from the chart, corresponding to point 2,

the wet bulb temperature is 58.3°F,

the relative humidity is 25%, and

the specific humidity is 0.0054 lbm vapor/lbm dry air.

The sensible heat added per lbm of dry air is given by the difference in enthalpy at point 1 and point 2.

Enthalpy at point 1 is 20.3 Btu/lbm of dry air.

Enthalpy at point 2 is 25.3 Btu/lbm of dry air.

Therefore, sensible heat added is 25.3-20.3

= 5 Btu/lbm of dry air.

• PROBLEM 10-26

2000 cfm of air at 88°F and 30% relative humidity is cooled to 63^0F, maintaining its specific humidity constant. Using the psychrometric chart, find the relative humidity of the cooled air and the amount of heat removed per minute.

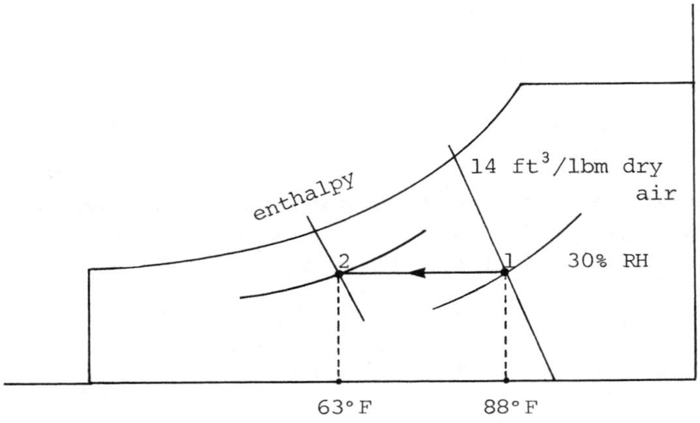

Solution: Referring to the figure, the 88°F dry bulb temperature line and 30% relative humidity line intersect at point 1. This point shows the condition of the entering air.

From that chart, it can be seen that the specific volume of air at point 1 is approximately 14 ft^3/lbm dry air.

Therefore, the mass flow rate of air is

$$m = \frac{2000}{14}$$

$$= 142.86 \text{ lbm dry air/min.}$$

To find the condition of the cooled air, a horizontal line is drawn through point 1 to cut the 63°F dry bulb temperature line at point 2.

The cooling process with constant specific humidity is represented by the line 1-2.

The condition of the cooled air is represented by point 2.

Reading from the chart, the relative humidity of the cooled air is 70%.

The amount of heat removed per minute is given by

$$q = m(h_1 - h_2)$$

where h = enthalpy of air in Btu/lbm dry air

From the chart ,

$$h_1 = 31.5 \text{ Btu/lbm dry air}$$

$$h_2 = 24.5 \text{ Btu/lbm dry air}$$

Therefore,

$$q = 142.86\ (31.5-24.5)$$

$$= 1000 \text{ Btu/min.}$$

• PROBLEM 10-27

2000 cfm of air at 90°F and 15% relative humidity is passed through an evaporative cooler (adiabatic humidifier).

(a) If the final temperature is 65°F, find the relative humidity of the exit air and the amount of water vapor added to the air per minute.

(b) Find the minimum temperature that could be achieved by this process.

Solve the problem with the help of psychrometric chart.

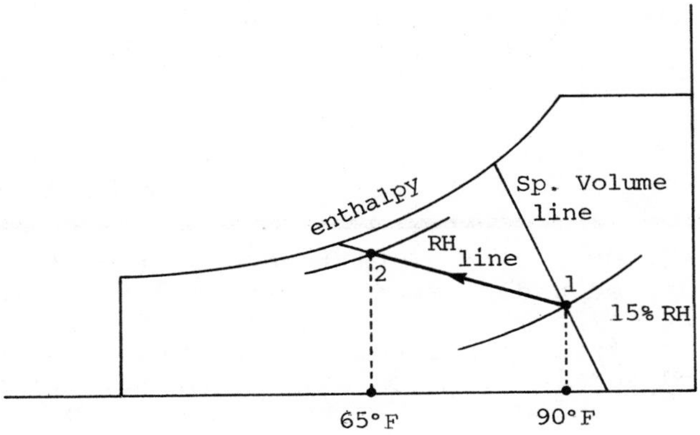

Solution: Referring to the figure, the 90°F dry bulb temperature line and 15% relative humidity line intersect at point 1. This point shows the condition of the entering air.

(a) From the chart, it can be seen that the specific volume of air at point 1 is 13.95 ft^3/lbm dry air. Therefore, the mass of flow rate of air is

$$m = \frac{2000}{13.95}$$

$$= 143.37 \text{ lbm dry air/min.}$$

Since the air is undergoing adiabatic humidification in the cooler, the cooling process should be of constant enthalpy. Point 2 is given by the intersection of the constant enthalpy line through point 1 and the 65°F dry bulb temperature line.

From the chart, the relative humidity at point 2 is

$$\phi_2 = 76\%$$

The amount of water vapor added to the air per minute is given by

$$m_v = m(\omega_2 - \omega_1)$$

From the chart,

$$\omega_2 = 0.0100 \text{ lbm vapor/lbm dry air}$$

$$\omega_1 = 0.0043 \text{ lbm vapor/lbm dry air}$$

Therefore,

$$m_v = 143.37(0.0100-0.0043)$$

$$= 0.817 \text{ lbm vapor/min.}$$

(b) The minimum temperature that could be achieved by this

process is the adiabatic saturation value, i.e., the wet bulb temperature of the initial state. From the chart, this temperature is 60°F.

• PROBLEM 10-28

Atmospheric air at 60°F with a relative humidity of 20 percent is humidified under steady state conditions to a specific humidity of 35 grains of vapor/lbm of dry air. Using the psychrometric chart, compare the processes given below with regard to the final relative humidity, final temperature, and amount of heat transfer per lbm of dry air:

(a) adiabatic,

(b) constant dry-bulb temperature, and

(c) constant relative humidity.

Take atmospheric air to be at a pressure of 14.7 psia and the humidifying of water to be at 60°F.

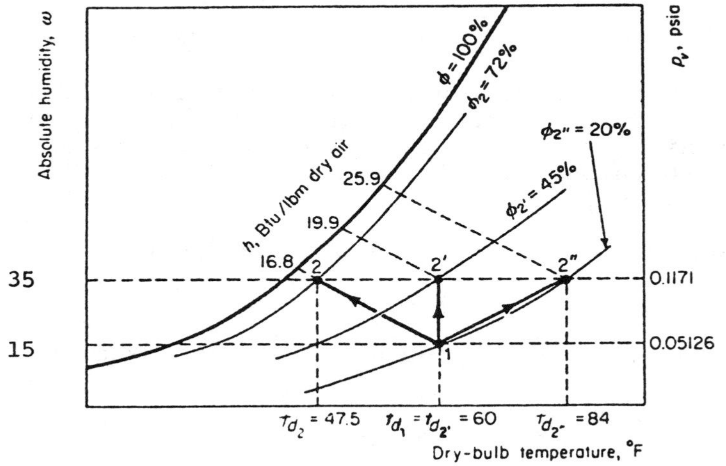

	φ(%)	T_{db}(°F)	Q(Btu)
Initial conditions	20	60	—
Adiabatic process	72	47.5	0
Constant-T_{db} process	45	60	3.1
Constant-φ process	20	84	9.1

Solution: The solution is shown on the psychrometric chart. Initial state is point 1. It is located at the intersection of the 60°F dry-bulb temperature line and 20% relative humidity line. Absolute humidity at point 1 is read from the chart as 15 grains vapor/lbm of dry air.

(a) The final state reached by the adiabatic process is point 2. It is on the same enthalpy line that passes theough point 1.

(b) The final state reached by the constant dry-bulb temperature process is point 2'. It is on the same dry-bulb temperature line as point 1.

(c) The final state reached by constant relative humidity process is point 2". It is on the same relative humidity line, 20%.

The three points 2, 2', and 2" lie on the 35 grains vapor/lbm of dry air humidity ratio line.

• PROBLEM 10-29

The figure below shows two streams of air being mixed together during an adiabatic steady flow process. Each stream has a pressure of 100 kPa. One stream has a temperature of 40°C, a 40% relative humidity and flows at the rate of 10 kg/min. The second stream has a temperature of 10°C, a 100% relative humidity and flows at the rate of 15 kg/min. Calculate the specific humidity and the final temperature of this mixture.

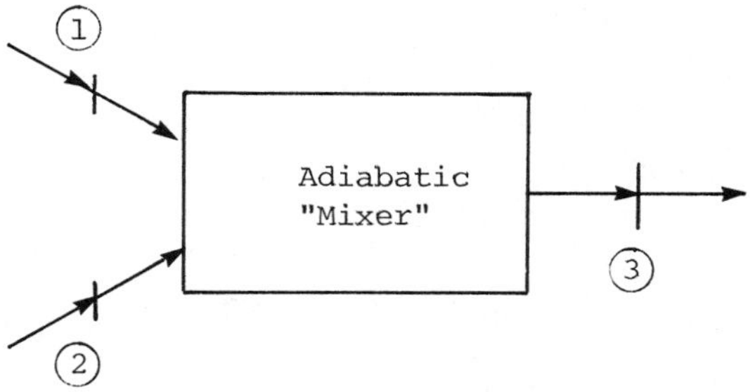

Solution: The humidity ratio (specific humidity) ω describes the quantity of water vapor in a mixture in terms of the amount of dry air present. It is defined as the ratio of the mass of water vapor present, m_v, to the mass of dry air, m_a.

$$\omega = \frac{m_v}{m_a}$$

$$= \frac{V/v_v}{V/v_a}$$

$$= \frac{v_a}{v_V}$$

$$= \frac{\rho_V}{\rho_a}$$

The humidity ratio can also be expressed as

$$\omega = \frac{R_u T / p_a M_a}{R_u T / p_V M_V}$$

$$= \frac{M_V p_V}{M_a p_a}$$

The ratio of molar masses for water to air is 0.622.

$$\therefore \quad \omega = 0.622 \, \frac{p_V}{p_a} = 0.622 \, \frac{p_V}{p_t - p_V} \qquad (1)$$

Using the equation of continuity,

$$m_1 + m_2 = m_3$$

In the above equation,

$$m_1 = m_{V_1} + m_{a_1} \qquad (2)$$

$$m_2 = m_{V_2} + m_{a_2} \qquad (3)$$

and

$$m_3 = m_{V_3} + m_{a_3} \qquad (4)$$

$$T_1 = 40°C \quad \text{(Given)}$$

From the steam tables, for this temperature the saturated water vapor pressure $p_{g_1} = 7.384$ kPa.

The relative humidity

$$\phi = \frac{p_V}{p_g}$$

$$\phi = 0.4$$

$$\therefore \; p_{V_1} = \phi_1 \times p_g$$

$$= 0.4 \times 7.384$$

$$= 2.954 \text{ kPa}$$

The humidity ratio for the first stream

$$\omega_1 = 0.622 \times \frac{2.954}{100-2.954}$$

$$= 0.0189$$

Similarly, the values for the second stream are

$$p_{g_2} = 1.2276 \text{ kPa}$$

$$p_{V_2} = 1.2276 \text{ kPa}$$

$$\omega_2 = 0.0077$$

Divide equation (2) by m_a.

$$\frac{m_1}{m_{a_1}} = \omega_1 + 1 \qquad (5)$$

$$\therefore\ m_{a_1} = \frac{m_1}{\omega_1 + 1}$$

$$= \frac{10.0}{0.0189 + 1}$$

$$= 9.814 \text{ kg/min}$$

From equation (1),

$$m_{V_1} = \omega_1 \times m_{a_1}$$

$$= 0.0189 \times 9.814$$

$$= 0.1855 \text{ kg/min}$$

$$m_{a_2} = \frac{m_2}{\omega_2 + 1}$$

$$= \frac{15.0}{0.0077 + 1}$$

$$= 14.885 \text{ kg/min.}$$

$$m_{V_2} = \omega_2 \times m_{a_2}$$

$$= 0.0077 \times 14.885$$

$$= 0.1146 \text{ kg/min}$$

$$m_{V_3} = m_{V_1} + m_{V_2} \quad \text{and}$$

$$m_{a_3} = m_{a_1} + m_{a_2}$$

Substituting the calculated values,

$$m_{V_3} = 0.300 \text{ kg/min}$$

and

$$m_{a_3} = 24.699 \text{ kg/min}$$

$$\therefore \omega_3 = \frac{m_{V_3}}{m_{a_3}}$$

$$= \frac{0.300}{24.699}$$

$$= 0.0121$$

(b) To calculate the final temperature:

From the first law of thermodynamics,

$$m_{a_3}h_3 = m_{a_1}h_1 + m_{a_2}h_2 \qquad (6)$$

In equation (6), h_1 and h_2 are the enthalpies at state 1 and state 2. They can be obtained from the psychrometric chart.

$$\left.\begin{aligned} h_1 &\cong 106.0 \text{ kJ/kg} \\ h_2 &\cong 49.5 \text{ kJ/kg} \end{aligned}\right\} \text{dry air}$$

Using equation (6),

$$h_3 = \frac{m_{a_1}h_1 + m_{a_2}h_2}{m_{a_3}}$$

$$= \frac{(9.814)(106) + (14.885)(49.5)}{24.699}$$

$$= 71.95 \text{ kJ/kg dry air}$$

Using the value of ω_3 calculated in part (a) and the value of h_3 just calculated, the temperature can be found (directly from the psychrometric chart) to be

$$T_3 \cong 21.0°C.$$

• PROBLEM 10-30

2000 cfm of an air stream at 60°F and 0.75 relative humidity is adiabatically mixed with 1200 cfm of another air stream at 95°F and 0.5 relative humidity. Determine (a) the mass flow rates of dry air in the two streams, and (b) temperature and relative humidity of the mixture.

Adiabatic mixing of two wet air streams

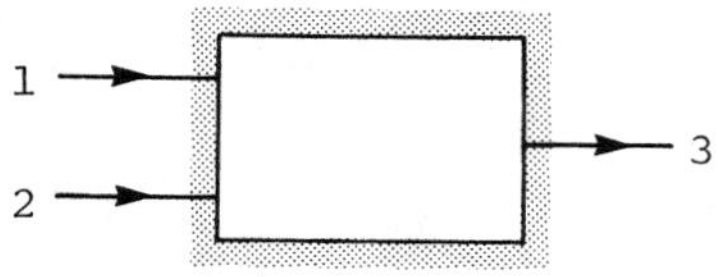

(a) The system

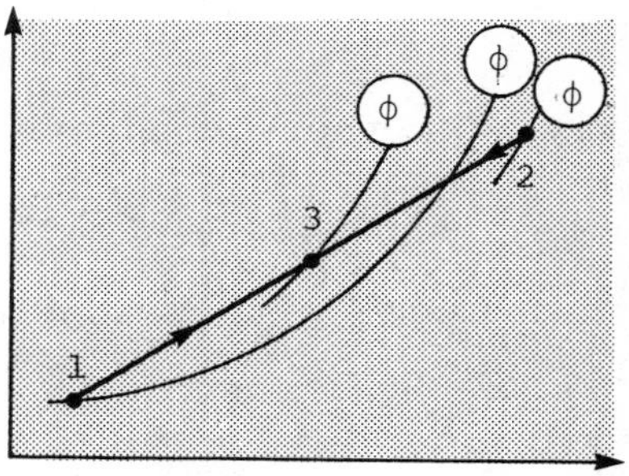

(b) The process representation as a psychrometric chart

Solution: (a) To calculate the mass flow rate of dry air, the specific volume of dry air and hence the partial pressure of dry air is required. In some psychrometric charts, the value of specific volume of dry air can be read directly.

For air at 60°F and 0.75 relative humidity, the specific volume of dry air is $v_1 = 13.27$ ft³/lbm dry air, and for air at 95°F and 0.5 relative humidity,

$$v_2 = 14.37 \text{ ft}^3/\text{lbm dry air}$$

If the specific volume of dry air is not given on the chart, it can be calculated as follows:

At 60°F the saturation vapor pressure is taken from the steam table as 0.2563 psia. From the definition of relative humidity, the vapor pressure is

$$p_v = \phi p_g$$

Therefore,
$$p_{v_1} = 0.75\ (0.2563)$$
$$= 0.1922 \text{ psia}$$

Then the partial pressure of dry air is

$$p_a = p_t - p_v$$

Therefore,
$$p_{a_1} = 14.7 - 0.1922$$
$$= 14.5078 \text{ psia}$$

From the ideal gas equation, the specific volume of dry air is

$$v_1 = \frac{R_a T_1}{p_{a_1}}$$

$$= \frac{53.35 \times 520}{14.5078 \times 144}$$

$$= 13.279 \text{ ft}^3/\text{lbm dry air}$$

Similarly, for the second stream,

$$p_{v_2} = 0.5(0.8162)$$

$$= 0.4081 \text{ psia}$$

Then

$$p_{a_2} = 14.7 - 0.4081$$

$$= 14.2919 \text{ psia}$$

and

$$v_2 = \frac{R_a T_2}{p_{a_2}}$$

$$= \frac{53.35 \times 555}{14.2919 \times 144}$$

$$= 14.387 \text{ ft}^3/\text{lbm dry air}$$

It can be seen that these values agree with the values taken from the psychrometric chart.

The mass flow rate of the dry air in the first stream is

$$m_{a_1} = \frac{2000}{13.279}$$

$$= 150.6 \text{ lbm dry air/min}$$

and the mass flow rate of dry air in the second stream is

$$m_{a_2} = \frac{1200}{14.387}$$

$$= 83.4 \text{ lbm dry air/min}$$

(b) The total mass of dry air in the mixture is

$$m_{a_3} = m_{a_1} + m_{a_2}$$

$$= 150.6 + 83.4$$

$$= 234 \text{ lbm dry air/min}$$

From the psychrometric chart,

$$\omega_1 = 0.00814 \text{ lbm vapor/lbm dry air}$$

$$h_1 = 23.5 \text{ Btu/lbm dry air}$$

$$\omega_2 = 0.01771 \text{ lbm vapor/lbm dry air}$$

$$h_2 = 42.5 \text{ Btu/lbm dry air}$$

The humidity ratio of the mixture is given by the continuity equation for water vapor,

$$m_{a_3}\omega_3 = m_{a_1}\omega_1 + m_{a_2}\omega_2$$

Substituting the values,

$$234\ \omega_3 = 150.6(0.00814) + 83.4(0.01771)$$

or $$\omega_3 = 0.01155 \text{ lbm vapor/lbm dry air}$$

$$= 80 \text{ grains vapor/lbm dry air}$$

The enthalpy of the mixture is given by

$$m_{a_3}h_3 = m_{a_1}h_1 + m_{a_2}h_2$$

Substituting the values,

$$234\ h_3 = 150.6(23.5) + 83.4(42.5)$$

or $$h_3 = 30.27 \text{ Btu/lbm dry air}$$

With the values of specific humidity and enthalpy, the state of the mixture can be fixed on the chart, and other properties of that state can then be read directly. The temperature and relative humidity of the mixture are 74°F and 66%.

• PROBLEM 10-31

An air-conditioning plant is designed for a room with the following conditions:

Outdoor conditions	40°F and 60% R.H
Required indoor conditions	70°F and 50% R.H
Amount of air circulation	15 ft^3/min/person
Room capacity	50

The required condition is achieved first by heating and then by adiabatic humidifying.

Find the following:

(a) heating capacity of the coil, and

(b) capacity of the humidifier.

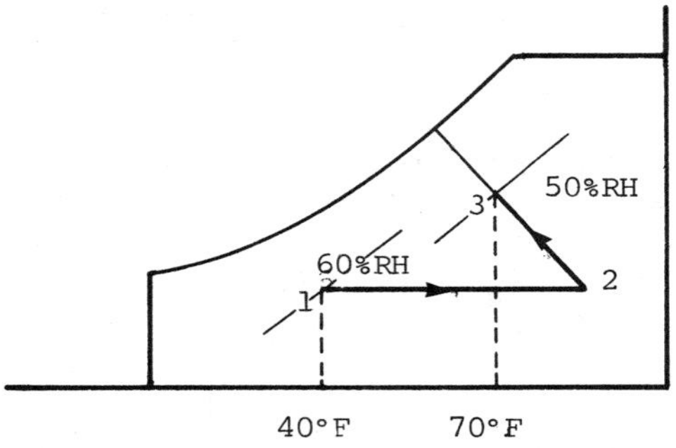

Solution: Referring to the figure, point 1 represents the outdoor conditions and point 3 represents the indoor conditions. Process 1-2 is the heating process in the heating coil and process 2-3 is the adiabatic humidification process. Point 2 is the intersection of the horizontal line (constant specific humidity) through point 1 and the enthalpy line through point 3. From the psychrometric chart,

$$h_1 = 13 \text{ Btu/lbm dry air}$$

$$\omega_1 = \omega_2 = 0.0031 \text{ lbm vapor/lbm dry air}$$

$$v_1 = 12.65 \text{ ft}^3\text{/lbm dry air}$$

$$h_2 = h_3 = 25.5 \text{ Btu/lbm dry air}$$

$$\omega_3 = 0.0078 \text{ lbm vapor/lbm dry air}$$

The mass of air circulated per minute is given by

$$m = \frac{\text{volume of air/min}}{\text{specific volume}}$$

$$= \frac{50 \times 15}{12.65}$$

$$= 59.3 \text{ lbm dry air/min}$$

(a) The heating capacity of the heating coil is given by

$$q = m(h_2 - h_1)$$

$$= 59.3(25.5-13)$$

$$= 741.25 \text{ Btu/min}$$

(b) The capacity of the humidifier is given by

$$m_v = m(\omega_3 - \omega_2)$$

$$= 59.3(0.0078-0.0031)$$

$$= 0.279 \text{ lbm/min.}$$

• PROBLEM 10-32

30,000 ft^3/hr of atmospheric air at a dry-bulb temperature of 95°F and wet-bulb temperature of 78°F is to be conditioned so that it enters a home at 72°F and 50 percent relative humidity. This is done by first cooling below its dew point temperature and then heating. Using steam tables, calculate (a) the amount of moisture removed, (b) the heat removed per hour in the cooling system, and (c) the heat added in the heating system in Btu/hr.

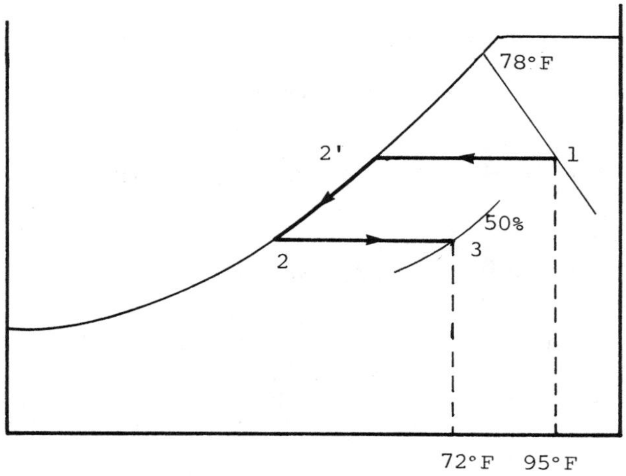

PSYCHROMETRIC CHART

Solution: The psychrometric chart shows the processes. At the initial state, i.e., at point 1, the DBT and WBT are 96°F and 78°F, respectively.

From the saturation steam tables, corresponding to the WBT of 78°F,

the vapor pressure is $p_{g_1} = 0.4764$ psia

The vapor pressure of the outside air may be obtained from the relation

$$p_{v_1} = p_{g_1} - \frac{(p_t - p_{g_1})(T_{d_1} - T_{w_1})}{2800 - 1.3T_{w_1}}$$

where

p_t = Total pressure of air = 14.696 psia

T_d = Dry bulb temperature (DBT)

T_w = Wet bulb temperature (WBT)

Therefore,

$$p_{v_1} = 0.4764 - \frac{(14.696-0.4764)(95-78)}{2800-1.3(78)}$$

$$= 0.3868 \text{ psia}$$

The specific humidity is given by

$$\omega_1 = 0.622 \frac{p_{v_1}}{p_t - p_{v_1}}$$

$$= \frac{0.622(0.3868)}{(14.696-0.3868)}$$

$$= 0.01681 \text{ lbm vapor/lbm dry air}$$

The mass of dry air per hour is given by

$$m_a = \left(\frac{p_t - p_{v_1}}{R_a \; T_{d_1}}\right)\left(\text{volume of air/hour}\right)$$

$$= \frac{(14.696-0.3868)}{53.35 \times 555}(30{,}000)(144)$$

$$= 2088 \text{ lbm/hr.}$$

At the final state, point 3, the DBT and relative humidity are 72°F and 50%.

From saturation steam tables, corresponding to 72°F, the saturation vapor pressure is

$$p_{g_3} = 0.3899 \text{ psia}$$

From the definition of relative humidity, the vapor pressure at state 3 is

$$p_{v_3} = (\phi)p_{g_3}$$

$$= 0.5(0.3899)$$

$$= 0.1950 \text{ psia}$$

The specific humidity at state 3 is

$$\omega_3 = 0.622 \frac{p_{v_3}}{p_t - p_{v_3}}$$

$$= 0.622\left(\frac{0.1950}{14.696-0.1950}\right)$$

$$= 0.00836 \text{ lbm vapor/lbm dry air}$$

The amount of moisture removed is given by

$$m_w = m_a(\omega_1-\omega_3)$$

$$= 2088(0.01681-0.00836)$$

$$= 17.7 \text{ lbm vapor/hr}$$

(b) The dew point temperature of the final state 3 is the temperature at state 2.

Therefore, the temperature at state 2 is the saturation temperature of vapor corresponding to the vapor pressure p_{v_3}.

From steam tables,

$$T_2 = 52.4°F$$

The enthalpy of an air-vapor mixture is given by

$$h = 0.24T + \omega h_v$$

where h_v = enthalpy of saturated vapor at temperature T.

The enthalpy at state 1 is

$$h_1 = 0.24(95) + 0.01681(1102.9)$$

$$= 41.34 \text{ Btu/lbm of dry air}$$

The enthalpy of state 2 is

$$h_2 = 0.24(52.4) + 0.00836(1084.4)$$

$$= 21.64 \text{ Btu/lbm of dry air.}$$

The amount of heat removed per hour is given by

$$Q_R = m_a[h_1-h_2-(\omega_1-\omega_2)h_{f_2}]$$

$$= 2088[41.34-21.64-(0.01681-0.00836)(20.56)]$$

$$= 40770 \text{ Btu/hr}$$

(c) The heat added in the heating section is given by

$$Q_A = (h_3-h_2)m_a$$

Enthalpy at state 3 is given by $h_3 = c_{pa}T_3 + \omega_3 h_{v_3}$

$$h_3 = 0.24(72) + 0.00836(1092.88)$$

$$= 26.42 \text{ Btu/lbm dry air}$$

Therefore,

$$Q_A = (26.42-21.64)(2088)$$

$$= 9980 \text{ Btu/hr.}$$

• PROBLEM 10-33

Atmospheric air at a dry bulb temperature of 95°F and wet bulb temperature of 78°F is to be conditioned so that it enters a home at 72°F and 50 percent relative humidity. This is done by first cooling below the dew point temperature and then heating. Using the psychrometric chart, calculate (a) the amount of water removed per lbm of dry air, (b) the heat removed by the cooling system in Btu/lbm of dry air, and (c) the heat added in the heating process in Btu/lbm of dry air.

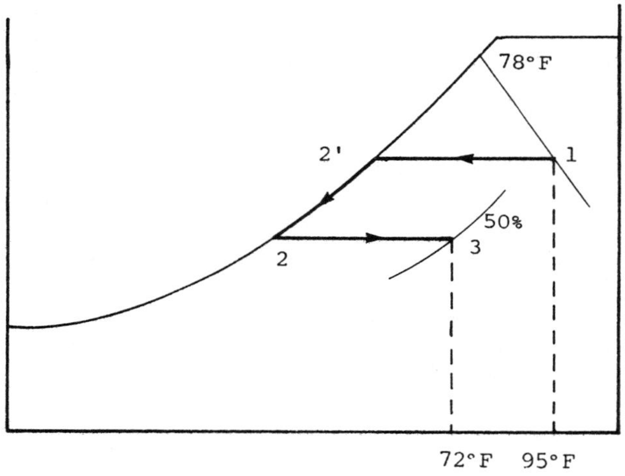

PSYCHROMETRIC CHART

Solution: Referring to the psychrometric chart, it can be seen that process 1-2 is the cooling process. In section 1-2', sensible cooling takes place, and in section 2'-2, dehumidification takes place because of cooling below the dew point temperature. State 2 is obtained by the projection of state 3 on the saturation line, because during the sensible heating process 2-3, the specific humidity remains constant.

Therefore, from the chart,

$$\omega_1 = \omega_{2'} = 0.0171 \text{ lbm vapor/lbm dry air}$$

$$\omega_2 = \omega_3 = 0.0081 \text{ lbm vapor/lbm dry air}$$

$$T_{2'} = 73°F; \quad T_2 = 52°F$$

(a) The quantity of water removed is given by the difference in the humidity ratios between state 2' and 2,

i.e.,

$$\omega_2' - \omega_2$$

$$= 0.0171 - 0.0081$$

$$= 0.009 \text{ lbm vapor/lbm dry air}$$

(b) The enthalpy at state 1 is read from the chart,

$$h_1 = 41.5 \text{ Btu/lbm dry air}$$

At state 2,

$$h_2 = 21.5 \text{ Btu/lbm dry air}$$

Therefore, the heat removed by the cooling system is

$$Q_R = h_1 - h_2 - (\omega_1 - \omega_2)h_{f_2}$$

$$= 41.5 - 21.5 - (0.0171 - 0.0081)(20.06)$$

$$= 19.82 \text{ Btu/lbm dry air}$$

(c) The enthalpy at state 3 is read from the chart.

$$h_3 = 27 \text{ Btu/lbm dry air}$$

Therefore, heat added in the heating process is

$$Q_A = h_3 - h_2$$

$$= 27 - 21.5$$

$$= 5.5 \text{ Btu/lbm dry air.}$$

• PROBLEM 10-34

A cooling tower cools 150,000 lbm/hr of water from 110°F to 85°F, by an unsaturated air mixture which enters the tower at 80°F and 60% relative humidity, and leaves at 100°F and 90% relative humidity. Determine the rate of air flow and the quantity of water evaporated per hour.

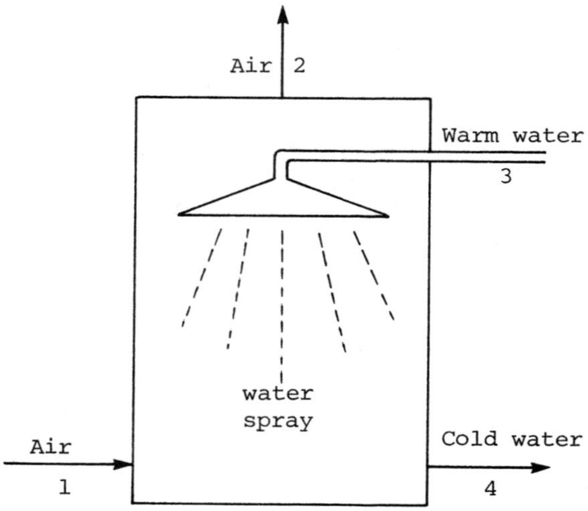

Fig. 1.

Solution: The relative humidity of an air-vapor mixture is defined as

$$\phi = \frac{p_v}{p_g}$$

where p_v = vapor pressure of the mixture

p_g = saturated vapor pressure

At the inlet section of air, the temperature and relative humidity are given as 80°F and 60%.

From saturated steam tables,

$$p_{g_1} = 0.5073 \text{ psia}$$

Therefore, from the definition of relative humidity,

$$p_{v_1} = 0.5073(0.6)$$

$$= 0.3044 \text{ psia}$$

The humidity ratio of air at the inlet is given by

$$\omega_1 = 0.622 \frac{p_{v_1}}{p_t - p_{v_1}}$$

$$= \frac{(0.622)(0.3044)}{(14.7-0.3044)}$$

$$= 0.01315 \text{ lbm vapor/lbm dry air}$$

At the outlet section of air, the temperature and relative humidity are given as 100°F and 90%.

From saturated steam tables,

$$p_{g_2} = 0.9503 \text{ psia}$$

Therefore,

$$p_{v_2} = (0.9)(0.9503)$$

$$= 0.8553 \text{ psia}$$

and

$$\omega_2 = 0.622 \frac{p_{v_2}}{p_t - p_{v_2}}$$

$$= 0.622 \frac{(0.8553)}{(14.7-0.8553)}$$

$$= 0.03843 \text{ psia.}$$

The gain in humidity ratio of air is due to the evaporation of water.

Therefore, the mass of water evaporated is

$$m_w = \omega_2 - \omega_1$$

$$= 0.03843 - 0.01315$$

$$= 0.02528 \text{ lbm/lbm of dry air}$$

Applying the continuity equation and the first law to the system,

$$(h_{a_1} + \omega_1 h_{v_1}) + m_{f_3} h_{f_3} = (h_{a_2} + \omega_2 h_{v_2}) + m_{f_4} h_{f_4}$$

where m_{f_3} = mass of water at inlet per lbm of dry air

m_{f_4} = mass of water at outlet per lbm of dry air

But $m_{f_4} = m_{f_3} - m_w$

and $h_a = c_{pa} T$

The above energy equation can be written as

$$c_{pa}(T_1 - T_2) + \omega_1 h_{g_1} + m_{f_3} h_{f_3} = \omega_2 h_{g_2} + (m_{f_3} - m_w) h_{f_4}$$

where c_{pa} = constant pressure specific heat of air

h_g = saturated vapor enthalpy

h_f = saturated water enthalpy

Substituting values into the above equation and evaluating m_{f_3},

$$0.24(80-100) + 0.01315(1096.4) + m_{f_3}(78.02)$$

$$= 0.03843(1105) + (m_{f_3}-0.02528)(53.08)$$

i.e., $24.94\ m_{f_3} = 31.51$

$$m_{f_3} = 1.263 \text{ lbm/lbm of dry air}$$

The rate of air flow is given by

$$= 150000\ \frac{(1+\omega_1)}{m_{f_3}}$$

$$= 150000\ \frac{(1+0.01315)}{1.263}$$

$$= 120327 \text{ lbm/hr}$$

The quantity of water evaporated is given by

$$(\omega_2-\omega_1) \times \frac{150000}{m_{f_3}}$$

$$= m_w \times \frac{150000}{m_{f_3}}$$

$$= (0.02528)\frac{(150000)}{1.263}$$

$$= 3002 \text{ lbm/hr.}$$

CHAPTER 11

CHEMICAL REACTIONS AND EQUILIBRIUM

THEORETICAL AIR, EXCESS AIR, AND AIR - FUEL RATIO

• PROBLEM 11-1

A coal sample has the following composition:

0.14 moles H_2/mole fuel

0.27 moles CO/mole fuel

0.03 moles CH_4/mole fuel

0.006 moles O_2/mole fuel

0.509 moles N_2/mole fuel

0.045 moles CO_2/mole fuel

Determine the air-fuel ratio if producer gas from this sample is burned with 50 percent excess air.

Solution: The combustion equation for one mole of fuel has to be determined, then from the stoichiometry of this equation the air-fuel ratio can be calculated.

For one mole of fuel the combustion equation for the combustible substances is

$$(0.14)H_2 + (0.07)O_2 \longrightarrow (0.14)H_2O$$

$$(0.27)CO + (0.135)O_2 \longrightarrow (0.27)CO_2$$

$$(0.03)CH_4 + (0.06)O_2 \longrightarrow (0.03)CO_2 + (0.06)H_2O$$

$$\begin{array}{l} \quad 0.265 \text{ moles } O_2 \text{ required/mole fuel} \\ \underline{-\ 0.006} \text{ moles } O_2 \text{ in fuel/mole fuel} \\ \quad 0.259 \text{ moles } O_2 \text{ required from air/mole fuel} \end{array}$$

∴ The overall combustion equation for one mole of fuel is

$$\text{fuel} + \text{air} \longrightarrow (A)H_2O + (B)CO_2 + (D)N_2$$

$$0.14H_2 + 0.27CO + 0.03CH_4 + 0.006O_2 + 0.509N_2 + 0.045CO_2$$
$$+ 0.259\,(O_2 + 3.76N_2) \longrightarrow 0.2H_2O + 0.345CO_2 + 1.482N_2$$

$$\left(\frac{\text{moles air}}{\text{mole fuel}}\right)_{\text{theoretical}} = (0.259 \text{ moles } O_2 + 0.259(3.76) \text{ moles } N_2)/\text{mole fuel}$$

$$= 1.233 \frac{\text{moles air}}{\text{mole fuel}} = \frac{\text{volume air}}{\text{volume fuel}}$$

For 50% excess air, $\frac{\text{moles air}}{\text{mole fuel}} = 1.233 \times 1.5$

$$= 1.85 \frac{\text{moles air}}{\text{mole fuel}}$$

On a mass basis the air-fuel ratio is

$$AFR = 1.85 \left(\frac{\text{mol wt air}}{\text{mol wt fuel}}\right)$$

$$AFR = 1.85\left[\frac{(28.96)}{0.14(2)+0.27(28)+0.03(16)+0.006(32)+0.509(28)+0.045(44)}\right]$$

$$= \frac{1.85(28.96)}{24.74} = 2.17 \text{ lbm air/lbm fuel}$$

Propane burns in dry 125 percent theoretical air (21% O_2, 79% N_2) and the reaction is given by:

$$C_3H_8 + 5O_2 + 18.8N_2 \longrightarrow 3CO_2 + 4H_2O + 18.8N_2$$

Calculate the dew point and the mole fractions of the combustion products when the air is at 1 atm pressure.

Solution: By using information obtained from the chemical equation stoichiometry, the mole fractions of the products can be obtained. The dew point is calculated by using the partial pressure of the H_2O vapor in the product gas in conjunction with steam tables.

The chemical equation for the reaction of propane with 125 percent theoretical air is :

$$C_3H_8 + 6.25O_2 + 23.5N_2 \longrightarrow 3CO_2 + 4H_2O + 1.25O_2 + 23.5N_2$$

This chemical equation was obtained by multiplying the oxygen and nitrogen on the reactant side by 1.25 and then balancing the equation by adding the appropriate amount of O_2 and N_2 to the product side.

The total number of moles of product gas = N_{TOT} = 3 + 4 + 1.25 + 23.5 = 31.75. The mole fractions of the products are :

$$X_{CO_2} = \frac{N_{CO_2}}{N_{TOT}} = \frac{3}{31.75} = 0.094$$

$$X_{H_2O} = \frac{N_{H_2O}}{N_{TOT}} = \frac{4}{31.75} = 0.126$$

$$X_{O_2} = \frac{N_{O_2}}{N_{TOT}} = \frac{1.25}{31.75} = 0.04$$

$$X_{N_2} = \frac{N_{N_2}}{N_{TOT}} = \frac{23.5}{31.75} = 0.74$$

The partial pressure of H_2O vapor in the product gas is :

$$P_{H_2O} = X_{H_2O}\, P_{TOTAL}$$

$$= (0.126)\ (1.5\ \text{atm})$$

$$= 0.189\ \text{atm}$$

From the steam tables, the saturation temperature corresponding to this pressure is approximately 138° F. If the product gas mixture is cooled to 138° F at constant pressure, the dew point is reached. If the mixture is further cooled, the water will condense out of the gas.

• PROBLEM 11-3

> The air used for the combustion of a hydrocarbon was supplied at 25°C and 100 kPa with a relative humidity of 48%. Determine (a) the carbon/hydrogen ratio of the fuel on a mass basis and (b) the percent theoretical air employed in the combustion process, if an analysis of the products of combustion yields the following volumetric composition on a dry basis:
>
> CO_2--13.0%; O_2--3.1%; CO--0.3%· N_2--83.6%

Solution: The chemical reaction written on dry basis is

$$C_aH_b + \alpha O_2 + \beta N_2 \rightleftharpoons 13CO_2 + 0.3CO + 3.1O_2 + 83.6N_2 + \gamma H_2O$$

(a) A balance for each of the elements involved will enable us to solve for the unknown coefficients.

C balance: $a = 13 + 0.3 = 13.3$

N balance: $2\beta = 2(83.6) \Rightarrow \beta = 83.6$

Also the nitrogen to oxygen ratio is

$$\frac{\beta}{\alpha} = 3.76 \Rightarrow \alpha = \frac{83.6}{3.76} = 22.23$$

O balance: $2\alpha = 26 + 0.3 + 6.2 + \gamma$

or

$$2(22.23) = 26 + 0.3 + 6.2 + \gamma$$

which gives

$$\gamma = 11.96$$

H balance: $b = 2\gamma = 2(11.96)$

or

$$b = 23.92$$

Thus the hydrocarbon is $C_{13.3}H_{23.92}$, and the carbon/hydrogen ratio on a mass basis is

$$\frac{m_C}{m_H} = \frac{N_C(MW_C)}{N_{H_2}(MW_H)}$$

$$= \frac{13.3\ (12)}{23.92\ (1)}$$

$$= 6.67$$

(b) The percent theoretical air is the same as the percent of theoretical oxygen. The chemical equation written with the values obtained is

$$C_{13.3}H_{23.92} + 22.23O_2 + 83.6N_2 \rightleftharpoons 13CO_2 + 0.3CO + 3.1O_2$$

$$+83.6N_2 + 11.96H_2O$$

and the equation for the combustion in oxygen only is

$$C_{13.3}H_{23.92} + 19.28O_2 \rightleftharpoons 13.3CO_2 + 11.96H_2O$$

Thus

$$\%T.A. = \frac{N_{O_2}\big|_{act.}}{N_{O_2}\big|_{theor.}} \times 100$$

$$= \frac{22.23}{19.28} \times 100$$

$$= 115.3\%$$

• PROBLEM 11-4

Propane is burned in 100% excess air. Combustion is complete and takes place at 100 kPa. Determine (a) the dew-point temperature of the products of combustion and (b) the moles of H_2O condensed per mole of fuel burned, if the products of combustion are cooled to $25^\circ C$.

Solution: The chemical reaction,

$$C_3H_8 + 5O_2 \rightleftharpoons 3CO_2 + 4H_2O$$

gives the amount of oxygen needed for the complete combustion of propane. But the oxygen in this case is supplied as air, and the reaction can be written

$$C_3H_8 + 5(2)O_2 + 5(2)(3.76)N_2 \rightleftharpoons 3CO_2 + 4H_2O + 5O_2 + 37.6N_2$$

(a) The mole fraction for the water vapor is

$$y_{H_2O} = \frac{n_i}{n_T} = \frac{P_i}{P_T} \tag{1}$$

or

$$y_{H_2O} = \frac{n_i}{n_T}$$

$$= \frac{4}{3+4+5+37.6}$$

$$= 0.0806 .$$

But $y_{H_2O} = \dfrac{P_{H_2O}}{P_T} \implies P_{H_2O} = y_{H_2O} P_T$

or

$$P_{H_2O} = 0.0806 \times 100$$

$$= 8.06 \text{ kPa} .$$

From steam tables the corresponding temperature is

$$T_{P.P.} = 41.53°C.$$

(b) At T = 25°C, the vapor pressure of water obtained from the steam tables is

$$P_V = 3.169 \text{ kPa}$$

From Eq. (1)

$$y_{H_2O} = \frac{3.169}{100} = 0.03169 .$$

But

$$y_{H_2O} = \frac{n_{H_2O}}{n_{H_2O} + n_p}$$

or

$$0.03169 = \frac{n_{H_2O}}{n_{H_2O} + 45.6}$$

or

$$n_{H_2O} = 1.4924 \text{ kmol/kmol } C_3H_8$$

$$n_{liq.} = n_T)_{H_2O} - n_v)_{H_2O}$$

$$= 4 - 1.4924$$

$$= 2.51 \text{ kmol } H_2O/\text{kmol } C_3H_8.$$

• PROBLEM 11-5

Hydrogen is burned with air at atmospheric pressure in an adiabatic burner to produce a flame of 2000K. Determine the percent theoretical air required, assuming complete combustion, when the hydrogen and the air are supplied at 25°C.

Solution: The first step in solving this problem is to write the necessary chemical equations that apply to this reaction.

The chemical reaction for hydrogen burned in oxygen only,

$$H_2 + \tfrac{1}{2}\, O_2 \rightleftharpoons H_2O$$

gives the amount of oxygen needed for the complete combustion of one mole of H_2, which is $\frac{1}{2}$. But the oxygen for the combustion of hydrogen is supplied as air, and the reaction can be written

$$H_2 + \tfrac{1}{2}\, yO_2 + \tfrac{1}{2}(3.76)yN_2 \rightleftharpoons H_2O + \alpha O_2 + \beta N_2$$

A balance for each of the elements involved will enable us to solve for the unknown coefficients.

Oxygen balance: $\frac{1}{2}y = 1 + 2\alpha \Longrightarrow \alpha = \frac{y-1}{4}$

Nitrogen balance: $\beta = 1.88y$

Substituting these values for the α and β, we obtain

$$H_2 + 0.5yO_2 + 1.88yN_2 \rightleftharpoons H_2O + \left(\frac{y-2}{4}\right)O_2 + 1.88yN_2$$

Applying the first law to this process,

$$\overset{o}{\not{Q}} - \overset{o}{\not{W}} = \sum_R n_i \bar{h} - \sum_P n_i \bar{h}$$

or

$$H_R = H_P \qquad (1)$$

where the subscripts R and P refer to the reactants and products, respectively, and the summations refer respectively to all the reactants or all the products. Then

$$H_P = 1\bar{h}_{H_2O} + 0.5y\bar{h}_{O_2} + 1.88y\bar{h}_{N_2}\Big|_{T=2000K} \qquad (2)$$

Using the table for enthalpies of formation of ideal gases at T=2000K,

$$\bar{h}_{H_2O} = \bar{h}^o_f\Big|_{298K} + \bar{h}\Big|_{2000K} = -241,827 + 72,689 = -169,138 \text{ kJ/kmol}$$

$$\bar{h}_{O_2} = \bar{h}^o_f\Big|_{298K} + \bar{h}\Big|_{2000K} = 0 + 59,199 = +59,199 \text{ kJ/kmol}$$

$$\bar{h}_{N_2} = \bar{h}^o_f\Big|_{298K} + \bar{h}\Big|_{2000K} = 0 + 56,141 = +56,141 \text{ kJ/mol}$$

At T=298K:

$$\bar{h}_{H_2} = 0, \ \bar{h}_{O_2} = 0, \text{ and } \bar{h}_{N_2} = 0$$

and thus $H_R = 0$.

From Equations (1) and (2),

$$H_P = 0 = 1(-169,138) + \left(\frac{y-2}{4}\right)(+59,199) + 1.88y(56,141).$$

Solving for y gives

$$y = \frac{169,138}{90,744}$$

$$= 1.86.$$

Thus

$$\% \text{ T.A.} = 1.86 \times 100 = 186\%.$$

• **PROBLEM 11-6**

Octane burns in theoretical air (21% O_2, 79% N_2) by the following combustion equation:

$$C_8H_{18} + 12.5O_2 + 12.5(3.76)N_2 = 8CO_2 + 9H_2O + 47N_2$$

What is the theoretical air-fuel ratio?

Solution: Using information obtained from reaction stoichiometry, the air-fuel ratio can be determined.

On a molar basis, the air-fuel ratio is:

$$R_{air-fuel} = \frac{\text{moles } O_2 + \text{moles } N_2}{\text{moles } C_8H_{18}} = \frac{12.5 + 47}{1}$$

$$= 59.5 \frac{\text{mole air}}{\text{mole fuel}} .$$

The air-fuel ratio on a mass basis is obtained by incorporating the mol wt of the fuel and the air.

$$\text{mol wt air} = 0.21(\text{mol wt } O_2) + 0.79(\text{mol wt } N_2) = 28.96 \text{ g/m}$$

$$\text{mol wt } C_8H_{18} = 114 \text{ g/mol}$$

$$R_{air-fuel} = 59.5 \frac{\text{mol air}}{\text{mol fuel}} \times \frac{28.96\text{g air/mol air}}{114\text{g fuel/mol fuel}}$$

$$= 15.1\text{g air/g fuel}$$

• **PROBLEM 11-7**

Theoretical air is composed of 21% O_2 and 79% N_2. Octane (C_8H_{18}) burns in air as described by the following reaction:

$$C_8H_{18} + 12.5O_2 + (3.76)(12.5)N_2 \longrightarrow$$
$$8CO_2 + 9H_2O + (3.76)(12.5)N_2 .$$

If octane is burned with 200% theoretical air, calculate the air/fuel ratio and the mole fractions of the combustion products. Also calculate the partial pressure of the products for a total pressure of 1 atm.

Solution: Once the chemical equation is written for the conditions of the problem (burning octane with 200% theoretical air), the solution can be obtained from its stoichiometry.

For 200% theoretical air the chemical reaction is :

$$C_8H_{18} + (2.0)(12.5)O_2 + (2.0)(3.76)(12.5)N_2 =$$
$$8CO_2 + 9H_2O + (12.5)O_2 + (2)(3.76)(12.5)N_2 \cdot$$

The mass of C_8H_{18} = 8(12 lb_m/mole) + 18(1 lbm/mole) =

114 lb_m/mole fuel.

The mol wt of air:

= 0.21 x mol wt O_2 + 0.79 x mol wt N_2 = 28.96.

The mass of air = (2)(12.5)(1+3.76)(28.96) =

3446 lb_m/mol fuel.

The air/fuel ratio is

$$R_{af} = \frac{\text{mass air}}{\text{mass fuel}} = \frac{3446}{114} = 30.2 \text{ lb}_m \text{ air/lb}_m \text{ fuel.}$$

The total number of moles of products is

N_T = moles CO_2 + moles H_2O + moles O_2 + moles N_2

$$= 8 + 9 + (12.5) + (2)(3.76)(12.5) = 123.5 \frac{\text{moles}}{\text{mole fuel}}$$

The mole fractions of each individual species can now be calculated:

$$X_{CO_2} = \frac{8}{123.5} = 0.065 = 6.5\%$$

$$X_{H_2O} = \frac{9}{123.5} = 0.073 = 7.3\%$$

$$X_{O_2} = \frac{12.5}{123.5} = 0.1 = 10.0\%$$

$$X_{N_2} = \frac{94}{123.5} = 0.762 = 76.2\%$$

The partial pressures can be calculated by using the equation $P_i = X_i P_{TOTAL}$. (With the partial pressure of H_2O dew point calculations can be made, i.e., the corresponding saturation temperature is the dew point).

$$P_{H_2O} = X_{H_2O} P_{TOTAL}$$

$$= (0.073)(1 \text{ atm})$$

$$= 0.073 \text{ atm}$$

$$P_{CO_2} = 0.065 \text{ atm}$$

$$P_{O_2} = 0.1 \text{ atm}$$

$$P_{N_2} = 0.762 \text{ atm}$$

• PROBLEM 11-8

Ethane reacts with a stoichiometric amount of air by the following combustion equation:

$$C_2H_6 + 3.5O_2 + 3.5(3.76)N_2 \longrightarrow 2CO_2 + 3H_2O + 3.5(3.76)N_2 .$$

Using the following enthalpy data, calculate the amount of heat transfer per mole of fuel if ethane enters at $60^\circ C$, the air enters at $4.4^\circ C$ and the products leave at $449^\circ C$.

Solution The amount of heat transferred is obtained through the use of a heat balance. With kinetic energy neglected, the energy (or heat) balance is

$$Q_{out} = \text{enthalpy in} - \text{enthalpy out} = -Q$$

$$= \sum_{\text{reactants}} \text{moles } (h_1 - h_0) - \Delta H_{reaction}$$

$$- \sum_{\text{products}} \text{moles } (h_2 - h_0)$$

where h_0 = enthalpy @ 25°C. h_1, h_2 are the initial and final enthalpies, respectively.

$$Q_{out} = (moles)_{C_2H_6} (h-h_0)_{C_2H_6} + (moles)_{O_2} (h_1-h_0)_{O_2}$$

$$+ (moles)_{N_2} (h_1-h_0)_{N_2} - \Delta H_{reaction} - (moles)_{CO_2}$$

$$\times (h_2-h_0)_{CO_2} - (moles)_{H_2O} (h_2-h_0)_{H_2O} - (moles)_{N_2}$$

$$\times (h_2-h_0)_{N_2}$$

DATA (Kcal/mol)				
	h25° c	h4.4° c	h449° c	h60° c
C_2H_6	1295	—	—	1507
O_2	939	873	—	—
N_2	940	875	2307	—
CO_2	1016	—	3059	—
H_2O	1073	—	2700	—
ΔH reaction = -154,695 Kcal/mol of czH6				

After substitution of the enthalpy values from the data and stoichiometric information from the chemical reaction, the heat balance becomes

$$Q_{out} = 1(1507-1295) + 3.5(873-939) + 13.1(875-940)$$

$$- (-154,695) - 2(3059-1016) - 3(2700-1073) -$$

$$13.1(2307-940)$$

$$= 126,950 \text{ kcal/mole}.$$

ANALYSIS OF THE PRODUCTS OF COMBUSTION

• PROBLEM 11-9

In order to determine the effects of various fuels on the environment, combustion products are often analyzed. A certain fuel that was burned in air was analyzed with the following results:

Determine the chemical equation and the air-fuel ratio based on these results.

SPECIES	MOLE: FRACTION = Xi
CO_2	0.12
O_2	0.02
CO	0.03
N_2	0.83
TOTAL	1.00

Solution: In this problem the fuel used is unknown. Therefore, the data given in the problem must be used to determine the chemical formula of the fuel. The fuel will be assumed to be a hydrocarbon of the form

$$C_aH_b .$$

It will also be assumed that the air used is theoretical (79% N_2, 21% O_2). The chemical equation, then, will be of the form

$$C_aH_b + A(O_2+3.76N_2) \rightleftharpoons B(CO_2) + C(H_2O) + D(CO) + E(O_2) + F(N_2).$$

From this reaction and the data given, the formula of the fuel can be calculated and the air-fuel ratio obtained.

Since the dry mixture product mole fractions are known, it is convenient to write the chemical equation on the basis of 100 moles of dry mixture. Therefore

$$B = 12, \quad D = 3, \quad E = 2, \quad F = 83.$$

By the conservation of N atoms,

$$A = \frac{83}{3.76} = 22.07.$$

By the conservation of O atoms,

$$C = 2A - 2B - D - 2E$$

$$C = 2(22.07) - 2(12) - 3 - 2(2)$$

$$= 13.14.$$

By the conservation of C atoms,

$$a = B + D = 12 + 3 = 15.$$

By the conservation of H atoms,

$$b = 2C = 2 \times 13.14 = 26.28.$$

$\therefore$ the fuel is an equivalent hydrocarbon

$$C_{15}H_{26.28}$$

The chemical reaction is

$$C_{23}H_{5.8} + 22.07(O_2+3.76N_2) \rightleftharpoons 12\ CO_2 + 13.14H_2O + 3CO + 2O_2 + 83N_2$$

Since the fuel's molecular configuration is not known, the air-fuel ratio on a molal basis would be meaningless. Therefore the air-fuel ratio is calculated on a mass basis. The molal mass of the effective fuel is

$$M = 12 \times (15) + (26.28) \times 1 = 206.8 \text{ g/gmol}$$

$\therefore$

$$\text{air-fuel ratio} = \text{AFR} = \frac{(\text{moles air})(\text{mol wt air})}{(\text{moles fuel})(\text{mol wt. fuel})}$$

$$= \frac{(4.76)(22.07)(28.97)}{(1)(206.8)} = 14.72 \text{ g air/g fuel}$$

$$= 14.72\ lb_m \text{ air}/lb_m \text{fuel}$$

ENTHALPY OF FORMATION

• **PROBLEM 11-10**

Heats of reaction can be calculated from the heats of formation of the reactant and product species. Using the following heats of formation, calculate the heat of reaction for the combustion of methane.

Heats of formation (@ 291 K and 14.7 psia)

$C + 2H_2 \longrightarrow CH_4(g) \quad \Delta H_f = 18{,}240$ cal/g mol

$C + O_2 \longrightarrow CO_2(g) \quad \Delta H_f = 94{,}450$ cal/g mol

$2H_2 + O_2 \longrightarrow 2H_2O(l) \quad \Delta H_f = 68{,}370$ cal/g mol

Solution: The heat of reaction is determined by subtracting the sum of the heats of formation of the reactants from the sum of the heats of formation of products. The chemical reaction is

$$CH_4 + 2O_2 \longrightarrow CO_2 + 2H_2O$$

$$\Delta H_{reaction} = (\Delta H_f)_{prod} - (\Delta H_f)_{react}$$

$$= (94{,}450 + 68{,}370) - (18{,}240 + 0)$$

(The ΔH_f of elements, i.e. oxygen, = 0)

$$\therefore \quad \Delta H_{reaction} = 144{,}580 \text{ cal/g mol } CH_4$$

(This value is the heat of reaction @ 316 K and 14.696 psia)

• **PROBLEM 11-11**

Using the bond energy table below, determine the enthalpy of ethane at STP. Assume that the enthalpy of solid carbon and H_2 gas is zero under these conditions.

BOND ENERGIES IN KCAL/G MOLE

Bond	Energy	Bond	Energy
H-H	104.2	H-I	71.4
C-C	83.1	C-N	69.7
Cl-Cl	58.0	C-O	84.0
Br-Br	46.1	C-Cl	78.5
I-I	36.1	C-Br	65.9
C-H	98.8	C-I	57.4
N-H	93.4	O-O	33.2
O-H	110.6	N≡N	226
H-Cl	103.2	C=C	147
H-Br	87.5	C≡C	194

C=O 164 in formaldehyde
171 in other aldehydes
174 in ketones,

Resonance energy in kcal/g mole
Benzene ring = 37
Naphthalene = 75
Carboxylic acids = 28
Esters = 24

Vaporization of carbon atoms = 171.7 $\frac{\text{kcal}}{\text{mo/c atom}}$

Solution: Due to the fact that the formation of C_2H_6 from H_2 (gas) and carbon (solid) takes place at constant pressure, the amount of heat added would be equal to the enthalpy increase. Therefore, from the stoichiometry of the formation reaction and the bond energy table, the enthalpy of formation may be calculated.

The formation reaction is:

$$2C(s) + 3H_2(g) = C_2H_6(g)$$

From the table:

vaporization of 2 carbon atoms :

Energy added = 2(171.7) = 343.4

Breaking of 3 H-H Bonds :

Energy added = 312.6 (3 x 104.2)

Total Energy added = 343.4 + 312.6 = 656

The energy released in the formation of the ethane molecule is :

formation of six C-H Bonds = 6(98.8) = 592.8

formation of one C-C bond = (1)(83.1) = 83.1

Total energy released = 675.9

The net energy is 656 - 675.9 = -19.9 kcal. Due to the fact that the elements were at the reference state, the enthalpy at 273°K is -19.9 kcal. This approximate value is in very close agreement with values obtained experimentally.

• PROBLEM 11-12

Gaseous hydrochloric acid dissociates in water as described by the following chemical reaction :

$$HCl(g) \longrightarrow H^+(aq) + Cl^-(aq)$$

Using the following heats of formation, calculate $\Delta H^o_{77^oF}$ for the reaction.

Heats of formation @ 77°F

$HCl - \Delta H_f = -87.54$ Btu/mole

$H^+ - \Delta H_f = 0$ Btu/mole

$Cl^- - \Delta H_f = -158.8$ Btu/mole

Solution: The heat of reaction is found by subtracting the sum of the heats of formation of the reactants from those of the products.

$$\Delta H^o_{298} = \sum_{\text{products}} \Delta H^o_f - \sum_{\text{reactants}} \Delta H^o_f$$

$$= (0 - 158.8) - (-87.54)$$

$$= -71.26 \text{ Btu}$$

• PROBLEM 11-13

Heats of formation are usually estimated by using bond dissociation energies. Determine the heat of formation for propane @ STP using the following bond energy data.

Data @ 298°K and 1 atm

Bond	Bond energy (kcal/mole)
C-C	80
C-H	99
H-H	103

heat of sublimation of carbon = 171.7 kcal/mole

Solution: The reaction is :

$$3C\ (solid) + 4H_2(g) \longrightarrow C_3H_8(g).$$

The ΔH for this reaction can be obtained by using the bond energies in the individual reactions and then adding or subtracting them as the case may be.

∴ From the data,

$$3C\ (solid) \longrightarrow 3C(g) \qquad \Delta H = 3(171.7)\ kcal$$

$$4H_2(g) \longrightarrow (4)(2)H(g) \qquad \Delta H = 4(103)\ kcal$$

$$3C(g) + 8H(g) \longrightarrow C_3H_8(g) \qquad \Delta H = -[2(80) + 8(99)]$$

(The negative sign is there since, in this reaction, the bonds are being formed. Two C-C bonds are formed and eight C-H bonds are formed.)

By adding the equations (and ΔH's),

$$3C\ (solid) + 4H_2(g) \longrightarrow C_3H_8(g) \qquad \Delta H = -24.9\ kcal$$

$$\therefore \quad \Delta H_{formation}\ (C_3H_8) = -\ 24.9\ kcal/mole$$

• PROBLEM 11-14

Using the following heat of solution data for ethanol, calculate the heat of dilution from the more concentrated to the more diluted solution, per mole of ethanol.

Data @ $77^{\circ}F$

$\Delta H = -4.45$ Btu/mole for $X_{C_2H_5OH} = 1/6$

$\Delta H = -6.66$ Btu/mole for $X_{C_2H_5OH} = 1/10$

Solution: The mole fractions given in the data can be used to determine the C_2H_5OH/H_2O ratio and, thereby, one can obtain the stoichiometry of the chemical equations. Once the equations are written, by sutraction the desired chemical equation, and therefore, the desired ΔH can be found.

When $X_{C_2H_5OH} = 1/6$, i.e. the ratio of (moles ethanol)/

(moles ethanol + moles H_2O) = 1/6

∴ The chemical reaction is

$$C_2H_5OH + 5H_2O \longrightarrow C_2H_5OH \cdot 5H_2O \qquad \Delta H = -4.45 \text{ Btu/mole}$$

When $X_{C_2H_5OH} = 1/10$,

$$C_2H_5OH + 9\,H_2O \longrightarrow C_2H_5OH \cdot 9H_2O \qquad \Delta H = -6.66 \text{ Btu/mole}$$

Subtracting the 2nd from the 1st equation gives:

$$C_2H_5OH \cdot 5H_2O + 4H_2O \longrightarrow C_2H_5OH \cdot 9H_2O \qquad \Delta H = -2.21 \text{ Btu/mole}$$

• PROBLEM 11-15

The normal boiling point of water is 9720 cal/mole. Calculate the heat of vaporization at $35^\circ C$ and 1 atm. Use the following Cp values to solve the problem.

C_p Values

for $H_2O(l)$; $C_p = 18.06$ cal $deg^{-1}mole^{-1}$ (independent of temperature)

for $H_2O(g)$; $C_p = 7.219 + 2.374(10^{-3})T + 2.67(10^{-7})T^2$ cal deg^{-1} $mole^{-1}$

Solution: In this problem, the equation

$$\Delta H_2 - \Delta H_1 = \int_{T_1}^{T_2} \Delta C_p \, dT \quad \text{is used to find } \Delta H_{vaporization}$$

at $35^\circ C$. The problem states,

$$H_2O(l) \longrightarrow H_2O(g) \qquad \Delta H^o_{373} = 9720 \text{ cal}$$

$$C_p = C_p \text{ products} - C_p \text{ reactants}$$

$$= 7.219 + 2.374(10^{-3})T + 2.67(10^{-7})T^2 - 18.06$$

$$= -10.84 + 2.374(10^{-3})T + 2.67(10^{-7})T^2$$

$$\therefore \quad H^o_{373} - H^o_{308} = \int_{308}^{373} \left[-10.84 + 2.374(10^{-3})T + 2.67(10^{-7})T^2\right] dt$$

$$= \left[-10.84T + 1.187 \times 10^{-3}T^2 + 8.9 \times 10^{-8} T^3\right]_{T_1}^{T_2}$$

$$\Delta H^o_{373} - \Delta H^o_{308} = -650$$

$$\therefore$$

$$\Delta H^o_{308} = +9720 + 650$$

$$= 10{,}370 \text{ cal/mole}$$

• PROBLEM 11-16

Benzene burns in air by the following reaction:

$$C_6H_6(l) + 7\tfrac{1}{2}\ O_2(g) \longrightarrow 6CO_2(g) + 3H_2O(l)$$

When the combustion is carried out at 77°F, 18000 Btu/lb (benzene) is evolved. Calculate $\Delta H_{77\ F}$ for this combustion per mole of benzene. Use 78.11 lb/lbmole as the molecular weight of benzene.

Solution: Using the thermodynamic relation $\Delta H = \Delta E + \Delta nRT$, the ΔH for the reaction can be obtained.

By definition, $\Delta E = qv$. For this reaction @ 77 F, qv =

$$-18000 \text{ Btu/lb}$$

or $-18000 \text{ Btu/lb} \times 78.11 \text{ lb/lbmole} = -1.40598 \times 10^6 \text{ Btu/lbmole}$

$$= qv$$

$$\therefore \quad \Delta H = -1.40598 \times 10^6 + \Delta nRT$$

For this reaction $\Delta n = 6 - 7\tfrac{1}{2} = -1\tfrac{1}{2}$

(The moles of liquid are not included since the liquid's pressure effects are negligible.)

$$\therefore$$

$$\Delta H = -1.40598 \times 10^6 - (1.5)(1.987)(460 + 77)$$

$$\Delta H = -1.4075 \times 10^6 \text{ Btu/lbmole}$$

• PROBLEM 11-17

The melting point of copper is 1083°C. If molten copper is cooled below the melting point to a temperature of 1073°C, nucleation of the solid copper occurs and solidification proceeds adiabatically. How much copper solidifies? Use the following data to solve the problem.

Data

Latent Heat of fusion of copper = 3,100 cal mole^{-1} @ 1,083°C

C_p of liquid copper = 7.5 cal deg^{-1} mole^{-1}

C_p of solid copper = $5.41 + 1.5 \times 10^{-3}T$ cal deg^{-1} mole^{-1}

Solution: Since no heat is added or let out from the system, solidification is caused only by the heat evolved in the process. The solidification stops when the temperature is raised to the true melting point by the heat evolved in the solidification process. Therefore the heat balance is between the heat evolved during solidification and the heat required to raise the temperature of the copper which is now a mixture of liquid and solid to the melting point. This heat is equal to

$$\int_{1346}^{1356} C_{p(1)}\, dT = \int_{1346}^{1356} 7.5\, dT$$

$$= 75.0 \text{ cal/mole of liq. Cu}$$

and

$$\int_{1346}^{1356} C_{p(s)}\, dT = \int_{1346}^{1356} (5.41 + 1.5 \times 10^{-3}T)\, dT$$

$$= \left[5.41T + 0.75 \times 10^{-3}T^2\right]_{1346}^{1356}$$

$$= 74.37 \text{ cal mole}^{-1} \text{ of solid copper}$$

For every mole of copper that solidifies, 3,100 cal of latent heat are evolved.

∴ The amount of Cu that is raised to the melting point is

$$\left[1 + \frac{3,100 - 74.37}{75}\right] = 41.34 \text{ mole of Cu}$$

The fraction of Cu that solidifies = 1/41.34 = 0.024

• PROBLEM 11-18

The reaction of chromic oxide with a strong stoichiometric amount of pure aluminium at 25°C is

$$2Al_{(s)} + Cr_2O_{3(s)} \rightleftharpoons 2Cr_{(s)} + Al_2O_{3(s)}$$

The reaction is exothermic and the maximum temperature attained by the products is 2,173°K. Using the following data, determine the heat lost to the surroundings per kilogram of aluminium. Solve the problem two different ways using the following two assumptions:

(a) The reaction takes place at 25°C, the heat generated is used to heat the products to 2,173°K, and the remaining is lost to the surroundings.

(b) The reaction takes place at 2,173°K i.e. heat is supplied to the reactants to bring them to a temperature of 2,173°K.

Data

Standard heats of formation:

$$Cr_2O_3 - \Delta H_f = -270 \text{ kcal/mole}$$

$$Al_2O_3 - \Delta H_f = -400 \text{ kcal/mole}$$

Heat capacities (cal $deg^{-1} mole^{-1}$)

$$C_{p(Al_2O_3(s))} = 27.38 + 3.08 \times 10^{-3} T - 8.20 \times 10^5 T^{-2}$$

$$C_{p(Cr(s))} = 5.84 + 2.36 \times 10^{-3} T - 0.88 \times 10^5 T^{-2}$$

$$C_{p(Cr(l))} = 9.40$$

$$C_{p(Al(s))} = 4.94 + 2.96 \times 10^{-3} T$$

$$C_{p(Al(l))} = 7.00$$

$$C_{p(Cr_2O_3)} = 28.53 + 2.20 \times 10^{-3} T - 3.74 \times 10^5 T^{-2}$$

Latent heats of fusion

$Cr_{(s)} = Cr_{(l)}$ m.p. = 2,123°K

heat of fusion = 4,600 cal $mole^{-1}$

$Al_{(s)} = Al_{(l)}$ m.p. = 932°K

heat of fusion = 2.5 kcal/mol

mol. wt of Al = 26.97 g/mol

Solution: Using assumption (a):

This assumption makes the problem relatively easy to solve. The enthalpy of the reaction is calculated from the heats of formation. The heat used to heat up the products is then calculated by using the equation

$$\Delta H = \int_{T_1}^{T_2} C_p \, dT.$$

These two values are then subtracted in order to obtain the heat dissipated to the surroundings.

The heat of reaction @ 298°K is

$$\Delta H^0_{298} = -400,000 - (-270,000)$$
$$= -130,000 \text{ cal of heat evolved.}$$

This evolved heat is partly used to heat 2 moles of chromium and 1 mole of Al_2O_3 to 2,173°K.

The heat required by the Al_2O_3 is

$$\Delta H^0_{(298\to 2,173^0K)} = \int_{298}^{2,173} C_{p(Al_2O_3)}dT$$

$$= \left[27.38T + 3.08 \times 10^{-3}\frac{T^2}{2} + 8.20 \times 10^5 T^{-1}\right]_{298}^{2,173}$$

$$= 51,350 + 7,140 - 2,375$$

$$= 56,115 \text{ cal mole}^{-1}$$

The heat required for the Cr is a little more complicated to calculate. This is due to the fact. that Cr melts at 2,123°K.

$$\therefore \quad \Delta H^0_{(298-2,173^0K)} = \int_{298}^{2,123} C_p(Cr(s))\ dT$$

$$+ 2 \text{ moles (heat of fusion)}$$

$$+ \int_{2,123}^{2,173} C_p(Cr(1))\ dT$$

$$\Delta H^0_{(298-2,173^0K)} = \int_{298}^{2,123} \left[11.68 + 4.72 \times 10^{-3}T - 1.76 \times 10^5 T^{-2}\right] dT$$

$$+ 2(4,600) + \int_{2,123}^{2,173} 18.80 \; dT$$

$$= 21,300 + 10,430 - 508 + 9,200 + 940$$

$$= 41,360 \text{ cal}$$

$\therefore$ The heat lost to the surroundings is:

$$\text{heat loss} = 130,000 - 56,100 - 41,400$$

$$= 32,500 \text{ cal}$$

This heat is for 2 moles of aluminum reacted, $\therefore$ the heat loss per kg is

$$\frac{32,500 \text{ cal}}{2 \text{ mole}} \times \frac{1,000 \text{ g/kg}}{26.97 \text{ g/mole}} = 603,000 \frac{\text{cal}}{\text{kg Al}}$$

For assumption (b), the heat required to raise the reactants to 1,373^{0}K must include the melting of Al which occurs at 932^{0}K.

The heat needed to raise the temperature of two moles of aluminium to 2,173^{0}K from 298^{0}K is

$$\Delta H^0_{(298\rightarrow 2,173^0K)} = \int_{298}^{932} C_{p(Al(s))} \; dT$$

$$+ \text{ 2 moles (heat of fusion)}$$

$$+ \int_{932}^{2,173} C_{p(Al(l))} \; dT$$

$$\Delta H^0_{(298 \to 2,173^0K)} = \int_{298}^{932} (4.94 + 2.96 \times 10^{-3}T)\, dT$$

$$+ 2(2,500) + \int_{932}^{2,173} (7)\, dT$$

$$= 30,940 \text{ cal}$$

The heat required for Cr_2O_3 is

$$\Delta H^0_{(298 \to 2,173)} = \int_{298}^{2,173} C_p\, dT$$

$$= \left[28.53T + 1.10 \times 10^{-3}T^2 + 3.74 \times 10^5 T^{-1}\right]_{298}^{2,173}$$

$$= 57,500 \text{ cal}$$

.˙. The total heat required to bring the reactants to a temperature of $2,173^0K$ is

$$\Delta H^0 = 30,940 + 57,500$$

$$= 88,440$$

Now the heat of reaction @ $2,173^0K$ must be determined.

$$\Delta H^0_{2,173} - \Delta H^0_{298} = \int_{298}^{932} \left[2C_{p(Cr(s))} + C_{p(Al_2O_3)} - 2C_{p(Al(s))} - C_{p(Cr_2O_3)}\right] dT$$

$$- (2 \times 2,500) + \int_{932}^{2,123} \left[2C_{p(Cr(s))} + C_{p(Al_2O_3)} - 2C_{p(Al(l))} - C_{p(Cr_2O_3))}\right] dT$$

$$+ (2 \times 4{,}600) + \int_{2{,}123}^{2{,}173} \left[2C_{p(Cr(l))} + C_{p(Al_2O_3)} - 2C_{p(Al(l))} - C_{p(Cr_2O_3(s))} \right] dT$$

$\therefore \quad \Delta H^{0}_{2{,}173} = -121{,}000$ cal

heat loss = 121,000 - 88,440

= 32,560 cal

Per kg of Al,

$$\text{heat loss} = \frac{32{,}560}{2} \times \frac{1{,}000}{26.97}$$

$$= 603{,}000 \text{ cal}$$

This heat loss is the same as the amount calculated earlier (where the first assumption of the reaction is occurring at 298°K).

• PROBLEM 11-19

A furnace operates with a gas inlet temperature of 650°C and an outlet temperature of 1,100°C. The inlet gas is composed of 10 percent CO, 20 percent CO_2, and 70 percent N_2 by volume. The combustion occurs with a stoichiometric amount of air. Using the following data, determine the maximum flame temperature and the heat supplied to the furnace in Btu/ft³ of exhaust gas.

Data

Standard heats of formation

CO; $\Delta H_f = -26{,}400$ cal/mole

CO_2; $\Delta H_f = -94{,}050$ cal/mole

Heat capacities (cal $deg^{-1}mole^{-1}$)

CO; $C_p = 6.79 + 0.98 \times 10^{-3}T - 0.11 \times 10^{5}T^{-2}$

O_2; $C_p = 7.16 + 1.00 \times 10^{-3}T - 0.40 \times 10^{5}T^{-2}$

CO_2; $C_p = 10.55 + 2.16 \times 10^{-3}T - 2.04 \times 10^5 T^{-2}$

N_2; $C_p = 6.66 + 1.02 \times 10^{-3}T$

Combustion reaction

$$2CO_{(g)} + O_{2(g)} \rightleftharpoons 2CO_{2(g)}$$

Solution: This problem involves a heat balance between the heat evolved in the reaction and the heating of the products and the surroundings. Assuming adiabatic conditions, the maximum flame temperature can be determined. The gas heat is partly transferred to the furnace and partly carried off in the exhaust. Calculation of the heat carried off in the exhaust will also enable us to find the heat supplied to the furnace. The heat of reaction at 25°C is determined by using Hess's law and the heats of formation of CO and CO_2.

Therefore,

$$\Delta H^0_{298} = [2 \times (-94{,}050) - 2 \times (26{,}400) - 0]$$
$$= -135{,}300 \text{ cal}$$

However, the reaction is occurring @ 650°C (923°K). Therefore, the equation

$$\Delta H^0 = \int \Delta C_p \, dT$$

must be used.

From the data, $\Delta C_p = 2C_{p(CO_2(g))} - 2C_{p(CO(g))} - C_{p(O_2(g))}$

$$= 0.36 + 1.36 \times 10^{-3}T - 3.46 \times 10^5 T^{-2}$$

$$\therefore \quad \Delta H^0_T = \Delta H_0 + 0.36T + 0.68 \times 10^{-3} T^2 + 3.46 \times 10^5 T^{-1}$$

(ΔH_0 = the integration constant)

To find ΔH_0, a substitution of ΔH^0_{298} is done

$$-135{,}300 = \Delta H_0 + 0.36(298) + 0.68 \times 10^{-3}(298)^2 + 3.46 \times 10^5(298)^{-1}$$

$$\Delta H_0 = -136{,}600$$

$$\therefore \quad \Delta H^0_T = -136{,}600 + 0.36T + 0.68 \times 10^{-3}T^2 + 3.46 \times 10^5 T^{-1}$$

For 923^0K,

$$\Delta H^0_{923} = -135{,}314 \text{ cal}$$

This heat will raise the temperature of the product and nitrogen gases and will be positive with respect to the exhaust gas.

The exhaust gas contains

2 mol CO_2 from the combustion reaction

2 mol CO_2 from the blast furnace gas

7 mol N_2 in the blast furnace gas

4 mol N_2 in the air (due to the stoichiometry of the reaction).

This gas is heated to the maximum flame temperature by the heat evolved by the combustion of 2 moles of CO @ 923^0K.

$$\therefore \quad \text{heat available} = \Delta H^0_{923} = \int_{923}^{T_{max}} C_{p(\text{exhaust gas})}\, dT$$

$$\text{heat available} = 135{,}314 \text{ cal} = \int_{923}^{T_{max}} \left[4C_{p(CO_2)} + 11C_{p(N_2)}\right] dT$$

For 4 moles of CO_2:

$$C_p = 42.2 + 8.64 \times 10^{-3}T - 8.16 \times 10^5 T^{-2}$$

For 11 moles of N_2:

$$C_p = 73.26 + 11.22 \times 10^{-3}T$$

$$\therefore \quad \int_{923}^{T_{max}} (115.46 + 1.986 \times 10^{-2}T - 8.16 \times 10^5 T^{-2})\, dT$$

$$= 135{,}314$$

$$\left[115.46T + 1.986 \times 10^{-2}\frac{T^2}{2} + 8.16 \times 10^5 T^{-1}\right]_{923}^{T_{max}} = 135{,}314$$

$$\therefore \quad 115.46T_m + \frac{1.986 \times 10^{-2}}{2} T_m^2 + 8.16 \times 10^5 T_m^{-1} = 251,227$$

Since T_m^{-1} will be small, the third term on the left hand side will be neglected to give a quadratic equation, which can be easily solved.

$$9.93 \times 10^{-3} T_m^2 + 115.46T_m - 251,227 \simeq 0$$

Using the quadratic equation,

$$T_{max} = \frac{-115.46 \pm \sqrt{(115.46)^2 - 4(9.93 \times 10^{-3})(-251,227)}}{2(9.93 \times 10^{-3})}$$

$$T_{max} = 1,874^{\circ}K = 1,601^{\circ}C$$

$\therefore$ The maximum flame temperature is $1,601^{\circ}C$.

The heat supplied to the furnace is the difference between the heat of reaction and the heat taken away in the exhaust gases.

The heat carried by the exhaust gases is the one that raises the exit temperature to $1,100^{\circ}C$ from an inlet temperature of $650^{\circ}C$.

This heat is

$$\int_{923}^{1,373} C_{p(exhaust)}\, dT = \left[115.46T + \frac{1.986 \times 10^{-2}}{2} T^2 + 8.16 \times 10^5 T^{-1}\right]_{923}^{1,373}$$

$$= 61,927 \text{ cal}$$

$\therefore$ The heat supplied to the furnace is

$$135,314 - 61,927 = 73,387 \text{ cal}$$

This heat is for 4 mol CO_2 and 11 mol N_2 = 15 moles of exhaust gas. Assuming ideal gas behavior, the gas volume at STP is 15 x 22.4 liter = 336 liter. At $1,100^{\circ}C$ and pressure of 1 atm, the gas expands to

$$336 \text{ liter} \times \frac{1,373^{\circ}K}{273^{\circ}K} = 1,690 \text{ liter}$$

$$= 60 \text{ ft}^3 \text{ of gas}$$

∴ The heat supplied to the furnace per ft^3 of exhaust gas is:

$$\frac{73{,}387 \text{ cal}}{60 \text{ ft}^3} = 1{,}223 \text{ cal/ft}^3 \text{ exhaust gas}$$

$$= 4.85 \text{ Btu/ft}^3 \text{ exhaust gas}$$

• PROBLEM 11-20

Psychrometric charts are indispensable when calculating the mass of water removed and the refrigeration required in certain systems. Using a psychrometric chart, determine these two quantities for the following system:

Initial state:

$t_i = 80^0F$

humidity = 40%

Final state:

$t_f = 50^0F$

humidity = 100%

Amount of airflow

2,000 cfm incoming air processed.

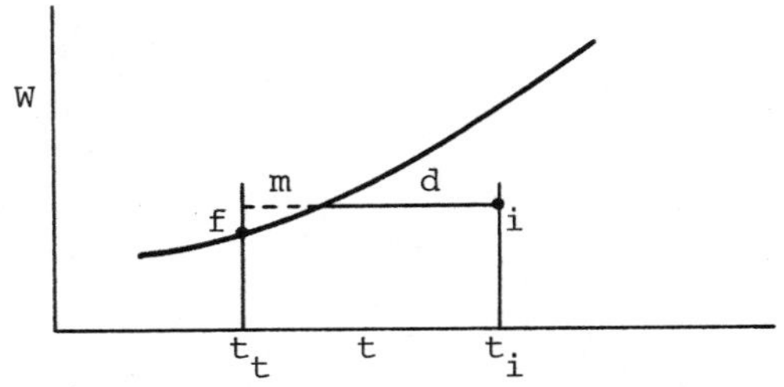

Fig.1

Solution: By using the psychrometric chart, the initial (and final) enthalpy, weight of moisture (per lb dry air) and volume are obtained. By using mass and energy balances, the mass of H_2O removed and the refrigeration required can be calculated.

PSYCHROMETRIC CHART

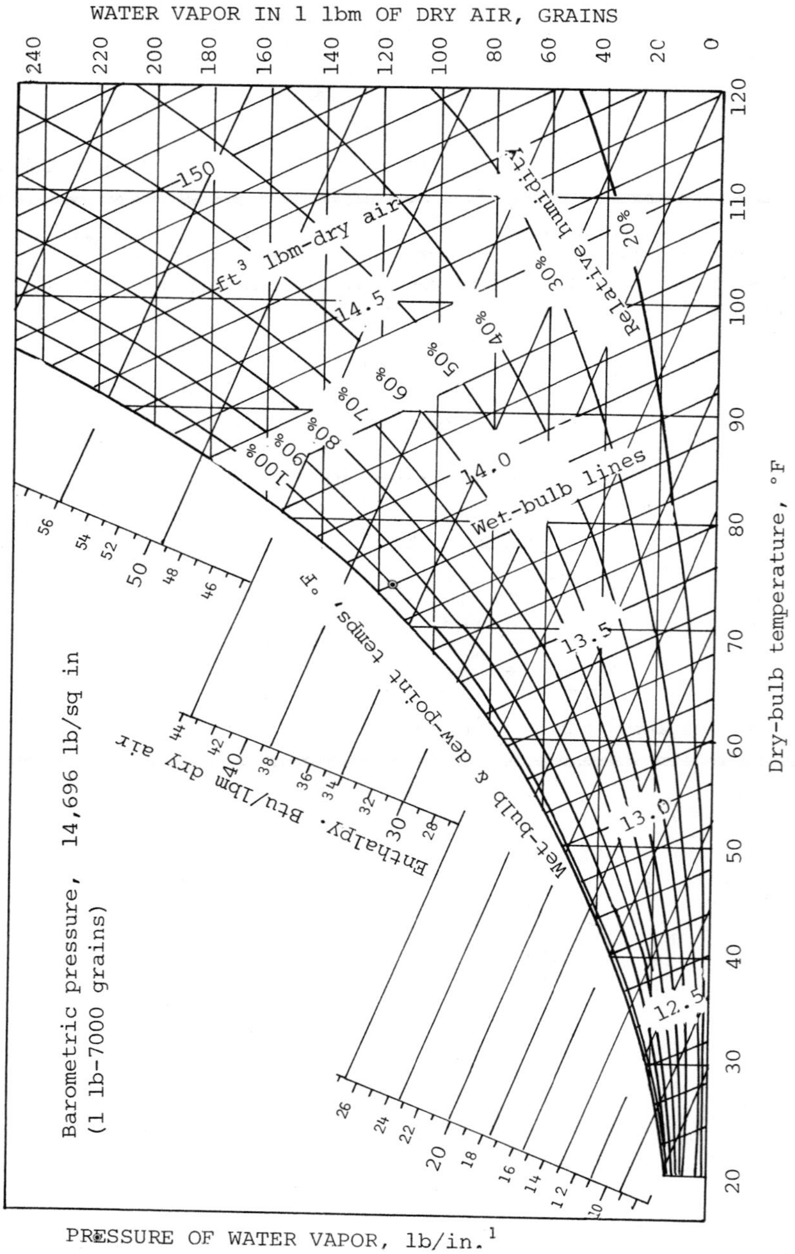

Initial state properties

$t_i = 80^0F$

humidity = 40%

enthalpy = h_i = 29 Btu/lb dry air

mass of moisture = m_i = 62 grains/lb dry air

volume = V_i = 13.78 ft³/lb dry air

Final state properties

$t_f = 50^0F$

humidity = 100%

h_f = 20.4 Btu/lb dry air

m_f = 53 grains/lb dry air

V_f = 13.0 ft³/lb dry air

Therefore, the amount of water to be separated out per pound of dry air is

$$m_{sep.} = m_i - m_f = 62 - 53$$
$$= 9 \text{ grains}$$

The energy balance gives, in conjunction with the mass balance on air and water, the refrigeration requirements (per lb of dry air) as the decrease in enthalpy:

$$-Q = h_i - h_f - (m_i - m_f)h_w$$

where h_w is the enthalpy of saturated H_2O liquid at 50^0F,

h_w = 18.1 Btu. Since 1 lbm = 7,000 grains, m_i and m_f are divided by 7,000.

Therefore,

$$-Q = 29 - 20.4 - \frac{9(18.1)}{7,000}$$

$$= 8.6 \text{ Btu/lbm dry air}$$

The total moisture removed is given by

$$M_T = \frac{2,000 \text{ cfm}}{V_i} \frac{(m_i - m_f)}{7,000}$$

$$= \frac{2,000 \text{ cfm}}{13.78 \text{ cf}} \frac{(9 \text{ grains})}{7,000 \text{ grains/lbm}} = 0.19 \text{ lbm/min}$$

and the refrigeration

$$(-Q)\cdot(\frac{cfm}{cf}) = \frac{2,000}{13.78} \times 8.6 = 1,248 \text{ Btu/min}$$

$$= 6.24 \text{ tons}$$

ADIABATIC FLAME TEMPERATURE

• PROBLEM 11-21

The combustion equation for octane burning in theoretical air (21% O_2 and 79% N_2) is

$$C_8H_{18}(l) + 12.5O_2 + 12.5(3.76)N_2 \rightarrow 8CO_2 + 9H_2O + 47N_2$$

Determine the adiabatic flame temperature for liquid octane burning with 200 percent theoretical air at 25°C. Use the following data to solve the problem:

h^0_f = Standard enthalpy of formation

(all enthalpies are in kcal/mol)

DATA

SPECIES	h° f (Kcal /mol)	h25°C	h139°C	h117/°C	h838°C
C_8H_{18}	-27093.8	——	——	——	——
CO_2	-42661.1	1015.6	8771	7355	5297
H_2O	-26218.1	1075.5	7153	6051	4395
N_2	0	940.0	5736	4893	3663
O_2	0	938.7	6002	5118	3821

Solution: Using the information obtained from the stoichiometry of the chemical equation (written for the 200 percent air combustion), a heat balance can be written. By trial and error, a set of enthalpies at a particular temperature can be found that satisfies the heat balance. The temperature to which this set of enthalpies belong is the adiabatic flame temperature.

The combustion equation for the reaction is

$$C_8H_{18}(l) + (2)(12.5)O_2 + (2)(12.5)(3.76)N_2 \longrightarrow 8CO_2 + 9H_2O + 2(12.5)(3.76)N_2 + (12.5)O_2$$

Due to the fact that the process is adiabatic

$$H_{reactants} = H_{products} \cdot$$

The enthalpy of the reactants is

$H_{reactants} = (h^0{}_f)_{C_8H_{18}} = -27{,}093.8$ kcal/mol. (Since all of the heat given off is due to the combustion of octane, $H_{reactants} = (h^0{}_f)_{C_8H_{18}}$). From the reaction stoichiometry, the enthalpy of the products is given by

$$H_{products} = 8(h^0{}_f + h_T - h_{25^\circ C})_{CO_2} + 9(h^0{}_f + h_T - h_{25^\circ C})_{H_2O} + 94(h^0{}_f + h_T - h_{25^\circ C})_{N_2} + 12.5(h_T - h_{25^\circ C})_{O_2}$$

$$= 8(-42{,}661.1 + (h_T)_{CO_2} - 1{,}015.6) + 9(-26{,}218.1 + (h_T)_{H_2O} - 1{,}075.5) + 94((h_T)_{N_2} - 940) + 12.5((h_T)_{O_2} - 938.7)$$

(The enthalpy of the products is the enthalpy of formation of each product species plus the enthalpy change. The enthalpy change $= h_T - h_{25^\circ C}$ since $h_2 = h_T$ and $h_1 = h_{25^\circ C}$. Each individual product enthalpy is multiplied by the number of moles produced.)

As a first guess, a value of $T = 1{,}393^\circ C$ is assumed (it is logical to try the highest value of T in the data table).

$$T = 1{,}393^\circ C$$

$$H_{products} = 8(-43{,}676.7 + 8{,}771) + 9(-27{,}293.6 + 7{,}153 + 94(5{,}736 - 940) + 12.5(6{,}002 - 938.7)$$
$$= 53{,}604.3$$

This value of T is too high since $H_{reactants} = 27,093.8$. Therefore, a lower value of T is attempted. For the next trial, $T = 1,171°C$ is assumed.

$$T = 1,171°C$$

$$H_{products} = 8(-43,677 + 7,355) + 9(-27,294 + 6,015) + 94(4,893 - 940) + 12.5(5,118 - 939)$$

$$H_{products} = -58,268$$

This value of T is too low. Therefore it is clear that $T_{adiabatic\text{-}flame}$ is between 1,393°C and 1,171°C. In order to obtain a fairly accurate answer quickly, an interpolation may be made.

$$A = (H_{prod})_{1,393°C} - (H_{prod})_{1,171°C} = 1.118723 \times 10^5$$

$$B = (H_{reactants}) - (H_{prod})_{1,171°C} = 31,174.2$$

$$\frac{B}{A} = 0.28$$

∴ $T_{adiabatic\text{-}flame}$ is approximately 28% of the way between 1,171 and 1,393°C, from the lower temperature.

$$\therefore \quad T_{a-f} = 0.28(1,393 - 1,171) + 1,171 = 1,233°C$$

Although correct, this solution is not practical due to product dissociation.

• PROBLEM 11-22

Carbon monoxide burns with a stoichiometric amount of air as described by the following equation:

$$CO(g) + \tfrac{1}{2}\left[O_2 + 3.76N_2\right](g) = CO_2(g) + 1.88N_2(g)$$

Initially, the carbon monoxide and air are @ STP. Determine the adiabatic flame temperature for this combustion. Use the following data to solve the problem and assume a basis of 1 lbmole of CO burned.

Data

enthalpy of air @ $25^0C = 0$

heat of combustion of CO = ΔH_C =
-121,800 Btu/lbmole

Mean molar heat capacities

Species	Temp (^0F)	$\bar{C}_p$ (Btu/lbmole^{0}F)
CO_2	$3,000^0F$	12.78
N_2	$3,000^0F$	7.86
CO_2	$4,400^0F$	13.4
N_2	$4,400^0F$	8.10

Solution: To solve this problem, an energy balance must be made. By trial and error, a temperature which fits the energy balance is found. This temperature is the adiabatic flame temp.

The actual reaction equation is

$$CO(g) + \tfrac{1}{2}O_2(g) = CO_2(g)$$

The energy balance is

$$\Delta H = Q = 0$$

$$\Sigma H_P = \Sigma H_R + \text{heating value of fuel.}$$

But $\Sigma H_R = 0$

$$\therefore \quad \Sigma H_P = \text{heating value of fuel}$$

$$= -(\text{heat of combustion of fuel})$$

$$= 121,800 \text{ Btu}$$

But,

$$\Sigma H_P = \Sigma n\bar{C}_P\ (t - 77) = 121,800$$

First trial : Try $t = 3{,}000^{\circ}F$

From the data,

For CO_2; $n\bar{C}_p\,(3{,}000 - 77) = 1 \times 12.78 \times 2{,}923$
$= 37{,}400$ Btu

For N_2; $n\bar{C}_p(3{,}000 - 77) = 1.88 \times 7.86 \times 2{,}923$
$= 43{,}200$ Btu

$$\Sigma\, n\bar{C}_p(t - 77) = 80{,}600 \text{ Btu} < 121{,}800$$

∴ The temperature chosen is too low.

Second trial: Let $t = 4{,}400^{\circ}F$

For CO_2; $n\bar{C}_p(4{,}400 - 77) = 1 \times 13.4 \times 4{,}323 = 57{,}800$ Btu

For N_2 ; $n\bar{C}_p(4{,}400 - 77) = 1.88 \times 8.10 \times 4{,}323 = 65{,}800$ Btu

$\Sigma n\bar{C}_p(t - 77) = 123{,}600$ Btu $> 121{,}800$ (a little too high)

By linear interpolation between these two temperatures,

$(123{,}600 - 121{,}800) = 1{,}800 \text{ Btu} = \Delta H_{4{,}400^{\circ}F\text{-flame temp}}$

$(123{,}600 - 80{,}600) = 43{,}000 \text{ Btu} = \Delta H_{4{,}400^{\circ}F-3{,}000^{\circ}F}$

$$\frac{1{,}800}{43{,}000} = 0.0418$$

$$\Delta t = 4{,}400 - 3{,}000 = 1{,}400^{\circ}F$$

$$4{,}400^{\circ}F - t_{flame} = (0.0418)(1{,}400) = 58.6^{\circ}F$$

$$t_{flame} \simeq 4{,}341^{\circ}F$$

The real adiabatic flame temperature is found by continued trials and is $4{,}330^{\circ}F$ (which is fairly close to the approximated value).

• PROBLEM 11-23

> Assuming a basis of one standard cubic foot of CO burned, determine the adiabatic flame temperature for the perfect combustion of CO with a stoichiometric amount of air, when the reactant gases are @ 60°F and 1 atm pressure. Also correct for CO_2 dissociation.

Solution: Let's assume 1.0 SCF of CO burned as a basis of calculation.

Process equation:

1 SCF		2.38 SCF		1 SCF		1.88 SCF
$CO(g)$	+	$\frac{1}{2}\left[O_2 + 3.76N_2\right](g)$	$\rightarrow$	$CO_2(g)$	+	$1.88N_2$
60°F		60°F		t = ?		t = ?

ΔH combustion for CO @ 60°F = -321.8 Btu

Reaction equation:

$$(1\ SCF)CO(g) + \tfrac{1}{2}(SCF)O_2(g) = (1\ SCF)CO_2(g)$$

Reference conditions: t = 60°F, P = 1 atm

Enthalpy of air @ 60°F = 0

Percent CO_2 dissociation (for P_{CO_2} = 0.35 atm)	Temp.
1.2	2,900°F
13.6	3,800°F
16.4	3,900°F

Species	Temp.	Enthalpy including dissociation effect
1 SCF of CO_2	2,900°F	96.5
1 SCF of CO_2	3,800°F	171
1 SCF of CO_2	3,900°F	184
1.88 SCF of N_2	2,900°F	107
1.88 SCF of N_2	3,800°F	145
1.88 SCF of N_2	3,900°F	150.5

The energy balance is made and a tempurature is found that will satisfy this balance.

The energy balance is

$$\Delta H = Q = 0$$

$$\Sigma H_P = \Sigma H_R - H^{60}_{combustion}$$

$$= 0 + 321.8 \text{ Btu}$$

CO_2 partial pressure estimation,

$$1 \text{ atm} \times \frac{1}{1+1.88} = 0.35 \text{ atm} = P_{CO_2}$$

Using the known data, three trials can be made.

@ $2900°F$, $\Sigma H_P = 96.5 + 107 = 204 < 321.8$

$\therefore$ this temperature is too low.

@ $3800°F$, $\Sigma H_P = 171 + 145 = 316 < 321.8$

also too low.

@ $3900°F$, $\Sigma H_P = 184 + 150.5 = 334 > 321.8$

$\therefore$ this temperature is too high.

By linear interpolation,

$$(3900 - 3800) = 100°F = \Delta t$$

$$(334 - 316) = 18 \text{ Btu} = \Delta H_{3900-3800}$$

$$(334 - 321.8) = 12.2 = \Delta H_{3900-flame}$$

$$3900 - T_{flame} = \frac{12.2}{18} \cdot (100) = 68$$

$$\therefore T_{flame} \simeq 3900 - 68 = 3832°F$$

The real adiabatic flame temperature is 3820°F, which is close to the calculated temperature.

HEAT OF REACTION

• PROBLEM 11-24

Methane burns in air by the following chemical reaction:

$$\tfrac{1}{2}CH_4 + O_2 + 3.76N_2 \longrightarrow \tfrac{1}{2}CO_2 + H_2O + 3.76N_2$$

This combustion can happen as a constant pressure or constant volume process. Calculate the maximum temperatures of combustion for these two processes. Assume that for the temperature range of interest, the specific heats are constant. Also assume that methane reacts with a stoichiometric amount of air and that initially, the methane and oxygen are at STP. The heat of combustion for one mole of CH_4 burned is equal to 48,418.7 kcal/mole.

Solution: From the stoichiometry of the equation, it can be seen that 5.28 moles of gas react and 5.28 moles of gas are produced. Therefore, it can be deduced that $(Q)_p = (Q)_v$ (where the subscripts p and v refer to the heat of combustion of a constant pressure and constant volume process, respectively). Thus, the heat of combustion can be used for both processes to calculate the maximum combustion temperature by using the equation

$$dQ = NCdT$$

$$\text{or} \quad Q = N\int_{T_1}^{T_2} CdT \qquad N = \#\text{ of moles}$$

It is known that

$$(C_v)_{CO_2} = 1.75 \text{ kcal/mol}$$

$$(C_v)_{H_2O} = 1.57 \text{ kcal/mol}$$

$$(C_v)_{N_2} = 1.27 \text{ kcal/mol}$$

$$(C_p)_{CO_2} = 2.25 \text{ kcal/mol}$$

$$(C_p)_{H_2O} = 2.07 \text{ kcal/mol}$$

$$(C_p)_{N_2} = 1.76 \text{ kcal/mol}$$

Hence, for a constant volume process:

$$(C_v)_{products} = (\tfrac{1}{2}(C_v)_{CO_2} + (C_v)_{H_2O} + 3.76(C_v)_{N_2})/5.28 \text{ moles}$$

$$= (\tfrac{1}{2}(1.75) + (1.57) + 3.76(1.27))/5.28$$

$$= 1.367 \text{ kcal/mol}$$

$$Q_v = N \int_{T_1}^{T_2} CdT$$

$\therefore$

$$\frac{48,418.7}{2} = 5.28 \times 1.367(T_2 - 273)$$

$$T_1 = 273^0\text{K}$$

$$T_2 = \frac{48,418.7}{2 \times 7.217} + 273$$

$$T_2 = 3627^0\text{K} = 3354^0\text{C}$$

For the constant pressure process:

$$Q_p = Q_v = N \int_{T_1}^{T_2} C_p dT$$

For the products:

$$C_p = (\tfrac{1}{2}(C_p)_{CO_2} + (C_p)_{H_2O} + 3.76(C_p)_{N_2})/5.38 \text{ moles}$$

$$= (\tfrac{1}{2}(2.25) + 2.07 + 3.76\ (1.76))/5.28$$

$$= 1.858 \text{ kcal/mol}$$

$\therefore$

$$\frac{48,418.7}{2} = 5.28 \times 1.858(T_2 - 273)$$

$$T_2 = \frac{48,418.7}{9.81 \times 2} + 273$$

$$= 2740^0\text{K} = 2467^0\text{C}$$

As can be seen, a higher temperature is obtained with the constant volume process. The efficiency of the constant volume process is therefore greater than the constant pressure process.

• PROBLEM 11-25

The combustion reaction of methane with oxygen is

$$CH_4 + 2O_2 \longrightarrow CO_2 + 2H_2O$$

The heat of reaction @ 18°C and one atmosphere is -383,648.1 Btu per mole. Using the following heat capacity information, calculate the heat of reaction @ T = 1000°C and P = 1 atm.

<u>heat capacity equations</u>

$$(C_p)_{CH_4} = 4.52 + (0.00737)T \text{ Btu/mole }^0R$$

$$(C_p)_{O_2} = 11.515 - (172)T^{-\frac{1}{2}} + (1530)T^{-1} \text{ Btu/mole }^0R$$

$$(C_p)_{CO_2} = 16.2 - (6.53 \times 10^3)T^{-1} + (1.41 \times 10^6)T^{-2} \text{ Btu/mole }^0R$$

$$(C_p)_{H_2O} = 19.86 - 597(T)^{\frac{1}{2}} + (7500)T^{-1} \text{ Btu/mole }^0R$$

Solution: The heat of reaction can be calculated using the equation

$$\Delta H = -\Delta N \int_{T_0}^{T} \Delta C_p dT$$

where Δ stands for products minus reactants.

The equation for the heat of reaction is

$$-Q_{reaction} = \Delta H = N_{reactants} \int_{T_0}^{T} C_{p\ react}\, dT - N_{products} \int_{T_0}^{T} C_{p\ products}\, dT$$

The reactants are 1 mole of CH_4 and 2 moles of O_2.

$$1 \text{ mole } CH_4 \longrightarrow C_p = 4.52 + (0.0073)T$$

$$\underline{2 \text{ moles } O_2 \longrightarrow 2C_p = 23.03 - (344)T^{-\frac{1}{2}} + 3060T^{-1}}$$

$$3 \text{ moles reactants} \longrightarrow N_{react}C_{p\ react} = 27.55 - (344)T^{-\frac{1}{2}}$$

$$+ (3060)T^{-1} + (0.0073)T$$

The products are one mole of CO_2 and two moles of H_2O.

$$1 \text{ mole } CO_2 \longrightarrow C_p = 16.2 - (6.53 \times 10^3)T^{-1} + (1.41 \times 10^6)T^{-2}$$

$$\underline{2 \text{ moles } H_2O \longrightarrow 2C_p = 39.72 - (1194)T^{-\frac{1}{2}} + (15 \times 10^3)T^{-1}}$$

$$3 \text{ moles products} \longrightarrow N_{prod}\ C_{p\ products} = 55.92 - (1194)T^{-\frac{1}{2}}$$
$$+ 8.47 \times 10^3 T^{-1} + (1.41 \times 10^6)T^{-2}$$

(To find C_p, divide by 3)

$$\Delta H = 3 \int_{T_0}^{T} (9.18 - (114.7)T^{-\frac{1}{2}} + 1020T^{-1} + 0.00246T)\ dT$$

$$-3 \int_{T_0}^{T} (18.64 - (378)(T)^{-\frac{1}{2}} + (2.823 \times 10^3)T$$

$$+ (0.47 \times 10^6)T^2)dT$$

$$= 3\left[(-9.46)(T - T_0) + 526.6(T^{\frac{1}{2}} - T_0^{\frac{1}{2}}) - 1.803 \times 10^3 \ln \frac{T}{T_0}\right.$$

$$\left. + 0.00246(T^2 - T_0^2) + 0.47 \times 10^6(\frac{1}{T} - \frac{1}{T_0})\right]$$

$$T = 1000^0C = 2292^0R \qquad T_0 = 18^0C = 524.4^0R$$

$\therefore$

$$\Delta H = 3[-16,721 + 13,152 - 2,659 + 12,247 - 691]$$

$$\Delta H = 15,984 \text{ Btu/mole of } CH_4$$

$\Delta H = \Delta H_2 - \Delta H_1$ where ΔH_2 is the heat of reaction @ 2292^0R and ΔH_1 is the heat of reaction @ 524.4^0R.

$$\therefore \quad \Delta H_2 = \Delta H + \Delta H_1 = 15{,}984 - 383{,}648$$

$$= -367{,}664 \text{ Btu/mole}$$

• PROBLEM 11-26

An isothermally run ($T = 77^0F$) hydrogen-oxygen fuel cell requires a heat interaction of -11.547 kcal/mol between the cell and its surroundings. Find the cell emf at this temperature.

Data Required for the Problem

Faraday's constant - F = 23,060 cal/V mol

Overall cell reaction:

$H_2 + \frac{1}{2}O_2 = H_2O$ (2 electrons transferred)

@ 1 atm and 77^0F, $\Delta H_{reaction} = -68.8$ kcal/mol

Solution: Using the equations

$\Delta H = Q - W$ and $W = -\Delta G$ (since no PV work is being done, only electrical work) and $\Delta G = -nFE$, the emf of the cell can be obtained.

$$\Delta H = Q - W, \quad Q = -11.547 \text{ kcal/mol}$$

$$W = Q - \Delta H$$

$$W = -\Delta G = Q - \Delta H$$

$$\Delta G = nFE = Q - \Delta H, \quad n = 2$$

$$nFE = -11.547 + 68.8 = 57.253 \text{ kcal/mol}$$

Therefore,

$$E = \frac{57{,}253 \text{ cal/mol}}{2 \times 23{,}060 \text{ cal/V mol}}$$

$$E = 1.24 \text{ V}$$

• PROBLEM 11-27

The reaction of sodium oxide with hydrochloric acid is described by the following chemical equation,

$$Na_2O(s) + 2HCl(g) \rightleftharpoons 2\ NaCl(s) + H_2O(1)$$

Calculate the heat of reaction @ 298 °K using the following data.

Data

Standard heats of formation

NaCl(s)	-98.6 ± 0.2 kcal/mole
$Na_2O(s)$	-100.7 ± 1.2 kcal/mole
HCl(g)	-22.0 ± 1.0 kcal/mole
$H_2O(1)$	-68.32 ± 0.01 kcal/mole

Solution: This problem requires the use of application of Hess's Law to obtain a solution.

The heat of reaction is equal to the difference between the enthalpies of the products and of the reactants.

$\therefore$

$$\Delta H^0_{298} = [2 \times (-98.6) + (-68.32)] - [(-100.7) + 2 \times (-22.0)]$$

$$= -120.82 \text{ kcal}$$

The errors however, are additive.

$$\therefore \quad \text{overall error} = 1.2 + (2 \times 0.1) + (2 \times 0.2) + 0.01$$

$$= \pm 1.81 \text{ kcal}$$

$\therefore$ The heat evolved when one mole of Na_2O and two moles of HCl react completely is 120.82 ± 1.81 kcal or ΔH^0_{298} = -120.82 ± 1.81 kcal.

• PROBLEM 11-28

Using the following data for cadmium, determine the absolute entropy of Cd at 298°K. Assume that T^3 law is valid below 12°C and also, there is no difference between C_p and C_v at these low temperatures.

Data

T, °K	C_p, cal/deg/g-atom cadmium	T, °K	C_p, cal/deg/g-atom cadmium
12	0.392	130	5.608
14	.592	140	5.684
16	.804	150	5.746
18	1.020	160	5.799
20	1.240	170	5.844
25	1.803	180	5.884
30	2.306	190	5.922
35	2.760	200	5.956
40	3.158	210	5.988
45	3.503	220	6.018
50	3.803	230	6.047
60	4.283	240	6.073
70	4.647	250	6.096
80	4.920	260	6.119
90	5.138	270	6.144
100	5.284	280	6.171
110	5.413	290	6.201
120	5.518	298.16	6.224

Solution: A mathematical integration is used to determine the quantity; (It can also be solved by graphical method.)

$$\int_{12}^{298} \frac{C_p}{T}\, dT$$

and the third power law is used to determine the quantity,

$$\int_{0}^{12} (C_p/T)dT = \int_{12}^{S_{12}}$$

The entropy at 298^0K is the addition of these two values,

$$\int_{298}^{S_{298}} = \int_{12}^{S_{12}} + \int_{12}^{298} \frac{C_p}{T}\,dT$$

The third power rule is

$$C_p = aT^3 \qquad (a = \text{constant}) \qquad (\text{for } T \leq 12^0\text{K})$$

To calculate $\int^{S}$ @ 12^0K,

$$\int_{12}^{S_{12}} = \int_{o}^{12} \frac{aT^3}{T}\,dT = \int_{o}^{12} aT^2\,dT$$

$$= \frac{aT^3}{3}\Bigg|_{o}^{12}$$

$$= \frac{C_p(@\ 12^0\text{K})}{3}$$

$$\therefore \quad \int_{S_{298}}^{S_{298}} = \frac{C_p(@\ 12^0\text{K})}{3} + \int_{12}^{298} \frac{C_p}{T}\,dT$$

Now the second integral has to be evaluated. The equation that is used is

$$\int_{a}^{b} YdX = \Sigma(X_b - X_a)(Y_a + Y_b)/2$$

For the case at hand

$$\int_{12}^{298} (C_p/T)dT = \Sigma(T_2 - T_1)((C_p/T)_2 + (C_p/T)_1)/2$$

where $(T_2 - T_1)$ refers to the small temperature intervals, taken from the data.

From the data,

T^0K	$\int_T^{T_2} (C_p/T)dT$	$\int_{12}^{T_2} (C_p/T)dT$	(The $\int_{12}^{T_2} (C_p/T)$ is just the summation of all the previous $\int_T^{T_2} (C_p/T)dT$)
12	0	0	
14	0.075	0.075	
16	0.093	0.168	
18	0.107	0.275	
20	0.119	0.394	
25	0.335	0.729	
30	0.372	1.101	
35	0.389	1.49	
40	0.395	1.885	
45	0.392	2.277	
50	0.385	2.662	
60	0.737	3.399	
70	0.689	4.088	
80	0.639	4.727	
90	0.593	5.32	
100	0.550	5.87	
110	0.515	6.385	
120	0.481	6.866	
130	0.446	7.312	
140	0.419	7.731	
150	0.395	8.126	
160	0.373	8.499	
170	0.353	8.852	
180	0.335	9.187	
190	0.319	9.506	
200	0.305	9.811	
210	0.291	10.102	
220	0.279	10.381	
230	0.268	10.649	
240	0.258	10.907	
250	0.248	11.155	
260	0.240	11.395	
270	0.138	11.533	
280	0.133	11.666	
290	0.217	11.883	
298	0.172	12.055	

$$\therefore \int_{298}^{S_{298}} = \int_{12}^{S_{298}} \int_{12}^{298} (C_p/T)dT$$

$$= \frac{0.392}{3} + 12.055$$

$$= 12.186 \text{ cal/deg/g-atom}$$

or for 1 g-atom $\int_{S_{298}} = 12.186$ eu

• PROBLEM 11-29

> The decomposition reaction of chlorine is
>
> $$Cl_2(g) \rightarrow 2Cl(g)$$
>
> Assuming that the entropy of 1 mole of $Cl_2(g)$ has an entropy (@ 298°K and 1 atm), of 53.2 eu, and that of 2 g atoms of Cl(g) (@ 25°C and 2 atm), is 76.2 eu, calculate the entropy increase for a constant volume process. Also decide whether $Cl_2(g)$ will decompose in an isolated system @ 25°C, 1 atm, assuming ΔE to be 57 kcal at all tempuratures.

Solution: For the conditions given, (Cl_2 @ 298°K, 1 atm, Cl @ 298°K, 2 atm) the volume would remain constant and the entropy change is 76.2 - 53.2 = 23.0 eu.

In an isolated system, there is no heat transfer to or from the surroundings. The decomposition of $Cl_2(g)$ requires a certain amount of energy in order to break the Cl - Cl bonds. The only source for this energy is the system itself. Therefore, the system will cool down since the temperature would drop. An absorption of 57,000 cal would cause the temperature to drop so that the entropy of 2Cl would be lower than that of Cl_2. Therefore, Cl_2 will not decompose in an isolated system.

• PROBLEM 11-30

Solid silver has a heat capacity given by the following equation:

$$\bar{C}_p(\text{cal mole}^{-1}\text{deg}^{-1}) = -0.023T + 2.5(10^{-3})T^2 - 1.9(10^{-5})T^3$$

This expression is valid for $273 \le T \le 333^\circ C$. Calculate the change in entropy when one mole of solid silver is heated from $273^\circ C$ to $333^\circ C$.

Solution: Using the relation $(\partial S/\partial T)_P = C_P/T$ and integrating, ΔS can be evaluated.

$$(\partial S/\partial T)_P = C_P/T$$

The change (increase) in entropy due to the temperature rise is

$$\Delta S = S_{60^\circ K} - S_{0^\circ K} = \int_0^{60} C_P dT$$

$$= \int_0^{60} [(-0.023T + 0.0025T^2 - 0.000019T^3)/T] dT$$

$$= 1.75 \text{ eu/mole}$$

According to the third law, the entropy @ $0^\circ K$ is equal to zero and therefore the entropy @ $60^\circ K$ is 1.75 eu/mole.

• PROBLEM 11-31

Ti solid reacts with chlorine gas by the following reaction :

$$Ti(s) + 2Cl_2(g) \longrightarrow TiCl_4(l)$$

Using the following standard entropy data, calculate the entropy change for the system @ $298^\circ K$.

Standard entropy data (@ $25^\circ C$)

$Ti(s)$ —— $S^0 = 7.2$ eu/mole

$Cl_2(g)$ —— $S^0 = 53.3$ eu/mole

$TiCl_4(l)$ —— $S^0 = 60.4$ eu/mole

Solution: The entropy change is given by the sum of the entropies of the products minus the sum of entropies of the reactants. That is,

$$\Delta S^0_{reaction} = S^0_{products} - S^0_{reactants}$$

$$= 60.4 - [7.2 + 2(53.3)] = -53.4 \text{ eu}$$

• **PROBLEM 11-32**

A particular substance has the following solid, liquid and gas heat capacities:

$$\text{Solid (for } T \leq 25^0\text{K)}; \; \bar{C}_p = 0.8T \text{ cal deg}^{-1} \text{ mole}^{-1}$$

From $25^0K \rightarrow 250^0K$ (melting point);

$$\bar{C}_p = 0.007T + 0.0006T^2 \text{ cal deg}^{-1} \text{ mole}^{-1}$$

$$\text{Liquid}; \; \bar{C}_p = 18 + 0.007T \text{ cal deg}^{-1} \text{ mole}^{-1}$$

Gas @ 1 atm (above 360^0K which is the boiling point);

$$\bar{C}_p = 15 \text{ cal deg}^{-1} \text{ mole}^{-1}$$

The heat of fusion is 2,000 cal/mole and the heat of vaporization is 6,850 cal/mole. Calculate the entropy @ 400^0K and 0.7 atm.

Solution: By using the equations

$$S = \int \frac{C_P}{T} dT \quad \text{for heating processes and } S = \frac{\Delta H}{T}$$

for phase change processes, the final entropy can be calculated by adding up the individual step entropies.

$$S(g, 400^0K) = \int_0^{25} 0.8(T/T)dT + \int_{25}^{250} (0.007T + 0.0006T^2)/T \, dT$$

$$+ 2,000/250 + \int_{250}^{360} ([18 + 0.007T]/T)dT +$$

$$6,850/360 + \int_{360}^{400} (15/T)dT$$

$$= 0.8(25) + 0.007(250 - 25) + \frac{0.0006}{2}(250^2 - 25^2)$$

$$+ 8 + 18(\ln 360 - \ln 250) + 0.007(360 - 250)$$

$$+ 19 + 15(\ln 400 - \ln 360)$$

$$= 76.05 \text{ eu}$$

This is the entropy @ 400^0K and 1 atm. In the expansion to 0.7 atm, the entropy increases by $R \ln(P_1/P_2)$

$$= 1.987 \ln(1/0.7)$$

$$= 0.71 \text{ eu}$$

$$\therefore \quad S(g, 400^0K, 0.7 \text{ atm}) = 76.05 + 0.71$$

$$= 76.76 \text{ eu}$$

• PROBLEM 11-33

Determine the relation between the parameters α (the coefficient of expansion = $[(1/V)(\partial V/\partial T)_P]$), β (compressibility = $[-(1/V)(\partial V/\partial P)_T]$), and the thermal pressure coefficient $\left(\left(\frac{\partial P}{\partial T}\right)_V\right)$. Show that according to the third law, the limiting value of β is unknown for a pure solid as $T \to 0^0$K.

Solution: Since $V = f(P,T)$,

$$dV = (\partial V/\partial P)_T\, dP + (\partial V/\partial T)_P\, dT.$$

For changes at constant volume, this becomes

$$0 = (\partial V/\partial P)_T(\partial P/\partial T)_V + (\partial V/\partial T)_P \text{ or}$$

$$(\partial P/\partial T)_V = -(\partial V/\partial T)_P/(\partial V/\partial P)_T$$

$$= (1/V)(\partial V/\partial T)_P/-(1/V)(\partial V/\partial P)_T$$

$$= \alpha/\beta$$

From the third law, $\lim_{T \to 0} (\partial P/\partial T)_V = \lim_{T \to 0} \alpha/\beta = 0$, which is in agreement with the previous relation, no matter what the value of β is.

• PROBLEM 11-34

The entropy values of four molecules @ 25°C and 760 mm, Hg, in decreasing order, are as follows:

ethylbenzene (g) - ΔS^0_{298} = 86.2 eu/mole

o-xylene (g) - ΔS^0_{298} = 84.3 eu/mole

p-xylene (g) - ΔS^0_{298} = 84.2 eu/mole

ethylbenzene (l) - ΔS^0_{298} = 60 eu/mole

Explain theoretically and justify their order.

Solution: Since all of the molecules have identical molecular weights, and are at the same temperature and pressure, the entropies can be compared by comparing states of aggregation and symmetries. The liquid has the least entropy since it is in a more ordered state. Concerning the gases, p-xylene is the most symmetrical (i.e. the entropy is minimum), and ethylbenzene (g) is the least symetrical (i.e. the entropy is maximum).

• PROBLEM 11-35

According to the third law, ΔS, ΔC_P and $(\partial \Delta S/\partial T)_P$ approach zero as T approaches 0°K. Using the following data, show that this is true.

Data

Chemical reaction; S_n (gray) — S_n (white)

Temperature, °K	Sn(gray) $\bar{S}$ eu mole^{-1}	Sn(gray) $\bar{C}_P$ cal deg^{-1} mole^{-1}	Sn(white) $\bar{S}$ eu mole^{-1}	Sn(white) $\bar{C}_P$ cal deg^{-1} mole^{-1}
10	0.12	0.36	0.14	0.45
20	0.29	0.84	0.86	1.1
50	1.9	2.7	2.7	3.7

Solution: From the data, at 10°K,

ΔS = 0.14 - 0.12 = 0.02 and ΔC_P = 0.45 - 0.36 = 0.09.

at 20°K ΔS = 0.07 and ΔC_P = 0.3. at 50° at 50°, ΔS = 0.8, ΔC_P = 1.0.

Therefore, it can be seen that as 0^0 is approached, ΔS and ΔC_P also approach zero.

The average $(\partial \Delta S/\partial T)_P$ between 20^0K and 50^0K is $((0.8 - 0.07)/(50 - 20)) = 0.02$. The average $(\partial \Delta S/\partial T)_P$ between 10^0K and 20^0K is $(0.07 - 0.02)/(20 - 10) = 0.005$.

Therefore, it can be seen that $(\partial \Delta S/\partial T)_P$ approaches zero 0^0K is approached.

• PROBLEM 11-36

If N_A molecules of argon and N_H molecules of helium are mixed, calculate the probabilities, W_A and W_H, of the individual gases and the probability, W_{AH}, of the mixture, and the entropy change due to mixing. Also develop an expression for the entropy change per mole of mixture formed, if the mole fractions are X_A and X_H.

Assume that both gases are ideal and that the process takes place at constant temperature and constant pressure.

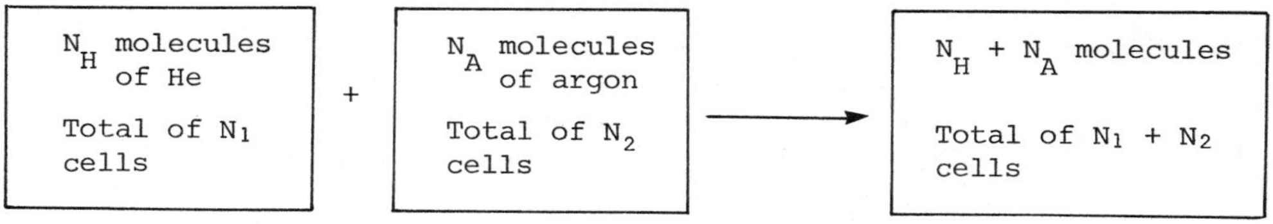

Solution: The following diagram describes the process:

The probability W, for N_A indistinguishable molecules in N_2 cells $= N_2^{N_A}/N_A! = W_A$. Similarly, $W_H = N_1^{N_H}/N_H!$. These equations are valid since the number of cells is much greater than the number of molecules. The number of ways of placing the total number of molecules in the total number of cells is equal to

$$(N_1 + N_2)(N_1 + N_2 - 1)(N_1 + N_2 - 2) \ldots$$

$$(N_1 + N_2 - N_A - N_H + 1)/N_A!\, N_H!$$

This can be approximated to

$$(N_1 + N_2)^{(N_A + N_H)}/N_A!\ N_H!$$

Hence, for the gas mixture,

$$W_{AH} = (N_1 + N_2)^{(N_H + N_A)}/N_A!\ N_B!\ .$$

The entropy change is

$$\Delta S = k \ln W_{final} - k \ln W_{initial}$$ where

k = Boltzmann's constant.

$$\therefore \Delta S = (k \ln W_{AH}) - (k \ln W_A + k \ln W_H)$$

$$= k \ln\left[(N_1 + N_2)^{(N_H + N_A)}/N_A!\ N_H!\right]$$

$$- \left[k \ln(N_1^{N_H}/N_H!) + k \ln(N_2^{N_A}/N_A!)\right]$$

$$= - k \ln \left[N_1^{N_H}\ N_2^{N_A}/(N_1 + N_2)^{(N_A + N_H)}\right]$$

This expression is modified to

$$\Delta S = - k \ln\left[\left(\frac{N_1^{N_H}}{(N_1 + N_2)^{N_H}}\right) \cdot \left(\frac{N_2^{N_A}}{(N_1 + N_2)^{N_A}}\right)\right]$$

$$= - k \ln (X_A^{N_A}\ X_H^{N_H}) = - k(N_A + N_H) \ln (X_A^{N_A}\ X_H^{N_H})^{1/(N_A + N_H)}$$

For 1 mole of mixture, $N_A + N_H = N_0$ (N_0 = Avogadro's number). Since $R = k\ N_0$,

$$\Delta S = - R \ln(X_A^{X_A}\ X_H^{X_H})$$

$$= - R(X_A \ln X_A + X_H \ln X_H)$$

• **PROBLEM 11-37**

Calculate the most probable distribution and the thermodynamic probability (Ω) for a system of eight molecules distributed among six available energy levels. The total system energy is 4 ergs and the individual levels have energies of 0, 1, 2, 3, 4, and 5 ergs, respectfully. Also determine the entropy of the system.

Solution: In order to illustrate the possible distributions, two conditions must be satisfied. The first is that the system's total energy is equal to four ergs. The second is that the system has eight molecules. There are five possible distributions that comply with these requirements.

The symbols used will be defined as follows:

Energy levels; $\varepsilon_0 = 0$ ergs, $\varepsilon_1 = 1$, $\varepsilon_2 = 2$, $\varepsilon_3 = 3$, $\varepsilon_4 = 4$, $\varepsilon_5 = 5$.

Number of molecules, n_i; thermodynamic probability = Ω

Using these symbols, the criterion is

$$\Sigma n_i \varepsilon_i = 4 \text{ ergs} \qquad \Sigma n_i = 8 \text{ molecules.}$$

Each distribution has a certain number of ways. This number is found by using the following equation:

$$\# \text{ of ways} = (\text{Total \# of molecules})!/\left[\pi(n_i!)\right]$$

The distribution with the most # of ways is the most probable distribution.

The five distributions for the problem at hand are:

Distribution	$\varepsilon_0=0$	$\varepsilon_1=1$	$\varepsilon_2=2$	$\varepsilon_3=3$	$\varepsilon_4=4$	$\varepsilon_5=5$	# of
	n_0	n_1	n_2	n_3	n_4	n_5	ways
(1)	7	0	0	0	1	0	8
(2)	6	1	0	1	0	0	56
(3)	6	0	2	0	0	0	28
(4)	5	2	1	0	0	0	168
(5)	4	4	0	0	0	0	70

As can be seen, the most probable distribution is number 4. As an illustration, if distribution number one is taken,

$$\Sigma_{ni}\varepsilon_i = (7)(0) + (1)(4) = 4 \text{ ergs}$$

$$\Sigma_{ni} = 7 + 1 = 8$$

$$\# \text{ of ways} = 8!/(7!)\cdot(1!) = 8$$

For the system,

$$\Omega = \Sigma(\# \text{ of ways})$$

$$= 8 + 56 + 28 + 168 + 70$$

$$= 330$$

$\therefore$ The entropy of the system is,

$$S = k \ln\Omega \text{ (This is the Boltzmann-Planck relation } k = \text{Boltzmann's constant.)}$$

$$= 1.38(10^{-16})\ln(330)$$

$$= 8.0 \times 10^{-16} \text{ erg/deg}$$

$$= 1.92 \times 10^{-16} \text{ cal deg}^{-1}$$

$$= 1.92 \times 10^{-16} \text{ eu}$$

SECOND LAW ANALYSIS OF REACTING SYSTEMS

• PROBLEM 11-38

Calculate the change in entropy for liquid water @ $-5^\circ C$ and 1 atm to ice at $-5^\circ C$ and 1 atm. Use the following data:

$$C_p \text{ for } H_2O(s) = 9 \text{ cal deg}^{-1} \text{ mole}^{-1}$$

$$C_p \text{ for } H_2O(l) = 18 \text{ cal deg}^{-1} \text{ mole}^{-1}$$

$$\Delta H_{fusion} \text{ @ } 0^\circ C \text{ and 1 atm is 1,440 cal/mole}$$

Solution: The ΔS for each step is calculated and the sum of all these terms gives the entropy change for the process. The entropy change is obtained by calculating the entropies of the following three steps:

(A) heating the $H_2O(l)$ from $5^\circ C \rightarrow 0^\circ C$

(B) phase transition $H_2O(l) \rightarrow H_2O(s)$ @ $0^\circ C$

(C) cooling $H_2O(s)$ from $0^\circ C \rightarrow -5^\circ C$

For step (A):

$$\Delta S_A = \int_{268}^{273} C_p dT/T = 18(\ln 273/268)\ \text{eu} = 0.333$$

For step (B):

$$\Delta S_B = -H_{fusion}/T = -1{,}440/273 = -5.27\ \text{eu}$$

ΔH_{fusion} is given for the reverse reaction, that is, $H_2O(s) \rightarrow H_2O(l)$, hence the negative sign is used.

For step (C):

$$\Delta S_C = \int_{273}^{268} C_p dT/T = 9 \ln\left(\frac{268}{273}\right) = -0.166$$

$$\Delta S_{TOT} = \Delta S_A + \Delta S_B + \Delta S_C$$

$$= 0.333 + (-5.27) + (-0.166)$$

$$= -5.1\ \text{eu}$$

• **PROBLEM 11-39**

Iron reacts with oxygen at high temperatures ($T > 910^\circ C$) with the following reaction:

$$Fe(\gamma) + \tfrac{1}{2}O_2(g) \rightleftharpoons FeO(s)$$

Calculate the entropy of this reaction at 1 atm. pressure and $1{,}200^\circ C$. Use the following data:

<u>Data</u>

(A) reaction @ $25^\circ C \leq T < 760^\circ C$: $Fe(\alpha)_1 + \tfrac{1}{2}O_2(g) = FeO(s)$

(B) reaction @ $T = 760^\circ C$: $Fe(\alpha)_1 = Fe(\alpha)_2$ (The subscripts 1 and 2 refer to the form of solid metal that is being dealt with. The (α) and (γ) also refer to the form of the solid lattice of the metal).

(C) reaction @ $760^\circ C \leq T \leq 910^\circ C$: $Fe(\alpha)_2 + \frac{1}{2}O_2(g) = FeO(s)$

(D) reaction @ $T = 910^\circ C$: $Fe(\alpha)_2 = Fe(\gamma)$

(E) reaction @ $910^\circ C \leq T$: $Fe(\gamma) + \frac{1}{2}O_2(g) = FeO(s)$

Standard entropies:

	S^0 cal deg^{-1} $mole^{-1}$
$Fe(\alpha)_1$	6.49
$O_2(g)$	49.02
$FeO(s)$	14.05

Enthalpies and Heat capacities:

For reaction (A): $\Delta C_p = 3.9 - 4.42 \times 10^{-3}T - 0.47 \times 10^{-5}T^{-2}$
(valid for temperature range $25^\circ C < T \leq 760^\circ C$)

For reaction (B): $\Delta H = +660$ cal/mole

For reaction (C):

$$\Delta C_p = -0.92 + 1.50 \times 10^{-3}T - 0.47 \times 10^{5}T^{-2}$$

(valid for temperature range $760^\circ C \leq T \leq 910^\circ C$)

For reaction (D): $\Delta H = +220$ cal/mole

For reaction (E): $\Delta C_p = 6.24 - 3.16 \times 10^{-3}T - 0.47 \times 10^{5}T^{-2}$

(valid for temperature range $910^\circ C \leq T < 1{,}378^\circ C$)

Solution: Using the equation

$$\Delta S = \int_{T_1}^{T_2} \frac{C_p}{T}\, dT$$

in conjunction with Hess's law and the data given, the entropy of the reaction under consideration, (reaction E) at the desired temperature ($1{,}200^\circ C$), can be obtained. If reaction B is subtracted from reaction A, reaction C is obtained. If reaction D is subtracted from C, the desired reaction (E) is obtained. Therefore, all that needs to be done is to substract the corresponding entropies (of reaction) and account for temperature change by using the equation shown above for ΔS dependence on temperature.

From the standard entropy data,

for reaction (A) @ 25°C,

$$\Delta S^0_{298} = S^0_{FeO(s)} - S^0_{Fe(\alpha)_1} - \tfrac{1}{2} S^0_{O_2(g)}$$

$$= -16.95 \text{ cal/deg}$$

The entropy change over the temperature interval 25°C to 273°C is

$$\Delta S^0_{1,033} - \Delta S^0_{298} = \int_{298}^{1,033} \frac{\Delta C_P}{T} \cdot dT$$

$$= \int_{298}^{1,033} \left[3.90T^{-1} - 4.42 \times 10^{-3} - 0.47 \times 10^5 T^{-3}\right] dT$$

$$= 4.85 - 3.25 - 0.25$$

$$= 1.35$$

$$\therefore \quad \Delta S^0_{1,033} = 1.35 + \Delta S^0_{298}$$

$$= 1.35 - 16.95$$

$$= -15.60 \text{ cal/deg}$$

at 760°C (1,033°K), the iron changes form from $Fe(\alpha)_1$ $Fe(\alpha)_2$. The entropy change is

$$\frac{\Delta H}{T} = \frac{660}{1,033} = 0.64 \text{ cal deg}^{-1} \text{ mole}^{-1}$$

∴ For reaction C (which equals reactions A - B)

$$\Delta S^0_{1,033} = (\Delta S^0_{1,033})_{\text{reaction A}} - (\Delta S^0_{1,033})_{\text{reaction B}}$$

$$= -15.6 - 0.64$$

$$= -16.24 \text{ cal/deg}$$

at 910°C, iron again changes form as shown by reaction D,

$$Fe(\alpha)_2 = Fe(\gamma)$$

The entropy change is

$$\Delta S^0_{1,183} = 220/1,183 = 0.19 \text{ cal/deg mole}$$

The entropy change for reaction C at 910° C is

$$\Delta S^{0}_{1,183} - \Delta S^{0}_{1,033} = \int_{1,033}^{1,183} \frac{\left[-0.92 + 1.5 \times 10^{-3}T - 0.47\times10^{-5}T^{-2}\right] dT}{T}$$

$$= -0.92 \ln \frac{1,183}{1,033} + 1.5 \times 10^{-3}(1,183-1,033)$$

$$+ 0.24 \times 10^{5} \times \left(\frac{1}{(1,183)^{2}} - \frac{1}{(1,033)^{2}}\right)$$

$$= 0.10$$

$$\therefore \quad \Delta S^{0}_{1,183} = 0.1 + \Delta S^{0}_{1,033}$$

$$= -16.24 + 0.1$$

$$= -16.14 \text{ cal/deg}$$

Equation E is found by subtracting reaction D from C,

(C) $\quad Fe(\alpha)_2 + \frac{1}{2}O_2 = FeO(s)$

(D) $\quad - \quad Fe(\alpha)_2 = Fe(\gamma)$

(E) $\quad Fe(\gamma) + \frac{1}{2}O_2 = FeO(s)$

$$(\Delta S^{0}_{E})_{1,183^{\circ}K} = (\Delta S^{0}_{C})_{1,183} - (\Delta S^{0}_{D})_{1,183}$$

$$= -16.19 - 0.19$$

$$= -16.33 \text{ cal/deg}$$

However, the temperature that ΔS^{0} is needed is at is $1,200^{\circ}$ C = $1,473^{\circ}$K.

$$\therefore \quad \Delta S^{0}_{1,473} - \Delta S^{0}_{1,183} = \int_{1,183}^{1,473} \frac{(\Delta C_P)_{\text{reaction E}}}{T} dT$$

$$\Delta S^{0}_{1,473} = \Delta S^{0}_{1,183} + 6.24 \ln \frac{1,473}{1,183} -$$

$$3.16 \times 10^{-3}(1,473 - 1,183) +$$

$$0.24 \times 10^{5} \quad \frac{1}{(1,473)^{2}} - \frac{1}{(1,183)^{2}}$$

$$= -16.33 + 0.45$$

$$\Delta S^{0}_{1,473} = -15.88 \text{ cal/deg} = \Delta S^{0}_{1,200^{\circ}C}$$

• PROBLEM 11-40

The temperature of spontaneous solidification for copper is 1,120 °K and the melting point is 1,356 °K. Calculate the Gibbs free - energy change at the spontaneous solidification temperature using the following data.

Data

Reaction: $Cu_{(l)} = Cu_{(s)}$

$$\Delta H^0 = -3{,}100 \text{ cal } (@\ 1{,}356\,^{\circ}K).$$

$$\Delta C_p = -2.09 + 1.5 \times 10^{-3} T$$

Solution: By using the Gibbs-Helmoltz equation along with the given data (to solve for the integration constant), the Gibbs free-energy can be calculated.

The Gibbs-Helmholtz equation is

$$\frac{\Delta G_T^0}{T} = - \int \frac{\Delta H^0}{T^2} \cdot dT$$

or

$$\Delta G_T^0 = -T \int \left[\frac{\Delta H_0}{T^2} + \frac{1}{T^2} \int \Delta C_p dT\right] dT$$

(The ΔH with the superscript zero is the enthalpy at 1 atm, while the ΔH with the subscript zero is a constant)

After substitution of ΔC_p,

$$\Delta G_T^0 = -T \int \left[\frac{\Delta H_0}{T^2} - \frac{2.09}{T} + 0.75 \times 10^{-3}\right] dT$$

$$= -T \int \left[\frac{\Delta H_0}{T^2} - \frac{2.09}{T} + 0.75 \times 10^{-3}\right] dT$$

$$\Delta G_T^0 = \Delta H_0 + 2.09T \ln T - 0.75 \times 10^{-3} T^2 + IT,$$

where ΔH_0 and I are integration constants. H comes from the integration of the Kirchoff equation. These constants can be evaluated either by knowing ΔG^0 at two temperatures or ΔG^0 and ΔH^0 at one temperature. For the problem at hand, the information that is given consists of ΔG^0 and ΔH^0 at one temperature.

at the melting point,

$$\Delta H^0 = -3,100 \text{ cal}$$

and $\Delta G^0 = 0$ (since at the melting point, it is an equilibrium process).

By using the equation

$$\Delta H^0_{1,356} = \Delta H_0 + \int C_p dT,\ \Delta H_0 \text{ can be calculated.}$$

$$\Delta H^0_{1,356} = -3,100 = \Delta H_0 + \int (-2.09 + 1.50 \times 10^{-3} T)\, dt$$

$$= \Delta H_0 - 2.09 \times 1,356 + 0.75 \times 10^{-3}(1,356)^2$$

$$\Delta H_0 = -1,650 \text{ cal}$$

Substituting this value into the expression obtained earlier for ΔG^0_T,

$$\Delta G^0_T = -1,650 + 2.09 T \ln T - 0.75 \times 10^{-3} T^2 + IT \text{ (cal/mole)}$$

Since $\Delta G^0_{1,356} = 0$, $T = 1,356^\circ K$

$$0 = -1,650 + 2.09(1,356)\ln(1,356) - 0.75 \times 10^{-3}(1,356)^2$$

$$+ I(1,356)$$

$I = -12.85$

$$\therefore \quad \Delta G^0_T = -1,650 + 2.09 T \ln T - 0.75 \times 10^{-3} T^2 - 12.85 T$$

(cal/mole)

$\therefore$ @ $1,120^\circ K$

$$\Delta G^0_{1,120} = -540 \text{ cal/mole}$$

• PROBLEM 11-41

Copper normally solidifies at a temperature of 1356° K, but can exist in the super-cooled liquid form up to a temperature of 1120°K, after which it starts solidifying spontaneously. Determine the entropy change for the solidification of copper at its temperature of spontaneous solidification (1120°K). Use the following data to solve the problem:

Data for $Cu(1) \rightleftharpoons Cu(s)$

$$C_{p\ Cu(1)} = 7.50 \text{ cal deg}^{-1} \text{ mole}^{-1}$$

$$C_{p\ Cu(s)} = 5.41 + 1.50 \times 10^{-3}T \text{ cal deg}^{-1} \text{ mole}^{-1}$$

$$\Delta H^0 = -3100 \text{ cal}$$

Solution: Using the equation

$$\Delta S = \int_{T_1}^{T_2} \frac{C_p}{T} dT$$

the entropy at the desired temperature can be calculated. However, the entropy change at one temperature should be known. At the melting point,

$$\Delta S^0_{1356} = \frac{\Delta H^0}{T} = \frac{-3100}{1356} = -2.28 \text{ cal deg}^{-1} \text{ mole}^{-1}$$

From the data

$$\Delta C_p = C_{pCu(s)} - C_{pCu(1)} = -2.09 + 1.5 \times 10^{-3}T \text{ cal deg}^{-1} \text{ mole}^{-1}.$$

The change in the entropy of reaction between 1120°K and 1356°K is given by

$$\Delta S^0_{1120} - \Delta S^0_{1356} = \int_{1356}^{1120} \frac{\Delta C_p}{T} dT$$

$$= \left[-2.09 \ln T + 1.5 \times 10^{-3} T\right]_{1356}^{1120}$$

$$= -2.09 \ln \frac{1120}{1356} + 1.5 \times 10^{-3} (1120 - 1356)$$

$$= 0.046 \text{ cal deg}^{-1} \text{ mole}^{-1}$$

$$\therefore \quad \Delta S^0_{1120} = -2.28 + 0.046$$
$$= -2.23 \text{ cal deg}^{-1} \text{ mole}^{-1}$$

• PROBLEM 11-42

Calculate the entropy change for

(a) H_2O (s, $-20^\circ C$, 1 atm) $\longrightarrow$ H_2O (s, $0^\circ C$, 1 atm)

(b) H_2O (s, $-20^\circ C$, 1 atm) $\longrightarrow$ H_2O (l, $20^\circ C$, 1 atm)

Assume $C_p(H_2O, l) = 18$ cal deg^{-1}mole^{-1}, $C_p(H_2O, s)$ = 9 cal deg^{-1}mole^{-1} and ΔH_{fusion} = 1440 cal deg^{-1}mole^{-1}, and also that the heat capacities are independent of temperature.

Solution: Since C_p is not a function of temperature, ΔS is given by

$$C_p \int \frac{1}{T}\, dT$$

(a) $$\Delta S = C_p \int_{T_1}^{T_2} \frac{dT}{T} = C_p \ln(T_2/T_1)$$
$$= C_p \ln\left(\frac{273}{253}\right)$$
$$= 9 \ln\left(\frac{273}{253}\right)$$
$$\Delta S = 0.68 \text{ eu/mole}$$

(b) $\Delta S = \Delta S_1$ (for heating $H_2O(s)$ From $-20^\circ C$ to $0^\circ C$)
$+ \Delta S_2$ (for melting @ $0^\circ C$)
$+ \Delta S_3$ (for heating $H_2O(l)$ from $0^\circ C$ to $+20^\circ C$)

$$\Delta S_1 = 9 \ln(273/253) = 0.68$$
$$\Delta S_2 = \Delta H/T = 1440/273 = 5.27$$
$$\Delta S_3 = 18 \ln(293/273) = 1.27$$
$$\Delta S = 0.68 + 5.27 + 1.27 = 7.22 \text{ eu}$$

The 3 individual entropies must be determined separately, since

$$\int_{253}^{293} C_p dT/T$$ cannot be found directly due to the

presence of both sensible and latent heat.

• PROBLEM 11-43

Methane reacts with water vapor at 25°C by the following reaction :

$$CH_4(g) + H_2O(g) \rightleftharpoons CO(g) + 3H_2(g)$$

Using the following data, calculate the standard Gibbs free-energy change for this reaction.

Data

	ΔH^0_{298} (kcal mole^{-1})	S^0_{298}(cal deg^{-1}mole^{-1})
$CH_4(g)$	-17.89	44.5
$CO(g)$	-26.40	47.3
$H_2(g)$	0	31.2
$H_2O(g)$	-57.80	45.1

Solution: The standard Gibbs free-energy can be obtained from the defining relation,

$$\Delta G^0 = \Delta H^0 - T\Delta S^0$$

$$\Delta H^0 = (\Delta H^0_{CO} + 3\Delta H^0_{H_2}) - (\Delta H^0_{CH_4} + \Delta H^0_{H_2O})$$

$$= (-26.40) + (0) - (-17.89) - (-57.80)$$

$$= 49.29 \text{ kcal/mole}$$

$$\Delta S^0 = (S^0_{CO} + 3S^0_{H_2}) - (S^0_{CH_4} + S^0_{H_2O})$$

$$= (47.3) + (3x31.2) - (44.5) - (45.1)$$

$$= 51.3 \text{ cal deg}^{-1}\text{mole}^{-1}$$

$$\therefore \quad \Delta G^0_{298} = 49,290 - 51.3T$$

$$= 49,290 - 15,280$$

$$= 34 \text{ kcal/mole}$$

A spontaneous reaction is always accompanied by a decrease in free energy. But since the standard free energy change is positive, the reaction will not proceed as indicated at this temperature. Therefore at 25°C, hydrogen and CO will react to form $CH_4 + H_2O$.

• PROBLEM 11-44

Determine the latent heat of vaporization of liquid carbon tetrachloride at its boiling point of 350°K. The vapor pressure of CCl_4 is a function of temperature and is given by:

$$gP = -2,400T^{-1} - 5.30 \log T + 23.60$$

(P = mmHg). Assume ideal gas behavior.

Solution: For the vaporization of a liquid, the volume of the liquid is negligible compared to that of the vapor. Therefore the volume change closely approximates the volume of the vapor. Since the gas behaves ideally, $\Delta V = V = \frac{RT}{P}$. Then the Clapeyron equation to calculate ΔH.

$$\frac{dT}{dP} = \frac{T\Delta V}{\Delta H}$$

$$\text{or} \quad \frac{dP}{dT} = \frac{\Delta H}{T\Delta V} = \frac{P\Delta H}{RT^2}$$

$$\text{or} \quad \frac{d\ln P}{dT} = \frac{\Delta H}{RT^2}$$

$$\text{or} \quad \frac{d\log P}{dT} = \frac{H}{4.575T^2}$$

This is one form of the Clausius-Clapeyron equation.

For the given problem,

$$\frac{d\log P}{dT} = 2,400T^{-2} - \frac{5.30}{2.303} T^{-1} \text{ , deg}^{-1}$$

$$\therefore \quad \Delta H = 4.575T^2 (2,400T^{-2} - 2.3T^{-1})$$

$\therefore$ @ 350°K,

ΔH = 7,300 cal/mole

• PROBLEM 11-45

Derive an expression for the temperature dependence on pressure. Also, determine the melting point of sodium 5 atm using the following data;

Data for sodium

mol wt = 23 g/mole
when P = 1 atm, melting point = 371° K

ΔH_{fusion} = 630 cal/mole
Increase in specific volume due to melting process = 0.0279 cc/g

Solution: The equation that describes the effect of pressure on a phase change in a one-component system is the Clapeyron equation. The derivation applied to the fusion reaction is as follows.

at equilibrium,

$$G(s) = G(l)$$

If the pressure and temperature of the system are changed infinitesimally, keeping the system at equilibrium,

$$dG_{(s)} = dG_{(l)}$$

Since $dG = VdP - SdT$

$$V_{(s)} \cdot dP - S_{(s)} \cdot dT = V_{(l)} \cdot dP - S_{(l)} \cdot dT$$

$$\therefore \quad \frac{dT}{dP} = \frac{V_{(l)} - V_{(s)}}{S_{(l)} - S_{(s)}} = \frac{\Delta V}{\Delta S}$$

At equilibrium, $\Delta S = \Delta H/T$

$$\therefore \quad \frac{dT}{dP} = \frac{T\Delta V}{\Delta H}$$

This is the expression for temperature dependence on pressure for systems at equilibrium.

For the case of sodium melting @ 1 atm,

$$\Delta H = \frac{630 \text{ cal/mole}}{23 \text{ g/mole}} = 27.4 \text{ cal/g}$$

$$T = 371^\circ K$$

$$\Delta V = 0.0279 \text{ cc/g}$$

$$\therefore \quad \frac{dT}{dP} = \frac{371 \times 0.0279}{27.4} = 0.378 \text{ deg cc cal}^{-1}$$

$$1 \text{ cal} = 41.293 \text{ cc atm}$$

$$\therefore \quad \frac{dT}{dP} = 0.378 \text{ (deg cc cal}^{-1}) \cdot \frac{1 \text{ cal}}{41.293 \text{ cc atm}}$$

$$= 0.00915 \text{ deg atm}^{-1}$$

Assuming this value is constant (not pressure dependent), for 5 atm

the increase in temperature $= (0.00915 \text{ deg atm}^{-1}) \times 5 \text{ atm}$

$= 0.04575 \text{ deg}$

$\therefore$ The melting point increases by only 0.04575 deg when the pressure is 5 atm.

$$T_{melt} \text{ @ } 5 \text{ atm} = 371.04575^\circ K$$

• PROBLEM 11-46

Ammonia is produced by the following reaction:

$$3H_2 + N_2 \longrightarrow 2NH_3$$

Determine the standard heat for the above reaction at a tempurature of 500°C, using the following data.

$\Delta H_{reaction}$ @ 25°C is equal to -22.08 kcal

	α	β	γ
NH_3	6.086	$8.812\ 10^{-3}$	$-1.506\ 10^{-6}$
N_2	6.524	$1.250\ 10^{-3}$	$-0.001\ 10^{-6}$
H_2	6.947	$=0.200\ 10^{-3}$	$0.481\ 10^{-6}$

Solution: Using the data and the following equation,

$$\Delta H_T^o = \Delta H_0 + \Delta\alpha T + \frac{\Delta\beta}{2} T^2 + \frac{\Delta\gamma}{3} T^3$$

the change in enthalpy at the desired temperature can be calculated.

From the reaction stoichiometry,

$$\Delta\alpha = \alpha_{products} - \alpha_{reactants}$$

$$= 2(6.086) - 6.524 - 3(6.947) = -15.193$$

$$\Delta\beta = 2(8.812x10^{-3}) - 3(-0.2x10^{-3}) - (1.25x10^{-3})$$

$$= 1.6974 \times 10^{-2}$$

$$\Delta\gamma = 2(-1.506x10^{-6}) - (-0.001x10^{-6}) - 3(0.481x10^{-6})$$

$$= 4.454 \times 10^{-6}$$

$$\therefore \quad \Delta H_T^o = \Delta H_0 - 15.193T + \frac{1.6974x10^{-2}}{2} T^2 - \frac{4.454x10^{-6}}{3} T^3$$

$$= \Delta H_0 - 15.193T + 8.487 \times 10^{-3} T^2 - 1.48 \times 10^{-6} T^3$$

From the data given, it is known that $H^o_{25^oC} = -22.08$ kcal

$= -22,080$ cal

$$\therefore \quad -22,080 = \Delta H_0 - 15.193(298) + 8.487 \times 10^{-3}(298)^2 - 1.48 \times 10^{-6}(298)^3$$

$$\Delta H_0 = -18,267 \text{ cal}$$

$\therefore$ The standard heat of reaction @ 500°C is

$$\Delta H^o_{773^oK} = -18,297 - 15.193(773) + 8.487 \times 10^{\ 3}(773)^2 - 1.48 \times 10^{-6}(773)^3$$

$$= -25,570 \text{ cal}$$

• **PROBLEM 11-47**

An important variable that has to be taken into account in rocket design is the coefficient of discharge. This coefficient is given by the following equation:

$$C_D = \left(\frac{2}{k+1}\right)^{(k+1)/2(k-1)} \cdot \left(\frac{k\cdot(\text{mol wt})}{R\cdot T_{\text{combustion}}}\right)^{\frac{1}{2}}$$

where k is a function of the particular fuel being used.

Calculate the mass rate of discharge and the engine operating time if a particular fuel is used in a rocket engine operating at a chamber pressure of 1500 psia and a throat cross-sectional area of 2 in^2. Use the following fuel data to solve the problem.

Data

Total fuel wt = 25 lbm

$R = 48\ lbf^2\ sec^2/lbm,\ lb\ mole\ ^{\circ}R$

k = 0.9

mol wt of fuel = 20.6

combustion temperature = $6750^{\circ}R$

Solution: Once C_D is calculated, the mass rate of flow and burning time can be calculated.

$$C_D = \left(\frac{2}{1.9}\right)^{(1.9/2(-0.1))} \cdot \left(\frac{0.9(20.6)}{48(6750)}\right)^{\frac{1}{2}}$$

$$C_D = 4.65 \times 10^{-3}\ lbm/lb_f\ sec$$

The mass rate of flow of gases is given by

mrf = C_D (cross sectional area)(chamber pressure)

$$mrf = (4.65 \times 10^{-3})(2)(1500)$$

$$= 13.95\ lb_m/sec$$

The combustion duration of the fuel is given by

$$t = \frac{25 lb_m}{13.95} = 1.792\ sec$$

• PROBLEM 11-48

The effect of inert gas on equilibrium composition can be determined by the computation of the mixture composition. Calculate the composition of the mixture at 3,000°K and 1 atm pressure, for a mixture initially composed of 0.5 mol of carbon monoxide and 2.38 mol of air.

Solution: The chemical equation for the ideal-gas reaction is:

$$0.5CO + 0.5O_2 + 1.88N_2 \longrightarrow xCO + yO_2 + zCO_2 + 1.88N_2$$

From the carbon and oxygen balances, $z = 0.5 - x$ and $y = \frac{1.5 - 2z - x}{2} = \frac{0.5 + x}{2}$ (where x is the number of moles of CO at equilibrium).

Total number of moles of mixture at equilibrium is

$$N_T = x + y + z + 1.88 = x + 0.5 - x + \frac{0.5+x}{2} + 1.88 = \frac{x + 5.26}{2}$$

The equilibrium constant is not dependent on the amount initially added, but only on the stoichiometry of the chemical reaction written with no excess species. The equation that describes the combustion of carbon monoxide is as follows:

$$CO + \tfrac{1}{2}O_2 + \tfrac{1}{2}(3.76)N_2 \longrightarrow CO_2 + \tfrac{1}{2}(3.76)N_2$$

$$K_p = P_{CO_2}/P_{CO}\, P_{O_2}{}^{\frac{1}{2}}$$

(N_2 is inert, therefore, it does not show in the K_p equation)
At 3,000°K and 1 atm pressure, $K_p = 3.06$.

Therefore, for the given problem,

$$P_{CO_2} = x_{CO_2}P_T = \frac{z}{N_T}P_T = \frac{(0.5 - x)}{\left(\frac{x + 5.26}{2}\right)}P_T$$

$$P_{CO} = x_{CO}P_T = \frac{x}{N_T}P_T = \frac{x}{\left(\frac{x + 5.26}{2}\right)}P_T$$

$$P_{O_2} = X_{O_2}P_T = \frac{y}{N_T}P_T = \frac{(0.5 + x)/2}{\left(\frac{x + 5.26}{2}\right)}P_T$$

$\therefore$ The expression for K_p is:

$$K_p = \frac{\left((0.5-x)/N_T\right)P_T}{(P_T)(x/N_T)\left(\left(\frac{0.5 + x}{2}\right)/N_T\right)^{\frac{1}{2}} P_T^{\frac{1}{2}}}$$

$$K_p = \frac{(0.5-x)\left(\frac{x + 5.26}{2}\right)^{\frac{1}{2}}}{x\left(\frac{0.5 + x}{2}\right)^{\frac{1}{2}}(1)^{\frac{1}{2}}} = 3.06$$

$$K_p = (0.5 - x)(x + 5.26)^{\frac{1}{2}} = 3.06x(0.5 + x)^{\frac{1}{2}}$$

By trial and error, a solution can be found. The answer obtained by this method is x = 0.24 mol of CO at the equilibrium state of 3,000°K and 1 atm pressure. It is apparent that the pressure of the system and the presence of inert gases must be taken into account when the equilibrium composition of a reacting ideal-gas mixture at a given temperature is evaluated.

• PROBLEM 11-49

For the reaction

$$CH_4 + 2O_2 + 7.56N_2 \longrightarrow (a)CO_2 + (1 - a)CO + 2(c)H_2O$$
$$+ 2(1 - c)H_2 + (\tfrac{3}{2} - \tfrac{1}{2}a - c)O_2$$
$$+ 7.56N_2$$

calculate the maximum combustion temperature of methane when the initial temperature is 21.1°C and the initial pressure is 1 atm. Assume the process is carried out at constant volume. Use variable specific heat with chemical equilibrium to solve the problem. Use the following data.

enthalpies @ 21.1°C

H_{CH_4} = 345,848 Btu/lb mole

H_{CO} = 121,188 Btu/lb mole

H_{H_2} = 102,465 Btu/lb mole

Solution: From the equilibrium constant and the energy balance, using a trial and error method, the maximum combustion temperature can be determined.

INTERNAL ENERGIES

	530°R	4680°R	4740°R	4800°R
CO	2915.8	49950.7	50721.4	51492.7
CO	2628.3	28280.7	28691.0	29101.7
H O	3149.7	39863.9	40522.7	41183.3
H	2539.6	26167.3	26563.7	26961.2
O	2623.6	29793.0	30234.3	30676.4
N	2628.3	27971.7	28379.3	28787.4

Moles of reactants $= 1 + 2 + 7.56 = 10.56 = N_R$

Moles of products $= a + (1 - a) + 2c + 2(1 - c)$

$+ (3/2 - a/2 - c) + 7.56$

$= a + 1 - a + 2c + 2 - 2c$

$+ 3/2 - a/2 - c + 7.56$

$= 4.5 - a/2 - c + 7.56$

$= 12.06 - a/2 - c = N_P$

The maximum temperature corresponds to the equilibrium temperature. Since N_P, a, c and T (T = max. temp.) are unknown, three more equations must be written.

For the CO reaction, $CO + \frac{1}{2}O_2 \rightarrow CO_2$,

$$K_{CO} = \frac{(p_{CO_2})}{(p_{CO})(p_{O_2})^{\frac{1}{2}}}\text{, the second equation.}$$

For the CO_2, H_2 reaction, called the water gas reaction, $CO_2 + H_2 \rightarrow H_2O + CO$,

$$K_{wg} = \frac{(p_{H_2O})(p_{CO})}{(p_{CO_2})(p_{H_2})}\text{, the third equation.}$$

Taking p as the total pressure at equilibrium and noting that at the beginning of combustion $p_1V = N_RRT_1$ and at the end of combustion $pV = N_PRT$,

$$p_{CO} = \frac{1 - a}{N_P} p = (1 - a)\frac{p_1 T}{N_R T_1},$$

$$p_{O_2} = (\frac{3}{2} - \frac{a}{2} - c) \frac{p_1 T}{N_R T_1},$$

and

$$p_{CO_2} = \frac{a p_1 T}{N_R T_1}$$

at T,

$$K_{CO} = \frac{\dfrac{a p_1 T}{N_R T_1}}{(1 - a)\dfrac{p_1 T}{N_R T_1}\sqrt{\left(\dfrac{3}{2} - \dfrac{a}{2} - c\right)\dfrac{p_1 T}{N_R T_1}}}$$

$$= \frac{a}{1 - a}\sqrt{\frac{N_R T_1}{\left(\dfrac{3}{2} - \dfrac{a}{2} - c\right)p_1 T}}$$

$$p_{H_2O} = \frac{2c p_1 T}{N_R T_1}$$

$$p_{H_2} = \frac{2(1 - c)p_1 T}{N_R T_1}$$

$$K_{wg} = \frac{\left(2c\dfrac{p_1 T}{N_R T_1}\right)\left((1 - a)\dfrac{p_1 T}{N_R T_1}\right)}{\left(a\dfrac{p_1 T}{N_R T_1}\right)\left(\dfrac{2(1 - c)p_1 T}{N_R T_1}\right)}$$

$$= \frac{c(1 - a)}{a(1 - c)} \quad .$$

Now the energy balance must be used. The energy given off by combustion is equal to the energy absorbed by the products. Therefore, the fourth necessary equation is

$$\Sigma N_p(U_{p\ final} - U_{p\ initial}) = H_{CH_4} - N_{CO}H_{CO} - N_{H_2}H_{H_2}.$$

This equation is based upon combustion taking place at the initial conditions; the products absorb the energy liberated, causing their temperature to increase from the initial to the final temperature, which is the maximum temperature of combustion.

The equilibrium energy and the number of moles present depend on the temperature. However, there are four equations and four unknowns (N_p, a, c and T). Hence, they can be evaluated.

From the combustion equation

$$CH_4 + 2O_2 + 7.56N_2 \longrightarrow aCO_2 + (1 - a)CO$$

$$+ 2cH_2O + 2(1 - c)H_2 + \left(\frac{3}{2} - \frac{a}{2} - c\right)O_2 + 7.56N_2$$

the energy equation can be written,

$$a(U_2^{CO_2} - U_1^{CO_2}) + (1 - a)(U_2^{CO} - U_1^{CO}) + 2c(U_2^{H_2O} - U_1^{H_2O})$$

$$+ 2(1 - c)(U_2^{H_2} - U_1^{H_2}) + \left(\frac{3}{2} - \frac{a}{2} - c\right)(U_2^{O_2} - U_1^{O_2})$$

$$+ 7.56(U_2^{N_2} - U_1^{N_2}) = H_{CH_4} - (1 - a)H_{CO} - 2(1 - c)H_{H_2}$$

or

$$a(U_2^{CO_2} - U_1^{CO_2}) + (1 - a)(U_2^{CO} - U_1^{CO}) + 2c(U_2^{H_2O} - U_1^{H_2O})$$

$$+ 2(1 - c)(U_2^{H_2} - U_1^{H_2}) + \left(\frac{3}{2} - \frac{a}{2} - c\right)(U_2^{O_2} - U_1^{O_2})$$

$$+ 7.56U_2^{N_2} = H_{CH_4} - H_{CO} - 2H_{H_2} + aH_{CO} + 2cH_{H_2} + 7.56U_1^{N_2}.$$

From the data given, all quantities on the right hand side of the equation are known.

$\therefore$ the equation becomes

$$7.56U_2^{N_2} = 39,600 + (a)121,188 + (c)204,930$$

From the internal energy table, substitutions can be made for the energy differences in the energy equation.

At 4680°R

$$a(47{,}034.9) + (1 - a)25{,}652.4 + (2c)36{,}714.2$$
$$+ 2(1 - c)23{,}627.7 + \tfrac{1}{2}(3 - a - 2c)27{,}169.4$$
$$+ 7.56(27{,}971.7)$$
$$= 7{,}707.8a + 325{,}661.9 - 996.4c$$
$$= 39.600 + 121{,}188a + 204{,}930c$$
$$+ 205{,}926.4c = -286{,}061.9 + 113{,}390.3a$$

Thus $c = 1.394 - 0.553a \; (= m - na)$

At 4740°R

$$a(47{,}805.6) + (1 - a)26{,}062.7 + (2c)37{,}373.0$$
$$+ 2(1 - c)24{,}024.1 + \left(\frac{3}{2} - \frac{a}{2} - c\right)27{,}610.7$$
$$+ 7.56 \times 28{,}379.3$$
$$= 7{,}937.6a + 329{,}526.8 - 912.9c$$
$$= 39{,}600 + 121{,}188a + 204{,}930c$$
$$+ 205{,}842.9c = -289{,}926.8 + 113{,}240.4a$$
$$c = 1.410 - 0.552a \; (= m - na)$$

At 4800°R

$$a(48{,}576.9) + (1 - a)26{,}473.4 + (2c)38{,}033.6$$
$$+ 2(1 - c)24{,}421.6 + \left(\frac{3}{2} - \frac{a}{2} - c\right)28{,}052.8$$
$$+ 7.56 \times 28{,}787.4$$
$$= 8077.1a + 334{,}395.8 - 828.8c = 39{,}600 + 121{,}188a$$
$$+ 204{,}930c - 205{,}758.8c = -294{,}795.8 + 113{,}110.9a$$
$$c = 1.438 - 0.551a (= m - na)$$

$K_{wgT} = \dfrac{c(1 - a)}{a(1 - c)}$ where $c = m - na$ above

Then $$K_{wg}a - (K_{wg} - 1)a(m - na) - m + na = 0$$

$$K_{wg}a - K_{wg}ma + K_{wg}a^2n + am - na^2 - m + na = 0$$

or $$n(K_{wg} - 1)a^2 + [n + m - K_{wg}(m - 1)]a - m = 0$$

At $4680^\circ R$, $K_{wg} = 6.214$

At $4740^\circ R$, $K_{wg} = 6.283$

At $4800^\circ R$, $K_{wg} = 6.351$

<u>At $4680^\circ R$</u>

$$0.553(6.214 - 1)a^2 + [0.553 + 1.394 - 6.214(1.394 - 1)]a - 1.394 = 0$$

$$2.88a^2 - 0.493a = 1.394$$

$$a^2 - 0.171a = 0.484$$

$$(a - 0.0855)^2 = 0.491$$

$$a - 0.0855 = \pm 0.702$$

$$a = 0.787$$

$$c = 1.394 - 0.553 \times 0.787$$

$$= 0.959$$

<u>At $4740^\circ R$</u>

$$0.552 \times 6.283a^2 + (0.552 + 1.410 - 6.283 \times 0.41)a - 1.410 = 0$$

$$2.91a^2 - 0.608a = 1.410$$

$$a^2 - 0.209a = 0.485$$

$$(a - 0.104)^2 = 0.496$$

$$a - 0.104 = \pm 0.705$$

$$a = 0.809$$

$$c = 1.410 - 0.552 \times 0.809$$

$$= 0.964$$

At 4800 ^{0}R

$$0.551 \times 6.351a^2 + (0.551 + 1.438 - 6.351 \times 0.438)a - 1.438 = 0$$

$$2.94a^2 - 0.791a = 1.438$$

$$a^2 - 0.269a = 0.487$$

$$(a - 0.134)^2 = 0.505$$

$$a - 0.134 = \pm 0.711$$

$$a = 0.845$$

$$c = 1.438 - 0.551 \times 0.845$$

$$= 0.973$$

For the CO reaction

$$K_{CO\,T} = \frac{a}{1 - a}\sqrt{\frac{N_R T_1}{e_{O_2} p_1 T}}$$

where N_R = moles of original mixture and e_{O_2} = moles of O_2 at equilibrium conditions.

$$K_{CO\,T} = \frac{a}{1 - a}\sqrt{\frac{N_R}{e_{O_2}}}\sqrt{\frac{T_1}{p_1}}\sqrt{\frac{1}{T}}$$

$$\log K_{CO\,T} + \frac{1}{2}\log T = \log\frac{a}{1 - a} + \frac{1}{2}\log N_R - \frac{1}{2}\log e_{O_2} + \frac{1}{2}\log T_1 - \frac{1}{2}\log p_1$$

where

$$e_{O_2} = \left(\frac{3}{2} - \frac{a}{2} - c\right)$$

Values of $K_{CO\,T}$ from tables: at 4680 ^{0}R = 15.95 and $\log_{10}K = 1.2027$

at 4740 ^{0}R = 13.65 and $\log_{10}K = 1.1351$

at 4800 ^{0}R = 11.48 and $\log_{10}K = 1.0599$

These values were determined with the pressure being expressed in atmospheres. The left side of the equation becomes:

$$\text{at } 4680^\circ R,\ 1.2027 + \tfrac{1}{2}\log 4680 = 3.0378$$

$$\text{at } 4740^\circ R,\ 1.1351 + \tfrac{1}{2}\log 4740 = 2.9730$$

$$\text{at } 4800^\circ R,\ 1.0599 + \tfrac{1}{2}\log 4800 = 2.9005$$

The right side of the equation can be evaluated from the values of a and c determined from the energy and the water gas equations. The constant terms are $\frac{1}{2}\log N_R + \frac{1}{2}\log T_1 - \frac{1}{2}\log p_1 = \frac{1}{2}\log 10.56 + \frac{1}{2}\log 530 - \frac{1}{2}\log 1 = 1.8739$.

The right side of the equation becomes

$$\log \frac{a}{1 - a} - \frac{1}{2}\log\left(\frac{3}{2} - \frac{a}{2} - c\right) + 1.8739.$$

At $4680^\circ C$

$$\log \frac{0.787}{1 - 0.787} - \frac{1}{2}\log\left(\frac{3}{2} - \frac{0.787}{2} - 0.959\right) + 1.8739$$

$$= \log 3.694 - \frac{1}{2}\log 0.248 + 1.8739$$

$$= 0.5675 + 0.3027 + 1.8739$$

$$= 2.7441$$

At $4740^\circ R$

$$\log \frac{0.809}{1 - 0.809} - \frac{1}{2}\log\left(\frac{3}{2} - \frac{0.809}{2} - 0.964\right) + 1.8739$$

$$= \log 4.235 - \frac{1}{2}\log 0.132 + 1.8739$$

$$= 0.6268 + 0.4397 + 1.8739$$

$$= 2.9404$$

At $4800^\circ R$

$$\log \frac{0.845}{1 - 0.845} - \frac{1}{2}\log\left(\frac{3}{2} - \frac{0.845}{2} - 0.973\right) + 1.8739$$

$$= \log 5.45 - \frac{1}{2}\log 0.105 + 1.8739$$

$$= 0.7364 + 0.4894 + 1.8739$$

$$= 3.0997$$

Interpolation or plotting can be used for the temperature determination. Plotting gives:

From the plotting, T is found to be $4747^{\circ}R$, which is a much lower temperature than that indicated by a constant specific heat. The value of a_e, is 0.966 and the value of c_e, is 0.814. The combustion equation becomes: $CH_4 + 2O_2 + 7.56N_2 \longrightarrow$

$0.966CO_2 + 0.034CO + 1.628H_2O + 0.372H_2 + 0.203O_2 + 7.56N_2$.

• PROBLEM 11-50

Calculate the equilibrium mixture of the carbon monoxide combustion reaction at 2504°C and 1 atm pressure. Assume that the CO reacts with a stoichiometric amount of air and that K_p for the reaction is equal to 49.365.

Solution: The complete reaction equation is:

$$2CO + O_2 + 3.77N_2 \longrightarrow 2CO_2 + 3.77N_2$$

If y stands for the fraction of the carbon which is in CO under equilibrium conditions, then the equilibrium mixture is composed of: 2y moles of CO, (2-2y) moles of CO_2, y moles of O_2: and 3.77 moles of N_2. Therefore, the total number of moles is $N_T = 2y + 2 - 2y + y + 3.77 = 5.77 + y$. The partial pressures of the four reacting species are:

$$P_{CO} = x_{CO}P_T = \frac{2y}{5.77+y}P_T$$

$$P_{CO_2} = x_{CO_2}P_T = \frac{2-2y}{5.77+y}P_T$$

$$P_{O_2} = x_{O_2}P_T = \frac{y}{5.77+y}P_T$$

$$P_{N_2} = x_{N_2}P_T = \frac{3.77}{5.77+y}P_T$$

using the equation $P_i = x_i P_{TOTAL}$.

Substituting these equalities into the K_p equation,

$$K_p = (P_{CO_2})^2/(P_{CO})^2P_{O_2} = \frac{(1-y)^2(5.77+y)}{y^3P_T} = 49.3647.$$

Assuming that P_T = 1 atm, this equation can be solved to attain a value for y, using a trail and error method. The answer obtained is y = 0.368. Therefore, the mole fractions are

$$x_{CO} = \frac{2y}{5.77+y} = 0.120$$

$$x_{CO_2} = \frac{2-2y}{5.77+y} = 0.206$$

$$x_{O_2} = \frac{y}{5.77+y} = 0.060$$

$$x_{N_2} = \frac{3.77}{5.77+y} = 0.614$$

The actual number of moles of each species can be calculated also.

moles CO = 2y = 0.736

moles CO_2 = 2-2y = 1.264

moles O_2 = y = 0.368 and moles N_2 = 3.77

The presence of N_2 will affect the extent of reaction but does not change the equilibrium constant. Excess oxygen causes the reaction to go further toward completion, but this excess will not affect the equilibrium constant since the equilibrium constant is independent of the amounts of reacting species that are actually present.

• PROBLEM 11-51

If K_p for $H_2(g) + I_2(g) \rightleftharpoons 2HI(g)$ at 25°C is 870, then assuming no solid iodine forms, calculate the number of moles of the following at equilibrium.

(a) HI formed when H_2 = 0.5 moles and I_2 = 0.5 moles

(b) I_2 formed when H_2 = 0.5 moles and HI = 1.5 moles.

Solution: (a) If x is the number of moles of H_2 (which is equal to the number of moles of I_2) consumed in the reaction, the following table can be constructed.

	H_2	I_2	HI	
Initial	0.5	0.5	0	moles
Consumed	x	x	-	moles
Created	-	-	2x	moles
Final	0.5 - x	0.5 - x	2x	moles

Using the equilibrium constant,

$$870 = K_p = K_n \quad (\text{since } \Delta n = 0)$$

$$K_n = \frac{(HI)^2}{(H_2)(I_2)} = \frac{(2x)^2}{(0.5 - x)^2} = 870$$

Taking the square root of both sides,

$$2x = 14.75 - 29.5x$$

$x = 0.468$ (The other root is $x = 0.536$ which is invalid since it implies that more H_2 and I_2 disappears than was present initially. Therefore, this root is discarded).

Therefore,

$2(0.468) = 0.936$ moles of HI are formed.

(b) If x = the number of moles of I_2 formed, the following table can be constructed.

	H_2	I_2	HI	
Initial	0.5	0	1.5	moles
Consumed	-	-	2x	moles
Created	x	x	-	moles
Final	x + 0.5	x	1.5 - 2x	moles

$$\therefore \quad \frac{(1.5 - 2x)^2}{(x)(0.5 + x)} = 870$$

After cross multiplication,

$$2.25 - 6x + 4x^2 = 870x^2 + 435x$$

$$866x^2 + 441x - 2.25 = 0$$

Using the quadratic equation,

$$x = \frac{-b \pm \sqrt{b^2 - 4ac}}{2a}$$

$$x = 0.005 \text{ moles of } I_2 \text{ formed.}$$

(The negative root is discarded.)

• PROBLEM 11-52

A mixture consisting of 50% CO and 50% O_2 on a molar basis enters a device at 100kPa and 25°C. It emerges from the device at 3000K and 100 kPa. Assuming that any oxygen emerging is diatomic, determine the magnitude and direction of the heat transfer for the steady state process.

Solution: The chemical reaction

$$0.5CO + 0.5O_2 \rightleftharpoons CO_2 + CO + O_2$$

gives the products that emerge from the device. Furthermore,

$$CO_2 \rightleftharpoons CO + \tfrac{1}{2}O_2$$

gives the equilibrium equation for the products. Let ε be the number of kmol of CO_2 dissociated, then

	$CO_2 \rightleftharpoons$	CO	$+ 0.5O_2$
Initial:	0	0.5	0.5
Change:	+ε	−ε	−0.5ε
Equilibrium:	ε	(0.5−ε)	(0.5 − 0.5ε)

Therefore the total number of kmol at equilibrium is

$$n = \varepsilon + (0.5 - \varepsilon) + (0.5 - 0.5\varepsilon) = 1 - 0.5\varepsilon,$$

and the equilibrium mole fractions are

$$y_{CO_2} = \frac{\varepsilon}{1-0.5\varepsilon}, \quad y_{CO} = \frac{0.5-\varepsilon}{1-0.5\varepsilon}, \quad y_{O_2} = \frac{0.5-0.5\varepsilon}{1-0.5\varepsilon}$$

From the table of the equilibrium constants, K at T = 3000K is

$$\ln K = -1.111 \Longrightarrow K = 0.329$$

Substituting these values along with P = 0.1 MPa into the following equation, gives :

$$K = 0.329 = \frac{y_{CO} \cdot y_{O_2}^{\frac{1}{2}}}{y_{CO_2}} \left(\frac{P}{P^0}\right)^{1+\frac{1}{2}-1}$$

$$= \frac{\left(\frac{0.5-\varepsilon}{1-0.5\varepsilon}\right)\left(\frac{0.5-0.5\varepsilon}{1-0.5\varepsilon}\right)^{\frac{1}{2}}}{\left(\frac{\varepsilon}{1-0.5\varepsilon}\right)} (1)^{\frac{1}{2}}$$

or in more simplified form

$$f(\varepsilon) = \left(\frac{0.5-\varepsilon}{\varepsilon}\right)^2 \left(\frac{0.5-0.5\varepsilon}{1-0.5\varepsilon}\right) = 0.1084$$

In the previous equation, the number of moles of each component must be greater than zero in order to obtain a physically meaningful root. Thus the root must lie in the range

$$0 \leq \varepsilon \leq 1$$

The solution is found by trial and error as shown in the table.

Assumed value for ε	$f(\varepsilon)$
0.32	0.1281
0.325	0.1173
0.3291	0.1084

Therefore the number of moles of each component at equilibrium is

$$n_{CO_2} = 0.3291, \; n_{CO} = 0.1709, \; n_{O_2} = 0.3355$$

and the overall process is

$$0.5CO + 0.5O_2 \rightleftharpoons 0.3291CO_2 + 0.1709CO + 0.3355O_2$$

The heat transfer for the reaction can be calculated using the first law and obtaining the enthalpies from the table of the enthalpies of formation. Let the subscripts R and P stand for the products and reactants, respectively ; from the first law, written for this case (on a mole basis)

$$Q + \sum_R n_i\bar{h} = \sum_P n_i\bar{h}$$

or solving for Q

$$Q = \left[n_{CO_2}\bar{h}_{CO_2} + n_{CO}\bar{h}_{CO} + n_{O_2}\bar{h}_{O_2}\right]_{T=3000K} - \left[n_{CO}\bar{h}_{CO} + n_{O_2}\bar{h}_{O_2}\right]_{T=298K} \qquad (1)$$

Using the tables of the enthalpies of formation with the formula

$$\bar{h}_i = \left[(h_f)_{298} + (\bar{h}^o_T - \bar{h}^o_{298})\right]_i$$

where the subscript $\underline{i}$ stands for the components at T=3000K,

$$\bar{h}_{CO_2} = -393,522 + 152,862 = -240,660 \text{ kJ/kmol}$$

$$\bar{h}_{CO} = -110,529 + 93,542 = -16,987 \text{ kJ/kmol}$$

$$\bar{h}_{O_2} = 0 + 98,098 = +98,098 \text{ kJ/kmol}$$

and at T=298K

$$\bar{h}_{CO} = -110,529$$

$$\bar{h}_{O_2} = 0$$

Substituting these values into equation (1), then

$$Q = \left[(0.3291)(-240,660)+(0.1709)(-16,987)+(0.3355)(98,098)\right] - \left[(0.5)(-110,529)\right]$$

$$= -6,072.09 \text{ kJ/kmol}$$

The negative sign indicates that the heat is added to the system.

EQUILIBRIUM CONSTANT

• PROBLEM 11-53

Carbon dioxide decomposes into carbon monoxide and oxygen by the following reaction:

$$CO_2 \rightleftharpoons CO + \tfrac{1}{2}O_2.$$

Calculate the equilibrium compositions and the extent of reaction at 5301°F and 1 atm. Assume that K_p under these conditions is equal to 0.647.

Solution: The equilibrium constant is related to the stoichiometric coefficients of a chemical equation. The CO combustion reaction may be rewritten using letters as the stoichiometric coefficients. The reaction will be written as follows:

$$aCO_2 \rightleftharpoons bCO + cO_2$$

The equilibrium constant will be

$$K_p = \frac{(x_{CO})^b \cdot (x_{O_2})^c}{(x_{CO_2})^a} P_{TOTAL}^{b+c-a}$$

For the given problem,

$a = 1$, $b = 1$, $c = 0.5$ and $P_{TOT} = 1$ atm. Therefore,

$$K_p = \frac{x_{CO}\, x_{O_2}^{\frac{1}{2}}}{x_{CO_2}} = 0.647$$

Initially, stoichiometric proportions were present in the mixture. However, as the reaction proceeds, CO_2 reacts and its stoichiometric coefficient no longer equals 1. The same is true for the products of the reaction. To compensate for this imbalance, an extent or degree of reaction ε is now written as follows.

$$CO_2 \longrightarrow (1-\varepsilon)CO_2 + \varepsilon CO + \frac{\varepsilon}{2} O_2$$

The total number of moles at equilibrium is

$$N_{TOTAL} = (1-\varepsilon) + \varepsilon + \frac{\varepsilon}{2} = 1 + \frac{\varepsilon}{2}$$

The mole fractions at equilibrium are

$$x_{CO_2} = \frac{1-\varepsilon}{1+\varepsilon/2}$$

$$x_{CO} = \frac{\varepsilon}{1+\varepsilon/2}$$

$$x_{O_2} = \frac{\varepsilon/2}{1+\varepsilon/2}$$

Therefore, the expression for K_p is:

$$K_p = \frac{\left(\frac{\varepsilon}{1+\varepsilon/2}\right)\left(\frac{\varepsilon}{1+\varepsilon/2}\right)^{\frac{1}{2}}}{\left(\frac{1-\varepsilon}{1+\varepsilon/2}\right)} = 0.647$$

$$K_p^2 = \frac{\varepsilon^3}{(1-\varepsilon)^2(2+\varepsilon)} = 0.4186$$

Solving for K_p by trial and error methods, the following solution is obtained:

$$\varepsilon = 0.578$$

With this value, the equilibrium concentrations are obtained.

$$x_{CO_2} = \frac{1-\varepsilon}{1+\varepsilon/2} = 0.327$$

$$x_{CO} = \frac{\varepsilon}{1+\varepsilon/2} = 0.448$$

$$x_{O_2} = \frac{\varepsilon/2}{1+\varepsilon/2} = 0.225$$

It was seen from this problem that not all of the CO_2 reacted and that a substantial portion of the equilibrium mixture contains CO_2.

• PROBLEM 11-54

Find the equilibrium constant for the reaction

$$CO + H_2O \longrightarrow CO_2 + H_2$$

at 77°F. Assume ideal gas behavior.

Solution: The equilibrium constant, K_p, can be determined from the following equation:

$$\Delta G^0 = -RT \ln K_p$$

where ΔG^0 = change in standard Gibbs function

R = gas constant

T = temperature

The change in the standard Gibbs function is given by

$$\Delta G^0 = \Delta G^0_{products} - \Delta G^0_{reactants}$$

The free energies of formation for all the constituents of the reaction are found from standard tables and are given below:

Component	ΔG^0_f cal/gm-mole (25°C)
CO	-32,810
H_2O	-54,640
H_2	0
CO_2	-94,260

Therefore,

$$\Delta G^0 = \Delta G^0_{products} - \Delta G^0_{reactants}$$

$$= (-94,260 - 0) - (-32,810 - 54,640)$$

$$= -6810 \text{ cal/gm-mole}$$

$$= -12,250 \text{ Btu/lbm-mole}$$

Solving for $\ln K_p$ gives

$$\ln K_p = -\frac{\Delta G^0}{RT} = \frac{12,250 \text{ Btu/lbm-mole} \times 778 \text{ ft}\cdot\text{lb/Btu}}{1545 \text{ ft}\cdot\text{lb/lbm-mole-}^{\circ}\text{R} \times 537^{\circ}\text{R}}$$

$$= 11.5$$

and $K_p = 98,000$

Ammonia decomposes by the following chemical reaction:

$$NH_3 \rightleftharpoons \tfrac{1}{2}N_{2(g)} + \tfrac{1}{2}H_{2(g)}$$

where the free energy of formation is

$$\Delta G^0 = 10,400 - 7.1T \log T - 3.79T \text{ cal}$$

Find the extent of dissociation of ammonia to form hydrogen and nitrogen at 523°K, 1.0 and 0.5 atm. Comment on the effect of pressure on ammonia dissociation. Assume ideal gas behavior.

Solution: The stability of ammonia gas depends on pressure. Three independent simultaneous equations are necessary to solve for the three unknowns p_{NH_3}, p_{H_2} and p_{N_2}.

For the decomposition reaction,

$$\Delta G^0 = 10,400 - 7.1T \log T - 3.79T \text{ cal}$$

@ 523°K

$$\Delta G^0 = -1677 \text{ cal}$$

$$\Delta G^0 = -RT \ln K_p$$

$$\therefore \quad K_p = \exp\left(\frac{+1677}{(1.99)(523)}\right)$$

$$K_p = 5.01$$

From the chemical reaction,

$$K_p = \frac{f_{H_2}^{3/2} \cdot f_{N_2}^{1/2}}{f_{NH_3}}$$

$$= p_{H_2}^{3/2} \cdot p_{N_2}^{1/2}/p_{NH_3} \quad \text{(due to ideal behavior)}$$

Since the dissociation of ammonia always results in the formation of 3 moles of H_2 for every one mole of N_2, $3p_{N_2} = p_{H_2}$.

The third relation is,

$$p_{N_2} + p_{H_2} + p_{NH_3} = p_{TOT}$$

For $p_{TOT} = 1$,

$$p_{N_2} + p_{H_2} + p_{NH_3} = 1$$

$\therefore$

$$4p_{N_2} + p_{NH_3} = 1 \quad \text{(substituting for } p_{H_2}\text{)}$$

Now substituting for p_{NH_3} in the equilibrium constant expression,

$$5.01 = \frac{(3p_{N_2})^{3/2}(p_{N_2})^{1/2}}{(-4p_{N_2} + 1)}$$

After cross multiplication,

$$5.2p_{N_2}^2 + 20.04p_{N_2} - 5.01 = 0$$

$$p_{N_2} = \frac{-20.04 \pm \sqrt{(20.04)^2 - 4(5.2)(-5.01)}}{2(5.2)}$$

$$p_{N_2} = 0.236$$

$$p_{H_2} = 3(0.236) = 0.708$$

$\therefore$ $p_{NH_3} = 1 - 0.236 - 0.708 = 0.056$

$\therefore$ @ 1 atm, 94.4% (by volume) of the NH_3 will dissociate.

For $p_{TOT} = 0.5$ atm,

$$p_{H_2} + p_{NH_3} + p_{N_2} = 0.5$$

$$4p_{N_2} + p_{NH_3} = 0.5$$

Plugging into the equilibrium constant expression,

$$5.2p_{N_2}^2 + 20.04p_{N_2} - 2.505 = 0$$

$$p_{N_2} = \frac{-20.04 \pm \sqrt{(20.04)^2 - 4(5.2)(-2.505)}}{2(5.2)}$$

$$p_{N_2} = 0.12$$

$$p_{H_2} = 0.36$$

$$p_{NH_3} = 0.02$$

$\therefore$ @ 0.5 atm, 96% (by volume) of the NH_3 dissociates.

The trend seen in this problem follows Le Chatelier's principle. Since 1 mole of gas reacts to give 2 moles of gas (H_2 + N_2) as the pressure is raised, the reverse reaction is favored and therefore, the dissociation decreases.

• PROBLEM 11-56

A certain steel containing 0.7 weight-percent carbon is in equilibrium with a methane-hydrogen gas mixture containing 99 percent hydrogen and 1 percent methane by volume at 1,173°K and 1 atm. Find the activity of carbon in the steel and the equilibrium volume percentages of a carbon monoxide-carbon dioxide mixture at equilibrium with the steel at the same conditions. Use the following data to solve the problem and assume all gases are ideal.

<u>Data</u>

For the reaction

$$C_{(s,\ graphite)} + 2H_{2(g)} \rightleftharpoons CH_{4(g)}$$

$$\Delta G^0 = -21{,}600 + 26.2T \text{ cal}$$

For the reaction

$$CO_{2(g)} + C_{(s,\ graphite)} \rightleftharpoons 2CO_{(g)}$$

$$\Delta G^0 = 40{,}800 - 41.7T \text{ cal}$$

<u>Solution</u>: This problem is a typical example of the principle of determining the equilibrium conditions of a certain reaction from the known conditions of a similar reaction. The carbon activity in the steel is found by the H_2 - CH_4 equilibrium gas composition. Using this activity, the molal analysis of a CO - CO_2 gas mixture can be obtained.

For the C - H_2 - CH_4 equilibrium,

$$@\ 1{,}173^{\circ}K \qquad \Delta G^0 = -21{,}600 + 26.2(1{,}173)$$

$$= 9{,}132.6 \text{ cal}$$

$$\ln K_p = \frac{-\Delta G^0}{RT}$$

$$\ln K_p = \frac{-9{,}132.6}{(1.99)(1{,}173)} = -3.9$$

$$K_p = 0.02$$

$$K_p = \frac{f_{CH_4}}{f^2_{H_2} \cdot a_C}$$

Since all gases are ideal,

$$K_p = \frac{P_{CH_4}}{P^2_{H_2} \cdot a_C}$$

Substituting the given equilibrium gas compositions,

$$P_{CH_4} = (0.01)\ 1\ \text{atm}$$

$$P_{H_2} = 0.99\ (1)\ \text{atm}$$

$\therefore$

$$K_p = \frac{0.01}{(0.99)^2 a_C} = 0.02$$

$$a_C = \frac{0.01}{0.02(0.99)^2} = 0.51$$

$\therefore$ The activity of the carbon in the steel (relative to graphite as the standard state) is 0.51.

The CO - CO_2 gas composition in equilibrium with the steel (carbon) is obtained from the reaction

$$CO_{2(g)} + C_{(s)} \rightleftharpoons 2CO_{(g)}$$

$$\Delta G^0 = 40{,}800 - 41.7T\ \text{cal}$$

@ 1,173°K

$$\Delta G^0 = 40{,}800 - 41.7(1{,}173)$$

$$= -8{,}114.1\ \text{cal}$$

$$K_p = \exp\left(\frac{+8{,}114.1}{1.99 \times 1{,}173}\right) = 32.3$$

From the chemical reaction,

$$K_p = f^2_{CO}/f_{CO_2} \cdot a_C$$

Since all gases are ideal,

$$K_p = P^2_{CO}/P_{CO_2} \cdot a_C$$

Substituting for K_p and a_C,

$$P^2_{CO}/P_{CO_2} = 16.47$$

but $$P_{CO} + P_{CO_2} = P_{TOT} = 1$$

$\therefore$

$$P^2_{CO} = 16.47(1 - P_{CO})$$

or

$$P^2_{CO} + 16.47P_{CO} - 16.47 = 0$$

Using the quadratic equation,

$$P_{CO} = \frac{-16.47 \pm \sqrt{(16.47)^2 - 4(-16.47)}}{2}$$

$P_{CO} = 0.946$ atm (The negative root is neglected)

$P_{CO_2} = 0.054$ atm

$\therefore$ The gas contains 94.6% CO and 5.4% CO_2 (by volume).

• PROBLEM 11-57

Carbon monoxide reacts with oxygen according to the following chemical equation:

$$CO + \tfrac{1}{2}O_2 = CO_2$$

A stoichiometric mixture of CO and O_2 enters a reactor at 100°C. CO_2, CO and O_2 leave the reactor in chemical equilibrium at 1,527°C and 2 atm. K_p for the reaction at 1,527%C is equal to $1 \times 10^{3.9}$ atm$^{-\frac{1}{2}}$. Calculate. the partial pressures of CO_2, CO and O_2 in the products.

Solution: Assuming ideal gas behavior, using the information obtained from reaction stoichiometry, mass conservation, and the K_p expression, the partial pressures of all the species can be calculated.

The expression for K_p is

$$K_p = \frac{P_{CO_2}}{P_{CO}\, P_{O_2}^{\frac{1}{2}}} = 1 \times 10^{3.9}\ \text{atm}^{-\frac{1}{2}}$$

Due to the ideal gas assumption,

$$P_{CO_2} + P_{CO} + P_{O_2} = P_{TOT} = 2$$

and

$$\frac{\text{initial \# atoms}_i}{\text{initial \# atoms}_j} = \frac{P_i}{P}$$

By the law of atomic conservation, carbon balance:

$$n_{CO_2(\text{initial})} + n_{CO(\text{initial})} = n_{CO_2(\text{final})} + n_{CO(\text{final})}$$

where n = number of atoms of carbon in each species present.

Oxygen balance:

$$2n_{CO_2(\text{initial})} + n_{CO(\text{initial})} + 2n_{O_2(\text{initial})} =$$

$$2n_{CO_2(\text{final})} + n_{CO(\text{final})} + 2n_{O_2(\text{final})}$$

Since $n_{CO_2(\text{initial})} = 0$, the balances are:

$$n_{CO(\text{initial})} = n_{CO_2(\text{final})} + n_{CO(\text{final})}$$

and

$$n_{CO(\text{initial})} + 2n_{O_2(\text{initial})} = 2n_{CO_2(\text{final})} + n_{CO(\text{final})} + 2n_{O_2(\text{final})}$$

If $n_{CO(\text{initial})}$ in the carbon balance is substituted in the oxygen balance, an expression for $n_{O_2(\text{initial})}$ is obtained.

$$n_{O_2(\text{initial})} = n_{O_2(\text{final})} + \tfrac{1}{2}n_{CO_2(\text{final})}$$

The feed stream consists of a stoichiometric ratio of CO to O_2. In other words, $\frac{n_{CO(initial)}}{n_{O_2(initial)}} = 2$ (a ratio of 2:1 from the chemical equation). Therefore,

$$\frac{n_{CO(initial)}}{n_{O_2(initial)}} = \frac{n_{CO_2(final)} + n_{CO(final)}}{n_{O_2(final)} + \frac{1}{2}n_{CO_2(final)}} = 2$$

Since the atomic ratios are proportional to the partial pressures,

$$\frac{P_{CO(final)}}{P_{O_2(final)}} = 2$$

or

$P_{CO} = 2P_{O_2}$ (The subscript "final" has been dropped since now there is no confusion regarding which pressure is being referred to.)

Since all of the pressures add up to 2,

$$P_{CO_2} + P_{CO} + P_{O_2} = 2$$

or $$P_{CO_2} + 3P_{O_2} = 2$$

Plugging these values into the K_p expression,

$$1 \times 10^{3.9} = \frac{P_{CO_2}}{(2P_{O_2}\ P_{O_2}{}^{\frac{1}{2}})} = \frac{P_{CO_2}}{2P_{O_2}{}^{3/2}}$$

$$16{,}000\ P_{O_2}{}^{3/2} = P_{CO_2}$$

But $3P_{O_2} = 2 - P_{CO_2}$

Therefore,

$$P_{CO_2} = 16{,}000\left(\frac{2 - P_{CO_2}}{3}\right)^{3/2}$$

This equation can be solved by trial and error.

If P_{CO_2} = 1.9 is tried, a value of P_{CO_2} = 243.5 is obtained. This shows that the first attempt was too high. If P_{CO_2} = 1.999 is tried, a value of P_{CO_2} = 0.2435 is obtained. Therefore, it is seen that this trial was too low. After a few trials, the correct value is obtained.

$$P_{CO_2} = 1.996 \text{ atm}$$

$$P_{O_2} = (2 - 1.996)/3 = 0.00133 \text{ atm}$$

$$P_{CO} = 2P_{O_2} = 0.00267 \text{ atm}$$

The extent of reaction is very high, and the small amounts of O_2 and CO in the product mixture are due to CO_2 dissociation at high temperatures.

• PROBLEM 11-58

What is the equilibrium composition of a mixture of carbon monoxide, carbon dioxide, and molecular oxygen at 3000°K and 30 psia? Assume the mixture contains 5 atoms of oxygen per atom of carbon.

Solution: The reaction is given by $CO_2 \rightleftharpoons CO + \frac{1}{2}O_2$ and the equilibrium constant for this dissociation reaction is given by

$$K(T) = \frac{x_{CO}\, x_{O_2}^{\frac{1}{2}}}{x_{CO_2}} \left(\frac{P}{P_0}\right)^{1 + \frac{1}{2} - 1}$$

where P = reaction pressure

P_0 = some reference pressure (atmospheric)

x_i = mole fraction of substance i

K = equilibrium constant

P_0 is arbitrarily chosen to be 1 atmosphere or 14.7 psia.

From a table of the equilibrium constant, it is found that at 3000°K, $\log_{10} K = -0.469$ or K = 0.340.

Thus, $\dfrac{x_{CO}\, x_{O_2}^{\frac{1}{2}}}{x_{CO_2}} = 0.340 \times \left(\dfrac{30}{14.7}\right)^{-\frac{1}{2}} = 0.238$

The above equation represents an equilibrium constraint on the system. A mole fraction constraint can also be written for the system,

$$x_{CO} + x_{CO_2} + x_{O_2} = 1$$

since the mole fractions must sum to unity. A third constraint for the system is the ratio of carbon atoms to oxygen atoms in the mixture: 1 carbon atom is present for every five oxygen atoms. So,

$$\frac{x_{CO_2} + x_{CO}}{2x_{CO_2} + x_{CO} + 2x_{O_2}} = \frac{1}{5}$$

The three constraints represent three simultaneous equations with three unknowns, which are x_{CO_2}, x_{CO} and x_{O_2}. These three equations can be solved using some numerical technique. The solution is found to be

$$x_{CO} = 0.0891$$

$$x_{O_2} = 0.615$$

$$x_{CO_2} = 0.296$$

which is the equilibrium composition of this system.

• PROBLEM 11-59

In a continuously fed catalytic ammonia converter 1 mol of nitrogen reacts with 3 mol of hydrogen according to the following chemical reaction:

$$N_2 + 3H_2 = 2NH_3$$

The converter is operated at a pressure of 100 atm and a temperature of 350°C. The equilibrium constant for this reaction K is equal to 14.4×10^{-6} at 500°C. The enthalpy of reaction ΔH^o is -25,800 cal/g-mol at the desired temperatures. All standard states are assumed to be pure components at 1 atm pressure. Assume ideal-gas and Lewis-Randall behavior. Calculate the equilibrium conversion of nitrogen to ammonia.

Solution: The equilibrium constant is given at a temperature of 500°C, therefore, the equilibrium constant (K) at the operating temperature (350°C) must be calculated. Once this value is known, K_m, the equilibrium constant based on mole fractions, can be determined and the equilibrium conversion obtained.

To calculate K at 350°C, the following equation is used:

$$\ln\left[\frac{(K)_{T_2}}{(K)_{T_1}}\right] = \int_{T_1}^{T_2} \frac{\Delta H^{\circ}}{RT^2}\, dT$$

Substituting the numerical values,

$$\ln\left[\frac{(K)_{623^{\circ}K}}{(K)_{773^{\circ}K}}\right] = \int_{773^{\circ}K}^{623^{\circ}K} \left[\frac{-25,800}{T^2}\right] dT$$

Integrating,

$$1.987\frac{\text{cal}}{\text{g-mol}^{\circ}K} \ln\left[\frac{(K)_{623^{\circ}K}}{14.4 \times 10^{-6}}\right] = \left[25,800\left(\frac{1}{623} - \frac{1}{773}\right)\right] \text{cal/g-mol}^{\circ}K$$

Simplifying,

$$\ln\left[\frac{(K)_{623^{\circ}K}}{14.4 \times 10^{-6}}\right] = \frac{8.036}{1.987} = 4.044$$

Hence,

$$(K)_{623} = 14.4 \times 10^{-6} \cdot e^{4.044} = 8.216 \times 10^{-4}$$

K is related to K_m by the expression

$$K = \frac{K_m K_p}{K_f^{\circ}}$$

Therefore,

$$K_m = \frac{K\ K_f^{\circ}}{K_p}$$

Since the standard-state conditions are all pure components at 1 atm, $f^{\circ} = 1$ atm and $K_f^{\circ} = \frac{f^2}{ff^3} = \frac{1}{f^2} = 1\ \text{atm}^{-2}$. K_p is directly related to the system pressure by the expression

$$K_p = \frac{p^2}{pp^3} = \frac{1}{p^2}$$

Since p = 100 atm, $K_p = (100 \text{ atm})^{-2} = 1 \times 10^{-4} \text{atm}^{-2}$

Now, K_m can be calculated.

$$K_m = \frac{K K_f^o}{K_p} = \frac{(8.216 \times 10^{-4})(1 \text{ atm}^{-2})}{1 \times 10^{-4} \text{ atm}^{-2}}$$

$$K_m = 8.216$$

Setting up a table of property values for the reacting mixture based on 1 mol of nitrogen feed and x mol of N_2 reacting.

Table 1

	N_2	H_2	NH_3	Total
Initial	1	3	0	4
Formed by reaction	-x	-3x	2x	-2x
Final	1-x	3-3x	2x	4-2x
Final mole fraction	$\left(\frac{1-x}{4-2x}\right)$	$\left(\frac{3-3x}{4-2x}\right)$	$\left(\frac{2x}{4-2x}\right)$	1.0

By using the calculated value of K_m, x can be obtained.

$$K_m = \frac{\left(Y_{NH_3}\right)^2}{Y_{N_2}\left(Y_{H_2}\right)^3}$$

Therefore,

$$8.216 = \frac{\left(\frac{2x}{TOTAL}\right)^2}{((1-x)/TOT)((3-3x)/TOT)} \quad \text{(where TOTAL=4-2x)}$$

$$8.216 = \frac{(4x^2)(4-2x)^2}{(1-x)(3-3x)^3}$$

The solution of this equation for x gives the equilibrium conversions of N_2 to NH_3. Since this is a fourth order equation, a trial and error method is adopted. Examination of the range of possible values for x shows that $0 \leq x \leq 1$. Since K_m is a relatively small number, it is quite possible that x cannot be a very small number (since there would be a small denominator resulting in a large K_m). A good first guess, therefore, is x = 0.5. For this value of x, K_m = 5.33. This shows that a higher value for x is needed. After a few trials, the exact value obtained is x = 0.54.

Table 2

Trial #	x	K_m	$x_{assumed}$ = high or low?
1	0.5	5.33	low
2	0.6	16.33	high
3	0.53	7.37	low
4	0.54	8.22	correct

Therefore, it is seen that the maximum conversion of N_2 to NH_3 under the given conditions is 0.54/1.0 = 0.54 or 54% conversion.

EQUILIBRIUM CONSTANT DEPENDENCE ON TEMPERATURE

• **PROBLEM** 11-60

Hydrogen reacts with iodine gas by the chemical reaction:

$$H_2(g) + I_2(g) \rightleftharpoons 2HI(g)$$

K_p for this reaction is equal to 870 @ 25°C and ΔH°_{25} = -2480 cal. Calculate K_p @ 40°C for the following two cases.

(a) If ΔH is constant for this temperature range.

(b) If ΔH varies with temperature.

Solution: K_p can be calculated by using the equation

$$d\ln K_p/dT = \Delta H^\circ/RT^2$$

After integration,

$$\log \frac{K_p\ (@T_2)}{K_p\ (@T_1)} = \frac{\Delta H^\circ}{2.303R}\left(\frac{T_2 - T_1}{T_1T_2}\right)$$

substitution into this equation yields:

$$\log K_p\ (@\ 313^\circ K) - \log 870 = \frac{-2480}{(2.303)(1.987)}\left(\frac{313 - 298}{(313)(298)}\right)$$

$$K_p = 712$$

Due to the fact that $\Delta H < 0$, K_p decreases with an increasing temperature.

If ΔH is not constant, it must be expressed as a function of temperature. Therefore

$$\Delta H_T = \Delta H_I t + \Delta a_T + (\Delta b/2)T^2 + (\Delta c/3)T^3 + \ldots .$$

$$\ln K_p = \int (1/RT^2)(\Delta H_I + \Delta aT + (\Delta b/2)T^2 + (\Delta c/3)T^3 + \ldots)dT + I$$

or

$$\ln K_p = -\frac{\Delta H_I}{RT} + \frac{\Delta a}{R}\ln T + \frac{\Delta b}{2R}T + \frac{\Delta c}{6R}T^2 + \ldots + I$$

This equation allows us to find K_p at any temperature within the range of valid parameters a, b, c, provided the parameters and the integration constants I, ΔH_I are known. The value of the integration constant I can be calculated by finding K_p (or ΔG°) at a particular temperature.

• PROBLEM 11-61

The sodium chloride formation reaction is

$$Na_{(1)} + \tfrac{1}{2}Cl_{2(g)} \rightleftharpoons NaCl_{(s)} .$$

The standard heat of formation of sodium chloride is equal to -98.6 kcal mole^{-1} and is temperature independent. When H_2 and HCl gas are in equilibrium with liquid sodium and solid NaCl, the partial pressure of chlorine gas is 1.672×10^{-43} mmHg @ $773^\circ K$. Using this information, determine the equilibrium partial pressure of chlorine @ $823^\circ K$.

Solution: Using the van't Hoff equation, K_p at the second temperature can be found. Due to the fact that ΔH_f is a constant, the approximate form is used. Before this calculation is performed, the known value of the partial pressure of chlorine is used to obtain K_p @ $773^{\circ}K$.

For the NaCl formation reaction,

$$K_p = \frac{a_{NaCl}}{a_{Na} \cdot f_{Cl_2}^{1/2}}$$

If sodium and NaCl are in their standard pure states and the Cl_2 behaves as an ideal gas,

$$K_p = \frac{1}{p_{Cl_2}^{1/2}}$$

$$p_{Cl_2}^{1/2} = 1.672 \times 10^{-43} \text{mmHg} = 2.2 \times 10^{-46} \text{atm}$$

$\therefore$

$$K_p = \frac{1}{(2.2 \times 10^{-46})^{\frac{1}{2}}}$$

$$= 6.74 \times 10^{22} \text{ @ } 500^{\circ}C$$

This value is now substituted into the van't Hoff equation (integrated form) as K_1,

$$\ln\left[\frac{(K_1)}{(K_2)}\right] = \frac{\Delta H}{R}\left(\frac{1}{T_2} - \frac{1}{T_1}\right)$$

$\therefore$

$$\ln(6.74 \times 10^{22}) - \ln K_2 = \frac{-98,600}{1.987}\left(\frac{1}{823} - \frac{1}{773}\right)$$

$$K_2 = 1.36 \times 10^{21}$$

Now,

$$p_{Cl_2} = \frac{1}{K_p^2}$$

$\therefore$

$$p_{Cl_2} = \frac{1}{(1.36 \times 10^{21})^2}$$

$$= 5.40 \times 10^{-43} \text{ atm.}$$

This problem can also be solved by calculating ΔG^0 @ $773\,^0K$ from K_{773} and solving for ΔS^0 in the equation

$$\Delta G^0 = \Delta H^0 - T\Delta S^0.$$

Assuming that ΔH^0 and ΔS^0 are temperature independent, then ΔG^0 @ 873 can be calculated, from which K_{873} can be obtained.

• PROBLEM 11-62

Hydrochloric acid gas reacts with oxygen by the following reaction :

$$2HCl(g) + \tfrac{1}{2}O_2(g) \rightleftharpoons H_2O(g) + Cl_2(g)$$

If $\Delta G^o_{298} = -9.098$ kcal and $\Delta H^o_{298} = -13.672$ kcal, calculate K_p and ΔG^o @ $400\,^oK$ using the following heat capacity data.

heat capacity data

(all heat capacities are in cal mole^{-1}deg^{-1})

$HCl(g)$, $\overline{C}^o_p = 6.7319 + 0.4325\,(10^{-3})T + 3.697(10^{-7})T^2$

$O_2(g)$, $\overline{C}^o_p = 6.0954 + 3.2533(10^{-3})T - 10.171(10^{-7})T^2$

$H_2O(g)$, $\overline{C}^o_p = 7.219 + 2.374(10^{-3})T + 2.67(10^{-7})T^2$

$Cl_2(g)$, $\overline{C}^o_p = 7.5755 + 2.4244(10^{-3})T - 9.65(10^{-7})T^2$

Also develop the expression for the variation of K_c [the equilibrium constant based on concentrations] with temperature.

Solution: From the heat capacity data, ΔH^o_I can be calculated. Using this value, K_p can be evaluated.

From the heat capacity data, Δa, Δb, and Δc can be evaluated and this leads to ΔC_p.

Therefore, $\Delta C^o_p = -1.7170 + 2.3067(10^{-3})T - 9.288(10^{-7})T^2$

Using the equation

$$\Delta H^o_T = \Delta H^o_I + \Delta aT + (\Delta b/2)T^2 + (\Delta c/3)T^3$$

at 298^oK, $\Delta H^o_I = -13{,}254$ cal. Since $\Delta G^o_{298} = -9098$ cal,

$$\ln K_p(@\ 298) = \frac{-9098}{(-1.987)(298.2)} = \frac{\Delta G}{RT} = 15.352$$

Using the equation

$$\frac{d \ln K_p}{dT} = \Delta H^\circ/RT^2$$

or

$$\ln K_p = \int \left[(1/RT^2)(\Delta H_I^\circ + \Delta aT + (\Delta b/2)T^2 + (\Delta c/3)T^3\right] dT + I$$

$$= \frac{-\Delta H_I^\circ}{RT} + \frac{\Delta a}{R} \ln T + \frac{\Delta b}{2R} T + \frac{\Delta c}{6R} T^2 \quad + I$$

$\therefore$

$$15.352 = \frac{13,254}{(1.987)(298.2)} - \frac{1.7170}{1.987} \ln 298.2 +$$

$$\frac{2.3067(10^{-3})}{2(1.987)} 298.2 - \frac{9.288(10^{-7})}{6(1.987)} (298.2)^2 + I$$

or $I = -2.263$

$\therefore$ at any temperature, K_p can be calculated.

$$\ln K_p = \frac{13,254}{1.987T} - \frac{1.7170}{1.987} \ln T + \frac{2.3067(10^{-3})}{2(1.987)} T$$

$$- \frac{9.288(10^{-7})}{6(1.987)} T^2 - 2.263$$

$\therefore$ at $T = 400^\circ K$, $\ln K_p = 1.3095 \times 10^4$.

$$\Delta G^\circ = -RT \ln K_p = -(1.987)(400)\ln(1.3095 \times 10^4)$$

$$= -7535 \quad \text{cal}$$

The variation of K_c with temperature is obtained by taking the logarithm on both sides of the equation, $K_p = K_c(RT)^{\Delta n}$, and taking the derivative with respect to temperature.

$$\frac{d \ln K_p}{dT} = d \ln K_c/dT + \Delta n/T$$

But $d \ln K_p = \Delta H^\circ/RT^2$

$$\therefore \frac{d \ln K_c}{dT} = \frac{\Delta H^\circ}{RT^2} - \Delta n/T = \left[\Delta H^\circ - \Delta n(RT)\right]/RT^2$$

$$\therefore \frac{d \ln K_c}{dT} = \Delta E^\circ/RT^2$$

• PROBLEM 11-63

Hydrogen and oxygen liquids are used as fuels for a rocket engine which is designed to operate at a chamber pressure of 15 atmospheres, and the gas feed temperature is -100 °F. Calculate the maximum temperature that can be attained in the combustion chamber when the dissociation is 0.02 and 0.2. Assume a constant pressure combustion and no OH product. Use table (1) for equilibrium constant values.

Logarithms to the Base 10 of the Equilibrium Constant K_p

Temperature (°K)	$H_2 = 2H$	$O_2 = 2O$	$H_2O(g) = H_2 + \frac{1}{2}O_2$	$H_2O(g) = OH + \frac{1}{2}H_2$	$CO_2 = CO + \frac{1}{2}O_2$	$CO_2 + H_2 = CO + H_2O(g)$	$N_2 = 2N$	$\frac{1}{2}O_2 + \frac{1}{2}N_2 = NO$
298	−71.210	−80.620	−40.047	−46.593	−45.043	−4.996	−119.434	−15.187
400	−51.742	−58.513	−29.241	−33.910	−32.41	−3.169	− 87.473	−11.156
600	−32.667	−36.859	−18.633	−21.470	−20.07	−1.432	− 56.206	− 7.219
800	−23.074	−25.985	−13.288	−15.214	−13.90	−0.617	− 40.521	− 5.250
1000	−17.288	−19.440	−10.060	−11.444	−10.199	−0.139	− 31.084	− 4.068
1200	−13.410	−15.062	− 7.896	− 8.922	− 7.742	+0.154	− 24.619	− 3.279
1400	−10.627	−11.932	− 6.344	− 7.116	− 5.992	+0.352	− 20.262	− 2.717
1600	− 8.530	− 9.575	− 5.175	− 5.758	− 4.684	+0.490	− 16.869	− 2.294
1800	− 6.893	− 7.740	− 4.263	− 4.700	− 3.672	+0.591	− 14.225	− 1.966
2000	− 5.579	− 6.269	− 3.531	− 3.852	− 2.863	+0.668	− 12.106	− 1.703
2200	− 4.500	− 5.064	− 2.931	− 3.158	− 2.206	+0.725	− 10.370	− 1.488
2400	− 3.598	− 4.055	− 2.429	− 2.578	− 1.662	+0.767	− 8.922	− 1.309
2600	− 2.833	− 3.206	− 2.003	− 2.087	− 1.203	+0.800	− 7.694	− 1.157
2800	− 2.176	− 2.475	− 1.638	− 1.670	− 0.807	+0.831	− 6.640	− 1.028
3000	− 1.604	− 1.840	− 1.322	− 1.302	− 0.469	+0.853	− 5.726	− 0.915
3200	− 1.104	− 1.285	− 1.046	− 0.983	− 0.175	+0.871	− 4.925	− 0.817
3500	− 0.458	− 0.571	− 0.693	− 0.577	+ 0.201	+0.894	− 3.893	− 0.692
4000	+ 0.406	+ 0.382	− 0.221	− 0.035	+ 0.699	+0.920	− 2.514	− 0.526
4500	+ 1.078	+ 1.125	+ 0.153	+ 0.392	+ 1.081	+0.928	− 1.437	− 0.345
5000	+ 1.619	+ 1.719	+ 0.450	+ 0.799	+ 1.387	+0.937	− 0.570	− 0.298

NOTE: For the reaction $aA + bB = cC + dD$, equilibrium constant K_p is defined as $K_p = pC^c pD^d / pA^a pB^b$, where p is the partial pressure in atmosphere.

Solution: The amount of dissociation will be defined as x in the equation

$$H_2 + \frac{1}{2}O_2 \longrightarrow (1 - x)H_2O + xH_2 + \frac{1}{2}xO_2$$

where $0 < x < 1$

The number of moles in the product N_p is then

$$N_p = (1 - x) + x + \frac{1}{2}x = \frac{2 + x}{2}$$

The equation $\frac{P_i}{P_{TOT}} = \frac{n_i}{n_{TOT}} = x_i$ relates the mole fraction of the products to the partial pressures so that

$$P_{H_2O} = \frac{2(1 - x)}{2 + x} P_{TOT}$$

$$P_{H_2} = \frac{2x}{2 + x} P_{TOT}$$

$$P_{O_2} = \frac{x}{2 + x} P_{TOT}$$

Now from table (1)

$$K_p = \frac{(P_{H_2})^1 (P_{O_2})^{1/2}}{(P_{H_2O})}$$

For x = 0.02,

$$P_{H_2} = \left(\frac{0.04}{2.02}\right)15 = 0.297 \text{ atm}$$

$$P_{O_2} = \left(\frac{0.02}{2.02}\right)15 = 0.149 \text{ atm}$$

$$P_{H_2O} = \left(\frac{2(1 - 0.02)}{2.02}\right)15 = 14.554 \text{ atm}$$

Then $K_p = \frac{(0.297)(0.149)^{\frac{1}{2}}}{(14.554)} = 0.00788$

$\log K_p = -2.103$

The temperature which corresponds to the maximum temperature for x = 0.02 is obtained by interpolating the data in table (1).

Therefore,

$$T \simeq 2553^\circ K$$

For x = 0.2

$$P_{H_2} = 2.73 \text{ atm}$$

$$P_{O_2} = 1.36 \text{ atm}$$

$$P_{H_2O} = 10.9 \text{ atm}$$

$$\therefore \quad K_p = 0.292$$

and

$$\log K_p = -0.534$$

From table (1)

$$T \simeq 3150^\circ K \quad \text{(approximately)}.$$

• PROBLEM 11-64

Carbon monoxide reacts with water by the following reaction :

$$CO + H_2O \rightleftharpoons CO_2 + H_2$$

If the gas feed stream contains 20 mole % H_2, 6 mole % CO, 2 mole % CO_2 and 72 mole % H_2O @ 477°C and the total pressure is 1 atm, calculate the conversion attained at 700, 800 and 900°K. Assume ideal gas behavior. Use the following entropies, heat capacity and heats of formation data to solve the problem.

units = calories; g mol, °K 77 8

	CO	H_2O	CO_2	H_2
H°_f, 298°K, 1atm	-26,416	-57,798	-94,052	—
S°, 298°K, 1atm	47.301	45.106	51.061	31.211
a	6.420	7.256	6.214	6.947
$b\times10^3$	1.665	2.298	10.396	-0.200
$c\times10^6$	-0.196	0.283	-3.545	0.481

Solution: From the data, ΔH, ΔS can be determined. From these quantities ΔG can be calculated. From ΔG, K is obtained and then conversion can be calculated. The heat of reaction @ 298°K and 1 atm is

$$\Delta H^\circ_{298} = (\Delta H_f)_{products} - (\Delta H_f)_{reactants}$$

$$= -94{,}052 + 26{,}416 + 57{,}798 = -9838 \text{ cal/g mole}$$

The entropy change of reaction @ $298^\circ K$

$$\Delta S^\circ_{298} = (\Delta S^\circ_{298})_{products} - (\Delta S^\circ_{298})_{reactants}$$

$$= 51.061 + 31.211 - 47.301 - 45.106 = -10.135 \text{ cal/g mole}^\circ K$$

$$\Delta a = (a)_{products} - (a)_{reactants}$$

$$= 6.214 + 6.947 - 6.420 - 7.256 = -0.515$$

$$\Delta b = (b)_{products} - (b)_{reactants}$$

$$= \left[10.396 - 0.200 - 1.665 - 2.298\right] \times 10^{-3} = 6.233 \times 10^{-3}$$

$$\Delta c = (c)_{products} - (c)_{reactants}$$

$$= \left[-3.545 + 0.481 + 0.196 - 0.283\right] \times 10^{-6} = -3.151 \times 10^{-6}$$

Using the following equations, ΔH°_0, ΔS°_0 and ΔG°_T are calculated.

(A) $\Delta H^\circ_0 = \Delta H^\circ_{298} - \Delta a(298) - \frac{\Delta b}{2}(298)^2 - \frac{\Delta c}{3}(298)^3$

(B) $\Delta S^\circ_0 = \Delta S^\circ_{298} - \Delta a \ln(298) - \Delta b(298) - \frac{\Delta c}{2}(298)^2$

(C) $\Delta G^\circ_T = \Delta H^\circ_0 + (\Delta a - \Delta S_0) - \Delta a T \ln(T) - \frac{\Delta b}{2}T^2 - \frac{\Delta c}{6}T^3$

$\therefore$

$$\Delta H^\circ_0 = -9838 + (0.515)(298) - (6.233\text{x}10^{-3}/2)(298)^2 + (3.151\text{x}10^{-6}/3)(298)^3 = -9934 \text{ cal/g mole}$$

$$\Delta S^\circ_0 = -10.135 + 0.515 \ln(298) - (6.233\text{x}10^{-3})(298) + (3.151\text{x}10^{-6}/2)(298)^2 = -8.92 \text{ cal/g mole}$$

$\therefore$

$$(\Delta G^\circ_T/T) = -(9934/T) + 8.41 + 0.515 \ln T - (6.233\text{x}10^{-3}/2)T + (3.151\text{x}10^{-6}/6)T^2$$

Using the equation

$$\ln K = -\Delta G^0/RT$$

the equilibrium constant can be determined.

T°K	ΔG°/T	ln K = −ΔG°/RT	K
700	-4.33	2.18	8.85
800	-2.72	1.37	3.93
900	-1.50	0.755	2.13

Assuming a basis of 100 moles of feed gas and x moles of carbon monoxide reacted, the moles of each species present at equilibrium are:

	moles
CO	6-x
H_2O	72-x
CO_2	2+x
H_2	20+x
Total	100

The equilibrium expression is

$$K = [CO_2][H_2] / [CO][H_2O]$$

substitution of the number of moles of each species at equilibrium gives

$$K = (20+x)(2+x)/(6-x)(72-x)$$

The quadratic equation may be solved to determine x as a function of K,

$$x = \frac{1-\left[1-(0.284)(K-0.0926)(K-1)/(K+0.282)^2\right]^{\frac{1}{2}}}{(0.0257)(K-1)/(K+0.282)}$$

The value of x is obtained for three different temperatures using the corresponding value of K.

Where x/6 indicates the fraction of the original CO that has reacted before equilibrium is reached.

Ethanol is produced from carbon monoxide gas and hydrogen gas as shown by the reaction

$$2CO_{(g)} + 4H_{2(g)} \longrightarrow C_2H_5OH_{(g)} + H_2O_{(g)}$$

Using the following data, show K as a function of temperature.

Data

$T^\circ K$	ΔF° cal/g mole
200	-39,662
400	-17,884
600	5,168

Heat Capacities (cal/gmol°K)

CO: $C_p = 6.60 + 1.2\text{x}10^{-3}T$

H_2: $C_p = 6.62 + 8.1\text{x}10^{-4}T$

C_2H_5OH: $C_p = 3.58 + 4.985\text{x}10^{-2}T - 16.99\text{x}10^{-6}T^2$

H_2O: $C_p = 8.22 + 1.5\text{x}10^{-4}T + 1.34\text{x}10^{-6}T^2$

Solution: By using the equations

$$\Delta F^\circ = -RT \ln K \quad \text{and}$$

$$I - \frac{\Delta H_0{}^\circ}{T} = (R \ln K - \Delta a \ln T - \frac{\Delta b}{2}T - \frac{\Delta c}{6}T^2) = y$$

A plot of y versus 1/T makes it possible to calculate $\Delta H_0{}^\circ$ from the slope and I from the intercept. An expression for K as a function of temperature can then be easily obtained.

The equation for C_p is in the form of

$$C_p = a + bT + cT^2.$$

The difference of the terms is calculated from the stoichiometry of the equation. The method used is:

$$a_{\text{products}} - a_{\text{reactants}} = \Delta a$$

For our reaction, $a_{\text{products}} = a(H_2O) + a(C_2H_5OH)$,

$a_{\text{reactants}} = 2a(CO) + 4a(H_2)$. The same method is used to calculate Δc and Δb.

The difference between terms in the C_p equations are calculated as follows:

$$\Delta a = 3.58 + 8.22 - 2(6.60) - 4(6.62)$$

$\Delta a = -27.88$ $\quad\quad$ $\Delta b = 0.04436$ $\quad\quad$ $\Delta c = -15.65 \times 10^{-6}$

From the data, R ln K can be calculated.

$$@\ T = 200\,^{\circ}K, \quad \Delta F^{\circ} = -39{,}662 = -RT \ln K$$

Therefore, $R \ln K = 39{,}662/200 = 198.3$

$$@\ T = 400\,^{\circ}K, \quad R \ln K = 17{,}884/400 = 44.7$$

$$@\ T = 600\,^{\circ}K, \quad R \ln K = -5{,}168/600 = -8.61$$

By plugging in these values and the values obtained for Δa, Δb, Δc, a value for y at each temperature is obtained.

$T\,^{\circ}K$	R ln K	y	1/T
200	198.3	341.9	0.05
400	44.7	203.2	0.0025
600	-8.61	157.5	0.00166

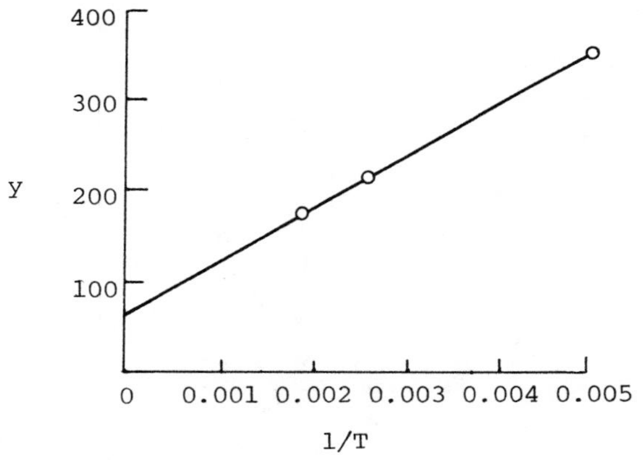

From the plot of y vs. $\frac{1}{T}$, a slope of 55,400 cal/g is obtained, and is equal to $-\Delta H_0{}^{\circ}$. The y intercept is 65.0 and is equal to I. By multiplying y by T and rearranging the equation, an expression for K as a function of T is obtained.

$$T\,(R \ln K + 27.88 \ln T - 0.02218T + 12.61 \times 10^{-6} T^2) =$$

$$65T + 55{,}400$$

$$\Delta F^{\circ} = -RT \ln K = -55{,}400 + 27.88T \ln T - 0.02218T^2 + 2.61 \times 10^{-6}T^3 - 65.0T$$

or

$$\ln K = \frac{55{,}400}{RT} - \frac{27.88}{R} \ln T - \frac{0.02218}{R} T + \frac{2.61\times10^{-6}}{R} T^2 + \frac{65.0}{R}$$

CHAPTER 12

FLOW THROUGH NOZZLES AND BLADE PASSAGES

STAGNATION PROPERTIES

• PROBLEM 12-1

Superheated steam, at 400 psia and 600°F, is flowing through a pipe with a velocity of 300 ft/sec. The flow starts from a point 10 ft. above the lowest part of the pipe line system. Determine the stagnation properties.

Solution: $P_1 = 400$ psia

$T_1 = 600°F$

At P_1 and T_1 from steam tables

Enthalpy $h_1 = 1307.4$ Btu/lb, entropy $S_1 = 1.5901$ Btu/lb°F and specific volume $v_1 = 1.4763$ ft³/lb.

Therefore the stagnation pressure is

$$P_0 = P_1 + \frac{V^2}{2gv_1} + \frac{Z}{v_1}$$

Therefore

$$P_0 = 400 + \frac{(300 \times 12)^2}{2\times(32.2\times12)\times[1.4763\times(12)^3]} + \frac{(10 \times 12)}{[1.4763\times(12)^3]}$$

$$= 406.62 \text{ psia.}$$

Stagnation enthalpy

$$h_0 = h_1 + \frac{V^2}{2Jg} + \frac{Z}{J}$$

$$= 1307.4 + \frac{(300)^2}{2\times778\times32.2} + \frac{10}{778}$$

$$= 1309.21 \text{ Btu/lb.}$$

And stagnation entropy $= S_0 = S_1 = 1.5901$ Btu/lb-^{0}F

Therefore for stagnation pressure $P_0 = 406.62$ psia and stagnation enthalpy $h_0 = 1309.21$ Btu/lb from steam tables, by interpolation.

Stagnation temperature is $\simeq 605^0$F and stagnation density

$$\rho_0 = \frac{1}{v_1} = \frac{1}{1.4643}$$

$$= 0.683 \text{ lb/ft}^3$$

• PROBLEM 12-2

A pipe has air flowing through it steadily with a mass flow rate of 35 lbm/s-ft^2. In the first section of the pipe, the pressure and temperature of the air are 60 psia and 100^{0}F. In another section of pipe further downstream, the pressure is 40 psia. Calculate the velocity and the Mach number of the airflow at the second section of the pipe. Assume the pipe has a constant area, no heat transfer, no change in potential energy, the flow is one-dimensional and air is an ideal gas with constant specific heats of $C_p = 0.24$ Btu/lbm^{0}R and $C_v = 0.171$ Btu/lbm^{0}R.

Solution: To calculate the velocity and the Mach number at the second section, the temperature at this section must be obtained. From the first law and the continuity equation,

$$h_1 + \frac{v_1^2}{2g_c}\left(\frac{\dot{m}}{A}\right)^2 = h_2 + \frac{v_2^2}{2g_c}\left(\frac{\dot{m}}{A}\right)^2$$

For an ideal gas,

$$h_1 - h_2 = Cp(T_1 - T_2)$$

$$v_1 = \frac{RT_1}{P_1}$$

$$v_2 = \frac{RT_2}{P_2}$$

Combining the above equations it is obtained

$$C_p(T_1-T_2) = \left(\frac{\dot{m}}{A}\right)^2 \left(\frac{R^2}{2g_c}\right) \left[\left(\frac{T_2}{P_2}\right)^2 - \left(\frac{T_1}{P_1}\right)^2\right]$$

Substituting the values, it reduces to

$$0.24 \frac{\text{Btu}}{\text{lbm}^0\text{R}} (560 - T_2)^0\text{R} = (35)^2 \frac{\text{lbm}^2}{\text{S}^2\text{ft}^4} \frac{(1.986/29)^2}{2(32.2)} \frac{\text{Btu}^2}{\text{lbm}^2\,{}^0\text{R}^2}$$

$$\frac{\frac{\text{lbf}\cdot\text{S}^2}{\text{lbm/ft}} \left[\frac{T_2{}^2}{(40\times144)^2} - \frac{560^2}{(60\times144)^2}\right] \frac{{}^0\text{R}^2}{\text{lbf}^2/\text{ft}^4}}{778 \text{ ft lbf/Btu}}$$

$$134.4 - 0.24T_2 = 69.41\left[3.014 \times 10^{-8}T_2^2 - 0.0042\right]$$

$$134.4 - 0.24T_2 = 2.09 \times 10^{-6}T_2^2 - 0.2916$$

$$2.09 \times 10^{-6}T_2^2 + 0.24T_2 - 134.692 = 0$$

$$T_2^2 + 1.14874 \times 10^5T_2 - 6.4469346 \times 10^7 = 0$$

$$T_2 = \frac{-1.14874 \times 10^5 \pm\sqrt{(1.14874\times10^5)^2 + 4(1)(6.4469\times10^7)}}{2 \times 1}$$

Therefore $T_2 = 554^0R$

For an ideal gas, the velocity of sound is,

$$c = \sqrt{kg_cRT} \qquad (k = 1.4 \text{ for air})$$

at $T_2 = 554^0R$,

$$C_2 = \left[\frac{1.4\times32.2\times1545\times554}{29}\right]^{\frac{1}{2}} \text{ ft/sec}$$

$$C_2 = 1153 \text{ ft/sec}$$

From the equation of continuity,

$$\frac{\dot{m}}{A} = \rho_2\overline{v}_2 = \frac{P_2}{RT_2}\,\overline{v}_2$$

Therefore $\overline{v}_2 = \dfrac{35\times1545\times554}{29\times40\times144}$

$$\overline{v}_2 = 179 \text{ ft/sec}$$

Therefore the Mach number is,

$$M_2 = \frac{\overline{v}_2}{c_2} = \frac{179}{1153} = 0.155$$

• PROBLEM 12-3

An air diffuser has an efficiency of 70 percent. The air enters at 333°K and 1.02 atm, and leaves at 2.8 atm. Calculate the pressure coefficient and the initial velocity. Assume

$$Cp_{air} = \text{constant} = 0.24 \text{ cal/g}^{0}\text{C} \quad \text{and } k_{air} = 1.4$$

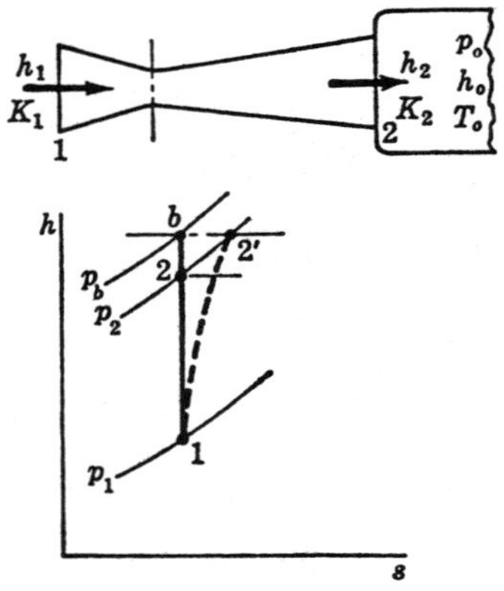

Fig. 1.

Solution: From the figure, it can be seen that $P_2 = P_2' = 2.8$ atm, where the prime refers to the actual state (including the efficiency). The theoretical process is an isentropic one and hence, the appropriate relations are used. T_2 is obtained by using the equation:

$$T_2 = T_1 \left(\frac{P_2}{P_1}\right)^{(k-1)/k} = 333\left(\frac{2.8}{1.02}\right)^{(1.4-1)/1.4}$$

$$= 444^{0}\text{K}$$

The actual temperature T_2' is obtained by using the diffuser efficiency, that is

$$e = \frac{T_2 - T_1}{T_2' - T_1} = 0.70 = \frac{444 - 333}{T_2' - 333}$$

$$T_2' = T_b = 492^{0}\text{K}$$

Using kinetic energy and an energy balance the initial velocity is obtained, that is

$$K_1 = \frac{V_1^{\,2}}{2g_0 J} = Cp(T_2' - T_1)$$

$$J = 427 \frac{(\text{meter})(\text{gram})}{\text{cal}}$$ (The value of J is obtained as shown below.)

$$J = 778 \frac{\text{ftlb}}{\text{Btu}}$$

$$J = 778 \frac{\text{ftlb}}{\text{Btu}} \times \frac{1\text{Btu}}{252\text{cal}} \times \frac{(0.3048)\text{meters}}{\text{ft}} \times (0.45359) \frac{\text{Kg}}{\text{lb}}$$

$$\times \frac{1000\text{g}}{\text{Kg}} = 427 \frac{\text{m}\cdot\text{g}}{(\text{a})}$$

$$V_1 = \left[2 \times 9.8 \text{ m/sec}^2 \times 427 \frac{\text{m}\cdot\text{g}}{\text{cal}} \times 0.24 \frac{\text{cal}}{\text{g}^0\text{K}} (492 - 333)^0\text{K}\right]^{\frac{1}{2}}$$

$$V_1 = 565 \text{ m/sec}$$

The pressure coefficient η_r, can be calculated by

$$\eta_r = \frac{P_2 - P_1}{P_b - P_1}$$ where P_b is the pressure along the

line 1 - b (see figure).

$$P_b = P_1 \left(\frac{T_2'}{T_1}\right)^{k/(k-1)} = 1.02 \left(\frac{492}{333}\right)^{3.5}$$

$$= 4 \text{ atm}$$

Therefore, $$\eta_r = \frac{2.8 - 1.02}{4 - 1.02} = 0.597$$

• PROBLEM 12-4

Using the steam tables, calculate the velocity in a nozzle at a point where the pressure is 40 Psia when the superheated steam flows from a boiler. The initial boiler conditions are

P(pressure) = 80 Psia, T(temperature) = 500^{0}F, and

V(velocity) = 0.

Solution: From the steam tables, knowing the initial conditions, it is obtained,

$$h_o = 1281.1 \text{ Btu/lbm}$$

$$S_o = 1.7346 \text{ Btu/lbm}^0\text{R}$$

This process is isoentropic. Therefore, the initial entropy is equal to the final entropy. At S = 1.7346 Btu/lbm^{0}R and P = 40 Psia by interpolation

$$T_f = 357^0 F$$

$$h_f = 1215.1 \text{ Btu/lbm}$$

$$V = \sqrt{2(h_o - h_f)g_c}$$

Therefore,

$$V = \sqrt{2 \times (1281.1 - 1215.1)\text{Btu/lbm} \times 778.26 \frac{\text{ft}\cdot\text{lb}}{\text{Btu}} \, 32.2 \frac{\text{lbm}\cdot\text{ft}}{\text{lb}\cdot\text{sec}^2}}$$

$$= 1819 \text{ ft/sec}$$

• PROBLEM 12-5

An adiabatically run air turbine has a nozzle of 4 in. diameter. The air flowing through the nozzle, has a pressure of 735 psia and a temperature of 350^{0}R. Calculate the air velocity as a function of P_2/P_1 and also the maximum output of air if k = 1.35.

Solution: The air velocity is calculated by using the velocity equation for flow through turbines, i.e.

$$V = \left(2g_c \frac{RT}{M} \frac{K}{K-1}\right)^{\frac{1}{2}} \left[1 - \left(\frac{P_1}{P_2}\right)^{(K-1)/K}\right]^{\frac{1}{2}}$$

$$V = 2.08 \times 10^3 \left[1 - \left(\frac{P_2}{P_1}\right)^{0.259}\right]^{\frac{1}{2}} \text{ ft/sec}$$

Tabulated results

P_2/P_1	V
1	0
0.9	341
0.8	492
0.7	616
0.6	733
0.5	843
0.4	955
0.3	1080
0.2	1220
0.1	1390
0	2080

To calculate maximum air output,

$$\left(\frac{P_2}{P_1}\right)_{critical} = \left(\frac{2}{1+K}\right)^{K/K+1} = 0.536$$

$$\left(\frac{P_2}{735}\right)_{critical} = 0.536$$

$$P_{2\ critical} = 394 \text{ psia}$$

$$\text{critical velocity}(V_c) = 2.08 \times 10^3 \left[1 - \left(\frac{394}{735}\right)^{0.259}\right]^{\frac{1}{2}} = 803 \text{ ft/sec}$$

$$\text{critical specific volume } (v_c) = \frac{RT_1/MP_1}{(P_2/P_1)_c^{\,1/K}} = \frac{0.177}{(P_2/P_1)_c^{\,1/K}}$$

$$= \frac{0.177}{\left(\frac{394}{735}\right)^{1/1.35}} = 0.28$$

$$\text{volume}_{critical} = 0.28 \text{ ft}^3/\text{lbm}$$

$$\text{critical mass velocity} = G_c = \frac{\text{velocity}_c}{\text{Spvolume}_c} = \frac{803}{0.28}$$

$$= 2868 \text{ lbm/ft}^2\text{sec}$$

$$\text{max. amount of air} = W_{max} = A \cdot G_c = \frac{\pi}{4} \times \left(\frac{4}{12}\right)^2 \times G_c$$

$$= 0.873 \times 10^{-3} \times 2868 = 2.5 \text{ lb/sec.}$$

NOZZLE EXIT CONDITIONS

• PROBLEM 12-6

Air is flowing tnrough a nozzle with a 90% efficiency and an expansion rate of 2.0 Kg/s. The inlet conditions are P = 550kPa and T = 680°K. If the exit pressure is 120kPa calculate the actual exit area, velocity and enthalpy. Assume K = 1.4.

Solution: The temperature T_2 is given by

$$T_2 = T_1\left(\frac{P_2}{P_1}\right)^{(k-1)/k} = 680\left(\frac{120}{550}\right)^{0.286} = 440^0K$$

The efficiency of the nozzle

$$\eta(\text{efficiency}) = \frac{h_0 - h_2'}{h_0 - h_2} = \frac{T_0 - T_2'}{T_0 - T_2} = 0.90$$

or

$$\frac{680 - T_2'}{680 - 440} = 0.9$$

Therefore the exit temperature $(T_2') = 464^0K$

The exit enthalpy$(h_2') = CpT_2' = 1.004\times464 = 465.8$ KJ/kg

The velocity$(V_2') = \sqrt{2(h_o - h_i)} = \sqrt{2Cp(T_o - T_2')}$

$$= \sqrt{2\times1004\times(680-464)} = 658 \text{ m/s}$$

Specific volume $= \frac{RT_2'}{P_2'} = \frac{287\times464}{120{,}000} = 1.109 \text{ m}^3\text{/kg}$

The exit area $= \frac{\dot{m}(\text{specific volume})}{V_2'} = \frac{(2)(1.109)}{658}$

$$= 3.37\times10^{-3}\text{m}^2$$

• PROBLEM 12-7

Air is flowing through a nozzle at a rate of 5 lb/sec. The inlet pressure and temperature is 200 psia and 400^{0}F respectively. The outlet pressure is 20 psia and the efficiency of the nozzle is 85%. Calculate the exit velocity and the exit areas for the nozzle.
Assume C_p = 0.24 Btu/lbm^{0}F and k = 1.4.

Solution:

$$T_2 = T_1\left(\frac{P_2}{P_1}\right)^{(k-1)/k}$$

$$T_2 = 860\left(\frac{20}{200}\right)^{0.286}$$

$$T_2 = 445^0R$$

The corrected temperature T_2' according to the nozzle efficiency is

$$C_p(T_1-T_2) = \eta C_p(T_1-T_2)$$

$$T_2' = T_1 - \eta(T_1-T_2)$$

$$= 860 - 0.85(860 - 445)$$

$$T_2' = 507^0R$$

Exit velocity $V_2 = \sqrt{2g_cC_p(T_1-T_2')}$

$$= \sqrt{2x32x0.24x778x(860-507)}$$

$$= 2060 \text{ ft/sec}$$

$$\text{Volume} = \frac{RT_2'}{P_2}$$

$$= \frac{1545 \text{ ft}\cdot\text{lb}_f/\text{lb mol. }^0R \times 507^0R}{20 \text{ lb}_f/\text{in}^2}$$

$$\text{Volume} = \frac{1545 \text{ ft}\cdot\text{lb}_f/\text{lb mol}^0R\ \frac{1\text{lb mol}}{29\text{lbs}} \times 507^0R}{20\ \frac{\text{lb}_f}{\text{in}^2}\ 144\text{in}^2/\text{ft}^2}$$

$$= \frac{1545x507}{20x144x29} = \frac{0.37x507}{20} = 9.37 \text{ ft}^3/\text{lb}$$

$$\text{Exit area} = \frac{W \text{ (volume)}}{\text{velocity}} = \frac{(5 \text{ lb/sec})(9.37 \text{ ft}^3/\text{lb})}{(2060 \text{ ft/sec})}$$

$$\text{Exit area} = 0.0227 \text{ ft}^2$$

• PROBLEM 12-8

A tube with an internal diameter 3 in. has air traveling through it. The entering air has a density of 0.409, a velocity of 250 ft/sec, and is at a temperature and pressure of 660 ^{0}K and 6.805 atm. Calculate the final conditions and exit velocity if the air is heated by 600 Btu/sec. Use the following data to solve the problem.

Data

mean $C_p(\text{at } 660^0R) = 0.24$

mean $C_p(0 < T < T_2) = 0.248$

Solution: $G = \rho_1 V_1 = 0.409 \times 250 = 102.25$ lb/ft^{2}sec

and,

$$GA = \frac{102 \times [\pi \times 3^2/4]}{144} = 5.0 \text{ lb/sec}$$

Therefore the amount of heat added per pound is,

$$\frac{600 \text{ Btu/sec}}{5.0 \text{ lb/sec}} = 120 \text{ Btu/lb}$$

P_2 can be solved for by using the equation,

$$P_2 + \frac{G^2}{g_c \rho_2} = P_1 + \frac{G^2}{g_c \rho_1} = (6.805\text{atm}) \times \left(14.696 \frac{\text{psia}}{\text{atm}}\right)$$

$$\times (144\text{in}^2/\text{ft}^2) + \frac{(102.25)^2}{(32.17)(0.409)}$$

$$= 15{,}195 \text{ psfa}$$

$$P_2 + \frac{(102.25)^2}{(32.17)(\rho_2)} = 15{,}195 \text{ psfa}$$

however, assuming ideal gas behavior

$$P_2 = \rho_2 R T_2, \quad R = 53.35$$

Therefore

$$53.35\rho_2 T_2 + \frac{325}{\rho_2} = 15{,}195 \tag{1}$$

from the data, mean $C_p = 0.24$ Btu/lb°F (at 660°R)

Therefore

$$h_2 + \frac{V_2^2}{2g_c} = 0.24 \times 200 + \frac{250^2}{2 \times 32 \cdot 17 \times 778} + 120$$

Therefore

$$h_2 + \frac{V_2^2}{2g_c} = 169.26$$

For $0 < T < T_2$ mean $C_p = 0.248$

$$0.248T_2 + \frac{G^2}{2g_c \rho_2^2 \times 778} = 0.248T_2 + \frac{(102.25)^2}{2(32)(\rho_2)^2 778}$$

$$= 169.26$$

Therefore

$$0.248T_2 + \frac{0.21}{\rho_2^2} = 169.26$$

or

$$0.248\rho_2 T_2 + \frac{0.21}{\rho_2} = 169.26\ \rho^2 \tag{2}$$

$$53.35\rho_2 T_2 + \frac{325}{\rho_2} = 15195 \quad (1)$$

divide eq.(1) by 215.1

$$0.248\rho_2 T_2 + \frac{1.51}{\rho_2} = 70.64 \quad (1a)$$

subtract eq.(2) from eq.(1a)

$$\frac{-1.3}{\rho_2} = 169.26\rho_2 - 70.64$$

or

$$-1.3 = 169.26\rho_2^2 - 70.64\rho_2$$

$$169.26\rho_2^2 - 70.64\rho_2 + 1.3 = 0$$

Using the quadratic equation,

$$\rho_2 = \frac{+70.64 \pm \sqrt{(-70.64)^2 - 4(169.26)(1.3)}}{2(169.26)}$$

$$\rho_2 = 0.019 \text{ lb/ft}^3$$

or

$$\rho_2 = 0.398 \text{ lb/ft}^3$$

Using the latter root, from equation (2)

$$0.248(0.398)T_2 + \frac{0.21}{0.398} = 169.96(0.398)$$

or

$$T_2 = 679.97^0\text{F}$$

Therefore

$$P_2 = \rho_2 R T_2 = (0.398)(53.35)(1139.97)$$

$$= 24{,}205 \text{ psfa}$$

$$= 168 \text{ psia}$$

$$\frac{V_2^2}{2g_c \times 778} = 169.26 - (0.248)(679.97)$$

or

$$\frac{V_2^2}{(2g_c)(778)} = 0.627$$

$$V_2^2 = 31{,}407$$

Therefore, $V_2 = 177$ ft/sec

or

$$V_2 = \frac{\rho_1 V_1}{\rho_1} = \frac{(0.409)(250)}{(0.398)}$$

$$= 256 \text{ ft/sec}$$

A nozzle has air flowing through it at a rate of 0.25 lb/sec. The inlet conditions are; $P_i = 35$ psia, $T_i = 650\,^0R$ and specific volume = 6.0 ft³/lb. The air enters with a velocity of 550 fps and leaves with a pressure of 18 psia. Compute the nozzle outlet cross-sectional area. Assume that the air expands inside the nozzle frictionlessly according to the relation $pv^{1.4}$ = constant and that the change in elevation between inlet and outlet is negligible.

Solution: The outlet specific volume (V_2) is found by using the equation, $p_1v_1^{1.4} = p_2v_2^{1.4}$, since v_1 and both pressures are known.

The outlet velocity V_2 can be calculated by using the expression,

$$W = -\int_1^2 vdp - \frac{V_2^2 - V_1^2}{2g_c} - \frac{g}{g_c}(z_2 - z_1)$$

From these values, the outlet area can be obtained by the use of the continuity equation,

$$A_2 = \frac{Mv_2}{V_2}$$

Using the equation $pv^{1.4}$ = const.,

$$v_2 = v_1\left(\frac{p_1}{p_2}\right)^{1/1.4} = 6(35/18)^{1/1.4} = 9.65 \text{ ft}^3/\text{lb}$$

Since there is no work done on or by the air, and the elevation change is negligible, the work expression reduces to,

$$\frac{V_2^2 - V_1^2}{2g_c} = -\int_1^2 vdp$$

V_1 is known and the right-hand side can be integrated since v is a function of p. This allows for the calculation of V_2.

Therefore $$\frac{V_2^2 - V_1^2}{2g_c} = -w - \int_1^2 vdp - \frac{g}{g_c}(z_2 - z_1)$$

or $$\frac{V_2^2 - V_1^2}{2g_c} = 0 - c^{1/1.4}\int_1^2 p^{-1/1.4}dp - 0$$

$$= -P_1^{1/1.4} \times v_1\left(\frac{1.4}{1.4-1}\right)\left[P_2^{(1-1/1.4)} - P_1^{(1-1/1.4)}\right]$$

$$= -\frac{1.4}{0.4}\, p_1 v_1 \left[\left(\frac{P_2}{P_1}\right)^{1-1/1.4} - 1\right]$$

$$= -\frac{1.4}{0.4}\,(35)(6.0)(144)\left[\left(\frac{18}{35}\right)^{1-1/1.4} - 1\right]$$

$$= 18{,}314 \text{ ft-lb/lb}$$

$$V_2 = \sqrt{2g_c(18{,}314) + V_1^2}$$

$$V_2 = \sqrt{2(32.2)(18{,}314) + (550)^2}$$

$$= 1217 \text{ ft/sec}$$

Therefore the exit nozzle area is

$$A_2 = \frac{MV_2}{V_2} = \frac{0.25 \times 9.65}{1217}$$

$$A_2 = 0.0019 \text{ ft}^2$$

• PROBLEM 12-10

A converging nozzle has air flowing through it. Calculate the stagnation temperature T_o and pressure p_o if at point A within the nozzle, $P_A = 40$ psia, $T_A = 2000\,^0R$, $V_A = 500$ ft/sec and A_A (cross-sectional area) = 0.2ft^2. Also calculate the sonic velocity, mach number at this section and the exit area A_B, exit pressure P_B, temperature T_B, and velocity V_B if the exit mach number is one. Assume air to be an ideal gas with $\gamma = 1.40$.

Solution: The stagnation temperature is

$$T_o = T_A + \frac{\gamma-1}{2\gamma R} V_A^2$$

Therefore,

$$T_o = 2000\,^0R + \frac{(1.4-1)(500)^2 \text{ft}^2/\text{sec}^2}{2\times1.4\times53.35\,\frac{\text{ft}\cdot\text{lb}}{\text{lbm}\,^0R}\times\frac{32\text{ lbm.ft}}{\text{lb sec}^2}}$$

$$= 2021\,^0R$$

The stagnation pressure is

$$p_o = P_A\left(\frac{T_o}{T_A}\right)^{\gamma/(\gamma-1)}$$

Therefore,

$$p_o = 40 \frac{lb}{in^2} \times \left(\frac{2021}{2000}\right)^{1.4/(1.4-1)}$$

$$= 41 \ lb/in^2$$

The sonic velocity is

$$C_A = \sqrt{\gamma R T_A}$$

$$C_A = \left(1.4 \times 53.35 \frac{ft \cdot lb}{lbm. {}^0R} \times 2000{}^0R \times 32.2 \frac{lbm \cdot ft}{lb \ sec^2}\right)^{\frac{1}{2}}$$

$$C_A = 2193 \ ft/sec$$

The mach number is,

$$M_A = \frac{V_A}{C_A} = \frac{500}{2193} = 0.228$$

The exit pressure is

$$\gamma_c = \frac{P_B}{P_o} = 0.528$$

Therefore,

$$P_B = 0.528 P_o = 0.528(41 psia) = 21.65 \ lb/in^2$$

The exit velocity is

$$V_B = C_B = \left(\frac{2\gamma}{\gamma+1} RT_o\right)^{\frac{1}{2}}$$

$$= \left(\frac{2 \times 1.4}{1.4+1} \times 53.35 \frac{ft \cdot lb}{lbm {}^0R} \times 32.2 \frac{lbm \ ft}{lbsec^2}\right)^{\frac{1}{2}}$$

$$= 2013 \ ft/sec$$

The exit temperature is,

$$T_B = \frac{2}{\gamma+1} T_o = \left(\frac{2}{1.4+1}\right)(2021{}^0R)$$

$$T_B = 1684{}^0R$$

To calculate the exit area, the mass rate of flow is required. Therefore,

$$\rho_A = \frac{P_A}{RT_A} = \frac{40 \frac{lb}{in^2} \times 144 \ in^2/ft^2}{53.35 \frac{ft \cdot lb}{lbm {}^0R} 2000{}^0R}$$

$$\rho_A = 0.054 \ lbm/ft^3$$

$$\rho_B = \frac{P_B}{RT_B} = \frac{21.65 \times 144}{53.35 \times 1684}$$

$$\rho_B = 0.035 \text{ lbm/ft}^3$$

Using the equation of continuity,

$$A_B = \frac{\rho_A A_A V_A}{\rho_B V_B} = \frac{0.054 \times 0.2 \times 500}{0.035 \times 2013} = 0.077 \text{ ft}^2$$

• PROBLEM 12-11

Find the throat area, exit area and the exit Mach number for a nozzle having an efficiency of 90%. The initial air pressure and temperature are 60 psia and 1500°R respectively. The air mass flow rate is 0.6 lb/sec and the exit pressure is 14.696 psia.

Solution: The air flow is assumed to be ideal. Therefore, the throat pressure is calculated by

$$\frac{P_c}{P_1} = \left(\frac{2}{k+1}\right)^{(k/k-1)}$$

Therefore,

$$P_c = 60\left(\frac{2}{1.4+1}\right)^{1.4/1.4-1} = 60 \times 0.53$$

$$= 31.8 \text{ psia}$$

The throat temperature is obtained by the use of the isentropic expansion equation.

$$\frac{T_c}{T_1} = \left(\frac{P_c}{P_1}\right)^{\frac{k-1}{k}}$$

Therefore,

$$T_c = 1500\left(\frac{31.8}{60}\right)^{1.4-1/1.4}$$

$$= 1251^0\text{R}$$

The throat velocity is

$$V_c = \sqrt{2gJc_pT_1(1-T_2/T_1)}$$

Therefore,

$$V_c = \left(2\times 32.2 \ \frac{\text{ft}}{\text{sec}^2}\times 778\frac{\text{ft}\cdot\text{lb}}{\text{Btu}}\times 0.24 \ \frac{\text{Btu}}{\text{lb}^0\text{R}}\times(1500-1251)^0\text{R}\right)^{\frac{1}{2}}$$

$$= 1730 \text{ ft/sec}$$

The throat specific volume is calculated by using the ideal gas equation

$$v_c = \frac{53.35 \text{ ft·lbf/lbm}^0\text{R} \times 1251^0\text{R}}{(31.8 \times 144)\text{lbf/ft}^2}$$

$$= 14.6 \text{ ft}^3/\text{lb}$$

The area of the throat is given by

$$\omega = \frac{A_1 V_1}{v_1} = \frac{A_2 V_2}{v_2}$$

Therefore,

$$0.6 \text{ lbm/sec} = \frac{A_c \times 1730 \text{ ft/sec}}{14.6 \text{ ft}^3/\text{lbm}}$$

$$A_c = 0.0051 \text{ ft}^2 = 0.729 \text{ inch}^2$$

The exit isentropic temperature is given by

$$\left(\frac{T_2}{T_1}\right) = \left(\frac{14.696}{60}\right)^{1.4-1/1.4}$$

Therefore,

$$T_2 = 1500(0.67)$$

$$= 1004^0\text{R}$$

The actual exit velocity is obtained by using the equation,

$$V_{2(\text{actual})} = \sqrt{2gJ(h_1 - h_2)\eta_n}$$

and

$$h_1 = C_p T_1$$

Therefore,

$$V_{2(\text{actual})} = \left[2 \times 32.2\text{ft/sec} \times 778\text{ft-lb/Btu} \times 0.24 \frac{\text{Btu}}{\text{lb}^0\text{R}} \times (1500 - 1004)^0\text{R} \times 0.90\right]^{\frac{1}{2}}$$

$$V_{2(\text{actual})} = 2317 \text{ ft/sec}.$$

The actual exit temperature is calculated by the equation,

$$\eta_N(h_1 - h_2)_{\text{ideal}} = (h_1 - h_2)_{\text{actual}}$$

or

$$\eta_N C_p(T_1-T_2)_{ideal} = C_p(T_1-T_2)_{actual}$$

Therefore,

$$0.90(1500-1004) = 1500 - T_{2actual}$$

$$T_{2actual} = 1054^0R$$

The exit specific volume is calculated by the ideal gas equation using $P_{exit} = 14.696$ psia and $T_{exit} = 1054^0R$.

Therefore,

$$v_{exit} = 53.35 \text{ ft-lbf/lb}^0R \times \frac{1054^0R}{14.696 \times 144 \text{ lbf/ft}^2}$$

$$v_{exit} = 26.4 \text{ ft}^3/\text{lb}$$

The exit area is obtained by the same method used before,

$$0.6 \text{ lb/sec} = \frac{A_{exit} \times 2317 \text{ ft/sec}}{26.4 \text{ ft}^3/\text{lb}}$$

$$A_{exit} = 0.0068 \text{ ft}^2 = 0.98 \text{ in}^2$$

The acoustic velocity at the exit is,

$$V_{exit} = \sqrt{gkRT_{actual}}$$

$$V_{exit} = (32.2 \text{ ft/sec}^2 \times 1.4 \times 53.35 \text{ ft}\cdot\text{lb/lb}^0R \times 1054^0R)^{\frac{1}{2}}$$

$$= 1592 \text{ ft/sec}$$

Therefore the Mach number is

$$M_{exit} = \frac{2317}{1592} = 1.45$$

• PROBLEM 12-12

Steam, flowing through a convergent nozzle, is subjected to isentropic expansion. The pressure and enthalpy at the inlet and outlet are given in the figure (1), the pressure and velocity changes across the length of the nozzle are also shown.
Derive an expression for the velocity of steam at the outlet in terms of enthapy and pressure ratio.

Convergence nozzle sections along
with (P) and (V) changes

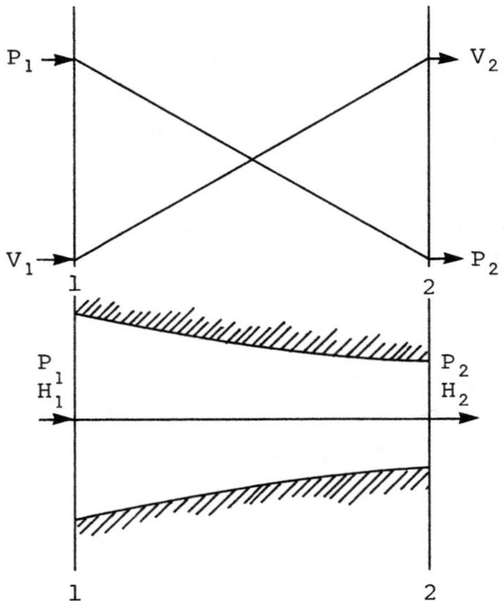

Fig. 1.

Solution (a): Consider the nozzle at sections 1-1 and 2-2. The energy balance equation for the steam flow rate of unit weight per second is given by

$$H_1 + \frac{V_1^2}{2gJ} + W \pm Q = H_2 + \frac{V_2^2}{2gJ} \qquad (1)$$

where H and V are enthalpy and velocity of steam and W and Q are work and heat transfer.

Since, the expansion through nozzle is considered as isentropic, and, also as there is no external work done during the flow of steam, both the heat transfer and work transfer have zero values

$$Q = 0$$

$$W = 0$$

Using these conditions in equation (1), we get,

$$H_1 + \frac{V_1^2}{2gJ} = H_2 + \frac{V_2^2}{2gJ}$$

$$\frac{V_2^2}{2gJ} = (H_1 - H_2) + \frac{V_1^2}{2gJ}$$

i.e. $$V_2 = \sqrt{2gJ(H_1-H_2) + V_1^2} \qquad (2)$$

Usually, the velocity of steam entering the nozzle (V_1) is very small as compared to the velocity at exit, and therefore, V_1 can be neglected.

$$V_2 \simeq \sqrt{2gJ(H_1 - H_2)} = \sqrt{2gJ(\Delta H)_{ise}}$$

$$= \sqrt{2 \times 9.81 \times 427(\Delta H)_{ise}}$$

i.e.
$$V_2 = 91.5\sqrt{\Delta H_{ise}} \qquad (3)$$

Where Δh_{ise} is the isentropic enthalpy drop per unit weight of steam when, the pressure drop is from p_1 to p_2.

This is the general energy equation irrespective of the shape.

(b) The isentropic flow of steam through the nozzle may be approximately represented by an equation.

$$pv^n = \text{constant} \qquad (4)$$

Where   n = 1·135 for saturated steam

= 1·3 for superheated steam

These values are approximate only because actually the value of n varies during the expansion.

Enthalpy of steam gets reduced during its isentropic expansion as it flows through the nozzle. The reduction in enthalpy results in an equal amount of increase in kinetic energy as given by eq.(2).

The work done during expansion is equal to the heat drop (which is equal to Rankine area).

i.e.
$$\frac{V_2{}^2}{2g} - \frac{V_1{}^2}{2g} = \left(\frac{p_1 v_1 - p_2 v_2}{1}\right)\frac{n}{n-1}$$

Where v_1 = (specific of steam at entry)

v_2 = (volume of steam at exit)

$V_1 \ll V_2$ and can be neglected

then
$$\frac{V_2{}^2}{2g} = \frac{n}{n-1}(p_1 v_1 - p_2 v_2)$$

$$= \frac{n}{n-1} p_1 v_1 \left(1 - \frac{p_2 v_2}{p_1 v_1}\right)$$

But $p_1 v_1{}^n = p_2 v_2{}^n$ by eqn. (4)

$$\frac{v_2}{v_1} = \left(\frac{p_1}{p_2}\right)^{\frac{1}{n}}$$

Substituting this in the above equation, we get

$$\frac{V_2^2}{2g} = \frac{n}{n-1} p_1 v_1 \left[1 - \frac{p_2}{p_1} \cdot \left(\frac{p_1}{p_2}\right)^{\frac{1}{n}}\right]$$

$$= \frac{n}{n-1} p_1 v_1 \left[1 - \left(\frac{p_2}{p_1}\right)\left(\frac{p_2}{p_1}\right)^{-\frac{1}{n}}\right]$$

$$= \frac{n}{n-1} p_1 v_1 \left[1 - \left(\frac{p_2}{p_1}\right)^{\frac{n-1}{n}}\right]$$

$$V_2 = \sqrt{2g \frac{n}{n-1} p_1 v_1 \left[1 - \left(\frac{p_2}{p_1}\right)^{\frac{n-1}{n}}\right]}$$

• PROBLEM 12-13

Superheated steam at 330 psia and 600°F, is flowing through a nozzle at a rate of 12,000 lb/hr. The final pressure at the exit is 5 psia. The velocity coefficient and the discharge coefficients are 0.92 and 0.95 respectively. Calculate a) the exit jet velocity and b) the areas at the throat and the exit.

Solution: Nozzles are designed at maximum rate of discharge. The pressure ratio for maximum discharge is defined as critical pressure ratio and is given by

$$\frac{P_t}{P_o} = \left(\frac{2}{n+1}\right)^{\frac{n}{n-1}}$$

For super heated steam $n = 1{\cdot}3$

$$\therefore \frac{P_t}{P_o} = 0.5457.$$

For the initial conditions

$$P_o = 330 \text{ psia} \quad T_o = 600°F$$

and mass flow rate w = 12000 lb/hr.

From steam tables

Enthalpy h_o = 1313 Btu/lb

$$\text{Entropy } S_o = 1.6153 \text{ Btu/lb}^0\text{F}$$

and $$P_t = P_o \times 0.5457$$

$$= 330 \times 0.5457 \simeq 180 \text{ psia.}$$

At P_t = 180 psia and S_o = 1.6153 Btu/lb^{0}F from tables h_{ts} = 1243·4 Btu/lb and specific volume v_{ts} = 2.8508 ft^3/lb. Also for P_2 = 5 psia and S_o = 1.6153

$$h_{2s} = 990.65 \text{ Btu/lb.}$$

a) The exit velocity is given by

$$\overline{V}_2 = C_{\overline{V}} \sqrt{2gJ(\Delta H)_{isen}}$$

where $(\Delta H)_{isen}$ = isentropic enthalpy drop

$$= h_o - h_{2s}$$

and $C_{\overline{V}}$ = velocity coefficient = 0.92.

Substituting the values

$$\overline{V}_2 = 0.92\sqrt{2\times32.2\times778\times(1313-990.65)}$$

$$\overline{V} \simeq 3697 \text{ ft/sec.}$$

b) The velocity at the throat is given by

$$\overline{V}_{ts} = \sqrt{2gJ(\Delta H)_{isen}}$$

where $$(\Delta H)_{isen} = h_o - t_{ts}$$

$$\overline{V}_{ts} = \sqrt{2\times32.2\times778\times(1313-1243.4)}$$

$$\overline{V}_{ts} = 1867.4 \text{ ft/sec}$$

The throat area is given by

$$a_t = \frac{w}{C_d} \times \frac{v_{ts}}{\overline{V}_{ts}}$$

where $C_d \rightarrow$ coefficient of discharge = 0.95

$$a_t = \frac{(12000/3600)}{0.95} \simeq \frac{2.8508}{1867.4}$$

$$= 0.00536 \text{ ft}^2 \simeq 0.772 \text{ in}^2.$$

Enthalpy at the exit is given by

$$h_2 = h_o - \eta_n(h_o - h_{2s})$$

where η_n is the nozzle efficiency = $(C_{\overline{V}})^2$.

Substituting the values

$$h_2 = 1313 - (0.92)^2 \times (1313 - 990.65)$$

$$\simeq 1040 \text{ Btu/lb.}$$

For P_2 = 5 psia and h_2 = 1040 Btu/lb

From tables specific volume $v_2 \simeq 67.6$

Therefore the exit area is given by

$$a_2 = w \times \frac{v_2}{\overline{V}_2} = \left(\frac{12000}{3600}\right) \times \frac{67.6}{3697}$$

$$\simeq 0.061 \text{ ft}^2 = 8.784 \text{ in}^2.$$

IMPULSE AND REACTION STAGES OF TURBINES

• PROBLEM 12-14

Calculate the internal efficiency and reheat factor for a three-stage turbine operating between an initial pressure of 100 psia, saturated steam, and a final pressure of 1 psia. Assume that the approach velocity is negligible, the stage efficiency is 65 percent and the process is isentropic.

Solution: The intermediate pressures, p_1, p_2 are fixed by dividing the overall enthalpy drop into equal steps.

The initial conditions are: (refer to the figure)

$$h_a = 1187.2 \text{ Btu/lb}$$

$$s_a = 1.6026 \text{ Btu/lb}^0\text{R}$$

at 1.0 psia, h_{3s} = 895 Btu/lb

and constant s = 1.6026 Btu/lb^{0}R

The enthalpy drop is divided into three parts:

$$h_{1s} = 1090 \text{ Btu/lb} \qquad P_1 = 28.0 \text{ psia}$$

$$h_{2s} = 993 \text{ Btu/lb} \qquad P_2 = 6.2 \text{ psia}$$

The internal efficiency is based on the work delivered to the shaft and does not consider the bearing losses.

$$h_1 = 1187 - 0.65(1187 - 1090) = 1124 \text{ Btu/lb}$$

$$s_1 = 1.650 \text{ Btu/lb}^0\text{R}$$

$$h_2' = 1024 \text{ Btu/lb}$$

$$h_2 = 1124 - (0.65)(1124 - 1024) = 1059 \text{ Btu/lb}$$

$$s_2 = 1.706 \text{ Btu/lb}^0\text{R}$$

$$h_3' = 953 \text{ Btu/lb}$$

$$h_3 = 1059 - (0.65)(1059 - 953) = 990 \text{ Btu/lb}$$

$$\text{Efficiency} = \frac{W_T}{h_a \quad -h_{3s}} = \frac{1187 - 990}{1187 - 895} = 0.675$$

$$\text{Reheat factor} = \frac{0.675}{0.65} = 1.04$$

• PROBLEM 12-15

Steam is flowing through a nozzle with a velocity of 1800 ft/sec at an angle of 18 deg with the rotational plane. The turbine blade has a peripheral velocity of 900 ft/sec and has the same entrance and exit angles. Compute the work done per pound of steam per second and the steam exit condition. Assume that ten percent of the initial kinetic energy relative to the blade is transformed into enthalpy by the friction of the water vapor passing over the blade.

Fig. 1.

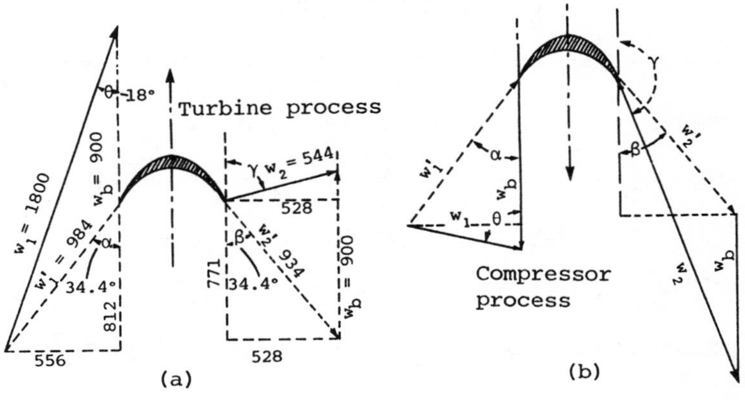

Solution: The work done is calculated as follows: (refer to figure A & B)

$$w_1\cos\theta = 1{,}800\ \cos 18^0 = 1712\ \text{ft/sec}$$

$$w_1\sin\theta = 1{,}800\ \sin 18^0 = 556\ \text{ft/sec}$$

Referring to Fig. A,

$$w_1' = \sqrt{(1712 - 900)^2 + (556)^2}$$

$\{(1712-900)$ is the actual steam velocity$\}$

$$w_1' = 984\ \text{ft/sec}$$

$$\alpha = \tan^{-1}\left(\frac{556}{812}\right) = 34.4^0$$

W_2' is calculated by

$$(W_2')^2/2g = (1 - \text{fraction of kinetic energy lost}) \times (W_1')^2/2g$$

$$(w_2')^2 = 0.9(w_1')^2 = 0.9(984)^2$$

$$w_2' = 934\ \text{ft/sec}$$

$$w_2'\cos\beta = 934\cos 34.4^0\ (\text{since } \alpha = \beta)$$

$$= 771\ \text{ft/sec}$$

$$w_2'\sin\beta = 934\sin 34.4^0 = 528\ \text{ft/sec}$$

Since W_b (peripheral velocity) is 900 ft/sec, W_2 is given by

$$W_2 = \sqrt{(900-771)^2 + (528)^2} = \sqrt{(129)^2 + (528)^2}$$

$$= 544\ \text{ft/sec}$$

$$\text{work} = (w_1\cos\theta - w_2\cos\gamma)(w_b/g)$$

$$= (1712 - 129) \times (900/32.2)$$

$$= 44{,}245\ \text{ft lb} = 56.9\ \text{Btu/(lb/sec)}$$

The exit condition is obtained as

$$H_2 - H_1 = \left\{(w_1^2 - w_2^2)/2g\right\} - W_{out}$$

$$= \left\{(1800^2 - 544^2)/64.4\right\} - 44{,}245$$

$$= 1470\ \text{ft}\cdot\text{lb} = 1.9\ \text{Btu}$$

The value of H_2 is 1.9 Btu higher than H_1 at the same pressure.

• PROBLEM 12-16

Superheated steam with an initial state of 70 psia and 400°F enters a symmetrical impulse stage turbine. The pressure of the steam after isentropic expansion is 10 psia. The velocity of the blade is 1000 ft/sec. The efficiency and the angle of the nozzle (α) are 92%, and 20° respectively. The ratio of relative velocity leaving the blade to the relative velocity entering is 0.95. If the blade outlet angle (β) is 30°, calculate (a) the work done by the stage and (b) the blade efficiency.

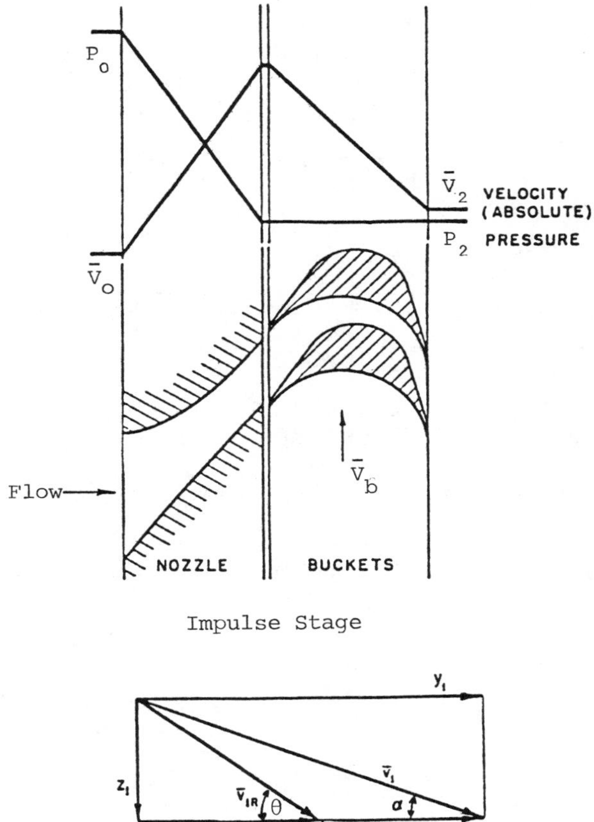

Impulse Stage

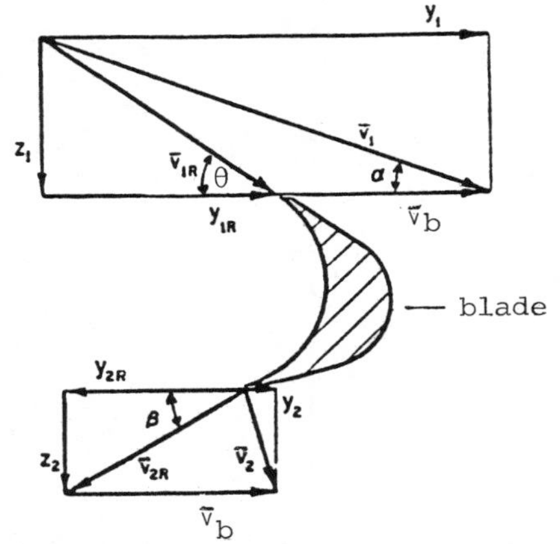

Velocity diagram for impulse stage

Solution: The impulse stage turbine setup along with the velocity diagram is shown in the figure.

At $P_o = 70$ psia and $T_o = 400^0F$ from steam tables $h_o = 1232$ Btu/lb and $S_o = 1.6951$ Btu/lb^{0}F.

Isentropic expansion occurs with the reduction of pressure to $P_1 = 10$ psia

Therefore at $P_1 = 10$ psia and $S_o = 1.6951$ Btu/lb^{0}F from steam tables $h_1 \simeq 1084$ Btu/lb. Now the velocity of the steam leaving the nozzle is given by

$$\overline{V}_1 = \sqrt{2gJ(\Delta H)_{isen} \times \eta_n}$$

where $(\Delta H)_{isen}$ = isentropic enthalpy drop

$= h_o - h_1$

and η_n = efficiency of the nozzle.

Substituting the values

$$\overline{V}_1 = \sqrt{2\times 32.2\times 778\times(1232-1084)\times 0.92}$$

$$\simeq 2612 \text{ ft/sec}$$

Then the other velocities can be calculated as the angles α and β and the bucket velocity coefficient are known.

The relations used are summarized below along with their values

$$z_1 = \overline{V}_1 \sin\alpha = 2612 \sin 20^0 = 893$$

$$y_1 = \overline{V}_1 \cos\alpha = 2612 \cos 20^0 = 2455$$

$$y_{1R} = y_1 - \overline{V}_b = 2455 - 1000 = 1455$$

$$\overline{V}_{1R} = \sqrt{z_1^2 + y_{1R}^2} = \left[(893)^2+(1455)^2\right]^{\frac{1}{2}} = 1707$$

$$\overline{V}_{2R} = C_b \overline{V}_{1R} = 0.95 \times 1707 = 1622$$

$$y_{2R} = \overline{V}_{2R} \cos\beta = 1622 \cos 30^0 = 1405$$

$$y_2 = y_{2R} + \overline{V}_b = 1405 + 1000 = 2405$$

$$z_2 = \overline{V}_{2R} \sin\beta = 1622 \sin 30^0 = 811$$

$$\overline{V}_2 = \sqrt{z_2^2 + y_2^2} = \left[(811)^2+(2405)^2\right]^{\frac{1}{2}} = 2538$$

$$\text{Blade angle}\theta = \text{Tan}^{-1}\left(\frac{z_1}{y_{1R}}\right) = \text{Tan}^{-1}\left(\frac{893}{1455}\right) \simeq 32^0$$

The work done per second per unit weight of fluid is given by,

Work = Force x Distance

$$W = (V_{2R}\cos\theta - V_{1R}\cos\beta)\frac{V_b}{g}$$

$$= (-1622\cos 32^0 - 1707\cos 30^0) \times \frac{1000}{32.2}$$

$$\simeq -88629 \text{ ft-lb/lb}$$

The negative sign has no significance here.

b) Blade efficiency is given by

$$\eta_b = \frac{W}{(\overline{V}_1^2/2g)} = \frac{(88629)(2)(32.2)}{(2612)^2} = 0.837$$

$$\eta_b \simeq 84\%$$

• PROBLEM 12-17

The isentropic enthalpy drop for a fluid flow through a simple impulse turbine stage is 60 Btu/lb. Pressure and velocity profiles along with the velocity component diagrams are shown in figures 1 and 2. Assume the approach velocity to be negligible. For the data given below, calculate

(a) the work done per pound of fluid flow;

(b) the axial thrust per pound of fluid flow per second; and

(c) the nozzle-bucket efficiency.

$C_{\overline{V}} = 0.9$ $\qquad \overline{V}_b = 750$ ft/sec

$C_b = 0.85$ $\qquad \alpha = 25^0$

and $\qquad \beta = 35^0$.

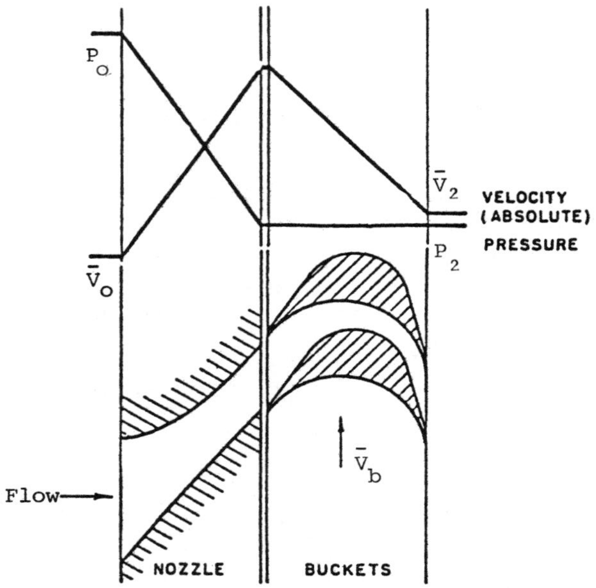

Fig. 1. Impulse Stage

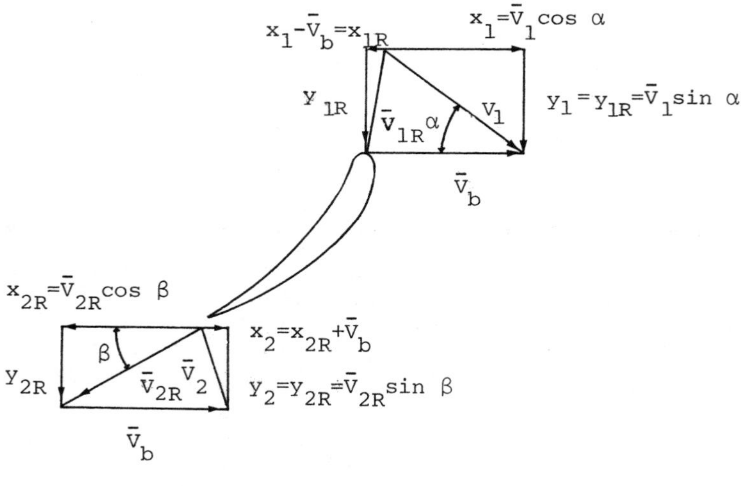

Fig. 2. Velocity components

Solution: Energy equation for nozzle, considering the flow rate of unit weight per second is given by

$$\frac{\overline{V}_1^{\,2}}{2gJ} + H_1 = \frac{V^2}{2gJ} + H + W \pm Q$$

Since the expansion through the nozzle is considered as isentropic and since no external work is done during the flow, both the heat transfer and the work done have zero values.

$$\therefore \quad \frac{\overline{V}_1^2}{2gJ} + H_1 = \frac{V^2}{2gJ} + H$$

As the approach velocity of fluid to the nozzle is very small compared to the velocity at exit V can be neglected.

$$\therefore \quad \frac{V_1^2}{2gJ} \simeq H - H_1 = (\Delta H)_{ise}$$

(isentropic drop)

Considering the velocity factor $C_{\overline{V}}$

$$\overline{V}_1 = C_{\overline{V}} \sqrt{2gJ(\Delta H)_{ise}} \qquad (1)$$

Substituting the values

$$\overline{V}_1 = 0.9\sqrt{2\times 32.2\times 778\times 60}$$

$$\simeq 1560 \text{ ft/sec}$$

Therefore the components

$$x_1 = \overline{V}_1\cos\alpha = 1560\cos 25^0 \simeq 1414 \text{ ft/sec}$$

$$y_1 = \overline{V}_1\sin\alpha = 1560\sin 25^0 = 659 \text{ ft/sec}$$

Therefore $\quad x_{1R} = x_1 - \overline{V}_b = 1414 - 750 = 664$ ft/sec

$$\overline{V}_{1R} = \sqrt{x_{1R}^2 + y_1^2} = \sqrt{(664)^2 + (659)^2}$$

$$= 935.5 \text{ ft/sec}$$

$$\overline{V}_{2R} = C_b\overline{V}_{1R} = 0.85 \times 935.5 \simeq 795 \text{ ft/sec}$$

and $\quad x_{2R} = -795 \times \cos 35^0 \simeq -651$ ft/sec

Negative tangential direction is indicated in x_{2R} and

$$y_2 = \overline{V}_{2R}\sin\beta = 795 \times \sin 35^0$$

$$\simeq 456 \text{ ft/sec}$$

(a) Work done per pound of the fluid flowing is given by

$$W_x = \frac{x_{1R} - x_{2R}}{g}\overline{V}_b$$

$$= \frac{664 + 651}{32.2} \times 750$$

$\simeq 30629$ ft lbf/lbm.

(b) The axial force on the bucket by the fluid flow is given by

$$F_A = \frac{W}{g}(y_1 - y_2) + p_1 a_1 - p_2 a_2$$

For a simple turbine, no pressure drop occurs and the area of cross-section would be the same throughout.

Therefore,

$$F_A = \frac{W}{g}(y_1 - y_2) = \frac{1}{32.2} \times (659 - 456)$$

$$= 6.3 \text{ lbf/lbm per sec.}$$

(c) Nozzle blade efficiency is given by

$$\eta_{nb} = \frac{W_x}{\left(\frac{\bar{V}_1}{C_{\bar{V}}}\right)^2 \Big/ 2g} = \frac{30629}{\left(\frac{1560}{0.9}\right)^2 \Big/ 2 \times 32.2} \simeq 0.66$$

• **PROBLEM 12-18**

A fluid is moving through a single stage impulse turbine with a weight flow rate of 20 lb/min. The absolute nozzle outlet velocity and the blade velocity are 1600 ft/sec and 900 ft/sec respectively. The nozzle angle is 10° while the blade angle at the outlet is 33°. Neglecting the turbulence and the frictional effects, calculate

a) the force exerted on the moving blades, and

b) the rate of mechanical energy transmitted.

Velocity diagram for impulse turbines

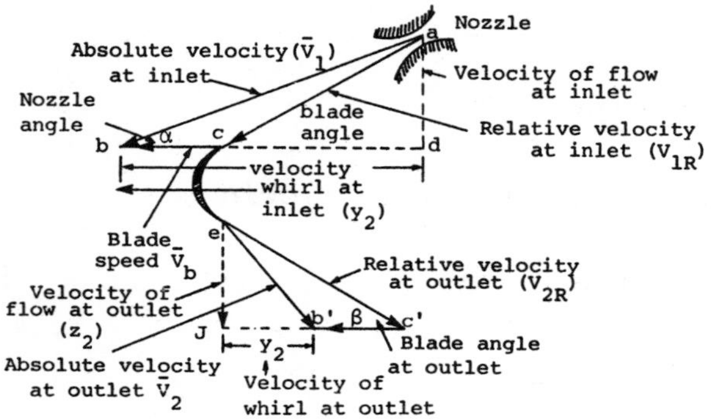

$bd = y_1 = \bar{V}_1 \cos\alpha$

$cd = y_{1R} = y_1 - \bar{V}_b$

$ca = \bar{V}_{1R} = \sqrt{z_1^2 + y_{1R}^2}$

$c'e = \bar{V}_{2R} = C_b \bar{V}_{1R}$

$Jc' = y_{2R} = \bar{V}_{2R} \cos\beta$

$Jb' = y_2 = y_{2R} + \bar{V}_b$

$Je = z_2 = \bar{V}_{2R} \sin\beta$

$eb' = \bar{V}_2 = \sqrt{z_2^2 + y_2^2}$

Solution: The velocity diagram for the single stage impulse turbine is shown in the figure.

Whirl velocity at the inlet is given by

$$y_1 = \overline{V}_1 \cos\alpha$$

where $\overline{V}_1$ - Absolute velocity of the fluid at the inlet = 1600 ft/sec.

and α - the nozzle angle = 10^0.

Therefore, $y_1 = 1600\cos 10^0 \simeq 1576$ ft/sec.

Relative velocity at the inlet is given by

$$\overline{V}_{1R}^2 = \overline{V}_1^2 + \overline{V}_b^2 - 2\overline{V}_1\overline{V}_b\cos\alpha \text{ (by law of cosine)}$$

$$= (1600)^2 + (900)^2 - 2 \times 1600 \times 900 \times \cos 10^0$$

Therefore, $\overline{V}_{1R} \simeq 731$ ft/sec.

Then relative velocity at the outlet is given by

$$\overline{V}_{2R} = C_b\overline{V}_{1R}$$

Since frictional effect is neglected $C_b = 1$. Therefore,

$$\overline{V}_{2R} = \overline{V}_{1R} = 731 \text{ ft/sec.}$$

$$y_{2R} = -\overline{V}_{2R}\cos\beta = -731\cos 33^0$$

$$= -613 \text{ ft/sec.}$$

Therefore, $y_2 = y_{2R} + \overline{V}_b = -613 + 900$

$$= 287 \text{ ft/sec.}$$

a) Force exerted on the moving blade is given by

F = Force exerted on the fluid in the negative direction

= mass × change in velocity

$= w \times (y_1 - y_2)$

$= \dfrac{20/60}{32.2} \times (1576 - 287)$

$\simeq 13.34$ lb.

b) Rate of mechanical energy transmitted is given by

$$E_T = \text{Force} \times (\text{Blade Velocity})$$

$= F \times V_b$

$= 13.34 \times 900$

$= 12006$ ft.lb/sec. $\simeq$ 15.43 Btu/sec.

MASS FLOW RATE THROUGH A NOZZLE

• PROBLEM 12-19

Derive an expression for the maximum discharge rate and maximum velocity at the exit for the isentropic expansion of steam through a nozzle.

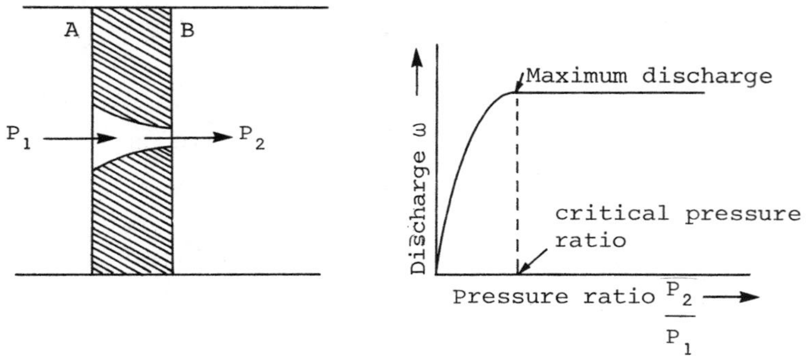

Fig. 1. Discharge as a function of pressure ratio

Solution: a) Consider an isentropic expansion of steam through a nozzle from pressure p_1 to p_2.

The velocity at the exit (V_2) is given by

$$V_2 = \sqrt{2g \frac{n}{n-1} p_1 v_1 \left[1 - \left(\frac{p_2}{p_1}\right)^{\frac{n-1}{n}}\right]} \quad (1)$$

The flow of steam through the nozzle is given by

$$m_s = \frac{A_2 V_2}{v_2} \quad (2)$$

where m_s = Mass of steam passing through the nozzle per second.

A_2 = Area at exit of convergent nozzle or at the throat of convergent divergent nozzle.

V_2 = Velocity at exit

v_2 = Volume of unit weight of steam at exit of nozzle.

Substituting the value of V_2 from equation (1) into equation (2)

$$m_s = \frac{A_2}{v_2}\sqrt{2g\,\frac{n}{n-1}\,p_1 v_1\left[1 - \left(\frac{p_2}{p_1}\right)^{\frac{n-1}{n}}\right]}$$

But $p_1 v_1{}^n = p_2 v_2{}^n$

$$v_2 = v_1\left(\frac{p_1}{p_2}\right)^{\frac{1}{n}} = v_1\left(\frac{p_2}{p_1}\right)^{-\frac{1}{n}}$$

Substituting this value of v_2 in the above equation,

$$m_s = \frac{A_2}{v_1}\left(\frac{p_2}{p_1}\right)^{+\frac{1}{n}}\sqrt{2g\,\frac{n}{n-1}\,p_1 v_1\left[1 - \left(\frac{p_2}{p_1}\right)^{\frac{n-1}{n}}\right]}$$

$$\therefore\ m_s = \frac{A_2}{v_1}\sqrt{2g\,\frac{n}{n-1}\,p_1 v_1\left[\left(\frac{p_2}{p_1}\right)^{\frac{2}{n}} - \left(\frac{p_2}{p_1}\right)^{\frac{n+1}{n}}\right]} \qquad (3)$$

The above equation shows that the flow is dependent on $\frac{p_2}{p_1}$ only as n is fixed.

Therefore for maximum discharge

$$\frac{dm_s}{d\left(\frac{p_2}{p_1}\right)} = 0$$

$$\therefore\ \frac{d}{d\left(\frac{p_2}{p_1}\right)}\left[\left(\frac{p_2}{p_1}\right)^{\frac{2}{n}} - \left(\frac{p_2}{p_1}\right)^{\frac{n+1}{n}}\right] = 0$$

i.e.,

$$\frac{2}{n}\left(\frac{p_2}{p_1}\right)^{\frac{2}{n}-1} - \frac{n+1}{n}\left(\frac{p_2}{p_1}\right)^{\frac{n+1}{n}-1} = 0$$

on simplification gives

$$\frac{p_2}{p_1} = \left(\frac{2}{n+1}\right)^{\frac{n}{n-1}} \qquad (4)$$

This pressure ratio which gives maximum discharge through the nozzle is known as critical pressure ratio

where $n = 1.135$ for saturated steam

and $n = 1.3$ for superheated steam.

Now substituting equation (4) in equation (3)

$$(m_s)_{max} = \frac{A_2}{v_1}\left[2g\frac{n}{n-1}p_1v_1\left[\left\{\left(\frac{2}{n+1}\right)^{\frac{n}{n-1}}\right\}^{\frac{2}{n}} - \left\{\left(\frac{2}{n+1}\right)^{\frac{n}{n-1}}\right\}^{\frac{n+1}{n}}\right]\right]^{\frac{1}{2}}$$

on simplification

$$= A_2\sqrt{2g\frac{n}{n-1}\left(\frac{p_1}{v_1}\right)\left(\frac{2}{n+1}\right)^{\frac{n+1}{n-1}}\left(\frac{n-1}{2}\right)}$$

i.e.

$$(m_s)_{max} = A_2\sqrt{g\cdot n\left(\frac{p_1}{v_1}\right)\left(\frac{2}{n+1}\right)^{\frac{n+1}{n-1}}} \tag{5}$$

Thus the mass flow of the steam is independent of the exit pressure but depends on initial pressure and throat area.

b) The maximum velocity of steam at the throat of the nozzle is obtained by substituting the value of the critical pressure ratio (eq. 4) in equation (1).

$$(V_2)_{max} = \sqrt{2g\frac{n}{n-1}p_1v_1\left[1-\left\{\left(\frac{2}{n+1}\right)^{\frac{n}{n-1}}\right\}^{\frac{n-1}{n}}\right]}$$

and on simplification

$$(V_2)_{max} = \sqrt{2g\frac{n}{n+1}p_1v_1}$$

• PROBLEM 12-20

Air behaving as an ideal gas at 25 Bar and 50°C enters a converging nozzle having the exit cross-sectional area $6\times10^{-4}m^2$ with negligible initial velocity. The flow is isentropic. Calculate the mass flow rate (Kg/sec) and the linear velocity (m/sec) at the exit if

a) the exit pressure is 15 Bar, and

b) the exit pressure is 12 Bar.

Properties of air: $C_p = 32$ KJ/kg.mol.°K

$C_V = 20.84$ KJ/kg.mol.°K

and $M = 29$ Kg/Kg.mol.

<u>Solution</u>: The critical pressure for the flow through nozzle is given by

$$P_c = P_1\left(\frac{2}{n+1}\right)^{\frac{n}{n-1}} \tag{1}$$

where $P_1 = 25$ Bar.

and $n = \frac{C_p}{C_V} = \frac{32}{20.84} \simeq 1.5355.$

Therefore $P_c = 25\left(\frac{2}{1.5355+1}\right)^{\frac{1.5355}{0.5355}} \simeq 12.66$ Bar.

a) The exit pressure is greater than P_c. Therefore the mass flow rate is subsonic and is given by

$$m_s = A_2\sqrt{2g_c\,\frac{n}{n-1}\,p_1\rho_1\left[\left(\frac{p_2}{p_1}\right)^{\frac{2}{n}} - \left(\frac{p_2}{p_1}\right)^{\frac{n+1}{n}}\right]} \tag{2}$$

where $\frac{p_2}{P_1} = \frac{15}{25} = 0.6$

and $\rho_1 = \frac{MP_1}{RT_1} = \frac{29(25\times10^5)}{(8314)(273+50)} \simeq 26.99$ Kg/m³

and $A_2 = 6\times10^{-4}\text{m}^2.$

$$m_s = 6\times10^{-4}\left\{(2)(1)\left(\frac{1.5355}{0.5355}\right)(25\times10^5)(26.99) \times\left[(0.6)^{\frac{2}{1.5355}} - (0.6)^{\frac{2.5355}{1.5355}}\right]\right\}^{\frac{1}{2}}$$

$\simeq 3.42$ kg/sec.

Velocity V is given by

$$V = \sqrt{2g_c \frac{n}{n-1} \frac{p_1}{\rho_1} \left[1 - \left(\frac{p_2}{p_1}\right)^{\frac{n-1}{n}}\right]}$$

$$= \sqrt{(2)(1)\left(\frac{1.5355}{0.5355}\right)\frac{(25\times10^5)}{26.99}\left[1 - (0.6)^{\frac{0.5355}{1.5355}}\right]}$$

$V \simeq 295$ m/sec.

b) Exit pressure = 12 Bar = 12×10^5 N/m^2.

Since the pressure is below the critical pressure

$$m = A_2\sqrt{g_c n(p_1\rho_1)\left(\frac{2}{n+1}\right)^{\frac{n+1}{n-1}}}$$

$$m = 6 \times 10^{-4}\sqrt{(1)(1.5355)(25\times10^5)(26.99)\left(\frac{2}{2.5355}\right)^{\frac{2.5355}{0.5355}}}$$

$\simeq 3.48$ kg/sec.

Throat velocity of the air is given by

$$V_{max} = \sqrt{2g_c \frac{n}{n+1} \frac{p_1}{\rho_1}}$$

$$= \sqrt{(2)(1)\left(\frac{1.5355}{2.5355}\right)\frac{(25\times10^5)}{(26.99)}}$$

$\simeq 335$ m/sec

• PROBLEM 12-21

Steam at 450 psia and 600°F, with negligible initial velocity is flowing through a nozzle. The nozzle efficiency and the area of the throat are 93% and 0.75 in^2 respectively. The exit steam is at 30 psia after the isentropic expansion in the nozzle. Calculate

a) the mass flow rate at equilibrium flow;

b) the mass flow rate at supersaturated flow; and

c) the exit area.

Solution: At Pressure $P_1 = 450$ psia

and Temperature $T_1 = 600^0F$

from the steam tables

Enthalpy $h_1 = 1302.5$ Btu/lb

Specific volume $v_1 = 1.2691$ ft^3/lb

and Entropy $S_1 = 1.5711$ Btu/lb^{0}F.

For Pressure $P_2 = 30$ psia and $S_1 = S_2 = 1.5711$ Btu/lb^{0}F from steam tables $h_2 \simeq 1076$ Btu/lb from Mollier diagram Quality of steam = 11.5% = 0.115, efficiency of the nozzle $\eta_n = 0.93$.

$$\therefore \quad 0.93 = \frac{h_1 - h_2'}{(h_1 - h_2)_s} = \frac{1302.5 - h_2'}{(1302.5 - 1076)}$$

$$\therefore \quad h_2' \simeq 1092 \text{ Btu/lb.}$$

and $$v_2' \simeq 12.9 \text{ ft}^3/\text{lbm.}$$

a) For equilibrium flow at the throat

$$P_{t(e)} = 0.545P_1 = 0.545 \times 450 \simeq 245 \text{ psia}$$

and $$S_{t(e)} = S_1 = 1.5711 \text{ Btu/lb-}^0\text{F}$$

From steam tables $h_{t(e)} = 1234.6$ Btu/lb.

$$v_{t(e)} = 1.9333 \text{ ft}^3/\text{lb.}$$

$$V_{t(e)} = 223.8\sqrt{h_1 - h_{t(e)}}$$

$$= 223.8\sqrt{1302.5 - 1234.6}$$

$$V_{t(e)} \simeq 1844 \text{ ft/sec.}$$

$$\text{mass flow rate } m = \frac{A_t \times V_{t(e)}}{v_{t(e)}}$$

$$= \frac{(0.75/144)(1844)}{1.9333}$$

$$\therefore m \simeq 4.97 \text{ lb/sec.} \qquad \text{(a)}$$

b) For supersaturated flow, velocity at the throat is given by

$$V_{t(s)} = \sqrt{2g \frac{n}{n-1} p_1 v_1 \left[1 - \left(\frac{p_2}{p_1}\right)^{\frac{n-1}{n}}\right]}$$

where n = 1.3 for superheated steam.

$$V_{t(s)} = \sqrt{(2)(32.2)\left(\frac{1.3}{0.3}\right)(450\times144)(1.2691)\left[1-\left(\frac{245}{450}\right)^{\frac{0.3}{1.3}}\right]}$$

$$\simeq 1733 \text{ ft/sec}$$

Now

$$v_{t(s)} = v_1\left(\frac{p_1}{p_t}\right)^{1/n} = (1.2691)\left(\frac{450}{245}\right)^{1/1.3}$$

$$\cong 2.026 \text{ ft}^3/\text{lb.}$$

$$\text{mass flow rate } m = \frac{A_t \times V_{t(s)}}{v_{t(s)}}$$

$$= \frac{(0.75/144)(1733)}{2.026}$$

$$\therefore m = 4.46 \text{ lb/sec} \qquad \text{(b)}$$

From (a) and (b)

$$\text{error for } m = \frac{(0.51)100}{4.97} = 10.3\%$$

c) At the exit

$$V_2' = 223.8\sqrt{h_1 - h_2'}$$

$$= 223.8\sqrt{1302.5 - 1092}$$

$$= 3247 \text{ ft/sec}$$

$$\text{Area at the exit } A_2' = \frac{mv_2'}{V_2'}$$

$$= \frac{4.46 \times 12.9}{3247}$$

$$= 0.01772 \text{ ft}^2$$

$$\therefore A_2' \cong 2.55 \text{ in}^2.$$

• PROBLEM 12-22

An ideal gas, at 42 psia and 250°F, enters a convergent conical channel having an inlet diameter of 6.5 in. and an outlet diameter of 0.5 in.

Neglecting the effect of friction, calculate

a) the maximum rate of flow through the channel at the entrance in lb/min and ft³/min;

b) the linear velocity at the outlet in ft/sec;

c) the outlet temperature; and

d) the rate of flow in lb/min if the outlet pressure is 30 psia.

The properties of gas are

molecular weight = 14.0

heat capacity C_p = 0.55.

Solution: The isentropic gas flow through the nozzle (conical channel) can be defined by

$$PV^n = \text{constant}$$

where
$$n = \frac{C_p}{C_V} \text{ and } b = \frac{1.985}{14} = 0.1418$$

For finding C_V; $C_V = C_p - b$

$$= 0.55 - \frac{1.985}{14}$$

$$= 0.408$$

$$\therefore \quad n = \frac{0.55}{0.48} = 1.146$$

For maximum discharge through nozzle

$$\frac{P_2}{P_1} = \left(\frac{2}{n+1}\right)^{\frac{n}{n-1}} = \left[\frac{2}{(1.146+1)}\right]^{\left(\frac{1.146}{1.146-1}\right)} = 0.5752$$

$$\therefore \quad P_2 = P_1 \times 0.5752 = 42 \times 0.5752 = 24.158 \text{ psia}$$

$$V_1 = \frac{(10.73)(250 + 460)}{14 \times 42} = 12.96 \text{ ft}^3/\text{lb.}$$

Specific volume at the outlet

$$v_2 = \frac{2}{n+1}\left(\frac{P_1 V_1}{P_2}\right) = \frac{2}{2.146}\left[\frac{42 \times 12.96}{24.158}\right]$$

$$\simeq 21 \text{ ft}^3/\text{lb.}$$

a) Maximum rate of flow through the nozzle is given by

$$m_{(max)} = A_2\sqrt{gn\left(\frac{p_1}{v_1}\right)\left(\frac{2}{n+1}\right)^{\frac{n+1}{n-1}}}$$

Substituting the values

$$m_{(max)} = \frac{\pi\times(0.5/12)^2}{4}\sqrt{(32.2)(1.146)\times\left(\frac{42\times144}{12.96}\right)\left[\frac{2}{1.146+1}\right]^{\frac{2.146}{0.146}}}$$

$$= 0.1066 \text{ lb/sec} \simeq 6.4 \text{ lb/min.}$$

b) Linear velocity at the outlet

$$V_2 = \frac{m_{(max)}v_2}{A_2} = \frac{0.1066\times 21}{\pi/4\times(0.5/12)^2}$$

$$\simeq 1642 \text{ ft/sec.}$$

c) Temperature at the outlet is given by

$$T_2 = T_1\left[\frac{P_2}{P_1}\right]^{b/C_p} = (250+460)\left[0.5752\right]^{\frac{0.1418}{0.55}}$$

$$\simeq 616^0\text{R} = 156^0\text{F}$$

d) General equation for the mass flow rate through the nozzle is given by

$$m = \frac{A_2}{V_1}\sqrt{2g\,\frac{n}{n-1}\,P_1V_1\left[\left(\frac{P_2}{P_1}\right)^{2/n} - \left(\frac{P_2}{P_1}\right)^{\frac{n+1}{n}}\right]}$$

Substituting the values knowing the pressure $P_2 = 30$ psia,

$$m = \frac{[\pi/4\times(0.5/12)^2]}{12.96}\left(2\times32.2\times\left(\frac{1.146}{0.146}\right)\times42\times12.96 \times\left[\left(\frac{30}{42}\right)^{2/1.146} - \left(\frac{30}{42}\right)^{\frac{2.146}{1.146}}\right]\right)^{\frac{1}{2}}$$

$$m \simeq 8.428\times10^{-3}\text{lb/sec} = 0.505 \text{ lb/min}$$

CHAPTER 13

HEAT TRANSFER

CONDUCTION

• PROBLEM 13-1

Determine the rate of heat flow per unit area through a composite wall, as shown in the figure. A 2 in. layer of fire brick ($k_1 = 1.0$ Btu/hr ft °F) is placed between two 0.25 in. thick steel plates ($k_3 = 30$ Btu/hr ft °F). The surface of the brick face adjoining the steel plate is rough and has only 30 percent of the brick area in contact with the steel plates. The average height of the asperities is 1/32 inch. If the temperatures on the two outer steel plates are 200°F and 800°F respectively, find the rate of heat flow per unit area.

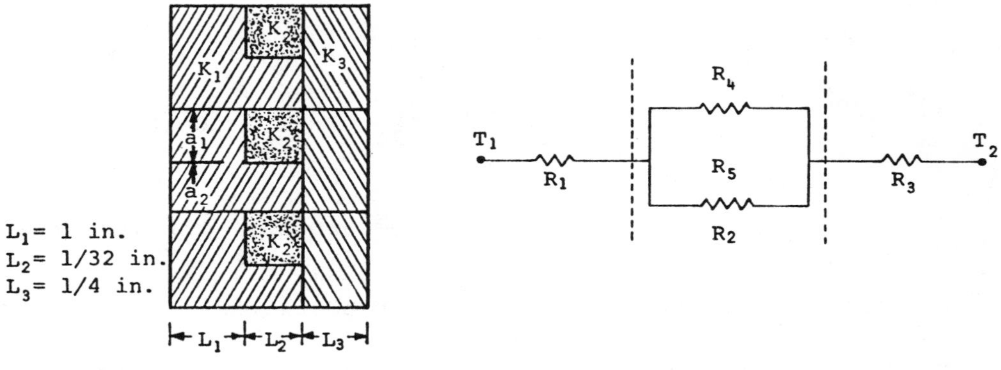

Fig. 1 Thermal circuit for a parallel-series composite wall. (T_1 is at the center.)

Solution: For the wall section shown it is assumed that the asperities are evenly distributed. Then the overall heat transfer coefficient for the composite wall is

$$u = \frac{1/2}{R_1 + \frac{R_4 R_5}{R_4+R_5} + R_3} \tag{1}$$

The thermal resistance of the steel plate (R_3), on the basis of unit area is

$$R_3 = \frac{L_3}{k_3} = \frac{0.25}{(12)(30)}$$

$$= 0.694 \times 10^{-3} \text{hr sq ft}^0\text{F/Btu}$$

The thermal resistance of the brick asperities, per unit area is

$$R_4 = \frac{L_2}{0.3k_1} = \frac{1/32}{12\times0.03\times1}$$

$$= 8.7 \times 10^{-3} \text{ hr sq ft}^0\text{F/Btu}$$

The air trapped in between the steel plate and the fire brick is very less and the effects of convection are negligible. Hence, the heat transfer through the air is assumed to take place by conduction alone. The thermal conductivity of air is taken at 300^0F and is equal to k_a=0.02 Btu/hr ft^{0}F. Then the thermal resistance of air (R_5) is

$$R_5 = \frac{L_2}{0.7\ k_a} = \frac{1/32}{12\times0.7\times0.02}$$

$$= 187 \times 10^{-3} \text{ hr sq ft}^0\text{F/Btu}$$

The factors 0.3 and 0.7 used in calculating R_4 and R_5 are the percent areas of the total areas for the two separate heat flow paths.

The total thermal resistance for the two paths, R_4 and R_5, is

$$R_2 = \frac{R_4 R_5}{R_4+R_5}$$

$$= \frac{8.7\times187\times10^{-6}}{(8.7+187)\times10^{-3}} = 8.3\times10^{-3}\text{hrsqft}^0\text{F/Btu}$$

Therefore, the thermal resistance of one-half the fire brick R_1 is

$$R_1 = \frac{1}{2}\frac{L_1}{k_1} = \frac{1}{2}\frac{2}{12\times1.0} = 83.5\times10^{-3}\text{hr sq ft}^0\text{F/Btu}$$

Then, the value of u, the overall heat transfer coefficient is determined by substituting the values of R_1, $R_2(R_4+R_5)$ and R_3 in equation 1,

$$u = \frac{1/2}{R_1+R_2+R_3}$$

$$= \frac{1/2}{83.5+8.3+0.69} = 5.4 \text{ Btu/hr sq ft}^0\text{F}$$

Heat transfer rate (q/A) is given by

$$q/A = u \,\Delta T$$

$$= 5.4(800-200) = 3250 \text{ Btu/hr sq ft}$$

The thermal resistance due to the roughness of the adjoining surfaces is called contact resistance.

• PROBLEM 13-2

> Determine the temperature distribution in a semi-infinite two-dimensional flat plate shown in the figure, if the base temperature is F(x) and the ambient temperature is T_∞.

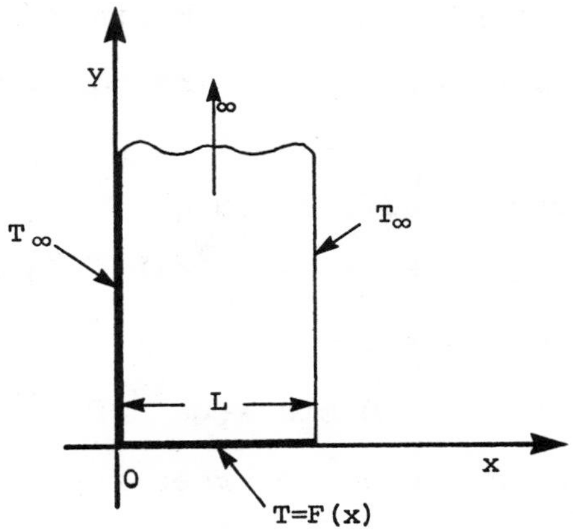

Solution: The controlling differential equation is

$$\frac{\partial^2 T}{\partial x^2} + \frac{\partial^2 T}{\partial y^2} = 0$$

and the given boundary conditions are

$$T(x,0) = F(x); \quad T(L,y) = T_\infty$$

$$T(0,y) = T_\infty \quad ; \quad T(x,\infty) = T_\infty$$

Since the boundary conditions are not homogeneous, the differential equation cannot be solved by the method of separation of variables. It requires the differential equation and three of the boundary conditions to be homogeneous. This can be achieved by a simple transformation

$$\theta = T - T_\infty$$

Writing the differential equation and boundary conditions in terms of θ,

$$\frac{\partial^2\theta}{\partial x^2} + \frac{\partial^2\theta}{\partial y^2} = 0 \quad (1)$$

$$\theta(x,0) = F(x) - T_\infty = f(x) \quad (2)$$

$$\theta(0,y) = 0 \quad (3)$$

$$\theta(L,y) = 0 \quad (4)$$

$$\theta(x,\infty) = 0 \quad (5)$$

The solution to the equation (1) by the method of separation of variables is

$$\theta(x,y) = (A \cos\lambda x + B \sin\lambda x)(Ce^{\lambda y} + De^{-\lambda y})$$

where

A, B, C, D and λ are constants.

Using the boundary condition (3)

$$\theta(0,y) = (A+0)(Ce^{\lambda y} + De^{-\lambda y}) = 0$$

Therefore $A = 0$

so, $$\theta(x,y) = B \sin\lambda x(Ce^{\lambda y} + De^{-\lambda y})$$

The constant B can be absorbed into the constants C and D.

Therefore,

$$\theta(x,y) = \sin\lambda x(Ce^{\lambda y} + De^{-\lambda y})$$

Using the boundary condition (5)

$$\theta(x,\infty) = \sin\lambda x(Ce^{\infty} + De^{-\infty}) = 0$$

From the above equation $C = 0$. Therefore the differential equation becomes

$$\theta(x,y) = \sin\lambda x(De^{-\lambda y})$$

Now using the boundary condition (4)

$$\theta(L,y) = De^{-\lambda y} \sin\lambda L = 0$$

Since $D \neq 0$, $\sin\lambda L = 0$

Therefore $\lambda L = n\pi \qquad n = 1,\ldots\infty$
or

$$\lambda = \frac{n\pi}{L} \qquad (6)$$

The solution $\theta(x,y) = De^{-\lambda y} \sin\lambda x$, is a particular solution of the equation (1).

The general solution is obtained by summing all the particular solutions.

Therefore $\theta(x,y) = \sum_{n=L}^{\infty} D_n e^{-\lambda_n y} \sin\lambda_n x$ is the general solution.

Using the non-homogeneous boundary condition (2)

$$f(x) = \sum_{n=L}^{\infty} D_n \sin\lambda_n x$$

This is a Fourier series. The value of D_n is

$$D_n = \frac{\int_0^L f(x)\sin\lambda_n x\,dx}{\int_0^L \sin^2\lambda_n x\,dx}$$

Simplifying, this reduces to

$$D_n = \frac{2}{L}\int_0^L f(x)\sin\lambda_n x\,dx$$

Substituting the value of D_n into the general solution,

$$\theta(x,y) = \frac{2}{L} \sum_{n=1}^{\infty} \left[\int_0^L f(\eta)\sin\lambda_n\eta\,d\eta\right] e^{-\lambda_n y} \sin\lambda_n x$$

where η is a dummy variable.

Equation (7) is the required temperature distribution.

● **PROBLEM 13-3**

The walls of a furnace 3 ft.× 4 ft.× 2.5 ft., are made from a refractory material $4\frac{1}{2}$ in. thick and having an average thermal conductivity of 0.8 Btu/hr ft°F.

The inner and outer surface temperatures are 400°F and 100°F, respectively. Determine the heat loss by conduction over a period of 24 hours.

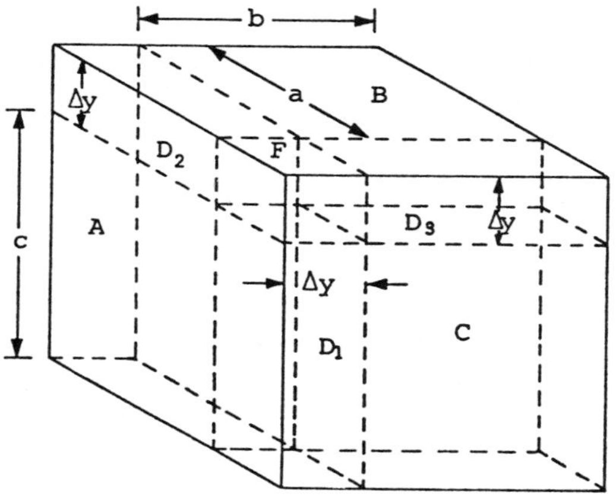

Fig. 1 Corner section of a furnace wall.

Solution: For an arbitrary number of plane sections having a total area of $\sum A$ and M edges, the shape factor is

$$S = \frac{\sum A}{\Delta y} + 0.54\ aM \tag{1}$$

where the shape factor for an edge section, s=0.54a has been experimentally determined. The quantities Δy and a are shown in the figure.

Similarly, the shape factor for corner sections has been experimentally determined. For N corners,

$$S = 0.15(\Delta y)N \tag{2}$$

Since the inside dimensions are greater than 1/5 the thickness of the wall, the combined shape factor for plane sections and corners is determined by combining equations (1) and (2), which gives

$$S = \left(\frac{2(3\times4) + 2(4\times2.5) + 2(3\times2.5)}{4.5/12}\right) + (4(0.54)[4+3+2.5])$$

$$+ \left(8(0.15)\ \frac{4.5}{12}\right)$$

$$= 157.5 + 20.5 + 0.45$$

The first, second and third terms represent the individual shape factor for the plane sections, the edge sections and the corners, respectively.

The heat flow per hour is given by

$$Q = Sk(t_1 - t_2)$$

$$q = 178.5(0.8)(400 - 100)$$

$$= 42,800 \text{ Btu/hr}$$

Therefore, after 24 hours, the heat loss is

$$Q = 42,800 \times 24$$

$$= 1,028,000 \text{ Btu.}$$

• PROBLEM 13-4

Find the solution for a region, with steady state heat conduction, having boundaries at x=0, x=a, y=0 and y=f(x) and boundary conditions as shown in the figure. Use the Galerkin method of partial integration, with respect to the y variable. Take the heat generation rate to be constant.

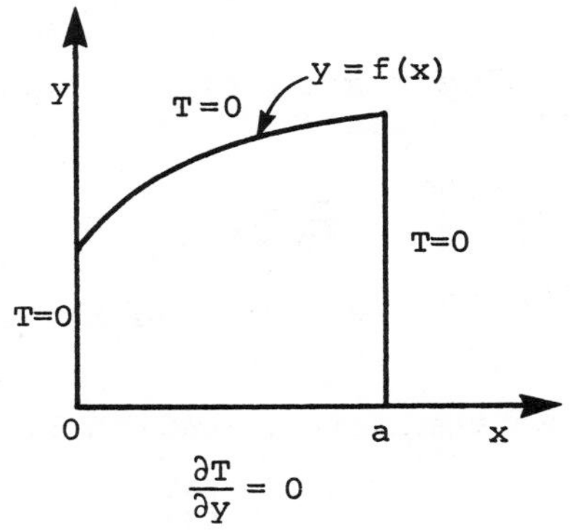

Solution: The appropriate equations and boundary conditions for this problem are

$$\frac{\partial^2 T}{\partial x^2} + \frac{\partial^2 T}{\partial y^2} + \frac{g}{k} = 0 \quad \text{in } 0 < x < a,\ 0 < y < f(x) \tag{1a}$$

$$T = 0 \qquad \text{at } x=0, x=a, \text{ and } y=f(x) \tag{1b}$$

$$\frac{\partial T}{\partial y} = 0 \qquad \text{at } y=0 \tag{1c}$$

Using the Galerkin method, partial integration of equation (1a) with respect to y, yields

$$\int_{y=0}^{f(x)} \left[\frac{\partial^2 T}{\partial x^2} + \frac{\partial^2 T}{\partial y^2} + \frac{g}{k}\right] \phi_i(y)dy = 0 \tag{2}$$

Now, taking a one-term trial solution

$$T_1(x,y) = X(x) \cdot \phi_1(y) \tag{3a}$$

where

$$\phi_1(y) = [y^2 - f^2(x)] \tag{3b}$$

The boundary conditions y=0 and y=f(x) are satisfied by this solution, but the function X(x) is not known. Substituting the trial solution into equation (2) and doing a partial integration with respect to the y variable, gives an ordinary differential equation which can be used to determine the function X(x),

$$2/5\ f^2X'' + 2ff'X' + (ff''+f'^2 - 1)X = -\frac{g}{2k} \text{ in } 0<x<a \tag{4a}$$

$$\text{for } X = 0 \quad \text{at} \quad x = 0 \quad \text{and} \quad x = a \tag{4b}$$

The function X(x) can be determined, once the function f(x), defining the form of the boundary, is specified. There are two special cases:

1. y = f(x) = b: The region is rectangular and the equation (4a) becomes

$$X'' - \frac{5}{2b^2}X = \frac{-5g}{4b^2k} \qquad \text{in } 0 < x < a \tag{5a}$$

$$X = 0 \quad \text{at } x = 0 \text{ and } x = a, \tag{5b}$$

and the one term approximate solution becomes

$$T_1(x,y) = (y^2 - b^2)X(x) \tag{6}$$

where $$X(x) = \frac{g}{2k}\left[1 - \frac{\cos h\left(\sqrt{2.5}\ \frac{x}{b}\right)}{\cos h\left(\sqrt{2.5}\ \frac{a}{b}\right)}\right]$$

2. $y = f(x) = \beta x$: For this case eq.(4a) becomes

$$x^2X'' + 5xX' + \frac{5(\beta^2-1)}{2\beta^2}\ X = \frac{5g}{4\beta^2 k} \quad \text{in } 0 < x < a \tag{7a}$$

$$x = 0 \quad \text{at} \quad x = 0 \quad \text{and} \quad x = a \tag{7b}$$

Equation (7a) is an Euler type equation that can be solved by finding a solution for X(x) in the form x^n. Substitution of $X = x^n$ into the homogenous part of eq.(7a), gives the expression

$$n^2 + 4n + \frac{5(\beta^2-1)}{2\beta^2} = 0 \tag{8a}$$

Hence

$$n_1,\ n_2 = -2 \pm \sqrt{4 - B} \tag{8b}$$

where $$B \equiv \frac{5(\beta^2-1)}{2\beta^2} \tag{8c}$$

Hence the complete solution for X(x) can be written as

$$X(x) = c_1x^{n_1} + c_2x^{n_2} - P(x) \tag{8d}$$

where P(x) is the particular solution of equation (7a)

$$P(x) = g/2k(\beta^2-1)$$

and the coefficients c_1 and c_2 are determined by the application of the boundary conditions given in equation (7b). Since the solution of X(x) is now known, the one term approximate solution is

$$T_1(x,y) = (y^2-\beta^2x^2)\ X(x)$$

• PROBLEM 13-5

A 3 inch schedule 40 pipe is covered with two layers of insulations. The inner layer (k_1=0.050) is 2 inches thick and the outer layer (k_2=0.037) is $1\frac{1}{4}$ inches thick. Calculate the heat loss, in Btu/hr per unit length, if the outer surface temperature of the pipe is 670°F and the outer surface temperature of the outer layer of insulation is 100°F.

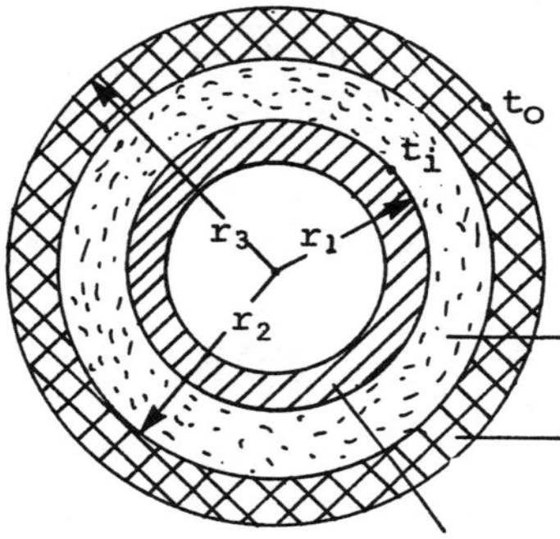

Solution: The outer diameter of the pipe is the inner diameter of the first layer of insulation. Therefore,

Outer diameter of pipe = 3.50 in., $r_1 = 1.75$ in.

Outer diameter of first layer = 3.50 + 4.00 = 7.50 in.

$r_2 = 3.75$ in.

Outer diameter of second layer = 7.50 + 2.50 = 10.0 in.,

$r_3 = 5.0$ in.

For the first layer of insulation, the mean radius is

$$r_{m_1} = \frac{r_2 - r_1}{\ln(r_2/r_1)}$$

$$= \frac{3.75 - 1.75}{\ln(3.75/1.75)} = 2.62 \text{ in.}$$

For the second layer of insulation, the mean radius is

$$r_{m_2} = \frac{r_3 - r_2}{\ln(r_3/r_2)}$$

$$= \frac{5.00 - 3.75}{\ln(5.00/3.75)} = 4.345 \text{ in.}$$

The thermal resistance of the first layer of insulation is

$$R_1 = \frac{r_2 - r_1}{2\pi k_1 r_{m_1}}$$

$$= \frac{3.75 - 1.75}{2\pi(0.05)(2.62)} = 2.43$$

The thermal resistance of the second layer of insulation

$$R_2 = \frac{r_3 - r_2}{2\pi k_2 r_{m_2}}$$

$$= \frac{5.00-3.75}{2\pi(0.037)4.345} = 1.24$$

The heat loss (q), per unit length, is given by

$$q = \frac{\Delta T}{R_1 + R_2}$$

$$= \frac{670-100}{2.43+1.24}$$

$$q = 155.3 \text{ Btu/hr} \quad \text{per foot length of pipe}$$

• **PROBLEM 13-6**

A right circular cylinder, having a constant thermal conductivity k and no heat generation, has all its surfaces at 0 except for the surface at z=L which has the temperature $T = T_0 J_0(2.405r/R)$. The temperature T is a function of the radial coordinate r, T_0 is a known constant and $J_0(2.405\ r/R)$ is the ordinary Bessel function of the first kind and zero order. Derive an exact analytical expression for the steady state temperature distribution within the cylinder.

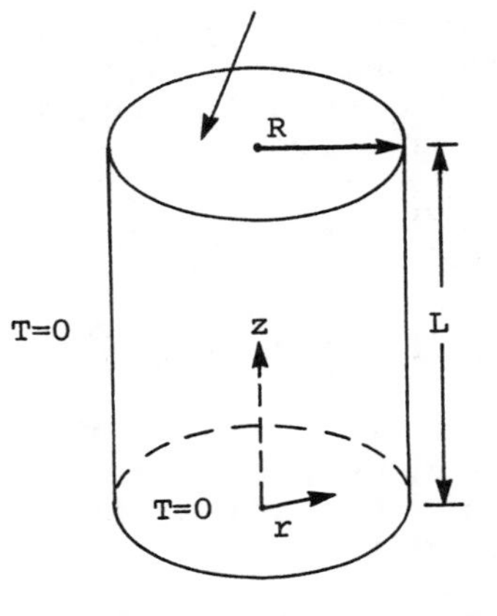

The circular cylinder

<u>Solution</u>: The most appropriate equation for this problem is the general conduction equation in the circular cylindrical coordinate system

$$\frac{\partial^2 T}{\partial r^2} + \frac{1}{r}\frac{\partial T}{\partial r} + \frac{1}{r^2}\frac{\partial^2 T}{\partial \theta^2} + \frac{\partial^2 T}{\partial z^2} + \frac{q'''}{k} = \frac{1}{\alpha}\frac{\partial T}{\partial \tau}$$

Dropping the generation term, the transient term and the circumferential conduction term, the equation reduces to

$$\frac{\partial^2 T}{\partial r^2} + \frac{1}{r}\frac{\partial T}{\partial r} + \frac{\partial^2 T}{\partial z^2} = 0 \qquad (1)$$

The boundary conditions are

(a) At $r = 0$ and $0 < z < L$ $\partial T/\partial r = 0$

(b) At $r = R$ and $0 < z < L$ $T = 0$

(c) At $z = 0$ and $0 < r < R$ $T = 0$

(d) At $z = L$ and $0 < r < R$ $T = T_0 J_0(2.405\ r/R)$

Equation (1) is solved by the separation of variables technique. Let the solution be of the form $T=Q(r)\ P(z)$. Substitute in eq.(1) and separate the functions

$$\frac{d^2Q/dr^2 + (1/r)dQ/dr}{Q} = \frac{-d^2P/dz^2}{P}$$

Since Q depends only on r and P depends only on z, the left-hand side depends only on r and the right-hand side depends only on z. The left-hand side of the equation must equal the right-hand side for all values of r and z in the conduction region, even though r and z can be varied independently of each other.

This equality can hold only if both sides of the equation are equal to the same constant, say $-\lambda^2$. This is called the separation constant. Equate both sides of equation (1) to $-\lambda^2$, which gives

$$\frac{d^2P}{dz^2} - \lambda^2 P = 0 \qquad (2)$$

$$\frac{d^2Q}{dr^2} + \frac{1}{r}\frac{dQ}{dr} + \lambda^2 Q = 0 \qquad (3)$$

Equation (2) is solved by the classical operator technique, and since the z domain is finite, the results are converted to the hyperbolic functions

$$P = A_1 \sinh \lambda z + A_2 \cosh \lambda z$$

Equation (3) is a Bessel equation whose solution is given as

$$Q = B_1J_0(\lambda r) + B_2y_0(\lambda r)$$

Hence,

$$T = [B_1J_0(\lambda r) + B_2y_0(\lambda r)](A_1\sinh\lambda z + A_2\cosh\lambda z) \qquad (4)$$

Applying boundary condition (a) to eq.(4), the derivative with respect to r gives a term $J_1(\lambda r)$ and $y_1(\lambda r)$. Since $J_1(0)=0$ and $y_1(0) \to -\infty$, $B_2=0$ is taken to satisfy boundary condition (a).

Let $B_1A_2 = C_2$
and
$B_1A_1 = C_1$

Equation (4) becomes

$$T = J_0(\lambda r)(C_1\sinh \lambda z + C_2 \cosh \lambda z) \qquad (5)$$

For boundary condition (b) to exist, it is required that at $r=R$, $T=0$ for all z. Hence,

$$0 = J_0(\lambda R)(C_1\sinh \lambda z + C_2\cosh \lambda z)$$

The functions of z cannot satisfy the condition, which must hold for all z in the region

$$J_0(\lambda R) = 0 \qquad (6)$$

Equation (6) is a transcendental equation for the positive roots of the equation, that is, for the values of $\lambda_n R$ that make J_0 equal to zero. To determine these roots, plot $J_0(\lambda R)$ versus λR. The points at which the curve cuts the λR axis are those values of λR which satisfy equation (6). Now equation (5) becomes

$$T = J_0(\lambda_n r)(C_1\sinh \lambda_n z + C_2\cosh \lambda_n z) \qquad (7)$$

Applying the boundary condition (c) to equation (7) gives $C_2=0$; hence, equation (7) becomes

$$T = C_1\sinh \lambda_n z J_0(\lambda_n r) \qquad (8)$$

There are an infinite number of solutions, because there are an infinite number of λ_n which satisfy all the conditions, except condition (d) which has not been considered as yet. Boundary condition (d) is: at $z=L$ and $0< r < R$

$$T = T_0J_0(2.405\ r/R) \qquad (9)$$

Setting z=L and multiplying the arguments in equation (8) of both sinh $\lambda_n z$ and $J_0(\lambda_n r)$ above and below by R and equating it to equation (9), yields

$$C_1 \sinh(\lambda_n RL/R) J_0(\lambda_n R\ r/R) = T_0 J_0(2.405\ r/R) \qquad (10)$$

This equation can only be solved if 2.405 is a value of $\lambda_n R$ that satisfies equation (6), else the solution of equation (8), in the form of equation (11) has to be used

$$T = \sum_{n=1}^{\infty} C_n \sinh \lambda_n z J_0(\lambda_n r) \qquad (11)$$

Now taking $\lambda_n R=2.405$, it is seen from equation (10) that

$$C_1 = \frac{T_0}{\sinh(2.405\ L/R)}$$

Hence, the steady state temperature distribution is

$$T(r,z) = T_0 \frac{\sinh(2.405\ z/R)}{\sinh(2.405\ L/R)} J_0(2.405\ r/R)$$

• PROBLEM 13-7

(a) A steam pipe, having an outside temperature of 180^0F, is buried in the earth (k=0.60 Btu/hr ft^{0}F) at a depth of 2 feet. The diameter of the pipe is 6 inches. If the soil surface temperature is at 50^0F, calculate the heat transfer rate per foot from the pipe.

(b) If the heat transfer rate, from the pipe in part (a), is to be reduced to 100 Btu/hr ft by adding insulation (k_a=0.03 Btu/hr ft^{0}F), while the physical system remains the same, determine the required outside diameter of the insulation.

Solution: The physical system is that of a horizontal pipe buried in a semi-infinite medium having an isothermal surface. The conduction shape factor for this system, having the restrictions $L \gg D$ and $D > 3r$ is

$$S = \frac{2\pi}{\cosh^{-1}(2z/D)}$$

The shape factor for this system is

$$S = \frac{2\pi}{\ln(2D/r)}$$

where D = Depth = 2 ft.
r = Radius = 3in. = 0.25ft.

Therefore

$$S = \frac{2\pi}{\ln(4/0.25)}$$

Shape factor $S = 2.26$

Heat loss $q = kS(T_1 - T_2)$

where T_1 = Outer surface temp=180 °F
T_2 = Ground surface temp=50 °F

Therefore

$$q = 0.6 \times 2.26(180 - 50)$$

$$q = 176.28 \text{ Btu/hr ft}$$

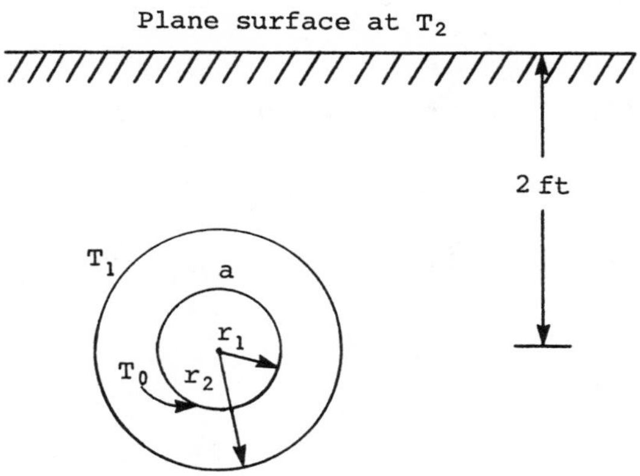

The buried steampipe.

(b) In this case, the outside surface temperature of the insulation is unknown. An expression for heat loss (q) in terms of the shape factor for the system is

$$q = kS(T_1 - T_2) \tag{1}$$

and the expression for the conduction heat transfer rate across 'a', in the absence of transients, heat generation, or heat flow in any other direction other than radial is given as

$$q = \frac{2\pi k_a(T_0 - T_1)}{\ln(r_2/r_1)} \quad (2)$$

where r_2 = outer radius of insulation

Since $r_2/r_1 = d_2/d_1 = d_2/0.5 = 2d_2$, equation (2) becomes

$$q = \frac{2\pi(0.03)(180 - T_1)}{\ln(2d_2)}$$

$$= \frac{0.1884(180 - T_1)}{\ln(2d_2)} \quad (3)$$

Rearranging equation (1) and substituting in equation (3) we get,

$$T_1 = T_2 + q/kS \quad (1)$$

$$q = \frac{0.1884(180 - T_2 - q/kS)}{\ln(2d_2)} \quad (3)$$

$$0 = 180 - T_2 - q/kS - q \ln 2d_2/0.1884$$

$$q = \frac{180 - T_2}{5.3\ln(2d_2) + 1/kS} \quad (4)$$

Since the depth D = 2ft., the shape factor is

$$S = \frac{2\pi}{\cosh^{-1}(2D/r_2)}$$

because in this case the restriction is only

$$L \gg r$$

The second restriction $D > 3r$, which was a valid restriction in part(a), is not applicable as the outer radius of the insulation is not known.

$$S = \frac{2\pi}{\cosh^{-1}(2/\tfrac{1}{2}d_2)}$$

$$= \frac{2\pi}{\cosh^{-1}(4/d_2)}$$

$$kS = \frac{0.6 \times 2\pi}{\cosh^{-1}(4/d_2)}$$

and $$1/kS = \frac{\cosh^{-1}(4/d_2)}{1.2\pi}$$

$$= 0.266 \cosh^{-1}(4/d_2)$$

Substituting this value of 1/kS into equation (4) gives

$$q = \frac{180 - T_2}{5.3\ln(2d_2)+0.266\cosh^{-1}(4/d_2)}$$

substituting the values

$$T_2 = 50^0F$$

$$\text{and } q = 100 \text{ Btu/hr ft}$$

$$100 = \frac{180 - 50}{5.3\ln(2d_2)+0.266\cosh^{-1}(4/d_2)} \qquad (5)$$

Equation (5) must be solved by the method of trial and error.

$$5.3\ln(2d_2) + 0.266\cosh^{-1}(4/d_2) = 1.3$$

1st trial

let $d_2 = 1$ ft.

$$5.3\ln(2) + 0.266\cosh^{-1}(4) = 4.22.$$

This value of d_2 is too high.

2nd trial

let $d_2 = 0.60$ ft.

$$5.3\ln(1.2) + 0.266\cosh^{-1}(6.67) = 1.65$$

The value of d_2 is still high.

3rd trial

let $d_2 = 0.55$

$$5.3\ln(1.1)+ 0.266\cosh^{-1}(7.27)= 1.22$$

This value is very close, but lower than the required value of d_2.

4th trial

let $d_2 = 0.56$

$$5.3\ln(1.12) + 0.266\cosh^{-1}(7.14) = 1.3$$

The outside diameter of the insulation should therefore be about $d_2 = 0.56$ ft. = 6.72 in.

• PROBLEM 13-8

The lateral surface of a copper rod is insulated and its two ends are maintained at a constant temperature of 70°F. The rod is 0.2 in. in diameter and 1 ft. long and its thermal conductivity is 220 Btu/hr ft°F. Conduction in the rod is one-dimensional (along the length). Calculate the maximum electrical current that may be carried by the rod, such that the temperature at any point should not exceed 250°F. Do the calculations for two values of electrical resistivity

a) Constant at 1.73×10^{-6} ohm-cm

b) equal to $1.73[1+0.002(t-70)]\times10^{-6}$ ohm-cm

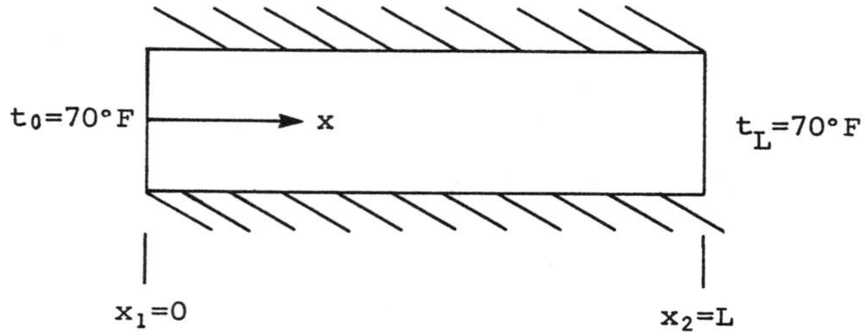

Solution: The resistance of the wire R is given as

$$R = \frac{\text{resistivity} \times \text{length}}{\text{cross-sectional area}}$$

$$= 1.73 \times 10^{-6} \times \frac{1}{2.54} \times \frac{12}{\frac{\pi(0.2)^2}{4}}$$

$$= 2.60 \quad 10^{-4} \text{ ohm.}$$

The differential equation applicable to this case is

$$\frac{d^2t}{dx^2} + \frac{q^*}{k} = 0$$

The boundary conditions are

$$\text{at } x = x_1 \qquad t = t_1$$

$$x = x_2 \qquad t = t_2$$

Using these conditions, the differential equation can be solved. Integrating twice gives

$$t + \frac{q^*}{k}\frac{x^2}{2} = Bx + C$$

Solving for the constants by inserting the boundary conditions,

$$B = \frac{t_2-t_1}{x_2-x_1} + \frac{q^*}{2k}(x_2+x_1)$$

$$C = \frac{x_2t_1-x_1t_2}{x_2-x_1} - \frac{q^*}{2k}x_1x_2$$

Inserting these constants in the integrated expression,

$$t = \left[t_i + \frac{t_2-t_1}{x_2-x_1}(x-x_1)\right] + \left[\frac{q^*(x_2-x_1)^2}{2k}\right]\left[\frac{x-x_1}{x_2-x_1} - \left(\frac{x-x_1}{x_2-x_1}\right)^2\right]$$

Substituting the numerical values into this equation,

$$250 = \left[70 + \frac{70-70}{1}(0.5)\right] + q^*\frac{(1)^2}{2\times 220}\left[\frac{0.5}{1} - \frac{0.5}{1}^{2}\right]$$

from which

$$q^* = 3.168\times 10^5 \text{ Btu/hr ft}^3$$

Also,

$$q^* = \frac{RI^2}{\text{Volume}}$$

Equating these two expressions for q^*,

$$3.168\times 10^5 = \frac{2.60\times 10^{-4}\times I^2\times 3.413}{\left[12\times\pi\times\frac{(0.2)^2}{4}\right]/1728}$$

from which the maximum current I is found to be 279 Amp.

(b) The given linear resistivity law yields a linear resistance

$$R = 2.60\times 10^{-4}[1 + 0.002(t-70)]$$

The heat generation will also depend linearly on temperature, with the rate constant $b=0.002\ 1/^{\circ}F$. This is because linearly dependent heat generation follows the relation

$$q^* = q_L^*[1+b(t-t_L)]$$

The differential equation in this case is

$$\frac{d^2t}{dx^2} + \frac{q_L^*}{k}[1+b(t-t_L)] = 0$$

The boundary conditions are

At $x=0$: $\frac{dt}{dx} = 0$

At $x=L$: $t = t_L$

This differential equation when solved gives the expression for q* and also the expression

$$t_0 = t_L + \frac{1}{b}\left(\frac{1}{\cos mL} - 1\right)$$

$$\text{where } m = \sqrt{b \frac{q_L^*}{k}}$$

Substituting the numerical values in this equation gives

$$250 = 70 + \frac{1}{0.002}\left[\frac{1}{\cos(0.5m)} - 1\right]$$

and

$$m = 1.489 \text{ 1/ft.}$$

Therefore,

$$q_L^* = (1.489)^2 \frac{220}{0.002}$$

$$= 2.44 \times 10^5 \text{ Btu/hr ft}^3$$

The quantity q_L^* is the dissipated energy corresponding to the coefficient in the above resistance law. Again, equating both the expressions for q_L^*

$$q_L^* = 2.44 \times 10^5 = \frac{2.60\times10^{-4}\times I^2\times3.413}{[12\times\pi\times\frac{(0\cdot2)^2}{4}]/1728}$$

or

$$I = 245 \text{ Amp.}$$

• PROBLEM 13-9

A fin of length L having an insulated tip, has a uniform initial temperature T_∞, equal to that of the ambient. The base temperature is suddenly changed to T_0 and is maintained at that temperature. Find a first order solution that gives the approximate temperature variation in the fin.

Solution: The solution involves the penetration depth, and its formulation may be given in two successive time domains. In the first domain, the penetration depth is less than or equal to the length of the fin, and in the second domain, the temperature of the tip rises from zero to a steady value.

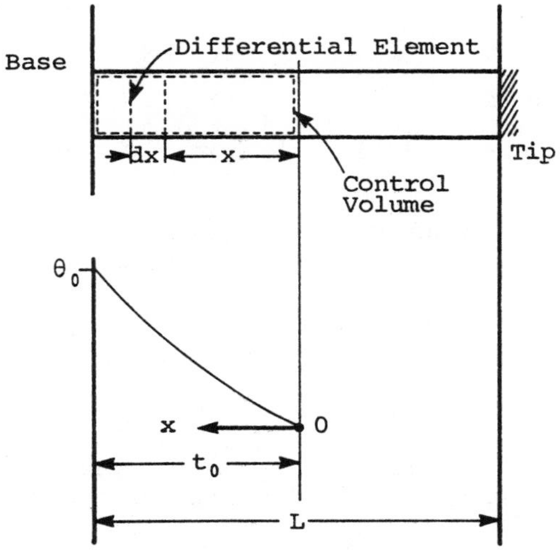

Fig. 1

Consider the lumped control volume and the differential system shown in Fig. 1, the integral formulation of the problem for the first time domain is

$$\frac{1}{a}\frac{d}{dt}\int_0^{\tau_0} \theta dx = \left(\frac{\partial \theta}{\partial x}\right)_{x=\tau_0} - m_2\int_0^{\tau_0} \theta dx, \tag{1}$$

where $\theta = T - T_\infty$ and x has its origin at the penetration depth.

It is convenient to select a spacewise parabolic, timewise unspecified Kantorovich profile which satisfies the boundary conditions of the problem and which is expressed in terms of the penetration depth

$$\frac{\theta(x,t)}{\theta_0} = \left(\frac{x}{\tau_0}\right)^2 \tag{2}$$

Insertion of equation (2) into equation (1) and subsequent integration gives the nonlinear differential equation

$$\frac{d\tau_0}{dt} + am^2\tau_0 = \frac{6a}{\tau_0},$$

which can be made linear in terms of $\tau_0^2/2$ as follows:

$$\frac{d(\tau_0^2/2)}{dt} + 2am^2(\tau_0^2/2) = 6a. \tag{3}$$

Equation (3) is to be satisfied by the condition

$$\tau_0(0) = 0 \tag{4}$$

and the solution is

$$\tau_0^2 = \frac{6}{m^2}\left(1 - e^{-2am^2t}\right), \tag{5}$$

This equation is now used to determine the penetration time, t_0, at which $\tau_0(t_0) = L$. It is given as

$$t_0 = \frac{1}{2am^2}\ln\left(\frac{1}{1-\mu^2/6}\right), \tag{6}$$

where $\mu = mL$.

Now, inserting equation (5) into equation (2) and rearranging, the temperature of the fin in the first domain is obtained,

$$\frac{\theta(x,t)}{\theta_0} = \frac{m^2x^2}{6[1 - \exp(-2am^2t)]} \tag{7}$$

The differential and lumped systems for the second time domain are shown in Fig. 2.

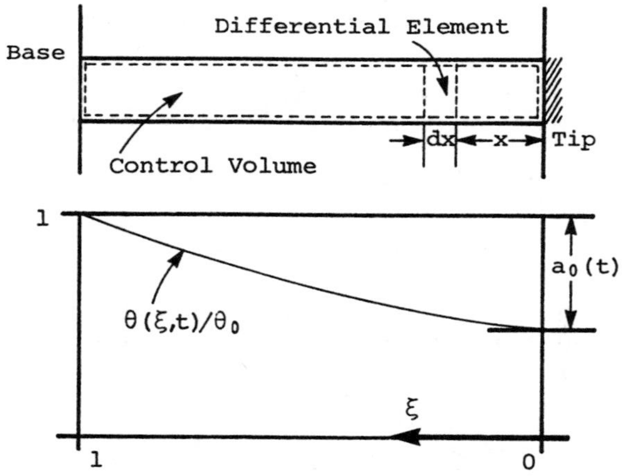

Fig. 2

Since the tip of the fin is insulated, rather than referring to figure (2), the integral formulation of the problem for the second time domain is obtained by replacing τ_0 by L in equation (3).

$$\frac{1}{a}\frac{d}{dt}\int_0^L \theta dx = \left(\frac{\partial\theta}{\partial x}\right)_{x=L} - m^2\int_0^L \theta dx.$$

Now, introducing the dimensionless variable $\xi = x/L$ and the parameter $\mu = mL$ in equation (8), which on rearranging gives

$$\frac{L^2}{a}\frac{d}{dt}\int_0^1 \theta d\xi = \left(\frac{\partial\theta}{\partial\xi}\right)_{\xi=1} - \mu^2 \int_0^1 \theta d\xi .$$

The first order Ritz profile is employed, a_0 is a time dependent parameter, and the function $a_0(t)$ is to be determined, therefore

$$\theta(\xi,t)/\theta_0 = 1 - (1 - \xi^2)a_0(t). \quad (10)$$

This is a first order Kantorovich profile. Inserting equation (10) into equation (9) and integrating, we get

$$\frac{da_0}{dt} + \frac{3a}{L^2}\left(1 + \frac{\mu^2}{3}\right) a_0 = \frac{3a}{L^2}\left(\frac{\mu^2}{2}\right). \quad (11)$$

The initial condition to be employed on equation (11) is

$$a_0(t_0) = 1 \quad (12)$$

Then the solution of equation (11) which satisfies eq. (12) is

$$a_0(t) = \frac{\mu^2/2}{1+\mu^2/3} + \frac{1-\mu^2/6}{1+\mu^2/3} \exp\left[-3\left(1 + \frac{\mu^2}{3}\right)\frac{a(t-t_0)}{L^2}\right]. \quad (13)$$

Introducing equation (13) into equation (10) gives the temperature of the fin in the second time domain,

$$\frac{\theta(\xi,t)}{\theta_0} = 1 - (1-\xi^2)\left\{\frac{\mu^2/2}{1+\mu^2/3} + \frac{1-\mu^2/6}{1+\mu^2/3}\exp\left[-3\left(1 + \frac{\mu^2}{3}\right)\frac{a(t-t_0)}{L^2}\right]\right\}. \quad (14)$$

As $t \to t_0$, equation (14) approaches the upper limit of the first time domain solution, equation (2) for $\tau_0 = L$, and as $t \to \infty$, it tends to the steady solution given by the equation

$$\frac{\theta(\xi)}{\theta_0} = 1 - \frac{\mu^2/2}{1+\mu^2/3}(1 - \xi^2) \quad (15)$$

The error of equation (14) is of the order of that obtained in eq.(15).

• PROBLEM 13-10

A wire, 5/8 in. diameter, at a temperature of 500^0F is suddenly exposed to a cooling medium which is at 110^0F. Evaluate the temperature response when the cooling medium is

a) water ($h = 15$ Btu/hr.ft^2. ^{0}F.) and

b) air ($h = 2$ Btu/hr.ft^2.^{0}F.)

Given the properties of the wire material

$$\rho = 560 \text{ lb/ft}^3 , \quad k = 216 \text{ Btu/hr.ft.}^0\text{F}$$

and $C_p = 0.09$ Btu/lb.^{0}F.

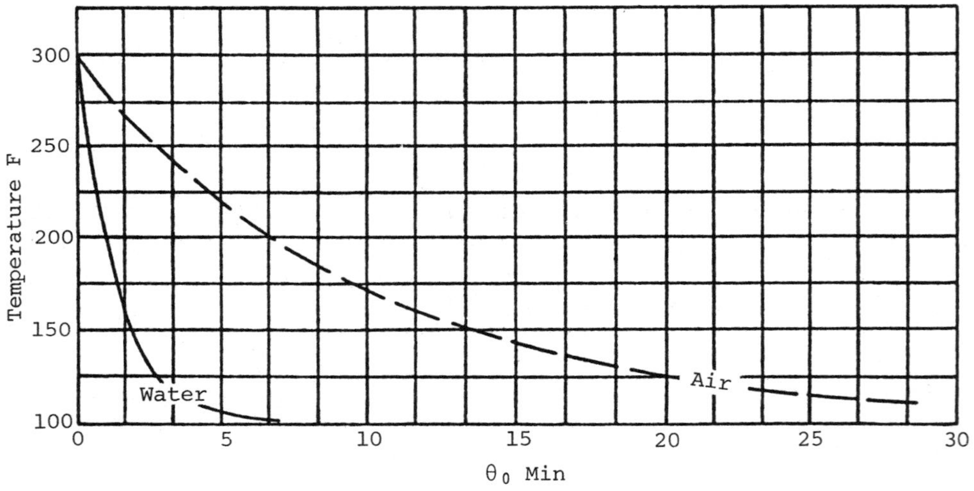

Cooling of wire in air and in water.

Solution: The Biot number is defined as

$$Bi = \frac{hV}{kA}$$

where
h - convective heat transfer coefficient
k - thermal conductivity of the wire material
V - volume of the wire
A - surface area of the wire

Therefore for water

$$Bi = \frac{(15) \times \pi/4\ D^2L}{216 \times \pi\ DL}$$

$$= \frac{15}{216} \times \frac{D}{4} = \frac{15}{216} \times \frac{(5/8 \times 12)}{4}$$

$$= 9.04 \times 10^{-4}$$

which is less than 0.1, hence the lumped parameter analysis is valid for the temperature history of the wire. The Biot number will be less for air as the cooling medium.

The temperature history can be found from the lumped parameter analysis equation as

$$\frac{T - T_\infty}{T_0 - T_\infty} = e^{-\frac{h\ A\ t}{\rho C_p\ V}} = e^{-\frac{h \times t}{\rho \times C_p} \times \frac{A}{V}}$$

where T is the temperature of the cooling wire at any instant of time t

T_0 is the temperature of the wire at time $t = 0$

T_∞ is the temperature of the cooling fluid and remains constant during the process of cooling.

Substituting the known values in the equation, yields

$$\frac{T - 110.0}{500 - 110.0} = \frac{T - 110.0}{390} = e^{-\frac{ht}{0.09 \times 560} \times \frac{A}{V}}$$

$$T - 110 = 390\ e^{-\frac{ht \times 4 \times 12}{0.09 \times 560 \times 5/8}}\ {}^\circ F$$

$$= 390\ e^{-1.5238 \times ht}\ {}^\circ F$$

For air $= 390\ e^{-1.5238 \times 2 \times t}\ {}^\circ F$

$$= 390\ e^{-3.04t}\ {}^\circ F$$

and for water $= 390\ e^{-22.8t}\ {}^\circ F$

Thus, the temperature history for cooling wire

in air $T_a = 110 + 390\ e^{-3.04t}\ {}^\circ F$ and

in water $T_w = 110 + 390\ e^{-22.8t}\ {}^\circ F$

Cooling curves are shown in the figure for both air and water.

• **PROBLEM 13-11**

A liquid is maintained at a uniform temperature T_i, above its melting temperature. One boundary of it is suddenly lowered and maintained at temperature T_0 below its melting temperature.

Evaluate the location of the solid liquid interface and also the temperature distribution throughout the system.

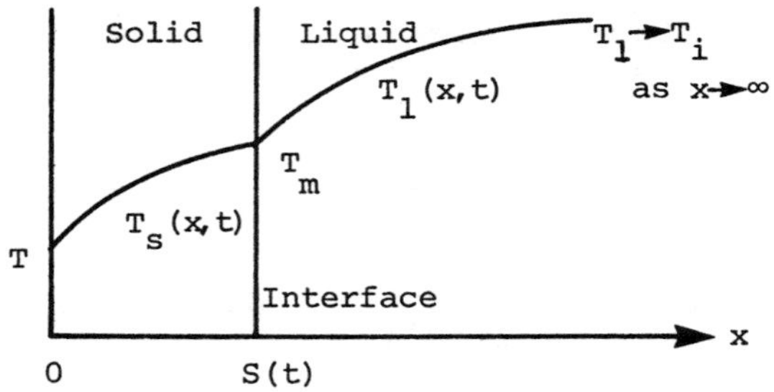

Solidification in a half-space.
Two phase problem.

Solution: The differential equation for the representation of the solid phase is

$$\frac{\partial^2 T_s}{\partial x^2} = \frac{1}{\alpha_s} \frac{\partial T_s(x,t)}{\partial t} \qquad \text{in } 0 < x < s(t),\ t > 0 \qquad (1)$$

$$T_s(x,t) = T_0 \qquad \text{at } x = 0,\ t > 0 \qquad (2)$$

and, for liquid phase

$$\frac{\partial^2 T_\ell}{\partial x^2} = \frac{1}{\alpha_l} \frac{\partial T_\ell(x,t)}{\partial t} \qquad \text{in } s(t) < x < \infty,\ t > 0 \qquad (3)$$

$$T_\ell(x,t) = T_i \qquad \text{for } t = 0, \text{ in } x > 0 \qquad (4)$$

$$T_\ell(x,t) \to T_i \qquad \text{as } x \to \infty,\ t > 0 \qquad (5)$$

conditions for and at the interface $x = s(t)$

$$T_s(x,t) = T_\ell(x,t) = T_m \quad \text{at } x = s(t),\ t > 0 \qquad (6)$$

$$k_s \frac{\partial T_s}{\partial x} - k_\ell \frac{\partial T_\ell}{\partial x} = \rho L \frac{ds(t)}{dt} \quad \text{at } x = s(t),\ t > 0 \qquad (7)$$

Now, assume a solution of the form

$$T_s(x,t) = T_0 + A \operatorname{erf}\left[x/2(\alpha_s t)^{\frac{1}{2}}\right] \tag{8}$$

The equation (1) for solid phase, and its boundary condition are satisfied.

Again, assume a solution for $T_\ell(x,t)$ as

$$T_\ell(x,t) = T_i + B \operatorname{erfc}\left[x/2(\alpha_l t)^{\frac{1}{2}}\right] \tag{9}$$

The differential equation (3) for liquid phase and initial and boundary conditions (5) and (4) are satisfied.

A and B are the constants. Substituting equations (8) and (9) into the interface equation (6) yields

$$T_0 + A \operatorname{erf}(\lambda) = T_i + B \operatorname{erfc}\left[\lambda\left(\frac{\alpha_s}{\alpha_\ell}\right)^{\frac{1}{2}}\right] = T_m \tag{10}$$

where

$$\lambda = \frac{s(t)}{2(\alpha_s t)^{\frac{1}{2}}} \quad \text{or} \quad s(t) = 2\lambda(\alpha_s t)^{\frac{1}{2}} \tag{11}$$

The constants A and B found from equation (10) are

$$A = \frac{T_m - T_o}{\operatorname{erf}(\lambda)}, \quad B = \frac{T_m - T_i}{\operatorname{erfc}[\lambda(\alpha_s/\alpha_\ell)^{\frac{1}{2}}]}$$

Now, the temperature distribution in the solid and liquid phases can be obtained by substituting the values of constants A and B into equations (8) and (9).

Thus

$$\frac{T_s(x,t) - T_o}{T_m - T_o} = \frac{\operatorname{erf}[x/2(\alpha_s t)^{\frac{1}{2}}]}{\operatorname{erf}(\lambda)} \tag{12}$$

$$\frac{T_\ell(x,t) - T_i}{T_m - T_i} = \frac{\operatorname{erfc}[x/2(\alpha_\ell t)^{\frac{1}{2}}]}{\operatorname{erfc}[\lambda(\alpha_s/\alpha_\ell)^{\frac{1}{2}}]} \tag{13}$$

In order to find an expression for the constant λ, expressions for s(t), $T_s(x,t)$ and $T_\ell(x,t)$, obtained from equations (11), (12) and (13) respectively, are substituted into equation (7), which results in

$$\frac{e^{-\lambda^2}}{\operatorname{erf}(\lambda)} + \frac{k_\ell}{k_s}\left(\frac{\alpha_s}{\alpha_\ell}\right)^{\frac{1}{2}} \frac{T_m - T_i}{T_m - T_o} \frac{e^{-\lambda(\alpha_s/\alpha_\ell)}}{\operatorname{erfc}[\lambda(\alpha_s/\alpha_\ell)^{\frac{1}{2}}]} = \frac{\lambda L\sqrt{\pi}}{C_{ps}(T_m - T_o)} \tag{14}$$

Thus, after evaluating λ, the interface temperature s(t), the temperature distribution $T_s(x,t)$ in the solid phase and $T_\ell(x,t)$ in the liquid phase can be obtained from equations (11), (12) and (13) respectively.

• PROBLEM 13-12

A solid metallic block of width 2b is initially at an uniform temperature T_o. Instantaneously the temperature, at time t=0, at both the end surfaces is raised to and maintained at T_1.

Derive an expression for the temperature distribution along its width as a function of time.

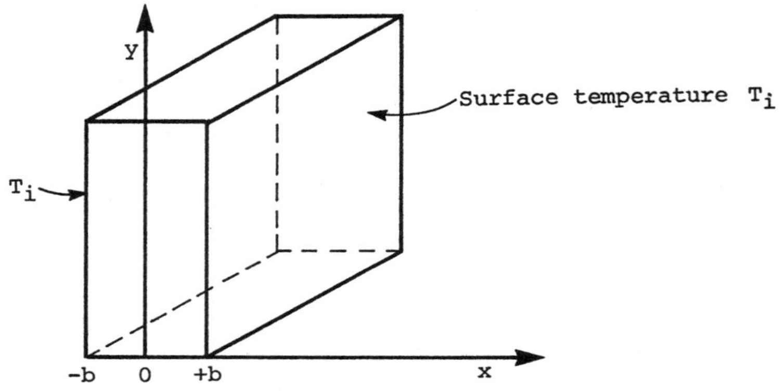

Fig. 1

Solution: The figure shows the cross section of the slate with temperature for time t > 0. The problem involves a three dimensional analysis.

For simplifying the problem non-dimensional parameters are introduced.

For temperature gradient

$$\theta = \frac{T-T_1}{T_o-T_1} \quad \text{non-dimensional temperature} \tag{1}$$

$$\ell = \frac{y}{b} \quad \text{non-dimensional width} \tag{2}$$

$$\tau = \frac{\alpha t}{b^2} \quad \text{non-dimensional time} \tag{3}$$

Now the problem reduces to the simpler partial differential equation

$$\frac{\partial\theta}{\partial\tau} = \frac{\partial^2\theta}{\partial\ell^2} \qquad (4)$$

with boundary conditions

$\theta = 1$ for time $\tau = 0$ Initial condition

$\theta = 0$ at $\ell = \pm 1$ for $\tau > 0$.

Equation (4) can be solved by variables separation method and the solution can be written as

$$\theta = ae^{-\beta^2\tau}(c\sin\beta\ell + d\cos\beta\ell) \qquad (5)$$

where a, c and d are some constants.

Since the problem is symmetric the above function should be even. This implies that $c = 0$ and hence the term $c\sin\beta\ell$ vanishes.

Substituting the boundary condition

$\theta = 0$ for $\tau > 0$

$0 = (ae^{-\beta^2\tau})d\cos\beta\ell$

This implies that $d\cos\beta\ell = 0$

since $ae^{-\beta^2\tau} \neq 0$

and $\cos\beta\ell = 0 \quad \because d \neq 0$

$\therefore$ the value of $\beta_n = (n + \frac{1}{2})\pi \qquad (6)$

where $n = 0, \pm 1, \pm 2,$

$\therefore$ The solution is

$\theta = (ae^{-\beta^2\tau})\ (d\cos\beta\ell)$

where $\beta = (n + \frac{1}{2})\pi$

The above equation can be written as

$\theta_n = A_n \times e^{-\beta_n{}^2\tau} \times \cos\beta_n\ell$

where A_n is another constant = a x d. For different values of n,θ will be different, hence for all integrals from

$$n = -\infty \quad \text{to} \quad n = +\infty$$

$$\theta = \sum_{n=0}^{\infty} A_n \; e^{-\beta_n^2 \tau} \cos\beta_n \ell \tag{7}$$

Now to find the value of A_n substitute the initial condition

i.e. $\theta = 1$ for time $\tau = 0$

$$1 = \sum_{n=0}^{\infty} A_n \cos\beta_n 1 \tag{8}$$

Multiplying both sides by $\cos\beta_m$ and integrating between the limits -1 and +1

$$\int_{-1}^{+1} \cos\beta_m 1 = \int_{-1}^{+1} \sum_{n=0}^{\infty} A_n \cos\beta_n \ell \cos\beta_m \ell$$

On the right hand side, except for m = n, all the other terms when m ≠ n are each equal to zero. When m = n it is equal to $\frac{A_n}{2}$.

On the left hand side

$$\int_{-1}^{+1} \cos\beta_m 1 = \frac{(-1)^m}{(m+\frac{1}{2})\pi}$$

$$\therefore \quad A_n = \frac{2\,(-1)^m}{(m+\frac{1}{2})\pi} \tag{9}$$

Substituting the value of A_n and β_n in equation (7)

$$\theta = 2\sum_{n=0}^{\infty} \frac{(-1)^m}{(m+\frac{1}{2})\pi} \times e^{-\left[(n+\frac{1}{2})\pi\right]^2 \tau} \times \cos\left[(n+\tfrac{1}{2})\pi\ell\right] \tag{10}$$

Now substituting the transformed parameters in equations (1), (2) and (3) and putting m = n

$$\frac{T-T_1}{T_o-T_1} = 2\sum_{n=0}^{\infty} \frac{(-1)^n}{(n+\frac{1}{2})\pi} \times e^{-(n\pi+\frac{\pi}{2})^2 \frac{\alpha t}{b^2}} \times \cos(n\pi+\tfrac{\pi}{2})\,\frac{y}{b} \tag{11}$$

This is the most generalized equation.

Solutions for heat conduction in rectangular parallelopipeds and finite cyclinders can be worked out similarly.

CONVECTION

• PROBLEM 13-13

Water at 80° F is being heated by a vertical plate. Determine the temperature at which the plate should be maintained if the rate of heat transfer from the plate to water is 5000 Btu/hr. The values of the constants for the number may be taken as a = 0.13 and m = 1/3.

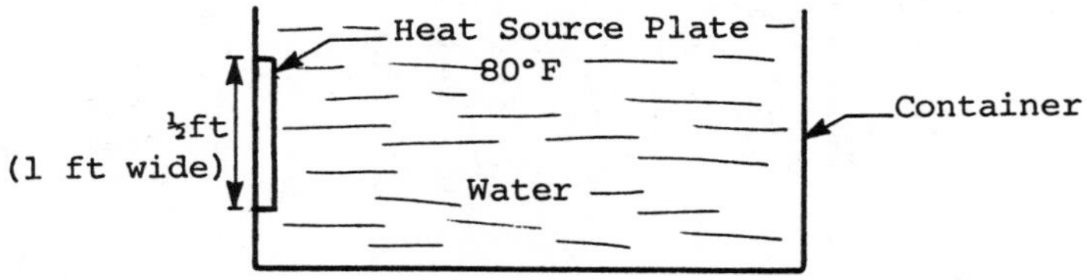

Solution: An iterative method is adopted to solve the problem. A plate temperature is assumed and using the Nusselt number, the convective heat transfer coefficient is obtained Subsequently, the plate temperature is re-calculated. The above procedure is repeated until the value

$$T_{p_{assumed}} \cong T_{p_{calculated}} \quad \text{is approached.}$$

The heat transferred from the plate is equal to the heat supplied to the plate

$$\text{Therefore,} \quad q = hA\Delta T \quad (\Delta T = T_p - T_w)$$

$$\text{or} \quad 5000 = h(\tfrac{1}{2} \times 1)(T_p - 80)$$

where subscripts p and w refer to plate and water, respectively

$$\text{or} \quad 10{,}000 = h(T_p - 80) \qquad (1)$$

The average film temperature at the plate-water interface is given by

$$T_f = \tfrac{1}{2}(T_p + T_w)$$

The turbulent (boundary layer type) free convection flow is given by the equation

$$\frac{h\ell}{k_f} = Nu = 0.13\ (Ra)^{1/3}$$

$$\text{or} \qquad h = 0.13\ \frac{K_f}{l}\ (Ra)^{1/3} \tag{2}$$

Also, $\qquad Ra = a_f L^3 \Delta T$

Hence, $$h = 0.13\ K_f\ a_f^{1/3}\ (T_p - T_w)^{1/3} \tag{3}$$

Equating (1) and (2), we get

$$T_p - 80 = \left(\frac{77{,}000}{K_f a_f^{1/3}}\right)^{3/4} \tag{4}$$

A value of T_p is assumed in order to calculate the film temperature, the values of a_f and k_f are obtained at this temperature (T_f), then T_p is calculated from eq. (3) and compared with the assumed value. If the two values differ substantially then this calculated value becomes the new assumed value and the procedure is repeated till we get nearly the same value.

Assume $T_p = 120°F$, then

$$T_f = \tfrac{1}{2}\ (120 + 80) = 100°F$$

From property tables of water at 100°F,

$$a_f = 547 \times 10^6$$

$$K_f = 0.363$$

Therefore, $a_f^{1/3} = 812.$

$$T_p - 80 = \left[\frac{77{,}000}{0.363(812)}\right]^{3/4}$$

$$\text{or} \qquad T_p = 144°F$$

Assume $T_p = 144°F$

$$T_f = \tfrac{1}{2}\ (144 + 80) = 112°F.$$

Therefore, $a_f = 697 \times 10^6$

$K_f = 0.367$

$a_f^{1/3} = 883$

$$T_p - 80 = \left[\frac{77{,}000}{0.367(883)}\right]^{3/4}$$

or $T_p = 140°F$ which is reasonably close to the assumed value.

Properties of Water

t(°F)	Saturation pressure (psia)	ρ (lbm/ft³)	μ (lb/hr ft)	k (Btu/hr ft °F)	c_p (Btu/lbm °F)	N_{Pr}	$a\dagger \times 10^{-6}$ (1/ft³ °F)
40	0.122	62.43	3.74	0.326	1.0041	11.5	
50	0.178	62.41	3.16	0.334	1.0013	9.49	
60	0.256	62.36	2.72	0.341	0.9996	7.98	154
70	0.363	62.30	2.37	0.347	0.9987	6.81	238
80	0.507	62.22	2.08	0.353	0.9982	5.89	330
90	0.698	62.12	1.85	0.358	0.9980	5.15	435
100	0.949	62.00	1.65	0.363	0.9980	4.55	547
110	1.28	61.86	1.49	0.367	0.9982	4.06	670
120	1.69	61.71	1.35	0.371	0.9985	3.64	804
130	2.22	61.55	1.24	0.375	0.9989	3.29	949
140	2.89	61.38	1.13	0.378	0.9994	3.00	1100
150	3.72	61.20	1.05	0.381	1.0000	2.74	1270
160	4.74	61.00	0.968	0.384	1.0008	2.52	1450
170	5.99	60.80	0.900	0.386	1.0017	2.33	1640
180	7.51	60.58	0.839	0.388	1.0027	2.17	1840
190	9.34	60.36	0.785	0.390	1.0039	2.02	2050
200	11.53	60.12	0.738	0.392	1.0052	1.89	2270
212	14.696	59.83	0.686	0.394	1.0070	1.76	2550
220	17.19	59.63	0.655	0.394	1.0084	1.67	2750
240	24.97	59.11	0.588	0.396	1.0124	1.51	3270
260	35.43	58.86	0.534	0.397	1.0173	1.37	3830
280	49.20	57.96	0.487	0.397	1.0231	1.26	4420
300	67.01	57.32	0.449	0.396	1.0297	1.17	5040
320	89.66	56.65	0.418	0.395	1.0368	1.10	5660
340	118.01	55.94	0.393	0.393	1.0451	1.04	6300
360	153.0	55.19	0.371	0.391	1.0547	1.00	6950
380	195.8	54.38	0.351	0.388	1.0662	0.97	7610
400	247.3	53.51	0.333	0.384	1.0800	0.94	8320
420	308.8	52.61	0.316	0.379	1.0968	0.92	9070
440	381.6	51.68	0.301	0.374	1.1168	0.90	9900
460	466.9	50.70	0.285	0.368			
480	566.1	49.67	0.272	0.362			

Checking for the Rayleigh number

$$R_{a_f} = a_f L^3 \Delta T$$

$$= 697 \times 10^6 \left(\tfrac{1}{2}\right)^3 (140-80) = 5.24 \times 10^9$$

Since $R_{a_f} > 10^9$, use of equation (2) is justified, and the required plate surface temperature is 140°F.

• **PROBLEM 13-14**

Consider a heating chamber with a 1 ft high vertical wall. The wall surface temperature is 450°F and the ambient temperature is 100°F. Find the convective heat transfer coefficient and the rate of heat transfer per unit surface area of the wall. Neglect radiation heat transfer.

Table 1.

Physical Properties of Air at 101.325 kPa (1 Atm Abs) (English Units)

T (°F)	ρ $\left(\frac{lb_m}{ft^3}\right)$	c_p $\left(\frac{btu}{lb_m \cdot °F}\right)$	μ (centipoise)	k $\left(\frac{btu}{h \cdot ft \cdot °F}\right)$	Pr	$\beta \times 10^3$ (1/°R)	$g\beta\rho^2/\mu^2$ (1/°R·ft³)
0	0.0861	0.240	0.0162	0.0130	0.720	2.18	4.39×10^6
32	0.0807	0.240	0.0172	0.0140	0.715	2.03	3.21×10^6
50	0.0778	0.240	0.0178	0.0144	0.713	1.96	2.70×10^6
100	0.0710	0.240	0.0190	0.0156	0.705	1.79	1.76×10^6
150	0.0651	0.241	0.0203	0.0169	0.702	1.64	1.22×10^6
200	0.0602	0.241	0.0215	0.0180	0.694	1.52	0.840×10^6
250	0.0559	0.242	0.0227	0.0192	0.692	1.41	0.607×10^6
300	0.0523	0.243	0.0237	0.0204	0.689	1.32	0.454×10^6
350	0.0490	0.244	0.0250	0.0215	0.687	1.23	0.336×10^6
400	0.0462	0.245	0.0260	0.0225	0.686	1.16	0.264×10^6
450	0.0437	0.246	0.0271	0.0236	0.674	1.10	0.204×10^6
500	0.0413	0.247	0.0280	0.0246	0.680	1.04	0.163×10^6

Solution: For a vertical plate at constant temperature and having a height of less than 3 ft, the average natural convective heat transfer coefficient is given by the following equation

$$Nu = \frac{hL}{k} = a\left(\frac{L^3\rho^2 g\,\beta\,\Delta T}{\mu^2}\ \frac{C_p\mu}{k}\right)^m$$

$$= a(GrPr)^m$$

where a and m are constants and can be found from the given table.

The physical properties of air are found at the average film temperature T_f

$$T_f = \frac{T_w + T_b}{2} = \frac{450 + 100}{2} = 275°F$$

Hence, from table 1, at 275°F

$$k = 0.0198 \text{ Btu/hr-ft-°F}$$

$$\rho = 0.0541 \text{ lbm/ft}^3$$

$$\mu = (0.0232 \text{ Cp})(2.4191) = 0.0562 \text{ lbm/ft-hr}$$

$$\beta = 1/(460 + 275) = 1.36 \times 10^{-3}/°R$$

$$Pr = 0.690 \text{ and } \Delta T = 450 - 100 = 350°F$$

Grashoff number is defined as

$$Gr = \frac{L^3 \rho^2 \, g \, \beta \Delta T}{\mu^2}$$

$$= \frac{(1.0)^3 (0.0541)^2 (32.174)(3600)^2 (1.36 \times 10^{-3})(350)}{(0.0562)^2}$$

$$= 1.84 \times 10^8$$

$$Gr \, Pr = (1.84 \times 10^8)(0.69)$$

$$= 1.27 \times 10^8$$

From table 2, for vertical plates, corresponding to $Gr = 1.27 \times 10^8$, the constants a and m are 0.59 and $\frac{1}{4}$, respectively. Therefore,

$$Nu = \frac{hL}{k} = 0.59 \, (1.27 \times 10^8)^{\frac{1}{4}}$$

$$\text{or} \quad h = 0.59 \, (1.27 \times 10^8)^{\frac{1}{4}} \left(\frac{0.0198}{1} \right)$$

$$\therefore \quad h = 1.24 \text{ Btu/hr-ft}^2\text{-°F}.$$

Table 2.

Constants for use with Eq. (1) for Nusselt Number

Physical Geometry	(Gr Pr)	*a*	*m*
Vertical planes and cylinders [vertical height $L < 1$ m (3 ft)]			
	$<10^4$	1.36	$\frac{1}{5}$
	$10^4 - 10^9$	0.59	$\frac{1}{4}$
	$>10^9$	0.13	$\frac{1}{3}$
Horizontal cylinders [diameter D used for L and $D < 0.20$ m (0.66 ft)]			
	$<10^{-5}$	0.49	0
	$10^{-5} - 10^{-3}$	0.71	$\frac{1}{25}$
	$10^{-3} - 1$	1.09	$\frac{1}{10}$
	$1 - 10^4$	1.09	$\frac{1}{5}$
	$10^4 - 10^9$	0.53	$\frac{1}{4}$
	$>10^9$	0.13	$\frac{1}{3}$
Horizontal plates			
Upper surface of heated plates or lower surface of cooled plates	$10^5 - 2 \times 10^7$	0.54	$\frac{1}{4}$
	$2 \times 10^7 - 3 \times 10^{10}$	0.14	$\frac{1}{3}$
Lower surface of heated plates or upper surface of cooled plates	$10^5 - 10^{11}$	0.58	$\frac{1}{5}$

The rate of heat transfer per unit wall surface area is given by

$$q = hA(T_w - T_b)$$

$$= 1.24 \times 1 \times (450-100) = 434 \text{ Btu/hr.}$$

• PROBLEM 13-15

A 3.5m × 2m vertical plate is subjected to a constant heat flux of 800 W/m². The back of the plate is insulated and the ambient air temperature is 30°C. Determine the average surface temperature of the plate, assuming that all the incident radiation is lost by free convection to the surrounding air.

Solution: In this problem, the plate surface temperature and the heat transfer coefficient are not known. The analysis is initiated with an assumed heat transfer coefficient and using this value, the surface temperature is calculated. Subsequently, using the Nusselt number, a new heat transfer coefficient is evaluated. This procedure is repeated till the assumed value nearly equals the calculated Nusselt number.

Physical Properties of Air at Atmopheric Pressure (SI Units)

T (°C)	T (K)	ρ (kg/m³)	c_p (kJ/kg · K)	μ × 10⁵ (Pa·s, or kg/m·s)	k (W/m · K)	Pr	β × 10³ (1/K)	gβρ²/μ² (1/K·m³)
-17.8	255.4	1.379	1.0048	1.62	0.02250	0.720	3.92	2.79×10^8
0	273.2	1.293	1.0048	1.72	0.02423	0.715	3.65	2.04×10^8
10.0	283.2	1.246	1.0048	1.78	0.02492	0.713	3.53	1.72×10^8
37.8	311.0	1.137	1.0048	1.90	0.02700	0.705	3.22	1.12×10^8
65.6	338.8	1.043	1.0090	2.03	0.02925	0.702	2.95	0.775×10^8
93.3	366.5	0.964	1.0090	2.15	0.03115	0.694	2.74	0.534×10^8
121.1	394.3	0.895	1.0132	2.27	0.03323	0.692	2.54	0.386×10^8
148.9	422.1	0.838	1.0174	2.37	0.03531	0.689	2.38	0.289×10^8
176.7	449.9	0.785	1.0216	2.50	0.03721	0.687	2.21	0.214×10^8
204.4	477.6	0.740	1.0258	2.60	0.03894	0.686	2.09	0.168×10^8
232.2	505.4	0.700	1.0300	2.71	0.04084	0.684	1.98	0.130×10^8
260.0	533.2	0.662	1.0341	2.80	0.04258	0.680	1.87	1.104×10^8

Assuming a value of $h = 10 W/m^2 °C$, heat transfer per unit area is

$$q = h\Delta T$$

or $$\Delta T = \frac{q}{h} = \frac{800}{10} = 80°C.$$

Therefore, $$T_f = \frac{80}{2} + 30 = 70°C \text{ or } 343°K.$$

The properties of air at 70°C are

$$\nu = 2.005 \times 10^{-5} m^2/s \text{ , } \beta = \frac{1}{T_f} = 2.92 \times 10^{-3} °K^{-1}$$

$$k = 0.0295 \text{ W/m°C} \quad \text{and} \quad Pr = 0.7$$

The Grashof number is defined as

$$Gr = \frac{g\beta q_w x^4}{k\nu^2}$$

$$Gr = \frac{9.8 \times (2.92 \times 10^{-3})(800)(3.5)^4}{(0.0295)(2.005 \times 10^{-5})^2}$$

$$= 2.9 \times 10^{14} \quad \text{(greater than } 10^9\text{)}$$

The flow of air around the plate is turbulent as the Grashof number is greater than 10^9. Hence, the Nusselt number is given by

$$Nu = 0.17\ (Gr\ Pr)^{1/4}$$

$$Nu = \frac{hx}{k} = 0.17\ (Gr\ Pr)^{1/4}$$

or $$h = \frac{0.0295}{3.5}\ (0.17)\ (2.9 \times 10^{14} \times 0.7)^{1/4}$$

$$= 5.41\ W/m^2\ °C.$$

Now, in a turbulent flow the value of h does not change appreciably, therefore it is reasonable to assume a constant value of h for further iterations.

$$\Delta T = \frac{q}{h} = \frac{800}{5.41} = 148°C$$

Therefore, $$T_f = \frac{148}{2} + 30 = 104°C$$

Properties of air at 104°C are

$$\nu = 2.354 \times 10^{-5}\ m^2/s\ ,\ \beta = \frac{1}{T_f} = 2.65 \times 10^{-3}$$

$$k = 0.0320\ W/m°C\ ,\ Pr = 0.695$$

Hence, $$Gr = \frac{(9.8)(2.65 \times 10^{-3})(800)(3.5)^4}{(0.0320)(2.354 \times 10^{-5})^2}$$

$$= 1.758 \times 10^{14}$$

or using the Nusselt number

$$h = \frac{k}{x}\ (0.17)(Gr\ Pr)^{1/4}$$

$$= \frac{(0.0320)(0.17)(1.758 \times 10^{14} \times 0.695)^{1/4}}{3.5}$$

$$= 5.17\ W/m^2°C$$

Thus, the new temperature difference is

$$\Delta T = \frac{800}{5.17} = 155°C$$

and the average wall temperature is

$$155 + 30 = 185°C.$$

• PROBLEM 13-16

Saturated steam at 30 psig and 50°F is flowing through a 2-in OD pipe. Calculate the rate of heat transfer when

(a) the pipe is surrounded by air at 55°F

(b) the pipe is surrounded by water at 55°F.

Assume the emissivity of the pipe surface as 0.9.

Solution: Transfer of heat takes place by convection only when the pipe is surrounded by water, and when surrounded by air, heat transfer is by convection and radiation.

From the table, corresponding to an absolute pressure of 30 + 14.7 ≅ 45 psia the saturation temperature of steam is 274.4°F. Therefore, the average film temperature at the pipe-fluid interface is

$$T_f = \frac{274.4 + 55}{2} = 164.7°F$$

The physical properties of air and water are obtained from the tables.

Physical Properties of Air at 1 Atm Abs

T (°F)	ρ $\left(\frac{lb_m}{ft^3}\right)$	c_p $\left(\frac{btu}{lb_m \cdot °F}\right)$	μ (centipoise)	k $\left(\frac{btu}{h \cdot ft \cdot °F}\right)$	Pr	β × 10^3 (1/°R)	$g\beta\rho^2/\mu^2$ (1/°R·ft³)
0	0.0861	0.240	0.0162	0.0130	0.720	2.18	4.39 × 10^6
32	0.0807	0.240	0.0172	0.0140	0.715	2.03	3.21 × 10^6
50	0.0778	0.240	0.0178	0.0144	0.713	1.96	2.70 × 10^6
100	0.0710	0.240	0.0190	0.0156	0.705	1.79	1.76 × 10^6
150	0.0651	0.241	0.0203	0.0169	0.702	1.64	1.22 × 10^6
200	0.0602	0.241	0.0215	0.0180	0.694	1.52	0.840 × 10^6
250	0.0559	0.242	0.0227	0.0192	0.692	1.41	0.607 × 10^6
300	0.0523	0.243	0.0237	0.0204	0.689	1.32	0.454 × 10^6
350	0.0490	0.244	0.0250	0.0215	0.687	1.23	0.336 × 10^6
400	0.0462	0.245	0.0260	0.0225	0.686	1.16	0.264 × 10^6
450	0.0437	0.246	0.0271	0.0236	0.674	1.10	0.204 × 10^6
500	0.0413	0.247	0.0280	0.0246	0.680	1.04	0.163 × 10^6

For air

$$\mu = 0.04943 \text{ lbm/hr-ft}$$

$$k = 0.0171 \text{ Btu/hr-ft-°F}$$

$$C_p = 0.241 \text{ Btu/lbm °F}$$

$$\beta = \frac{1}{(164.7 + 460)} = 1.6 \times 10^{-3} \quad \frac{1}{°R}$$

$$Pr = 0.697, \ \rho = 0.0636 \ lbm/ft^3$$

Properties of Water

t(°F)	Saturation pressure (psia)	ρ (lbm/ft³)	μ (lb/hr ft)	k (Btu/hr ft °F)	c_p (Btu/lbm °F)	N_{Pr}	$a^\dagger \times 10^{-6}$ (1/ft³ °F)
40	0.122	62.43	3.74	0.326	1.0041	11.5	
50	0.178	62.41	3.16	0.334	1.0013	9.49	
60	0.256	62.36	2.72	0.341	0.9996	7.98	154
70	0.363	62.30	2.37	0.347	0.9987	6.81	238
80	0.507	62.22	2.08	0.353	0.9982	5.89	330
90	0.698	62.12	1.85	0.358	0.9980	5.15	435
100	0.949	62.00	1.65	0.363	0.9980	4.55	547
110	1.28	61.86	1.49	0.367	0.9982	4.06	670
120	1.69	61.71	1.35	0.371	0.9985	3.64	804
130	2.22	61.55	1.24	0.375	0.9989	3.29	949
140	2.89	61.38	1.13	0.378	0.9994	3.00	1100
150	3.72	61.20	1.05	0.381	1.0000	2.74	1270
160	4.74	61.00	0.968	0.384	1.0008	2.52	1450
170	5.99	60.80	0.900	0.386	1.0017	2.33	1640
180	7.51	60.58	0.839	0.388	1.0027	2.17	1840
190	9.34	60.36	0.785	0.390	1.0039	2.02	2050
200	11.53	60.12	0.738	0.392	1.0052	1.89	2270
212	14.696	59.83	0.686	0.394	1.0070	1.76	2550
220	17.19	59.63	0.655	0.394	1.0084	1.67	2750
240	24.97	59.11	0.588	0.396	1.0124	1.51	3270
260	35.43	58.86	0.534	0.397	1.0173	1.37	3830
280	49.20	57.96	0.487	0.397	1.0231	1.26	4420
300	67.01	57.32	0.449	0.396	1.0297	1.17	5040
320	89.66	56.65	0.418	0.395	1.0368	1.10	5660
340	118.01	55.94	0.393	0.393	1.0451	1.04	6300
360	153.0	55.19	0.371	0.391	1.0547	1.00	6950
380	195.8	54.38	0.351	0.388	1.0662	0.97	7610
400	247.3	53.51	0.333	0.384	1.0800	0.94	8320
420	308.8	52.61	0.316	0.379	1.0968	0.92	9070
440	381.6	51.68	0.301	0.374	1.1168	0.90	9900
460	466.9	50.70	0.285	0.368			
480	566.1	49.67	0.272	0.362			

For water

$$Pr = 2.43, \ \mu = 0.936 \ lb/hr \ ft$$

$$\rho = 60.906 \ lbm/ft^3, \ k = 0.385 \ Btu/hr \ ft°F$$

$$C_p = 1.0012 \ Btu/lbm°F, \ \beta = 1.6 \times 10^{-3} \ \frac{1}{°R}$$

Rayleigh number is the product of Grashof and Prandtl numbers,

$$Ra = (Gr \cdot Pr)$$

For air, $Gr = \dfrac{g\rho^2\beta\Delta TL^3}{\mu^2}$

$$= \frac{32.2 \times (0.0636)^2\ 1.6 \times 10^{-3}}{(0.04943)^2} \times \left(\frac{2}{12}\right)^3 \times (3600)^2 \times$$

$$\times\ (274.4-55) = 1.1228 \times 10^6$$

For water, $Gr = \dfrac{32.2 \times (60.906)^2 \times 1.6 \times 10^{-3}}{(0.936)^2} \left(\dfrac{2}{12}\right)^3 (3600)^2$

$$\times\ (274.4-55)$$

$$= 2.87 \times 10^9$$

Therefore, $Ra = 1.1228 \times 10^6 \times 0.697 = 0.782 \times 10^6$ for air

$= 2.87 \times 10^9 \times 2.43 = 6.974 \times 10^9$ for water.

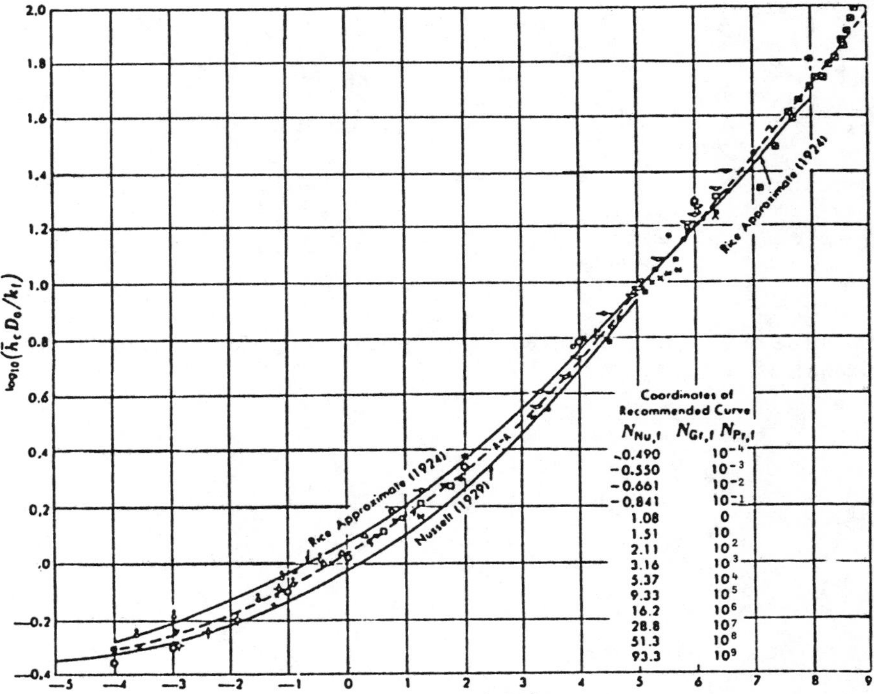

Free-convection heat transfer correlation for horizontal cylindrical surfaces.

Knowing the values of the Rayleigh number for air and water, the corresponding values of the Nusselt number can be obtained from the graph. For air,

$$Ra = 0.782 \times 10^6$$

$\log(0.782 \times 10^6) = 5.893$ and corresponding to this value, $\log(Nu) = 1.2$

$$\text{hence} \quad Nu = 15.84$$

For water

$$Ra = 6.974 \times 10^9$$

$\log(6.974 \times 10^9) = 9.843$ and corresponding to this value, $\log(Nu) = 1.98$ which gives

$$Nu = 95.5$$

Next, the convective heat transfer coefficient for water and air are calculated.

$$Nu = \frac{h_c D_o}{k}$$

For air, $h_c = \dfrac{15.84 \times 0.0171}{2/12} = 1.625 \text{ Btu/hr-ft}^2\text{-}^\circ\text{F}$

For water, $h_c = \dfrac{95.5 \times 0.385}{2/12} = 220.6 \text{ Btu/hr-ft}^2\text{-}^\circ\text{F}$.

The rate of heat transfer per unit length of pipe - when submerged in water:

$$q_w = h_c A \Delta T$$

$$= \frac{220.6 \times \pi \times 2 \times (274.4-55)}{12}$$

$$= 25{,}342 \text{ Btu/hr-ft}$$

When exposed to air:

by convection, $q_1 = \dfrac{1.625 \times \pi \times 2 \times (274.4-55)}{12}$

$$= 186.6 \text{ Btu/hr-ft}$$

by radiation, $q_2 = \varepsilon A \sigma (T_1^4 - T_2^4)$

where,

$$\sigma = \text{Stefan-Boltzman constant}$$

$$= 0.171 \times 10^8 \text{ Btu/hr ft}^2{}^\circ\text{R}^4$$

$$T_1 = 274.4 + 460 = 734.4^\circ\text{R}$$

$$T_2 = 55 + 460 = 515^\circ\text{R}$$

$$\varepsilon = \text{emissivity of the pipe surface} = 0.9$$

$$q_2 = 0.9 \times \frac{\pi \times 2 \times 1}{12} \times 0.171 \left[\left(\frac{734.4}{100}\right)^4 - \left(\frac{515}{100}\right)^4\right]$$

$$= 177.2 \text{ Btu/hr-ft}$$

The total heat transferred in air

$$= q_1 + q_2$$

$$= 186.6 + 177.2$$

$$= 363.8 \text{ Btu/hr-ft}$$

It is interesting to note that the rate of heat transfer in air is only 1.44 percent of the rate of heat transfer when the pipe is submerged in water.

• PROBLEM 13-17

A spherical ball, 1 in. in radius and at a temperature of 800°F, is suddenly quenched in a large pool of liquid which is maintained at 280°F. Estimate the surface temperature of the ball after one hour. The average convective heat transfer coefficient h = 2 Btu/hr ft²°F. The properties of the ball material are:

$k = 25$ Btu/hr ft°F $\rho = 492$ lbm/ft³

$Cp = 0.11$ Btu

Solution: Biot number (Bi), the dimensionless parameter, compares the relative values of internal conduction resistance and surface convective resistances to heat transfer.

$$\text{Biot number - Bi} = \frac{hx}{k} < 0.1$$

where h is the coefficient of convective heat transfer

k is the coefficient of heat conductivity

x is the characteristic dimension of the body.

For a sphere, the characteristic dimension is given by

$$x = \frac{\text{volume of sphere}}{\text{surface area of sphere}}$$

$$= \frac{4\pi r^3/3}{4\pi r^2}$$

$$= \frac{r}{3} = \frac{1}{3} \text{ in.}$$

Now, substituting values in the expression for the Biot number,

$$Bi = \frac{(2) \times \left(\frac{1}{3\times 12}\right)}{(25)} = 0.00222$$

Since Bi is less than 0.1, the problem can be solved by using the lumped parameter analysis.

Hence, $$\frac{T-T_\infty}{T_o-T_\infty} = e^{-\left(\frac{hA}{C\rho v}\right)t}$$

$$\frac{hA}{C\rho v} = \frac{2}{0.11 \times 492 \times (1/36)} \text{ per hr}$$

$$= 1.333 \text{ per hr}$$

Therefore,

$$\frac{T-280}{800-280} = e^{-(1.333)1.0}$$

or $$T = 417°F$$

• PROBLEM 13-18

A 1/12 in. dia metal wire is placed in still air at 66°F. Compute the rate of heat generation required to maintain the surface temperature of the wire at 1734°F. The heat loss due to radiation may be neglected. Use the given chart.

Solution: The mean film temperature at the air-wire interface is

$$T_f = \frac{1734 + 66}{2} = 900°F$$

Properties of air at 900°F are:

$$k = 0.032 \text{ Btu/hr-ft-°F}$$

$$a = \frac{g\beta\rho^2 C_p}{\mu^2 k} = 0.0251 \times 10^6 \ (1/\text{ft}^3\text{-°F})$$

$$Gr \times Pr = \frac{\rho^2 \beta g \Delta T D^3}{\mu^2} \times \frac{C_p \mu}{k} = \frac{g\beta\rho^2 C_p}{\mu k} \times (\Delta T) \times (D^3)$$

$$= 0.0251 \times 10^6 \times (1734-66) \times \left(\frac{1}{12 \times 12}\right)^3$$

$$= 14.02$$

$$\log (Gr \times Pr) = \log (14.02) = 1.146$$

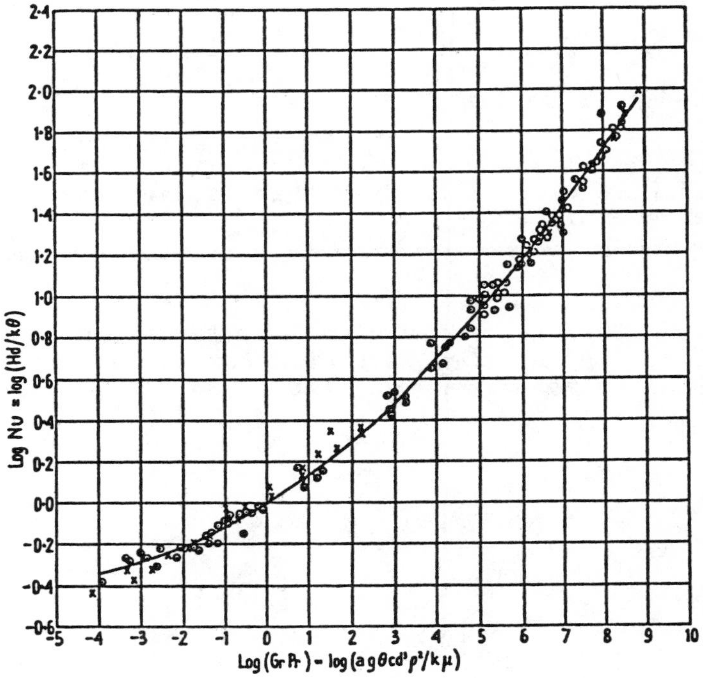

Natural convection for horizontal cylinders. ⊙s are experimental points for gases, Xs are experimental points for liquids.

From the graph, log Nu = log(0.15)·

$$Nu = \frac{hD}{k} = 1.412$$

or $$h = \frac{1.412k}{D} = \frac{1.412 \times 0.032}{\left(\frac{1}{12\times12}\right)} = 6.51$$

Hence,

$$q = h \times A \times \Delta T$$

$$= 6.51 \times \left(\pi \times \frac{1}{12\times12}\right) \times \left(1734-66\right)$$

$$\cong 237 \text{ Btu/hr ft}$$

• PROBLEM 13-19

Consider the heat transfer involved in turbulent fluid flow in a pipe. It is known that the dependent variables are:

k - thermal conductivity

G - mass fluid velocity

d - pipe diameter

μ - viscosity

c_p - specific heat

Use dimensional analysis to discover the physical relationship involved, and from this, define the heat transfer coefficient.

Solution: The basic dimensional system to be used is the MLθ (mass, length, time) system. First, each dependent variable must be non-dimensionalized. So, if T = temperature and H = heat, then

$$k - \left(\frac{H}{\theta LT}\right) \qquad G - \left(\frac{M}{\theta L^2}\right)$$

$$d - (L) \qquad \mu - \left(\frac{M}{L\theta}\right)$$

$$c_p - \left(\frac{H}{MT}\right)$$

For purposes of simplification, the constant $K_H - \left(\frac{ML^2}{H\theta^2}\right)$

is included, since M and H appear in it. Now the heat transfer coefficient may be expressed as

$$h = f(k,G,d,\mu,c_p,K_H) \tag{1}$$

Taking an infinite series of this,

$$h = (C_1 k^{a_1} G^{b_1} d^{e_1} \mu^{f_1} c_p^{i_1} K^{m_1}) + (C_2 k^{a_2} G^{b_2} d^{e_2} \mu^{f_2} c_p^{i_2} K^{m_2}) + \ldots \tag{2}$$

The law of dimensional homogeneity states that each grouping must have the same overall dimensions. Therefore, the first group is taken as a complete representation. Since $h - \left(\frac{H}{\theta L^2 T}\right)$, substituting all the dimensional formulae into eq.(2) gives

$$\frac{H}{\theta L^2 T} = C_1 \left(\frac{H}{\theta LT}\right)^a \left(\frac{M}{\theta L^2}\right)^b (L)^e \left(\frac{M}{L\theta}\right)^f \left(\frac{H}{MT}\right)^i \left(\frac{ML^2}{H\theta^2}\right)^m \tag{3}$$

Taking each dimension separately and collecting exponents,

ΣH: $1 = a + i - m$

$\Sigma\theta$: $-1 = -a - b - f - 2m$

ΣL: $-2 = -a - 2b + e - f + 2m$

ΣT: $-1 = -a - i$

ΣM: $0 = b + f - i + m$

Solving these five simultaneous equations yields:

$m = 0, \quad b = e+1, \quad a = 1-i, \quad \text{and} \quad a + e + f = 0$

Now, if the variables as shown in eq.(2) are given these exponents and rearranged, the result is

$$\frac{hd}{k} = C_1 \left(\frac{c_p\mu}{k}\right)^i \left(\frac{dG}{\mu}\right)^e$$

or

$$\frac{hd}{k} = f\left[\left(\frac{c_p\mu}{k}\right),\left(\frac{dG}{\mu}\right)\right]$$

$\left(\frac{hd}{k}\right)$ is called the Nusselt number (Nu), $\left(\frac{c_p\mu}{k}\right)$ is the Prandtl number (Pr), and $\left(\frac{dG}{\mu}\right)$ is the Reynolds number (Re).

Thus, in terms of the non-dimensional parameters is

$$Nu = f\left[Pr,\ Re\right].$$

• **PROBLEM 13-20**

A plate loses heat to a stream of air by convection. The plate is 2 ft. in length, and it is initially at a surface temperature of 500°F. The ambient air temperature is 100°F, and the air flow rate is observed to be 150 ft/sec. Assuming a unit (1 ft.) width, calculate

(a) the heat transferred from the laminar boundary layer region; and

(b) the heat transferred from the turbulent boundary layer region.

Then assume that the boundary layer is completely turbulent.

Find

(c) the heat transfer involved; and

(d) the error this assumption results in.

Solution: The mean film temperature is

$$T_m = \frac{100 + 500}{2} = 300^\circ F$$

At this temperature, the properties of air are

$\nu = 1.1026\ ft^2/hr$ $\quad k = 0.01995\ Btu/hr\text{-}ft\text{-}^\circ F$

and

$Pr = 0.701$

(a) The Reynolds number over the entire length of the plate is

$$Re_L = \frac{UL}{\nu} = \frac{(150)(3600)(2)}{1.1026}$$

$$= 9.8 \times 10^5$$

If the Reynolds number is used for computing the Nusselt number the resulting coefficient of heat transfer will be an average value, or one that is for the entire length. Similarly, the heat transfer calculated using the average coefficient will be the heat transfer over the entire length, or the total heat transfer. This is equal to the sum of the heat transfer from both the laminar and turbulent boundary layer regions, or

$$q_T = q_{Lam} + q_{turb} \tag{1}$$

Now, the length of the laminar boundary layer L_{cr} can be found, knowing the critical Reynolds number.

$$Re_{cr} = \frac{UL_{cr}}{\nu} \tag{2}$$

If the Nusselt number is found over the laminar boundary layer region, then the coefficient of heat transfer of that region may be found, as

$$Nu_{Lam} = \frac{h_{Lam}L_{cr}}{k} \tag{3}$$

Then the heat transfer of that region is easily determined. Proceeding to that end, first consider the plate as a whole. For mixed flow (where there are both laminar and turbulent regions) the Nusselt number is

$$Nu_L = \left[0.037\ Re_L^{0.8} - 872\right] Pr^{1/3}$$

with the constraint

$$5 \times 10^5 < Re_L < 10^7$$

As this is satisfied,

$$Nu_L = \left[0.037(9.8\times10^5)^{0.8} - 872\right](0.701)^{1/3}$$

$$= 1265.97$$

Then the average heat transfer coefficient is

$$h_{av} = \frac{Nu_L k}{L} = \frac{(1265.97)(0.01995)}{2}$$

$$= 12.63 \text{ Btu/hr-ft}^2\text{-}^0\text{F}$$

This is used for the calculation of the total heat transferred, or

$$q_T = h_{av}A(T_s - T_\infty)$$

$$= 12.63(2)(1)(500 - 100)$$

$$= 10{,}104 \text{ Btu/hr}$$

(a) The length of the laminar boundary layer is found from eq.(2).

$$L_{cr} = \frac{Re_{cr}\nu}{U} = \frac{(5\times10^5)(1.1026)}{(150)(3600)}$$

$$= 1.021 \text{ ft.}$$

Now, for laminar flow, the Nusselt number is found as

$$Nu_L = 0.664\ Re_L^{\frac{1}{2}}\ Pr^{1/3}$$

where the subscript L refers to the length of the laminar boundary layer. The condition

$$0.6 \le Pr \le 50$$

is satisfied. Then

$$Nu_L = 0.664(5\times10^5)^{\frac{1}{2}}(0.701)^{1/3}$$

$$= 417.09$$

Then the heat transfer coefficient in the laminar region is found using eq.(3).

$$h_{Lam} = \frac{Nu_{Lam}k}{L_{cr}} = \frac{(417.09)(0.01995)}{1.021}$$

$$= 8.15 \text{ Btu/hr-ft}^2\text{-}^0\text{F}.$$

Finally, the heat transfer out of the laminar region is

$$q_{Lam} = h_{Lam}A_{Lam}(T_s - T_\infty)$$

$$= (8.15)(1)(0.817)(500 - 100)$$

$$= 2,663.3 \text{ Btu/hr}.$$

(b) Referring to eq.(1), the heat transferred from the turbulent boundary layer region is easily found as

$$q_{turb} = q_T - q_{Lam}$$

$$= 10,104 - 2,663.3$$

$$= 7440.7 \text{ Btu/hr}$$

(c) If the boundary layer is turbulent from the leading edge on the Nusellt number is given by

$$Nu_L = 0.037 \, Re_L^{0.8} \, Pr^{1/3}$$

Substituting,

$$Nu_L = 0.037(9.8\times10^5)^{0.8}(0.701)^{1/3}$$

$$= 2040.6$$

The heat transfer coefficient is then

$$h_L = \frac{Nu_L k}{L} = \frac{(2040.6)(0.01995)}{2}$$

$$= 20.36 \text{ Btu/hr-ft}^2\text{-}^0\text{F}$$

Therefore, the total heat transferred

$$q_T = (20.36)(2\times1)(500 - 100)$$

$$= 16,288 \text{ Btu/hr}$$

(d) The difference between the two values of the total heat transfer may be expressed as a percent error:

$$\% \text{ error} = \frac{16{,}288 - 10{,}104}{10{,}104} \times 100\%$$

$$\simeq 61\%$$

The overall turbulence assumed results in erroneous results and hence is to be avoided.

• PROBLEM 13-21

A plate at 60°C, is cooled by forced convection from an airstream. The steady flow velocity of the air stream is observed to be 2m/sec with the temperature and pressure as 27°C and 1 atm., respectively. Find the heat transfer per unit width from the leading edge to a distance of (a) 20 cm and (b) 40 cm. Also find (c) the drag force over the 40 cm distance.

Solution: When referring to a length of plate, the heat transfer must be calculated using a coefficient of heat transfer that applies over the length, or the average coefficient. Therefore, the average Nusselt number correlation is used.

(a) First, the Reynolds number must be calculated. The mean film temperature is

$$T_m = \frac{27 + 60}{2} = 43.5\,^0\text{C}$$

At this temperature, the air tables give

$$\nu = 17.36 \times 10^{-6}\ \text{m}^2/\text{sec} \qquad k = 0.02749\ \text{W/m-}^0\text{C}$$

$$\text{Pr} = 0.7 \quad \text{and } C_p = 1.006\ \text{KJ/kg}^0\text{C}.$$

(a) Then at a length of 20 cm,

$$\text{Re}_{(x)} = \frac{UL}{\nu} = \frac{(2)(0.2)}{17.36\times 10^{-6}}$$

$$\simeq 23{,}041$$

This is a laminar flow. As the condition

$$0.6 \le \text{Pr} \le 50$$

is satisfied, the average Nusselt number may be calculated as

$$\begin{aligned} Nu_L &= 0.664\ Re_L^{1/2}\ Pr^{1/3} \\ &= 0.664(23{,}041)^{1/2}\ (0.7)^{1/3} \\ &\simeq 89.49 \end{aligned}$$

From this, the average heat transfer coefficient is found to be

$$\begin{aligned} h_L &= \frac{Nu_L k}{L} = \frac{(89.49)(0.02749)}{0.2} \\ &\simeq 12.3\ W/m^2\text{-}^0C \end{aligned}$$

Then the heat transferred from this region is

$$\begin{aligned} q &= h_L A(T_s - T_\infty) \\ &= 12.3(0.2)(1)(60\text{-}27) \\ &\simeq 81.19\ W \end{aligned}$$

(b) The same process is repeated, but the plate length is now taken to be 40 cm. Thus

$$\begin{aligned} Re_L &= \frac{UL}{\nu} = \frac{(2)(0.4)}{17.36\times10^{-6}} \\ &= 46{,}083 \end{aligned}$$

The flow is still laminar, so the same Nusselt number expression is used.

$$\begin{aligned} Nu_L &= 0.664\ Re_L^{1/2}\ Pr^{1/3} \\ &= 0.664(46{,}083)^{1/2}(0.7)^{1/3} \\ &= 126.56 \end{aligned}$$

This gives an average heat transfer coefficient of

$$\begin{aligned} h_L &= \frac{Nu_L k}{L} = \frac{(126.56)(0.02749)}{0.4} \\ &= 8.7\ W/m^2\text{-}^0C \end{aligned}$$

Finally, the heat transferred is

$$q = h_L A(T_s - T_\infty)$$

$$= 8.7(0.4)(1)(60-27)$$

$$= 114.8 \text{ W}$$

(c) The drag force F_D is

$$F_D = \tau_0 A$$

where τ_0 is the wall shear stress. This may be evaluated knowing the relation

$$\tau_0 = \frac{1}{2} D_D \rho U^2$$

where C_D is the coefficient of drag. This is given by

$$C_D = \frac{1.328}{Re_L^{1/2}}$$

For a length of 40 cm, the coefficient of drag is

$$C_D = \frac{1.328}{(46{,}083)^{1/2}} = 0.00619$$

At the mean temperature, the air tables give

$$\rho = 1.115 \text{ kg/m}^3$$

Then

$$\tau_0 = \frac{1}{2}(0.00619)(1.115)(2)^2$$

$$= 0.0138 \text{ N/m}^2$$

The drag force is, then,

$$F_D = (0.0138)(0.4)(1)$$

$$= 0.0055 \text{ N}$$

Water enters a reactor through a length of pipe in which the necessary preheating is accomplished. The reactor has a maximum power rating of 150 W per meter of pipe, and its operating temperature is 350 °K. The flow is measured at 5 kg/hr, and it enters the pipe at a mean bulk temperature of 290 °K. If the internal diameter of the pipe is 0.005 m, calculate (a) the length of pipe over which the necessary heat transfer may be accomplished, and (b) the maximum exit temperature of the water.

Solution: (a) The heat balance over the length of pipe L is given by

$$q\pi dL = \dot{m}C_p \; \Delta T_b \tag{1}$$

Solving for L,

$$L = \frac{\dot{m}C_p \Delta T_b}{q\pi d} \tag{2}$$

Now, the mean bulk temperature of the water is

$$T_m = \frac{290 + 350}{2} = 320\,^{\circ}K$$

Properties of water at this temperature are

$$\rho = 989 \text{ kg/m}^3 \qquad \nu = 0.59 \times 10^{-6} \text{ m}^2\text{/sec}$$

$$C_p = 4.174 \text{ kJ/kg}\,^{\circ}K \qquad k = 0.641 \text{ W/m}^2\text{-}^{\circ}K$$

The heat flow per meter of pipe is 150 watts. It is desired to express this per unit area of pipe, so

$$q = \frac{150 \text{ W/m}}{\pi d} = \frac{150}{\pi(0.005)}$$

$$= 9549.3 \text{ W/m}^2$$

Substituting into eq.(2) gives the required length as

$$L = \frac{\left(\frac{5}{3600}\right)(4.174)(1000)(350-290)}{(9549.3)\pi(0.005)}$$

$$= 2.32 \text{ m}$$

(b) The Reynolds number is

$$Re = \frac{Ud}{\nu}$$

Since

$$\dot{m} = \rho U \frac{\pi}{4} d^2$$

or

$$Ud = \frac{4\dot{m}}{\rho \pi d}$$

the Reynolds number may be calculated as

$$Re = \frac{4\dot{m}}{\rho \pi d \nu}$$

$$= \frac{4\left(\frac{5}{3600}\right)}{(989)\pi(0.005)(0.59\times10^{-6})}$$

$$= 606$$

This is a laminar flow. Now, if the flow is assumed to be fully developed, the Nusselt number will approach the value 4.364 by an asymptotic curve. Then

$$h = \frac{kNu}{d} = \frac{4.364k}{d} \qquad (3)$$

Since the heat flow per unit area in a pipe is defined as

$$q/A = h\Delta T_b,$$

the change in bulk temperature along a length is

$$\Delta T_b = \frac{(q/A)}{h} \qquad (4)$$

Substituting eq.(3) into eq.(4) yields

$$\Delta T_b = \frac{(q/A)d}{4.364k}$$

With the given parameters, this becomes

$$\Delta T_b = \frac{(9549.3)(0.005)}{4.364(0.641)}$$

$$= 17.07^0K$$

Then the exit temperature is

$$T_{b_2} = 350 + 17.07$$

$$= 367.07^0K$$

• PROBLEM 13-23

A tube is heated by means of forced convection from an airstream. The tube has a length of 1000 ft., and the wall surface temperature is 60°F. The flow is measured at a speed of 30 ft/sec, and it moves through an area measuring 3 in. across. If the air is at a mean bulk temperature of 70°F and a pressure of 29.4 psia, calculate

(a) the pressure drop over the tube length,

(b) the rate of heat flow from the air, and

(c) the coefficient of heat transfer by which this occurs.

Neglect the effects of any disturbance at the pipe entrance.

Solution: Since the temperature difference is small (ΔT = 70-60 = 10°F), the properties of air may be evaluated at the mean bulk temperature. The air tables list the properties as

μ = 0.0441 lbm/ft-hr $\qquad C_p$ = 0.24 Btu/lbm-°F

Pr = 0.71 $\qquad$ k = 0.0149 Btu/hr-ft-°F

Density may be found from the equation of state as

$$\rho = \frac{P}{RT}$$

$$= \frac{(29.4)(144)}{(53.3)(70+460)}$$

$$= 0.15 \text{ lbm/ft}^3$$

Then the Reynolds number is given by

$$Re = \frac{\rho U d}{\mu}$$

Substituting the values,

$$Re = \frac{(0.15)(30)(3600)(3/12)}{0.0441}$$

$$= 91{,}837$$

This is a turbulent flow.

(a) For this case, the pressure drop is defined as

$$\Delta p = 4f \frac{L}{d} \rho \frac{U^2}{2}$$

where the friction factor for a turbulent flow is

$$f = \frac{0.08}{Re^{1/4}}$$

$$= \frac{0.08}{(91{,}837)^{1/4}} = 0.0046$$

and

$$\Delta p = 4(0.0046)\left(\frac{1000}{3/12}\right)\left(\frac{0.15}{32.2}\right) \times \frac{(30/12)^2}{2}$$

$$= 1.071 \text{ psi}$$

(b) For calculating the rate of heat transfer, the following relation may be used:

$$q = \frac{QfC_p AU\Delta T}{2Pr}$$

where $C_p = \nu \times C = (0.15)(0.24) = 0.036 \text{ Btu/ft}^3\text{-}^0\text{F}$

and

$$Q = \frac{Pr^{1/2}}{1 + \frac{750(Pr)^{1/2}}{Re} + \frac{7.5(Pr)^{1/4}}{Re^{1/2}}}$$

Substituting,

$$Q = \frac{(0.71)^{1/2}}{1 + \frac{750(0.71)^{1/2}}{91{,}837} + \frac{7.5(0.71)^{1/4}}{(91{,}837)^{1/2}}}$$

$$= 0.818$$

and

$$A = \pi dL = \pi\left(\frac{3}{12}\right)(1000) = 785.4 \text{ ft}^2.$$

Substituting the values,

$$q = \frac{(0.818)(0.0046)(0.036)(785.4)(30)(70-60)}{2(0.71)}$$

$$\simeq 22.48 \text{ Btu/sec}$$

$$= 80928 \text{ Btu/hr.}$$

(c) Since $q = hA\Delta T$,

$$h = \frac{q}{A\Delta T}$$

$$= \frac{80928}{(785.4)(70-60)}$$

$$= 10.3 \text{ Btu/hr-ft}^2\text{-}^0\text{F}$$

Note: the heat flux can also be found from the correlation of Dittus-Boelter:

$$Nu_d = 0.023\ Re_d^{0.8}\ Pr^{0.4}$$

where as the process involves heating.

This is applicable as the difference of the pipe surface temperature and the bulk fluid temperature is small.

With this method, values of

$$q = 87{,}493\ \text{Btu/hr}$$

and

$$h = 11.14\ \text{Btu/hr-ft}^2\text{-}^0\text{F}$$

are obtained.

• PROBLEM 13-24

> A pipe is cooled by forced convection from a stream of water flowing at the rate of 20 gal/min. The pipe is 10 ft. long and has an inner diameter of 1 in. The wall surface temperature of the pipe is maintained at 210 °F. If the water has an entrance temperature of 50 °F, calculate the exit temperature. Use analogies of
>
> (a) Reynolds,
> (b) Colburn,
> (c) Prandtl, and
> (d) von Kármán.
>
> Assume the flow is fully developed.

Solution: Consider a pipe length dx. The heat balance between the pipe and the water is

$$\rho U \frac{\pi}{4} d^2 c_p (T|_{x+\Delta x} - T|_x) = h\pi d\Delta x(T_s - T)$$

where T is the mean bulk temperature. Letting $\Delta x \to 0$ and rearranging yields

$$\frac{dT}{dx} + \frac{h}{\rho U c_p}\,\frac{4}{d}\,(T - T_s) = 0$$

The group $\frac{h}{\rho U c_p}$ represents the Stanton number. This equation may be solved by the separation of variables into

$$\frac{dT}{T - T_s} + St\,\frac{4}{d}\,dx = 0$$

Integrating over a given length L yields

$$\int_{T_o}^{T_L} \frac{dT}{T - T_s} + St\,\frac{4}{d}\int_{o}^{L} dx = 0$$

or

$$\ln\left(\frac{T_L - T_s}{T_o - T_s}\right) + St\,\frac{4L}{d} = 0 \qquad (1)$$

If the Stanton number can be found, this equation may be used to find the exit temperature T_L.

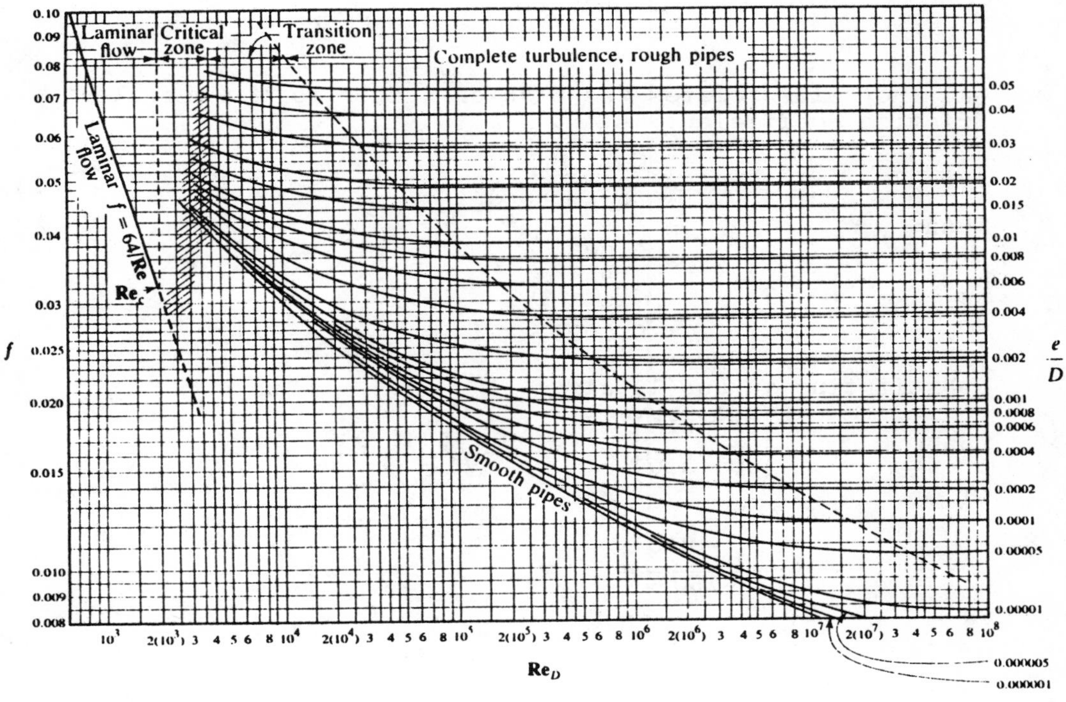

Moody Diagram

For a given Reynolds number, the associated friction factor may be found from the accompanying Moody diagram (see Figure 1). Then the Stanton number may be found from an appropriate analogy. The exit temperature is solved for from eq.(1).

Assume a mean temperature of 70°F. At this temperature, the water tables give values of

$$\nu = 1.06 \times 10^{-5} \text{ ft}^2/\text{sec.}$$

$$Pr = 6.82$$

The velocity is found as

$$U = \frac{(20\text{gal/min})(1\text{min}/60\text{sec})(1\text{ft}^3/7.48\text{gal})}{\frac{\pi}{4}\left(\frac{1}{12}\text{ft}\right)^2}$$

$$= 8.17 \text{ ft/sec}$$

Then the Reynolds number is

$$Re = \frac{Ud}{\nu} = \frac{(8.17)(1/12)}{1.06 \times 10^{-5}}$$

$$= 64,230$$

Using the smooth pipe line on the Moody diagram, the friction factor is read as 0.005.

(a) Reynolds relates the Stanton number to the turbulent friction coefficient as

$$St = \frac{C_f}{2} \tag{2}$$

Then

$$St = \frac{0.005}{2}$$

$$= 0.0025$$

Substituting in eq.(1) gives

$$\ln\left(\frac{T_L - 210}{50 - 210}\right) + \frac{(0.0025)(4)(10)}{1/12} = 0$$

or

$$\frac{T_L - 210}{-160} = e^{-1.2}$$

Solving for T_L gives

$$T_L = 161.8^\circ F.$$

(b) Colburn expresses the Stanton number as

$$St = \frac{C_f}{2} (Pr)^{-2/3} \qquad (3)$$

which gives

$$St = \frac{0.005}{2} (6.82)^{-2/3}$$

$$= 0.000695$$

Substituting in eq.(1) and solving gives

$$T_L = 210 - 160e^{-\left[\frac{(0.000695)(4)(10)}{1/12}\right]}$$

$$= 95.4^0F.$$

(c) The analogy of Prandtl is

$$St = \frac{C_f/2}{1+5\sqrt{C_f/2}(Pr-1)}$$

$$= \frac{0.005/2}{1+5\sqrt{0.005/2}(6.82-1)}$$

$$= 0.00102$$

Then eq.(1) yields

$$T_L = 210 - 160e^{-\left[\frac{(0.00102)(4)(10)}{1/12}\right]}$$

$$= 111.9^0F$$

(d) Finally, the von Karman relation is given by

$$St = \frac{C_f/2}{1+5\sqrt{C_f/2}\{(Pr-1)+\ln[1+\frac{5}{6}(Pr-1)]\}}$$

$$= \frac{0.005/2}{1+5\sqrt{0.005/2}\{(6.82-1)+\ln[1+\frac{5}{6}(6.82-1)]\}}$$

$$= 0.000863$$

and so

$$T_L = 210 - 160e^{-\left[\frac{(0.000863)(4)(10)}{1/12}\right]}$$

$$= 104.3^0F.$$

These values of T_L are summarized below.

$$\text{Reynolds} - T_L = 161.8^\circ F$$

$$\text{Colburn} - T_L = 95.4^\circ F$$

$$\text{Prandtl} - T_L = 111.9^\circ F$$

$$\text{von Kármán} - T_L = 104.3^\circ F$$

Only the Reynolds analogy proved to show a great discrepancy from the others. Based on the other three, the average outlet temperature is

$$T_L = \frac{95.4+111.9+104.3}{3} = 103.87^\circ F$$

Then the mean bulk fluid temperature is

$$T_m = \frac{50+103.87}{2} \cong 77^\circ F.$$

• PROBLEM 13-25

A steel cylinder contains liquid at a mean bulk temperature of 80°F. Steam condensing at 212°F on the outside surface is used for heating the liquid. The coefficient of heat transfer on the steam side is 1,000 Btu/hr-ft²-°F. The liquid is agitated by the stirring action of a turbine impeller. Its diameter is 2 ft., and it moves at an angular velocity of 100 rpm. The cylinder is 6 ft. long, with a diameter of 6 ft. and a wall thickness of 1/8 in. The thermal conductivity of steel may be taken as 9.4 Btu/hr-ft²-°F. Properties of the liquid, taken as constant, are:

$c_p = 0.6$ Btu/lbm-°F $\qquad$ $k = 0.1$ Btu/hr-ft-°F

$\rho = 60$ lbm/ft³

The viscosity at 130°F is 653.4 lbm/ft-hr, and at 212°F is 113.74 lbm/ft-hr. Calculate the time required to raise the mean bulk temperature of the liquid to 180°F.

Solution: If an energy balance is taken over the cylinder, the result is

$$q = UA\Delta T_L = \dot{m}c_p\Delta T_b$$

where

$$\Delta T_L = \frac{T_{b_2}-T_{b_1}}{\ln\left(\frac{T_s-T_{b_1}}{T_s-T_{b_2}}\right)}$$

where T_s is the steam temperature. Rearranging and substituting,

$$\frac{1}{\dot{m}} = \frac{c_p}{UA} \ln\left(\frac{T_s-T_{b_1}}{T_s-T_{b_2}}\right) \tag{1}$$

Now, the overall heat transfer coefficient (based on the inside surface area) is defined as

$$\frac{1}{U_i} = \frac{1}{h_i} + \frac{A_i x}{A_m k} + \frac{A_i}{A_o h_s}$$

where m denotes a mean value, and x is the wall thickness. However, since the walls are relatively thin, the approximation

$$A_i \simeq A_o \simeq A_m$$

may be used, giving

$$\frac{1}{U_i} = \frac{1}{h_i} + \frac{x}{k} + \frac{1}{h_s} \tag{2}$$

The unknown quantity here is the inside heat transfer coefficient h_i. This may be found from the appropriate Nusselt number configuartion, which is

$$Nu = \frac{h_i d_T}{k} = 0.73\ Re^{0.65}\ Pr^{1/3} \left(\frac{\mu_b}{\mu_w}\right)^{0.24} \tag{3}$$

where w refers to the inside wall surface temperature value and d_T is the total hydraulic diameter.

Now, if the Reynolds and Prandtl numbers are known, h_i may be found from eq.(3). With this, U_i may be found from eq.(2). Finally, if eq.(1) is used, the required length of time will be

$$\Delta t(hr) = \frac{1}{\dot{m}} \left(\frac{hr}{lbm}\right) \times \text{weight}(lbm)$$

so rewriting eq.(1) yields

$$\Delta t = \frac{(wt)c_p}{UA} \ln\left(\frac{T_s-T_{b_1}}{T_s-T_{b_2}}\right) \tag{4}$$

Calculations will be done at the mean temperature of

$$T_m = \frac{80 + 180}{2} = 130\,^0F$$

The Reynolds number is

$$Re = \frac{\rho U d}{\mu}$$

but given the angular velocity, $U = \omega d$ is used. Then

$$Re = \frac{(60)(100)(60)(2)^2}{653.4}$$

$$= 2204.$$

The Prandtl number is

$$Pr = \frac{\mu c_p}{k}$$

$$= \frac{(653.4)(0.6)}{0.1}$$

$$= 3920.4$$

From eq.(3),

$$h_i = 0.73(2204)^{0.65}(3920.4)^{1/3}\left(\frac{653.4}{113.74}\right)^{0.24}\left(\frac{0.1}{6}\right)$$

$$= 43.5 \text{ Btu/hr-ft}^2\text{-}^0F$$

Then, from eq.(2),

$$U_i = \frac{1}{\frac{1}{43.5} + \frac{(1/8)/12}{9.4} + \frac{1}{1{,}000}}$$

$$= 39.85 \text{ Btu/hr-ft}^2\text{-}^0F$$

Now, since $\rho = \text{wt/vol}$,

$$\text{wt} = (\rho)(\text{vol})$$

$$= (60)\pi\frac{(6)^2}{4}(6)$$

$$= 10{,}179 \text{ lbm}$$

The wall surface temperature is taken to be approximately equal to that of the condensing stream.

Substituting the values in eq.(4),

$$\Delta t = \frac{(10{,}179)(0.6)}{(39.85)\pi(6)(6)} \ln\left(\frac{212 - 80}{212 - 180}\right)$$

$$= 1.92 \text{ hr}$$

A compressible gas flows over a flat plate. Properties of the gas are closely similar to those of air. The flow is at a temperature and pressure of 700°F and 30 psia, respectively. The plate is 1 in. in length and is assumed to be perfectly insulated. If the gas is moving at a speed of 500 ft/sec, calculate the surface temperature of the plate. (Note: the speed is too great to neglect the effects of viscous dissipation.)

Solution: Heat transfer takes place by forced convection, and the high-speed flow results in viscous drag which cannot be neglected. This is similar to the aerodynamic heating effects on high-speed aircrafts, rockets and missiles where mechanical energy is transformed to thermal energy. For the given problem, properties must be evaluated at a reference temperature which is given by

$$T^* = 0.5(T_s + T_\infty) + 0.22(T_r - T_\infty) \quad (1)$$

where T_r is the recovery temperature of the surface that would be attained if it is allowed to come to equilibrium with the flow.

A related variable is the recovery factor. This is defined as

$$r = \frac{T_r - T_\infty}{U^2/2g_c c_p} \quad (2)$$

For laminar flow, it is given as

$$r = Pr^{*\,1/2} \quad (3)$$

while for turbulent flow, it is

$$r = Pr^{*\,1/3} \quad (4)$$

Now, for this problem, the plate is perfectly insulated. This simplifies the problem, as it can be assumed that $T_s = T_r$ Substituting this into eq.(1) yields

$$T^* = 0.72\ T_r + 0.28\ T_\infty \quad (5)$$

An iterative procedure is used to calculate the recovery temperature as follows:

to begin with, a value of $T_r = 800°F$ is assumed.

Substituting in eq.(5) yields

$$T^* = 0.72(800) + 0.28(700)$$

$$= 772°F.$$

At this temperature, the properties of air are:

$\mu^* = 0.0795$ lbm/ft-hr $\qquad$ $Pr^* = 0.68$

$C_p^* = 0.256$ Btu/lbm-^{0}F

Since $$\rho^* = \frac{P}{RT^*} = \frac{(30)(144)}{(53.3)(772+460)}$$

$$= 0.0657 \text{ lbm/ft}^3$$

The Reynolds number is

$$Re = \frac{\rho UL}{\mu} = \frac{(0.0657)(500)(3600)(1/12)}{0.0795}$$

$$= 123{,}962$$

which is a laminar flow, and hence eq.(3) is used.

$$r = (0.68)^{1/2}$$
$$= 0.825$$

Substituting this into eq.(2) and rearranging gives a new value of the recovery temperature as

$$T_r = T_\infty + \frac{U^2 r}{2g_c c_p}$$

$$= 700 + \frac{(500)^2(0.825)}{2(32.2)(778)(0.256)}$$

$$= 716^0\text{F}.$$

The value of 778 ft-lb/Btu is used as a conversion factor.

There is a difference between the assumed and the calculated T_r. Hence, 716^{0}F is assumed for the second iteration for the recovery temperature. Substituting in eq.(5) gives

$$T^* = 711.5^0\text{F}$$

The air tables give corresponding values of

$\mu^* = 0.0773$ lbm/ft-hr $\qquad$ $Pr^* = 0.7016$

$c_p^* = 0.254$ Btu/lbm-^{0}F

Then
$$\rho^* = 0.069 \text{ lbm/ft}^3$$
and
$$Re = 134{,}254$$

As the flow is still laminar, eq.(3) is used, giving

$$r = 0.838$$

Then eq.(2) gives

$$T_r = 716.5^\circ F$$

As there is not much difference between the assumed and the calculated recovery temperature, this is acceptable. As the surface temperature is equal to the recovery temperature,

$$T_s = 716.25^\circ F.$$

This is the average value.

RADIATION

• PROBLEM 13-27

The temperature of a tungsten filament of a light bulb is 6000°R. Calculate the energy emitted by the bulb in the visible wavelength spectrum from 0.4 μm to 0.7 μm, considering it as a grey body.

Solution: The given data is as follows:

$$\lambda_1 = 0.4 \ \mu m$$

$$\lambda_2 = 0.7 \ \mu m$$

$$T = 6000^\circ R$$

Therefore

$$\lambda_1 T = 0.4 \times 6000 = 2400 \ \mu m^\circ R$$

$$\lambda_2 T = 0.7 \times 6000 = 4200 \ \mu m^\circ R$$

From tabulated values of λT and $E_{b(0 \to \lambda T)}/\sigma T^4$ it can be determined that:

For

$$\lambda_1 T = 2400 \ \mu m^\circ R \qquad \frac{E_{b(0 - 2400)}}{\sigma T^4} = 0.0053$$

$$\lambda_2 T = 4200 \ \mu m^\circ R \qquad \frac{E_{b(0 - 4200)}}{\sigma T^4} = 0.1269$$

TABLE: Energy Radiation

λT, μm-°R	$\frac{E_{b\lambda} \times 10^5}{\sigma T^5}$, ($\mu$m-°R)$^{-1}$	$\frac{E_{b(0-\lambda T)}}{\sigma T^4}$	λT, μm-°R	$\frac{E_{b\lambda} \times 10^5}{\sigma T^5}$, ($\mu$m-°R)$^{-1}$	$\frac{E_{b(0-\lambda T)}}{\sigma T^4}$
1,000.0	0.000039	0.0000	10,400.0	5.142725	0.7183
1,200.0	0.001191	0.0000	10,600.0	4.921745	0.7284
1,400.0	0.012008	0.0000	10,800.0	4.710716	0.7380
1,600.0	0.062118	0.0000	11,000.0	4.509291	0.7472
1,800.0	0.208018	0.0003	11,200.0	4.317109	0.7561
2,000.0	0.517405	0.0010	11,400.0	4.133804	0.7645
2,200.0	1.041926	0.0025	11,600.0	3.959010	0.7726
2,400.0	1.797651	0.0053	11,800.0	3.792363	0.7803
2,600.0	2.761875	0.0098	12,000.0	3.633505	0.7878
2,800.0	3.882650	0.0164	12,200.0	3.482084	0.7949
3,000.0	5.093279	0.0254	12,400.0	3.337758	0.8017
3,200.0	6.325614	0.0368	12,600.0	3.200195	0.8082
3,400.0	7.519353	0.0507	12,800.0	3.069073	0.8145
3,600.0	8.626936	0.0668	13,000.0	2.944084	0.8205
3,800.0	9.614973	0.0851	13,200.0	2.824930	0.8263
4,000.0	10.463377	0.1052	13,400.0	2.711325	0.8318
4,200.0	11.163315	0.1269	13,600.0	2.602997	0.8371
4,400.0	11.714711	0.1498	13,800.0	2.499685	0.8422
4,600.0	12.123821	0.1736	14,000.0	2.401139	0.8471
4,800.0	12.401105	0.1982	14,200.0	2.307123	0.8518
5,000.0	12.559492	0.2232	14,400.0	2.217411	0.8564
5,200.0	12.613057	0.2483	14,600.0	2.131788	0.8607
5,400.0	12.576066	0.2735	14,800.0	2.050049	0.8649
5,600.0	12.462308	0.2986	15,000.0	1.972000	0.8689
5,800.0	12.284687	0.3234	16,000.0	1.630989	0.8869
6,000.0	12.054971	0.3477	17,000.0	1.358304	0.9018
6,200.0	11.783688	0.3715	18,000.0	1.138794	0.9142
6,400.0	11.480102	0.3948	19,000.0	0.960883	0.9247
6,600.0	11.152254	0.4174	20,000.0	0.815714	0.9335
6,800.0	10.807041	0.4394	21,000.0	0.696480	0.9411
7,000.0	10.450309	0.4607	22,000.0	0.597925	0.9475
7,200.0	10.086964	0.4812	23,000.0	0.515964	0.9531
7,400.0	9.721078	0.5010	24,000.0	0.447405	0.9579
7,600.0	9.355994	0.5201	25,000.0	0.389739	0.9621
7,800.0	8.994419	0.5384	26,000.0	0.340978	0.9657
8,000.0	8.638524	0.5561	27,000.0	0.299540	0.9689
8,200.0	8.290014	0.5730	28,000.0	0.264157	0.9717
8,400.0	7.950202	0.5892	29,000.0	0.233807	0.9742
8,600.0	7.620072	0.6048	30,000.0	0.207663	0.9764
8,800.0	7.300336	0.6197	40,000.0	0.074178	0.9891
9,000.0	6.991475	0.6340	50,000.0	0.032617	0.9941
9,200.0	6.693786	0.6477	60,000.0	0.016479	0.9965
9,400.0	6.407408	0.6608	70,000.0	0.009192	0.9977
9,600.0	6.132361	0.6733	80,000.0	0.005521	0.9984
9,800.0	5.868560	0.6853	90,000.0	0.003512	0.9989
10,000.0	5.615844	0.6968	100,000.0	0.002339	0.9991
10,200.0	5.373989	0.7078			

Therefore the energy emitted in the visible wavelength range is:

$$0.1269 - 0.0053$$

$$= 0.1216$$

or 12.16% of the energy is released as visible light.

• PROBLEM 13-28

Compute the heat absorbed by a body which is exposed to an electric heater releasing energy at the rate of 1850 W/m. The absorbing body accepts 95% of the radiation falling above 2.7μm and 30% of radiation below 2.7μm. The diameter of the heating element is 25 mm while the two bodies are 10 cm apart.

<u>Solution</u>: The irradiation upon the surface is given by the equation

$$q^{-} = [I^{-}][2 \sin \gamma_1][\pi/2]$$

The intensity $I = [\dot{Q}/\pi DL][1/\pi]$

$$= [1850/\pi(0.025)1][1/\pi]$$

and $2 \sin \gamma_1 = 2.5/10$

Therefore $q^{-} = [1850/0.025\pi][1/\pi][2.5/10][\pi/2]$

$$= 2944 \text{ W/m}^2$$

Using the Stefan-Boltzmann Law

$$\sigma T^4 = \dot{Q}/\pi DL$$

$$T = \left[\frac{\dot{Q}}{(\pi DL)(\sigma)}\right]^{\frac{1}{4}}$$

$$= \left[\frac{1850}{(\pi 0.025)(1)(5.6697\times10^{-8})}\right]^{\frac{1}{4}}$$

$$= 803\text{K}$$

Accordingly, $\lambda T = (2.7\mu\text{m})(803\text{K})$

$$= 2168 \ \mu\text{mK}$$

and $f_e = 0.095$

Thus the absorbed flux αq^- is

$$\alpha q^- = [(0.95)(0.30)+(0.905)(0.95)][2944]$$

$$= 2615 \text{ W/m}^2$$

• PROBLEM 13-29

The annular space between two concentric aluminium spheres is evacuated to provide insulation to the system. The radii of the inner and outer spheres are 0.75 ft and 1.0 ft respectively. The inner sphere contains liquefied oxygen and the outer sphere is maintained at 45°F. The boiling temperature of oxygen is -297°F and the emissivity of aluminium is ε=0.03. Determine the rate of heat flow to the oxygen by radiation.

Solution: The rate of heat loss from the outer sphere to the inner sphere due to radiation is given by:

$$q_1 = \frac{A_1 \sigma (T_1^4 - T_2^4)}{\frac{1}{\varepsilon_1} + \frac{A_1}{A_2}\left(\frac{1}{\varepsilon_1} - 1\right)}$$

Where A_1 = Area of the outer sphere

A_2 = Area of the inner sphere

$\varepsilon_1 = \varepsilon_2$ = Emissivity of aluminium

T_1 = Temperature of the outer sphere

T_2 = Temperature of the inner sphere

R_1 = Radius of the outer sphere

R_2 = Radius of the inner sphere

$$A_1 = 4\pi R_1^2 = 4\left(\frac{22}{7}\right)(1.0)^2 = 12.57 \text{ ft}^2$$

$$A_2 = 4\pi R_2^2 = 4\left(\frac{22}{7}\right)(0.75)^2 = 7.07 \text{ ft}^2$$

$$\varepsilon_1 = \varepsilon_2 = 0.03$$

The temperature of the oxygen will remain unchanged due to the phase change which occurs

$$T_2 = 460 - 297 = 163°R$$

$$T_1 = 460 + 45 = 505°R$$

Substituting the numerical values and calculating.

$$q_1 = \frac{12.57\ (0.1714 \times 10^{-8})[(505)^4 - (163)^4]}{\frac{1}{0.03} + \frac{12.57}{7.07}\left(\frac{1}{0.03} - 1\right)}$$

$$= \frac{1386.02}{33.33 + 57.48}$$

$$= \frac{1386.02}{90.81}$$

$$q_1 = 15.26 \text{ Btu/hr}$$

The rate of heat loss from the outer sphere to the oxygen by radiation is 15.26 Btu/hr.

• PROBLEM 13-30

Estimate the velocity of flue gases flowing through a 6 in. diameter and 36 in. long duct such that its (flue gas) temperature drops by 200°F from 1200°F. The outside of the duct is perfectly insulated, the average temperature and emissivity of the inside surface are 900°F and 0.8, respectively. The contents of the flue gas and the specific heat of the gas are given below. Assume heat exchange occurs by radiation alone.

$CO_2 \longrightarrow 10\%$

(Vapor) $H_2O \longrightarrow 20\%$

$C_p \longrightarrow 0.007$ Btu/ft³-°F.

Solution: The radiant heat transfer depends upon the rate of flow for a given set of temperatures for the tube.

The net radiation heat flux from gas to duct wall is given by

$$A\varepsilon_{av}\sigma[E_{(c+w)1}T_1^4 - E_{(c+w)2}T_2^4]$$

where ε_{av} is the average emissivity $= \frac{0.8 + 1}{2} = 0.9$

σ - Stefan Boltzmann constant $= 0.1714 \times 10^{-8}$

T - Absolute temperature in Rankine

$E_{(c+w)}$ - effective emissivity of the flue gas at a temperature

$$p_w \ell = 0.2 \times 0.4 = 0.08 \text{ ft-atm.}$$

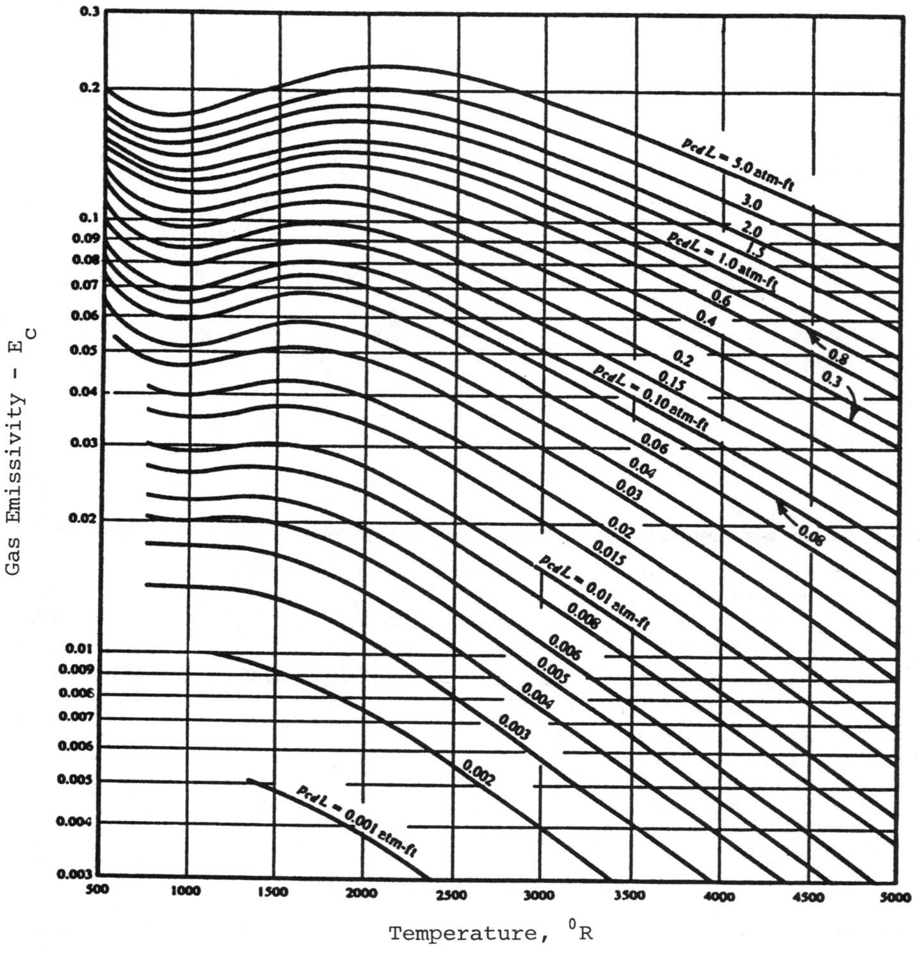

Fig. 1 Emissivity of carbon dioxide for total pressure 1 atmosphere.

From figure 1, the emissivity of carbon dioxide at a mean temperature of gas $\frac{1200 + 1000}{2} = 1100°F$ and of duct 900°F can be read as

$$E_c(1100) = 0.057 \text{ and}$$

$$E_c(900) = 0.055$$

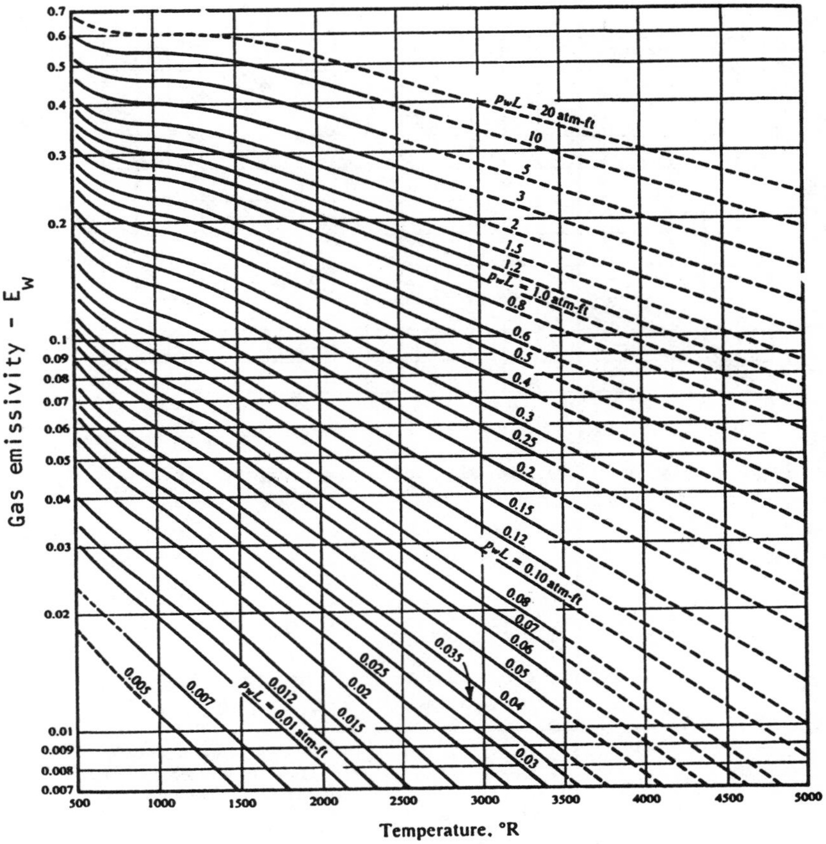

Fig. 2 Emissivity of water vapour for total pressure 1 atmosphere.

Similarly, for water vapor, from figure 2.

$$E_w(1100) = 0.061 \text{ and}$$

$$E_w(900) = 0.069$$

Applying the correction factor from figure 3., i.e., multiplying the values by correction factor 1.15, the corrected values are

$$E_w(1100) = 0.07 \text{ and}$$

$$E_w(900) = 0.079$$

Subscripts 1 and 2 correspond to inlet and outlet of the duct, respectively. The value of $E_{(c+w)}$ can be found from the charts figures 1, 2 and 3 corresponding to the product of pressure and characteristic length of the duct.

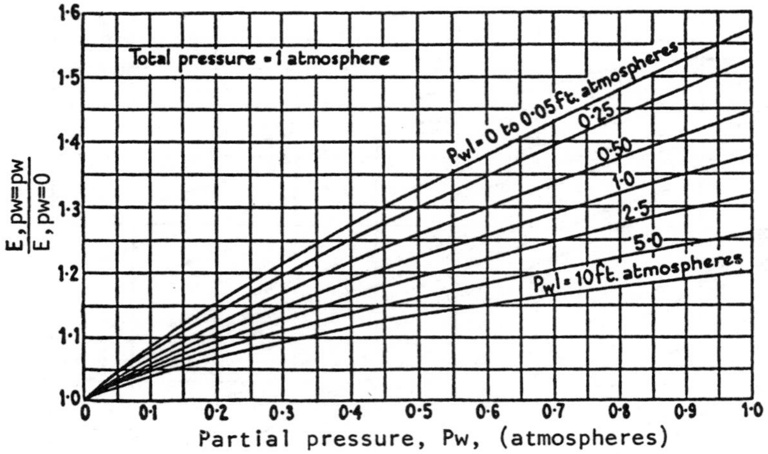

Fig. 3 Ratio of emissivity of water vapour for $p_w = p_w$ to that for $p_w = 0$

Equivalent Thickness l for Non-Luminous Gas Radiation Layers of Different Shapes

Shape	Characteristic dimension Z	*Factor by which Z is to be multiplied to give equivalent l for hemispherical radiation*	
		Calculated by various workers	*3·4 × (volume/area)*
Sphere	Diameter	0·60	0·57
Cube	Side	0·60	0·57
Infinite cylinder radiating to walls	Diameter	0·90	0·85
Ditto, radiating to centre of base	Diameter	0·90	0·85
Cylinder, height = diameter, radiating to whole surface	Diameter	0·60	0·57
Ditto, radiating to centre of base	Diameter	0·77	0·57
Space between infinite parallel planes	Distance apart	1·80	1·70
Space outside infinite bank of tubes with centres on equilateral triangles, tube diameter = clearance	Clearance	2·80	2·89
Ditto, but tube diameter = one-half clearance	Clearance	3·80	3·78
Ditto, with tube centres on squares, and tube diameter = clearance	Clearance	3·50	3·49
Rectangular parallelepiped, 1 × 2 × 6 radiating to: 2 × 6 face	Shortest edge	1·06	1·01
1 × 6 face	,,	1·06	1·05
1 × 2 face	,,	1·06	1·01
all faces	,,	1·06	1·02
Infinite cylinder of semicircular cross-section radiating to centre of flat side	Diameter	0·63	0·52

The characteristic length of the duct is given by (see table)

$$\frac{3.4 \times \text{volume}}{\text{surface area}} = \frac{3.4 \times \pi r^2 \ell}{2\pi r\ell + 2\pi r^2}$$

$$= \frac{1.7r\,\ell}{(\ell + r)} = \frac{1.7 \times 6 \times 36}{(36 + 6)} = 4.8 \text{ in.}$$

or 0.4 ft

Now, the product of the partial pressure of the gas and the characteristic length can be evaluated.

$$p_c = 0.1 \times 0.4 = 0.04 \text{ ft atm.}$$

The total emissivity of the gas at 1100°F and 900°F can be obtained by combining the individual constituent of gas emissivities,

$$E_{(c+w)}(1100) = 0.055 + 0.07 = 0.127$$

$$E_{(c+w)}(900) = 0.057 + 0.079 = 0.134$$

Introducing the values in the equation for net radiant heat transfer yields

$$q = 0.9 \times 0.173 \times 10^{-8} \times \pi \frac{6}{12} \times \frac{36}{12} \times \left[0.127 \times (1560)^4 - 0.134(1360)^4\right]$$

$$= 2155 \text{ Btu/hr.}$$

Let v be the velocity of flow of the flue gas. Then heat transfered from the gas for a temperature drop of 200°F is

$$C_p Q \times \Delta T$$

$$= 0.007 \times \pi r^2 v \times 200$$

which should be equal to the net radiant heat transfer

$$\therefore 2140 = 0.007 \times \pi r^2 v \times 200$$

or

$$v = \frac{2140}{200 \times 0.007 \times (0.4)^2}$$

$$v = 3040.9 \text{ ft/hr}^2$$

• **PROBLEM 13-31**

Determine the geometric shape factor for radiant heat transfer between a very small disc of area dA_1 and a large parallel disc of area A_2. The large disc is placed directly above the smaller disc. The radius of the larger disc is R and the perpendicular distance between the two discs is L. See figure (1).

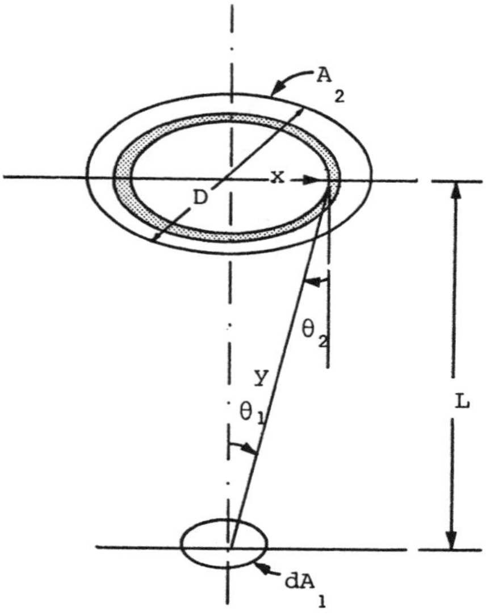

Figure (1)

Solution: The geometric shape factor is given by:

$$F_{12} = \frac{1}{dA_1} \int_{A_1}\int_{A_2} \frac{\cos\theta_1 \cdot \cos\theta_2}{\pi y^2} \, dA_1 \, dA_2 \qquad (1)$$

But $\theta_1 = \theta_2$ since they are alternate angles. Consider a differential area of radius x and thickness δx. Refer to figure (1).

Then,

$$dA_2 = 2\pi x \cdot dx$$

Therefore equation (1) simplifies to

$$F_{12} = \int_{A_2} \frac{\cos^2\theta \cdot 2\pi x}{\pi y^2} \, dx \qquad (2)$$

From the geometry it is clearly seen that

$$y^2 = x^2 + L^2, \text{ using the Pythagorean theorem}$$

$$y = \sqrt{x^2 + L^2}$$

Also

$$\cos\theta = \frac{\text{adjacent}}{\text{Hypotenuse}}$$

$$\cos\theta = \frac{L}{y}$$

but $\quad y = \sqrt{x^2 + L^2}$

Therefore $\cos\theta = \dfrac{L}{\sqrt{x^2 + L^2}}$

Substituting the values of $\cos\theta$ and y into equation(2) reduces it to

$$F_{12} = \int_0^R \frac{L^2}{x^2 + L^2} \times \frac{2\pi x}{\pi \cdot (x^2 + L^2)} dx$$

The limits of integration are so taken since x varies from 0 to R.

$$F_{12} = \int_0^R \frac{2xL^2}{(x^2 + L^2)^2} dx$$

In order to integrate use the substitution technique.

That is,

Let $\quad x^2 + L^2 = Z$

Differentiating

$$2xdx = dZ$$

Therefore

$$F_{12} = \int_0^R \frac{L^2}{Z^2} dZ$$

$$F_{12} = L^2 \left[-\frac{1}{Z}\right]_0^R$$

Substituting back the expression for Z,

$$F_{12} = -L^2 \left[\frac{1}{x^2 + L^2}\right]_0^R$$

Evaluating the limits,

$$F_{12} = -L^2\left[\frac{1}{R^2 + L^2}\right] - \frac{1}{L^2}$$

$$F_{12} = 1 - \frac{L^2}{R^2 + L^2}$$

$$F_{12} = \frac{R^2}{R^2 + L^2}$$

• **PROBLEM 13-32**

Determine the geometric shape factor between a small area dA_1 in a vertical plane and a rectangular surface (a × b) in a horizontal plane. The area dA_1 is directly below one corner of the rectangle and the distance between them is H.

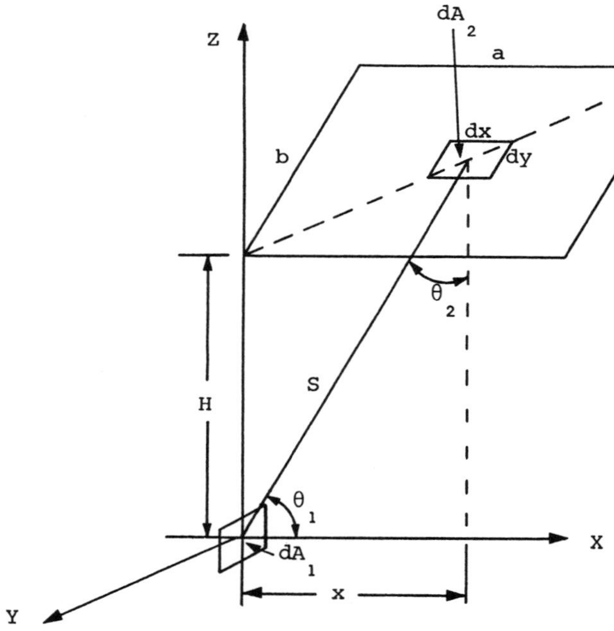

Solution: From the figure

$$\cos\theta_1 = \frac{x}{S}$$

$$\cos\theta_2 = \frac{H}{S}$$

$$S^2 = x^2 + y^2 + H^2$$

$$dA_2 = dx \cdot dy$$

The limits of x and y are 0 to a and o to b respectively.

From the definition of the shape factor:

$$F_{12} = \int_{A_2} \frac{\cos\theta_1 \cdot \cos\theta_2}{\pi S^2} dA_2$$

$$F_{12} = \int_{A_2} \frac{\frac{x}{S} \quad \frac{H}{S}}{\pi S^2} dA_2$$

$$= \int_0^a \int_0^b \frac{xH}{\pi S^4} dx\ dy$$

$$= \int_0^a \int_0^b \frac{xH}{\pi(x^2 + y^2 + H^2)^2} dx\ dy$$

$$= \frac{H}{\pi} \int_0^b \left[\int_0^a \frac{x}{(x^2 + y^2 + H^2)^2} dx \right] dy$$

Let $x^2 + y^2 + H^2 = Z$

$$2xdx = dZ$$

Substituting,

$$= \frac{H}{\pi} \int_0^b \left[\frac{1}{2} \int_0^a \frac{2x}{(x^2 + y^2 + H^2)} dx \right] dy$$

$$= \frac{H}{\pi} \int_0^b \left[\frac{1}{2} \int_0^a \frac{dZ}{Z^2} \right] dy$$

$$= \frac{H}{\pi} \int_0^b \left[-\frac{1}{2} \cdot \frac{1}{Z} \right]_0^a dy$$

$$= \frac{H}{\pi} \int_0^b \left[- \frac{1}{2(x^2 + y^2 + H^2)} \right]_0^a dy$$

$$= \frac{H}{\pi} \int_0^b \left[\frac{1}{2} \left(\frac{1}{y^2 + H^2} - \frac{1}{a^2 + y^2 + H^2} \right) \right] dy$$

$$= \frac{H}{2\pi} \int_0^b \left(\frac{1}{y^2 + H^2} - \frac{1}{y^2 + a^2 + H^2} \right) dy$$

This is of the form:

$$\int \frac{dx}{x^2 + a^2} = \frac{1}{a} \tan^{-1} x/a$$

Therefore

$$F_{12} = \frac{H}{2\pi} \left[\frac{1}{H} \tan^{-1}\left(\frac{y}{H}\right) - \frac{1}{\sqrt{a^2 + H^2}} \tan^{-1} \left(\frac{y}{\sqrt{a^2 + H^2}}\right) \right]_0^b$$

$$F_{12} = \frac{H}{2\pi} \left[\frac{1}{H} \tan^{-1}\left(\frac{b}{H}\right) - \frac{1}{\sqrt{a^2 + H^2}} \tan^{-1} \left(\frac{b}{\sqrt{a^2 + H^2}}\right) \right]$$

$$F_{12} = \frac{1}{2\pi} \left[\tan^{-1} \left(\frac{b}{H}\right) - \frac{H}{\sqrt{a^2 + H^2}} \tan^{-1} \left(\frac{b}{\sqrt{a^2 + H^2}}\right) \right]$$

• PROBLEM 13-33

A spherical body, in space, is at a distance of 1 astronomical unit from the sun. Assume the body to be at a uniform temperature and having negligible internal heat generation. Determine the quality of the surface required such that the temperature of the body remains at 300°K.

Solution: The steady state internal heat transfer from a spherical body of radius R with uniform temperature and uniform surface finish is expressed as

$$Q = \varepsilon(T_w)\sigma T_w^4 \ (4\pi r^2) - \alpha(T_w, T_s)(I_s d_{ws})(\pi r^2)$$

where subscripts w and s refer to the spherical body and the sun, respectively. ε and α are the emissivity and absorptivity, respectively.

The irradiance on a surface normal to the solar radiation at a distance of 1 astronomical unit and outside the earth's atmosphere is known as the solar constant and is given by

$$I_s d_{ws} = 130 \ W/m^2$$

The value of Q is zero as there is no internal heat generation or dissipation to the outside of the sphere. Therefore the equation simplifies to

$$\varepsilon(T_w)\ \sigma(T_w)^4(4\pi r^2) = \alpha(T_w\ T_s)(I_s d_{ws})(\pi r^2)$$

or

$$\frac{\alpha}{\varepsilon} = \frac{4\sigma T_w^4}{I_s d_{ws}}$$

$$= \frac{4 \times (5.667 \times 10^{-8}) \times (300)^4}{(1380)}$$

$$= 1.33$$

Again, the ratio of absorptivity and emissivity is also expressed as

$$\frac{\alpha}{\varepsilon} = \frac{F_1\alpha_1 + (1 - F_1)\alpha_2}{F_1\varepsilon_1 + (1 - F_1)\varepsilon_2} = 1.33$$

The view factor F_1 can be expressed as

$$F_1 = \frac{1.33 \qquad \alpha_2}{\alpha_1 - 1.33\varepsilon_1 - \alpha_2 + 1.33\varepsilon_2}$$

Table 1 Total Emittances and Solar Absorptances of Surfaces

	Total Normal Emittance	Extraterrestrial Solar Absorptance
Alumina, flame sprayed	0.80 (− 10°F)	0.28
Aluminum foil, as received	0.04 (70°F)	
Aluminum foil, bright dipped	0.025 (70°F)	0.10
Aluminum, vacuum deposited on duPont mylar	0.025 (70°F)	0.10
Aluminum alloy, 6061, as received	0.03 (70°F)	0.37
Aluminum alloy, 75S-T6 weathered 20,000 hr on a DC6 aircraft	0.16 (150°F)	0.54
Aluminum, hard anodized, 6061-T6, 35 amp/ft² at 45 volts in 20°F sulfuric acid solution, 1 mil thick	0.84 (− 10°F)	0.92
Aluminum, soft anodized *Reflectal* aluminum alloy, 5 amp/ft² for 2 hr in 40°F, 10% H_2SO_4 solution	0.79 (− 10°F)	0.23
Aluminum, 7075-T6, sandblasted with 60 mesh silicon carbide grit	0.30 (70°F)	0.55
Aluminized silicone resin paint Dow Corning XP-310	0.20 (200°F) 0.22 (800°F)	0.27
Beryllium	0.18 (300°F) 0.21 (700°F) 0.30 (1100°F)	0.77
Beryllium, anodized	0.90 (300°F) 0.88 (700°F) 0.82 (1100°F)	

The basic material for the sphere may (refer to table) be assumed as aluminium for which $\varepsilon=0.1$ and $\alpha=0.03$, and the surface may be painted with white potassium zirconium silicate for which $\alpha=0.13$ and $\varepsilon=0.86$.

Introducing these values in the equation for F_1 yields

$$F_1 = \frac{1.33(0.86) - 0.13}{0.10 - 0.04 - 0.13 + 1.33(0.86)}$$

$$= 0.943$$

• PROBLEM 13-34

A solar energy collector, aperture area $15m^2$, is installed on top of a house at an angle of 25° from the horizontal and located at latitude 35°N. The angle of acceptance is 24°. The normal radating beam on a day at a particular hour was 900 W/m^2. Calculate the solar flow to the panel.

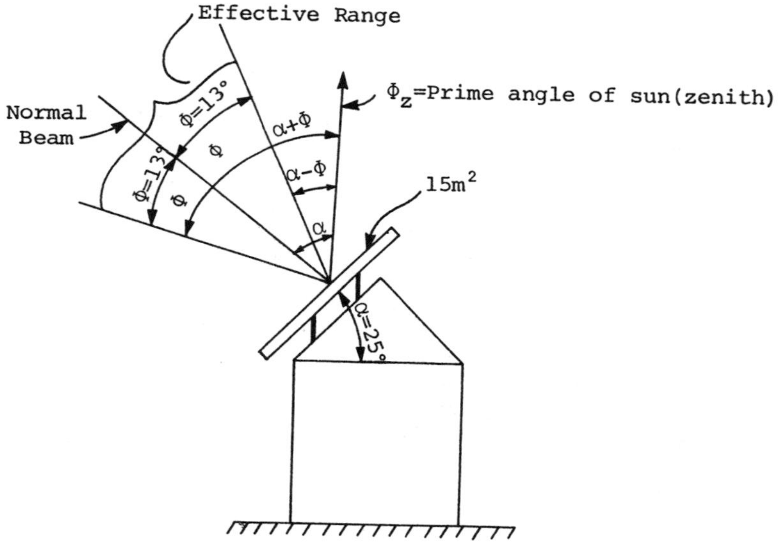

Fig. 1

Solution: As shown in figures (1) and (2), the following condition must be satisfied for energy from the incident beam of the sun to be effectively absorbed:

$$(\alpha-\Phi) \leq \tan^{-1}(\tan\Phi_z \cos\gamma) \leq (\alpha + \Phi) \quad (1)$$

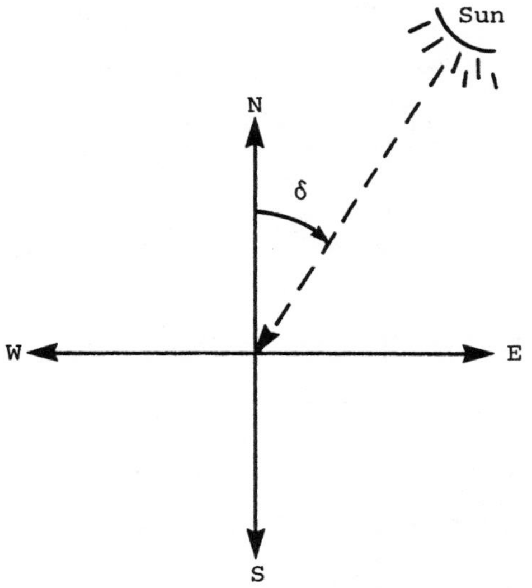

Fig. 2 Solar incident angle measured counter-clockwise from North to South (azimuth angle).

To check for the effectiveness, a decision factor (F) is introduced such that

$$F = \begin{cases} 1 \text{ if equation (1) is valid} \\ 0 \text{ otherwise} \end{cases}$$

For the angle of zenith angle Φ_z,

$$\cos\Phi_z = \cos\delta \cos\phi \cos\omega + \sin\delta \sin\phi$$

gives $\cos\Phi_z = 0.851$ and $\Phi_z = 31.6°$

Now, solar azimuthal angle is

$$\sin\gamma = \frac{\cos\delta \sin\omega}{\sin\Phi_z} = \frac{\cos(17.9) \times \sin(-30)}{\sin(31.6)}$$

$$\sin\gamma = -0.908 \therefore \gamma = -65.2°$$

For the solar panel, $\alpha - \Phi = 25 - 12 = 13°$

and $\alpha + \Phi = 25 + 12 = 37°$

$$\therefore \tan^{-1}(\tan\Phi_z \cos\gamma) = \tan^{-1}[\tan 31.6 \cos(-65.2)]$$

$$= 14.5°$$

Since 14.5° is between 13° and 37°, the decision factor is 1.

Angle of incidence for the beam radiation on the aperture is

$$\cos\theta = \cos(L - \alpha)\cos\delta \ \cos\omega + \sin(L - \alpha)\sin\delta$$

$$= \cos(35\text{-}25)\cos 17.9 \cos 30 + \sin(35\text{-}25)\sin 17.9$$

$$= 0.865$$

The effective energy rate of the beam radiant incident on the solar panel is

$$G_e = G_{bn} \times F \times \cos\theta$$

$$= 900 \times 1 \times 0.865 = 778.5 \text{ W/m}$$

$\therefore$ for aperture area of 15m^2, effective beam radiation

$$= 778.5 \times 15 = 11677.5 \text{ W}$$

$$= 11.68 \text{ kW}.$$

• PROBLEM 13-35

> If a thin high thermal conductivity grey plate is introduced parallely between two infinite parallel grey plates of equal area, obtain an equation which provides the reduction in radiant heat transfer between the plates.

Solution: The total energy absorbed by the second plate can be obtained by summing up energies absorbed from any beam on repeated reflection. (Refer to figure (1))

$$Q_{1\to 2} = A\sigma T_1^4 \left[e_1 e_2 + e_1 e_2 (1 - e_1)(1 - e_2) + \ldots\right]$$

where e is the emissivity.

Similarly the total energy absorbed by first plate is:

$$Q_{2\to 1} = A\sigma T_2^4 \left[e_1 e_2 + e_1 e_2 (1 - e_1)(1 - e_2) + \ldots\right]$$

The net total energy transfer is:

$$Q_{12} = A\sigma(T_1^4 - T_2^4)\left[e_1 e_2 + e_1 e_2 (1 - e_1)(1 - e_2) + \ldots\right]$$

which can be simplified to

$$Q_{12} = A\sigma e_1 e_2 (T_1^4 - T_2^4) \sum_{i=0}^{\infty} \left[(1 - e_1)(1 - e_2)\right]^i \qquad (1)$$

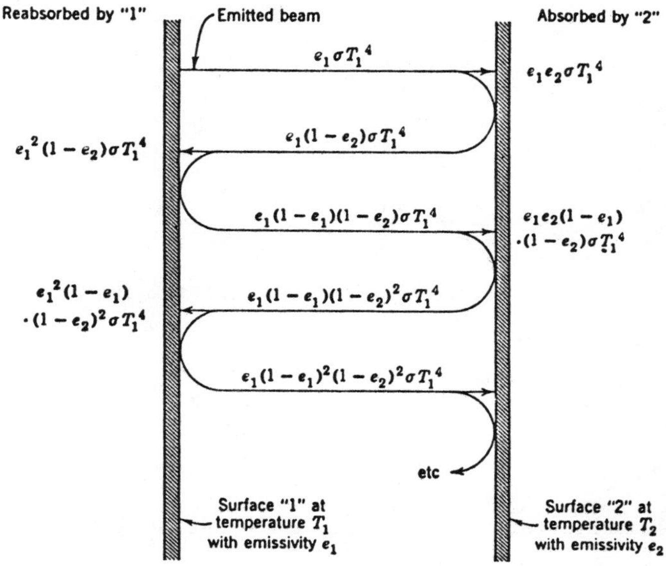

Schematic diagram showing what happens to radiation emitted from surface "1".

Fig. 1.

It is known that

$$\sum_{n=0}^{\infty} x^n = \frac{1}{1 - x}$$

Therefore:

$$\sum_{i=0}^{\infty} \left[(1 - e_1)(1 - e_2)\right]^i = \frac{1}{1 - (1 - e_1)(1 - e_2)}$$

$$= \frac{1}{1 - (1 - e_2 - e_1 + e_1 e_2)}$$

$$= \frac{1}{1 - 1 + e_2 + e_1 - e_1 e_2}$$

$$= \frac{1}{e_1 e_2\left(\frac{1}{e_1} + \frac{1}{e_2} - 1\right)}$$

Substituting in equation (1) yields:

$$Q_{12} = A\sigma e_1 e_2(T_1^4 - T_2^4) \quad \frac{1}{e_1 e_2\left(\frac{1}{e_1} + \frac{1}{e_2} - 1\right)}$$

$$= \frac{A\sigma(T_1^4 - T_2^4)}{\left(\frac{1}{e_1} + \frac{1}{e_2} - 1\right)}$$

Analogously,

$$Q_{23} = \frac{A\sigma(T_2^4 - T_3^4)}{\left(\frac{1}{e_2} + \frac{1}{e_3} - 1\right)}$$

To obtain the solution, T_2 must be written in terms of T_1 and T_3.

At steady state:

$$Q_{12} = Q_{23}$$

$$\frac{A\sigma(T_1^4 - T_2^4)}{\left(\frac{1}{e_1} + \frac{1}{e_2} - 1\right)} = \frac{A\ (T_2^4 - T_3^4)}{\left(\frac{1}{e_2} + \frac{1}{e_3} - 1\right)}$$

$$\frac{T_1^4}{\frac{1}{e_1} + \frac{1}{e_2} - 1} - \frac{T_2^4}{\frac{1}{e_1} + \frac{1}{e_2} - 1} = \frac{T_2^4}{\frac{1}{e_2} + \frac{1}{e_3} - 1} - \frac{T_3^4}{\frac{1}{e_2} + \frac{1}{e_3} - 1}$$

$$T_2^4 \left[\frac{1}{\frac{1}{e_2} + \frac{1}{e_3} - 1} + \frac{1}{\frac{1}{e_1} + \frac{1}{e_2} - 1}\right] = \frac{T_1^4}{\frac{1}{e_1} + \frac{1}{e_2} - 1} + \frac{T_3^4}{\frac{1}{e_2} + \frac{1}{e_3} - 1}$$

$$T_2^4 \left[\frac{\left(\frac{1}{e_1} + \frac{1}{e_2} - 1\right) + \left(\frac{1}{e_2} + \frac{1}{e_3} - 1\right)}{\left(\frac{1}{e_2} + \frac{1}{e_3} - 1\right)\left(\frac{1}{e_1} + \frac{1}{e_2} - 1\right)}\right] = \frac{T_1^4}{\frac{1}{e_1} + \frac{1}{e_2} - 1} + \frac{T_3^4}{\frac{1}{e_2} + \frac{1}{e_3} - 1}$$

$$T_2^4 = \frac{\left[T_1^4\left(\frac{1}{e_2} + \frac{1}{e_3} - 1\right) + T_3^4\left(\frac{1}{e_1} + \frac{1}{e_2} - 1\right)\right]}{\left(\frac{1}{e_1} + \frac{1}{e_2} - 1\right) + \left(\frac{1}{e_2} + \frac{1}{e_3} - 1\right)}$$

Recall that:

$$Q_{12} = \frac{A\sigma(T_1^4 - T_2^4)}{\frac{1}{e_1} + \frac{1}{e_2} - 1}$$

Substituting the value of T_2:

$$Q_{12} = \frac{A\sigma\left[T_1^4 - \left\{\frac{T_1^4\left(\frac{1}{e_2} + \frac{1}{e_3} - 1\right) + T_3^4\left(\frac{1}{e_1} + \frac{1}{e_2} - 1\right)}{\left(\frac{1}{e_1} + \frac{1}{e_2} - 1\right) + \left(\frac{1}{e_2} + \frac{1}{e_3} - 1\right)}\right\}\right]}{\left(\frac{1}{e_1} + \frac{1}{e_2} - 1\right)}$$

$$Q_{12} = \frac{A\sigma}{\left(\frac{1}{e_1} + \frac{1}{e_2} - 1\right)}\left[\frac{T_1^4\left(\frac{1}{e_1} + \frac{1}{e_2} - 1\right) - T_3^4\left(\frac{1}{e_1} + \frac{1}{e_2} - 1\right)}{\left(\frac{1}{e_1} + \frac{1}{e_2} - 1\right) + \left(\frac{1}{e_2} + \frac{1}{e_3} - 1\right)}\right]$$

$$Q_{12} = \frac{A\sigma(T_1^4 - T_3^4)}{\left(\frac{1}{e_1} + \frac{1}{e_2} - 1\right) + \left(\frac{1}{e_2} + \frac{1}{e_3} - 1\right)}$$

The ratio of radiant energy transfer with a middle plate to that without one is:

$$\frac{Q_{12}}{Q_{13}} = \frac{\left(\frac{1}{e_1} + \frac{1}{e_3} - 1\right)}{\left(\frac{1}{e_1} + \frac{1}{e_2} - 1\right) + \left(\frac{1}{e_2} + \frac{1}{e_3} - 1\right)}$$

• PROBLEM 13-36

Compute the rate of radiant heat transfer to a spherical meat ball, 8 in. dia., at a temperature of 70°F, placed in a cubical oven, of side 2 ft., at 400°F. The emissivity of the walls of the oven is 0.8. The meat ball is wrapped in an aluminium foil having an emissivity of 0.1.

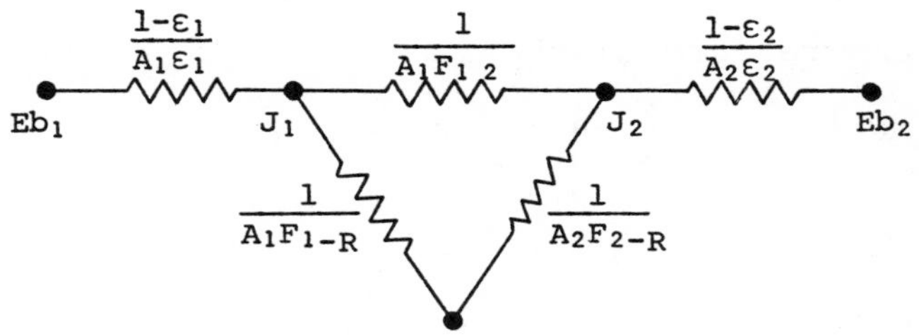

Fig. Electrical analogy for a two-gray surface system enclosed by reradiating walls.

Solution: Using the electrical analogy, the problem can be represented in the form of an electrical circuit as shown above. The notations used are as explained below.

E_b is the radiosity of the heat source (oven) and the meat ball

A is the surface area involved in the radiation heat transfer

F_{i-j} is the shape factor

ε is the emissivity of the surfaces

The subscripts 1, 2 and R correspond to the heater surface, meat ball and the other 5 walls of the oven, respectively.

The net radiant heat transfer rate can be computed by solving the electrical circuit using the equation

$$q = \frac{A_1 \sigma(T_1^4 - T_2^4)}{\frac{1-\varepsilon_1}{\varepsilon_1} + \left[\frac{1}{F_{1-2} + \frac{1}{\frac{1}{F_{1-R}} + \frac{A_1}{A_2 F_{2-R}}}}\right] + \frac{1-\varepsilon_2}{\varepsilon_2}\frac{A_1}{A_2}}$$

$T_1 = 400 + 460 = 860°R$

$T_2 = 70 + 460 = 530°R, \quad \sigma = 0.171 \times 10^{-8}$

$\varepsilon_1 = 0.8, \quad \varepsilon_2 = 0.1$

The shape factor F_{2-1} can be explained as follows:

The radiations of the meat ball fall on all the walls of the oven, therefore,

$$F_{2-1} = \frac{1}{6} \quad \text{and}$$

applying the reciprocal theorem

$$A_2 F_{2-1} = A_1 F_{1-2}$$

or

$$F_{1-2} = \frac{A_2}{A_1} F_{2-1}$$

$$= \frac{\pi\left(\frac{8}{12}\right)^2}{2 \times 2} \times \frac{1}{6} = 0.058$$

Again, the view factor $F_{1-R} = 1.0 - F_{1-2}$

$$= 1 - 0.058 = 0.942$$

and $F_{2-R} = \frac{5}{6}(1.0) = \frac{5}{6} = 0.833$

Now, $$\left[\frac{1}{F_{1-2} + \frac{1}{\frac{1}{F_{1-R}} + \frac{A_1}{A_2 F_{2-R}}}}\right] = \left[\frac{1}{0.058 + \frac{1}{\frac{1}{0.942} + \frac{4}{\pi\left(\frac{8}{12}\right)^2} \times \frac{1}{0.833}}}\right]$$

$$= 3.569$$

$$\frac{1-\varepsilon_1}{\varepsilon_1} = \frac{1-0.8}{0.8} = 0.25$$

$$A_1 = 2 \times 2 = 4 \text{sq.ft.}$$

$$\frac{1-\varepsilon_2}{\varepsilon_2} = \frac{1-0.1}{0.1} = 9 \qquad \frac{A_1}{A_2} = \frac{4}{\pi \left(\frac{8}{12}\right)^2} = 2.865$$

$$T_1^4 - T_2^4 = 860^4 - 530^4 = 4.68103 \times 10^{11}$$

Substituting the values in the equation,

$$q = \frac{(4) \times (0.171 \times 10^{-8})(4.68103 \times 10^{11})}{(0.25) + (3.569) + (9 \times 2.865)}$$

$$q \cong 108 \text{ Btu/hr.}$$

• PROBLEM 13-37

The temperature of two 1 m² square boards, placed parallel and 0.5 m apart, are $T_1 = 1000°K$ and $T_2 = 400°K$, with their respective emissivities $\varepsilon_1 = 0.8$ and $\varepsilon_2 = 0.5$. Formulate the node relations, by network analysis, when:

(a) the boards are enclosed in a housing at 300°K, and

(b) a re-radiating wall, perfectly insulated at its outer surface, connects the two surfaces.

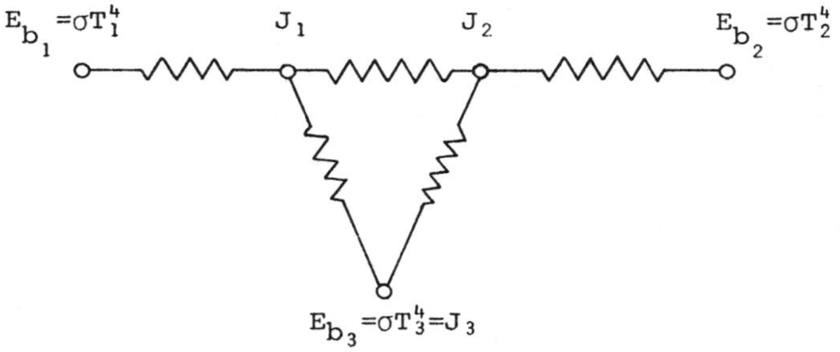

Fig. 1 Radiation network of the three body system.

Solution: This is a three-body problem, i.e., the two boards, surfaces 1 and 2, and the receptacle, surface 3. The equivalent electrical network of the system is shown in fig.1.

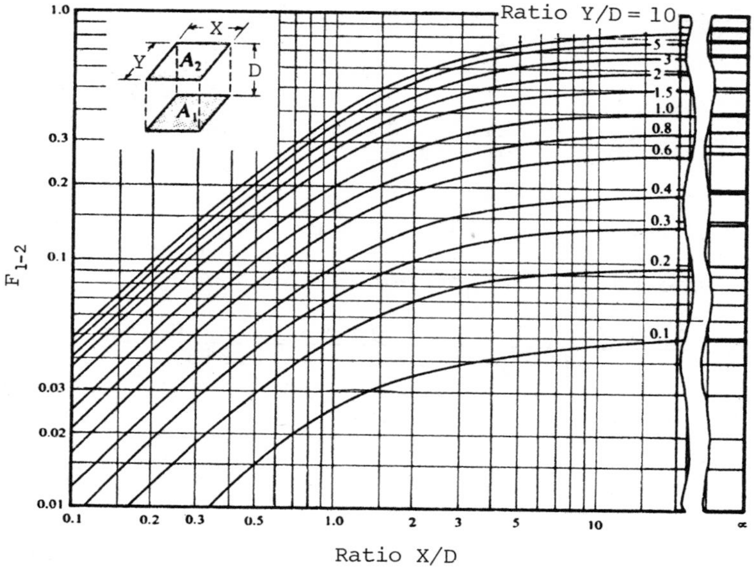

Referring to fig. 2, the ratios needed to determine the shape factors are:

$$Y/D = 1.0/0.5 = 2.0, \quad X/D = 1.0/0.5 = 2.0$$

and the shape factors are:

$$F_{1-2} = 0.46 = F_{2-1}$$

$$F_{1-1} = 0 = F_{2-2}$$

$$F_{1-3} = 1 - F_{1-2} = 1 - 0.46 = 0.54$$

$$F_{2-3} = 1 - F_{2-1} = 1 - 0.46 = 0.54$$

(a) The energies radiated per unit time and per unit area by the surfaces are:

$$E_{b1} = \sigma T_1^4 = (5.669 \times 10^{-8})(1000°K)^4 = 56690 \text{ W/m}^2$$

$$E_{b2} = \sigma T_2^4 = (5.669 \times 10^{-8})(400°K)^4 = 1451 \text{ W/m}^2$$

$$E_{b3} = \sigma T_3^4 = (5.669 \times 10^{-8})(300°K)^4 = 459 \text{ W/m}^2$$

Since the area of the receptacle is very large, the radiation shape factor from the receptacle surface to the boards will reach zero.

Using the concept of reciprocity yields:

$$A_1F_{1-3} = A_3F_{3-1}, \quad F_{3-1} = \frac{A_1F_{1-3}}{\infty} = 0$$

$$A_2F_{2-3} = A_3F_{3-2}, \quad F_{3-2} = \frac{A_2F_{2-3}}{\infty} = 0$$

For surfaces which may see themselves, the general relation is:

$$\sum_{j=1}^{n} F_{ij} = 1.0$$

Applying this relation yields:

$$F_{3-1} + F_{3-2} + F_{3-3} = 1.0, \quad F_{3-3} = 1.0$$

The relations for nodes 1, 2, and 3 are expressed by:

$$J_i - 1 - \varepsilon_i \sum_j F_{ij} J_j = \varepsilon E_{bi}$$

Node 1: $J_1 - (1 - \varepsilon_1)(F_{1-1}J_1 + F_{1-2}J_2 + F_{1-3}J_3) = \varepsilon_1 E_{b1}$

Node 2: $J_2 - (1 - \varepsilon_2)(F_{2-1}J_1 + F_{2-2}J_2 + F_{2-3}J_3) = \varepsilon_2 E_{b2}$ (1)

Node 3: $J_3 - (1 - \varepsilon_3)(F_{3-1}J_1 + F_{3-2}J_2 + F_{3-3}J_3) = \varepsilon_3 E_{b3}$

Substituting in the corresponding values for equation set (1) yields:

$$J_1 - (1 - 0.8)\left[(0)J_1 + (0.46)J_2 + (0.54)J_3\right] = (0.8)(56690)$$

$$J_2 - (1 - 0.5)\left[(0.46)J_1 + (0)J_2 + (0.54)J_3\right] = (0.5)(1451)$$

$$J_3 - (1 - \varepsilon_3)\left\lfloor(0)J_1 + (0)J_2 + (1.0)J_3\right\rfloor = \varepsilon_3(459)$$

Since the receptacle is very large, the radiation emitted toward it will be completely absorbed. But, the receptacle surface will still radiate heat per unit time and per unit area. Therefore, node three gives $J = 459\ W/m^2$

Simplifying the node relations yields:

$$J_1 - 0.092J_2 - 0.108J_3 = 45,352$$

$$-0.23J_1 + J_2 - 0.27J_3 = 725.5$$

$$J_3 = 459$$

Solving for J_1 and J_2 yields:

$$J_1 = 46462.87\ W/m^2 = 46463\ W/m^2$$

$$J_2 = 11535.885\ W/m^2 = 11536\ W/m^2$$

The energies radiated for boards 1 and 2 are calculated as:

$$q_1 = \frac{A_1 \varepsilon_1}{(1 - \varepsilon_1)}(E_{b1} - J_1) = \frac{(1.0)(0.8)}{(1 - 0.8)}(56690 - 46463) = 40908 \text{ W}$$

$$q_2 = \frac{A_2 \varepsilon_2}{(1 - \varepsilon_2)}(E_{b2} - J_2) = \frac{(1.0)(0.5)}{(1 - 0.5)}(1451 - 11536) = -10085 \text{ W}$$

The total energy assimilated by the receptacle is:

$$q_3 = q_1 + q_2 = 40908 - 10085 = 30823 \text{ W}$$

(b) The area of the plate joined to the board exteriors is 4.0 m^2.

Applying the concept of reciprocity yields:

$$A_1F_{1-3} = A_3F_{3-1}, \quad F_{3-1} = \frac{A_1F_{1-3}}{A_3} = \frac{(1.0)(0.54)}{4.0} = 0.135$$

$$A_2F_{2-3} = A_3F_{3-2}, \quad F_{3-2} = \frac{A_2F_{2-3}}{A_3} = \frac{(1.0)(0.54)}{4.0} = 0.135$$

and $F_{3-1} + F_{3-2} + F_{3-3} = 1.0$, $F_{3-3} = 1.0 - 0.135 - 0.135 = 0.73$

The relations for nodes 1, 2, and 3 are the same as in part (a).

Substituting in the corresponding values yields:

$$J_1 - (1 - 0.8)[(0)J_1 + (0.46)J_2 + (0.54)J_3] = (0.8)(56690)$$

$$J_2 - (1 - 0.5)[(0.46)J_1 + (0)J_2 + (0.54)J_3] = (0.5)(1451)$$

$$J_3 - (1 - \varepsilon_3)[(0.135)J_1 + (0.135)J_2 + (0.73)J_3 = \varepsilon_3 J_3$$

Simplifying the three equations yields:

$$J_1 - 0.092J_2 - 0.018J_3 = 45{,}352$$

$$-0.23J_1 + J_2 - 0.27J_3 = 725.5$$

$$-0.135J_1 - 0.135J_2 + 0.27J_3 = 0$$

Solving the three equations simultaneously for J_1, J_2, and J_3 yields:

$$J_1 \cong 51{,}424 \text{ W/m}^2$$

$$J_2 \cong 22{,}535 \text{ W/m}^2$$

$$J_3 \cong 36{,}980 \text{ W/m}^2$$

The energies radiated from the boards are:

$$q_1 = \frac{A_1\varepsilon_1}{1-\varepsilon_1}(E_{b1} - J_1) = \frac{(1.0)(0.8)}{1-0.8}(56690 - 51424) = 21064 \text{ W}$$

$$q_2 = \frac{A_1\varepsilon_1}{1-\varepsilon_1}(E_{b2} - J_2) = \frac{(1.0)(0.5)}{1-0.5}(1451 - 22535) \cong -21064 \text{ W}$$

It is obvious that the energies radiated from the boards compliment each other since the plate connected to them is protected from heat loss. The plate temperature may be calculated from

$$J_3 = E_{b3} = \sigma T_3^4 = 36{,}980 \text{ W/m}^2$$

$$T_3 = \left(\frac{36{,}980 \text{ W/m}^2}{5.669 \times 10^{-8}}\right)^{\frac{1}{4}} = 899 \text{ K}$$

• PROBLEM 13-38

Determine the net energy transferred for a square channel (fig. 1) at each surface of different material. The properties of the surfaces are given in table 1.

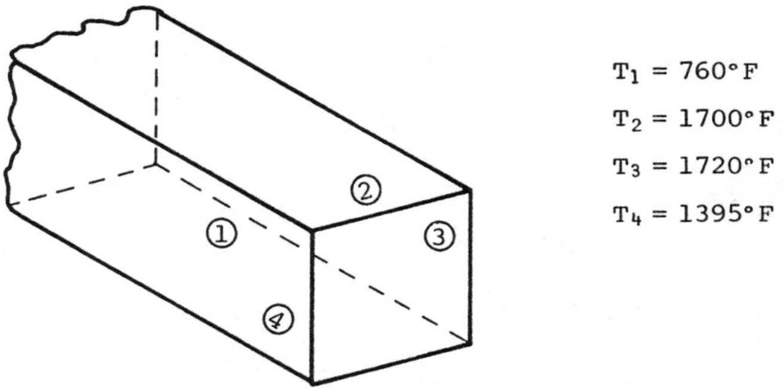

Fig. 1 Channel for semigray problem.

Table 1

Surface Number	Material	Temperature	Emissivity
1	Monel Metal	760°F	0.44
2	Iron, Polished	1700°F	0.34
3	Nickel, Oxidized	1720°F	0.71
4	Mild Steel	1395°F	0.27

Solution: The problem to be solved is a Four-Node System. Each surface will have the node energy depicted as:

(1,0,0,0), (0,1,0,0,), (0,0,1,0), and (0,0,0,1).

The radiation shape factors of each surface will be equal to its corresponding emissivity:

$$F_{11} + F_{12} + F_{13} + F_{14} = \varepsilon_1$$

or, $0.0598 + 0.0909 + 0.2336 + 0.0557 = 0.440$

$$F_{21} + F_{22} + F_{23} + F_{24} = \varepsilon_2$$

$$0.0683 + 0.0491 + 0.1765 + 0.0461 = 0.34$$

$$F_{31} + F_{32} + F_{33} + F_{34} = \varepsilon_3$$

$$0.1552 + 0.1791 + 0.2880 + 0.0877 = 0.7100$$

$$F_{41} + F_{42} + F_{43} + F_{44} = \varepsilon_4$$

$$0.074 + 0.0632 + 0.1135 + 0.0189 = 0.27$$

Next, the emissive powers of the walls are

$$E_{b1} = \varepsilon_1 \sigma T_1^4 = 0.44(.1714 \times 10^{-8})(760°F + 460°R)^4$$
$$= 1.67 \times 10^3 \text{ Btu/hr. ft}^2$$

$$E_{b2} = \varepsilon_2 \sigma T_2^4 = 0.34(.1714 \times 10^{-8})(1700°F + 460°R)^4$$
$$= 1.268 \times 10^4 \text{ Btu/hr.ft}^2$$

$$E_{b3} = \varepsilon_3 \sigma T_3^4 = 0.71(.1714 \times 10^{-8})(1720°F + 460°R)^4$$
$$= 2.748 \times 10^4 \text{ Btu/hr.ft}^2$$

$$E_{b4} = \varepsilon_4 \sigma T_4^4 = 0.27(.1714 \times 10^{-8})(1395°F + 460°R)^4$$
$$= 5.48 \times 10^3 \text{ Btu/hr. ft}^2$$

The energy transferred by each surface may be represented by:

$$q_j = \sum_{k=1}^{4} F_{kj} E_{bk} - \varepsilon_j E_{bj} \qquad (1)$$

Expanding eq. (1) yields:

$$q_1 = F_{11} E_{b1} + F_{21} E_{b2} + F_{31} E_{b3} + F_{41} E_{b4} - \varepsilon_1 E_{b1}$$

$$= 0.0598(1.67 \times 10^3) + 0.0683(1.268 \times 10^4) + 0.1552(2.748 \times 10^4)$$
$$+ 0.0744(5.48 \times 10^3) - 0.44(1.67 \times 10^3) = 4.9 \times 10^3 \text{ Btu/hr.ft}^2$$

$$q_2 = F_{12}E_{b1} + F_{22}E_{b2} + F_{32}E_{b3} + F_{42}E_{b4} - \varepsilon_2 E_{b2}$$

$$= 0.0909(1.67 \times 10^3) + 0.0491(1.268 \times 10^4) + 0.1791(2.748 \times 10^4)$$

$$+ 0.0632(5.48 \times 10^3) - 0.34(1.268 \times 10^4) = 1.73 \times 10^3 \text{ Btu/hr.ft}^2$$

$$q_3 = F_{13}E_{b1} + F_{23}E_{b2} + F_{33}E_{b3} + F_{43}E_{b4} - \varepsilon_3 E_{b3}$$

$$= 0.2336(1.67 \times 10^3) + 0.1765(1.268 \times 10^4) + 0.2880(2.748 \times 10^4)$$

$$+ 0.1135(5.48 \times 10^3) - 0.71(2.748 \times 10^4) = -8.35 \times 10^3 \text{ Btu/hr.ft}^2$$

$$q_4 = F_{14}E_{b1} + F_{24}E_{b2} + F_{34}E_{b3} + F_{44}E_{b4} - \varepsilon_4 E_{b4}$$

$$= 0.0557(1.67 \times 10^3) + 0.0461(1.26 \times 10^4) + 0.0877(2.748 \times 10^4)$$

$$+ 0.0189(5.48 \times 10^3) - 0.27(5.48 \times 10^3) = 1.71 \times 10^3 \text{ Btu/hr.ft}^2$$

CHAPTER 14

STATISTICAL THERMODYNAMICS

• PROBLEM 14-1

(a) **Show** that the partition function appropriate to an isothermal-isobaric ensemble is

$$\Delta(N,P,T) = \sum\sum \Omega(N,V,E)e^{-E/kT}e^{-PV/kT}$$

(b) Derive the principal thermodynamic connection formulas for this ensemble.

Solution: An ensemble is a (mental) collection of a very large number of systems, each constructed to be a replica on a thermodynamic level of the actual thermodynamic system whose properties are being investigated. For example, consider a system of pressure P that contains N molecules of a single component and is immersed in a large heat bath at a temperature T. In this case, the ensemble consist of π systems, all of which are constructed to duplicate the thermodynamic state (N,P,T) and the environment of the original system. Define:

H_i = enthalpy measured from system i

$\bar{N} = \sum n_i$, where n_i is the number of systems with enthalpy H_i

$\bar{H} = \sum n_i H_i$

The constraints are

$$\phi_i = \sum n_i - \bar{N} = 0$$

i) $\alpha' d\phi_1 = \sum \alpha dn_i = 0$

where the parameter α is called the Lagrange multiplier

$$\phi_2 = \sum n_i H_i - \bar{H} = 0.$$

ii) $\beta d\phi_2 = \sum \beta H_i dn_i = 0.$

For each value of N, there will be a different set of energy states. Let the number of states associated with the distribution $n = \Omega(n)$. Then

$$\Omega(n) = \frac{\bar{N}!}{\prod_i n_i} \qquad (1)$$

Let the total number of states over all $n = C$. Then,

$$C = \sum_n \Omega(n) \qquad (2)$$

and the probability $\omega(n)$, of a given distribution is given by

$$\omega(n) = \frac{\Omega(n)}{C} \quad . \qquad (3)$$

Since the most probable distribution set is desired, maximize ω using equations (1) and (3):

$$\ell n\ \omega(n) = \ell n\ \bar{N}! - \sum_i \ell n\ n_i! - \ell n\ C.$$

Using Stirling's approximation

$$\ell n\ \omega(n) = N\ \ell n\ \bar{N} - \bar{N} - \sum_i n_i\ \ell n\ n_i + \sum n_i - \ell n\ C.$$

But $\bar{N} = \sum n_i$,

$$\therefore \quad \ell n\ \omega(n) = N\ \ell n\ \bar{N} - \sum_i n_i\ \ell n\ n_i - \ell n\ C.$$

$$\frac{d\ \ell n\ \omega(n)}{dn} = -\sum_i (n_i \frac{dn_i}{n_i} + dn_i\ \ell n\ n_i)$$

$$= -\sum_i (1 + \ell n\ n_i) dn_i$$

Apply Lagrange's method of undetermined multipliers;

$$\sum_i (-1 - \ell n\ n_i - \alpha' - \beta H_i) dn_i = 0.$$

Thus, $(1 + \alpha') + \ell n\ n_i + \beta H_i = 0$.

Let $\alpha = 1 + \alpha'$ then

$$\ell n\ n_i = -\alpha - \beta H_i$$

or

$$n_i = e^{-\alpha} e^{-\beta H_i} \quad . \qquad (4)$$

Recall that $\sum n_i = \bar{N}$. Therefore,

$$\bar{N} = \sum_i e^{-\alpha} e^{-\beta H_i}$$

$$= e^{-\alpha} \sum_i e^{-\beta H_i} \tag{5}$$

Let the probability of the system having enthalpy of H_i in the maximum distribution n be P_i

$$\therefore \quad P_i = \frac{n_i}{\bar{N}}$$

From equations (4) and (5)

$$P_i = \frac{e^{-\alpha} e^{-\beta H_i}}{e^{-\alpha} \sum_i e^{-\beta H_i}}$$

$$= \frac{e^{-\beta H_i}}{\sum e^{-\beta H_i}}$$

$$= \frac{e^{-\beta H_i}}{\Delta} \tag{6}$$

where Δ is the partition function. Now

$$\bar{H} = \sum_i P_i H_i \tag{7}$$

$$\therefore \quad \bar{H} = \frac{\sum_i H_i e^{-\beta H_i}}{\sum_i e^{-\beta H_i}}$$

$$= \frac{\sum H_i \; e^{-\beta H_i}}{\Delta}$$

Differentiate equation (7) to obtain

$$d\bar{H} = \sum_i P_i dH_i + \sum_i H_i dP_i \tag{8}$$

From the combined first and second laws of thermodynamics

$$dH_i = TdS + V_i dP \tag{9}$$

But $$\left(\frac{\partial H_i}{\partial P}\right)_N = V_i$$

$$\therefore \quad dH_i = \left(\frac{\partial H_i}{\partial P}\right)_N dP = V_i dP \qquad (10)$$

Also, from equation (6)

$$\ell n\ P_i + \ell n\ \Delta = -\beta H_i$$

Rearranging this to solve for H_i yields

$$H_i = -\frac{1}{\beta}(\ell n\ P_i + \ell n\ \Delta) \qquad (11)$$

Using the expressions for dH_i and H_i in equation (8) gives

$$d\bar{H} = \sum_i P_i V_i dP - \sum_i \frac{1}{\beta}(\ell n\ P_i + \ell n\ \Delta) dP_i$$

$$= \bar{V}dP - \sum_i \frac{1}{\beta}\ \ell n\ P_i\ dP_i - \frac{1}{\beta}\ \ell n\ \Delta \sum dP_i$$

$$= \bar{V}dP - \sum_i \frac{1}{\beta}\ \ell n\ P_i\ dP_i - 0$$

But $$d\left(\sum P_i\ \ell n\ P_i\right) = \sum_i P_i \frac{dP_i}{P_i} + \sum_i dP_i\ \ell n\ P_i$$

$$= 0 + \sum_i dP_i\ \ell n\ P_i$$

$$= \sum_i dP_i\ \ell n\ P_i$$

$$\therefore \quad d\bar{H} = -\frac{1}{\beta}\ d\left(P_i\ \ell n\ P_i\right) + \bar{V}dP \qquad (12)$$

and from equation (9)

$$dH = TdS + VdP$$

Comparing equations (9) and (12) imply that

$$TdS = -\frac{1}{\beta}\ d\left(P_i\ \ell n\ P_i\right)$$

From the cannonical ensemble, β is defined as

$$\beta = \frac{1}{kT}.$$

But $$\Delta = \sum_i e^{-\beta H_i}$$

$$\therefore \quad \Delta = \sum_i e^{-E_i/kT} e^{-PV/kT}$$

Summing over all levels yields

$$\Delta = \sum_E \sum_V \Omega(N,V,E) e^{-E/kT} e^{-PV/kT}$$

(b) The derivation of the thermodynamic functions are as follows

$$dS = -kd\left(\sum_i P_i \ln P_i\right)$$

$$= -kd\left[\frac{\sum_i e^{-\beta H_i}}{\Delta} \ln\left(\frac{e^{-\beta H_i}}{\Delta}\right)\right]$$

$$= \frac{1}{\beta T} d\left[\frac{\sum_i e^{-\beta H_i}}{\Delta}(+\beta H_i + \ln \Delta)\right]$$

$$S = \frac{1}{T} \frac{\sum_i H_i e^{-\beta H_i}}{\Delta} + \frac{1}{\beta T} \frac{\ln \Delta \sum_i e^{-\beta H_i}}{\Delta}$$

$$= \frac{\bar{H}}{T} + k \ln \Delta \quad . \qquad (13)$$

$$G = H - TS$$

or $$S = \frac{H}{T} - \frac{G}{T} \qquad (14)$$

From equation (13)

$$\frac{-G}{T} = k \ln \Delta$$

or $$G = -kT \ln \Delta(N,P,T)$$

$$dG = -SdT + VdP + \mu dN$$

and $$\left(\frac{\partial G}{\partial T}\right)_{P,N} = S$$

$$\left(\frac{\partial G}{\partial P}\right)_{T,N} = V$$

$$\left(\frac{\partial G}{\partial N}\right)_{T,P} = \mu$$

$$\therefore \quad S = k \frac{\partial}{\partial T}\Big(T \ln \Delta(N,P,T)\Big)_{P,N}$$

$$= k\left[T\left(\frac{\partial \ln \Delta(N,P,T)}{\partial T}\right)_{P,N} + \ln \Delta\right]$$

$$= kT\left(\frac{\partial \ln \Delta}{\partial T}\right)_{P,N} + k \ln \Delta$$

From equation (14)

$$H = kT^2\left(\frac{\partial \ln \Delta}{\partial T}\right)_{P,N}$$

• PROBLEM 14-2

Calculate the molecular translational partition functions in a volume of 1 cm^3 at 298 °K for the following molecules a) H_2, b) CH_4, c) C_8H_{18}.

Solution: The molecular translational partition function is given by

$$q_{trans.} = \left[\frac{2\pi mkT}{h^2}\right]^{3/2} V$$

where h is Planck's constant, m is the mass of the molecule and V is the volume. Taking the mass out of the square bracket, gives

$$q_{trans.} = \left[\frac{2\pi kT}{h^2}\right]^{3/2} Vm^{3/2}$$

$$= \left[\frac{2\pi(1.38\times10^{-23}JK^{-1})(298°K)}{(6.63\times10^{-34}J\ Sec)^2}\right]^{3/2} (1\ cm^3)\left(\frac{1\ m}{100\ cm}\right)^3 m^{3/2}$$

$$= 1.42 \times 10^{64}\left(J^{-1}S^{-2}\right)^{3/2} m^{3/2}(\text{meters})^3 \qquad (1)$$

a) For H_2:

$$\text{Mass per molecule of } H_2 = \frac{(2.016\ g\ mol^{-1})\left(\frac{1\ kg}{1000\ g}\right)}{6.02 \times 10^{23}\ mol^{-1}}$$

$$= 3.348 \times 10^{-27}\ kg$$

From equation (1)

$$q_{trans.} = 1.42 \times 10^{64}\left(J^{-1}s^{-2}\right)^{3/2}\left(3.348 \times 10^{-27}\ kg\right)^{3/2}$$

$$= 2.750 \times 10^{24}\left(J^{-1}s^{-2}\right)^{3/2}\ kg^{3/2}(met)^3$$

$$= 2.750 \times 10^{24}\left(\frac{sec^2}{kg(met)^2}\ \frac{1}{sec^2}\right)^{3/2}\ kg^{3/2}(met)^3$$

$$= 2.750 \times 10^{24}\ kg^{-2/3}\ met^{-3}\ kg^{3/2}\ met^3$$

$$= 2.750 \times 10^{24}$$

b) For CH_4:

$$\text{mass per molecule of } CH_4 = \frac{(16.04\ g\ mol^{-1})\left(\frac{1\ kg}{1000\ g}\right)}{6.02 \times 10^{23}\ mol^{-1}}$$

$$= 2.664 \times 10^{-26}\ kg$$

$$\therefore\ q_{trans.} = (1.42 \times 10^{64})\left(2.664 \times 10^{-26}\right)^{3/2}$$

$$= 6.175 \times 10^{25}$$

c) For C_8H_{18}:

$$\text{Mass per molecule of } C_8H_{18} = \frac{(114.22\ g\ mol^{-1})\left(\frac{1kg}{1000\ g}\right)}{6.02 \times 10^{23}\ mol^{-1}}$$

$$= 1.897 \times 10^{-25}\ kg$$

$$\therefore\ q_{trans.} = (1.42 \times 10^{64})\left(1.897 \times 10^{-25}\right)^{3/2}$$

$$= 1.173 \times 10^{27}$$

PROBLEM 14-3

Using the Euler-Maclaurin summation formula

$$\sum_{n=a}^{\infty} f(n) = \int_a^{\infty} f(x)dx + \frac{1}{2}f(a) - \frac{1}{12}f'(a) + \frac{1}{720}f'''(a) + \ldots,$$

evaluate the rotational partition function at high temperatures.

Solution: The rotational partition function for a diatomic molecule is given by

$$q_{rot.}(T) = \sum_{J=0}^{\infty} (2J + 1)e^{-\beta\bar{B}J(J+1)/kT}$$

where J = the rotational quantum number.

Let $\beta\bar{B}/k = \Theta$

$$\therefore \quad q_{rot.}(T) = \sum_{J=0}^{\infty} (2J + 1)e^{-\Theta_{rot}J(J+1)/T} \qquad (1)$$

The Euler-Maclaurin summation formula is

$$\sum_{J=0}^{\infty} f(J) = q_{rot} = \frac{1}{\sigma}\int_0^{\infty} f(x)dx + \frac{1}{2}f(0) - \frac{1}{12}f'(0)$$

$$+ \frac{1}{720}f'''(0) + \ldots \qquad (2)$$

$$\text{where} \quad f(J) = (2J + 1)e^{-J(J+1)\Theta_{rot}/T} \qquad (3)$$

and σ is symmetry number.

Let $a = \frac{\Theta_{rot}}{T}$. Take the ℓn of both sides of equation (3) and differentiate it to obtain

$$\ell n\ f(J) = \ell n(2J + 1) - a(J^2 + J)$$

$$\ell n\ f'(J) = 2 - a(2J + 1)a.$$

$$\text{Then} \quad \frac{f'(J)}{f(J)} = \frac{2}{2J + 1} - \frac{a(2J + 1)a}{a(J^2 + J)}$$

$$\therefore \quad f'(J) = \left[\frac{2}{2J+1} - \frac{(2J+1)a}{J^2+J}\right]\left[(2J+1)e^{-(J^2+J)a}\right]$$

$$= \left[2 - a(2J + 1)^2\right]e^{-(J^2+J)a}.$$

Taking natural logarithm

$$\ell n\ f'(J) = \ell n\left[2 - a(2J+1)^2\right]\ell n\ e^{-(J^2+J)a}$$

$$= \ell n\left[2 - a(2J+1)^2\right] - (J^2+J)a$$

$$\frac{f''(J)}{f'(J)} = \left[\frac{-4a(2J+1)}{2-a(2J+1)^2} - (2J+1)a\right]\left[2-a(2J+1)^2\ e^{-(J^2+J)a}\right]$$

$$\therefore\ f''(J) = \left[-4a(2J+1) - (2J+1)a\left[2-a(2J+1)^2\right]e^{-(J^2+J)a}\right]$$

$$= \left[-4a(2J+1) - 2a(2J+1) + a^2(2J+1)^3\right]e^{-(J^2+J)a}$$

$$= \left[a^2(2J+1)^3 - 6a(2J+1)\right]e^{-(J^2+J)a}$$

Taking ℓn of both sides

$$\ell n\ f''(J) = \ell n\left[a^2(2J+1)^3 - 6a(2J+1)\right]\ell n\ e^{-(J^2+J)a}$$

$$= \ell n\left[a^2(2J+1)^3 - 6a(2J+1)\right] - (J^2+J)a$$

Evaluating the third derivative

$$\frac{f'''(J)}{f''(J)} = \frac{a^3 3(2J+1)^2 \times 2 - 6a \times 2}{a^2(2J+1)^3 - 6a(2J+1)} - (2J+1)a$$

$$f'''(J) = \left[6a^2(2J+1)^2 - 12a - a^3(2J+1)^4 + 6a^2(2J+1)^2\right]e^{-(J^2+J)a}$$

$$\therefore\ f'''(J) = \left[-a^3(2J+1)^4 + 12a^2(2J+1)^2 - 12a\right]e^{-(J^2+J)a}$$

The terms under the Euler-Maclaurin summation formula will now be evaluated. Let J = x. Thus

$$\int_0^\infty f(x)\,dx = \int_0^\infty (2x+1)e^{-(x^2+x)a}\,dx.$$

Let

$$U = x^2 + x$$

$$dU = (2x+1)dx$$

$$\therefore\ \int_0^\infty f(x)\,dx = \int_0^\infty e^{-aU}\,dU$$

$$= -\frac{1}{a}\int_0^\infty (-a)e^{-aU}\,dU$$

$$= -\frac{1}{a}e^{-aU}\Big|_{U=0}^{U=\infty}$$

$$= \frac{1}{a}$$

Also $f(0) = (1)e^0$

$$= 1$$

$$f'(0) = \left[2 - a(1^2)\right]e^0$$

$$= 2 - a$$

$$f'''(0) = [-a^3 + 12a^2 - 12a]$$

$$= a[-a^2 + 12a - 12].$$

Therefore from eqn (2)

$$\sum_{J=0}^{\infty} f(J) = q_r = \frac{1}{\sigma}\left[\frac{1}{a} + \frac{1}{2}(1) - \frac{1}{12}(2-a) + \frac{a}{720}(-a^2+12a-12)\right]$$

$$= \frac{1}{\sigma}\left[\frac{1}{a} + \frac{1}{2} - \frac{1}{6} + \frac{a}{12} - \frac{a^3}{720} + \frac{12a^2}{720} - \frac{12a}{720} + \ldots\right]$$

$$= \frac{1}{\sigma}\left[\frac{1}{a} + \frac{1}{3} + \frac{48a}{720} + \frac{a^2}{60} - \frac{a^3}{720} + \ldots\right]$$

$$= \frac{1}{\sigma}\left[\frac{1}{a} + \frac{1}{3} + \frac{1a}{15} + \frac{a^2}{60} - \frac{a^3}{720} + \ldots\right]$$

$$= \frac{1}{\sigma a}\left[1 + \frac{a}{3} + \frac{a^2}{15} + \frac{a^3}{60} - \frac{a^4}{720} + \ldots\right]$$

But $\quad a = \dfrac{\Theta_{rot}}{T}$

Therefore,

$$q_{rot} = \frac{T}{\sigma\Theta_{rot}}\left[1 + \frac{1}{3}\left(\frac{\Theta_{rot}}{T}\right) + \frac{1}{15}\left(\frac{\Theta_{rot}}{T}\right)^2 + \frac{1}{60}\left(\frac{\Theta_{rot}}{T}\right)^3 - \frac{1}{720}\left(\frac{\Theta_{rot}}{T}\right)^4 + \ldots\right]$$

For $T >> \Theta_{rot}$, then $q_{rot} = \dfrac{T}{\sigma\Theta_{rot}}$, which is the classical high temperature result.

• PROBLEM 14-4

Calculate a) the rotational partition function q_{rot}, b) the entropy contribution from rotation and c) the rotational contribution to the heat capacity at constant volume, C_{Vr} for HD gas at 96 °K. Take Θ_r = 64 °K. d) What is the val-

ue of E in cal $mole^{-1}$ deg^{-1} for HD at 96 °K ? e) Find the fraction of HD molecules in each of the first four rotational energy levels at 32 °K, 96 °K and 256 °K. The value of θ_{vib} is 6100 °K.

Solution: a) At low temperatures, a direct summation must be carried out in order to calculate $q_r(T)$

$$q_r(T) = \sum_{J=0}^{\infty} (2J + 1)e^{-J(J+1)\Theta_r/T} \quad (1)$$

where Θ_r is the characteristic temperature given by

$$\Theta_r = \frac{h^2}{8\pi^2 Ik}.$$

I is the moment of inertia about the center of mass, and J is the rotational quantum number. Expanding equation (1) gives

$$q_r = 1 + 3e^{-2\Theta/T} + 5e^{-6\Theta/T} + 7e^{-12\Theta/T} + 9e^{-20\Theta/T} + \ldots$$

$$= 1 + 0.790 + 0.092 + 0.002 + 0.000015$$

$$= 1.884$$

b) $E_r = NkT^2\left(\frac{\partial \ \ell n \ q_r}{\partial T}\right)$

Let $q_r = x$. Therefore,

$$NkT^2 \frac{\partial \ \ell n \ q_r}{\partial T} = NkT^2 \frac{1}{x}\frac{dx}{dT}$$

$$= \frac{NkT^2}{q_r}\left[\frac{6\Theta_r}{T^2}e^{-2\Theta_r/T} + \frac{30\Theta_r}{T^2}e^{-6\Theta_r/T} + \frac{84\Theta_r}{T^2}e^{-12\Theta_r/T}\right]$$

$$= \frac{R}{q_r}\left\{6\Theta_r e^{-2\Theta_r/T} + 30\Theta_r e^{-6\Theta_r/T} + 84\Theta_r e^{-12\Theta_r/T}\right\} \quad (2)$$

$$R = 1.987 \text{ cal/mole °K}$$

$$q_r = 1.884$$

$$\Theta_r = 64 \text{ °K}$$

Substitute these values into equation (2) and solve for E_r.

As a result, $E_r = 145.7$ cal/mole

c) $C_{Vr} = \left(\frac{\partial E}{\partial T}\right)_V$

$$= Rq_r\left(\frac{12\Theta_r^2}{T^2}e^{-2\Theta/T} + 180\,\frac{\Theta^2}{T^2}e^{-6\Theta/T} + 1008\,\frac{\Theta^2}{T^2}e^{-12\Theta/T}\right)$$

$$- R\left(6\Theta_r e^{-2\Theta_r/T} + 30\Theta_r e^{-6\Theta_r/T} + 84\Theta e^{-12\Theta_r/T}\right)$$

$$\left(6\,\frac{\Theta_r}{T^2}e^{-2\Theta_r/T} + 30\,\frac{\Theta_r}{T^2}e^{-6\Theta_r/T} + 84\,\frac{\Theta_r}{T^2}e^{-12\Theta_r/T}\right)/q_r^2$$

$$= \frac{1}{q_r^2}\left[Rq_r\,\frac{\Theta_r^2}{T^2}\left(12e^{-2\Theta_r/T} + 180e^{-6\Theta_r/T} + 1008e^{-12\Theta_r/T}\right)\right.$$

$$\left. - \frac{R\Theta_r^2}{T^2}\left(6e^{-2\Theta_r/T} + 30e^{-6\Theta_r/T} + 84e^{-12\Theta_r/T}\right)^2\right]$$

$$= \frac{11.3106 - 1.9068}{q^2}$$

$$= 2.65 \text{ cal/deg mole}$$

d) $E_{total} = E_{trans} + E_{rot} + E_{V_i} + E_{elec.}$ (3)

$$E_{trans.} = (3/2)NkT$$

$$= \frac{3}{2}\left(6.02\times10^{23}\text{ mole}^{-1}\right)\left(1.38\times10^{-16}\text{ erg deg}^{-1}\right)$$

$$\left(\frac{1\text{ cal}}{4.18\times10^{7}\text{ erg}}\right)(96\ ^\circ\text{K})$$

$$= 286.2 \text{ cal mole}^{-1}$$

$$E_{rot} = 145.7 \text{ cal mole}^{-1}$$

$$E_{Vi} = Nk\left[\frac{\Theta_{Vi}}{2} + \frac{\Theta_{Vi}}{\left(e^{\Theta_{Vi}/T} - 1\right)}\right]$$

The value of $\Theta_{Vi} = 6100\ ^\circ$K

$\therefore$ $E_{Vi} = 1.987$ cal mole $^\circ\text{K}^{-1}$(3050 °K)

$$= 6060.35 \text{ cal mole}^{-1}.$$

$$E_{elec} \simeq 0.$$

Using the above values in equation (3) gives

$$E_{tot} = (286.2 + 145.7 + 6060.35)\text{cal mole}^{-1}$$

$$= 6492.3 \text{ cal mole}^{-1}.$$

e) Fraction of HD molecules in each of the first four rotational energy levels is estimated using the Boltzmann distribution and it is given by

$$P(\varepsilon)d\varepsilon = \frac{\omega_j e^{-\varepsilon_j/kT}}{q} \qquad j = 1, \ldots, 4$$

$$= \frac{(2J+1)e^{-J(J+1)\Theta_r/T}}{q(T)}$$

The following results are tabulated as

	T = 32 °K	96 °K	256 °K
J = 0	0.948	0.531	0.230
J = 1	0.052	0.420	0.419
J = 2		0.049	0.257
J = 3			0.080

T(°K)	q(T) (°K)
32	1.055
96	1.884
256	4.345

• PROBLEM 14-5

For the $^{35}Cl_2$ molecule, the following data is available. The equilibrium internuclear distance = 1.988×10^{-8} cm. The reduced mass = $17.4894 \text{g mol}^{-1}$. The fundamental vibrational frequency = $1.6947 \times 10^{13} \text{s}^{-1}$. Neglecting the electronic contributions, calculate the a) molar heat capacity at constant pressure, b) enthalpy functions, c) Gibbs free energy function, d) and the entropy of $^{35}Cl_2$ at 25 °C and 1 atm.

Solution: The translational contributions to the thermodynamic functions of an ideal gas are as follows

Internal Energy:

$$\left(\frac{U^o - U_0^o}{T}\right)_{trans} = kT\left(\frac{\partial \ \ell n \ Q_{trans}}{\partial T}\right)_{V,N} = \frac{3}{2}R$$

where U_0^o is the internal energy at standard conditions, Q is the molar partition function and R is the gas constant.

a) In the same manner, the enthalpy function and the molar heat capacity are given by

$$\left(\frac{H^o - H_0^o}{T}\right)_{trans} = \left(C_P^o\right)_{trans} = \frac{3}{2}R + R$$

$$= \frac{3}{2}(8.314J \ K^{-1} \ mol^{-1}) + (8.314J \ K^{-1} \ mol^{-1})$$

$$= 20.78J \ K^{-1} \ mol^{-1}.$$

b) The Gibbs free energy function is given by

$$\left(-\frac{G^o - H_0^o}{T}\right)_{trans} = -R \ \ \ell n\left(\frac{q_{trans}}{N}\right)$$

$$= -R \ \ \ell n\left[\frac{V(2\pi mkT)^{3/2}}{Nh^3}\right]$$

where V for an ideal gas is given as V = RT/P. N is Avogadro's number and h is Plank's constant.

$$\therefore \quad \left(\frac{G^o - H_0^o}{T}\right)_{trans} = -141.00J \ K^{-1} \ mol^{-1}.$$

The rotational contributions to the enthalpy functions and molar heat capacity are

$$\left(\frac{H^o - H_0^o}{T}\right)_{rot} = kT\left(\frac{\partial \ \ell n \ Q_{trans}}{\partial T}\right)_N$$

$$= \left(C_P^o\right)_{rot}$$

$$= R$$

$$= 8.314J \ K^{-1} \ mol^{-1}$$

The rotational contribution to the Gibbs free energy function is given by

$$\left(\frac{G^o - H_0^o}{T}\right)_{rot} = -R\,\ell n\left(\frac{q_{rot}}{N}\right)$$

$$q_{rot} = \frac{8\pi^2 IkT}{h^2}$$

where I is the moment of inertia given by $I = \mu r^2$. μ is the reduced mass of the $^{35}Cl_2$ molecule and r is the equilibrium internuclear distance which is 1.988×10^{-8} cm

$$\therefore \quad I = 17.4894 \text{ g mol}^{-1} \times (1.988 \times 10^{-8} \text{ cm})^2$$

$$= 6.912 \times 10^{-15} \text{ g cm}^2 \text{ mol}^{-1}$$

$$q_{rot} = \frac{8\pi^2 \left[6.912)10^{-15}\text{g cm}^2\text{mol}^{-1}\right]\left[\frac{1\text{kg}}{1000\text{g}}\right]\left[\frac{1\text{m}}{100\text{cm}}\right]^2 \left[1.38\times10^{-23}\text{JK}^{-1}\right]\left[298°\text{K}\right]}{(6.63 \times 10^{-34} \text{ J}\cdot\text{s})^2}$$

$$= \frac{8\pi^2(6.912\ 10^{-22}\text{kg m}^2\text{mol}^{-1})(4.11\times10^{-21})}{4.396\ 10^{-67}\ \text{m}^2\ \text{kg}\ \text{s}^{-2}\cdot\text{s}^2}$$

$$= 5.102 \times 10^{26} \text{ mol}^{-1}.$$

Therefore the Gibbs free energy function becomes

$$\left(\frac{G^o - H_0^o}{T}\right)_{rot} = -8.314 \text{ J K}^{-1} \text{ mol}^{-1}\ \ell n\left(\frac{5.102 \times 10^{26} \text{ mol}^{-1}}{6.02 \times 10^{23} \text{ mol}^{-1}}\right)$$

$$= -56.06 \text{ J K}^{-1} \text{ mol}^{-1}.$$

The vibrational contribution to the enthalpy function is given by

$$\left(\frac{H^o - H_0^o}{T}\right)_{vib} = R\frac{\Theta_{vib}/T}{\left(e^{\Theta_{vib}/T} - 1\right)} \qquad (1)$$

where Θ_{vib} is the characteristic temperature of vibration given by

$$\Theta_{vib} = \frac{h\nu}{k}$$

h is Planck's constant and ν is the fundamental vibrational frequency, in this case given as $1.6947 \times 10^{13}\ s^{-1}$. For $^{35}Cl_2$ the value of

$$\frac{\Theta_{vib}}{T} = 2.74$$

From equation (1),

$$\left(\frac{H^o - H_0^o}{T}\right)_{vib} = 8.314\ J\ K^{-1}\ mol^{-1}\left[\frac{2.74}{e^{2.74} - 1}\right]$$

$$= 8.314\ J\ K^{-1}\ mol^{-1}(0.189)$$

$$= 1.573\ J\ K^{-1}\ mol^{-1}$$

The vibrational contribution to the heat capacity is given as

$$C^o_{vib} = R\frac{\left(\Theta_{vib}/T\right)^2 e^{\Theta_{vib}/T}}{\left(e^{\Theta_{vib}/T} - 1\right)^2}$$

$$= 8.314\ J\ K^{-1}\ mol^{-1}\left[\frac{(7.50)(15.48)}{209.87}\right]$$

$$= 8.314\ J\ K^{-1}\ mol^{-1}(0.554)$$

$$= 4.606\ J\ K^{-1}\ mol^{-1}$$

The vibrational contribution to the Gibbs free energy function is given as

$$G_{vib} = R\ \ell n\left(1 - e^{-\Theta_{vib}/T}\right)$$

$$= 8.314\ J\ K^{-1}\ mol^{-1}\ \ell n(1 - e^{-2.74})$$

$$= 8.314\ J\ K^{-1}\ mol^{-1}\ \ell n(0.935)$$

$$= -0.555\ J\ K^{-1}\ mol^{-1}$$

The total contributions to the thermodynamic functions are as follows;

$$C^o_P = \left(C^o_P\right)_{trans} + \left(C^o_P\right)_{rot} + \left(C^o_P\right)_{vib}$$

$$= (20.78 + 8.31 + 4.60)J\ K^{-1}\ mol^{-1}$$

$$= 33.66 \text{ J K}^{-1} \text{ mol}^{-1}$$

$$\left(\frac{H^o - H_0^o}{T}\right) = \left(\frac{H^o - H_0^o}{T}\right)_{trans} + \left(\frac{H^o - H_0^o}{T}\right)_{rot} + \left(\frac{H^o - H_0^o}{T}\right)_{vib}$$

$$= (20.78 + 8.31 + 1.57) \text{J K}^{-1} \text{ mol}^{-1}$$

$$= 30.66 \text{ J K}^{-1} \text{ mol}^{-1}$$

$$\left(\frac{G^o - H_0^o}{T}\right) = \left(\frac{G^o - H_0^o}{T}\right)_{trans} + \left(\frac{G^o - H_0^o}{T}\right)_{rot} + \left(\frac{G^o - H_0^o}{T}\right)_{vib}$$

$$= (-141.00 + (-56.06) - 0.55) \text{J K}^{-1} \text{ mol}^{-1}$$

$$= -191.89 \text{ J K}^{-1} \text{ mol}^{-1}$$

d) The entropy is given in terms of the thermodynamic functions. Thus

$$S^o = \left(\frac{H^o - H_0^o}{T}\right) - \left(\frac{G^o - H_0^o}{T}\right)$$

$$= 30.66 + 191.89$$

$$= 222.55 \text{ J K}^{-1} \text{ mol}^{-1}.$$

• PROBLEM 14-6

Calculate the constant-pressure heat capacity, C_p and entropy, S of ideal gaseous fluoroform, CHF_3, at 25°C and 1 atm. The following data are available

C-H bond length: 1.096 Å

C-F bond length: 1.330Å

Each of the bond angles (F-C-F and F-C-H) is very close to the tetrahedral value of 109° 28'. The vibrational wave numbers are $\omega_1 = 3{,}035.6 \text{ cm}^{-1}$, $\omega_2 = 1{,}209 \text{ cm}^{-1}$, $\omega_3 = 703.2 \text{ cm}^{-1}$, $\omega_4(2) = 1{,}351.5 \text{ cm}^{-1}$, $\omega_5(2) = 1{,}152.4 \text{ cm}^{-1}$ and $\omega_6(2) = 509.4 \text{ cm}^{-1}$. The last three modes are doubly degenerate.

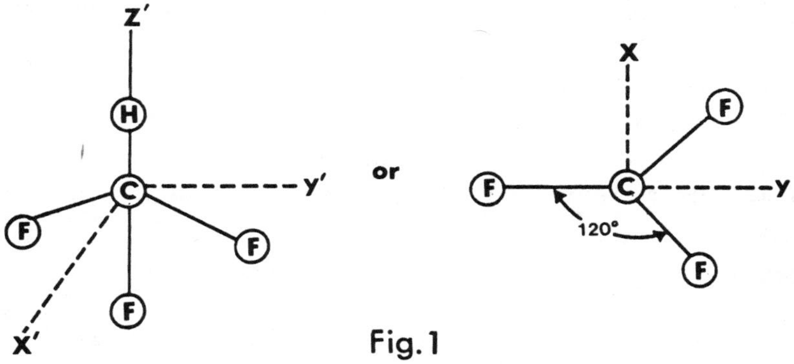

Fig. 1

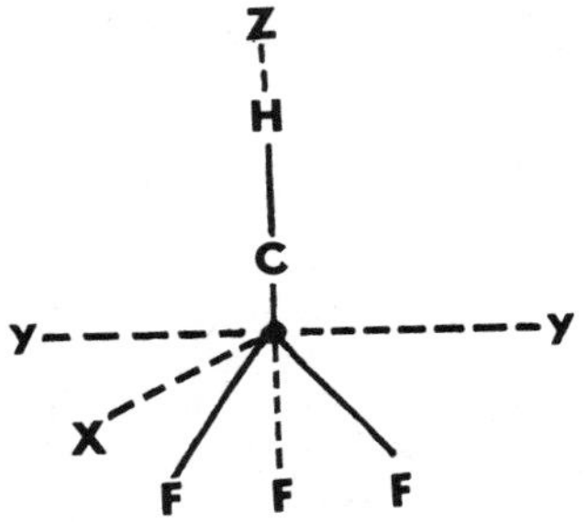

Fig. 3

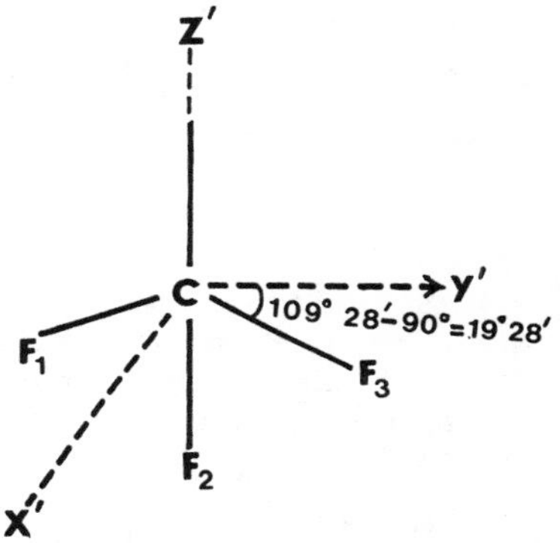

Fig. 2

Solution: Assume that the electronic contributions to entropy are negligible at the 25°C. Therefore the general partition function $Q = Q_t Q_r Q_v$. The fluoroform molecule has the structure shown in figure 1.

ROTATIONAL CONTRIBUTION:

The rotational contribution to heat capacity is given by

$$C_{P_{rot}} = (3/2)R$$

where R is the gas constant.

$$\therefore \quad C_{P_{rot}} = 3/2 \ (1.987 \text{ cal mole}^{-1} \ °K^{-1})$$

$$= 2.980 \text{ cal mole}^{-1} \ °K^{-1} \ .$$

Find the entropy contribution by first calculating the principal moments of inertia. To do this, calculate the center of mass of the molecule.

Reducing the tetrahedral structure of the molecule as in fig. 2 to a linear molecule gives

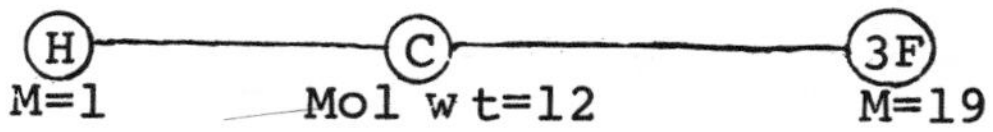

The molecule CHF_3 is a symmetric top and therefore the

center of mass is located on the Z-axis and is given by Z'_{cm}

$$Z'_{cm} = \frac{1}{M} \sum_i m_i z_i .$$

Here, M is the molecular mass of CHF_3, m is the mass of the atoms and z_i is the perpendicular distance.

Therefore from the bond distances and angles

$$Z'_{cm} = \frac{1}{70 \text{ gm}} [(1.096\text{Å})(1.008) - (3 \times 19.00 \times 1.330 \sin 19°28')]$$

To convert 28' to its decimal degree equivalent use the relation $28 \text{ ft} \times \frac{1 \text{ degree}}{60 \text{ ft}} = .467$ degree. Hence 19°28' becomes 19.467°.

$$Z'_{cm} = -0.345\text{Å}$$

Now, construct the principal axes x,y,z parallel to x', y', z' and having their origin at the center of mass: The principal moments of inertia about the new principal axes are I_x, I_y, I_z. But $I_x = I_y$ because of the symmetry of the molecule. See Fig. (3).

Calculate the moment of inertia about the z and x axes;

$$I_z = \sum_i m_i (x_i^2 + y_i^2)$$

$$= \frac{19(1.330\text{ Å})^2}{6.023 \times 10^{23}} \times 10^{-16} \frac{\text{cm}^2}{\text{Å}^2} \times (2 \cos^2 19°28' \cos^2 60°$$

$$+ 2 \cos^2 19°28' \cos^2 30°$$

$$+ \cos^2 19°28')$$

$$149 \times 10^{-40} \text{ gm cm}^2$$

$$I_x = I_y = \sum_i m_i (y_i^2 + z_i^2)$$

$$= \frac{19}{6.023 \times 10^{23}} \times 10^{-16} \times [3(.345 - 1.330 \sin 19°28')^2$$

$$+ 2(1.330)^2 \cos^2 19°28' \cos^2 30°]$$

$$+ \frac{12.00}{6.023 \times 10^{23}} \times 10^{-16} \times (0.345)^2$$

$$+ \frac{1.008}{6.023 \times 10^{23}} \times 10^{-16} \times (1.096 + 0.345)^2$$

$$= 82 \times 10^{-40} \text{ g cm}^2$$

Therefore the entropy contribution per mole for rotation is given by

$$S_r = R \ln Q_{rot.} + C_{P_r}$$

$$= R \ln Q_{rot.} + (3/2)R \qquad (1)$$

where Q_{rot} is the rotational partition function given by

$$Q_{rot} = \frac{\pi^{1/2}}{\sigma}\left(\frac{8\pi^2 I_x kT}{h^2}\right)^{1/2}\left(\frac{8\pi^2 I_y kT}{h^2}\right)^{1/2}\left(\frac{8\pi^2 I_z kT}{h^2}\right)^{1/2} \qquad (2)$$

σ is the degree of freedom, I_x, I_y, I_z are the principle moments of inertia and h is Planck's constant.
For these molecules, $\sigma = 3$.
From equation (2)

$$Q_{rot} = \frac{\pi^{1/2}}{3}\left[\frac{8\pi^2(82\times10^{-40})(1.38\times10^{-16})(298°K)}{\left(6.626 \times 10^{-27}\right)^2}\right]$$

$$\left[\frac{8\pi^2(149\times10^{-40})(1.38\times10^{-16})(298°K)}{\left(6.626 \times 10^{-27}\right)^2}\right]^{1/2}$$

$$= 16030.5$$

From equation (1)

$$S_{rot} = 1.987 \text{ cal mole}^{-1}\ °K^{-1} \ln 16030.5$$

$$+ 3/2(1.987 \text{ cal mole}^{-1}\ °K^{-1})$$

$$= 22.2 \text{ cal mole}^{-1}\ °K^{-1}$$

TRANSLATIONAL CONTRIBUTION: The heat capacity contribution per mole is given by

$$C_{P_{(t)}} = \frac{5}{2}R$$

$$= \frac{5}{2}(1.987 \text{ cal mole}^{-1}\ °K^{-1})$$

$$= 4.967 \text{ cal mole}^{-1}\ °K^{-1}$$

Therefore, the entropy contribution per mole is given by

$$S_{trans} = R\,\ell n\,Q_{trans.} + \frac{5}{2}R \qquad (3)$$

But $$Q_{trans.} = \left(\frac{2\pi mkT}{h^2}\right)^{3/2} V$$

where V is the volume given by

$$V = \frac{RT}{PN}.$$

Consequently, equation (3) becomes

$$S_{trans} = R\,\ell n\left[\left(\frac{2\pi mkT}{h^2}\right)^{3/2} \frac{RT}{PN}\right] + \frac{5}{2}R \qquad (4)$$

$$= 1.987\,\ell n\left[\frac{2\pi(70)(1.38\times10^{-16})(298)}{(6.023\times10^{23})(6.626\times10^{-27})^2}\right]^{3/2}$$

$$\times\left[\frac{(82.05)(298)}{1(6.023\times10^{23})}\right] + \frac{5}{2}(1.987)$$

$$= 38.6 \text{ cal mole}^{-1}\text{ K}^{-1}$$

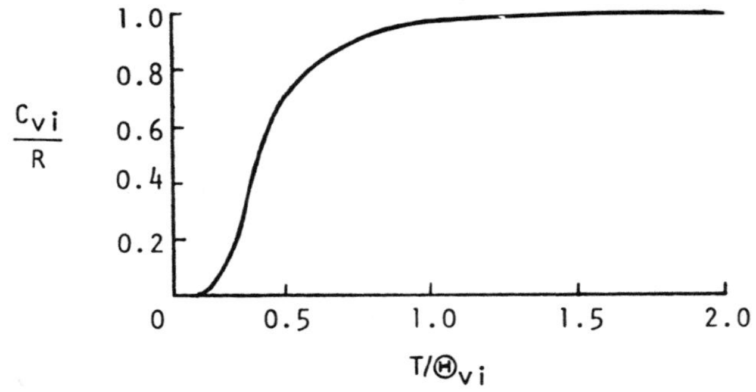

Vibrational contribution to heat capacity: as $T/\Theta_{vi} \rightarrow \infty, C_{vi} \rightarrow R$. **Fig.4**

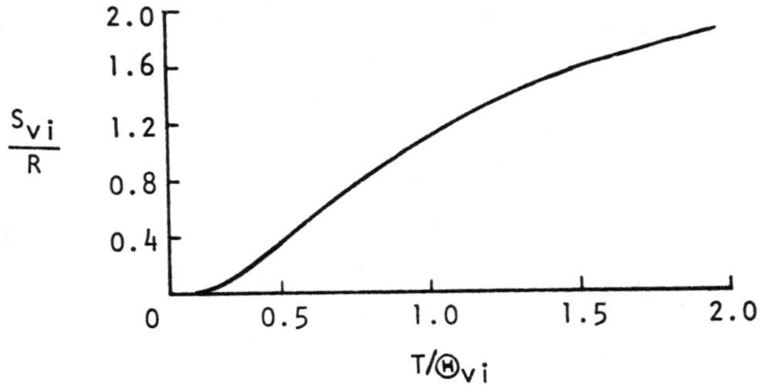

Vibrational contribution to entropy: as $T/\Theta_{vi} \to \infty, S_{vi} \to \infty$.

Fig. 5

VIBRATIONAL CONTRIBUTION: The entropy contribution is given by

$$S_{Vi} = \sum_{i=1}^{6} \left[\frac{Nk\,\Theta}{T\left(e^{\Theta_{vi}/T} - 1\right)} - Nk\left(\ln 1 - e^{-\Theta_{vi}/T}\right) \right]$$

where Θ is the vibrational characteristic temperature given as

$$\Theta_{vib} = \frac{hc}{k}\omega_{vi} \qquad (5)$$

$$= 1.439\omega_{vi}$$

ω_{vi} represents the vibrational wave numbers.

Graphs of $\frac{C_{V_{trans}}}{R}$ vs $\frac{T}{\Theta_{vi}}$ and $\frac{S_{vi}}{R}$ vs $\frac{T}{\theta_{vi}}$ are plotted in fig. 4 and fig. 5 respectively and the entropy contribution S_{vt} and the specific contribution C_{V_i} can be calculated using the wave numbers.

From equation (5)

$$\Theta_{vi} = \frac{hc}{k}\omega_{vi}$$

For the first wave number

$$\Theta_{V_1} = \frac{hc}{k}\omega_1$$

$$= 1.44(3035.6)$$

$$= 4.37 \times 10^3$$

$$\therefore \quad \frac{T}{\Theta_{V_1}} = \frac{298}{4.37 \times 10^3}$$

$$= 0.068$$

$$\omega_2 = 1{,}209\ \text{cm}^{-1}$$

$$\Theta_{V_2} = 1.44(1209)$$

$$= 1740.9$$

$$\therefore \quad \frac{T}{\Theta_{V_2}} = \frac{298}{1740.9}$$

$$= 0.171$$

Similarly $$\frac{T}{\Theta_{V_3}} = 0.294$$

$$\frac{T}{\Theta_{V_4}} = 0.154$$

$$\frac{T}{\Theta_{V_5}} = 0.180$$

and $$\frac{T}{\Theta_{V_6}} = 0.407.$$

Now, using figs 4 and 5 and values of the reduced vibrational temperatures $\frac{T}{\Theta_{vi}}$, the different values of $C_{P_{vi}}$ and S_{Vi} the contributions to thermodynamic properties, can be read off the graph. They are tabulated as follows

$T^*_{vi} = \frac{T}{\Theta_{vi}}$	$\frac{C_{vi}}{R}$	$\frac{S_{vi}}{R}$
0.068	0	0
0.171	0.098	0.011
0.294	0.50	0.173
0.154	0.135	0.010
0.180	0.251	0.060
0.407	0.130	0.531
	1.114	0.786

T^*_{vi} is the reduced vibrational temperature. The total heat capacity and entropy are:

Total $C_P = C_{P_{rot.}} + C_{P_{trans.}} + C_{Vi}$

$$= (2.980 + 4.967 + 1.114) \text{ cal mole}^{-1} \text{ °K}^{-1}$$

$$= 9.06 \text{ cal mole}^{-1} \text{ °K}^{-1}$$

and Total $S = S_{rot.} + S_{trans.} + S_{vi}$

$$= (22.2 + 38.6 + 0.786) \text{ cal mole}^{-1} \text{ °K}^{-1}$$

$$= 61.58 \text{ cal mole}^{-1} \text{ °K}^{-1}$$

• PROBLEM 14-7

CO_2 is a linear molecule with moment of inertia, $I = 71.67 \times 10^{-40}$ g cm^2, and four degrees of vibrational freedom corresponding to wave numbers of $\bar{\nu}_1 = 2349$ cm^{-1}, $\bar{\nu}_2 = 1320$ cm^{-1} and $\bar{\nu}_3 = \bar{\nu}_4 = 667$ cm^{-1} (doubly degenerate). Assume that CO_2 is an ideal gas, calculate the heat capacity at constant volume, C_V, per mole of CO_2 at intervals of 200 °K from 0 to 1000 °K.

Solution: The heat capacity at constant volume is defined as

$$C_V = \left(\frac{\partial U}{\partial T}\right)_V \tag{1}$$

where U is the internal energy given by

$$U = NkT^2\left(\frac{\partial \ \ln Q}{\partial T}\right)_V \tag{2}$$

N is the Avogadro's number and Q is the molar vibrational partition function. But

$$Q_{vib} = \left(1 - e^{-hc\bar{\nu}/kT}\right)^{-1} \tag{3}$$

where h is Planck's constant, c is the speed of light and $\bar{\nu}$ is the wave number. Let

$$\theta = \frac{hc\bar{\nu}}{k} \tag{4}$$

then, equation (3) can be written as

$$Q_{vib} = \left(1 - e^{-\theta/T}\right)^{-1}$$

or $\qquad \ell n\ Q_{vib} = -\ell n(1 - e^{-\theta/T})$.

Equation (2) then becomes

$$U = \frac{Nk\theta}{e^{\theta/T} - 1}$$

The expression for the heat capacity in equation (1) changes to

$$C_V = \frac{R\left(\frac{\theta}{T}\right)^2 e^{\theta/T}}{\left(e^{\theta/T} - 1\right)^2} \qquad (5)$$

From equation (4),

$$\theta = \frac{(6.63\times10^{-34} \text{J s})(3\times10^{10}\ \text{cm s}^{-1})\bar{\nu}}{(1.38\times10^{-23}\ \text{J K}^{-1})}$$

$$= 1.438\ \text{cm °K}\ \bar{\nu} \qquad (6)$$

The heat capacity has contributions from the three modes of motion namely translational, rotational and vibrational modes, neglecting the electronic contributions. Therefore

$$C_V = C_{V,trans.} + C_{V,rot.} + C_{V,\ vib.}$$

$$= C_{V,trans.} + C_{V,rot.} + C_V(2349\ \text{cm}^{-1}) + C_V(1320\ \text{cm}^{-1})$$

$$+ 2C_V(667\ \text{cm}^{-1}) \qquad (7)$$

The translational contributions to the molar heat capacity is given by equations (1) and (2)

$$C_{V,trans.} = \left(\frac{\partial U_{trans.}}{\partial T}\right)_V$$

$$= \frac{\partial}{\partial T}\left[kT^2\left(\frac{\partial\ \ell n\ Q_{trans.}}{\partial T}\right)_V\right]$$

$$= \frac{\partial}{\partial T}\left(\frac{3}{2}\ RT\right)$$

$$= \frac{3}{2}R$$

$$= \frac{3}{2}\left(8.314\ \text{J °K}^{-1}\right)$$

$$= 12.47\ \text{J}\cdot\text{K}^{-1}$$

The rotational contributions to the molar heat capacity is given by

$$C_{V,rot.} = \left(\frac{\partial U_{rot.}}{\partial T}\right)_V$$

But $$U_{rot.} = NkT^2\left(\frac{\partial \ln q_{rot.}}{\partial T}\right)_N$$

and $$q_{rot.} = \frac{8\pi^2 IkT}{\sigma h^2}.$$

$$\therefore \quad U_{rot.} = RT^2\left\{\left[\frac{\partial \ln(8\pi^2 Ik/\sigma h^2)}{\partial T}\right] + \frac{\partial \ln T}{\partial T}\right\}$$

$$= RT^2 \frac{1}{T}$$

$$= RT$$

and $$C_{V,rot.} = \left(\frac{\partial (RT)}{\partial T}\right)_V$$

$$= R$$

$$= 8.314\ \text{J}\cdot\text{K}^{-1}$$

The four degrees of vibrational freedom in CO_2 will now be used in calculating q_{vib} at intervals of 200 °K from 0 to 1000 °K. For wave number $\bar{\nu}_1 = 2349\ \text{cm}^{-1}$ and from equation (6)

$$\theta = (1.438\ \text{cm °K})(2349\ \text{cm}^{-1})$$

$$= 3380\ \text{°K}$$

Using equation (5) with values of T = 0, 200, 400, 600, 800 and 1000 °K, the corresponding values of C_V are tabulated as follows:

T	0	200	400	600	800	1000
C_V $\text{J}\cdot\text{K}^{-1}$	0	1.09×10^{-4}	0.127	0.950	2.235	3.466

For wave number $\bar{\nu}_2 = 1320\ \text{cm}^{-1}$

$$\theta = (1.438 \text{ cm °K})(1320 \text{ cm}^{-1})$$

$$\theta = 1899 \text{ °K}$$

and the corresponding table is

T	0	200	400	600	800	1000
C_V $J \cdot K^{-1}$	0	0.0564	1.653	3.833	5.304	6.209

For wave number, $\bar{\nu}_3 = 667 \text{ cm}^{-1}$

$$\theta = (1.438 \text{ cm °K})(667 \text{ cm}^{-1})$$

$$= 959.7 \text{ °K.}$$

The corresponding table is

T, °K	0	200	400	600	800	1000
C_V $J \cdot K^{-1}$	0	1.604	5.225	6.746	7.384	7.705

Using equation (7)

at $T = 200$ °K ,

$$C_V = 12.47 + 8.314 + 1.09 \times 10^{-4} + 0.0564 + 2(1.604) \text{J K}^{-1}$$

$$= 24.04 \text{ J K}^{-1} .$$

At $T = 400$ °K ,

$$C_V = 12.47 + 8.314 + 0.127 + 1.653 + 2(5.225) \text{J K}^{-1}$$

$$= 33.07 \text{ J K}^{-1}$$

Similarly at $T = 600$ °K ,

$$C_V = 39.06 \text{ J K}^{-1}$$

At $T = 800$ °K ,

$$C_V = 43.09 \text{ J K}^{-1}$$

and at $T = 1000$ °K

$$C_V = 45.87 \text{ J K}^{-1}$$

Spectroscopic studies give the moments of inertia of water molecule as $I_A = 1.022 \times 10^{-40}$ g cm^2, $I_B = 1.918 \times 10^{-40}$ g cm^2, $I_C = 2.940 \times 10^{-40}$ g cm^2 and the vibrational frequencies as $V_1 = 3657$ cm^{-1}, $V_2 = 1595$ cm^{-1} and $V_3 = 3756$ cm^{-1}. Calculate the entropy of water vapor at a temperature of 25 °C and a pressure of 1 atm, given that the symmetry number of the molecule is 2 and assuming ideal gas conditions. Discuss why the calorimetric value of entropy $\frac{S}{R} = 22.29 \pm 0.03$ is less than the calculated value.

Solution: The molar partition function for an assembly of independent indistinguishable molecules is given by

$$Q = \frac{q^N}{N!}$$

where q is the individual molecular partition function given in terms of the translational, rotational, vibrational and electronic contributions. That is

$$q = q_{trans.} q_{rot.} q_{vi.} q_{elec.}$$

Also $$Q = Q_{trans.} Q_{rot.} Q_{vi.} Q_{elec.}$$

The molar translational contribution to entropy is given by

$$S_{trans.} = Nk \, \ln\left[\frac{V}{N\Lambda^3}\right] + \frac{5}{2}Nk \qquad (1)$$

where $$\Lambda = \frac{h}{(2\pi mkT)^{1/2}} \qquad (2)$$

h is the Planck's constant and m is mass of the water molecule given by

$$m = \frac{M}{N}$$

$$= \frac{18 \text{ gm mole}^{-1}}{6.02\times10^{23} \text{ mole}^{-1}}$$

$$= 2.99 \times 10^{-23} \text{ gm}$$

Since ideality is assumed,

$$V = \frac{RT}{P}$$

$$= \frac{(8.314 \text{ N m °K}^{-1}\text{mole}^{-1})(298 \text{ °K})}{101325 \text{ N m}^{-2}}$$

$$= (0.02445 \text{ m}^3)\left(\frac{100 \text{ cm}}{1 \text{ m}}\right)^3$$

$$= 2.445 \times 10^4 \text{ cm}^3 \text{ mole}^{-1}$$

From equation (2),

$$\Lambda = \frac{6.63 \times 10^{-27} \text{ erg sec}}{\left[2\pi(2.990\times10^{-23} \text{ g})(1.38\times10^{-16} \text{ erg °K}^{-1})(298 \text{ °K})\right]^{1/2}}$$

$$= 2.38 \times 10^{-9} \frac{\text{erg sec}}{(\text{g erg})^{1/2}} = 2.38 \times 10^{-9} \frac{\text{erg sec}}{\left(\text{g} \frac{\text{g cm}^2}{\text{sec}^2}\right)^{1/2}}$$

$$= 2.38 \times 10^{-9} \frac{\frac{\text{g cm}^2}{\text{sec}^2}\text{sec}}{\text{g} \frac{\text{cm}}{\text{sec}}}$$

$$= 2.38 \times 10^{-9} \text{ cm.}$$

From equation (1)

$$\frac{S_{trans.}}{Nk} = \frac{S_{trans.}}{R} = \ln\left[\frac{2.445\times10^4 \text{ cm}^3 \text{ mole}^{-1}}{(6.02\times10^{23} \text{ mole}^{-1})(2.38\times10^{-9} \text{ cm})^3}\right] + \frac{5}{2}$$

$$= 14.915 + \frac{5}{2}$$

$$= 17.415$$

The rotational contribution to entropy is given by

$$\frac{S_{rot}}{R} = \ln Q_{rot} + \frac{3}{2} \qquad (3)$$

where $$Q_{rot} = \frac{\pi^{1/2}}{\sigma}\left(\frac{T^3}{\theta_A\theta_B\theta_C}\right)^{1/2} \qquad (4)$$

Here σ is the symmetry number and θ is the characteristic temperature. For substance A,

$$\theta_A = \frac{h^2}{8\pi^2 k \, I_A}$$

where I is moment of inertia

$$\therefore\ \theta_A = \frac{(6.63 \times 10^{-27}\ \text{ergsec})^2}{8\pi^2(1.38\times10^{-16}\ \text{erg}\ °K^{-1})(1.022\times10^{-40}\ \text{g cm}^2)}$$

$$= 39.4\ °K.$$

For substance B,

$$\theta_B = \frac{h^2}{8\pi^2 k\ I_B}$$

$$= \frac{(6.63\times10^{-27}\ \text{ergsec})^2}{8\pi^2(1.38\times10^{-16}\ \text{erg}\ °K^{-1})(1.918\times10^{-40}\ \text{g cm}^2)}$$

$$= 20.99\ °K.$$

Similarly,

$$\theta_C = \frac{h^2}{8\pi^2 k\ I_C}$$

$$= \frac{(6.63 \times 10^{-27}\ \text{ergsec})^2}{8\pi^2(1.38\times10^{-16}\ \text{erg}\ °K^{-1})(2.940\times10^{-40}\ \text{g cm}^2)}$$

$$= 13.69\ °K$$

From equation (4) with $\sigma = 2$,

$$Q_{rot} = \frac{\pi^{1/2}}{2}\left[\frac{(298\ °K)^3}{(39.4)(20.99)(13.69)}\right]^{1/2}$$

$$= 42.85$$

From equation (3)

$$\frac{S_{rot}}{R} = \ln 42.85 + \frac{3}{2}$$

$$= 5.258$$

The vibrational contribution to entropy is given by

$$\frac{S_{vi}}{R} = \sum_{i=1}^{3} \frac{\theta_i/T}{e^{\theta_i/T}-1} - \ln\left(1 - e^{-\theta_i/T}\right) \qquad (5)$$

where $\theta_i = \frac{h\nu_i}{k}$,

and ν is the frequency given by

$$\nu_i = cVi$$

where c is the speed of light and Vi is the vibrational frequency. Therefore

$$\theta_i = \frac{hcVi}{k}$$

$$= \frac{(6.63\times10^{-27} \text{ erg sec})(3\times10^{10} \text{ cm s}^{-1})}{1.38 \times 10^{-16} \text{ ergs } {}^\circ K^{-1}} Vi$$

$$= 1.438 \text{ cm } {}^\circ K \, Vi$$

$V_1 = 3657 \text{ cm}^{-1}$, $V_2 = 1595 \text{ cm}^{-1}$ and $V_3 = 3756 \text{ cm}^{-1}$

$$\therefore \quad \theta_1 = 1.438 \ (3657 \text{ cm}^{-1})$$

$$= 5261.7 \ {}^\circ K.$$

Similarly,

$$\theta_2 = 2294.9$$

and $\theta_3 = 5404.1$

From equation (5)

$$\frac{S_{Vi}}{R} = \sum_{i=1}^{3} \frac{\theta_i/T}{e^{\theta_i/T}-1} - \ln\left(1 - e^{-\theta_i/T}\right)$$

$$= \frac{\theta_1/T}{e^{\theta_1/T}-1} - \ln\left(1 - e^{-\theta_1/T}\right) + \frac{\theta_2/T}{e^{\theta_2/T}-1} - \ln\left(1 - e^{-\theta_2/T}\right)$$

$$+ \frac{\theta_3/T}{e^{\theta_3/T}-1} - \ln\left(1 - e^{-\theta_3/T}\right)$$

$\frac{\theta_1}{T} = \frac{5261.7 \ {}^\circ K}{298 \ {}^\circ K} = 17.657$, $\quad \frac{\theta_2}{T} = \frac{2294.9 \ {}^\circ K}{298 \ {}^\circ K} = 7.701$

$$\frac{\theta_3}{T} = \frac{5404.1 \ {}^\circ K}{298 \ {}^\circ K} = 18.135$$

$$\frac{S_{Vi}}{R} = 4.004\times10^{-7} + 3.3937\times10^{-3} + 2.5462\times10^{-7}$$

$$\frac{S_{Vi}}{R} = 0.004$$

Assume $\frac{S_{elec.}}{R} \simeq 0$

Therefore $\frac{S_{total}}{R} = 1/R \left[S_{trans.} + S_{rot.} + S_{Vi}\right]$

$$= (17.415 + 5.258 + 0.004)$$

$$= 22.677.$$

The argument for the difference between the calculated and calorimetric values of entropy is as follows.

Ice has oxygen atoms tetrahedrally situated with a hydrogen atom in between each O-O position of the tetrahedron. Each water molecule has two hydrogens and therefore two possible orientations with respect to the rest of the crystal. With N molecules, there are 2^{2N} possible configurations. However only a few are acceptable with respect to possible species.

1 way for 4H to be close to O => $(OH_4)^{+2}$

4 ways for 3H to be close to O => $(OH_3)^{+}$

6 ways for 2H to be close to O => OH_2

4 ways for 1H to be close to O => OH^{-}

1 way for no H to be close to O => O^{-2}

16 total ways but only six yield for H_2O molecule.

Therefore, fraction of ways acceptable $= \frac{6}{16} = \frac{3}{8}$ and total

$$\text{acceptable ways} = \frac{3}{8}^{2N} \times 2^{2N}$$

$$= \left(\frac{3}{2}\right)^{N}$$

$$= \Omega$$

But from Boltzmann's formula

$$S = kN \ln \Omega$$

and $\frac{S}{R} = \ln \frac{3}{2}$

$$= 0.41$$

Therefore the calorimetric value with correction is

$$\frac{S}{R} = (22.29 \pm 0.03) + 0.41$$

$$= 22.70 \pm 0.03$$

and $$\frac{S}{R} = 22.68$$

which is now comparable with the calculated value.

• PROBLEM 14-9

Figure 1 shows the potential energy curve for the dissociation reaction

$$N_2(g) \rightarrow 2N(g)$$

N_2 and N have degeneracy numbers in the electronic ground levels of one and four respectively. Calculate the equilibrium constant for the dissociation reaction at 5000 °K assuming the rigid rotor and harmonic oscillator approximation. The ground state of N is a doublet denoted by $^2P_{3/2,1/2}$ with a separation of $3.8854(10^4)\,cm^{-1}$.

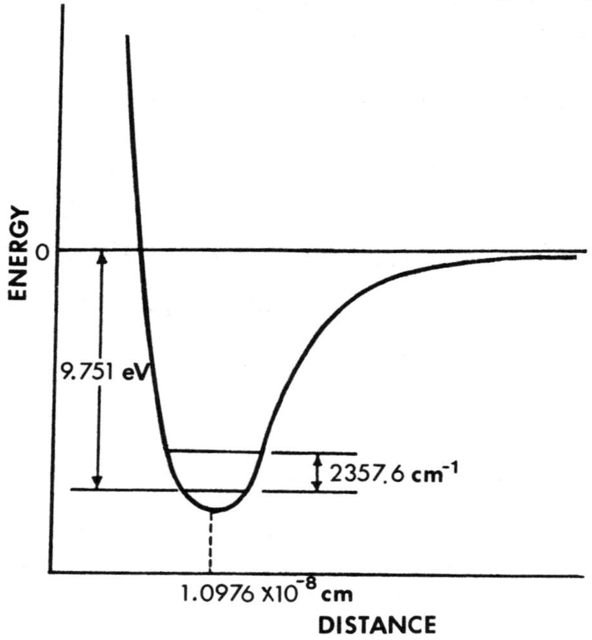

Fig. 1

Solution: From figure 1, the energy of dissociation of N_2 is $\Delta E_0 = 9.751$ eV. The fundamental vibration frequency $\bar{\nu} = 2357.6\ cm^{-1}$, and the internuclear distance is 1.0976×10^{-8} cm. The equilibrium constant expression for the reaction has the form

$$K_P = \left[\frac{\left(\frac{q}{N}\right)^2_{N(g)}}{\left(\frac{q}{N}\right)_{N_2(g)}}\right] e^{-\Delta\varepsilon_0/RT} \qquad (1)$$

where q is the partition function given by

$$q = q_{trans.} \times q_{rot.} \times q_{vi.} \times q_{elec.}$$

From equation (1)

$$K_P = \left[\frac{\left(\frac{q_{trans}}{N}\right)_{N(g)}}{\left(\frac{q_{trans}}{N}\right)_{N_2(g)}}\right] \times q_{rot.} \times q_{vi.} \times q_{elec.} \times e^{-\Delta\varepsilon_0/RT}$$

$$= \frac{\left[\frac{\left(2\pi m_N kT\right)^{3/2} RT}{Nh^3 P}\right]^2}{\left[\frac{\left(2\pi m_{N_2} kT\right)^{3/2}}{Nh^3 P}\right]} \left(\frac{h^2\sigma}{8\pi^2 IkT}\right)_{N_2(g)} \left(1 - e^{-\theta_{vi}/T}\right)_{N_2(g)}$$

$$\times \left(q_{elec}\right)^2_{N(g)} \times e^{-\Delta\varepsilon_0/RT} \qquad (2)$$

where $\theta_{vi} = \frac{hc\bar{\nu}}{k}$

here c is the speed of light and $\bar{\nu}$ is the vibration frequency. σ is the symmetry number and N is the Avogadro's number.

From equation (2)

$$q_{trans} = \frac{[(2\pi mkT)^{3/2} RT/Nh^3P]^2_{N(g)}}{[2\pi mkT)^{3/2} RT/Nh^3P]_{N_2(g)}} \qquad (3)$$

$$m_{N(g)} = \frac{1}{2} m_{N_2(g)} = \frac{14 \text{ g mole}^{-1}}{6.02\times10^{23} \text{ mole}^{-1}}$$

$$= 2.33 \quad 10^{-23} \text{ g}$$

$$q_{trans} = 8.393 \times 10^8$$

$$q_{rot} = \left(\frac{h^2\sigma}{8\pi^2 IkT}\right)_{N_2(g)} \tag{4}$$

where I = moment of inertia given by

$$I = \mu r_e^2$$

where μ is the reduced mass and r is the internuclear distance

$$\therefore \qquad I = \left(\frac{m_1 m_2}{m_1 + m_2}\right) r_e^2$$

$$= \frac{\left(\dfrac{14.008 \text{ g mole}^{-1}}{6.023\times10^{23} \text{ mole}^{-1}}\right)^2}{\left(\dfrac{28.016 \text{ g mole}^{-1}}{6.023\times10^{23} \text{ mole}^{-1}}\right)} \times (1.098\times10^{-8} \text{ cm})^2$$

$$= 1.402 \times 10^{-39} \text{ g cm}^2$$

Substitution of these values into equation (4) gives

$$q_{rot} = 1.150 \times 10^{-3}$$

$$q_{vi} = \left(1 - e^{-\theta_{vi}/T}\right)_{N_2(g)}$$

$$\frac{\theta_{vi}}{T} = \frac{h\bar{\nu}}{kT}$$

$$= \frac{hc\bar{\nu}}{kT}$$

$$= 6.7915 \times 10^{-1}$$

$$q_{vi} = .4923$$

$e^{-\Delta\varepsilon_0/RT}$ is computed as follows:

$$\Delta\varepsilon_0 = 9.751 \frac{\text{eV}}{\text{molec}} \times 6.023(10^{23}) \frac{\text{molec}}{\text{mole}} \times \frac{1.602(10^{-19})\frac{\text{J}}{\text{eV}}}{4.184 \text{ J/cal}}$$

$$= 225{,}023 \text{ cal/mole}$$

$$\frac{\Delta\varepsilon_0}{RT} = \frac{225023 \text{ cal/mole}}{1.987 \text{ cal/°K mole} \times 5000 \text{ °K}} = 22.650$$

$$e^{-\Delta\varepsilon_0/RT} = 1.457 \times 10^{-10}$$

q_{elec} is calculated as follows:

$$q_{elec} = g_0 e^{-\varepsilon_0/kT} + g_1 e^{-\varepsilon_1/kT} + g_2 e^{-\varepsilon_2/kT} + \ldots$$

where g_j is the electronic degeneracy and ε_j is the electronic energy of level j taken relative to the ground level. The ground state of N is a doublet ($^2P_{3/2,1/2}$) separated by 7603 cm^{-1}. Thus, the first term has a degeneracy of 4 while the second term has a degeneracy of 2. Hence

$$q_{elec} = 4e^{-(\varepsilon_0/hc)(hc/kT)} + 2e^{-(\varepsilon_1/hc)(hc/kT)}.$$

Given that the ground state has a separation of 7603 cm^{-1}, $\varepsilon_0 = 0$, while $\varepsilon_1/hc = 7603 \text{ cm}^{-1}$. Therefore

$$q_{elec} = 4e^0 + 2e^{-(3.8854(10^4)\text{cm}^{-1})(hc/kT)}.$$

Now

$$\frac{hc}{kT} = \frac{(6.63\times10^{-27})\text{ erg sec} \times (3\times10^{10})\text{cm sec}^{-1}}{(1.38\times10^{-16})\text{erg K}^{-1} \times 5000 \text{ °K}}$$

$$= 2.882(10^{-4})\text{cm}$$

$$q_{elec} = 4 + 2.74 \times 10^{-5} \cong 4$$

From equation (2)

$$K_P = (8.393\times10^8)(1.150\times10^{-3})\times(0.4923)\times16\times(1.457\times10^{-10})$$

$$= 1.108 \times 10^{-3} \text{ atm.}$$

• PROBLEM 14-10

For the dissociation reaction

$$Cl_2(g) \rightleftarrows 2Cl(g)$$

at 1200 °K, calculate the equilibrium constant K_P by statistical thermodynamics. The equilibrium internuclear distance is 0.199 nm, the fundamental vibration frequency of Cl_2 is at $\bar{\nu} = 565\ cm^{-1}$, and the energy of dissociation of Cl_2 is 2.48 eV.

Solution: The equilibrium constant K_P of a chemical reaction can be calculated from the partition functions, Q of the reactants and products by using the relation

$$\Delta G° = -RT\ \ell n\ K_P \tag{1}$$

Using the expression for Helmholtz free energy, partition functions and Stirling formula, equation (1) becomes

$$\Delta G° = -RT\ \ell n(Q°/L) \tag{2}$$

where L = the Avogadro's number and $Q°$ = the partition function of an ideal gas in the standard state, and is given by

$$Q° = Q_{int}\frac{(2\pi mkT)^{3/2}}{h^3}(RT) \tag{3}$$

Here, Q_{int} indicates the product of the rotational, vibrational and electronic contributions to Q°.

For the general reaction

$$aA + bB \rightleftarrows cC + dD,$$

Equation (2) gives

$$\Delta G° = -RT\ \ell n\frac{(Q_C°/L)^c(Q_D°/L)^d}{(Q_A°/L)^a(Q_B°/L)^b}\exp(-\Delta\varepsilon_0°/kT)$$

where $\exp(-\Delta\varepsilon_0°/kT)$ = the dissociation energy term.

The equilibrium constant expression is then

$$K_P = \frac{(Q_C°/L)^c(Q_D°/L)^d}{(Q_A°/L)^a(Q_B°/L)^b}\exp(-\Delta\varepsilon_0°/kT)$$

Now, write the K_P expression for the dissociation reaction $Cl_2 \rightleftarrows 2Cl$ as

$$K_P = \frac{[Q°(Cl)]^2}{[Q°(Cl_2)]L}\exp(-\Delta\varepsilon_0°/kT) \tag{4}$$

From Equation (3)

$$K_P = \left(\frac{2\pi kT}{h^2}\right)^{3/2} \frac{m_{Cl}^3}{m_{Cl_2}^{3/2}} \left(\frac{RT}{PL}\right) Q_{rot} Q_{vib} Q_{electronic}$$

But, $\quad m_{Cl} = \frac{1}{2} m_{Cl_2}$

$$= \frac{35.5 \text{ g mole}^{-1}}{6.02\times10^{23} \text{ mole}^{-1}}$$

$$= 5.89 \times 10^{-23} \text{ g}$$

$R = 82.06$ cc atm K^{-1}.
Take note of the units of R.
Thus the translational partition function

$$Q_{trans} = \left(\frac{2\pi kT}{h^2}\right)^{3/2} \frac{m_{Cl}^3}{m_{Cl_2}^{3/2}} \frac{RT}{PL}$$

$$= \left[2\pi \frac{(1.38\times10^{-16} \text{ erg K}^{-1})(1200°K)}{(6.63\times10^{-27} \text{ erg sec})^2}\right]^{3/2}$$

$$\times \frac{(5.89\times10^{-23})^3}{\left(2(5.89\ 10^{-23})\right)^{3/2}} \frac{(82.06 \text{ cc atm K}^{-1} \text{ mole}^{-1})(1200°K)}{(1 \text{ atm})6.02\times10^{23} \text{ mole}^{-1}}$$

$$Q_{trans} = 9.298 \times 10^7$$

The rotational partition function,

$$Q_{rot.} = \frac{8\pi^2 IkT}{\sigma h^2}$$

where h = the Planck's constnat, σ is the symmetry number = 2 for a homonuclear molecule. I is the moment of inertia given by

$$I = \mu r^2$$

$$= \frac{m_1 m_2}{m_1 + m_2} r^2$$

Observe that the molecule is homonuclear.

$$\therefore \quad I = \frac{m^2}{2m} r^2$$

$$= \frac{1}{2} m_{Cl} r^2$$

r is the interatomic distance

$$\therefore \quad I = 116.5 \times 10^{-40} \text{ g cm}^2$$

Consequently,

$$Q_{rot.} = \frac{8\pi^2(116.5\times10^{-40} \text{ g cm}^2)(1.38\times10^{-16} \text{ erg K}^{-1})(1200°K)}{2(6.63 \times 10^{-27}\text{erg s})^2}$$

$$= 1732.7.$$

The vibrational partition function,

$$Q_{vib} = \left(1 - e^{-hc\tilde{\nu}_0/kT}\right)^{-1}$$

where c = the speed of light and $\tilde{\nu}_0$ is the fundamental vibrational frequency. The term

$$\frac{hc\tilde{\nu}_0}{kT} = \frac{(6.63\times10^{-34}\text{J s})(3\times10^8\text{m s}^{-1})(565 \text{ cm}^{-1})(\frac{100 \text{ cm}}{1 \text{ m}})}{(1.38 \times 10^{-23}\text{J K}^{-1})(1200 °K)}$$

$$= .67861.$$

$$\therefore \quad Q_{vib} = \left(1 - e^{-.67861}\right)^{-1}$$

or $\quad Q_{vib} = 2.030.$

The electronic partition function

$$Q_{elect.} = 4 + g(e^{-\varepsilon/kT})$$

where g = the statistical weight of the degenerate level and is equal to the number of superimposed levels. The ground state of Cl_2 is singly degenerate and the ground state of Cl is a doublet $(^2P_{3/2,1/2})$, separated by 881 cm^{-1}

$$\therefore \quad Q_{elect.}(Cl) = 4 + 2 \exp(-\varepsilon/kT)$$

$$\varepsilon/kT = (\varepsilon/hc)\ (hc/kT)$$

$$\frac{hc}{kT} = \frac{6.63\times10^{-27} \text{ erg sec}\times3\times10^{10} \text{ cm/sec}}{1.38\times10^{-16} \text{ erg/°K}\times1200°K} = 1.20 \times 10^{-3} \text{ cm}$$

$$\varepsilon/kT = 881 \text{ cm}^{-1} \times 1.20 \times 10^{-3} \text{ cm} = 1.056$$

$$\therefore \quad Q_{elect}(Cl) = 4 + 2e^{-1.056}$$

$$= 4.696$$

$$Q_{elect.}(Cl)^2 = 22.05$$

The dissociation energy term

$$\frac{\Delta\varepsilon_0^\circ}{kT} = \frac{(2.48 \text{ eV})\left(\frac{1.602\ 10^{-19}\ J}{eV}\right)}{(1.38\times10^{-23}\ J°K^{-1})(1200\ °K)}$$

$$= 23.90$$

$$e^{-23.90} = 4.17 \times 10^{-11}$$

From (4)

$$K_p = \frac{(Q_{trans.}Q_{elec.})^2_{Cl}}{(Q_{trans.}Q_{rot.}Q_{vib.})_{Cl_2}} \exp(-\Delta\varepsilon_0^\circ/kT)$$

$$= \frac{9.298\times10^7\times22.05\times4.17\times10^{-11}}{1,732.7\times2.032}$$

$$K_p = 2.43 \times 10^{-5}$$

• PROBLEM 14-11

What is the superposition approximation? Give a physical and a mathematical description. In what context is it used?, and when does it fail?

Solution: The superposition principle can be written as

$$g_3(r) = g(r_{12})g(r_{23})g(r_{13})$$

where $g_3(r)$ is a three particle distribution function and by definition

$$g_3(r) = \frac{f_3}{\rho^3}.$$

f_3 is proportional to the probability of particles located at positions $d\underline{r}_1$, $d\underline{r}_2$, $d\underline{r}_3$.

The superposition approximation indicates that the three-body problem is related to the three separate two-body (g_2) radial distribution function by a simple product. The approximation is used in connection with the Yvon, Born and Green (YBG) equation,

$$\frac{\partial g(r_{12})}{\partial r_1} + g(r_{12})\frac{\partial \phi(r_{12})}{\partial r_1} + \rho \int \frac{\partial \phi(r_{13})}{\partial r_1} g_3(r)dr_3 = 0,$$

to determine the equation of state of fluids. This approximation fails at high densities.

• PROBLEM 14-12

Every unit area of a dilute monomolecular film on the surface of a liquid contains N identical molecules each of mass m. Answer the questions below, expressing them in terms of mass m, number of molecules N, T, and universal constants; assume that each molecule moves independently of one another and of the solvent molecules. a) Determine the two-dimensional speed distribution function f(v) for these molecules, normalized so that

$$\int_0^\infty f(v)dv = 1$$

b) Calculate the average velocities $\bar{v}$, $\overline{v^2}$, $\overline{v^3}$. c) A line segment is placed on the edge of the surface layer. Calculate the number of collisions, per unit length per unit time, with the line. d) Calculate the average kinetic energy of those molecules escaping through a small gap in the partition.

Solution: a) The two dimensional speed distribution function is given by

$$f(v) = \left(Ce^{-mv^2/2kT}\right)v \tag{1}$$

where m is the mass of the molecules, v is the speed and k is the Boltzmann constant. The constant C is determined by the normalization condition,

$$\int_0^\infty f(v)dv = 1 \tag{2}$$

since the possible values of v run from 0 to ∞. A distribution function obeying equation (2) is said to be normalized. Substituting equation (1) into equation (2) yields

$$\int_0^\infty Ce^{-mv^2/2kT} \quad vdv = 1$$

or
$$C\int_0^\infty e^{-mv^2/2kT} vdv = 1 \tag{3}$$

The integration is performed as follows: Let $x = v^2$, then $dx = 2vdv$ and $\frac{1}{2}dx = vdv$. Also let $a = \frac{m}{2kT}$. Therefore, the equation becomes

$$\frac{1}{2}C \int_0^\infty e^{-ax}dx = 1.$$

It is now in a familiar standard form and easily integrated to yield $\frac{C}{2}\left(-\frac{1}{a}\right)e^{-ax}\Big|_0^\infty = 1$. After replacing a by $\frac{m}{2kT}$ the equation becomes

$$-\frac{kT}{m}C\ e^{-mv^2/2kT}\Big|_0^\infty = 1$$

$$-C\frac{kT}{m}(0) + C\frac{kT}{m} = 1$$

$$C\frac{kT}{m} = 1$$

and $$C = \frac{m}{kT}$$

From equation (1), the normalized two dimensional speed distribution functinn becomes

$$f(v) = \frac{m}{kT}e^{-mv^2/2kT}\ vdv$$

b) (i) The mean speed $\bar{v}$ is given by

$$\bar{v} = C\int_0^\infty vf(v)dv$$

$$= \frac{m}{kT}\int_0^\infty\left(e^{-mv^2/2kT}\right)v^2dv$$

$$= \frac{m}{kT}\cdot\frac{\sqrt{\pi}}{4}\left(\frac{2kT}{m}\right)^{3/2}$$

$$= \left(\frac{\pi kT}{2m}\right)^{1/2}$$

(ii) $$\overline{v^2} = C\int_0^\infty v^2 f(v)dv$$

$$= \frac{m}{kT} \int_0^\infty e^{-mv^2/2kT} \, v^3 dv$$

$$= \frac{m}{kT} \cdot \frac{1}{2} \left(\frac{2kT}{m} \right)^2$$

$$= \frac{2kT}{m}$$

(iii) $$\overline{v^3} = C \int_0^\infty v^3 f(v) dv$$

$$= \frac{m}{kT} \int_0^\infty e^{-mv^2/2kT} \, v^4 dv$$

$$= \frac{m}{kT} \frac{3\sqrt{\pi}}{8} \left(\frac{2kT}{m} \right)^{5/2}$$

$$= 3\sqrt{\frac{\pi}{2}} \left(\frac{kT}{m} \right)^{3/2}$$

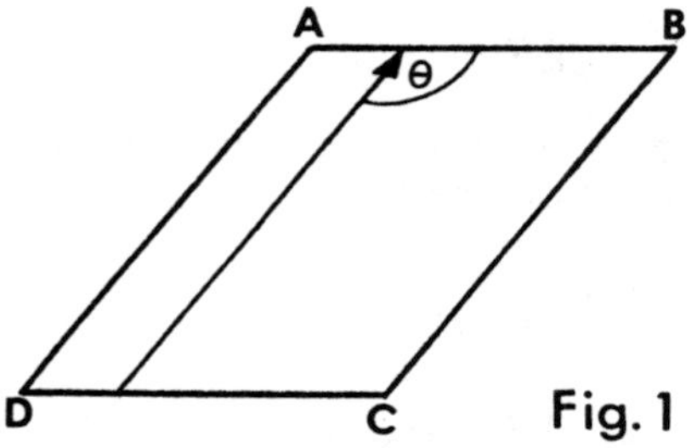

Fig. 1

c) Fig. 1 shows a line segment AB which contains molecules. The molecules have speeds between v and v + dv and a velocity vector between angles θ and θ + dθ. They collide if they are in the area ABCD.

$$\overline{AD} = v.$$

This area is given by

$$(\overline{AB})(\overline{AD}) \sin \theta$$

and since there is a unit line segment the area becomes

$$v \sin \theta.$$

As a result, the number of molecules in this area is $Nv \sin \theta$. The number of molecules in the range v, v + dv and θ, θ + dθ is given by

$$Nv \sin \theta \cdot \frac{m}{kT} e^{-mv^2/2kT} \, v dv \, \frac{d\theta}{2\pi}$$

$$= \frac{Nm \sin\theta \, d\theta \, e^{-mv^2/2kT} \, v^2 \, dv}{2\pi kT} \qquad (3)$$

Equation (3) gives the number of collisions in the given v and θ range. To obtain the total number of collisions Z, integrate equation (3) as follows:

$$Z = \frac{Nm}{2\pi kT} \int_0^{\pi} \sin\theta \, d\theta \int_0^{\infty} e^{-mv^2/2kT} \, v^2 dv$$

$$= N\left(\frac{kT}{2\pi m}\right)^{1/2}$$

d) The number of molecules colliding with the gap is equal to the number of molecules escaping, since any molecule striking the gap will escape. Therefore the average **kinetic** energy of the escaping molecules $\bar{\varepsilon}$, is equal to the total kinetic energy E, divided by the number of molecules colliding with the gap. That is,

$$\bar{\varepsilon} = \frac{E}{Z} \qquad (4)$$

But $E = \frac{1}{2}mv^2 Z$

$$= \frac{Nm}{2\pi kT} \cdot \frac{1}{2}mv^2 \int_0^{\pi} \sin\theta \, d\theta \int_0^{\infty} e^{-mv^2/2kT} \, v^2 \, dv$$

$$= \frac{Nm}{2\pi kT} \cdot \frac{1}{2}m \int_0^{\pi} \sin\theta \, d\theta \int_0^{\infty} e^{-mv^2/2kT} \, v^4 \, dv$$

$$= \frac{3N}{\sqrt{\pi m}}\left(\frac{kT}{2}\right)^{3/2}$$

From equation (4)

$$\bar{\varepsilon} = \frac{\frac{3N}{\sqrt{\pi m}}\left(\frac{kT}{2}\right)^{3/2}}{N\left(\frac{kT}{2\pi m}\right)^{1/2}}$$

$$= \frac{3kT}{2}$$

• **PROBLEM 14-13**

A set of ideal gas molecules, each of mass m, are restricted to two dimensions. The distribution law for each component of velocity is given by

$$\frac{dN_{v_x}}{N_{total}} = A\,e^{(-mv_x^2/2kT)}\,dv_x$$

a) Show that the distribution law with respect to speed v, is given by

$$\frac{dN_v}{N_{total}} = 2\pi A^2 e^{-mv^2/2kT}\,v\,dv$$

and evaluate the constant A.
b) Determine the average speed $\bar{v}$ of the molecules, in terms of mass m of the molecules, temperature T, and universal constants.

Solution: a) These molecules are confined to two dimensions, thus the probability of locating a molecule with velocity, v_x in the x-direction, is given by

$$\frac{dN_{v_x}}{N_{total}} = A\,e^{-mv_x^2/2kT}\,dv_x \qquad (1)$$

Likewise for molecules with velocity, v_y in the y-direction,

$$\frac{dN_{v_y}}{N_{total}} = A\,e^{-mv_y^2/2kT}\,dv_y \qquad (2)$$

Now the probability of simultaneously finding a molecule with velocity v_x, between v_x and $v_x + dv_x$ and with velocity v_y, between v_y and $v_y + dv_y$ is the product of the separate probabilities. Therefore,

$$\frac{dN_{v_xv_y}}{N_{total}} = \left(\frac{dN_{v_x}}{N_{total}}\right)\left(\frac{dN_{v_y}}{N_{total}}\right)$$

$$= \left(A\,e^{-mv_x^2/2kT}\,dv_x\right)\left(A\,e^{-mv_y^2/2kT}\,dv_y\right)$$

$$= A^2 \exp\left[-m\left(\frac{v_x^2 + v_y^2}{2kT}\right)\right]dv_x\,dv_y$$

$$= A^2 e^{-mv^2/2kT} v\,dv\,d\theta \quad (3)$$

Equation (3) is written in polar coordinates in velocity space, where θ is the angle such that $\tan\theta = \frac{v_y}{v_x}$ and v^2 replaces $v_x^2 + v_y^2$. The distribution law with respect to speed v (that is, the number of molecules with speeds between v and v + dv) is obtained by integrating equation (3) at all angles θ. Therefore,

$$\frac{dN_v}{N_{total}} = \int_0^{2\pi} A^2 e^{-mv^2/2kT} v\,dv\,d\theta$$

$$= A^2 e^{-mv^2/2kT} v\,dv \int_0^{2\pi} d\theta$$

$$= 2\pi A^2 e^{-mv^2/2kT} v\,dv \quad (4)$$

The constant A is determined by using the normalization condition given by

$$\int_{v=0}^{\infty} \frac{dN_v}{N_{total}} = 1$$

$$\therefore \quad \int_0^{\infty} 2\pi A^2 e^{-mv^2/2kT} v dv = 1$$

$$\text{or} \quad 2\pi A^2 \int_0^{\infty} e^{-mv^2/2kT} v dv = 1 \quad (5)$$

Let $U = -\frac{mv^2}{2kT}$

Then, $dU = -\frac{m}{2kT} 2v\,dv$

$$= -\frac{m}{kT} v\,dv$$

Eqn (5) becomes

$$-\frac{kT}{m} 2\pi A^2 \int_0^{\infty} e^U\,dU = 1$$

$$- \frac{kT}{m} 2\pi A^2 \ e^U \Big|_0^\infty = 1 \tag{6}$$

Substituting $U = - \frac{mv^2}{2kT}$ back into equation (6) yields

$$- \frac{kT}{m} 2\pi A^2 e^{-mv^2/2kT} \Big|_0^\infty = 1$$

$$- \frac{kT}{m} 0 + \frac{kT}{m} 2\pi A^2 = 1$$

$$2\pi A^2 \ \frac{kT}{m} = 1$$

$$\therefore \quad A^2 = \frac{m}{2\pi kT}$$

Alternatively, to solve for A^2, each of the separate integrals could be solved for A and this answer squared. Eqn. (4) then becomes

$$\frac{dN_v}{N_{total}} = 2\pi \left(\frac{m}{2\pi kT} \right) e^{-mv^2/2kT} \ v \ dv$$

$$= \frac{m}{kT} \ e^{-mv^2/2kT} \ v \ dv$$

b) The average speed $\bar{v}$ is given by

$$\bar{v} = \int_0^\infty v \ \frac{dN_v}{N_{total}}$$

$$= \frac{m}{kT} \int_0^\infty e^{-mv^2/2kT} \ v^2 \ dv$$

$$= \frac{m}{kT} \int_0^\infty v \ e^{-mv^2/2kT} \ v \ dv$$

$$= \frac{m}{kT} \int_0^\infty x \ e^{-mx^2/2kT} \ x \ dx \tag{7}$$

Integrate by parts using

$$\int udv = uv - \int vdu \tag{8}$$

From equation (7),

Let $U = x$ and $dv = e^{-mx^2/2kT}\, x\, dx$

$\therefore \quad dU - dx$ and $v = -\frac{2kT}{2m} e^{-mx^2/2kT}$

Using equation (8), equation (7) becomes

$$\bar{v} = \frac{m}{kT} \cdot \left(-x \frac{kT}{m}\right) e^{-mx^2/2kT} \Big|_0^\infty + \frac{m}{kT} \cdot \int_0^\infty \frac{kT}{m} e^{-mx^2/2kT}\, dx$$

$$= \frac{m}{kT} \cdot \left(-x \frac{kT}{m}\right) e^{-mx^2/2kT} \Big|_0^\infty + \frac{m}{kT} \cdot \frac{kT}{m} \int_0^\infty e^{-mx^2/2kT}\, dx$$

$$= 0 + \int_0^\infty e^{-mx^2/2kT}\, dx$$

$$= \frac{1}{2}\sqrt{\frac{\pi}{\frac{m}{2kT}}} \quad \text{in polar coordinates.}$$

$$= \frac{\sqrt{\pi}}{2\sqrt{\frac{m}{2kT}}}$$

$$= \frac{\sqrt{\pi}}{\sqrt{\frac{4m}{2kT}}}$$

$$= \frac{\sqrt{\pi}}{\sqrt{\frac{2m}{kT}}}$$

$$= \left(\frac{\pi kT}{2m}\right)^{1/2}$$

• PROBLEM 14-14

In one of the experiments on gravitational sedimentation equilibrium, the number of gamboge particles in water at 20°C were monitored. (Gamboge is a yellow pigment not soluble in water.) The following data was obtained:

Height in μm:	0	25	50	75	100
Mean no. of particles:	203	166	136	112	91

Assuming that the gamboge particles had a mean volume equal to $9.78 \times 10^{-21}\ m^3$ and a density equal to 1351 kg/m^3, calculate the Boltzmann constant.

Solution: Gravitational sedimentation implies that the downward velocity, V_G due to gravitational forces alone equals the upward velocity V_D due to diffusion alone.

Let component 1 = water
and component 2 = particle

The gravitational downward force = $m_2 g$. The bouyant diffusional upward force = $m_2 \frac{1}{\rho_2} \rho_1 g$. g is the acceleration due to gravity and ρ is the density. Another upward force is that due to Stoke's law, given by

$$f = 6\pi\mu a V_G$$

where a is the radius and μ is the coefficient of viscosity of the medium.

At equilibrium, the forces balance

$$\text{and } \Delta F = 0 = -m_2 g\left(1 - \frac{\rho_1}{\rho_2}\right) - 6\pi\mu a V_G$$

$$\text{or } \quad V_G = \frac{m_2 g\left(1 - \rho_1/\rho_2\right)}{6\pi\mu a}$$

$$= \frac{m_2 g'}{6\pi\mu a} \tag{1}$$

where $g' = g(1 - \rho_1/\rho_2)$.

Determination of V_D:

The rate of diffusion is the upward z-direction is given by

$$j_z = CV_D = -\mathcal{D}_{12} \frac{dC}{dZ} \tag{2}$$

where C is the concentration and $\mathcal{D}$ is the diffusion coefficient given by

$$\mathcal{D}_{12} = \frac{kT}{6\pi\mu a}$$

Therefore, $$V_D = -\frac{kT}{6\pi\mu a} \frac{dC}{CdZ} \tag{3}$$

At equilibrium $V_G = V_D$ and equation (3) becomes

$$\frac{dC}{C} = -\frac{m_2 g'}{kT} dZ$$

Integration yields

$$\ln C = \frac{-m_2 g' Z}{kT} + \bar{C}$$

From which

$$C = C_0 \exp\left[-\frac{m_2 g' Z}{kT}\right] \qquad (4)$$

where $C = C_0$ at $Z = 0$.

Equation (4) is the familiar Boltzmann's equation and it indicates that the equilibrium distribution of the particles obeys this equation. The Boltzmann's constant can then be determined from the equation. To do this, plot $\ln C$ vs h, where h is the height in the z-direction. From equation (4)

$$\ln C = \ln C_0 - \frac{m_2 g' h}{kT}$$

By using a linear regression calculation, or by graphically plotting the data, the slope can be found. Using linear regression calculation the formula for the slope is given by:

$$\text{Slope} = \frac{\sum x \sum y - n \sum xy}{(\sum x)^2 - n \sum x^2}$$

The letter n refers to the number of data item which in this case equals 5. Since the plot involves $\ln C$ versus h, the x in the above equation will the h and the y the $\ln C$ term. The following table represents our data.

h (μm)	0	25	50	75	100
C (mean number of particles)	203	166	136	112	91
$\ln C$	5.313	5.112	4.913	4.718	4.511

$\sum x = 0+25+50+75+100 = 250$ μm, $(\sum x)^2 = 62500\,(\mu m)^2$, $\sum y = 24.567$,

$$\sum xy = x_1y_1+x_2y_2+x_3y_3+x_4y_4+x_5y_5 = 0+127.8+245.65+353.85+451.1$$
$$= 117.84\mu m$$

$$\sum x^2 = x_1^2+x_2^2+x_3^2+x_4^2+x_5^2 = 0+625+2500+5625+10{,}000 = 18750\,(\mu m)^2$$

$$\text{Slope} = \frac{((250)(24.567) - 5(1178.4))\,\mu m}{(62500 - 5(18750))\,(\mu m)^2} = -7.99(10^{-3})\frac{1}{\mu m}$$

$$\text{Slope} = \frac{-m_2 g'}{kT} = -7.99 \times 10^{-3}\ \frac{1}{\mu m}$$

$$\therefore \quad k = \frac{m_2 g'}{(7.99 \times 10^{-3})\frac{1}{\mu m}T} \qquad (5)$$

$$m_2 = V_2 \rho_2$$

$$= (9.78 \times 10^{-21} \text{ m}^3)(1351 \text{ kg m}^{-3})$$

$$= 1.321 \times 10^{-17} \text{ kg}$$

$$g' = g\left(1 - \frac{\rho_1}{\rho_2}\right)$$

$$= 9.78 \frac{\text{m}}{\text{sec}^2}\left(1 - \frac{998.230}{1351}\right)$$

$$= 2.55 \text{ m sec}^{-2}$$

Using these values in equation (5) yields

$$k = \frac{(1.321\times10^{-17} \text{ kg})(2.55 \text{ m s}^{-2})}{(7.99\times10^{-3} \text{ µm})\left(\frac{10^6 \text{ µm}}{1 \text{ m}}\right)(293 \text{ °K})}$$

$$= 1.44 \times 10^{-23} \text{ J/°K}$$

or $k = 1.44 \times 10^{-16}$ ergs/°K

• PROBLEM 14-15

Molecules of a gas are crossing a given plane of unit area in unit time. Show that the average total kinetic energy of the molecules is 2kT.

Solution: Let the number of particles in the gas be N, and their velocity be v. Also, let the number of molecules with velocities between v and v + dv be dN. The number of particles emerging across the plane is dN' and is proportional to dN. The emitted beam has a mean square velocity of $\overline{v'^2}$ and is given by

$$\overline{v'^2} = \frac{\int_0^\infty v^2 dN'}{\int_0^\infty dN'}$$

$$= \frac{\int_0^\infty v^3 dN}{\int_0^\infty v dN} \qquad (1)$$

Of particular interest are the fraction of the molecules having a speed in the range v to v + dv, independent of the direction. If the origins of the velocity vectors of all the molecules in a sample of the gas are brought to the origin of a coordinate system, molecules having speed vectors ending in a spherical shell of radius v around the origin with thickness dv are wanted. The volume of this shell is $4\pi v^2 dv$, and thus the fraction of the molecules with velocities v in the range v to v + dv is given by

$$f(v)dv = \left(\frac{m}{2\pi kT}\right)^{3/2} e^{-mv^2/2kT}\ 4\pi v^2 dv$$

which is the Maxwell equation. Substituting the Maxwell equation into equation (1) gives

$$\overline{v'^2} = \frac{4\pi N_0 \left(\frac{m}{2\pi kT}\right)^{3/2} \int_0^\infty v^5 \exp\left[-\frac{mv^2}{2kT}\right] dv}{4\pi N_0 \left(\frac{m}{2\pi kT}\right)^{3/2} \int_0^\infty v^3 \exp\left[-\frac{mv^2}{2kT}\right] dv}$$

$$= \frac{\int_0^\infty v^5 \exp\left[-\frac{mv^2}{2kT}\right] dv}{\int_0^\infty v^3 \exp\left[-\frac{mv^2}{2kT}\right] dv}$$

$$= \frac{\left[\frac{8k^3T^3}{m^3}\right]}{\left[\frac{2k^2T^2}{m^2}\right]}$$

$$= \frac{4kT}{m}$$

Kinetic energy is given by

$$E = \frac{1}{2}m\ \overline{v'^2}$$

$$= \frac{1}{2}m\left(\frac{4kT}{m}\right)$$

$$= 2kT\ .$$

INDEX

Numbers on this page refer to PROBLEM NUMBERS, not page numbers

Numbers on this page refer to PROBLEM NUMBERS, not page numbers

Numbers on this page refer to PROBLEM NUMBERS, not page numbers

Numbers on this page refer to PROBLEM NUMBERS, not page numbers

Numbers on this page refer to <u>PROBLEM NUMBERS</u>, not page numbers

Numbers on this page refer to PROBLEM NUMBERS, not page numbers

Numbers on this page refer to PROBLEM NUMBERS, not page numbers

Numbers on this page refer to PROBLEM NUMBERS, not page numbers